Leiths

COOKERY BIBLE

Leiths

COOKERY BIBLE

**PRUE LEITH and
CAROLINE WALDEGRAVE**

Third edition edited by Susan Spaull

BLOOMSBURY

First edition published in 1991
This edition published in 2003

Copyright © 1991 and 1996 Prue Leith and Caroline Waldegrave
This revised edition © 2003 Caroline Waldegrave

The moral right of the authors has been asserted

Bloomsbury Publishing Plc, 38 Soho Square, London W1D 3HB

A CIP catalogue record is available from the British Library

ISBN 0-7475-7189-9

Typeset by Hewer Text Limited, Edinburgh
Printed by Tien Wah Press, Singapore

Photographs by Jason Lowe
Home economists: Angela Boggiano and Susan Spaull
Assisted by: Anna-Lisa Aldridge, Suzan Brown and Hélène Robinson-Moltke
Book design: Here + There

Contents

Acknowledgements

This book is officially by Prue Leith and me. In fact this is not really the case. It is the result of twenty-seven years in the life of Leiths School of Food and Wine. Teachers, students and friends alike have all contributed. Recipes have been unashamedly adapted from magazines, newspaper articles and other cookery books, including all the Leiths titles.

When we see or hear of a recipe that appeals to us, we test it and adapt it as we see fit. It then undergoes a more rigorous testing as it is cooked by ninety-six students, all of whom follow it to the letter. We certainly know if we have got it wrong. It then gets rewritten and becomes part of the *Bible*.

We have acknowledged other people's recipes when we can but sometimes, I am afraid, we no longer know where they first came from and hope their creators will forgive us. Prue and I are not trying to take credit for these recipes; we have simply tried to build up the collection we rather grandly call our *Bible*.

Past and present staff have contributed enormously to this end. I would like to thank the following people for their contributions: Fiona Burrell, Suzan Brown, Sara Blount, Alison Cavaliero, Emma Crowhurst, Maxine Clarke, Roz Denny, Puff Fairclough, Richard Harvey, C. J. Jackson, Be Kassapian, Charlotte Lyon, Claire MacDonald, Eithne Neame, Janey Orr, Susan Spaull, Sarah Staughton, Karen Sorenson, Barbara Stevenson, and Caroline Yates. For the new edition of this book I would particularly like to thank Jenny Stringer and Viv Pidgeon. Their advice has been invaluable.

The new edition would never have been produced without Sue Spaull who has updated much of the information in the book, provided us with new recipes, cooked the food for many of the photographs and remained consistently enthusiastic throughout the whole production process.

We would also like to thank Helen Campbell, our extremely patient and brilliant editor, Chiki Sarkar at Bloomsbury who has worked so hard to get this new edition into production, and Angela Boggiano who cooked many of the dishes for the photographs that were taken by Jason Lowe.

Caroline Waldegrave, OBE

Foreword

There are not many cookbooks whose recipes have been tested over and over again by 100 students and 15 teachers. However, this book has evolved over the past 30 years and can probably claim to include the most tried, tested and true set of instructions ever offered to the keen cook, greedy gourmet or addicted recipe reader.

What we have tried to do in this book is to reproduce the style of cooking taught at Leiths School. Frankly, we threw out recipes, however classic and time-honoured, if the teachers and students did not like the results. This has meant the demise of nut cutlets and many an uninspiring stew. It has also meant the inclusion of dozens of 'new classics' – the fresh, imaginative cooking that has been such an inspiration to today's chefs. It has meant that Oriental, Indian, South American and vegetarian dishes have come into their own. It has meant due regard for healthy eating, alongside the *haute cuisine* of rich butter sauces and high-cholesterol puddings and the hearty, homely cooking of the modern brasserie.

What we have guarded determinedly against is gimmickiness or pretentiousness. Thus, we have included a fruit coulis only when it improves the flavour as well as the appearance of a dessert. We have kept garnishes, decorations and trimmings to the edible and relevant minimum.

The whole point of cooking, it seems to us, is to lift food from the merely nutritive to the positively pleasurable. There was never a good cook with a Calvinist heart. By which I don't mean that good cooks are profligate, extravagant or wasteful. Waste is as painful to a true cook as second-rate ingredients are.

Another thread running through the recipes, however simple or grand, is the love of doing things well. For there really is great satisfaction for the cook (more, perhaps, even than for the diner) in a perfectly balanced and executed meal. There is no buzz quite like that of surveying a buffet, every dish of which you have got exactly right, before the marauding guests descend. That feeling of pride and pleasure is worth all the hard work.

But of course this book is more a practical manual than a paean to the joy of creativity. It is essentially the tool by which such pleasures (and profit) are reached. It will be, we hope, the mentor and guide of newly fledged cooks, and will become the trusted old friend and helpmeet of experienced chefs. Caroline Waldegrave and her team of teachers have put into it everything we think a professional might turn to for reference, and enough to turn the amateur into a professional.

Above all, I hope that this book will spread the gospel: good cooking is enjoyable and rewarding for everyone – not least the cook.

Prue Leith

Introduction

Conversion Tables

Metric	Imperial	Metric	Imperial
7–8 g	¼ oz	15 g	½ oz
20 g	¾ oz	30 g	1 oz
55 g	2 oz	85 g	3 oz
110 g	4 oz (¼ lb)	140 g	5 oz
170 g	6 oz	200 g	7 oz
225 g	8 oz	255 g	9 oz
285 g	10 oz	310 g	11 oz
340 g	12 oz (¾ lb)	370 g	13 oz
400 g	14 oz	425 g	15 oz
450 g	16 oz (1 lb)	560 g	1¼ lb
675 g	1½ lb	900 g	2 lb
785 g	1¾ lb		
1 kg	2 lb 4 oz	1.15 kg	2 lb 8 oz
1.35 kg	3 lb	1.8 kg	4 lb
2.3 kg	5 lb	2.7 kg	6 lb
3.2 kg	7 lb	3.6 kg	8 lb
4 kg	9 lb	4.5 kg	10 lb

Lengths

Imperial	Metric
½ in	1 cm
1 in	2.5 cm
2 in	5 cm
6 in	15 cm
8 in	20 cm
12 in	30 cm

Approximate American/European Conversions

	USA	Metric	Imperial
Flour	1 cup	125 g	$4\frac{1}{2}$ oz
Caster and granulated sugar	1 cup	170 g	6 oz
Brown sugar	1 cup	170 g	6 oz
Butter/margarine/lard	1 cup/2 sticks	225 g	8 oz
Sultanas/raisins/currants	1 cup	140 g	5 oz
Ground almonds	1 cup	100 g	$3\frac{1}{2}$ oz
Uncooked rice	1 cup	170 g	6 oz
Grated cheese	1 cup	110 g	4 oz
Chopped nuts	1 cup	100 g	$3\frac{1}{2}$ oz

1 American pint = 16 fl oz = 450 ml

1 Imperial pint = 20 fl oz = 570 ml

1 tablespoon = 3 teaspoons = 15 ml

1 lb = 16 oz = 450 g

2 lb 4 oz = 1,000 g | 1 kg

1 average bottle of wine   75 cl | 750 ml

1 average bottle of spirits   70 cl | 700 ml

1 lt = 1,000 ml = 100 cl = 10 dl = $1\frac{3}{4}$ imperial pints

Australian

250ml = 1 cup

20ml = 1 tablespoon

5ml = 1 teaspoon

Australian cup measures

	Metric	Imperial
1 cup flour	140g	5oz
1 cup sugar (crystal or caster)	225g	8oz
1 cup brown sugar, firmly packed	170g	6oz
1 cup icing sugar, sifted	170g	6oz
1 cup butter	225g	8oz
1 cup honey, golden syrup, treacle	340g	12oz
1 cup fresh breadcrumbs	55g	2oz
1 cup packaged dry breadcrumbs	140g	5oz
1 cup crushed biscuit crumbs	110g	4oz
1 cup rice, uncooked	200g	7oz
1 cup mixed fruit or individual fruit, such as sultanas	170g	6oz
1 cup nuts, chopped	110g	3oz
1 cup coconut, desiccated	85g	3oz

Oven Temperatures

°C	°F	Gas mark	USA
70	150	¼	
80	175	¼	
100	200	½	COOL
110	225	½	
130	250	1	VERY SLOW
140	275	1	
150	300	2	SLOW
170	325	3	MODERATE
180	350	4	
190	375	5	MODERATELY HOT
200	400	6	FAIRLY HOT
220	425	7	HOT
230	450	8	VERY HOT
240	475	8	
250	500	9	
270	525	9	EXTREMELY HOT
290	550	9	

Wine Quantities

Imperial	ml	fl oz
Average wine bottle	750	25
1 glass wine	100	3
1 glass port or sherry	70	2
1 glass liqueur	45	1

Dictionary of Cooking Terms and Kitchen French

Abats: French for offal (hearts, livers, brains, tripe, etc.). Americans call them 'variety meats'.

Bake blind: To bake a pastry case while empty. In order to prevent the sides falling in or the base bubbling up, the pastry is usually lined with paper and filled with 'blind beans'. See below.

Bain-marie: A roasting tin half-filled with hot water in which terrines, custards, etc. stand while cooking. The food is protected from direct fierce heat and cooks in a gentle, steamy atmosphere. Also a large container that will hold a number of pans standing in hot water, used to keep soups, sauces, etc. hot without further cooking.

Bard: To tie bacon or pork fat over a joint of meat, game bird or poultry, to be roasted. This helps to prevent the flesh from drying out.

Baste: To spoon over liquid (sometimes stock, sometimes fat) during cooking to prevent drying out and to promote flavour.

Bavarois: Creamy pudding made with eggs and cream and set with gelatine.

Beignets: Fritters.

Beurre manié: Butter and flour in equal quantities worked together to a soft paste, and used as a liaison or thickening for liquids. Small pieces are whisked into boiling liquid. As the butter melts it disperses the flour evenly through the liquid, thereby thickening it without causing lumps.

Beurre noisette: Browned butter; see Noisette.

Bisque: Shellfish soup, smooth and thickened.

Blanch: Originally, to whiten by boiling, e.g. to boil sweetbreads or brains briefly to remove traces of blood and to remove strong flavours, or to boil almonds to make the brown skin easy to remove, leaving the nuts white. Now commonly used to mean parboiling, as in blanching vegetables when they are parboiled prior to freezing, or precooked so that they have only to be reheated before serving.

Blanquette: A stew made without initial browning of the meat. Usually used for lamb, chicken or veal. The sauce is often thickened with an egg and cream liaison.

Blind beans: Dried beans, peas, rice and pasta used to fill pastry cases temporarily during baking.

Bouchées: Small puff pastry cases like miniature vol-au-vents.

Bouillon: Broth or uncleared stock.

Bouquet garni: Parsley stalks, small bay leaf, fresh thyme, celery stalk, sometimes with a blade of mace, tied together with string and used to flavour stews, etc. Removed before serving.

Braise: To bake or stew slowly on a bed of vegetables in a covered pan.

Brunoise: Vegetables cut into very small dice.

Canapé: A small bread or biscuit base, sometimes fried, spread or covered with savoury paste, egg, etc., used for cocktail titbits or as an accompaniment to meat dishes. Sometimes used to denote the base only, as in champignons sur canapé.

Caramel: Sugar cooked to a toffee.

Cartouche: Piece of greaseproof paper dampened and placed directly on top of vegetables when sweating or used dry for baking blind.

Châteaubriand: Roast fillet steak from the thick end for 2 people or more.

Chine: To remove the backbone from a rack of ribs. Carving is almost impossible if the butcher has not 'chined' the meat.

Clarified butter: Butter that has been separated from milk particles and other impurities which cause it to look cloudy when melted, and to burn easily when heated.

Collops: Small slices of meat, taken from a tender cut such as neck of lamb.

Concassé: Tomatoes cut into small even squares or diamonds.

Concasser: To chop roughly.

Consommé: Clear soup.

Coulis: Essentially a thick sauce, made from puréed cooked or raw fruit (e.g. summer berries) or vegetables (e.g. tomatoes).

Court bouillon: Liquid used for cooking fish.

Cream: To beat ingredients together, such as butter and fat when making a sponge cake.

Crêpes: Thin French pancakes.

Crépin: Pig's caul.

Croquettes: Stiff purée of mashed potato and possibly poultry, fish or meat, formed into small balls or patties, coated in egg and breadcrumbs and deep-fried.

Croustade: Bread case dipped in butter and baked until crisp. Used to contain hot savoury mixtures for a canapé, savoury or as a garnish.

Croûte: Literally crust. Sometimes a pastry case, as in fillet of beef en croûte, sometimes toasted or fried bread, as in Scotch woodcock or scrambled eggs on toast.

Croûtons: Small evenly sized cubes of fried bread used as a soup garnish and occasionally in other dishes.

Dariole: Small castle-shaped mould used for moulding rice salads and sometimes for cooking cake mixtures.

Déglacer: To loosen and liquefy fat, sediment and browned juices stuck at the bottom of a frying pan or saucepan by adding liquid (usually stock, water or wine) and stirring while boiling.

Deglaze: See Déglacer.

Dégorger: To extract the juices from meat, fish or vegetables, generally by salting then soaking or washing. Usually done to remove indigestible or strong-tasting juices.

Dépouiller: To skim off the scum from a sauce or stock: a splash of cold stock is added to the boiling liquid. This helps to bring scum and fat to the surface, which can then be skimmed more easily.

Dropping consistency: The consistency where a mixture will drop reluctantly from a spoon, neither pouring off nor obstinately adhering.

Duxelles: Finely chopped raw mushrooms, sometimes with chopped shallots or chopped ham, often used as a stuffing.

Egg wash: Beaten raw egg, sometimes with salt, used for glazing pastry to give it a shine when baked.

Emulsion: A stable suspension of fat and other liquid, e.g. mayonnaise, hollandaise.

Entrecôte: Sirloin steak.

Entrée: Traditionally a dish served before the main course, but usually served as a main course today.

Entremet: Dessert or sweet course, excluding pastry sweets.

Escalop: A thin slice of meat, sometimes beaten out flat to make it thinner and larger.

Farce: Stuffing.

Fecule: Farinaceous thickening, usually arrowroot or cornflour.

Flamber: To set alcohol alight. Usually to burn off the alcohol, but frequently simply for dramatic effect. (Past tense flambé or flambée; English: to flame).

Flame: See Flamber.

Fleurons: Crescents of puff pastry, generally used to garnish fish or poultry.

Fold: To mix with a gentle lifting motion, rather than to stir vigorously. The aim is to avoid beating out air while mixing.

Frappé: Iced, or set in a bed of crushed ice.

Fricassé: White stew made with cooked or raw poultry, meat or rabbit and a velouté sauce, sometimes thickened with cream and egg yolks.

Fumet: Strong-flavoured liquid used for flavouring sauces. Usually the liquid in which fish has been poached, or the liquid that has run from fish during baking. Sometimes used of meat or truffle-flavoured liquors.

Glace de viande: Reduced brown stock, very strong in flavour, used for adding body and colour to sauces.

Glaze: To cover with a thin layer of shiny jellied meat juices (for roast turkey), melted jam (for fruit flans) or syrup (for rum baba) or beaten egg (bread and pastries).

Gratiner: To brown under a grill after the surface of the dish has been sprinkled with breadcrumbs and butter and, sometimes, cheese. Dishes finished like this are sometimes called gratinée or au gratin.

Hors d'oeuvre: Usually simply means the first course. Sometimes used to denote a variety or selection of many savoury titbits served with drinks, or a mixed first course (hors d'oeuvres variés).

Infuse: To steep or heat gently to extract flavour, as when infusing milk with onion slices.

Julienne: Vegetables or citrus rind cut in thin matchstick shapes or very fine shreds.

Jus or jus de viande: God's gravy, i.e. juices that occur naturally in cooking, not a made-up sauce. Also juice.

Jus lié: Thickened gravy.

Knock down or knock back: To punch or knead out the air in risen dough so that it resumes its pre-risen bulk.

Knock up: To separate slightly the layers of raw puff pastry with the blade of a knife to facilitate rising during cooking.

Lard: To thread strips of bacon fat (or sometimes anchovy) through meat to give it flavour, and, in the case of fat, to moisturize very lean meat.

Lardons: Small strips or cubes of pork fat or bacon generally used as a garnish.

Liaison: Ingredients for binding together and thickening sauce, soup or other liquid, e.g. roux, beurre manié, egg yolk and cream, blood.

Macédoine: Small diced mixed vegetables, usually containing some root vegetables. Sometimes used of fruit meaning a fruit salad.

Macerate: To soak food in a syrup or liquid to allow flavours to mix.

Mandolin: Frame of metal or wood with adjustable blades set in it for thinly slicing cucumbers, potatoes, etc.

Marinade: A liquid containing oil, aromatic vegetables, herbs and spices, and an acid such as wine, lemon juice or vinegar.

Marinate: To soak meat, fish or vegetables before cooking in acidulated liquid containing flavourings and herbs. This gives flavour and tenderizes the meat.

Marmite: French word for a covered earthenware soup container in which the soup is both cooked and served.

Medallions: Small rounds of meat, evenly cut. Also small round biscuits. Occasionally used of vegetables if cut in flat round discs.

Mirepoix: The bed of braising vegetables described under **Braise**.

Mortifier: To hang meat, poultry or game.

Moule-à-manqué: French cake tin with sloping sides. The resulting cake has a wider base than top, and is about 5 cm|2 in high.

Napper: To coat, mask or cover, e.g. éclairs nappés with hot chocolate sauce.

Needleshreds Fine, evenly cut shreds of citrus zest (French julienne) generally used as a garnish.

Noisette: Literally 'nut'. Usually means nut-brown, as in beurre noisette, i.e. butter browned over heat to a nut colour. Also hazelnut. Also boneless rack of lamb rolled and tied, cut into neat rounds.

Nouvelle cuisine: Style of cooking that promotes light and delicate dishes often using unusual combinations of very fresh ingredients, attractively arranged.

Oyster: Small piece of meat found on either side of the backbone of a chicken. Said to be the best-flavoured flesh. Also a bivalve mollusc.

Panade or panada: Very thick mixture used as a base for soufflés or fish cakes, etc., usually made from milk, butter and flour.

Paner: To egg and crumb ingredients before frying.

Papillote: A wrapping of paper in which fish or meat is cooked to contain the aroma and flavour. The dish is brought to the table still wrapped up. Foil is sometimes used, but as it does not puff up dramatically, it is less satisfactory.

Parboil: To half-boil or partially soften by boiling.

Parisienne: Potato (sometimes with other ingredients) scooped into small balls with a melon baller and usually fried.

Pass: To strain or push through a sieve.

Pâte: The basic mixture or paste, often used of uncooked pastry, dough, uncooked meringue, etc.

Pâté: A savoury paste of liver, pork, game, etc.

Pâtisserie: Sweet cakes and pastries. Also a cake shop.

Paupiette: Beef (or pork or veal) olive, i.e. a thin layer of meat, spread with a soft farce, rolled up, tied with string and cooked slowly.

Piquer: To insert in meats or poultry a large julienne of fat, bacon, ham, truffle, etc.

Poussin: Baby chicken.

Praline: Almonds cooked in sugar until the mixture caramelizes, cooled and crushed to a powder. Used for flavouring desserts and ice cream.

Prove: To put dough or yeasted mixture to rise before baking.

Purée: Liquidized, sieved or finely mashed fruit or vegetables.

Quenelles: A fine minced fish or meat mixture formed into small portions and poached. Served in a sauce, or as a garnish to other dishes.

Ragoût: A stew.

Réchauffée: A reheated dish made with previously cooked food.

Reduce: To reduce the amount of liquid by rapid boiling, causing evaporation and a consequent strengthening of flavour in the remaining liquid.

Refresh: To hold boiled green vegetables under cold running water, or to immerse them immediately in cold water to prevent their cooking further in their own steam, and set the colour.

Relax or rest: Of pastry: to set aside in a cool place to allow the gluten (which will have been stretched during rolling) to contract. This lessens the danger of shrinking in the oven. Of batters: to set aside to allow the starch cells to swell, giving a lighter result when cooked.

Render: To melt solid meat fat (e.g. beef, pork) slowly in the oven.

Repere: Flour mixed with water or white of egg used to seal pans when cooking a dish slowly, such as lamb ragoût.

Revenir: To fry meat or vegetables quickly in hot fat in order to warm them through.

Roux: A basic liaison or thickening for a sauce or soup. Melted butter to which flour has been added to form a smooth paste.

Rouille: Garlic and oil emulsion used as flavouring.

Salamander: A hot oven or grill used for browning or glazing the tops of cooked dishes, or a hot iron or poker for branding the top with lines or a criss-cross pattern.

Salmis: A game stew sometimes made with cooked game, or partially roasted game.

Salsa: Chunky sauce made from chopped, uncooked vegetables usually including tomatoes and onions.

Sauter: Method of frying in a deep-frying pan or sautoir. The food is continually tossed or shaken so that it browns quickly and evenly.

Sautoir: Deep-frying pan with a lid used for recipes that require fast frying and then slower cooking (with the lid on).

Scald: Of milk: to heat until just below the point of boiling, when some movement can be seen at the edges of the pan but there is no overall bubbling. Of muslin, cloths, etc.: to immerse in clean boiling water, generally to sterilize.

Seal or seize: To brown meat rapidly usually in fat, for flavour and colour.

Season: Of food: to flavour, generally with salt and pepper. Of iron frying pans, griddles, etc.: to prepare new equipment for use by placing over high heat, generally coated with oil and sprinkled with salt. This prevents subsequent rusting and sticking.

Slake: To mix flour, arrowroot, cornflour or custard powder to a thin paste with a small quantity of cold water.

Soft ball: The term used to describe sugar syrup reduced by boiling to sufficient thickness to form soft balls when dropped into cold water and rubbed between finger and thumb.

Supreme: Choice piece of poultry (usually from the breast).

Sweat: To cook gently, usually in butter or oil, but sometimes in the food's own juices, without frying or browning.

Tammy: A fine muslin cloth through which sauces are sometimes forced. After this treatment they look beautifully smooth and shiny. Tammy cloths have generally been replaced by blenders or liquidizers, which give much the same effect.

Tammy sieve: A fine mesh strainer, conical in shape, used to produce the effect described under **Tammy**.

Terrine: Pâté or minced mixture baked or steamed in a loaf tin or earthenware container.

To the thread: Of sugar boiling. Term used to denote degree of thickness achieved when reducing syrup, i.e. the syrup will form threads if tested between a wet finger and thumb. Short thread: about 1 cm|½ in; long thread: 5 cm|2 in or more.

Timbale: A dish that has been cooked in a castle-shaped mould, or a dish served piled high.

Tomalley: Greenish lobster liver. Creamy and delicious.

Tournedos: Fillet steak. Usually refers to a one-portion piece of grilled fillet.

To turn vegetables: To shape carrots or turnips to a small barrel shape. To cut mushrooms into a decorative spiral pattern.

To turn olives: To remove the olive stone with a spiral cutting movement.

Velouté: See under **Sauces**, p. 115.

Vol-au-vent: A large pastry case made from puff pastry with high raised sides and a deep hollow centre into which chicken, fish, etc. is put.

Well: A hollow or dip made in a pile or bowlful of flour, exposing the tabletop or the bottom of the bowl, into which other ingredients are placed prior to mixing.

Zest: The skin of an orange or lemon, used to give flavour. It is very thinly pared without any of the bitter white pith.

Classic Garnishes

Américane: For fish. Slices of lobster tail and slices of truffles.

Anglaise: Braised vegetables such as carrots, turnips and quartered celery hearts (used to garnish boiled salted beef).

Aurore: A flame-coloured sauce obtained by adding fresh tomato purée to a béchamel sauce: used for eggs, vegetables and fish.

Bolognese: A rich sauce made from chicken livers and/or minced beef flavoured with mushrooms and tomatoes. Usually served with pasta.

Bonne femme: To cook in a simple way. Usually, of chicken, sautéed and served with white wine gravy, bacon cubes, button onions and garnished with croquette potatoes. Of soup, a simple purée of vegetables with stock. Of fish, white wine sauce, usually with mushrooms; and served with buttered mashed potatoes.

Boulangère: Potatoes and onions sliced and cooked in the oven in stock. Often served with mutton.

Bouquetière: Groups of very small carrots, turnips, French beans, cauliflower florets, button onions, asparagus tips, etc. Sometimes served with a thin demi-glace or gravy. Usually accompanies beef or lamb entrées.

Bourgeoise: Fried diced bacon, glazed carrots and button onions. Sometimes red wine is used in the sauce. Used for beef and liver dishes.

Bourguignonne: Button mushroom and small onions in a sauce made with red wine (Burgundy). Used for beef and egg dishes.

Bretonne: Haricot beans whole or in a purée. Sometimes a purée of root vegetables. Usually served with a gigot (leg) of lamb.

Chasseur: Sautéed mushrooms added to a sauté of chicken or veal.

Chiffonnade: Chopped lettuce or sorrel cooked in butter to garnish soup.

Choron: Hollandaise sauce with prawns and tomato.

Clamart: Garnish of artichoke hearts filled with buttered petits pois. Sometimes a purée of peas, or simply buttered peas.

Doria: A garnish of cucumber, usually fried in butter.

DuBarry: Denotes the use of cauliflower; potage DuBarry is cauliflower soup. Also, cooked cauliflower florets masked with Mornay sauce and browned under grill, used for meat entrées.

Flamande: Red cabbage and glazed small onions used with pork and beef.

Florentine: Spinach purée, or leaf spinach. Also a 16th-century name for a pie.

Hongroise: Normally implies the addition of paprika.

Indienne: Flavoured with curry powder.

Jardinière: Garnished with fresh vegetables.

Joinville: Slices of truffle, crayfish tails and mushrooms with a lobster sauce, used for fish dishes.

Lyonnaise: Denotes the use of onions as garnish – the onions are frequently sliced and fried.

Meunière: Of fish, lightly dusted with flour, then fried and served with beurre noisette and lemon juice; also frequently (but not classically) chopped fresh parsley.

Milanese: With a tomato sauce, sometimes including shredded ham, tongue and mushrooms. Frequently served with pasta.

Minute: Food quickly cooked, either fried or grilled. Usually applied to a thin entrecôte steak.

Mornay: With a cheese sauce.

Nantua: With a lobster sauce.

Napolitana: Tomato sauce and Parmesan cheese (for pasta). May also mean a three-coloured ice cream.

Niçoise: Name given to many dishes consisting of ingredients common in the South of France, such as tomatoes, olives, garlic, fish, olive oil.

Normande: Garnish of mussels, shrimps, oysters and mushrooms. Or creamy sauce containing cider or Calvados, and sometimes apples.

Parmentier: Denotes the use of potato as a base or garnish.

Paysanne: Literally, peasant. Usually denotes the use of carrots and turnips sliced across in rounds.

Portuguaise: Denotes the use of tomatoes or tomato purée.

Princesse: Denotes the use of asparagus (usually on breast of chicken).

Printanière: Early spring vegetables cooked and used as a garnish, usually in separate groups.

Provençal: Denotes the use of garlic, and sometimes tomatoes and/or olives.

Rossini: With collops of foie gras and truffles tossed in butter, served with a rich meat glaze.

St Germain: Denotes the use of peas, sometimes with pommes Parisienne.

Soubise: Onion purée, frequently mixed with a Béchamel sauce.

Vichy: Garnish of small glazed carrots.

Menu Planning

Once a menu is planned, cooking becomes much easier. It is making the decisions that can be so daunting. Here are a few hints that may help. One of the most important things is to make the menu relevant to the people for whom you are cooking; giving a rugby team grilled aubergines with pesto would be as absurd as giving a ladies' lunch party carbonnade of beef with savoury crumble. The menu should stay in style throughout. The figurative leap from the South of France, with aubergine flan, to the Nursery, with steak and kidney pudding, apart from being badly balanced, would also give your guests an uncomfortable culture shock. One of the many skills of cooking is to think of the people for whom you are cooking and choose a menu that you know they will like. Here are a set of guidelines that can help:

- Never repeat the same basic ingredients in a menu – for example, do not have pastry in two courses or serve smoked salmon in the first and main courses. However, it is perfectly acceptable to have a fish first course, such as a seafood salad, followed by a fish main course.
- Try to devise a menu that is full of colour. This is particularly important when planning a buffet party. For a conventional lunch or dinner party, always think about the appearance of the main course plate.
- Think about the balance of the menu. Do not be so inclined to generosity that you daunt your guests. If there is to be a great number of courses then serve a sorbet halfway through to refresh the palate. If you decide to serve a very rich pudding, always offer a light alternative.
- The texture of a meal is important – it should vary.
- Try not to have too many exciting and exotic tastes in one menu. If you get carried away, sometimes the basic flavour of a delicious ingredient can be drowned. If the menu is to include a highly seasoned dish, don't follow it with a subtle dish – your guests simply won't be able to appreciate it.
- Most people love sauces, so if you serve a sauce be generous.
- We would always recommend serving a salad with any rich meal.

At Leiths there is always much discussion about the order of a meal. In England we conventionally serve the pudding followed by the cheese. In France it is more usual to serve the cheese before the pudding – the theory being that the red wine is finished with the cheese and then the pudding is served with a sweet white wine. We rather like the French approach for both its wine appreciation factor and also for its practicality in that it means that the host or hostess can nip off to the kitchen and do any last-minute cooking necessary for the pudding.

Finally, we would say don't overtax yourself. A dinner party is meant to be fun. Don't try to cook three hot courses and sit down to each successive course feeling slightly more flushed. Prepare as much as you can in advance – work out a timetable of how you are going to cope, and enjoy the meal with your guests.

Planning a Large Party

Cooking for a party can be daunting, but if you are well prepared it can also be terrific fun and it is deeply satisfying to look at perfectly presented food and realize that the occasion is going to be a success.

Forward Planning

1 Decide where you are going to have the party, decide on a convenient date and book the venue.
2 Decide on the type of party – cocktail party, buffet, sit-down dinner, dancing or disco.
3 Work out how many people can come to the party. Allow 3 square metres|10 square feet per person for a sit-down party and 2 square metres|6 square feet for a drinks party.
4 If chairs have to be removed to allow space for dancing, make sure that you hire stackable chairs.
5 Is the kitchen area big enough? Are there good reheating facilities or should you hire extra ovens?
6 Are there adequate toilet facilities or will you need to hire a portacabin?
7 Think about the colour scheme, particularly if you are having a marquee that has to be ordered well in advance.
8 Get invitations printed – and expect one-third refusals.
9 If the party is a commercial event, organize a licence and extend your employer's liability insurance.
10 If the party is for charity, set up a committee to organize the tombola, programme advertising, and most importantly the sale of tickets.

Medium-Term Planning

1 Plan the menu (see page 18).
2 Work out the hire list. Once you know the menu it is simple to work out how many knives, forks, plates, coffee cups and glasses you will need and how many chairs and tables to hire, but don't forget any of the following:
4 or 5 extra place settings
serving dishes and cloths
butter dishes
serving trays for food and glasses
serving spoons and forks
1½ glasses per head for a cocktail party
menu holders (if required)

cake stand (for a wedding)
coffee urns for a big party
table mats
knife and board for lemons
ice buckets
water jugs
corkscrews
coffee pots, milk jugs, sugar bowls, teaspoons
punch bowl and ladle
tablecloth and napkins
cocktail shakers
ashtrays, plenty, all the same size
dustbins in which to chill wine
salt and pepper pots (check that they are full)
bread baskets
plate stackers (for piling up plates of ready plated food)
fruit baskets
coat rail and hangers
candlesticks
drugget (cloth for the floor behind the bar)
stand for the seating plan
extra ovens or hot cupboards

Establish that the hired linen is returned dirty and agree a delivery time.

3 Hire a van to deliver food if necessary – start saving boxes to deliver food in.

4 Plan the wine to go with the menu (see pages 90–5). Allow a bottle per head and hope to have some left over. Order on sale or return and only chill wine as you need it so that the labels don't drop off. Many wine firms will supply ready-chilled wine and glasses.

5 Book a master of ceremonies if necessary.

6 Book staff if necessary. The general rule is that for silver service, one waitress can cope with 8 people, and for butler service one waitress can look after 10 people. At a buffet, one waitress can look after 25 people. One barman can cope with 30 people if it is a full bar and with 50 people for a simple bar. Decide whether you need to hire kitchen staff, kitchen porters, cloakroom ladies, security staff or any other help. Decide on the kind of staff you want.

7 Think about parking arrangements. Do you need to give car registration numbers to security? Find out from what time you can have access and from what time you can lay the tables. Check what time you need to leave the building and the latest time you can have the hired equipment collected in the morning. Check how the equipment can be delivered to the right place – is there a goods lift, etc?

8 Hire and order flower arrangements and table decorations as necessary.

9 Order the band, discotheque, casino, etc. Discuss electrical requirements.

10 Go to the party venue and make a plan of action so that you can establish if there are any gaps in your forward-planning scheme.

A Week Before the Party

1 Order the food (see catering quantities pages 25–9) to arrive 2 days before the party. Don't forget to order sandwiches for the staff.
2 Order the ice. Champagne is generally served colder than other wine. Make sure that the containers for ice are delivered before the ice arrives.
3 Order other drinks, such as orange juice, mineral water and whisky.
4 Talk over the plan of the party with a friend to make sure there are no gaps.

A Day Before the Party

1 Prepare as much of the food as you can. Separate into small batches to cool as quickly as possible and chill well. The easiest way to cook in large quantities is to do one process at a time. If making sandwiches make all the fillings, soften all the butter, butter all the bread and then put the sandwiches together.
2 Get all the equipment you need to take, such as:
matches
loo paper, cloakroom soap and towels, flowers for loos
clingfilm
absorbent kitchen paper
kitchen foil
dustbin liners (lots)
knives, whisks, fish slices, etc.
carving knife and fork
electric carving knife
oven gloves
tea towels
washing-up liquid
mop and bucket
broom and dustpan and brush
J-cloths
plenty of boxes for taking home dirty equipment
first-aid box
pins
screwdriver
needles and cotton
rubber gloves
chopping boards
scissors
lemons
petty cash (for tipping people)
tea bags, milk, sugar for staff
cold drinks for staff

On the Day of the Party

1 Get someone to the venue reasonably early to check off the deliveries, sign slips, persuade people to take equipment to the right place and generally organize the setting-up and laying of tables, the seating plan, the flowers, the microphone, the lighting, the table decorations, tidying the cloakroom and warding off potential problems.

2 Meanwhile, finish off all the cooking, pack up the food, undecorated, and deliver it with all the equipment and garnishes.

3 Set up an efficient working kitchen, work tidily and stick to a time plan.

4 Serve the food by the agreed method and enjoy the party.

Planning a Buffet Party

If you are going to be cooking for a buffet party, here are a few hints that may be helpful when planning your menu and arranging your food.

- The larger the choice of dishes, the more generous you have to be, and therefore if you are cooking for a small number the increased costs can be significant.
- Think about ease of both serving and eating – if there are not many places for guests to sit down it should be a fork buffet.
- Think about what the food will look like once people have started to fill their plates. We decorate the underplates with fresh flowers or bunches of herbs and leave the dishes themselves very simply garnished. Do not put too many flowers on the table – let the food speak for itself.
- Have more than one service point with only about 16 sets of knives, forks and plates in any one pile – the crockery must not dominate the table. If you are cooking for 100 people, you will need at least 4 service points. Think carefully about the appearance of the food – it should be a good mixture of colours.
- Try to make the table look attractive by using height. Place the food on cake stands and put boxes under the tablecloths.
- Don't decorate the front of the tablecloth with garlands of flowers – they'll get crushed and look untidy.
- Always think about what the buffet will look like at the end of the meal.
- If possible change the tablecloth in between courses – if not, then certainly after coffee.
- Use linen napkins to hide spills.
- Never underestimate the number of helpers you'll need – people helping themselves often have eyes bigger than their stomachs. For 100 people you will need 4 people serving the food.
- Make sure that there is easy access to all service points and that there is a choice of all the dishes beside each pile of plates.
- It is possible to buy (from disposable products suppliers) little plastic holders so that the wine glasses can be attached to plates.
- Don't use linen napkins – they are too cumbersome at a buffet.
- Precut and slice most of the food but for the sake of appearance leave some whole.

- Never put out all the food – keep some back so that the last shall be first. Always hide the vegetarian dishes – you could run out and genuine vegetarians would not be able to have any.
- Try to avoid individual portions as they dictate how many people can have how much of a certain dish – you may well calculate tastes incorrectly.
- If people have to queue you'll find that only about two-thirds of the guests will come back for puddings, and only about half will come back again for coffee. Obviously you have to cater for full take-up but don't be over-generous.

Catering Quantities

Few people accurately weigh or measure quantities as a control-conscious chef must do, but when catering for large numbers it is useful to know how much food to allow per person. As a general rule, the more people you are catering for the less food per head you need to provide, e.g. 225 g | 8 oz stewing beef per head is essential for 4 people, but 170 g | 6 oz per head would feed 60 people.

Soup

Allow 290 ml | ½ pint soup per head, depending on the size of the bowl.

Poultry

Chicken and Turkey: Allow 340 g | 12oz per person, weighed when plucked and drawn. An average chicken serves 4 people on the bone and 6 people off the bone.

Duck: A 2.7 kg | 6 lb bird will feed 3–4 people; a 1.8 kg | 4 lb bird will feed 2 people. 1 duck makes enough pâté for 6 people.

Goose: Allow 3.6 kg | 8 lb for 4 people; 6.9 kg | 15 lb for 8 people.

Game

Pheasant: Allow 1 bird for 2 people (roast); 1 bird for 3 people (casseroled).

Pigeon: Allow 1 bird per person.

Grouse: Allow 1 young grouse per person (roast); 2 birds for 3 people (casseroled).

Quail: Allow 2 small birds per person or 1 large boned stuffed bird served on a croûton.

Partridge: Allow 1 bird per person.

Venison: Allow 170 g | 6 oz lean meat per person; 1.8 kg | 4 lb cut of haunch weighed on the bone for 8–9 people.

Steaks: Allow 170 g | 6 oz per person.

Lamb or Mutton

Casseroled: 225 g | 8 oz per person (boneless, with fat trimmed away).

Roast leg: 1.35 kg | 3 lb for 3–4 people; 1.8 kg | 4 lb for 4–5 people; 2.7 kg | 6 lb for 7–8 people.

Roast shoulder: 1.8 kg | 4 lb shoulder for 5–6 people; 2.7 kg | 6 lb shoulder for 7–8 people.

Grilled best end cutlets: 3–4 per person.

Grilled loin chops: 2–3 per person.

Beef

Stewed: 225 g | 8 oz boneless trimmed meat per person.

Roast (off the bone): If serving men only, 225 g | 8 oz per person; if serving men and women, 200 g | 7 oz per person.

Roast (on the bone): 340 g | 12 oz per person.

Roast whole fillet: 1.8 kg | 4 lb piece for 8–10 people.

Grilled steaks: 170–225 g | 6–8 oz per person depending on appetite.

Pork

Casseroled: 170 g | 6 oz per person.

Roast leg or loin (off the bone): 200 g | 7 oz per person.

Roast leg or loin (on the bone): 340 g | 12 oz per person.

Fillet: 340 g | 12 oz will feed 2–3 people.

Grilled: 1 × 170 g | 6 oz chop or cutlet per person.

Veal

Stews or pies: 225 g | 8 oz pie veal per person.

Fried: 1 × 170 g | 6 oz escalope per person.

Minced Meat
170 g | 6 oz per person for shepherd's pie, hamburgers, etc.
110 g | 4 oz per person for steak tartare.
85 g | 3 oz per person for lasagne, cannelloni, etc.
110 g | 4 oz per person for moussaka.
110 g | 4 oz per person for spaghetti.

Fish

Whole large fish: (e.g. sea bass, salmon, whole haddock), weighed uncleaned, with head on: 340–450 g | 12 oz–1 lb per person.

Cutlets and steaks: 170 g | 6 oz per person.

Fillets: (e.g. sole, lemon sole, plaice): 3 small fillets per person (total weight about 170 g│6 oz).

Whole small fish: (e.g. trout, slip soles, small plaice, small mackerel, herring) 225–340 g│8–12 oz weighed with heads for main course; 170 g│6 oz for first course.

Fish off the bone: (in fish pie, with sauce, etc.) 170 g│6 oz per person.

Shellfish

Prawns: 55–85 g│2–3 oz per person as a first course; 140 g│5 oz per person as a main course.

Mixed shellfish: 55–85 g│2–3 oz per person as a first course; 140 g│5 oz per person as a main course.

Vegetables

Weighed before preparation and cooking, and assuming 3 vegetables, including potatoes, served with a main course: 110 g│4 oz per person, except (per person):

French beans: 55 g│2 oz.

Peas: 55 g│2 oz.

Spinach: 340 g│12 oz.

Potatoes: 3 small (roast); 170 g│6 oz (mashed); 10–15 (Parisienne); 5 (château); 1 large or 2 small (baked); 110 g│4 oz (new).

Rice

Plain, boiled or fried: 55 g│2 oz (weighed before cooking) or 1 breakfast cup (measured after cooking).

In risotto or pilaf: 30 g│1 oz per person (weighed before cooking) for first course; 55 g│2 oz per person for main course.

NOTE: As a general rule men eat more potatoes and less 'greens' than women!

Salads

Obviously, the more salads served, the less guests will eat of any one salad. Allow 1 large portion of salad, in total, per head – e.g. if only one salad is served make sure there is enough for 1 helping each. Conversely if 100 guests are to choose from 5 different salads, allow a total of 150 portions – i.e. 30 portions of each salad.

Tomato salad: 450 g│1 lb tomatoes (average 6 tomatoes), sliced, serves 4 people.

Coleslaw: 1 small cabbage, finely shredded, serves 10–12 people.

Grated carrot salad: 450 g|1 lb carrots, grated, serves 6 people.

Potato salad: 450 g|1 lb potatoes (weighed before cooking) serves 5 people.

Green salad: Allow a loose handful of leaves for each person (i.e. a large Cos lettuce will serve 8, a large Webb's will serve 10, a Dutch hothouse 'butterhead' will serve 4).

Sandwiches

2 slices of bread make 1 round of sandwiches.

Cucumber: 1 cucumber makes 15 rounds.

Egg: 1 hardboiled egg makes 1 round.

Ham: Allow 20 g|3/4 oz for each round.

Mustard and cress: For egg and cress sandwiches, 1 punnet makes 20 rounds.

Tomatoes: 450 g|1 lb makes 9 rounds.

Smoked salmon: Allow 20 g|3/4 oz for each round.

Cocktail Parties

Allow 10 cocktail canapés per head.
Allow 14 cocktail canapés per head if served at lunchtime when guests are unlikely to go on to a meal.
Allow 4–5 canapés with pre-lunch or pre-dinner drinks.
Allow 12 cocktail canapés, plus 4 miniature sweet cakes or pastries per head for a lunchtime wedding reception.

Puddings

Cooking apples: Allow 225 g|8 oz per head for puddings.

Fruit salad: Allow 8 oranges, 2 apples, 2 bananas and 450 g|1 lb grapes for 8 people.

Mousses: Allow 290 ml|1/2 pint double cream inside and 290 ml|1/2 pint to decorate a mousse for 8 people.

Strawberries: Allow 110 g|4 oz per head.

Miscellaneous

Brown bread and butter: 1 1/2 slices (3 triangular pieces) per person.

French bread: 1 large loaf for 8 people; 1 small loaf for 4 people.

Cheese: After a meal, if serving one blue-veined, one hard and one soft cheese: 85 g|3 oz per person for up to 8 people; 55 g|2 oz per person for over 20 people.

At a wine and cheese party: 110 g|4 oz per person for up to 8 people; 85 g|3 oz per person for up to 20 people; 55 g|2 oz per person for over 20 people. Inevitably, if catering for small numbers, there will be cheese left over but this is unavoidable if the host is not to look mean.

Biscuits: 3 each for up to 10 people; 2 each for up to 30 people; 1 each for over 30 people.

Butter: 30 g|1 oz per person if bread is served with the meal; 45 g|1½ oz per person if cheese is served as well.

Cream: 1 tablespoon per person for coffee; 3 tablespoons per person for pudding or dessert.

Milk: 570 ml|1 pint for 18–20 cups of tea.

Sliced bread: A large loaf, thinly sliced, generally makes 16–18 slices.

Butter: 30 g|1 oz soft butter will cover 8 large bread slices.

Sausages: 450 g|1 lb is the equivalent of 32 cocktail sausages; 16 chipolata sausages; 8 pork sausages.

Bouchées: 675 g|1½ lb packet of puff pastry makes 60 bouchées.

Chicken livers: 450 g|1 lb chicken livers will be enough for 60 bacon and chicken liver rolls.

Dates: 50 fresh dates weigh about 450 g|1 lb.

Prunes: A prune (with stone) weighs about 10 g|⅓ oz.

Mushrooms: A button mushroom weighs about 7 g|¼ oz.

Bacon: A good sized rasher weighs about 30 g|1 oz.

Button onions: A button onion weighs about 15 g|½ oz.

Choux pastry: 6-egg choux paste makes 150 baby éclairs. They will need 570 ml|1 pint cream for filling and 225 g|8 oz chocolate for coating.

Shortcrust pastry: 900 g|2 lb pastry will line 150 canapé size tartlet tins. Calculate the amount of pastry required to line a flan ring by subtracting 2 from the diameter measurement in inches. The resulting number gives the amount of flour required in ounces.

Food Presentation

If food looks delicious, people are predisposed to find that it tastes delicious. If you have spent a long time cooking, it is a shame just to dump the food on a plate. At Leiths School we have gradually developed a set of rules which can be used as guidelines when presenting food. Fashion may dictate the method – be it nouvelle cuisine or chunky bistro food – but the guidelines are the same.

- **Keep it simple:** Over-decorated food often looks messed about – no longer appetizing, but like an uncertain work of art. The more cluttered the plate, the less attractive it inevitably becomes.
- **Keep it fresh:** Nothing looks more off-putting than tired food. Sprigs of herbs used for garnish should always be absolutely fresh. Pot herbs now widely available in super-markets make this easy to ensure. Salad wilts when dressed in advance; sautéed potatoes become dull and dry when kept warm for hours, and whipped cream goes buttery in a warm room, so don't risk it.
- **Keep it relevant:** A sprig of fresh watercress complements lamb cutlets nicely. The texture, taste and colour all do something for the lamb. But scratchy sprigs of parsley, though they might provide the colour, are unpleasant to eat. Gherkins cut into fans do nothing for salads, tomato slices do not improve the look of a platter of sandwiches – they rather serve to confuse and distract the eye. It is better by far to dish up a plate of chicken mayonnaise with a couple of suitable salads to provide the colour and contrast needed, than to decorate it with undressed tomato waterlilies or inedible baskets made out of lemon skins and filled with frozen sweetcorn.
- **Centre height:** Dishes served on platters, such as chicken sauté, meringues, profiteroles or even a bean salad, are best given 'centre height' – arranged so the mound of food is higher in the middle with sides sloping down. Coat carefully and evenly with the sauce, if any. Do not overload serving platters with food, which makes dishing up difficult. Once breached, an over-large pile of food looks unattractive.
- **Contrasting rows:** Biscuits, petits fours, little cakes and cocktail canapés all look good if arranged in rows, each row consisting of one variety, rather than dotted about. Pay attention to contrasting colour, taking care, say, not to put 2 rows of chocolate biscuits side by side, or 2 rows of white sandwiches.
- **Diagonal lines:** Diamond shapes and diagonal lines are easier to achieve than straight ones. The eye is more conscious of unevenness in verticals, horizontals and rectangles.
- **Not too many colours:** As with any design, it is easier to get a pleasing effect if the colours are controlled – say, just green and white, or just pink and green, or chocolate and coffee colours or even 2 shades of one colour. Coffee icing and hazelnuts give a cake an elegant look. Adding multi-coloured icings to a cake, or every available garnish to a salad, tends

to look garish. There are exceptions of course: a colourful salad Niçoise can be as pleasing to the eye as a dish of candy-coated chocolate drops.

- **Contrasting the simple and the elaborate:** If the dish or bowl is elaborately decorated, contrasting simple food tends to show it off better. A Victorian fruit epergne with ornate stem and silver carving will look stunning filled with fresh strawberries. Conversely, a plain white plate sets off attractive food to perfection.

- **Uneven numbers:** As a rule, uneven numbers of, say, rosettes of cream on a cake, baked apples in a long dish, or portions of meat on a platter look better than even numbers. This is especially true of small numbers. Five and three invariably look better than four, but there is little difference in effect between 11 and 12.

- **A generous look:** Tiny piped cream stars, or sparsely dotted nuts, or mean-looking chocolate curls on a cake look amateurish and stingy.

- **Avoid clumsiness:** On the other hand, the temptation to cram the last spoonful of rice into the bowl, or squeeze the last slice of pâté on to the dish leads to a clumsy look, and can be daunting to the diner.

- **Overlapping:** Chops, steaks, sliced meats, even rashers of bacon, look best evenly overlapping. This way, more of them can be fitted comfortably on the serving dish than if placed side by side.

- **Best side uppermost:** Usually the side of a steak or a cutlet that is fried first looks the best, and should be placed uppermost. Bones are generally unsightly and, if they cannot be clipped off or removed, they should be tucked out of the way.

- **Individual plating:** Until the advent of nouvelle cuisine in the 1970s it was considered a caterer's short-cut trick to plate dishes individually. Suddenly it became the only way to present food. When plating individually the same rules apply to presentation. Keep it simple and keep it relevant. We add two extra caveats. First, think of the rim of the plate as a picture frame: do not put any food on the 'frame'. Second, stick to your original idea. If a dish has been plated up and then changed, it will inevitably look messy.

Serving Style

How much formal convention is followed at an informal family table or at a simple supper with friends depends of course on the character and personal style of the host or hosts. But it is useful to know how things ought to be done, so that, at an elegant dinner party or if cooking for someone else, the cook at least won't make any blunders.

Laying the Table

As a rule, cutlery is laid so that the diner works from the outside in – his first-course knife will be furthest from the plate, and on the right, because he is to pick it up with his right hand. His first-course fork will be on his left, and furthest from his plate. Similarly, if the first course is soup, the soup spoon will be on the right (because most people are right-handed), at the extreme outside of the cutlery collection.

If a knife-and-fork first course is followed by soup, the soup spoon will be in second place, and so on, working inwards to dessert spoon and fork, or cheese knife. Dessert or pudding cutlery is sometimes put across the top of the diner's place, the spoon above or beyond the fork and the handles pointing towards the hand that will pick them up – i.e. spoon handle towards the right hand, fork handle towards left hand.

Logic prevails in the same way with glasses, which are set out just beyond the knife tip, in a diagonal row, with the first one closest to the knife tip and the last one furthest away. The bread plate is placed on the diner's left, to the left of the cutlery. Napkins either go on this plate, or in the middle of the diner's place if the first course is not yet on the table. Individual ashtrays, fingerbowls, salt cellars are placed within comfortable reach.

The commonest mistakes made in laying tables are to fail to leave enough space between the banks of cutlery for the dinner plate to fit comfortably (leaving the guest foraging under his plate for a knife or fork), to line up the tips of the cutlery instead of the bases, which gives an untidy unprofessional look, and to arrange flowers or candles in such a way that diners cannot see each other across the table. Low flowers are best, and candles should be checked to make sure they do not confuse sight lines. Nothing is so irritating as having to peer round an obstruction to carry on a conversation.

The Etiquette of Serving

At a formal dinner convention holds that women are served before men, starting with the most important female guest and ending with the hostess. Usually the top female guest will be seated on the right of the host. The men are then served, the most important male guest (who will be seated at the right of the hostess) being served first, then the others and, lastly, the host. Once everyone is served the hostess starts to eat which is a signal for everyone else to begin.

How Much to Serve

A daunting plateful tends to take away the appetite, so do not over-help guests to food. Take trouble to arrange things neatly and attractively on the plate. Place the first spoonful (say the meat) to one side, not in the middle, then work round with vegetables and garnishes, keeping them separate. Slops and drips look bad, so take time when spooning a sauce to let any excess run off the spoon before moving away from the main dish, and make sure the serving dish and diner's plate are as close together as possible.

If waiting formally, by the diner's side, hold the platter with one hand almost over his plate and use a spoon and fork in the other hand to serve him. This is called 'silver service'. If the diner is helping himself, hold the platter very low close to the table and close to his plate, to the side of it, so he can manage the awkward business of turning and wielding spoon and fork. This is called 'butler service'. With silver service the server serves food to the diners' left. With butler service diners are offered food to their right. Plates are always cleared from the diners' right. But in awkward or crowded corners it is better to forget convention and do whatever is least likely to disturb conversation.

Serving Wine

The wine should be served at the same time as the food, or even before, but not too long afterwards – waiting is a strain and drinking is permitted straight away even if eating is not. The host tastes the wine – if he has not already done so – then everyone is served, ladies then men.

Good waiters, or hosts, do not constantly top up glasses, but do so positively when they are down to about a third. Glasses should not be filled more than two thirds full – the idea is to leave room for the drinker to be able to get his nose into the glass to smell it without getting the tip wet! It also means he can swill the wine about, which encourages the release of its bouquet.

Clearing the Table

This should happen as unobtrusively as possible. Nothing should be touched until everyone has finished his food and indicated the fact by putting knife and fork firmly together. Then the plates are removed, but not stacked one on top of other or scraped within sight of the diners. Such unattractive operations should be performed out of sight. When the plates are cleared, everything connected with the just-removed course is cleared too – salt and pepper, mustard, sauces, salad dishes and, if the savoury courses are now over, bread plates and bread and butter. Nothing connected with the pudding should go on the table before everything pertaining to the previous course is off it. The same goes for coffee – it should not appear, nor should the bitter mints or petits fours, until the pudding has vanished, with its sauce jugs, cream, etc.

Healthy Eating

Healthy recipes form an integral part of this book, in that you will find some that are low in saturated fat, sugar and salt. However this is not a health book as it is designed to cover all aspects of cooking.

Nutritionists seem to have changed their advice dramatically over the past few years and this can be very confusing. But in fact they are responding to the considerable advance in knowledge made recently as well as to changing social conditioning. In the earlier part of the twentieth century, the national diet was high in inexpensive carbohydrate foods like bread and potatoes and often dangerously low in the more costly protein foods like meat. The more affluent post-war years have seen a great change in the way the nation eats, however, and now the danger is seen to be not so much in an excess of protein as in too much saturated fat in the diet. Saturated fat comes from high-protein foods like meat and cheese as well as from more obvious sources like butter and cream. Moreover, we no longer eat enough carbohydrate to provide adequate dietary fibre.

We are told now to reduce our intake of saturated fat, but we are also sometimes told that a small increase in polyunsaturated fat may be a good thing. What is the difference between these two types of fat? It is a matter of the chemical structure of the fatty acids that make them up. Fatty acids are long chains of carbon atoms joined by a chemical bond, which may be either double or single. A fatty acid with no double bonds is called saturated; where there is only one double bond it is known as monounsaturated, and where there are two or more, polyunsaturated. Most fats are made up of a mixture of many fatty acids. For example, the fat in butter is 63 per cent saturated, 3 per cent polyunsaturated and 34 per cent monounsaturated fatty acids. So when you hear that butter is a saturated fat, this really means that it is higher in saturated fat than in any other kind. Unsaturated bonds can be converted back into single (saturated) bonds by a process called hydrogenation; a food that undergoes this process, therefore, will become higher in saturated fats. Hydrogenation is used in some food-refining processes to make liquid fats solidify.

Why are saturated fats considered to be bad for us? Medical research suggests that a high level of saturated fat in the blood blocks and damages the arteries and impedes blood circulation. This increases the risk of cardiovascular disease, which is one of the major killers in this country. Polyunsaturated fat makes the blood less 'sticky' and so prevents it from attaching itself to arterial walls and causing blockages. Thus it has a beneficial effect on health, unless you eat so much of it that your weight starts to become a health problem. Monounsaturated fat has no effect on the blood.

Saturated fat is also thought to be a factor in the level of cholesterol in the blood. Cholesterol is a common source of confusion. It is a substance associated with fat and can originate in two ways.

Blood (serum) cholesterol is manufactured by the human liver and is an essential part of all healthy cells. The liver makes enough cholesterol for our needs, and in some people a high level of saturated fat in the diet makes the liver produce more cholesterol than is needed by the body.

Dietary cholesterol is cholesterol found in foods. Animal foods that are high in saturated fat are also high in cholesterol; some low-fat foods contain high levels as well. You should be concerned about eating too much fat overall, but not about eating prawns, brains, liver and kidney which, although high in cholesterol, are low in other fats. The important point is still to reduce the proportion of saturated fats in your diet.

All fat is fattening, that is, high in calories: 1 gram of fat releases about 9 calories, while 1 gram of carbohydrate releases only about 4. Calories are a unit of heat energy, but if the food you eat releases more calories than you need, your body will store the extra energy as body fat. If you are trying to lose weight, cutting fats out of your diet is therefore the best way. You would find it hard, and it would be foolish, to cut them out entirely, however, as some intake of fat is essential to several metabolic processes.

It is recommended that no more than 30–35 per cent of daily calories should come from fats of any sort, even if you are not trying to lose weight. Fat in the diet comes from many sources, from the obvious fatty foods such as butter, cream and cheese to hidden sources such as many ready-prepared and processed foods. Meat products, such as sausages, pork pies and so on, are generally high in fat, and especially high in saturates. Some cuts of meat are very fatty and, again, the fat is mostly saturated. The leanest meats are chicken – especially when skinned – turkey, rabbit, game, liver and kidney. Many fish, such as tuna, salmon, herrings and mackerel, are oily, but the fat is mainly monounsaturated and polyunsaturated. If you buy fish canned in oil, however, drain away the oil as it may be high in saturated fat unless, for example, soya oil is used. White fish and shellfish are low in fat.

Nutritionists also advise us to reduce the amount of sugar we eat. Too much sugar has no direct link with heart disease, but sugar is quite fattening and obesity is a major cause of heart disease. Sugar is also bad for your teeth. The calories released by sugar are 'empty', that is, they provide no nutritional advantages.

The basic message is to cut down on fat – saturated fat in particular – sugar, salt and processed foods. And to increase your intake of fresh fruit, vegetables and cereals if you want to eat healthily.

At home, avoid using saturated fats in cooking. This means do not use butter, lard, cream, dripping, coconut oil, blended cooking fat, mixed blended vegetable oil, solid vegetable fat, or margarines unless they are labelled 'high in polyunsaturated fat'. For general cooking purposes use sunflower or grapeseed oil as they are both high in polyunsaturated fat. Corn oil is also a good choice but it has a strong flavour, and safflower is high in polyunsaturated fat but very expensive. For special occasions, buy walnut oil, as it is fairly high in polyunsaturated fat and tastes delicious, as does extra virgin olive and hazelnut oil, which is high in monounsaturated fatty acids. Extra virgin olive oil, which is high in monounsaturated fatty acids can also be used. Use a polyunsaturated margarine instead of butter, but most low-fat spreads are not suitable for cooking, because they tend to separate on contact with heat.

When cooking conventionally, cream is often an important part of a recipe. Cream is high in saturated fat, so use low-fat natural yoghurt, buttermilk, low-fat soft cheese (quark), tofu, fromage frais and cottage cheese in place of cream.

Greek yoghurt is higher in fat than ordinary natural yoghurt but makes a very good cream substitute for special occasions when you would normally serve cream as an accompaniment.

Unfortunately none of these substitutes is capable of remaining stable if boiled, so they must be added at the last minute. Cottage cheese must be whizzed or sieved before use and the others should be slaked. Greek yoghurt can be momentarily boiled.

Skimmed or semi-skimmed milk can easily be substituted for full-fat milk and after a couple of weeks you will not notice the difference. Nuts are a high-fat food although their fat is mainly monounsaturated and polyunsaturated. There are two exceptions: coconut contains saturated fat and chestnuts are very low in fat.

Of all the foods high in saturated fats, cheese is the one many people find hardest to give up. On the whole try to eat low-fat cheese such as quark or cottage cheese, but for a treat have Brie and, for a real treat, farmhouse Cheddar. Looking at labels on cheese can be confusing, as in other parts of Europe the fat content is measured at a different stage in the manufacturing process. They measure the amount of fat in the 'dry matter', that is, the fat content of the cheese minus water. Many French cheeses, like Brie, have a high water content. Here in Britain the amount of fat given per 100 g is the amount of fat you actually eat. When you see a Brie labelled in the French way as containing 45 per cent fat, it is only about 23 per cent fat by British standards: that is, the same as the rather bland Edam that dieters have always been told to eat.

A change to healthy eating can involve imitating conventional recipes in a healthier way, making shepherd's pie with more vegetables and less mince, for example. But there are some dishes that you cannot imitate. What is the point of a yoghurt-based crème brûlée? Or a carob, polyunsaturated oil, wholemeal flour and raw sugar chocolate cake? Either you allow yourself the occasional treat, or you try to find equally sophisticated puddings that are low in fat. You want, after all, to keep to your new way of eating. Learning to eat healthily takes time and patience: it is much better to go slowly and stick to it than be too dramatic and too restrictive and then give it up. Begin by allowing yourself occasional treats: after 6 months you will not want them any more! The gentle and almost subversive route to health is a smooth path.

Fat Contents of Various Foods

Bacon

	Fat (g/100 g)
Collar joint, boiled, lean and fat	27.0
Collar joint, boiled, lean only	9.7
Gammon, boiled or grilled, lean and fat	18.9
Gammon, boiled or grilled, lean only	5.5
Rashers, grilled, lean only	18.9
Rashers, back, lean and fat	33.8
Rashers, streaky, lean and fat	36.0
Rashers, middle, lean and fat	35.1

Beef

Brisket, boiled, lean and fat	23.9
Forerib, roast, lean and fat	28.8
Forerib, roast, lean only	12.6
Rump steak, grilled, lean and fat	12.1
Rump steak, grilled, lean only	6.0
Stewing steak, lean and fat	11.0

Lamb

Breast, roast, lean and fat		37.1
Breast, roast, lean only		16.6
Chops, grilled, lean and fat	without bone	29.0
Chops, grilled, lean only		12.3
Leg, roast, lean and fat		17.9
Leg, roast, lean only		8.1

Pork

Chops, grilled, lean and fat	without bone	24.2
Chops, grilled, lean only		10.7
Leg, roast, lean and fat		19.8
Leg, roast, lean only		6.9

Veal

Cutlets, grilled	5.0
Fillet, roast	11.5

Chicken

Roast, meat and skin	14.0
Roast, meat only	5.5

Grouse

Roast	3–5

Partridge

Roast	4–7

Pheasant

Roast	5–10

Pigeon

	Fat (g/100 g)
Roast	5–13

Turkey

Roast, meat and skin	6.5
Roast, meat only	2.7

Rabbit, Hare

Stewed	3–7

Offal

Kidneys	5–7
Liver, grilled, etc.	5

Cooking Fat

	Total fat content (g/100 g)
Butter	82.0
Margarine	82.0
Gold	40.7
Cream, single	21.2
Cream, soured	18.0
Cream, whipping	35.0
Cream, double	48.2

Cheese

Camembert, Brie, etc.	23.2
Cheddar, Cheshire, Gruyère, Emmental, etc.	33.5
Danish Blue, Roquefort, etc.	29.2
Edam, Gouda, St Paulin, etc.	22.9
Parmesan	29.7
Stilton	40.0
Cream cheese	47.4
Low-fat cottage cheese (see carton)	0–4
Medium-fat curd cheese	25
Medium-fat Mozzarella, etc.	25

Fish

Cod, steamed	5.0
Herring, grilled	13.0
Kipper, baked	6.2
Mackerel, grilled	6.2
Salmon, steamed	13.0
Sardines, canned (drained)	13.0
Trout, steamed	3.0
Tuna, canned (includes oil)	22.0
Tuna, canned (drained, estimated value)	8.0

Nutrition

by Karen Sorensen, Guy's and St Thomas' Hospital Trust

Food plays a vital role in all our lives. At its most basic, it provides the nutrients essential to existence and general health. A regular intake of food is required by the body to work, grow and repair itself.

Food also influences physical and mental well-being, and plays an important part in social activities. It is used to celebrate and commiserate, to reward and to give pleasure, and as a sign of affection and caring.

A balanced variety of foods needs to be eaten for the body to function most efficiently, as well as fulfilling these wider functions. All foods are made up of the same main constituents: protein, fat, carbohydrate, vitamins and minerals, in differing amounts. All these elements, known as nutrients, must be included in the diet, although specific requirements for each nutrient vary according to individual needs, circumstances and activity.

Energy Requirements

Normal Requirements

Energy provides fuel for the body, and is often referred to by one of its measurements – calories.

The energy requirement for each individual is the amount of energy taken in from food that balances the amount of energy used by the body to maintain its normal processes. This amount differs from person to person, and is affected by a variety of factors, such as age, gender and level of physical activity. Almost three-quarters of the energy utilized by the body is used in basic involuntary activities such as breathing, keeping the heart beating and maintaining body temperature. This is often known as the Basal Metabolic rate or BMR. Additional energy is used during processes such as digestion of food and physical activity. It is the latter which can affect weight loss or weight gain.

Periods of intense growth, such as childhood, adolescence and pregnancy, significantly increase energy needs. As an example, a one-year-old child needs about 1000 calories per day, an adolescent boy about 2700 calories per day, and an adult male about 2500 calories per day. Women have slightly lower requirements on average than men.

Fat and Carbohydrate as Energy Sources

The main energy sources in the diet are fat and carbohydrate. Protein can be used as an energy source, but this is a complex process, and protein is needed first by the body for its growth and repair functions.

Carbohydrate foods such as bread, potatoes, rice, pasta and cereals provide the majority of energy in the British diet, along with spreading fats and fat in food. A healthy diet contains a higher proportion of energy from starchy carbohydrate foods, especially those high in fibre. Weight for weight, fat has more than twice the energy of carbohydrate or protein. This makes it an excellent energy source where requirements are particularly high, but it needs to be taken in moderation in a normal diet.

Protein

Structure and Function

Protein foods are made up of amino acids, which are small organic compounds. When food containing protein is digested, it is broken down into its constituent amino acids. Amino acids are usually classified into those which the body can synthesize or make itself and are therefore non essential, and those which have to be obtained from the diet and are known as essential amino acids. There are nine essential amino acids.

The body requires a variety of protein foods to supply its needs. Some of these foods (generally from animal sources) contain all the essential amino acids, and are known as high biological value (HBV) protein. Foods which have small amounts of some essential amino acids are known as low biological value protein (LBV), and these are usually proteins from vegetable sources. However, a combination of plant protein foods, such as beans and bread, can provide a meal which in total has a high biological value. This principle is essential in planning a well-balanced vegetarian or vegan diet.

Protein is essential to life. The body needs protein to provide for repair and growth of tissues, and to provide vital supplies of nitrogen and other chemicals.

Normal Requirements

Individual requirements for protein vary from person to person, although requirements are usually expressed as figures for population groups.[1] Protein in the body is constantly being broken down and resynthesized, especially during periods of growth, such as childhood, adolescence and pregnancy.

Unlike fat and carbohydrate, protein in excess of immediate requirements cannot be stored by the body. Any protein foods not used as a protein source will be converted to provide a further energy source for the body. Protein foods need to be eaten daily to fulfil the body's requirements for protein.

The current Dietary Reference Values for Protein[2] suggest protein intakes of 45 g (women) and 55.5 g (men) of protein per day for an adult between 19 and 50. Older adults and pregnant and lactating women have slightly higher requirements. There are separate figures for children, who have proportionally higher needs, because of their increased rate of growth.

The average protein intake in the UK is significantly higher than this. A person consuming a modest 570 ml|1 pint of milk, 55 g|2 oz of cheese at lunch, and 110 g|4 oz (uncooked weight) of meat or fish at dinner is already consuming 56 g of protein, before the substantial contribution from bread and cereals is taken into account.

Sources of Protein in Foods

Meat, fish, poultry, offal, eggs, cheese, milk, yoghurt
Beans, peas, lentils, nuts and seeds
Bread, flour, cereals, pasta, rice

Carbohydrate

Structure and Function

Dietary carbohydrate is made up of sugars and starches. Carbohydrates contribute to the taste and texture of food, and provide essential supplies of dietary fibre.

Sugars and starches are made up of chemical units called saccharides. Sugars are either made up of one unit (monosaccharides or simple sugars, such as glucose, fructose) or of two units (disaccharides, such as sucrose, lactose). Starches contain many saccharide units (polysaccharides). Some foods contain non-starch polysaccharides which cannot be digested, and it is these which constitute dietary fibre.

The main role of carbohydrate in the diet is as an energy source. Carbohydrates are digested by the body and broken down to form glucose, which is absorbed into the bloodstream. It is this glucose which acts as the fuel for the body, in the same way that petrol is the fuel for a car.

Sugars

Sugar in the diet provides an easily and quickly absorbed form of energy. Much has been made of the adverse, though well-documented, effects of sugar, such as dental caries. It is more useful to look at sugars as part of the overall diet. Sugars can be divided into those which are naturally present in food as part of cells (intrinsic sugars), such as the sugar in fruit, and those which are not (extrinsic sugars). Milk, which contains an extrinsic sugar (lactose), is an exception to this rule. Knowing this allows us to look at the overall quality of a diet. Naturally occurring sugars (intrinsic and milk sugars) should form a higher proportion of the sugar in the diet than non-milk extrinsic sugars, such as sucrose (table sugar). A diet high in added sugar is likely to be poor in other nutrients, and the small volume in which it is consumed and its attractive sweetness make it easy to eat too much sugar, which may lead to obesity.

Sugars have important properties in cooking, keeping gluten soft in cakes, providing a medium for yeast in baking, and strengthening the structure of egg white.

Starch is the main carbohydrate present in all foods, and forms a major part of our diet. In cooking, starch swells, and the starch cells burst and gelatinize, improving digestibility, palatability and texture. Starch is composed of complex links of glucose units, and these are broken down to provide energy.

Non-Starch Polysaccharides

Non-starch polysaccharides are more commonly (and less accurately) known as dietary fibre. They are a form of carbohydrate which cannot be digested by the body. From this characteristic come the beneficial effects of fibre in improving bowel function, reducing constipation and the risk of bowel diseases. Some foods, particularly oats and pulses, contain soluble forms of fibre, such as pectin, and these have been shown to be effective in controlling glucose and cholesterol levels in the blood.

Foods high in fibre are filling and add bulk to the diet, which is particularly helpful for those trying to cut down on fat, or to lose weight.

Normal Requirements

Starch (complex carbohydrates) should provide the main source of energy in the diet. Individual requirements vary, depending on levels of activity, for example. However, general health recommendations suggest that an overall increase in carbohydrate intake, particularly from cereals, fruit and vegetables, is beneficial. At least half the energy from food should come from starchy foods. Meals should contain plenty of potatoes, rice, pasta, bread or cereals.

To give an example: an average woman who requires 2000 calories per day, obtaining half her energy intake from carbohydrate, would be eating 5 tablespoons breakfast cereal, 4 slices of bread, a large portion of spaghetti, 3 portions of fresh fruit, 2 portions of vegetables (one beans or peas), 290 ml | ½ pint semi-skimmed milk, as well as other foods to make up a normal diet.

Sources of Carbohydrate in Food

Bread, breakfast cereals, rice, pasta, potatoes (wholegrain varieties are best sources of fibre)
Fruit, vegetables, milk
Sugar, confectionery, cakes and biscuits, preserves

Fats

Structure and Function

Fat acts as an energy source, and forms the major part of adipose tissue, the fatty layer beneath the skin which protects body tissue and organs and helps to maintain body temperature. Fat in the diet consists of triglycerides (which are composed of fatty acids), cholesterol and phospholipids. Some fatty acids are essential to the body, and fat also acts as a carrier for fat-soluble vitamins.

Triglycerides form the largest component of dietary fat, and are made up of three (hence tri-) fatty acids and glycerol. It is the different types of fatty acid, and their chemical make-up, which determine their nutritional properties, as well as whether they are liquid or solid at room temperature. The essential fatty acids (linoleic and linolenic acids) are those which the body cannot make itself. All fatty acids are used in the body for a variety of important processes, such as immune function.

Fatty acids are distinguished chemically into saturated, monounsaturated and poly-unsaturated fatty acids.

Fats containing saturated fatty acids are mainly solid at room temperature, and are usually found in foods from animal sources.

Unsaturated fatty acids are generally found in foods of vegetable origin, and are liquid at room temperature.

Monounsaturated fatty acids are found primarily in olive oil.

Cholesterol is a complex steroid compound which is not only essential, but is synthesized by the body itself. Plasma (blood) cholesterol is not affected by cholesterol in the diet, but by the total fat in the diet.

Fat in food provides flavour, smooth texture and fullness.

Normal Requirements

Some fat is necessary in the diet, to provide the essential fatty acids, but this can easily be obtained from foods which contain fat naturally, such as milk, meat and oily fish. It is not necessary to add fat to foods for spreading and cooking, but fat does make food more palatable, and small amounts of it can be used in a healthy diet. Too much fat in the diet, especially fat with a high proportion of saturated fatty acids, is linked to a high incidence of coronary heart disease.

Choosing more foods from vegetable sources, and replacing some red meat with chicken and fish will reduce the overall fat intake. Further information about changes which can usefully be made in the normal diet is available in the chapter on Healthy Eating.

Sources of Fat in Food

Butter, margarine, oil, lard, fat on meat, nuts, seeds, milk, cheese, cream, eggs, oily fish, pastry, cakes, biscuits, crisps, and fried foods.

Vitamins

Vitamins are a group of organic compounds, so called because they are vital to life, essential in the body in small amounts. They perform specific roles in the metabolic process: energy metabolism, blood clotting, absorption of other nutrients.

Vitamins are divided into two groups; those which are fat-soluble, and are found in association with fat, and those which are water-soluble. Special care must be taken in preparation and cooking to preserve the water-soluble vitamins.

Vitamin requirements for groups of the population are defined in the tables below.[3] Vitamins are found in a wide range of food sources. A well-balanced diet based on a wide variety of foods including plenty of fresh fruit and vegetables, should provide adequate vitamin intakes for most people. Supplementary vitamins are only necessary in exceptional cases.

The growing role of antioxidant vitamins, particularly those in fresh fruit and vegetables, has led to the 'Take Five' initiative internationally – encouraging intake of at least 5 portions of fruit and vegetables per day.

A number of vitamins have now been recognized as having strong antioxidant properties. These are Vitamin C, Vitamin E and beta-carotene. Antioxidants neutralize the effect in the body of free radicals, substances produced during the body's normal processes, but potentially harmful to the body if not mopped up. Free radicals are believed to play a role in cardiovascular disease, ageing and cancer. Women planning a pregnancy and in the early stages of pregnancy should take folic acid supplements.

Water-soluble Vitamins

Vitamin	Functions	Sources in Food
Vitamin C	Maintains connective tissue, e.g. skin, gums. Important role in wound healing. Antioxidant.	Potatoes, green vegetables, fruits, especially citrus.
Vitamin B1 (Thiamine)	Release of energy from carbohydrate.	Milk, wholemeal bread, fortified bread and cereals, meat, especially offal.
Vitamin B2 (Riboflavin)	Utilization of energy from food.	Milk, dairy produce, meat, especially liver, yeast extracts.
Vitamin B3 (Niacin)	Utilization of energy from food.	Meat, especially liver, fish, wholemeal cereals.
Vitamin B6 (Pyridoxine)	Metabolism of amino acids and formation of haemoglobin.	Occurs widely in foods, especially meats and fish, eggs, wholegrain cereals.
Vitamin B12	Growth and metabolism. Red blood cells.	Occurs only in animal products. Offal, fish, eggs, milk and dairy foods.
Folic acid	Many functions in body. Important for reduction of risk of neural tube defect	Offal, green leafy vegetables, fortified bread and cereals.

Fat-soluble Vitamins

Vitamin	Functions	Sources in food
Vitamin A (Retinol) Only in animal products, but body can convert beta-carotene in fruit and vegetables into Retinol.	Essential for healthy skin and tissues. Resistance to disease, light perception.	Fish liver oils, offal, eggs, carrots, green and yellow vegetables, margarine (fortified by law).
Vitamin D Produced by action of sunlight on skin, in addition to dietary sources.	Controls and maintains absorption of calcium, essential for healthy bones and teeth.	Margarine (fortified by law), fatty fish, eggs, fortified cereals, butter.

Vitamin	Functions	Sources in food
Vitamin E	Antioxidant, protects cell membranes.	Plant sources, especially wheatgerm and green vegetables.
Vitamin K	Blood clotting.	Green vegetables, egg yolk, liver.

Minerals and Trace Elements

Minerals are naturally occurring chemicals essential in small quantities for the body to function normally. Trace elements are needed in even smaller quantities, and usually act in enzyme systems.

Like vitamins, minerals and trace elements occur in a wide variety of foods, and normal requirements should be obtained from a balanced, varied diet which provides adequate energy.

Mineral	Functions	Sources in food
Iron	Formation of haemoglobin which transports oxygen around the body. Deficiency can lead to anaemia.	Meat, especially offal. Cereal products, egg yolk and green leafy vegetables. Absorption improved in combination with foods containing Vitamin C.
Calcium	Gives strength to teeth and bones, in combination with phosphorus. Required for muscle contraction, nerve activity, normal blood clotting.	Milk and dairy produce, green leafy vegetables, fish with edible bones, flour, bread.
Sodium	Essential for muscle and nerve activity. High intake related to increased blood pressure.	Table salt, bread, cereals, meat products, e.g. bacon, ham. Processed foods.
Potassium	Complements sodium in function of cells, and fluid balance.	Fruit, fruit juices, vegetables, meat and milk.
Magnesium	Enzyme function and energy utilization.	Wide range of foods, especially those of vegetable origin.
Zinc	Wound healing. Component of many enzymes.	Meat, dairy produce, eggs and oysters.

Water

Water is an essential component of all the cells and tissues in the body. An adult body consists of about 60 per cent water. Water is the main constituent of body fluids, such as blood and urine, and acts as a solvent for minerals and vitamins. Lack of fluid, especially in the elderly, can be a major cause of constipation. Fluid is therefore an essential part of any diet. Intake can be in the form of plain water, or as drinks, sauces, etc. Normal fluid intake should be not less than 1.5 litres|2½ pints per day, which is about 6–8 cups.

Special Diets

All special diets require modification of one or more components of the diet. It is essential that professional help and advice are sought when preparing special diets for medical conditions. Changes in the diet need expert supervision to ensure that all nutrients continue to be provided.

A few of the most common diets are outlined below. Local hospital Dietetic Department can give further advice on the cooking modifications needed for these and other therapeutic diets.

Weight-reducing, diabetic and lipid-lowering diets

All medical conditions which need these diets require a change to a healthy lifestyle, which includes a diet based on fresh foods and high in fibre and low in fat. The emphasis should be on wholegrain bread and cereals, fresh fruit and vegetables, with moderate portions of lean meat and fish. These dietary modifications are all based on healthy eating principles, and as such can easily be followed by partners and the rest of the family. Drastic changes should be avoided, as this generally means the diet is difficult to keep to. The appropriate changes made to diet and lifestyle can be incorporated into the normal diet permanently.

Gluten-free diet

This diet is specifically for the treatment of coeliac disease. It requires complete avoidance of gluten, a protein found in wheat, rye, barley and oats. All foods containing these, even in small amounts, must be avoided. Gluten-free flour, bread, pasta and biscuits are available on prescription and from supermarkets: the flour can be used to make gluten-free versions of many foods. Rice, soya, corn and potato flour are naturally gluten-free, and can also be used. Gluten is the component of flour which gives it stretchiness and air-holding qualities, and it takes time to adapt to gluten-free flours.

Many manufactured products contain gluten, and labels must be carefully checked. If in doubt, omit it.

Dietary Change on Religious and Moral Grounds

Many people choose to follow a specific set of dietary rules for ethnic, cultural, moral and religious reasons. These may be dictated by religious texts, such as the Koran for Muslims. They may also involve special methods of preparation and/or slaughter of animals, or the avoidance of certain foods together at the same meal. It is very important when cooking for other people to find out if they have any such dietary restrictions, and to adhere strictly to them.

The information given below outlines the generally accepted guidelines for the most widely used of these diets. There are also a number of religious festivals, which may provide the opportunity for special foods, or fasting for periods of time.

Hindu

Orthodox or strict Hindus are vegetarian. Many, particularly women, do not eat eggs, and will only eat vegetarian cheese, which does not contain animal rennet. Hindus never eat beef, as the cow is considered a sacred animal. Some non-Orthodox Hindus may eat chicken, mutton and occasionally fish. Milk, yoghurt and butter are permitted.

Muslim

Muslims can only eat meat which is halal and has been killed according to Islamic law. This can be obtained from a halal butcher. Pork is strictly forbidden, as are all of its products. Care must be taken with cooking fats, which must be of vegetable origin, or from halal sources.

Fish, eggs, milk and dairy products are allowed. Alcohol is strictly avoided by most Muslims, and should not be used in cooking.

At certain times of the Islamic calendar, such as Ramadan, Muslims will fast during the hours of daylight, and eat late at night and early in the morning. There are a number of important festivals, which are celebrated by special food customs.

Jewish

Jews can only eat meat from animals which have been ritually slaughtered and prepared to render them kosher. Pork is forbidden, but kosher lamb, beef and goat are acceptable.

Fish which have fins and scales are allowed, but shellfish are not. Chicken, turkey, duck, goose, partridge and pheasant are allowed, but other game birds are not.

The other important aspect of the Jewish diet is that meat and dairy foods must be kept apart in cooking, and must not be eaten at the same meal.

Vegetarian

Some people choose not to eat meat, poultry or fish in their diet. Within this group, there are a number of variations. Protein foods need to be combined in vegetarian meals, to provide all the essential amino acids.

Demi-vegetarians while not strictly vegetarian, will eat fish, but not meat.

Lacto-vegetarians will eat milk, cheese and dairy products. Cheese should not be made with animal rennet. Seemingly vegetarian foods, such as vegetable soups made with meat stock, are not acceptable.

Lacto-ovo-vegetarians eat eggs in addition to the above foods.

A vegan diet avoids animal foods of any sort, including dairy foods, and relies entirely on plant foods. Protein is obtained from foods such as soya beans and nuts. A vegan diet is deficient in Vitamin B12, which is only present in animal products, or in synthetic form. A number of yeast extracts fortified with Vitamin B12 are available, which can be used in a variety of ways to fortify the diet.

Food Additives

Many people express concern about additives in food. Certainly, a diet based mainly on a variety of fresh ingredients, well prepared and freshly cooked, is ideal. However, many food products rely on some form of additives, such as preservatives, to ensure that they are safe to eat. The range of foods available would be severely restricted if these were not used in moderation. Similarly, many foods would look unpalatable after processing if some colouring were not added to them.

The legislation governing additives in the UK is extensive, and all foods containing additives are labelled as such. 'E' numbers show that an additive is accepted as safe throughout the European Community. Many of these are derivatives of natural products, like red colouring derived from beetroot (E162).

The key is to base the diet on fresh foods, using processed foods in moderation.

Conclusion

For all its life-giving and therapeutic properties, food is to be enjoyed. If a variety of food is eaten, chosen from a range of food groups, in appropriate portions, anyone's diet can provide for both the body's fundamental physical requirements and the important psychological aspects of the enjoyment of food. The recipes in this book are designed to provide a happy balance of these two interlinked roles of food in our lives.

References
1 Dietary Reference Values for Food Energy and Nutrients for the United Kingdom; Department of Health. 1991.
2 Ibid.
3 Ibid.

Food Safety

Food safety and hygiene are essential in the kitchen as many foods may contain harmful organisms. The cook must be aware of these bacteria and of how to prevent them multiplying to dangerous levels in food which would cause food poisoning.

The vulnerable groups who are particularly at risk are pregnant women, babies, the elderly and those with underlying illness which results in impaired resistance to infection. These special groups are advised to avoid pâtés and soft ripened cheeses of the Brie, Camembert and blue vein types, and to reheat cooked chilled meals and ready-to-eat poultry until piping hot rather than eat them cold.

Preventing the Growth of Bacteria

Bacteria will grow to toxic levels if given the chance. What they need to do their evil work is warmth, time and moisture – ideal conditions, from the bugs' point of view, would be lukewarm food left out in a hot kitchen for several hours. A tiny (and therefore harmless) colony of bacteria could multiply rapidly to such an extent that anyone eating that food could become very ill and require hospitalization. If the victim was a baby (with an immune system not fully developed) or an elderly person or invalid (whose immunity might be impaired), death could result.

Fortunately, some simple precautions can be taken to prevent food poisoning. These are as follows.

Buying: Buy only very fresh food from suppliers you can trust.

Washing: Wash all food if it is to be eaten raw. It is good practice to wash all fruits and vegetables, even if they are to be peeled, as they could contaminate other foods. Wash free-range eggs just before cooking – salmonella is more likely to be present on the egg shell than in the egg.

Refrigeration: Refrigerate all meat, fish and chicken, all dairy products and eggs. Until the discovery of salmonella in eggs, refrigeration of eggs was not thought to be necessary. The danger is still small, but why take any unnecessary risks? Besides, eggs lose their freshness and become stale much more quickly when they are not stored in a refrigerator.

Keep food refrigerated as much as you can. Never leave it on the side in the kitchen waiting to be used, and never leave cold, cooked food at room temperature for more than an hour or so.

Although the original cooking will have destroyed any bacteria, food can be re-infected and, if left in a warm atmosphere, can become harmful.

Do not put hot food in the refrigerator. It will warm up the atmosphere inside and encourage the growth of any bacteria present in other foods in the cabinet.

As far as possible, always keep raw and cooked food separated until serving. Bacteria can enter the kitchen on raw food, and can then be transferred to cooked food where they might easily be left to multiply in peace if the food is not to be re-cooked.

Cooking: Cook food sufficiently to kill any bacteria that may be present. In particular chicken, chopped meats, rolled joints, burgers and re-formed steaks must be cooked thoroughly as food-poisoning bacteria may be present in the centres of these. If cooking for the very young, the very old, pregnant women or the infirm, egg yolks should be cooked hard. (Soft-cooked eggs may not have reached a sufficiently high temperature to kill salmonella.)

Raw meat and fish: Consumption of raw meat and fish carries a risk of food poisoning. Meat and fish that are traditionally served raw, such as sushi and steak tartare, must be of the freshest, best quality, and should be prepared and eaten on the day they are purchased. Some traditional dishes, such as gravad lax, smoked salmon, or Parma ham, although they are raw, can be kept safely under refrigeration because they have been cured either with salt or smoke, or both.

Reheating: If reheating food, make sure that you serve it really hot, i.e. near boiling point, even right in the middle.

Do not pour hot sauces on to cold food unless you are going to reheat it right through at once. Don't add warm food to cold food. Don't mix yesterday's soup with today's without reboiling. Always reheat any mixture immediately if adding two things of different temperatures together. Remember that the cool one might contain a few bacteria, and the hot one will provide enough heat to start them multiplying, but not enough to kill them.

Reboil stocks, soups and sauces frequently in hot weather. Even in winter, reboil them every three days. In theory, you can keep the same stockpot on the go for ever if you reboil it every time you add anything to it. And remember that the stronger the stock, the firmer the jelly it will set to, and the better it will keep in the refrigerator. If reheating aspic, bring to the boil, then let it cool enough to use.

Keeping food warm: If food must be kept warm, first make sure that it is heated through sufficiently to kill all bacteria; then keep it really hot, not lukewarm. Do not pour a warm sauce over, say, cold poached eggs and keep them warm in a hot cupboard or warming drawer.

Freezing: Do not refreeze completely thawed food without cooking it first. Although the freezing and thawing do not harm, it is easy to forget just how many periods at room temperature the food has had, and it is therefore impossible to guess how large the concentration of bacteria may be. Never refreeze chicken that has been frozen and thawed.

Cooking from frozen: Do not cook large items (such as whole chickens) when frozen. When the bird looks cooked, the inside (where salmonella is most likely to be present on the surface of the cavity) may still be lukewarm and raw. For the same reason, it is unwise to stuff large birds. The stuffing may prevent the heat from penetrating the cavity and killing any bacteria present.

Thawing: Thaw food slowly in the refrigerator or in a leakproof plastic bag under cold water. Do not try to thaw things fast by putting them in a warming drawer or under hot water. The outer layer will stay at incubating temperature too long. However, microwaving to thaw is safe because it is so fast that the bacteria do not have time to breed. But cook the food as soon as it is thawed, just in case your microwave has warmed it up too much.

Cooling: Cool large quantities of food fast. If a stew is left to cool in a heavy pan, the centre of it will provide perfect bacteria breeding conditions: warmth, moisture and time. And a stir with a non-sterile wooden spoon could easily provide the parent bacteria to start the colony. Commercial caterers cool food in a blast chiller, but small kitchens do not have this luxury. So either tip the stew into shallow flat containers to cool, or cool the pot fast by standing it in a bowl in the sink, and continuously running the cold tap into the bowl, to keep the waterjacket round the pan cool. Give it an occasional stir to speed things up.

Nor should you leave hot food covered with a heavy lid. Open food cools quicker. If you want to avoid the food drying out or forming a skin, place some wet greaseproof paper (which is thin enough not to hinder cooling) flat on the surface of the food.

Wrapping: Take care when wrapping hot food in clingfilm – if there are any air spaces between the food and the film, greenhouse-like incubating conditions will be produced. Instead, wrap the food loosely in kitchen foil, and refrigerate as soon as it is cold.

Utensils: Don't use the same knife or board for raw and cooked food without washing it between jobs. If you have just jointed a raw chicken and then slice cooked beef with the same knife, you could transfer bacteria from the chicken to the beef. The micro-organisms in the chicken will get cooked to death, but they could grow with impunity in the beef. Caterers have separate refrigerators and boards for storing and preparing hot and cold food, and large-production kitchens very often have separate kitchen areas and separate cooks. The home cook, however, who is dealing with small quantities of food that are cooked, eaten or refrigerated fast, need not go to such lengths but should practise good food hygiene and take sensible precautions, always washing utensils thoroughly after use.

Keep the kitchen area clean. This means frequently washing tools in near-boiling water, scrubbing boards and surfaces with detergent, washing out the refrigerator weekly with weak bleach, and making sure that tea-towels and cloths are changed as soon as they are dirty or damp. A damp cloth left over a warm cooker, or a crack in the wooden handle of a much-used knife, provides the perfect incubating conditions for germs.

'Off' foods: Don't ever serve food that smells or looks at all peculiar. Although salmonella is completely tasteless and has no discernible odour, unpleasant odours or appearance are an indication of age and poor condition, and food-poisoning organisms are likely to be present along with the ones causing the obvious deterioration. Always err on the safe side and throw out any food that looks or smells dubious – don't take risks.

Salmonella in eggs: Consumption of raw eggs or uncooked dishes made from them, such as homemade mayonnaise, mousse and ice cream, carries the risk of food poisoning. However, if you do use raw eggs to make these dishes, make sure you use only the freshest, that the dishes are eaten as soon as possible after making and that they are never left for more than 1 hour at room temperature.

For healthy people there is little risk from eating cooked eggs, however they have been prepared – boiled, fried, scrambled or poached. Vulnerable people such as the elderly, the sick, babies, toddlers and pregnant women should only eat eggs that have been thoroughly cooked until the white and yolk are solid. These vulnerable people should avoid egg recipes which require light cooking, such as meringues and hollandaise sauce.

Lightly cooked egg dishes should be eaten as soon as possible after cooking and if the dishes are not for immediate use they should be stored in the refrigerator after cooling. Pasteurized egg, which is free from harmful bacteria, is often used by caterers in these dishes and is available as a useful alternative in the home.

Poisonous foods: Some foods are naturally poisonous and must be treated with care. For example, red kidney beans must be boiled for 10 minutes to destroy an enzyme which is potentially fatal. Cooking the beans until soft at a low temperature is not sufficient to do this, so, if using a 'slow cooker', give the beans a good boil before putting them into the pot.

Green potato skins, rhubarb leaves and many wild mushrooms are mildly poisonous and can cause gastric upsets in some people. Indeed, a few wild mushrooms are lethal. Do not cook mushrooms unless purchased from a reputable supplier and you are certain they are safe. Do not gather and cook wild mushrooms unless you have the knowledge to distinguish between the safe and poisonous varieties.

Choosing and Storing Produce

This chapter has been written to offer a few guidelines on how to recognize good-quality food and how best to store it. For freezability please see the chapter on freezing (see page 69). When shopping we would always suggest buying organic ingredients although they are more highly priced than non-organic ingredients. The purse inevitably dictates your final decision.

Meat

When choosing meat, the general principle is to look for signs that it has come from a young animal. It should not be too fatty, the joints should be reasonably small, it should be of a firm texture and not have too much gristle, although obviously there are different expectations about the quantity of acceptable fat and gristle depending on the particular cut of meat. Meat should never be slimy; it should be moist but not gelatinous (with the exception of veal) and it should not smell. Any exposed bones should be pinkish-blue in colour and the paler the fat the better.

Always allow meat to breathe, so if it comes tightly wrapped up, pierce the clingfilm and refrigerate for not more than 2–3 days. Raw meat should always be stored at the bottom of the refrigerator so that no raw blood can drop on to cooked food – this can be a cause of food poisoning.

Beef

Generally you should look for a deep, dull red piece of meat rather than a bright, orange-red joint. This is difficult in a supermarket because managers assume that their customers want 'bright' meat so there is much use of clever lighting as well as the widespread use of adding anti-oxidants. The fat on beef should be a pale creamy yellow colour. When choosing beef, ask for meat from a traditional beef herd.

Veal

The flesh should be pale pink, soft but not flabby, and finely grained. There should be a very little creamy white fat. Do not worry if there is a lot of gelatinous tissue around the meat as this is a natural characteristic of a very immature animal.

Lamb

The colour of the meat varies with the breed of lamb. The fat should be creamy white (if it is yellow it indicates old age) and it should not be oily. All joints should be plump and compact rather than long and thin. The skin should be pliable; not hard and wrinkled. Welsh or English lamb is considered to be superior to New Zealand lamb.

Pork

The meat should be pale pink, close-grained and firm to the touch. It should not have enlarged glands or abscesses (pigs kept too close together, reasonably enough, bite each other). The fat should be firm and white, not oily, and without a greyish tinge. There should be an even covering of fat. Try to find free-range pork; it has an excellent flavour.

Offal

Offal has often been called 'awful offal' in the past, but at last it is gaining the recognition it deserves as a delicacy. It tends to be low in fat and high in iron and is very healthy. All offal must be eaten very fresh.

Liver

It should not have a strong smell; it should be shiny and a little bloody.

Calves' liver: It should be a pale milky brown colour with a fine even texture. Dutch liver is considered better than English.

Lambs' liver: This is darker in colour than calves'.

Pigs' liver: This is dark and close-textured. It is used in pâtés and terrines.

Ox liver: This is dark bluish-brown with a very strong flavour. Used occasionally in stews and pies but it is very inferior to other sorts of liver and is best avoided.

Kidney

Kidneys are sold loose or still in their suet. To store kidneys, remove them from the suet and refrigerate for a maximum of 24 hours. Make sure that they are not tightly wrapped in clingfilm – they must be allowed to breathe.

Veal kidneys: These are delicious. They should be a pale milky brown with a creamy white suet. They look rather like a bunch of grapes.

Lambs' kidneys: These are medium brown, faintly bluish, firm-textured and kidney-bean-shaped.

Pigs' kidneys: These are pale brown with a rather strong flavour, similar in shape to lambs' kidneys.

Ox kidneys: These look like huge veal kidneys but are much darker in colour. They are only suitable for pies and puddings.

Sweetbreads: As with all offal, the calves' sweetbreads are the best, then the lambs' and then the ox breads. Pigs' sweetbreads are not sold.

Ox Cheek: This is sold for brawns and stews.

Heart

Heart is highly nutritious, but needs slow cooking to tenderize it. It is also very lean, and requires a sauce or plenty of basting to keep it moist. Hearts must be cleaned of all sinew and the tubes removed before cooking.

Ox heart: This is large, very tough, strongly flavoured, coarse and muscular and bluish-red. It is generally used chopped or minced with other ingredients – perhaps for a pie.

Lambs' hearts: The smallest and most tender of the hearts, but stuffing to add flavour, slow cooking and careful basting are still necessary to moisten and tenderize the naturally lean and tough flesh.

Feet and trotters

Calves' feet: These are seldom sold to the public. They are good for stock and calf's foot jelly due to the high concentration of gelatine present in the feet. Pigs' trotters are high in gelatine, and good for setting stocks, and for brawn. They can be boned, stuffed, braised, served hot with mustard sauce, or hot or cold with vinaigrette. Sheep's trotters and ox feet are not sold. Cow heel is treated before sale, and looks and tastes similar to tripe. It consists of the whole foot and heel of the animal.

Tripe

Tripe can come from all cud-chewing animals, being the first and second stomachs, but in practice only ox tripe is sold. The first stomach (blanket tripe) is smooth, the second honeycombed.

Tripe is sold parboiled, but needs further long boiling to tenderize it. It is wise to ask the butcher how much more boiling it will need. Grey, slimy, flabby, strong-smelling tripe should be avoided. It should be thick, firm and very white. Tripe can be stewed, boiled or deep-fried. A specialist taste, it's either loved or loathed!

Oxtail

Oxtail is sold skinned and usually jointed. Choose large fat tails, with plenty of meat on them. Cow tails, which are skinny and rather tasteless, are sometimes passed off as oxtail. The meat should be dark and lean, and the fat creamy white and firm. Oxtail is high in gelatine content, so it cooks to a tender, almost sticky, stew. It is good for soups and very rich in flavour.

Tongue

To get a pig's tongue you must buy the whole head, while calves' tongues are very rarely available. Ox and lambs' tongues can be bought, however.

Ox tongue: It should feel soft to the touch, though it may have a rough, pigmented skin.

Lambs' tongues: They are very small and are generally sold by the kilo. They should be pale pink: the roughish skin may be light or dark grey.

Blood

Pigs' blood is used in the making of black pudding. It is mixed with fat, and stuffed into intestines like a sausage.

NOTE: Brains, oxtail and marrow-bones were not eaten for a time because of the BSE controversy. We have included recipes for them.

Game

If you want to roast your game, try to buy young tender birds or animals. You can recognize a young bird by its smooth legs and pliable feet and beak. If it has already been plucked, feel it for pliability in the breastbone. See the end of this section (page 58) for a seasonal table of game.

If it has not been hung already, you should hang game, undrawn (except for rabbits, which are paunched, or gutted, as soon as they are killed), in a cool, dry place. Birds are hung by the neck and animals by the feet. The hanging time varies according to the animal and the weather, but a rough guide is given below with a brief description of each bird or animal. The less well hung it is, the easier it is to pluck and draw. If the game is already prepared, store it loosely wrapped in the bottom of the refrigerator.

Grouse

Hanging time: anything from 2–10 days.
After 2 days it does not have a strong flavour but after 10 it will be very gamey. Red or Scottish grouse is best. Allow one grouse per head.

Partridge

Hanging time: 3–4 days.
We think that a partridge, particularly the grey British as opposed to the French red leg, is the nicest of all game birds. Plucked birds should have a pale skin and plump breast. Allow one partridge per head (some people can eat 2).

Pheasant
Hanging time: 3–8 days.
As with most game birds the hen pheasant is juicier than the cock. Pheasant is fairly mild in terms of 'gameyness'. Allow one pheasant to 2–3 people.

Pigeon and squab
These are in season all the year round. Squab are fledgling pigeons. The pigeon breast should be moist, glistening dark red meat. It is difficult to judge the age of a pigeon by its appearance so you have to trust the game dealer. Allow one pigeon per head or 3 breasts each.

Quail
Eat quail fresh – preferably 24 hours after being killed. Most of today's quails are farmed and should look plump for their size. They have a slightly gamey flavour. Allow 2 quails per person.

Snipe
Hanging time: 4 days.
This is a small bird with a long bill which is sometimes served pushed into the body of the bird, like a skewer, drawing the head through the legs before roasting. It is traditionally roasted ungutted and served on a croûte. Snipe are very hard to find unless you shoot them yourself.

Wild duck, teal and widgeon
Wild duck varies in size from the large mallard to the tiny teal. All wild ducks should be eaten fresh. It tends to be rather dry and can have a fishy flavour. This can be overcome by stuffing the cavity with an orange, by marinating or by parboiling the plucked bird.

Woodcock
Like the snipe, it is also roasted undrawn. It is very rarely available to buy: you have to be given woodcock as a present by a rather good shot.

Venison
Hanging time: 3–10 days.
Venison should be a good deep red colour with a firm texture and should not be slimy. It should be moist but not gelatinous with very little fat, and it therefore needs to be cooked carefully. Venison that has been hung for 3 days tastes like rather delicious beef. However, once it has been hung for 10 days it has a very gamey flavour.

Game Seasons

Feathered Game

Grouse	12 August–10 December
Partridge	1 September–1 February
Pheasant	1 October–1 February
Pigeon and squab	In season all year round
Quail	Available all year round
Snipe	August–January
Wild duck, teal and wigeon	Various, starting September and finishing 20 February
Woodcock (Scotland)	1 September–31 January
(England and Wales)	1 October–31 January

Furred Game

Venison — Seasons are complicated (see *Statutory deer close seasons*, below), but frozen wild venison is often available all year round and farmed venison is available throughout the year.

Statutory Deer Close Seasons

		England and Wales	Scotland
Red	Stags	1 May–31 July	21 October–30 June
	Hinds	1 March–31 Oct	16 February–20 Oct
Sika	Stags	1 May–31 July	21 October–30 June
	Hinds	1 March–31 Oct	16 February–20 Oct
Fallow	Bucks	1 May–31 July	1 May–31 July
	Does	1 March–31 Oct	16 February–20 Oct
Roe	Bucks	1 Nov–31 March	21 Oct–31 March
	Does	1 March–31 Oct	1 April–20 Oct

Muntjac and Chinese water deer have no statutory close seasons. The British Deer Society recommends that to avoid orphaning muntjac fawns dependent upon the mother's milk, only immature and heavily pregnant females (at which time a previous fawn will be independent) should be culled.

Hunting seasons

Staghunting	Autumn stags	early August–end October
	Hinds	1 November–end February
	Spring stags	March–end April
Rabbit	Wild or farmed available all year	
Hare	September–March	

Rabbit

Hanging time: 24 hours.

Wild or farmed rabbit is available all the year round. Rabbits are paunched (gutted) as soon as they are killed. Wild rabbit is gamier and less tender than farmed, whose pale flesh is rather like chicken. If the rabbit has not been skinned, look for smooth, sharp claws and delicate soft ears.

Hare

Hanging time: 5–6 days, unpaunched.

If the hare has not been skinned, look for smooth sharp claws and delicate soft ears. A leveret (young hare) has a hardly noticeable hare lip – this becomes deeper and more pronounced in an older animal. If the hare has been skinned, look for deep claret flesh. Only young tender joints of hare are suitable for roasting, and even they need much basting. Older hares and the tougher joints are traditionally jugged.

Poultry

If the bird has been sold with giblets remove them as soon as you get home, and unwrap the bird so that it can breathe. Store at the bottom of the refrigerator for not more than 2–3 days.

Chickens

The more you spend on a chicken, the better it will probably taste. A frozen supermarket bird, battery-raised and fed on fishmeal until the moment of slaughter, has little chance of tasting good, however well cooked. Try to buy free-range birds. They may look scrawnier than the plump-breasted oven-ready bird but the flavour is far superior.

Poussins: These are 4–6 weeks old. They serve one person and look appetizing but have very little flavour.

Double poussins: These are 6–10 weeks old. They serve 2 people and have quite a good flavour.

Spring chickens: These are 10–12 weeks old. They serve 3 people and have a similar flavour to that of double poussins.

Roasters: These are usually over 3 months old and can have an excellent flavour as long as they have been reasonably raised. They normally serve 4 people.

Corn-fed chickens: These are normally free-range chickens fed on corn. They are yellow in colour and have a very good flavour. The French corn-fed chickens generally seem to have a better flavour than the English ones.

Poulet noir: This is a French black-legged chicken. It is more like a guinea fowl than a chicken in both shape and texture. The poulet noir is more expensive than a conventional chicken but is really worth the occasional burst of extravagance.

Boiling fowls: These are very rare today. They require long, slow cooking and have an excellent flavour.

Duck

Most ducks sold today are ducklings of 7–9 weeks. A 1.8 kg|4 lb duck feeds only 2–3 people. Young duck is delicious, but do not buy frozen duck as you will not be able to judge the pliability of the breastbone, which is the tell-tale sign of age. The skin of a fresh duck should be dry, soft and smooth. It should not be slimy and should not smell strongly. The Aylesbury duck is a very superior bird.

Goose

This is at its best when it weighs 4.6 kg|10 lb, i.e. when it is 6–9 months old. A goose can be utterly delicious but make sure that you choose a young bird as old geese can be very tough. Fresh goose has a clean white skin, which is soft and dry to the touch.

Turkey

Try to buy fresh rather than frozen turkeys as they tend to have a better flavour. The flesh should be snow-white and firm, and the skin dry and soft. A turkey can often smell a little high. Remove all the giblets as soon as possible because they deteriorate quickly, and wipe the bird inside and out before storing.

Guinea fowl

This is normally a little smaller than the average-sized chicken and looks rather scrawny. The taste is that of a very delicious, slightly gamey chicken. Be warned: it needs careful cooking as it should have very little fat.

Dairy Products

Eggs

Chicken eggs: There is no nutritional difference between a battery and a free-range egg, but somehow the idea of a battery egg is depressing. If the box says 'farm eggs' it simply means battery-farmed eggs. You cannot judge the freshness of an egg from its outward appearance so buy eggs from somewhere with a rapid turnover. You can test for freshness by breaking an egg into a saucer: the yolk should be well domed and there should be 2 distinct layers of egg white, the inner circle being rather gelatinous and the outer circle a little thinner. When an egg is stale, the yolk is flatter and the 2 layers of white intermingle. Store eggs pointed end downwards so that the air pocket in the rounded end is uppermost. Keep according to the use by date, for a maximum of 3 weeks in the refrigerator. If the eggs have been separated, the whites can be frozen and the yolks kept refrigerated for 2–3 days. Cover them with a little cold water to prevent a hard crust from forming, then cover with clingfilm.

Eggs can be tainted easily so keep them well separated from other foods. The easiest thing is to keep them in the egg box in which they have been bought.

Goose, duck, plover, gull, turkey and quail eggs: All eggs should be stored in the same way as chicken eggs. The following eggs are now available fresh from farms, from specialist shops and from the occasional supermarket.

Turkey, goose and duck eggs: These have too strong a flavour to be eaten in the normal way as eggs but are useful for cooking. Goose eggs make particularly good sponge cakes.

Quail, guinea fowl and gull eggs: These make very good first courses served with celery salt, paprika, brown bread and butter. Quail eggs take 3 minutes to boil, guinea fowl eggs take 5, and gull eggs are always sold ready cooked and are only in season in May and June.

Milk and Cream

Always refrigerate dairy products as quickly as possible and keep it covered as it can easily be tainted by other foods in the refrigerator. An open bottle or carton will go off more quickly than an unopened one. Be guided by the use-by date.

Milk is standardized by its fat content. All milk should have been pasteurized to kill harmful bacteria.

Skimmed milk: A thin, slightly grey-coloured milk from which virtually all the fat has been removed. It goes off a little more quickly than 'fattier' milks.

Semi-skimmed milk: As skimmed milk but with a little more fat.

'Regular' milk: This is the standard milk with about 3.5 per cent fat.

'Raw' milk: This unpasteurized milk is not available for legal sale.

Homogenized milk: This has been pasteurized and then spun in a centifuge to distribute the fat evenly throughout the milk.

Long-life milk: This is milk that has been sterilized or heat-treated to give it a long shelf life unrefrigerated. It is a useful emergency stopgap but has a boiled flavour. Once opened, treat as fresh.

Butter

This is either salted or unsalted and made from pasteurized milk. Whether you buy salted or unsalted depends on your personal taste, but unsalted butter is better (although more expensive) for cooking as it contains less sediment and is consequently less likely to burn. It should be used for all butter sauces.

Unsalted butter does not keep as long as salted butter. It must always be refrigerated and should be kept tightly wrapped to prevent it drying out or becoming tainted by other foods in the refrigerator.

Cheese

It is difficult to choose cheese in a supermarket if it has been tightly wrapped in clingfilm and is deceptively coloured by supermarket lighting.

Hard cheese (e.g. Cheddar, Double Gloucester): Try to find a mature cheese that has a rind. It should have a good strong smell but should not smell of whey (i.e. sour milk) and nor should it smell of ammonia. If there is no odour at all, it is probably too bland. It should feel hard rather than soft and should not be sweaty, or have any mould or be cracked.

Soft fresh cheeses (e.g. cottage cheese, curd cheese): They should look and smell fresh and the packaging should be undamaged.

Soft matured cheeses (e.g. Brie, Camembert): There are a huge number of soft matured cheeses available but many of them are rather dull. We think that the best are Brie and Camembert, but fear that the imitation Somerset Brie bears little resemblance to the real thing. Buy a soft runny cheese. If it has a strong smell of ammonia do not buy it as it will have an unpleasant flavour.

Firm matured cheeses (e.g. Pont l'Eveque, Reblochon): These cheeses can vary from the rather tasteless (Port Salut) to the utterly delicious and very strong Pont l'Eveque. Firm matured cheeses should be pale, creamy and fairly firm in texture.

Blue cheeses (e.g. Stilton, Roquefort): These cheeses can be soft or firm, and should have strong blue veins with no brown blotches.

Storing cheese

Ideally cheese should be kept in a larder, but as few houses have one, the next best thing is to wrap it tightly in greaseproof paper then in clingfilm and keep it in the refrigerator. Remove at least 1 hour before serving. If kept in the warmth of a centrally heated house it will sweat.

Yoghurt

There are many different types of yoghurt widely available. Most yoghurt is labelled 'low fat' as it is made from skimmed milk. Greek yoghurt, which is widely available in supermarkets as well as delicatessens, is a little higher in fat than most yoghurts but the taste is delicious.

Storage

Store in the refrigerator for 3–4 days. Note that Greek yoghurt tends to go off more quickly than other yoghurts.

Fish

For fish classifications and methods of preparation see the chapter on fish (page 304).

Fish must be purchased and eaten when it is still very fresh. Some fish is frozen on board trawlers, so do not be put off buying a frozen fish as it may well be significantly fresher than a 'fresh' fish. It is easy to tell if fish is fresh, firstly by its smell – if it has a strong fishy smell it is probably quite stale. Scaly fish should have plenty of scales and all fish should have bright eyes, red gills and firm flesh. If you press your finger into a fish and the flesh does not spring back into place immediately, it is probably not fresh.

Shellfish are often sold live in order to guarantee freshness – if buying raw shellfish, opt for frozen rather than for dead raw shellfish. Chinese supermarkets are often the best place to buy good-quality raw frozen shellfish. If you want to buy cooked shellfish it must be very fresh. Some fishmongers will buy and cook lobsters and crayfish to order. Cooked 'shell-on' prawns are delicious but they must be bought from a reputable source and eaten on the day of purchase. If you just need a few cooked prawns for a recipe, I would recommend that you buy frozen ones and defrost them slowly sprinkled with a little lemon juice and freshly ground black pepper.

Storing Fish

Store fish, gutted, for as short a time as possible. Refrigerate it, lightly covered with clingfilm, and eat on the day of purchase. Smoked fish will keep for a couple of days and vacuum-packed smoked fish will stay fresh for much longer (check the sell-by date), but as with all 'long-life' products it must be treated as fresh once opened. To store live shellfish, such as crabs, lobsters, mussels and oysters, put them curved side down to prevent them losing their juices on a tray in the bottom of the refrigerator and cover with a damp cloth. They can be kept overnight.

Vegetables and Herbs

See the vegetable chapter (page 273) for detailed descriptions and uses for vegetables and herbs.

Choosing

The most important thing about choosing vegetables is that they should be young and fresh. Old-fashioned gardeners and many producers take pride in their enormous turnips and giant parsnips but, in fact, nothing can be nicer than a tiny roasted parsnip or a minute braised turnip. The only vegetables that are good when reasonably old (but not stale) are carrots. Young carrots can be rather flavourless compared to large, deep orange ones. Very old carrots, however, are horrid as they have woody cores.

To choose good-quality vegetables: It is obvious from a carrot's wrinkled skin that it is old, or from a lettuce's limp leaves that it has wilted. As a general rule of thumb, the vegetables you choose should be small (of their type), brightly coloured, unwrinkled, unblemished and should look 'alert' – for example, pea pods should snap open. Fruit vegetables, such as tomatoes, avocado pears and aubergines, can be large but they should still look and feel ripe. They should also feel heavy for their size.

Storing

Unwrap any vegetables that have been sold tightly wrapped in clingfilm. Store them in the warmest part of the refrigerator (i.e. the salad compartment) or in a larder. To prevent dehydration, you should store root vegetables (which like to be in the dark) in brown paper bags, and above-ground vegetables in polythene bags. Make sure that the vegetables are not squeezed into too small a space. If there is no room in the refrigerator and the vegetables have to be kept in a warm room do not put them in polythene bags as they will sweat and rot. Small packets of fresh herbs will keep in their cartons for a day or two. Large bunches can be kept in polythene bags or, like flowers, in jugs of water. Watercress is best kept leaves downwards in a jug of water.

Fruit

Choosing

It is fairly easy to choose good-quality fresh fruit – it should look bright-skinned and, usually, should be heavy for its size. It should also have a fairly strong scent without being overpowering. Some fruits, such as pears, are very rarely perfect in the shops as they are only perfectly ripe for one day and should therefore be purchased in advance and ripened at home.

Storing

Soft fruit: Do not store for more than 2 days in the refrigerator. Do not prepare until ready for use – an unhulled strawberry will keep longer than a hulled one. If the fruit cannot be used in time, freeze and use for dishes such as ice creams, purées and pies.

Citrus fruits and hard fruits: Ideally these should be kept refrigerated in polythene bags. If there is no room in the refrigerator, do not leave them in polythene bags as they will rot. To store these fruits for more than a week: wrap each piece of fruit individually in newspaper and place in a box in a cool place. Some fruits (especially if under-ripe), such as quinces, apples and pears, will keep well like this for 2–3 months. Citrus fruits can be kept for 2–3 weeks. Seville oranges will only keep for 1 week but may be frozen. (Freezing will not spoil the marmalade.)

Bananas and avocado pears: Do not refrigerate but leave in a cool place. To ripen firm avocado pears, place in a paper bag and keep in a warm place.

Stone fruits (e.g. apricots, plums, grapes, etc.): Store in a cool place, preferably the refrigerator.

NOTE: Strong-smelling fruit, such as cut pineapple or melon, must be well wrapped if kept in the refrigerator as their fragrance will taint cheese, butter and milk.

Storecupboard Ingredients

This section describes our store room at Leiths School – i.e. the basic dry ingredients that are useful to have to hand, and where necessary we have made a few notes.

Mustard

Buy in small pots – once opened, mustard deteriorates quite rapidly. We have smooth Dijon mustard. Dry English mustard is also useful for cheese sauces, mayonnaise and some spicy recipes.

Vinegar

We keep white wine vinegar as a basic ingredient although balsamic and flavoured ones, e.g. herb vinegars, are a welcome additional ingredient. Malt vinegar is very useful for cleaning and the occasional recipe.

Flours

We have 100 per cent wholemeal (once opened it goes off quite quickly so keep in a sealed container), 85 per cent wholemeal, strong flour (including 'oo' grade for making pasta), plain flour, granary flour, self-raising flour, cornflour, arrowroot and rice flour.

Oils

Sunflower is good for general cooking use; extra virgin olive oil for special salads; and sesame oil for Chinese dishes. We usually have some hazelnut, walnut and sometimes pinenut oil in the refrigerator. The expensive oils tend to deteriorate quite quickly and so should be bought in small jars.

Pasta

Dried pasta keeps well in sealed containers and we always have a selection of different shapes. The versatility and reliability of dried pasta makes it a useful standby ingredient.

Dried Herbs and Spices

Ideally, all herbs and spices should be fresh, but in practice this is not possible. Store them out of the sunlight and buy in small jars from a supermarket with a quick turnover as they go stale quite quickly. At Leiths we have the following dried herbs and spices:

Herbs	Spices
Bay leaves	Whole and ground nutmeg
Herbes de Provence	Whole and ground cinnamon
Rosemary	Whole and ground mace
Tarragon	Whole and ground cardamon
Oregano	Vanilla pods
	Juniper berries
	Allspice
	Cloves
	Coriander
	Cumin
	Turmeric
	Mixed spice
	Saffron
	Chilli
	Paprika
	Cayenne

Bottles

Soy sauce, Worcestershire sauce, Heinz tomato ketchup, vanilla extract, rosewater, orange blossom water, passata (sieved tomatoes), stem ginger in syrup, capers, olives.

Cans

Plum tomatoes, flageolet beans, kidney beans, chick peas, tuna fish, sardines, anchovies, smoked oysters, red peppers, green peppercorns, water chestnuts and sweetcorn.

Grains

Basmati rice (brown and white), long-grain rice, risotto rice, pudding rice, brown rice, couscous, cracked wheat (bulghur), semolina and polenta.

Nuts

Almonds, ground, nibbed, flaked and whole; walnuts, pieces and halved; hazelnuts, whole; pinenuts, whole; pistachios, Brazil nuts, pecans.

Seeds

Sesame, poppy, mustard, pumpkin.

Jams

Apricot, redcurrant jelly – for glazing. Honey.

Sugars

Granulated, caster, icing, preserving, demerara, lump and muscovado. Treacle and golden syrup.

Chocolate

High-quality chocolate, coca powder.

Dried Fruit

Raisins, currants, sultanas, apples, apricots, prunes, mixed peel, figs and mango.

Coffee and Tea

Freshly ground, decaffinated and instant coffee, Earl Grey, infusions and Indian tea.

Creative Leftovers

Most of us spend some time foraging in the refrigerator or store cupboard looking for inspiration. Some types of dishes are particularly suitable for leftover cooking such as:

Soups: leftover vegetables

Soufflés: cheeses

Flans: vegetables

Pies: cooked meats

Stir-fries: cooked meats

Warm salads: cooked chicken, turkey, etc.

Gougères: cooked game, chicken, fish

Stuffed pancakes: fish, meat, vegetables

Risottos: fish, meat, vegetables

Pilaffs: fish, meat, vegetables

Rice, noodle and pasta salads: fish, meat, chicken

Pasties: cooked meat

Ice creams: 'tired' fruit

The important thing when cooking with leftovers is not to try to be too clever – don't be tempted to use too many different ingredients in one recipe. Use store cupboard ingredients to make leftover cooking more exciting and instant cooking easier.

Freezing Food

Freezing is a method of preserving food – not indefinitely, but for some weeks or months. Bacterial action, which causes spoilage, is prevented by keeping the food at extremely low temperatures. Note that some deterioration in the taste, texture and colour of food will take place if it is kept frozen for longer than the recommended times. Providing that the following simple instructions for freezing are followed religiously, many foods can be stored successfully without any loss of nutritional value or quality.

Rapid Freezing

The quicker the freezing process, the smaller the ice crystals formed in the food will be. Large ice crystals, resulting from slow freezing, damage the cell walls of the food itself, and consequently, when it is thawed, liquid will be lost, including some soluble nutrients. Meat, in particular, will lose moisture on thawing if frozen too slowly, and will be dry when cooked.

Packing the Freezer

In order to facilitate rapid freezing, only small amounts of unfrozen food should be put into the freezer at one time. Large quantities of food at room temperature would raise the temperature in the freezer and, inevitably, the freezing process would be slower. For the same reason, food should not be packed in large parcels, and the items should be separated in the freezing compartment, allowing the air to circulate around them. Once they are frozen, however, they can be – and indeed should be for economy's sake – packed tightly together with as little space between them as possible. A full freezer costs less to run than a half-empty one. Many freezers contain a fast-freeze compartment for the actual freezing process, and larger compartments for storage.

Wrapping the Food

Because the cold atmosphere of a freezer is very drying, and direct contact with the icy air causes 'freezer burn' (dry discoloured patches) on some foods, most foods need careful wrapping before freezing. Heavyweight polythene bags are the cheapest and best wrappers, because it is possible to see through them, and they take various shapes of food without creating too much air space. However, an airtight container will suffice. Foil is sometimes used, as are rigid plastic containers, old yoghurt cartons, bowls with lids, etc.

Whatever container you use, it must be robust enough to withstand some rough handling in the freezer, and it must be possible to label it clearly. Freezer labels, or polythene bags with white labels on which it is possible to write with a freezer pen, are best. Once the food is packed into the container, as closely wrapped as possible, it should be labelled with the contents and the date, and frozen immediately. Liquids can be poured into polythene bags set in square containers and frozen. Once solid, the bag is lifted out of the outer container and thus stored. This means fewer kitchen containers are out of use in the freezer, and liquids can be stored in space-saving rectangular shapes. Liquids in plastic tubs or containers should be frozen with a 2.5 cm | 1 in gap between bowl and lid to allow for expansion. Food should be used up in the right order – for example, peas frozen the previous week should not be eaten before the batch that was frozen 2 months ago. To facilitate this, a record or inventory of what is in the freezer can be kept on it, in it or near it, with additions and subtractions made each time food is put in or taken out.

Open Freezing

If frozen in a mass, fruit and vegetables will emerge from the freezer in a solid block. This can be inconvenient for thawing in a hurry, or if only a small quantity of the food is needed, and the fruit and vegetables may also lose their individual shape and texture. For this reason, many foods are frozen on open trays so that each raspberry, pea, broad bean or sprig of cauliflower is individually frozen before packing into bags. The frozen produce will then be free-flowing and separate. Use this method for sausages, beefburgers, breadcrumbs, bread rolls, etc. as well as for fruit and vegetables. Decorated cakes and puddings can be open-frozen, then packed when the decoration is hard enough to withstand the tight wrapping around it.

Mass Freezing

If the food to be frozen is not suitable for open freezing, make sure that the block is not too thick. This will make cooking and thawing easier and quicker. For example, meatballs in tomato sauce should be laid one deep in a plastic box, not piled one on top of each other; spinach should be in a flattish pack so that it can be cooked from frozen (a thick block would mean overcooked outside leaves while the middle was still frozen). Air should be excluded as far as possible. This is especially important with casseroles, where the chicken or meat should be coated or covered completely by the sauce. Otherwise, the meat may become dry and fall apart on reheating.

Thawing

Thawing should be as slow as possible. Rapid thawing leads to loss of moisture and subsequent dryness or tastelessness of the food. However, it is sometimes imperative to thaw food in a hurry. To do this, put it into an airtight polythene bag and immerse it in cold, not hot, water. Hot water tends to cook the outside of the food and encourages bacterial activity which would cause the food to go bad if not completely cooked immediately. Meat should be thawed completely, and should be at room temperature before it is cooked.

Re-freezing Frozen Food

Freezing does not kill bacteria present in food; it simply inhibits growth. So when food is removed from the freezer the bacteria in it will multiply normally. When put back, the now considerably increased population of bacteria will cease breeding, to start afresh when the food is brought back into the warmth. For this reason, frozen food manufacturers caution purchasers not to refreeze the product once it has been thawed. They are justly nervous that if the food is taken in and out of the freezer, it could contain germs in dangerous concentrations. However, the cook may still regard the product as being perfectly fresh because it has just emerged from the freezer. The foods most likely to cause illness are commercial ice cream and seafood, as both deteriorate rapidly.

Foods that Cannot be Frozen Successfully

Although most food will be prevented from going bad if kept at freezing point, some foods cannot be frozen successfully as their texture is ruined by freezing. This is particularly true of foods with a high water content. However, some of these may be frozen if wanted for soups or purées, in which case they should normally be frozen in purée form. Examples are bananas, cucumbers, lettuce and watercress.

Emulsions such as mayonnaise or hollandaise sauce do not freeze successfully as they separate when thawed.

Yoghurt, milk and cream can be frozen but will not be totally smooth when thawed. Double cream freezes better if whipped first. Storage time: 4 months.

Eggs cannot be frozen in the shell, but both whites and yolks freeze well, either lightly beaten together or separated. Storage time: 9 months.

Jelly, both savoury and sweet, loses its texture if frozen, so is not recommended.

Mousses and soufflés set with gelatine tend to go rubbery.

Strawberries keep their colour and flavour well, but become soft on thawing.

Melon is too watery to remain crisp when thawed. It is best frozen in balls in syrup, but even this is not totally satisfactory.

Tomatoes emerge mushy when thawed, but are good for soups and sauces. One bonus of freezing tomatoes whole is that they can be easily peeled if placed, still frozen, under running hot water. They can, of course, be frozen as purée or juice.

Fats, or foods with a high fat content, freeze less successfully as a rule than less fatty foods. They have a tendency to develop a slightly rancid flavour if stored for more than 3 months.

Foods that Freeze Successfully

Most foods freeze well if some care is taken with wrapping, etc. But some foods freeze so well that no one would ever know that they had been frozen. Baked or raw pastries, breads, bread or biscuit doughs, cakes and sandwiches containing not-too-wet fillings are good examples. As a general rule, raw food keeps better and longer than cooked. But cooked food, especially if well covered in a sauce, or under a potato or pastry crust, keeps well.

Vegetables freeze well if they are to be eaten cooked. They cannot be frozen if intended to be eaten raw. In order to prevent enzyme activity, green vegetables are boiled briefly, then cooled rapidly, before freezing. They may be frozen without this 'blanching' but their storage time would be reduced, and it is foolish to lose food through lazy freezing. Only the best vegetables, very fresh, should be used. They should be washed, or picked over, or otherwise prepared as if for immediate cooking. A large saucepan of water is brought to a rapid boil, and the vegetables (not more than 450 g | 1 lb or so at a time) lowered into it. Accurate timing of the blanching process is important: the minutes are counted from the time the water reboils. As soon as the time is up, the vegetables are lifted out, and immediately cooled in a sink full of cold water, if possible. Once stone-cold, the vegetables are lifted out, drained well, patted dry if necessary, and frozen. The same blanching water can be used for several batches of vegetables. Some vegetables (onions, mushrooms, potatoes) may be cooked completely in butter or blanched in oil instead of water. They are allowed to cool normally before freezing.

Fruits: Only freeze fruit that is in prime condition. Unripe, over-ripe or blemished fruit gives poor results. Three methods, as follows, are generally used to freeze raw fruit. (Cooked fruit may also be frozen whole or puréed.) Storage time: 9 months.
   Open Freezing: Suitable for most soft fruit such as raspberries and currants. Spread the fruit out on a baking sheet or tray and place in the freezer uncovered. When hard, pack into polythene bags or a rigid container, with or without adding sugar.
   Dry Sugar Pack: Suitable for most fruit to be used in cooked puddings. Prepare the fruit, toss it in sugar and freeze, with any juices that may have run from it during preparation. Care should be taken to exclude air, which may cause discoloration of the fruit.

Purée: Suitable for most fruits. Stew the fruit and mash, liquidize or sieve. Allow the purée to cool. Pack into containers, leaving head space, cover, label and freeze. Raw purées freeze well, too. Storage time: 1 year.

Herbs: should be frozen dry in small polythene bags or packets, or chopped finely, put into ice trays and just covered with water. The frozen cubes can be transferred to labelled bags. Storage time: 3 months.

Meat and Fish: Special care should be taken in wrapping to prevent freezer burn. Storage time: raw beef, 1 year, other raw meat, 6 months; cooked meat, 3 months; raw fish, 3 months; cooked fish, 3 months.

Cakes and Bread: Both raw and cooked doughs and pastries freeze well. Storage time: 1 month.

Stocks: Reduce stocks by boiling rapidly until very concentrated. Freeze in ice trays and when thawed use as stock cubes. Storage time: 3 months.

The following vegetables freeze successfully:

Vegetable	Preparation	Blanching time in minutes	Storage time in months
Asparagus	Do not tie in bunches	2–3	12
Artichoke (globe)	Remove stalks and outer tough leaves	5	12
Artichoke (Jerusalem)	Freeze once cooked into a purée	5	9
Beans, broad	Sort by size	$1\frac{1}{2}$	12
Beans, French	Trim ends	2–3	12
Beans, runner	Slice thickly	$1\frac{1}{2}$–2	6
Beetroot	Freeze completely cooked and skinned. Slice if large	–	6
Broccoli	Trim stalks	$2\frac{1}{2}$–4	12
Brussels sprouts	Choose small, firm sprouts. Remove outer leaves	3–4	12
Carrots	Choose small young ones with good colour. Scrape, Freeze whole	3	12
Cauliflower	Break heads into florets	3–4	6
Celery	Will be soft when thawed, but good for soups and stews	2	12
Corn on the cob	Remove husks and silks	4–6	12
Kale	Remove stalks	1	6
Leeks	Slice thinly; chop in chunks or leave whole	1–3	12
Mushrooms	Do not peel. Freeze unblanched for up to 1 month. For longer storage, cook in butter	$1\frac{1}{2}$	3
Onions	Store unblanched onions, sliced or chopped, for up to 3 months. Sliced or chopped onions can be blanched in water or oil. Button onions can be blanched whole	1–3	2
Mangetout and Fresh Peas	Choose young, very fresh peas	1	12
Potatoes	New	4	12
	Chips: blanch in oil		
	Boiled or mashed: freeze cooked and cold	–	3
Root vegetables	Cut into chunks; blanch, or cook completely	3	12
Spinach	Move about in water to separate leaves	1	12
Tomatoes	Make into a tomato sauce (see p. 128–9)	–	12

Essential Equipment

When buying kitchen equipment, the basic rule for standard items is to buy the best that you can possibly afford. Good kitchen equipment will probably last for 15 years and is worth the investment. When buying small or specialist equipment that may be used once only, be as economical or extravagant as your purse dictates.

The following is not intended to be a complete list of the kitchen equipment available, but includes all the utensils that the home cook could possibly want, while excluding certain specialist items like preserving and cake-decorating equipment, barbecues, smokers and storage equipment.

Utensils

The following items of equipment are essential for any cook:

1 cook's knife with 20 cm | 8 in blade
1 cook's knife with 7.5 cm | 3 in blade
1 filleting knife with 14 cm | 5 in blade
1 fruit knife
1 serrated bread knife
1 palette knife
1 stockpot
1 large saucepan 21 cm | 8 in diameter with lid
1 medium saucepan 19 cm | 7 in diameter with lid
1 small saucepan 12 cm | 5 in diameter
1 frying pan with 25 cm | 10 in diameter base
1 colander
2 wooden spoons
1 fish slice
1 rubber spatula

1 sieve (bowl strainer)
1 vegetable peeler
1 set of scales
1 measuring jug
1 pair kitchen scissors
3 gradated pudding basins
1 cheese grater
2 wooden or plastic chopping boards
1 rolling pin
1 pastry brush
1 set of measuring spoons
2 roasting tins; 1 small, 1 large
1 salad bowl
1 whisk
2 baking sheets
1 wire rack
2 large stainless steel bowls
20 cm | 8in flan ring
20 cm | 8in cake tin
1 lb loaf tin

Wine

by Richard Harvey M.W.

In Britain we are fortunate in having the widest selection of wines from the most varied outlets in the world. Being only a minor producer of wine, we are less prone to the natural chauvinism that exists in most wine-growing regions and countries. The assiduous research of the buyers for British importers has resulted in an enormous range of wines now being available not only in specialist wine shops but also in most supermarkets and off-licences. So where should you go to buy wine, whether it's for everyday consumption or a special occasion?

Where to Buy

Supermarkets

These account for most of the retail wine sales in the UK. They have been responsible for bringing wine to many new consumers, with the result that, today, no matter where you live, there is a wide range of wines available. By virtue of their size, the major supermarket groups have great buying power with the result that they can offer the customer very competitive prices. However, their size is also a disadvantage in that normally they are required to buy from the larger producers, and therefore cannot realistically offer the often more characterful wines made by smaller growers.

The second, and more important, disadvantage to buying in a supermarket is the lack of any personal advice. Many stores have overcome this to a small extent by the use of information slips on the shelves, or on back labels of the bottles, but this is rarely sufficient for the really interested consumer. The supermarkets, therefore, are the place to buy everyday drinking wines at affordable prices at the lower end of the price scale as well as their own-label champagnes and fortified wines.

Retail Chains

These groups have suffered most from the development and rapid growth of wine sales through the supermarkets over the last 20 years. Although these stores can offer personal advice, it is all too rarely knowledgeable. The notable exceptions are Oddbins and Majestic, both of which offer a wide and interesting range of wines, with knowledgeable and enthusiastic staff on hand to advise the customer.

Specialists

The specialist wine merchants, with perhaps only one or two outlets, or even working from home, have proliferated over the last 20 years, since the major brewery groups bought up most of the existing wine-merchant businesses in the 1960s. Some of these specialists offer the most comprehensive range of wines available, such as Lay and Wheeler of Colchester, or perhaps specialize in the wines of a particular country or region, such as Yapp's of Mere which sells wines mainly from the Rhône and Loire Valleys of France. What these specialists can offer is expert advice, since often, especially in the case of a one-man band, you will be buying from the person who has actually visited the vineyard and selected the wine. Whilst these specialists often cannot compete in price with the supermarkets at the lower end of the scale, what they can offer are wines, often only available in small quantities, that have a really individual character. These are certainly the places to buy once you have exhausted the super-markets' more basic ranges.

Mail Order

This area was for a long time the domain principally of the Wine Society, founded in 1874. It remains the leading operator in this field, but has been joined by many of the specialist merchants mentioned above. This is a good way to buy wine if you do not live near a good wine shop, and many of the wine lists sent out by firms who offer this service are extremely informative. However, the consumer has to bear the cost of delivery, either directly or indirectly, and this can add to the cost significantly for small orders of the less expensive wines. Also, the minimum quantity that you can order is a dozen bottles, although usually these can be mixed.

Auctions

Wine auctions have also developed considerably during the last 20 years, although they have existed since the nineteenth century. The majority of wine sold at auction is fine claret and vintage port, but other smaller auctions around the country also offer a range of everyday wine. It is important to check on the wine and ensure that it has been well stored, and is not simply stock that a wine merchant has been unable to sell. The other disadvantage is that normally lot sizes are in the order of 2 to 5 dozen cases. However, for individual purchasers, or groups of purchasers, who know specifically which fine wine they want to buy, the major London auction houses can be cheaper than a traditional merchant.

Abroad

Since January 1993, there have been no limits on personal imports from the European Union. This has opened up a new market for people to bring back as much wine as they wish, either direct from the vineyard, or purchased from shop or supermarket. The result has been a burgeoning of both French and British-owned wine shops in the French Channel ports, which offer a generally superior selection and service to most French supermarkets.

What to Buy

Having decided where to buy, the next question is what to buy. Normally, the first criterion in the mind of the consumer is the price. So it is worth examining how the cost of a bottle of wine is determined. In the United Kingdom, we have high rates of excise duty based on the alcoholic strength of the product (and a higher rate for sparkling wines). Because this tax is not related to the cost of the wine, a significantly high percentage of the selling price of less expensive wines is made up by the fixed costs, as the table below shows.

How the Retail Price is Made Up

Retail price	£4.00	£6.00	£8.00
Duty	45%	35%	30%
Shipping, distribution and retailing	30%	25%	20%
Wine	25%	40%	50%

It is apparent therefore that the less expensive wines offer the lowest value in terms of wine for money.

Reading the Label

In the absence of any personal advice from an expert, the consumer's buying choice must be based on the information given on the label. This can sometimes be very informative, although only a minimum of information has to be given by law: the country of origin of the wine, the quantity in the bottle (a standard bottle is now 75 centilitres), the alcoholic strength, the name and address of the bottle responsible, and, for wines produced within the EC, the quality of the wine. This latter designation is important as it distinguishes quality wines produced from a specified region from table wines that have no specific geographical designation.

Wine Labels

Country	Description of table wine	Description of regional wine	Description of quality wine	Description of top-quality wine
France	Vin de Table	Vin de Pays	VDQS (Vin Délimité de Qualité Supérieure)	AOC (Appellation d'Origine Contrôlée)
Italy	Vino da Tavola	IGT Indicazione Geographica Tipica	DOC (Denominazione di Origine Controllata)	DOCG (Denominazione di Origine Controllata e Garantita)
Germany	Deutscher Tafelwein	Landwein	QbA (Qualitätswein bestimmter Anbaugebiete)	QmP (Qualitätswein mit Prädikat)
Spain	Vino de Mesa	Vino de la Tierra	DO (Denominación de Origen)	DOC (Denominación de Origen Calificada)
Portugal	Vinho de Mesa	Vinho Regional	Indicacaode Proveniencia Regulamentada	Denominacao de Origen

The name and address of the bottler is also a good guide to the quality of the wine within the bottle, and it is worth looking for wines labelled as being bottled by the grower, or at the domaine, estate or château. Apart from giving greater assurance of authenticity, such wines will normally have more individual character than blends put together by large merchant houses or co-operatives. Most French, Italian, German and Spanish wines are named after the region, or village, in which they are produced. The grape variety is sometimes indicated, especially if it is not the norm for the area or, as in Germany, if the same named wine can be produced from different varieties. Most of the Vin de Pays (see chart above) produced in France now indicate the specific grape variety. The quality-wine laws of France and Italy specify the permissible varieties for any particular quality wine.

By contrast, the wines produced in what is called the New World (United States, Australia, New Zealand, South Africa and South America) are usually named after the grape variety, as a producer may make several wines in the same region from a number of different grape varieties, and the concept of the *terroir*, vineyard, is considered of less importance.

What is Wine?

Wine is the alcoholic drink resulting from the fermentation of the sugars in the grape by natural yeasts. The alcoholic content of most wines is between 8 per cent and 15 per cent alcohol by volume. The wine may be white, pink (rosé) or red. It may be the produce of only one year (a vintage wine) or a blend of wines produced in different years (a non-vintage wine).

The style of any particular wine is influenced by the following factors: the climatic conditions in which the grapes are grown; the soil in which the vine's roots develop; the particular grape variety grown; the methods used to cultivate the vine; the techniques used to make the wine; and any particular variations that occur from year to year. Climatic conditions mean that grapes which receive higher levels of sunshine will have higher degrees of sugar, and thus the resulting wines will be higher in alcohol (generally described as fuller wines).

Conversely, wines produced from grapes grown in cooler climates will be lower in alcohol, higher in acidity, and normally described as being lighter. Cooler climates are generally better suited to the production of white wines, which require a balance of acidity to give them a fresh, crisp style.

White wine is produced only from the juice of the grape, which is usually colourless, so that either white or black grapes can be used. Red wine achieves its colour from the skins remaining in contact with the juice for a period of time. In addition to colour, the skins also give tannin to the wine – a natural acid, which diminishes in time but can often make young red wines appear quite tough and dry. Rosé wines are produced from a very brief contact with the red grape skins.

Sweetness in wines is achieved either by not fully fermenting the grape sugars into alcohol, thereby leaving residual sugar in the wine, or by adding a concentrate of unfermented grape juice to the wine prior to bottling, which is the usual practice for German and English wines. Almost all red wines are dry, but white and rosé wines can be dry, medium or sweet. Sparkling wines are produced by inducing a second fermentation in the wine and retaining the carbon dioxide gas that is produced naturally. Champagne, the best-known sparkling wine, can only be produced in the delimited Champagne region of north-eastern France by secondary fermentation in the bottle. Wines made by this method elsewhere will usually show the term *méthode traditionelle* on the label.

Fortified wines are made by the addition of grape spirit either during or after fermentation. This spirit is normally brandy, the distillate of wine. These wines are usually between 15 and 20 per cent alcohol by volume and include: sherry, which can be dry, medium or sweet; port, which is normally sweet (although a little dry white port is made); Madeira; Marsala; and the sweet Muscat wines from the South of France.

Some Useful Terms

Sec – dry
Demi-sec – medium-sweet
Doux – sweet
Moelleux – sweet
Liquoreux – sweet
Brut – very dry (sparkling wine)
Blanc de Blancs – white wine produced only from white grapes
Supérieur – normally 0.5°; or 1.0° higher in alcohol

Italy

Secco – dry
Amarone – dry (literally bitter)
Abboccato – medium-sweet
Amabile – medium-sweet
Dolce – sweet
Recioto – wine made from selected (i.e. riper) bunches of grapes
Riserva – wine that has undergone a longer period of ageing
Classico – wines that come from the best part of the denomination

Germany

Kabinett – grower's selection of riper grapes
Spätlese – late-picked grapes with more sugar
Auslese – selected bunches of very ripe grapes
Beerenauslese – selected berries
Trockenbeerenauslese – selected berries with the greatest concentration of sugar
Trocken – dry
Halbtrocken – medium-dry (most German wines are medium to sweet)

Spain

Crianza – wine that has not been aged in cask
Reserva – wine aged in cask
Gran Reserva – wine aged in cask for a longer period

Major Wine-producing Areas

White Wines

France produces many of the greatest white wines of the world, both dry and sweet. The Loire Valley produces mostly crisp, dry white wines, such as Muscadet and the Sauvignon-based Sancerre and Pouilly-Fumé, with their fresh, almost tart, gooseberry flavour. Burgundy is the home of the classic white wines produced from the Chardonnay grape – from Chablis in the north to Mâcon and Pouilly-Fuissé in the south, with the finest, most concentrated and richest wines coming from Meursault and Puligny-Montrachet in the middle, just south of the town of Beaune. Alsace produces fine, fruity wines, which, because they come mostly from German grape varieties, are often confused with German wines. They are mostly dry with a wonderful, intense, spicy flavour. Bordeaux, although producing some good dry white wine in Entre-Deux-Mers and Graves, is best known for the lusciously sweet dessert wines made in Sauternes and Barsac, from grapes that have achieved a super-rich concentration of sugars.

Germany is best known for its slightly sweet, delicate and fruity white wines, the best of which are made from the Riesling grape. They also produce drier styles, called trocken or halbtrocken, but these can appear rather hard and acidic to British tastes.

Italy produces a vast range of white wines, mostly inexpensive and easy to drink, like Soave, Frascati and Orvieto. More interesting wines can be found in the north of the country, often from French grape varieties.

Spain has now turned much of its production from heavy, oaked, alcoholic white wines to fresher, crisper styles.

Portugal is best known for Vinho Verde, traditionally a light, slightly acidic wine, which is usually white and sweetened for the British market.

Eastern Europe: Austria and Hungary, in particular, are making fine white wines, particularly sweeter styles from well-ripened grapes. Tokaji from Hungary, one of the world's great sweet wines, is making a comeback.

Australia makes very good, ripe, buttery wines from Chardonnay grapes, and lighter, more lemony-tasting wines from Semillon, as well as experimenting with many other varieties, often blended together.

New Zealand produces very fine examples of Chardonnay and particularly good Sauvignon, the equal of Sancerre of Pouilly-Fumé.

California also makes Chardonnay- and Sauvignon-based wines which are generally fuller and fatter than those of New Zealand, due to the hotter climate

Chile makes very good Sauvignon Blanc and Chardonnay.

South Africa is producing increasing quantities of good-quality Chardonnay, Sauvignon Blanc and Chenin Blanc.

Red Wines

France traditionally recognized as producing the finest red wines in the world, be they Bordeaux or Burgundy, now faces competition from around the world. Claret, the English term for red wines from Bordeaux, is made predominantly from the Cabernet-Sauvignon grape in the Médoc and Graves, and the Merlot grape in St-Emilion and Pomerol. The wines are, at their best, deeply coloured, tannic when young, with the characteristic blackcurranty flavour of the Cabernet. Bordeaux is an enormous wine-producing region which also offers a vast variety of good-value red wines, often under a château label. Burgundy, in contrast, produces only a fraction of the quantity of wine made in Bordeaux, and is generally expensive. The finest wines, from the Pinot Noir grape, produced in well-known villages such as Nuits-St-Georges, Gevrey-Chambertin or Beaune, are softer and generally lighter than those of Bordeaux, with a raspberry fruitiness which matures quicker than the more tannic Cabernet. Beaujolais, France's best-known red wine, has been devalued by the excessive production of wine sold as Nouveau, but true Beaujolais is an easily drinkable, fruity wine from the Gamay grape. The Rhône Valley makes deeply coloured, rich spicy reds from the Syrah grape, such as Hermitage, and, further south, wines like Châteauneuf-du-Pape have a full, peppery alcoholic flavour derived from the Grenache grape. The South of France, in the past the source of vast quantities of unexciting table wines, is now producing many interesting wines, such as Corbières, Minervois and Vin de Pays.

Italy generally makes better red wines than white, whether traditional ones such as Chianti, Barolo or Barbaresco or new wines made outside the DOC laws and labelled simply as Vino da Tavola. The traditional wines were made to accompany the local cuisine, and can often appear somewhat tannic and astringent to the unaccustomed palate, without the balance of a cuisine based predominantly on olive oil.

Spain is best known for Rioja. This, like most Spanish reds, is a full, soft wine, with the pronounced oaky flavour that comes from being aged in oak barrels.

Portugal produces many interesting red wines from local grape varieties.

Bulgaria has become known for inexpensive red wines, particularly Cabernet Sauvignon. The better ones have a geographical designation.

Australia's best red wines come from the Cabernet Sauvignon and Shiraz (Syrah) grapes. They are rich, very concentrated wines with masses of ripe fruit flavours.

California also produces some very fine wines from the Cabernet Sauvignon, which, with the warmer temperatures, tend to be softer and riper than those from Bordeaux, with less tannin.

South Africa is making fine red wines from Cabernet and Merlot. Those made from Cinsault and Pinotage are usually less interesting.

South America, notably Chile and Argentina, is making increasingly good red wines from Cabernet Sauvignon, Merlot and Malbec.

Rosé Wines

Rosé wines are little appreciated in Britain – the most common being slightly sweet. There are, however, some fine dry rosé wines produced in France – the best, such as Tavel, coming from the southern Rhône. Other very good examples are made in the Languedoc, but those from Côtes de Provence are usually over-priced in relation to their quality.

Sparkling Wines

Whilst few people would dispute the supremacy of the best producers of champagne, there are also some very good sparkling wines made by secondary fermentation in the bottle (*méthode traditionelle*), which are available at a third of the price of champagne. Saumur and Vouvray in the Loire make fine examples from the local Chenin and Cabernet grapes. Spain produces good wines in the Penedes region south of Barcelona, labelled as Cava. There are also some very good sparkling wines made in Italy, Australia and California, both inexpensive and top-quality.

Fortified Wines

Sherry denotes a wine that can only come from a delimited area around the town of Jerez in Andalucía, in Spain. Although similar-style wines are made in Cyprus and South Africa, for example, they do not have the classic flavours associated with true sherry. The drier styles, fino, manzanilla and amontillado, make excellent aperitifs, whereas the full, sweeter oloroso-based wines are better after a meal.

Port is the traditional after-dinner drink. The most common styles, ruby and tawny (relating to their colour), are being overtaken in favour by higher-quality Vintage Character (an older ruby-style), 10-, 20- and 30-year-old tawnies, and vintage and late-bottled vintage ports. This last style is wine from a single year which does not need decanting, an essential requirement for a vintage or crushed port, which has matured for years in the bottle.

Madeira and Marsala are fortified wines which today are somewhat out of favour as drinks, although appreciated in the kitchen. The sweet, fortified Muscat wines from the South of France, such as Beaumes-de-Venise, are popular as dessert wines in the United Kingdom, although in France they are drunk as aperitifs (as with many sweet wines, and even port).

Storing Wine

Any wines which are going to be kept for longer than a few weeks must be stored correctly. There is no greater disappointment than holding high expectations of a bottle of wine which has been maturing for years, only to find it virtually undrinkable. Today very few houses have traditional underground cellars, and purpose-built ones are extremely expensive. However, it is not too difficult to replicate ideal conditions in some part of most homes. The following are the most important factors to bear in mind.

Temperature: The ideal temperature for storing wine for any length of time is around 12°C. Equally important, though, is to maintain a constant temperature; far better to keep the wine at a steady 10°C or 14°C than to fluctuate between 8°C and 16°C, ending up at an average 12°C, which is what can happen if the wine is stored in a centrally heated room, where the temperature rises and falls during each twenty-four-hour period. As a general rule, wine stored at a higher temperature will mature sooner than if stored at cooler temperature.

Humidity: The ideal humidity for storing wine is 100 per cent; unfortunately this quickly damages the cartons and labels. The best compromise is a relative humidity of around 75–80 per cent at 12°C.

Light: Ultra-violet damages wine, therefore it should always be stored in a dark area.

Smell: Wine can become tainted by smell, through the cork, so a clean atmosphere is important.

Vibration: The maturation of wine can be upset by vibration, so any movement must be avoided if possible.

Storing Position: Finally, and most importantly, it must be remembered that all wine bottles with corks must be stored on their sides, if they are to be kept for any length of time. This ensures that the wine keeps the cork moist which would otherwise start to dry out and contract and allow air into the bottle. The wine will soon oxidize, and become undrinkable.

Tasting Wine

Tasting wine must be viewed as an objective exercise, whereas drinking wine is much more subjective, a question of personal like or dislike. The reason for tasting, rather than just drinking, a wine is to assess its qualities. The taster's aim should be to provide someone who has not tasted a particular wine with as accurate a description as possible. Personal prejudices have to be put aside. Learning to taste is easy; all that is required is a little concentration and an idea of the elements to look for. Tasting wine involves the senses of sight and smell as well as taste.

The Appearance of a Wine

Clarity

Wine should look clear and bright. If it is cloudy, there is either an intrinsic fault with the wine or it has been badly handled, causing sediment in the bottle to have become mixed with the wine.

Some wines will contain small bubbles of carbon dioxide gas; *pétillance*, as this is known, is encouraged deliberately by some producers, particularly of white wines, to enhance freshness. It is achieved by not allowing all the carbon dioxide produced during fermentation to escape. The best-known example is Muscadet de Sèvre et Maine; if it is labelled 'Sur Lie', it means that the wine has not been racked off the yeast sediment following the alcoholic fermentation, but has been filtered and bottled early, directly from the vat, while some carbon dioxide is still being created.

Sugar-like crystals, often found on the cork or in the bottom of a bottle, are simply tartrates which have been precipitated by cold; they are entirely harmless.

Colour

Colour can give a good indication of the style of wine to be tasted. White wines will vary from pale, watery white to deep, golden yellow, covering all shades in between. The palest-coloured wines usually come from cooler wine-producing regions, such as the Moselle or Loire valleys. Chablis will usually have a pronounced greenish tinge. Many Australian and Californian Chardonnays will be straw-yellow in colour, as a result of the hotter climate in which they are produced. Sweet wines produced from over-ripe, or 'botrytized', grapes will often be a beautiful golden yellow. However, it would be wrong to assume that all sweet wines will be this colour; many sweet German wines, for example, are quite pale. A golden-yellow colour can also be an indication of age; white wines become more yellow as they mature, finally turning brown, which could indicate that they have become oxidized (i.e. they are too old), or, in extreme cases, maderized (i.e. they have taken on the burnt caramel colour of Madeira).

Red wines, when young, will usually be purplish in colour. Light reds, particularly some Italian wines such as Valpolicella and Bardolino, often have a cherry-red colour. Normally, ruby-red is more typical, the deeper-coloured wines again usually indicating warmer climates. As red wines age they take on a more brick-red hue, finally turning tawny and brown. Unlike white wines, these tawny-coloured reds may not be completely oxidized; long ageing in cask prior to bottling is traditional for many Italian wines, and the Pinot Noir grape of Burgundy produces wines which take on an orangey-brown colour much sooner than, for instance, Cabernet Sauvignon-based wines.

The Bouquet or Smell of a Wine

It is possible to obtain a reasonably good indication of a wine's style from its smell. Any faults not apparent on sight will also be noticeable in the smell. The most common fault, other than an oxidized wine, will be one that is corked. This is the result of a cork which may have been infected with cork weevil, as a result of a failure in the sterilization process which all wine corks undergo, or more likely cork taint. The wine will smell musty and woody, although there may be no visual indication on the cork itself. A fault which is becoming less and less common, thankfully, is the smell of sulphur, caused by excessive use of sulphur dioxide as an anti-oxidant and anti-yeast agent during the wine-making process.

To gain the most from a wine's bouquet, it is essential to swirl the wine around the glass, which will help release the aromas. Many of the primary elements of the wine – fruit flavours, sweetness, acidity and alcohol – may be noticed. Certain grape varieties have very distinctive aromas – Cabernet Sauvignon of blackcurrants, Sauvignon Blanc of gooseberries or elderflowers. Sweetness on the nose may not necessarily indicate residual sugar in the wine, as it is not a volatile element. Acidity and alcohol will often be apparent.

Terms Describing the Bouquet of a Wine

Fruity: Attractive fruit quality, as in blackcurrants (Cabernet Sauvignon) or gooseberries (Sauvignon Blanc)

Grapey: Often produced by wines with some residual sugar

Floral: Flowery aromas such as elderflower (Sauvignon Blanc) or roses (Gewürztraminer)

Grassy: Sappy, green smell

Stalky: Green, woody (Cabernet Franc)

Vegetal: Mature Pinot Noir

Dumb or closed: Little smell, often from a young or undeveloped wine

Corked: See above

Oxidized: See above

Acetic: Vinegar smell from excess volatile acidity

Sulphury: See above

The Taste of Wine

Taste should be a confirmation and development of sight and smell. When tasting wine it is important to swirl it well around the mouth. The human tongue picks up sweetness at the tip and acidity at the back. It also helps to draw in air through the teeth to aerate the wine and thereby appreciate its development.

The Primary Elements of Taste

Sweetness: Often detected first

Acidity: Can carry right through

Alcohol: Constitutes part of the body of a wine: a light wine may still be high in alcohol, although a full-bodied wine is rarely low in alcohol

Fruit: This can be carried through from the nose but may be more or less intense on the palate

Tannin: Tannic acid is found in young red wines, as a result of the skin maceration required to obtain colour. It will leave a dry, slightly bitter taste in the mouth, although the same effect can be the result of wine which has been allowed to age too long, and has lost its fruit and started to dry out.

A wine in which all these elements are in balance will appear complete, although it must be remembered that a young red wine may have noticeably high levels of tannin until it reaches maturity.

Terms Describing the Taste of a Wine

Sweetness

Dry: Wine with all its grape sugars fermented out

Sweet: Wine containing residual grape sugars

Acidity

Fresh, crisp, green, sharp, tart: Noticeable or excessive acidity

Flat, flabby: Lack of acidity

Alcohol

Body: A light, medium or full-bodied wine is determined by the amount of alcohol and extract

Extract: The soluble solids in a wine

Thin: Wine with little extract or body

Big: Wine with plenty of extract and alcohol

Heavy: Wine with too much extract and alcohol

Fruit

Ripe: Wine made from mature grapes

Rich: Wine full of fruit, alcohol and extract

Nutty: Often the taste of full, dry white wines

Spicy: Often found in wines from the Syrah grape

Peppery: Often found in wines from the Grenache grape

Neutral: Bland, little fruit flavour

Mouldy, musty, woody: 'Off' flavours – perhaps corked wine

Tannin

Hard, tough: Excess of tannin

Round, smooth, soft, supple: Little tannin

Finally, it is important to appreciate the length of time the taste remains after swallowing or spitting out the wine. This is known as the after-taste or finish and its length is a good indicator of quality – a wine can be described as having good length. When little taste remains after swallowing, a wine is described as short.

Serving Wine

The enjoyment of wine is greatly enhanced if it is served correctly. This requires a little forethought, particularly as far as serving temperature is concerned.

Temperature

White and rosé wines are best served around 7°C. The best way to chill wine is to put the bottle into a refrigerator for a couple of hours. If the wine is going to be drunk sooner, then 15 minutes in a bucket of ice and water, or in a freezer, will achieve the same result. However, it is important to remember that too cold a temperature will deaden the bouquet and flavour of a wine.

Sparkling wines should be served well chilled, 5–7°C; the low temperature helps to reduce the pressure of carbon dioxide gas in the bottle.

Light fortified wines, such as pale dry, fino or manzanilla sherry should also be served well chilled. It is also not uncommon to serve light tawny port chilled; otherwise, fortified wines are best served at ambient room temperature.

Red wines are traditionally served at what is called 'room' temperature. This term originated before central heating, and nowadays there is a tendency to serve red wine too warm. But there is also a fashion for serving some light red wines, particularly those from the Loire Valley, chilled. Certainly, lighter styles such as these, or Beaujolais, or Valpolicella and Bardolino from Italy, are best served cool, around 12°C. Fuller-bodied red wines are best served warmer, around 16°C. It is dangerous to try to raise a red wine's temperature quickly; if the wine is 'cooked' or 'boiled' it will be completely spoilt. If a red wine cannot be allowed to rise to ambient room temperature naturally and slowly, it can be put in a bucket of warm, not hot water, but it should never be put under boiling water, in an oven or on a radiator.

Opening

Many red wines benefit from being opened some time before serving. As a general rule, the younger and more full-bodied the wine, the longer it will need to breathe. Old wines should only be opened up to an hour before drinking, as they can deteriorate very quickly once they have come in contact with air. Otherwise a couple of hours is generally sufficient.

Corkscrews

The best corkscrew for opening bottles of wine will have a broad wide spiral which ensures good purchase on the cork, whereas a thick screw can pull out a hole through the middle of a cork.

Decanting

Red wines which have been made to mature in the bottle will begin to throw a sediment after a number of years. It is therefore always safer to decant a wine more than 10 years old, in order to separate the wine from the deposit in the bottle. Decanting also helps to aerate a wine as it is being poured, and so also serves to soften full-bodied, young red wines.

Glasses

The enjoyment of any wine is enhanced by serving it in good glasses. The best glasses for wine are the simplest, made of clear, thin glass, narrower at the lip than in the bowl to concentrate the bouquet, and with a stem long enough to keep the hand away from the bowl. Glasses, especially for red wine, should be generous in size; they should be no more than two-thirds filled to allow space for the bouquet to develop as the wine is swirled around the glass. Finally, it is important to ensure that glasses are clean and not carrying any smell of detergent.

Keeping Opened Wine

Once a wine has been opened the exposure to the air means that it will start to oxidize and deteriorate. The length of time any opened wine can be kept depends not only on the wine itself, but also on the amount left in the bottle in proportion to the air. A bottle with only one glassful taken from it will last for 3 or 4 days, whereas a bottle with one glassful remaining in it may not be drinkable the following day. White wines which have been opened should always be kept in the refrigerator, and red wines keep better in a cool place. Wines made from certain grape varieties, notably Pinot Noir and Gamay, do not really keep at all well, whereas others, such as Nebbiolo, can actually improve the day after being opened.

Various products claim to maintain freshness in an opened bottle of wine; the best system is an inert gas spray which, being heavier than air, forms a blanket on top of the wine.

Wine and Food

Most wines taste different when tasted on their own or drunk with food. Different elements in each react with each other. Traditionally, matching wine and food had little to do with anything other than geographical association. For centuries, the purpose of wine production was simply to provide wine for meals. While different areas discovered that certain grape varieties and styles were better suited to their climate and soil than others, wines were primarily being made to suit the local foods.

The increasing consumption of wine without food has contributed to the popularity of New World wines with their ripe, sweet fruit flavours and soft tannins. A lot of these wines have a variety of flavours which often conflict with the different flavours in many dishes; they are at their best accompanying simple roast or grilled foods. Many Italian red wines, on the other hand, can taste rather dry and astringent on their own, but soften dramatically when drunk with food, especially a cuisine based on olive oil. German wines, generally light in body and slightly sweet, are best drunk on their own.

There are two specific criteria for matching wine with food. First, the two must complement each other: a strong-tasting food will kill a light wine, just as a rich, full-bodied wine will overwhelm light food. Muscadet and Chablis are perfect with shellfish but would be killed by game. Equally important is contrast. A wine with good acidity and dryness can be a perfect match for oily food – Sancerre, or New Zealand Sauvignon Blanc, with smoked salmon, for example – while claret, with its dry tannins, is the perfect complement to the sweet fattiness of lamb.

Certain combinations which have developed over the years can seem strange. The most striking is drinking Sauternes with foie gras; one of the richest foods accompanied by rich, strong, sweet white wine. An equally good match would be a strong, dry, spicy white from Alsace.

When selecting wine to match a specific dish, it is important to remember that it is not just a question of choosing the wine to match the particular type of meat or fish; the sauce in which they are cooked can have greater effect on the wine. Cream- or butter-based sauces demand wines with acidity rather than alcohol to help cut the richness: Sauvignon grape-based wines, Bourgogne Aligote or Muscadet for white wines; cool-climate red wines, such as those from the Loire Valley, Beaujolais, or even light Burgundy. Dishes rich in oil need dry, full-bodied wines, such as whites or rosés from southern France, or Bordeaux or Piedmontese red wines. Hot, spicy foods will kill just about any wine, and are best accompanied by water or beer.

One of the hardest ingredients with which to match wine is vinegar, its natural antithesis. Any dish with a dressing containing vinegar will be detrimental to wine. The best solution for salad dishes is to serve a full-bodied, dry white wine with low acidity. Chocolate is also difficult, but not impossible – a fortified Muscat, such as Beaumes de Venise with its orangey sweetness, can make a good match, as can rich Australian Liqueur Muscat, or Malaga from Spain.

Strong, dry cheeses are usually best eaten with red wine, but this is not the ideal accompaniment to all cheese. Creamy blue cheeses can often be delicious with sweet white wine. Port may be fine for Stilton, but only if it is drunk with it, not poured into it.

If you are serving different wines during a meal, and especially if they are its focal point, it is important to serve them in the right order:

Dry before sweet
Light before full-bodied
Young before old

Food	Style of Wine	Suggestion
Fish Dishes		
Terrine	Light dry white	Chablis
Soups	Crisp dry white	Sancerre/Pouilly-Fumé
Mayonnaise		New Zealand Sauvignon
Buttery sauce		Burgundy
Smoked	Spicy white	Alsace
Chinese-style		Tokay/Riesling
Barbecued		
Chicken Dishes		
Mayonnaise	Clean, dry white	Soave
Buttery sauce		
Chinese-style	Full white	Mâcon, Australian Chardonnay
Roast	Light, fruity red	Beaujolais
Casseroled		
Barbecued/Indian/	Fuller red	Côtes du Rhône
Tandoori		
Veal		
Buttery sauce	Light, fruity red	Valpolicella
Roast		
Casserole	Fuller red	Chianti Classico
Pork		
Buttery sauce	Light red	Beaujolais Villages
Spicy/		
Chinese style		
Stewed/Cassoulet	Full red	Corbières
Roast	Medium red	Burgundy
Barbecued		

Lamb

With Hollandaise	Light to medium red	Chinon/Bourgueil
Stewed Roast	Fuller red	Claret/Rioja
Spiced/curried/ barbecued	Spicy red	Crozes-Hermitage

Beef

With Hollandaise	Medium red	Burgundy
Casserole Roast	Fuller red	Rhône/Châteauneuf du Pape
Spiced/barbecued	Full, spicy red	Australian Shiraz Australian/Californian Cabernet

Venison	Rich red	Australian Shiraz
Duck	Medium red	Burgundy
Game birds	Full red	Claret
Cold Collations/ Salmis	Rosé or light red	Tavel Rosé Valpolicella
Pâtés/terrines	Spicy red	Côtes du Rhône
Foie gras	Sweet white	Sauternes Alsace Gewurztraminer/Tokay

Soups

Light	Fortified	Dry sherry/Madeira
Creamy	Dry white	Burgundy

Vegetable dishes	Light dry wine	Soave

Cheese		
Soufflé		Alsace Tokay
Soft, creamy	Light, sweet wine	Loire (Coteaux du Layon)
Blue		
Hard	Medium red	Burgundy

Puddings		
Plain fruit	Slightly sweet white	German Spätlese/Auslese
Light fruit puddings	Sweet white	Coteaux du Layon
Ice creams/sorbets		Italian Moscato
Rich creamy puddings	Rich, sweet, white	Sauternes
Hot soufflés	Sweet	Champagne
Chocolate puddings	Fortified	Muscat de Beaumes de Venise
		Australian Liqueur Muscat

Wine Style	**Style of Food**
Very dry white (Muscadet, Sauvignon grape wines, Chablis)	Shellfish, salmon, oily fish
Dry white (Soave, Frascati, Chardonnay wines, Burgundy)	White fish
Spicy dry white (Alsace, some dry German and English wines)	Smoked fish
Medium dry white (Moselle, Vouvray, Vinho Verde)	Chicken
Medium sweet white (German Spätlese/Auslese, Italian Moscato)	Soft, creamy cheese Fruit and fruit puddings

Sweet white (Sauternes, Barsac, Muscat de Beaumes de Venise)	Foie gras Rich puddings Chocolate puddings
Rosé (Tavel, Provence)	Bouillabaisse Cold meats
Light red (Beaujolais, Valpolicella)	Chicken, veal Pork
Soft red (Burgundy)	Pork, duck
Medium red (Claret, Côtes du Rhône, Chianti, Rioja)	Lamb Game birds
Full red (Châteauneuf du Pape, Cabernet-Sauvignon wines)	Beef
Very full red (Crozes-Hermitage, Barolo, Australian Shiraz)	Rich stews Venison

A Dictionary of Tasting Terms

Appearance

Bright: All wines in sound condition should be bright.

Colour: White wines can be:

Pale: Usually indicating they come from a cool climate.

Straw-yellow: A deeper colour from a hot climate.

Green: Usually indicates a young wine.

Purple: The colour of young red wine, turning ruby or cherry red before becoming brick red or tawny with age.

Deep-coloured: Wines that usually come from hot climates.

Smell

Bouquet: The particular smell of a wine.

Fruity: Attractive fruit quality, not necessarily:

Grapey: Aroma produced by certain grape varieties.

Grassy: Green, woody smell often found in young wine.

Dumb or Closed: Little smell, usually from a young or undeveloped wine.

Corked: Distinct smell of cork – the result of a diseased or tainted cork leading to a wine becoming:

Oxidized: ... or worse.

Maderized: White wine turned brown in colour.

Acetic/vinegary: Excess volatile acidity.

Sulphury: Excess of sulphur used in the wine's production.

Taste

Acidity: Natural component of wine. High-acid wines are described as crisp, green, sharp, tart. Low-acid wines taste flat or flabby and lack freshness.

Alcohol: Indicated by the weight of a wine. Low-alcohol wines tend to be light.

Extract: The soluble solids in a wine. Wines with plenty of extract and alcohol are described as having plenty of body, or as being big or full-bodied wines. These tend to come from hot climates and will usually have more alcohol and extract than those from cool climates.

Heavy: Wine with too much alcohol and extract.

Thin: Wine with little extract or flavour.

Flavour: The particular taste of a wine. Useful terms in this area are:

Fruity: Not necessarily grape tastes.

Nutty: Found in full, dry white wines.

Peppery: Raw taste often found in young red wine, but also from certain grape varieties.

Spicy: Rich taste found in certain grape varieties.

Ripe: Wine made from mature grapes – or a wine ready to drink.

Rich: Full fruit flavour with alcohol and extract, not necessarily sweet.

Round: No rough edges.

Smooth: No rough edges.

Soft: No rough edges.

Supple: No rough edges.

Neutral: Bland flavour.

Oxidized: Flat, stale taste – the result of the wine's exposure to air.

Mouldy: Off flavour.

Musty: Off flavour.

Woody: Off flavour.

Dry: Wine with all grape sugars fermented out.

Sweet: Wine with high sugar content.

Tannin: Tannic acid derived from grape skins during fermentation therefore found only in young red wines. Leaves dry taste in mouth and around teeth. Wine with an excess of tannin is described as hard or tough.

Finish: The end-taste of a wine. The time it lasts is described as length.

Recipes

Stocks

Behind every great soup and behind many a sauce stands a good strong stock. Stock is flavoured liquid, and the basic flavour can be fish, poultry, meat or vegetable. Stock cubes and bouillon mixes are usually over-salty and lack the intense flavour of properly made stock, making food taste the same. As an emergency measure, or to strengthen a rather weak stock, they are useful. But a good cook should be able to make a perfect stock.

Making a Stock

The secret of stocks is slow, gentle simmering. If the liquid is the slightest bit greasy, vigorous boiling will produce a murky, fatty stock. Skimming, especially for meat stocks, is vital: as fat and scum rise to the surface they should be lifted off with a basting spoon.

Rich, brown stocks are made by first frying or baking the bones, vegetables and scraps of meat until a good, dark, even brown. Only then does the cook proceed with the gentle simmering. Care must be taken not to burn the bones or vegetables: one burned carrot can ruin a pot of stock. Brown stocks are usually made from red meats or veal, but can be made with poultry or fish bones and sometimes only from vegetables for vegetarian dishes.

White stocks are more delicate and are made by simmering only. They are based on white poultry or vegetables or fish.

The longer brown meat stocks are simmered the better flavoured they will be. A stockpot will simmer all day in a restaurant, being skimmed or topped up with water as the chef passes it, and only strained before closing time. However, it is important not to just keep adding bits and pieces to the stockpot and to keep it going on the back burner for days, because the pot will become cluttered with cooked-out bones and vegetables that have long since given up any flavour. At least 3, and up to 8 hours over the gentlest flame, or in the bottom oven of an Aga, is ample cooking time.

Fish stocks should never be simmered for more than 30 minutes. After this the bones begin to impart a bitter flavour to the liquid. For a stronger flavour the stock can be strained, skimmed of any scum or fat, and then boiled down to reduce and concentrate it.

Similarly, vegetable stocks do not need long cooking. As they contain very little fat, even if the vegetables have been browned before simmering, they are easily skimmed, and can then be boiled rapidly after straining to concentrate the flavour. 30 minutes simmering is generally enough.

The bones

Most households rarely have anything other than the cooked bones from a roast available for stocks. These will make adequate stock, but it will be weaker than that made with raw bones. Raw bones are very often free from the butcher, or can be had very cheaply. Get them chopped into manageable small pieces in the shop. A little raw meat, the bloodier the better, gives a rich, very clear liquid.

Water

The water must be cold, as if it is hot the fat in the bones will melt immediately and when the stock begins to boil much of the fat will be bubbled into the stock. The stock will then be murky, have an unattractive smell and a nasty flavour. Cold water encourages the fat to rise to the surface; it can then be skimmed.

Jellied stock

Veal bones produce a particularly good stock that will set to a jelly. A calf's foot added to any stock will have the same jellifying effect. Jellied stock will keep longer than liquid stock, but in any event stocks should be reboiled every 2 or 3 days if kept refrigerated, or every day if kept in a larder, to prevent them going bad.

Salt

Do not add salt to stock. It may be used later for something that is already salty, or boiled down to a concentrated glaze (glace de viande), in which case the glaze would be over-salted if the stock contained salt. (Salt does not boil off with the water, but remains in the pan.)

Storage

A good way of storing a large batch of stock is to boil it down to a syrupy consistency, and to add water only when using. Freeze the glaze in ice cube trays, then turn the frozen cubes into a plastic box in the freezer. They will keep for at least a year if fat-free.

Brown Stock

MAKES 1 LITRE|1¾ PINTS

1 kg|2¼ lb beef or veal marrow bones or chicken carcasses, cut into 5 cm|2 in pieces

2 medium onions, unpeeled, cut into 2.5 cm|1 in pieces or into eighths through the root

2 medium carrots, peeled and cut into 2.5 cm|1 in pieces

2 sticks of celery, cut into 2.5 cm|1 in pieces

1 turnip, cut into 2.5 cm|1 in pieces

½ small celeriac, peeled and cut into 2.5 cm|1 in pieces

110 g|4 oz button mushrooms

1 bulb of Florence fennel

2 tablespoons vegetable oil

1 tablespoon tomato purée

a handful of fresh parsley stalks

1 bay leaf

½ teaspoon black peppercorns

1 sprig of fresh thyme about 2 litres|3½ pints cold water

1 Preheat the oven to 220°C|425°F|gas mark 7.

2 Trim any excess fat from the bones. Place in a roasting tray and roast in the oven for

about 1 hour until a rich russet-brown. Turn the bones occasionally to ensure that they roast and brown evenly on all sides. During the browning process most of the remaining fat will melt and collect in the roasting tray.

3 Shallow-fry the vegetables in vegetable oil until they are caramelized to a rich golden-brown. It is essential that they do not burn.

4 Add the tomato purée to the vegetables just before they are fully browned to caramelize it to a deeper red-brown colour.

5 Remove any burnt vegetable pieces as they will taint the stock with a bitter flavour.

6 Place the bones and vegetables in a deep, narrow pot and cover with cold water.

7 Bring slowly to the boil, skimming off the scum as it rises to the surface. There should be little fat as most of it was rendered down during the roasting and browning process.

8 When the water comes to a poach, pour cold water into the pan to solidify the fat and scum and skim well to remove the fat and scum, ensuring that the remaining liquid is as clear as possible.

9 Add more cold water to cover all the ingredients, then bring back to the boil. Poach the ingredients for 4–5 hours for chicken bones or 5–6 hours for beef or veal bones, skimming occasionally.

10 Strain the stock but do not press the vegetables in the sieve as this could make the stock cloudy.

11 Reduce the stock to the required strength, skimming regularly.

12 To store the stock, reduce to a glaçe, then cool.

White Chicken Stock

MAKES 1 LITRE|1¾ PINTS

2 chicken carcasses, broken up

1 veal knuckle bone

2 onions, cut into 2.5 cm|1 in pieces

1 medium carrot, cut into 2.5 cm|1 in pieces

2 sticks of celery, cut into 2.5 cm|1 in chunks

1 leek, green leaves removed, cut into 2.5 cm|1 in pieces

55 g|2 oz button mushrooms

a handful of fresh parsley stalks

1 bay leaf

½ teaspoon black peppercorns

1 sprig of fresh thyme

about 2 litres|3½ pints cold water

1 Trim any excess fat from the bones.

2 Place the prepared bones in a deep, narrow pot. Cover with cold water and slowly bring to a poach.

3 Skim off the scum and fat that rise to the surface, using a ladle.

4 When the water starts to boil, pour cold water into the pan to solidify the fat and scum. Skim well to remove the fat and scum, ensuring that the remaining liquid is as clear as possible.

5 Add the vegetables, herbs and peppercorns to the pot and cover all the ingredients with cold water.

6 Bring back to a poach, then regulate the heat so that the stock poaches 3–4 hours, gently throughout the cooking period. Skim occasionally.

7 Make sure that the ingredients remain covered with water. As the liquid evaporates, top the pot up with cold water as this will help to draw any remaining fat and scum to the surface.

8 Once the stock is cooked, strain carefully through a fine sieve, to remove all remaining fragments, into a storage container or a clean wide pan for reducing. Do not force the liquid through the sieve by pressing the ingredients as this may result in a cloudy stock.

9 Reduce the stock to the required strength, skimming regularly to remove any further impurities that collect on the surface. To store the stock, continue to reduce it to a glace, then cool.

Glace de Viande

Brown stock (see page 102), absolutely free of fat

1 In a heavy saucepan reduce the brown stock by boiling over a steady heat until thick, clear and syrupy.

2 Pour into small pots. When cold cover with clingfilm.

3 Keep in the refrigerator until ready for use.

NOTE: Glace de viande keeps for several weeks and is very useful for enriching sauces.

Ham Stock

The best-flavoured ham stock is generally the well-skimmed liquor from boiling a ham or gammon (see page 479), but this recipe works well with a cooked ham bone.

1 cooked ham bone
1 onion, cut into 2.5 cm|1 in dice
1 carrot, cut into 2.5 cm|1 in dice
1 stick of celery cut into 2.5 cm|1 in dice

1 bay leaf
fresh parsley stalks
black peppercorns

1 Place all the ingredients together in a large saucepan. Cover with cold water and bring gradually to the boil. Skim off any fat and/or scum. Simmer for 2–3 hours, skimming frequently and topping up the water level if necessary.

2 Strain and use as required.

NOTE: Ham stock is usually salty and should not be reduced.

Turkey Stock (1)

Ideally all stocks are made from raw bones. However, no one is likely to have raw turkey bones. If you are making stock before Christmas you will have to make it from the giblets. This recipe can be used for making goose, pheasant and chicken stock as well. Never add liver to a stock pot; it will make the stock taste bitter.

the neck of the turkey

giblets, well washed, without the liver

1 onion, sliced

1 stick of celery, sliced

1 carrot, sliced

1 parsley stalk, bruised

1 sprig of fresh thyme

2 bay leaves

10 black peppercorns

1 Put all the ingredients into a large saucepan. Cover generously with cold water and bring slowly up to the boil. Skim off any fat.
2 Simmer slowly for 2–3 hours, skimming frequently and topping up the water level if necessary.
3 Strain and cool.

Turkey Stock (2)

This recipe for making stock uses the cooked turkey bones.

cooked turkey bones

1 onion, sliced

a stick of celery, sliced

1 carrot, sliced

1 parsley stalk, bruised

1 sprig of fresh thyme

2 bay leaves

10 black peppercorns

1 Put all the ingredients into a large saucepan. Cover generously with cold water and bring slowly to the boil. Skim off any fat and/or scum.
2 Simmer slowly for 2–3 hours, skimming frequently and topping up the water level if necessary.
3 Strain and cool.

Aspic

1 litre | 1¾ pints well-flavoured white stock (see page 103)

powdered gelatine, as necessary

2 egg shells, crushed

2 egg whites

1 Lift or skim any fat from the stock. Sterilize all the equipment and the egg shells.
2 Put the stock into a large saucepan and sprinkle on the gelatine, if using. If the stock is liquid when chilled, use 45 g | 1½ oz gelatine; if the stock is set when chilled, gelatine will not be necessary. Dissolve over a low heat, then allow to cool.

3 Put the shells and egg whites into the stock. Place over the heat and whisk steadily with a balloon whisk until the mixture begins to boil. Stop whisking immediately and remove the pan from the heat. Allow the mixture to subside. Take care not to break the crust formed by the egg white.

4 Bring the aspic just to the boil again, and again allow to subside. Repeat this once more (the egg white will trap the sediment in the stock and clear the aspic). Allow to cool for 2 minutes.

5 Fix a double layer of fine muslin over a clean basin. Place a large spoonful of the crust into the sieve then carefully strain the aspic through it. Do not try to hurry the process by squeezing the cloth, or murky aspic will result.

Court Bouillon

1.1 litre|2 pints water
150 ml|¼ pint white wine vinegar
1 carrot, sliced
1 onion, sliced

1 stick of celery
12 black peppercorns
2 bay leaves
salt

1 Place half of the water with all the remaining ingredients in a large saucepan and simmer for 20 minutes.

2 Add the remaining water then allow to cool, and strain.

White Fish Stock

1 onion, sliced
1 carrot, sliced
1 stick celery, sliced
1 leek sliced
450 g|1lb fishbones, skins, fins, heads or tails of white fish

parsley stalks
bay leaf
1 sprig fresh thyme
6 black peppercorns

1 Put all the ingredients together into a saucepan, with water to cover, and bring to the boil. Turn down to simmer and skim off any scum.

2 Simmer for 20 minutes if the fish bones are small, 30 minutes if large. Strain.

NOTE: The flavour of fish stock is impaired if the bones are cooked for too long. Once strained, however, it may be strengthened by further boiling and reducing.

White Vegetable Stock

MAKES 1 LITRE | 1¾ PINTS

1 kg | 2¼ lb aromatic vegetables or trimmings, to include:

2 onions, cut into 1 cm | ½ in dice

2 carrots, peeled and cut into 1 cm | ½ in dice

1 leek, green leaves removed and cut into 1 cm | ½ in dice

2 sticks of celery, cut into 1 cm | ½ in dice

a few mushroom stalks

2 litres | 3½ pints cold water

a handful of fresh parsley stalks

1 sprig of fresh thyme

1 bay leaf

½ teaspoon black peppercorns

1 Place all the ingredients in a saucepan and simmer for 30 minutes, skimming regularly, then strain.

Brown Vegetable Stock

MAKES 1 LITRE | 1¾ PINTS

2 tablespoons vegetable oil

2 onions, unpeeled

2 carrots

1 turnip

2 sticks of celery

1 small parsnip

55 g | 2 oz mushrooms or mushroom stalks and peelings

1 clove of garlic

1 teaspoon tomato purée

a handful of fresh parsley stalks

1 bay leaf

1 sprig of fresh thyme

12 black peppercorns

2 litres | 3½ pints cold water

1 Heat the oil in a large, heavy saucepan and cook the vegetables slowly and evenly on all sides until a russet-brown colour. If you are making a large quantity of stock, do not overcrowd the pan with vegetables or they will sweat rather than brown. Instead, brown the vegetables in batches and return them to the pan before adding the remaining ingredients.

2 Remove any overbrowned or burnt pieces of vegetable before adding all the remaining ingredients to the pan.

3 Cover with water and stir. Bring to the boil, then simmer for 1 hour, skimming occasionally.

4 Strain and reduce to the required strength.

Shellfish Stock

1 onion, sliced

1 carrot, sliced

1 stick of celery, sliced

a selection of crustacean and mollusc shells, such as prawn shells, mussel shells, lobster or crab cases

1 bouquet garni (see page 9)

6 black peppercorns

1 Put all the ingredients into a saucepan. Cover with water and bring to the boil, then reduce the heat and simmer for 30 minutes. Skim regularly. Strain and reduce to two-thirds of the original quantity by boiling rapidly. Use as required.

Fish Glaze

Fish glaze (glace de poisson) is simply very well-reduced, very well-strained fish stock, which is used to flavour and enhance fish sauces. It can be kept refrigerated for about 3 days or frozen in ice cube trays and used as required.

Brown Fish Stock

This is not a classic stock but can be used when a stronger flavour is required.

MAKES 1 LITRE | 1¾ PINTS

2 tablespoons vegetable oil

2 shallots, peeled and cut into 1 cm | ½ in dice

½ bulb of Florence fennel, cut into 1 cm | ½ in dice

½ carrot, peeled and cut into 1 cm | ½ in dice

1 stick of celery, cut into 1 cm | ½ in dice

1 litre | 1¾ pints cold water

fish bones, skins, fins, crustacean and mollusc shells, cleaned and cut into 5 cm | 2 in pieces

1 bouquet garni

1 clove of garlic

½ teaspoon tomato purée

1 Heat the oil in a large, heavy saucepan and add the vegetables. Cook over a very low heat until the vegetables are soft and evenly browned. Do not allow them to burn.

2 Remove the pan from the heat and add the fish bones, trimmings and shells, the bouquet garni, garlic and tomato purée. Cover with cold water.

3 Bring to the boil, then simmer for 30 minutes, skimming regularly.

Savoury Sauces

Larousse defines a sauce as a 'liquid seasoning for food', and this covers anything from juices in a frying pan to complicated and sophisticated emulsions.

Flour-thickened sauces

The commonest English sauces are those thickened with flour, and these are undoubtedly the most practical for the home cook. The secret is not to make them too thick (by not adding too much flour), to beat them well and to simmer for 2 minutes after they have boiled to make them shine. They will also look professionally shiny if they are finished by whizzing in a blender, or if they are 'mounted' with a little extra butter, gradually incorporated in dice, at the end.

The butter and flour base of a sauce is called a roux. In a white roux, the butter and flour are mixed over a gentle heat without browning; in a blond roux, they are allowed to cook to a biscuit colour; and in a brown roux, they are cooked until distinctly brown.

Another way of thickening a sauce with flour is to make a beurre manié. Equal quantities of butter and flour are kneaded to a smooth paste and whisked into a boiling liquid. As the butter melts the flour is evenly distributed throughout the sauce, thickening the liquid without allowing lumps to form. Cornflour and arrowroot are also useful thickeners. They are 'slaked' (mixed to a paste with cold water, stock or milk), added to a hot liquid and allowed to boil to thicken it for a couple of minutes.

Emulsions

Emulsions are liquids that contain tiny droplets of oil or fat evenly distributed in suspension.

Stable emulsions

Mayonnaise is the best known of the cold and stable emulsion sauces, in which oil is beaten into egg yolks and held in suspension. If the oil is added too fast the sauce will curdle.

Warm emulsions

The most stable warm emulsions, like cold emulsions, are based on egg yolks. The best known is hollandaise, in which butter is beaten into egg yolks over a gentle heat. Great care has to be taken not to allow the sauce to curdle.

Eggless emulsions

These have become the more fashionable butter sauces. The classic is beurre blanc. Eggless emulsions split very easily, so great care should be taken to follow the recipe precisely.

Unstable emulsions

French dressing will emulsify if whizzed or whisked together, but will separate back to its component parts after about 15 minutes.

Egg yolks are whisked over heat and the flavouring ingredient is gradually whisked in. The suspension is temporary and most sabayons collapse after 30–40 minutes.

Egg yolk can be mixed with cream to form a liaison. It is then used to thicken and enrich sauces. The yolks must not boil or the sauce will curdle.

Sauce Table

Flour-thickened		Emulsions		Combinations and other
Mother	Daughter	Mother	Daughter	
White sauce	Anchovy	**Mayonnaise**	Aïoli	Apple sauce
	Béchamel		Rémoulade	Tomato sauce
	Cardinale		Tartare	Mint sauce
	Crème		Andalouse	Cumberland sauce
	Egg		Elizabeth	Cranberry sauce
	Cheese		Watercress	Bread sauce
	Onion			Horseradish cream
	Parsley	**Hollandaise**	Béarnaise	Onion sauce
	Green		Choron	Red pepper sauce
			Moutarde	Black bean sauce
Blond (velouté)	Aurore		Mousseline	Pesto
	Poulette			Ginger and tomato sauce
	Suprême	**Beurre blanc**	Chicken	Uncooked pasta sauce
	Mushroom		Fish	Exotic sauce
			Orange	Salsa Pizzaiola
			Saffron	Salsa
Brown	Chasseur	**French dressing**		
	Robert			**Savoury butters**
	Madeira			Almond, Anchovy,
	Mustard Sauce			Garlic, Green,
	Bordelaise			Maître d'hotel,
	Poivrade			Mint and Mustard
	Diane			
	Reforme			**Sabayons**
	Périgueux			Leek and watercress
				Liaisons
				As in Blanquette de Veau
				Reduction and pan sauces
				Wild mushroom sauce

Horseradish Cream

150 ml | ¼ pint double cream

1–2 tablespoons finely grated fresh horseradish

2 teaspoons white wine vinegar

½ teaspoon made English mustard

salt and freshly ground white pepper

sugar to taste

1 Put all the ingredients into a bowl and whisk to the required consistency.

Uncooked Pasta Sauce

This sauce should be served on the day after it has been made in order to allow the flavours to develop. It can be served with hot or cold pasta.

6 large tomatoes, peeled and finely chopped

1 red onion, finely chopped

2 cloves of garlic, finely chopped

4 tablespoons chopped fresh basil

1 tablespoon chopped fresh parsley

6 tablespoons extra virgin olive oil

juice of ½ lemon

salt and freshly ground black pepper

1 Put the tomatoes into a sieve and drain them for 30 minutes.

2 Mix the tomatoes with the onion, garlic and herbs. Add the oil and lemon juice. Season to taste with salt and pepper.

Ginger and Tomato Sauce

This is a very simple sauce that can be used to accompany fish, chicken, pasta and vegetable dishes. This quantity fills 2 sauceboats.

1 × 400 g | 14 oz can of tomatoes

3 spring onions

2 teaspoons very finely peeled and chopped fresh root ginger

1 large clove of garlic

2 tablespoons fresh lime juice

2 teaspoons caster sugar

1 fresh chilli, deseeded (under cold running water) and chopped

2 tablespoons roughly chopped fresh coriander

salt and freshly ground black pepper

1 Simply process or liquidize together all the ingredients.

White Sauce

This is a quick and easy basic white sauce.

20 g | ¾ oz butter
20 g | ¾ oz plain flour
a pinch of dry English mustard

290 ml | ½ pint creamy milk
salt and freshly ground white pepper

1 Melt the butter in a heavy saucepan. Remove from the heat.
2 Add the flour and the mustard and stir over the heat for 1 minute. Remove the pan from the heat, gradually stir in the milk and mix well.
3 Return the sauce to the heat and stir continuously until boiling.
4 Simmer for 2 minutes and season with salt and pepper.

Béchamel Sauce

290 ml | ½ pint creamy milk
1 slice of onion
1 blade of mace
a few fresh parsley stalks
4 white peppercorns

1 bay leaf
20 g | ¾ oz butter
20 g | ¾ oz plain flour
salt and freshly ground white pepper

1 Place the milk with the onion, mace, parsley, peppercorns and bay leaf in a saucepan and slowly bring to simmering point.
2 Remove from the heat and leave for the flavour to infuse for 8–10 minutes.
3 Melt 20 g | ¾ oz of the butter in a heavy saucepan, remove from the heat, stir in the flour and cook over heat for 1 minute.
4 Remove from the heat. Strain the infused milk and gradually stir into the flour.
5 Return the sauce to the heat and stir continuously until boiling.
6 Simmer, stirring well, for 2 minutes.
7 Season to taste with salt and pepper.

NOTE: To make a professionally shiny Béchamel sauce, pass through a tammy strainer before use or whizz in a blender.

Mornay Sauce (Cheese Sauce)

20 g | ¾ oz butter
20 g | ¾ oz plain flour
a pinch of dry English mustard
a pinch of cayenne pepper
290 ml | ½ pint milk

55 g | 2 oz Gruyère or strong Cheddar cheese, finely grated
15 g | ½ oz Parmesan cheese, freshly grated (optional)
salt and freshly ground black pepper

1 Melt the butter in a heavy saucepan and stir in the flour, mustard and cayenne pepper. Cook, stirring, for 1 minute.
2 Remove the pan from the heat. Gradually stir in the milk.
3 Return the pan to the heat and stir until boiling. Simmer, stirring well, for 2 minutes. Remove from the heat.
4 Add all the cheese, and mix well, but do not reboil.
5 Season to taste with salt and pepper.

Parsley Sauce

290 ml ½ pint creamy milk

1 slice of onion

a good handful of fresh parsley

4 black peppercorns

a bay leaf

20 g | ¾ oz butter

20 g | ¾ oz plain flour

salt and freshly ground black pepper

1 Put the milk, onion, parsley stalks (but not leaves), peppercorns and bay leaf into a saucepan and slowly bring to simmering point.
2 Remove from heat and leave for the flavour to infuse for about 10 minutes.
3 Melt the butter in a heavy saucepan and remove from the heat. Stir in the flour, return to the heat and cook, stirring, for 1 minute.
4 Remove from the heat. Strain the infused milk and gradually stir into the flour.
5 Return the sauce to the heat and stir continuously until boiling, then simmer for 2 minutes. Season to taste with salt and pepper.
6 Chop the parsley leaves very finely and stir into the hot sauce. Serve immediately.

Soubise Sauce

For the Soubise

30 g | 1 oz butter

225 g | 8 oz onions, very finely chopped

20 g | ¾ oz plain flour

290 ml | ½ pint milk

4 tablespoons double cream

For the Béchamel sauce

20 g | ¾ oz butter

1 bay leaf

1 Make the soubise: melt the butter in a heavy saucepan. Add the onions and cook over a very low heat, covered with a piece of dampened greaseproof paper and a lid to create a steamy atmosphere. Stir every few minutes. The onions should become very soft and transparent, but on no account brown.
2 Now prepare the Béchamel: melt the butter in a saucepan and remove from the heat. Add the bay leaf and flour and return to the heat, stirring, for 1 minute. Remove from

the heat and gradually stir in the milk. Return to the heat and bring slowly to the boil, stirring continuously. Simmer for 2 minutes.

3 Remove the bay leaf and mix the sauce with the soubise. Add the cream.

NOTE: This sauce can be liquidized in a blender or pushed through a sieve if a smooth texture is desired.

Green Sauce

20 g | ¾ oz butter
20 g | ¾ oz plain flour
290 ml | ½ pint milk

salt and freshly ground black pepper
2 bunches of watercress, trimmed and chopped

1 Melt the butter in a heavy saucepan, remove from the heat and stir in the flour. Return to the heat and cook, stirring for 1 minute.

2 Remove from the heat and gradually stir in the milk. Mix well. Return to the heat and stir continuously until boiling. Simmer for 2 minutes.

3 Add the watercress to the sauce. Cook for 1 minute. Season to taste.

4 Liquidize the sauce thoroughly. Do not keep it warm for too long or the colour will dull.

English Egg Sauce

3 hardboiled eggs, peeled
45 g | 1½ oz butter
45 g | 1½ oz plain flour
570 ml | 1 pint fish or white stock or milk (see pages 106, 103)

3 tablespoons cream
4 tablespoons chopped fresh parsley
salt and freshly ground white pepper

1 Using a stainless steel knife, chop the eggs into pea-sized dice.

2 Melt the butter in a heavy saucepan. Remove from the heat and stir in the flour. Return to the heat and cook for 1 minute. Remove from the heat, gradually stir in the stock or milk.

3 Return the sauce to the heat and stir continuously until boiling, then simmer for 2–3 minutes, stirring occasionally.

4 Just before serving, add the remaining ingredients and season to taste. This sauce does not keep warm well.

NOTE: The liquid in which fish or chicken is cooked is suitable as stock. Chicken stock will do for veal, fish or chicken dishes, but fish stock is of course only good for fish dishes.

Velouté Sauce

20 g | ¾ oz butter
20 g | ¾ oz plain flour
290 ml | ½ pint white stock, strained and well
   skimmed (see page 103)

2 tablespoons double cream
salt and freshly ground white pepper
a few drops of lemon juice

1 Melt the butter in a heavy saucepan, remove from the heat and add the flour. Return to the heat and cook, stirring, over a low heat until straw coloured. Remove from the heat. Gradually stir in the stock.

2 Return to the heat. Bring to the boil, stirring, and simmer until slightly syrupy for at least 2 minutes. Stir in the cream. Season to taste with salt, pepper and lemon juice.

Chicken Velouté Sauce

20 g | ¾ oz butter
20 g | ¾ oz plain flour
100 ml | 3½ fl oz milk, infused with bay leaf, celery,
   onion and peppercorns

100 ml | 3½ fl oz white stock, made with chicken
   bones (see page 103)

1 Melt the butter in a small saucepan. Remove from the heat and add the flour. Return to the heat and cook over a low heat until straw-coloured about 3–5 minutes.

2 Gradually stir in the milk and stock and bring up to the boil stirring all the time. Simmer for 2 minutes and use as required.

Espagnole Sauce

A small amount of flour is added to this sauce for texture and to give body to the sauce. Brown the flour by placing it in a baking tin in the oven preheated to 150°C | 300°F gas mark 2 for about 20 minutes, stirring occasionally, until the flour is light brown.

SERVES ABOUT 4

4 tablespoons vegetable oil
1 tablespoon carrot, cut into 1 cm | ½ in dice
2 tablespoons of celery, cut into 1 cm | ½ in dice
2 tablespoons onion, cut into 1 cm | ½ in dice
2 teaspoons plain flour, browned

½ teaspoon tomato purée
570 ml | 1 pint brown stock (see page 102)
a few button mushrooms
1 bouquet garni (2 parsley stalks, 1 bay leaf and 1
   blade of mace, tied together with string)

1 Heat the oil in a sauté pan. Add the carrot and celery and fry over a medium-low heat until they begin to soften and shrivel. Add the onion and continue to fry until the vegetables are evenly cooked to a light brown colour.

2 Stir in the flour and continue to cook slowly, stirring continuously, until the vegetables are a deep brown. Add the tomato purée and cook to caramelize.

3 Remove the pan from the heat. Stir in three-quarters of the stock to make a smooth sauce. Add the mushrooms and bouquet garni.

4 Return to the heat and bring to the boil. Skim thoroughly to remove any fat and scum. Add a splash of cold stock to the boiling liquid to help bring the scum and fat to the surface.

5 Transfer the sauce and vegetables to a small saucepan and simmer for about 2 hours, skimming as required. The vegetables should be covered with liquid at all times. Add more stock as necessary.

6 Pass through a chinois. Do not press the vegetables or they might break up and make the sauce cloudy.

7 Boil to reduce as required.

Demi-glace Sauce

Demi-glace sauce is a refined Sauce Espagnole. Simmer together equal quantities of sauce espagnole and brown stock. Reduce by boiling to half original quantity. Skim off impurities as they rise to the surface. Pass through a fine chinois (conical strainer), reboil and check seasoning.

Madeira Sauce

3 tablespoons Madeira	290 ml | ½ pint sauce espagnole (see page 115)
1 teaspoon glace de viande (see page 104)	a nut of butter

1 Place the Madeira and glace de viande together in a small heavy saucepan. Boil until reduced by half.

2 Add the sauce espagnole and heat.

3 Beat in the nut of butter.

Sauce Robert

1 tablespoon chopped onion	3 gherkins, finely diced
a little butter	1 teaspoon Dijon mustard
150 ml | ¼ pint white wine vinegar or white wine	1 teaspoon chopped fresh parsley
290 ml | ½ pint demi-glace sauce (see above)	

1 Soften the onion in the butter in a heavy saucepan over a low heat. Add the vinegar and boil until the liquid has reduced to 1 tablespoon.

2 Place the demi-glace sauce in a saucepan. Stir in the reduction and simmer for 10–15 minutes.

3 Immediately before serving, add the gherkin, mustard and parsley.

Aïoli

This is a speciality of Provençe.

6 cloves of garlic, peeled and crushed
3 egg yolks
3 tablespoons fresh white breadcrumbs
salt and freshly ground white pepper

4 tablespoons white wine vinegar
290 ml | ½ pint good-quality olive oil
1 tablespoon boiling water

1 Put the garlic, egg yolks, breadcrumbs, salt, pepper and vinegar into a food processor. Whizz to a paste.
2 With the motor running, add the oil slowly to make a thick, emulsified sauce. Add the boiling water. Season to taste and use as required.

Mayonnaise

2 egg yolks
salt and freshly ground white pepper
1 teaspoon dry English mustard

290 ml | ½ pint olive oil, or 150 ml | ¼ pint each olive
   and salad oil
a squeeze of lemon juice
1 tablespoon white wine vinegar

1 Put the yolks into a bowl with a pinch of salt and the mustard and beat well with a wooden spoon.
2 Add the oil, literally drop by drop, beating with a wooden spoon all the time. The mixture should be very thick by the time half the oil is added.
3 Beat in the lemon juice.
4 Resume pouring in the oil, going more quickly now, but alternating the dribbles of oil with small quantities of vinegar.
5 Season to taste with salt and pepper.

NOTE: If the mixture curdles, another egg yolk should be beaten in a separate bowl, and the curdled mixture beaten into it drop by drop.

Elizabeth Sauce

This sauce was invented by the staff at the Cordon Bleu School for the Coronation of Queen Elizabeth II in 1953 and has become a classic.

1 small onion, chopped

2 teaspoons oil

2 teaspoons curry powder

½ teaspoon tomato purée

3 tablespoons water

1 small bay leaf

4 tablespoons red wine

salt and freshly ground black pepper

2 teaspoons apricot jam

1 slice of lemon

1 teaspoon lemon juice

290 ml|½ pint mayonnaise (see page 117)

2 tablespoons double cream

1 Cook the onion gently in the oil covered with a piece of dampened greaseproof paper and a lid, until soft.
2 Add the curry powder and fry gently for 1 minute.
3 Add the tomato purée, water, bay leaf, wine, salt, pepper, jam, lemon slice and juice and simmer until a thick paste.
4 Strain the mixture, pushing as much as possible through the sieve. Leave to cool.
5 When cold, use this sauce to flavour the mayonnaise to the desired strength.
6 Half-whip the cream and fold into the sauce.

NOTE: This sauce is also delicious made with Greek yoghurt instead of mayonnaise.

Watercress Mayonnaise

1 bunch of watercress

290 ml|½ pint mayonnaise (see page 117)

salt and freshly ground black pepper

1 Pick over the watercress to remove the stalks and any yellowed leaves. Blanch and refresh. Dry thoroughly and chop very finely.
2 Add to the mayonnaise and season to taste with salt and pepper.

NOTE: Cooked and very well-drained spinach can be used instead of watercress.

Tartare Sauce

150 ml | ¼ pint mayonnaise (see page 117)
1 tablespoon chopped capers, rinsed
1 tablespoon chopped gherkins, rinsed
1 tablespoon chopped fresh parsley

1 shallot, finely chopped
a squeeze of lemon juice
salt and freshly ground black pepper

1 Mix all the ingredients together. Check the seasoning.

Rémoulade Sauce

150 ml | ¼ pint mayonnaise (see page 117)
1 teaspoon Dijon mustard
½ tablespoon finely chopped capers
½ tablespoon finely chopped gherkin

½ tablespoon finely chopped fresh tarragon or chervil
1 anchovy fillet, finely chopped

1 Mix all the ingredients together.

NOTE: Rémoulade sauce is a mayonnaise with a predominantly mustard flavour. The other ingredients, though good, are not always present.

Hollandaise Sauce

3 tablespoons wine vinegar
6 black peppercorns
1 bay leaf
1 blade of mace

2 egg yolks
salt
110 g | 4 oz unsalted butter
lemon juice

1 Place the vinegar, peppercorns, bay leaf and water mace in a small heavy saucepan and reduce by simmering to 1 tablespoon. Strain immediately into a cold bowl.
2 Cream the egg yolks with a pinch of salt and a nut of the butter in a small heatproof bowl and half a teaspoon of reduction. Set in a roasting pan of gently simmering water. Using a wooden spoon, beat the mixture until slightly thickened, taking care that the water immediately around the bowl does not boil. Mix well.
3 Stir over the heat until slightly thickened. Beat in the butter bit by bit, increasing the temperature as the sauce thickens and you add more butter, but take care that the water does not boil. If the sauce becomes oily in appearance or too thick, add a little more reduction or a few drops of cold water.

4 When the sauce has become light and thick remove from the heat and beat or whisk for 1 minute. Check the seasoning and add lemon juice, and salt if necessary. Keep warm by standing the bowl in hot water. Serve warm.

NOTE: Hollandaise sauce will set too firmly if allowed to get cold and it will curdle if overheated. It can be made in larger quantities in either a blender or a food processor: simply put the eggs and salt into the blender and blend lightly. Add the hot reduction and allow to thicken slightly. Set aside. When ready to serve, pour in warm melted butter, slowly allowing the sauce to thicken as you pour.

Béarnaise Sauce

3 tablespoons white wine vinegar	2 egg yolks
6 black peppercorns	salt and freshly ground black pepper
1 bay leaf	110 g	4 oz unsalted butter
1 small shallot, chopped	1 teaspoon chopped fresh tarragon
1 sprig of fresh tarragon	1 teaspoon chopped fresh chervil
1 sprig of fresh chervil	a nut of glace de viande (see page 104)

1 Place the vinegar, peppercorns, bay leaf, shallot, tarragon and chervil in a heavy saucepan and reduce over a medium heat to 1 tablespoon. Strain immediately into a cold bowl.
2 In a small heatproof bowl cream the egg yolks with a pinch of salt, half a teaspoon of the reduction and a nut of butter. Set the bowl over, not in, a saucepan of gently simmering water and using a wooden spoon, beat the mixture until slightly thickened.
3 Beat in the remaining butter bit by bit, increasing the temperature as the sauce thickens and you add more butter, but take care that the water does not boil immediately round the bowl. If the sauce becomes oily in appearance or too thick, add a little more reduction or a few drops of cold water.
4 When all the butter is added, stir in the tarragon, chervil and glace de viande. Check for seasoning.

NOTE: See the note at the end of Hollandaise Sauce (above) for cooking in larger quantities.

Herby Hollandaise Sauce

1 shallot, finely chopped	2 egg yolks
2 tablespoons of chopped fresh tarragon	110 g	4 oz unsalted butter
2 tablespoons of chopped fresh chervil or parsley	a pinch of salt
4 tablespoons white wine vinegar	a pinch of cayenne pepper
6 white peppercorns	lemon juice
1 bay leaf	

1 Put the shallot, tarragon and chervil or parsley stalks, the wine vinegar, peppercorns and bay leaf into a small saucepan and simmer until the liquid is reduced to about 1 tablespoon. Strain into a small bowl.

2 In a small heatproof bowl cream the eggs with a pinch of salt, half a teaspoon of the reduction and a nut of butter.

3 Fit the bowl over a saucepan of water, making sure that the water does not touch the bottom of the bowl. (Alternatively set the bowl in one end of a roasting pan full of water. Place the empty end of the pan over enough heat to make the water bubble only in that area, leaving the water immediately around the bowl hot but not bubbling.) Bring the water under and around the bowl to simmering point, stirring the egg yolk mixture with a wooden spoon all the time. Allow to thicken slightly and then gradually add the butter, a piece at a time. When all the butter is absorbed you should have a sauce the consistency of soft mayonnaise.

4 Stir in the chopped herbs. Add salt, cayenne and a very little lemon juice to taste. Serve in a warmed sauceboat.

NOTE: See the note at the end of Hollandaise Sauce (see page 120) for cooking in larger quantities.

Herb and Cream Hollandaise Sauce

The addition of cream to the Hollandaise Sauce means that it is stabilized and can be gently reheated, though it will curdle if allowed to boil. This recipe has glace de poisson in it, so is only suitable for fish dishes.

2 egg quantity Hollandaise Sauce (see page 119)
1 teaspoon fish glaze (see page 108)
85 ml | 3 fl oz double cream

1 tablespoon chopped fresh mixed herbs, such as chives, chervil, tarragon, fennel

1 Make the Hollandaise Sauce and stir in the fish glaze, double cream and herbs.

2 Reheat over a very low heat as and when required.

Beurre Blanc

225 g | 8 oz unsalted butter, chilled
1 tablespoon chopped shallot
3 tablespoons white wine vinegar

3 tablespoons water
salt and ground white pepper
a squeeze of lemon juice

1 Cut the butter in 3 lengthways, then across into thin slices. Keep cold.

2 Put the shallot, vinegar and water into a heavy sauté pan or small shallow saucepan. Boil slowly until reduced to about 2 tablespoons. Strain and return to the saucepan.

3 Lower the heat under the pan. Using a wire whisk and plenty of vigorous continuous whisking, gradually add the butter, piece by piece. The process should take about 5 minutes and the sauce should become thick, creamy and pale – rather like a thin hollandaise. Season to taste with salt, pepper and lemon juice.

Fish Beurre Blanc

225 g|8 oz unsalted butter, chilled
1 shallot, finely chopped
5 tablespoons very strong fish stock (see page 106)

1 tablespoon white wine vinegar
salt and freshly ground white pepper
a squeeze of lemon

1 Cut the butter in 3 lengthways, then across into thin slices. Keep cold.
2 Put the shallot, stock and vinegar into a small heavy saucepan and boil slowly until reduced to 2 tablespoons. Strain and return to the pan.
3 Keep the stock hot, not boiling. Using a wire whisk and plenty of continuous whisking, gradually add the butter, piece by piece. The process should take about 5 minutes and the sauce should become thick, creamy and pale, rather like a thin Hollandaise. Season to taste with salt, pepper and lemon juice.

Chicken Beurre Blanc

225 g|8 oz unsalted butter, chilled
1 shallot, finely chopped
5 tablespoons very strong white stock, made with chicken bones (see page 103)

1 tablespoon white wine vinegar
salt and freshly ground white pepper
a squeeze of lemon juice

1 Cut the butter in 3 lengthways, then across into thin slices. Keep cold.
2 Put the shallot, stock and vinegar into a small heavy saucepan and boil slowly until reduced to 2 tablespoons. Strain and return to the pan.
3 Keep the stock hot but not boiling. Using a wire whisk and plenty of continuous whisking, gradually add the butter, piece by piece. The process should take about 5 minutes and the sauce should become thick, creamy and pale, rather like a thin Hollandaise. Season to taste with salt, pepper and lemon juice.

Lime Beurre Blanc

225 g|8 oz unsalted butter, chilled
75 ml|3 fl oz white wine
juice of 2 limes
finely grated zest of 1 lime

1 tablespoon chopped fresh parsley
1 tablespoon double cream
salt and freshly ground white pepper

1 Cut the butter into small, even pieces. Keep cold.
2 Put the wine and zest into a small saucepan, bring to the boil and reduce to 3 tablespoons.
3 Lower the heat under the pan. Using a wire whisk and plenty of vigorous continuous whisking, gradually add the butter piece by piece. This process should take about 5 minutes, and the sauce should become thick and creamy.
4 Add the lime juice, parsley and cream and season to taste with salt and pepper.

French Dressing (Vinaigrette)

1 tablespoon wine vinegar
salt and freshly ground black pepper
3–4 tablespoons salad oil

1 Place the vinegar with a pinch of salt and a few grinds of pepper into a small bowl. Whisk in the oil gradually to form an emulsion.

NOTES: This dressing can be flavoured with crushed garlic, mustard, a pinch of sugar, chopped fresh herbs, etc., as desired.

If kept refrigerated, the dressing has a slightly thicker consistency.

Tomato Dressing

1 tomato
4 tablespoons oil
1 tablespoon water

1 tablespoon tarragon vinegar
a small pinch of dry English mustard
a small pinch of caster sugar

1 Chop the tomato and whizz in a blender with the remaining ingredients.
2 When well emulsified push through a sieve. If the dressing looks as though it might separate add a little very cold water.

Soy, Garlic and Olive Dressing

This dressing is delicious with cold meats and particularly good with cold butterfly leg of lamb (see page 494). Scatter the olives and rosemary over the meat and hand the sauce separately.

1 small clove of garlic, unpeeled
2 teaspoons olive oil
290 ml | ½ pint plain yoghurt
1 tablespoon light soy sauce
2 teaspoons sesame oil
salt and freshly ground black pepper

To serve
55 g | 2 oz black olives, pitted
1 tablespoon roughly chopped fresh rosemary

1 Preheat the oven to 200°C | 400°F | gas mark 6.
2 Brush the clove of garlic with a little of the olive oil, place on a baking sheet and bake in the oven for 15 minutes. Peel the garlic and mash well.
3 Mix together the mashed garlic, yoghurt, soy sauce, sesame oil and remaining olive oil. Season to taste with salt and pepper. Serve with the olives and rosemary as required.

Tapenade

110 g | 4 oz black olives, pitted

2 tablespoons capers, rinsed

1 medium clove of garlic, chopped

85 ml | 3 fl oz olive oil

freshly ground black pepper

1 Put the olives, capers and garlic into a food processor and process until smooth. While the motor is still running, pour in the oil. Season with pepper.

Pesto Sauce

2 cloves of garlic

2 large cups of fresh basil leaves

55 g | 2 oz pinenuts

55 g | 2 oz Parmesan cheese, freshly grated

150 ml | ¼ pint olive oil

salt

1 In a blender or mortar, grind the garlic and basil together to a paste.

2 Add the nuts and cheese, process. Add the oil with the motor running, season.

3 Keep in a covered jar in a cool place.

Parsley Pesto

2 cloves of garlic

a large handful of freshly picked parsley, roughly chopped

30 g | 1 oz blanched almonds

150 ml | ¼ pint olive oil

55 g | 2 oz Cheddar cheese, finely grated

salt and freshly ground black pepper

1 Process or liquidize the garlic and parsley together to a paste.

2 Whizz in the nuts, then add the olive oil slowly with the motor still running. Whizz in the cheese quickly. Season to taste with salt and pepper.

3 Keep in a covered jar in a cool place.

Dill Pesto

a large handful of fresh dill

55 g | 2 oz blanched almonds

2 cloves of garlic

30 g | 1 oz Parmesan cheese, freshly grated

150 ml | ¼ pint extra virgin olive oil

salt and freshly ground black pepper

1 Put the dill, almonds and garlic into a food processor and whizz to a paste. Add the cheese and continue to blend until well mixed.

2 With the motor running, gradually pour the oil into the herb mixture in a steady stream. It should be well emulsified. Season to taste with salt and pepper.

3 Keep in a covered jar in a cool place.

Rocket Pesto

55 g | 2 oz rocket

55 g | 2 oz blanched almonds

85 ml | 3 fl oz olive oil

55 g | 2 oz Parmesan cheese, freshly grated

salt and freshly ground black pepper

1 Put all the ingredients into a blender and process until smooth. Season to taste with salt and pepper. If the paste begins to look oily and too thick, add 1 tablespoon water.

Red Pesto

2 cloves of garlic

1 small bunch of fresh basil

55 g | 2 oz pinenuts

55 g | 2 oz sundried tomatoes, chopped

150 ml | ¼ pint olive oil

55 g | 2 oz Pecorino cheese, finely grated

salt and freshly ground black pepper

1 In a food processor or blender, whizz the garlic and basil together to a paste.

2 Add the nuts and sundried tomatoes and whizz again, then add the oil slowly with the motor still running. Add the cheese and whizz quickly.

3 Season to taste with salt and pepper. Keep in a covered jar in a cool place.

Mustard Sauce for Gravad Lax

1 tablespoon Dijon mustard

6 tablespoons oil

2 tablespoons wine vinegar

1 tablespoon chopped fresh dill

1 teaspoon caster sugar

salt and freshly ground black pepper

1 Put the mustard into a small bowl and gradually whisk in the oil, then the vinegar.

2 Mix in the dill and sugar and season to taste with salt and pepper. Keep in a covered jar in a cool place.

Wild Mushroom Sauce

30 g | 1 oz butter

2 shallots, chopped

110 g | 4 oz wild mushrooms, such as horn of plenty, chanterelles, etc.

55 g | 2 oz flat mushrooms, sliced

425 ml | ¾ pint brown stock (see page 102)

100 ml | 3½ fl oz dry white wine

170 g | 6 oz unsalted butter, chilled and cut into small pieces

1 Melt the butter in a sauté pan, add the shallots and cook until soft. Increase the heat and cook until golden-brown.

2 Add the mushrooms and cook for 1–2 minutes. Remove the mushrooms with perforated spoon and reserve.

3 Add the stock and wine. Boil the stock and wine until reduced to about 150 ml|¼ pint. Lower the heat under the pan.

4 Using a small wire whisk and plenty of vigorous continuous whisking, gradually add the butter, piece by piece. This process should take about 5 minutes and the sauce should become thick and creamy.

5 Return the mushrooms to the sauce, check the seasoning and serve.

Mushroom Sauce

2 handfuls of mixed fresh herbs, such as tarragon, parsley, chervil
150 ml|¼ pint white stock (see page 103)
220 ml|8 fl oz double cream

30 g|1 oz butter
110 g|4 oz button mushrooms
110 g|4 oz oyster mushrooms
salt and freshly ground black pepper

1 Drop the herbs into a saucepan of boiling salted water. Bring back to the boil, then strain through a sieve. Pour cold water on to the herbs and squeeze out any excess moisture. Put into a blender.

2 Put the stock and cream into a saucepan, bring up to the boil and simmer until a coating consistency is achieved. Pour into the blender and liquidize with the herbs until smooth and green.

3 Melt the butter in a sauté pan and cook the mushrooms until soft and any liquid has evaporated. Add the herb sauce to the pan and reheat. Season to taste with salt and pepper.

Salsa Pizzaiola

This recipe has been taken from *A Taste of Venice* by Jeanette Nance Nordio.

1 onion, chopped
2 tablespoons olive oil
3–4 cloves of garlic, crushed
1 kg|2¼ lb canned chopped plum tomatoes
2 tablespoons tomato purée

2 teaspoons dried oregano
1 teaspoon dried basil
1 bay leaf
2 teaspoons sugar
salt and freshly ground black pepper

1 In a saucepan, sweat the onion in the oil until transparent.

2 Add the garlic and cook for 1 further minute, then stir in the tomatoes with their liquid, the tomato purée, oregano, basil, bay leaf, and sugar. Season to taste with salt and pepper. Bring to the boil, then cook very gently for about 1 hour.

3 Remove the bay leaf and check the seasoning. This sauce should be quite thick and rough but you may purée it if you wish.

Tomato, Basil and Olive Oil Sauce

55 ml | 2 fl oz olive oil

1 clove of garlic, bruised

2 medium tomatoes, peeled, deseeded and finely
   chopped

4 large fresh basil leaves

salt and freshly ground black pepper

1 Place the oil and the garlic in a small saucepan and set over a low heat to infuse for a few
minutes.
2 Remove the garlic and add the tomatoes and basil. Season to taste with salt and pepper.
3 Serve warm.

Tomato and Mint Salsa

1 shallot, finely diced

1 tablespoon wine vinegar

3 tablespoons extra-virgin olive oil

4 tomatoes, peeled, deseeded and finely chopped

1 clove of garlic, crushed

1 tablespoon chopped fresh mint

salt and freshly ground black pepper

1 Mix together the shallot, vinegar and oil and allow to stand for 10 minutes.
2 Add the tomatoes, garlic and mint and season to taste with salt and pepper.

Warm Red Salsa

SERVES 10

2 red peppers

2 large tomatoes, peeled, deseeded and finely diced

1 tablespoon chopped fresh basil

1 tablespoon olive oil

juice of ½ lemon

juice of ½ orange

salt and freshly ground black pepper

1 Preheat the oven to 180°C | 350°F | gas mark 4.
2 Place the peppers on a baking sheet and roast in the oven for about 30 minutes, or until
the peppers are soft and the skins will come off easily.
3 Leave the peppers until cold, then cut them in half and remove and discard the seeds,
membrane and skin. Dice the flesh finely and mix with the remaining ingredients.
Season to taste with salt and pepper.
4 Just before serving, heat through very gently until just warm.

Thick Onion and Mint Sauce

1 large Spanish onion
55 g | 2 oz butter
2 tablespoons chopped fresh mint

salt and freshly ground black pepper
a pinch of caster sugar (optional)

1 Chop the onion very finely. Cook very slowly in the butter covered with a piece of dampened greaseproof paper and a lid until very soft but not coloured. Push through a sieve, or liquidize in a blender.

2 Mix in the mint and season to taste with salt and pepper, and sugar if necessary.

Exotic Sauce

This sauce has been adapted from a recipe by Josceline Dimbleby. It is a very useful accompaniment to fish, chicken or veal.

2 large green chillies, finely chopped
450 g | 1 lb tomatoes, peeled and chopped
2–3 cloves of garlic, crushed
1 teaspoon ground cardamom
2 teaspoons caster sugar

1 tablespoon tomato purée
juice of ½ lemon
1 tablespoon chopped fresh coriander
110 g | 4 oz button mushrooms, thinly sliced
salt and freshly ground black pepper

1 Put the chilli peppers, tomatoes, garlic, cardamom, sugar, tomato purée and lemon juice into a saucepan. Bring to the boil, then simmer for 10 minutes.

2 Add the coriander and mushrooms. Season to taste with salt and pepper.

NOTE: If this sauce is too thick it can be thinned to the required consistency with water.

Tomato Sauce (1)

1 large onion, finely chopped
3 tablespoons oil
10 tomatoes, roughly chopped

salt and freshly ground black pepper
a pinch of caster sugar
150 g | ¼ pint white stock (see page 103)
1 teaspoon fresh thyme leaves

1 Sweat the onion in the oil in a saucepan. Add the tomatoes, salt, pepper and sugar, and cook for a further 25 minutes. Add the stock and cook for 5 minutes.

2 Liquidize the sauce and push through a sieve. If it is too thin, reduce, by boiling rapidly, to the desired consistency. Take care: it will spit and has a tendency to catch.

3 Add the thyme. Check the seasoning.

Tomato Sauce (2)

1 × 400 g|14 oz can of tomatoes
1 small onion, chopped
1 small carrot, chopped
1 stick of celery, chopped
½ clove of garlic, crushed
1 bay leaf

2 parsley stalks
salt and freshly ground black pepper
juice of ½ lemon
a dash of Worcestershire sauce
1 teaspoon caster sugar
1 teaspoon chopped fresh basil or thyme

1 Put all the ingredients together in a heavy saucepan, cover and simmer over a medium heat for 30 minutes.

2 Liquidize and sieve the sauce and return it to the pan.

3 If it is too thin, reduce by boiling rapidly. Check the seasoning, adding more salt or sugar if necessary.

Red Pepper Sauce

1 onion, finely chopped
1 tablespoon sunflower oil
2 tomatoes, chopped
1 red pepper, peeled (by singeing over a flame), cored, deseeded and cut into strips

1 clove of garlic, crushed
1 bouquet garni (see page 9)
6 tablespoons water
salt and freshly ground black pepper

1 Cook the onion in the oil in a saucepan until just beginning to soften. Add the tomatoes, red pepper, garlic and bouquet garni. Add the water and season lightly with salt and pepper. Cover and cook over a low heat for 20 minutes.

2 Liquidize until smooth, then push through a sieve. Chill.

Black Bean Sauce

3 tablespoons fermented black beans
1 tablespoon sunflower oil
2 spring onions, chopped
1 clove of garlic, sliced
2.5 cm|1 in piece of fresh root ginger, peeled and sliced

2 tablespoons soy sauce
2 tablespoons sherry
1 teaspoon sugar
290 ml|½ pint water
2 teaspoons sesame oil

1 Wash the beans several times. Drain.

2 Heat the oil in a saucepan, add the spring onions, garlic and ginger and cook for 1 minute.

3 Add the soy sauce, sherry, beans, sugar and water. Bring slowly to the boil, then simmer for 15 minutes to allow the flavour to infuse.

4 Stir in the sesame oil. Use as required.

Rouille

The traditional accompaniment to Bouillabaisse (see page 149).

3 cloves of garlic, roasted and crushed

1 red chilli pepper, deseeded and chopped

1 green pepper, halved, deseeded, grilled and peeled

1 red pepper, halved, deseeded, grilled and peeled

6 tablespoons olive oil

2 tablespoons fresh white breadcrumbs

salt and freshly ground pepper

Tabasco sauce

1 Blend the garlic, chilli and green and red peppers in a liquidizer until smooth.

2 With the motor still running, very slowly pour the oil on to the purée. Add the breadcrumbs to bind the sauce.

3 Season to taste with with salt, pepper and Tabasco.

Apple Sauce

450 g | 1 lb cooking apples

finely grated zest of ¼ lemon

3 tablespoons water

2 teaspoons sugar

1 Peel, quarter, core and chop the apples.

2 Place in a heavy saucepan with the lemon zest, water and sugar. Cover with a lid and cook very slowly until the apples are soft. Add extra sugar if required. Serve hot or cold.

Mint Sauce

a large handful of fresh mint

2 tablespoons caster sugar

2 tablespoons hot water

2 tablespoons wine vinegar

1 Wash the mint and shake it dry. Remove the stalks and chop the leaves finely. Place in a bowl with the sugar.

2 Pour on the hot water and leave for 5 minutes to dissolve the sugar. Add the vinegar and leave to soak for 1–2 hours.

Cranberry and Orange Sauce

SERVES 8

juice of 2 oranges

225 g | 8 oz sugar

450 g | 1 lb cranberries

1 Put the orange juice and sugar together in a saucepan. Allow the sugar to dissolve over a gentle heat.

2 Add the cranberries and simmer very slowly until just tender.

3 Serve cold.

Bread Sauce

This is a very rich sauce. The quantity of butter may be reduced, and the cream is optional.

1 large onion, peeled

6 cloves

290 ml | ½ pint milk

1 bay leaf

10 white peppercorns, or a pinch of freshly ground white pepper

a pinch of freshly grated nutmeg

salt

55 g | 2 oz fresh white breadcrumbs, sieved

55 g | 2 oz butter

2 tablespoons single cream (optional)

1 Cut the onion in half. Stick the cloves into the onion pieces and put with the milk and bay leaf into a saucepan.

2 Add the peppercorns, nutmeg, and a good pinch of salt. Bring to the boil very slowly, then remove from the heat and leave to infuse for 30 minutes. Strain.

3 Reheat the milk and add the breadcrumbs, butter and the cream, if using. Mix and return to the saucepan.

4 Reheat the sauce carefully without boiling. If it has become too thick, beat in more hot milk. It should be creamy. Check the seasoning.

Cumberland Sauce

2 oranges

1 lemon

225 g | 8 oz redcurrant jelly

1 shallot, chopped

150 ml | ¼ pint port

½ teaspoon Dijon mustard

a pinch of cayenne pepper

a pinch of ground ginger

1 Peel 1 orange and the lemon, removing only the outer skin. Cut the zest into fine shreds.

2 Squeeze the fruit juice and strain into a pan. Then add the remaining ingredients with the needleshreds. Simmer for 10 minutes and cool.

Chicken and Rosemary Jus

MAKES ABOUT 570 ML | 1 PINT

450 g | 1 lb chicken wings

2 tablespoons sunflower oil

1 leek, sliced

1 small carrot, sliced

1 stick of celery, sliced

2 shallots, sliced

2 tomatoes, halved and deseeded

2 cloves of garlic, bruised

4 sprigs of fresh thyme

1 bay leaf

1 sprig of fresh parsley

6 black peppercorns

290 ml | ½ pint dry white wine

425 ml | ¾ pint dry red wine

3 litres | 5¼ pints well-flavoured white stock, made with chicken bones (see page 103)

1 Brown the chicken wings thoroughly in the oil in a large saucepan. Lift out and set aside.

2 Add the leek, carrot, celery and shallots to the pan and fry over a low heat until golden-brown. Add the tomatoes and garlic and cook for a further 2–3 minutes. Add the herbs and peppercorns.

3 Add the white and red wine and bring to the boil, then lower the heat and simmer gently until the wine is reduced by two-thirds. Return the browned chicken wings to the pan. Add cold water to cover.

4 Add the stock and cook very slowly for 2–3 hours, skimming frequently. Do not allow the liquid to boil.

5 Strain into a clean saucepan, discarding the bones and vegetables. Bring to the boil, then lower the heat and simmer until the liquid is reduced to 570 ml | 1 pint. Strain through a fine sieve and season to taste with salt and pepper.

Savoury Butters

Flavoured butters are good served with grilled or fried fish or shellfish, or with plainly grilled chicken or meat dishes. They are also excellent with hot toast or bread. After preparation the butter should be shaped into a cylinder, rolled up in clingfilm or damp greaseproof paper and chilled in the refrigerator. It can then be sliced and used as required. If it is to be kept for more than 2 days it should be frozen.

Almond Butter

55 g│2 oz butter, softened
30 g│1 oz ground almonds

a squeeze of lemon juice
salt and freshly ground white pepper

1 Beat the butter to a light cream. Mix the almonds with the lemon juice and beat this paste into the softened butter. Season to taste with salt and pepper. Chill.

Anchovy Butter

2 anchovy fillets
½ clove of garlic
55 g│2 oz butter, softened

freshly ground black pepper
anchovy essence

1 Pound the anchovies and garlic and mix well with the butter. Season with pepper and anchovy essence. Chill.

Garlic Butter

55 g│2 oz butter, softened
1 large clove of garlic, crushed with salt

2 tablespoons lemon juice
salt and freshly ground black pepper

1 Beat all the ingredients together. Chill.

Green Butter

2 sprigs of watercress
1 small bunch of fresh tarragon
1 sprig of fresh parsley

55 g | 2 oz butter, softened
1 shallot, minced
salt and freshly ground black pepper

1 Blanch the watercress, tarragon and parsley for 30 seconds in boiling salted water. Refresh under cold running water. Drain well and pat dry. Chop very finely.
2 Cream the butter and beat in the shallot, watercress and herbs. Season to taste with salt and pepper. Chill.

Maître d'Hôtel Butter

55 g | 2 oz butter, softened
2 teaspoons lemon juice

1 teaspoon finely chopped fresh parsley
salt and freshly ground black pepper

1 Cream the butter, stir in the lemon juice and parsley and season to taste with salt and pepper. Mix well and chill.

Mint and Mustard Butter

55 g | 2 oz butter, softened
1 teaspoon Dijon mustard

1 tablespoon finely chopped fresh mint
salt and freshly ground black pepper

1 Cream the butter until very soft and beat in the mustard and mint.
2 Season with salt and pepper. Chill.

Soups

Gazpacho (1)

This recipe assumes that the cook has a blender.

SERVES 6

900 g | 2 lb fresh, very ripe tomatoes, peeled

1 large mild Spanish onion

2 red peppers

1 small cucumber

1 thick slice of white bread, crust removed

1 egg yolk

2 large cloves of garlic

6 tablespoons olive oil

1 tablespoon tarragon vinegar

450 g | 1 lb canned tomatoes

1 tablespoon tomato purée

freshly ground black pepper

plenty of salt (preferably sea salt)

To serve

a large bowl of croûtons (see page 156)

1 Chop or dice finely a small amount of the fresh tomato, onion, red pepper and cucumber and put into separate small bowls for garnish. Roughly chop the remaining vegetables to prepare them for the blender.

2 Put the bread, egg yolk and garlic into the blender. Turn it on and add the oil in a thin steady stream while the motor is running. You should end up with a thick, mayonnaise-like emulsion.

3 Add the vinegar and then gradually add all the soup ingredients in batches and blend until smooth.

4 Sieve the soup to remove the tomato seeds and check for seasoning.

NOTES: Gazpacho should be served icy cold with the small bowls of chopped vegetables and fried croûtons handed separately. Sometimes crushed ice is added to the soup at the last minute.

If you prefer a thinner soup, dilute it with iced water or tomato juice.

wine: CRISP DRY WHITE

Gazpacho (2)

This recipe by Christopher Buey is from *The Taste of Health* and is lower in fat than the previous recipe.

SERVES 4

285 g | 10 oz tomatoes
½ cucumber
½ green pepper
½ red pepper
1 medium onion
570 ml | 1 pint canned or fresh tomato juice
1 clove of garlic
2 tablespoons tarragon vinegar

salt and freshly ground black pepper
2 tablespoons olive oil
ice cubes

To garnish

1 tablespoon chopped fresh herbs, such as parsley, chervil, tarragon, chives

1 Cut all the vegetables into chunks. Set aside a little of each for the garnish.
2 Place half the tomato juice in a food processor or blender with the vegetables and garlic, and liquidize for 2–3 minutes. Gradually add the remaining tomato juice, the vinegar, salt and pepper and finish with the olive oil.
3 Add the ice cubes to the soup and refrigerate for 10 minutes.
4 Remove the ice cubes and serve the soup garnished with the reserved chopped raw vegetables and herbs.

wine: **CRISP DRY WHITE**

Cucumber and Melon Gazpacho

SERVES 6

2 large cucumbers, peeled and deseeded
1 medium Galia melon, peeled and deseeded
1 bunch of rocket
3 sprigs of fresh dill
3 sprigs of fresh mint
2 tablespoons tarragon vinegar
1 small clove of garlic, peeled
1 small green chilli, deseeded

290 ml | ½ pint carrot juice or mixed vegetable juice
150 ml | ¼ pint Greek yoghurt
6 tablespoons olive oil
salt and freshly ground black pepper

To garnish

ice, crushed sprigs of fresh dill

1 Finely dice ¼ of 1 cucumber and 1 slice of melon and reserve.
2 Chop the remaining cucumber and melon roughly and put into a blender with the rocket, dill, mint, vinegar, garlic, chilli and half the carrot or mixed vegetable juice. Liquidize to a smooth paste and gradually blend in the remaining juice, yoghurt and oil. Season to taste with salt and pepper. Refrigerate until cold.
3 To serve: pour into 6 individual soup bowls and garnish with the reserved cucumber and melon, crushed ice cubes and sprigs of dill.

wine: **FINO SHERRY**

Lebanese Cucumber and Yoghurt Soup

SERVES 4

1 large cucumber, peeled
290 ml | ½ pint single cream
150 ml | ¼ pint plain yoghurt

2 tablespoons tarragon vinegar
1 tablespoon chopped fresh mint
salt and freshly ground white pepper

1 Grate the cucumber coarsely.
2 Stir in the remaining ingredients and season to taste with salt and pepper.
3 Chill in the refrigerator for 2 hours before serving.

NOTE: This soup may be garnished with cold croûtons; chopped fresh chives; a spoonful of soured cream added just before serving; chopped gherkins; a few pink shrimps. It is also good flavoured with garlic.

wine: **DRY WHITE**

Chilled Beetroot Soup with Soured Cream

SERVES 4

675 g | 1½ lb raw beetroots, washed
salt and freshly ground black pepper
570–860 ml | 1–1½ pints white stock (see page 103)
1–2 teaspoons ground cumin or caraway seeds
caster sugar

salt and freshly ground black pepper
290 ml | ½ pint soured cream

To garnish
chopped fresh herbs

1 Place the whole raw beetroots in a large saucepan of cold water, and season with salt and pepper. Bring to the boil and cook until *al dente* (about 1 hour, depending on the size of the beetroots).
2 Drain and leave to cool.
3 Peel the beetroots, cut roughly into small pieces and liquidize in a food processor or blender.
4 Push the purée through a fine sieve, then add the stock to give a thick consistency which will still easily run from a spoon.
5 Season the soup to taste with ground cumin or caraway, sugar, salt and pepper. Chill.
6 Ladle the beetroot soup into three-quarters of an ice-cold soup plate, holding the plate at an angle. Then ladle the soured cream into the remaining (uppermost) quarter of the plate, gently lowering the plate as you do so.
7 Feather the cream into the beetroot soup at the 'join', using a cocktail stick or thin skewer. Sprinkle with herbs. Serve cold.

wine: **SPICY WHITE**

Iced Curried Consommé

SERVES 4

1 × 340 g | 12 oz can of jellied consommé

170 g | 6 oz cream cheese

1 teaspoon curry powder

1 squeeze of lemon juice

1 Reserve 1 cupful of consommé for the top.

2 In a food processor or blender, liquidize the remaining consommé with the cheese, curry powder and lemon juice. Pour into cocotte dishes.

3 Chill in the refrigerator until set.

4 Spoon over the remaining consommé (which should be cool, on the point of setting) and chill again until ready to serve.

NOTE: Some canned consommé will not set. Test it by chilling for 1 hour. If the soup is still liquid, melt 1 teaspoon powdered gelatine in the consommé and allow to cool. Consommé with 'serve hot' on the label is generally non-setting.

wine: DRY WHITE

Iced Vichyssoise Soup

SERVES 4

55 g | 2 oz butter

1 medium onion, finely chopped

300 g | 10 oz white part of leek, finely sliced

110 g | 4 oz potatoes, peeled and sliced

salt and freshly ground white pepper

290 ml | ½ pint white stock (see page 103)

290 ml | ½ pint creamy milk

2 tablespoons single cream

chopped fresh chives

1 Melt the butter in a heavy saucepan and add the onion and leek.

2 Sweat the vegetables for 15 minutes or so. They must soften without browning.

3 Add the potatoes, salt and pepper and the stock. Simmer until the potatoes are soft.

4 Liquidize the soup in a food processor or blender and push it through a sieve.

5 Add the milk and cream. (Check the consistency before adding all the milk.)

6 Check the seasoning. Chill in the refrigerator.

7 Add the chives just before serving, and perhaps an extra swirl of cream.

NOTE: The soup is good hot, too. Reheat without boiling.

wine: WHITE BURGUNDY

Simple Vegetable Soup

SERVES 8

45 g | 1½ oz butter

225 g | 8 oz onions, chopped

450 g | 1 lb carrots, chopped

110 g | 4 oz celery, chopped

225 g | 8 oz potatoes, chopped

860 ml | 1½ pints water

salt and freshly ground black pepper

425 ml | ¾ pint milk

1 Melt the butter in a large heavy pan with 2 tablespoons water. Stir in the onions, carrots and celery. Cover with a piece of damp greaseproof paper and lid. Cook over a slow heat until soft but not coloured, stirring occasionally (about 45 minutes).

2 Remove the greaseproof paper. Add the potatoes and water. Season with salt and pepper and simmer, without a lid, for 15 minutes.

3 Liquidize the soup in a food processor or blender, with the milk, then sieve.

4 Pour into the rinsed-out pan. Season to taste and add water if the soup is too thick. Reheat without boiling.

wine: **DRY WHITE/LIGHT RED**

Creamy Vegetable Soup

SERVES 4

30 g | 1 oz butter

225 g | 8 oz onions, very thinly sliced

225 g | 8 oz leeks, thinly sliced

1 small head of celery, thinly sliced

1 large potato, peeled and thinly sliced

570 ml | 1 pint white stock (see page 103)

salt and freshly ground white pepper

nutmeg, freshly grated

290 ml | ½ pint creamy milk

1 tablespoon single cream

1 Melt the butter in a very large, heavy saucepan. Stir in the onions, leeks and celery and sweat covered with a piece of damp greaseproof paper with the lid on, stirring occasionally, until the whole mass is soft (about 45 minutes).

2 Add the potatoes and stock, bring to the boil, stirring, and boil for 1 minute. Add the salt, pepper and nutmeg to taste and simmer gently for 20 minutes.

3 Liquidize the soup in a blender or food processor and pass through a sieve.

4 Reheat, and add the cream. Warm the milk and combine with the vegetables.

NOTE: Do not add all the milk if the soup looks too thin.

wine: **DRY WHITE OR LIGHT RED**

Roasted Tomato Soup with Basil Cream

SERVES 6

1 kg|2¼ lb ripe tomatoes, preferably plum tomatoes

2 large red onions, peeled and cut into eighths

6 fresh basil stalks, leaves reserved for garnish

2 tablespoons balsamic vinegar

1 teaspoon caster sugar

2 tablespoons olive oil

1 litre|1¾ pints vegetable or white chicken stock
(see page 103)

2 tablespoons Madeira

salt and freshly ground black pepper

For the garnish

15 g|½ oz fresh basil

100 ml|3½ fl oz single cream

1 Preheat the oven to 200°C|400°F|gas mark 6.
2 Cut the tomatoes in half lengthways and place cut side up in a single layer in a roasting pan. Tuck the onions and basil stalks around the tomatoes.
3 Sprinkle the vegetables with the vinegar, sugar and olive oil. Place in the top third of the oven (the hottest part) and roast for 1 hour or until softened and browned.
4 Place the vegetables in a large saucepan. Add the stock and Madeira, then simmer for 30 minutes or until the vegetables fall apart.
5 Let the soup cool slightly, then liquidize and pass through a sieve. Season to taste with salt and pepper.
6 Prepare the garnish: process the basil leaves and cream in a liquidizer or food processor.
7 Warm the soup gently. Drizzle with the basil cream and garnish with the basil.

wine: **LIGHT, SPICY RED**

Minestrone

SERVES 4–6

85 g|3 oz dried haricot beans or 225 g|8 oz canned
beans, drained

1 tablespoon oil

2 cloves of garlic, crushed

1 large onion, sliced

2 carrots, diced

1 stick of celery, chopped

2 medium potatoes, peeled and diced

1.1 litres|2 pints vegetable, chicken or ham stock
(see pages 103, 104, 107)

1 bouquet garni (3 leaves fresh basil, 2 parsley
stalks, bay leaf, tied together with string)

1 tablespoon tomato purée

110 g|4 oz white cabbage

3 large tomatoes, peeled and chopped

55 g|2 oz broken spaghetti or other small pasta

salt and freshly ground black pepper

freshly grated Parmesan cheese

1 Soak the beans in cold water for 3–4 hours.
2 Heat the oil in a heavy saucepan, add the onion, carrot and celery and cook for 2 minutes, stirring. Add the potato and cook until the oil has been absorbed and the vegetables are soft. Add the garlic and cook for a further minute.

3 Add the stock, bring to the boil, add the bouquet garni, tomato purée and drained beans. Simmer for 45 minutes.

4 Add the cabbage, tomato and pasta and continue to simmer for a further 15 minutes, or until the beans are soft and the spaghetti is tender.

5 Just before serving remove the herbs and check the seasoning. Serve sprinkled with Parmesan cheese.

wine: **LIGHT RED**

Soupe au Pistou

This is a Mediterranean peasant soup which calls for fresh basil and very fresh garlic.

SERVES 6–8

450 g | 1 lb dried haricot beans, soaked overnight

2 tablespoons oil (preferably olive)

225 g | 8 oz potatoes, peeled and diced

2 leeks, thinly sliced

2 carrots, thinly sliced

110 g | 4 oz green beans, sliced or chopped

1.7 litres | 3 pints white stock (see page 103)

½ teaspoon coarsely ground black pepper

2 tablespoons vermicelli or other small pasta

4 ripe tomatoes, peeled and chopped

1 teaspoon salt

For the pistou

4 cloves of garlic, crushed

4 tablespoons chopped fresh basil

3 tablespoons olive oil

To serve

grated Gruyère cheese

1 Cook the beans in boiling water for about 1 hour, until half tender.

2 Heat the oil and add the potatoes, leeks and carrots. Cover and cook over a low heat until the vegetables are soft.

3 Add the half-cooked dried beans, the green beans, stock and pepper. Simmer until the haricot beans are soft (about 1½ hours). Add the pasta and tomatoes, season with salt and cook for a further 10 minutes, or until the pasta is tender. Allow to cool a little before adding the pistou.

4 Make the pistou: put the garlic and the basil in a mortar or blender and pound to a paste. Add the oil, drop by drop (as when making mayonnaise), mixing all the time, to form an emulsion. Just before serving, stir the pistou into the soup. Hand the cheese separately.

NOTE: Recipes for this soup vary along the Mediterranean according to local tradition and season. Courgettes, cabbage and onions sometimes make their appearance. The Italian version of pesto (page 124), from which pistou is derived, is sometimes added to the soup, which is itself a version of Italian minestrone.

wine: **LIGHT RED**

Jerusalem Artichoke Soup

SERVES 4

55 g | 2 oz butter

1 medium onion, sliced

675 g | 1½ lb Jerusalem artichokes

570 ml | 1 pint milk, scalded

570 ml | 1 pint water

salt and freshly ground white pepper

1 Melt the butter in a saucepan and gently cook the onion in it until soft but not coloured.

2 Peel the artichokes and leave in a bowl of cold acidulated water (water with lemon juice or vinegar added) to prevent discoloration.

3 Slice the artichokes and add to the pan. Continue cooking, covered, for about 10 minutes, giving an occasional stir.

4 Add the milk and water, season well with salt and pepper and simmer for a further 20 minutes. Do not allow it to boil, or it will curdle.

5 Liquidize in a food processor or blender and push through a sieve. Check for seasoning – this soup needs plenty of salt and pepper.

wine: **SPICY DRY WHITE**

Chestnut Soup

SERVES 4–6

1 onion, finely chopped

1 carrot, finely chopped

30 g | 1 oz butter

675 g | 1½ lb fresh chestnuts, peeled

1 bouquet garni (see page 9)

860 ml-1 litre | 1½ pints white stock (see page 103)

150 ml | ¼ pint single cream

salt and freshly ground black pepper

To garnish

1 Cox's apple, diced

15 g | ½ oz butter

1 teaspoon caster sugar

finely chopped fresh parsley

1 Sweat the onion and carrot in the butter until tender. Add the chestnuts and sweat for a further 5 minutes.

2 Add the bouquet garni and stock. Bring up to the boil, then simmer for 20–30 minutes or until the chestnuts are tender.

3 Liquidize the soup and strain into a clean saucepan. Add the cream, bring up to scalding point (just below the boil) and season to taste with salt and pepper.

4 Meanwhile, prepare the garnish: fry the apple in the butter, add the sugar and let the apple caramelize. Add the parsley.

5 Serve garnished with the apple.

NOTE: If fresh chestnuts are not available use 1 large can whole, peeled chestnuts.

wine: **DRY WHITE OR LIGHT RED**

Lettuce and Dill Soup

SERVES 4–6

3 lettuces, washed

30 g | 1 oz butter

225 g | 8 oz onion, very thinly sliced

400 g | 14 oz potatoes, peeled and thinly sliced

1 litre | 2 pints white stock (see page 103)

salt, freshly ground white pepper and freshly grated nutmeg

1 bunch of fresh dill, roughly chopped

2 tablespoons single cream

1 Shred the lettuces finely. Melt the butter in a large, heavy saucepan and add the onion and potato. Cover and sweat for 10 minutes.

2 Add the stock, bring to the boil, season with salt, pepper and nutmeg and simmer gently for 5 minutes.

3 Add the lettuce, and simmer for 10 minutes.

4 Add the dill, and simmer for 1 minute.

5 Liquidize the soup in a food processor or blender and push through a sieve into rinsed-out pan.

6 Bring back to the boil and add the cream.

wine: **LIGHT DRY WHITE**

Stilton Soup

SERVES 4

1 medium onion, finely chopped

2 sticks of celery, finely chopped

55 g | 2 oz butter

45 g | 1½ oz plain flour

5 tablespoons dry white wine

1 litre | 1¾ pints white stock (see page 103)

290 ml | ½ pint milk, warmed

225 g | 8 oz Stilton cheese, grated or crumbled

2 tablespoons single cream

salt and freshly ground black pepper

1 Soften the onion and celery in the butter over a low heat, covered with a piece of damp greaseproof paper and a lid. Add the flour and cook for 1 minute.

2 Remove from the heat and stir in the wine. Return to the heat and bring to the boil to reduce the wine by half. Stir in the stock, bring to the boil, then simmer for 25 minutes.

3 Taste. Add the milk and simmer for 2 minutes. Do not boil. Remove from the heat and whisk in the Stilton. Liquidize in a food processor or blender and push through a sieve.

4 Add the cream and salt and pepper. Reheat the soup, taking care not to let it boil, or it will curdle and become stringy.

NOTES: White port, well chilled, is delicious with this soup.

The soup can be served chilled. In this event streak the cream into the soup just before serving, giving it an attractive marbled appearance.

wine: **LIGHT RED**

Mushroom Soup

SERVES 4

55 g | 2 oz butter

340 g | 12 oz flat mushrooms, chopped

3 tablespoons chopped fresh parsley

½ clove of garlic, crushed

2 large slices of bread, crusts removed, crumbled

860 ml | 1½ pints white stock (see page 103)

a pinch of freshly grated nutmeg or ground mace

salt and freshly ground black pepper

75 ml | 2½ fl oz single cream

1 Melt the butter in a very large, heavy saucepan.

2 Add the mushrooms and most of the parsley. Cook over a low heat, stirring, until soft. Add the garlic and the bread. Stir until the bread and mushrooms are well mixed, then add the stock, nutmeg or mace and salt and plenty of pepper to taste. Bring to simmering point, then cook slowly for 10 minutes.

3 Liquidize the soup in a food processor or blender or put it through a vegetable mill. If the soup is to be served cold, allow to cool, sprinkle on the parsley and swirl in the cream. Alternatively, add the parsley and cream and reheat.

wine: **SPICY WHITE**

Clear Borscht

SERVES 6

900 g | 2 lb raw beetroots

1.7 litres | 3 pints white stock (see page 103)

6 black peppercorns

8 coriander seeds

½ teaspoon fennel seeds

1 parsley stalk, bruised

1 onion, chopped

1 carrot, peeled and chopped

1 clove of garlic, unpeeled

salt and freshly ground black pepper

4 teaspoons malt vinegar

1 tablespoon caster sugar

1 Wash and peel the beetroots and cut each one into quarters.

2 Put the beetroot into a large clean saucepan with the stock.

3 Put the peppercorns, coriander and fennel seeds into a small piece of muslin and tie up. Add to the pan with the parsley stalk. Bring to the boil, then simmer for 1 hour.

4 Add the onion, carrot, garlic, salt and pepper and cook very slowly for a further 20 minutes. Add the vinegar and sugar. Check the seasoning.

5 Strain the soup through a muslin-lined sieve into a clean saucepan. Reheat and pour into individual soup bowls.

wine: **SPICY WHITE**

Lentil Soup

SERVES 4

340 g|12 oz orange lentils

1 litre|2 pints water

1 small bacon bone

1 bay leaf

55 g|2 oz onion, sliced

1 parsley stalk

3–4 tablespoons single cream

To garnish

chopped fresh mint

1 Wash the lentils and drain them. Put them into a saucepan with the water, bacon bone, bay leaf, onion and parsley stalk, and boil for about 30 minutes.

2 When the lentils are soft, remove the bone and flavourings. Liquidize in a food processor or blender, then sieve the soup.

3 Return the soup to the rinsed-out pan with the cream and heat through. Serve sprinkled with a little mint.

wine: **LIGHT RED**

Corn Chowder

SERVES 4

110|4 oz rindless streaky bacon, chopped

30 g|1 oz butter

3 sticks of celery, chopped

1 large onion, chopped

1 large yellow pepper, cored, deseeded and finely chopped

1 bay leaf

1 large potato, peeled and diced

30 g|1 oz plain flour

570 ml|1 pint milk

4 ears of boiled sweetcorn or 340 g|12 oz cooked sweetcorn kernels

salt and freshly ground black pepper

To garnish

chopped fresh parsley

1 Fry the bacon in the butter. When brown but not crisp add the celery, onion, yellow pepper and bay leaf. Reduce the heat and cook slowly until the onion looks soft and transparent. Add the potato after 5 minutes.

2 Remove the pan from the heat; mix in the flour, cook for 1 minute and then add the milk.

3 Return the pan to the heat; stir until boiling.

4 Cut the kernels from the ears and add them to the soup. Scrape the cobs with a sharp knife to extract all the juice and add this too. Season to taste with salt and pepper. Simmer for 5 minutes or until the vegetables are soft but not broken. Remove the bay leaf and discard.

5 Serve sprinkled with parsley.

wine: **DRY WHITE**

Watercress and Potato Soup

SERVES 4

30 g | 1 oz butter

1 medium onion, chopped

225 g | 8 oz potatoes, diced

570 ml | 1 pint white stock (see page 103)

2 bunches of watercress, leaves chopped

290 ml | ½ pint creamy milk, scalded

salt and freshly ground black pepper

a pinch of freshly grated nutmeg

To garnish

chopped fresh chives

1 Melt the butter, add the onion and cook over a low heat until soft but not coloured. Add the potatoes and stock and simmer for 10–15 minutes or until the potatoes are tender. Stir the watercress into the hot soup.

2 Liquidize the soup with the watercress in a food processor or blender and push it through a sieve. Pour into the rinsed-out pan.

3 Add enough of the milk to get the required consistency and season to taste with salt, pepper and nutmeg. Reheat until the soup is just below boiling point.

4 Serve garnished with chives.

wine: **CRISP DRY WHITE**

Carrot and Coriander Soup

SERVES 4

675 g | 1½ lb carrots, peeled and sliced

1 onion, finely chopped

15 g | ½ oz butter

1 bay leaf

860 ml | 1½ pints white stock (see page 103) or water

salt and freshly ground black pepper

1 tablespoon chopped fresh parsley

1 tablespoon chopped fresh coriander

4 tablespoons double cream

1 Put the carrots and onion into a large, heavy saucepan with the butter. Sweat for 10 minutes or until beginning to soften. Add the bay leaf, stock, salt and pepper. Bring to the boil, then simmer as slowly as possible for 25 minutes. Remove the bay leaf.

2 Liquidize the soup with the parsley and coriander in a food processor or blender and push through a sieve into a clean saucepan. Check the consistency. If a little thin, reduce by rapid boiling, if a little thick, add extra water.

3 Add the cream and season to taste with salt and pepper.

wine: **CRISP DRY WHITE**

Pea and Ham Soup

SERVES 4

1 tablespoon vegetable oil

1 onion, thinly sliced

1 stick of celery, chopped

1 ham hock, about 250 g|9 oz

250 g|9 oz split peas

1.1 litres|2 pints water

6 black peppercorns

4 sprigs of fresh thyme

1 bay leaf

1 Heat the oil in a deep saucepan over a medium heat, add the onion and celery and cook until softened.

2 Add the ham hock, peas, water, peppercorns, thyme and bay leaf. Simmer for $1-\frac{1}{2}$ hours or until the peas have broken up and the ham is falling from the bone.

3 Remove the peppercorns, thyme and bay leaf and discard.

4 Remove the ham hock. Trim away any fat, then cut the meat into 2.5 cm|1 in pieces. Set aside.

5 Purée the soup in a food processor or liquidizer, then return to the rinsed-out pan.

6 Add the ham and warm through to serve. Do not boil.

wine: **LIGHT RED**

Prawn Bisque

SERVES 4

900 g|2 lb shell-on cooked prawns

2 tablespoons oil

110 g|4 oz butter

2 shallots, chopped

juice of ½ lemon

3 tablespoons brandy

1 litre|1¾ pints well-flavoured fish or shellfish stock (see page 108)

1 bay leaf

1 parsley stalk

1 blade of mace

45 g|1½ oz plain flour

salt and freshly ground white pepper

Tabasco sauce

3 tablespoons single cream

1 Peel all but 4 of the prawns, and reserve the shells. Wash the prawns, remove the dark veins and reserve any roe.

2 In a large, heavy saucepan heat the oil, add 30 g|1 oz of the butter and fry the prawn shells for 2 minutes. Add the shallots, lemon juice and brandy and continue to cook for a further 2 minutes. Add the stock, bay leaf, parsley stalk and blade of mace and cook for 30 minutes (this will help to give the bisque flavour and colour).

3 Meanwhile, blend or pound together all the peeled prawns with about 45 g|1½ oz butter and any reserved roe.

4 Melt the remaining butter in a saucepan. Add the flour and cook for 30 seconds. Strain in the stock and bring slowly to the boil, stirring constantly. Simmer for 2 minutes, strain in the pan juices, and whisk in the prawn butter.

5 Season with salt, pepper and Tabasco. Add the cream and the reserved prawns.

NOTE: If there is no roe to be found, whisk 1 tablespoon tomato purée into the bisque to give it a better colour.

wine: **LIGHT DRY WHITE**

Lobster Bisque

SERVES 4

1 × 675 g|1½ lb live lobster
2 tablespoons oil
110 g|4 oz butter
2 shallots, chopped
juice of ½ lemon
3 tablespoons brandy
1 bay leaf
1 parsley stalk

1 blade of mace
1 litre|1¾ pints fish, shellfish or vegetable stock (see pages 106, 108, 107)
45 g|1½ oz plain flour
3 tablespoons single cream
salt and freshly ground white pepper
a pinch of cayenne pepper

1 Preheat the oven to 180°C|350°F|gas mark 4.
2 Kill the lobster by pushing a sharp knife through its nerve centre (marked by a well defined cross on the back of the head).
3 Lay the lobster flat on a board and split it in half lengthways. Remove and discard the little sac from the head and the thread-like intestine. Remove the coral (if any) and reserve.
4 In a large flameproof casserole, heat the oil with 30 g|1 oz of the butter. Sauté the lobster, flesh side down, for 5 minutes. Add the shallot, lemon juice and brandy. Cover and place in the oven for 15 minutes.
5 Remove all the meat from the lobster, adding the greenish creamy paste from the body.
6 Break up the shells in the pan, add the bay leaf, parsley stalk, mace and stock, and simmer for 30 minutes. Set aside. (This will help to give the bisque flavour and colour.)
7 Meanwhile, blend or pound together all but a small chunk of the lobster meat with about 45 g|1½ oz butter and the coral. Cut the reserved meat into neat dice and set aside for garnish.
8 Strain the stock. Melt the remaining butter, add the flour and cook for 30 seconds. Add the stock and bring slowly to the boil, stirring all the time. Simmer for 2 minutes, add the pan juices and whisk in the lobster butter.
9 Add the cream and finally the lobster pieces. Check the seasoning. Serve sprinkled with a pinch of cayenne pepper.

wine: **LIGHT DRY WHITE**

Preparing a Lobster

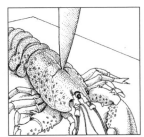

Push a sharp knife through the lobster's nerve centre

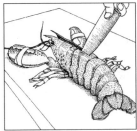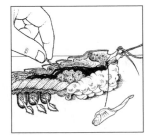

Split the lobster in half and remove the stomach sac

Remove the thread-like intestine and the greeny black roe

Bouillabaisse

Recipes for this Mediterranean stew are many and varied according to the availability of fish and vegetables. The sad truth is that it is only possible to make a real bouillabaisse on or near the Mediterranean coast. Imitations made at home never have quite the freshness and authenticity of the original.

This recipe is an adaptation of many recipes but we have relied mostly on Jane Grigson's in *Fish Cookery*.

SERVES 10

150 ml | ¼ pint good-quality olive oil

2 onions, chopped

2 cloves of garlic, crushed

white part of 2 leeks, chopped

1 small bulb of Florence fennel, sliced

1 small green chilli, deseeded and chopped

2 very large tomatoes, peeled and chopped

7 filaments of saffron, dissolved in 4 tablespoons hot
water

cayenne pepper

salt

3 litres | 5 pints fish stock (see page 106)

1 small bunch of fresh parsley

2.7 kg | 6 lb fresh fish, cleaned

To serve

10 slices of French bread, toasted lightly in the oven,
fried in olive oil and rubbed with garlic

a bowl of rouille (see page 130)

a bowl of aïoli (garlic mayonnaise – see page 117)

1 Put the oil into a large, heavy saucepan. Add the onions, garlic, leeks, fennel and chilli. Sweat for 5 minutes.

2 Add the tomatoes, saffron liquid, cayenne pepper, salt, stock and parsley. Bring to the boil and boil hard to enable the oil and water to emulsify. Reduce to a simmer.

3 Gradually add the fish. Conger eel will take about 20 minutes to cook; crayfish about 15 minutes; unfilleted white fish about 10 minutes, and most shellfish 5 minutes.

4 Remove the fish to a warmed serving dish, split the crayfish head in two and slice the tail. Leave the shellfish unshelled. Check the seasoning of the soup.

5 Bring the soup to the boil and boil hard for a few moments to emulsify the liquid, then strain into a warmed soup tureen. Serve immediately with the fish, hot bread, rouille and aïoli.

NOTE: Use a selection of the following fish: rascasse, bay scallops, mussels, monkfish, conger eel, John Dory, gurnard, crayfish, lobster, Dublin Bay prawns, scampi.

Traditionally the fish are cooked and served unfilleted but they can be skinned and filleted if preferred. The cooking time would need to be reduced accordingly.

wine: ROSÉ

New England Clam Chowder

SERVES 4

3 rashers of rindless streaky bacon, chopped

55 g | 2 oz butter

1 large or 2 medium onions, chopped

1 stick of celery, chopped

1 leek, chopped

48 clams (soft- or hard-shelled)

425 ml | ¾ pint water

3 medium potatoes, peeled and finely diced

425 ml | ¾ pint creamy milk

a pinch of dried thyme

a small piece of bay leaf

salt and freshly ground black pepper

30 g | 1 oz plain flour

4 tablespoons double cream

1 Put the bacon into a heavy saucepan and fry in its own fat until crisp and slightly brown.

2 Add half the butter and the onion, celery and leek. Cover with a dampened piece of greaseproof paper and a lid then cook slowly until the vegetables are softened but not coloured.

Soup au Pistou

Italian Seafood Salad

Pea and Ham soup

Adding Butter to Brioche
and Kneading

Brioche Stuffed with Wild Mushrooms

Bouillabaisse

Onion Tart

Spinach and Bacon Salad
with Red Chilli and Mango

Greek Parsley Pasta

Tartare of Salmon and Tuna

Grilled Sardines with
Warm Greek Salad

Fritto Misto

Dry-Fried Prawns with Coriander

Grilled Chilli Squid with Lime

Pork and Liver Terrine

3 While the vegetables are cooking, scrub the clams well, using a brush to remove any sand. Put the clean clams into a second saucepan and pour on the water. Cook slowly until the shells have opened wide (about 10 minutes).

4 Lift out the clams and reserve their liquid. Remove the clams from their shells and chop the flesh. Strain the cooking liquid through a fine cloth to remove any sand.

5 Add the potato, milk, thyme and bay leaf to the onion mixture and season with salt and pepper. If the potatoes are not covered by the liquid, top up with a little water. Cover the pan and simmer gently until the potatoes are almost tender (about 12 minutes).

6 Meanwhile, melt the remaining butter, remove from the heat and stir in the flour. Return to the heat and cook gently for 30 seconds. Remove the pan from the heat and stir in the strained liquid reserved from poaching the clams. Return to the heat and stir steadily until the mixture boils. Simmer for 2 minutes. Add the clams.

7 Stir the thickened clam liquid into the chowder. Check the seasoning. Stir in the cream and serve immediately.

NOTE: Canned clams can be used as a substitute for fresh. They should be added once the soup has cooked, and simmered for 3–4 minutes before serving. If using canned clams, substitute good fish stock for water.

wine: **CRISP DRY WHITE**

Hot and Sour Soup

SERVES 6

For the marinade
1 teaspoon light soy sauce
1 teaspoon cornflour
½ teaspoon sesame oil
1 chicken breast, boned, skinned and thinly sliced

For the aromatics
2 tablespoons white wine vinegar
2 tablespoons light soy sauce
1 bunch of spring onions, sliced on the diagonal
1 teaspoon sesame oil
1 teaspoon Sichuan peppercorns, ground
2 fresh red chilies, deseeded and finely chopped
5 cm|2 in piece of fresh root ginger, peeled and finely julienned

1 large handful of fresh coriander leaves, roughly chopped

For the soup
3 tablespoons sunflower oil
2 litres|3½ pints water
4 tablespoons light soy sauce
1 small can of bamboo shoots, drained
55 g|2 oz shiitake mushrooms, sliced
85 g|3 oz fresh beansprouts
3 tablespoons cornflour
250 g|9 oz firm tofu, cut into 1 cm|½ in cubes
55 g|2 oz peeled prawns
2 eggs, lightly beaten

1 Mix together the ingredients for the marinade, add the chicken and refrigerate for 20 minutes.

2 Place the aromatics at the bottom of a warmed soup tureen.

3 Heat the sunflower oil in a wok until smoking, then add the chicken and marinade. Stir-fry until the chicken is a light golden-brown. Remove from the wok and set aside.

4 Add the water and soy sauce to the work and bring to the boil. Add the bamboo shoots and the mushrooms, lower the heat and simmer for 2 minutes.

5 Return the chicken to the wok, add the beansprouts and simmer for 2 minutes.

6 Slake the cornflour with enough cold water to make a smooth paste and add to the wok. Stir gently as the soup thickens.

7 Add the tofu and prawns and simmer until heated through.

8 Drizzle the beaten eggs into the simmering soup and stir gently.

9 Pour the hot soup straight on to the aromatics in the soup tureen. Stir.

10 Allow the soup to infuse for 5 minutes, then serve.

wine: **SPICY WHITE**

Cock-a-Leekie Soup

This is an unthickened chicken broth, and it should have plenty of chicken and leeks in it.

SERVES 6

1.35 kg│3 lb chicken	6 leeks, cut into matchstick lengths
2 teaspoons salt	6 no-soak, stoned prunes
freshly ground black pepper	
1 bay leaf	**To garnish**
a few parsley stalks	chopped fresh parsley

1 Joint the chicken and place the pieces in a pan with 2 litres│3 ½ pints water. Reserve the giblets. Add salt and pepper, the bay leaf, giblets (except the liver) and parsley. Bring to the boil and skim. Cover and simmer for about 45 minutes.

2 Skim the fat from the soup, add the leeks and prunes and simmer for a further 45 minutes.

3 Remove the chicken, giblets, bay leaf and parsley stalks. Skin the chicken and cut the flesh into small, neat dice. Add the diced chicken to the soup.

4 Check the seasoning and serve hot with a little parsley sprinkled over at the last minute.

NOTES: You may prefer to reserve the chicken breast and use it for another dish, rather than adding it to the soup. Chicken portions (thighs and drumsticks) can be bought more cheaply than whole chickens, but this means no giblets. Best of all, use a boiling fowl, but remember this will need a total of 3 hours simmering, with the water being topped up as necessary.

If there is no time to soak the prunes they may be cooked whole in the soup and the stones removed afterwards.

wine: **LIGHT RED**

Beef Consommé

SERVES 6

1.75 litres | 3 pints very well-flavoured brown stock (see page 102)

225 g | 8 oz lean shin of beef, minced

salt and freshly ground black pepper

3 egg whites and shells

5 tablespoons medium sherry or Madeira

1 Sterilize your equipment and egg shells in boiling water.

2 Place the stock, beef and sherry in a large clean metal saucepan. Season very well with salt and pepper.

3 Put the crushed egg shells and the whites into the stock. Place over the heat and whisk steadily with a balloon whisk until the mixture steams. Stop whisking immediately, bring to the boil, then remove the pan from the heat. Allow the mixture to subside. Take care not to break the crust formed by the egg white.

4 Bring the consommé just up to the boil again and then again allow to subside. Repeat this once more. (The egg white will trap the sediment in the stock and clear the soup.) Allow to cool for 2 minutes.

5 Fix a double layer of fine muslin over a clean basin. Place a large spoonful of the crust into the sieve and carefully strain the soup through it. Do not try to hurry the process by squeezing the cloth as this will produce murky soup: it must be allowed to drip through at its own pace. Warm the consommé gently before serving.

NOTES:

To serve the consommé en gelée (jellied), pour the liquid into a shallow pan or tray to cool and refrigerate until set. Chop roughly with a knife and spoon into ice-cold soup cups. Serve with a wedge of lemon and toast.

Garnishes for Consommé

Aux pointes des Asperges

Place cooked asparagus tips at the bottom of a warmed tureen and pour the soup over.

À la julienne

Add mixed carrot, turnip, leek and celery cut into julienne strips to the consommé and cook until tender. Chopped fresh chervil or parsley is sometimes added at the last minute.

Lady curzon

Chill the consommé in ovenproof cups. Flavour 2 tablespoons double cream with curry powder, salt and pepper and pour over each consommé. Place under a hot grill to brown the top. Put into a warm oven to heat the soup.

Aux profiteroles

Season choux pastry with Parmesan, mustard and cayenne, pipe in pea-size pieces and bake until crisp. Place in the bottom of a hot tureen, pour the soup over and serve immediately before the profiteroles can become soggy.

Aux quenelles

Poach small chicken quenelles in stock. Float these in the consommé and sprinkle with chopped fresh chervil or parsley.

Aux vermicelli

Cook vermicelli in stock until tender. Rinse well, place in a warmed tureen and pour the soup over. (Other small-size pastas are also used.)

wine: DRY SHERRY

Consommé Royale

SERVES 6

1 egg white	salt and freshly ground white pepper
4 tablespoons double cream	beef consommé (page 153)

1 Mix the egg white with a fork and beat in the cream, salt and pepper.
2 Place in a heatproof dish and stand in a pan of gently simmering water until set.
3 Cool, cut into neat strips and add to the consommé just before serving.

wine: DRY SHERRY

French Onion Soup

SERVES 4–6

55 g | 2 oz butter	salt and freshly ground black pepper
450 g | 1 lb onions, sliced	55 g | 2 oz Gruyère cheese, grated
½ clove of garlic, crushed	1 teaspoon Dijon mustard
1 teaspoon plain flour	4–6 slices of French bread
1.1 litres | 2 pints good stock, preferably brown (see page 102)	

1 Melt the butter in a large, heavy saucepan and slowly cook the onions: this should take at least 1 hour and the onions should become meltingly soft and greatly reduced in quantity. Cook until they are evenly golden-brown all over and transparent. Add the garlic after 45 minutes.
2 Stir in the flour and cook until golden brown.
3 Add the stock and stir until boiling. Season with salt and pepper and simmer for 20–30 minutes.
4 Preheat the oven to 200°C | 400°F | gas mark 6.

5 Place the soup into an ovenproof tureen. Mix the Gruyère cheese with the mustard and pepper. Spread this on the bread slices and place on top of the soup. Put the soup (uncovered) in the oven until well browned and bubbling.

wine: **LIGHT RED**

Spiced Parsnip Soup

SERVES 4

1 medium onion, finely chopped
2 tablespoons olive oil
340 g | 12 oz parsnips, peeled and diced
1 teaspoon ground coriander
1 teaspoon ground cumin

½ teaspoon chilli flakes
850 ml | 1½ pints white chicken stock (see page 103)
salt and freshly ground black pepper
150 ml | ¼ pint single cream

1 Place the onion in a saucepan with the oil and cover with a piece of dampened greaseproof paper and a lid. Cook over a low heat until the onion begins to soften.
2 Add the parsnips and cook, covered, until just soft.
3 Stir in the coriander, cumin and chilli flakes and cook for 1 further minute.
4 Add the stock and salt and pepper and bring to the boil, then lower the heat and simmer for 20 minutes. Allow to cool.
5 Purée the soup in a food processor or liquidizer and return to the rinsed-out pan. Add the cream and reheat without boiling. Season to taste with salt and pepper.

wine: **SPICY WHITE OR BEER**

Cullen Skink

SERVES 4

340 g | 12 oz smoked haddock
570 ml | 1 pint milk and water mixed
½ onion, sliced
1 small blade of mace
30 g | 1 oz butter
½ onion, finely chopped

450 g | 1 lb potatoes, peeled and chopped
1 tomato, peeled, deseeded and diced
1 tablespoon chopped fresh parsley
salt and freshly ground black pepper
4 tablespoons double cream

1 Wash the haddock, scrape off any scales and lay it skin side up in a flameproof dish.
2 Pour in the milk and water and add the sliced onion and mace. Cover with a piece of dampened greaseproof paper. Place over a medium heat and poach for about 5 minutes. Let stand for 10 minutes.
3 Meanwhile, melt the butter in a saucepan, add the chopped onion and potatoes and cook very slowly until soft.

4 Remove the fish from the poaching liquid, then remove the skin and any bones. Flake the fish into bite-sized pieces and set aside.

5 Strain the cooking liquid on to the potatoes and simmer for a further 5 minutes.

6 Purée the soup in a food processor or liquidizer, then push through a sieve into the rinsed-out pan. Reheat and add the flaked fish, tomato and parsley. Season to taste with salt and pepper.

7 Pour the cream into the bottom of a warmed soup tureen, pour on the hot soup and serve immediately.

wine: **CRISP DRY WHITE**

Salmon Laksa

SERVES 4

2 fresh red chillies, deseeded and finely chopped

2 cloves of garlic, crushed

1 stick of lemon grass, peeled and finely chopped

2.5 cm│1 in piece of fresh root ginger, peeled and grated

1.1 litres│2 pints white fish stock (see page 106)

2 teaspoons nam pla (Thai fish sauce)

grated zest and juice of 2 lemons

1 bunch of coriander, stalks left whole and leaves chopped

4 spring onions, thinly sliced

110 g│4 oz vermicelli

170 g│6 oz salmon, skinned and cut into bite-sized chunks

150 ml│¼ pint coconut milk

chilli powder to taste

1 Place half of the chillies, garlic, lemon grass and ginger in the stock in a saucepan and add the nam pla, lemon zest and coriander stalks. Poach for 20 minutes to infuse the stock.

2 Strain the infusion. Add the remaining chilli, garlic, lemon grass and ginger to the stock along with the spring onions. Bring to the boil, add the vermicelli and cook for 1 minute. Turn the heat down to a poach, add the salmon and continue to cook gently until the noodles are soft and the fish is cooked.

3 Stir in the coconut milk and season to taste with salt, pepper, chilli powder and lemon juice as required. Garnish with the coriander leaves.

wine: **SPICY WHITE**

Croûtons

2 slices of bread, crusts removed, from an unsliced slightly stale white loaf

oil for frying

salt

1 Cut the bread into 5 mm│¼ in cubes.

2 Heat the oil in a frying pan until a cube of bread will brown in 30 seconds. Fry the bread cubes until golden-brown.

3 Drain on absorbent kitchen paper and then sprinkle with salt.

Traditional First Courses

Caviar

30 G | 1 OZ PER PERSON

Leave the caviar in its pot. Chill, and stand it on a napkin. Serve 1 teaspoon on each individual plate, and offer, from another platter, wedges of lemon, chopped hardboiled egg white and sieved yolk (in separate piles), chopped fresh parsley and very finely chopped raw onions. Serve with hot toast or blinis.

wine: **CRISP DRY WHITE**

Blinis

MAKES FIFTEEN

225 g | 8 oz wholemeal or buckwheat flour
225 g | 8 oz plain flour
salt
3 eggs
45 g | 1½ oz fresh yeast

2 teaspoons sugar
720 ml | 1¼ pints warm milk
1 tablespoon melted butter
oil for frying

1 Sift the flours into a bowl, add the salt and any bran left in the sieve.
2 Make a well in the centre and drop in 2 whole beaten eggs and 1 egg yolk, reserving 1 egg white.
3 Cream the yeast with the sugar and add the milk. Mix well.
4 Pour the yeasty milk gradually into the flours and mix to a smooth batter. Add the melted butter.
5 Cover with a sheet of greased clingfilm or a cloth and leave in a warm place for 1 hour.
6 Just before cooking, whisk the remaining egg white to medium peaks and fold it into the mixture.
7 Grease a heavy frying pan lightly with oil. Heat it gently over steady heat. When the frying pan is hot, pour enough of the batter on to the surface to make a blini the size of a saucer. When bubbles rise, turn it over and cook the other side to a light brown.
8 Keep the blinis warm in a cool oven between sheets of greaseproof paper.

To serve

Caviar: Place a spoonful of caviar (or Danish lumpfish roe) on top of the warm blini and surround with soured cream. Serve immediately.

Smoked Salmon: Spread the warm blini liberally with soured cream and place a roll of smoked salmon on top. Serve immediately.

Pickled Herring: Mix herring fillets with soured cream. Top the warm blini with the herring and soured cream mixture. Serve immediately.

NOTES: If using dried yeast use half the amount called for, mix it with 3 tablespoons of the liquid (warmed to blood temperature) and 1 teaspoon sugar. Leave until frothy (about 15 minutes), then proceed. (If the yeast does not froth it is dead and unusable.)

Blinis are very good made with buckwheat flour in place of some or all of the wholemeal flour. They can also be made with all white flour.

wine: **VERY DRY OR SPICY WHITE**

Brown Shrimps

110 G | 4 OZ PER PERSON

Serve the shrimps in piles, unpeeled, on individual plates with hot bread, good butter, lemon wedges and salt and freshly ground pepper. The guests peel their own shrimps. Provide finger bowls.

wine: **CRISP DRY WHITE**

Potted Shrimps

1 SMALL POT PER PERSON

Warm the pots gently in a low oven, and when the butter is just melted, or at least soft, turn out on to individual plates. Offer toast (no butter) and lemon wedges separately, and a knife and fork to eat them with. This is the traditional way of serving shrimps, but today they are sometimes turned out cold and eaten, like pâté, on toast. They are better just warm, however. Do not rechill them once melted.

wine: **CRISP DRY WHITE**

Gull's Eggs

2 PER PERSON

Gull's eggs are normally sold ready-cooked. Serve in a basket lined with lettuce leaves or a napkin, and offer sea or rock salt, celery salt or oriental salt, freshly ground black pepper and cayenne pepper separately. Serve brown bread and butter. The guests peel the eggs and eat them with their fingers.

NOTE: Plover's and quail's eggs may be served in the same way. Plover's eggs (4 per person): boil for 6 minutes. Quail's eggs (6 per person): boil for 2 minutes.

wine: **DRY WHITE**

Oysters

9–12 PER PERSON

Serve 6 each if there is a big meal to come, but oyster lovers like a lot! Order the oysters and ask for them to be opened only when you collect them, or as late as possible. Keep refrigerated until serving but no longer than 24 hours. If the fishmonger has not loosened the oysters from the bottom shell, do so with a sharp knife. Check that there are no bits of shell or grit on the saucer-shaped bottom shells, but leave any sea water or juices with them. Discard the top shells. Put the oysters on to oyster plates, or failing them, on to dinner plates covered by a napkin to keep them from tipping or rolling. Hand Tabasco sauce, or chilli pepper, freshly ground black pepper, white pepper, wedges of lemon and vinegar separately, and serve with brown bread and butter. The diner eats the oysters with a fork, and drinks the juice from the shell as from a cup.

wine: **DRY WHITE**

Oursins (Sea Urchins)

3 PER PERSON

Serve exactly as oysters, with the same accompaniments, but with a teaspoon for the guest to extract the flesh. The fishmonger cuts off the top of the shell, like the top of a boiled egg.

wine: **DRY WHITE**

Smoked Salmon

85 G|3 OZ PER PERSON

Arrange slices in a single layer on dinner plates. Garnish with lemon wedges and hand buttered brown bread separately. To slice smoked salmon: use a salmon or ham knife. Put the fish skin-side down on a board. Slice the top thin layer of smoked skin-like flesh off, then feel for the row of lateral bones whose tips will be sticking like pins straight up in a row between the 2 fillets of flesh, in a line running the length of the fish. Pull them out, one by one, with tweezers or pliers. Then slice the flesh horizontally in paper-thin pieces. The slices should be long and wide. It is customary to remove the central stripe of brownish flesh, but this is not strictly necessary. Keep covered with clingfilm or painted with salad oil to prevent drying out.

wine: SPICY WHITE

Smoked Trout

1 FISH PER PERSON

Use kitchen scissors to cut the smoked skin carefully round the neck and tail before loosening it with the fingers and peeling it off, leaving head and tail intact. Serve on individual plates with lemon wedges, handing buttered brown bread and horseradish sauce separately.

wine: SPICY WHITE

Smoked Mackerel

½ FISH PER PERSON

Peel the fish and carefully lift the fillets off the backbone. There will be 4 of them. Arrange 2 per person on individual plates with lemon wedges and hand mustard, mayonnaise or horseradish sauce separately. Serve with buttered brown bread.

wine: SPICY WHITE

Asparagus

6 FAT OR 12 THIN SPEARS PER PERSON

Cut off the woody ends. Peel the fibrous stalks. Wash well. Boil stalk end down in an asparagus cooker (the stalks stand in the water, the tips cook in the steam), or simmer lying down in salted water in a frying pan, until the stalk is tender halfway down. Drain well. Serve from a platter lined with a napkin to absorb the moisture. Hand melted clarified butter, Hollandaise or Beurre Blanc separately if hot, vinaigrette if cold.

wine: LIGHT DRY WHITE

Globe Artichokes

1 PER PERSON

Score the stem of the artichoke next to the base using a sharp knife. Twist and pull the stalk off the artichoke very close to the base so that it will stand without rolling. Trim the tips of the bottom few rows of leaves off straight if they are hard or cracked and if the tip spines are prickly. Leave the smaller higher leaves. Boil for 35–45 minutes in salted water with a cut-up lemon. When an inner leaf will pull out easily, drain the artichokes upside down. When cool enough to handle, prise open the middle leaves and lift out the central cluster of tiny leaves. Using a teaspoon, scrape out the fibrous choke and discard it. Serve the artichokes on individual plates on a folded napkin. Give each guest a small pot of clarified melted butter if the artichokes are hot, or vinaigrette dressing if cold. The guest pulls the leaves off the flowerhead, dips the flesh end into the butter or sauce with his fingers, eats the softer part and discards the leaves.

wine: LIGHT DRY WHITE

Egg Mayonnaise

SERVES 4

290 ml | ½ pint mayonnaise (see page 117) water
6 hardboiled eggs (see page 162), shelled

To garnish
chopped fresh parsley or paprika pepper

1 Thin the mayonnaise slightly by adding a little water, to achieve a thick coating consistency.
2 Cut the eggs in half lengthways and arrange, cut side down, on a plate. Pat dry with kitchen paper. Carefully coat each egg with mayonnaise.

3 Garnish half the eggs with a neat sprinkling of chopped parsley. Garnish the other half with paprika pepper.

NOTE: Other suitable garnishes for egg mayonnaise include thin strips of anchovy fillet in a criss-cross pattern, pitted black olives, rings of radish or watercress leaves.

wine: **CRISP DRY WHITE**

Hardboiled Eggs

There are two tried and tested methods for hardboiling an egg:

1 If you are cooking a lot of eggs, lower them carefully into a saucepan of boiling water and simmer for 12 minutes.
2 If you are just boiling one or two eggs put them into a saucepan of cold water, bring the water up to the boil and then simmer for 10 minutes.
3 Once the eggs are cooked, drain and put to cool in a bowl of cold water.

NOTES: If you have an egg pricker, prick the rounded end of the raw egg to allow the air under the shell to escape. This will prevent cracking when boiling.
Fresh eggs take longer to cook than stale eggs. Add 30 seconds if the eggs are new-laid and 30 seconds if they are straight from the refrigerator.

Pâte de Foie Gras and Artichoke Heart Salad

SERVES 6

2 handfuls of bitter salad leaves
French dressing (see page 123)

4 warm artichoke hearts
110 g │ 4 oz pâté de foie gras

1 Wash, pick over and pull to smallish pieces the bitter salad leaves. Dry well. Toss in some of the French dressing and arrange on 6 side plates.
2 Slice the still warm artichoke hearts and toss in the remaining French dressing. Pile them on top of the salad leaves.
3 Slice the foie gras very thinly and arrange the slices on top of the artichoke hearts. Serve immediately.

wine: **MEDIUM DRY WHITE**

Snails with Garlic Butter

SERVES 4

170 g │ 6 oz butter
juice of ½ lemon
2 tablespoons chopped fresh parsley
6 cloves of garlic

salt
24 shelled snails and 24 shells

To serve
French bread

1 Soften the butter and beat in the lemon juice and parsley. Crush the garlic with salt and beat this into the butter. Leave in a cool place.

2 Using a teaspoon handle, push a snail, tail first, into each shell. Fill the remaining cavity of the shell with the garlic butter, scraping off the top neatly. Keep in the refrigerator until needed.

3 Preheat the oven to 200°C|400°F|gas mark 6. Place a snail, butter upwards, in each indentation of 4 snail dishes and cook in the oven for 8 minutes or until the butter starts to sizzle, but no longer. (Overcooking snails toughens them.)

4 Serve immediately with fresh French bread.

NOTE: Because preparing fresh snails is a specialized and lengthy process, ready-to-use snails are bought in cans, even by top French restaurants. Shells are bought separately and can be reused.

wine: **LIGHT WHITE**

Fillet of Beef Carpaccio

SERVES 6

675 g|1½ lb fillet steak, cut across the grain into very thin slices

salt and freshly ground black pepper
½ teaspoon horseradish cream
lemon juice

For the sauce

3 tablespoons plain yoghurt
3 tablespoons double cream
3 tablespoons mayonnaise (see page 117)
1 tablespoon made English mustard

To garnish

rocket leaves
shavings of Parmesan cheese

1 Flatten the slices of beef between 2 sheets of clingfilm or damp greaseproof paper, using a mallet or rolling pin. Carefully remove all the sinews.

2 When the slices are as thin as possible, spread them over plates without letting them overlap.

3 Mix together the first 4 sauce ingredients.

4 Flavour to taste with the remaining ingredients.

5 Garnish with the rocket and Parmesan. Serve the sauce separately.

wine: **MEDIUM RED**

Vegetable, Fruit and Salad First Courses

Stuffed Mushrooms

SERVES 4

4 large flat mushrooms about 7.5 cm│3 in in
  diameter

salt and freshly ground black pepper

70 g│2½ oz pancetta or streaky bacon, diced

2 shallots, finely chopped

½ clove of garlic, crushed

55 g│2 oz fresh white breadcrumbs

1 tablespoon chopped fresh parsley

1 tablespoon Sercial Madeira or dry sherry

1 tablespoon freshly grated Parmesan cheese

1 Preheat the oven to 180°C│350°F│gas mark 4.

2 Wipe the mushrooms and peel them if necessary. Cut off the stems, dice and set aside.

3 Put the mushrooms in a single layer into a shallow ovenproof dish. Season with salt and pepper.

4 Sauté the pancetta or bacon for 1 minute over a medium–high heat, then reduce the heat to medium and add the shallots. Cook for a further 4 minutes, stirring frequently.

5 Add the diced mushroom stalks and continue to cook until the pancetta is lightly browned and the shallots are golden (about 2 minutes).

6 Add the garlic and cook for 1 further minute. Remove from the heat.

7 Stir in the breadcrumbs, parsley and Madeira or sherry. Season to taste with salt and pepper.

8 Heap the stuffing mixture into the mushroom caps, pressing down lightly. Sprinkle with the Parmesan cheese.

9 Bake in the oven for 20–25 minutes, or until the mushrooms are tender when pierced with a skewer and the stuffing is golden-brown. Serve warm.

wine: **LIGHT RED**

Tomato, Avocado and Mozzarella Salad

55 g│2 oz tomatoes per person

¼ avocado per person, sliced

55 g│2 oz mozzarella cheese per person, sliced

shredded fresh basil

French dressing (see page 123)

black olives

salt and freshly ground black pepper

1 Dip the tomatoes into boiling water for 10 seconds and then into cold water. Peel, and slice across the width into ⅛ in thick slices, discarding both ends.

2 Arrange the tomato, avocado and cheese in overlapping slices on a serving dish.

3 Add the basil to the dressing. Pour over the salad and sprinkle with a few olives. Season well with salt and plenty of pepper.

wine: **DRY WHITE**

French Country Salad

SERVES 4

1 curly frisée lettuce

110 g│4 oz piece of rindless bacon or lardons

2 slices of thick white bread

2 tablespoons olive oil

French dressing made with plenty of garlic (see page 123)

1 Wash and trim the lettuce. Spin dry.

2 Cut the bacon and bread into 2 cm│¾ in cubes.

3 Fry the bacon in oil in a frying pan over medium heat until it begins to brown. Remove and keep warm. Add the bread to the pan and fry until brown and crisp.

4 Toss together and serve immediately.

wine: SPICY WHITE

Melon, Cucumber and Tomato Salad

SERVES 6

6 tomatoes, peeled, deseeded and cut into slivers

1 cucumber, cubed

1 medium ripe melon, deseeded and cut into chunks

French dressing (see page 123)

1 tablespoon chopped fresh mint

1 Mix all the ingredients together with the French dressing and mint. Serve well chilled.

wine: DRY WHITE

Grilled Pepper Salad

SERVES 4

2 large red peppers

2 large green peppers

2 large yellow peppers

3 hardboiled eggs, quartered

6 anchovy fillets

2 tablespoons extra virgin olive oil

freshly ground black pepper

1 Cut the peppers into quarters and remove the stalks, inner membranes and seeds. Preheat the grill to its highest setting.

2 Grill the peppers, skin side uppermost, until the skin is black and blistered. Place in a plastic bag to cool. Remove the skin. Cut into strips.

3 Arrange the peppers on individual plates and garnish with the hardboiled eggs and the anchovy fillets. Pour over the olive oil and sprinkle with a little pepper.

wine: SPICY DRY WHITE

Salade Tiède

SERVES 4

1 tablespoon olive oil
110 g | 4 oz piece of rindless bacon, diced
150 ml | ¼ pint olive oil
4 slices of white bread, cut into 1 cm | ½ inch cubes
salt
225 g | 8 oz chicken livers, cleaned
5 spring onions, sliced on the diagonal
1 tablespoon tarragon vinegar

1 small frisée lettuce
1 bunch of watercress
1 small radicchio
French dressing (see page 123)

To garnish
1 bunch of chervil, roughly chopped

1 Heat 1 tablespoon of the oil in a frying pan and cook the bacon until it is evenly browned all over. Lift it out with a slotted spoon and keep it warm in a low oven.
2 Heat 150 ml | ¼ pint oil in another frying pan and cook the bread until golden-brown. Drain well and sprinkle with a little salt. Keep the croûtons warm in the oven.
3 Tip most of the oil out of the frying pan and cook the livers over medium heat until fairly firm to the touch. They should be light brown on the outside and pink in the middle. Place in a sieve over a bowl to drain away any blood.
4 Add the spring onions and fry for 30 seconds.
5 Add the tarragon vinegar to the pan then the livers. Shake the livers and spring onions in the vinegar for 10 seconds.
6 Toss the salad leaves in the well-seasoned French dressing and divide it between 4 dinner plates.
6 Scatter the croûtons, the bacon, the spring onions and livers over the salad. Sprinkle the salad with the chervil and serve immediately.

wine: **SPICY DRY WHITE**

Panzanella

SERVES 6

225 g | 8 oz stale Italian bread, crusts removed
1 large red onion, roughly chopped
1 cucumber, peeled, deseeded and chopped
10 fresh basil leaves, roughly chopped
2 tablespoons capers, rinsed and drained
18 black olives, stoned

450 g | 1 lb beef tomatoes, peeled and finely chopped
salt and freshly ground black pepper
110 ml | 4 fl oz good-quality olive oil
1–2 tablespoons red wine vinegar

To garnish
5 fresh basil leaves
radicchio leaves

1 Cut the bread into small pieces and place in a bowl.

2 Put the onion on top of the bread followed by the cucumber, basil leaves, capers, olives and tomatoes.

3 Cover and refrigerate for at least 2 hours.

4 Transfer to a large bowl. Add salt and pepper to taste, then the oil and vinegar. Toss very well, sprinkle over the remaining basil leaves, then garnish with a few radicchio leaves.

wine: DRY WHITE

Warm Mediterranean Salad with Polenta

SERVES 10 (AS A FIRST COURSE)

1 litre│1¾ pints white stock (see page 103)	2 large courgettes
200 g│7 oz polenta (coarse cornmeal)	1½ tablespoons chopped fresh oregano
140 g│5 oz Parmesan cheese, grated	140 g│5 oz prosciutto, thinly sliced
salt and freshly ground black pepper	½ head of radicchio, washed
85 ml│3 fl oz olive oil, infused with a sliced clove of garlic	140 g│5 oz mesclun, washed
	2 teaspoons balsamic vinegar
2 medium aubergines	30 g│1 oz fresh Parmesan cheese

1 Use the stock to cook the polenta according to the manufacturer's instructions, or heat the stock in a large saucepan until simmering. Slowly pour in the polenta, stirring all the time until thick. Reduce the heat to as low as possible, cover the pan and cook, stirring frequently, for 30–40 minutes. Pre-cooked polenta will take about 5 minutes to cook. Add 125 g│4½ oz of the Parmesan cheese and season with pepper. Cover and set aside to cool slightly.

2 Pour the polenta on to a damp baking sheet and smooth the surface with a wet spatula. The polenta should be about 1 cm│½ in thick.

3 Preheat the grill.

4 Cut the aubergines into long strips 1 cm│½ in wide and salt them lightly. Leave for 30 minutes, then rinse and dry. Brush with the flavoured oil and grill until soft.

5 Slice the courgettes on the diagonal into 5 mm│¼ in pieces. Brush with the flavoured oil and grill on both sides until just cooked and lightly browned. Toss with the oregano.

6 When the polenta is cool, cut into diamond shapes, place on a lightly greased baking sheet, brush with the flavoured oil and grill under the hot grill. When brown and crisp turn the shapes over, brush with more oil and grill on the other side. Dust with the remaining grated Parmesan cheese.

7 Heat some of the remaining flavoured oil in a frying pan, add the prosciutto and fry briskly until crisp and brown.

8 Arrange the radicchio and mesclun on 10 individual serving plates. Distribute the aubergine, courgettes and prosciutto between the plates. Mix 2 tablespoons of the flavoured oil with the vinegar and sprinkle over the salads. Scatter with shavings of Parmesan cheese. Put 2 warm polenta shapes on each plate.

wine: **CHILLED LIGHT RED**

Bruschetta

To make bruschetta simply cut thick slices of French bread on the diagonal. Fry them in olive oil that has been infused with garlic until crisp on both sides. Drain well on absorbent paper. The toast should be crisp on the outside but still soft in the middle. Top with a large variety of toppings such as:

Parma ham, rocket and Parmesan cheese
Grilled haloumi cheese and beef tomatoes
Grilled red and yellow peppers with olive oil
  and basil

Grilled marinated aubergines with sun-
  dried tomatoes

Smoked Chicken and Noodle Salad

SERVES 6

1 smoked chicken	**For the dressing**
225 g|8 oz egg noodles	2 tablespoons sesame oil
3 tablespoons vegetable oil	2 tablespoons light soy sauce
110 g|4 oz rindless streaky bacon, cut into thin	2 tablespoons balsamic vinegar
strips	1 tablespoon clear honey
2 parsnips, peeled and coarsely grated	a pinch of cayenne pepper
2 cloves of garlic, crushed	1 cm|½ in piece of fresh root ginger, peeled and grated
110 g|4 oz mangetout, topped and tailed	zest of ½ lemon
1 tablespoon sesame seeds, to garnish	salt and freshly ground black pepper

1 Skin and bone the chicken and pull the meat into bite-sized pieces.

2 Cook the noodles according to the manufacturer's directions. Drain and refresh under cold running water, then place in a large bowl.

3 Mix together all the dressing ingredients and pour over the noodles.

4 Heat the oil in a large frying pan, add the bacon and fry until brown.

5 Add the parsnips and cook until beginning to soften, then add the garlic and cook for 1 further minute. Add the mangetout and cook for a further 2 minutes, or until the mangetout have just wilted. Remove from the heat and allow to cool.

6 Add the chicken, bacon and mangetout to the noodles and mix thoroughly. Season to taste with salt and pepper.

7 To serve, pile into a serving bowl and sprinkle with the sesame seeds.

wine: **SPICY WHITE OR LIGHT RED**

Bacon and Quail's Egg Salad

SERVES 4

3 rashers of rindless streaky smoked bacon

2 tablespoons oil for frying

1 slice of bread

2 handfuls of very young spinach or beet leaves

1 handful of young dandelion leaves, or watercress if
  not available

French dressing (see page 123)

12 raw quail's eggs

1 Cut the bacon across into thin strips. Brown them rapidly in the oil. Remove and drain on absorbent kitchen paper. Cut the bread into small dice and fry in the hot fat until evenly browned. Remove with a perforated spoon and drain on absorbent kitchen paper.

2 Wash and pick over the spinach and dandelion leaves and pull them into small pieces, discarding any stalks or thick ribs. Dry well. Toss in the dressing and arrange on 4 individual plates.

3 Get a frying pan or shallow sauté pan of water bubbling on the heat. Break the quail's eggs carefully on to a plate. Slide the eggs into the pan. Reduce the heat and poach for 1 minute. Remove from the pan and slip into a bowl of warm water until ready for use.

4 Arrange 3 well-drained eggs per person on the salads. Add a sprinkling of bacon, then the fried croûtons, still warm, and serve immediately.

wine: DRY WHITE

Pinenut and Duck Breast Salad

SERVES 4

2 handfuls of bitter salad leaves, such as mâche,
  watercress, chicory, radicchio

2 tablespoons French dressing, made with walnut oil

1 tablespoon olive oil

1 duck breast, skinned and halved horizontally

55 g | 2 oz pinenuts

1 Wash and pick over the bitter salad leaves and pull them into small pieces. Dry well. Toss in the French dressing and arrange on 4 individual plates.

2 Heat the oil in a frying pan. Add the duck breast pieces and fry fairly fast to brown on both sides – about 3 minutes in all. They are done when they feel firm when pressed and are pink, not blue, when cut. Lift out on to a board.

3 Put the pinenuts into the frying pan and shake over the heat until pale brown and crisp.

4 Cut the duck diagonally into thin slices and scatter over the salad with the pinenuts. Serve immediately.

wine: LIGHT/SOFT RED

Wild Mushrooms in a Cage

SERVES 4

For the vegetable sauce

100 g | 3½ oz unsalted butter

¼ onion, peeled and diced

½ leek, cleaned and diced

½ stick of celery, diced

30 g | 1 oz carrots, peeled and diced

30 g | 1 oz cabbage, shredded

¼ teaspoon crushed garlic

¼ teaspoon crushed black peppercorns

150 ml | ¼ pint dry white wine

290 ml | ½ pint water

2 tablespoons double cream

4 slices of wholemeal bread

45 g | 1½ oz unsalted butter

2 shallots, finely chopped

100 g | 3½ oz selection of wild mushrooms, such as
morels, trompettes, oyster, chanterelles, etc.,
washed and roughly chopped if large

70 ml | 2½ fl oz Madeira

70 ml | 2½ fl oz dry white wine

150 ml | ¼ pint double cream

salt and freshly ground black pepper

100 g | 3½ oz flour quantity puff pastry (see page
566)

beaten egg to glaze

To garnish

fresh chervil leaves

1 Preheat the oven to 200°C | 400°F | gas mark 6.

2 First prepare the vegetable sauce: melt 30 g | 1 oz of the butter in a medium saucepan and add the diced vegetables and garlic. Sweat gently, covered, for about 10 minutes, or until soft. Add the peppercorns and wine. Bring to the boil, then simmer, uncovered, until reduced by half.

3 Add the water and bring to the boil, skimming frequently. Simmer gently for 20–25 minutes. Pass through a fine sieve. Skim off any fat that rises to the top and reserve the stock.

4 Cut out 4 × 9 cm | 3½ in diameter circles of wholemeal bread. Brush with 30 g | 1 oz melted butter and place in a patty tin. Press another patty tin, of the same size, on top and place in the oven for 10 minutes. Remove the top tin and continue to dry out the croustades in the oven.

5 Melt 15 g | ½ oz of the butter in a sauté pan, add the shallots and cook over a low heat for 2 minutes. Then add the wild mushrooms and cook for 1 further minute. Add the Madeira and white wine and cook until reduced by half, then add the cream and continue reducing until the mushrooms are coated with the cream. Check the seasoning and allow to cool.

6 Fill the croustades with the mushroom mixture.

7 Roll out the pastry very thinly and cut out 4 circles 6.5 cm | 2½ in in diameter. Make 1 cm | ½ in parallel gashes into the pastry at regular intervals from the centre to the rim.

8 Brush the pastry with beaten egg and put on top of the mushrooms, pulling downwards to stick on to the croustade. Chill in the refrigerator for 30 minutes.

9 Brush the 'cages' with egg wash and bake 15 minutes.

10 Boil the stock until reduced by half, add the double cream and reduce again until thickened. Whisk in the remaining butter, adding a little at a time to form an emulsion. Check the seasoning.

11 To serve: pour a little sauce on to a serving plate, remove the 'cages' from the oven and place on the centre of the plate. Garnish with the chervil. Serve immediately.

wine: **CRISP DRY WHITE**

Quail's Eggs en Croustade

SERVES 4

8 quail's eggs

4 thin slices of bread

unsalted butter

1 shallot, finely chopped

1 rasher of rindless streaky bacon, finely chopped

85 g | 3 oz flat mushrooms, finely chopped

chopped fresh parsley

salt and freshly ground black pepper

beurre blanc (see page 121)

1 Preheat the oven to 170°C | 325°F | gas mark 3.

2 Cut the bread into circles with a large fluted pastry cutter and press very firmly into large patty tins. Brush with melted unsalted butter. Bake in the preheated oven for 15 minutes. Remove from the tins, turn upside down and bake for a further 10 minutes or until crisp and lightly browned.

3 Meanwhile, prepare the duxelles: cook the shallot and bacon in butter. Add the mushrooms and cook for a further 2 minutes. Boil away the liquid. Add the parsley and season to taste with salt and pepper. The mixture should be very dry.

4 Bring a saucepan of water to simmering point. Break 2 quail's eggs at a time on to a saucer, then tip carefully into the saucepan and poach for about 2 minutes. Repeat with the remaining eggs.

5 Divide the duxelles mixture between the croustades. Place 2 eggs on top of each and coat with the beurre blanc.

wine: **LIGHT RED**

Toasted Goat's Cheese with Sesame Seeds

SERVES 6

6 small or 3 medium goat's cheeses (crottins)

85 g | 3 oz sesame seeds, lightly toasted

6 slices of wholemeal toast, cut into circles just larger than the cheeses

2 heads of radicchio, washed and dried

For the dressing

2 tablespoons olive oil

2 teaspoons white wine vinegar

1 clove of garlic, crushed

2 tablespoons chopped fresh chives

salt and freshly ground black pepper

1 Preheat the oven to 200°C|400°F|gas mark 6.
2 If you are using 3 medium goat's cheeses, cut them in half horizontally. Roll the cheeses in the sesame seeds until completely coated.
3 Place the circles of toast on a baking sheet and place the cheeses on top. Bake in the oven for 5–10 minutes, until the cheese is soft and on the point of melting.
4 Meanwhile, combine all the ingredients for the dressing and mix well. Separate the radicchio into leaves and toss in the dressing. Arrange on 6 individual serving plates and place the hot toast and cheese on each leaf. Serve immediately.

wine: **VERY DRY WHITE**

Camembert Fritters

SERVES 3

1 Camembert cheese, chilled
1 egg, beaten
dried white breadcrumbs
oil for deep-frying

To garnish
salad leaves

1 Cut the chilled Camembert into small wedges and roll each first in beaten egg, then in breadcrumbs. Chill again for 30 minutes.
2 Heat oil in a deep-fryer until a cube of bread will brown in 20 seconds: if it starts to sizzle immediately, the oil is ready.
3 Deep-fry the Camembert wedges until very pale brown. Drain well on absorbent kitchen paper.
4 Garnish the fritters with the salad and serve immediately.

NOTE: These are delicious served with gooseberry sauce (see page 320).

wine: **LIGHT RED**

Grilled Aubergines with Pesto

SERVES 6

2 medium aubergines, sliced
salt
150 ml|¼ pint French dressing (see page 123)

2 teaspoons French mustard
parsley pesto sauce (see page 124)

1 Sprinkle the aubergine slices liberally with salt and leave to degorge for 30 minutes.
2 Make the French dressing and season with the mustard.
3 Preheat the grill.
4 Rinse the aubergines, drain and dry well. Brush them on both sides with French dressing.
5 Grill the aubergines for about 5 minutes on each side, or until soft and pale brown.

6 Spread one side of the aubergine with the parsley pesto sauce and return to the grill for 1 minute.

7 Arrange on a round plate.

wine: LIGHT RED OR ROSÉ

Celeriac Rémoulade

SERVES 4

3 tablespoons mayonnaise (see page 117)

½ teaspoon Dijon mustard

2 teaspoons finely chopped gherkin

2 teaspoons finely chopped fresh tarragon or chervil

2 teaspoons finely chopped capers

1 anchovy fillet, finely chopped

450 g | 1 lb celeriac

1 Mix together all the ingredients except the celeriac.

2 Peel the celeriac and cut into very fine matchstick lengths. Blanch briefly in boiling acidulated water, refresh and drain well. Mix with the sauce, before it has time to discolour.

3 Turn into a clean dish.

NOTE: Rémoulade sauce is a mayonnaise with a predominantly mustard flavour. The other ingredients, though good, are not always present.

wine: SPICY DRY WHITE

Mushrooms à la Grecque

SERVES 4

290 ml | ½ pint water

1 tablespoon tomato purée

2 tablespoons olive oil

2 tablespoons dry white wine

2 shallots, finely chopped

1 clove of garlic, crushed

6 coriander seeds, well crushed

1 teaspoon dried fennel seed

freshly ground black pepper

a small pinch of salt

a pinch of caster sugar

a good squeeze of lemon juice

450 g | 1 lb button mushrooms, wiped and trimmed

2 teaspoons chopped fresh parsley

1 Place all the ingredients except the mushrooms and parsley in a saucepan and simmer gently for 15–20 minutes.

2 Add the mushrooms and simmer for 10 minutes, then remove.

3 Reduce the liquid by boiling to about 190 ml | ⅓ pint. Put the mushrooms back and allow to cool.

4 Check the seasoning and tip into a shallow bowl or dish. Sprinkle with the parsley.

wine: LIGHT RED

Mushroom Roulade

SERVES 4–6

450 g | 1 lb mature flat mushrooms, roughly chopped

30 g | 1 oz butter

30 g | 1 oz plain flour

1 teaspoon tomato purée

1 teaspoon mushroom ketchup (optional)

a pinch of freshly grated nutmeg

salt and freshly ground black pepper

4 eggs, separated

For the filling

225 g | 8 oz cream cheese

4 tablespoons fromage frais or plain yoghurt

4 medium spring onions, thinly sliced

1 tablespoon chopped fresh mixed herbs, such as
  parsley, thyme, sage, chervil

salt and freshly ground black pepper

1 Preheat the oven to 200°C | 400°F | gas mark 6. Place the mushrooms in a food processor with 1 tablespoon water. Process until very finely chopped.

2 Melt the butter in a large saucepan, add the flour and cook for 30 seconds.

3 Add the mushrooms and stir well. Cook, stirring occasionally, until the mushrooms are dry. (They will, at first, exude a lot of liquid which needs to be evaporated. This may take up to 20 minutes.) Meanwhile, line a large roasting pan with a double sheet of lightly greased greaseproof paper or non-stick baking parchment, allowing the edges to stick up above the sides of the pan.

4 Remove the mushrooms from the heat and add the tomato purée, mushroom ketchup, nutmeg, and salt and pepper to taste. Allow to cool. Stir in the egg yolks and turn into a large bowl.

5 In another large bowl whisk the egg whites with a balloon whisk until they hold their shape. Take a spoonful of egg white and add to the mushroom mixture, stirring it in to loosen the mixture.

6 Fold the remaining egg whites into the mixture and carefully spread the mixture into the prepared roasting pan, taking care not to lose any air.

7 Bake in the oven for about 12 minutes, or until the roulade is firm to the touch.

8 Meanwhile, prepare the filling. Using a wooden spoon, combine the cream cheese with the fromage frais, stirring well to ensure no lumps are left. Add the spring onions, herbs, salt and pepper.

9 When the roulade is cooked, turn it on to a piece of greaseproof paper, trim the edges, spread over the filling and roll it up carefully, letting it rest on the seam. Wrap tightly with the greaseproof paper and place in the refrigerator for about 30 minutes, or until cold.

wine: **LIGHT RED**

Brioche Stuffed with Wild Mushrooms

SERVES 4

110 g | 4 oz flour quantity brioche dough (1) (see
   page 761), sugar omitted

For the filling

340 g | 12 oz wild mushrooms, sliced
20 g | ¾ oz butter

1 tablespoon chopped fresh parsley
a squeeze of lemon juice
salt and freshly ground black pepper
4 tablespoons double cream
a little beaten egg to glaze

1 Grease and flour a large brioche mould or 4 small moulds. Roll three-quarters of the dough into a ball and put it into the mould. Make a dip in the centre. Roll the remaining dough into a ball and press into the prepared dip. Press a wooden spoon handle through the smaller of the 2 balls into the brioche base to anchor the top in place during baking.

2 Cover with greased clingfilm and leave in a warm place until risen to the top of the mould (about 30 minutes).

3 Preheat the oven to 220°C | 425°F | gas mark 7.

4 Meanwhile, make the filling: fry the mushrooms in the butter over a low heat for 1 minute. Add the parsley, lemon juice, salt, pepper and cream. Taste and set aside.

5 Brush the brioche with beaten egg and bake in the oven for 25 minutes. Remove the 'top knot' and some of the inside brioche dough.

6 Heat up the mushroom mixture and spoon it into the brioche cavity. It does not matter if it does not all fit in as the final dish looks very attractive served with some of the filling on the side of the plate. Replace the top and serve immediately.

wine: **SPICY DRY WHITE**

Spinach Roulade

SERVES 4

4 eggs, separated
15 g | ½ oz butter
450 g | 1 lb fresh spinach, or 170 g | 6 oz frozen leaf
   spinach, cooked and puréed
salt and freshly ground black pepper
a pinch of freshly grated nutmeg

For the filling

15 g | ½ oz butter
170 g | 6 oz mushrooms, chopped
15 g | ½ oz plain flour
150 | ¼ pint milk
4 tablespoons double cream
1 tablespoon chopped fresh parsley
salt and freshly ground black pepper

1 Line a roasting pan with a double sheet of lightly greased greaseproof paper or non-stick baking parchment. Allow the edges to stick above the sides of the tin.

2 Prepare the filling: melt the butter in a saucepan and gently cook the mushrooms in it. Remove the pan from the heat, add the flour and mix well. Return the pan to the heat and cook for 30 seconds. Add the milk and bring to the boil, stirring continuously until you have a very thick creamy sauce. Add the cream and parsley and season to taste with salt and pepper.

3 Preheat the oven to 190°C|375°F|gas mark 5.

4 Make the roulade: gradually beat the egg yolks and butter into the spinach and season with salt, pepper and nutmeg. Whisk the egg whites until stiff but not dry and fold them into the spinach. Pour the mixture into the prepared roasting pan and spread it flat. Bake in the oven for 10–12 minutes, or until it feels dry to the touch.

5 Put a piece of greaseproof paper on top of a tea towel. Turn the roulade out on to the paper and remove the original piece of paper. Warm the filling then spread the filling on to the roulade and roll it up as you would a Swiss roll, removing the paper as you go. Serve whole on a warmed dish. Slice to serve.

NOTE: This roulade can also be served at room temperature.

wine: **SOFT RED**

Spinach Roulade with Smoked Salmon and Crème Fraîche

SERVES 4

15 g|½ oz butter
450 g|1 lb fresh spinach, or 170 g|6 oz frozen leaf
  spinach, cooked and puréed
4 eggs, separated
salt and freshly ground black pepper
a pinch of freshly grated nutmeg

For the filling
290 ml|½ pint crème fraîche
110 g|4 oz smoked salmon, chopped freshly ground
  black pepper
2 teaspoons chopped fresh dill plus sprigs for garnish

1 Preheat the oven to 190°C|375°F|gas mark 5. Line a large roasting pan with a double sheet of lightly greased greaseproof paper or non-stick baking parchment, allowing the edges to stick up above the sides of the pan.

2 Heat the butter in a saute pan over medium heat. Stir in the spinach and heat for 1 minute to dry it. Place on a plate to cool.

3 Make the roulade: beat the egg yolks into the spinach and season with salt, pepper and nutmeg. Whisk the egg whites until stiff but not dry and fold them into the spinach. Season. Pour the mixture into the prepared roasting pan and spread it flat. Bake for 10–12 minutes, or until it feels dry to the touch.

4 Mix together the filling ingredients.

5 Turn the roulade out on to a piece of greaseproof paper. Spread the filling on to the roulade and roll it up as you would a Swiss roll, removing the paper as you go. Serve on a warmed dish.

NOTE: Extra soured cream can be served separately with this dish.

wine: **DRY WHITE**

Spinach and Ricotta Strudels

These strudels can be made easily with bought filo pastry.

SERVES 6

450 g | 1 lb fresh spinach, cooked and finely chopped
170 g | 6 oz ricotta cheese
1 egg, lightly beaten
salt and freshly ground black pepper
freshly grated nutmeg
340 g | 12 oz flour quantity filo or strudel pastry (see page 563)
melted butter

1 Preheat the oven to 200°C | 400°F | gas mark 6.

2 Mix the spinach with the ricotta cheese, egg, salt, pepper, and nutmeg to taste.

3 Cut the strudel sheets into 13 cm | 5 in squares. Brush each square immediately with melted butter. Lay 2 or 3 squares on top of each other.

4 Put a spoonful of the spinach mixture on each piece of pastry. Fold the sides of the pastry over slightly to prevent the filling escaping during cooking, then roll the strudels up rather like a Swiss roll.

5 Brush with more melted butter, place on a greased baking sheet and bake in the oven for 15 minutes.

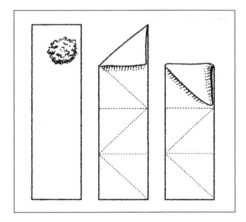

Put a spoonful of filling in the top right-hand corner and fold the pastry into successive triangles

NOTE: Alternatively, the strudel pastry can be cut into long strips, a spoonful of the filling placed in the top right-hand corner and the pastry folded into successive triangles as illustrated.

wine: SPICY DRY WHITE OR LIGHT RED

Spinach Moulds

SERVES 6

30 g | 1 oz butter
675 g | 1½ lb spinach leaves, destalked and washed
225 g | 8 oz ricotta cheese
30 g | 1 oz Gruyère cheese, grated
30 g | 1 oz fresh Parmesan cheese, grated

2 eggs
4 tablespoons single cream
freshly grated nutmeg
salt and freshly ground black pepper

1 Lightly butter 6 ramekins.
2 Blanch 10 spinach leaves, refresh, drain and dry well.
3 Arrange the leaves inside the ramekin dishes, overlapping the edges.
4 Cook the remaining spinach leaves for 2 minutes, then drain very well by pressing between 2 plates. Chop finely. Preheat the oven to 200°C | 400°F | gas mark 6.
5 Mix together the cheese, eggs, cream, nutmeg, salt and pepper.
6 Fill the ramekins with alternate layers of the cheese mixture and the chopped spinach. Fold the spinach leaves over the top to cover.
7 Cover each ramekin with a disc of greaseproof paper. Set in a roasting pan half-filled with hot water (a bain-marie) and bake in the oven for 25–30 minutes until set. Remove from the oven and allow to rest for 2 minutes before unmoulding.

wine: **DRY WHITE**

Spinach and Bacon Salad with Red Chilli and Mango

SERVES 6

1 mango, peeled, stoned and cut into chunks
½ fresh red chilli, deseeded and finely chopped
110 g | 4 oz feta cheese, crumbled
5 tablespoons sunflower oil
140 g | 5 oz piece of rindless streaky bacon, cut into chunks
2 thick slices of white bread, crusts removed and cut into cubes

salt
225 g | 8 oz young spinach leaves, thoroughly washed

For the dressing
6 tablespoons olive oil
2 tablespoons sherry vinegar
salt and freshly ground black pepper

1 Make the dressing: whisk together the oil and vinegar. Season with salt and pepper.
2 Mix together the mango, chilli and cheese.
3 Heat 1 tablespoon of the oil in a large frying pan, add the bacon and fry until crisp. Remove from the pan with a slotted spoon and drain on absorbent kitchen paper.
4 Heat the remaining oil in the pan, add the bread cubes and fry until golden-brown on all sides. Remove the croûtons from the pan with a slotted spoon and drain on absorbent kitchen paper. Sprinkle lightly with salt.

5 Wipe out the pan, add the bacon and the dressing and reheat briefly.

6 Put the spinach leaves and mango mixture into a large bowl. Add the bacon and hot dressing and toss thoroughly.

7 To serve, turn the salad into a serving bowl and sprinkle with the croûtons.

wine: **ROSE**

Carrot and Gruyère Timbales

SERVES 4

170 g | 6 oz carrots, grated

85 g | 3 oz Gruyère cheese, grated

1 egg, beaten

salt and freshly ground black pepper

½ teaspoon dry English mustard

2 tablespoons double cream

butter

To serve

tomato sauce 1 (see page 128)

1 Preheat the oven to 190°C | 375°F | gas mark 5.

2 Blanch the carrot in boiling water for 30 seconds. Refresh under cold running water and drain well on absorbent kitchen paper. Mix together the carrot, cheese, egg, salt, pepper, mustard and cream. Beat well.

3 Butter 4 dariole moulds and pour in the carrot and cheese mixture. Cover with lids or kitchen foil and put the moulds into a roasting pan half filled with hot water (a bain-marie).

4 Bake in the oven for 20 minutes. Carefully turn the moulds out on to a warmed serving dish or individual plates. Hand the tomato sauce separately.

wine: **LIGHT RED**

Courgette Timbales

SERVES 6

450 g | 1 lb courgettes

salt and freshly ground black pepper

2 eggs

1 egg yolk

55 g | 2 oz fresh white breadcrumbs, sieved

290 ml | ½ pint milk

1 tablespoon chopped fresh thyme

To serve

tomato sauce 2 (see page 129)

1 Preheat the oven to 170°C | 325°F | gas mark 3.

2 Oil and line 6 ramekins with circles of greased greaseproof paper.

3 Top, tail and grate the courgettes. Sprinkle sparingly with salt. Leave to degorge in a sieve for 30 minutes. Rinse and dry well on absorbent kitchen paper.

4 Lightly beat the eggs and egg yolk together. Add the breadcrumbs, milk, thyme and courgettes. Season well with salt and pepper.

5 Pour the mixture into the prepared ramekins. Cover with greased greaseproof paper and place in a roasting pan half-filled with hot water (a bain-marie). Bake in the centre of the oven for 40 minutes, or until the timbales are set.

6 Turn out on to warmed individual serving plates and serve warm, with the tomato sauce handed separately.

wine: DRY WHITE

Vegetable Terrine

SERVES 8

10 large fresh spinach leaves, blanched and refreshed

550 g | 1 lb 2 oz large carrots, peeled and thinly sliced

salt and freshly ground black pepper

grated zest and juice of ½ lemon

3 tablespoons water

4 level 5 ml | 4 teaspoons powdered gelatine

1 large ripe avocado

1 Line an oiled loaf tin first with clingfilm, then with the spinach leaves, overlapping them neatly without any gaps.

2 Cook the carrots in a minimum quantity of water until tender, then drain and whizz them in a food processor until they are absolutely smooth. Season the carrots and add the lemon zest.

3 Put the water into a small saucepan, sprinkle on the gelatine and set aside for 5 minutes to become spongy.

4 Dissolve the gelatine over a gentle heat until it is liquid and clear, then stir into the carrot purée.

5 Spoon half the carrot purée into the prepared loaf tin, smooth it down, cover the tin and leave the terrine to set in the refrigerator.

6 Peel and slice the avocado, sprinkle it with lemon juice and arrange on top of the carrot purée. Cover it with the remaining carrot purée, smooth the top down and fold over the spinach leaves carefully to seal the terrine. Cover with clingfilm and refrigerate the terrine again until set.

7 To serve: place a large serving plate over the loaf tin. Turn the tin and plate over together. Give a sharp shake, and remove the tin. Slice the terrine with a serrated knife.

wine: MEDIUM DRY WHITE

Leek Terrine with Stilton Dressing and Griddled Scallops

SERVES 8

27 tiny leeks, cleaned and boiled in salted water until
tender
4 tablespoons olive oil
1 tablespoon wine vinegar
1 teaspoon made English mustard
55 g | 2 oz Stilton cheese, crumbled

salt and freshly ground black pepper
radicchio leaves

To serve
8 scallops, cleaned (see page 198)
unsalted butter

1 Cut the leeks in half lengthways. Lay them lengthways in a 450 g | 1 lb loaf tin, making sure they lie head-to-tail, half of them one way, half the other.
2 Put another loaf tin on top to press them down, turn both tins upside-down so the water can drain out, turn over again, and put a 900 g | 2 lb weight on top to press the leeks. Leave for 4 hours.
3 Meanwhile, prepare the dressing: mix together the oil, vinegar, mustard and Stilton cheese and season with salt and pepper.
4 Cut the scallops in half horizontally. Season with pepper.
5 Unmould the terrine and carefully cut into slices. Lay a slice on each of 8 individual serving plates. Quickly fry or griddle the scallops in butter and arrange beside the terrine. Surround with the radicchio leaves and serve with the dressing.

wine: **DRY WHITE**

Pears with Stilton and Poppy Seed Dressing

SERVES 4

For the filling
85 g | 3 oz Stilton cheese
85 g | 3 oz cream cheese
4 ripe dessert pears, washed but not peeled

For the dressing
3 tablespoons oil
1 tablespoon lemon juice

2 teaspoons poppy seeds, toasted
salt and freshly ground black pepper
pinch of sugar

To garnish
1 small bunch of watercress

1 Put all the dressing ingredients together in a screw-top jar and shake until well emulsified. Check the seasoning.
2 Beat together the Stilton and cream cheese until soft. Arrange onto 4 plates. Spoon into a piping bag fitted with a large plain nozzle.

3 Using an apple corer, remove the centre of the pears. Pipe in the cheese mixture. Refrigerate until ready to serve (at least 2 hours).

4 Slice each pear across into thin round slices. Arrange on to 4 plates. Spoon over the poppy seed dressing and garnish with watercress.

NOTE: To toast the poppy seeds, place in a heavy saucepan over a medium heat for a couple of minutes.

wine: **SPICY DRY WHITE**

Grape and Grapefruit Cocktail

SERVES 4

2 grapefruit

110 g | 4 oz white grapes

1 teaspoon sugar

1 tablespoon sunflower oil

1 tablespoon chopped fresh mint

salt and freshly ground black pepper

To garnish

30 g | 1 oz flaked almonds, toasted

To serve

brown bread and butter

1 Halve the grapefruit and, using a grapefruit knife, remove all the segments, leaving the membranes attached to the shell. Put the segments, with the juice, into a bowl. Reserve the grapefruit shells.

2 Dip the grapes into boiling water for 4 seconds, then peel them. Cut them in half lengthways and discard any pips. Add the grapes to the grapefruit with the sugar, oil, mint, salt and pepper. Leave for at least 30 minutes.

3 Pull the membrane from the grapefruit shells and fill the shells with the grapes and grapefruit mixture.

4 Scatter the almonds on top. Serve with brown bread and butter.

NOTE: If the grapes are soft-skinned and nice looking do not bother to peel them.

wine: **MEDIUM WHITE**

Fish First Courses

Gravad Lax

This Scandinavian pickled salmon is best made with a whole fish. The recipe is for a 2.25 kg|5 lb salmon which would serve 15–20 people, but it can be made with a pound or two of salmon fillet. The fillet should come from a large fish – the larger the fish the oilier and better flavoured. Freeze the salmon for 24 hours before pickling.

SERVES 20

1 salmon, filleted into 2 sides and pin-boned (see
   page 307) but not skinned
vegetable oil
about 3 tablespoons granulated sugar
1½ tablespoons coarse sea salt
1 tablespoon brandy

1 tablespoon chopped fresh dill
crushed white peppercorns

To serve
mustard sauce (see page 125)
brown bread and butter

1 Smear the sides of salmon all over with oil. Put one of them skin side down on a board.

2 Mix together the sugar and salt and pack this mixture in a layer on the flesh side of the fillet. Sprinkle with brandy to moisten and cover the top with dill – there should be enough dill to cover the sugar|salt completely. Sprinkle with the peppercorns.

3 Put the second side on top of the first, skin side up, so that you have a salmon sandwich with a thick sugar and dill filling.

4 Wrap the whole thing up very tightly in 2–3 layers of kitchen foil and put it in a tray or dish with a good lip. Put another tray on top and weight it down with something heavy such as a couple of large cans of fruit. Chill in the refrigerator.

5 Unwrap the parcel, taking care not to lose any of the juice, turn the whole sandwich over and rewrap. Weight down again and refrigerate for a further 4 hours.

6 The gravad lax will be ready when it has been marinating for at least 12 hours.

7 Scrape the marinade from the fish then slice the salmon thinly and serve with the juices that have run from the fish. Hand mustard sauce and brown bread and butter separately.

wine: **VERY DRY WHITE**

Potato Cakes with Smoked Salmon

MAKES 8

450 g | 1 lb floury potatoes, peeled
55 g | 2 oz butter, melted
1 egg yolk
salt and freshly ground black pepper
plain flour

For the filling

1 tablespoon creamed horseradish
2 tablespoons mayonnaise (see page 250)

2 tablespoons soured cream
grated zest of ½ lemon
salt and freshly ground black pepper
225 g | 8 oz smoked salmon, cut into strips

To garnish

55 g | 2 oz salmon roe
1 small bunch of fresh chives, snipped

1 Preheat the oven to 180°C | 350°F | gas mark 4.

2 Cut the potatoes into 5 cm | 2 in chunks then boil until just tender. Drain.

3 Mash the potatoes, add the butter and egg yolk and stir until well mixed. Season with salt and pepper.

4 Divide the mixture into 8 equal pieces and with floured hands shape into flattish circles about 9 cm | 4½ in in diameter.

5 Place on a lightly oiled baking sheet and bake in the oven for 20 minutes, then turn over and bake for a further 20 minutes.

6 Meanwhile, prepare the filling: mix together the horseradish, mayonnaise, soured cream and lemon zest, and season to taste with salt and pepper.

7 Top the potato cakes with the filling and the smoked salmon. Garnish with salmon roe and chives.

wine: VERY DRY WHITE

Moules Marinière

SERVES 4

1.8 kg | 4 lb mussels
2 medium onions, very finely chopped
2 shallots, chopped
2 cloves of garlic, chopped
55 g | 2 oz butter
1 tablespoon chopped fresh parsley

150 ml | ¼ pint water
150 ml | ¼ pint dry white wine
salt and freshly ground black pepper

To garnish

extra chopped fresh parsley

1 Clean the mussels by scrubbing them well under a running tap. Pull away the 'beards' (seaweed-like threads). Throw away any mussels that are cracked or that remain open when tapped.

2 Sweat the onion, shallot and garlic in 15 g | ½ oz of the butter for 10 minutes. Add the parsley, water and wine and cook for a further 5 minutes. Add the mussels, put on the lid and leave to steam over a low heat until the shells open, shaking the pan occasionally (about 5 minutes). Tip the mussels into a colander set over a bowl.

3 Throw away any mussels that have not opened. Pour the mussel liquid from the bowl into a saucepan. Boil to reduce well. Lower the heat and whisk in the remaining butter, then season to taste with pepper.

4 Transfer the mussels to a warmed soup tureen or wide bowl, pour over the sauce and sprinkle with parsley.

NOTES: Moules marinière recipes vary from port to port in France. In Normandy cream is sometimes added to the sauce instead of, or as well as, butter. Sometimes the juice is thickened by the addition of beurre manié. Herbs other than parsley are frequently used in sophisticated restaurants. Sometimes one mussel shell from each mussel is removed and discarded after cooking, as is the 'rubber band' found round the mussel. The mussels are served in the remaining shells, neatly piled on a dish.

Extra soup plates or bowls should be provided to take the pile of discarded shells.

wine: **VERY DRY WHITE**

Baked Mussels Provençale

SERVES 4

1 kg | 2¼ lbs mussels	170 g | 6 oz butter
290 ml | ½ pint water	2 small cloves of garlic, crushed
1 onion, chopped	1 shallot, finely chopped
a few sprigs of fresh parsley	3 tablespoons finely chopped fresh parsley
1 bay leaf	2 tablespoons grated Gruyère cheese
	2 tablespoons dried wholemeal breadcrumbs

1 Scrub the mussels well, discarding any that are cracked or will not close when tapped.

2 Heat the water, onion, parsley and bay leaf in a large saucepan. When simmering add the mussels and cover. Shake the pan occasionally until the mussels have opened (about 5 minutes).

3 Strain through a colander, discarding any mussels which have not opened.

4 Completely open the mussel shells, throwing away the top halves. Remove the 'rubber band' around each mussel.

5 Preheat the oven to 200°C | 400°F | gas mark 6.

6 Cream the butter and stir in the garlic, shallot and chopped parsley. Spread each mussel with the garlic butter and place on a flat ovenproof serving dish. Mix the cheese with the breadcrumbs and sprinkle the mixture over each shell.

7 Bake in the oven until hot and browned (about 10 minutes).

NOTE: The water in which the mussels were stewed will make an excellent base for a fish sauce or soup.

wine: **VERY DRY WHITE**

Grilled Oysters

SERVES 4

24 oysters

150 ml | ¼ pint single cream

freshly grated Parmesan cheese

cayenne pepper

melted butter

dried white breadcrumbs

1 Open the oysters: wrap a tea-towel around your left hand. Place an oyster on your palm with the flat side upwards. Slip a short, wide-bladed kitchen or oyster shucking knife under the hinge and push it into the oyster. Press the middle fingers of your left hand on to the shell and with your right hand jerk up the knife and prise the two shells apart. Free the oyster from its base.

2 Preheat the grill.

3 Rinse and dry the bottom oyster shells, spoon a little cream into each and replace the oysters. Sprinkle with Parmesan cheese, a very little cayenne, melted butter and breadcrumbs. Grill for 3–4 minutes or until hot and lightly browned.

wine: **CHAMPAGNE OR VERY DRY WHITE**

Steamed Clams

4–6 soft-shelled clams per person, depending on size

1 Clean the clams thoroughly with a brush under cold running water.

2 Place the clams on a flat heatproof dish.

3 Put the dish in a steamer and allow to steam for 7–8 minutes or until the shells open.

wine: **DRY WHITE**

Goujons with Tartare Sauce

110 g | 4 oz white fish fillets, skinned, per person

oil for deep-frying

seasoned plain flour

beaten egg

dried white breadcrumbs

salt

To serve

tartare sauce (see page 119)

lemon wedges

1 Cut the fish, across the grain or on the diagonal if possible, into finger-like strips.

2 Heat the oil in a deep-fryer until a cube will brown in 20 seconds.

3 Dip the fish into the seasoned flour, then into the beaten egg, and toss to coat the breadcrumbs. Twist the strips then place on a wire rack for at least 5 minutes to allow the coating to set.

4 Fry a few goujons at a time until crisp and golden-brown. Drain well on absorbent kitchen paper and sprinkle with salt. Serve with tartare sauce and lemon wedges.

wine: **VERY DRY WHITE**

Ceviche

SERVES 4

450 g | 1 lb fillet of monkfish, halibut or salmon, skinned and cut into thin slices or small strips

1 onion, sliced

juice of 2 lemons or 4 limes

1 tablespoon good-quality olive oil

a pinch of cayenne pepper

1 fresh chilli pepper, deseeded and finely chopped (optional)

1 tablespoon chopped fresh dill or chives

1 avocado, peeled and diced

1 tomato, peeled and diced

½ yellow pepper diced

salt and freshly ground black pepper

1 Put the fish, onion, lemon juice, oil, cayenne pepper, chilli, if using, and half the dill or chives into a dish and leave in a cool place for 6 hours, giving an occasional stir. (If the fish is really thinly sliced, as little as 30 minutes will do; it is ready as soon as it looks 'cooked' – opaque white rather than glassy.)

2 Remove the onion from the marinade and discard.

3 Season the fish with salt and pepper. Arrange on a serving dish with the avocado, tomato and pepper, and sprinkle liberally with the remaining dill or chives.

wine: **VERY DRY WHITE**

Brandade

SERVES 4–6

450 g | 1 lb salt cod

lemon juice

6 black peppercorns

2 thick slices of white bread, crusts removed

4–5 tablespoons olive oil

2 cloves of garlic, roasted and crushed

juice of 1 lemon

salt and freshly ground black pepper

4–5 tablespoons mayonnaise (see page 117)

To garnish

1 tablespoon capers, rinsed and drained

1 Soak the salt cod in cold water for 24 hours. Change the water twice to ensure that as much salt as possible is extracted.

2 Drain the salt cod on absorbent kitchen paper and poach the fish in fresh water with the lemon juice and peppercorns. Leave it to cool in its own juice.

3 Drain the cod. Remove the skin and bones.

4 Soak the bread in a little water with 1 tablespoon of the olive oil. Squeeze dry.

5 Put the salt cod, bread and garlic into a food processor, then gradually add the remaining oil, whizzing until thoroughly incorporated.

6 Add the lemon juice and salt and pepper to taste.

7 Stir in the mayonnaise and season with more salt and pepper if required.

8 Pile into a serving dish and garnish with the capers.

wine: **LIGHT RED**

Tuna Fish and Pasta Salad

SERVES 8

85 g | 3 oz pasta shells
salt and freshly ground black pepper
oil and lemon for cooking
150 ml | ¼ pint French dressing (see page 123)
1 × 200 g | 7 oz can of flageolet beans, rinsed and drained
1 × 200 g | 7 oz can of borlotti beans, rinsed and drained

1 × 200 g | 7 oz can of red kidney beans, rinsed and drained
1 bunch of spring onions, chopped diagonally
1 box of mustard and cress
1 tablespoon chopped fresh chives
1 tablespoon finely chopped fresh parsley
a squeeze of lemon juice
1 × 200 g | 7 oz can of tuna fish, drained
15 small black Niçoise olives, pitted

1 Cook the pasta shells in plenty of boiling salted water, with 1 tablespoon oil and 1 slice of lemon, until just tender (about 10 minutes.)

2 Drain and rinse the pasta well.

3 Soak the pasta in the French dressing for 30 minutes, seasoning well with salt and pepper.

4 Mix the pasta with the beans, spring onions, half the mustard and cress, half the chives and parsley and the lemon juice.

5 Add the tuna fish and gently mix so as not to break it up.

6 Pile into a serving dish and scatter over the remaining herbs and mustard and cress and the olives.

wine: **VERY DRY WHITE**

Smoked Salmon and Pasta Salad

SERVES 4

170 g | 6 oz fresh green and white tagliatelle
170 g | 6 oz good-quality smoked salmon, cut into
   thin strips
French dressing (see page 123)

To garnish

4 sprigs of fresh dill

1 Cook the pasta in plenty of rapidly boiling water. When cooked, drain and rinse with cold water. Leave to cool.
2 Mix the pasta and smoked salmon with the dressing. Arrange on 4 individual serving plates and garnish each with a sprig of fresh dill.

wine: **VERY DRY WHITE**

Marinated Salmon and Melon Salad

A simple, light and refreshing first course.

SERVES 6

225 g | 8 oz piece fresh salmon, skinned
juice of 1 lime
2 teaspoons canned green peppercorns, well rinsed
2 handfuls of bitter salad leaves

1 small melon
French dressing (see page 123)
salt and freshly ground black pepper

1 Slice the salmon finely and marinate overnight in the lime juice and green peppercorns. Turn occasionally.
2 Wash and spin-dry the salad leaves.
3 Cut the melon in half. Scoop out the seeds. Cut into quarters, cut off the skin and slice thinly. Toss the salad leaves in the French dressing, arrange on 6 small serving plates and cover with salmon and melon. Season well with salt and pepper.

wine: **DRY WHITE**

Cleaning and Preparing Squid

 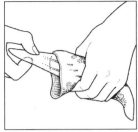

Remove the squid entrails and cartilage

Cut off the head and scrape away the membrane

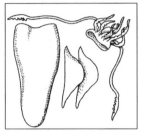

Body, fins and tentacles

Italian Seafood Salad

SERVES 6

450 g | 1 lb fresh small squid

a few slices of onion

a few parsley stalks

1 bay leaf

2 slices of lemon

salt

1 medium leek

1 medium carrot

55 g | 2 oz peeled, cooked prawns

55 g | 2 oz cooked cockles

55 g | 2 oz white button mushrooms, thinly sliced

For the dressing

1 tablespoon good-quality olive oil

2 tablespoons mild salad oil

1 teaspoon wine vinegar

1 teaspoon lemon juice

salt and freshly ground black pepper

1 small clove of garlic, crushed

1 tablespoon finely chopped fresh parsley

1 Clean and skin the squid, see diagram on page 190. Remove the blood (ink) and the entrails under cold running water – they will come out easily. Remove the clear plastic-like piece of cartilage (the quill) that runs the length of the body on the inside. Cut off and throw away the head (it is the round middle bit with two large eyes). Scrape off the pinkish-purple outside skin – a fine membrane – from the body and the tentacles. Don't worry if you cannot get all the tentacles completely clear of it. Wash the body and tentacles to remove all traces of ink: you should now have a perfectly clean, white, empty squid.

2 Cut it into diamond shapes. Score the bodies with a sharp knife into a diamond pattern. Put them into a saucepan and just cover with water. Add the onion, parsley stalks, bay leaf, lemon slices and a pinch of salt. Simmer gently until the squid is tender. This will probably take 1–2 minutes. Drain well.

3 Wash the leek and discard the tough outside leaves and the dark green part. Shred the remainder finely and plunge it into boiling salted water for 30 seconds until just tender but still bright green. Rinse under cold running water to set the bright colour. Drain.

4 Peel the carrot. Using a potato peeler, shred it into long thin ribbons.

5 Combine the ingredients for the dressing in a screw-top jar and shake well.

6 Put the squid into a bowl. Add the prawns, cockles, mushrooms, carrot strips, leek and dressing. Toss. Chill well in the refrigerator before serving.

NOTE: Other seafood can be used too.

Fresh cockles: Leave for 1 hour in salty water and turn often to rid them of sand before cooking as for mussels.

Mussels: Scrub well under running water. Pull away the 'beards' and discard any that are broken or which will not close when tapped. Put into a heavy pan with a little white wine, cover, and shake over heat for 5 minutes until the shells have opened. Discard any that remain closed. Remove the mussels from the shells and discard the 'rubber bands'.

Frozen cooked prawns: Thaw slowly, season with lemon juice, salt and freshly ground black pepper.

Frozen raw 'scampi': Simmer in a court bouillon for 3–4 minutes.

Raw whole prawns: Simmer in a court bouillon for 4 minutes. (The shells will be bright red when they are cooked.) Shell carefully. If using any whole for garnish, remove the legs and any roe after cooking.

wine: DRY WHITE

Squid Salad with Cucumber and Cumin

SERVES 4

450 g | 1 lb squid
150 ml | ¼ pint water
150 ml | ¼ pint dry white wine
1 onion, chopped
1 bay leaf

For the salad

1 cucumber
6 spring onions, thinly sliced

For the dressing

1 teaspoon Dijon mustard
2 tablespoons crème fraiche, or Greek yoghurt
2 tablespoons olive oil
½ teaspoon ground cumin
salt and freshly ground black pepper
grated zest and juice of 1 lime
1 tablespoon chopped fresh mint and chives

1　Clean the squid (see page 190). Chop the tentacles into 2.5 cm | 1 in lengths. Score the outside surface of the body in a lattice pattern. Cut the body into wide strips or rings.
2　Place the water, wine, onion and bay leaf into a saucepan and bring to the boil, then simmer for 10 minutes. Strain and bring back to the boil, then add the squid and remove from the heat. Leave to stand for 1–2 minutes, or until the squid is tender and opaque, then lift out and allow to cool.
3　Peel the cucumber and cut into half lengthways. Using a teaspoon, remove the seeds and then slice the cucumber about the same size as the squid.
4　Make the dressing by mixing all the ingredients together. Check the seasoning.
5　Toss the squid, cucumber, and spring onion in the dressing.

wine: DRY WHITE

Grilled Chilli Squid with Lime

SERVES 4

16 small squid, prepared (see page 190)
salt
1 tablespoon chilli oil
Tabasco sauce

For the dressing

1 red chilli, deseeded and chopped
grated zest and juice of 1 lime
3 tablespoons grapeseed oil

1 tablespoon chopped fresh coriander
1 tablespoon chopped fresh parsley
½ teaspoon Sichuan peppercorns
1 teaspoon sugar
salt and freshly ground black pepper

To serve

225 g | 8 oz bulghur (cracked wheat)
salt and freshly ground black pepper

1　Preheat the grill to its highest setting.
2　Season the squid bodies and tentacles with salt. Brush with the chilli oil and add a splash of Tabasco sauce. Set aside.

3 Make the dressing: put all the ingredients into a blender and whizz until well mixed. Season to taste with salt and pepper.

4 Cook the bulghur wheat according to the manufacturer's directions. Dry on absorbent kitchen paper. Season well with salt and pepper.

5 Grill the squid bodies and tentacles for 2–3 minutes or until the bodies have puffed up and turned opaque.

6 To serve: divide the bulghur wheat between 4 individual plates, arrange 4 squid on each and spoon over the dressing. Serve warm.

NOTE: Any grain, such as quinoa or couscous, may be used instead of bulghur wheat.
The squid can be cooked on a hot griddle rather than grilled if preferred.

wine: MEDIUM DRY WHITE

Fish Quenelles

SERVES 4

675 g | 1½ lb fish fillet, such as sole, salmon or pike
salt
2 egg whites
freshly ground white pepper
cayenne pepper
290 ml | ½ pint double cream

290 ml | ½ pint court bouillon or fish stock (see page 106)
Fish Beurre Blanc (see page 122)

To garnish
slivers of peeled tomatoes
whole fresh chervil leaves

1 Process the fish well in a food processor, adding salt and a little egg white if necessary.

2 Remove from the processor. Pass through a fine sieve. Weigh the fish. You should have about 500 g | 1 lb 4 oz, if it weighs less, use proportionately less cream. Place in a large bowl set in a roasting pan of ice. Beat well and gradually add first the egg white and then the cream, making sure that the mixture remains fairly firm. Taste and season with salt, pepper and cayenne – it should be well seasoned.

3 Heat the court bouillon or stock.

4 Using 2 wet dessertspoons, mould the mixture into 12 egg shapes and drop them into the hot court bouillon or stock. Poach for 3–5 minutes, or until the quenelles feel firm to the touch.

5 Flood the base of 4 individual serving plates with the beurre blanc and arrange 3 quenelles on each plate. Garnish with the tomatoes and chervil leaves.

NOTE: In this recipe much of the beating is done over ice. This is to prevent the mixture from separating, which it may do in a food processor, especially if you are working with large quantities in hot weather.

wine: VERY DRY WHITE

Scallop Mousse with Crayfish Sauce

This recipe has been adopted from Michel Guérard's *Cuisine Gourmande*.

SERVES 4

450 g | 1 lb cleaned scallops

salt and freshly ground white pepper

1 egg

340 ml | 12 fl oz double cream

30 g | 1 oz butter, melted

For the sauce

1 litre | 1¾ pints court bouillon (see p. 106)

20 freshwater crayfish

2 tablespoons olive oil

2 small carrots, peeled and diced

½ onion, chopped

1 shallot, chopped

1 unpeeled clove of garlic, crushed

1 bouquet garni (see page 9)

2 tablespoons Armagnac

2 tablespoons port

200 ml | 7 fl oz dry white wine

2 tomatoes, deseeded and diced

1 tablespoon tomato purée

salt and freshly ground black pepper

290 ml | ½ pint double cream

1 teaspoon chopped fresh tarragon

To garnish

a few sprigs of lamb's lettuce

1 Remove the tough muscle (found opposite the roe) from the scallops (see page 198). Process the scallops briefly in a food processor with salt and pepper. When smooth, add the egg and process to combine. Refrigerate until fairly firm (about 30 minutes).

2 Now process in the cream. The mousse should be fairly thick. Check the seasoning.

3 Preheat the oven to 150°C | 300°F | gas mark 2. Line the bases of 4 ramekins with discs of baking parchment then brush with melted butter. Fill with the scallop mousse and cover the mousse with a second disc of baking parchment.

4 Place in a roasting pan half-filled with hot water (a bain-marie) and cook for 30 minutes. Remove from the oven and keep warm in the bain-marie.

5 Make the sauce: place the court bouillon in a sauté pan and bring to the simmer. Add the crayfish and poach for 3–5 minutes, or until the shells turns orange and the tails curl under. Remove the crayfish. Shell them and remove the black vein but do not throw away the shells. Reserve the tail meat.

6 Pound the shells in a mortar (or grind in a food processor). Add to the sauté pan with the vegetables, garlic and bouquet garni. Cook slowly without browning. Add the Armagnac and port and simmer until reduced by half.

7 Add the wine, tomatoes and tomato purée. Simmer for 20 minutes, then reduce to one-third by rapid boiling. Push the sauce through a fine sieve, pressing well.

8 Add the cream and tarragon and simmer slowly for 10 minutes. Stir every so often to prevent the sauce from catching. Add the crayfish to warm.

9 Turn out the warm mousses on to individual serving plates.

10 Coat each mousse with the hot sauce and garnish with the crayfish and lettuce.

wine: DRY WHITE

Arranged Seafood Salad with Basil Aïoli

This first course is quite extravagant, but ideal for an easy dinner party. For a main course dish, simply increase the amount of seafood.

SERVES 8

For the basil aïoli

2 cloves of garlic, crushed

2 egg yolks

a generous handful of basil leaves

salt and freshly ground white pepper

290 ml | ½ pint grapeseed oil

2 tablespoons lemon juice

a selection of seafood, such as:

16 small oysters, shucked

16 tiger prawns, cooked, peeled and deveined

225 g | 8 oz smoked salmon

225 g | 8 oz smoked halibut

225 g | 8 oz smoked mussels

225 g | 8 oz slender asparagus spears

Tabasco sauce

juice of 1 lemon

freshly ground black pepper

To garnish

sprigs of basil

1 Make the basil aïoli: put the garlic, egg yolks and basil into a liquidizer or food processor. Season with a little salt and pepper. Whizz until well puréed. With the motor running, pour the oil in a thin stream on to the egg yolks. When a thick emulsion has formed, add the lemon juice and season to taste with salt and pepper. Pour into a small dish and set aside.

2 Prepare the seafood: remove the top shell of the oysters and cut the smoked salmon and halibut into long strips. Arrange the fish and asparagus in an attractive pattern on a large platter.

3 Season the oysters with a dash of Tabasco. Season the smoked fish with a little lemon juice and pepper.

4 Garnish with sprigs of basil and hand the basil aïoli separately.

wine: **CRISP DRY WHITE**

Avocados Stuffed with Crab

SERVES 4

170 g | 6 oz white crabmeat

1 stick of celery, finely chopped

3 tablespoons mayonnaise (page 117)

1 tablespoon single cream

1 teaspoon finely grated lemon zest

salt and freshly ground black pepper

2 ripe avocados

French dressing (see page 123)

1 Pick over the crabmeat and remove any pieces of inedible cartilage.
2 Cut the avocados in half lengthways, remove the stones and immediately brush the cut surface with French dressing to prevent discoloration.
3 Mix the crabmeat and celery with the mayonnaise lightened by the addition of the cream and lemon zest. Season to taste with salt and pepper and pile into the avocado halves.

wine: VERY DRY WHITE

Mushroom and Prawn Salad

SERVES 4

170 g | 6 oz peeled, cooked prawns
lemon juice
freshly ground black pepper
170 g | 6 oz button mushrooms, sliced

For the French dressing

3 tablespoons olive oil
1 tablespoon lemon juice

½ clove of garlic, crushed
salt and freshly ground black pepper
2 teaspoons chopped fresh mint

To garnish

1 teaspoon chopped fresh parsley

1 Sprinkle the frozen prawns liberally with lemon juice and black pepper and leave to defrost.
2 Mix together the ingredients for the French dressing and add the mushrooms. Leave to marinate in the refrigerator for 6 hours.
3 Add the prawns, mix well and put into a clean serving dish. Garnish with the parsley.

wine: VERY DRY WHITE

Mango and Lobster Salad

SERVES 4

2 ripe mangoes
2 × 450 g | 1 lb cooked lobsters

4 handfuls of bitter salad leaves, such as endive, lamb's lettuce and radicchio
French dressing (see page 123)

1 Cut a thick slice from each side of the mangoes, keeping as close to the stone as possible.
2 Carefully peel off the skin and slice the flesh horizontally.
3 Cut the heads and claws off the lobsters and remove the shell, rather like peeling a large prawn. Cut the body flesh into neat slices or collops. Crack the claws but leave whole.
4 Wash and dry the salad leaves. Toss in some of the French dressing and arrange on 4 individual plates.

5 Arrange alternate slices of lobster and mango on each diner's plate. Pour over the remaining French dressing and garnish with a claw.

wine: **DRY WHITE**

Scallop and Rocket Salad

SERVES 4

12 scallops	balsamic vinegar
seasoned plain flour	fresh chives
hazelnut oil	a large handful of rocket, washed

1 Clean the scallops (see page 198). Remove the muscular white frill found opposite the roe. Rinse off any black matter. Slice them in half horizontally, trying to keep the roe attached to the scallop.

2 Dip the scallops into seasoned flour. Heat some oil in a frying pan and fry the scallops quickly on both sides until lightly browned and just cooked. Sprinkle over some vinegar.

3 Tip the scallops on to the rocket leaves. Toss lightly and place on 4 individual plates.

wine: **DRY WHITE**

Alex Floyd's Prawn Cocktail

SERVES 4

For the prawns

12 Tiger prawns, deveined, but not peeled

1 small carrot, peeled and finely sliced

2 sticks celery, finely sliced

1 small onion, finely chopped

white of 1 small leek

75 ml | 2 ½ fl oz dry white wine

10 black peppercorns, crushed

1 bay leaf

2 tablespoons white wine vinegar

coarse sea salt

2 litres | 4 pints water

1 lemon, sliced

1 sprig of parsley

dill stalks

For the sauce

6 tablespoons mayonnaise

1 tablespoon Heinz tomato ketchup

dash of Worcester sauce

dash of Tabasco

1 tablespoon Cognac

lemon juice

pinch of cayenne

salt

For the salad

2 little gem lettuce, thinly sliced

1 spring onion, finely sliced

2 plum tomatoes, skinned and cut into fine dice

1/3 cucumber, peeled, deseeded and cut into fine dice

lemon juice

To serve

1 egg white

1 tablespoon ground paprika

4 lemon wedges

1 sprig of dill

For the prawns

1 Place all the ingredients, except for the prawns, into a deep saucepan. Bring to the boil and simmer 15–20 minutes. Bring back to the boil and plunge in the prawns for 2–3 minutes. Remove and cool. Peel the prawns leaving on the tails if desired.
2 Prepare the cocktail sauce by mixing together all the sauce ingredients. Season to taste with a little salt, lemon juice and paprika then set aside.
3 Prepare the salad by tossing together all the salad ingredients, season lightly with a little salt and lemon juice. Gently divide the salad between 4 prepared goblets (see below).

To serve

4 Prepare the goblets by lightly beating the egg white with a fork and dip the rim into the egg white and then into the paprika, set aside.
5 To finish, divide the prawns equally between the goblets, season with a little lemon juice, spoon over the cocktail sauce, garnish with a little dill and serve with a wedge of lemon.

wine: **VERY DRY WHITE**

Scallop and Asparagus Salad

SERVES 4

225 g | 8 oz young asparagus, trimmed
salt and freshly ground black pepper
12 scallops
endive, picked over
radicchio, torn

lamb's lettuce
French dressing (see page 123)
unsalted butter
lemon juice

1 Cook the asparagus in boiling salted water until just tender. Drain well.
2 Clean the scallops, removing the muscular white frill found opposite the roe. Rinse off any black matter. Separate the roes from the body and slice both in half horizontally.

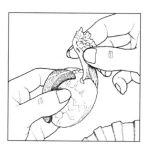

Remove the muscular white frill found opposite the scallop roe

3 Toss the well-washed salad leaves in French dressing and divide between 4 plates.
4 Arrange the still warm asparagus on top of the salad leaves.

5 Fry the scallops quickly in a little butter. Cool slightly, and add the lemon juice, salt and pepper.

6 Divide the scallops, with their pan juices, between the 4 plates.

wine: **CRISP DRY WHITE**

Shell Salad

SERVES 4

8 cooked king prawns

1 avocado, sliced

2 oranges, cut into segments

110 g | 4 oz cooked mangetout

110 g | 4 oz cooked cauliflower florets

French dressing (see page 123)

1 tablespoon chopped fresh chives

1 tablespoon chopped fresh parsley

salt and freshly ground black pepper

1 Mix all the ingredients together, season and serve, well chilled, on individual plates.

wine: **VERY DRY WHITE**

Tartare of Salmon and Tuna

This recipe is taken from *New American Classic Cookery* by Jeremiah Towers.

SERVES 4

1 cucumber

salt and freshly ground white pepper

120 ml | 4 fl oz fresh lemon juice

2 tablespoons sesame oil

225 g | 8 oz salmon fillet, skinned

225 g | 8 oz tuna fillet, skinned, all dark meat removed

2 tablespoons olive oil

4 tomatoes, peeled, deseeded and finely chopped

To garnish

rocket and chopped fresh chives

1 Cut the cucumber into very thin slices lengthways. Whisk salt and pepper into half the lemon juice; then whisk in the sesame oil. Toss the cucumber slices in the sauce and leave to stand for 1 hour.

2 Finely chop the salmon and tuna separately. Into each chopped fish stir half the remaining lemon juice, a tablespoon of olive oil and salt and pepper to taste.

3 To serve: curl the cucumber into tubes. Place two on each plate. Spoon the 2 fish tartares into the cucumber tubes.

4 Toss the chopped tomato with the rocket and divide between the plates. Garnish with chives.

wine: **VERY DRY WHITE**

Tempura

SERVES 4

1 small aubergine

salt

oil for deep-frying

1 medium courgette, cut into batons

110 g | 4 oz baby sweetcorn, halved lengthways

225 g | 8 oz scampi, seasoned with lemon juice and
   freshly ground black pepper

For the batter

110 g | 4 oz plain flour

110 g | 4 oz cornflour

2 small egg yolks

340 ml | 12 fl oz water

a pinch of salt

For the sauce

2 teaspoons sesame oil

2 tablespoons red wine vinegar

2 tablespoons soy sauce

3 tablespoons ginger syrup (from a jar of preserved
   ginger)

2 tablespoons clear honey

1 small bunch of spring onions, shredded

1 Slice the aubergine thinly, score the flesh lightly and place in a colander, sprinkling each layer with salt. Leave to degorge for 30 minutes.

2 Mix together all the ingredients for the sauce, except for the spring onions.

3 Heat oil in a deep-fryer until a crumb will sizzle vigorously in it.

4 Wash the aubergines well and pat dry on absorbent kitchen paper.

5 When the oil is hot, mix the batter ingredients together – it should not be smooth.

6 Dip the prepared aubergine, courgette, sweetcorn and scampi into the batter and deep-fry in small batches. Drain well on kitchen paper and sprinkle lightly with salt. Arrange on a large warmed serving dish.

7 Scatter the shredded spring onions on top of the tempura and hand the sauce separately.

wine: SPICY DRY WHITE

Mousses and Soufflés

Gelatine

Many recipes for mousses and cold soufflés call for gelatine.

Gelatine, available powdered and in leaves, is obtained from pig skin. It is easy to use if the procedure below is carefully followed.

How to use powdered gelatine

1 Pour a small amount of liquid into a saucepan.
2 Slowly sprinkle on the required amount of gelatine.
3 Leave the gelatine to 'sponge' i.e. swell, for 3–5 minutes.
4 Melt the gelatine over a very low heat. Do not allow to boil. Do not stir. It should become clear and warm.
5 Pour into the mousse|soufflé base. Stir briskly: if the base is too cold the gelatine can set quickly in strings. Gelatine is generally poured from a height to help cool it down.
6 When the mousse has reached setting-point other light ingredients such as cream or whisked egg whites can be added. If the cream or egg whites are added too early the base mix will not support their weight and the soufflé will separate into layers. If the cream or whites are added too late the mixture has to be beaten hard to incorporate the additions and the result is heavy.

Setting-point is when the base mixture will support its own weight and when a spoon is drawn through the mixture the bottom of the mixing bowl will remain visible for 2–3 seconds.

NOTE: Acids weaken the setting power of gelatine so when following a recipe such as lemon soufflé an increased amount of gelatine is called for.

How to use leaf gelatine

1 Soak the leaves in a small amount of cold water for 5 minutes. Squeeze gently to remove excess water.
2 Add to the warm base then dissolve over a gentle heat until liquid.
3 Use as powdered gelatine.

Gelatine conversion table

3 level teaspoons	11 g	$\frac{1}{3}$ oz	3 leaves

Agar Agar

Agar agar, a seaweed, is cooked, pressed, freeze-dried and then flaked or powdered for use as a setting agent in vegetarian cooking. It is also useful in warm weather because it doesn't melt unless boiled. 1 teaspoon powdered agar agar has the setting power of 1 tablespoon powdered gelatine. Agar agar's setting qualities are affected by the nature of the food to which it is added, and so required quantities will vary, but as a general rule 1 teaspoon powder or 1 tablespoon powdered gelatine will set 570 ml | 1 pint, and twice the quantity should be used to set a firm jelly.

How to use agar agar

1 Soak the agar agar in the full liquid measurement specified in the recipe, in a saucepan; leave powder for 5 minutes, flakes for 10–15 minutes.
2 Dissolve the agar agar in the pan over a medium heat, stirring continuously. Turn up the heat and boil for 2–3 minutes, continuing to stir to prevent sticking. Use as required. (Agar agar may be re-boiled without impairing its setting ability.)
3 If properly prepared, agar agar sets quickly on contact with anything much cooler than itself. Therefore, the ingredients to which it is added must be no colder than room temperature. To test whether it is ready for use, spoon a small quantity on to a cold plate: a skin should form very quickly, and wrinkle if a finger is pulled over the surface.

Tuna Fish Mousse

SERVES 4

2 teaspoons powdered gelatine
285 g | 10 oz canned tuna fish
150 ml | ¼ pint mayonnaise (see page 117)
salt and freshly ground black pepper
lemon juice
1 tablespoon chopped fresh parsley

150 ml | ¼ pint Greek yoghurt
oil for greasing

To garnish
thin slices of cucumber
pitted black olives

1 Put 2 tablespoons cold water into a small saucepan, sprinkle on the gelatine and set aside for 5 minutes to become spongy.
2 Oil a mould and leave upside down to drain.
3 Pour off the oil from the tuna fish and flake the fish with a fork. Mash to a pulp. Stir in the mayonnaise, salt, pepper, lemon juice and parsley.
4 Place the gelatine over a gentle heat; when it is liquid and clear, stir into the tuna mixture.
5 Fold in the yoghurt. Pour into the mould. Refrigerate until set.
6 To turn out, invert a serving dish over the mould and then turn both the dish and the mould over together. Give both a sharp shake, and remove the mould.
7 Garnish with cucumber slices and olives.

NOTE: If the mousse is to stand for more than 1 hour after garnishing, the cucumber slices should first be degorged, i.e. salted, allowed to stand for 30 minutes, rinsed well and patted dry. If this is not done the cucumber will weep when left on the sides of the mousse.

wine: SPICY DRY WHITE

Egg Mousse

SERVES 4

2 teaspoons powdered gelatine

6 hardboiled eggs

6 tablespoons mayonnaise (see page 117)

2 teaspoons anchovy essence

3 tablespoons double cream, lightly whipped

salt and freshly ground white pepper

cayenne pepper

To garnish

thin slices of cucumber

1 Put 2 tablespoons cold water into a small saucepan and sprinkle over the gelatine. Set aside for 5 minutes to become spongy.

2 Oil a soufflé dish or mould and leave it upside down to drain.

3 Chop the eggs and mix them with the mayonnaise, anchovy essence and cream, and season with salt, pepper and cayenne.

4 Place the gelatine over a gentle heat and when liquid and clear, stir it into the mixture.

5 Pour into the mould or dish. Refrigerate until set.

6 Loosen the mousse round the edge, using fingers or thumb, and turn out on to a serving plate. Garnish with cucumber slices.

NOTE: If the mousse is to stand for more than 1 hour after garnishing, the cucumber slices should first be degorged, i.e. salted, allowed to stand for 30 minutes, rinsed well and patted dry. If this is not done the cucumber will weep when left on the sides of the mousse.

wine: ROSÉ

Smoked Haddock Mousse

SERVES 6

225 g | 8 oz smoked haddock

150 ml | ¼ pint milk

2 slices of onion

1 bay leaf

6 white peppercorns

15 g | ½ oz butter

15 g | ½ oz plain flour

1 teaspoon powdered gelatine

2 hardboiled eggs

150 ml | ¼ pint double cream, lightly whipped

3 tablespoons mayonnaise (see page 117)

salt and freshly ground white pepper

1 teaspoon anchovy essence

To garnish

thin slices of cucumber

1 Preheat the oven to 180°C | 350°F | gas mark 4. Oil a 10 cm | 4 in soufflé dish and leave it upside down to drain.

2 Place the haddock in an ovenproof dish. Pour over the milk and add the onion, bay leaf and peppercorns. Cover and poach in the oven for 20–30 minutes, or until the haddock is cooked.

3 Strain the milk into a bowl and taste to check for saltiness. Skin the haddock.

4 Melt the butter in a saucepan and add the flour. Stir over a gentle heat for 1 minute. Remove from the heat and gradually add the milk the fish was cooked in. Return to the heat and bring gently to the boil, stirring continuously. You should now have a very thick white sauce. Remove from the heat and set aside to cool.

5 Put 3 tablespoons cold water into a small saucepan and sprinkle over the gelatine. Set aside for 5 minutes to become spongy.

6 Meanwhile, chop the hardboiled eggs. Flake the fish carefully, removing any bones.

7 Mix the cream and mayonnaise with the cooled sauce, the eggs and the fish. Season to taste with salt, pepper and anchovy essence.

8 Place the gelatine over a gentle heat until liquid and clear. Using a large metal spoon, stir the gelatine thoroughly into the fish mixture. Add the cream. Pour into the prepared soufflé dish. Cover and refrigerate until set, preferably overnight.

9 To turn the mousse out, invert a wetted plate over the top of the dish. Turn dish and plate over together and give a sharp shake. The mousse should come out immediately. (Wetting the plate makes it easier to shift the mousse, should it not turn out in the centre.) Garnish with cucumber slices.

NOTE: If the mousse is to stand for more than 1 hour after garnishing, the cucumber slices should first be degorged, i.e. salted, allowed to stand for 30 minutes, rinsed well and patted dry. If this is not done the cucumber will weep when left on the sides of the mousse.

wine: CRISP DRY WHITE

Cucumber Mousse

SERVES 4

1 large cucumber, peeled if preferred
110 g | 4 oz cream cheese
150 ml | ¼ pint double cream, whipped, or plain yoghurt or soured cream
2 tablespoons chopped fresh herbs, such as mint, tarragon, parsley and chives
salt and freshly ground white pepper

a pinch of freshly grated nutmeg
juice of 1 lemon
150 ml | ¼ pint white or vegetable stock (see pages 103, 107)
3 level teaspoons powdered gelatine

1 Grate the cucumber, reserving about 2.5 cm | 1 in to slice for decoration. Put the grated cucumber into a sieve. Leave to drain for 15 minutes.

2 Oil a soufflé dish or mould, and leave upside down to drain.

3 Beat together the cream cheese and whipped cream, yoghurt or soured cream. Mix in the grated cucumber and herbs. Season well with salt, pepper and nutmeg. Add the lemon juice.

4 Put the stock into a small saucepan, sprinkle over the gelatine and set aside for 5 minutes until spongy. Then place over a gentle heat until the gelatine is liquid and add to the cucumber mixture, mixing gently but thoroughly.

5 Pour into the prepared mould and refrigerate.

6 To turn the mousse out, invert a wetted plate over the mould and turn plate and mould over together. Give a sharp shape to dislodge the mousse. Garnish with cucumber slices.

NOTES: If a velvety texture is required, blend the cucumber with the yoghurt or cream in a blender. This mousse does not keep well. Eat within 24 hours.

wine: DRY WHITE

Red Pepper Bavarois with Red Pepper Salad

SERVES 8

3 red peppers, quartered and deseeded

3 small cloves of garlic, finely chopped

1 onion, thinly sliced

1 tablespoon olive oil

salt and freshly ground black pepper

290 ml | ½ pint milk

4 large egg yolks

4 level teaspoons powdered gelatine

150 ml | ¼ pint double cream

150 ml | ¼ pint low-fat plain yoghurt

1 teaspoon chilli sauce

To serve

red pepper salad (see page 301)

1 Preheat the grill to its highest setting. Grill the peppers, skin side up, until they are blistered and blackened. Place in a plastic bag to cool. The steam will help loosen the skins. Discard the skins, then chop the pepper flesh.

2 Cook the peppers, garlic and onion over low heat in the olive oil until soft but not brown. Allow to cool, then purée in a food processor and push through a sieve. Season with salt and pepper.

3 Put the milk into a saucepan and heat until scalding. Beat the egg yolks. Pour the milk on to the egg yolks, stirring all the time. Return the mixture to the saucepan and heat gently until it coats the back of a wooden spoon. Do not allow to boil. Strain into the red pepper purée.

4 Put 3 tablespoons cold water into a small saucepan, sprinkle over the gelatine and leave for 5 minutes until spongy. Lightly oil a charlotte mould or 20 cm | 9 in cake tin. Place the gelatine over a gentle heat until liquid and clear. Add it to the purée. Allow to cool and thicken.

5 Whip the cream lightly and mix it with the yoghurt and the chilli sauce.

6 Fold the cream mixture into the red pepper custard and pour into the prepared mould. Refrigerate until set.

7 Dip the mould quickly into very hot water and turn out on to a serving plate. Serve with the red pepper salad.

wine: MEDIUM DRY WHITE

Avocado Mousse with Prawns

SERVES 4

2 teaspoons powdered gelatine
2 ripe avocados
lemon juice
salt and freshly ground black pepper
290 ml | ½ pint Greek yoghurt

85 g | 3 oz peeled, cooked prawns
French dressing (see page 123)

To serve
brown bread and butter

1 Lightly oil a ring mould.
2 Put 3 tablespoons cold water into a small saucepan, sprinkle over the gelatine and set aside for 5 minutes until spongy.
3 Meanwhile, peel the avocados and mash or purée until smooth. Add the lemon juice, salt and pepper.
4 Place the gelatine over a gentle heat until liquid and clear, then stir into the avocado mixture. Fold in the yoghurt, using a large metal spoon.
5 Pour into the prepared mould and refrigerate until set. Dip the mould quickly into very hot water and turn out on to a round serving plate. Mix the prawns with the French dressing and pile into the centre of the mousse. Serve with brown bread and butter.

wine: **SPICY DRY WHITE**

Smoked Trout Mousse

SERVES 4

2 large smoked trout, about 200 g | 7 oz cleaned fish
150 ml | ¼ pint double cream, lightly whipped
a squeeze of lemon juice
½ teaspoon horseradish cream (see page 111)
freshly ground black pepper

4 slices of smoked salmon

To serve
brown bread and butter

1 Cut the heads and tails off the trout. Skin the fish and remove the bones. Mince or pound the flesh and mix with the cream, lemon juice, horseradish and pepper to taste.
2 Shape the mixture into a shallow mound on a serving plate. Cover neatly with the slices of smoked salmon.
3 Serve with brown bread and butter.

NOTE: Individual mousses can be made by covering small mounds of mousse with a slice of smoked salmon.

wine: **SPICY DRY WHITE**

Cheese Soufflé

SERVES 4 AS A FIRST COURSE – SERVES 2 AS A MAIN COURSE

melted butter for greasing

dried white breadcrumbs

40 g | 1¼ oz butter

30 g | 1 oz plain flour

½ teaspoon dry English mustard

a pinch of cayenne pepper

290 ml | ½ pint milk

85 g | 3 oz strong Cheddar or Gruyère cheese, finely grated

4 eggs, separated

salt and freshly ground black pepper

1 Preheat the oven to 200°C | 400°F | gas mark 6. Place a baking sheet on the shelf in the top third of the oven.

2 Brush a 15 cm | 6 in soufflé dish or 4 ramekins with melted butter. Dust lightly with the breadcrumbs.

3 Melt 40 g butter in a saucepan and stir in the flour, mustard and cayenne pepper. Cook for 45 seconds. Add the milk gradually and cook, stirring, until the mixture boils. Boil for 2 minutes. The mixture will get very thick and leave the sides of the pan. Remove from the heat.

4 Stir in the cheese, egg yolks, salt and pepper. Taste; the mixture should be very well seasoned.

5 Whisk the egg whites until just stiff, and mix a spoonful into the cheese mixture. Then fold in the remainder and pour into the soufflé dish. It should be about two-thirds full. Run your finger around the top of the soufflé mixture. This gives a 'top hat' appearance to the cooked soufflé.

6 Bake in the oven for 25–30 minutes for a large soufflé or 8–10 minutes for individual soufflés. Serve immediately. (Do not test to see if the soufflé is done until two-thirds of the way through the cooking time. Then open the oven just wide enough to get your hand in and give the soufflé a slight shove. If it wobbles alarmingly, cook for a further 5 minutes.)

wine: **SPICY DRY WHITE**

Courgette Soufflé

SERVES 6 AS A FIRST COURSE – SERVES 3–4 AS A MAIN COURSE

melted butter, for greasing

625 g | 1 lb 6 oz small dark green courgettes

salt and freshly ground black pepper

55 g | 2 oz unsalted butter

45 g | 1½ oz plain flour

150 ml | ¼ pint milk, infused with 1 slice of onion

30 g | 1 oz fresh Parmesan cheese, grated

30 g | 1 oz Cheddar cheese, grated

2 egg yolks

4 egg whites

To serve

tomato sauce 1 (see page 128)

1 Preheat the oven to 180°C|350°F|gas mark 4. Brush 6 ramekins with melted butter.
2 Trim the courgettes. Slice 450 g|1 lb of them very thinly. Place in a colander or sieve and sprinkle with a little salt. Mix in well and allow to drain for at least 1 hour.
3 Cut the remaining courgettes into 5 mm|¼ in dice. Salt lightly then leave to drain.
4 Rinse the sliced courgettes and put in a pan with 150 ml|¼ pint water. Bring to the boil, then simmer for 5 minutes. Liquidize in a blender or food processor until smooth.
5 Melt 45 g|1½ oz of the butter in a medium saucepan, add the flour and cook over a gentle heat for about 1 minute, stirring occasionally. Remove from the heat and allow to cool slightly.
6 Gradually add the flavoured milk and courgette purée to the flour and butter. Bring to the boil, then cook over a gentle heat for about 15 minutes, stirring occasionally. Add more water to the sauce if it gets too thick. Remove from the heat.
7 Beat in the egg yolks, allow to cool slightly and then add the grated cheeses.
8 Melt the remaining butter in a small pan and cook the rinsed, drained and diced courgettes until slightly brown and crisp.
9 Season the sauce well with salt and pepper. Whisk the egg whites until medium peaks are formed. Fold carefully into the courgette sauce.
10 Half fill each prepared ramekin with the soufflé mixture. Divide the diced courgettes between the ramekins and cover with the remaining mixture.
11 Place the ramekins in a roasting pan half-filled with hot water (a bain-marie) and bake at the top of the oven for 25–30 minutes, or until well risen and brown on the top. Serve immediately with the tomato sauce.

wine: DRY WHITE

Twice-baked Cheese Soufflés

These little soufflés are wonderfully rich. They can be cooked a few hours before serving and then re-baked at the last minute.

SERVES 6

290 ml|½ pint milk	a pinch of cayenne
1 slice of onion	110 g|4 oz strong Cheddar cheese, grated
a pinch of freshly grated nutmeg	4 eggs, separated
45 g|1½ oz butter	salt and freshly ground black pepper
40 g|1¼ oz plain flour	200 ml|7 fl oz double cream
a pinch of dry English mustard	

1 Generously butter 6 timbale moulds or ramekins.
2 Preheat the oven to 180°C|350°F|gas mark 4. Heat a bain marie. Heat the milk slowly with the onion and nutmeg. Remove the onion.
3 Melt the remaining butter in a saucepan and stir in the flour, mustard and cayenne. Gradually add the milk, off the heat, stirring until smooth.

4 Return to the heat and stir until the sauce boils and thickens. Remove from the heat, cool slightly and add three-quarters of the cheese and the egg yolks. Season with salt and pepper.

5 Whisk the egg whites to medium peak, and fold into the cheese mixture. Spoon into the cups to fill two-thirds full. Stand the cups in a roasting pan of boiling water half-filled with hot water (a bain-marie) and bake for 15 minutes, or until set. Allow to sink and cool.

6 Run a knife round the soufflés to loosen them. Turn them out on to your hand, giving the cups a sharp shake. Put them, upside down, on to an overproof serving dish.

7 Twenty minutes before serving, sprinkle the remaining cheese on top of the soufflés. Season the cream with salt and pepper and pour all over the soufflés, coating them completely. Put the dish into a hot oven, 220°C|425°F|gas mark 7, for 10 minutes or until the soufflé tops are pale gold. Serve immediately before they sink.

wine: **SPICY DRY WHITE**

Smoked Haddock and Spinach Soufflé

This is more of a 'pudding' than a soufflé.

SERVES 4

melted butter for greasing	6 black peppercorns
2 tablespoons fresh white breadcrumbs	450 g│1 lb fresh spinach
170 g│6 oz smoked haddock fillet	30 g│1 oz butter
290 ml│½ pint milk	30 g│1 oz plain flour
1 bay leaf	a pinch of dry English mustard
½ small onion	salt and freshly ground black pepper
	4 large eggs, separated

1 Preheat the oven to 200°C|400°F|gas mark 6 and place a baking tray on the middle shelf. Brush a 1.2 litre│2 pint soufflé dish with the melted butter and coat with the breadcrumbs.

2 Lay the smoked haddock in a shallow ovenproof dish and pour on the milk. Add the bay leaf, onion and peppercorns, cover lightly with a lid or foil and bake in the oven for 20 minutes, or until the fish is cooked.

3 Strain the milk through a sieve and reserve. Skin the fish and mash the haddock finely with the back of a fork, then set it aside.

4 Rinse and shake excess water from the spinach and put it into a large non-aluminium saucepan. Set it over a medium heat and cook gently for 3–4 minutes or until tender. Drain very well, cool a little, then chop finely.

5 Melt the butter in a saucepan, stir in the flour and mustard powder. Cook for 30 seconds. Remove the pan from the heat and gradually add the reserved and the remaining milk.

Return the pan to the heat and bring the sauce to the boil. Simmer for 1 minute, then remove from the heat and season with salt and pepper.

6 Allow the sauce to cool slightly, then beat in the egg yolks. Stir in the mashed haddock and spinach.

7 Whisk the egg whites to medium peak. Fold 2 large spoonfuls into the sauce to slacken it, then gently fold in the remaining egg whites. Spoon the mixture into the prepared soufflé dish, place on the heated baking tray and bake in the oven for 25 minutes, or until well risen and rich brown in colour. Serve immediately.

wine: **VERY DRY WHITE**

Twice-baked Individual Goat's Cheese Soufflés

SERVES 6

290 ml | ½ pint milk
1 slice of onion
45 g | 1½ oz butter
45 g | 1½ oz plain flour
110 g | 4 oz soft goat's cheese, cut into small cubes
a pinch of chopped fresh thyme

3 eggs, separated
salt and freshly ground white pepper

To serve
4 tablespoons single cream
4 tablespoons freshly grated Parmesan cheese

1 Preheat the oven to 180°C | 350°F | gas mark 4.

2 Heat the milk slowly with the onion in a saucepan. Remove from the heat just before it boils and leave to infuse for 15 minutes, then strain.

3 Melt the butter in a saucepan and use a little of it to brush 6 ramekins or timbales.

4 Stir the flour into the remaining butter. Cook, stirring, for 45 seconds. Off the heat, gradually blend in the infused milk, whisking until smooth.

5 Return to the heat and stir until the sauce boils and thickens. Remove from the heat, add the cheese, thyme and egg yolks and season to taste with salt and pepper.

6 Whisk the egg whites until stiff but not dry and mix a spoonful into the mixture to loosen. Fold in the remaining egg whites. Spoon into the prepared ramekins or timbales until two-thirds full.

7 Place in a roasting pan and pour in enough hot water to come halfway up the sides of the moulds. Bake in the oven for 15–20 minutes or until set. Remove and allow to cool.

8 Turn the oven temperature up to 220°C | 425°F | gas mark 7.

9 Run a knife around the soufflés to loosen them. Turn them out into individual shallow ovenproof dishes. Top each soufflé with a tablespoon of cream and a sprinkling of Parmesan cheese.

10 Return the soufflés to the oven for 10 minutes or until the tops are puffed up and golden. Serve immediately.

wine: **SPICY DRY WHITE**

Warm Arbroath Smokies Mousse

SERVES 6

3 large Arbroath smokies
3 eggs
285 g│10 oz fromage frais
juice of ½ lemon
salt and freshly ground black pepper
melted butter

To serve
tomato, basil and olive oil sauce (see page 127)
sprigs of fresh dill

1 Preheat the oven to 160°C│325°F│gas mark 3.
2 Place the smokies in an ovenproof dish and cook in the oven for 10 minutes.
3 Remove from the oven and carefully remove the skin and bones.
4 Place the flesh in a food processor and process until smooth. Add the eggs one at a time and continue to blend. Gradually add the fromage frais, lemon juice and seasonings to taste. Be careful with the salt.
5 Brush 6 ramekins with melted butter and line the bases with circles of greased greaseproof paper.
6 Divide the fish mixture between the dishes and place them in a roasting pan half filled with hot water (a bain-marie). Cover each mousse with a disc of greaseproof paper.
7 Bake in the centre of the oven for 35–40 minutes, or until set.
8 Meanwhile, make the sauce.
9 Remove the mousses from the oven and allow to rest for 2 minutes. Remove the greaseproof paper discs. Run a knife around the edges of the ramekins and turn the mousses out on to warmed individual serving plates.
10 Spoon a tablespoon of the warm sauce over each mousse. Garnish with a sprig of dill.

wine: **SPICY DRY WHITE**

Pâtés and Terrines

Sardine and Lemon Pâté

SERVES 6–8

110 g | 4 oz butter
225 g | 8 oz canned sardines
110 g | 4 oz cream cheese
½ teaspoon French mustard
juice of ½ lemon
salt and freshly ground black pepper

To garnish
6 black olives, pitted

To serve
hot toast

1 Beat the butter until soft and creamy.
2 Add the sardines with their oil and beat.
3 Add the cream cheese, mustard, lemon, salt and plenty of pepper and mix well. (Alternatively all the above ingredients can be combined in a food processor.)
4 Pile on to a dish and garnish with olives. Serve with hot toast.

wine: VERY DRY WHITE

Smoked Trout Pâté

This recipe is a low-fat version of smoked trout mousse (page 206). It is also delicious made with smoked salmon.

SERVES 4

2 smoked trout about 200 g | 7 oz cleaned fish
170 g | 6 oz low-fat cottage cheese, very well drained
1 teaspoon grated horseradish

freshly ground black pepper
lemon juice

1 Skin and bone the trout.
2 Blend all the ingredients together in a food processor. Alternatively, mince the trout or chop very finely. Sieve the cottage cheese and beat in the trout. Add the horseradish, pepper and lemon juice to taste.
3 Pile into a dish and refrigerate for 3 hours.

wine: SPICY DRY WHITE

Kipper Pâté

SERVES 4

340 g | 12 oz kipper fillets
85 g | 3 oz unsalted butter, softened
85 g | 3 oz cream cheese
freshly ground black pepper

creamed horseradish
lemon juice

To garnish
4 black olives, slivered

1 Skin and mince the kipper fillets.
2 Beat the butter until very creamy (but do not melt it) and beat in the cream cheese. Add the kippers and beat well.
3 Season well with pepper, horseradish and lemon juice.
4 Pile into a dish and garnish with olive slivers.

wine: SPICY DRY WHITE

Chicken Liver Pâté

SERVES 6

225 g | 8 oz butter
1 large onion, very finely chopped
1 large clove of garlic, crushed
450 g | 1 lb chicken livers, or 225 g | 8 oz duck livers
and 225 g | 8 oz chicken livers

1 tablespoon brandy
salt and freshly ground black pepper
85 g | 3 oz clarified butter (see page 385), if the pâté
is to be stored

1 Melt half the butter in a large, heavy frying pan and gently fry the onion until soft and transparent.
2 Add the garlic and continue cooking for 1 further minute. Remove with a slotted spoon leaving the butter in the pan. Set aside.
3 Discard any discoloured pieces of liver as they will be bitter. Rinse under water. Pat dry.
4 Add the livers to the pan and fry, turning to brown them lightly on all sides, until cooked. Flame the brandy and add to the livers.
5 When the flames subside, add salt and plenty of pepper. Allow to cool slightly.
6 Combine the livers and onions in a food processor with the remaining butter. Put it into an earthenware dish or pot.
7 If the pâté is to be kept for more than 3 days, cover the top with a layer of clarified butter.

NOTE: If making large quantities of chicken liver pâté simply bake all the ingredients together under foil or a lid in the oven preheated to 190°C | 375°F | gas mark 5 for 40 minutes. Cool for 15 minutes, then proceed from step 6.

wine: FULL RED

Smooth Duck Pâté

SERVES 6

1   2.3 kg | 5 lb ovenready duck

1 bay leaf

1 carrot, sliced

1 onion, peeled and sliced

1 blade of mace

10 black peppercorns

1 stick of celery, sliced

1 tablespoon chopped fresh sage

salt and freshly ground black pepper

60–85 g | 2½ –3 oz butter, softened

grated zest and juice of 1 orange

85 g | 3 oz clarified butter (see page 385)

1 Put the duck into a saucepan with the bay leaf, carrot, onion, mace, peppercorns and celery and cover with water. Bring to the boil, then poach for 1½ –2 hours until the duck is tender, when the legs will feel wobbly. Remove from the heat and allow to cool.

2 Remove the duck from the stock. Strain the stock and reserve. Remove the flesh from the duck, discarding the fat, skin and bones. Cut up the flesh and place in a food processor with the sage, salt and pepper. Whizz until smooth. Add the butter, orange zest and juice and 5 tablespoons of the reserved stock. Check the seasoning.

3 Spread the pâté flat in a serving dish and leave to cool. When completely cold, melt the clarified butter and pour it over the top of the pâté.

wine: **RED MEDIUM**

Chicken Parfait with Chicken Livers and Mushrooms

SERVES 6–8

butter for greasing

300 g | 11 oz white chicken meat, finely minced

salt and freshly ground white pepper

a generous pinch of ground ginger

a generous pinch of ground cardamon

1 egg white, lightly beaten

55 g | 2 oz flour quantity panade, sieved (see next recipe)

340 ml | 12 fl oz double cream, lightly whipped

140 g | 5 oz chicken livers

1–2 tablespoons oil

150 g | 5 oz mushrooms, washed and diced

570 ml | 1 pint aspic (see page 105), flavoured with 3 tablespoons Madeira

3 tablespoons chopped fresh parsley

1 Grease a 1 litre | 1¾ pint mould or loaf tin and line the base with a piece of greased greaseproof paper.

2 Sprinkle the chicken with salt, pepper and the spices. Chill in the refrigerator for at least 2 hours.

3 Preheat the oven to 150°C | 300°F, gas mark 2.

4 Put the chicken into a bowl. Set in a bowl of ice, beat in the egg white and then add the panada.

5 Push the mixture through a drum sieve and then beat in the lightly whipped cream, a spoonful at a time, over ice.

6 Remove all the membrane and blood vessels from the chicken livers and cut into small pieces. Fry quickly in a little oil, season with salt and pepper and allow to cool.

7 Fry the mushrooms in a little more oil and season with salt and pepper. Drain and allow to cool. Mix together the mushrooms and chicken livers.

8 Put half the chicken mixture into the prepared mould and spread flat. Cover with the chicken liver and mushroom mixture. Add the remaining chicken mixture and spread flat. Cover the mould with greased greaseproof paper or foil and place in a roasting pan half filled with very hot water (a bain-marie). Bake in the centre of the oven for about 40 minutes.

9 Allow the parfait to cool, then turn out carefully on to a plate and remove the lining paper. Coat carefully with one third of the Madeira-flavoured aspic and sprinkle with parsley. Allow to set and coat with a second layer of Madeira aspic.

10 Chill the remaining Madeira aspic until firm, then dice. Serve the parfait on a bed of the diced aspic.

wine: **SPICY WHITE OR LIGHT RED**

Panade for Chicken Parfait

100 ml | 3½ fl oz milk
20 g | ¾ oz butter
salt and freshly ground white pepper

freshly grated nutmeg
55 g | 2 oz plain flour, sifted
1 egg

1 Bring the milk, butter and seasoning up to the boil in a small saucepan. Add all the flour at once and mix well off the heat. Beat until it comes away from the sides of the pan.

2 Allow the panada to cool slightly, then beat in the egg. Transfer to a bowl and leave to cool completely.

3 Push the cold panade through a sieve. Use as required.

Terrine de Ratatouille Niçoise

SERVES 10–12

20 large spinach leaves, blanched and refreshed
salt and freshly ground black pepper
2 red peppers
2 yellow peppers
2 green peppers
2 aubergines
1 bulb of Florence fennel, separated into layers
3 medium courgettes
olive oil

For the mousse

olive oil
½ onion, roughly chopped
2 cloves of new season garlic, crushed
3 red peppers, chopped
2 tomatoes, chopped

2 tablespoons tomato purée
12 fresh basil leaves
1 sprig of fresh thyme
1 tablespoon caster sugar
150 ml | ¼ pint dry white wine
290 ml | ½ pint water
6 leaves of gelatine, soaked in cold water
   (see page 201)

For the basil sauce

25 fresh basil leaves
150 ml | ¼ pint mayonnaise (see page 117)
150 ml | ¼ pint single cream
lemon juice to taste
salt and freshly ground black pepper

1 Line a 900 g | 2 lb terrine first with clingfilm, then with the spinach leaves, overlapping them neatly without any gaps. Season lightly with salt and pepper.

2 Prepare the vegetables as follows. Cook the peppers in olive oil in the oven preheated to 220°C | 425°C | gas mark 7 for 20–25 minutes. Cool, then remove the skins and seeds. Cut the aubergines into quarters lengthways. Cook in olive oil in the oven for 20 minutes. Blanch the fennel in boiling water for 5–8 minutes. Refresh in iced water and pat dry. Cut the courgettes into quarters lengthways and shape neatly into pencil thickness. Blanch and refresh, then dry.

3 Prepare the mousse: heat a little oil in a large saucepan, and add the onion, garlic, peppers, tomatoes and tomato purée. Add the herbs and sugar, and cook for 4–5 minutes.

4 Add the wine and cook until reduced by half. Add the water and cook gently on the edge of the stove until the vegetables are well cooked (about 15–20 minutes). Pass through a sieve. You should have 725 ml | 1¼ pt.

5 Warm the sauce and add the soaked gelatine. Remove the pan from the heat.

6 Allow to cool completely but not set. Check the seasoning.

7 Prepare the terrine: pour 2 tablespoons of the mousse into the bottom of the spinach-lined terrine. Cut the yellow peppers to fit and cover the terrine from end to end. Season the vegetables with salt and pepper as you go.

8 Pour another 2 tablespoons of the mousse on top, then add the aubergine, skin side down first to make a good colour contrast, then another 2 tablespoons of mousse followed by the courgettes. Repeat the process, alternating layers of mousse and vegetable in the following sequence: red pepper, fennel, green pepper, aubergine, yellow pepper. Finish with a layer of mousse.

9 Fold over the spinach leaves carefully to seal the terrine, then cover with clingfilm. Press the terrine with a weight and leave for 8–24 hours in the refrigerator.

10 Prepare the basil sauce: place all the ingredients in a blender and liquidize. Check the seasoning and consistency.

11 Pour a little sauce on to a plate, cut a slice of terrine and place it on the sauce. Serve chilled.

wine: ROSÉ OR DRY WHITE

Pork and Liver Terrine

Make this terrine the day before serving.

SERVES 6–8

110 g | 4 oz pig's liver, minced
225 g | 8 oz rindless belly of pork, minced
225 g | 8 oz lean veal, minced
2 shallots, finely chopped
1 clove of garlic, crushed
2 teaspoons brandy

a pinch of ground allspice
salt and freshly ground black pepper
225 g | 8 oz thin rashers of rindless streaky bacon
110 g | 4 oz chicken livers, cleaned
2 bay leaves

1 Preheat the oven to 170°C | 325°F | gas mark 3.

2 Mix together the pig's liver, belly pork, veal, shallots, garlic, brandy and allspice. Season with salt and pepper.

3 Stretch the bacon rashers with the back of a knife and use to line a medium terrine or loaf tin.

4 Tip in half the prepared mixture and spread it flat.

5 Trim any discoloured parts from the chicken livers, then place in an even layer over the mixture and top up with the other half of the mixture. Lay the bay leaves on the surface.

6 Cover with a piece of greased greaseproof paper then cover with foil. Stand the terrine in a roasting pan half-filled with hot water (a bain-marie) and bake in the oven for $1-1\frac{1}{4}$ hours. The mixture should feel fairly firm to the touch.

7 Remove from the roasting pan, place a weight on the terrine (a can of fruit in a second terrine will do) and leave to cool. Refrigerate until needed, and turn out on to a plate to serve.

wine: FULL RED

Alex Floyd's Foie Gras Terrine

SERVES 10

Literally translated foie gras means fattened liver. There is a general misconception that foie gras inevitably means goose liver (this may simply be because oie is French for goose). In fact both duck and goose liver can be used. To make this terrine the liver must be left at room temperature until it is soft.

2 fattened duck livers (foie gras), total weight about
  1 kg|2¼ lb
20 g|¾ oz coarse sea salt (you need 20 g salt for every kilo of foie gras)

freshly ground white pepper
1 glass of white port
1 glass of Cognac or Armagnac

1 When the duck liver is soft and pliable, remove as many veins as you can without breaking up the lobes.

2 Preheat the oven to 170°C|325°F|gas mark 3.

3 Put the livers into a roasting pan. Sprinkle with the salt and pepper. Pour over the port and Cognac or Armagnac. Turn the livers so that they are evenly seasoned. Leave at room temperature for 1 hour to marinate.

4 Place in the oven for 12 minutes or until blood temperature. If the foie gras gets too hot it is ruined. If it does not reach the correct temperature it is of course not cooked. A thermometer to monitor temperature control is useful.

5 Remove from the oven. Lay the lobes on a clean kitchen cloth. Reserve the pan juices.

6 Press the lobes into a terrine and refrigerate for 24 hours. Serve as required.

NOTE: Tip all the pan juices into a bowl and leave in the refrigerator to set. Remove from the refrigerator and lift off the fat. Discard the pan juices (they will be bitter, salty and alcoholic). Let the fat reach room temperature. This fat can then be whizzed with room-temperature unsalted butter and used to enhance the meat flavour of different sauces.

wine: SPICY DRY WHITE

Venison Terrine and Cumberland Sauce

SERVES 8

225 g|8 oz back pork fat
225 g|8 oz lean pork
225 g|8 oz lean venison
1 onion, finely chopped
1 clove of garlic, crushed
8 juniper berries, crushed
½ teaspoon ground mace
½ teaspoon ground allspice
4 tablespoons red wine

2 tablespoons brandy
salt and freshly ground black pepper
2 eggs
285 g|10 oz rashers of streaky bacon, cut very thin and stretched with a knife

To serve
Cumberland sauce (see page 131)

1 Cut half the pork fat into small cubes. Mince the pork, remaining fat and venison and mix with the onion, garlic, diced fat, juniper berries, spices, wine, brandy, salt, pepper and eggs. Beat very well and check for seasoning.

2 Stretch the bacon slices by stroking along the length with a table knife. Line a 1 litre|1¾ pint terrine with bacon and fill with the mixture. Cover with the remaining bacon.

3 Refrigerate for at least 3 hours for the flavour to develop – the longer the better.

4 Preheat the oven to 170°C|325°F|gas mark 3.

5 Put the terrine into a roasting pan half-filled with hot water (a bain-marie). Cook in the oven for 1–1½ hours. It is cooked when the terrine shrinks away from the side of the dish and a skewer inserted in the centre comes out piping hot.

6 Weight the terrine and allow to cool. Keep the terrine in the refrigerator for a couple of days to mature the flavour.

7 Serve the terrine with Cumberland sauce.

wine: **FULL RED**

Wild Boar Terrine

SERVES 10

900 g|2 lb boned loin of wild boar, fat removed

1 small onion, chopped

1 clove of garlic, crushed

salt and freshly ground black pepper

1 teaspoon ground allspice

5 juniper berries

a good pinch of ground cloves

1 teaspoon green peppercorns

1 teaspoon chopped fresh thyme

1 bay leaf

55 g|2 oz fresh white breadcrumbs

150 ml|¼ pint strong red wine, preferably Rioja

560 g|1¼ lb pork fat

1 egg, beaten

30 g|1 oz black truffles, finely chopped

55 g|2 oz shelled pistachios, skinned and roughly chopped

400 g|14 oz pork fat, thinly sliced

To garnish

1 fresh bay leaf

1 sprig of fresh thyme

1 Trim the wild boar of fat and sinew and cut into strips. Place in a bowl with the onion, garlic, 2 teaspoons salt, the spices, herbs, breadcrumbs and wine. Leave to marinate for 24 hours.

2 Discard the wine, then put the wild boar and all the marinade ingredients through the finest blade of the mincer or whizz in small batches in a food processor until very finely chopped but not puréed. Chill thoroughly in the refrigerator.

3 Preheat the oven to 160°C|325°F|gas mark 3.

4 Cut two-thirds of the pork fat into strips with which to line the terrine and dice the remainder. Work the egg, truffles, pistachios and diced pork fat into the wild boar mixture. Season with plenty of salt and pepper.

5 Line the terrine with the fat strips and fill with the stuffing. Fold over the excess fat and

cover with the sliced pork fat. Garnish with the bay leaf and thyme. Cover with a double layer of oiled greaseproof paper then cover with kitchen foil. Seal the edges by twisting the foil over the rim of the tin.

6 Cook in a bain-marie (a roasting pan half-filled with hot water) in the bottom of the oven for about 1 hour. The terrine is ready when a skewer inserted into the centre of the terrine for a few seconds comes out hot.

7 When the terrine is cooked, remove from the bain-marie. Weight the top down and leave to cool. Refrigerate for several hours before serving.

NOTES: Wild boar are considered a delicacy up to the age of 18 months when they became very tough and strong-flavoured. They can live up to 30 years but only the head of old boar is ever cooked.

A marcassin (young boar up to the age of 6 months) is highly esteemed for its flesh. A bête rousse is a boar from 6–12 months old.

All wild boar must be marinated for 24 hours before cooking.

wine: **SPICY WHITE**

Pâté en Croûte

SERVES 10

For the filling

1 shallot, very finely chopped

15 g | ½ oz butter

4 oz | 110 g chicken livers, membranes and blood
  vessels removed

2 tablespoons brandy

6 oz | 170 g lean veal, minced

6 oz | 170 g lean pork, minced

6 oz | 170 g pork fat, minced

1 egg, beaten

1 oz | 30 g fresh white breadcrumbs

1 teaspoon dried mixed herbs

1½ teaspoons ground allspice

salt and freshly ground black pepper

1 pig's caul, about 45 cm | 18 in square

290 ml | ½ pint aspic (see page 105), seasoned with
  Madeira or tarragon vinegar

To garnish

110 g | 4 oz lean ham

110 g | 4 oz lean veal

2 tablespoons brandy

1 tablespoon chopped fresh thyme

For the pastry

450 g | 1 lb plain flour

1 teaspoon salt

225 g | 8 oz butter, cubed

1 egg

2–3 tablespoons very cold water

beaten egg, to glaze

1 Make the filling: sweat the shallot in the butter until soft but not coloured. Add the chicken livers and sauté gently.

2 Warm the brandy in a ladle, set alight with a match and then pour over the chicken livers and allow to flambé until the flames subside.

3 Whizz the mixture in a food processor until smooth, then set aside to cool.

4 Mix all the meats together with the pork fat, egg, breadcrumbs, herbs, allspice and seasoning. Mix in the liver purée. Leave to marinate overnight.

5 Meanwhile, prepare the garnish: cut the ham and veal into strips 1 cm $\vert$ $\frac{1}{2}$ in thick and marinate in the brandy with the thyme overnight in the refrigator.

6 Make the pastry: sift the flour with the salt into a bowl. Rub in the fat until the mixture resembles coarse breadcrumbs.

7 Beat the egg with 2–3 tablespoons of water. Stir into the flour with a knife and bring together to form a stiff but not dry dough, adding more water if necessary.

8 Roll out a large rectangle no thinner than a £1 coin. Chill for 20 minutes.

9 Assemble the pâté: cut a long strip 10 cm $\vert$ 4 in wide off the edge of the pastry and reserve for the top. Place the remaining rectangle of pastry on a baking sheet.

10 Lay the piece of pig's caul over the pastry, to cover it entirely.

11 Take one-third of the meat filling and lay it in a neat rectangle about 20 × 7.5 cm $\vert$ 8 × 3 in on the pastry. Arrange half the garnish strips of ham and veal on top and season with salt and pepper. Repeat with another layer of meat. Arrange the remaining garnish on top and cover with the remaining meat.

12 Cut the corners out of the pastry, wet the edges and lift the pastry up to the sides of the meat, forming a terrine shape. Seal at the corners and crimp. Cut the reserved strip of pastry down to the exact size and lay over the top. Decorate the edges by crimping. Make 4 steam holes in the pastry on top at the sides.

13 Meanwhile, preheat the oven to 220°C $\vert$ 425°F $\vert$ gas mark 7.

14 Glaze the pastry all over with beaten egg. Garnish with pastry trimmings cut into decoration shapes. Chill in the refrigerator for 30 minutes.

15 Glaze the pastry again with beaten egg. Bake in the top of the oven for 15 minutes, then turn down the oven temperature to 170°C $\vert$ 325°F $\vert$ gas mark 3, transfer the pâté en croûte to the bottom of the oven and bake for a further 1–1 $\frac{1}{2}$ hours. It is cooked when a skewer inserted into the centre of the terrine comes out hot. Remove from the oven and place on a cooling rack until completely cold.

16 Using a plastic baster, drip the aspic into the steam holes to fill up any air pockets inside the pastry. If there are any holes in the pastry before adding the aspic, block them with softened butter.

17 Chill the pâté en croûte again for at least 1 hour before serving.

wine: **SPICY RED**

Pain de Poisson

SERVES 4

285 g | 10 oz sole, salmon or pike

1 egg white

225 ml | 8 fl oz double cream

salt and freshly ground white and black pepper

cayenne pepper

1 egg

55 g | 2 oz fresh white breadcrumbs

2 tablespoons chopped fresh parsley

1 tablespoon mixed chopped fresh tarragon and chives

To serve

Hollandaise sauce (see page 119)

1 Preheat the oven to 150°C | 300°F | gas mark 2.

2 Skin the fish and remove any bones. Cut into pieces and chop finely in a food processor. Add 1 egg white and process well. Remove to a bowl and gradually beat in approximately two-thirds of the cream. Everything should be very cold. If not, place the bowl over iced water as the cream is added. Season well with salt, white pepper and cayenne. Place in the refrigerator.

3 Whisk the egg and add the remaining cream. Add the breadcrumbs and herbs. Season with salt and black pepper.

4 Oil a 450 g | 1 lb loaf tin and line the base with a piece of greaseproof paper cut to size and also lightly oiled.

5 Spread the fish mixture round the base and sides of the tin to about 1 cm | ½ in thickness.

6 Place the herb mixture in the middle and cover with the remaining fish.

7 Cover with a double sheet of damp greaseproof paper. Place in a roasting pan half-filled with hot water (a bain-marie) and bake in the oven for 1–1¼ hours.

8 Allow to cool in the tin slightly, then turn out and serve with Hollandaise sauce.

wine: DRY WHITE

Fish Terrine with Chive and Lemon Dressing

SERVES 6

1 large carrot, peeled and cut into batons

45 g | 1½ oz French beans, topped and tailed

680 g | 1½ lb sole fillets, skinned

3 egg whites, lightly beaten

salt and freshly ground black pepper

290 ml | ½ pint double cream

15 g | ½ oz butter

2 teaspoons canned green peppercorns, rinsed and drained

For the dressing

1 large bunch of fresh chives

150 ml | ¼ pint soured cream

290 ml | ½ pint mayonnaise (see page 117)

salt and freshly ground black pepper

juice of ½ lemon

To garnish

sprigs of watercress

1 Steam the carrots and beans over boiling water until very tender. Rinse under cold running water and drain on absorbent kitchen paper.

2 Preheat the oven to 180°C|350°F|gas mark 4. Pound the sole fillets in a food processor with a little egg white. Season with salt. Place in a large bowl set in a roasting pan of ice. Beat well and gradually add first the remaining egg whites and then the cream, making sure that the mixture remains fairly firm. Beat in the pepper. Taste: the mixture should be well seasoned.

3 Lightly butter a medium loaf tin or terrine, line the base with greaseproof paper and spoon in a quarter of the fish mixture. Spread it flat with a spatula. Arrange 4 parallel lines of green beans down the length of the tin. Cover with a second quarter of the fish mixture. Spread flat. Arrange 4 parallel lines of carrot batons immediately above the beans. Cover with a third quarter of the fish mixture. Spread flat. Arrange 4 parallel lines of green peppercorns immediately above the carrots. Cover with the remaining fish mixture and smooth over with a spatula. Cover with a piece of damp greaseproof paper.

4 Stand the terrine in a roasting pan half-filled with hot water (a bain-marie). Bake in the oven for 35 minutes. Remove from the oven, leave to cool and refrigerate overnight.

5 Make the sauce: put the chives and soured cream into a blender and whizz until pale green. Remove from the blender, mix with the mayonnaise and season to taste with salt, pepper and lemon juice.

6 To serve: invert a plate or wooden board over the terrine and turn the whole thing over. Give a gentle shake and remove the tin. Cut into even slices. Serve with the chive dressing and garnish with watercress.

NOTE: If you do not have a food processor the fish should be pushed through a sieve before adding the egg whites (quite a task).

wine: **VERY DRY WHITE**

Pâté of Fish Tricolour

If whiting is not available, any other white fish can be used.

SERVES 4

For the fish mousse

675 g | 1½ lb whiting fillets, skinned

2 egg whites

1 teaspoon salt

½ teaspoon freshly ground white pepper

425 ml | ¾ pint double cream

For the fish

170 g | 6 oz salmon fillet

4 large sole fillets (about 140 g | 5 oz each), skinned
and lightly pounded

For the herb mousse

4–5 shallots, roughly chopped

225 ml | 8 fl oz dry white wine

a pinch of freshly ground white pepper

½ teaspoon salt

110 g | 4 oz spinach leaves

1 small bunch of watercress leaves, chopped

2 teaspoons chopped fresh tarragon, or chives

2 tablespoons chopped fresh parsley

For the sauce

1 large tomato, peeled, deseeded and roughly
chopped

½ teaspoon good paprika pepper

a pinch of cayenne pepper

1 teaspoon salt

a pinch of freshly ground white pepper

1 tablespoon good red wine vinegar

1 egg yolk

225 ml | 8 fl oz virgin olive oil

To prepare the fish mousse:

1 Preheat the oven to 140°C | 275°F | gas mark 1.

2 Place the whiting in a food processor and process for 1 minute with the egg whites, salt
and pepper, slowly pouring in half the cream with the motor still running.

3 Fold the remaining cream into the fish mixture.

To prepare the herb mousse:

4 Put the shallots, wine, pepper and salt into a saucepan and bring to the boil, then reduce
by boiling rapidly to 3 tablespoons. Add the spinach and cook until the liquid is
reduced to 1 tablespoon.

5 Put into a clean food processor with the watercress, tarragon or chives and the parsley.
Process until smooth, then mix with 3 tablespoons of the whiting mousse.

To assemble the terrine:

6 Grease a 1.7 litre | 3 pint mould or 2 × 450 g | 1 lb loaf tins with butter and line the
bottom with greaseproof paper. Line the bottom and sides of the mould with 1 cm | ½
in of the fish mousse.

7 Cut the salmon fillet into 1 cm | ½ in slices and line the fish mousse with a layer of the
salmon slices.

8 Sprinkle with salt and pepper and spread a thin layer of fish mousse on top.

9 Place half the pounded sole fillets over the fish mousse.

10 Place the herb mousse in the centre.

11 Cover with the remaining sole fillets, spread with some more fish mousse and slices of salmon.

12 Thinly cover the last layer of salmon with the remaining fish mousse, smooth the top and cover with non-stick baking parchment. Place damp greaseproof paper over the top.

13 Place the mould or loaf tins in a roasting pan three-quarters filled with hot water (a bain-marie). Bake in the oven for $1\frac{1}{2}$ hours. Remove from the oven and allow to cool.

To prepare the sauce:

14 Combine all the sauce ingredients, except the oil, in a food processor and blend until smooth. Add the oil slowly with the machine running as for mayonnaise. Check the seasoning. If the sauce is too thick, thin down to a creamy consistency with a little lukewarm water.

To serve:

15 Unmould the cooled terrine and cut into 5 mm $|\frac{1}{4}$ in slices. Spread about 2 tablespoons of the sauce on to the base of each of 4 individual serving plates. Arrange a slice of the terrine on top of the sauce.

The finished layers of the terrine

NOTE: This terrine is quite difficult to slice – if you have an electric carving knife it makes slicing much easier.

wine: **VERY DRY WHITE**

Melba Toast

6 slices of white bread

1 Preheat the grill to its highest setting. Preheat the oven to 150°C|300°F|gas mark 2.

2 Grill the bread on both sides until lightly browned.

3 While still hot, quickly cut off the crusts and split the bread in half horizontally.

4 Put the toast in the oven uncooked side up and leave until golden brown.

NOTE: Melba toast can be kept for a day or two in an airtight tin but it will lose its flavour if kept longer, and is undoubtedly best served straight from the oven.

Savoury Tarts and Flans

Savoury tarts and flans are very versatile. They can be served as a main course for lunch or supper accompanied by a salad and crusty bread. Smaller portions of individual tarts make an excellent first course for a formal dinner.

Aubergine Flan

SERVES 8

340 g | 12 oz flour quantity lemon pastry (see page 560)

For the filling

1 medium (340 g | 12 oz), aubergine, sliced
6 tablespoons olive oil
2 medium onions, thinly sliced
3 cloves of garlic, crushed
6 large tomatoes, peeled and chopped
a pinch of chopped fresh thyme
a pinch of chopped fresh rosemary
a pinch of cayenne pepper
salt and freshly ground black pepper
4 eggs
150 ml | ¼ pint single cream
85 g | 3 oz Cheddar cheese, grated
30 g | 1 oz Parmesan cheese, freshly grated
12 black olives, pitted

1 Sprinkle the aubergine slices lightly with salt and leave in a colander for 30 minutes to extract any bitter juices.

2 Roll out the pastry and use to line a loose-bottomed flan ring about 27.5 cm | 11 in in diameter. Chill in the refrigerator for about 45 minutes to allow the pastry to relax and prevent shrinkage during baking.

3 Preheat the oven to 200°C | 400°F | gas mark 6.

4 Bake the pastry case blind (see page 557). Remove from the oven and turn the temperature down to 170°C | 325°F | gas mark 3.

5 Rinse the aubergines well and pat dry. Fry them in about 2 tablespoons of the oil until golden-brown. Drain on absorbent kitchen paper.

6 Heat the remaining oil, add the onions and fry until lightly browned. Add the garlic and fry for a further 30 seconds. Add the tomatoes, thyme, rosemary, cayenne, salt and pepper. Cook for 5–6 minutes or until a thick pulp. Allow to cool.

7 Beat the eggs, and stir in the cream and cheeses. Mix with the tomato mixture. Season to taste with salt and pepper.

8 Spoon half the mixture into the baked flan case, cover with the fried aubergines and then spoon in the remaining tomato mixture with the olives. Bake in the oven for 40 minutes, or until set.

wine: **LIGHT RED OR ROSÉ**

Onion Tart

SERVES 4

170 g | 6 oz flour quantity rich shortcrust pastry (see page 559)

55 g | 2 oz butter

1 tablespoon olive oil

675 g | 1½ lb onions, sliced

2 eggs

2 egg yolks

150 ml | ¼ pint double cream

salt and freshly ground black pepper

freshly grated nutmeg

1 Preheat the oven to 200°C | 400°F | gas mark 6.
2 Roll out the pastry and use to line a 20 cm | 8 in flan ring. Refrigerate for 20 minutes to relax – this prevents shrinkage during baking.
3 Melt the butter in a large frying pan, add the oil and onions and cook very slowly until soft and lightly coloured (up to 30 minutes). Remove from the heat and leave to cool.
4 Bake the pastry case blind (see page 557), then reduce the oven temperature to 150°C | 325°F | gas mark 2.
5 Mix together the eggs, cream and onions. Season to taste with salt and pepper. Pour into the prepared flan case and sprinkle with nutmeg. Bake until golden and just set (about 30–40 minutes).

wine: SPICY DRY WHITE OR LIGHT RED

Leek and Bacon Flan with Mustard

SERVES 4–6

170 g | 6 oz flour quantity rich shortcrust pastry (see page 559)

For the filling

55 g | 2 oz rindless bacon, finely chopped

15 g | ½ oz butter

white part of 300 g | 10 oz leeks, washed and finely chopped

1 egg, beaten

150 ml | ¼ pint double cream

3 tablespoons Parmesan cheese, freshly grated

salt and freshly ground black pepper

2 tablespoons good-quality coarse-grain mustard

1 Roll out the pastry and use to line a 20 cm | 8 in flan ring. Refrigerate for 30 minutes to relax – this prevents shrinkage during baking.
2 Preheat the oven to 200°C | 400°F | gas mark 6.
3 Bake the pastry case blind (see page 557). Remove from the oven and reduce the temperature to 170°C | 325°F | gas mark 3.
4 Cook the bacon, in its own fat, until it begins to brown.
5 Add the butter and the leeks. Cover with a piece of dampened greaseproof paper and cook over low heat until the leeks are soft. Drain well and allow to cool.

6 Mix together the egg, cream and cheese. Add the leeks and bacon. Season with salt and pepper.

7 Spread a thin layer of mustard on the base of the flan and then pour in the filling. Bake in the oven for 40–45 minutes or until the filling is set.

wine: **VERY DRY WHITE**

Leeks en Croûte with Red Pepper Sauce

SERVES 4

30 g | 1 oz butter

900 g | 2 lb leeks, trimmed and thinly sliced

3 tablespoons double cream

salt and freshly ground black pepper

450 g | 1 lb flour quantity puff pastry (see page 566)

4 fresh basil leaves

1 egg yolk

To serve

red pepper sauce (see page 129)

1 Melt the butter in a sauté pan and add the leeks. Cook over a low heat for about 15 minutes, or until the leeks have softened. Add the cream and cook until the juices have evaporated. Season with salt and pepper and allow to cool completely.

2 Flour a work surface lightly. Roll the pastry out to the thickness of a £1 coin. Using a 10 cm | 4 in and a 13 cm | 5 in cutter, cut out 4 rounds of each size. If you need to re-roll the pastry, lay the scraps on top of each other and re-roll.

3 Take the 4 smaller circles and divide the leeks between them, leaving a 1 cm | ½ in border clear. Top each mound of leeks with a basil leaf. Dampen the edges lightly with water.

4 Take the larger circles of pastry and carefully place over the filling, ensuring no air is trapped inside. Press the edges lightly together, knock up and scallop the edges.

5 Brush with the egg yolk, then, using the back of a sharp knife, mark a criss-cross pattern on the top.

6 Put the leeks en croûte on a baking sheet and chill in the refrigerator for 30 minutes.

7 Meanwhile, preheat the oven to 200°C | 400°F | gas mark 6.

8 Bake the leeks en croûte in the oven for 15–20 minutes, or until they are risen and brown.

9 To serve: put a leeks en croûte on indivdual plates and spoon a little sauce around the edge.

wine: **DRY WHITE**

Creamy Fish Flan with Burnt Hollandaise

SERVES 4

170 g | 6 oz flour quantity shortcrust pastry (see page 559)

1 small onion, very finely chopped

30 g | 1 oz butter

30 g | 1 oz plain flour

1 bay leaf

290 ml | ½ pint milk

salt and freshly ground black pepper

1 egg

225 g | 8 oz white fish, cooked and flaked

1 tablespoon chopped fresh parsley

a squeeze of lemon juice

55 g | 2 oz butter quantity hollandaise sauce (see page 119)

1 Preheat the oven to 190°C | 375°F | gas mark 5. Roll out the pastry and use to line a 20 cm | 8 in flan ring. Refrigerate for 20 minutes to relax – this prevents shrinkage during baking.

2 Bake blind (see page 557), then remove from the oven.

3 Reduce the oven temperature to 180°C | 350°F | gas mark 4.

4 Cook the onion in the butter in a saucepan until soft but not coloured. Add the flour and bay leaf. Cook, stirring, for 1 minute. Remove from the heat, stir in the milk, and bring slowly to the boil, stirring continuously. Taste and season as necessary with salt and pepper. Simmer for 2 minutes, remove the bay leaf and allow to cool for 5 minutes.

5 Separate the egg and beat the yolk into the sauce. Stir in the fish, parsley and lemon juice to taste. Whisk the egg white until stiff but not dry and fold into the mixture. Pour into the pastry case. Bake in the centre of the oven for about 25 minutes.

6 Preheat the grill 10 minutes before the flan is cooked.

7 Prepare the Hollandaise sauce and spoon over the flan. Put the flan under the hot grill until the top is nicely browned. Serve immediately.

NOTE: If the fish has been poached in milk, reserve the cooking liquor for the white sauce.

wine: VERY DRY WHITE

Spinach and Olive Tart

This recipe has been adapted from Roger Vergé's *Entertaining in the French Style*.

SERVES 8

285 g | 10 oz flour quantity herb wholemeal pastry (see page 560)

2 tablespoons olive oil

2 onions, finely chopped

450 g | 1 lb fresh spinach, cooked and chopped

3 cloves of garlic, crushed

3 eggs

3 tablespoons double cream

salt and freshly ground black pepper

340 g | 12 oz small black Niçoise olives in oil, pitted

1 teaspoon fresh thyme leaves

1 Preheat the oven to 200°C|400°F|gas mark 6.

2 Heat the oil in a large frying pan, add the onions, and cook over a low heat for about 15 minutes until beginning to soften and brown. Add the garlic and continue to cook for a further minute. Stir in the spinach. Remove from the heat and leave to cool.

3 Beat the eggs with the cream. Add the onion and spinach mixture. Mix well and season lightly to taste.

4 Roll out the pastry and use to line the base of a 30 cm|12 in loose-bottomed flan ring. Refrigerate for 20 minutes to relax.

5 Bake the pastry case blind (see page 557) in the centre of the preheated oven.

6 Reduce the oven temperature to 180°C|350°F|gas mark 4.

7 Pour the spinach and onion mixture into the flan case and spread it evenly over the base. Bake in the centre of the oven for 20 minutes. Remove the flan ring to allow the sides of the pastry to cook and sprinkle the olives evenly over the tart. Sprinkle with the fresh thyme leaves and bake for a further 5 minutes.

8 Serve hot or cold.

wine: ROSÉ

Mushroom and Ricotta Tart

SERVES 8

225 g|8 oz flour quantity herb wholemeal pastry (see page 560)

225 g|8 oz medium mushrooms, stalks removed

30 g|1 oz butter

juice of ½ lemon

900 g|2 lb ricotta cheese

2 teaspoons canned green peppercorns, rinsed and crushed

1 clove of garlic, crushed

3 eggs

4 tablespoons double cream

4 tablespoons chopped fresh mixed herbs, such as chives, parsley, dill, sage

salt and freshly ground black pepper

1 Preheat the oven to 400°F|200°C|gas mark 6.

2 Roll out the pastry and use to line a 28 cm|11 in flan ring. Refrigerate for 20 minutes to relax.

3 Bake the pastry case blind (see page 557), then remove from the oven and turn the temperature down to 170°C|325°F|gas mark 3.

4 Cook the mushrooms in half the butter and the lemon juice for about 5 minutes. Remove from the heat and leave to cool.

5 Beat together the ricotta cheese, peppercorns, garlic, eggs, cream and herbs. Season to taste with salt and pepper.

6 Carefully spoon the mixture into the flan case and smooth it flat.

7 Place the mushrooms, stalk side down, on top of the filling. Brush with the remaining butter, melted, and bake in the centre of the oven for 30 minutes. Serve hot.

wine: LIGHT RED

Artichoke and Green Olive Pie

SERVES 6–8

10 large globe artichoke hearts, cooked

30 g | 1 oz butter

10 shallots, finely diced

2 small cloves of garlic, crushed

chopped fresh thyme

chopped fresh sage

4 tablespoons dry white vermouth or white wine

150 ml | $\frac{1}{4}$ pint double cream

170 g | 6 oz green olives, pitted and chopped

salt and freshly ground black pepper

225 g | 8 oz flour quantity puff pastry (see page 566)

1 egg, beaten, to glaze

1 Preheat the oven to 190°C | 375°F | gas mark 5.
2 Cut the artichoke hearts into 5 mm | $\frac{1}{4}$ in cubes and cook slowly in the butter, with the shallots, garlic, thyme and sage, for 5 minutes.
3 Add the vermouth or wine and reduce by half, by boiling. Add the cream and reduce to a coating consistency. Stir the sauce every so often to prevent it from catching on the bottom of the saucepan.
4 Add the olives and season to taste with salt and pepper. Leave to cool.
5 Roll out the pastry and use half to line a 20 cm | 8 in flan ring. Pile in the artichoke and olive mixture and cover the pie with the remaining pastry.
6 Brush with beaten egg and bake in the centre of the oven for 15–20 minutes or until golden brown.

NOTE: If fresh artichokes are not available, canned artichoke bottoms may be used.

wine: **DRY WHITE**

Caramelized Onion and Thyme Quiche

SERVES 6

170 g | 6 oz rich shortcrust pastry (see page 559)

For the filling

55 g | 2 oz butter

1 kg | $2\frac{1}{4}$ lb onions, sliced

1 teaspoon caster sugar

4 eggs

200 ml | 7 fl oz milk

200 ml | 7 fl oz single cream

4 tablespoons finely grated Parmesan cheese

2 teaspoons chopped fresh thyme

salt and freshly ground black pepper

1 Preheat the oven to 200°C | 400°F | gas mark 6.
2 Roll out the pastry and use to line a 20 cm | 8 in flan ring, 4 cm | $1\frac{1}{2}$ in deep. Chill until firm, then bake blind (see page 557).
3 Turn the oven temperature down to 170°C | 325°F | gas mark 3.
4 Make the filling: melt the butter in a large sauté pan and stir in the onions. Cover with a dampened piece of greaseproof paper and cook over a low heat until softened. Remove the paper and stir in the sugar. Continue to cook until the onions are golden-brown. This can take up to 1 hour.

5 Beat the eggs in a large bowl and stir in the milk and cream. Strain through a sieve to remove any eggy threads, then stir in the cheese and thyme. Season to taste with salt and pepper.

6 Using a slotted spoon, remove the solids from the filling. Place in the bottom of the pastry case. Pour over enough of the egg and cream mixture to fill the pastry case to the rim.

7 Bake in the bottom third of the oven for about 40 minutes or until set. Serve warm or cold.

wine: **SPICY WHITE**

Quiche Lorraine

SERVES 4–6

170 g | 6 oz flour quantity rich shortcrust pastry (see page 559)

For the filling

15 g | 1½ oz butter

1 onion, finely chopped

110 g | 4 oz streaky bacon, diced

225 ml | 8 fl oz milk

225 ml | 8 fl oz single cream

3 medium eggs, beaten

3 yolks

85 g | 3 oz strong Cheddar or Gruyère cheese, grated

salt and freshly ground black pepper

1 Roll out the pastry and use to line a 20 cm | 8 in flan ring, 4 cm | 1½ in deep. Refrigerate until firm.

2 Preheat the oven to 200°C | 400°F | gas mark 6. Bake the pastry case blind (see page 557).

3 Melt the butter in a small saucepan and stir in the onion. Cover with a dampened piece of greaseproof paper and a lid. Cook over a low heat until the onion is soft but not coloured.

4 Remove the lid and the paper and stir in the bacon. Cook over a medium heat until the bacon is cooked through but not browned.

5 Remove the onion and the bacon from the pan with a slotted spoon and place on a plate. Leave to cool.

6 Mix together the milk, cream, beaten eggs and yolks. Pass through a sieve to remove any eggy threads.

7 Stir in the onion and bacon mixture and the cheese. Season to taste with salt and pepper.

8 Turn the oven temperature down to 150°C | 300°F | gas mark 2.

9 Using a slotted spoon, remove the solids from the filling mixture and distribute evenly over the bottom of the baked pastry case. Pour enough of the cream mixture into the pastry case to fill it to the top.

10 Bake in the lower third of the oven for about 40 minutes until the filling is set firm but not browned.

11 If the pastry is still very pale, the flan ring can be removed and the quiche returned to the oven for a further 5 minutes. Serve warm or cold.

wine: **SPICY, DRY WHITE**

Spinach Flan

SERVES 4–6

170 g | 6 oz rich shortcrust pastry (see page 559).

For the filling

30 g | 1 oz butter

1 medium onion, finely chopped

150 ml | ¼ pint milk

150 ml | ¼ pint single cream

3 eggs, beaten

340 g | 12 oz spinach, cooked, drained and finely chopped

55 g | 2 oz strong Cheddar or Gruyère cheese, finely grated

salt and freshly ground black pepper

freshly grated nutmeg

1 Preheat the oven to 200°C | 400°F | gas mark 6.

2 Roll out the pastry and use to line a 20 cm | 8 in flan ring, 4 cm | 1½ in deep. Chill until firm. Bake blind (see page 557).

3 Preheat the oven to 170°C | 325°F | gas mark 3.

4 Melt the butter in a small saucepan and stir in the onion. Cover with a piece of dampened greaseproof paper and a lid and cook over a low heat until softened. Allow to cool.

5 Mix together the milk, cream and eggs. Pass through a sieve to remove any eggy threads.

6 Stir the onion, spinach and cheese into the egg and cream mixture. Season.

7 Use a slotted spoon to remove the solids from the mixture and place in the baked pastry case. Pour over enough egg and cream mixture to fill the pastry case to the top.

8 Bake for 30–40 minutes in the lower third of the oven. Serve warm or cold.

wine: **LIGHT RED**

Pasta, Polenta and Gnocchi

Pasta should always be cooked *al dente*, i.e. firm to the bite. Remember that fresh or homemade pasta, which already contains moisture, cooks 4 times faster than the dried commercial equivalents. The cooking time also depends on the thickness. Dried vermicelli cooks in 2–3 minutes, while dried lasagne takes 15–16.

Egg Pasta

400 g | 14 oz strong '00' flour
4 large eggs
1 tablespoon oil

1 Sift the flour on to a wooden board. Make a well in the centre and put in the eggs and oil.
2 Using the fingers of one hand, mix together the eggs and oil and gradually draw in the flour, to make a very stiff dough.
3 Knead until smooth and elastic (about 15 minutes). Wrap in clingfilm and leave to relax in a cool place for 1 hour.
4 Roll out one small piece of dough at a time until paper-thin. Cut into the required shape.
5 Allow to dry (unless making ravioli), hanging over a chair back if long noodles, or lying on a wire rack or dry tea towel if small ones, for at least 30 minutes before cooking. Ravioli is dried after stuffing.

NOTE:If more or less pasta is required the recipe can be altered on a pro-rata basis, for example a 340 g | 12 oz quantity of flour calls for a pinch of salt, 3 eggs and 1 scant tablespoon of oil.

Green Pasta

225 g | 8 oz spinach, cooked
340 g | 12 oz strong '00' flour
a pinch of salt

2 eggs
1 tablespoon double cream

1 Chop or liquidize the spinach and push through a sieve to get a fairly dry paste.
2 Sift the flour with the salt on to a board. Make a well in the centre and put in the eggs,

spinach and cream. Using the fingers of one hand, mix together the eggs, spinach and cream, gradually drawing in the flour, to make a stiff dough.

3 Knead until smooth and elastic (about 15 minutes). Wrap in clingfilm and leave to relax in a cool place for 30 minutes.

4 Roll out one small piece of dough at a time until paper-thin. Cut into the required shape. Allow to dry (unless making raviol), hanging over a chair back if long noodles, or lying on a wire rack or clean tea-towel if small ones, for at least 30 minutes before cooking. Ravioli is dried after stuffing.

Half-hour Pasta

With a food processor and a pasta machine you can be eating pasta half an hour after you thought about it. Use the same ingredients as for the traditional egg pasta recipe opposite. While the dough is resting make your favourite quick pasta sauce and sit down to enjoy the best fast food there is.

400g|14 oz strong '00' flour
4 eggs
4 tablespoons olive oil

1 Put the flour and the flavouring of your choice (see box) into a food processor and blend well. Beat the eggs and oil together, and with the motor running, gradually add them to the flour until the mixture resembles breadcrumbs. Remove from the processor. Bring a small amount of the mixture together with your fingertips. It should come together easily, but not be too wet. If it does feel wet, add a little extra flour.

2 Knead the dough briefly to bring it together, wrap it in clingfilm and leave it to relax for 10 minutes. Pass it through the widest setting of the pasta machine three or four times, then roll it through the different settings of the machine until you can get it through the narrowest gauge. Allow the pasta to dry until the surface no longer feels tacky. Cut the pasta into the required shape and drop it straight into a large saucepan of boiling salted water.

3 Cook until *al dente*, then drain and serve with the sauce of your choice.

Flavoured Pasta

Follow the recipe for egg pasta (see page 234) and add the flavourings with the eggs.

Tomato Pasta: Add about 2 teaspoons tomato purée.

Herb Pasta: Add plenty of chopped very fresh herbs to taste, such as parsley, thyme, tarragon.

Beetroot Pasta: Add 1 small cooked, puréed beetroot.

Chocolate Pasta: Add 55 g|2 oz melted plain chocolate.

Saffron Noodles

½ teaspoon saffron filaments, dry-fried
225 g | 8 oz strong '00' flour
2 eggs
3 egg yolks

1 tablespoon olive oil
freshly ground white pepper

1 Place the saffron in a small bowl and pour over 2 teaspoons of boiling water. Leave to cool.

2 Put all the ingredients into a food processor and process until the mixture forms a dough. (If a food processor is not available, sift the flour into a bowl, add the salt and pepper, make a well in the centre and add the eggs, oil and saffron liquid. Gradually mix the flour into the liquid, using your hand. Eventually draw it together into a ball of dough and knead until smooth, about 15 minutes.

3 Roll the pasta as thinly as possible. Dust with flour and roll up like a Swiss roll. Cut as thinly as possible. Unravel the pasta, dust with flour and place on a tray to dry slightly. (This is much easier if you have a pasta machine.)

Cracked Black Pepper Pasta with Truffle Oil and Parmesan

SERVES 6

675 g | 1½ lb strong '00' flour
2 tablespoons black peppercorns
6 eggs
2 tablespoons olive oil

To garnish

170 g | 6 oz Parmesan cheese, in a piece
4 tablespoons truffle-flavoured oil
3 tablespoons olive oil

1 Make the pasta: put the flour and peppercorns into a food processor and process until the peppercorns are finely chopped. They should not look like ground pepper, but if the pieces are too large they will not go through the pasta machine.

2 Mix the eggs and oil together, and with the motor still running, gradually add them to the flour until the mixture resembles breadcrumbs. Bring a small amount of the mixture together with your fingertips. It should come together easily, but not be too wet. If it does feel wet, add a little more flour.

3 Knead the dough briefly to bring it together, wrap it in clingfilm and leave to relax for at least 10 minutes. Feed the dough through the widest setting of a pasta machine 3–4 times before rolling it in the usual way down to the narrowest setting. Cut the pasta to the required shape, either using the machine or by hand. Unroll it and leave to dry, either over a clean broom handle or on a dry tea towel.

4 Bring a large saucepan of salted water to the boil and drop in the pasta. Give it a stir to prevent it from sticking and boil until the pasta is *al dente*. This will take anything from 2 to 5 minutes, depending on the thickness of the pasta.

5 Meanwhile, make shavings of Parmesan by running the blade of a swivel-headed vegetable peeler over the surface of the cheese.

6 When the pasta is cooked, drain it thoroughly and transfer to a large warmed serving dish. Pour over the truffle oil and olive oil and toss together. Sprinkle the Parmesan over the top and serve immediately.

wine: **DRY WHITE**

Ravioli

SERVES 4

400 g|14 oz flour quantity egg pasta (see page 234)

For the meat filling

170 g|6 oz cooked meat, minced

15 g|½ oz butter

2 teaspoons fresh white breadcrumbs

2 teaspoons chopped fresh parsley

2 teaspoons brown stock (see page 102)

1 teaspoon tomato purée

salt and freshly ground black pepper

a pinch of freshly grated nutmeg

a pinch of ground cinnamon

1 small egg, beaten

freshly grated Parmesan cheese

melted butter or oil or tomato sauce 2 (see page 129)

1 Fry the meat in the butter in a saucepan for 5 minutes. Stir in the breadcrumbs, parsley, stock, tomato purée, salt, pepper, nutmeg and cinnamon. Check the seasoning.

2 Add enough egg to bind the mixture together. Allow to cool.

3 Roll out the pasta to a very thin rectangle. Cut in half. Keep well covered to prevent drying out.

4 Take one sheet of pasta and place half-teaspoons of filling at 3 cm|1½ in intervals, in even rows, all over it. Cover with the other sheet of pasta and press together firmly all round each mound of filling taking care to exclude any air. Cut between the rows, making sure that all the edges are sealed. Allow to dry on a wire rack until leathery.

5 Simmer the ravioli in near-boiling salted water for 5–10 minutes, or until just tender. Drain well. Serve with butter, oil or tomato sauce, and hand grated Parmesan cheese separately.

wine: **LIGHT RED**

Rabbit Ravioli

SERVES 4

For the filling
450 g|1 lb rabbit
1 tablespoon oil
3 onions, finely chopped
1 teaspoon soft dark brown sugar
1 tablespoon balsamic vinegar
290 ml|½ pint white stock (see page 103)
3 tablespoons finely chopped fresh thyme
juice of ½ lemon
a pinch of cayenne
salt and freshly ground black pepper

For the pasta
200 g|7 oz strong white '00' flour
a pinch of salt
2 eggs, beaten
2 teaspoons oil

For the sauce
150 ml|¼ pint dry white wine
150 ml|¼ pint white stock (see page 103)
2 tablespoons dry sherry
200 ml|7 fl oz double cream
1 tablespoon grainy mustard
salt and freshly ground white pepper

1 Skin, bone and mince the rabbit finely and set aside.
2 Heat the oil in a heavy frying pan and sweat the onions until soft and translucent.
3 Add the sugar, increase the heat and stir until the onions are a dark golden brown. Add the vinegar and remove from the pan.
4 Add more oil to the pan if it seems dry and brown the minced rabbit meat thoroughly.
5 Return the onions to the pan with the stock, thyme, lemon juice, cayenne and salt and pepper. Simmer for about 45 minutes, or until all the liquid has evaporated and the rabbit is tender. Taste and add extra salt and pepper if necessary. Leave to cool.
6 Meanwhile, make the pasta: sift the flour and salt on to the work surface. Make a well in the centre and drop in the eggs and oil.
7 Using the fingers of one hand, mix together the eggs and oil and gradually draw in the flour. The mixture should be a very stiff dough.
8 Knead until smooth and elastic (about 15 minutes). Wrap in clingfilm and leave to relax in a cool place for 1 hour.
9 Roll the pasta out as thinly as possible and stamp out circles using a 7.5 cm|3 in round cutter. Put a heaped teaspoon of the rabbit mixture in the centre of half the circles, wet the edges and cover with the remaining pasta circles. Press the edges together firmly to seal well and eliminate any air bubbles. Leave to dry on a wire rack for 30 minutes.
10 To make the sauce: put the wine into a saucepan and boil rapidly to reduce by one third, then add the stock and sherry and boil again to reduce by half.
11 Add the cream and reduce again by about half or until the sauce is of coating consistency. Add the mustard and season to taste with salt and pepper.
12 Cook the pasta in a large saucepan of boiling salted water until tender (about 4–6 minutes).
13 To serve: drain the pasta well, arrange on 4 warmed individual serving plates and pour over the sauce.

wine: **MEDIUM RED**

Crab and Prawn Ravioli

SERVES 4

1 quantity egg pasta dough (see page 234)

110 g|4 oz cooked shell-on prawns

110 g|4 oz cooked crabmeat

1 egg white

2 teaspoons finely chopped fresh chives

2 teaspoons lemon juice

salt and freshly ground black pepper

For the sauce

1 tablespoon vegetable oil

1 small onion, roughly chopped

1 clove of garlic, crushed

1 whole star anise

3 tablespoons brandy

2 tomatoes, chopped

1 bay leaf

1 teaspoon tomato purée

1 litre|1¾ pints shellfish stock or brown fish stock
   (see page 108)

150 ml|¼ pint double cream

chopped fresh chives, to garnish

1 Wrap the pasta dough in clingfilm and set aside to relax.

2 Remove the prawns from their shells, reserving the shells for the sauce.

3 Put the prawns and crabmeat into a food processor and process until smooth. Add the egg white, chives, lemon juice, salt and pepper and process again until well mixed. Taste and season with more salt and pepper if necessary. Refrigerate.

4 Make the sauce: heat the oil in a heavy saucepan and fry the prawn shells and the onion until beginning to brown. Add the garlic and star anise. Cook for a further 30 seconds.

5 Add the brandy, tomatoes, bay leaf and tomato purée. Add the stock and simmer for 20 minutes.

6 Roll out the pasta as thinly as possible, through a pasta machine or by hand with a rolling pin, to a strip approximately 15 cm × 80 cm|6 in × 32 in. Brush lightly with water.

7 Place teaspoonfuls of the filling in even rows at intervals of 4 cm|1½ in over half of the pasta. Fold the other half of the pasta over the mounds of filling. Press together, firming around each mound and making sure that all the air is excluded. Cut between the mounds, making sure that the edges of the ravioli are sealed.

8 Strain the sauce and reduce to 150 ml|¼ pint by boiling rapidly. Add the cream and reduce to the consistency of single cream. Season to taste with salt and pepper.

9 Cook the ravioli in a saucepan of boiling salted water for 3–4 minutes until *al dente*.

10 Place the ravioli on a warmed serving dish, pour over some of the sauce, and garnish with the chives. Hand the remaining sauce separately.

wine: **LIGHT WHITE**

Ravioli with Spinach and Ricotta Filling

SERVES 4

400 g | 14 oz flour quantity egg pasta
(see page 234)

For the filling

450 g | 1 lb spinach, cooked and chopped
110 g | 4 oz ricotta cheese
1 egg

salt and freshly ground black pepper
freshly grated nutmeg
freshly grated Parmesan cheese

To serve

pesto sauce (see page 124)

1 Mix the spinach with the ricotta cheese, add the egg and beat well. Season to taste with salt, pepper, nutmeg and Parmesan cheese.
2 Roll the pasta to a very thin rectangle. Cut in half. Keep well covered to prevent drying out.
3 Take one sheet of pasta and place half-teaspoons of filling, in even rows, all over it. Brush round the piles of filling with a little water. Cover loosely with the other sheet of pasta and press firmly round each mound of filling. Check carefully that there are no pockets of air.
4 Cut between the rows, making sure that all the edges are sealed. Allow to dry on a wire rack for 30 minutes.
5 Cook in a saucepan of simmering salted water for 4–5 minutes until tender. Drain well and serve with the pesto sauce.

wine: **MEDIUM RED**

Macaroni Cheese

SERVES 4

170 g | 6 oz macaroni
20 g | ¾ oz butter
20 g | ¾ oz plain flour
cayenne pepper
a pinch of dry English mustard

425 ml | ¾ pint milk
salt and freshly ground black pepper
170 g | 6 oz strong Cheddar cheese, grated
1 tablespoon fresh white breadcrumbs

1 Cook the macaroni, uncovered, in plenty of rapidly boiling salted water. The water must boil steadily to keep the macaroni moving freely and prevent it from sticking to the saucepan; the lid is left off to prevent boiling over. Cook the macaroni until it is just tender. Drain well and rinse under boiling water.
2 Melt the butter in a second saucepan and add the flour, cayenne pepper and mustard. Cook, stirring, for 1 minute. Remove from the heat. Gradually pour in the milk and mix well. Return to the heat and stir until boiling. Simmer, stirring all the time, for 2 minutes.

3 Stir in all but 1 tablespoon of the cheese. Season the sauce to taste with salt and pepper. Stir the macaroni into the sauce and reheat if necessary. Turn the mixture into an ovenproof dish.

4 Preheat the grill to its highest setting.

5 Mix the reserved cheese with the breadcrumbs and sprinkle evenly over the sauce; make sure that all the sauce is covered or it will form brown blisters under the grill.

6 Grill fairly quickly until the top is browned and crisp.

wine: **LIGHT FRUITY RED**

Spaghetti Carbonara

SERVES 4

450 g │ 1 lb spaghetti	4 egg yolks
salt	6 tablespoons single cream
1 tablespoon oil	55 g │ 2 oz Parmesan cheese, freshly grated
100 g │ 3½ oz streaky bacon, cut into small strips	freshly ground black pepper

1 Cook the spaghetti in plenty of rapidly boiling salted water.

2 Heat the oil in a fairly large frying pan, add the bacon and fry lightly over a medium heat until the fat has melted and the bacon has cooked. Remove the pan from the heat and set aside. Keep warm.

3 Meanwhile, whisk the egg yolks in a bowl, then whisk in the cream and half the Parmesan cheese, and season generously with pepper.

4 When the spaghetti is still firm to the bite (*al dente*), drain it; transfer it to the pan with the bacon, place over a medium heat and pour the egg mixture over it. Stir quickly and serve immediately, with the remaining Parmesan cheese handed separately.

wine: **LIGHT RED**

Spaghetti con Vongole

SERVES 4

900 g │ 2 lb baby clams in their shells	salt and freshly ground black pepper
6 tablespoons olive oil	1 tablespoon chopped fresh parsley
2 cloves of garlic, peeled and bruised	450 g │ 1 lb spaghetti
4 large tomatoes, peeled and chopped	

1 Wash and scrub the clams thoroughly.

2 Heat 1 tablespoon oil in a large saucepan, add the clams, cover and shake until they have opened. Discard any that have remained closed. Remove the clams and strain the juices. Reserve both.

3 Heat 4 tablespoons of the remaining oil in the pan, add the garlic and cook until golden-brown; remove and discard. Add the tomatoes, clam juice, salt and pepper and cook for about 30 minutes. Add the clams and cook over a low heat for 1–2 minutes. Add the parsley.

4 Meanwhile, cook the spaghetti in plenty of rapidly boiling salted water until *al dente*. Drain and mix with the sauce. Serve immediately and provide finger bowls.

wine: **DRY WHITE**

Spaghetti en Papillote

This is an unusual way to serve spaghetti, which keeps it moist and succulent.

SERVES 4

150 ml | ¼ pint good-quality olive oil	225 g | 8 oz spaghetti
1 large clove of garlic, peeled	450 g | 1 lb fresh tomatoes, peeled, deseeded and slivered
1 × 400 g | 14 oz can of tomatoes, drained	
salt and freshly ground black pepper	2 tablespoons finely chopped fresh parsley
¼ teaspoon chilli powder	28 large black Greek olives, pitted

1 Heat all but 2 tablespoons of the oil in a heavy saucepan. Add the garlic and leave to infuse over a gentle heat for 2 minutes. Remove and add the drained tomatoes, taking care as the oil will spit. Simmer for 20 minutes, stirring occasionally. Season with salt, pepper and the chilli powder.

2 Process or liquidize in a blender until smooth, then return to the pan. Simmer for a further 10 minutes until reduced to a thick, shiny sauce.

3 Preheat the oven to 190°C | 375°F | gas mark 5.

4 Cook the spaghetti in plenty of rapidly boiling salted water until *al dente*.

5 Meanwhile, place 4 × 30 cm | 12 in circles of double greaseproof paper on the work surface.

6 Drain the spaghetti, mix it with the fresh tomatoes, the remaining oil, half the parsley, the olives and the tomato sauce. Mix well and check the seasoning.

7 Divide the spaghetti mixture between the 4 circles of greaseproof paper. Close each parcel up, trap a little air in the parcel and secure the edges firmly by twisting and turning them together.

8 Place in a shallow, damp roasting pan and bake in the oven for 15 minutes.

9 Remove from the oven and place on warmed dinner plates. Open the parcels with scissors and sprinkle the remaining parsley over each serving.

wine: **MEDIUM RED**

Greek Parsley Pasta

SERVES 4

400 g | 14 oz flour quantity egg pasta (see page 234)
1 bunch of flat-leaf parsley, washed and dried
1 quantity pesto sauce (see page 124)

For the sauce

Tomato, Basil and Olive Oil Sauce (see page 127)

1 Roll the pasta out to a very thin rectangle on a lightly floured board. Cut in half. Keep well covered to prevent it from drying out.

2 Take one sheet of pasta and arrange individual parsley leaves at 3 cm | 1 ½ in intervals, in even rows, all over it. Cover loosely with the other sheet of pasta and press down firmly. Roll again until the parsley can be seen between the layers of pasta.

3 Using a pastry cutter, cut between the rows, making sure that all the edges are sealed.

4 Make the sauce.

5 Simmer in boiling salted water for 2–3 minutes or until just tender. Drain well and toss in warm sauce.

wine: **MEDIUM RED**

Pasta Roulade with Tomato Sauce

SERVES 4

30 g | 1 oz butter
1 kg | 2¼ lb spinach, cooked and chopped
225 g | 8 oz ricotta cheese
85 g | 3 oz pinenuts, toasted
freshly grated nutmeg

salt and freshly ground black pepper
1 tablespoon roughly chopped fresh basil
400 g | 14 oz flour quantity egg pasta (see page 234)
tomato sauce 1 (see page 128)
freshly grated Parmesan cheese

1 Melt the butter in a saucepan, add the spinach and cook for 1 minute, stirring continuously to prevent sticking. Add the ricotta, pinenuts, nutmeg, salt, pepper and basil. Remove from the heat and leave to cool.

2 Roll out the pasta into a large thin rectangle. Spread the spinach filling evenly over the surface, then roll up like a Swiss roll. Wrap the roll in a clean 'J'-cloth or piece of muslin and tie the ends with string, like a Christmas cracker.

3 Cook in a large saucepan or fish kettle of salted simmering water for about 20 minutes.

4 Preheat the oven to 200°C | 400°F | gas mark 6.

5 Slice the roulade thickly and arrange in an ovenproof dish. Pour over the tomato sauce, sprinkle with Parmesan cheese and reheat in the oven for 20 minutes.

wine: **MEDIUM RED**

Tagliatelle with Oyster Mushrooms and Sage

SERVES 3–4

225 g│8 oz tagliatelle

salt and freshly ground black pepper

55 g│2 oz butter

450 g│1 lb oyster mushrooms, sliced

1 tablespoon chopped fresh sage

1 Cook the tagliatelle in plenty of rapidly boiling salted water until tender. Drain well and keep warm.

2 Melt the butter in a large saucepan and cook the oyster mushrooms for 1–2 minutes until soft. Add the tagliatelle and sage, season to taste with salt and pepper and serve immediately.

wine: DRY WHITE

Tricolour Pasta Salad

SERVES 4–6

225 g│8 oz pasta twists

1 red pepper, cored, deseeded and quartered

450 g│1 lb broccoli

6 tablespoons French dressing (see page 123)

2 tablespoons chopped fresh parsley

1 Cook the pasta in plenty of rapidly boiling salted water until just tender. Rinse under cold running water until completely cold, then drain well.

2 Grill the pepper until the skin is well charred, scrape off the skin and cut the flesh into 5 mm│¼ in wide strips.

3 Cut the broccoli into small florets and cook in boiling water for 1 minute. Rinse under cold running water and drain well.

4 Toss the pasta, peppers and broccoli in the French dressing and parsley. Serve chilled.

wine: LIGHT DRY WHITE

Lasagne Verdi Bolognese

SERVES 4

140 g | 5 oz fresh pasta or 8 leaves of bought lasagne

freshly grated Parmesan cheese

For the meat sauce

1 tablespoon olive oil

340 g | 12 oz lean minced beef

1 onion, finely diced

1 stick of celery, finely diced

4 cloves of garlic, chopped

30 g | 1 oz plain flour

290 ml | ½ pint brown stock (see page 102)

100 ml | 3½ fl oz dry white wine

salt and freshly ground black pepper

1 tablespoon chopped fresh parsley

1 teaspoon chopped fresh marjoram

a pinch of ground cinnamon

1 tablespoon tomato purée

For the cream sauce

45 g | 1½ oz butter

1 bay leaf

45 g | 1½ oz plain flour

570 ml | 1 pint creamy milk

salt and freshly ground black pepper

freshly grated nutmeg

1 Prepare the pasta according to manufacturer's instructions.

2 Heat the oil in a saucepan and brown the mince well. Add the vegetables and garlic and fry, stirring continuously, for 2 minutes.

3 Stir in the flour. Cook until brown. Pour in the stock and wine and add the salt, pepper, parsley, marjoram, cinnamon and tomato purée. Bring to the boil, stirring. Simmer slowly for 1–1½ hours, stirring occasionally, until the sauce is very thick and syrupy.

4 Make the cream sauce: melt the butter in a saucepan, add the bay leaf and flour and cook, stirring, for 1 minute. Remove from the heat.

5 Gradually add the milk and return to the heat. Bring to the boil, stirring continuously, until you have a thick, creamy sauce. Simmer for 2 minutes. Season to taste with salt and pepper and remove the bay leaf.

6 Preheat the oven to 190°C | 375°F | gas mark 5. Place a thin layer of meat sauce into an ovenproof dish and cover with a layer of pasta, then spoon on a thin layer of meat sauce. Cover with a layer of cream sauce. Arrange a layer of pasta on top of this. Continue the layers in this manner, finishing with cream sauce. Sprinkle with grated Parmesan cheese.

7 Bake for 20–25 minutes until bubbling and just brown on top.

wine: **MEDIUM RED**

Cannelloni

SERVES 4

200 g | 7 oz flour quantity egg pasta (see page 234)
290 ml | ½ pint tomato sauce 2 (see page 129)
45 g | 1½ oz strong Cheddar or Gruyère cheese, or
  30 g | 1 oz Parmesan cheese, grated

For the filling

2 teaspoons olive oil
340 g | 12 oz lean minced beef
1 onion, chopped

1 stick of celery, chopped
1 clove of garlic, crushed
2 teaspoons tomato purée
2 teaspoons plain flour
180 ml | 6 fl oz brown stock (see page 102)
1 bay leaf
1 tablespoon chopped fresh parsley
1 tablespoon port or Madeira
salt and freshly ground black pepper

1 Cut the pasta into 10 × 10 cm | 4 × 4 in squares. Allow to dry until leathery.

2 Heat the oil in a saucepan and add the mince. Brown well all over. Add the onion, celery, garlic and tomato purée and cook for 2 minutes.

3 Add the flour and cook for 30 seconds. Remove the pan from the heat, add the stock, bay leaf and parsley, stir well and return to the heat. Bring slowly to the boil, stirring continuously.

4 Season with salt and pepper, cover and simmer for 1 hour. Then add the port or Madeira and continue to simmer for 10 minutes. Check the sauce every so often and if it is getting too dry add a little extra stock. Remove the bay leaf.

5 Preheat the oven to 200°C | 400°F | gas mark 6. Preheat the grill to its highest setting.

6 Cook the pasta in rapidly boiling salted water until just tender (about 5 minutes if home-made, 12 minutes if bought). Drain well and pat dry with a tea-towel or cloth.

7 Divide the meat mixture between the pasta strips and roll them up to form the cannelloni. Place them in a greased ovenproof dish.

8 Pour over the tomato sauce and sprinkle with grated cheese. Bake for 15 minutes, then place under the grill until nicely browned.

NOTES: For a blander version, trickle over a little white sauce or double cream before grilling the finished dish. Commercially made cannelloni are usually tube-shaped, and the filling is inserted with a teaspoon.

wine: LIGHT RED

Gnocchi alla Romana

SERVES 4–6

1 litre | 1¾ pints milk
1½ teaspoons salt
freshly grated nutmeg
225 g | 8 oz coarse-ground semolina

3 egg yolks
85 g | 3 oz Parmesan cheese, freshly grated
85 g | 3 oz butter

1 Lightly oil a baking tray.

2 In a large saucepan, bring the milk, salt and plenty of nutmeg to the boil, then remove from the heat and sprinkle over the semolina, stirring continuously with a wooden spoon.

3 Reduce the heat and return the pan to the heat. Continue to cook, uncovered, for 10–15 minutes, stirring occasionally to prevent burning and sticking, until the spoon is able to stand upright, unsupported, in the mixture. Remove from the heat and allow to cool slightly.

4 Beat in the egg yolks, 30 g|1 oz of the cheese and 30 g|1 oz of the butter. Check the seasoning.

5 Pile onto the prepared tray and smooth over with a wet spatula to about 5 mm|¼ in thick. Refrigerate for about 1–1½ hours until firm.

6 Preheat the oven to 225°C|450°F|gas mark 8. Melt the remaining butter and lightly brush a shallow ovenproof dish with a little of it.

7 Cut the semolina into circles, using a 4 cm|1½ in plain pastry cutter. Arrange the circles slightly overlapping in the prepared dish.

8 Pour over the rest of the melted butter and sprinkle with the remaining cheese. Bake in the oven for 15–20 minutes, or until crisp and golden-brown.

wine: **LIGHT RED**

Lemon and Garlic Gnocchi with Warm Borlotti Beans

SERVES 4

1 quantity well-seasoned gnocchi (see page 246)

3 cloves of garlic, unpeeled

oil

110 g|4 oz fine fresh white breadcrumbs

finely grated zest of 1 lemon

3 tablespoon chopped fresh parsley

freshly ground black pepper

150 ml|¼ pint extra virgin olive oil

2 cloves of garlic, peeled

1 small red chilli, deseeded

1 egg, beaten

oil for frying

2 tablespoons chopped fresh basil

2 × 400 g|14 oz cans of borlotti beans, drained

juice of 1 lemon

salt and freshly ground black pepper

1 Preheat the oven to 200°C|400°F|gas mark 6.

2 Make the gnocchi and leave to chill in a shallow square tin which has been rinsed with water.

3 Paint the cloves of garlic with a little oil and fry for about 10 minutes, then peel and crush.

4 Mix together the crushed garlic, breadcrumbs, lemon zest and parsley, and season with black pepper.

5 Heat the extra virgin olive oil, remove from the heat, add the garlic and chilli and leave to infuse for 30 minutes. Strain.

6 Divide the chilled gnocchi into 8 even pieces. Dip into beaten egg, then coat evenly in the breadcrumb mixture.

7 Heat enough oil in a frying pan to come halfway up the gnocchi and then fry until golden-brown on both sides. Drain well and keep warm in the oven.

8 Heat the infused oil and when hot, quickly fry the basil. When it turns bright green reduce the heat, add the borlotti beans and heat through. Add the lemon juice, salt and pepper to taste.

9 Divide the warmed beans between 4 warmed dinner plates, and put 2 gnocchi on each plate.

wine: **SPICY DRY WHITE**

Spinach Gnocchi

SERVES 6

170 g | 6 oz fresh spinach, cooked and chopped	salt and freshly ground black pepper
225 g | 8 oz ricotta cheese	freshly grated nutmeg
85 g | 3 oz Parmesan cheese, freshly grated	plain flour
1 egg	45 g | 1½ oz butter, melted

1 Combine the spinach, ricotta and half the Parmesan cheese in a bowl with the egg, salt, pepper and plenty of nutmeg. Mix thoroughly.

2 Bring a large saucepan of salted water to simmering point.

3 Meanwhile, shape the spinach mixture into egg shapes, using a tablespoon and the palm of your hand. Roll the gnocchi lightly in flour. Place them in the simmering water a few at a time and poach gently until they rise to the surface (about 2–3 minutes).

4 Preheat the grill. Remove the gnocchi from the pan with a slotted spoon, allowing excess liquid to drain off. Arrange in an ovenproof dish.

5 Pour over the melted butter, and sprinkle with the remaining Parmesan cheese. Place under the hot grill for a few minutes until the cheese is bubbly and golden-brown. Serve immediately.

wine: **DRY WHITE**

Fried Gnocchi

SERVES 6

570 ml | 1 pint milk
1 onion, sliced
1 clove
1 bay leaf
6 parsley stalks
110 g | 4 oz semolina
200 g | 7 oz strong Cheddar cheese
2 tablespoons freshly grated Parmesan cheese

1 tablespoon chopped fresh parsley
salt and freshly ground black pepper
a pinch of dry English mustard
a pinch of cayenne pepper
oil for deep-frying
beaten egg
dried white breadcrumbs

1 Infuse the milk in a saucepan with the onion, clove, bay leaf and parsley stalks over a very gentle heat for 7 minutes. Bring up to boiling point, then strain.

2 Sprinkle in the semolina, stirring continuously, and cook, still stirring, until the mixture is thick (about 1 minute). Remove the pan from the heat and add the cheeses, parsley, salt, pepper, mustard and cayenne. Taste: the mixture should be well seasoned. Spread this mixture into a neat round on a wet plate and refrigerate for 30 minutes.

3 Cut the gnocchi paste into 8 equal wedges. Refrigerate again.

4 Heat oil in a deep-fryer until a crumb will sizzle vigorously in it. Dip the gnocchi into beaten egg and coat with breadcrumbs.

5 Deep-fry in hot oil until golden-brown (about 2 minutes). Drain well on absorbent kitchen paper. Sprinkle with salt and serve.

NOTES: A thin tomato sauce (see page 128) is good with fried gnocchi.

If you do not like the idea of deep-frying, bake the gnocchi in the oven preheated to 190°C | 375°F | gas mark 5 for 20 minutes, then grill until well-browned on both sides.

wine: LIGHT RED

Fried Polenta

Polenta is a classical dish of Northern Italy. It can be eaten as soon as it is cooked, served with roasts, grills, casseroles or poultry. Or it can be left to cool, sliced and then grilled or fried. Fried polenta is particularly good served with sautéed wild mushrooms.

SERVES 4–6

2 litres | 3½ pints white stock (see page 106)
teaspoon salt

285 g | 10 oz polenta (coarse cornmeal)
oil for frying

1 Put the stock and salt into a large saucepan and bring to the boil.

2 Remove from the heat and sprinkle on the polenta, whisking quickly to prevent lumps from forming. Reduce the heat.

3 Return the pan to the heat and cover it as the mixture will bubble and spatter.

4 Continue cooking until the polenta is very thick (about 35–40 minutes), stirring often to prevent sticking and burning. Pre-cooked polenta will take 8–10 minutes to cook.

5 The polenta can be served at this stage piled high on a plate, or it can be fried as below.

6 Lightly oil a shallow tin 28 × 18 cm | 11 × 7 in. Spread the mixture out evenly, allow to cool, and refrigerate for about 1 hour.

7 Turn the polenta out of the tin, and cut into 4 cm | 1½ in slices.

8 Fill a large deep frying pan with enough oil to come 2 cm | ¾ in up the sides of the pan. Heat until very hot.

9 Add the polenta slices, being careful not to overcrowd the pan as this will make turning difficult, reduce the heat and fry gently until golden-brown on both sides. Remove with a fish slice, taking care to drain off excess oil.

wine: **LIGHT RED**

Rice and Potatoes

Farinaceous staples – rice and potatoes – are fundamental to the diet worldwide. Here we give information and cooking instructions.

Rice
by Roz Denny

It is said that around two-thirds of the world's population are nourished daily with rice. Unlike any other major food, rice is central to the cultures, and in some cases the religion, of many countries, particularly in Asia. The cultivation of rice requires great skills of irrigation which in turn has demanded levels of social organization unknown in the West. Rice farmers had to cooperate amicably if their paddy fields were to receive sufficient water for the two or more crops a year needed to sustain their families and fellow villagers. Small wonder, then, that the rice-growing nations of the world hold rice in great esteem and consider it central to their exciting and sophisticated cuisines. Unfortunately, we in the West have barely exploited the potential of rice in the kitchen, relegating it frequently to a small side accompaniment on a plate and requiring only that it should not stick!

In fact, the beauty of rice is that it has very many qualities, and it is well worth learning to discriminate between different types and brands. Texture and flavour play an important part in assessing the culinary worth of rice. This depends on the variety and growing conditions. Good rice can be compared to fine wine in that it can take on the characteristics of the soil and climate where it is grown. Unfortunately, there is no equivalent of an *appellation contrôlée* for rice sold in the West and therefore little way of knowing which is the best quality. Even higher prices are no guide. Whilst cheaper supermarket own-brand rices may well be of poorer quality than well-known brands, a well-advertised brand may lack finesse of flavour and simply be milled to a consistent, bland, non-stick standard. You are merely paying more for marketing and advertising costs.

The best guide to buying quality rices is to seek out brands bought by rice-eating people – Indians, Chinese, Thais, Arabs, and so on. Another assurance of quality is to look for the country of origin on the pack. Rice sold without a country of origin may well be a blend of grains milled to a basic standard with little to commend it to the cook.

Types of Rice

Estimates on the varieties of rice grown vary, but there are believed to be approximately 7,000, all with their own individual styles of taste, texture, colour and cooking quality. Rice is categorized botanically into either long-grain (*Oryza indica*) or short-grain (*Oryza japonica*). Indica rices (e.g. basmati) are higher in amylose starch, which keeps the grains more separate after cooking, whilst Japonica rices (e.g. sushi or risotto) are higher in amylopectin, which makes them appear more starchy. And some grains fall in between the two categories. Long-grain rices are generally more slender and longer. Short-grain rices have plumper grains and cook to a more starchy consistency, either more creamy or more sticky.

Long-Grain Rices

Originally called Patna, after the popular rice grown in India, but little rice is now sold as such. Generally it will be classified simply as long-grain. One of the biggest exporters of long-grain rice is the USA. American long-grain rice is a high-quality grain giving excellent results, sometimes said to have a natural 'popcorn' flavour. The best American long-grain is grown in Arkansas, on the delta of the Mississippi, but production is also prolific in California and Texas. Long-grain rice may also come from Spain, India, Surinam, Thailand and Australia.

When rice is sold with the bran layer intact it is known as wholegrain or brown rice.

Uses: General accompaniment for casseroles and curries. Good for chilli con carne, Caribbean dishes, salads and pilafs.

Basmati

The Prince of Rices. An elegant long-grain rice with a legendary flavour. The name basmati means 'the fragrant one' in Hindi, and good basmati will smell deliciously aromatic even in its uncooked state. The smell of basmati cooking is even better. There are very many varieties and qualities of basmati, which is grown in Iran, Pakistan and Northern India. The best comes from the state of Haryana in the foothills of the Himalayas and is sold under a brand name for export to the Middle East, Europe and the USA. Good basmati will lengthen to three times its dried length once cooked and retain a white, delicate, separate fluffiness.

Basmati is also available as wholegrain or brown basmati.

Uses: For curries, pilafs and kedgerees as well as salads, casseroles, koulibiacs, to serve with sauces and even as rice puddings.

Thai rice

Thailand, known as the rice bowl of Asia, is the world's greatest exporter of rice. (The great rice-eating nations of China, Japan and India produce most of their own rice to support their billion-plus populations and export relatively little.) Many rices are produced in Thailand but rice known specifically as Thai rice is lightly sticky or glutinous, displaying some characteristics of short-grain rices, yet retaining a good bite to the grain. This is the rice Chinese cooks like to serve at home and it is becoming increasingly popular in the West. High-quality Thai rices have a silky sheen and a wonderful natural fragrance, like a milky, sweet nuttiness, often likened to the smell of jasmine flowers. It can be sold as Thai Fragrant or specifically Thai Jasmine.

Uses: An ideal accompaniment to all Thai and Indonesian dishes as well as Indian food, Chinese and other Oriental dishes. It is excellent, too, as a stir-fry rice as the light stickiness separates out during re-frying. It also makes excellent rice puddings and rice cakes, and is good as a sushi rice.

Short-Grain Rices

Japonica varieties include risotto and pudding rices (both from Italy) and sticky rices from China and Japan.

Risotto rices

As with basmati, there are different qualities of risotto rices, and choosing the right one can make or break a dish. Risotto rices are grouped into superfini and semifini qualities. The most highly rated risotto rices are Carnaroli and Arborio, which are superfini quality, although the semifino Vialone Nano grain is highly prized by risotto connoisseurs because of its smaller, firmer grain. A good risotto grain should absorb up to five times its volume in stock and impart a creaminess to the dish while still retaining a good *al dente* bite. When risotto is left to cool it becomes solid and can be shaped into rissoles or savoury cakes. The arborio grain is particularly suitable for this use. Risottos are made differently from pilafs in that hot stock is stirred gradually into the rice, allowing each addition to be absorbed, thus encouraging the starch in the grain to give a natural creaminess to the dish.

Uses: Risottos, paella, puddings, rissoles/fritters, cakes.

Paella rice

The Moors brought rice-growing into Spain and from there it was introduced into the lush valleys of the Po river in Italy during medieval times. Paella rice is similar to risotto rice in that it is a medium-short grain rice with a creamy texture. A classic paella is shaken, not stirred, in the pan, so the right grain should be not quite as creamy as a risotto rice. However, true paella rices, such as Valencia and Bomba, are not easy to buy in the UK and USA and an arborio grain is fine as a substitute.

Pudding rice

Most of this short-grain rice comes from Italy, although at one stage the Carolinas in North America were abundant producers, hence the one-time term Carolina rice, which is not now used in the industry. Pudding rice imparts a lot of creaminess to a dish, but the grain breaks down completely on cooking and so has little else to offer the cook in the way of flavour or texture. Increasingly, chefs and cooks are experimenting with using other more flavoursome grains such as risotto, Thai or basmati rices in desserts.

Uses: Puddings either baked in a slow oven or stirred in a saucepan, to be served hot or cold.

Other Rices

Wild rice

Botanically not a true rice at all, but an aquatic grass that is native to Canada and the USA, producing dark brown grains with a delicious nutty flavour and texture. During cooking, good wild rice imparts a wonderful smell like that of new-mown grass. This is a grain that helped sustain the early settlers of North America and consequently is particularly popular in the USA around Thanksgiving and Christmas, served with turkey and game as a 'dressing' or stuffing. The best-quality wild rice has long, unbroken, dark brown, glossy grains and is grown organically around lakes in Canada where it is still hand-harvested by native Americans in canoes. Again, look for good branded wild rice rather than grains sold loose or as own-label. 'Wild' rice is also cultivated and these grains are smaller and paler in colour. Cultivated grains can be passed through a system of rollers that scratches the outside of the grain (known as scarified rice), enabling water to enter the grain quicker during cooking and so shorten the otherwise long cooking time. This grain is increasingly sold blended with basmati or white long-grain rice.

Uses: As a dressing|stuffing for turkey, also good with fish, mixed with white rice as an accompaniment, and for salads.

Red Camargue rice

A hybrid rice discovered as a happy accident by a member of the Griotto family of rice farmers in the traditional rice-growing region of the Camargue, southern France. It has a reddish-brown colour and a rather pleasant flavour slightly reminiscent of buckwheat. The texture is nutty but breaks down somewhat in cooking. It is good as an accompaniment and should be treated as a cross between wild rice and brown rice.

Uses: Similar to wild rice, for stuffings, as an accompaniment and in salads.

Glutinous black rice

This rice from South East Asia is used primarily as a pudding rice, cooked with sugar, coconut milk and lemon grass. It has a nice nutty texture and a delicious, sweet, milky taste.

Uses: As a dessert served with sliced mango, star fruits, etc.

Wehani rice

A reddish-brown, nutty-style rice from the USA, developed by the Lundburg family in California. It should be treated as brown rice and is good as an accompaniment or for stuffings and puddings.

Easy-cook Rices

The rice-milling process called par-boiling is actually based on an ancient Persian technique of treating rice grains so that they could be stored for longer. In Europe we call these rices 'easy-cook'; in the USA the term used is 'instant'. After the removal of the outer bran layer, rice grains are subjected to short bursts of intense steam which hardens the outside of the grain, causing the gelatinization of the starch. The process also has the benefit of driving the vitamins on the outside of the grain into the centre, thus making it marginally more nutritious. Manufacturers claim this makes the rice non-stick, but par-boiling deprives the grain of a lot of its natural flavour, and some would say makes the rice seem quite chewy. Easy-cook rice takes longer to cook than some varieties and the par-boiling makes the grains look yellowish, although the rice is more resistant to careless cooking. An easy-cook basmati rice seems to survive the process quite well, and much of the original flavour continues to shine through.

Cooking Methods

Allow 55 g|2 oz uncooked rice per person

Choosing the right grain for a dish is the secret of successful rice cooking. It is hard to make a pilaf with a risotto rice, or a risotto with an easy-cook rice. Also, many grains need differing amounts of water and cooking times: most brown rice, for example, needs considerably longer cooking than white. The best guide is to follow instructions on the pack. There are two main methods (see below) of cooking rice, apart from risotto and pudding rices: the open-pan method is quick and easy and so ideal for inexperienced cooks. For specific rice recipes, see pages 257–9. Note that all rice benefits from a standing time of about 5 minutes after cooking and draining so that excess water is absorbed back into the grain. Allow for this before serving. In addition, basmati rice benefits from rinsing and sometimes a little pre-soaking. This is not essential but does give a lighter, more traditional result (see page 256).

Open-Pan/Fast Boiling

Suitable for basmati, easy-cook basmati, brown basmati and other brown rices, long-grain, wild rices and wild rice blends.

Allow 1.2 litres|2 pints water and 1 teaspoon salt for each 110 g|4 oz rice.

1. Bring a saucepan of water to a rolling boil. Add salt, then stir in the rice.
2. Return to a medium boil and cook for the following times.

- Basmati and Thai rices: 10 minutes
- American long-grain: 12 minutes
- Easy-cook basmati and easy-cook long-grain: 15 minutes
- Brown basmati and wild rice with white rice blends: 20–25 minutes
- Brown long-grain rices: 25–30 minutes
- Wild rice: 40–50 minutes

3. Drain in a large sieve and briefly rinse in cool water. Allow to stand in the sieve for 5 minutes before forking through with melted butter or oil.

Covered Pan/Absorption Method

Suitable for Thai rice, sushi rice, basmati (rinsed), brown basmati, brown rice, wild rice, wild rice with white rice blends, easy-cook rices. A measured amount of water is absorbed during cooking, so there is no need to drain. Follow the instructions below according to the rice variety.

1. Put rice, water and salt to taste into a saucepan. bring to the boil, stir once, then cover and lower the heat to a gentle simmer. Do not lift the lid.

2. After the calculated cooking time (see below) remove from the heat, still uncovered, and allow to stand 5 minutes before forking through with butter or oil.

For each (225 ml | 8 fl oz) cup of rice allow:

- Thai and Sushi rice: $1\frac{1}{4}$ cups water. Cook for 10–12 minutes.
- Basmati rice: $1\frac{1}{2}$ cups water. Cook for 10–12 minutes.
- Brown basmati, wild rice with white rice blends, easy-cook rices: 2 cups water. Cook for 20–25 minutes.
- Wild rice and brown long grain rice: $2\frac{1}{2}$–3 cups water. Cook for 40–50 minutes.

Rinsing and Soaking Basmati

For a traditional, light and fluffy grain.

- Place the rice in a deep bowl. Cover with cold water and stir well with your hand. Tip out the water (the grains sink to the bottom, so there is no need for a sieve).
- Fill with more cold water, and repeat the process three more times until the water becomes clearer.
- Fill again with cold water and leave to stand for 10–15 minutes. This also helps shorten the cooking time slightly. Drain well before cooking.

Rice and Your Health

Rice is an excellent food for a well-balanced, healthy diet. For a start, it is a complex carbohydrate starchy food, and as such one of the foods nutritionists and doctors tell us we must eat more of. In fact, half our daily calorie intake should come from starchy foods such as rice. A good 50 g | 2 oz portion (uncooked weight) which swells to 150 g | 5 oz cooked weight provides approximately 170 calories, with useful amounts of B group vitamins, a small amount of easy-to-digest protein, the minerals iron and zinc and useful amounts of fibre. The starchy carbohydrate in rice does not give the body immediate energy. Rather, the energy is released slowly into the bloodstream. In other words, it is better-value energy and keeps us going longer. Rice is therefore an invaluable food for athletes.

Boiled Rice

55 g│2 oz long-grain white rice per person, rinsed
salt

1 Fill a large saucepan with salted water (1 cup of rice will need at least 6 cups of water, but the exact quantities do not matter as long as there is plenty of water). Bring to the boil.
2 Tip in the rice and stir until the water returns to the boil.
3 Boil for 10 minutes and then test: the rice should be neither hard nor mushy, but firm to the bite: *al dente*.
4 Drain the rice in a colander or sieve. Rinse briefly with cold water. Allow to stand for 5 minutes.

Boiled Brown Rice

Brown rices vary enormously, and though this method is suitable for the majority of them, some may require longer, slower cooking.

55 g│2 oz brown rice per person
salt

1 Cook the rice in a large amount of boiling salted water for 20 minutes. Drain well. Allow to stand for 5 minutes.

Basmati Rice (1)

Allow 55 g│2 oz rice per head. Rinse and soak the rice (see page 256). Put it into a saucepan and add enough cold water to cover, a pinch of salt, a cinnamon stick, 1 teaspoon lightly fried mustard seeds, and the crushed seeds from 2–3 cardamom pods. Bring to the boil, cover and simmer until the rice is cooked and the water absorbed (about 10 minutes). Remove the cinnamon stick.

Basmati Rice (2)

Allow 55 g│2 oz rice per head. Rinse and soak the rice (see page 256). Put into a saucepan with a pinch of salt. Add enough cold water to just cover the rice. Bring to the boil, then reduce heat to the simmer, cover and cook for 10 minutes, then remove from the heat. After about 5 minutes the rice should be perfectly cooked and all the water absorbed.

Steamed Rice

375 g | 13 oz long-grain white rice
450 ml | ¾ pint water
1 tablespoon vegetable oil

1 Wash the rice in several changes of water until the water is no longer milky. Drain well.
2 Put the rice into a cake tin or a Pyrex pie dish. Add the water and oil. Put the tin or dish on a steaming stand in a wok.
3 Steam, covered, over a high heat for about 25 minutes in a cake tin or 35 minutes in a Pyrex dish. The rice should be firm but cooked through. Fluff up and serve.

Fried Rice

SERVES 4

8 tablespoons long-grain rice
55 g | 2 oz pinenuts (optional, browned)
4 tablespoons oil

2 spring onions, finely chopped
salt and freshly ground black pepper

1 Bring a large saucepan of salted water to the boil and tip in the rice. Stir, bring back to the boil, and cook for 10 minutes or until the rice is just tender.
2 Fry the pinenuts in 1 tablespoon of the oil until lightly browned all over.
3 Rinse briefly with cold water to remove the excess starch and drain well. While it is draining, turn it over occasionally with a fork to allow trapped steam to escape.
4 Pour the remaining oil into the frying pan with the spring onions. Put in the rice, which should now be quite dry. Fry, turning all the time to brown evenly. Season to taste with salt and pepper.
5 Stir in the pinenuts.

NOTE: 'Easy-cook' or polished rice is much easier to fry evenly.

Chinese Fried Rice

This recipe can be changed to use up leftovers in the refrigerator as long as the essential ingredients – rice, spring onions and egg – are included.

SERVES 4–6

3 tablespoons sunflower oil

1   110 g|4 oz can of bamboo shoots, drained

½ cucumber, diced

110 g|4 oz petits pois, cooked

6 spring onions, cut into small rounds, white and
   green parts separated

2 eggs, lightly beaten with ¼ teaspoon salt

steamed rice (see page 258)

½ teaspoon salt

225 g|8 oz lean bacon, grilled and diced

225 g|8 oz cooked chicken, diced

1 tablespoon light soy sauce, plus extra to taste

1 Heat a wok, add 1 tablespoon of the oil and when hot add the bamboo shoots and cucumber. Stir-fry for 30 seconds, then remove and mix with the petits pois. Wipe the wok clean.

2 Heat the remaining oil, add the white spring onions and stir-fry for 30 seconds. Add the eggs and allow to set very slightly. Add the rice. Stir-fry vigorously, mixing the eggs thoroughly into the rice. When the mixture is hot add the salt, bacon and chicken.

3 Add the bamboo shoots, cucumber and peas and stir again until very hot. Add the soy sauce and green spring onions. Stir and add extra soy sauce to taste.

wine: **SPICY WHITE**

Sweet Sushi Rice Salad

SERVES 6

1 quantity sweet vinegar rice (see page 352)

110 g|4 oz smoked salmon, thinly sliced and
   shredded

½ cucumber, peeled, deseeded and diced

2 spring onions, thinly sliced

110 g|4 oz fine asparagus spears, blanched

1 tablespoon capers, rinsed

juice of 1 lemon

salt and freshly ground black pepper

1 Put the rice into a large bowl, add the smoked salmon, cucumber, spring onions, asparagus and capers. Toss together.

2 Add the lemon juice, salt and pepper. Toss together and pile into a serving dish. Chill for 15 minutes, then serve.

Brown Rice Pilaf with Sesame Seeds

SERVES 4–6

225 g | 8 oz brown rice

1 small onion, finely chopped

30 g | 1 oz butter

720 ml | 1¼ pints white or vegetable stock (see pages 103, 107)

salt and freshly ground black pepper

3 tablespoons sesame seeds, toasted

1 tablespoon chopped fresh mixed herbs

paprika pepper

1 Soak the rice in cold water for 30 minutes.

2 Cook the onion in the butter in a saucepan until soft but not coloured.

3 Add the rice and fry, stirring, until it is slightly transparent (about 1 minute).

4 Add the stock, salt and pepper. Bring to the boil, then cover and cook very slowly for 45 minutes, by which time the liquid should be completely absorbed and the rice tender. Add the seeds and herbs.

5 Serve sprinkled with a little paprika.

wine: **LIGHT, FRUITY RED**

Risotto with Three Cheeses

SERVES 4–6

110 g | 4 oz Gorgonzola cheese, rind removed

110 g | 4 oz mozzarella cheese

150 ml | ¼ pint warm milk

85 g | 3 oz butter

1 tablespoon olive oil

450 g | 1 lb arborio rice

860 ml | ½ pints white stock (see page 103)

salt and freshly ground black pepper

30 unsalted pistachio nuts, shelled, blanched and skinned, or toasted pinenuts

110 g | 4 oz Parmesan cheese, freshly grated

1 Cut the Gorgonzola and mozzarella cheeses into small cubes. Place in a bowl, pour over the milk and leave to stand for 20 minutes.

2 Heat the butter and oil in a flameproof casserole over a medium heat. When the butter is melted, add the rice and cook over a very low heat for 4 minutes.

3 Meanwhile, heat the stock and gradually add it to the rice, stirring continuously but gently until all the stock has been absorbed. This will take about 30 minutes.

4 Add the milk with the cheeses to the pan and stir continuously until well amalgamated (about 5 minutes).

5 Check for seasoning and add the nuts and Parmesan cheese. Leave to stand for 5 minutes before serving.

NOTE: Risotto is best made at the last minute.

wine: **LIGHT RED**

Risotto alla Milanese

SERVES 4

85 g | 3 oz unsalted butter

1 large onion, finely chopped

400 g | 14 oz risotto (arborio) rice

150 ml | ¼ pint dry white wine

1.75 litres | 3 pints white stock (see page 103)

about 15 saffron strands

salt and freshly ground black pepper

30 g | 1 oz unsalted butter

55 g | 2 oz Parmesan cheese, freshly grated

1 Melt the butter in a large saucepan and gently cook the onion until soft and lightly coloured. Add the rice and wine and bring to the boil, cook until the wine is absorbed (about 3 minutes), then reduce the heat and stir gently and continuously.

2 Meanwhile, reheat the stock in a second pan and add the saffron. Allow the stock to simmer gently.

3 Start adding the hot stock to the rice a little at a time, stirring gently. Allow the stock to become absorbed after each addition. Keep stirring constantly. Season with salt and pepper, and keep adding the stock until the rice is cooked but still *al dente* (about 30 minutes).

4 Remove the pan from the heat, add the butter and the Parmesan cheese and mix well with a wooden spoon until the butter is melted and the cheese absorbed. Allow to stand for five minutes before serving with additional grated Parmesan cheese handed separately if desired.

wine: LIGHT RED

Summer Vegetable Risotto

SERVES 4 AS A MAIN COURSE OR 8 AS A FIRST COURSE

30 g | 1 oz butter

1 large onion, chopped

1.2 litres | 2 pints boiling vegetable stock (see page 107)

a large pinch of saffron strands (optional)

110 g | 4 oz each of any 4 of the following: fresh peas, asparagus, broad beans, French beans, runner beans, carrots, courgettes

340 g | 12 oz risotto rice

110 ml | 4 fl oz white wine

6 tablespoons freshly grated Parmesan cheese, plus extra for shavings

salt and freshly ground black pepper

1 tablespoon chopped fresh parsley

1 Melt the butter in a large sauté pan. Stir in the onion. Cover with a piece of dampened greaseproof paper and a lid. Cook over a low heat until soft.

2 Place the stock in a saucepan and bring to a simmer. Add the saffron, and keep hot.

3 Prepare the vegetables: cut the asparagus and beans into 2.5 cm | 1 in lengths. Peel and slice the carrots thinly. Cut the courgettes into 6 mm | ¼ in cubes.

4 Tip the rice into the pan with the onion and stir for 1 minute to coat all the grains.
5 Pour in the wine and stir until it has evaporated.
6 Stir a ladleful of the hot stock into the rice. When the stock has nearly evaporated, stir in another ladleful.
7 When half the stock has been added, tip in all the vegetables, except the courgettes. Continue to add the stock, stirring in a ladleful at a time.
8 When nearly all the stock has been added, stir in the courgettes. The risotto is done when the rice is cooked through but still has some 'bite'.
9 Stir in the grated cheese and season to taste with salt and pepper. Allow to stand for 5 minutes.
10 Serve garnished with the parsley and shavings of Parmesan cheese.

wine: **LIGHT RED**

Potatoes

In Britain potatoes are often classified according to when they are harvested:
First earlies (new): end May–July
Second earlies (new): August–March
Main crop: September–May

The growing season for early potatoes is short. They are harvested when the tubers are immature; the skin is not 'set' and can be rubbed off easily, and they should be eaten soon after purchase as they do not keep well.

Main crop varieties are lifted when fully mature and will keep through to next year's harvest if correctly stored.

Buying and Storing

Look for potatoes that are well-shaped, firm and free from blemishes. Avoid those with green patches as these indicate exposure to light and the production of toxins (non-deadly poisons) under the skin. Buy new potatoes in small quantities as they do not keep well.

Always remove potatoes from the plastic bag in which they have been sold.

Main crop potatoes will keep well if they are stored, unwashed, in a dark, cool, frost-free, airy place away from smells. Light turns potatoes green, and warmth and dampness can cause them to sprout, shrivel and rot.

Selection of Potato Varieties

Name	Crop	Uses	Comments
Cara	Main	Baking, roasting	Large; oval; white skin; pink eyes; cream flesh; fluffy texture when cooked.
Charlotte	Second early	Salads, steaming boiling	Pale yellow skin and flesh; good flavour waxy texture when cooked.
Desirée	Main	Baking, roasting	Red skin; pale yellow flesh; fluffy when cooked.
Estima	Second early	Baking, chipping boiling, mashing	Pale yellow skin and flesh; creamy texture when cooked.
Golden Wonder	Main	Salads, baking mashing	Brown skin; pale yellow flesh; floury texture when cooked.
Kerr's Pink	Main	Baking, roasting, mashing	Pale skin with pink patches; floury texture when cooked.
King Edward	Main	Roasting, mashing	Large; pale skin with red eyes; creamy flesh; floury texture when cooked.
La Ratte	Second early	Salads, steaming	Yellow skin; cream flesh; waxy texture when cooked.
Maris Bard	First early	Salads, boiling, baking when mature	White skin and flesh; waxy texture when cooked.
Maris Piper	Main	Chipping, roasting, mashing	Thin white skin; cream coloured flesh; floury texture when cooked.

Name	Crop	Uses	Comments
Nadine	Second early	Boiling, roasting	Light skin; oval; white flesh; waxy texture when cooked.
Pentland Javelin	First early	Salads, boiling, steaming	Smooth white skin; white flesh; waxy texture when cooked.
Pink Fir Apple	Main	Salads, boiling	Pink skin; pinky-yellow flesh; waxy texture when cooked.
Romano	Main	Baking, boiling, roasting, chipping	Red skin; creamy flesh; waxy texture when cooked.
Santé	Main	Boiling, chipping, roasting	White skin; creamy flesh; floury texture when cooked.
Wilja	Second early	Boiling, baking, chipping	Rough yellow skin; pale yellow firm flesh; slightly dry but firm texture when cooked.

Fondant Potatoes

SERVES 4

900 g | 2 lb potatoes
55 g | 2 oz butter
2 bay leaves

200 ml | 7 fl oz white stock (see page 103)
salt and freshly ground black pepper

1 Wash and peel the potatoes and trim into 8-sided barrel shapes.
2 Melt the butter in a sauté pan, add the potatoes and brown lightly on all sides.
3 Add the bay leaves, stock, salt and pepper and cover with damp greaseproof paper. Cook over a low heat for about 40 minutes, or until the stock is absorbed and the potatoes tender.

4 Carefully lift the potatoes out of the pan and place in a warmed serving dish. Pour over any remaining butter and juices from the sauté pan.

NOTE: These are best made in a heavy-based aluminium pan.

Roast Potatoes

SERVES 4
900 g | 2 lb potatoes
salt
4 tablespoons dripping or oil

1 Preheat the oven to 200°C | 400°F | gas mark 6.
2 Wash and peel the potatoes and, if they are large, cut them into 5 cm | 2 in pieces.
3 Bring them to the boil in salted water. Simmer for 5 minutes. Drain well, return to the pan and shake the potatoes to roughen their surfaces.
4 Melt the dripping or oil in a roasting pan and when hot add the potatoes, turning them so that they are coated all over. Season with salt and pepper.
5 Roast, basting occasionally, and turning the potatoes over halfway through cooking. See note below.

NOTES: Potatoes can be roasted at almost any temperature, usually taking 1 hour in a hot oven, or 1½ hours in a moderate one. They should be basted and turned over once or twice during cooking, and they are done when a skewer glides easily into them. Potatoes roasted in the same pan as meat have the best flavour, but will not be as crisp as potatoes roasted only in fat.

The water in which the potatoes were parboiled can be saved and used for making gravy if no stock is available.

Château Potatoes

SERVES 4
900 g | 2 lb small, even-sized potatoes
oil or beef dripping
salt and freshly ground black pepper

1 Wash and peel the potatoes. Trim each one into a barrel shape.
2 Preheat the oven to 190°C | 375°F | gas mark 5.
3 Heat a few spoons of oil or dripping in a sauté pan. Add the potatoes and brown gently on all sides, shaking the pan constantly, until they are just brown. Season with salt and pepper.

4 Cover the pan and cook in the oven for about 30 minutes or until the potatoes are tender. (Alternatively, they can be cooked on the hob, but care must be taken that they do not burn: shake the pan frequently. Do not remove the lid as this allows the steam to escape, and the potatoes will fry rather than cook gently.)

Baked Potatoes with Chives and Soured Cream

SERVES 1

1 medium potato, well scrubbed

2 tablespoons soured cream

1 teaspoon chopped fresh chives

salt and freshly ground black pepper

1 Preheat the oven to 200°C|400°F|gas mark 6.
2 Prick the potatoes with a fork to prevent them from bursting in the oven.
3 Bake for 1 hour, or until a skewer glides easily through the largest potato.
4 Mix together the soured cream and chives and season with salt and pepper.
5 Split the potatoes without cutting them quite in half and fill with the soured cream mixture. Serve immediately.

NOTE: There is some controversy about preparing potatoes for baking: oiling and wrapping them in foil gives a soft shiny skin, wetting them with water and sprinkling them with salt gives a dull but very crisp skin.

Baked New Potatoes en Papillote

SERVES 4

675 g|1½ lb new potatoes

1 tablespoon olive oil

salt and freshly ground black pepper

1 sprig of fresh rosemary

1 clove of garlic, unpeeled

1 Preheat the oven to 200°C|400°F|gas mark 6.
2 Put the potatoes on a large piece of greaseproof paper. Turn them lightly in the oil and season with salt and pepper.
3 Add the rosemary and garlic and wrap the potatoes up in the greaseproof paper, sealing the parcel tightly so that the steam does not escape.
4 Bake for about 50 minutes, or until tender.

Boulangère Potatoes

SERVES 4

45 g | 1 oz butter

675 g | 1½ lb floury potatoes, very thinly sliced

1 small onion, very thinly sliced

salt and freshly ground black pepper

200 ml | 7 fl oz white stock (see page 103)

1 Preheat the oven to 170°C | 325°F | gas mark 3.

2 Butter a pie dish and arrange the potatoes in layers with the onion, adding a little salt and pepper as you go.

3 Arrange the top layer of potatoes in overlapping slices.

4 Dot with the remaining butter and pour in the stock. Press the potatoes down firmly – they should be completely submerged in the stock.

5 Bake for about 2 hours, or until the potatoes are tender and the top browned.

Dauphinoise Potatoes

SERVES 6–8

1 onion, thinly sliced

30 g | 1 oz butter

1 clove of garlic, crushed (optional)

290 ml | ½ pint double cream

100 ml | 3½ fl oz crème fraîche

425 ml | ¾ pint milk

1 kg | 2¼ old floury potatoes, peeled and thinly sliced

salt and freshly ground black pepper

1 Preheat the oven to 170°C | 325°F | gas mark 3.

2 Cook the onions in the butter until soft but not brown. Add the garlic and cook for a further minute.

3 Heat the creams and milk and season well. Add the sliced potatoes and onion | garlic. Simmer for 30 minutes or until the potatoes start to soften.

4 Turn the potatoes into a lightly buttered dish, and bake for 1 hour, or until tender.

Pommes Anna

SERVES 4

675 g | 1½ lb potatoes, peeled and thinly sliced

55 g | 2 oz butter, clarified (see page 385)

salt and freshly ground black pepper

freshly grated nutmeg

1 Preheat the oven to 200°C | 400°F | gas mark 6. Brush a heavy non-stick ovenproof pan with the clarified butter and heat over medium heat.

2 Arrange a neat layer of overlapping potato slices on the bottom of the pan. Brush the potatoes with butter and season well with salt, pepper and nutmeg.

3 Continue to layer the potatoes, butter and seasoning until all the potatoes have been used. Finish with butter and seasoning.

4 Set the pan over direct medium heat for 5 minutes to brown the bottom layer of potatoes.

5 Remove from the heat and cover with greased paper and a lid or kitchen foil. Bake for about 45 minutes or until the potatoes are tender.

6 Invert a serving plate over the pan and turn the potatoes out so that the neat first layer is on top.

Individual Pommes Anna

SERVES 4

450 g | 1 lb small potatoes, peeled and very thinly sliced

45 g | 1½ oz unsalted butter, melted

salt and freshly ground black pepper

freshly grated nutmeg

1 Preheat the oven to 200°C | 400°F | gas mark 6. Brush 12 individual patty tins with the melted butter.

2 Arrange one slice of potato on the bottom of each patty tin and then neatly overlap the slices with more melted butter and seasoning. You need 8 layers of potatoes.

3 Bake at the top of the oven for 30 minutes, or until golden-brown and tender.

4 Remove the potatoes from the patty tins and serve immediately.

Mashed Potatoes

This recipe is for very soft mashed potatoes. If you want a stiffer consistency, add less milk.

SERVES 4

675 g | 1½ lb potatoes, peeled

salt and freshly ground black pepper

85–150 ml | 3–5 fl oz milk

55 g | 2 oz butter

a little freshly grated nutmeg

1 Boil the potatoes in salted water until tender. Drain thoroughly.

2 Return them to the dry saucepan. Heat carefully, stirring to allow the potato to steam-dry. Push the hot potatoes through a sieve or mouli.

3 Place the potato to one side of the pan. Set the exposed part of the pan over direct heat and pour in the milk. Add the butter, salt, pepper and nutmeg. Tilt the pan to allow the milk to heat and the butter to melt.

4 When the milk is steaming beat it into the potato. Check the seasoning.

VARIATION: Add 2 peeled cloves of garlic to the cooking water in step 1. Mash the garlic in with the potatoes. Substitute olive oil for the butter.

Sauté Potatoes

SERVES 4

675 g | 1½ lb even-sized floury potatoes

salt and freshly ground black pepper

2 tablespoons oil

45 g | 1½ oz butter

1 sprig of rosemary

1 tablespoon chopped fresh parsley or rosemary

1 Cook the whole potatoes in their skins until tender in boiling salted water. Drain and peel using rubber gloves to protect your hands. Break into 2.5 cm | 1 in irregular chunks.

2 Heat the oil in a large sauté or frying pan, add the butter and the sprig of rosemary and wait until the foam subsides. Add all the potatoes at once.

3 Season with salt and pepper and shake the potatoes gently over the heat while they fry slowly until pale brown. Turn them only occasionally or they will break up too much. They should in any case be fairly dry and crumbly. This should take up to 40 minutes.

4 When delicately brown and crisp, drain on kitchen paper add the parsley or rosemary and tip into a warmed serving dish.

Pommes Parisienne

SERVES 4

6 large potatoes, peeled

2 tablespoons oil

a knob of butter

salt

1 Scoop the potatoes into small balls, using a melon baller. As you prepare the balls, drop them into a bowl of cold water to prevent discoloration. Float a plate on top to keep them submerged.

2 Heat the oil in a sauté pan and add the butter. Dry the potato balls well and toss them in the pan until completely coated with fat. Fry very slowly until they are browned and tender, shaking the pan frequently to prevent them from sticking.

3 Drain well, sprinkle with salt and serve immediately.

NOTE: Allow 15 Parisienne potatoes per head. The larger the potatoes, the easier it is to scoop them into balls.

Chips

SERVES 4

657 g | 1½ lb potatoes

oil for deep-frying

salt

1 Cut the potatoes into 5 × 1 cm | 2 × ½ in sticks. Keep them in a bowl of cold water until ready for cooking. This will prevent any discoloration and remove excess starch, which tends to stick the chips together.

2 Heat oil in a deep-fryer to a medium temperature – when a crumb of bread is dropped in it should sizzle gently.

3 Dry the potatoes carefully and place a few at a time in the chip basket – too many will stick together.

4 Fry for 7–8 minutes until soft. Remove from the oil.

5 Heat the oil again, until a crumb of bread will sizzle and brown in just 20 seconds.

6 Repeat the frying process in the hotter oil until the chips are well browned and crisp.

7 Drain the chips on absorbent kitchen paper. Sprinkle with salt.

8 Serve immediately. Do not cover the chips or they will lose their crispness.

NOTE: Chips are cooked in two stages because if the fat is hot enough to crisp and brown them, the middle of the potato will not be cooked. On the other hand, if the oil is cooler, although the chip will cook through, it will be soggy. The second frying, to create the crisp brown outside, should be done just before serving.

Game Chips

SERVES 4

450 g | 1 lb large potatoes
oil for deep-frying
salt

1 Wash and peel the potatoes. If you want even-sized chips trim each potato into a cylinder shape.

2 Slice them very thinly across the cylinder, preferably on a mandolin. Soak in cold water for 30 minutes to remove the excess starch – this will prevent them from discolouring or sticking together. Dry well.

3 Heat oil in a deep-fryer until a cube of bread will brown in 20 seconds.

4 Dry the chips very thoroughly on a tea towel.

5 Lower a basket of chips into the hot oil. They are cooked when they rise to the surface and are golden-brown.

6 Drain on absorbent kitchen paper, sprinkle with salt and serve immediately.

NOTE: Commercial plain potato crisps will do very well as game chips. Simply heat them, uncovered, in a moderate oven.

Matchstick Potatoes (Pommes Allumettes)

SERVES 4

450 g | 1 lb potatoes
oil for deep-frying
salt

1 Wash and peel the potatoes. Cut them into tiny even matchsticks and soak in cold water for 15 minutes. This is to remove the excess starch and will prevent the potatoes from sticking together. Dry them very thoroughly on a tea towel.

2 Heat oil in a deep-fryer until a crumb will sizzle vigorously in it. Fry the chips in a chip basket for 2–3 minutes, until golden brown and crisp. Drain on absorbent kitchen paper.

3 Sprinkle with salt and serve immediately.

Game Chip Baskets Filled with Chestnuts

SERVES 4

675 g│1½ lb potatoes
oil for deep-frying
45 g│1½ butter
30 g│1 oz pinenuts

1 × 400 g│14 oz can of whole unsweetened
  chestnuts
a handful of raisins
1 small bunch of white grapes, halved and any pips
  removed

1 Peel the potatoes. Slice thinly, using a mandolin or a patterned cutter so that the finished basket will look like woven straw.

2 Dip a small wire strainer or sieve into the oil to get it well greased. Heat oil in a deep-fryer until a crumb will sizzle vigorously in it.

3 Line the strainer with potato slices overlapping each other. Using a small ladle to prevent the chips floating away from the strainer as you cook them, deep-fry the 'basket' until golden and crisp.

4 Drain well on absorbent kitchen paper.

5 Melt the butter and add the pinenuts. Brown them lightly, then add the chestnuts, raisins and grapes. Fry until hot.

6 Fill the baskets with this mixture just before serving.

NOTE: A gadget for making the baskets is available in shops selling to the catering trade, but the sieve and ladle method works perfectly well.

Traditional Rösti Potatoes

SERVES 4

1 onion, finely chopped
55 g│2 oz rindless streaky bacon, finely chopped
45 g│1½ oz butter

1 tablespoon oil
675 g│1½ lb large waxy potatoes, peeled
salt and freshly ground black pepper

1 Cook the onion and bacon in half of the butter in a 23 cm│9 in non-stick frying pan over a low heat until the onion is transparent and soft but not coloured. Remove from the heat.

2 Cut the potatoes into 5 cm chunks. Place in a saucepan and cover with cold, salted water. Bring to the boil and simmer for 5 minutes. Drain, cool slightly then grate the potatoes coarsely. Fork in the onion and bacon and season with salt and pepper.

3 Heat the remaining butter and the oil in the frying pan. Add the potato mixture. Pat it lightly into a flat cake.

4 Fry over a low heat while shaking the pan to keep the potatoes from sticking until the underside is crusty and golden-brown (about 15 minutes). Shake the pan from time to time to ensure that the cake does not stick.

5 Place a plate larger than the frying pan over the pan, turn both plate and pan over and tip the rösti out on to the plate. Slip it immediately back into the pan for 15–20 minutes to cook the other side. Serve on a large flat dish, cut into wedges like a cake.

NOTES: Finely grated raw carrots are sometimes added to the mixture. The potato cake can be baked in the oven preheated to 190°C|375°F|gas mark 5 for about 30 minutes rather than fried.

Individual Rösti Potatoes

SERVES 4–6

1 Spanish onion, finely chopped
2 tablespoons oil
55 g|2 oz rindless streaky bacon, diced

675 g|1½ lb large waxy potatoes, peeled
salt and freshly ground black pepper
30 g|1 oz butter, melted

1 Cook the onion in half the oil until soft but not coloured.

2 Preheat the oven to 200°C|400°F|gas mark 6.

3 Cut the ham into short thin strips. Grate the potatoes coarsely. Season with salt and leave to stand for 20 minutes. Season with pepper and mix with the onion and ham.

4 Divide the mixture into 12 and place in patty tins. Spoon over the melted butter and bake for about 25 minutes, or until golden-brown.

NOTES: To make 1 large Rösti using this method, fry the potatoes in the butter for 5 minutes on both sides (step 4) then bake in an oven preheated to 190°C|375°F gas mark 5 for about 40 minutes or until cooked through.

Vegetables

Vegetables in Britain are usually served as an accompaniment to a main meat course. It is worth considering them, however, as first courses on their own, or as main courses if served in sufficient variety or with a sauce. For a salad or first course they may be served raw or cooked, warm or cold, and with a dressing.

To Prepare Vegetables

Always wash vegetables before preparing them. Vegetables are an excellent source of vitamins and minerals but these can easily be leached if the vegetables are cut up too far in advance of cooking, if they are left to soak in cold water (vitamin C in particular is lost in this way), if they are cut up with a blunt knife, which damages the cells, or if they are cooked with bicarbonate of soda in an attempt to preserve colour.

Cooking Vegetables

Boiling: is a general term for cooking food submerged in liquid by one of several techniques: from fast, agitated bubbling – a rolling boil – to a gentle simmer, when bubbles will appear in one part of the pan only, or to the barest tremble of the liquid, which is poaching. Boil each type of vegetable separately: bring the water to a good boil and drop in the vegetables. Use enough water to barely cover them and add 1 teaspoon salt for each 570 ml | 1 pint water. Boil as rapidly as possible, but bear in mind that delicate vegetables like broccoli can break up if too rapidly boiled.

Rapid boiling in an open pan protects the vivid colours of some vegetables, such as runner beans, while enhancing the colours of others, such as artichokes. When covered, discoloration can be caused by acids from the vegetables, which collect in the condensation on the lid and fall back into the water. The best method is to bring the water to the boil without the vegetables, add the vegetables and cover with a lid to bring them back to the boil as fast as possible, then remove the lid.

Vegetables that would be damaged by vigorous boiling are cooked by the more gentle simmering methods. Vegetables unlikely to discolour, like potatoes, carrots, parsnips, beetroot and other root vegetables, are traditionally cooked in a covered pan to preserve heat and contain fuel costs. Hence the adage: 'If it grows in the light, cook it in the open; if it grows in the dark, keep it covered.'

Refreshing: Once cooked, refresh the vegetables by rinsing them briefly under cold running water, then put them into a warmed serving dish. Refreshing prevents further cooking by the heat retained in the vegetables, and thus sets the colour. Vegetables that hold their colour well, such as carrots, or small quantities of vegetables, such as French beans for 4 people, do not need refreshing, but for large quantities it is vital, especially if there is to be any delay before serving. They can be reheated briefly before serving by any of the following methods: by being dipped in boiling water; by rapid steaming; by being given 30–60 seconds in a microwave oven; by being tossed quickly in butter over high heat. Slow reheating in the oven will discolour most green vegetables, frozen peas being the exception, although even these will eventually lose their brilliant hue.

Blanching: Some foods, especially vegetables and fruit, are immersed in boiling water without being fully cooked. It is also used to destroy enzymes in vegetables destined for the freezer and to prevent discoloration and to semi-cook or soften food, e.g. fennel in salad. This method of cooking vegetables is commonly used in restaurants where some advance preparation is vital. It is worth doing when coping with a large selection of vegetables.

NOTE: As the cooking liquid contains most of the vitamins and minerals it should, if possible, be preserved and used for soups or sauces.

Sweating: Put the prepared vegetables into a heavy saucepan with 1 tablespoon butter or oil. Place a piece of dampened greaseproof paper directly on top of the vegetables. Cover tightly with a lid. Cook over a very low heat. Stir occasionally until the vegetables are tender.

Steaming: Steaming in a proper steamer is an excellent method of cooking root vegetables, but is less successful with green ones as their bright colour is sometimes lost. It is nutritionally superior to boiling – although vegetables take longer to cook, there is no leaching of vitamins or minerals into the water.

Stir-frying: This cooking method, much beloved of Chinese cooks, is excellent for green vegetables. It preserves vitamins and minerals, and the vegetables remain bright in colour. The disadvantage is that you must stir the vegetables continuously while they cook, but the cooking time is short.

Slice the vegetables as thinly as you can, then put into a hot deep-sided frying pan (a Chinese wok is perfect) with a splash of oil. Toss the vegetables in the hot oil over a fierce heat. Shake the pan, and stir and turn the vegetables continuously until they are just tender. Sprinkle with salt and serve.

Dried Pulses

Dried peas and beans (lentils, split peas, chickpeas, green peas, black-eyed peas, haricot beans, lima beans, butter beans, brown beans, red kidney beans, etc.) are generally cheaper than their fresh or canned equivalents, are easy to cook and are very nutritious. They should be bought from grocers with a good turnover, and as a rule, small butter beans are better than large ones.

Most pulses need soaking until softened and swollen before cooking. Soaking can be done overnight but do not soak for more than 12 hours in case the beans start germinating or fermenting. If there is no time for preliminary soaking, unsoaked pulses may be cooked either in a pressure cooker or simmered for a long time in a saucepan; but remember that enough water must be used to allow the beans first to swell and then to cook. Preliminary soaking is less hazardous. As a general rule, 450 g|1 lb dried peas or beans, unsoaked, will need 1 litre|2 pints water and will cook in 30 minutes at 7 kg|15 lb pressure.

To cook the pulses, cover them with fresh cold water, bring to the boil, then simmer for 10 minutes. Change the water and simmer until tender. Boiling times vary according to the age and size of the pulses: new season's pulses will cook faster. Small lentils may take as little as 15 minutes and large haricot beans or chickpeas can take as long as 2 hours.

NOTE: Red kidney beans must be boiled fast for at least 10 minutes to destroy dangerous toxins.

Cabbage with Caraway

SERVES 4

30 g|1 oz butter
2 onions, sliced
450 g|1 lb white cabbage, finely shredded

1 teaspoon caraway seeds
1 teaspoon vinegar or lemon juice
salt and freshly ground black pepper

1 Melt the butter in a frying pan and add the sliced onions. Cover with a piece of dampened greaseproof paper and a lid. Cook over a low heat until soft but not coloured.
2 Put the cabbage into a saucepan of boiling salted water. Simmer for about 5 minutes until tender, then drain well.
3 Add the caraway seeds and vinegar to the onion and cook gently for 1 further minute.
4 Stir this into the drained cabbage and season well with salt and pepper.

Spring Cabbage with Cream and Nutmeg

SERVES 4–6

675 g|1½ lb spring cabbage
salt and freshly ground black pepper
a pinch of freshly grated nutmeg
15 g|½ oz butter
2 tablespoons soured cream

1 Shred the cabbage finely and rinse it under cold running water. Place in boiling salted water and return to the boil. Boil rapidly for 3–5 minutes until slightly soft but crunchy.
2 Drain the cabbage well, then return it to the heat to evaporate excess moisture, shaking the pan and tossing the cabbage so that it dries but does not burn.
3 Sprinkle with pepper and nutmeg. Toss in the butter. Remove from the heat and stir in the soured cream.

Brussels Sprouts and Chestnuts

SERVES 4

450 g | 1 lb very small Brussels sprouts

225 g | 8 oz fresh chestnuts

30 g | 1 oz butter

salt and freshly ground black pepper

freshly grated nutmeg

1 Wash and trim the sprouts, paring the stalks and removing the outside leaves if necessary.

2 Make a slit in the skin of each chestnut and put them into a saucepan of cold water. Bring to the boil, then simmer for 15 minutes and remove from the heat. Remove 1–2 nuts at a time and peel. The skins come off easily if the chestnuts are hot but not too well cooked.

3 Melt the butter in a frying pan, and slowly fry the chestnuts, which will break up a little, until brown.

4 Bring a large saucepan of salted water to the boil, and tip in the sprouts. Boil fairly fast until they are cooked, but not soggy: their flavour becomes unpleasant if they are boiled too long. Drain them well.

5 Mix the sprouts and chestnuts together gently, adding the butter from the frying pan. Season with salt, pepper and nutmeg.

Vichy Carrots

SERVES 4

450 g | 1 lb carrots

2 teaspoons butter

½ teaspoon salt

1 teaspoon caster sugar

freshly ground black pepper

1 teaspoons each chopped fresh mint and parsley

1 Peel the carrots and cut them into sticks or even-sized barrel shapes; or if they are very young leave them whole.

2 Put all the remaining ingredients except the pepper and herbs into a saucepan, half-cover them with water and boil until the water has almost evaporated and the carrots are tender. Then turn down the heat and allow the carrots to glaze in the remaining butter and sugar, watching to make sure they do not burn.

3 Season with pepper and mix in the herbs.

NOTE: It is important not to oversalt the water. When the water has evaporated the entire quantity of salt will remain with the carrots.

Glazed Vegetables

SERVES 6–8

450 g | 1 lb large potatoes
450 g | 1 lb carrots
450 g | 1 lb turnips
12 button onions
1 tablespoon bacon or pork dripping
½ teaspoon caster sugar

salt and freshly ground black pepper
55 g | 2 oz butter
110 g | 4 oz button mushrooms
juice of ½ lemon
1 tablespoon chopped fresh parsley

1 Wash and peel the potatoes, carrots and turnips. Peel the potatoes and cut into 2.5 cm | 1 in chunks. Dry them in a clean cloth. Trim the carrots and turnips and cut into chunks.

2 Cook the vegetables in boiling salted water for 3 minutes. Drain and refresh under the cold tap. Pat dry.

3 Peel the onions. (Dipping them into boiling water for 1 minute makes this easier.)

4 Preheat the oven to 200°C | 400°F | gas mark 6.

5 Put the prepared vegetables in a roasting pan and baste with the dripping. Roast, shaking the pan occasionally and turning the vegetables over, for 45 minutes.

6 Melt the butter over medium heat and toss the mushrooms in it. Shake the pan to make sure that every mushroom is coated with butter. When they are beginning to brown, add the lemon juice and allow this to sizzle and evaporate a little. Add salt, pepper and the parsley.

7 When the vegetables are tender, put the roasting pan over direct heat, add the sugar and shake the pan until the vegetables are browned to a good even colour. Season with salt and pepper. Keep warm.

8 Stir the mushrooms into the roasted vegetables and serve on a heated dish.

NOTE: The root vegetables can be 'pot roasted' on top of the hob instead of cooked in the oven. Toss the vegetables in the fat in a heavy casserole or saucepan. Cover with a lid, and turn the heat down low. Cook for 20 minutes or until the vegetables are tender, giving the casserole or pan a shake every now and then to prevent sticking. When the vegetables are cooked, brown them with the sugar, and fry the mushrooms as described above.

Provençal Tomatoes

SERVES 4

4 medium tomatoes
30 g | 1 oz butter
1 onion, finely chopped
½ clove of garlic, crushed
4 heaped tablespoons stale white breadcrumbs
salt and freshly ground black pepper

a pinch of freshly grated nutmeg
2 teaspoons chopped fresh parsley
1 teaspoon chopped fresh tarragon

To garnish
chopped fresh parsley

1 Preheat the oven to 200°C|400°F|gas mark 6.
2 Cut the tomatoes in half horizontally. Spoon out and strain the tomato pulp.
3 Melt the butter in a frying pan and stir in the onion. Cover with a piece of dampened greaseproof paper and a lid and cook over a low heat until soft. Add the garlic and cook for 1 further minute.
4 Mix the breadcrumbs, salt, pepper, nutmeg, herbs, and the onion mixture together with a fork. Add enough strained tomato to make a moist but not soggy stuffing.
5 Pile the mixture into the tomatoes.
6 Put the tomatoes into an ovenproof dish and bake in the oven for about 20 minutes, or until the breadcrumbs are golden.
7 Sprinkle with the parsley.

Baked Tomatoes

SERVES 4

4 tomatoes
olive oil
salt and freshly ground black pepper

1 Preheat the oven to 190°C|375°F|gas mark 5.
2 Remove the stalks from the tomatoes. Using a sharp knife cut a shallow cross in the rounded end of each tomato.
3 Drizzle with a little olive oil and season with salt and pepper.
4 Put the tomatoes into a roasting dish and bake for about 20 minutes, until soft but still holding their shape.

Bashed Neeps

SERVES 4

675 g|1½ lb swedes
30–55 g|1–2 oz butter
salt and freshly ground black pepper

freshly grated nutmeg
caster sugar (optional)

1 Peel the swedes and cut them into chunks.
2 Boil the swedes in salted water until tender.
3 Drain very well.
4 Mash with a potato masher. Beat in the butter and salt, pepper and nutmeg, and a little sugar if necessary.

NOTE: The Scots call a swede a neep (or turnip). Very confusing.

Celeriac and Potato Mash

SERVES 4

2 medium potatoes

225 g | 8 oz celeriac

150 ml | ¼ pint milk

55 g | 2 oz butter

salt and freshly ground white pepper

1 Wash and peel the potatoes and cut into 50 m | 2 in chunks. Place them in a saucepan of cold salted water. Bring to the boil, cover and simmer for about 25 minutes until tender.

2 Meanwhile, wash the celeriac, peel it and cut into chunks. Place in a saucepan with the milk. Add enough water to cover then simmer slowly for about 20–30 minutes, or until tender.

3 Drain the celeriac and mash with a potato masher.

4 Drain the potatoes and mash or sieve them. Place the potatoes and celeriac together in a clean heavy saucepan. Beat over a low heat, adding the butter as you mix. Season to taste with salt and pepper.

5 Pile into a serving dish and serve immediately.

Pea Purée

SERVES 4

1 medium onion

45 g | 1½ oz butter

150 ml | ¼ pint white stock (see page 103)

450 g | 1 lb defrosted frozen or podded fresh peas

salt and freshly ground black pepper

225 g | 8 oz mashed potatoes (see page 268)

1 Chop the onion finely and put it with the butter, stock and peas into a saucepan. Add a little salt and pepper. Place a piece of dampened greaseproof paper directly on top of the onions. Cover the saucepan and sweat over low heat until soft.

2 Add the peas and cook until tender.

3 Liquidize the peas with any remaining juice in a blender or food processor, or push through a sieve. Turn into a bowl.

3 Gradually beat the potato into the peas. The purée should be soft but hold its shape. Check the seasoning and turn into a warmed dish.

Carrot and Chervil Purée

SERVES 4

450 g | 1 lb carrots

570 ml | 1 pint white or vegetable stock (see pages 103, 107)

2 cardamom pods, crushed

1 bay leaf

2 tablespoons crème fraîche

1 tablespoon chopped fresh chervil

salt and freshly ground black pepper

1 Peel and slice the carrots. Cook in the stock with the cardamom and bay leaf for 20 minutes, or until very soft.

2 Remove from the heat and allow to cool slightly, then remove the cardamom pod and bay leaf. Drain well but reserve a little of the liquor.

3 Whizz the carrots with the crème fraîche in a blender or food processor to make a purée. If too firm, add a little of the reserved cooking liquor. Add the chervil and season to taste with salt and pepper.

Californian Vegetables

SERVES 4

12 small new potatoes, washed but not peeled

12 baby carrots, or 3 carrots peeled and sliced on the diagonal

¼ red pepper, deseeded and cut into 4 strips

¼ yellow pepper, deseeded and cut into 4 strips

4 baby sweetcorn

4 button turnips

16 French beans, topped and tailed

4 broccoli florets

2 small courgettes, each cut into 6 diagonal slices

12 radishes

12 strips of cucumber, deseeded

30 g | 1 oz butter

freshly ground black pepper

1 Cook the potatoes and carrots in boiling salted water until just tender. Drain.

2 Blanch all the remaining vegetables except the cucumber in boiling salted water for 2 minutes. Drain.

3 Melt the butter in a sauté pan, add the cucumber and toss all the vegetables in it until lightly glazed. Pile on to a warmed serving dish or divide between 4 individual serving plates and serve immediately.

Stir-fried Vegetables

This recipe can be adapted according to what you have in your refrigerator but most people would expect it to include mangetout and baby sweetcorn.

SERVES 4–6

2 tablespoons sunflower oil

1 × 2.5 cm | 1 in piece of fresh root ginger, peeled and cut into thick slices

1 clove of garlic, bruised

110 g | 4 oz baby sweetcorn, cut in half lengthways

3 sticks of celery, cut into julienne strips

2 carrots, peeled and cut into julienne strips

1 red pepper, peeled (after singeing over a flame), deseeded and cut into strips

110 g | 4 oz mangetout, topped and tailed

3 spring onions, sliced on the diagonal

85 g | 3 oz Chinese leaves, finely shredded

2 tablespoons soy sauce

2 teaspoons sesame oil

1 Heat the oil in a heavy wok. Add the ginger and garlic and fry gently for 1–2 minutes. Remove.

2 Add the baby sweetcorn, celery and carrots. Stir-fry for 1–2 minutes.

3 Add the red pepper, mangetout, spring onions and Chinese leaves. Stir-fry until the Chinese leaves begin to wilt. Add the soy sauce and sesame oil and serve immediately.

Petits Pois à la Française

SERVES 4

225 g | 8 oz peas, shelled (use frozen peas if fresh are not available)

1 large mild onion, very thinly sliced

1 small lettuce, shredded

150 ml | ¼ pint water

30 g | 1 oz butter

a handful each of fresh mint and parsley

½ clove of garlic, crushed (optional)

salt and freshly ground black pepper

1 teaspoon caster sugar

1 Mix the peas, onion and lettuce together in a flameproof casserole. Add the water, butter, mint, parsley, garlic (if using), salt, pepper and sugar.

2 Cover tightly. Put a double layer of greaseproof paper over the casserole before pressing down the lid to make a good seal.

3 Cook for about 30 minutes over a very low heat until the peas are almost mushy or, better still, bake in the oven preheated to 170°C | 325°F | gas mark 3 for 1–2 hours.

NOTE: The liquid may be thickened by the addition of beurre manié (see page 109) if preferred, but care should be taken not to mash the peas while stirring.

Vegetable Stew

SERVES 6

110 g | 4 oz dried haricot beans

55 g | 2 oz butter

3 small whole onions, peeled

2 leeks, washed and cut up

2 courgettes, cut into chunks

2 medium carrots, peeled and cut into chunks

2 sticks of celery, cut into chunks

3 small tomatoes, peeled and quartered

290 ml | ½ pint vegetable stock (see page 107)

3 new potatoes, cut into chunks

salt and freshly ground black pepper

¼ cauliflower, broken into florets

2 teaspoons plain flour

2 teaspoons chopped fresh parsley

2 teaspoons fresh chopped mint

To serve

brown rice (see page 257)

1 Soak the haricot beans for 4 hours. Cook them in fresh boiling water until tender (1–2 hours). Drain well.

2 Melt half the butter, add the onions and cook them over a low heat for 1 minute, then add the leeks, courgettes, carrots, celery and tomatoes. Pour on the stock and bring to the boil. Add the potatoes, season with salt and pepper and simmer for about 30 minutes. Add the cauliflower and beans and continue to simmer for about 15 minutes until all the vegetables are tender.

3 Mix the remaining butter and the flour to a smooth paste (beurre manié). Slip a little at a time down the side of the pan and into the mixture, stirring gently. When all the beurre manié has been added you should have a smooth, slightly thickened sauce for the vegetables. Simmer the stew for 3 minutes to cook the flour. Add the parsley and mint. Check the seasoning. Serve with brown rice.

Braised Celery

SERVES 4

15 g | ½ oz butter
1 small onion, finely chopped
1 carrot, finely chopped
1 head of celery, cut into batons
290 ml | ½ pint white stock (see page 103)

1 bay leaf
salt and freshly ground black pepper
15 g | ½ oz butter
15 g | ½ oz plain flour

1 Preheat the oven to 180°C | 350°F | gas mark 4.
2 Melt the butter in a heavy roasting pan and cook the onions and carrots in it until soft but not coloured.
3 Add the celery, stock, bay leaf, salt and pepper and bring to the boil.
4 Cover with a lid or kitchen foil and bake for about 30 minutes until tender.
5 Mix the butter and the flour to a smooth paste (beurre manié).
6 When the celery is tender, place the roasting pan over direct heat. When the liquid boils, stir in a little of the beurre manié to thicken the sauce. Do not add too much at a time. Stir until boiling.
7 Simmer for 2 minutes to cook the flour. Check the seasoning.
8 Remove the bay leaf. Transfer the celery and liquid to a warmed serving dish.

Baked Fennel with Sun-dried Tomatoes and Goat's Cheese

SERVES 4

4 even-sized bulbs of fennel
30 g | 1 oz butter
1½ teaspoons chopped fresh parsley
juice of 1 lemon
1 tablespoon olive oil
4 tablespoons water

1 onion, finely diced
6 whole sun-dried tomatoes, soaked in boiling water
   for 10 minutes
30 g | 1 oz pinenuts
140 g | 5 oz goat's cheese log, such as Roubillac
salt and freshly ground black pepper

1 Preheat the oven to 180°C | 350°F | gas mark 4.
2 Discard any damaged outside leaves from the fennel and cut the bulbs lengthways in half. Carefully remove some of the dense core.
3 Put the fennel halves into an ovenproof dish, cut side uppermost. Melt the butter in a saucepan and add the parsley and lemon juice. Pour over the fennel, add the water and cover tightly with a lid or kitchen foil. Bake in the oven for about 1 hour or until tender.
4 Heat the oil in a small saucepan, add the onion and cook over a low heat until soft and transparent. Slice the sun-dried tomatoes finely and mix with the pinenuts, diced goat's cheese and onion.

5 Increase the oven temperature to 200°C|400°F|gas mark 6.

6 Remove the fennel from the oven, take off the foil and pile the cheese mixture on top. Return to the oven for 15–20 minutes.

7 Serve immediately.

NOTE: There is no need to soak sun-dried tomatoes that have been packed in oil.

Ratatouille

SERVES 4

2 small aubergines

2 courgettes

olive oil

1 large onion, sliced

1 clove of garlic, crushed

1 medium green pepper, cored, deseeded and sliced

1 small red pepper, cored, deseeded and sliced

6 tomatoes, peeled, quartered and deseeded

salt and freshly ground black pepper

a pinch of ground coriander

1 tablespoon chopped fresh basil (optional)

1 Wipe the aubergines and courgettes and cut into bite-sized chunks. Degorge (sprinkle with salt and leave to drain for about 30 minutes). Rinse away the salt and dry the vegetables well.

2 Melt a little oil in a large heavy saucepan and add the onions and garlic. When soft but not brown, add the aubergine and fry until pale brown, adding more oil if necessary. Add the peppers and courgettes, cover and cook over a low heat for 25 minutes.

3 Add the tomatoes, salt if necessary, pepper and coriander. Cook, covered, for about 20 minutes.

4 To serve sprinkle with basil. Serve hot or well chilled.

NOTE: If you are making large quantities of ratatouille try this catering trick. Deep-fry the aubergines, peppers and courgettes in oil. Drain them and put into the saucepan with the onions, which you have gently fried in olive oil, and the tomatoes. Cook, covered, for 10 minutes with the flavourings. Deep-frying saves a lot of time, but the oil must be clean.

wine: **SPICY RED**

Red Ratatouille

SERVES 4

1 medium aubergine

olive oil

2 red onions, finely sliced

1 clove of garlic, crushed

1 large red pepper, cored, deseeded and diced

400 g|14 oz can of chopped tomatoes

a pinch of caster sugar

salt and freshly ground black pepper

a pinch of ground coriander

1 tablespoon chopped fresh purple basil (optional)

1 Wipe the aubergine, cut into bite-sized chunks and degorge (sprinkle with salt and leave to drain for about 30 minutes). Rinse away the salt and dry the aubergine well.

2 Heat a little oil in a large heavy saucepan, add the onions and fry until soft but not brown. Add the garlic and cook for a futher minute. Add the aubergine and fry until pale brown. Add the red pepper and fry over a low heat for another couple of minutes until the pepper softens a little.

3 In a seperate sauté pan, heat enough oil to cover the base of the pan. Add the tomatoes, cooked onion and garlic, sugar, salt, pepper and coriander. Cover with a lid and simmer gently for about 20 minutes until the vegetables have softened but not broken up. (If the ratatouille is too wet, remove the lid and reduce the juices.)

4 Check the seasoning and serve sprinkled with purple basil, if using.

Red Cabbage

SERVES 4

450 g | 1 lb red cabbage finely sliced

225 g | 8 oz dessert apples, peeled, cored and grated

140 g | 5 oz red onion, sliced

75 ml | 5 tablespoons red wine

150 ml | ¼ pint of water

2 tablespoons dark brown sugar

ground nutmeg, cinnamon cloves, to taste

1 Place all ingredients except the sugar and spices in a heavy based ovenproof saucepan.

2 Stir well and cook over low to medium heat on the hob for 1 hour, stirring frequently to ensure it does not catch.

3 Top up with water if it gets too dry.

4 When cabbage is cooked stir in sugar and spices to taste and continue to cook for a further 30 minutes.

Roast Parsnips

SERVES 4

675 g | 1½ lb parsnips

salt

oil

salt and freshly ground black pepper

1 Preheat the oven to 200°C | 400°F | gas mark 6.

2 Wash and peel the parsnips. Cut them in half lengthways.

3 Boil in salted water for 5 minutes. Drain well.

4 Heat 1 cm | ½ in of oil in a roasting pan in the oven. When the oil is hot, add the parsnips. Season with salt and pepper.

5 Roast the parsnips, basting and turning during cooking, until they are crisp and golden brown (about 30 minutes).

Cauliflower Cheese

SERVES 4–6

1 large or 2 small cauliflowers

salt

290 ml | ½ pint mornay sauce (see page 112)

1 teaspoon dried white breadcrumbs

1 tablespoon grated Cheddar cheese

1 Break the cauliflower into florets and cook in boiling salted water until just tender. Drain well.
2 Preheat the grill.
3 Reheat the mornay sauce. Put the cauliflower into an ovenproof dish and coat with the sauce.
4 Sprinkle with the breadcrumbs and cheese and place under the hot grill until brown.
5 If prepared in advance and chilled, bake in a preheated 170°C | 350°F | gas mark 4 oven for 20–25 minutes or until heated through and browned on top.

Vegetable Mornay

SERVES 6

1 small cauliflower

salt

225 g | 8 oz shelled fresh or frozen peas

450 g | 1 lb carrots, peeled and cut into batons

3 tomatoes, peeled and halved

570 ml | 1 pint Mornay Sauce (see page 112)

To finish

dried white breadcrumbs

grated cheese

1 Break the cauliflower into florets and cook them in boiling salted water until just tender but not soft. Drain well.
2 Boil the peas. Boil the carrots in salted water until just tender. Preheat the oven to 200°C | 400°F | gas mark 6.
3 Put all the vegetables into an ovenproof dish.
4 Heat the mornay sauce and pour it over the vegetables. Sprinkle with the breadcrumbs and cheese.
5 Bake until bubbling and brown on top. If necessary, the finished dish can be placed briefly under a hot grill.

Salsify (or Scorzonera) in Mornay Sauce

Salsify and scorzonera are classified as different vegetables but they taste very alike and are treated similarly, the only practical difference being that salsify is peeled before cooking and scorzonera afterwards. In fact both may be peeled before cooking, but the flavour of scorzonera boiled in its skin is considered to be superior.

SERVES 4

12 roots of salsify or scorzonera

salt

lemon juice (for salsify only)

290 ml | ½ pint Mornay Sauce (see page 112)

grated cheese

dried white breadcrumbs

1 For salsify, wash, peel and cut each root into 3–4 pieces.
2 Place in a pan with a little salted water and a squeeze of lemon juice and simmer, with a tightly closed lid, for 12–20 minutes, or until tender, topping up with water if necessary.
3 Drain well and arrange in a serving dish.
4 Coat with the hot Mornay Sauce, sprinkle with the breadcrumbs and cheese and brown under a hot grill.

NOTE: For scorzonera, wash and cut each root into 3–4 pieces. Place unpeeled in a pan of boiling salted water and simmer until tender (15–20 minutes). Drain well and peel off the skin. Proceed as for salsify.

Hot Raw Beetroot

SERVES 4

450 g | 1 lb raw beetroot

55 g | 2 oz butter

salt and freshly ground black pepper

a squeeze of lemon juice

1 Peel the beetroot and put it through the julienne blade of a food processor or grate it on a coarse cheese grater or mandolin.
2 Melt the butter. Toss the beetroot in it for 2 minutes until hot but by no means cooked. Season with salt, pepper and lemon juice.

NOTE: Raw beetroot in a mustard vinaigrette is also very good.

Cooked Cucumber with Dill

SERVES 4

2 cucumbers

salt and freshly ground white pepper

30 g | 1 oz butter

a squeeze of lemon juice

2 teaspoons chopped fresh dill

1 Peel and de-seed the cucumbers and cut them into 1 cm|½ in cubes.
2 Drop them into boiling salted water and cook for 30 seconds.
3 Rinse under cold running water and drain well.
4 Melt the butter in a frying pan and when foaming add the cucumber.
5 When the cucumber is beginning to turn pale brown, reduce the heat, season with pepper and lemon juice. Shake briefly to glaze. Add the dill.

Spinach Bhajee

SERVES 4

3 tablespoons oil

1 medium onion, finely chopped

1 green chilli pepper, deseeded and chopped

1 clove of garlic, crushed

2.5 cm|1 in piece of fresh root ginger, peeled and grated

2 teaspoons ground coriander

1 teaspoon ground cumin

6 cardamom pods

1 tomato, deseeded and sliced

900 g|2 lb fresh spinach, cooked and roughly chopped

salt and freshly ground black pepper

1 Heat the oil in a saucepan and fry the onion until golden. Add the chilli, garlic, ginger and spices and cook together very slowly and carefully for 1 minute.
2 Add the tomato and stir over a low heat for about 2 minutes. Add the spinach and cook for a further 4 minutes. Season with salt and pepper. If necessary, boil away any extra liquid.

Cauliflower Fritters

SERVES 4

1 large cauliflower

salt and freshly ground black pepper

oil for deep-frying

150 ml|¼ pint fritter batter (see page 570)

To serve

290 ml|½ pint tomato sauce 1 (see page 128)

1 Cut the cauliflower into florets. Boil them in salted water for 3 minutes.
2 Drain the florets well. When dry, season with pepper.
3 Heat oil in a deep-fryer until a cube of bread browns in 20 seconds.
4 Dip each piece of cauliflower into the seasoned fritter batter and drop carefully into the hot oil.
5 The batter will puff up and the cauliflower is ready when golden–brown. Drain well, sprinkle with salt and serve immediately with tomato sauce.

French Beans with Almonds

SERVES 4

450 g | 1 lb whole French beans, topped and tailed
salt
20 g | ¾ oz butter

30 g | 1 oz flaked almonds
a squeeze of lemon juice
freshly ground black pepper

1 Cook the beans in a saucepan of boiling salted water until just tender.
2 Meanwhile, melt the butter and, when foaming, add the almonds. Fry until golden-brown, cool for 30 seconds, then add the lemon juice.
3 Drain the beans well and mix with the buttery almonds. Sprinkle with pepper.

Broad Beans and Bacon

SERVES 4

3 rashers of rindless streaky bacon
450 g | 1 lb shelled broad beans
7 g | ¼ oz butter, melted

salt and freshly ground black pepper
1 tablespoon chopped fresh savory or thyme

1 Dice the bacon and fry in its own fat until crisp and brown but not brittle.
2 Boil the beans in salted water for 8 minutes.
3 Drain well and toss in the melted butter. Season with salt and pepper, then stir in the diced bacon, any bacon fat, and the savory or thyme.

NOTE: Large, tough broad beans are delicious if the inner skins are removed after boiling. Boil the beans as usual, then leave under cold running water until cool enough to handle. Slip off the skins and put the bright green beans into a frying pan with the butter, bacon and savory or thyme. Toss carefully to reheat – they are inclined to break up.

Mjadara

This is a Middle Eastern peasant dish. It is good served with a salad of finely shredded cabbage dressed with yoghurt, lemon and garlic.

SERVES 4

225 g | 8 oz brown lentils, soaked for 2 hours
1 litre | 1¾ pints water
salt and freshly ground black pepper
2 tablespoons olive or vegetable oil
1 large onion, thinly sliced
55 g | 2 oz long-grain rice

To garnish
1 raw red onion, thinly sliced
1 raw tomato, thinly sliced

1 Drain the lentils and cook in salted water in a large saucepan for about 1 hour, or until just tender but not mushy.

2 Meanwhile, heat the oil in a frying pan and cook the onion over a very low heat until soft and just brown.

3 Stir the rice into the lentils, making sure that there is enough water to cook it. Cook for about 10–12 minutes, or until the rice is tender. At the end of the cooking time the water should be absorbed by the rice and lentils. If it is not, strain in a colander.

4 Stir the onion into the rice and lentils and season with salt and pepper. Transfer to a warmed flat dish. Garnish with the onion and tomato.

Vegetable Couscous

Couscous is made from wheat. It is similar to semolina, but coarser.

SERVES 4

110 g | 4 oz chickpeas
110 g | 4 oz couscous
425 ml | ¾ pint vegetable stock (see page 107)
salt and freshly ground black pepper
4 button onions, peeled
2 leeks, roughly chopped
1 carrot, peeled and roughly chopped
1 stick of celery, roughly chopped
2 courgettes, roughly chopped
4 tomatoes, peeled and coarsely chopped
1 teaspoon chopped fresh mint

2 teaspoons chopped fresh parsley
a pinch of dried oregano
a pinch of saffron or a few shreds soaked in
1 tablespoon water

For the sauce

2 tablespoons hot vegetable stock
1 teaspoon ground cumin
1 teaspoon ground coriander
½ teaspoon chilli powder
2 tablespoons tomato purée

1 Soak the chickpeas for 3 hours. Drain them, then simmer for 1–2 hours in fresh water until tender. Drain well.

2 Cook the couscous according to the manufacturer's directions. Keep warm.

3 Put the stock, salt, pepper and onions into a large saucepan. Bring slowly to the boil and add the leeks, carrots and celery.Simmer for 30 minutes.

4 Add the courgettes to the vegetables. Cook for 2 minutes.

5 Add the tomatoes, mint, parsley and oregano to the vegetable mixture and again cover and cook for 2 minutes.

6 Add the chickpeas and the saffron, with its water if soaked, to the vegetables, and heat for 2 minutes.

7 For the spiced sauce, mix the 2 tablespoons of hot stock with the cumin, coriander, chilli powder and tomato purée.

8 Spread the couscous over a flat serving dish and pile the vegetables, with a cupful or so of stock, on top. Serve the spiced sauce separately.

Zucchini Fritters

This is one of Italy's most popular courgette recipes, hence the use of the Italian word for courgettes (also used in the USA).

SERVES 4

450 g | 1 lb courgettes (zucchini)
salt and freshly ground black pepper
plain flour

oil for deep-frying
2 egg whites

1 Cut the courgettes into thin chip-like strips. Sprinkle with salt and leave to degorge for 30 minutes. Rinse, drain and pat dry.
2 Season the flour well with salt and pepper.
3 Heat the oil in a deep-fryer until a cube of bread will brown in 20 seconds.
4 Whisk the egg whites until stiff but not dry.
5 Put the courgettes into a sieve. Add the seasoned flour and toss them in it. Then turn them in the egg white.
6 Fry a few at a time in the hot oil until brown. Drain on absorbent kitchen paper. Season with salt and pepper. Serve immediately.

Seaweed

This recipe has been adapted from Yan-Kit So's excellent *Classic Chinese* cookbook. She says: 'This Northern dish uses a special kind of seaweed which is not readily available elsewhere. However, the adapted ingredients used below do produce the desired delicious result.'

SERVES 4

450 g | 1 lb spring greens
oil for deep-frying

¼ teaspoon salt
2 teaspoons caster sugar

1 Remove and discard the tough stalks from the spring greens. Wash, then dry thoroughly.
2 Fold 6–7 leaves, or however many you can handle at a time, into a tight roll and, using a sharp knife, slice very finely into shreds. Lay out on a tray to dry. The drier the better.
3 Heat oil in a deep-fryer until a cube of stale bread will brown in 40 seconds. Add half the spring greens and fry for 30 seconds or until bright green and crisp. Remove with a large strainer and drain on a tray lined with kitchen paper. Deep-fry the remaining spring greens.
4 Sprinkle with salt and sugar and mix thoroughly.

Salads

Green Salad

1 lettuce (any kind)
French dressing (see page 123)
Choice of the following:
cucumber
fennel
celery

chicory
spring onions
watercress
green beans
peas
1 teaspoon chopped fresh mint, parsley or chives

1 Prepare the salad ingredients.
Lettuce: Wash, drain and shake to dry. Do not twist or wring the leaves together, which bruises them, but tear each lettuce leaf individually into a bite-sized pieces and place in a salad bowl.
Cucumber: Peel or not, as desired. Slice thinly.
Fennel: Wash and shave into thin slices.
Celery: Wash and chop together with a few young leaves.
Belgian Endive: Wipe with a damp cloth. Remove the tough core with a sharp knife and cut each head on the diagonal into 3–4 pieces.
Spring onions: Wash and peel. Remove any tough stalks or dry outer leaves. Chop half the green stalks finely. Keep the white part with the rest of the salad.
Watercress: Wash and pick over, discarding the thick stalks and any yellow leaves.
Beans and peas: Cook in boiling salted water until just tender and cool under cold running water. Drain well and pat dry in a tea towel.
2 Add the herbs and the spring onion tops to the dressing.
3 Mix the salad ingredients together and just before serving toss them in French dressing.

Herb Omelette Salad

SERVES 2–4

For the omelette

5 eggs

1 tablespoon olive oil

1 tablespoon chopped fresh parsley

salt and freshly ground black pepper

For the salad

2 red peppers, quartered and deseeded

2 large tomatoes, peeled and cut into strips

1 cucumber, peeled, deseeded and cut into strips

1 head of lettuce

1 bunch of fresh chives, roughly chopped

12 fresh basil leaves, chopped

For the dressing

1 clove of garlic, crushed

2 anchovy fillets, mashed

1 teaspoon Dijon mustard

2 tablespoons wine vinegar

8 tablespoons olive oil

salt and freshly ground black pepper

To garnish

10 small black olives, pitted

1 Make the omelettes: in a bowl, mix together the eggs, parsley, salt and pepper.

2 Lightly grease the base of an omelette pan with a little of the oil. When hot, add enough of the omelette mixture to thinly cover the base of the pan. The omelette mixture should be the thickness of a pancake. Cook the omelette for about 1 minute. Slide on to a plate and leave to cool. Continue to cook the remaining omelette mixture in the same way.

3 When cool, cut the omelettes into 1 cm | $\frac{1}{2}$ strips.

4 Meanwhile, prepare the salad: place the peppers skin-side up under a hot grill. When the skins are black, place the peppers in a plastic bag to cool. Peel away the skins then cut the flesh into 1 cm | $\frac{1}{2}$ in strips.

5 Prepare the dressing: whizz the ingredients in a blender. Season with salt and pepper.

6 Save a handful of the salad ingredients for garnish then mix together the remaining salad ingredients, the omelette strips and the herbs. Add the dressing and toss well.

7 Pile on to a serving dish and scatter over the garnish.

wine: **LIGHT TO MEDIUM RED**

Bitter Leaf Salad

slightly bitter leaves: watercress; young kale; curly endive; young spinach; chicory; lamb's lettuce; radicchio; rocket; frisée

For the dressing

3 tablespoons salad oil

1 tablespoons olive oil

1 tablespoon red wine vinegar

1 teaspoon French mustard

salt and freshly ground black pepper

1 Mix the dressing ingrèdients together using a small whisk.

2 Wash and dry the salad leaves, discarding any tough stalks.

3 Toss the salad in the dressing and tip into a clean bowl.

Caesar Salad

SERVES 4

2 large cloves of garlic, slivered

150 ml | ¼ pint olive oil

1 tablespoon white wine vinegar

squeeze of lemon juice

a pinch of dry English mustard

freshly ground black pepper

1 egg, boiled in its shell for 1 minute

2 anchovy fillets, rinsed and finely chopped

2 slices of bread, crusts removed, cubed

1 cos lettuce, torn into bite-size pieces

4 tablespoons freshly grated Parmesan cheese

1 Mix the garlic with the oil. Leave to stand for 10 minutes. Strain off 3 tablespoons of the oil to make the dressing.

2 Add it to the vinegar, lemon juice, mustard, pepper and egg. Whisk well. Add the anchovies.

3 Pour the remaining oil and the garlic into a frying pan. There should be at least 1 cm | ½ in oil. Heat slowly. When the garlic shreds begin to sizzle, remove, add the bread cubes and fry, turning frequently with a fish slice or spoon, until the croûtons are crisp and brown. Using a perforated spoon, lift out the croûtons and drain and allow to cool on absorbent kitchen paper.

4 Toss the lettuce in the dressing. Sprinkle over the croûtons and cheese.

Tomato and Basil Salad

SERVES 4

6 tomatoes, peeled and sliced

8–10 fresh basil leaves, roughly chopped

French dressing (see page 123)

1 Arrange the tomato slices on a plate.

2 Mix the dressing and basil together and spoon over the tomatoes.

Carrot and Mint Salad

SERVES 4

½ teaspoon caster sugar

a large pinch of ground cumin

French dressing (see page 123)

8 large carrots

2 tablespoons chopped fresh mint

salt and freshly ground black pepper

1 Mix the sugar and cumin with the dressing.

2 Peel the carrots and grate coarsely into the French dressing.

3 Add the mint and toss the salad well. Check the seasoning.

Fennel and Walnut Salad

SERVES 6

2 large or 3 small bulbs of Florence fennel

110 g|4 oz fresh shelled walnuts, roughly chopped

1 tablespoon chopped fresh marjoram

French dressing made with walnut oil (see page 123)

1 Remove the feathery green tops of the fennel and set aside. Wash, then finely slice the fennel heads, discarding any tough outer leaves or discoloured bits.

2 Blanch the fennel in boiling water for 1 minute to soften slightly. Refresh under cold running water until cool. Drain well on absorbent kitchen paper, or dry in a tea towel.

3 Mix together the fennel, nuts and marjoram and moisten with a little French dressing. Pile into a salad bowl.

4 Chop the green fennel leaves and scatter them over the salad.

Fennel, Red Onion and Red Pepper Salad

SERVES 4–6

For the dressing

1 tablespoon wine vinegar

3 tablespoons salad oil

a pinch of dry English mustard

salt and freshly ground black pepper

½ medium red onion, very finely sliced

1 large or 2 small heads of fennel

1 red pepper

For the salad

½ medium red onion

1 red pepper

1 large or 2 small heads of fennel

1 Whisk the dressing ingredients together.

2 Stir the onion into the dressing.

3 Remove and discard the seeds and membrane from the pepper. Cut the flesh into quarters. Place, skin side up, under a very hot grill. Grill until very black. Place in a plastic bag to cool. Skin and cut the flesh into strips.

4 Remove the feathery green tops of the fennel and set aside. Thinly slice the fennel heads, discarding any tough outer leaves. Blanch in boiling salted water for 1 minute. Refresh under cold running water. Drain well.

5 Toss everything in the dressing and tip into a clean salad bowl. Chop the green fennel leaves and scatter over the salad.

Japanese-Style Cucumber and Carrot Salad

This recipe is by Madhur Jaffrey from *The Taste of Health*.

SERVES 4–6

1 large cucumber

1 small carrot

1 tablespoon unhulled sesame seeds

2 tablespoons soy sauce

$1\frac{1}{2}$ tablespoons distilled white vinegar

1 Peel the cucumber and cut it diagonally into wafer-thin, long, oval shapes. Put them into a bowl.

2 Peel the carrot and cut this similarly. Put into the bowl with the cucumber.

3 Put the sesame seeds into a small cast-iron frying pan and place over a low heat. Cook, shaking the pan, until the sesame seeds begin to brown evenly (just a few minutes). When the seeds start popping, they are ready. You can also spread the sesame seeds out on a tray and roast them under a hot grill. They should turn just a shade darker.

4 Pour the soy sauce and vinegar over the salad, and mix thoroughly. Sprinkle on the sesame seeds and mix again. Serve immediately.

Chinese Cabbage and Apple Salad

SERVES 4

450 g | 1 lb Chinese cabbage (Chinese leaves)

2 dessert apples

chopped fresh parsley

1 tablespoon wine vinegar

3 tablespoons chopped fresh mint

2 tablespoons soured cream

salt and freshly ground black pepper

For the dressing

3 tablespoons oil

1 Whisk together all the dressing ingredients. Season well with salt and pepper.

2 Shred the cabbage finely. Slice the apples but do not peel them.

3 Toss the cabbage and apple in the dressing.

4 Tip into a salad bowl and sprinkle with plenty of parsley.

Mushroom and Coriander Seed Salad

SERVES 4

225 g | 8 oz button mushrooms

French dressing (see page 123)

2 teaspoons coriander seeds, lightly toasted

1 onion, sliced

sunflower oil

freshly ground black pepper

1 Wipe the mushrooms, slice fairly thinly and leave to marinate in the French dressing.

2 Crush the coriander seeds very well in a pestle and mortar and add to the mushrooms. Leave for 2 hours.

3 Cook the onion until soft but not brown in a minimum amount of oil in a non-stick frying pan. Remove from the heat and cool, then add to the mushrooms and season well.

Spinach Salad with Bacon and Yoghurt

SERVES 4

450 g | 1 lb fresh young spinach

6 rashers of rindless streaky bacon

For the dressing

2–3 tablespoons plain yoghurt

2 tablespoons oil

2 teaspoons wine vinegar

1 teaspoon French mustard

½ clove of garlic, crushed

salt and freshly ground black pepper

caster sugar to taste

1 Preheat the grill.

2 Wash the spinach and remove the stalks. Dry thoroughly.

3 Grill the bacon for about 2 minutes on each side until brown and crispy. Cool, then chop.

4 Mix all the dressing ingredients together.

5 Toss the spinach and bacon in the dressing just before serving.

Salade Niçoise

SERVES 3–6

For the dressing

1 tablespoon wine vinegar

3 tablespoons olive oil

salt and freshly ground black pepper

½ clove of garlic, crushed

1 tablespoon finely chopped fresh mixed herbs

½ red onion, thinly sliced

3 tomatoes, peeled and quartered

225 g│8 oz cooked French beans

1 × 200 g│7 oz can of tuna fish

1 red pepper, cored, deseeded and sliced

1 lettuce heart

6 anchovy fillets, split lengthways

2 hardboiled eggs, quartered lengthways

8 black olives

450 g│1 lb small new potatoes, cooked

1 Put all the dressing ingredients into a large bowl and whisk well. Stir in the sliced onions.

2 Arrange the salad ingredients carefully on to a platter or individual plates. Drizzle over the dressing.

Bean and Bean Salad

SERVES 4

450 g│1 lb fresh French beans, topped and tailed

450 g│1 lb cooked or canned haricot beans or butter beans

1 tablespoon lemon juice

salt and freshly ground black pepper

1 small clove of garlic, crushed

3 tablespoons salad oil

2 tablespoons chopped fresh basil or spring onion tops

1 Boil the French beans in salted water until just tender. Drain and refresh under cold running water to prevent further cooking and preserve their colour. Drain well.

2 Drain the haricot or butter beans if they are canned and rinse away any starchy water. When they are dry mix them with the cooked French beans and put into a dish.

3 Mix together the ingredients for the dressing. Pour over the salad.

NOTE: All types of beans are good – fresh broad beans (especially if the inner skins are removed after cooking), dried lima beans, canned flageolets, etc.

Watercress Salad with Croûtons

SERVES 4–5

For the dressing

3 tablespoons oil

1 tablespoon wine vinegar

salt and freshly ground black pepper

½ clove of garlic, crushed

1 teaspoon chopped fresh parsley

a pinch of sugar (optional)

oil for deep-frying

4 slices of white bread, crusts removed, cubed

2 bunches of watercress, trimmed

1 Whisk together all the dressing ingredients.

2 Make the croûtons: heat oil in a deep-fryer until a cube of bread will brown in 20 seconds. Fry the bread cubes until golden-brown and crisp. Drain well on absorbent kitchen paper. Sprinkle lightly with salt.

3 Just before serving toss the watercress in the French dressing, tip into a clean salad bowl and sprinkle the croûtons on top.

Salad of Roast Tomatoes and Spring Onions

SERVES 4

10 medium ripe tomatoes

olive oil

salt and freshly ground black pepper

caster sugar to taste

sprigs of fresh thyme

2 tablespoons of oil

½ bunch of spring onions, trimmed and cleaned, sliced on the diagonal

For the dressing

1 teaspoon Dijon mustard

2 teaspoons tarragon vinegar

2 teaspoons white wine vinegar

2 tablespoons olive oil

To garnish

3 tablespoons vegetable oil

½ bunch of flat-leaf parsley, chopped

1 Preheat the oven to 200°C|400°F|gas mark 6. Cut the tomatoes in half vertically and scoop out the seeds. Drain the tomatoes thoroughly on absorbent kitchen paper.

2 Brush a baking sheet with oil. Arrange the tomatoes cut side up on the sheet. Season with salt, pepper and sugar. Scatter with sprigs of thyme and drizzle over more oil.

3 Roast for 10–15 minutes until the tomato flesh just gives when touched.

4 Arrange 5 tomato halves, cut side down, on each individual serving plate.

5 Place the oil in a frying pan and sauté the spring onions for about 2 minutes. Scatter over the roasted tomatoes.

6 Whisk the dressing ingredients together, check the seasoning, and drizzle over the tomatoes. Sprinkle with parsley.

NOTE: This dish is ideally made with plum tomatoes.

Pasta and Red Pepper Salad

SERVES 4

2 red peppers
225 g | 8 oz pasta, preferably spirals
salt
1 tablespoon oil

110 g | 4 oz broccoli
French dressing (see page 123)
chopped fresh sage

1 Preheat the grill to its highest setting.
2 Cut the peppers into quarters and remove the stalk, inner membrane and seeds.
3 Grill the peppers, skin side uppermost, until the skin is black and blistered. Place in a plastic bag to cool. Remove all the skin. Cut the flesh into strips.
4 Cook the pasta in plenty of boiling salted water with oil. Drain well and leave to cool.
5 Cook the broccoli in boiling salted water. Refresh under cold running water. Drain well and leave to cool.
6 Toss the pasta, pepper, broccoli, French dressing and sage together.

Rice Salad

Almost any vegetables can be added to cold cooked rice to make a salad, but it is important to have approximately equal quantities of rice and vegetables, or the result may be lifeless and stodgy. The dressing should moisten, not soak, the dish.

SERVES 8

For the dressing

4 tablespoons salad oil
1 tablespoon vinegar
½ small onion, very finely chopped
salt and freshly ground black pepper

225 g | 8 oz long-grain rice
110 g | 4 oz frozen peas

1 red pepper, cored, deseeded and chopped
1 small stick of celery, chopped
¼ cucumber, peeled and chopped
2 tomatoes, peeled and cut into strips
2 tablespoons finely chopped fresh parsley, mint, chives or dill

1 Whisk together all the dressing ingredients.
2 Boil the rice in plenty of water until just tender (about 10 minutes). Add the peas 4 minutes before the end of cooking. Rinse in cool water and drain well.
3 While the rice is still warm, stir in the dressing. Spread the rice thinly on a tray and allow to cool.
4 Mix everything together and add salt and pepper if necessary.

New Potato Salad

SERVES 4

675 g | 1½ lb even-sized new potatoes

salt

1 sprig of fresh mint

4 tablespoons French dressing (see page 123)

150 ml | ¼ pint soured cream

1 tablespoon mayonnaise (page 117)

2 tablespoons chopped fresh chives

1 Scrape the skins from the potatoes, if desired, then cut if large. Boil with the mint in a saucepan of salted water until just tender. Drain.

2 Toss the potatoes in the French dressing while still hot. Leave to cool.

3 Mix the soured cream with the mayonnaise. Add half the chives.

4 Turn the potatoes in this creamy dressing and tip into a salad bowl.

5 Sprinkle with the remaining chives.

NOTE: There is always controversy about peeling new potatoes. The best, very new, pale ones need little more than washing. Most need scraping, and some – usually large, dark and patently not very new – need peeling after cooking.

New Potatoes Vinaigrette

SERVES 4

675 g | 1½ lb small new potatoes

salt

1 small bunch of fresh mint

French dressing (see page 123)

1 tablespoon chopped fresh chives

1 shallot, finely chopped

1 Wash the potatoes and scrape them, but do not peel. Cook in boiling salted water with a sprig of mint until tender. Chop 8–10 mint leaves finely.

2 Mix the French dressing with the chopped mint, chives and shallot.

3 Drain the potatoes well and toss immediately in the French dressing. Leave to cool and toss again just before serving. Decorate with fresh mint leaves.

Coleslaw with Raisins and Walnuts

SERVES 4

225 g | 8 oz firm white cabbage, very finely shredded

3 small carrots, coarsely grated

3 tablespoons mayonnaise (see page 117)

1 teaspoon French mustard

1 teaspoon sugar

salt and freshly ground black pepper

1 tablespoon raisins

1 tablespoon chopped walnuts

1 Toss the cabbage and carrots together in a bowl.

2 Mix the mayonnaise with all the remaining ingredients and combine it with the cabbage and carrots.

NOTE: Mayonnaise for coleslaw is delicious made with cider vinegar.

Avocado, Apple and Lettuce Salad

SERVES 4

1 dessert apple
French dressing (see page 123)

1 ripe avocado
1 small Cos or round lettuce

1 Cut the unpeeled apple into chunks, and put straight into the French dressing.
2 Peel and cut the avocado into cubes and turn carefully with the apple in the French dressing until completely coated.
3 Arrange the lettuce on 4 plates and top with the avocado and apple.

Red Pepper Salad

SERVES 4

4 red peppers
1 clove of garlic
½ teaspoon salt
3 tablespoons extra virgin olive oil

4 anchovy fillets
1 teaspoon chopped fresh oregano
3 tablespoons pitted black olives

1 Preheat the grill to its highest setting. Cut the peppers into quarters and remove the membrane and seeds. Grill the skin side of the peppers until they are blistered and blackened all over. Place in a plastic bag to cool. The steam will help loosen the skins. Remove the skins. Cut the flesh into strips.
2 Crush the garlic with the salt and add the oil and anchovies. Mash well together. Add the oregano and toss in the red pepper strips. Mix with the olives.

Quinoa and Lime Salad

SERVES 8

225 g│8 oz quinoa
720 ml│1¼ pints water
salt

4 small cloves of garlic, crushed
1 tablespoon each chopped fresh flat-leaf parsley,
   basil and coriander

For the dressing

juice of 3 limes
125 ml│4 fl oz groundnut oil
salt and freshly ground black pepper
1 tablespoon caster sugar
1 tablespoon dry-roasted Sichuan peppercorns,
   ground

To serve

10 Kalamata olives, pitted and slivered
140 g│5 oz cooked kidney beans
1 head of radicchio
1 small bunch of fresh basil or coriander

1 Rinse and drain the quinoa well before use to remove bitterness. It can then be lightly toasted in oil to enhance the flavour, if you wish.

2 Cook the quinoa according to the manufacturer's directions. Drain well and allow to cool.

3 Make the dressing: put the ingredients into a blender and process until smooth, then season well to make a strong-flavoured dressing.

5 Mix the dressing with the quinoa and mix in most of the olives and the kidney beans, reserving a few for garnish.

6 Line a serving bowl with the radicchio leaves, spoon in the quinoa, scatter over the reserved olives and kidney beans and garnish with basil or coriander leaves.

NOTES: Quinoa is a South American grain which looks like tapioca. It is available in health food shops.
  The dressing is also very good with hot or cold pasta. It should be made on the day that it is eaten as it loses some of its brilliant green colour if kept overnight.

Three-pea Salad

SERVES 8

110 g | 4 oz brown lentils
110 g | 4 oz chickpeas, soaked for 3 hours
110 g | 4 oz split green peas
150 ml | ¼ pint French dressing (see page 123)
1 teaspoon chopped fresh mint
1 tablespoon chopped fresh parsley
1 teaspoon French mustard
salt

1 Cook the lentils, chickpeas and split green peas in separate saucepans of boiling water. The lentils and split peas will take between 30 to 75 minutes, and the chickpeas up to 2 hours. Rinse them all under cold running water and drain well.

2 Whisk the dressing until well emulsified. Add the herbs and mustard and shake again. Mix with the lentils, chickpeas and peas and pile into a serving dish.

NOTE: Other pulses, such as soya beans, red kidney beans and haricot beans, are good treated similarly.

Tabbouleh

Recipes for this are legion. The important thing is that the salad should be green and have a good lemon flavour.

SERVES 4

110 g | 4 oz bulghur (cracked wheat)
1 tomato, peeled, deseeded and chopped
½ cucumber, deseeded and chopped
10 fresh mint leaves, finely chopped
a good handful of fresh parsley, finely chopped

1 shallot, finely chopped
3 tablespoons olive oil
salt and freshly ground black pepper
lemon juice

1 Cook the bulghur according to manufacturer's directions. Drain and wrap in a clean tea towel. Squeeze out the moisture. Spread the wheat on a tray to dry further.
2 Mix all the ingredients together, adding salt, pepper and plenty of lemon juice to taste.

Cracked Wheat and Chickpea Salad

SERVES 4

170 g | 6 oz fine cracked wheat
1   400 g | 14 oz can of chickpeas, drained and rinsed
200 g | 7 oz red pesto (see page 125)

4 tablespoons roughly chopped fresh coriander
4 sun-dried tomatoes, very finely chopped
salt and freshly ground black pepper

1 Cook the cracked wheat according to the manufacturer's directions.
2 Mix together the cracked wheat and chickpeas with the pesto, coriander and sun-dried tomatoes. Season to taste with salt and pepper.

Fish and Shellfish

Fish are classified according to the location where they are spawned either in fresh water or in the sea. Freshwater fish are divided into coarse fish, fished mainly for sport and generally thrown back live into the rivers, and game fish, which are caught both for sport and commercially. Much freshwater fish in fact comes from fish farms. Many freshwater fish, such as bass, sturgeon, sea trout and salmon, spend most of their adult lives in the sea, swimming back up the rivers to spawn, but they are still classified as freshwater fish despite the fact that most of them are caught by trawl in the sea. Coarse river fish, such as roach, gudgeon and tench, are not sold commercially and are seldom eaten except by anglers' families. It is increasingly difficult today to get locally caught fish. Fish is frozen or deep-chilled on trawlers and immediately exported.

Fish is a valuable source of protein, vitamin D (in oily fish), calcium and phosphorus (found especially in the edible bones of whitebait, sardines, etc.), iodine, fluorine and some of the B vitamins. Fish contains very little fat, and even oily fish seldom has more than 20 per cent fat content. The fat in fish is polyunsaturated and contains essential fatty acids that cannot be obtained elsewhere.

Like meat, fish is composed of muscle fibres that vary in length and thickness according to type. For example, lobster has long and coarse fibres and herring very fine fibres.

The fibres are generally shorter than in meat and are packed in flakes with very little connective tissue between them. The fat is dispersed among the fibres. The connective tissue is very thin and is quickly converted to gelatine when cooked.

Because of its structure, fish is naturally more tender than meat, and over-vigorous or overlong cooking will cause dryness and disintegration as the connective tissue dissolves and the flakes fall apart. The protein in the fibres coagulates, the fish begins to shrink and the juices are extracted – in dry heat there is a more rapid loss of juices. In moist heat soluble nutrients and flavouring minerals are lost into the liquid. Overcooked fish is dry, tough and tasteless.

Fish does not keep well and should be eaten as fresh as possible. Fish live in cold water, they are cold-blooded and their enzymes work at very low temperatures. Thus they continue, unlike meat, to deteriorate in the refrigerator.

Fish should be cooked quickly by grilling or frying, or slowly by poaching. If frying or grilling, the fish should be protected from the fierce heat by a coating of seasoned flour, beaten egg, breadcrumbs or a batter. If poaching, use a well-seasoned court bouillon and then use this liquid to make the sauce so that none of the flavour is lost. Drain fish well after it has been poached, and do not keep it warm as it will dry out and become tough and tasteless.

Preparation for Cooking

Removing the scales

Some fish have dry scales which should be removed before cooking. To do this, scrape the back of a large knife the wrong way along the fish (from tail to head). This can be a messy business as the scales tend to fly about; place the fish in a plastic carrier bag to prevent this. However, unless you are buying fish from a wholesale market, the fishmonger will do it for you.

Remove the scales with the back of a knife

Gutting and cleaning

The fishmonger will probably clean the fish, but if you are to do it yourself you will need a very sharp knife. If the fish is to be stuffed or filleted it does not matter how big a slit you make to remove the entrails. Start just below the head and slit through the soft belly skin. After pulling out the innards, wash the fish under cold water. If it is large, and of the round type, make sure all the dark blood along the spinal column is removed. Now carefully cut away the gills. Take care not to cut off the head if you want to serve the fish whole. If you do not, cut off head and tail now. To remove the fins, cut the skin round them, take a good grip (if you salt your fingers well it will stop them slipping) and yank sharply towards the head. This will pull the fin bones out with the fin.

Remove the innards and wash thoroughly

Skinning a whole flat fish

Fish skin is easier to remove after cooking. But sometimes the fish must be skinned beforehand. Most whole fish are not skinned or filleted before grilling, but sole (and lemon sole, witch and plaice) are skinned on at least the dark side, and sometimes on both sides. To do this, make a crossways slit through the skin at the tail, and push a finger in. You will now be able to run the finger round the edge of the fish loosening the skin. When you have done this on both edges, salt your fingers to prevent slipping, take a firm grip of the skin at the tail end with one hand, and with the other hold the fish down. Give a quick strong yank, peeling the skin back towards the head. If necessary, do the same to the other side.

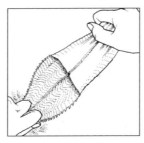

Remove the skin from a flat fish in one piece

Filleting flat fish

Flat fish are generally filleted into four quarter fillets. To do this, lay the fish on a board with the tail towards you. Cut through the flesh to the backbone along the length of the fish. Then, with a sharp pliable knife, cut the left-hand fillet away from the bone, keeping the blade almost flat against the bones of the fish. Then swivel the fish round so the head is towards you and cut away the second fillet in the same way. Turn the fish over and repeat the process on the other side. (If you are left-handed, tackle the right-hand fillet first.)

To fillet a flat fish, stroke the flesh away from the bones

Filleting and skinning round fish

Round fish are filleted before skinning. They do not have to be gutted if they are going to be filleted. If they are to be cooked whole, they are cooked with the skin, but this may be carefully peeled off after cooking, as in the case of a whole poached salmon. To fillet a round fish, lay it on a board and cut through the flesh next to the dorsal fin along the backbone from the head to the tail. Insert a sharp pliable knife between the flesh and the bones, and slice the fillet away from the bones, working with short strokes from the backbone and from the head end. Remember to keep the knife as flat as possible, and to keep it against the bones. When the fillet is almost off the fish you will need to cut through the belly skin to detach it completely. Very large round fish can be filleted in four, following the flat fish method, or the whole side can be lifted as described here, and then split in two once off the fish.

To skin a fish fillet

Put it skin side down on a board. Hold the tip down firmly, using a good pinch of salt to help get a firm grip. With a sharp, heavy, straight knife, cut through the flesh, close to the tip, taking care not to go right through the skin. Hold the knife at a 30° angle to the fish fillet. Use a gently sawing motion, cut the flesh from the skin.

To bone small fish

Split the fish open completely through the belly, clean thoroughly and lay, skin side up, on a board. With the heel of your hand, press down firmly on the backbone of the fish. This will loosen it. Turn it over, cut through the backbone near the head, and pull it out with all the side bones, or nearly all the side bones, attached to it.

Pinboning fish

This is done to remove all the small bones that run along the flanks of the fish through the flesh.

Fish should be pinboned either before or after cooking. Run the tips of the fingers of one hand over the surface of the flesh to locate the ends of the small bones. Pull the bones out with tweezers or pliers.

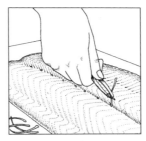

Remove the bones with tweezers or pliers

Skinning eel

Cut through the skin round the neck and slit the skin down the length of the body. Hang the eel up by its head – a stout hook through the eyes is best. Using a cloth to get a good grip, pull hard to peel off the skin from neck to tail.

Stuffing fish

Round fish are more suitable for stuffing whole than flat fish, as there is more space in the body cavity after gutting. Stuffings usually contain breadcrumbs, which swell during cooking, so care should be taken not to overfill the fish. Fish fillets can be sandwiched with stuffing, or rolled up round the mixture. Well-flavoured expensive fish is less often stuffed than the more bland varieties, which benefit from the additional flavour of an aromatic filling.

Seasonal Table of Commercial Fish Available in the U.K.

Fish Family	Season	Category	Type
Salmonidae			
Salmon – farmed	all year	Oily/Fresh and Seawater	Mainly Pelagic
Salmon – wild	May–Sept		
Trout – farmed	all year	Round	
Trout – wild	various		
Others include:			
Char			
Pacific salmon species			
Gadidae		White/Seafish	Mainly Demersal
Cod	June–Feb		
Haddock	May-June	Round	
Coley	August–Feb		
Pollack	May-Sept		
Ling	June–Feb		
Whiting	June–Feb		
Hake	June–March		
Scombridae		Oily/Seafish	Pelagic Shoaling
Mackerel	All year		
Tuna	All year	Round	
Clupeidae		Oily/Seafish	Pelagic Shoaling
Herring	May–Dec		
Anchovy	June–Dec	Round	
Sardine	Jan/Feb/April/ Nov/Dec		
Sprat	Oct–March		
Bothidae		White/Seafish	Demersal
Turbot	April–Feb		
Brill	June–Feb	Flat	
Pleuronect		White/Seafish	Demersal
Plaice	May–Feb		
Halibut	June–March	Flat	
Lemon sole	May–March		
Solidae		White/Seafish	Demersal
Dover/Slip soles	May–Feb	Flat	
Rajidae		White/Seafish	Demersal
Skate	May–Feb	Flat	
Lophiidae		White/Seafish	Demersal
Monkfish	All year	Round	
Zeidae		White/Seafish	Pelagic
John Dory	All year	Round	
Triglidae		White/Seafish	Demersal
Gurnard	July–Feb	Round	

Fish Family	Season	Cateogry	Type
Mullidae **Red mullet**	May–Nov	White/Seafish Round (Highest oil content of all white fish)	Demersal
Muglidae **Grey mullet**	Sept–Feb	White/Seafish Round	Demersal and Pelagic
Moronidae **Seabass** **Others include:** **Wrasse** **Ocean perch** **Rockfish**	August-March	White/Seafish Round Round	Pelagic/ Shoaling
Imported Species Inc. **Mahi mahi** **Red snapper** **Croakers** **Orange roughy** **Barracudas** **Grouper** **Sea bream** **Pomfrets etc . . .**	All year (previously frozen)	Round	
Deepsea Dwellers **Marlin** **Swordfish** **Shark family** **Includes:** **Porbeagle** **Tope** **Mako** **also** **Huss**	All year (previously frozen)	Various Round (mainly white)	Various
Shellfish			
Crustacea **Crabs** **Brown edible** **Spider** **Many other** **species** **Lobster** **Rock/Spiny** **Prawns** **Various** **species** **Others include:** **Crayfish** **Dublin Bay prawn (scampi)**	 April–Dec April–Oct April–Nov All year worldwide		
Molluscs Bivalve			
Mussel **Oyster** **Scallop** **Clam** **Cockle**	Sept–March All year Sept–March All year May–Dec		

Fish Family	Season	Category	Type
Gastropods			
Univalve			
Whelk	Feb–August		
Winkle	Sept-April		
Cephalopods			
Octopus	May–Dec		
Squid	May–Oct		
Cuttlefish	May–Dec		

Definitions of Terms

Demersal: fish that live and feed on the seabed

Pelagic: fish that live and feed on the surface of the water

Crustacea: shellfish that are multijointed, legs and pincers

Molluscs subdivided into three categories

Bivalve: hinged/double shell (mussel/oyster)

Gastropod: (univalve) single shell (whelk/winkle)

Cephalopod: shellfish with modified internal shell (octopus/squid)

Shellfish

Edible shellfish can be divided into two main categories:

Crustaceans
Lobsters, crabs, crawfish, langoustines, prawns and shrimps, which have 5 pairs of legs and live encased in a jointed, multi-hinged shell.

Molluscs

Gastropods (univalves) or single-shelled creatures, including whelks and winkles, and **bivalves** or double-hinged shelled creatures, such as mussels, oysters and scallops. These are also known as filter-feeders.

Cephalopods, creatures with tentacles and a modified internal shell – octopus, squid and cuttlefish.

The shellfish industry is a multi-million-pound business and is growing. In the UK shellfish can only be marketed and sold commercially if harvested from an area that has met with government approval and has been designated as safe by scientific research. It is unwise to gather these species yourself from any area you are not completely confident about. This is particularly important where bivalves or filter-feeders are concerned as they filter a considerable amount of water through their systems each day and in doing so they can pick up any toxins and bacteria in the water. This does not affect the shellfish but, if the water is polluted, could have an adverse effect on the consumer.

Freshness is of paramount importance in shellfish, so always buy from a reputable supplier. For instructions on preparation, see individual recipes on pages 149, 190, 198 and 353.

Grilled Fish Cutlets

This recipe is suitable for brill, cod, halibut, haddock, turbot or salmon cutlets. The pieces of fish should, if possible, be cut to a uniform thickness.

SERVES 4

4 × 170 g|6 oz fish cutlets
melted butter
freshly ground black pepper
juice of ½ lemon

To garnish
sprigs of fresh parsley or watercress
lemon wedges

1 Preheat the grill. Brush the cutlets and the bottom of the grill pan with melted butter. Season the cutlets with pepper and lemon juice. Lay them in the grill tray (not on the wire tray where they might stick).
2 Grill them until pale brown. Turn over and brush with more melted butter. Season again with pepper and lemon juice and grill for a further 3 minutes or until cooked. They will feel firm to the touch, and the flesh will flake easily.
3 Serve on a warmed dish with the pan juices poured over, garnished with parsley or watercress and lemon wedges.

wine: **CRISP DRY WHITE**

Fish in Batter

SERVES 4

4 cutlets or steaks of any white fish
oil for deep-frying
2 teaspoons oil
55 g|2 oz plain flour
a pinch of salt

1 egg yolk
3 tablespoons warm water

To serve
lemon wedges

1 Heat the oil in a deep-fryer until a cube of bread will brown in 40 seconds.
2 Mix the 2 teaspoons oil with the flour in a shallow bowl and add the salt, egg yolk and water.
3 Dip the fish into this batter, hold it with tongs and lower it into the hot oil. Increase the temperature of the oil.
4 Fry for 4–10 minutes depending on the thickness of the fish pieces.
5 Drain well on absorbent kitchen paper and sprinkle lightly with salt. Serve with lemon wedges.

wine: **VERY DRY WHITE**

Poached Fish, Hot or Cold

Use fish either whole or in a large piece. If the fish weighs over 1.35 kg | 3 lb, double the court bouillon quantities.

For the fish
see above

For the court bouillon
about 1.1 litres | 2 pints water
1 teaspoon salt
150 ml | ¼ pint white wine vinegar
1 medium onion, sliced
1 bunch of fresh parsley
1 sprig of fresh thyme
1 bay leaf
6 black peppercorns

For cold fish
watercress, trimmed
cucumber slices, blanched
mayonnaise (see page 117)

For hot fish
lemon wedges
boiled potatoes
melted butter

1 Simmer together all the court bouillon ingredients for 20 minutes. Strain and cool.
2 Put the fish into the cold court bouillon and heat gently, bringing up to poaching temperature. Do not allow the water to simmer or boil – it should barely move. Poach until the flesh of the fish has turned from translucent to opaque. The length of time will depend on the thickness of the fish and the quantity of the fish being cooked. If the fish is to be served hot, poach it for 4 minutes per 450 g | 1 lb, then carefully lift it out. Skin it if necessary, garnish with lemon wedges, surround with hot potatoes and pass the melted butter separately.
3 When the fish is cooked, remove it carefully from the court bouillon and leave to get cold. When cold, skin the fish, garnish it with watercress and cucumber and hand the mayonnaise separately.

NOTE: Starting with a cooled court bouillon is considered to produce moister flesh, but it is not always practicable. If the fish has to be put into a hot court bouillon, allow 6 minutes per 450 g | 1 lb and remove immediately from the pan.

wine: DRY WHITE

Spicy Fish Curry

Any firm white fish will do for this curry. Be very careful not to overcook the fish or it will begin to fall apart and look unattractive. This is a fairly mild curry but can be made hotter by using an extra green chilli pepper.

675 g | 1½ lb monkfish, filleted and skinned
1 large onion, chopped
1 green pepper, cored, deseeded and sliced
1 green chilli, deseeded and chopped
sunflower oil
1 × 1 cm | ½ in piece of fresh root ginger, peeled and cut into slivers
1 clove of garlic, crushed
1 teaspoon ground cumin

1 teaspoon ground coriander
1 teaspoon ground cinnamon
1 teaspoon ground turmeric
450 ml | ¾ pint water
salt and freshly ground black pepper
110 g | 4 oz Greek yoghurt

To garnish
roughly chopped fresh mint

1 Cut the monkfish into 2.5 cm | 1 in cubes.
2 Fry the onion, pepper and chilli in a little oil in a frying pan and allow to soften without browning for 2–3 minutes. Add the ginger, garlic and dry spices and cook for a further 2 minutes. Stir regularly and add a little extra oil if the mixture is getting too dry.
3 Remove the pan off the heat. Add the water and bring to the boil. Season well with salt and pepper. Add the fish and simmer for 10 minutes. Remove the fish with a slotted spoon. Reduce the sauce, by boiling rapidly, to a syrupy consistency.
4 Beat the yoghurt with a little water, add some of the hot fish juices, mix well and return to the pan. Bring to the boil but do not allow to get too hot. Return the fish to the pan.
5 Pile into a warmed serving dish and serve garnished with the mint.

wine: SPICY DRY WHITE

Fish Pie

SERVES 6

900 g | 2 lb haddock, whiting or cod fillet or a mixture of any of them
425 ml | ¾ pint milk
½ onion, sliced
6 black peppercorns
1 bay leaf
salt and freshly ground black pepper

5 hardboiled eggs, quartered
1 tablespoon chopped fresh parsley
30 g | 1 oz butter
30 g | 1 oz plain flour
2 tablespoons double cream
675 g | 1½ lb mashed potatoes (see page 268)

1 Preheat the oven to 180°C | 350°F | gas mark 4.
2 Lay the fish fillets in a roasting pan, skin side up.
3 Heat the milk with the onion, peppercorns, bay leaf and a pinch of salt.

4 Pour over the fish. Cover the fish with greaseproof paper and cook in the oven for about 15 minutes, until the fish is firm and creamy-looking.

5 Strain off the milk and reserve it for the sauce. Remove the skin and bones from the fish. Flake the fish into a pie dish and add the eggs. Sprinkle over the parsley.

6 Melt the butter in a saucepan, remove from the heat stir in the flour. Return to the heat and cook for 1 minute. Remove from the heat and gradually add the reserved milk.

7 Return to the heat and stir, bringing slowly to the boil. Season to taste with salt and pepper. Stir in the cream and pour over the fish, mixing the sauce in carefully with a palette knife or spoon.

8 Spread a layer of mashed potatoes on the top and mark with a fork in a criss-cross pattern. Or pipe the potatoes on top of the pie. Place on a baking sheet and brown in the oven for about 10 minutes or brown under a hot grill. If the pie has been made in advance reheat in the oven for 20–30 minutes.

wine: **DRY WHITE**

Eel Pie

SERVES 6

340 g | 12 oz flour quantity puff pastry (see page 566)

900 g | 2 lb fresh spinach, cooked and chopped

freshly grated nutmeg

freshly ground black pepper

900 g | 2 lb smoked eel, skinned and boned

For the sauce

55 g | 2 oz unsalted butter

15 g | ½ oz plain flour

150 ml | ¼ pint milk

2 egg yolks

beaten egg to glaze

1 Preheat the oven to 200°C | 400°F | gas mark 6.

2 Take one-third of the pastry and roll it out to a 15 × 20 cm | 6 × 8 in rectangle. Place on a wet baking sheet and prick all over with a fork. Bake for about 20 minutes until golden-brown. Transfer the pastry to a wire rack to cool but do not turn the oven off.

3 Season the spinach with nutmeg and pepper.

4 Make the sauce: melt 15 g | ½ oz of the butter, remove from the heat and add the flour. Return to the heat and cook for 30 seconds. Remove from the heat and stir in the milk gradually. Return to the heat and stir until boiling. Boil for two minutes.

5 Cool slightly, then beat in the remaining butter and the egg yolks. Season with pepper.

6 Arrange half the spinach on the cooked pastry base and cover with the eel. Spread the sauce over the eel and cover with the remaining spinach.

7 Roll the remaining pastry on a floured board into a 'blanket' large enough to overlap the edges of the pie. Lay it gently over the spinach. Using a sharp knife, cut off the corners to the size of the pie. Reserve the pastry trimmings.

8 Lift one side of the overlapping pastry and brush the underside with a little beaten egg. Tuck the 'blanket' neatly underneath the cooked base. Repeat with the other three sides.

9 Shape the trimmings into leaves. Brush the whole pie with beaten egg. Arrange the pastry leaves on top and brush again. Chill until the pastry is firm.

10 Bake in the oven for 30–40 minutes. Serve hot or cold.

NOTE: To counteract the saltiness of the smoked eel, salt is not added to the sauce or to the spinach.

wine: **DRY WHITE**

Turbot with Spring Onions and Ginger Sauce

Any firm white fish such as halibut, haddock, monkfish or turbot can be used for this recipe – the firmer the fish, the easier it is to cook.

SERVES 3–4

450 g | 1 lb turbot fillet
sesame oil for frying
2 cloves of garlic, bruised
1 cm | ½ in piece of fresh root ginger, peeled and
  sliced
8–10 spring onions, shredded

For the marinade

1 tablespoon soy sauce mixed with 1 tablespoon dry
  sherry

For the sauce

½ teaspoon ground ginger
½ teaspoon caster sugar
1 tablespoon soy sauce
1 tablespoon dry sherry

1 Cut the fish fillets into strips 5 cm × 1 cm | 2 in × ½ in.

2 Add the fish to the marinade and leave it to stand for 30 minutes.

3 Mix all the ingredients for the sauce together and set aside.

4 Heat a sauté pan (preferably non-stick), add a little oil, and when hot add the garlic and ginger. Cook quickly until the garlic is lightly browned. Remove with a slotted spoon. Lower the heat and add the fish, in its marinade, and fry briefly. Pour in the sauce, stir and add the spring onions. Serve immediately.

wine: **SPICY DRY WHITE**

Turbot Sausages with Watercress Sauce

SERVES 4

340 g | 12 oz turbot fillet, skinned
110 g | 4 oz whiting or haddock fillet, skinned
2 egg whites
290 ml | ½ pint double cream
salt and freshly ground black pepper
cayenne pepper

For the sauce

30 g | 1 oz butter
30 g | 1 oz plain flour

290 ml | ½ pint fish stock (see page 106)
150 ml | ¼ pint double cream
1 bunch of watercress, trimmed, blanched and
  refreshed
salt and freshly ground black pepper

To garnish

watercress leaves

1 Keeping everything as cool as possible, process the fish with a little egg white in a food processor until smooth and season with salt. Place in a large bowl and set in a roasting pan of ice. Beat well, and gradually add the remaining egg whites, then the cream, salt, pepper and cayenne.
2 Roll the mixture up in clingfilm in the shape of sausages.
3 Poach for 10–15 minutes in simmering water. Remove the clingfilm.
4 Make the sauce: melt the butter in a saucepan, remove from the heat and add the flour. Return to the heat and cook for 30 seconds. Remove from the heat. Gradually add the stock and cream. Return to the heat and bring to the boil, then simmer for 4 minutes. Add the watercress and whizz briefly. Season to taste with salt and pepper. Garnish with watercress leaves and serve with the sauce.

wine: **VERY DRY WHITE**

Haddock Filling for Gougère

SERVES 4

45 g | 1 oz butter
30 g | 1 oz plain flour
pinch of cayenne
290 ml | ½ pint milk
freshly ground black pepper
4 tablespoons double cream

2 tablespoons chopped fresh parsley
340 g | 12 oz smoked haddock fillet, cooked and
  flaked
4 tomatoes, peeled, deseeded and cut into slivers
1 gougère case (see page 377)

1 Melt the butter in a saucepan. Remove from the heat and add the flour and cayenne. Return to the heat and cook for 1 minute.
2 Remove from the heat, add the milk gradually then add the pepper and cream. Return to the heat and stir until boiling. Simmer for 1–2 minutes. Stir in the parsley.
3 Stir in the haddock and tomatoes. Use to fill a gougère case (see page 377).

wine: **DRY WHITE**

Haddock with English Egg Sauce

SERVES 4

675 | 1½ lb haddock fillets
570 ml | 1 pint milk
1 onion, sliced
1 bouquet garni (see page 9)
salt and freshly ground black pepper

To serve

570 ml | 1 pint English egg sauce (see page 114),
    made with the reserved cooking liquor

1 Preheat the oven to 170°C | 325°F | gas mark 3.
2 Wash the fish, lay it skin side up in a roasting pan.
3 Pour in the milk and add the onion, bouquet garni, salt and pepper.
4 Cover the dish with greased paper or a lid and bake in the oven for 30 minutes, or until the fish is opaque and firm.
5 Remove the fish, skin, drain and remove any bones. Reserve the fish liquor for the sauce. Arrange the fish on a flat ovenproof dish.
6 Cover again with the paper and keep warm while you make the sauce.
7 Pour the sauce over the fish and serve.

NOTE: Cooking times for baking fillets of fish depend on the size of the fillets, the type of roasting pan and the heat of the milk as well as the oven temperature.

wine: **DRY WHITE**

Haddock with Tomatoes and Chives

SERVES 4

4 × 170 g | 6 oz haddock fillets
salt and freshly ground black pepper
290 ml | ½ pint fish stock (see page 106)
150 ml | ¼ pint dry white wine
30 g | 1 oz butter
30 g | 1 oz plain flour

150 ml | ¼ pint double cream
2 large tomatoes, peeled, deseeded and cut into
    slivers
1 tablespoon chopped fresh parsley
1 tablespoon chopped fresh chives

1 Preheat the oven to 180°C | 350°F | gas mark 4. Wash the haddock fillets and season with salt and pepper.
2 Lay the fish skin side up in an ovenproof dish. Pour over the strained stock and the wine. Cover with buttered greaseproof paper or foil and bake in the oven for 15–20 minutes.
3 Lift out the fish. Strain the cooking liquor into a small heavy saucepan and boil rapidly until reduced to 290 ml | ½ pint.

4 Melt the butter in another saucepan, remove from the heat and add the flour. Return to the heat and stir for 1 minute. Remove from the heat and gradually add the reduced fish liquor. Return to the heat, bring slowly to the boil, and simmer for 2 minutes. Remove from the heat. Season to taste with salt and pepper and add the cream, tomatoes, parsley and chives.

5 Skin the fish and lay it in a serving dish. Pour over the sauce.

wine: **VERY DRY WHITE**

Roast Cod with Garlic

SERVES 4

4 × 170 g|6 oz cod fillets, unskinned
150 ml|5 fl oz good-quality olive oil
4 cloves of garlic, unpeeled, bruised
salt and freshly ground black pepper
seasoned flour

To serve
lemon wedges

1 Preheat the oven to 200°C|400°F|gas mark 6.

2 Pinbone the cod fillets if necessary (see page 307).

3 Heat the oil in a roasting tin. Add the garlic and bake in the oven for 15 minutes. Remove the tin from the oven and increase the oven temperature to its highest setting. Remove the garlic and set aside.

4 Season the fish with salt and pepper and dip them, skin side down, into the seasoned flour. Shake off excess.

5 Set the oil in the tin over direct heat and add the cod, skin side down. Let it sizzle for 2 minutes.

6 Turn the cod skin side uppermost, and roast in the oven for 3 minutes or until cooked (it should be opaque and firm).

7 To serve: place the cod, skin side uppermost, on a serving dish with the baked garlic and lemon wedges.

wine: **LIGHT RED**

Halibut au Gratin

SERVES 4

4 × 170 g|6 oz halibut steaks

For the court bouillon

570 ml|1 pint water

2 tablespoons white wine vinegar

1 carrot, sliced

1 onion, sliced

4 cloves

salt

6 black peppercorns

1 parsley stalk

1 sprig of fresh thyme

1 bay leaf

For the sauce

30 g|1 oz butter

20 g|¾ oz plain flour

150 ml|¼ pint milk

For the topping

dried breadcrumbs

30 g|1 oz Gruyère or strong Cheddar cheese, grated

1 Make up the court bouillon: combine all the ingredients, bring to the boil, simmer for 20 minutes, then allow to cool.

2 Preheat the oven to 180°C|350°F|gas mark 4. Place the halibut steaks in a buttered dish. Strain on the court bouillon and cover with a piece of greaseproof paper, foil or a lid. Poach in the oven or over a gentle heat for 10–15 minutes. Reduce the oven temperature to 80°C|175°F|gas mark ¼.

3 Lift out the fish. Strain the fish liquor into a saucepan and reduce it by rapid boiling to 150 ml|¼ pint.

4 Skin the halibut and remove the bones. Drain well. Place the fish steaks on an ovenproof serving dish, cover, and return to the oven.

5 Preheat the grill.

6 Make the sauce: melt the butter in a small saucepan, remove from the heat and stir in the flour. Return to the heat and cook for 1 minute, then remove from the heat. Gradually stir in the reduced fish liquor and milk. Return to the heat and bring slowly to the boil, stirring until you have a smooth creamy sauce. Simmer for 2 minutes. Season to taste with salt and pepper.

7 Spoon the sauce over the fish. Sprinkle with breadcrumbs and grated cheese.

8 Grill until well browned.

wine: VERY DRY WHITE

Mackerel with Gooseberry Sauce

SERVES 4

4 × 225 g | 8 oz mackerel

For the gooseberry sauce

340 g | 12 oz young gooseberries

30 g | 1 oz caster sugar

30 g | 1 oz butter

a pinch of ground ginger

To garnish

lemon wedges

1 Preheat the grill.
2 Clean the mackerel, cut off the fins and make 2 or 3 diagonal slashes into the flesh through the skin.
3 Prepare the gooseberry sauce: top and tail the berries and place them in saucepan with a little water and the sugar. Simmer until tender.
4 Push the gooseberries through a sieve. Beat in the butter and ginger and taste for sweetness. It maybe necessary to add extra sugar.
5 Grill the mackerel for about 5 minutes on each side, depending on size, or until cooked.
6 Arrange the mackerel on a warmed serving dish. Garnish with lemon wedges. Hand the sauce separately.

wine: **SPICY WHITE**

Monkfish with Herby Hollandaise

SERVES 4

800 g | 1¾ lb monkfish, skinned, boned and filleted

For the court bouillon

1.1 litres | 2 pints water

5 tablespoons white wine vinegar

1 carrot, sliced

1 onion, sliced

1 bunch of fresh parsley

1 bay leaf

1 stock of celery

6 black peppercorns

¼ teaspoon salt

To finish

Herby Hollandaise Sauce (see page 120)

sprigs of fresh chervil

1 Remove any membrane from the fish.
2 Combine all the court bouillon ingredients with 570 ml | 1 pint water into a saucepan and bring to the boil. Simmer for 20 minutes. Strain add the remaining water and cool.
3 Put the fish into a saucepan and pour over the court bouillon. Cover and bring slowly to simmering point, then reduce the heat until it barely moves; it must not boil. Poach the fish for 10 minutes.
4 Lift out the fish. Remove any remaining membrane and pat the fish dry.

5 Slice the fish and arrange on a warmed serving dish. Coat with the Herby Hollandaise and garnish with the chervil.

wine: **VERY DRY WHITE**

Monkfish Salad with Exotic Sauce

This recipe has been adapted from *The Josceline Dimbleby Collection*. It is ideal for a cold buffet.

SERVES 10

4 tablespoons olive oil	1 teaspoon caster sugar
1.25 kg│2½ lb monkfish, skinned, boned and cubed	1 tablespoon tomato purée
2 large green chillies, deseeded and chopped	juice of ½ lemon
2–3 cloves of garlic, crushed	salt
450 g│1 lb tomatoes, peeled and chopped	1 good bunch of fresh coriander
1 teaspoon ground cardamom	110 g│4 oz button mushrooms, thinly sliced

1 Heat the oil in a large frying pan and cook the fish over a medium heat for 5–7 minutes, turning gently. Turn off the heat, remove the fish with a slotted spoon and set aside in a bowl. Leave the fish juices in the pan.

2 Pour any juices that have drained from the fish into the bowl back into the pan. Bring the juices to the boil and add the chillies, garlic, tomatoes, cardamom, sugar, tomato purée and lemon juice. Stir and allow to simmer over a low heat for 7–10 minutes until the tomato is soft. Season to taste with salt and turn off the heat.

3 Chop about three-quarters of the coriander and stir into the hot sauce. Pour the sauce over the fish in the bowl and gently mix in. Stir the mushrooms into the mixture. Leave until cold.

4 When the salad has cooled, pile it into a clean serving dish. Pull the whole leaves off the remaining sprigs of coriander and scatter them over the fish.

NOTE: The sauce can be made separately and used with chicken or veal dishes.

wine: **DRY WHITE**

Girardet's Red Mullet with Rosemary Sauce

SERVES 4

4 × 140–200 g | 5–7 oz red mullet
55 g | 2 oz butter
2 medium shallots, finely chopped
1 sprig of fresh rosemary, cut into 4
100 ml | 3½ fl oz dry white wine
290 ml | ½ pint double cream

juice of ½ lemon
salt and freshly ground black pepper
2 tablespoons olive oil

To garnish
sprigs of fresh rosemary

1 Prepare the mullet. Cut off the head and tail and remove the scales. Using a sharp kitchen knife, cut down either side of the backbone. Lift off the 2 fillets and remove the pin-sized bones along the centre of the fillets. Chop the heads, bones and trimmings.

2 Make the stock: melt half the butter in a heavy saucepan, add the fish trimmings, and the shallots. Simmer for 2–3 minutes.

3 Add the shallot and continue to simmer for a further 2 minutes, stirring constantly. Add the rosemary, wine and an equal quantity of water and simmer for a further 7 minutes. Remove the rosemary and discard.

4 Pass the stock through a fine sieve into a clean saucepan. Set the pan over a high heat and reduce the stock by boiling rapidly to half its original quantity.

5 Pour the reduced stock on to the cream in a bowl. Return to the pan and continue to reduce until the sauce is thick enough to coat the back of a wooden spoon, stirring frequently to prevent the sauce from catching.

6 Remove the pan from the heat and gradually beat in the remaining butter, a little at a time. Add the lemon juice and season to taste with salt and pepper. Keep warm.

7 Cook the fish fillets: heat 2 heavy frying pans. Pour half the oil into each pan and arrange 4 fillets, skin side up, in each pan. Season generously with salt and pepper. Cook gently for 2 minutes.

8 To serve: cover 4 warmed dinner plates with the sauce; place 2 fillets on each plate, skin uppermost, and garnish with the rosemary.

wine: **SPICY WHITE**

Red Mullet with Fennel and Chives

This is a very low-fat dish.

SERVES 4

4 × 250 g│9 oz red mullet, filleted (see page 306)
the fish trimmings
1 litre│1¾ pints water
1 stick of celery, sliced
1 onion, sliced
1 bay leaf

3 slices of lemon
6 black peppercorns
100 ml│3½ fl oz dry white wine
1 small bulb of Florence fennel, chopped, leaves
    reserved
1 bunch of fresh chives, chopped

1 Remove any scales and pinbones from the mullet fillets (see pages 305 and 307).

2 Clean the fish trimmings and put into a large saucepan with the water, celery, onion, bay leaf, lemon slices and peppercorns. Bring gradually up to the boil, then reduce the heat and simmer very gently for 20 minutes.

3 Strain, pushing the trimmings well into the bottom of the sieve to extract as much flavour as possible, into a large flat saucepan.

4 Put the mullet fillets into the saucepan, skin side uppermost, with the white wine and fennel, and simmer very slowly for 2 minutes.

5 Remove the fish with a fish slice and keep warm on a serving dish. Boil the stock rapidly until reduced to 150 ml│¼ pint.

6 To serve: add the chives and pour over the fillets. Garnish with a few of the fennel leaves.

wine: **MEDIUM DRY WHITE OR ROSÉ**

Grilled Tuna Fish Steaks with Green Chilli Pesto

Tuna is wonderful if carefully cooked. If overdone it becomes very dry and rather cardboard-like in texture.

SERVES 4

4 × 170 g│6 oz tuna steaks, skinned (see page 307)

For the marinade
6 tablespoons olive oil
2 tablespoons balsamic vinegar
freshly ground black pepper

For the chilli pesto
2 green chillies
1 bunch of fresh coriander

55 g│2 oz pinenuts, toasted
2 cloves of garlic, crushed
55 g│2 oz Parmesan cheese, freshly grated
6 tablespoons olive oil
salt and freshly ground black pepper

To garnish
sprigs of fresh coriander

1 Put the tuna steaks in a flat dish and pour over the marinade ingredients. Cover and refrigerate for $\frac{1}{2}$ hour.
2 Preheat the grill to its highest setting.
3 Make the chilli pesto: slit the chillies carefully and remove the seeds. Put the chillies, coriander, pinenuts and garlic into a blender. Blend well, add the Parmesan cheese, and with the motor still running pour on the oil in a thin stream until well emulsified. Season to taste with salt and pepper. Let down with a little water if too thick.
4 Lift the tuna steaks from the marinade, place on the grill rack and grill for about 3 minutes on each side, until cooked (they should be opaque, lightly browned and firm but still moist). Alternately, cook for 2–3 minutes per side on a hot griddle.
5 To serve: place the tuna steaks on a serving dish, spoon the chilli pesto on top and garnish with coriander.

NOTE: Take care when handling chillies: the volatile oil contained in the juice can burn sensitive skin badly. It is a good idea to wear rubber gloves when chopping chillies.

wine: **VERY DRY WHITE**

Oriental Red Snapper Salad

SERVES 4

1.35 kg | 3 lb whole red snapper, filleted and skinned
2 tablespoons olive oil

1 teaspoon curry powder
freshly ground black pepper

For the marinade

1 teaspoon salt
2 teaspoons sugar
1 teaspoon peeled and grated fresh root ginger
1 teaspoon dry English mustard
$\frac{1}{2}$ teaspoon ground turmeric

For the salad

110 g | 4 oz beanshoots
1 red pepper, deseeded and cut into strips
225 g | 8 oz mangetout, blanched
225 g | 8 oz baby sweetcorn, blanched
110 g | 4 oz broccoli spears, blanched

1 Pinbone the red snapper fillets if necessary (see page 307).
2 Mix all the marinade ingredients together. Coat the snapper with the marinade and leave, covered, in the refrigerator for at least 2 hours.
3 Heat the oil in a wok or large frying pan and fry the marinated snapper fillets for 2–3 minutes or until just cooked through.
4 Toss the salad ingredients together with the fish and serve immediately.

NOTE: This can also be served with a hot salad. Just toss the prepared vegetables into the wok after frying the fish and heat through well. Sprinkle with a little sesame seed oil and light soy sauce.

wine: **SPICY DRY WHITE**

Salmon with Fish Mousseline and Tomato Sauce

SERVES 4

4 × 170 g│6 oz tail-end slices of fresh salmon

110 g│4 oz fresh salmon trimmings

2 egg yolks

150 ml│¼ pint double cream

1 tablespoon Pernod

1 tablespoon very finely chopped fresh chives

salt and freshly ground white pepper

freshly grated nutmeg

For the sauce

1 shallot, very finely chopped

225 ml│8 fl oz dry white wine

2 large tomatoes, peeled and deseeded

tomato purée

15 g│½ oz butter

To garnish

1 small bunch of fresh chervil

1 Prepare the salmon slices: cut them in half horizontally and remove any grey flesh. Place each one between two pieces of clingfilm and batter them slightly so that they increase their size by about a quarter.

2 You should now have 8 thin pieces of salmon shaped like flattened triangles.

3 Now prepare the mousse filling. Put the salmon trimmings into a food processor with the egg yolks. Process quickly, then add half the cream and process again. Season with the Pernod, chives, salt, pepper and nutmeg. Chill in the refrigerator for 20 minutes.

4 Preheat the oven to 180°C│350°F│gas mark 4.

5 Divide the filling between the 8 pieces of salmon and roll them up.

6 Put the salmon cones into a lightly greased baking dish. Sprinkle with the shallot, pour over the wine, cover and bake for 10 minutes.

7 Meanwhile, cut the tomatoes into julienne strips and leave to drain in a sieve.

8 Remove the salmon fillets to a warm place while you make the sauce.

9 Reduce the cooking liquor by boiling rapidly, then add a little tomato purée and the remaining cream. The sauce should be fairly thin.

10 Melt the butter in a frying pan and heat the tomatoes through very quickly.

11 Partially flood the base of 4 dinner plates with the sauce. Slice the salmon and arrange on the plates. Garnish with the warm tomatoes and the chervil leaves.

The pieces of salmon should be shaped like flattened triangles

wine: **VERY DRY WHITE**

Salmon in Filo Pastry with Watercress

This recipe is similar to a Moroccan B'stilla dish.

SERVES 6

110 g | 4 oz watercress, trimmed

8 eggs

55 ml | 2 fl oz single cream

100 ml | 3½ fl oz fish stock (see page 106)

salt and freshly ground black pepper

olive oil

400 g | 14 oz filo pastry

1 tablespoon cumin seeds, dry-fried

900 g | 2 lb salmon fillets, skinned

1 tablespoon lemon juice

1 Place the watercress in a sieve and immerse in boiling water to blanch it. Remove after 2 seconds and refresh under cold running water. Drain well.

2 Place the watercress, eggs, cream, fish stock, salt and pepper in a blender and liquidize until smooth and pale green. Pour into a small saucepan and stir over a low heat until the mixture is creamy and nearly set.

3 Preheat the oven to 400°F | 200°C | gas mark 6.

4 Brush an ovenproof dish large enough to take the salmon in one layer with oil. Line the base and sides of the dish with a sheet of filo pastry (there will be a lot of overlap). Brush the pastry with oil. Cover with a further 5 sheets of oiled filo.

5 Sprinkle with the cumin seeds and spoon over half the watercress mousseline.

6 Lay the salmon on top of the watercress in a single layer. Sprinkle with pepper and lemon juice. Spoon over the remaining watercress mousseline. Smooth the surface.

7 Arrange 4 sheets of filo pastry on top of the watercress cream, brushing with oil as you go. Fold over the overlapping piece of pastry, trim to get a good fit, brush with more oil and cover with the last sheet of filo. Brush with oil. Score the surface of the pastry into diamond shapes.

8 Bake for 35–40 minutes until golden brown. Serve hot or cold.

wine: **CRISP DRY WHITE**

Noisettes of Salmon with Saffron Sauce and Dill Pesto

SERVES 4

4 × 170 g | 6 oz salmon cutlets, cut 3.5 cm | 1½ in thick

1 tablespoon oil

salt and freshly ground black pepper

1 quantity dill pesto (see page 124)

For the saffron sauce

100 ml | 3½ fl oz dry white wine

1 shallot, finely chopped

½ teaspoon saffron filaments

150 ml | ¼ pint double cream

salt and freshly ground black pepper

To garnish

sprigs of fresh dill

1 Prepare the salmon noisettes: carefully remove the bones from the cutlets. Using a sharp knife, slice the skin away from the flesh halfway round the cutlet. Curve the skinned piece of fish into the centre and wrap the other half of the cutlet round the outside. Smooth the skin around the sides of the noisette. Tie with string. Press the noisettes between 2 plates and chill in the refrigerator for at least 1 hour.

2 Preheat the grill to its highest setting.

3 Make the saffron sauce: put the wine, shallot and saffron into a saucepan. Bring to the boil, then lower the heat and simmer until the wine is reduced to half its original quantity. Add the cream and reduce until syrupy by boiling rapidly. Season to taste with salt and pepper.

4 Brush the salmon noisettes on both sides with oil and season with salt and pepper. Grill the salmon noisettes for about 4 minutes on each side or until cooked (they should be opaque and firm).

5 To serve: remove the string and skin and arrange the salmon noisettes on 4 dinner plates. Spoon a little of the saffron sauce around one side and a little pesto around the other. Garnish each salmon noisette with a sprig of dill.

wine: VERY DRY WHITE

Summer Salmon en Papillote with Lime and Chives

SERVES 4

8 × 85 g | 3 oz thin slices of salmon fillet	55 g | 2 oz butter, melted
oil	2 tablespoons dry white wine
8 tomatoes, peeled and thinly sliced	Lime Beurre Blanc (see page 122)
salt and freshly ground black pepper	
2 limes	**To garnish**
1 small bunch of fresh chives, very finely chopped	4 small sprigs of watercress

1 Preheat the oven to 220°C | 425°F | gas mark 7. Cut out 4 × 20 cm | 8 in circles of kitchen foil. Brush with oil.

2 Sandwich the fillets of salmon with the tomato slices. Season well with salt and pepper.

3 Place each salmon sandwich on one half of a circle of foil.

4 Slice one of the limes into eighths and squeeze the juice from the second lime.

5 Put 2 slices of lime and a sprinkling of chives on each salmon sandwich and sprinkle with the lime juice, melted butter and wine.

6 Fold over the foil to make a parcel rather like an apple turnover. There must be space inside for circulation of air. Twist and press hard to make a good seal.

7 Place a baking sheet in the oven for 5 minutes to heat. Put the papillotes on the baking sheet, taking care that they do not touch each other. Bake in the oven for 12 minutes.

8 Unwrap the parcels and place the salmon on warmed dinner plates. Garnish with small sprigs of watercress. Hand the sauce separately.

wine: VERY DRY WHITE

Salmon Mayonnaise

The recipe is for boned salmon mayonnaise. It is an excellent idea to bone the salmon for a large party as it makes it easy to serve.

1 whole salmon, cleaned

For the court bouillon
150 ml | ¼ pint white wine vinegar
3 bay leaves
1 onion, sliced
1 large bunch of fresh parsley
1 carrot, peeled and sliced

12 black peppercorns
1 teaspoon salt

To garnish
cucumber slices, blanched
lemon wedges
1 bunch of watercress, trimmed
290 ml | ½ pint mayonnaise (see page 117)

1 Half fill a fish kettle with water and add the remaining court bouillon ingredients. Simmer together for 20 minutes. Strain and cool.

2 Put the salmon into the cold court bouillon and bring slowly to the boil. Poach gently for 5 minutes per 450 g | 1 lb.

3 Check it every 10 minutes or so and when the salmon is cooked, remove it carefully and leave to get cold. Test to see if the salmon is cooked by removing the dorsal fin. It should fall away easily. Look inside the fish to see if the flesh is opaque. Remove the fish from the cooking liquid and place on a tray to cool.

4 Remove the fins. Skin the top half of the salmon, leaving the head and tail intact. Lift off the 2 top fish fillets and turn them over on to a serving plate so that they are skinned side down. Remove any remaining little bones.

5 Cut the backbone out from the fish and remove any remaining little bones. Lift the bottom fillets and turn them over on the top fillets to reassemble the fish. Remove the skin.

6 Garnish the salmon as you wish, using cucumber slices, lemon wedges and watercress. Hand the mayonnaise separately.

NOTE: Starting with a cooled court bouillon is considered to produce moister flesh, but it is not always practicable. If the fish has to be put into a hot court bouillon allow about 6 minutes for every 450 g | 1 lb and remove as soon as it is cooked.

wine: **VERY DRY WHITE**

Salmon en Croûte

SERVES 10

1 × 2.3 kg|5 lb salmon, filleted and skinned
450 g|1 lb flour quantity puff pastry (see page 566)
a few tablespoons fine semolina
butter
lemon juice
tarragon leaves
freshly ground white pepper and salt
beaten egg, to glaze

For the sauce

55 g|2 oz butter
20 g|¾ oz plain flour
290 ml|½ pint fish stock (see page 106)
55 ml|2 fl oz dry white wine
1 teaspoon chopped fresh tarragon or parsley
2 tablespoons double cream
salt and freshly ground white pepper

1 Preheat the oven to 230°C|450°F|gas mark 8.

2 Roll out a third of the pastry into a long, narrow rectangle, about the thickness of a £1 coin. Cut it to roughly the size and shape of the original salmon.

3 Place on a baking sheet, and prick all over with a fork. Leave to relax in a cool place for 15 minutes. Bake it in the oven until the pastry is brown and crisp. If, when you turn it over, it is soggy underneath, put it back in the oven, upside down, for a few minutes. Allow to cool.

4 Sprinkle the cooked pastry evenly with semolina to prevent the fish juices making the pastry soggy.

5 Reassemble the salmon fillets on the cooked pastry, dotting them with plenty of butter and sprinkling with lemon juice, tarragon, salt and pepper as you go. Trim away the excess cooked pastry, leaving a border of 1 cm|½ in.

6 Roll out the remaining pastry into a large sheet, slightly thinner than the base, and lay it over the salmon. Cut round the fish, leaving a good 2.5 cm|1 in border beyond the edge of the bottom layer of pastry. Carefully tuck the top sheet under the cooked pastry, shaping the head and tail of the fish carefully.

7 Brush with beaten egg. Using the back of a knife, mark the pastry to represent fish scales, with the rounded end of a teaspoon. Cut some pastry trimmings into fine strips and use them to emphasize the tail fins and gills, and use a circle of pastry for the eye. Brush again with beaten egg.

8 Bake in the oven for 15 minutes to brown and puff up the pastry, then turn down the oven temperature to 150°C|300°F|gas mark 2 for a further 30 minutes to cook the fish. Cover the crust with damp greaseproof paper if the pastry looks in danger of over-browning. To test if the fish is cooked, push a fine skewer through the pastry and fish from the side: it should glide in easily.

9 Make the sauce, melt half the butter in a saucepan, remove from the heat and add the flour. Return to the heat and cook, stirring, until the butter and flour are pale biscuit-coloured. Remove from the heat, then gradually add the stock and wine. Return to the heat and stir until boiling and smooth. Boil rapidly until you have a sauce of coating consistency.

10 Add the tarragon or parsley and the cream. Season to taste with salt and pepper. Beat in the remaining butter, piece by piece. Pour into a warmed sauceboat.

11 Slide the salmon en croûte on to a board or salmon dish.

12 Hand the sauce separately.

wine: **CRISP DRY WHITE**

Salmon Koulibiac

This is a simple version of a classic dish normally made with brioche dough.

SERVES 4

110 g	4 oz long-grain rice	1 tablespoon chopped fresh parsley
170 g	6 oz flour quantity rough puff pastry (see page 565)	juice of ½ lemon
55 g	2 oz butter	285	10 oz cooked salmon, flaked
1 onion, finely diced	2 hardboiled eggs, roughly chopped
30 g	1 oz mushrooms, chopped	salt and freshly ground black pepper
	1 egg, beaten with a pinch of salt, to glaze

1 Preheat the oven to 200°C | 400°F | gas mark 6.

2 Cook the rice in a large saucepan of boiling water for 10–12 minutes. Drain in a colander or sieve and refresh with cold water. Stand the colander on the draining board. With the handle of a wooden spoon, make a few draining holes through the pile of rice to help the water and steam escape. Leave until cool.

3 Roll a third of the pastry into a rectangle as thick as a £1 coin. Leave to relax in the refrigerator for 10 minutes.

4 Place the pastry on a baking sheet. Prick lightly all over with a fork. Bake in the oven for about 15 minutes, until golden-brown. Transfer to a wire rack and leave to cool but do not turn the oven off. Rinse the baking sheet under cold running water until cool.

5 Melt the butter over a medium heat and add the onion. When nearly cooked add the mushrooms and cook gently for 5 minutes. Allow to cool.

6 Put the cooked rice into a bowl and fork in the onion, mushrooms, parsley, lemon juice, salmon, eggs and plenty of salt and pepper.

7 Place the cooled pastry base on the baking sheet and pile on the rice mixture. Shape it with your hands into a neat mound, making sure that it covers the fish completely.

8 Roll the remaining pastry into a blanket large enough to cover the mixture with an overlap of 2.5 cm | 1 in. Using a sharp knife, cut the corners off the blanket at right angles to the cooked base. Working carefully with a palette knife, lift the base and tuck the pastry blanket underneath it. Brush with beaten egg to seal. Repeat with the other 3 sides. Chill until the pastry is firm.

9 Meanwhile, shape the discarded pastry corners into leaves, making the veins and stem with the back of a knife.

10 Brush the koulibiac with more beaten egg, decorate with the pastry leaves and brush again with egg. Bake in the oven for 30 minutes, until the pastry is golden-brown. Serve hot or cold.

NOTES: If a sauce is required, serve plain soured cream, seasoned with salt and pepper.

This is also delicious made with cooked chicken instead of salmon.

wine: **CRISP DRY WHITE**

Flat Salmon Pie

SERVES 4

450 g | 16 oz flour quantity pâte à pâte (see page 565)

55 g | 2 oz Gruyère or Cheddar cheese, grated

30 g | 1 oz Parmesan cheese, grated

85 g | 3 oz unsalted butter, melted

55 g | 2 oz fresh white breadcrumbs

225 g | 8 oz smoked salmon, chopped

2 tablespoons chopped fresh dill

1 large clove of garlic, crushed

150 ml | ¼ pint soured cream

freshly ground black pepper

lemon juice

beaten egg to glaze

1 Roll out the pâte à pâte into 2 rectangles, one to fit a Swiss roll tin, the other slightly larger.

2 Preheat the oven to 200°C | 400°F | gas mark 6.

3 Lightly grease a baking sheet. Put the smaller rectangle of pastry on it and prick all over with a fork. Chill until firm. Bake for 25 minutes until cooked. Loosen it on the baking sheet so that it does not stick and leave to cool.

4 Mix together the Gruyère or Cheddar cheese, the Parmesan, the melted butter and the breadcrumbs. Sprinkle half of this mixture all over the pastry, leaving 1 cm | ½ in clear round the edge.

5 Scatter the smoked salmon on top of the cheese mixture. Then scatter over the dill.

6 Mix the garlic with the soured cream and spread all over the salmon. Season well with pepper but not salt.

7 Sprinkle evenly with lemon juice and top with the remaining cheese mixture. Wet the edge of the bottom piece of pastry lightly with beaten egg and put the top sheet of pastry in place, pressing the edges to seal it well.

8 Use any pastry trimmings to decorate the pie and brush all over with beaten egg.

9 Bake until the pastry is crisp and pale brown about 25 minutes. Serve hot or cold.

NOTE: Off-cuts and trimmings of smoked salmon are cheaper than slices, and do well for this dish.

wine: **SPICY WHITE**

Salmon Fish Cakes

SERVES 4

450 g | 1 lb cooked salmon, flaked

340 g | 12 oz mashed potatoes (see page 268)

salt and freshly ground black pepper

30 g | 1 oz butter, melted

1 tablespoon chopped fresh parsley

2 eggs, beaten

dried white breadcrumbs

6 tablespoons oil for frying

290 ml | ½ pint parsley sauce (see page 113)

To serve

lemon wedges

1 Mix the salmon and potato together. Season well with salt and pepper.
2 Add the melted butter, parsley and enough beaten egg to bind the mixture until soft but not sloppy. Allow to cool.
3 Flour your hands and shape the mixture into 8 flat cakes 2.5 cm | 1 in thick. Brush with beaten egg and coat with breadcrumbs.
4 Heat the oil in a frying pan and fry until the fish cakes are brown on both sides.
5 Serve with parsley sauce and lemon wedges.

wine: DRY WHITE

Grilled Gravad Lax with Saffron Noodles

SERVES 6

900 g | 2 lb salmon fillets

170 g | 6 oz sea salt

170 g | 6 oz caster sugar

15 g | ½ oz white peppercorns, freshly ground

1 bunch of fresh dill, chopped

To serve

saffron noodles (see page 236)

55 g | 2 oz butter, melted

salt and freshly ground black pepper

200 ml | 7 floz crème fraîche

To garnish

1 bunch of fresh chives, chopped

1 Make sure all the bones are removed from the salmon.
2 Mix the salt, sugar and pepper together. Lay half the dill in the bottom of a non-metallic dish large enough to hold the salmon fillets. Sprinkle half the salt and sugar mixture evenly over the dill.
3 Place the salmon fillets, flesh side down, on top of the cure. Cover with the remaining dill, salt and sugar. Cover tightly and refrigerate for 24 hours.
4 Remove the salmon from the cure, scrape off the dill and cure, and pat the fish dry with kitchen paper. Remove the skin and slice the fish on the diagonal into pieces 5 mm | ¼ in thick.
5 Preheat the grill and place a sheet of well-buttered kitchen foil on the top of the grill pan.

Place the salmon slices on the foil and grill very quickly on one side so that the salmon is barely cooked.

6 Meanwhile, boil the noodles in plenty of boiling salted water for about 5–6 minutes until *al dente*. Drain well, toss with melted butter and season with salt and pepper.

7 Place a pile of noodles on 6 warmed dinner plates and arrange 3 slices of grilled salmon on top. Spoon on the crème fraîche and sprinkle with the chives. Serve immediately.

wine: **MEDIUM DRY WHITE**

Salmon and Plaice Ravioli with Basil Sauce

The egg whites and cream can be added in the food processor but they must be very cold and not over-beaten. If too warm the mixture will split (curdle). The fish must be very fresh.

SERVES 4

1 egg quantity pasta dough (see page 234)

For the filling
85 g | 3 oz salmon fillet, skinned
85 g | 3 oz plaice fillet, skinned
5 mm | ¼ in piece of fresh root ginger, peeled and grated
a squeeze of lemon juice
salt and freshly ground white pepper
1 egg white

170 ml | 16 fl oz double cream, chilled
½ teaspoon ground mace

For the sauce
170 ml | 6 fl oz extra virgin olive oil
1 large clove of garlic, peeled and very thinly sliced
2 tomatoes, peeled, deseeded and finely diced
1 squeeze of lemon juice
10 fresh basil leaves, torn

1 Make the pasta and leave to relax, covered in clingfilm.

2 Put the salmon, plaice, ginger and lemon juice into a food processor and pound well or chop finely, then push through a sieve. (This is quite a task.) Weigh the fish to ensure there is 170 g | 6 oz.

3 Put the fish into a bowl. Season with salt and pepper and set in a roasting pan of ice to keep the mixture chilled. Beat well, gradually adding the egg white, then the cream, making sure that the mixture does not become too runny. If the mixture becomes slack, do not add anymore cream. It should hold its shape. Season to taste with mace, and more salt and pepper if necessary. Refrigerate until ready to use.

4 Roll out the pasta very thinly. Brush lightly with water. Place teaspoonfuls of filling at intervals of 3 cm | 1½ in in even rows over half the pasta. Fold the other half of the pasta over the mounds of fish mousseline. Press together, firming all round each mound of filling. Cut between the rows, making sure that the edges are sealed. Set aside.

5 Put a large saucepan of salted water on to boil.

6 Make the sauce: heat the oil in a saucepan, add the garlic and leave to cook very slowly for about 3–4 minutes.

7 Add the tomatoes, lemon juice, salt and pepper. Warm through for 2 minutes, then add the basil.

8 Cook the ravioli in the simmering water for 3–4 minutes. Drain well.

9 Serve the ravioli with the basil and olive oil sauce drizzled over the top.

wine: DRY WHITE

Oriental Baked Salmon

SERVES 8

1 × 2.7 kg│6 lb salmon, divided into 2 fillets, skinned oil for brushing

2 bunches of spring onions, finely chopped

2.5 cm│1 in piece of fresh root ginger, peeled and very finely chopped

7.5 cm│3 in piece of fresh galangal, peeled and very finely chopped

2 fresh green chillies, deseeded and very finely chopped

6 sticks of lemon grass, peeled and very finely chopped

110 g│4 oz fresh coriander, chopped

4 tablespoons nam pla (Thai fish sauce)

4 tablespoons rice wine or dry white vermouth

1 Preheat the oven to 180°C│350°F│gas mark 4.

2 Lightly oil a casserole large enough to hold the salmon fillets when laid flat. Alternatively, lightly oil a sheet of kitchen foil large enough to encase the fillets.

3 Pinbone the salmon fillets, and place one fillet, skinned side down, in the casserole or on the foil. Sprinkle over the remaining ingredients, covering the fillet completely. Lay the second fillet, skinned side up, on top to make a sandwich. Cover the casserole or make a sealed parcel with the foil, pressing the edges together firmly.

4 Place the casserole or foil parcel (on a baking sheet) in the preheated oven and cook for 35–40 minutes or until the salmon is cooked. The flesh should be opaque and firm.

5 To serve, slice the salmon into wedges.

wine: SPICY WHITE

Soy-glazed Salmon with Crunchy Hot and Sour Salad

SERVES 4

4 170 g│6 oz salmon steaks

1 tablespoon sunflower oil

For the marinade

5 tablespoons light soy sauce

1 tablespoon sesame oil

1 teaspoon clear honey

For the salad hot and sour dressing

3 tablespoons rice wine vinegar

1 fresh red chilli, finely chopped

1 tablespoon caster sugar

For the salad

140 g│5 oz cashew nuts

1 teaspoon sea salt crystals (Malden if available)

1 teaspoon black mustard seeds

225 g│8 oz beansprouts

110 g│4 oz mangetout, roughly chopped

1 small can of water chestnuts, drained and sliced

grated zest and juice of ½ lime

1 tablespoon chopped fresh coriander

1 Place the salmon steaks in a dish. Combine the marinade ingredients and pour over the salmon steaks. Refrigerate for up to 1 hour.
2 Make the hot and sour dressing: place the vinegar, chilli and sugar in a small saucepan and heat gently without boiling until the sugar has dissolved. Leave to cool, then add the sunflower oil.
3 Gently fry the cashew nuts in a heavy frying pan until lightly browned, then add the sea salt and mustard seeds and fry for 1 minute or until the seeds begin to pop. Set aside.
4 In a hot pan, fry the salmon steaks for 4 minutes on each side – no extra oil should be necessary.
5 Combine the remaining salad ingredients and toss in the dressing. Serve piled on to each plate, sprinkled with the cashew nut mixture and topped with the soy-glazed salmon.

wine: **SPICY WHITE**

Grilled Sardines

SERVES 4

16 small or 8 large fresh sardines
oil
freshly ground black pepper
lemon juice

To garnish
chopped fresh parsley

1 Clean the sardines: slit them along the belly and remove the entrails. Rinse the fish under cold running water and with a little salt gently rub away any black matter in the cavity. Cut off the gills.
2 Preheat the grill. Score the fish with 3–4 shallow diagonal cuts on each side, brush with oil, season with pepper and sprinkle with lemon juice.
3 Grill for about 2 minutes on each side, brushing with the hot oil and the juices that run from the fish.
4 Lay the sardines on a warmed serving platter. Pour over the juices from the grill pan, sprinkle with parsley and serve immediately.

wine: **CRISP DRY WHITE**

Grilled Sardines with Warm Greek Salad

SERVES 4

8 × 110 g | 4 oz sardines, scaled and gutted

2 tablespoons extra virgin olive oil

1 teaspoon coarse sea salt

freshly ground black pepper

For the salad

8 small tomatoes, halved and deseeded

2 courgettes, cut into 2.5 cm | 1 in slices

1 large onion, thickly sliced

4 unpeeled cloves of garlic

3 tablespoons extra virgin olive oil

6 sprigs of fresh thyme

salt and freshly ground black pepper

1 tablespoon balsamic vinegar

12 Kalamata olives, pitted

110 g | 4 oz feta cheese, diced

1 tablespoon chopped fresh basil

1 Preheat the oven to 200°C | 400°F | gas mark 6.

2 Rinse and dry the sardines. Make 3 diagonal slashes on both sides of each sardine. Arrange the sardines on a baking sheet, drizzle with the oil and season with salt and pepper. Cover and set aside in the refrigerator.

3 Make the salad: put the tomatoes on to a baking sheet and add the courgettes, onions and garlic. Pour the oil over the vegetables and add the sprigs of thyme. Season with salt and pepper. Roast for 25 minutes or until the vegetables are soft and lightly browned.

4 Meanwhile, preheat the grill to its highest setting.

5 Grill the sardines for 2–3 minutes on each side or until cooked. The flesh should be opaque and firm.

6 Lift the roasted vegetables into a large mixing bowl. Discard the thyme. Toss the vegetables with the vinegar, olives, cheese and basil. Spoon on to a serving dish and arrange the sardines on top.

wine: **SPICY WHITE**

Deep-fried Whitebait

SERVES 4

450 g | 1 lb whitebait

oil for deep-frying

seasoned plain flour

salt

To serve

lemon wedges

cayenne pepper

1 Sort through the whitebait, discarding any broken fish.

2 Heat the oil in a deep-fryer until a cube of bread browns in 20 seconds.

3 Put the whitebait into a sieve and spoon over the seasoned flour. Shake and toss carefully until every fish is coated. Do this in batches if necessary.

4 Place a small handful of whitebait (too many will stick together) into the hot oil and fry for no more than 2 minutes. Remove and repeat until all the fish are fried. They should be crisp and pale brown.

5 Drain on absorbent kitchen paper. Sprinkle with salt. Serve immediately with lemon wedges and offer cayenne pepper.

NOTE: If for any reason the whitebait cannot be served immediately, they should be spread out in a thin layer on a baking sheet and kept, uncovered, in a just-warm oven until wanted. They will become soggy if piled up or covered.

wine: **VERY DRY WHITE**

Sea Bass with Black Bean Sauce

Black beans can be bought from Chinese supermarkets in tins or vacuum packs. If you like, the sauce can be thickened at the end with 2 teaspoons cornflour.

SERVES 8

1 bunch spring onions
1 tablespoon sunflower oil
1 × 1.8 kg | 4 lb sea bass, cleaned and scaled
salt and freshly ground black pepper
4 slices of lemon

To serve
black bean sauce (see page 129)

1 Prepare the spring onion bows. Choose large cylindrical spring onions that do not have especially bulbous roots. Cut off a large part of the green tops and the roots. With a small, sharp knife, cut vertical lines halfway through the onions at both ends. Leave in icy water for 2 hours, by which time they will have opened out.

2 Preheat the oven to 190°C | 375°F | gas mark 5.

3 Brush a large piece of kitchen foil with the oil. Place the fish on it, season with salt and pepper, cover with the lemon slices, wrap up loosely, but secure the edges firmly, and place on a baking sheet

4 Bake in the oven for 40 minutes.

5 Remove from the foil wrapping to a warmed serving dish, garnish with the spring onion bows, dribble over a little of the sauce and hand the rest separately.

wine: **CRISP DRY WHITE**

Sea Bass with Wild Rice

SERVES 4–6

1 × 1.25 kg|3 lb sea bass, cleaned and scaled
lemon juice
freshly ground black pepper
55 g|2 oz brown rice, soaked overnight
55 g|2 oz wild rice
30 g|1 oz pinenuts, toasted
30 g|1 oz sultanas
1 tablespoon chopped fresh dill

oil for greasing
1 onion, sliced
1 bay leaf
2 tablespoons dry white wine

To garnish
bunch of watercress, trimmed

1 Preheat the oven to 190°C|375°F|gas mark 5.
2 Season the inside of the sea bass with a little lemon juice and pepper. Wash both the rices very well and cook them according to the manufacturers' instructions. Drain and rinse them under cold running water until they are completely cold. Drain them well. Add the pinenuts, sultanas and dill. Season to taste with salt and pepper.
3 Put the sea bass on a sheet of well-oiled kitchen foil and stuff the cavity with the rice mixture. Scatter the onion over the fish, add the bay leaf and sprinkle on the wine. Draw the foil up to make a parcel.
4 Place the parcel on a large baking sheet and bake for 40 minutes. Serve hot or cold, garnished with watercress.

wine: **CRISP DRY WHITE**

Skate with Brown Butter and Capers

SERVES 4

900 g|2 lb skate wings
570 ml|1 pint court bouillon (see page 106)
75 g|3 oz unsalted butter

1 tablespoon lemon juice
1 tablespoon capers, rinsed and roughly chopped

1 Wash the skate and divide into 4 portions.
2 Place the skate in the cold court bouillon in a shallow pan. Cover with a lid and bring slowly to the boil. Poach very gently for 15–20 minutes.
3 Remove the fish and drain on absorbent kitchen paper. Gently scrape away any skin. Place the skate on a warmed serving dish and keep warm in a low oven while you make the sauce.
4 Pour off the court bouillon, reheat the pan and melt the butter. Mix the lemon juice with 1 tablespoon water. When the butter is foaming and a rich golden brown, remove the pan from the heat, add the lemon juice and capers and pour over the skate.

wine: **VERY DRY WHITE**

Skate with Spinach and Bacon

SERVES 2

55 g | 2 oz button mushrooms, sliced

15 g | ½ oz butter

juice of ½ lemon

salt and freshly ground black pepper

15 g | ½ oz fresh flat-leaf parsley, chopped

1 skate wing, filleted into 2

4 rashers of rindless streaky bacon

1 small piece of pig's caul, about 30 cm | 12 in square

oil

2 cloves of garlic

2 tablespoons balsamic vinegar

2 tablespoons water

150 ml | ¼ pint white stock, made with chicken bones (see page 103)

For the spinach

30 g | 1 oz butter

1 clove of garlic, crushed

pinch of freshly grated nutmeg

450 g | 1 lb fresh spinach, large stalks removed

1 Preheat the oven to 200°C | 400°F | gas mark 6.

2 Sauté the mushrooms in the butter. Add the lemon juice and season to taste with salt and pepper. Stir in half of the parsley.

3 Divide the mushroom mixture between the 2 fillets and roll up. Wrap in the bacon and then in the caul. Secure, if necessary, with a cocktail stick.

4 Heat a little oil in a flame proof casserole. Add the garlic and skate parcels, with the secured ends in contact with the pan. Sauté until the parcels are browned all over.

5 Cover and bake for 15–20 minutes. Remove the cocktail sticks, if used.

6 Put the casserole back on the heat. Add the vinegar and 2 tablespoon water and reduce by half. Then add the chicken stock and reduce by half again. Add the remaining parsley.

7 Heat the butter in a frying pan until pale brown. Add the garlic and cook for 30 seconds. Stir the spinach and cook until it wilts. Season with nutmeg. Squeeze dry then chop roughly.

8 Put the spinach on 2 plates, arrange the skate on top and pour over the reduced vinegar and stock.

wine: **DRY WHITE**

Sole au Gratin

SERVES 4

4 small soles, filleted and skinned

6 tablespoons sunflower oil

1 lemon, quartered

2 large sprigs of fresh tarragon

30 g | 1 oz butter, melted

6 tablespoons grated Cheddar cheese

6 tablespoons dried white breadcrumbs

To garnish

lemon wedges

springs of fresh parsley

1 Arrange the sole fillets, skinned side downwards, in a shallow dish. Pour over the oil. Lightly squeeze the lemon quarters over the soles, and leave them in the dish. Place the tarragon over the fish and leave to marinate for 24 hours in the refrigerator.
2 Preheat the grill to a high setting.
3 Brush a large baking tray with a good lip with the melted butter. Arrange the sole fillets on top. Dust evenly with the cheese and crumbs and grill until golden-brown.
4 Arrange on warmed dinner plates and garnish with the lemon wedges and parsley.

wine: DRY WHITE

Sole Bonne Femme

SERVES 4

70 g | 2½ oz butter
1 shallot, finely chopped
170 g | 6 oz mushrooms, thinly sliced
290 ml | ½ pint hot fish stock (see page 106), made from the trimmings
100 ml | 3½ fl oz dry white wine

½ teaspoon lemon juice
3 medium soles, skinned and filleted
salt and freshly ground white pepper
15 g | ½ oz plain flour
150 ml | ¼ pint double cream

1 Preheat the oven to 180°C | 350°F | gas mark 4.
2 Melt 15 g | ½ oz of the butter in a frying pan, add the shallots and cook over a low heat for 10 minutes, or until the shallots are soft. Add the mushrooms and cook for a further 5 minutes. Add the stock and wine and reduce, by boiling rapidly, to half its original quantity. Add the lemon juice.
3 Put the shallots and mushrooms into the bottom of an ovenproof dish. Season the inside of the fillets with salt and pepper. Arrange the sole fillets, folding the ends underneath, on top. Cover with a lid and bake in the oven for 10–15 minutes.
4 Lift the fillets on to a plate and keep warm. Strain the cooking liquor into a saucepan and reserve the mushrooms as a garnish.
5 Reduce the fish liquor to 125 ml | 4 fl oz by boiling rapidly.
6 Melt 30 g | 1 oz of the remaining butter, remove from the heat and add the flour. Return to the heat and cook for 30 seconds. Remove from the heat and gradually add the fish fumet (reduced fish stock). Stir well, return to the heat and bring slowly to the boil, stirring continuously until very thick.
7 Cut the remaining butter into small cubes. Gradually beat the double cream into the fish sauce – if it looks as though it might curdle, beat it vigorously. Remove the sauce from the heat and gradually beat in the cubes of butter to make it shiny. The sauce should now be of coating consistency, but if it is too thick a little milk can be added. Season to taste with salt, pepper and lemon juice.
8 Reheat the mushrooms. Arrange the fish fillets on a warmed serving dish. Coat the fish with the cream sauce, spoon the mushrooms down the centre and serve.

NOTE: Small crescents of puff pastry are a traditional garnish for this dish.

wine: CRISP DRY WHITE

Sole with Mustard and Bacon

SERVES 4

2 tablespoons butter

1 large onion, finely chopped

1 lemon or Dover sole fillets

Dijon mustard

4 thin rashers of rindless smoked back bacon

290 ml | ½ pint fish stock (see page 106)

8 tomatoes, chopped

10 fresh sage leaves, roughly chopped

salt and freshly ground black pepper

3 tablespoons Greek yoghurt

fish glaze to season (see page 108)

1 Melt the butter in a saucepan and stir in the onions. Cover with a piece of dampened greaseproof paper and a lid. Sweat until soft, stirring occasionally.

2 Spread the skinned side of each sole fillet with a very little mustard. Fold into neat parcels, skinned side inside. Stretch the bacon slices by stroking with a table knife.

3 Cover each sole parcel with a bacon rasher and set aside.

4 Meanwhile, make the sauce: add the stock, to the softened onion, tomatoes, sage, salt and pepper and simmer for 20–30 minutes. Remove from the heat and allow to cool.

5 Pre-heat the grill.

6 Liquidize the sauce ingredients very well in a blender until smooth; then pass through a sieve. Return to the rinsed-out pan and boil rapidly, stirring frequently, to a purée. Remove from the heat. Add the yoghurt and taste. It may be necessary to add a little extra fish glaze.

7 Grill the fillets of sole, bacon side up, for 4 minutes. Arrange on a warmed serving dish and hand the sauce separately.

wine: **FULL DRY WHITE**

Fillets of Sole Meunière

SERVES 4

3 lemon soles, skinned and filleted

seasoned plain flour

55 g | 2 oz butter, clarified (see page 385)

1 tablespoon chopped fresh mixed herbs, including parsley

2 tablespoons lemon juice

To serve

lemon wedges

1 Wash the sole fillets, dry thoroughly, and roll in the seasoned flour.

2 Melt half the butter in a heavy frying pan and when foaming add the fillets skinned side uppermost. Cook over a medium heat until lightly browned, turn over and brown on the other side.

3 Place the fish on to a plate and keep warm. Mix the lemon juice with 1 tablespoon of water.

4 Wipe the pan very well, removing any bits of fish. Melt the remaining butter in the pan, heat until a delicate brown, cool slightly and add the herbs and lemon juice. Shake the pan to emulsify the sauce. Pour over the fish and serve immediately with the lemon wedges.

wine: DRY WHITE

Sole Colbert

In this recipe, the backbone of the fish is loosened while it is raw and removed after cooking.

SERVES 4

4 × 340 g 12 oz Dover soles	oil or deep-frying
seasoned plain flour	110 g 4 oz Maître d'Hôtel Butter (see page 134)
beaten egg	
dried white breadcrumbs	**To serve**
	lemon wedges

1 Skin and trim the soles, leaving the heads on. With a small sharp knife make a cut on the side of the fish that had the black skin, down the centre through the flesh to the backbone. Working from the centre of the fish, lift the fillets, loosening them with a knife, and snip the bone just below the head and above the tail.
2 Dip the fish in seasoned flour, shaking away any excess. Brush with beaten egg and press on the breadcrumbs. Be sure to egg-and-crumb the underside of the raised fillets.
3 Heat the oil in a deep fryer until a cube of bread will brown in 30 seconds. Fry the whole fish until a good golden-brown, holding it down with a fish slice to prevent it curling up. Drain well on absorbent kitchen paper. Sprinkle with salt.
4 Allow to settle for 1–2 minutes. Then carefully pull out the backbone, cutting round the breadcrumb coating to prevent too much of it being pulled off.
5 Fill the cavity with slivers of maître d'hôtel butter. Serve immediately with lemon wedges.

NOTE: For a light lunch dish or first course 'slip' soles are suitable. They weigh 170–225 g 6–8 oz.

wine: DRY WHITE

Grilled Dover Sole

1 Dover sole per person	salt and freshly ground black pepper
melted butter	lemon juice

1 Make a cut in the belly (near the head) of each fish and remove the entrails. Wash the fish thoroughly in cold water.
2 Now skin the fish: place the fish on a piece of greaseproof paper and pour a little pile of salt beside it. Snip off the fins with scissors. Make a cut across the black skin just above the tail with a sharp knife, being careful to cut only the skin and not the flesh. Dip your thumb and index finger in the salt and then gently work them under the black skin from the tail upwards until you have raised enough of the skin to be able to take a firm grasp of it. The salt prevents the skin slipping out of your grasp. Using a tea towel to help get a

Grilled Tuna Fish Steaks
with Green Chilli Pesto

Noisettes of Lamb with Red Ratatouille
and Pommes Dauphinoise

Roast Cod with Garlic

Paella

English Roast Chicken

Coq Au Vin

Scallops with Pea and Mint Puree
and Deep-Fried Leek and Ginger

Braised Lamb Shanks with Flageolet Beans

Veal and Ham Raised Pie

Rogan Josh

Calves' Liver with Parsnip Crisps

Roast Beef

Carbonnade de Boeuf

Red Onion and Polenta Tatin

firm grip, pull the skin off the fish in one sharp tug. Repeat on the other (pale) side. This will prove rather more difficult, and is not strictly necessary.

3 Preheat the grill. Brush both the grill pan and one side of the fish with melted butter. Season with salt, pepper and lemon juice and place under the hot grill for about 4 minutes. Turn over and brush the second side with butter. Grill again.

NOTES: This method of skinning a flat fish does not work very well for lemon soles.

Alternatively, the fish can be grilled by dipping them in melted butter and then seasoned flour, which makes them crisper.

wine: **DRY WHITE**

Chaudfroid of Sole

This is one of the great classics of French cuisine.

SERVES 2

1 sole about 675 g | 1½ lb soles, filleted and skinned (see page 306, 307)

2 tablespoons double cream
salt and freshly ground white pepper

For the stock and aspic jelly

1 onion
1 carrot
1 stick of celery
heads, bones and skins of the soles
1 bay leaf
6 white peppercorns
100 ml | 3½ fl oz dry white wine
55 g | 2 oz powdered gelatine
2 egg whites and 2 egg shells, crushed

For the chaudfroid sauce

290 ml | ½ pint milk
6 peppercorns
1 blade of mace
1 slice of onion
30 g | 1 oz butter
20 g | ¾ oz flour
1 level teaspoon powdered gelatine
75 ml | ⅛ pint aspic jelly (see above)
1 tablespoon double cream
salt and freshly ground white pepper

For the farce

85 g | 3 oz uncooked salmon, minced
½ egg white

To garnish

paper-thin truffle or mushroom slices

1 Make the stock: cut the onion, carrot and celery into dice and put into a saucepan with the fish heads, bones and skins. Add the bay leaf, peppercorns, wine, and season well. Add 2 pints cold water and bring to the boil, then skim and allow to simmer for 30 minutes. Strain the stock and leave to cool.

2 Preheat the oven to 170°C | 325°F | gas mark 3.

3 Make the farce: put the salmon into a bowl. Whisk the egg white until frothy and beat slowly into the salmon with the cream. Set over ice. Season to taste with salt and pepper.

4 Wash and dry the sole fillets. Gently bat the fillets between two pieces of clingfilm until they are of even thickness. Divide the farce equally between them, spreading it on the skinned side. Roll or fold up each fillet into a neat parcel.

5 Put the rolled fillets into a buttered ovenproof dish and add a cupful of the stock. Cover with buttered kitchen foil or greaseproof paper. Bake in the oven for 12 minutes, or until the fish and the farce is cooked (it should be opaque and firm). Strain off and reserve the liquid; leave the fish to cool, uncovered.

6 Make the chaudfroid sauce: heat the milk with the peppercorns, mace and onion. Strain and mix with the reserved cooking liquid.

7 Melt the butter in a saucepan and add the flour. Cook, stirring, for 1 minute. Remove from the heat and add the milky liquid. Bring back to the boil, stirring continuously, and allow to simmer for 2 minutes. Strain through a tammy sieve or piece of muslin. Leave to cool, stirring occasionally to prevent a skin from forming.

8 Make the aspic: put the stock into a large saucepan, sprinkle on the gelatine and set the pan over a low heat.

9 Put the crushed egg shells into a bowl, add the egg whites and whisk until frothy. Pour into the cold stock and keep whisking steadily (preferably with a balloon whisk) until the mixture begins to steam. Stop whisking immediately and allow the mixture to come just to the boil. Remove the pan from the heat. Allow the mixture to subside. Take care not to break the crust formed by the egg white.

10 Bring the aspic up to the boil again and allow to subside again. Repeat this once more (the egg white will trap the sediment in the stock and clear the aspic).

11 Fix a double layer of fine scalded muslin over a clean basin, lift the egg white crust to the sieve and then check to see how clear the stock is. If not quite clear carefully strain the aspic through it. Strain the aspic again. Do not try to hurry the process by squeezing the cloth, or the aspic will be murky. Set aside a little of the aspic to use for coating the garnish.

12 Soak the gelatine for the sauce in about 4 tablespoons of the cleared cool aspic in a small saucepan for 5 minutes, then melt over a low heat. Stir the liquid gelatine into the sauce with the cream. Season to taste with salt and pepper. Squeeze through a piece of sterlized muslin.

13 Lay the sole parcels on a wire rack with a tray underneath. As the sauce thickens, spoon some over each parcel, covering the top and sides. Refrigerate the coated fillets until the sauce is set. Wash the tray and place it back under the wire rack.

14 Garnish the fish parcels with truffle or mushroom slices which have been dipped in aspic. When the aspic is cold and on the point of setting, carefully coat each fillet with it. Refrigerate to set. Repeat the coating if necessary: the aspic layer should be thin, but very shiny. Trim with a hot sharp knife.

15 Pour the remaining aspic into a shallow tray and allow to set in the refrigerator, then cut it into tiny squares with a sharp knife.

16 Arrange the fillets on a serving dish. Garnish with the chopped aspic and keep cool until ready to serve.

NOTE: If the aspic is less than crystal-clear do not use it to garnish. Chopping it only seems to emphasize its murkiness.

wine: DRY ROSÉ

Lemon Sole with Cucumber

SERVES 4

1 large cucumber, peeled, halved lengthways,
deseeded and thickly sliced

3 × 675 g | 1½ lb lemon soles, filleted and skinned
(see pages 306, 307)

seasoned plain flour

55 g | 2 oz clarified butter

2 tablespoons lemon juice plus 1 tablespoon water

1 Blanch the cucumber in a saucepan of boiling salted water for 30 seconds. Refresh, drain and dry well.

2 Dip the sole fillets in seasoned flour. Lay them on a plate but do not allow them to touch each other or they will become soggy.

3 Heat half the butter in a frying pan. When foaming, put in a batch of fillets taking care to place the side that was next to the bone down. Turn them over when golden-brown (about 1 minute on each side). Dish on to a shallow platter and keep warm. Fry the remaining fillets in the same way.

4 Melt the remaining butter in the pan. Add the cucumber and fry quite briskly for 1 minute. Add the lemon juice and water to the hot pan. Bring to the boil and tip over the fish. Serve immediately.

wine: DRY WHITE

Lemon Sole with Burnt Hollandaise

SERVES 4

12 lemon sole fillets, skinned (see page 307)

570 ml | 1 pint fish stock (see page 106), cooled

150 ml | ¼ pint Hollandaise sauce (see page 119)

3 tablespoons double cream

1 Preheat the oven to 180°C | 350°F | gas mark 4.

2 Roll the sole fillets up, skinned side inside. Lay them in an ovenproof dish or roasting pan and pour over enough stock to nearly cover the fish. Cover and poach in the oven for 10–15 minutes. Alternatively, poach carefully on the hob.

3 While the fish cooks, preheat the grill and make the hollandaise sauce, which must be very thick.

4 Drain the fish well and arrange on a heatproof serving dish. Mix the sauce with the cream and coat each fillet with a spoonful. Brown quickly under the grill and serve immediately.

wine: DRY WHITE

Grilled Brill Fillets with Anchovy Butter

SERVES 4

55 g | 2 oz unsalted butter, softened
4 anchovy fillets
1 teaspoon lemon juice
salt and freshly ground black pepper
8 × 85 g | 3 oz brill fillets, skinned (see page 307)

To serve

rocket and radicchio leaves
1 quantity French dressing (see page 123), made
  with walnut oil
1 bunch of fresh chives, chopped

1 Preheat the grill to its highest setting. Put the butter into a food processor with the anchovy fillets and lemon juice. Whizz to a smooth paste and season with pepper.
2 Fold each brill fillet into 3 with the skinned side inside. Season with salt and pepper and grill the fillets for 4–5 minutes until cooked through (they should be opaque and firm). Brush each fillet generously with the anchovy butter to give a good shine.
3 To serve: toss the salad in the French dressing and divide between 4 dinner plates. Arrange 2 brill fillets on each plate and sprinkle with the chopped chives. Serve immediately.

wine: **CRISP DRY WHITE**

Trout with Almonds

SERVES 4

4 medium rainbow trout
seasoned plain flour
85 g | 3 oz clarified butter (see page 385)
55 g | 2 oz flaked almonds
lemon juice

chopped fresh parsley
salt and freshly ground black pepper

To garnish

lemon wedges

1 Preheat the oven to 170°C | 325°F | gas mark 3.
2 Clean the trout very well (if not properly cleaned they will taste very bitter). Dip them in seasoned flour and shake off any excess.
3 Fry briefly on both sides in all but 15 g | ½ oz of the butter. Transfer to an ovenproof dish, pouring over the butter from the pan. Bake for 15 minutes, or until firm to the touch.
4 Fry the almonds in the remaining butter. Add the lemon juice and parsley and shake over the heat until emulsified.
5 Arrange the trout on a warmed serving dish, pour over the almonds and butter, then sprinkle with lemon juice, salt and pepper. Garnish with lemon wedges and sprinkle with parsley.

NOTE: The trout may be cooked entirely in the frying pan, but they must be fried slowly, about 7 minutes a side.

wine: **DRY WHITE**

Trout en Papillote

SERVES 2

55 g | 2 oz butter

1 tablespoon very finely shredded white of leek

1 tablespoon very finely shredded carrot

55 g | 2 oz button mushrooms, thinly sliced

1 teaspoon chopped fresh tarragon or fennel leaves

salt and freshly ground black pepper

4 × 110 g | 4 oz unskinned trout fillets, pinboned
  (see page 307)

lemon juice

2 tablespoons dry white wine

oil for brushing

1 Preheat the oven to 220°C | 425°F | gas mark 7. Place a baking sheet in the oven.

2 Fold a large sheet of greaseproof paper in half and cut out 2 semi-circles, with a radius of 20 cm | 8 in. Open out to form circles. Papillotes are generally made from circular papers but are better made from heart-shaped pieces if whole small fish or long fillets of fish are to be wrapped.

3 Melt half the butter and add the leek and carrot. Cook slowly without browning for 5 minutes, then add the mushrooms. Cook for 2 more minutes, then add the tarragon or fennel, and season with salt and pepper. Allow to cool.

4 Brush the inside of the paper circles with a little oil, leaving the edges clear. Sandwich the trout fillets, skin side outside, with the vegetables. Place a sandwich on one side of each paper circle. Squeeze a few drops of lemon on each and sprinkle on the wine. Dot with the remaining butter and add salt and pepper.

5 Fold the free half of the papillote paper over to make a parcel rather like an apple turnover. Fold the edges of the 2 layers of paper over twice together, twisting and pressing hard to seal.

6 Put the papillotes on the hot baking sheet, taking care that they do not touch each other. Bake in the oven for 12 minutes.

7 Slash the parcels then serve immediately on warmed dinner plates.

NOTES: Halibut, haddock, salmon, indeed almost any fish, can be cooked in this way. Whole trout weighing 340 g | 12 oz will take 15 minutes to cook. Breast of chicken, boned and skinned, is also good *en papillote*, and takes 20 minutes in a piece, 15 minutes if in slices.

For a richer dish serve with beurre blanc (see page 121).

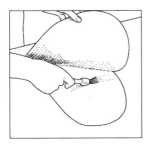

Brush the paper with a little oil

Fold the edges of the paper together; twist and press to make a really good seal

wine: DRY WHITE

Steamed Trout Fillets in Lettuce

Fish, shellfish and tender cuts of meat, often wrapped in pastry or vegetable leaves, are quickly steamed. Food in one or more stacked rattan or metal baskets with a lid is placed over steaming liquid in a pan or wok for quick cooking.

Plate steaming is an excellent method of cooking small quantities of fish in their own juices. Put the fish fillets or steaks on a lightly buttered plate, season well and cover with another upturned buttered plate or buttered kitchen foil. Set the covered plate on top of a pan of gently boiling water or on a trivet inside a large frying pan of bubbling water and cook for 8–10 minutes, depending on the thickness of the fish.

SERVES 4

2 shallots, very finely chopped
1 tablespoon oil
170 g | 6 oz mushrooms, finely chopped
a squeeze of lemon juice

salt and freshly ground black pepper
8 large lettuce leaves or cabbage leaves
4 large trout, pink-fleshed if possible, filleted,
    skinned and pinboned (see pages 306, 307)

1 Sweat the shallots in the oil, stirring constantly. Add the mushrooms, lemon juice, salt and pepper. Sauté until the mushrooms give off their juices, then boil hard until all the juice has evaporated.

2 Blanch the lettuce in a large quantity of boiling salted water for 15 seconds, until just limp. Refresh in a bowl of cold water, then spread out on tea towels or absorbent kitchen paper to dry.

3 Trim the fillets and remove any bones with tweezers. By running your finger against the grain of the flesh, you can feel where they are. Pat the fillets dry and season with salt and pepper. Place a spoonful of the mushroom mixture on each fillet and roll up. Wrap in a lettuce leaf and place seam down in a steamer. Continue with the other fillets. Steam until tender (about 10 minutes).

wine: **DRY WHITE**

Steamed Trout Fillets with Tomato and Ginger Sauce

SERVES 4

8 × 110 g|4 oz trout fillets, skinned and pinboned
  (see page 307)
1 tablespoon oil
lemon juice
salt and freshly ground white pepper

For the tomato and ginger sauce

6 fresh ripe tomatoes, roughly chopped
1 teaspoon tomato purée
1 tablespoon ginger syrup from a jar of preserved
  stem ginger
1 slice of fresh root ginger, peeled

15 g|½ oz butter
salt and freshly ground black pepper
a squeeze of lemon juice
a pinch of caster sugar

For the watercress and coriander garnish

15 g|½ oz butter
1 bunch of watercress, leaves and young shoots only
1 small bunch of coriander, leaves only
1 tablespoon double cream
salt and freshly ground black pepper

1 Put the trout fillets on a sheet of lightly oiled kitchen foil. Brush the fish with oil and sprinkle with the lemon juice, salt and pepper. Cover with foil and refrigerate until ready to cook.

2 Liquidize the tomatoes and tomato purée in a blender and then pass through a sieve. Add the ginger syrup, fresh ginger and butter and simmer for 15 minutes. Add salt, pepper, lemon juice and the sugar.

3 Prepare the watercress and coriander garnish: melt the butter. Add the watercress and coriander and cook for 2 minutes. Drain well in a colander. Return the leaves to the saucepan, add the cream, salt and pepper and set aside until ready to serve.

4 Cook the fish: lay the parcels of fish on a wire rack and steam over a pan of boiling water on top of the stove for 3–4 minutes.

5 Place a spoonful of the watercress mixture on each warmed dinner plate. Arrange 2 trout fillets on top and surround with the sauce. Serve immediately.

wine: **SPICY DRY WHITE**

Trout in Filo Pastry with Lime Beurre Blanc

SERVES 4

4 × 225 g|8 oz trout, filleted, skinned and pinboned
  (see pages 306, 307)
85 g|3 oz butter
1 large carrot, cut into julienne strips
1 leek, cut into julienne strips

4 sheets of filo pastry (see page 563)
4 tablespoons dry white wine
salt and freshly ground black pepper
lime beurre blanc (see page 122)

1 Preheat the oven to 200°C|400°F|gas mark 6.

2 Cut the trout into 2.5 cm|1 in wide strips and divide them into 4 equal portions.

3 Melt a little of the butter in a frying pan, add the carrot and leek and cook until soft but not coloured.

4 Melt the remaining butter. Cut each filo sheet in half and brush with butter. Sandwich the halves together.

5 Divide the vegetables between the 4 filos and then place the fish on top of the vegetables. Sprinkle 1 tablespoon of the wine over each, brush with melted butter and season with salt and pepper.

6 Draw the edges of the pastry to form pouches.

7 Place each pouch on a lightly greased baking sheet, dab with melted butter and bake in the oven for 8–10 minutes, or until the pastry is crisp and golden brown.

8 Serve immediately with the lime beurre blanc.

wine: **VERY DRY WHITE**

Boned Stuffed Trout

SERVES 2

2 × 225 g | 8 oz trout, cleaned (see page 305)

55 g | 2 oz butter

1 tablespoon very finely shredded white of leek

1 tablespoon very finely shredded carrot

55 g | 2 oz button mushrooms, very thinly sliced

1 teaspoon chopped fresh thyme

lemon juice

2 tablespoons dry white wine

salt and freshly ground black pepper

55 g | 2 oz feta cheese, diced

To garnish

lemon wedges

1 small bunch of watercress

1 Preheat the oven to 200°C | 400°F | gas mark 6.

2 Melt the butter in a saucepan and gently cook the leek and carrot for 2 minutes. Add the mushrooms and cook for 1 further minute. Add the thyme, lemon juice and wine and cook until the liquid has evaporated. Season to taste with salt and pepper. Allow to cool. Add the feta cheese.

3 Stuff the trout with this mixture and lay in a lightly greased roasting pan. Cover and bake for 15 minutes.

4 Remove to a warmed serving dish and garnish with lemon wedges and watercress.

wine: **DRY WHITE**

Japanese Fish Cooking

Sushi

The word sushi, literally translated, means 'happy children', which goes some way to describing the special love the Japanese have for this dish, which is served at special occasions; it is not an everyday food or one that is generally cooked in the home.

The base of sushi is sweet vinegar-flavoured rice served in various forms (for sushi recipes see page 352).

Sushi nori maki (literally, 'seaweed roll') is cooked rice rolled in nori seaweed, often with a selection of fish fillings.

Sushi nigiri (literally, 'grip') is a piece of fish lying over or 'gripping' the rice.

Plain sushi is the vinegar-flavoured rice served on its own in a bowl with fish or meat forked through it. This is the traditional way of serving it.

Sashimi

This consists of sheets or slices of raw fish, which is sold ready-prepared. Most Japanese supermarkets in the UK sell frozen fish especially for sashimi. As the fish is frozen while still very fresh, it tastes superb and is well worth trying. Fish traditionally served as sashimi include squid, young tuna, scallops, prawns, sea bream and yellow tail.

The fish used for sashimi in Japan is always very fresh, prepared and handled carefully by fishermen and fishmongers alike. Sashimi is kept separately from other fish at the market, to prevent cross-contamination.

Hygiene legislation in the UK now states that fish that is prepared for raw dishes, such as sushi, ceviche, gravad lax, etc. must be frozen for at least 24 hours prior to consumption, to ensure that any harmful bacteria present are kept to a minimum.

Sashimi is eaten dipped in soy sauce and traditionally served with wasabi and shredded daikon and garnished with shiso leaves.

Tempura

Literally translated, tempura means 'fritter'. Fish, meat or vegetables are dipped in a batter, then deep-fried (see page 200).

Tepin-yaki

Literally translated, tepin-yaki means 'iron-grill'. In a Japanese restaurant this method of cooking is performed in front of the diner by a highly trained tepin-yaki chef. He will demonstrate chopping, tossing, cooking and presentation techniques to the customers seated around the hot grill.

Teri-yaki

Literally translated, teri-yaki means 'shine-grill'. The food, whether it is fish, chicken or other meat, is marinated first in soy, sugar and mirin, then grilled on a hot plate.

Sweet Vinegar Rice

This is the recipe for the rice used in sushi. As with any cooked rice dish, keep refrigerated and eat within 24 hours of cooking.

MAKES ENOUGH FOR 15 PIECES OF SUSHI

225 g | 8 oz Japanese sushi short-grain rice
450 ml | ¾ pint water
1 piece of kombu seaweed

75 ml | 2½ fl oz rice wine vinegar
1 tablespoon caster sugar
2 teaspoons salt

1 Put the rice into a sieve and rinse under running cold water for 1 minute, to remove excess starch.
2 Put into a saucepan, cover with the water, add the kombu and allow to soak for 45 minutes.
3 After the soaking time, cover the saucepan with a well-fitting lid and bring to the boil. Reduce the heat and continue to cook the rice for 10–12 minutes or until cooked through.
4 Meanwhile, put the vinegar into a small saucepan, add the sugar and salt and heat slowly until dissolved. Remove from the heat and allow to cool.
5 When the rice is cooked, turn it on to a flat plate and remove and discard the kombu.
6 Pour the sweetened vinegar over the rice, toss with a fork and allow to cool. Use as required.

Traditional Nori Sushi Rolls

Smoked or raw fish can be included in this simple roll as desired.

MAKES ABOUT 40

2 eggs
1 tablespoon light soy sauce
freshly ground black pepper
1 tablespoon oil
½ cucumber, peeled
4–5 sheets of nori seaweed
1 quantity sweet vinegar rice (see above)

For dipping
3 tablespoons dark soy sauce
1 red chilli, deseeded and chopped
wasabi paste or powder

1 Beat the eggs and soy sauce together and season with pepper. Heat the oil in a frying pan, add the egg mixture and cook over a low heat until the egg is cooked and resembles an omelette. Remove from the pan and allow to cool.
2 Cut the cucumber into long pencil lengths. Cut the omelette into strips.
3 Lay a sushi mat or large piece of clingfilm on work surface. Place the sheets of nori on the mat and press a layer of rice over half of each sheet up to the edges.

4 Arrange a couple of cucumber and omelette strips on the rice, then roll up firmly as for a Swiss roll, using the sushi mat or clingfilm to help you. Refrigerate for 15 minutes.

5 Cut each roll crosswise into about 8 even slices and arrange on a plate.

6 Mix the soy sauce and chilli together and hand separately in a little dish. Hand the wasabi separately too.

Dressed Crab

SERVES 3

1 900 g|2 lb live crab
salt

hardboiled egg yolks, sieved
chopped fresh parsley

To season
lemon juice
salt and freshly ground black pepper
mustard
fresh white breadcrumbs

To serve
mayonnaise (see page 117)
tartare sauce (see page 119)
brown bread and butter

1 Pierce the crab between the eyes with a skewer.

2 Place the crab in a pan of well-salted water (about 4 tablespoons to 2.5 litres|4 pints water), cover and bring to the boil. Simmer, allowing 15 minutes to each 450 g|1 lb crab. Remove from the pan and allow to cool.

3 Lay the crab on its back. Twist off the legs and claws. Cracking round the natural line (visible near the edge), remove the pale belly shell and discard it. Remove and throw away the small sac at the top of the crab body and the spongy lungs which line the edge (they look rather like grey fish gills).

 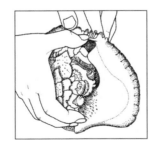 

Twist off the legs and claws; remove and throw away the pale belly shell; discard the spongy lungs and small stomach sac

4 Have 2 bowls ready, one for white meat, one for brown. Lift out the body of the crab, cut into 2–4 pieces and carefully pick out all the meat that you can. This is fiddly and could take up to 15 minutes. If you have a lobster pick it can be very useful. Wash and dry the shell.

5 Crack the large claws, remove the meat and put it into the white-meat bowl.

6 With a lobster pick or toothpick poke out the remaining meat from the legs, and add it to the white meat in the bowl.

7 Dress the crab: cream the brown meat, season with lemon juice, salt, pepper and mustard. Add enough breadcrumbs to bind the mixture. Arrange this down the centre of the shell. Season the white meat with salt then pile up at each side. Garnish with neat lines of egg yolk and parsley.

8 Place on a serving plate with the claws. Serve with mayonnaise or tartare sauce and brown bread and butter.

wine: **VERY DRY WHITE**

Langoustines in Filo with Herb Butter

SERVES 4

12 langoustines

85 g | 3 oz unsalted butter

6 cloves of garlic, 4 bruised and 2 crushed

1 tablespoon finely chopped fresh parsley

4 slices of white bread

4 sheets of filo pastry (see page 563)

salt and freshly ground black pepper

1 egg, beaten, to glaze

To serve

1 lemon, cut into wedges

1 Bring a saucepan of water to the boil. Put the langoustines into the water and bring back to simmering point. Remove the langoustines and allow them to cool.

2 Remove the head, shells and legs from the langoustines. Remove the digestive tract (the black vein running down the back).

3 Gently melt the butter in a pan and add the 4 bruised cloves of garlic. Turn off the heat and allow them to infuse for as long as possible – at least 30 minutes. Remove the garlic cloves and add the crushed garlic and the parsley.

4 Preheat the oven to 170°C | 325°F | gas mark 3.

5 Cut 4 × 5 cm | 2 in rounds from the bread and dry out in the oven until crisp.

6 Cut a sheet of filo in half and trim each half into 17.5 cm | 7 in squares.

7 Brush each square with the herb butter and place one on top of the other at an angle.

8 Put a piece of the crisp bread in the middle. Dip 2 langoustines into the herb butter. Place them on the bread and season with salt and pepper.

9 Gather the corners of the pastry together to form a pouch. Brush with beaten egg. Repeat for the other 3 parcels. Refrigerate until required.

10 Turn up the oven temperature to 220°C | 425°F | gas mark 7. Place the parcels on a baking sheet and bake in the oven for 5 minutes or until they are a rich brown.

11 Remove from the oven and serve immediately with lemon wedges.

wine: **VERY DRY WHITE**

Boiled Lobster

SERVES 4

2 × 900 g | 2 lb live lobsters

For the court bouillon

1 litre | 2 pints water
225 g | 8 oz carrots, sliced
1 medium onion, sliced
1 bay leaf
1 sprig of fresh thyme
30 g | 1 oz salt

150 ml | ¼ pint white wine vinegar
1 bunch of fresh parsley
10 black peppercorns

To serve hot

Hollandaise Sauce (see page 119), or melted butter

To serve cold

mayonnaise (see page 117)

1 Combine all the court bouillon ingredients in a saucepan and simmer for 30 minutes. Strain. Bring the court bouillon back to the boil.

2 Next kill the lobsters. See recipe below for instructions. Put the lobsters' head first into the court bouillon.

3 Cover and simmer for 8 minutes per 450 g | 1 lb. Lift the lobsters out. Allow to cool before splitting if to be served cold.

4 Split the lobsters in half, remove the grit sac and the intestine, a thin grey or black line running the length of the body.

5 Serve with hollandaise sauce or melted butter if to be eaten hot, with mayonnaise if cold.

NOTE: A fresh live lobster turns bright red when cooked and the tail tightens considerably.

wine: **DRY WHITE**

Grilled Lobster with Red Butter Sauce

SERVES 4

4 small live lobsters
unsalted butter, melted
cayenne pepper

For the butter sauce

1 shallot, finely chopped
150 ml | ¼ pint dry white wine
1 teaspoon fish glaze (see page 108)

110 g | 4 oz unsalted butter, chilled and diced
the coral from the lobster
3 tablespoons double cream
tomato purée (optional)
salt and freshly ground white pepper

To garnish

watercress, trimmed

1 Begin to prepare the butter sauce: put the shallot into a small saucepan with the wine. Cook slowly until the liquid is reduced to half its original quantity. Strain into a clean saucepan. Add the fish glaze and set aside.

2 Next kill the lobsters. Push a sharp strong knife through the nerve centre of each lobster. This is a well-defined cross on the back of its head. When the middle of the cross is pierced the lobster will die instantly, although it will still move alarmingly.

3 Lay the lobsters out flat and split in half lengthways. Remove the grit sac and the threadlike intestine running the length of the body. Do not mistake the roe (or coral), which may or may not be present, for the intestine, which is tiny. The roe, when cooked, will be bright red and has an excellent flavour. Reserve it for the sauce. Do not throw away the soft grey green flesh near the head either – it is the liver (or tomalley) and quite delicious.

4 Preheat the grill.

5 Brush the lobsters with butter and season with cayenne pepper. Place in the grill pan, cut side uppermost first, and grill for 5–10 minutes on each side, depending on size, until the lobster shell is a good bright red.

6 Meanwhile continue with the butter sauce. Mix 1 teaspoon of the butter with the lobster coral. Set aside.

7 When the lobsters are cooked, crack the claws, without removing them from the body if possible, with a claw cracker or by covering with a cloth and hitting gently with a rolling pin. Keep the lobsters warm while finishing the sauce.

8 Warm up the reduced wine and fish glaze. Using a wire whisk and plenty of vigorous continuous whisking, add the butter piece by piece. The process should take about 2 minutes and the sauce should thicken considerably. Do not allow it to get too hot.

9 Whisk in the coral and cream, and any pan juices from the grill pan. Add a little tomato purée to brighten up the colour it necessary. The coral should make the sauce a pink colour. If this does not happen turn up the heat a little until the sauce changes colour. Season to taste with salt and pepper.

10 Arrange the lobsters on a large oval dish. Garnish with watercress and hand the sauce separately.

wine: DRY WHITE

Lobster Fricassée with Tarragon Cream Sauce

SERVES 2

2 × 450 g | 1 lb live lobsters	290 ml | ½ pint crème fraîche
45 g | 1½ oz unsalted butter	2 sprigs of fresh tarragon
1 shallot, finely chopped	salt and freshly ground black pepper

1 Kill the lobsters. Cut the lobsters in half lengthways. Remove the grit sac and the threadlike intestine running the length of the body. Crack the claws.

2 Melt the butter in a sauté pan and add the shallot. Cook gently until softened and slightly brown.

3 Add the lobster halves, shell side down, and pour the crème fraîche over them. Add the tarragon stems, stripped of their leaves (reserve these), and simmer over a low heat until the cream comes to the boil. Cover the pan and turn the heat down to very low. Cook for 10 minutes.

4 Remove the lobsters from the cream. Carefully pull the tail meat out of the shells in one piece. Remove the claw meat. Place all the meat in a medium saucepan and set aside.

5 Crack or cut up all the lobster shells and add to the cream in the sauté pan. Bring to the boil over a medium heat. Remove from the heat and pass the sauce through a very fine sieve into the saucepan containing the lobster meat. Season with salt, pepper and the reserved tarragon leaves.

6 Heat the fricassée through very gently and serve.

7 If making this in advance, allow the fricassée to cool, and refrigerate. About 10 minutes before serving, heat through very gently in a saucepan.

wine: **CRISP DRY WHITE**

Dry-fried Prawns with Coriander

This has been adapted from a recipe by Yan-Kit So.

SERVES 4

450 g | 1 lb raw, medium shell-on prawns, weighed
  without heads

5 cloves of garlic

2.5 cm | 1 in piece of fresh root ginger

3–4 tablespoons oil

1 tablespoon dry sherry

3 spring onions, chopped

1 tablespoon chopped fresh coriander

For the marinade

½ teaspoon salt

1 teaspoon sugar

1–2 tablespoons light soy sauce

2 teaspoons Worcestershire sauce

2 teaspoons oil

freshly ground black pepper

1 Shell the prawns. Using a small sharp knife, slit along the backs of the prawns and remove the black vein. Cut off the legs. Wash and pat dry.

2 Mix together all the marinade ingredients and add the prawns. Leave to stand for at least 30 minutes.

3 Bruise the garlic with a rolling pin, remove the skin and leave the cloves flattened but whole. Peel the ginger and bruise it with a rolling pin.

4 Heat a wok or heavy sauté pan until it is very hot. Add the oil and swirl it about. Fry the garlic and ginger for about 1 minute, remove and discard.

5 Add the prawns. Spread them out in a single layer and fry for about 1 minute. Reduce the heat if they begin to burn. Turn over to fry the other side for about 1 minute. Turn up the heat if necessary. Splash in the sherry. The prawns are cooked when they have turned red and curled up. Sprinkle with the spring onion and coriander. Stir once or twice and serve immediately.

wine: **DRY WHITE**

Prawn Pilaf

SERVES 4

790 g | 1¾ lb cooked shell-on prawns
570 ml | 1 pint water
100 ml | 3½ fl oz dry white wine
salt and freshly ground black pepper
1 slice of lemon
3–4 parsley stalks
55 g | 2 oz butter

1 medium onion, finely chopped
225 g | 8 oz long-grain rice, washed
2 hardboiled eggs, chopped

To garnish
1 tablespoon chopped fresh parsley

1 Peel all but 3 of the prawns. Reserve the prawns and put the shells into a saucepan with the water, wine, salt, pepper, lemon slice and parsley stalks. Bring to the boil, then simmer for 15 minutes. Strain and reserve the liquor.

2 Melt half of the butter in a saucepan and cook the onion gently until soft. Add the rice and fry slowly until it looks opaque. Add the reserved liquor. Bring to the boil, stirring with a fork. Cover and simmer gently for 25 minutes, until the rice is tender and the water absorbed. Remove from the heat and allow to stand for 10 minutes.

3 Meanwhile, melt the remaining butter, add the peeled prawns and eggs and heat through. Season with salt, pepper and lemon juice. Fork the shelled prawns and eggs into the pilaf rice. Pile into a warmed serving dish and sprinkle with plenty of parsley. Put the unshelled prawns on top and serve.

NOTES: Ideally, prawn pilaf should be made with raw shell-on prawns, but they are often difficult to get hold of. If you can get them, simply cook the prawns for 4 minutes in the water and wine. Remove from the liquid and then follow the recipe as before.

If the pilaf is to be kept warm, do not garnish with the parsley and whole prawns until serving. The parsley dries out and the prawns turn chalky-white.

wine: DRY WHITE

Prawns in Coconut Sauce

SERVES 4

450 g | 1 lb raw shell-on prawns
2 teaspoons coriander seeds
½ teaspoon black peppercorns
a few fenugreek seeds
2 tablespoons oil
a few mustard seeds
2 cloves of garlic, cut into slivers
3 shallots, chopped
1 teaspoon peeled and grated fresh ginger root
150 ml | ¼ pint water

1 teaspoon paprika pepper
a pinch of cayenne pepper
a pinch of ground turmeric
salt
2 teaspoons lemon juice
110 g | 4 oz creamed coconut

To garnish
fresh coriander leaves

1 Peel the prawns and remove the black veins. Rinse them out quickly under cold running water and pat them dry with kitchen paper. Cover and refrigerate.

2 Heat a small cast-iron frying pan over a medium heat. When hot, put in the coriander seeds, peppercorns and fenugreek seeds. Stir for about 1 minute or until lightly roasted. Remove from the heat and grind in a clean grinder. Set aside.

3 Heat the oil in a large frying pan. When hot, put in the mustard seeds. As soon as they begin to pop (this takes just a few seconds), stir once and add the garlic and shallot. Stir and fry until the shallot is lightly browned. Put in the ginger and stir once. Now add the water, the paprika, cayenne, turmeric, salt, the ground spice mixture and the lemon juice. Bring to the boil, then simmer for 5 minutes.

4 Add the prawns and stir until they just turn opaque. Stir in the creamed coconut. As soon as the liquid begins to bubble, turn off the heat and serve garnished with coriander leaves.

wine: **FULL DRY WHITE**

Fried Scallops with Garlic

SERVES 4

16 scallops

55 g | 2 oz garlic butter (see page 133)

salt and freshly ground black pepper

juice of $\frac{1}{2}$ lemon

a little chopped fresh parsley

1 Remove the hard muscle from the scallops (opposite the coral or roe, see page 198).

2 Melt the garlic butter in a frying pan. Add the scallops and pepper. Fry over a high heat for 30 seconds on each side.

3 Remove from the heat, add the lemon juice and parsley and sprinkle with salt. Serve immediately.

wine: **LIGHT DRY WHITE**

Coquilles St Jacques

SERVES 4

150 ml | $\frac{1}{4}$ pint dry white wine

1 bay leaf

$\frac{1}{4}$ onion

8 large or 12 small scallops

450 g | 1 lb mashed potatoes (see page 268)

30 g | 1 oz butter

30 g | 1 oz plain flour

1 tablespoon double cream

lemon juice

salt and freshly ground black pepper

dried white breadcrumbs

a little extra butter to finish

To serve

4 scallop shells

1 Put the wine with 150 ml | ¼ pint water, the bay leaf and onion into a saucepan. Bring to the boil. Turn down the heat, add the scallops and poach very gently for 5 minutes.

2 Lift the scallops from the liquid. Pull away the hard muscle (opposite the coral or roe, see page 198) and cut each scallop into 2 or 3 pieces.

3 Divide the scallops between the 4 scallop shells. Pipe or spoon the mashed potato around the edge of the shells.

4 Preheat the grill.

5 Melt the butter in a saucepan, remove from the heat and add the flour. Return to the heat and cook for 30 seconds. Remove from the heat and strain over the liquid in which the scallops were cooked. Stir until the sauce is thick and smooth. Add the cream and season with lemon juice, salt and pepper.

6 Spoon over the scallops. Sprinkle with the crumbs, dot with butter and brown under the grill.

wine: **VERY DRY WHITE**

Fried Scallops with Bacon

SERVES 4

12 scallops

4 rashers of rindless back bacon

1 tablespoon chopped fresh parsley

lemon juice

salt and freshly ground black pepper

1 Clean the scallops, pull away the hard muscle (opposite the coral or roe) and discard (see page 198). Cut in half horizontally.

2 Cut the bacon into slivers and fry until beginning to brown. Reduce the heat and add the scallops. Fry quickly for 30 seconds on each side.

3 Remove from the heat, add the parsley and lemon juice, season with salt and pepper and serve immediately.

wine: **DRY WHITE**

Didier Oudill's Braised Scallops in their Shells

This recipe has been taken from Michel Guérard's *Cuisine Gourmande*.

SERVES 4

12 scallops in their shells

75 g | 2¾ oz butter

125 g | 4½ oz flour quantity flaky pastry (see page 566)

salt and freshly ground black pepper

½ beaten egg to glaze

To garnish

55 g | 2 oz butter

110 g | 4 oz leeks, cut into julienne strips

110 g | 4 oz carrots, cut into julienne strips

110 g | 4 oz button mushrooms, cut into julienne strips

salt and freshly ground black pepper

1 teaspoon chopped fresh tarragon

1 tablespoon chopped shallot

1 Open the scallops with a strong knife and detach the scallop from the lower shell. Scoop out the scallops with a spoon, catching all their juice in a strainer lined with a fine cloth and placed over a bowl. Pull away and discard the membrane or frill and the black stomach parts. Wash the scallops thoroughly in cold running water, and dry them on a cloth. Separate the corals and cut the white parts in 2 across the middle to obtain 24 rounds.

2 Scrub 8 of the shells (tops and bottoms) under running water and set aside.

3 Heat the butter in a saucepan and cook the leeks and carrots for 5 minutes. Then add the mushrooms and cook for a further 3 minutes. Add salt, pepper and the tarragon. Cover and simmer for 2 minutes.

4 Roll out the pastry and cut it into 8 strips 25 × 2.5 cm | 10 × 1 in. Preheat the oven to 250°C | 480°F | gas mark 9.

5 Divide half the vegetable garnish among the 8 curved shells and sprinkle with the shallot.

6 Put the coral and 3 rounds of the white part of the scallop on each shell and season with salt and pepper.

7 Cover the scallops with the remaining vegetables, sprinkle them with the strained scallop juice and divide the butter between them.

8 Put 8 empty shells on top of the filled shells and edge each with a strip of the pastry, brushed with beaten egg, to seal completely. Bake in the preheated oven for 10–12 minutes, according to the size of the scallops, and serve in the shells.

NOTE: A low-fat version of this recipe can be prepared without the butter. Steam the vegetables for the garnish instead of frying them.

wine: **DRY WHITE**

Scallops with Pea and Mint Purée and Deep-Fried Leek and Ginger

SERVES 4

1 leek, cut into julienne strips

1   5 cm | 2 in piece of fresh root ginger, peeled and cut into julienne strips

seasoned flour

oil for deep-frying

salt

olive oil

20 large scallops, prepared (see page 198)

juice of 1 lemon

For the pea purée

285 g | 10 oz frozen peas

pinch of sugar

2 large sprigs of fresh mint

4 tablespoons crème fraîche

salt and freshly ground black pepper

1 teaspoon chopped fresh mint

1 Make the pea purée: simmer the peas in the sugared water with the sprigs of mint until just tender. Drain reserving the cooking liquid and discard the mint. Process the peas until smooth in a food processor or blender. Pass through a sieve. Add the crème fraîche. Adjust the consistency with the reserved cooking liquid. Season to taste with salt and pepper.

2 Toss the leek and ginger in seasoned flour.

3 Heat the oil in a deep-fryer until a a cube of bread will brown in just 30 seconds. Deep-fry the leek and ginger until just golden. Drain well on absorbent kitchen paper, sprinkle with salt and keep warm.

4 Heat some olive oil in a frying pan and fry the scallops on both sides until brown on the outside but translucent inside. Add a little extra oil to the pan with the lemon juice.

5 Stir the chopped mint into the pea purée. Divide the purée between 4 dinner plates. Arrange the scallops on top of or around the purée and garnish with the deep-fried leeks and ginger.

wine: **DRY WHITE**

Fried Scampi

SERVES 4

675 g | 1½ lb scampi	beaten egg
salt and freshly ground black pepper	dried white breadcrumbs
lemon juice	
oil for deep-frying	**To garnish**
seasoned plain flour	deep-fried parsley (see page 823)

1 If using frozen scampi sprinkle with pepper and lemon juice and defrost slowly in the refrigerator.

2 Heat the oil in a deep-fryer until a cube of bread will brown in 20 seconds.

3 Dip the scampi in seasoned flour. Dip into beaten egg, then turn carefully in the breadcrumbs, to coat thoroughly. Deep-fry until golden-brown. Drain on absorbent kitchen paper. Sprinkle with salt.

4 Garnish with fried parsley and serve immediately.

wine: **VERY DRY WHITE**

Stuffed Squid Provençal

SERVES 4

12 small squid	2 egg yolks
2 tablespoons olive oil	salt and freshly ground black pepper
1 onion, finely chopped	2 tablespoons brandy
4 spring onions, finely chopped	150 ml | ¼ pint dry white wine
2 clove of garlic, crushed	425 ml | ¾ pint tomato sauce 2 (see page 129)
6 tomatoes, peeled, deseeded and roughly chopped	3 anchovies, soaked in milk, drained and chopped
2 tablespoons chopped fresh mixed herbs	1 tablespoon capers, rinsed and chopped
3 tablespoons finely chopped fresh parsley	12 black olives, pitted
2 tablespoons fresh white breadcrumbs	

1 Preheat the oven to 150°C|300°F|gas mark 2.
2 Prepare the squid (see page 190), keeping the tentacles for the stuffing.
3 Start the stuffing. Heat half the oil in a saucepan and sweat the onions, spring onions and garlic, adding the roughly chopped tentacles to the pan for the last minute, to cook them lightly.
4 Mix together the tomatoes, mixed herbs, 2 tablespoons of the parsley, the breadcrumbs and the cooled onion mixture. Bind the stuffing with the egg yolks, beat well and season with salt and pepper.
5 Fit a piping bag with a medium plain nozzle and fill with the stuffing. Pipe into the whole squid, being careful not to overfill, or the squid will burst during cooking. Seal the ends of each squid with a cocktail stick.
6 Heat the remaining oil in a frying pan and brown the squid evenly all over. Then flame with the brandy. When the flames subside, remove the squid from the frying pan, and place in a casserole dish.
7 Add the wine to the frying pan and boil to reduce by half. Add the tomato sauce, the anchovies, capers and olives, and bring to the boil. Pour over the squid.
8 Cover the casserole dish and cook in the oven for 1 hour or until the squid are tender.
9 Using a slotted spoon, remove the squid from the casserole dish to a serving dish and keep warm while finishing the sauce.
10 If the sauce is too thin, reduce by boiling rapidly in a saucepan. Check the seasoning, and spoon over the squid. Garnish with the olives and the remaining parsley.

wine: ROSÉ

Stir-fried Squid

SERVES 4

900 g|2 lb fresh or frozen squid	2 sticks of lemon grass, bruised
1 tablespoon sunflower oil	4 spring onions, sliced
1 clove of garlic, bruised	1–2 teaspoons sugar
1 cm|½ in piece of fresh ginger root, peeled and thinly sliced	1 tablespoon Shaoxing wine, vermouth or dry sherry
	salt and freshly ground black pepper

1 Clean the squid (see page 190). Score the outside of the squid in a diamond pattern. Pat dry.
2 Heat the oil in a wok, add the garlic, ginger and lemon grass and cook slowly for 1 minute. Remove the flavourings. Add the squid and stir-fry over a very high heat for 30 seconds.
3 Reduce the heat, add the spring onions and cook over a low heat for 30 seconds.
4 Add the sugar and wine and cook for a further 30 seconds. Season with salt and pepper.

wine: SPICY WHITE

Fritto Misto

SERVES 4

450 g | 1 lb mixed raw prawns, crayfish tails, crab
    meat, sole, whiting and whitebait (prepared
    weight)
lemon juice
salt and freshly ground black pepper
oil for deep-frying

For the batter

5 g | ¼ oz fresh yeast

150 ml | ¼ pint tepid water
110 g | 4 oz plain flour
a pinch of salt
1 tablespoon olive oil
1 egg white

To garnish

deep-fried parsley (see page 823)

1 Make the batter: mix the yeast with the water. Sift the flour and salt into a bowl. Make a well in the centre and pour in the frothing yeast liquid and oil.
2 Beat the mixture with a wooden spoon, gradually drawing in the flour. Leave in a warm place to rise for 30 minutes.
3 Sprinkle the fish with lemon juice and pepper and leave for 30 minutes or so.
4 Beat the egg white until stiff and fold it into the batter.
5 Drain the fish and dry on absorbent kitchen paper. Dip into the batter, coating each piece completely.
6 Heat the oil until a cube of bread will brown in 30 seconds. Deep-fry the fish pieces, a few at a time, until the batter is golden-brown. Drain on absorbent kitchen paper, sprinkle with salt and pile on to a warmed serving dish. Garnish with deep-fried parsley.

wine: **DRY WHITE**

Seafood Feuilletées with Spinach

225 g | 8 oz flour quantity puff pastry (see page 566)
1 egg, beaten, to glaze

For the filling

450 g | 1 lb fresh very young spinach
30 g | 1 oz butter
290 ml | ½ pint fish stock (see page 106)
85 g | 3 oz raw tiger prawns
3 small sole fillets

110 g | 4 oz scallops, prepared (see page 198)
340 g | 12 oz peeled cooked prawns
freshly grated nutmeg

For the sauce

2 shallots, finely chopped
225 g | 8 oz chilled unsalted butter
1 teaspoon fish glaze (see page 108) (optional)
100 ml | 3½ fl oz dry white wine
1 tablespoon double cream
juice of ¼ lemon
salt and freshly ground white pepper

1 Preheat the oven to 220°C | 425°F | gas mark 7.
2 Roll the pastry into a large rectangle 1 cm thick. Trim the edges and cut it into 4 diamonds.
3 Place the diamonds on a baking sheet and brush with egg glaze. Using a sharp knife, trace a line about 1 cm | ½ in from the edge of each diamond, without cutting all the way through the pastry. A small diamond is thus traced, which will form the lid for the

pastry case. Make a design inside this diamond with the knife. Flour the blade of a knife and use this to knock up the sides of the pastry. Chill in the refrigerator until firm.

4   Bake the pastry cases for 20–30 minutes, or until puffed up and brown. Using a knife, outline and remove the lids and scoop out any uncooked dough inside. Return to the oven for 2 minutes to dry out.

5   Transfer the cases and lids to a wire rack and leave to cool. Reduce the oven temperature to 130°C|250°F gas mark 1.

6   Wash the spinach very well and remove the stalks. Fry quickly in half the butter until just beginning to wilt.

7   Put the fish stock into a large shallow pan. Bring up to scalding point (just below boiling), add the tiger prawns and poach for 1 minute, then add the sole fillets and poach for 1 further minute until just cooked. Remove the fish from the pan with a slotted spoon. Strain the stock and reduce to a glaze. Reserve. Fry the scallops in the remaining butter until just cooked. Set aside.

8   Make the sauce: sweat the shallots very slowly in 15 g|½ oz of the butter in a saucepan. Add the fish glaze and white wine. Strain. Add the cream and reduce again. Cut the remaining cold butter into small pieces and gradually whisk it into the pan over a low heat. Remove the pan from the heat from time to time so that the butter thickens the sauce without melting. Work fairly quickly, however, as otherwise you may find that the sauce is only just warm (it does not reheat well). Add the lemon juice. Taste, add extra fish glaze if necessary and season with salt and pepper.

9   While the sauce is being made the feuilletées can be assembled and reheated. Reheat the spinach in the butter and season with salt, pepper and nutmeg. Pile some spinach inside each pastry case. Cut the sole fillets into 3–4 diagonal pieces. Arrange with the other seafood on the spinach.

10 Just before serving, spoon a generous tablespoon of sauce over each feuilletée. Set a lid on top. Hand the remaining sauce separately in a warmed sauce-boat.

wine: DRY WHITE

Pot au Feu de la mer

SERVES 6

170 g|6 oz monkfish, cubed	8 spring onions, trimmed and cut into julienne strips
170 g|6 oz sole fillets, skinned and sliced	1 medium carrot, peeled and cut into julienne strips
675 ml|1½ pints fish stock (see page 106)	1 large stick of celery, cut into julienne strips
4 large scallops, muscle removed (see page 198), halved	4 large cap mushrooms, quartered
	150 ml|¼ pint double cream
110 g|4 oz whole scampi	salt and freshly ground black pepper
6 tablespoons dry white wine	

1   Poach the monkfish and sole in the hot fish stock for 2 minutes. Remove and keep warm in a very low oven. Add the scallops and scampi to the stock and poach for 1 minute. Remove and keep warm.

2 Add the wine to the stock and reduce, by boiling rapidly, to 290 ml | ½ pint.

3 Meanwhile, blanch the spring onions, carrots and celery in boiling salted water for 1 minute, then drain well. Blanch the mushrooms until just cooked.

4 Add the cream to the reduced stock and boil to reduce to a creamy consistency. Season to taste with salt and pepper. Add the fish.

5 Arrange the fish in its sauce on 4 dinner plates and garnish with a scattering of warm julienne vegetables and the mushrooms.

wine: DRY WHITE

Paella

There are hundreds of recipes for paella. We have chosen a good selection of shellfish, but if you are unable to find all the ingredients don't worry. A true paella is made with Valencian rice, but long-grained rice is a good substitute.

SERVES 6

1 litre	1¾ pints strong, well-flavoured shellfish stock (see page 108)	16 langoustines
a pinch of saffron strands	450 g	1 lb live mussels
5 tablespoons dry sherry	225 g	8 oz shell-on prawns
55 g	2 oz butter, clarified (see page 385)	1 450 g	1 lb single portion poussin
1 large Spanish onion, finely chopped	2 cloves of garlic, crushed
1 450 g	1 lb cooked lobster meat, removed from the shell	225 g	8 oz long-grain rice
	6 plum tomatoes, peeled, deseeded and chopped
	salt and freshly ground black pepper

1 Heat the stock with the saffron and the sherry. Sweat the onions with half of the butter.

2 Prepare the shellfish and chicken: cut the lobster meat into thick slices and dice the claw meat. Set aside. Devein the langoustines. Scrub and pick over the mussels, remove the beards and make sure that the shells are shut. Peel and devein the prawns. Cut the poussin into quarters.

3 Heat the remaining butter in a *paellera* or large frying pan. Brown the poussin quarters well, then set aside on a plate.

4 Add the onion, garlic and rice and cook for 2–3 minutes, or until the rice is opaque.

5 Add the stock to the pan, with the poussin. Cover the pan and cook very slowly for 15–20 minutes, or until the rice is nearly cooked. (If the rice begins to stick, but needs longer cooking, add a little more water.)

6 Add the langoustines and mussels to the pan. Cook for 3–4 further minutes until the mussel shells have opened and the langoustines and poussin are cooked.

7 Stir the lobster meat and tomatoes into the rice and heat for 2 further minutes, or until the lobster is very hot.

8 Season the paella very well with salt and pepper. Serve very hot.

wine: VERY DRY WHITE

Braised Octopus with Glazed Onions and Aïoli

SERVES 4

900 g | 2 lb octopus, cleaned

1 tablespoon oil

30 g | 1 oz butter

1 onion, thinly sliced

1 carrot, thinly sliced

2 cloves of garlic, crushed

2 tablespoons brandy

100 ml | 3½ fl oz red wine

150 ml | 5 fl oz fish stock (see page 106)

salt and freshly ground black pepper

900 g | 2 lb button onions

55 g | 2 oz butter

1 tablespoon sugar

To serve

1 quantity aïoli (see page 117)

1   Blanch the octopus in boiling water for 2 minutes, then drain. Peel the dark skin off the main body of the octopus and scrape the skin off the tentacles with a knife. If using baby octopus they will not need peeling. Beat thoroughly with a rolling pin. Cut the tentacles and body into 5 cm | 2 in pieces. Set aside.

2   Preheat the oven to 325°C | 170°F | gas mark 3.

3   Heat the oil and butter in a large flame-proof casserole. When the butter is foaming, brown the octopus pieces a few at a time. Lift on to a plate.

4   Add the onion and carrot to the casserole, reduce the heat and cook slowly until soft. Add the garlic and cook for 2 further minutes. Put the octopus on top of the vegetables. Reserve the ink, if any.

5   Heat the brandy in a ladle or small saucepan, ignite and pour, flaming, over the octopus and vegetables. When the flames have died down, pour over the wine and stock and season lightly with salt and pepper. Bring to the boil and cover with a lid. Cook in the oven for 2 hours or until the octopus is completely tender.

6   Meanwhile, blanch the onions in boiling water for 3 minutes, then drain and peel. Taking care when removing the skin not to cut too much of the top off, or the onions will disintegrate during cooking.

7   Heat the butter and sugar in a second large flameproof casserole, add the onions, cover and set over a low heat. Shake the pan from time to time, but avoid removing the lid too often. When the onions are well browned all over, put into the oven and cook for 30 minutes or until tender.

8   When the octopus is cooked, lift out of the casserole and stir into the glazed onions. Keep warm. Strain the remaining contents of the octopus casserole into a saucepan, bring to the boil and reduce by boiling rapidly if necessary until syrupy. Add the reserved ink. Season to taste with salt and pepper.

9   Pour the reduced cooking liquid on to the octopus and onions.

10 To serve: divide the octopus, onions and sauce between 4 individual plates. Put a spoonful of aïoli on top of each and serve immediately.

wine: DRY WHITE

Poultry and Game

Small birds such as quail are invariably cooked whole, perhaps stuffed, and perhaps boned (see pages 370–1). But medium-sized ones, like chickens and guinea fowl, are often cut into 2, 4, 6 or 8 pieces. Use a knife to cut through the flesh and poultry shears or scissors to cut the bones.

Jointing a Chicken

To Joint a Medium-sized Bird into 8 Pieces to Serve 4 People:

By jointing a chicken into 8 pieces each person will be served with a piece of dark meat and a piece of white breast meat. Before jointing remove any trussing strings then singe the bird if necessary. Wipe clean with kitchen paper to remove hairs and pin feathers. Use a cook's knife to cut through the flesh and poultry shears or kitchen scissors to cut the bones and cartilage.

1 Place the bird, breast side, down on a board with the parson's nose facing you.
2 Using a large cook's knife, make a cut down the backbone through the skin from one end to the other.
3 Locate the soft pockets of flesh called the oysters on either side of the backbone at the top of the legs. Cut round them with the tip of the knife to loosen them from the carcass, then loosen them with the fingertips and thumbs so that they come away freely from the bone. This way, the oyster will will remain intact with the legs as they are pulled from the carcass.
4 Turn the bird over so that it is breast-side up, pull the skin covering the breast meat towards the breastbone, then cut through the skin between the breast and the leg, cutting as close to the leg as possible, using the blade of the knife, not the tip.
5 Continue cutting the skin around the leg to make a cut perpendicular to the backbone next to the loosened oyster. Bend the leg out from the body and down towards the chopping board to release it from the socket.
6 Use a knife to cut the cartilage and tendons around the ball joint.
7 Remove the leg by grasping it firmly and pulling it towards the back of the chicken. When the oyster piece is completely loosened it should come away with the leg.
8 Repeat the process with the other leg.
9 Using a sharp knife, cut cleanly through the skin and flesh between the 2 breasts, slightly one side of the breastbone.
10 Using poultry shears or kitchen scissors, cut along the length of the breastbone and through the wishbone at the neck end.
11 Using scissors, cut along the fat line running along the edge of each breast, cutting through the ribs then around and underneath the wings to the neck of the chicken. Do

not separate the breast meat from the breastbone as the bone will help to keep the meat moist during cooking. Cut out the wishbone in each piece. Save the carcass for stock.

12 Tuck the wings behind the breasts in the 'sunbathing position'. Place the breasts next to each other to form a heart shape. Using a large, sharp knife, cut through the meat on a slant, from the cleavage of the heart to the elbow joint of the wing. You now have 2 wing-breast portions and 2 longer diamond-shaped breast portions. Leave the wing tips (pinions) intact as they help to hold the wing in position while the chicken cooks. They are trimmed at the middle joint once the chicken is cooked.

13 Place the legs skin side up on the board. Locate the joint between the drumstick and thigh by pressing against the meat with your finger to find the notch.

14 Using the large knife, cut down through the joint on both legs, the knife should cut through the joint easily. If it does not, you have hit the bone and you are cutting in the wrong place.

16 You now have 8 equal portions of chicken, 4 with white meat and 4 with dark meat.

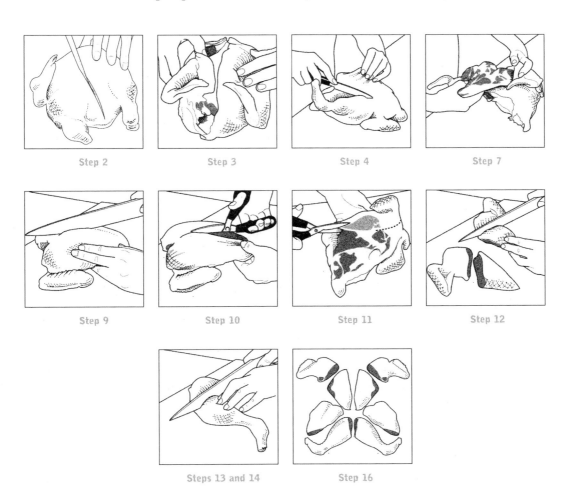

Step 2   Step 3   Step 4   Step 7

Step 9   Step 10   Step 11   Step 12

Steps 13 and 14   Step 16

To Joint a Bird into 4

1 First pull out any trussing strings, then pull the leg away from the body. With a sharp knife cut through the skin joining the leg to the body, pull the leg away further and cut through more skin to free the leg.

2 Bend the leg outwards and back, forcing the bone to come out of its socket close to the body.

3 Turn the bird over, feel along the backbone to find the oyster (a soft pocket of flesh at the side of the backbone, near the middle). With the tip of the knife, cut this away from the carcase at the side nearest the backbone and farthest from the leg.

4 Then turn the bird over again, and cut through the flesh, the knife going between the end of the thigh bone and the carcass, to take off the leg, bringing the oyster with it.

5 Using poultry shears or a heavy knife, split the carcass along the breastbone.

6 Cut through the ribs on each side to take off the fleshy portion of the breast, and with it the wing. Trim the joints neatly to remove scraps of untidy skin.

For six joints, proceed as above but split the legs into thigh portions and drumsticks.

To Split a Bird in Half

Simply use a sharp knife to cut right through flesh and bone, just on one side of the breastbone, open out the bird and cut through the other side, immediately next to the backbone. Then cut the backbone away from the half to which it remains attached. The knobbly end of the drumsticks and the fleshless tips to the pinions can be cut off before or after cooking.

Boning a Whole Bird

1 Place the chicken breast side down on a board. Cut through the skin to the backbone along the length of the chicken.

2 Feel for the fleshy oyster at the top of each thigh and cut round it against the bone, loosening further with the fingers and thumb.

3 Working down one side of the chicken, cut and scrape the flesh from the carcass, using a small sharp knife held as close as possible to the bone. Take care not to cut through the skin.

4 Cut the flesh from either side of the shoulder blade, then using scissors or poultry shears cut through the bone at the base of the wing next to the body of the chicken.

5 Continue cutting along one side of the body until the rib-cage is exposed. Once you have reached the centre of the breastbone, start again on the other side of the chicken from step 3 above.

6 When the flesh has been scraped from the carcass on both sides, hold the chicken by the carcass, allowing the meat to hang down off the breastbone, and carefully cut the flesh away from the tip of the breastbone. Avoid puncturing the skin.

7 Lay the boned chicken skin side down on the board.

8 Using a knife, cut through the skin just above the feet joints to remove the knuckle end of the drumsticks.

9 Working from the inside thigh end, scrape one leg bone clean, pushing the flesh down towards the end of the drumstick until you can pull the thigh bone through and remove it. Push the boned skin and flesh of the legs inside the bird. Repeat on the other leg.

10 To bone the wings, cut off the pinions (tips) at the middle joint with a heavy knife.

11 Scrape the wing bones clean from the inside as you did the leg bones.

12 Trim away any excess fat and any remaining bone from inside the bird with a sharp knife.

13 Keep the neck flap of skin intact to fold over the end once the chicken is stuffed.

Boning a chicken

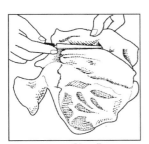 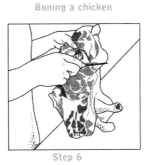 

Step 5   Step 6   Step 9

To Prepare and Draw a Game Bird for the Oven

Some birds are easier to pluck than others, ducks being notoriously tedious. All birds are easier to pluck if still warm when tackled. Work away from draughts, as the feathers fly about, and pluck straight into a dustbin. Tug the feathers, working from the tail to the head, pulling against the way the feathers grow. If the bird is very young or if there is a lot of fat, pull downwards towards the tail to avoid tearing the flesh.

Once plucked, the bird should be singed. This can be done with a burning taper, or directly over a gas flame, but care should be taken to singe only the down and small feathers, and not to blacken the flesh. The bird should then be rubbed with a clean tea-towel to remove any remaining stubble. It is now ready for drawing.

Surprisingly, birds keep better, when hanging, with their insides intact. Once eviscerated they must be cooked within a day or two. So when you are ready to cook the bird, take it down, and proceed as follows.

1 Pluck it, starting from the tail end.

2 Cut round the feet, at the drumstick joint, but do not cut right through the tendons. Pull the legs off the bird, drawing the tendons out with them. If the bird is small this is easy enough – just bend the foot back until it snaps, and pull, perhaps over the edge of a table. Turkeys are more difficult: snap the feet at the drumstick joint by bending them over the end of the table, then hang the bird up by the feet from a stout hook, and pull on the bird. The feet plus tendons will be left on the hook, the turkey in your arms. All too often birds are sold with the tendons in the legs, making the drumsticks tough when cooked.

3 Now for the head and neck. Lay the bird breast side down on a board. Make a slit through the neck skin from the body to the head. Cut off the head and throw it away. Pull back the split neck skin, leaving it attached to the body of the bird (it will come in useful to close the gap if you are stuffing the bird). Cut the neck off as close to the body as you can.

4 Put a finger into the neck hole, to the side of the stump of neck left on the bird, and move the finger right round, loosening the innards from the neck. If you do not do this you will find them difficult to pull out from the other end.

5 With a sharp knife slit the bird open from the vent to the parson's (or pope's) nose, making a hole large enough to just get your hand in. Put your hand in, working it so the back of your hand is up against the arch of the breastbone, and carefully loosen the entrails from the sides of the body cavity, all the way round. Pull them out, taking care not to break the gall bladder, the contents of which would embitter any flesh they touched. Covering the gutting hand with a cloth helps extract the intestines intact. The first time you do this it is unlikely that you will get everything out in one motion, so check that the lungs and kidneys come too. Have another go if necessary. Once the bird is empty, wipe any traces of blood off with kitchen paper.

The neck and feet go into the stockpot with the heart and the cleaned gizzard. To clean the gizzard, carefully cut the outside wall along the natural seam so that you can peel it away from the inner bag of grit. Throw the grit bag away, with the intestines and the gall bladder. Do not put the liver in the stockpot: it may make the stock bitter. It may be fried and served with the dish, or fried, chopped and added to the sauce, or kept frozen until enough poultry liver has been collected to make pâté. But if the liver is to be used, carefully cut away the discoloured portion of it where it lay against the gall bladder (it will be bitter) and trim off any membranes.

Trussing a Bird

A bird is trussed to keep it in a compact, neat shape, usually after stuffing. Trussing large birds is unnecessary as the bird is to be carved up anyway, and trussing serves to prevent the inside thigh being cooked by the time the breast is ready. Small birds, especially game birds where underdone thighs are desirable, are trussed, but their feet are left on. Their feet may simply be tied together for neatness sake, and the pinions skewered under the bird.

Or they may be trussed in any number of ways, one of which is described below.

1 Arrange the bird so that the neck flap is folded over the neck hole, and the pinions turned under and tucked in tight. They will, if folded correctly, hold the neck flap in place, but if the bird is well stuffed the neck flap may have to be skewered or sewn in place.

2 Press the legs down and into the bird to force the breast into a plumped-up position. Thread a long trussing needle with thin string and push it through the wing joint, right through the body and out of the other wing joint.

3 Then push it through the body again, this time through the thighs. You should now be back on the side you started.

4 Tie the two ends together in a bow to make later removal quick.

5 Then thread a shorter piece of string through the thin end of the two drumsticks and tie them together, winding the string round the parson's nose at the same time to close the vent. Sometimes a small slit is cut in the skin just below the end of the breastbone, and the parson's nose is pushed through it.

Barding

Poultry liable to dry out during cooking is often barded: lay fatty bacon or rindless pork back fat strips over the body of the bird, and secure or tie in place. The barding is removed during cooking to allow the breast to brown.

Roasting Tables

If using a fan (convection) oven, reduce the cooking times by 15 per cent or lower the oven temperature by 20°C|40°F.

Meat		Temperature			Cooking time	
		°C	°F	Gas	per kg	per lb
Chicken		220	425	7	45 mins	20 mins
	NOTE: Few chickens, however small, will be cooked in much under an hour					
Turkey	Small (under 6 kg|13 lb)	200	400	6	30 mins	12 mins
	Large	180	350	4	35 mins	15 mins
	NOTE: For more detailed timings see chart on page 374.					
	(Few turkeys, however small, will be cooked in under 2 hours.)					
Duck, goose	Small (under 2.3 kg|5 lb)	190	375	5	45 mins	20 mins
	Large	180	350	4	55 mins	25 mins
Pigeon		200	400	6	22–35 mins in total	
Grouse		190	375	5	25–35 mins in total	
Guinea fowl		190	375	5	70 mins in total	
Partridge		190	375	5	20–25 mins in total	
Pheasant		190	375	5	45–60 mins in total	
Wild duck		200	400	6	40 mins in total	
Woodcock		190	375	5	20–30 mins in total	
Quail		180	350	4	20 mins in total	
Snipe		190	375	5	15–20 mins in total	

Thawing and Cooking Times for Turkeys

Although the thawing time in this table can be relied on, the cooking times are dependent on an accurate oven. For safety's sake, plan the timing so that, if all goes right, the bird will be ready 1 hour before dinner. This will give you leeway if necessary. To test if the turkey is cooked, press a skewer into the thickest part of the thigh. The juices should run clear. When the bird is cooked, open the oven door to cool the oven, then put the turkey on a serving dish and return it to the oven to keep warm.

Thawing in a warm room (over 18°C|65°F) or under warm water is not recommended, as warmth will encourage the growth of micro-organisms, which might result in food poisoning.

Weight of bird when ready for the oven regardless of whether it is boned, stuffed or empty	Thawing time at room temperature 18°C/65°F	Thawing time in refrigerator 5°C/40°F	Cooking time at 200°C/400°F gas mark 6	Cooking time at 180°C/350°F gas mark 4
	hours	hours	hours	hours
4–5 kg|8–10 lb	20	65	2½–3 hrs	–
5–6 kg|10–13 lb	24	70	3–3¾ hrs	–
6–7 kg|13–16 lb	30	75	30 mins then	3¼–4
8–9 kg|16–20 lb	40	80	30 mins then	4–4½
9–11 kg|20–24 lb	48	96	1 hr then	4–4½

Chicken Elizabeth

The Cordon Bleu School devised this dish for the Coronation celebration in 1953.

SERVES 4

1 × 1.35 kg|3 lb chicken, cleaned but not trussed
1 bay leaf
6 peppercorns
salt
2 parsley stalks

1 lemon slice and 2 teaspoons fresh thyme leaves
225 ml|8 fl oz Elizabeth sauce (see page 118)

To serve
rice salad (see page 299)
1 bunch of watercress

1 Place the chicken in a saucepan with the flavourings. Cover with water, leaving the very top of the breast protruding. Cover with a piece of greaseproof paper and a lid.
2 Poach for 1¼–1½ hours or until the chicken is tender and the drumsticks feel loose and wobbly. Remove the chicken from the pan and set aside to cool.
3 Remove the flesh from the chicken bones, and when quite cold mix with the sauce, reserving a little of it.

4 Pile the chicken into a serving-dish and coat with the reserved sauce. Serve with the rice salad and garnish with watercress.

NOTE: It is easier to strip chicken from the bones while the bird is still lukewarm. But on no account should the sauce be added to the flesh until the chicken is completely cold.

wine: VERY DRY WHITE

Poached Chicken with Parsley Sauce

SERVES 4

1 × 1.35 kg | 3 lb chicken, cleaned but not trussed

For the court bouillon

1 onion, sliced

1 carrot, peeled and sliced

2 parsley stalks

salt

6 black peppercorns

1 stick of celery

2 bay leaves

For the parsley sauce

30 g | 1 oz butter

30 g | 1 oz plain flour

150 ml | $\frac{1}{4}$ pint milk

2 tablespoons single cream (optional)

2 tablespoons chopped fresh parsley

salt and freshly ground black pepper

1 Put the chicken into a large saucepan with the onion, carrot, parsley stalks, salt, peppercorns, celery and bay leaves. Submerge the bird in water, leaving the very top of the breast protruding.

2 Bring to the boil, then reduce the heat and cover with a piece of greaseproof paper and a well-fitting lid. Simmer gently for $1\frac{1}{4}$ hours or until the chicken is cooked, when the legs feel loose and wobbly.

3 Remove the chicken from the pan and strain the stock.

4 Carefully skim the stock of all the fat. When you have spooned off as much grease as possible, lay successive sheets of absorbent kitchen paper on the surface of the liquid to remove the remaining fat.

5 Now start the parsley sauce: melt the butter in a saucepan, remove from heat and add the flour. Return to the heat and cook for 1 minute. Remove from the heat.

6 Gradually add the milk and 150 ml | $\frac{1}{4}$ pint of the chicken stock. Return to the heat and bring to the boil, stirring continuously.

7 Simmer for 2 minutes, then add the cream, if using, and set aside.

8 Skin the chicken and remove the bones, leaving the flesh in large pieces.

9 Reheat the sauce and add the parsley. Season if necessary with salt and pepper. Add more stock if the sauce is too thick. Add the chicken to the sauce, turn gently to coat, and tip into a serving dish.

NOTE: Do not add the parsley to the sauce in advance as it will lose its colour.

wine: DRY WHITE

Curried Chicken and Ham Pie

SERVES 4

55 g | 2 oz butter

1 onion, chopped

2 teaspoon curry paste

½ teaspoon ground turmeric

45 g | 1½ oz plain flour

290 ml | ½ pint stock, reserved after cooking the chicken

150 ml | ¼ pint creamy milk

5 ml | 1 teaspoon chopped fresh parsley

1 teaspoon chopped fresh mint

a pinch of crushed cardamom seeds

a pinch of dry English mustard

salt and freshly ground black pepper

a squeeze of lemon juice

2 hardboiled eggs, chopped

110 g | 4 oz ham, cut into 1 cm | ½ in dice

1 1.35 kg | 3 lb chicken, poached, boned and cut into large chunks

225 g | 8 oz flour quantity wholemeal pastry (see page 560)

1 egg, beaten with a pinch of salt and a teaspoon water, to glaze

1 Preheat the oven to 200°C | 400°F | gas mark 6.

2 Melt the butter in a saucepan and add the onion. Cover with a dampened piece of greaseproof paper and a lid. Cook gently until soft but not coloured.

3 Stir in the curry paste and turmeric and cook for 1 minute. Remove from the heat.

4 Add the flour, then return to the heat and cook over a low heat for 1 minute. Remove the pan from the heat. Add the stock gradually and stir well. Return to the heat and bring slowly to the boil, stirring continuously until the sauce is thick and shiny.

5 Add the milk and stir again until the sauce returns to the boil.

6 Add the parsley, mint, cardamom seeds, mustard, salt and pepper. Simmer for 2–3 minutes.

7 Taste, adding more salt if necessary, and add the lemon juice. Allow to cool.

8 Stir in the hardboiled eggs, the ham and the chicken. Pour the mixture into a pie dish.

9 Roll the pastry on a floured board to a rectangle about 5 mm | ¼ in thick.

10 Cut a band of pastry slightly wider than the edge of the pie dish. Brush the rim of the dish with water and press on the band of pastry. Brush with a little beaten egg or water and lay the pastry lid over the pie. Cut away any surplus pastry from the sides with a knife.

11 Press the pie edges together and mark a pattern with the point of a small knife, or pinch with the fingers into a raised border. Shape the pastry trimmings into leaves for decoration. Make a small hole in the pastry to allow the steam to escape.

12 Brush the pastry with beaten egg and decorate with the pastry leaves. Brush again with egg.

13 Bake for 30–35 minutes until golden-brown.

NOTE: If the pie is not to be baked as soon as it has been assembled it is essential that the curry sauce and the chicken are both completely cold before they are combined. Keep the pie refrigerated or frozen until ready to bake. If frozen, thaw in the refrigerator before baking.

wine: SPICY DRY WHITE OR ROSE

Chicken and Sweetbread Filling for Feuilletées

SERVES 4

a pair of calves' sweetbreads or 225 g | 8 oz lamb's
  sweetbreads

45 g | 1½ oz butter

1 small onion, very finely chopped

55 g | 2 oz button mushrooms, sliced

30 g | 1 oz plain flour

150 ml | ¼ pint creamy milk

1 tablespoon dry sherry

150 ml | ¼ pint white stock, made with chicken bones
  (see page 103)

1 tablespoon chopped fresh parsley

a squeeze of lemon juice

225 g | 8 oz cooked chicken, cut into chunks

salt and freshly ground black pepper

1 large vol-au-vent case (see page 567) or 4
  feuilletée cases

1 Soak the sweetbreads in cold water for 4 hours. Change the water every time it becomes pink (probably 4 times). There should be no blood at all when the sweetbreads are ready for cooking.

2 Place them in a saucepan of cold water and bring to the boil. Reduce the heat and poach for 2 minutes.

3 Drain the sweetbreads and rinse under cold running water. Dry well. Pick them over, removing all the skin and membrane, and cut into small bite-sized pieces.

4 Melt the butter in a saucepan, add the onion. Cover with a dampened piece of greaseproof paper and a lid, and cook over a low heat until soft but not coloured (this may take 10 minutes).

5 Stir in the mushrooms and leave over a low heat for 1 minute. Remove and mushrooms with a slotted spoon.

6 Stir the flour into the pan and cook for 1 minute. Remove from the heat and stir in the milk, sherry and stock. Return to the heat and bring slowly to the boil, stirring continuously. Simmer for 1 minute.

7 Add the parsley, lemon juice, chicken pieces, sweetbreads, mushrooms, salt and pepper.

8 Tip the mixture carefully into the vol-au-vent case and reheat in the oven for 5 minutes.

wine: SPICY DRY WHITE

Gougère

A gougère is a cheese choux pastry case which may be filled with a variety of mixtures such as haddock (see page 316), chicken or game (see below).

SERVES 4

105 g | 3¾ oz plain flour

a pinch of salt

freshly ground black pepper

cayenne pepper

85 g | 3 oz butter

220 ml | 7 ½ fl oz water

3 eggs, lightly beaten

55 g | 2 oz strong Cheddar cheese, cut into 5 mm |
¼ in cubes

425 ml | ¾ pint filling (see following recipe)

2 teaspoons browned breadcrumbs

1 tablespoon grated cheese

1 Preheat the oven to 200°C | 400°F | gas mark 6.

2 Sift the flour with the salt, pepper and cayenne 3 times.

3 In a large saucepan slowly heat the butter in the water and when completely melted bring to a rolling boil. When the mixture is bubbling all over, tip in the flour, remove from the heat and beat well with a wooden spoon until the mixture leaves the sides of the pan. Allow to cool to room temperature.

4 Beat in the eggs gradually until the mixture is smooth and shiny and of a dropping consistency – you may not need the last few spoonfuls of egg. Stir in the diced cheese.

5 Spoon the mixture round the edge of a flattish greased 30 cm|10 in ovenproof dish leaving a space for the filling in the centre. Bake for 25 minutes until the choux is well risen and golden.

6 Pile the filling into the centre and sprinkle with the breadcrumbs and grated cheese. Return to the oven and bake for about 15 minutes, until the filling is hot.

Chicken or Game Filling for Gougère

SERVES 4

30 g|1 oz butter
1 medium onion, thinly sliced
110 g|4 oz large mushrooms, sliced
20 g¾ plain flour

290 ml|½ pint white stock, made with chicken bones (see page 103)
salt and freshly ground black pepper
2 teaspoons chopped fresh parsley
340 g|12 oz cooked game or chicken, shredded

1 Melt the butter in a saucepan and soften the onion over a low heat. Add the mushrooms. Cook for 5 minutes. Remove from the heat.

2 Stir in the flour. Return to the heat and cook until straw-coloured, 3–5 minutes.

3 Remove the pan from the heat and stir in the stock. Return to the heat. Bring to the boil, stirring continuously. Season to taste with salt and pepper. Simmer for 2 minutes.

4 Add the parsley and game or chicken and use as required.

wine: **LIGHT RED**

Chicken Kiev

SERVES 4

110 g|4 oz butter, softened
1 clove of garlic, crushed
1 tablespoon chopped fresh parsley
a squeeze of lemon juice
salt and freshly ground black pepper

4 chicken supremes
seasoned plain flour
beaten egg
dried white breadcrumbs
oil for deep-frying

1 Mix the butter with the garlic, parsley, lemon juice, salt and pepper. Divide into 4 equal pieces, shape into rectangles and chill well in the refrigerator.

2 Remove the skin and bone from the chicken breasts. You should have 4 equal pieces of chicken. Using a sharp knife, split the breasts almost in half horizontally and open them out so that you have a chicken escalope. Put them between sheets of wet greaseproof paper and, using a rolling pin, carefully beat the chicken pieces to flatten the meat out thinly.

3 Place a piece of the chilled parsley butter in the centre of each chicken piece. Fold the chicken over so that the butter is completely wrapped. Dust lightly with seasoned flour. Dip into beaten egg, then roll carefully in breadcrumbs. Chill in the refrigerator for 30 minutes.

4 Brush with more beaten egg and roll again in breadcrumbs. Leave to chill for a further 30 minutes.

5 Heat the oil in a deep-fryer until a cube of bread will brown in 40 seconds. Fry the chicken pieces in the oil for 12 minutes. Drain well on absorbent kitchen paper and serve.

NOTES: Crushed garlic is frequently added to the butter inside the chicken. Though frowned on by classic chefs, this is quite delicious. Other flavourings, such as chopped tarragon, smooth liver pâté, mashed anchovies, or a duxelles of mushrooms, can be good too. But the butter is the essential ingredient, providing flavour, moisture and drama all at once.

If desired, the small wing bone at the shoulder end of the breast can be left in place. When the chicken escalope is rolled up, the bone protrudes from the parcel, giving the breast the appearance of a drumstick.

wine: **LIGHT RED**

Balti Chicken

Balti curries from northern Pakistan are easy-to-make one-dish meals. Choose a combination of meat and vegetables and use Balti curry paste for spice and flavour. Serve with pulses or basmati rice.

SERVES 4

1 onion, chopped

4 tablespoons vegetable oil

110 g|4 oz new potatoes, cut into 1 cm|½ in dice

2 small green peppers, deseeded and cut into
   2 cm|¾ in dice

1 × 400 g|14 oz can of chopped tomatoes

450 g|1 lb boned and skinned chicken breast, cut
   into bite-sized pieces

salt and freshly ground black pepper

4 tablespoons Balti curry paste

2 tablespoons water

To garnish

2 tablespoons chopped fresh coriander

4 tablespoons Greek yoghurt

1 Fry the onion in half the oil for about 10 minutes until starting to soften.

2 Add the potatoes and green peppers and fry until lightly browned.

3 Place the vegetables in a saucepan. Add the tomatoes with their juice and simmer for 10 minutes.

4 Season the chicken with salt and pepper and brown lightly in the remaining oil.

5 Stir in the Balti paste and cook for 30 seconds. Add the water, then add the chicken to the vegetables.

6 Simmer for about 15 minutes until the chicken and vegetables are cooked through.

7 Serve garnished with the coriander and yoghurt.

wine: **SPICY WHITE OR BEER**

Chicken Biryani

SERVES 4

For the marinade

½ teaspoon ground cumin

½ teaspoon ground coriander

½ teaspoon paprika

¼ teaspoon ground turmeric

¼ teaspoon ground cloves

½ teaspoon ground cardamom

1 teaspoon ground cinnamon

1 fresh green chilli (optional)

1 medium onion

5 cloves of garlic

30 g | 1 oz fresh coriander leaves

1 tablespoon peeled and finely chopped fresh root
   ginger

½ tablespoon tomato purée

salt

225 ml | 8 fl oz plain yoghurt

450 g | 1 lb boned and skinned chicken breast, cut
   into bite-sized pieces

For the rice

2 tablespoons ghee, butter or oil

½ medium onion, finely chopped

400 g | 14 oz Basmati rice, washed and drained

500 ml | 18 fl oz white stock, made with chicken
   bones (see page 103)

½ teaspoon saffron powder, dissolved in 2 teaspoons
   hot water

To garnish

55 g | 2 oz cashew nuts, toasted

225 g | 8 oz onions, deep-fried

1 Prepare the marinade: process all the ingredients, except the chicken, in a food processor or liquidizer until smooth. Marinate the chicken in the spicy yoghurt mixture for at least 4 hours in the refrigerator, stirring from time to time.

2 Prepare the rice: grease a large casserole dish.

3 Heat half the ghee, butter or oil in a saucepan, add the onion and fry until golden-brown. Add the rice and fry over a low heat for 5 minutes until the grains are translucent. Add the stock and bring to the boil. Cover the pan and simmer for 10 minutes.

4 Meanwhile, heat the remaining ghee, butter or oil in a frying pan, add the chicken pieces and fry for 1 minute. Pour in the marinade and simmer for 5 minutes. Preheat the oven to 160°C | 325°F | gas mark 3.

5 Place one-third of the rice in the bottom of the casserole dish. Put half the chicken over the rice and cover with half the remaining rice. Put in the remaining chicken and cover with the remaining rice.

6 Measure the marinade liquid and add hot water if necessary to make it up to 225 ml | 8 fl oz. Add the saffron liquid to the marinade and pour over the casserole. Cover and bake for 45 minutes.

7 Garnish with the cashew nuts and onions just before serving.

wine: SPICY WHITE OR BEER

Sri Lankan Chicken Curry

SERVES 4

For the garam masala

1½ teaspoons coriander seeds

2 teaspoons cumin seeds

1 teaspoon fennel seeds

1¼ teaspoon black peppercorns

5 cm|2 in cinnamon stick

6 cloves

seeds from 5 cardamom pods

¼ teaspoon fenugreek seeds

For the curry

3 tablespoons vegetable oil

1 medium onion, finely chopped

1 1.3 kg|3 lb chicken, jointed into 8 pieces (see page 368)

1 teaspoon peeled and chopped fresh root ginger

1 teaspoon chilli powder (optional)

salt

½ teaspoon ground turmeric

55 g|2 oz creamed coconut, roughly chopped

290 ml|½ pint water

1 Heat the whole garam masala spices in a dry heavy frying pan over a low heat until they are lightly roasted. Shake the pan from time to time to ensure even roasting – if the spices are burnt the curry will taste bitter. Cool, then grind the spices to a fine powder.

2 Make the curry: heat the oil in a medium saucepan, add the onion and fry until golden-brown. Using a slotted spoon, remove the onion and reserve.

3 Brown the chicken on the skinned side, a few pieces at a time, adding more oil to the pan if necessary.

4 Stir in the ground roasted spices, the onion and all the remaining ingredients except the creamed coconut and the water.

5 Add the creamed coconut and the water and bring rapidly to the boil. Stir until the creamed coconut is dissolved. Cover, lower the heat and simmer for about 1 hour or until the chicken is cooked.

NOTE: To vary the flavour of this curry you could omit the creamed coconut and add 150 ml|¼ pint Greek yoghurt or 4 fresh tomatoes instead. A combination of yoghurt and tomatoes is delicious.

wine: **SPICY WHITE OR BEER**

Green Chicken Curry

SERVES 4

1 tablespoon vegetable oil

2 cloves of garlic, sliced

2 tablespoons green curry paste (see page 382)

290 ml|½ pint thick coconut milk

2 tablespoon nam pla (Thai fish sauce)

1 teaspoon caster sugar

3 small green Thai aubergines, quartered if large, or 1 medium purple aubergine, chopped

4 chicken breasts, boned, skinned and cut into strips

20 sweet basil leaves (horapa)

3 kaffir lime leaves, shredded

1 Heat the oil in a large frying pan, add the garlic and fry until golden-brown. Add the green curry paste, then gradually blend in the coconut milk, nam pla and sugar.

2 Add the aubergines and cook for 7 minutes then add the chicken and cook for a further 5 minutes. You may need to add extra water to the pan if it becomes too dry.

3 Stir in the basil leaves and lime leaves.

NOTE: If using bought curry paste use only 1 tablespoon.

wine: **SPICY WHITE OR BEER**

Green Curry Paste

15 fresh green chillies, deseeded and roughly chopped

2 sticks of lemon grass, peeled and chopped

4 shallots

1 piece of galangal│laos (Thai ginger)

2.5 cm│1 in piece of krachai (optional)

2–3 roots of fresh coriander

2 teaspoons ground cumin

3 kaffir lime leaves, chopped

1 teaspoon shrimp paste

6 whole black peppercorns

1 Pound or blend all the ingredients to a paste.

2 Store in a jar in the refrigerator for up to 1 week.

Chicken in Creamy Garlic Sauce

SERVES 4

30 g│1 oz clarified butter (see page 385)

1 × 1.35 kg│3 lb chicken, jointed into 8 pieces

5 large cloves of garlic, unpeeled

5 tablespoons wine vinegar

290 ml│½ pint dry white wine

2 tablespoons brandy

2 teaspoons Dijon mustard

1 heaped teaspoon tomato purée

290 ml│½ pint very fresh double cream

2 tomatoes, peeled and deseeded

1 Heat the butter in a large sauté pan and brown the chicken pieces on the skin side. Add the garlic and cover the pan. Cook over a low heat for 20 minutes, or until the chicken is tender. Remove the chicken and keep warm. Pour off all the fat from the pan.

2 Add the vinegar to the pan with the garlic, stirring well and scraping any sediment from the bottom. Boil rapidly until the liquid is reduced to about 2 tablespoons.

3 Add the wine, brandy, mustard and tomato purée, mix well and boil to a thick sauce (about 5 minutes at a fast boil).

4 In a large, heavy saucepan boil the cream until reduced by half, stirring frequently to prevent burning. Remove from the heat and fit a small wire sieve over the saucepan. Push the vinegar sauce through this, pressing the garlic cloves well to extract their pulp.

5 Stir the sauce and season to taste with salt and pepper. Cut the tomato into thin strips and stir into the sauce. Arrange the chicken on a hot serving dish, and spoon over the sauce.

NOTES: The deliciousness of this dish – and it is delicious – depends on the vigorous reduction of the vinegar and wine. If the acids are not properly boiled down the sauce will be too sharp.

Five cloves of garlic seems a lot, but the resulting smooth sauce does not taste particularly strongly of garlic.

wine: **LIGHT RED**

Chicken with Tomato and Coriander

SERVES 4

2 onions, finely chopped	1 × 400 g 14 oz can of tomatoes
4 tablespoons oil	1 bay leaf
1 × 1.35 kg 3 lb chicken, jointed into 8 pieces	2 teaspoons tomato purée
seasoned plain flour	salt and freshly ground black pepper
1 clove of garlic, crushed	2 tablespoons roughly chopped fresh coriander

1 Place the onions with 2 tablespoons oil in a small saucepan. Cover with a piece of dampened greaseproof paper and a lid. Sweat over low heat, stirring occasionally, until soft

2 Dip the chicken pieces in the seasoned flour.

3 Heat the oil in a large sauté pan and brown the chicken on the skin side. With a slotted spoon, take up the pieces and place them in a roasting dish or casserole.

4 Preheat the oven to 180°C 350°F gas mark 4.

5 Add the onions to the sauté pan. Add the garlic and cook for 1 further minute. Add the tomatoes, bay leaf and tomato purée. Season to taste with salt and pepper. Bring slowly to the boil, stirring continuously.

6 Pour the mixture over the chicken pieces. Cover with a piece of dampened greaseproof paper. Cover and cook in the oven for 45–50 minutes, or until the chicken is tender. Turn off the oven.

7 Lift the chicken pieces out of the sauce. Trim them and arrange on a warmed serving dish. Keep warm in the turned-off oven.

8 Skim any fat off the sauce, then boil rapidly to a syrupy consistency. Stir the sauce well to amalgamate the tomatoes and to prevent the sauce from catching. Add three-quarters of the coriander. Check the seasoning and pour the sauce over the chicken. Garnish with the remaining coriander.

wine: **LIGHT RED**

Coq au Vin

If there is time, marinate the chicken joints in the wine with the bouquet garni for a few hours or overnight – this will improve their taste and colour. Dry the joints well before frying or browning will be difficult.

SERVES 4

1.35 kg│3 lb chicken, jointed into 8 pieces (pages 368–9)

290 ml│½ pint red wine

1 small clove of garlic, peeled and bruised

1 bouquet garni (1 bay leaf, 1 sprig each of thyme and parsley and 1 stick of celery, tied together with string)

8 button onions

100 g│4 oz rindless bacon, cut into 2 cm × 6 mm│¾ × ¼ in lardons

55 g│2 oz clarified butter (page 385)

12 button mushrooms

salt and freshly ground black pepper

570 mlg│1 pint White Chicken Stock (see page 103)

1 clove garlic, crushed

20 g│¾ oz plain flour

To garnish

1 tablespoon finely chopped fresh parsley

1 Place the chicken pieces in a large plastic bag with the wine, bruised garlic and bouquet garni. Tie the top and marinate in the refrigerator for a few hours or overnight.

2 To remove the skins from the onions, blanch them in boiling water for 1 minute, then refresh in cold water. Trim the roots level with the bulbs, then peel.

3 Blanch the bacon in boiling water for 30 seconds to remove the excess salt. Drain and dry well.

4 Put half the butter into a large, heavy saucepan and brown the onions, bacon and mushrooms. Remove and reserve.

5 Remove the chicken from the marinade, reserving the marinade and the bouquet garni and discarding the garlic. Pat the chicken dry and season with salt and pepper.

6 Add the remaining butter to the pan and brown the chicken on the skin side over a medium-low heat. Tip off all the fat and reserve.

7 Return the vegetables and bacon pieces to the pan and add the wine from the marinade and enough stock nearly to cover the chicken pieces.

8 Add the crushed garlic and bouquet garni.

9 Cover with a piece of damp greaseproof paper and a tightly fitting lid and simmer slowly for about 45 minutes, until the onions and chicken are tender. Test each piece of chicken by cutting into the underside near the bone and pressing the meat to make sure the juices run clear.

10 Discard the bouquet garni. Lift out the vegetables and bacon and put them on to a warmed serving dish. Keep warm while you make the sauce.

11 Place the cooking liquid in a jug and reserve.

12 Mix the flour with enough of the reserved fat to make a paste or roux. Cook the roux in a small pan over a medium heat until light brown.

13 Use a bulb baster to remove the liquid from the bottom of the jug, leaving the fat behind. Add the liquid to the roux off the heat, stirring to make a smooth sauce.

14 Return to the heat, bring to the boil and boil for 2 minutes. Adjust the thickness of the sauce to coating consistency either by boiling further or by adding water, as required. Taste and adjust the seasoning.

15 Trim the chicken pieces, arrange in a warmed deep serving platter and spoon the sauce over the chicken. Garnish with the parsley.

Clarified Butter

Method 1: Put the butter into a saucepan with a cupful of water and heat until melted and frothy. Allow to cool and set solid, then lift the butter, now clarified, off the top of the liquid.

Method 2: Heat the butter until foaming without allowing it to burn. Pour it through fine muslin or a double layer of clean 'J' cloth.

Method 3: Melt the butter in a heavy saucepan and skim off the froth with a slotted spoon. Pour the clear butter into a bowl leaving behind the white solids.

NOTE: Clarified butter will act as a seal on pâtés or potted meats, and is useful for frying as it will withstand great heat before burning.

Chicken Sauté Normande

SERVES 4

45 g | 1 oz clarified butter (see above)

1 shallot, chopped

1 × 1.35 kg | 3 lb chicken, jointed into 8 pieces

1 tablespoon Calvados

2 teaspoons plain flour

225 ml | 8 fl oz dry cider

150 ml | ¼ pint white stock, made with chicken bones (see page 103)

salt and freshly ground black pepper

1 bouquet garni (1 bay leaf, parsley stalks and 4 sprigs of fresh thyme, tied together with string)

2 tablespoons double cream

To garnish

2 dessert apples, peeled, cored and cut into wedges

15 g | ½ oz butter

a pinch of caster sugar

chopped fresh parsley

1 Heat the butter in a large sauté pan. Add the shallot and sauté for 2–3 minutes. Remove the shallot and reserve.

2 Add the chicken and brown the pieces on the skin side. Pour off excess fat.

3 Add the Calvados, light it with a match and shake the pan until the flames subside. Remove the chicken pieces.

4 Stir in the flour and cook for 3–5 minutes until straw-coloured. Remove from the heat. Add the cider and the cooked shallot. Blend well and add the stock. Return to the heat and bring slowly to the boil, stirring continuously. Season with salt and pepper and add the bouquet garni. Simmer for 2 minutes.

5 Replace the chicken, cover and simmer gently for 45 minutes until cooked through.

6 Meanwhile, prepare the garnish: fry the apple wedges in the butter with the sugar until golden-brown on each side. Keep warm.

7 When the chicken is cooked, lift it out and trim the pieces neatly. Arrange on an ovenproof platter and keep warm.

8 Strain the sauce into a clean saucepan and reduce by boiling rapidly to the required consistency. Add the cream and season to taste with salt and pepper.

9 Garnish with the apple and sprinkle with the parsley.

wine: **LIGHT FRUITY RED**

Chicken Paprika

SERVES 4

1 × 1.35 kg│3 lb chicken	1 bay leaf
1 tablespoon oil	2 slices of lemon
15 g│½ oz butter	1 parsley stalk
1 onion, thinly sliced	salt and freshly ground black pepper
2 tablespoons paprika pepper	150 ml│¼ pint white sauce (see page 112)
1 × 200 g│7 oz can of tomatoes	
100 ml│3½ fl oz dry white wine	**To garnish**
570 ml│1 pint white stock, made with chicken bones (see page 103)	1 tablespoon soured cream
	chopped fresh parsley

1 Wash the chicken and wipe dry. Preheat the oven to 200°C│400°F│gas mark 6.

2 Heat the oil in a frying pan and when hot add the butter. When the butter is foaming, add the chicken and brown on the skin side only. Take it out and put into a casserole.

3 Fry the onion in the oil and butter and when just beginning to brown, reduce the heat and add the paprika. Cook for 2–3 minutes. Stir in the tomatoes, wine and stock. Add the bay leaf, lemon slices and parsley stalk. Season well with salt and pepper. When boiling, pour over the chicken.

4 Cover and bake in the oven for about 1 hour or until the chicken is cooked.

5 When the chicken is cooked, take it out of the casserole and remove the bay leaf, parsley stalk and lemon slices. Carefully skim off the fat with a spoon, or soak up and lift off the fat by laying absorbent kitchen paper on the surface of the sauce. Liquidize the sauce in a blender, then push it through a sieve.

6 Beat the paprika sauce into the prepared white sauce until completely incorporated and smooth.

7 Joint the chicken neatly into 8 pieces and arrange on a warmed serving dish. Heat the sauce and spoon it over the chicken. Trickle over the soured cream and sprinkle with parsley.

wine: **LIGHT RED**

Tarragon Chicken

SERVES 4

1 × 1.35 kg | 3 lb chicken with giblets
55 g | 2 oz clarified butter (see page 385)
1 slice of lemon
4 sprigs of fresh tarragon
salt and freshly ground black pepper

150 ml | ¼ pint white stock, made with chicken bones
  (see page 103)
20 g | ¾ oz plain flour
150 ml | ¼ pint double cream
salt and freshly ground black pepper
a squeeze of lemon juice

1 Preheat the oven to 200°C | 400°F | gas mark 6. Wipe the chicken inside and out. Place a small nut of the butter, the lemon slice and half the tarragon leaves inside the cavity. Season inside and out with salt and pepper.
2 Melt the remaining butter in a flameproof casserole the size of the chicken and brown the bird on all sides. Place the giblets (except the liver) in the casserole and pour over the stock. Cover with a lid and cook in the oven for 1¼ hours or until the juices run clear, rather than pink, when the thigh is pierced with a skewer.
3 Remove the chicken, draining the juices back into the casserole. Joint the chicken neatly and put the pieces into a covered dish. Keep warm.
4 Skim all the fat from the stock. Mix 15 ml | 1 tablespoon of this fat with the flour in a cup. When thoroughly blended pour more of the stock into the cup and mix well. Return this to the casserole and stir over direct heat until boiling. Simmer for 5 minutes.
5 Strain into a clean saucepan and add the remaining tarragon, chopped. Simmer for 1–2 minutes, then stir in the cream. Taste and season with salt, pepper and lemon juice.
6 Spoon over the chicken pieces and serve.

wine: CRISP DRY WHITE

Poussins with Pernod

SERVES 4

4 single-portion poussins
seasoned plain flour
459 g | 1½ oz clarified butter (see page 385)
2 shallots, finely chopped
5 tablespoons Pernod

To garnish
lemon wedges
chopped fresh parsley

1 Bone the poussins completely (see pages 370–1).
2 Open the poussins out; put them between 2 pieces of wet greaseproof paper and flatten them with a wooden mallet or rolling pin.
3 Dip them in the seasoned flour and shake off any excess.
4 Melt 30 g | ½ oz butter in a large sauté pan, add the poussins and brown them on each side. Reduce the heat and continue to sauté the poussins until cooked.
5 Sweat the shallots in the remaining butter until soft. Remove from the pan.

6 Increase the heat and pour the Pernod into the pan with the chicken. When hot, set alight with a match and turn off the heat. When the flames subside, scrape the pan with a spoon to loosen any sediment stuck to the bottom. Stir in the shallots.

7 Take out the poussins; arrange on a warmed serving dish. Boil up the pan juices and pour, sizzling, over the poussins. Garnish with lemon wedges and parsley and serve immediately.

NOTE: Two-portion poussins are called 'double' poussins, whereas one-portion birds are 'single' birds.

wine: **SPICY DRY WHITE**

Chicken Jambonneaux Stuffed with Wild Mushrooms

SERVES 4

4 chicken drumsticks with the thighs attached
salt and finely ground black pepper
6 tablespoons dry sherry or Madeira
30 g | 1 oz butter, clarified (see page 385)
290 ml | ½ pint white stock, made with chicken bones (see page 103)

85 g | 3 oz shiitake mushrooms, finely chopped
30 g | 1 oz fresh white breadcrumbs
1 tablespoon finely chopped fresh parsley
1 tablespoon chopped fresh thyme
1 teaspoon dry sherry or Madeira
salt and freshly ground black pepper

For the stuffing

1 onion, very finely chopped
15 g | ½ oz butter
1 rasher of rindless streaky bacon, finely diced
55 g | 2 oz fresh wild mushrooms, finely chopped

To serve

Madeira sauce (see page 116)

To garnish

small sprigs of watercress

1 Make the stuffing: sweat the onion in the butter in a frying pan until soft but not brown. Add the bacon and stir over medium heat until the bacon is cooked.

2 Add all the mushrooms and continue to cook until all the excess liquid released from the mushrooms has evaporated. Turn the mixture into a bowl to cool.

3 Cut the knobbly joint off the bottom of each drumstick. Using the point of a sharp knife, remove the bones from the leg by cutting around the flesh next to the bone, starting from the thigh end and working to the end of the drumstick. Season the chicken with salt and pepper.

4 Stir the breadcrumbs, herbs and the sherry or Madeira into the mushroom mixture and season to taste with salt and pepper.

5 Stuff the chicken legs with the mushroom mixture. Fold the chicken over to encase the stuffing and secure by tying with string.

6 Preheat the oven to 200°C | 400°F | gas mark 6.

7 Heat the clarified butter in a sauté pan over a medium heat and brown the chicken well on all sides.

8 Place the chicken in an ovenproof dish and pour over the sherry or Madeira and the stock. Cover and bake for 30 minutes, or until the juices run clear from the chicken when it is pierced with a skewer. Tip the cooking liquor into a glass bowl. Remove any fat and add the Madeira sauce. Reduce, by boiling rapidly, until syrupy.

9 Place the chicken on a warmed serving plate. Spoon over a little of the Madeira sauce and garnish with the watercress. Hand the remaining sauce separately.

wine: **DRY WHITE OR ROSÉ**

Chicken Fricassee with Mushrooms

SERVES 4

1 × 1.35 kg | 3 lb chicken, cleaned but not trussed
1 onion, sliced
1 carrot, peeled and sliced
1 stick of celery, sliced
6 black peppercorns
2 bay leaves
2 stalks of fresh parsley

For the sauce

55 g | 2 oz butter
250 g | 9 oz button mushrooms, sliced
40 g | 1 1/3 oz plain flour
1 egg yolk
2 tablespoons double cream
salt and freshly ground white pepper
a squeeze of lemon juice
1 tablespoon chopped fresh parsley

1 Place the chicken in a large saucepan with the onion, carrot, celery, peppercorns, bay leaves and parsley. Cover with cold water, leaving the very top of the chicken breast protruding. Place a piece of greaseproof paper directly on the chicken then cover with a lid.

2 Poach for 1 1/4 hours, or until the chicken is cooked through (the legs should feel loose and wobbly).

3 Remove the chicken from the pan and strain the stock.

4 Using a large spoon, carefully skim the stock of the fat. Place successive sheets of absorbent kitchen paper on the surface of the stock to remove the remaining fat. Boil the stock until reduced to 570 ml | 1 pint.

5 Remove the chicken from the bones and cut into 5 cm | 2 in pieces.

6 Make the sauce: melt 15 g | 1/2 oz of the butter in a frying pan and cook the mushrooms for about 5 minutes until tender. Remove with a slotted spoon and reserve.

7 Melt the remaining butter in the frying pan. Remove from the heat and stir in the flour to make a smooth paste. Return to the heat and cook over a medium heat for about 5 minutes until a light straw colour.

8 Remove the pan from the heat and gradually stir in the reduced stock to make a smooth sauce.

9 Return to the heat and bring to the boil, stirring. Simmer for 2 minutes.

10 Mix the egg yolk with the cream. Gradually stir a few tablespoons of the hot sauce into the egg and cream mixture. When it is warm (do not allow to boil), stir it into the hot sauce. Heat gently to thicken, but do not allow to boil.

11 Add the chicken to the sauce and warm through without boiling. Season to taste with salt, pepper and lemon juice. Just before serving, sprinkle with the parsley.

wine: **DRY WHITE**

Boned Stuffed Chicken

The filling for Boned Duck (see page 408) is also delicious in a boned chicken.

SERVES 6

1 × 1.35 kg | 3 lb chicken
55 ml | 2 fl oz oil

For the stuffing

15 g | ½ oz butter
1 small onion, finely chopped
225 g | 8 oz good-quality sausagemeat
2 tablespoons fresh white breadcrumbs

1 small dessert apple, chopped
1 teaspoon chopped fresh sage
2 tablespoons chopped fresh parsley
1 egg
salt and freshly ground black pepper

To garnish

1 bunch of watercress

1 Bone the chicken without removing the legs or wings (see pages 370–1).
2 Make the stuffing: melt the butter in a saucepan, add the onion and cook until soft but not coloured. Allow to cool. Mix together the sausagemeat, onion, breadcrumbs, apple, sage, parsley and egg and season well with salt and pepper. Beat very well.
3 Use this stuffing to fill the boned chicken. Draw up the sides and wrap the chicken in a piece of muslin or sterilized 'j'-cloth saturated with the oil. Tie the chicken at either end so that it resembles a Christmas cracker.
4 Preheat the oven to 200°C | 400°F | gas mark 6.
5 Place the chicken breast-side up on a wire rack over a roasting pan and bake in the oven for 1½ hours.
6 Unwrap the chicken and serve hot or cold, garnished with the watercress.

wine: **DRY WHITE OR ROSE**

Boned Chicken Stuffed with Ricotta and Sun-Dried Tomatoes

SERVES 6

1 × 1.8 kg | 4 lb chicken
55 ml | 2 fl oz oil

For the stuffing:

170 g | 6 oz ricotta cheese
1 egg
85 g | 3 oz fresh white breadcrumbs

55 g | 2 oz sun-dried tomatoes, cut into slivers
30 g | 1 oz black olives, pitted
1 tablespoon roughly chopped fresh basil
salt and freshly ground black pepper

To garnish

fresh basil leaves

1 Bone the chicken completely, including the legs and wings (see pages 370–1).
2 Preheat the oven to 200°C | 400°F | gas mark 6.
3 Make the stuffing: beat the ricotta cheese, add the egg and beat again. Add the breadcrumbs, sun-dried tomatoes, olives and basil. Season to taste with salt and pepper.

4 Use the stuffing to fill the boned chicken. Draw up the sides and wrap the chicken up in a piece of muslin or a clean 'J'-cloth saturated with oil. Tie the chicken at either end so that it looks rather like a Christmas cracker.

5 Place the chicken breast-side up on a wire rack over a roasting pan and bake for 1–1½ hours.

6 Unwrap the chicken and serve hot or cold garnished with fresh basil leaves.

wine: **LIGHT RED OR ROSÉ**

Boned Stuffed Poussin

SERVES 1

1 single-portion poussin
45 g | 1½ oz butter
½ tablespoon chopped onion
110 g | 4 oz chicken breast, boned and skinned
30 g | 1 oz dried apricots, chopped
2 tablespoons mixed chopped fresh tarragon and parsley

15 g | ½ oz unsalted pistachio nuts, skinned and chopped
salt and freshly ground black pepper
85 g | 3 oz mixed finely diced onion, carrot, turnip and celery (mirepoix)
220 ml | 8 fl oz white stock, made with chicken bones (see page 103)
1 bay leaf
1 small bunch of watercress

1 Bone the poussin without removing the legs or wings (see pages 370–1).

2 Make the stuffing: melt 15 g | ½ oz of the butter in a small pan, add the onion and cook over a low heat until soft but not coloured. Remove from the heat and allow to cool.

3 Chop the chicken breast very finely or whizz briefly in a food processor. Turn into a bowl. Add the cooled onion, apricots, tarragon, parsley and pistachio nuts. Mix and season very well with salt and pepper.

4 Lay the poussin, skin side down, flat on a work top. Place the stuffing in the middle and sew the poussin up using a trussing needle and/or very fine string.

5 Melt half the remaining butter in a flameproof casserole. When it is foaming, add the poussin and brown lightly all over, then remove from the casserole.

6 Add the remaining butter to the casserole with the mirepoix of diced vegetables. Fry until the vegetables are lightly browned.

7 Set the poussin on top of the vegetables. Add the stock, bay leaf, salt and pepper. Bring to the boil, cover and simmer gently for 40–50 minutes.

8 When the poussin is cooked (when pierced with a skewer the juices that run out should be clear, not pink), place it on a plate and remove the thread or string. Keep warm.

9 Sieve the sauce then discard the vegetables. Boil to reduce to a syrupy consistency. Season to taste with salt and pepper.

10 Garnish the poussin with watercress and serve the sauce separately.

wine: **LIGHT RED**

Boned Stuffed Poussins with Shiitake Mushrooms and Wild Rice

SERVES 4

4 single-portion poussins

85 g | 3 oz shiitake mushrooms, sliced

30 g | 1 oz butter

4 spring onions, chopped

85 g | 3 oz rice, cooked

30 g | 1 oz wild rice, cooked

30 g | 1 oz pistachio nuts, roughly chopped

1 egg, beaten

salt and freshly ground black pepper

a little oil

15 g | ½ oz butter

1 small onion, finely chopped

1 small carrot, finely chopped

1 stick of celery, finely chopped

290 ml | ½ pint white stock, made with chicken bones
(see page 103)

1 bay leaf

To garnish

1 bunch of watercress

1 Bone the poussins without removing the legs or wings (see pages 370–1).

2 Make the stuffing: cook the mushrooms slowly in the butter, with the spring onions, for 3 minutes. Allow to cool. Add to the rices with the pistachio nuts. Bind with the beaten egg and season to taste with salt and pepper.

3 Lay the poussins, skin side down, flat on a board. Divide the stuffing between them and sew them up, using cotton or very fine string. Try to shape them to their original form. Tie their legs together loosely.

4 Heat the oil in a flameproof casserole, add the butter and when foaming add the poussins, 2 at a time, and brown lightly all over. Remove to a plate.

5 Add the onion, carrot and celery to the pan and fry until lightly browned. Set the poussins on top of the vegetables. Add the stock, bay leaf, salt and pepper. Bring to the boil, then cover and simmer for 40–50 minutes.

6 When the poussins are cooked, remove to a warmed serving plate. Remove the cotton or string.

7 Meanwhile, make the sauce: skim the fat from the surface of the cooking juices. Strain the sauce into a clean saucepan. Boil rapidly to a syrupy consistency. (Check that the sauce is not too strong – if necessary it can be thickened with a little beurre manié and need not be reduced). Season with salt and pepper.

8 Arrange the poussins on a warmed serving dish. Garnish with the watercress.

9 Heat the sauce, pour into a warmed sauceboat and serve separately.

wine: **LIGHT RED**

French Roast Chicken

SERVES 4

1 × 1.35 kg | 3 lb roasting chicken with giblets

butter

freshly ground black pepper and salt

1 slice of onion

1 bay leaf

a few parsley stalks

For the gravy

1 scant tablespoon plain flour

290 ml | ½ pint white stock, made with chicken bones
(see page 103) or vegetable water

1. Preheat the oven to 200°C|400°F|gas mark 6.
2. Smear a little butter all over the chicken. Season inside and out with pepper only (no salt). Put the bird breast side down in a roasting pan.
3. Put all the chicken giblets (except the liver) and the neck into the pan with the chicken. Add the onion, bay leaf and parsley stalks. Pour in a cup of water. Roast for 30 minutes.
4. Take out of the oven, season all over with salt, turn the chicken right side up and baste it with the fat and juices from the pan. Return to the oven.
5. Check the chicken periodically. It will take 60–80 minutes. It is cooked when the leg bones wobble loosely and independently from the body. Baste occasionally as it cooks, and cover with kitchen foil or greaseproof paper if it is browning too much. Remove the cooked chicken to a warmed serving dish and keep warm while making the gravy.
6. Place the roasting pan with its juices over a low heat. Skim off most of the fat.
7. Mix a tablespoon of the fat with the flour to make a paste.
8. Add the stock or vegetable water and whisk the paste into the stock. Stir until the sauce boils. Simmer for 2–3 minutes. Check the seasoning. Strain into a warmed gravy-boat and serve with the chicken.

wine: **LIGHT RED**

English Roast Chicken

SERVES 4

1 × 1.35 kg|3 lb roasting chicken
15 g|½ oz butter
freshly ground black pepper

For the stuffing

30 g|1 oz butter
1 onion, very finely chopped
55 g|2 oz fresh white breadcrumbs
1 small cooking apple, grated
2 teaspoons chopped mixed fresh herbs
grated zest of ½ lemon
½ egg, beaten
salt and freshly ground black pepper

To garnish

4 chipolata sausages
4 rashers of rindless streaky bacon

For the gravy

1 scant tablespoon plain flour
290 ml|½ pint white stock, made from the chicken neck and giblets (see page 103)

To serve

bread sauce (see page 131)

1. Preheat the oven to 200°C|400°F|gas mark 6.
2. Start to make the stuffing: melt the butter in a saucepan, cover with a piece of dampened greaseproof paper and a lid, then fry the onion until soft but not coloured. Allow to cool.
3. Put the breadcrumbs, apple, herbs and lemon zest together in a mixing bowl.
4. Add the softened onion and enough beaten egg to bind the mixture together. Do not make it too wet. Season to taste with salt and pepper.
5. Stuff the chicken from the neck end, making sure the breast is well plumped. Draw the neck skin flap down to cover the stuffing. Secure with a skewer if necessary.
6. Smear a little butter all over the chicken and season with salt and pepper. Roast for about 1½ hours, or until the juices run clear when the thigh is pierced with a skewer.

7 Meanwhile, make each chipolata sausage into 2 cocktail-sized ones by twisting gently in the middle. Cut each bacon rasher into short lengths and roll them up.

8 After the chicken has been roasting for 1 hour, put the sausages and bacon rolls into the roasting pan, wedging the bacon rolls so that they cannot come undone.

9 Baste occasionally and check that the sausages and bacon are not sticking to the side of the pan and getting burnt.

10 When the chicken is cooked, lift it out on to a warmed serving dish. Trim off the wing tips and tops of the drumsticks, surround with the bacon rolls and sausages and keep warm while you make the gravy.

11 Slowly pour off all but 15 ml | 1 tablespoon of the fat from the roasting pan, taking care to keep any juices. Add the flour and stir over heat until staw-coloured. Add the stock and stir until the sauce boils. Simmer for 3 minutes. Check the seasoning. Strain into a warmed gravy-boat.

12 Serve the chicken with bread sauce and the gravy.

NOTES: English chicken is usually stuffed from the neck end.

The chicken looks neater if it is trussed after stuffing, but it is more difficult to get the thighs cooked without the breast drying out if this is done.

wine: **LIGHT RED**

Chicken Baked in a Brick

If you have no chicken brick an earthenware casserole with a well-fitting lid will do, but the brick, which is chicken-shaped, is particularly good as it fits the chicken closely, with little space for the evaporation of juices. It is a modern version of the ancient method of covering a gutted bird, feathers and all, in wet clay, then baking it. When the hardened clay was broken off, the feathers came away with it, leaving the chicken cooked, succulent and tender. Modern bricks, not made of wet clay, are designed for plucked birds!

SERVES 4

1 × 1.35 kg | 3 lb chicken
a handful of fresh herbs
lemon

melted butter or olive oil
salt and freshly ground black pepper

1 Clean the chicken. Place the herbs and lemon inside the body cavity.

2 Brush the chicken with the butter or oil and season with salt and pepper. Place in a chicken brick.

3 Cover with the lid. Place in a cold oven. Heat the oven to 230°C | 450°F | gas mark 8 and bake for 2 hours. Serve the juices with the chicken.

NOTES: If the chicken is to be served cold, remove the lid when cooked and leave to cool.

The chicken can also be put into a preheated oven. It will then take about 1½ hours.

The manufacturers of chicken bricks generally advise the user not to wash the brick in detergent. Simply rinse in very hot water and put back in the warm oven to dry out.

wine: **DRY WHITE OR ROSE**

Chicken with Prunes

SERVES 4

1 × 1.35 kg | 3 lb chicken with giblets

30 g | 1 oz butter

a few slices of onion

1 slice of lemon

salt and freshly ground black pepper

1 bay leaf

a few slices of carrot

For the sauce

15 g | ½ oz butter

12 shallots, blanched and peeled

12 cooked prunes, stoned

1 tablespoon sugar

1 tablespoon wine vinegar

To garnish

1 bunch of watercress

1 Preheat the oven to 200°C | 400°F | gas mark 6.

2 Wipe the chicken inside and out. Place half the butter, half the onion and the lemon in the breast cavity. Place breast side down in a roasting dish with 5 m | ¼ in water. Spread the remaining butter over the chicken and season with salt and pepper. Add the giblets (except the liver), the bay leaf, the remaining onion and the carrot to the water.

3 Roast for 1–1¼ hours, basting 3 or 4 times and turning the bird over halfway through. The chicken is cooked when the juices run clear from the thigh when pierced with a skewer.

4 Meanwhile, prepare the sauce: melt the butter and when foaming add the shallots. Season with salt and pepper. Cover and cook slowly, shaking the pan occasionally to prevent them from burning but allowing them to brown all over. Add the prunes to the pan and reduce the heat to a minimum.

5 Slowly melt the sugar in a heavy saucepan, tilting and turning it as necessary to get an even pale caramel colour. Add the vinegar – be sure to stand back as it will hiss and splutter. Add 75 ml | 5 tablespoons of the chicken stock from the bottom of the roasting pan. Simmer until the caramel is dissolved. Check the seasoning.

6 Joint the chicken and arrange on a warmed serving dish. Spoon over the prunes and shallots and glaze with the caramel sauce. Garnish with watercress.

wine: **FULL RED**

Lemon Poussins

SERVES 4

2 small lemons

2 double poussins

55 g | 2 oz clarified butter (see page 385)

2 teaspoons sugar

paprika pepper

salt and freshly ground black pepper

To garnish

sprigs of watercress

4 lemon wedges

1 Prick the lemons all over with a fork. Cut in half and put one inside the cavity of each poussin. Tie the drumsticks together with string.

2 Melt the butter in a large saucepan.

3 Add the whole poussins and cover the pan.

4 Cook over a low heat for 30 minutes, turning the poussins to brown lightly on all sides. They should now be partially cooked, and the butter in the pan should be brown but not burnt.

5 Take out the birds and split them in two. Trim the wing tips and the knuckles.

6 Preheat the grill. Lay the portions of poussin cut side up in the grill pan. Brush them with some butter from the saucepan. Sprinkle with half the sugar and plenty of paprika and pepper. Grill slowly for about 5 minutes or until a really good brown.

7 Turn the poussins over and brush again with butter and sprinkle with sugar, paprika and pepper. Grill for a further 5 minutes until cooked through and very dark – almost, but not quite, charred. Sprinkle with salt.

8 Arrange on a warmed dish, pour over the juices from the grill pan and garnish with sprigs of watercress and lemon wedges.

wine: **SPICY DRY WHITE**

Lemon Chicken with Cream Cheese and Herbs

SERVES 6

6 large chicken breasts, boned and skinned

4 tablespoons good-quality olive oil

finely grated zest of 2 lemons

3 sprigs of fresh rosemary, chopped

140 g | 5 oz cream cheese with herbs

salt and freshly ground black pepper

1 Trim the chicken of any fat and cut into bite-sized pieces. Put into a bowl with 2 tablespoons of the oil, the lemon zest and rosemary. Cover and marinate for at least 30 minutes or overnight in the refrigerator.

2 Heat the remaining oil in a large, heavy sauté pan. Lift the chicken pieces from the marinade, add to the pan a few at a time and fry, turning, until browned.

3 When all the chicken is browned, return it to the pan. Cover and cook over a medium heat without boiling for about 4 minutes or until the chicken is tender. Add the cream cheese, season to taste with salt and pepper and reheat briefly without boiling. If the sauce becomes too thick, add a little water. Serve immediately.

wine: **DRY WHITE**

Mustard Grilled Chicken

Although this is called grilled chicken it is partially baked to ensure that the chicken is cooked without becoming burnt.

SERVES 4

30 g | 1 oz butter, softened

2 tablespoons Dijon mustard

1 teaspoon sugar

1 teaspoon paprika pepper

1 × 1.35 kg | 3 lb chicken

juice of 1 lemon

salt and freshly ground black pepper

To garnish

a few sprigs of watercress

1 Mix together the butter, mustard, sugar and paprika.

2 Preheat the oven to 200°C|400°F|gas mark 6.

3 Joint the chicken into 8 pieces. Remove any small feathers.

4 Spread the underside of each chicken piece with half the mustard mixture. Sprinkle with half the lemon juice. Season with salt and pepper. Bake for 15–20 minutes.

5 Turn the chicken over and spread again with the mustard mixture. Sprinkle with the remaining paprika, lemon juice and sugar. Season with pepper. Bake for a further 15 minutes.

6 Preheat the grill. Cut off the wing tips and the knuckles.

7 Arrange the joints under the grill in such a way that the larger joints are closest to the strongest heat and the breast joints are near the edge of the grill.

8 Grill until dark and crisp but be very careful not to let the joints burn.

9 Arrange the joints neatly on a warmed flat serving dish. Pour over the juices from the pan and garnish with sprigs of watercress.

wine: LIGHT RED

Spatchcock Grilled Chicken

SERVES 4

4 single-portion poussins
salt and freshly ground black pepper
a pinch of cayenne pepper
lemon juice
55 g|2 oz butter
15 g|½ oz Parmesan cheese, grated

To garnish

sprigs of watercress
French dressing (see page 123)

1 Split the poussins down one side of the backbone with a pair of poultry shears or kitchen scissors. Cut down the other side of the backbone to remove it. Open out the chickens and flatten well on a board by pressing with the heel of your hand. Skewer the birds in position, i.e. flat and open.

2 Season well with salt, pepper and cayenne and sprinkle with lemon juice. If possible, leave for 1 hour.

3 Preheat the grill. Brush the cut side of the poussins with melted butter. Grill for about 12 minutes or until a good golden-brown, brushing frequently with the pan juices. Turn over, brush again and grill for a further 7 minutes or until the poussin is cooked.

4 Brush once more with the hot butter and sprinkle with the Parmesan cheese. Grill until golden-brown and crisp. Arrange on a warmed serving dish and garnish with sprigs of watercress dipped in French dressing.

wine: LIGHT RED

Chicken Chaudfroid

This is a cold chicken coated with a white sauce, glazed with aspic jelly, and garnished with slices of truffle or mushroom. The chicken should be cooked the day before serving because the stock in which it is cooked becomes the aspic jelly. The recipe calls for a whole chicken but poached chicken supremes can be used in its place. When making clear jellies, all the equipment should be scalded to ensure it is absolutely clean and fat-free.

SERVES 4

1 × 1.35 kg | 3 lb chicken, not trussed
1 onion, sliced
½ carrot
2 bay leaves
1 sprig of fresh parsley
6 black peppercorns
2.5 ml | ½ teaspoon salt

For the aspic jelly

860 ml | 1½ pints white stock, made with chicken bones (see page 103)
55 g | 2 oz powdered gelatine
5 tablespoons dry white wine
5 tablespoons dry sherry
1 tablespoon tarragon vinegar
3 egg whites, frothed
3 egg shells, crushed and sterlized

For the chaudfroid sauce

1 bay leaf
4 black peppercorns
1 slice of onion
1 blade of mace
1 sprig of fresh parsley
425 ml | ¾ pint milk
30 g | 1 oz butter
30 g | 1 oz plain flour
salt
150 ml | ¼ pint aspic jelly (see above)
15 g | ½ powdered gelatine
5 tablespoons double cream

To garnish

1 bunch of chervil
1 punnet of mustard and cress

1 Place the chicken in a saucepan, just cover with cold water, and add the vegetables, herbs, peppercorns and salt. Bring to the boil, cover and simmer gently until the chicken is tender (about 1¼ hours). When it is cooked, a skewer will glide easily into the thigh, and the drumstick should feel loose.

2 Remove the bird from the pan, allow it to cool, cover loosely with clingfilm, and refrigerate overnight. Strain the stock, taste and season very well with salt and pepper and leave to cool. If possible, refrigerate it (this will set the fat and make it easier to remove the next day). Reduce the stock, if necessary, to give a strong flavour.

3 The next day make the aspic jelly: remove all the fat from the chicken stock. Put the stock (which should be about 860 ml | 1½ pints) and gelatine into a clean pan. Add the wine, sherry and vinegar.

4 Put the egg whites and the crushed shells into the stock. Place over the heat and whisk steadily with a balloon whisk until a crust begins to form. Stop whisking when the mixture starts to steam. Allow the mixture to come just to the boil. Remove the pan from the heat and allow the mixture to subside. Take care not to break the crust formed by the egg whites. Leave to cool for 1 minute.

5 Bring the aspic just to the boil again, and again allow to subside. Repeat this once more (the egg white will trap the sediment in the stock and clear the aspic). Leave to cool for 2 minutes.

6 Fix a double layer of fine muslin or white kitchen paper over a clean bowl and carefully strain the aspic through the egg-white crust. When all the liquid is through, check and if it is not quite clear, strain the aspic again. Do not try to hurry the process by squeezing the cloth, or murky aspic will result. Allow to cool.

7 Make the chaudfroid sauce: place the bay leaf, peppercorns, onion slice, mace and parsley sprig in a saucepan with the milk. Set over a low heat and bring slowly to the boil. Remove from the heat and leave to cool for 20 minutes.

8 Melt the butter in a saucepan, remove from the heat, add the flour. Return to the heat and cook for 1 minute. Remove from the heat and slowly, stirring all the time, strain the milk into the pan. Return the pan to the heat and bring slowly to the boil, stirring continually until you have a slightly thickened, shiny sauce. Season well with salt and simmer gently for 2–3 minutes.

9 Put 3 tablespoons liquid aspic into a small saucepan and sprinkle the gelatine over the aspic. Allow to soak for 5 minutes, then heat gently until liquid and clear. Strain this into the white sauce with the cream. Taste and add more salt if necessary. The sauce must be very smooth and shiny: it can be strained through a tammy strainer or blended in a liquidizer to give it a good sheen. Stir the sauce as it cools and begins to set. When it is the consistency of thick cream it is ready to use for coating.

10 Prepare the chicken: skin and joint it very neatly into 4 or 8 pieces, removing the wing tips and drumstick knuckles. Place the pieces on a wire rack with a clean tray underneath.

11 Coat each chicken joint very carefully with the cold, nearly set chaudfroid sauce. Allow to set and if necessary give it a second coating, scraping extra sauce (which will need reheating slightly to return it to coating consistency) from the tray underneath the wire rack.

12 When nearly set, dip the chervil leaves in a little aspic and arrange in a formal simple pattern on each chicken piece. Allow to set. Wash the tray and replace under the chicken.

13 Coat with some of the cool but still liquid aspic. Allow to set. Give a second and perhaps third coating, allowing each coating to set before attempting the next.

14 Pour the remaining aspic on to a shallow tray. Allow to set, then cut it into neat dice. Use it to cover a large flat serving dish and make a slight dome in the centre. Arrange the chicken chaudfroid around this and surround with small clumps of mustard and cress.

NOTES: Chaudfroid is classically decorated with sliced truffles. These are delicious if fresh but disappointing as well as expensive if bought in tins.

If the aspic is less than crystal-clear it is wise not to chop it, which seems to emphasize its murkiness.

wine: **CRISP DRY WHITE**

Chicken Breasts with Grilled Red Pepper Mousseline and Black Olive Tapenade

SERVES 4

4 boneless and skinless chicken breasts

1 red pepper

½ tablespoon chopped fresh basil

1 teaspoon finely chopped fresh parsley

1 egg white

75 ml | 2½ fl oz double cream

1 teaspoon ground mace

salt and freshly ground white pepper

1 tablespoon tapenade (see page 124)

570 ml | 1 pint white stock, made with chicken bones
(see page 103)

To serve

tomato sauce 1 (see page 128)

1 Remove the small loose fillets from the chicken breasts, chop roughly and place in a food processor.

2 Grill or roast the red pepper until the skin blackens. Allow to cool, then remove the skin, membrane and seeds. Cut the flesh into medium dice. Add to the food processor with the basil and parsley.

3 Briefly whizz the mixture, then add the egg white and cream while the machine is still running. The mixture should be smooth, but be careful not to over-process.

4 Season well with the mace, salt and pepper. Chill in the refrigerator until ready to use.

5 Cut a small pocket in the side of each chicken breast and spread a little tapenade inside it. Put a spoonful of the red pepper mousseline mixture into the pocket and pull the edges together to seal.

6 Place the stuffed chicken breasts in a large shallow pan or a roasting pan. Heat the chicken stock to boiling point and pour over the chicken. Poach over a gentle heat so that the stock barely simmers for about 15 minutes or until the chicken breasts are firm to the touch. Remove from the stock and allow to cool.

7 Serve the chicken breasts sliced with the warm tomato sauce.

NOTE: The chicken keeps its shape better if wrapped in clingfilm and then poached until firm.

wine: **LIGHT RED**

Chicken Breasts with Parma Ham and Spinach

SERVES 4

4 chicken breasts, boned, skinned and any fat
  removed

4 thin slices of best-quality Parma ham

8 large spinach leaves, blanched and refreshed

For the dressing

4 tablespoons good-quality olive oil

4 tablespoons salad oil

2 tablespoons tarragon vinegar

1 tablespoon chopped fresh parsley

1 tablespoon chopped fresh dill

1 teaspoon coarse-grain mustard

salt and freshly ground black pepper

1 Wrap each chicken breast in 1 slice of Parma ham and then in the spinach. Wrap each individually in clingfilm.
2 Place the chicken breasts in a saucepan side by side, not on top of each other, and pour over hot water to cover.
3 Cover the saucepan with a lid and bring back to the boil, then turn down the heat and poach gently for 18–20 minutes, or until the breasts feel just firm to the touch, then lift the chicken breasts out of the saucepan and drain.
4 Meanwhile, make the dressing: combine all the ingredients together in a liquidizer or food processor and process to a green purée.
5 Flood 4 plates with some of the dressing. Remove the clingfilm from the chicken breast. Slice each chicken breast on the diagonal and arrange overlapping slices in a semi-circle on the dressing.

NOTE: This can be served hot or cold.

wine: **CRISP DRY WHITE**

Chicken with Mushrooms and Coriander

SERVES 4

4 chicken breasts, skinned and boned

15 g | ½ oz cornflour

1 large onion, thinly sliced

1–2 tablespoons sunflower oil

2 teaspoons coriander seeds, very well crushed

225 g | 8 oz flat mushrooms, sliced

150 ml | ¼ pint white stock, made with chicken bones (see page 103)

salt and freshly ground black pepper

2 tablespoons medium sherry

To garnish

fresh coriander leaves

1 Trim any fat from the chicken breasts and cut the flesh into large cubes. Toss in the cornflour and set aside.
2 Fry the onion in 1 tablespoon of the oil and when beginning to soften add the coriander seeds, increase the heat and allow the onion to brown and the seeds to toast (1–2 minutes).
3 Add the chicken and fry for 3 minutes. Remove the chicken and onions from the pan and set aside. Add the remaining oil and the mushrooms and cook until beginning to soften. Return the chicken and onions to the pan. Add the stock and season with salt and pepper. Stir well and simmer for 4–5 minutes.
4 Add the sherry and boil for 30 seconds. Pile on to a warmed serving dish and garnish with coriander.

wine: **LIGHT RED**

Chicken Breasts with Leek and Watercress Sauce

SERVES 4

4 chicken breasts, boned and skinned

30 g | 1 oz truffle, thinly sliced (optional)

15 g | ½ oz butter

85 g | 3 oz white of leeks, finely chopped

1 small shallot, finely chopped

1 small bunch of watercress, carefully picked over

2 tablespoons white port

290 ml | ½ pint white stock, made with chicken bones (see page 103)

2 egg yolks

75 ml | 2½ fl oz double cream

1 Using a sharp knife, make a horizontal incision in the thickest part of each chicken breast and insert slices of truffle, if using.

2 Melt the butter, add the leek and shallot and cook slowly until soft but not brown. Add half of the watercress, the port and stock and simmer for 10 minutes.

3 Add the chicken breasts and poach, covered, for 12 minutes. Turn the chicken over halfway through cooking. Remove from the pan, returning any watercress or leeks stuck to the breasts to the saucepan. Keep warm while you make the sauce.

4 Chop the remaining watercress very finely.

5 Reduce the poaching liquid, by boiling rapidly, to concentrate its flavour, and liquidize in a blender until very smooth. Pour into a clean saucepan. Bring to just below boiling point.

6 Mix the egg yolks with the cream, add a little of the hot sauce to the yolks, stir and return to the saucepan. Stir over medium heat until thickened. It is essential that the sauce does not get near boiling point or it will curdle. Stir in the remaining watercress to improve the colour.

7 Arrange the chicken breasts, split in 2 if liked, on warmed dinner plates. Spoon over the sauce.

wine: DRY WHITE

Chicken Breasts with Ginger

SERVES 4

4 chicken breasts, boned and skinned

1 large onion, very finely chopped

2 cloves of garlic, crushed

5 cm | 2 in piece of fresh root ginger, peeled and very finely chopped

5 cardamom pods, cracked

1 teaspoon ground turmeric

4 tablespoons light soy sauce

4 tablespoons dry sherry (optional)

1 Place the chicken breasts in a bowl with the onion, garlic, ginger, cardamom pods, turmeric, soy sauce and sherry. Cover the bowl and refrigerate for 2–24 hours so that the chicken can absorb the flavour. Turn the chicken once or twice.

2 Preheat the oven to 200°C|400°F|gas mark 6.

3 Line a flat baking dish with kitchen foil and arrange the breasts on it. Pour over the marinade and seal the chicken tightly in the foil so that none of the juice can escape.

4 Bake for 30 minutes.

wine: DRY WHITE

Chicken Breasts with Red Pepper Sauce

SERVES 4

4 chicken breasts, skinned and boned

3 tablespoons finely shredded white of leek

2 tablespoons finely shredded carrot

salt and freshly ground black pepper

To serve

red pepper sauce (see page 129)

To garnish

watercress leaves

1 Remove any fat from the chicken breasts.

2 Mix the leek and carrot together, season with salt and pepper and use as a stuffing.

3 Put the stuffing between the main part of the chicken breasts and the loose fillet. Wrap each breast in a piece of clingfilm.

4 Poach the chicken breasts in water for 15 minutes. Remove from the saucepan, unwrap and leave to get completely cold.

5 Flood the base of 4 dinner plates with the red pepper sauce.

6 Put a chicken breast on each plate and garnish with watercress leaves.

wine: DRY WHITE OR ROSÉ

Chicken Curry with Almonds

This is a fairly mild curry. Extra spices can be added if liked.

SERVES 8

8 chicken breasts, skinned and boned

4 tablespoons sunflower oil

85 g|3 oz blanched almonds

2 teaspoons ground cardamom

1 teaspoon ground cloves

1 teaspoon ground chilli

4 teaspoons ground cumin

4 teaspoons ground coriander

2 teaspoons ground turmeric

2 onions, finely chopped

2 cloves of garlic, crushed

2.5 cm|1 in piece of fresh root ginger, peeled and finely chopped

1   400 g|14 oz can of tomatoes, chopped

salt and freshly ground black pepper

150 ml|¼ pint water

2 tablespoons Greek yoghurt

To garnish

a few fresh coriander leaves

1 Preheat the oven to 190°C|375°F|gas mark 5.
2 Remove any fat or gristle from the chicken breasts. Set aside.
3 Put 1 tablespoon of the oil into a saucepan and fry the almonds until golden-brown but not burnt. Set aside. Add the remaining oil and in it slowly cook the spices for 1 minute.
4 In a blender, liquidize the almonds and cooked spices with enough water to make a smooth paste.
5 Rinse out the saucepan, add 2 more tablespoons oil and in it fry the onions, garlic and ginger until the onions are golden-brown.
6 Reduce the heat and add the tomatoes, spice and almond paste, salt, pepper and water. Stir well and simmer for 2–3 minutes.
7 Tip the sauce into an ovenproof dish. Add the chicken breasts and spoon over some of the sauce. Cover with kitchen foil and bake for 40 minutes, or until the chicken is cooked.
8 Transfer the chicken to a warmed serving dish. Swirl the yoghurt into the sauce. Pour over the chicken breasts and garnish with coriander.

wine: SPICY RED

Chicken with Coriander and Saffron Sauce

SERVES 4

1 sachet powdered saffron
30 g|1 oz butter
2 onions, chopped
2 cloves of garlic, crushed
150 ml|¼ pint Greek yoghurt
1 × 400 g|14 oz can of chopped tomatoes

5–6 tablespoons chopped fresh coriander
salt and freshly ground black pepper
4 chicken breasts, skinned and boned

To garnish
a few fresh coriander leaves

1 Heat the saffron in a small dry saucepan for 3 seconds. Pour on 3 tablespoons of hot water and stir to dissolve.
2 Melt the butter in a sauté pan and fry the onions and garlic for 5–8 minutes, until lightly golden. Stir in the saffron liquid. Add the yoghurt, 1 tablespoon at a time, stir and fry until it is well incorporated into the sauce. Add the tomatoes, coriander, salt and pepper.
3 Put the chicken breasts into the pan and bring slowly to the boil. Cover and simmer over a low heat for 30 minutes, or until the chicken is tender.
4 Remove the lid, lift out the chicken breasts and keep warm.
5 Reduce the sauce by boiling rapidly, stirring occasionally to prevent it catching, until thickened. Pour over the chicken breasts, garnish with coriander and serve immediately.

wine: SPICY DRY WHITE

Lemon Chicken with Mint and Yoghurt Sauce

SERVES 4

4 chicken breasts, skinned and boned

For the marinade

grated zest and juice of 1 lemon

1 tablespoon chopped fresh parsley

1 tablespoon fresh thyme leaves or ¼ teaspoon dried thyme

1.25 ml ¼ teaspoon ground coriander

1 tablespoon sunflower oil

For the sauce

150 ml | ¼ pint yoghurt

1 tablespoon chopped fresh mint

salt and freshly ground black pepper

1 clove of garlic, crushed

To garnish

1 small bunch of watercress

1 Mix together the marinade ingredients and leave the chicken breasts in it in the refrigerator overnight or as long as possible.

2 Preheat the oven to 200°C 400°F gas mark 6.

3 Place the chicken and the marinade in a roasting pan and cook for 30 minutes.

4 Meanwhile, mix all the sauce ingredients together.

5 When the chicken is cooked, arrange on a warmed serving dish, garnish with watercress and serve the sauce separately.

wine: **FULL DRY WHITE**

Chicken with Black Bean Sauce

SERVES 4

4 large chicken breasts, skinned and boned

2 teaspoons cornflour

3 tablespoons fermented black beans

2 tablespoons sunflower oil

2 spring onions, chopped

1 clove of garlic, bruised

2.5 cm | 1 in piece of fresh root ginger, peeled and sliced

2 tablespoons soy sauce

2 tablespoons dry sherry

1 teaspoon sugar

290 ml | ½ pint water

2 teaspoons sesame oil

To garnish

2 spring onions, chopped

1 Trim any fat off the chicken breasts and cut into bite-sized pieces. Mix with the cornflour and set aside.

2 Wash the beans several times as they are very salty.

3 Heat 1 tablespoon of the sunflower oil in a small saucepan, add the spring onions, garlic and ginger and cook over a low heat for 1 minute. Remove and discard.

4 Add the soy sauce, sherry, sugar, black beans and water. Bring to the boil, then simmer slowly for 10 minutes.

5 Heat the remaining sunflower oil in a wok and quickly stir-fry the chicken. Add the black bean sauce and cook over a very low heat for a further 5 minutes.

6 Add the sesame oil and pile on to a warmed serving dish. Garnish with the spring onions.

wine: **SPICY DRY WHITE**

Chicken Fried Rice

4 chicken breasts, skinned and boned

170 g | 6 oz basmati rice, soaked in cold water for 30 minutes

oil

1 onion, chopped

1 clove of garlic, crushed

2.5 cm | 1 in piece of fresh root ginger, peeled and finely chopped

1 green chilli, finely chopped

½ teaspoon ground turmeric

1 teaspoon chopped fresh lemon grass or 2 teaspoons dried lemon grass

290 ml | ½ pint white stock made with chicken bones (see page 103)

salt and freshly ground black pepper

1 tablespoon sesame seeds

To garnish

sprigs of fresh coriander

1 Remove any fat from the chicken and cut the flesh into bite-sized pieces.
2 Drain and rinse the rice.
3 Fry the chicken lightly in a little oil in a large sauté pan. Remove from the pan. Add the onion and cook for 10 minutes. Add the garlic, ginger, chilli and rice and fry until the rice becomes slightly opaque. Add the turmeric and cook for 1 minute.
4 Return the chicken to the sauté pan. Add the lemon grass and enough stock to just cover the rice. Season with salt and pepper.
5 Bring to the boil, then simmer slowly, adding more stock if necessary, until the rice is cooked (about 30 minutes).
6 Stir in the sesame seeds. Pile into a warmed serving dish and garnish with the coriander.

wine: **DRY WHITE**

Oriental Chicken with Sesame Seeds

SERVES 4–6

4 boneless chicken breasts

2 tablespoons vegetable or groundnut oil

a large pinch of ground turmeric

1 teaspoon tomato purée

For the marinade

1 small clove of garlic, crushed

1 cm | ½ in piece of fresh root ginger, peeled and grated

3 tablespoons soy sauce

1 tablespoon sesame oil

½ tablespoon clear honey

½ tablespoon wine vinegar or sherry

For the vegetables

55 g | 2 oz mangetout, blanched

55 g | 2 oz baby sweetcorn, blanched

55 g | 2 oz button mushrooms, blanched

1 red pepper, cored, deseeded and cut into strips on the diagonal

55 g | 2 oz French beans, blanched

1 tablespoon sesame seeds, toasted

1 Skin the chicken breasts and cut the flesh into strips.
2 Mix together the ingredients for the marinade and add the chicken. Chill for 1 hour.
3 Heat the oil in a wok, add the chicken and stir-fry, with its marinade, until firm (4–5 minutes).
4 Add all the vegetables and when thoroughly heated, pile into a warm serving dish and scatter over the warm toasted sesame seeds.

wine: FULL DRY WHITE

Stir-fried Chicken with Cashews

450 g | 1 lb boneless and skinless chicken meat, or 4 chicken breasts, skinned

2.5 cm | 1 in piece of fresh root ginger, peeled and sliced

2 small cloves of garlic, bruised

2 teaspoons cornflour

1 tablespoon soy sauce

1 tablespoon dry sherry

150 ml | ¼ pint white stock, made with chicken bones (see page 103)

1 tablespoon sunflower or grapeseed oil

To garnish

55 g | 2 oz unsalted cashew nuts

2 spring onions, sliced on the diagonal

1 Trim the chicken of all fat and cut into 3 cm | 1½ chunks.
2 Put into a bowl with the ginger and garlic, cover and leave to stand for 10 minutes.
3 Mix the cornflour with the soy sauce, sherry and stock. Set aside.
4 Heat the oil in a wok. Add the cashew nuts and stir-fry until lightly browned. Remove with a slotted spoon.
5 Add the chicken to the wok with the ginger and garlic and stir-fry until the chicken is cooked and tender (4–5 minutes).
6 Add the liquid ingredients and stir until well blended and thickened. Add a little water if it seems too thick. Check the seasoning. Pile into a warmed serving dish and sprinkle with the cashew nuts and spring onions.

Note: For stir-frying choose a carbon iron wok with a round base and one long wooden handle. The best size is about 35 cm | 14 in. The advantage of stir-frying is that there is a large surface area all at the same temperature, so the food cooks fast and retains all its flavour, colour and texture. The trick is to stir with a Chinese ladle, strainer or spoon with one hand while shaking and jerking the wok with the other. When stir-frying vegetables add the firmest vegetables first, and the more tender ones a few minutes later.

wine: FULL DRY WHITE

Warm Chicken Salad

This salad can be adapted according to what salad ingredients you have in the refrigerator. It can easily be made into a complete meal with the addition of hot new potatoes. The essential ingredients (other than the chicken) are the rocket, chives, walnut oil and balsamic vinegar. It is also very good made with breast of pheasant instead of chicken.

SERVES 4

4 chicken breasts, skinned

salad leaves, such as frisée, lamb's lettuce, gem lettuce, rocket

110 g | 4 oz baby sweetcorn

110 g | 4 oz broccoli

seasoned plain flour

salt and freshly ground black pepper

sunflower oil

110 g | 4 oz shiitake or chestnut mushrooms

1 bunch of fresh chives, chopped

2 tablespoons sunflower oil

2 tablespoons walnut oil

1 tablespoon balsamic vinegar

1 Remove any fat from the chicken breasts, cut the flesh into bite-sized pieces.

2 Put the salad leaves into a large salad bowl.

3 Cook the sweetcorn and broccoli in a small amount of boiling salted water. Drain.

4 Coat the chicken pieces lightly with seasoned flour and fry in hot sunflower oil for about 5 minutes, until browned on both sides. Reduce the heat and continue to fry until the chicken is cooked. Meanwhile, fry the mushrooms in a second pan.

5 Lift the chicken pieces on to absorbent kitchen paper.

6 Transfer all the ingredients to the salad bowl, mix together, season well with salt and pepper and serve immediately.

wine: **CRISP DRY WHITE**

Boned Duck with Apricot and Pistachio Stuffing

SERVES 4

1 duck, boned (see pages 370–1)

1 large chicken breast, boned and skinned

½ small onion, chopped

110 g | 4 oz dried apricots, sliced

chopped fresh tarragon and parsley

30 g | 1 oz unsalted pistachio nuts, skinned

salt and freshly ground black pepper

1 Preheat the oven to 200°C | 400°F | gas mark 6.

2 Carefully remove any excess fat from the duck, especially from the vent end.

3 Put the chicken breast and onion in a food processor and whizz briefly. Add the apricots, tarragon, parsley and pistachio nuts. Mix well and season with salt and pepper.

4 Stuff the duck and wrap it in a piece of lightly oiled muslin or a clean 'J'-cloth. Tie it at either end so it looks like a Christmas cracker.

5 Place the duck breast-side up on a wire rack in a roasting pan. Prick lightly all over and rub with salt. Roast for 1¼ hours. Serve cold or hot with Cumberland sauce (see page 131).

wine: **SOFT LIGHT RED**

Roast Duckling

SERVES 3

1 large oven-ready duckling	1 stick of celery, finely chopped
salt and freshly ground black pepper	1 small onion, finely chopped
30 g│1 oz granulated sugar	45 g│1½ oz flaked almonds, toasted
1 tablespoon wine vinegar	
150 ml│¼ pint duck or strong white stock (see page 103)	**To garnish**
grated zest and juice of 1 orange	1 whole orange, segmented
2 teaspoons brandy	1 bunch of watercress

1 Preheat the oven to 200°C│400°F│gas mark 6.

2 Prick the duck all over with a fork and sprinkle lightly with salt. Place the duck on a wire rack in a roasting pan, roast in the oven for 45 minutes–1 hour. It needs no fat, but it is a good idea to lay it legs up for the first 15 minutes and turn it right side up for the remaining time.

3 Remove the duck from the oven, drain well, and joint it. Put the pieces into a clean roasting pan, skin side up. Reserve the roasting juices.

4 Return to the oven and continue cooking until the joints are cooked through (a further 20 minutes or so). Do not baste. Remove the duck joints to an ovenproof plate and keep warm. (If the skin is not truly crisp the duck can be returned to the oven for 10 minutes like this without the sauce.)

5 Put the sugar and vinegar into a heavy saucepan. Dissolve the sugar over a low heat, then boil until the sugar caramelizes: it will go dark brown and bubbly, with large slow bubbles. Pour on the stock; it will hiss and splutter, so take care. Stir until the caramel lumps disappear. Add the orange zest and juice, the roasting juices from the duck (but no fat) and the brandy.

6 Skim the sauce to remove any fat, and strain into a saucepan. Add the celery and onion, and boil until the celery is just beginning to soften but is still a little crunchy (about 5 minutes). Check the sauce for seasoning. You should have a thin, fairly clear liquid with plenty of chopped celery and onion in it. Add the orange segments to the sauce

7 Serve the sauce separately, or poured round, not over, the duck. Surround the duck with the orange segments, scatter over the almonds and garnish with watercress.

wine: **FULL RED**

Jointing a Duck

Cutting out the backbone

Cutting through the breast

Pieces of duck

Dividing the breast

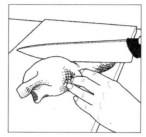
Dividing legs and breast

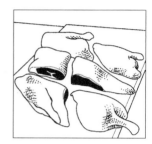
Pieces of duck

Roast Duck with Apple Sauce

SERVES 3

1.8 kg|4 lb oven-ready duck
salt and freshly ground black pepper
½ onion
½ orange
1 teaspoon plain flour

290 ml|½ pint duck or strong white stock, made
   with chicken bones (see page 103)

To serve
apple sauce (see page 130)

1 Preheat the oven to 200°C|400°F|gas mark 6. Wipe the duck clean inside and out. Season the cavity well with salt and pepper. Place the onion and orange inside the duck. Prick the skin all over and sprinkle with salt.

2 Put the duck upside down on a rack in a roasting pan and roast for 30 minutes. Then pour off the fat. Turn the duck over and continue roasting until cooked (about 1 hour). Test by piercing the thigh with a skewer – if the juices run out pink the duck needs further cooking.

3 Tip the juices from the cavity into a bowl and reserve them. Joint the duck into 6 pieces and arrange on a serving dish; or leave the duck whole for carving at the table. In any event keep it warm, without covering, as this would spoil the crisp skin.

4 Make the gravy: pour off all but 1 tablespoon of the fat in the roasting pan. Stir over a low heat, scraping the bottom of the pan to loosen all the sediment. Whisk in the flour, cook until brown and add the juices from inside the duck, and the stock, and whisk until smooth. Simmer, stirring, for 2 minutes. Season to taste with salt and pepper.

5 Strain the gravy into a warmed gravy-boat. Fill a second gravy-boat with hot or cold apple sauce, and serve with the duck.

wine: LIGHT RED

Caramelized Breast of Duck with Honey, Lime and Ginger Sauce

SERVES 4

4 × 200 g|7 oz boned duck breasts
salt and freshly ground black pepper
2 teaspoons caster sugar
2 limes
150 ml|¼ pint sugar syrup (see page 665)
2 tablespoons olive oil
30 g|1 oz unsalted butter

3 tablespoons clear honey
170 ml|6 fl oz dry white wine
225 ml|8 fl oz brown stock, made with duck bones if available (see page 102)
30 g|1 oz fresh root ginger, peeled and cut into fine slivers

1 Preheat the oven to 225°C|450°F, gas mark 8.

2 Score the duck skin in fine diagonal lines. Rub salt, pepper and the sugar into the skin.

3 Using a potato peeler, pare the zest of the 2 limes very thinly so there is no pith on the back of the zest. Cut into matchstick-size strips. Blanch in boiling sugar syrup for 15 seconds, then refresh in cold water, drain and remove.

4 Remove all the pith from the limes. Save any juice. Cut the limes into neat segments, discarding any membrane, and reserve.

5 Heat the oil in a large, heavy frying pan, add the butter and when sizzling place the duck breasts skin side down in the pan and fry until brown. Turn the breasts over and place them skin side up on a wire rack over a roasting pan. Brush with half the honey and bake in the oven until just firm, about 7 minutes.

6 Meanwhile, pour all but 1 tablespoon of the fat from the frying pan. Add the wine, lime juice and the remaining honey and boil until reduced by half.

7 Add the stock and ginger and bring back to the boil. Allow to simmer until the sauce begins to thicken.

8 Remove the duck breasts from the oven, slice and arrange on 4 plates. Add any cooking juices to the sauce and simmer for 1–2 further minutes or until syrupy. Strain and pour over the duck. Garnish with the lime segments and zest.

wine: SPICY RED

Duck Breasts with Green Peppercorn Sauce

SERVES 4

4 large duck breasts, skinned
45 g | 1½ oz clarified butter

For the sauce
150 ml | ¼ pint dry white wine
3 tablespoons brandy
8 tablespoons white stock, made with chicken bones
  (see page 103)
290 ml | ½ pint double cream
2 tablespoons wine vinegar
1 teaspoon sugar

1 tablespoon port
20 g | ¾ oz canned green peppercorns, well rinsed
20 g | ¾ oz canned red pimiento, cut into tiny dice
salt and freshly ground black pepper

To garnish
30 g | 1 oz unsalted butter
2 firm dessert apples, peeled, cored and cut into
  eighths
a little caster sugar

1 Make the sauce: put the wine and brandy into a heavy saucepan and boil gently for about 5 minutes or until reduced by two-thirds.

2 Add the stock and boil for 5 minutes. Add the cream and boil for about a further 5 minutes, stirring occasionally so that it does not catch on the bottom of the pan, until the sauce has reduced by about a third and is of pouring consistency (i.e. about as thick as single cream).

3 Put the vinegar and sugar into a small saucepan. Boil for 30 seconds or until the mixture smells caramelized and is reduced to about 1 tablespoon. Add the reduced cream sauce. Stir well. It may be necessary to replace the pan over the heat to re-melt the caramel. Add the port, peppercorns and pimiento. Season with salt and pepper. Set aside.

4 Cook the duck breasts and the apple garnish: melt the 45 g | 1½ oz unsalted butter in a large, heavy frying pan. When it stops foaming, add the duck breasts and fry fairly fast on both sides. Reduce the heat and fry slowly for 8–10 minutes, until browned but pink in the centre.

5 Melt the butter for the garnish in a second frying pan and fry the apples very slowly with a little sugar until golden-brown.

6 Serve the duck breasts garnished with the apples and hand the sauce separately.

NOTE: An alternative way to cook the duck breasts is to sprinkle the unskinned breasts with a little salt, roast in a hot oven for 15–20 minutes and then place them under a grill for a good crisp skin.

wine: **LIGHT RED**

Peking Duck

The pancakes can be bought from oriental grocers, or follow the instructions below for making them.

SERVES 6

1 × 2.3 kg|5 lb duck
3 tablespoons brandy
5 tablespoons clear honey
3 tablespoons light soy sauce
1 bunch of spring onions
10 cm|4 in piece of cucumber

For the Chinese pancakes

250 g|9 oz plain flour, plus extra for dusting
200 ml|7 fl oz boiling water
3 tablespoons sesame oil

For the sauce

1 tablespoon sesame oil
2.5 cm|1 in piece of fresh root ginger, peeled and sliced
2 tablespoons soya paste
200 g|7 oz plum jam
1 teaspoon chilli powder
30 g|1 oz caster sugar

1 Place the duck in a colander in a saucepan. Pour over a kettleful of boiling water to loosen the skin. Pat dry, inside and out, with absorbent kitchen paper.

2 Brush the brandy over the duck – the alcohol has a drying effect on the skin and will help to make it really crispy. Tie a piece of string around the wings and hang the duck up in a cool airy place. Put a bowl or tray underneath to catch any drips.

3 Leave the duck for 4 hours, or until the skin is very dry. Mix together the honey and soy sauce and brush over the duck. Leave to dry for 1 hour, then brush again and leave to dry for 1 hour, then brush again and leave to dry for a further 3 hours.

4 Meanwhile, make the pancakes: sift the flour into a mixing bowl and gradually add the water to make a soft dough. Place on a lightly floured surface and knead well until smooth. Place in a bowl, cover with a clean damp tea-towel and leave to rest for 30 minutes.

5 Knead the dough again for 5 minutes, and dust with a little flour if it is sticky. Roll out to a roll about 2.5 cm|1 in in diameter. Cut the roll into 16 2.5 cm|1 in segments, then roll each segment into a smooth ball.

6 Work with 2 dough balls at a time. Dip one side of one ball in the sesame oil. Place the oiled side on top of the other ball, then flatten the balls together slightly with the palm of your hand. Lightly flour your work surface, then roll out to a circle of about 15 cm|6 in diameter. Repeat with the remaining balls of dough.

7 Heat a heavy frying pan over a low heat. Place a double pancake in the pan and cook for about 1 minute, or until dry on one side. Turn over and cook for 1 minute on the other side. Pull the pancakes apart and stack on a plate. Cooking the pancakes together will keep them moist, making them easier to roll around the filling.

8 Make the sauce: heat the oil in a small pan and fry the ginger for 2 minutes to lightly flavour the oil. Remove the ginger with a slotted spoon. Add the soy paste, plum jam,

chilli powder and sugar and heat gently until smooth. Pour into a serving bowl and set aside.

9 Preheat the oven to 190°C|375°F|gas mark 5. Place the duck on a rack in a roasting pan and roast in the oven for 1½ hours. It is essential that the duck be placed on a rack, otherwise the fat in the pan will stop the skin browning underneath. Do not open the door during the cooking time.

10 Meanwhile, cut the spring onions into 5 cm|2 in pieces, and shred lengthways into thin strips. Cut the cucumber in half and then into batons. Arrange on a warmed serving dish.

11 Transfer the duck to a board. Remove the skin and cut into squares. Carve the meat into slices and place both on a serving dish. To serve: dip the meat and crispy skin in the plum sauce and brush over a pancake. Put the meat, skin, spring onion, and cucumber in the middle and roll up to eat.

NOTE: Instead of making the plum sauce, you can use hoisin sauce. Flavour the oil with the ginger, then add 125 ml|4 fl oz hoisin sauce and heat gently.

wine: **FULL DRY WHITE**

Roast Goose Mary-Claire

SERVES 6

1 × 4.5 kg|10 lb oven-ready goose
salt and freshly ground black pepper
½ lemon

55 g|2 oz shredded beef suet
85 g|3 oz fresh white breadcrumbs
1 egg

For the stuffing

30 g|1 oz butter
1 onion, finely chopped
285 g|10 oz chicken breast, minced (or cut in 4 if using a food processor)
1 tablespoon chopped fresh sage
340 g|12 oz dessert apples, peeled and chopped
10 dried apricots, soaked for 2 hours, drained and chopped
55 g|2 oz unsalted pistachio nuts, lightly chopped

To finish

1 tablespoon clear honey

For the gravy

570 ml|1 pint potato water or goose stock
2 tablespoons Calvados

To garnish

1 bunch of watercress

1 Wipe the goose all over. Season the inside with salt and pepper and rub with the cut lemon.

2 Preheat the oven to 190°C|375°F|gas mark 5.

3 Make the stuffing: melt the butter in a saucepan, add the onion and cook for about 10 minutes until soft but not coloured. Allow to cool.

4 Mix together the chicken, onion, sage, apple, apricots, pistachio nuts and suet. Add enough of the breadcrumbs to make a firm but not solid stuffing. Season to taste with salt and pepper. Add the egg and beat really well.

5 Fill the goose cavity with the stuffing. Weigh the stuffed goose, to establish the cooking time. Allow 15 minutes per 450 g|1 lb plus an extra 15 minutes.

6 Prick the goose all over with a fork and sprinkle with salt. Place on a wire rack over a roasting pan. Roast, basting occasionally, but do not worry if you forget as a goose is very fatty. Every so often you will have to remove fat from the roasting pan with a baster. Do not throw the fat away as it is wonderful for cooking. If the goose gets too dark, cover it with kitchen foil.

7 Ten minutes before the bird is cooked, brush the honey evenly over the skin. This will help to make it crisp. When the goose is cooked, place on a serving plate and return to the turned-off oven.

8 Make the gravy: carefully spoon off all the fat in the roasting pan, leaving the cooking juices behind. Scrape off and discard any burnt pieces stuck to the bottom of the pan. Add the potato water or stock and, if you can, a little of the stuffing. Bring to the boil, whisk well and simmer for about 15 minutes. Increase the heat and boil until syrupy, add the Calvados, season to taste with salt and pepper and boil for 30 seconds. Taste and strain into a warmed gravy-boat.

9 Garnish the goose with watercress.

wine: **MEDIUM RED**

Confit d'oie (Preserved Goose)

This recipe, still common in France, is for goose flesh preserved in fat. The pieces of goose are lifted from the jar and wiped clean of fat before being served either cold or reheated, or used in composite dishes. The confit takes 3 days to complete. Use a very fat goose, but if you cannot get one, use 2 average or 3 small ducks instead.

1 × 4.5 kg|10 lb goose
900 g|2 lb salt
7 g|¼ oz saltpetre (optional, if available)
4 cloves, crushed

2 bay leaves, pounded
a pinch of dried thyme
1.8 kg|4 lb goose fat
450 g|1 lb lard

1 Cut the goose into quarters.

2 Mix together the salt, saltpetre, cloves, bay leaves and thyme and rub some of this over the whole surface of the goose.

3 Put the goose into a large (about 1.8 kg|4 lb) glazed earthenware pot and add the remaining spiced salt. Cover and leave for 24 hours in the refrigerator.

4 Slowly melt the goose fat in a large saucepan. Remove the goose pieces from the salt, wipe clean and put into the fat. Place over a low heat and cook very gently for 3 hours. To test if the goose is cooked, prick it with a skewer. The juices that run out should be clear, and the flesh should feel tender.

5 Drain the pieces of goose and remove the bones. Strain a thick layer of fat in which the goose was cooked into a large glazed earthenware jar.

6 When this fat has completely solidified arrange the pieces of goose on top, making sure they do not touch the wall of the jar.

7 Cover the pieces of goose with just-liquid cool goose fat. Put into a cool place.

8 Leave for 2 days. Strain some more liquid goose fat into the jar to seal any holes which may have occurred.

9 When this is set, melt the lard and pour a layer about 1 cm | ½ in thick over the surface. When this is set, put a circle of greaseproof paper on top, pressing it down to exclude any air. Cover the top of the jar with a double thickness of paper and tie with string. You can keep the confit d'oie in this way for at least a month in the refrigerator.

wine: **FULL RED**

Roast Turkey

A large square of fine muslin (butter-muslin) is needed for this recipe.

SERVES 12

1 × 5.35 kg | 12 lb oven-ready turkey

For the oatmeal stuffing

1 large onion, finely chopped

20 g | ¾ oz butter

340 g | 12 oz medium oatmeal

1 teaspoon rubbed dried sage, or 4 fresh sage leaves, chopped

170 g | 6 oz shredded beef suet

salt and freshly ground black pepper

For the sausagemeat and chestnut stuffing

450 g | 1 lb sausagemeat

450 g | 1 lb unsweetened chestnut purée

110 g | 4 oz fresh white breadcrumbs

1 large egg, beaten

salt and freshly ground black pepper

To prepare the turkey for the oven

170 g | 6 oz butter

giblets

½ onion

2 bay leaves

a few parsley stalks

290 ml | ½ pint water

To garnish

1 chipolata sausage per person

1 rindless streaky bacon rasher per person

For the gravy

30 g | 1 oz plain flour

570 ml | 1 pint turkey stock (see page 105) or vegetable water

1 Weigh the turkey. Calculate the cooking time with the help of the chart on page 374.

2 Make the oatmeal stuffing: cook the onion in the butter until beginning to soften. Allow to cool. Mix with the oatmeal, sage and shredded suet. Add enough water just to bind the mixture together, and taste and season as required. Stuff into the cavity of the turkey.

3 Make the sausagemeat and chestnut stuffing: mix together the sausagemeat, chestnut purée, breadcrumbs and beaten egg. Taste and season as required. Stuff this into the neck end of the turkey, making sure that the breast is well plumped. Draw the skin flap down to cover the stuffing. Secure with a skewer.

4 Preheat the oven to 180°C | 350°F | gas mark 4.

5 Melt the butter and in it soak a very large piece of butter-muslin (about 4 times the size of the turkey) until all the butter has been completely absorbed.

6 Season the turkey well with salt and pepper. Place it in a large roasting pan with the giblets (except the liver) and neck. Add the onion, bay leaves and parsley stalks and pour in the water. Completely cover the bird with the doubled butter-muslin and roast for the calculated time (a 5.3 kg | 12 lb turkey should take 3–3½ hours).

7 Meanwhile, prepare the garnishes: make each chipolata sausage into 2 cocktail-sized ones by twisting gently in the middle. Stretch each bacon rasher slightly with the back of a knife, cut into 2 lengthways and roll up. Put the sausages and bacon rolls into a second roasting pan, with the bacon rolls wedged in so that they cannot unravel. Thirty minutes before the turkey is ready, put the sausages and bacon in the oven.

8 When the turkey is cooked, the juices that run out of the thigh when pierced with a skewer should be clear. Remove the muslin and lift the bird on to a serving dish. Surround with the bacon and sausages and keep warm while making the gravy.

9 Pour the juices and fat from the pan into a jug. Skim off 45 ml | 1½ fl oz fat and return to the roasting tin. Stir in the flour. Cook the flour over medium heat until deep straw colour.

10 Remove from the heat. Gradually stir in the stock or vegetable water. Bring to the boil, stirring, and boil for 2 minutes or until syrupy. Check the seasoning. Strain into a warmed gravy-boat.

wine: **MEDIUM RED**

Christmas Turkey Stuffed with Ham

SERVES 20

2.3 kg | 5 lb piece of boiled bacon or ham, skinned
6.7 kg | 15 lb turkey, boned (see pages 370–1)

For the stuffing

30 g | 1 oz butter
1 large onion, finely chopped
900 g | 2 lb pork belly, minced
450 g | 1 lb unsweetened canned chestnut purée or
    mashed cooked fresh chestnuts
225 g | 8 oz fresh white breadcrumbs
2 eggs, lightly beaten
1 teaspoon dried sage
2 tablespoons chopped fresh parsley
salt and freshly ground black pepper

For roasting

55 g | 2 oz butter
1 onion, sliced
3 bay leaves
2 parsley stalks
425 ml | ¾ pint water

For the gravy

45 g | 1½ oz plain flour
about 860 ml | 1½ pint turkey stock (see page 105)
1 bunch of watercress

1　Preheat the oven to 200°C|400°F|gas mark 6.
2　Make the stuffing: melt the butter in a saucepan, add the onion and cook until soft but not coloured. Allow to cool.
3　When cold, mix with all the other stuffing ingredients.
4　Open the turkey out flat on a board, skin side down. Spread the stuffing on the turkey and put the ham or bacon on top.
5　Draw up the sides and sew together with a needle and fine string. Turn the bird right side up and tie it into an even, rounded shape.
6　Smear the butter all over the turkey and put it into a roasting pan. Add the giblets (except the liver) and the neck. Add the onion, bay leaves and parsley stalks. Pour in the water.
7　Roast for 1 hour, then lower the temperature to 180°C|350°F|gas mark 4 and roast for a further 3 hours. Baste occasionally as the turkey cooks and cover with kitchen foil or greaseproof paper if it is browning too much.
8　When the turkey is cooked, the juices will run clear when a skewer is inserted. Lift it out on to a serving dish and keep warm while you make the gravy.
9　Pour the juices and the fat from the pan. Return 55 ml|2 fl oz fat to the pan and stir in the flour. Cook the flour over medium heat until a deep straw colour.
10　Remove from the heat and gradually add the stock. Return to the heat and bring to the boil, stirring. Boil for 1 minute or until syrupy. Check the seasoning.
11　Garnish the turkey with the watercress and serve the gravy separately.

NOTES: This turkey is delicious served cold with a herby mayonnaise.

The turkey may be stuffed the day before cooking. If this is done, care should be taken that both the turkey and stuffing are well chilled before the bird is stuffed. Refrigerate until ready to cook.

If the turkey is roasted covered in 2 layers of muslin completely saturated in melted butter there is no need for basting during cooking, and when the cloths are removed the bird will be brown and crisp.

wine: **MEDIUM RED**

Jugged Hare

SERVES 6

1 hare, skinned and jointed, with its blood	570 ml|1 pint brown stock (see page 102)
2 tablespoons oil	salt and freshly ground black pepper
225 g|8 oz mirepoix of carrot, onion and celery	1 tablespoon redcurrant jelly
1 bouquet garni (1 bay leaf, 2 parsley stalks, 1 sprig of fresh thyme, tied together with string)	3 tablespoons port

1　Wash and wipe dry the pieces of hare, removing any membranes. Heat the oil in a large saucepan and fry the joints until well browned, adding more oil if the pan becomes dry. Lift out the joints and brown the mirepoix.
2　Return the hare to the pan. Add the bouquet garni, stock, salt and pepper. Cover and simmer for 2 hours, or until the hare is very tender.

3 Arrange the joints in a casserole.

4 Strain the stock into a saucepan. Add the redcurrant jelly and port and simmer for 5 minutes. Remove the pan from the heat.

5 Mix the blood with a cupful of the hot stock. Pour back into the pan without allowing the sauce to boil. The blood will thicken the sauce slightly.

6 Taste the sauce, adding salt and pepper if necessary. Pour over the hare joints in the casserole and serve.

NOTE: The sauce depends on the hare's blood to thicken it. If very little blood (less than 150 ml $\frac{1}{4}$ pint) comes with the hare, the basic stock must be thickened with a little beurre manié – flour and butter kneaded together in equal quantities – and whisked in small blobs into the boiling stock. This must be done before the addition of the blood, which would curdle if boiled.

wine: **FULL RED**

Venison Casserole

SERVES 4

675 g $1\frac{1}{2}$ lb venison

For the marinade

5 tablespoons sunflower oil

1 onion, sliced

1 carrot, sliced

1 stick of celery, sliced

1 clove of garlic, crushed

6 juniper berries

1 slice of lemon

1 bay leaf

290 ml $\frac{1}{2}$ pint red wine

2 tablespoons red wine vinegar

6 black peppercorns

For the casserole

1 tablespoon sunflower oil

30 g 1 oz butter

110 g 4 oz onions, peeled

1 clove of garlic, crushed

110 g 4 oz button mushrooms

2 teaspoons plain flour

150 ml $\frac{1}{4}$ pint brown stock (see page 102)

1 tablespoon cranberry jelly

salt and freshly ground black pepper

55 g 2 oz fresh cranberries

15 g $\frac{1}{2}$ oz sugar

110 g 4 oz cooked whole chestnuts

To garnish

chopped fresh parsley

1 Cut the venison into 5 cm 2 in pieces, trimming away any membrane, sinew and fat.

2 Mix the ingredients for the marinade together in a bowl and add the venison. Mix well, cover and leave in the refrigerator overnight.

3 Preheat the oven to 170°C $325°F$ gas mark 3.

4 Lift out the venison pieces and pat dry with absorbent kitchen paper. Strain the marinade, reserving the liquid for cooking.

5 Heat half the oil in a heavy saucepan and brown the venison pieces in small batches. Place them in a casserole. If the bottom of the pan becomes brown or too dry, pour in a little of the strained marinade, swish it about, scraping off the sediment stuck to the bottom, and pour over the venison pieces. Then heat a little more oil and continue browning the meat.

6 When all the venison has been browned, repeat the déglaçage (boiling up with a little marinade and scraping the bottom of the pan).

7 Now melt the butter in a saucepan and fry the onions and garlic until the onions are pale brown all over. Add the garlic and mushrooms and continue cooking for 2 minutes. Remove the onions, garlic and mushroom with a slotted spoon and place in the casserole.

8 Remove from the heat, stir in the flour and cook until brown. Remove from the heat, add the remaining marinade and the brown stock, return to the heat and stir until boiling, again scraping the bottom of the pan. When boiling, pour over the venison.

9 Add the cranberry jelly. Season with salt and pepper.

10 Cover the casserole and cook in the oven for about 2 hours or until the venison is very tender.

11 Meanwhile, cook the cranberries briefly with the sugar in 2–3 tablespoons water until just soft but not crushed. Strain off the liquor. Lift the venison, mushrooms and onions with a slotted spoon into a serving dish.

12 Boil the sauce fast until reduced to a shiny, almost syrupy consistency. Add the chestnuts and cranberries and simmer gently for 5 minutes.

13 Pour the sauce over the venison and serve garnished with chopped parsley.

wine: **FULL RED**

Braised Venison

SERVES 8–10

2.7 kg│6 lb haunch of venison	1 tablespoon chopped fresh thyme
30 g│1 oz butter	1 teaspoon chopped fresh sage
1 tablespoon oil	150 ml│¼ pint red wine
2 onions, sliced	about 290 ml│½ pint brown stock (see page 102)
225 g│8 oz carrots, sliced	30 g│1 oz butter
4 sticks of celery, sliced	30 g│1 oz plain flour
salt and freshly ground black pepper	1 tablespoon cranberry jelly
1 bay leaf	

1 Preheat the oven to 150°C│300°F│gas mark 2.

2 Prepare the venison by trimming away any tough membranes, sinews and fat.

3 Heat the butter and oil in a large flameproof casserole and brown the venison well on all sides. Remove from the casserole.

4 Add the onions, carrots and celery, and fry for 5 minutes until lightly browned.

5 Season with salt and pepper, add the bay leaf and a sprinkling of thyme and sage. Lay the venison on top of the half-cooked vegetables. Add the wine and enough stock to come about a quarter of the way up the meat.

6 Bring to simmering point, then cover tightly and cook in the oven for 1½ hours, or until tender.

7 When cooked lift out the meat, carve and place on a warmed serving dish. Keep warm, covered with a lid or kitchen foil.

8 Strain the liquid from the vegetables into a saucepan. Reduce to 420 ml | ¾ pint.

9 Mix the butter and flour together to make a beurre manié. Add this to the liquid bit by bit, stirring, and bring to the boil. Stir in the cranberry jelly and correct the seasoning.

10 Just before serving spoon a thin layer of sauce over the venison to make it look shiny and appetizing; serve the remaining sauce in a sauceboat.

wine: **FULL SPICY RED**

Peppered Venison Steak

SERVES 4

4 140 g | 5 oz venison collops (steaks) cut from the fillet	30 g | 1 oz unsalted butter
2 tablespoons black peppercorns	2 tablespoons brandy
1 tablespoon oil (preferably olive)	150 ml | ¼ pint double cream
	salt

1 Wipe the steaks and trim off any gristle and fat.

2 Crush the peppercorns coarsely in a mortar or under a rolling pin and press them into the surface of the meat on both sides.

3 Cover the steaks and chill for 2 hours for the flavour to penetrate the meat.

4 Heat the oil in a heavy pan, add the butter and when it is foaming fry the steaks until done to your liking (about 2 minutes per side for blue, 3 minutes for rare, 3½ minutes for medium and 4 minutes for well done). Remove any excess fat from the pan.

5 Pour in the brandy and set it alight. Add the cream and a pinch of salt. Mix the contents of the pan thoroughly, scraping up any sediment stuck to the bottom.

6 Place the steaks on a warmed serving platter.

7 Boil up the sauce again, then simmer to a syrupy consistency or add water if too thick and pour over the meat. Serve immediately.

NOTE: If the venison is very fresh and you want a gamier taste, marinate it for 2 days in equal quantities of red wine and oil, flavoured with a sliced onion, 6 juniper berries and a bay leaf. Dry well before frying.

wine: **FULL RED**

Roast Pheasant

A piece of apple can be placed in the pheasant cavity, to help keep the flesh moist and improve the flavour.

SERVES 4

2 medium oven-ready pheasants	**For the gravy**
salt and freshly ground black pepper	1 tablespoon flour
2 strips of pork fat	1 tablespoon butter, softened
butter	1 tablespoon ruby port
	1 teaspoon redcurrant jelly

1 Wipe the pheasants and remove any remaining feathers.
2 Preheat the oven to 200°C|400°F|gas mark 6.
3 Season the birds inside.
4 Tie the pork fat over the breasts (this is called barding and is to prevent drying out during cooking). Tie the legs together loosely.
5 Spread a little butter over the rest of the birds and season with salt and pepper.
6 Place in a roasting pan, pour 5 mm|¼ in water into the pan and roast for about 40–50 minutes, basting frequently.
7 When cooked, lift the pheasants out of the pan and keep warm while you make the gravy.
8 Mix together the flour and the butter. Add the port and redcurrant jelly to the roasting juices.
9 Place the roasting pan over heat and whisk small pieces of the flour/butter paste into the liquid. Heat, stirring until the liquid boils.
10 Add a little more water or stock if it is too thick. Boil for 2 minutes, then season well and strain into a warmed gravyboat.
11 Serve the pheasants on a warmed serving platter. Serve the gravy separately.

wine: **FULL RED**

Galantine of Pheasant

SERVES 6

1 large oven-ready pheasant	**For the stock**
225 g|8 oz raw chicken meat, minced	1 carrot, sliced
170 g|6 oz sausagemeat	1 onion, sliced
2 shallots, chopped	1 stick of celery, chopped
2 tablespoons Madeira	6 black peppercorns
1 tablespoon chopped fresh parsley	1 bay leaf
salt and freshly ground black pepper	1 parsley stalk
2 slices of cooked tongue, cut into strips	salt
1 field mushroom, sliced	a pinch of dried thyme
	To garnish
	1 bunch of watercress

1   Bone the pheasant completely, including the legs and wings (see pages 316–17). Cut off any excess fat from the vent end.

2   Place the bones in a saucepan of water with the stock ingredients, bring to the boil, cover and simmer gently for about 1 hour.

3   Meanwhile, prepare the farce (stuffing): mix together the chicken meat, sausagemeat, shallots, Madeira and parsley. Season with salt and pepper.

4   Open the pheasant out on a board, skin side down. Push the meat around gently so that it is evenly distributed on top of the skin. Spread with half the farce and lay on the tongue strips and the mushroom slices. Season and cover with the remaining farce. Fold over the sides of the bird and stitch them together with a needle and fine string. Wrap the bird in a piece of muslin and tie the ends together.

5   Strain the stock. Place the pheasant in a heavy saucepan and pour over the stock. Bring to the boil, cover tightly with a lid and simmer slowly for $1\frac{1}{2}$ hours, turning the pheasant over once during cooking.

6   Lift out the bird and, when cool, tighten the muslin cloth round it and refrigerate overnight.

7   Unwrap the cold pheasant, wipe off any grease and slice. Arrange the slices on a flat serving plate and garnish with watercress.

wine: **MEDIUM RED**

Pheasant Breasts with Pancetta and Rosemary

4 pheasant breasts, skinned and boned
salt and freshly ground black pepper
4 sprigs of fresh rosemary, chopped
110 g | 4 oz pancetta, thinly sliced

To garnish
1 small bunch of watercress

To serve
Cumberland sauce (see page 131)

1   Preheat the oven to 200°C | 400°F | gas mark 6.

2   Wipe the pheasant breasts and season lightly with salt and pepper.

3   Sprinkle the rosemary on each breast and cover them with the pancetta, folding the overlap underneath.

4   Wrap the pheasant breasts in a lightly oiled large piece of kitchen foil in a single layer. Place on a baking sheet and bake in the oven for 5 minutes. Uncover the parcel and bake for a further 10 minutes or until the pheasant is cooked and the pancetta lightly browned.

5   Remove to a warmed serving dish. Garnish with the watercress and hand the Cumberland sauce separately.

wine: **DRY WHITE**

Whiskied Pheasant

This recipe is one that Nicola Cox has demonstrated at Leiths School; it was, rightly, very popular.

SERVES 2

55 g | 2 oz butter
1 plump oven-ready pheasant
1 onion, finely chopped
55 ml | 2 fl oz whisky
salt and freshly ground black pepper
200–300 ml | ⅓– ½ pint double cream

1 tablespoon Dijon mustard
1 lemon

To garnish
1 bunch of watercress

1 Preheat the oven to 190°C | 375°F | gas mark 5.
2 Melt the butter in a flameproof casserole and gently fry the onion until golden. Remove from the pan and reserve. Add the pheasant and brown on all sides.
3 Pour over the whisky and set alight, shaking the pan until the flames subside. Season with salt and pepper, return the onions to the pan then cover the casserole closely and cook in the oven for 40–50 minutes, until the pheasant is tender.
4 Remove and joint the pheasant; keep warm.
5 Place the pan over a high heat and boil the juices to reduce to 2–3 tablespoons, stirring all the time; then gradually add the cream, boiling down until you have a sauce of coating consistency.
6 Remove the pan from the heat, add the mustard and season to taste with salt and pepper. Add the lemon juice, pour over the pheasant and serve garnished with the watercress.

wine: **FULL RED**

Mustard Rabbit

Preparation for this dish begins a day in advance.

SERVES 4

1 rabbit, skinned and cleaned
7 teaspoons French mustard
1 teaspoon chopped fresh tarragon
45 g | 1½ oz butter or bacon dripping
85 g | 3 oz bacon or salt pork, diced
1 onion, finely chopped

1 clove of garlic, crushed
1 teaspoon plain flour
570 ml | 1 pint white stock (see page 103)

To garnish
chopped fresh parsley

1 If the rabbit's head has not been removed, cut it off with a sharp heavy knife. Then joint the rabbit into 6 neat pieces.
2 Soak the rabbit in cold salted water for 3 hours. Drain and dry well. (This is to whiten the rabbit.)

3 Spread 6 teaspoons mustard mixed with the tarragon over the rabbit pieces and refrigerate overnight.

4 The next day, preheat the oven to 170°C|325°F|gas mark 3.

5 Heat the butter or dripping in a frying pan and brown the rabbit pieces all over. Remove them with a slotted spoon and place in a casserole.

6 Add the bacon and onion to the pan and cook over a low heat until the onions are soft and just browned. Stir in the garlic and cook for 1 minute. Remove from the heat and stir in the flour. Return to the heat and cook for 1 minute.

7 Remove the pan from the heat and gradually stir in the stock. Return to the heat and bring the sauce slowly to the boil, stirring continuously.

8 Pour this sauce over the rabbit. Cook in the oven for about 1½ hours, or until the rabbit is tender.

9 Lift the rabbit on to a warmed serving dish. Add 1 teaspoon mustard to the sauce and check the seasoning. Boil for 1 minute. If the sauce is now rather thin, reduce it by boiling rapidly until shiny and rich in appearance. Pour the sauce carefully over the rabbit pieces.

10 Sprinkle with the parsley.

wine: **FULL RED**

Warm Pigeon Breast and Cracked Wheat Salad

SERVES 4

8 pigeon breasts, skinned

110 g|4 oz cracked wheat (bulghur)

2 tablespoons sesame oil

½ red chilli, deseeded and finely chopped

2.5 cm|1 in piece of fresh root ginger, peeled and grated

110 g|4 oz shiitake mushrooms, sliced

110 g|4 oz Parma ham, sliced

140 g|5 oz plum jam

5 spring onions, sliced on the diagonal

55 g|2 oz sun-dried tomatoes in oil, drained and sliced

salt and freshly ground black pepper

lemon juice

30 g|1 oz pinenuts, toasted

½ cucumber, deseeded and finely chopped

2 tablespoons oil

For the marinade

2 tablespoons Chinese five-spice powder

1 tablespoon light soy sauce

To garnish

2 tablespoons snipped chives

1 Mix together the marinade ingredients and coat the pigeon breasts on both sides. Put into a shallow dish, cover and leave to marinate for at least 30 minutes or overnight in the refrigerator.

2 Prepare the cracked wheat according to the manufacturer's directions. Drain thoroughly, squeeze out any remaining water and spread out to dry on absorbent kitchen paper.

3 Heat the sesame oil in a wok or large frying pan, add the chilli, ginger, mushrooms and Parma ham and stir-fry over a high heat for 2–3 minutes. Add the jam, spring onions and sun-dried tomatoes and bring to the boil. Add the cracked wheat and season to taste with salt, pepper and lemon juice. Heat thoroughly and stir in the pinenuts and cucumber. Keep warm.

4 Heat the oil in a frying pan, add the pigeon breasts in batches and fry for 3 minutes. Turn and cook for 2 further minutes until browned but pink inside.

5 To serve: place 2 pigeon breasts on each of 4 individual plates and spoon a portion of the cracked wheat salad beside each serving. Sprinkle with the chives.

wine: **SPICY DRY WHITE**

Roast Woodcock

SERVES 4

4 woodcock

4 rashers of rindless streaky bacon

salt and freshly ground black pepper

4 rounds of white bread 13 cm|5 in in diameter, toasted on one side (see croûtes, page 434)

1 teaspoon plain flour

150 ml|¼ white stock, made with chicken bones (see page 103)

a squeeze of lemon juice

To garnish

1 bunch of watercress

1 Pluck the woodcock. Remove the heads and draw the gizzards through the neck openings, but do not draw the entrails. Truss neatly.

2 Preheat the oven to 180°C|350°F|gas mark 4.

3 Cover each bird with a rasher of bacon and season well with salt and pepper. Place in a roasting pan and roast for about 25 minutes, removing the bacon after 15 minutes to allow the breasts to brown thoroughly.

4 Spread the entrails on the untoasted side of the bread rounds and place a bird on top of each. Keep warm while you prepare the gravy.

5 Tip off all but a scant tablespoon of the fat from the roasting pan.

6 Add the flour to the pan and cook over heat for 1 minute until a russet brown.

7 Pour in the stock and bring to the boil, stirring continuously with a spoon, scraping the bottom of the pan to loosen the sediment as it comes to the boil.

8 Season with salt, pepper and lemon juice. Simmer for 2 minutes. Strain the gravy into a warmed gravy-boat.

9 Place the woodcock on a warmed serving dish and garnish with sprigs of watercress.

wine: **FULL RED**

Roast Partridge with Port and Grapes

This is a low-fat recipe; if required, a little cream can be added to the sauce to enrich it.

SERVES 4

4 small partridges
1 dessert apple
1 onion, chopped

1 tablespoon port
55 g | 2 oz seedless grapes

1 Preheat the oven to 375°F | 190°C | gas mark 5.
2 Clean the partridges. Cut the apple into quarters and put a quarter inside each partridge.
3 Put the onion into a roasting pan. Pour on 425 ml | ¾ pint water.
4 Put the partridges on a wire rack in the roasting pan. Roast in the oven, basting occasionally with water, for 25–30 minutes.
5 Remove from the oven. Transfer the partridges to a warmed serving platter and keep warm. Tip the apple and any meat juices from the partridges into the roasting pan. Bring to the boil and stir vigorously to pulverize the apple. Simmer for 2–3 minutes.
6 Push through a sieve, pressing well to extract all the flavour, into a clean saucepan. If it is too thin, boil rapidly to reduce to a syrupy consistency.
7 Add the port and boil for 30 seconds; add the grapes and allow them to warm through.
8 Serve the partridges with the sauce separately in a warmed sauceboat.

wine: **RED BURGUNDY**

Partridge with Pears

SERVES 4

110 g | 4 oz pancetta or rindless smoked streaky
   bacon, in one piece
3 tablespoons olive oil
12 shallots, peeled and blanched
2 plump partridges, halved and claws removed
plain flour, seasoned with salt, freshly ground black
   pepper and ground mace
2 tablespoons brandy
150 ml | ¼ pint dry white wine
150 ml | ¼ pint white stock (see page 103)

1 small clove of garlic, crushed
thinly pared zest of ½ lemon
1 tablespoon finely chopped fresh rosemary

To garnish

2 medium pears (ideally Comice)
15 g | ½ oz unsalted butter

To serve

wild rice

1 Cut the pancetta or bacon into 1 cm | ½ in chunks and blanch in a pan of boiling water for 30 seconds. Drain and pat dry with absorbent kitchen paper.
2 Heat half the oil in a heavy flameproof casserole and fry the bacon until brown. Remove from the pan with a slotted spoon and reserve.

3 Next add the shallots, shaking the casserole to brown them evenly. When brown remove from the casserole with a slotted spoon and reserve with the bacon.

4 Coat the partridges lightly with the seasoned flour and place in the casserole, skin side down, adding more oil if the dish is too dry. Remove when brown and tip off all the oil.

5 Add the brandy, set alight with a match and shake the casserole until the flames subside.

6 Add the wine, stock, garlic, lemon zest, rosemary and partridges. Season with salt and pepper and bring to the boil, then cover and simmer very slowly for 35–40 minutes. Add the shallots and bacon 10 minutes before the end of the cooking time.

7 Meanwhile, prepare the garnish: peel, quarter and core the pears and cut each quarter into 3 slices lengthways. Melt the butter in a frying pan and when foaming add the pear slices and fry over a medium heat until golden-brown on both sides.

8 When the partridges are ready, lift them out of the casserole, trim them neatly and keep them warm on a serving dish, surrounded by the bacon, shallots and pear slices.

9 Strain the sauce into a clean saucepan and boil rapidly to reduce to a syrupy consistency. Pour over the partridges and serve with wild rice.

wine: **MEDIUM RED**

Partridge with Lentils

2 partridges, drawn, trussed and barded
salt
30 g | 1 oz lard or oil
30 g | 1 oz rindless unsmoked bacon, chopped
30 g | 1 oz onion, chopped
110 g | 4 oz Puy lentils, soaked in cold water for 1 hour and drained

grated zest of ½ lemon
1 bay leaf
110 g | 4 oz Gyula sausage or similar dried, smoked pork sausage
290 ml | ½ pint white stock, made with chicken bones (see page 103)

1 Preheat the oven to 170°C | 325°F | gas mark 3.

2 Sprinkle the partridges with salt. Melt the lard in a large frying pan and fry the partridges until they are golden-brown all over. Remove from the pan.

3 Fry the bacon and onion in the same pan until golden-brown.

4 Put the lentils into a large casserole with the lemon zest and bay leaf. Add the partridges, sausage, bacon and onion. Pour over enough stock to just cover the lentils. Cover with a lid and cook in the oven until the partridges are tender (about 45 minutes). If the partridges are ready before the lentils, remove them and the sausages from the pan.

5 When the lentils are tender, bring the liquid to the boil.

6 Carve the partridges and cut the sausages into thin slices. Place the lentils in a deep serving dish, put the partridge pieces on top and garnish with the sliced sausage.

wine: **MEDIUM RED**

Guinea Fowl Braised with Caramel and Oranges

SERVES 4

2 guinea fowl

2 teaspoons sunflower oil

55 g | 2 oz shallots, finely chopped

30 g | 1 oz granulated sugar

1 tablespoon wine vinegar

175 ml | 6 fl oz white stock (see page 103)

juice of 2 oranges, strained

salt and freshly ground black pepper

To garnish

1 orange, segmented

1 small bunch of watercress

1 Preheat the oven to 190°C | 375°F | gas mark 5.

2 Remove any feathers from the guinea fowl and wipe clean inside with a damp cloth.

3 Heat the oil in a flameproof casserole. Add the guinea fowl and brown them all over. Remove them from the casserole.

4 Reduce the heat, add the shallots to the casserole and cook for 2 minutes. Remove from the pan. Add the sugar and vinegar, dissolving the sugar over a low heat, then boil the liquid until the sugar caramelizes. Pour on the stock – it will hiss and splutter, so take care – and stir over a low heat until the caramel lumps disappear. Add the orange juice. Season well with salt and pepper. Return the guinea fowl and the shallots to the casserole and bring the cooking liquor to the boil.

5 Cover the casserole and place in the oven for 1 hour.

6 Remove the guinea fowl and joint them as you would a chicken (see pages 368–9). Arrange the pieces on a warmed serving plate. Skin as much fat as possible from the cooking liquor. Strain it into a clean saucepan, skim it again and boil rapidly for 3 minutes. Add the orange segments.

7 Garnish the guinea fowl with the watercress, and serve the sauce separately in a warmed sauceboat.

wine: **MEDIUM RED**

Soy-glazed Guinea Fowl with Shiitake Mushrooms

SERVES 6

20 g | ¾ oz dried shiitake mushrooms

250 ml | 9 fl oz boiling water

2 tablespoons sunflower oil

2 guinea fowl, each jointed into 8 pieces

2 cloves of garlic, crushed

15 g | ½ oz fresh root ginger, peeled and sliced

100 ml | 3½ fl oz dry Madeira or sherry

240 g | 8½ oz vacuum-packed whole peeled chestnuts

1 tablespoon clear honey

8 tablespoons dark soy sauce

500 ml | 18 fl oz white chicken stock (see page 103)

2 teaspoons cornflour

2 tablespoons water

1 Cover the shiitake mushrooms with the boiling water and leave for 20–30 minutes.

2 Heat the oil in a frying pan and brown the guinea fowl, skin side down, over a medium heat for about 8 minutes, until golden-brown. Remove from the pan and set aside.

3 Add the garlic and ginger to the pan and cook for 1 minute, then add the Madeira or sherry, scraping the sediment from the bottom of the pan. Boil to reduce by half.

4 Return the guinea fowl to the pan with the chestnuts, honey, soy sauce, stock and the mushrooms with their soaking liquid. Bring to simmering point, then cover and cook over a low heat for 45 minutes or until the guinea fowl is cooked through (the juices should run clear when the meat is pierced with a skewer).

5 Joint the guinea fowl and arrange on plates with the chestnuts and mushrooms. Bring the pan juices to the boil over a medium heat. Slake the cornflour with the water, then whisk the paste into the pan juices to thicken. Bring to the boil, stirring, then spoon over the guinea fowl and serve immediately.

NOTE: If preparing this dish ahead, reheat it in the oven preheated to 180°C|350°F|gas mark 4 for 30 minutes.

wine: **SPICY RED**

Quail with Chestnuts and Calvados

8 small quail

freshly ground black pepper

2 dessert apples, peeled, cored and diced

1 onion, sliced

1 bay leaf

3 tablespoons Calvados

1   140 g|5 oz can of unsweetened chestnuts

white stock, made with chicken bones (see page 103)

1 Preheat the oven to 200°C|400°F|gas mark 6.

2 Season the quail with pepper and stuff with the apple.

3 Place the quail in a roasting pan with the onion, bay leaf, Calvados and 4 of the chestnuts. Add enough chicken stock to come a quarter of the way up the quail. Cover with kitchen foil and roast for 15 minutes. Remove the foil and roast for a further 10 minutes.

4 Transfer the quail to a warmed serving dish and keep warm in the turned-off oven.

5 Strain the cooking liquid into a saucepan. Skim off any fat from the liquid, then reduce by boiling until syrupy. You should have about 290 ml|½ pint.

6 Add the remaining chestnuts and warm through in the sauce.

7 Spoon the sauce over the quail.

wine: **LIGHT RED**

Cold Game Pie

This pie takes 2 days to complete.

SERVES 6–8

1 grouse	290 ml|½ pint red wine
1 partridge	1 litre|1¾ pints white stock, made with chicken
1 pigeon	bones (see page 103)
2 hare joints	4 bay leaves
110 g|4 oz venison	a little fresh thyme
1 large carrots	parsley stalks
2 large onions	salt and freshly ground black pepper
2 sticks celery	30 g|1 oz powdered gelatine
110 g|4 oz butter	450 g|1 lb quantity pâte à pâte (see page 565)
4 tablespoons oil	beaten egg

1 Split the birds in half. Cut the venison into small cubes. Chop the carrot, onion and celery roughly.

2 Heat about 1 tablespoon each of butter and oil in a heavy frying pan, and when the butter is foaming, add a good handful of the chopped vegetables. Keep the heat at a medium temperature – enough to fry and brown the vegetables without burning the butter. Keep turning the vegetables to get an even colour all over. When they are all done, lift them out with a slotted spoon and transfer to a large, deep saucepan.

3 Add more oil and butter to the frying pan and brown the venison, the hare and finally the birds. If the bottom of the pan becomes sticky and brown, deglaze it with half a glass of the wine or stock: pour in the liquid and boil up, stirring with a metal spoon or fish slice and scraping the bottom of the pan to loosen the sediment. Tip this liquid in with the browned ingredients and continue frying the meats.

4 When all the ingredients are browned and transferred to the deep saucepan, deglaze the pan again, pouring the juices in with the meats. Add the remaining wine, the stock, and, if necessary, a little water (the ingredients must be just covered). Add the herbs, salt and pepper. Cover with a lid and simmer for 1½ hours or until everything is tender.

5 Strain off the liquid and leave until completely cold. Skim thoroughly, then transfer to a saucepan and boil to reduce to about 570 ml\|1 pint. Add the gelatine to the liquid and leave to soak.

6 When the meat is cool enough to handle, remove all the bones from the birds and hare and cut the flesh into small pieces (about the size of the cubes of venison). Discard the cooked vegetables, the bay leaves and parsley stalks. Let the meat cool completely.

7 Preheat the oven to 190°C\|375°F\|gas mark 5. Lightly grease a 1.8 kg\|4 lb pie mould or a loose-bottomed cake tin.

8 Roll two-thirds of the pastry into a round big enough to cover the base and sides of the mould or tin. Dust the pastry with a little flour. Now fold it in half, away from you. Place one hand on the fold of the semi-circle and with the other gently push and pull

the sides so that you form a 'bag' roughly the shape and size of the pie mould or cake tin. Open out the bag and fit it into the greased mould or tin.

9 Fill the pie with the meat. Roll out the remaining pastry into a round big enough to cover the top of the pie. Dampen the bottom edge, then press this 'lid' on to the pastry case, pinching the edges together.

10 Decorate with pastry trimmings, shaped into leaves, and make a neat pea-sized hole in the middle of the top. Chill until the pastry is firm.

11 Brush with beaten egg. Bake for 40 minutes.

12 Remove the pie carefully from the mould or tin and stand it on a flat baking sheet. Brush the pie all over with beaten egg and return to the oven for a further 20 minutes. Remove and allow to cool.

13 Heat up the stock to melt the soaked gelatine. Allow to cool.

14 Using a small funnel, pour the cooled, but not quite set, stock into the pie through the hole in the pastry lid. Allow the liquid to seep down into the pie, then pour in some more: this can be a slow process, but the pie should take about 570 ml | 1 pint of liquid, and it is important that you add it to prevent the filling becoming crumbly and dry.

NOTE: If buying such small quantities of hare and venison proves difficult, use 225 g | 8 oz lean chuck steak instead.

wine: FULL RED

Cold Pheasant Pie

Preparation for this dish must start 2–3 days in advance.

SERVES 6

For the forcemeat

110 g | 4 oz poultry livers

1 pheasant, boned (see pages 370–1) and skinned

450 g | 1 lb pork belly, derinded

3 shallots, finely chopped

2 fresh sage leaves, finely chopped

1 teaspoon chopped fresh thyme

1 clove of garlic, crushed

2 teaspoons salt

1 teaspoon coarsely ground black pepper

1 tablespoon brandy

3 tablespoons dry white wine

For the jelly

1 stick of celery

1 carrot, sliced

1 slice of onion

1 bay leaf

1 sprig of fresh parsley

1 sprig of fresh marjoram

bones, giblets (except the liver) and skin of the pheasant

15 g | ½ oz powdered gelatine

For the pastry crust

450 g | 1 lb flour quantity pâte à pâte (see page 565)

a piece of pig's caul about 30 cm | 12 in square

beaten egg to glaze

1 Trim any discoloured parts and sinew from the livers.

2 Reserve 1 pheasant breast, the pheasant liver and 1 other poultry liver. Mince the rest of the pheasant meat with the remaining livers and the pork belly. Add the shallot, sage, thyme, garlic, salt, pepper, brandy and wine. Mix well and put into a deep bowl.

3 Lay the breast meat and livers on top, and cover. Refrigerate for 24 hours.

4 Make the stock by simmering the jelly ingredients (except the gelatine) in 1 litre|2 pints water for 2 hours. Strain through muslin or a double 'J'-cloth and chill overnight.

5 Make up the pâte à pâte. Chill until firm but still pliable.

6 Use two-thirds of the pastry of it to line a 20 cm|8 in raised pie mould or loose-bottomed cake tin.

7 Line the pastry shell with the pig's caul, allowing the sides to hang down over the edge.

8 Put half the minced mixture into the mould. Cut the pheasant breast into strips and lay them on top of the forcemeat.

9 Lay the livers on top of the pheasant strips. Cover with the remaining forcemeat, pressing down well to eliminate any air pockets.

10 Draw the caul up over the forcemeat to envelop it.

11 Preheat the oven to 190°C|375°F|gas mark 5.

12 Use the remaining pastry to cover and elaborately decorate the top of the pie. Press the edges of the top firmly to the base pastry. Make a hole in the middle of the pastry top to allow steam to escape.

13 Brush with beaten egg.

14 Bake the pie for 15 minutes, then turn the oven temperature down to 150°C|300°F|gas mark 2, and bake for a further $1\frac{3}{4}$ hours. Remove the pie from the oven and allow to cool overnight.

15 Remove all traces of fat from the stock. Pour it into a saucepan. Boil until there is 290 ml|$\frac{1}{2}$ pint of liquid left.

16 Place 75 ml|$\frac{1}{2}$ fl oz cold water in a small saucepan. Sprinkle over the gelatine. Allow to stand for 5 minutes. Heat gently until clear, then pour into the warm stock.

17 Leave until cold but not set – it should be syrupy. Carefully pour, little by little, into the pie, through the hole in the pastry. A small funnel will make this operation easier. Continue until the liquid level is visible, and will no longer gradually sink. If by some mischance the pastry case has a hole in it allowing the liquid to leak out, plug the hole with softened butter.

18 Chill the pie until the liquid is set: about 2 hours.

NOTE: If pouring the liquid into the pie proves difficult, carefully make, with the top of a knife, another hole in the cooked pastry towards the edge, and pour the liquid through this.

wine: **FULL RED**

Croûtes for Roast Game Birds

When roasting small game birds, such as snipe or woodcock, the 'trail', or entrails, is left inside and only the gizzard removed. After roasting, the liver and juices are spread on the uncooked side of a slice of bread which has been fried or toasted on one side only. The roasted bird is served on this croûte.

Larger birds like pheasant and grouse are drawn before roasting, but the liver may be returned to the body cavity to cook with the bird. This, plus any other scrapings from the inside of the bird, is spread on the uncooked side of the croûte, which is then cut in half on the diagonal and served as a garnish to the whole roast bird.

Fried Crumbs for Roast Game Birds

55 g | 2 oz butter
4 tablespoons dried white breadcrumbs

Melt the butter and fry the crumbs very slowly until they have absorbed most of it, and are golden and crisp. Serve in a warmed bowl, handed with the sauce or sauces.

NOTE: Fresh white breadcrumbs can be used, but rather more butter will be needed as they are very absorbent, and great care should be taken to fry slowly so that the crumbs become crisp before they turn brown.

Meat and Offal

The younger the animal, and the less exercise it has taken, the more tender its meat will be, but its flavour will be less pronounced. For example a week-old calf will be tender as margarine, and about as flavourless. An ox that has pulled a cart all its long life will be quite the reverse – good on flavour, but tough as old boots. A relatively young, and therefore tender, animal will have white or pale fat, rather than yellow; the meat will be less dark, and the bones more pliable than in an older, tougher animal. So rump steak with a bright red hue and white fat may well be more tender than the dark flesh and yellow fat of older meat, but it will probably lose in flavour what it gains in texture.

Because tenderness is rated highly today, the most expensive cuts of meat are those from the parts of the animal's body that have had little or no exercise. For example, the leg, neck and shoulder cuts of beef are tougher (and therefore cheaper) than those taken from the rump or loin.

But apart from the age of the animal, there are other factors that affect tenderness. Meat must not be cooked while the muscle fibres are taut due to rigor mortis, which can last, depending on the temperature at which the carcase is stored, for a day or two. The state of the animal prior to slaughter can also affect the tenderness of the meat; for example, if it is relaxed and peaceful the meat is likely to be more tender. Injections of certain enzymes (proteins that produce changes in the meat without themselves being changed) given to the animal before slaughter will produce the same result artificially.

Another factor affecting tenderness is the length of time that meat is stored before cooking. If hung in temperatures of 2°C|35°F it will, due to enzyme activity, become increasingly tender. Temperatures should not be higher than this, because although the enzyme activity would be greater, the risk of spoilage due to bacterial action would become high. For beef, 7 days is the minimum hanging time, while 3 weeks or a month are more desirable. However, with the commercial demands for quick turnover, the weight-loss during storage and the expense of storing, good hanging is rare these days. Some enzyme activity continues if the meat is frozen, and the formation, and subsequent melting, of ice-crystals (which, in expanding, bruise the fibres of the meat) mean that freezing meat can be said to tenderize it. However, the inevitable loss of juices from the meat, and subsequent risk of dryness after cooking is a disadvantage that outweighs the minimal tenderizing effect.

Hanging is most important in beef, as the animals are comparatively old, perhaps 2 or 3 years, when killed. It is less important for carcases of young animals, such as calves and lambs, as their meat is relatively tender anyway.

Because, inevitably, some bacterial action (as well as enzyme action) must take place during hanging, the flavour of well-hung meat is stronger, or gamier, than that of under-hung meat. The colour will also deepen and become duller with hanging. But the prime reason for hanging meat is to tenderize it, rather than to increase or change its flavour. This is not so with game, including venison, which is hung as much to produce a game flavour as to tenderize the meat.

The last, and probably most important, factor that affects the ultimate tenderness of meat is the method of cooking. Half-cooked or rare meat will be tender simply because its fibres have not been changed by heat, and will still retain the softness of raw meat. But as the heat penetrates the whole piece of meat the fibres set rigidly and the juices cease to run. Once the whole piece of meat is heated thoroughly, all the softness of raw meat is lost and it is at its toughest. This explains the natural reluctance of chefs to serve well-done steaks – it is almost impossible to produce a tender well-done grilled steak.

Muscle tissue is made up of long thin cells or muscle fibres bound together by sheets of connective tissue. Individual fibres can be as long as the whole muscle. Bundles of fibres are organized in groups to form an individual muscle. The lengthways structure of muscles is known as the grain of the meat. It is easier to carve and also to chew in the direction of the grain, which is why meat is cut across the grain.

The connective tissue is the harness of the muscle and is visible as gristle, tendons, etc. Connective tissue is made up of three main proteins: collagen, which can be converted by long, slow cooking into gelatine; elastin, which is elastic and not changed by heat; and reticulen, which is fibrous and not changed by heat. This is seen in stewing, when long, slow cooking gradually softens the flesh. A joint from an older animal, which has done much muscular work during its lifetime and is coarse-grained and fibrous, can be made particularly tender by prolonged gentle cooking. This is because much of the connective tissue present in such a joint, if subjected to a steady temperature of, say, 100°C|200°F, will convert to gelatine, producing a soft, almost sticky tenderness.

Tender cuts of meat such as sirloin steak have relatively few connective tissues and as they cook the meat fibres shrink and lose moisture. If overcooked, the juices finally dry up and a once tender piece of meat becomes tough and dry.

Joints with finer graining and little connective tissue, such as rump or sirloin, will never become gelatinous, and are consequently seldom cooked other than by roasting or grilling, when their inherent tenderness (from a life of inaction) is relied on. But they will never be as tender as the slow-cooked shin or oxtail, which can be cut with a spoon.

It is possible to tenderize meat before cooking it. This can be done by cutting, pounding and grinding to break down the structure of the muscle bundles. It can also be done by marinating. The acid in citrus fruit or wine produces protein-digesting enzymes that can break down muscle and connective tissue.

Methods of Cooking Meat

Roasting

1 Weigh the joint and establish the length of cooking time (see below).
2 Preheat the oven (electric ovens take longer to heat up than gas ovens).
3 Prepare the joint for roasting; see the relevant recipe.

4 Heat some dripping in a roasting pan and if the meat is lean, brown the joint over direct heat so that it is well coloured. Pork and lamb rarely need this but many cuts of beef do.

5 Place the joint in the pan, on a grid if you have one available, as this aids the circulation of hot air; roast for the time calculated.

6 Allow the meat to stand for at least 15 minutes at room temperature before carving. This allows the fibre of the meat to relax and absorb some of the juices.

Roasting Times

Obviously a long thin piece of meat weighing 2.3 kg|5 lb will take less time to cook than a fat round piece of the same weight, so that the times below are meant only as a guide. The essential point is that meat must reach an internal temperature of 60°C|140°F to be rare, 70°C|150°F to be medium pink, and 80°C|170°F to be well done. A meat thermometer stuck into the thickest part of the meat, and left there during cooking, eliminates guesswork.

Beef: Beef is generally roasted at 220°C|425°F|gas mark 7 for 20 minutes to brown the meat (or it may be fried all over in fat before being transferred to the oven). Whatever the method, calculate the cooking time after the browning has been done, and allow 15 minutes per 450 g|1 lb for rare meat, 20 minutes for medium and 25 for well done, roasting the meat in an oven preheated to 160°C|325°F|gas mark 3.

Lamb: Put the lamb into the hottest of ovens for 20 minutes, then allow 20 minutes to 450 g|1 lb at 190°C|375°F|gas mark 5. This will produce very slightly pink lamb. If lamb without a trace of pinkness is wanted, allow an extra 20 minutes after the calculated time is up.

Pork: Pork must be well cooked. Roast for 25 minutes at 220°C|425°F|gas mark 7, then turn the heat to 190°C|375°F|gas mark 5 and roast for 25 minutes per 450 g|1 lb

Veal: Brown in hot fat over direct heat. Or roast for 20 minutes at 220°C|425°F|gas mark 7. Then allow 20 minutes per 450 g|1 lb at 180°C|350°F|gas mark 4.

Meat		Temperature			Cooking time	
		°C	°F	Gas	per kg	per lb
Beef	Brown	220	425	7	20 mins+	
	Rare roast	160	325	3	35 mins	15 mins
	Medium roast	160	325	3	45 mins	20 mins
	Well done roast	160	325	3	55 mins	25 mins
Pork	Roast	190	375	5	55 mins	25 mins
Veal	Brown	220	425	7	20 mins+	
	Roast	180	350	4	45 mins	20 mins
Lamb	Brown	220	425	7	20 mins+	
	Roast	190	375	5	55 mins	20 mins

Cuts of Meat

Beef

For roasting: sirloin, fore rib, fillet

For pot-roasting: topside, silverside, brisket, thick flank

For stewing, braising and boiling, and for salting and boiling: chuck, shin, brisket, flank, neck, topside, silverside

For grilling and frying: fillet, rump and sirloin. But the names for steaks can be confusing:

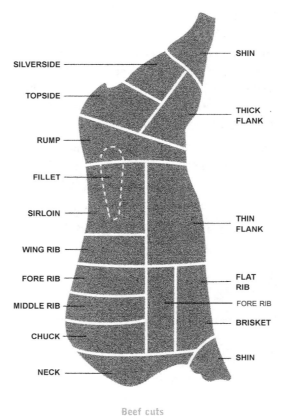

Beef cuts

Rump steaks (rumsteak or bifsteak in French): These are thick (about 2 cm | ¾ in) slices cut across the grain of the rump, and then, if for individual servings, cut into smaller pieces.

Fillet steak: This comes in various guises. Cut across into thick (2.5 cm | 1 in) slices, it becomes tournedos. A piece for 2 people, weighing perhaps 225 g | 8 oz cut from the thick end (but with all the coarser meat trimmed from it), can be grilled, spitted or roasted as a châteaubriand. Medallions are thin slices cut across the fillet.

Sirloin steaks: The name sirloin covers steak from the upper side of the true sirloin, wing rib and fore rib. The French entrecôte means only the true tender sirloin, which is cut in individual steaks or as T-bone steaks (on the rib, with the sirloin on one side of the T and the fillet or undercut on the other). French côte de boeuf or English rib of beef are thick steaks on the rib bone, from the slightly less tender wing rib or fore rib. Porterhouse is a double-sized T bone, or double-sized wing rib.

For pies: chuck, brisket, thick flank, shin (foreleg), shin or leg (hind leg)

Veal

The cuts of veal, and their names, more closely resemble those of a lamb or sheep than those of grown-up beef.

As veal is more tender than beef, most of the animal is suitable for quick cooking (roasting, frying). But as there is little fat on a calf, care must be taken to moisten the meat frequently during cooking to prevent dryness. Because of the absence of fat, veal is seldom grilled.

Much Dutch veal is milk-fed and expensive. It has a pale pink colour and the best cuts are exceptionally tender. But the taste is mild to the point of insipidity, and it needs good seasoning, usually plenty of lemon, pepper or a good sauce. English veal is cheaper, has more flavour, and generally has a slightly more reddish hue. This is because the animals are killed at an older age then their Dutch fellows, and are generally, though not always, grass-fed. But veal should never look bloody or really red.

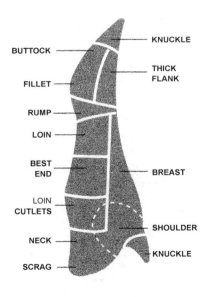

Veal cuts

For roasting: leg, loin, best end, breast

For braising and stewing: leg, shoulder, middle neck, scrag, breast

For frying: cushion (fillet), loin chops, best end cutlets, rump, round (buttock)

For stock: knuckle, foot or scrag end of neck

NOTE: The more tender cuts from the forequarter, from a top-quality milk-fed calf, may also be boned out and sliced for escalopes.

Venison

Venison is the meat of deer. Good deer meat should be dark red with a fine grain and firm white fat.

When preparing venison remove as much of the membrane as possible. Venison is very low in fat so it is often recommended that the meat be marinated before cooking. If roasting, the meat can be barded with bacon to help retain moisture.

For roasting: haunch, saddle, either whole or in fillets

For grilling and frying: steaks from the fillet or chops made from the saddle

For stewing: shoulder, neck, flank

For braising in one piece: shoulder, haunch

For mincing: flank, neck

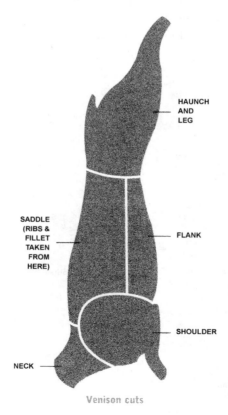

Venison cuts

Pork

Pork used to be eaten mainly in winter, or as bacon, because of the difficulty of keeping it fresh. But with modern methods of refrigeration, pork is eaten all the year round.

The flesh should be pale pink, not red or bloody. Pork killed for the fresh meat market is generally very young and tender, carrying little fat. Suckling pigs, killed while still being milk-fed, may be roasted or barbecued whole, and are traditionally served with the head on, and with an apple or an orange between the jaws.

Crackling is the roasted skin of pork. The skin must be scored deeply with a sharp knife before roasting. Salt is rubbed on the skin, making it crisp and bubbly when cooked.

For roasting: any part of the pig (bar the head, trotters and knuckle) is suitable

For grilling and frying: spare rib chops, loin chops, chump chops from the saddle, best end cutlets, belly bones or American spare ribs (usually with a marinade), fillet, tenderloin, trotters

For boiling: leg, belly, hand and spring, trotters

For pies: any meat is suitable

For sausages: any fatty piece, especially belly

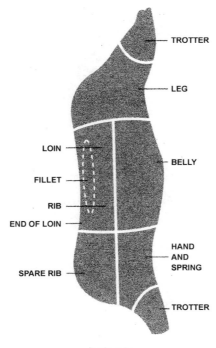

Pork cuts

Bacon

Bacon pigs are killed when heavier than pigs destined for the fresh pork market, so the comparable cuts of bacon should contain more fat than those of fresh pork.

Almost the whole of the pig is salted in brine for up to a week then matured. Green bacon is sold at this stage. Smoked bacon is hung in cool smoke for up to a month. Gammon is bacon from a hind leg, and ham is bacon from a hind leg that has been brined or cured in dry salt separately from the rest of the pig. Gammon is cured while still attached to the body. Hams are salted and possibly smoked according to varying local traditions. Parma ham and Bayonne ham, for example, are salted and smoked but not cooked further before eating. English hams are generally cooked before eating hot or cold. The most famous are the well-hung Bradenham ham and the sweet milk York ham. American Virginia hams are said to owe their sweet flavour to the fact that the hogs are fed on peanuts and peaches, and the hams are cured in salt and sugar and smoked over apple and hickory wood for a month. Westphalian ham from Germany is eaten raw in thin slices like Parma ham. Paris ham is similar to English York ham.

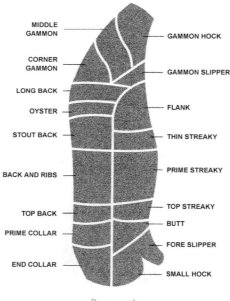

MIDDLE GAMMON — GAMMON HOCK
CORNER GAMMON — GAMMON SLIPPER
LONG BACK
OYSTER — FLANK
STOUT BACK — THIN STREAKY
BACK AND RIBS — PRIME STREAKY
TOP BACK — TOP STREAKY
— BUTT
PRIME COLLAR — FORE SLIPPER
END COLLAR — SMALL HOCK

Bacon cuts

Since good refrigeration is now widely available, pork need no longer be salted as a preservative measure. Today pork is turned into bacon mainly for the flavour. Smoked bacon keeps slightly longer than green (unsmoked) but, again, modern smoking is done more for the flavour than for preservation.

Commercially produced bacon is generally mild. Bacon cured at home, without chemical preservatives, vacuum packs, etc., is likely to have more flavour and saltiness, but needs soaking before cooking.

Smoked and green bacon flesh look similarly reddish-pink. It should not be dry, hard, dark or patchy in colour. Smoked rind is yellowish-brown; green bacon rind is white.

English bacons vary according to manufacturer and price, some being saltier than others, so care should be taken if boiling without prior soaking. It is wise to soak large pieces to be cooked whole, such as gammons or forehocks. Smaller cuts, steaks and rashers, rarely need soaking.

Danish pigs are all cured in the same manner, giving a good quality, mild-tasting, not very salty bacon.

For boiling and stewing: all cuts are suitable, but the lean pieces (forehock, gammon, collar) are sometimes casseroled or stewed whole, tied with string

Streaky and flank: are used diced for soups, or to add flavours to stews

For frying or grilling: all cuts are suitable but rashers are usually cut from the back, streaky or collar. Steaks are cut from the gammon or prime back

For baking (usually boiled first): large lean pieces are generally used (whole gammon or ham, whole gammon hock, large piece of back, whole boned and rolled forehock or either of the collars)

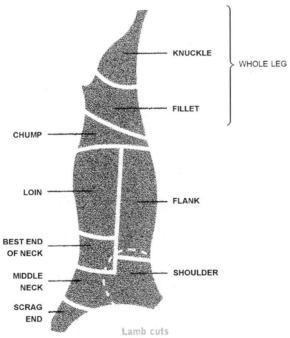

Lamb cuts

Lamb and Mutton

Animals weighing more than 36 kg|80 lb are graded as mutton. Real mutton is seldom available in butchers' shops since all the animals are killed young enough to be called lamb. But there is a difference between the small sweet joints of the new season's spring lamb, and the larger lambs killed later in the year.

Really baby lambs, killed while still milk-fed, are extremely expensive, with very pale, tender flesh. A leg from such a lamb would feed only 2 or perhaps 3 people at most.

British lamb is very fine in flavour, but good imported New Zealand lamb is usually cheaper. As a general rule, New Zealand lamb joints come from smaller animals than the full-grown English lambs, but it should be remembered that 3 grades of New Zealand lamb are imported into Britain, ranging from excellent to very tough. All New Zealand lamb comes into the country frozen, so it stands to reason that some lambs have been more recently killed than others. The best time to buy New Zealand lamb is from Christmas through to the summer months.

Lamb should be brownish-pink rather than grey in colour, but not bloody. Because the animal is killed young, almost all the cuts are tender enough for grilling, frying or roasting, but the fattier, cheaper cuts are used for casseroles and stews too.

For roasting: saddle or loin, best end of neck (rack of lamb), shoulder, leg, breast

For braising: chump chops, loin, leg

For grilling and frying: best end cutlets, loin chops, chump chops, steaks from fillet end of leg

For boiling and stewing: knuckle, scrag and middle neck, breast, leg

Butchery and Meat Preparation

Most cuts of meat are available ready prepared from the shop or market. But it is useful to know how to bone and tie certain French and English cuts that a busy butcher may be unwilling to tackle.

Boning

Boning is easier than most people imagine. A short sharp knife is essential. Tunnel-boning, where the bone is extracted without opening out the meat, is more difficult than open-boning where the flesh is split along the bone, the bone worked out and the meat rolled up and tied or sewn. But, whether tunnel-boning or open-boning, it is essential to work slowly and carefully, keeping the knife as close to the bones as possible, and scraping the meat off the bone rather than cutting it. Any meat extracted inadvertently with the bone can be scraped off and put back into the joint.

With most bones it is possible, when tunnel-boning, to work from both ends – for example, a leg of lamb can be worked on where the knuckle bone sticks out of the thin end, and the leg bone out of the fillet end. But in most cases it is simpler to cut neatly through the flesh, along the length of the bone, from the side nearest to the bone, and work the bone out all along its length. After all, some sewing or tying is necessary at the ends of the joints even if tunnel-boned, and it is simpler to sew up the length of the joint.

Trainee butchers are taught to use the knife in such a way that should it slip it will not hurt them. This means never pulling the knife directly towards the body. In addition, the knife is held firmly like a dagger when working, with the point of the knife down. But the safest precaution that cooks can take is to see that their knives are sharp. Blunt knives need more pressure to wield, and are therefore more inclined to slip.

Rolling and tying

Once a joint, such as loin, is boned, remove most of the fat and lay it, meat side up, on the board. Season it or spread sparingly with stuffing. Roll it up from the thick end and use short pieces of thin cotton (not nylon) string to tie round the meat at 2.5 cm | 1 in intervals. These can easily be cut off when serving, or the carver can slice between them when cutting the meat into thick slices.

Tie with short pieces of string or cotton

Sewing up whole joints after stuffing

Use a larding needle or large darning or upholstery needle. Some of these are curved slightly which makes the job easier. Use thin old-fashioned white string, not nylon which will melt under heat. If the string is not very thin it can be 'untwined' quite easily and used as required. Leave a good length of string at the beginning and end, but do not tie elaborate knots, which are difficult to undo when dishing the meat. Simple, large, fairly loose stitches are best – the whole length of string can be pulled out in one movement when dishing.

Larding

Some very lean or potentially tough meat is larded before roasting. This helps keep the meat moist and adds flavour. The technique is most commonly used for slow-roasted dishes like boeuf à la mode or roast veal. A special larding needle is used.

To lard a joint, cut the larding fat (usually rindless back pork fat) into thin strips and put one of them into the tunnel of the needle, clamping down the hinge to hold it in place. The fat should extend a little way out of the needle. Thread through the meat, twisting the needle gently to prevent the fat pulling off. Then release the clamp, and trim the 2 ends of fat close to the meat. Repeat this all over the lean meat at 2.5 cm | 1 in intervals.

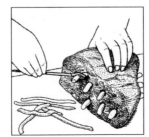

To lard: thread with strips of pork fat

Preparing Beef

Steaks for grilling or frying
Cut across the grain of the meat, if possible into thickish slices. Trim neatly, and cut rump slices into 2–3 individual steaks.

Minute steaks
Cut large thin steaks. Put them between 2 sheets of paper or clingfilm and bat gently with a cook's mallet or rolling pin to flatten the meat.

Tournedos steaks
Cut 2.5 cm | 1 in slices across the trimmed fillet.

For stewing
Remove the gristle, but not all the fat (it will add moisture and flavour). Cut into 4 cm | 1½ in cubes. Too-small pieces become dry and tough during cooking.

For stroganoff
Cut into small strips about the thickness of a pencil across the grain of the meat.

For roasting
If the meat has no fat on it, tie a piece of pork fat, or fatty bacon, round it. Tie up as described on page 445.

Preparing Lamb

Butterfly joints
To make a butterfly joint, open-bone a leg of lamb. Hold a sharp, sturdy butcher's knife like a dagger and cut, from the knuckle end, down the non-fleshy side of the leg and gradually work out the three bones.

To make a butterfly joint, work from the knuckle end. Gradually ease out the three bones

Lamb 'en ballon'
This is stuffed boned shoulder of lamb that is tied up to look like a balloon (see page 494 for a recipe). To reassemble the shoulder, spread the stuffing on one half of the boned lamb and fold the other half close up over to cover it. If the shoulder has been tunnel-boned, push the stuffing into it. Turn the shoulder over, skinned side up. Tie the end of a 3 m | 9 ft piece of string firmly round the shoulder, making a knot in the middle at the top. Take the string

around again, but this time at right angles to the first line, again tying at the first knot. Continue this process until the 'balloon' is trussed about 8 times. Tuck in any loose flaps of meat or skin.

   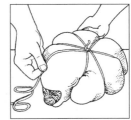

To assemble lamb en ballon, stuff a boned shoulder and tie

Saddle

This consists of both loins of lamb, left attached at the backbone, in the same way as a baron of beef.

First remove the skin: with a small knife lift a corner of the skin, hold this firmly and tug sharply to peel off. Trim off any very large pieces of fat from the edges of the saddle, but leave the back fat. Tuck the flaps under the saddle. Cut out the kidneys but keep them (they can be brushed with butter and attached to the end of the saddle with wooden skewers 30 minutes before the end of the roasting time). Using a sharp knife, score the back fat all over in a fine criss-cross pattern.

The pelvic or aitch bone, protruding slightly from one end of the saddle, can be removed, or left in place and covered with a ham frill when the saddle is served.

Rack of lamb/best end cutlets

Skin the best end: lift a corner of the skin from the neck end with a small knife, hold it firmly, and peel it off. Chine if the butcher has not already done so. This means sawing carefully through the chine bone (or spine) just where it meets the rib bones. Take care not to saw right through into the eye of the meat. Now remove the chine bone completely. Chop off the cutlet bones so that the length of the remaining bones is not more than twice the length of the eye of the meat. Remove the half-moon shaped piece of flexible cartilage found buried between the layers of fat and meat at the thinner end of the best end. This is the tip of the shoulder blade. It is simple to work out with a knife and your fingers. Remove the line of gristle to be found under the meat at the thick end.

  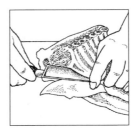 

For cutlets: skin and chine Remove the shoulder blade and gristle

 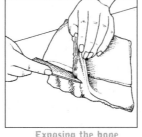 

Cutting through the fat   Exposing the bone   Scraping bones clean

For an English trim, cut through the fat 2.5 cm│1in from the ends of the bones. Remove the fat, then, using a small sharp knife, scrape the exposed bones until they are clean

If thin small cutlets are required, cut between each bone as evenly as possible, splitting the rack into 6–7 small cutlets. If fatter cutlets are required, carefully ease out every other rib bone. Then cut between the remaining bones into thick cutlets. Now trim the fat from the thick end of each cutlet, and scrape the rib bones free of any flesh or skin.

Noisettes

These are boneless cutlets, tied into a neat round shape with string. They are made from the loin or best end. Skin the meat: lift a corner of the skin with a small knife, holding it firmly with a cloth to get a good grip, and pull it off.

Chine the meat (see above). Now remove first the chine bone and then all the rib bones, easing them out with a short sharp knife. Remove the half-moon-shaped piece of flexible cartilage found buried between the layers of fat and meat at the thinner end of the best end. This is the top of the shoulder blade. Remove the line of gristle to be found under the meat at the thick end.

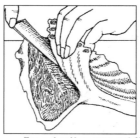 

For noissettes: ease out the bones, then roll, tie and cut

Trim off any excess fat from the meat and roll it up tightly, starting at the meaty thick side and working towards the thin flap. Tie the roll neatly with separate pieces of string placed at 4 cm│1½ in intervals. Trim the ragged ends of the roll to neaten them. Now slice the roll into pieces, cutting accurately between each string. The average English best end will give 4 good noisettes. The string from the noisette is removed after cooking.

Collops

These are small slices of meat taken from the best end neck of lamb. They are a very extravagant cut (see page 482 for recipe). Lay the best end neck down and prepare the meat partly as for noisettes (see above), i.e. remove the chine bone, gristle and shoulder blade.

With a sharp knife (and making small cuts close to the rib bones), ease the bones, in one piece, away from the meat. Gradually separate the whole 'eye' of the meat (the fat-free cylinder) from the bones. Using a sharp flexible knife, remove all fat and membranes from the meat. Finally, slice into meat rounds or 'collops'.

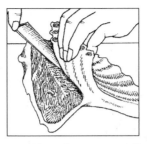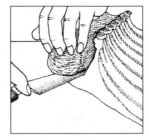

For collops: ease out the bones and separate the eye

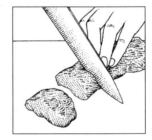

Remove fat and membrane, and slice

Crown roast

Two racks (best ends) are needed. The rack is prepared similarly to one for rack of lamb but the rib bones are left slightly longer, and the rack is not split into cutlets.

Remove the fat from the prepared rack. Bend each best end into a semi-circle, with the fatty side of the ribs inside. To facilitate this it may be necessary to cut through the sinew between each cutlet, from the thick end for about 2.5 cm | 1 in. But take care not to cut into the fleshy eye of the meat. Sew the ends of the racks together to make a circle, with the meaty part forming the base of the crown. Tie a piece of string round the 'waist' of the crown. A crown roast is traditionally stuffed, but this can result in undercooked inside fat if it has not been removed.

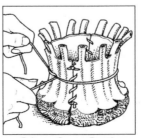

Removing the fat   Tying a Crown Roast

Guard of honour (rack of lamb)

Prepare 2 best end racks exactly as for the crown roast, above. Hold the 2 best ends, one in each hand, facing each other with the meaty part of the racks on the board, and the fatty sides on the outside. Jiggle them so that the rib bones interlock and cross at the top. Stuff the arch if required. Sew or tie the bases together at intervals.

To assemble a guard of honour:
tie the prepared racks together

Preparing Pork and Bacon

Chops

Chops are trimmed of rind, and the fat snipped or cut across (from the outside towards the meat). This is because as the fat shrinks during cooking, it tends to curl the chops out of shape.

To prepare chops: snip the fat at even intervals

Gammon steaks or bacon chops

Snip the surrounding fat as described above. Bacon chops (really thick rashers from the prime back) are sometimes cooked with the rind left on, but snipping is essential to prevent curling.

American or chinese spare ribs

These are made from pork belly (not English spare rib). They can be cut before or after cooking. Simply cut between each belly bone, splitting the meat into long bones.

To Score Crackling

It is vital that crackling should be scored evenly and thoroughly, each cut, which should penetrate the skin and a little of the fat below it, being even and complete. Unscored crackling is tough and difficult to carve. Make the cuts not more than 1 cm|½ in apart all over the skin. Score the crackling after boning but before rolling and tying the joint.

Carving Meat

The most important factor in good carving is a really sharp knife, a fork with a safety guard, and a board or flat plate unencumbered by vegetables and garnishes. Common sense usually dictates how joints are to be tackled. Meat off the bone is simple: just cut in slices of whatever thickness you prefer, across the grain of the meat. Pork, beef and veal are traditionally carved in thinner slices than lamb.

Legs

The legs of pork, lamb, bacon (gammon or ham), veal and venison are carved similarly. Put the leg meaty side up on the board or plate and grasp the knuckle bone with one hand, or pierce the joint firmly with a carving fork. Cut a small shallow 'V' or scoop out the middle of the top of the meat. Carve slices of meat from both sides of the 'V'. Then turn the leg over and take horizontal slices from the other side.

Legs can also be cut in diagonal slices from the knuckle end. This is more common with hams, but both methods are used for all legs.

To carve a leg of lamb:
carve slices of meat from both sides of the 'V'

Alternatively, carve diagonally
from the knuckle end

Loins

Loins and best end of pork, veal and lamb are often roasted on the bone to prevent shrinkage, but to carve them it is easier to remove the meat off the rib cage and slice to the desired thickness. To carve a loin of pork, the crackling can be removed in one piece. The meat is then sliced and the crackling can be cut, with scissors, in the same number of pieces as there are slices of meat. If boned, the meat is cut similarly, but in thinner slices, about 5 mm|¼ in thick. Beef strip loin (boned sirloin) is cut in the same way, thinly in Britain, thickly in America.

To carve a loin of pork: remove
bones and crackling before slicing

To carve a sirloin on the bone:
slice from the top and undercut

Sirloin of beef on the bone is tackled from the top and bottom, the slices cut as thinly as possible on the top, the undercut or fillet slices being carved more thickly. Each diner should be given a slice or two from both top and bottom.

Saddle of lamb

The chump end of the saddle is cut in thin angles across the grain of the meat, at right angles to the backbone. But the main part of the saddle, lying each side of the backbone, is cut in thin strips or narrow slices down the length of the saddle. This can be done on the bone, but it is easier if you lift the whole side of the saddle off in one piece and cut into long slices.

To carve a saddle: cut in thin strips,
down the length of the saddle

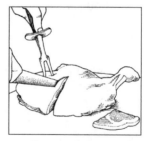

To carve a shoulder
of lamb: cut like a cake

Crown roast and guard of honour

Remove the string and split into cutlets.

Shoulder of lamb

A shoulder is simple to carve as long as you know where the bones are. Place it fatty side up and cut like a cake on the side opposite to the bone.

Small forerib of beef

A single forerib of beef is cooked on the bone and then cut off the bone in one piece. Instead of slicing into thin horizontal slices it can be cut into shorter fatter vertical slices.

Place the roast on its side and make a 5 cm|2 in cut along the length of the rib. Stand the meat up, rib side down. Carve several slices and lift off and place on a warm serving dish. Turn the rib back on its side and make a second 5 cm|2 in cut along the length of the rib. Carve.

To carve a small forerib of beef: remove from the bone and slice horizontally

To carve a large forerib of beef

Steak and Kidney Pudding

Steaming gives the suet pastry its distinctive soft, open texture. The easiest way to cook the pudding is to put its container in a saucepan with hot water that comes halfway up the sides of the container. The pan is covered and the pudding cooked over low heat to steam gently for a long time, and water is added to the pan as necessary. Take care to cover the pudding with a double thickness of kitchen foil, pleated to allow for expansion of the crust, and put a band of folded foil under the basin with ends projecting up the sides to act as handles.

SERVES 4

675 g|1½ lb chuck steak
225 g|8 oz ox kidney
plain flour
suet pastry made with 340 g|12 oz self-raising flour
  (see page 561)

butter for greasing
salt and freshly ground black pepper
2 teaspoons very finely chopped onion
2 teaspoons chopped fresh parsley

1 Cut the beef into cubes about 2.5 cm|1 in square.
2 Cut the kidneys into smaller cubes, discarding any sinews.
3 Place both beef and kidney in a large sieve. Pour over the flour and shake until the meat is lightly coated.
4 On a floured surface, roll out two-thirds of the suet pastry into a round about 1 cm|1½ in thick. Flour the surface lightly to stop it sticking together when folded. Fold the pastry over to form a half-moon shape. Place the pastry with the straight side away from you and roll it lightly so that the straight side becomes curved and the whole rounded again. Now separate the layers, and you should have a bag, roughly the shape of a 1 kg|2¼ lb pudding basin. Use it to line the lightly greased basin, easing

the pastry where necessary to fit, and trimming off the top so that 1 cm | ½ in sticks up over the edge.

5 Fill the lined basin with the meat, sprinkling plenty of salt, pepper, onion and parsley in between the layers.

6 Add water to come three-quarters of the way up the meat.

7 Roll the remaining third of suet pastry 5 mm | ¼ in thick, and large enough to just cover the pudding filling. Put in place, wet the edges and press them together securely.

8 Cover the pudding with a double piece of greaseproof paper, pleated down the centre to allow room for the pastry to expand, and a similarly pleated piece of kitchen foil. Tie down with string.

9 Place in a saucepan of boiling water with a tightly closed lid, or in a steamer, for 4–5 hours, taking care to top up with boiling water occasionally so as not to boil dry.

10 Remove the paper and foil and serve the pudding from the bowl.

NOTES: Traditionally, steak and kidney puddings served from the bowl are presented wrapped in a white linen napkin.

As the filling of the pudding may, with long cooking, dry out somewhat, it is worth having a gravy boat of hot beef stock handy to moisten the meat when serving.

A delicious addition to steak and kidney pudding is to add a small can of smoked oysters to the meat filling.

wine: **FULL RED**

Steak and Kidney Pie

SERVES 4

675 g	1½ lb chuck steak	425 ml	¾ pint brown stock (see page 102)
225 g	8 oz ox kidney	salt and freshly ground black pepper
oil or dripping	1 tablespoon chopped fresh parsley
1 onion, finely chopped	225 g	8 oz flour quantity rough puff pastry (see
30 g	1 oz plain flour	page 565)
	beaten egg

1 Trim away the excess fat from the steak and cut the beef into cubes about 2.5 cm | 1 in square. Cut the kidneys into smaller cubes, discarding any sinew.

2 Heat the oil or dripping in a frying pan and fry a few beef cubes at a time until browned all over, putting them into a flameproof casserole as they are done. Fry the onion in the same fat until soft and brown.

3 Stir in the flour and cook for 1 minute. Gradually add the stock, stirring continuously and scraping any sediment from the bottom of the pan. Bring to the boil, then simmer for 1 minute. Pour over the meat in the casserole, season with salt and pepper and simmer slowly until the meat is tender (about 2 hours). Add the parsley.

4 If the sauce is too greasy, skim off the fat; if it is too thin, remove the meat to a pie dish and boil the sauce rapidly until syrupy. Pour the sauce over the meat and leave until completely cold.

5 Preheat the oven to 200°C|400°F|gas mark 6.

6 Roll out the pastry to ¼ cm|⅛ in thickness. Cut a long strip just wider than the rim of the pie dish, brush the lip of the dish with water and press down the strip.

7 Brush the strip with water and lay over the sheet of pastry. Press it down firmly. Cut away any excess pastry.

8 Cut a 1 cm|½ in hole in the centre of the pie-top and cover with a leaf-shaped piece of pastry (the hole is to allow the escape of steam).

9 Decorate the top with more pastry leaves. Brush all over with egg. Chill in the refrigerator until the pastry is firm.

10 Bake in the oven for 30 minutes, or until the pastry is well risen and golden-brown.

wine: **FULL RED**

Shepherd's Pie (1)

SERVES 4–5

675 g|1½ lb minced beef
1 onion, finely chopped
1 carrot, finely chopped
1 stick of celery, finely chopped
oil for frying
2 teaspoons plain flour
570 ml|1 pint brown stock (see page 102)
1 bay leaf

1 teaspoon Worcestershire sauce (optional)
1 teaspoon tomato purée
salt and freshly ground black pepper

For the topping
900 g|2 lb mashed potato (see page 268)
butter

1 Fry half the mince in a large frying pan. Brown well all over. Remove with a slotted spoon and place in a saucepan. Brown the remaining mince and place in the saucepan.

2 Fry the onion, carrot and celery in the frying pan until just beginning to brown. Tip off a little of the fat and place in another saucepan.

3 Add the flour and cook over low heat until lightly browned.

4 Add the stock and bring slowly to the boil, stirring continuously.

5 Now add the bay leaf, Worcestershire sauce, tomato purée, salt and pepper. Mix with the browned mince.

6 Set the saucepan over a medium heat to simmer. Cover and leave to cook for 1–1½ hrs. Check it every so often and add extra water if it becomes too dry.

7 Preheat the oven to 200°C|400°F|gas mark 6.

8 Remove the bay leaf from the mince and tip the meat into a pie dish. If the liquid is very runny, boil the liquid until syrupy.

9 When slightly cooled, spread or pipe the potato over the top.

10 Fork it up to leave the surface rough, or draw the fork over the surface to mark with a pattern.

11 Place in the oven for 30 minutes, or until the potato is brown and crusty.

wine: MEDIUM RED

Shepherd's Pie (2)

This is a low-fat dish – the mince is a component part, rather than a principal ingredient.

SERVES 4

2 teaspoons grapeseed oil

110 g│4 oz lean minced beef

1 onion, finely chopped

2 large carrots, finely chopped

2 sticks of celery, finely chopped

2 teaspoons tomato purée

½ teaspoons ground allspice

2 teaspoons plain flour

290 ml│½ pint brown stock (see page 102)

1 bay leaf

salt and freshly ground black pepper

110 g│4 oz cooked chickpeas

For the topping

675 g│1½ lb potatoes, peeled and cut into chunks

150 ml│¼ pint skimmed milk

30 g│1 oz low-fat spread (optional)

freshly grated nutmeg

salt and freshly ground black pepper

1 Heat the oil in a large non-stick sauté pan. Add the mince and brown well all over. Reduce the heat and add the onion, carrot and celery. When the vegetables have softened, add the tomato purée, allspice and flour. Cook for 1 minute.

2 Remove from the heat, add the stock and stir well. Return to the heat and bring gradually to the boil, stirring continuously. Add the bay leaf, season with salt and pepper and simmer for 30 minutes.

3 Meanwhile, prepare the mashed potatoes. Cook the potatoes in boiling water until soft. Drain them and return to the empty saucepan. Mash over a medium heat allowing them to dry out as you do so but taking care that the mashed potato does not stick to the bottom of the pan and burn. Push the mound of potato to one side of the pan and pour the milk into the exposed side of the pan. Put this side over direct heat and get the milk boiling. Add the low-fat spread and allow it to melt. Now beat the milk and low-fat spread into the potato. Season with nutmeg, salt and pepper.

4 Preheat the oven to 200°C│400°F│gas mark 6.

5 Add the chickpeas to the pan of meat and vegetables and simmer for 2–3 minutes. Remove the bay leaf. With a large slotted spoon, transfer the meat and vegetables to a pie dish. Boil the gravy until reduced to a syrupy consistency. Pour it over the meat and vegetables and mix well. Leave to cool for 5 minutes.

6 Pile the potato on top of the pie filling and fork it up roughly. Reheat in the oven for 20 minutes.

wine: MEDIUM RED

Spaghetti Bolognese

SERVES 4

340 g | 12 oz spaghetti

For the sauce

85 g | 3 oz unsmoked bacon

340 g | 12 oz lean minced beef

2 tablespoons olive oil

medium onion finely diced

1 clove of garlic, crushed

110 g | 4 oz mushrooms, sliced

100 ml | 3½ fl oz red wine

290 ml | ½ pint brown stock (see page 102)

1   100 g | 14 oz can of tomatoes

1 teaspoon tomato purée

1 teaspoon dried basil

1 teaspoon chopped fresh marjoram or oregano

salt and freshly ground black pepper

4 tablespoons freshly grated Parmesan cheese

1 Dice the bacon and fry slowly in its own fat, in a large frying pan, until lightly browned. Remove from the pan and set aside. Add a little oil if necessary, and brown the mince.

2 With a slotted spoon, lift the mince into a saucepan. Place 1 tablespoon of the oil in the frying pan. Add the onion and celery. Cook over a low heat, stirring occasionally, until soft and lightly coloured. Add the garlic and mushrooms and cook for 5 minutes. Tip into the pan of meat.

3 Pour the wine into the frying pan and bring to the boil, scraping the bottom of the pan with a wooden spoon to loosen all the sediment. Stir in the stock, tomatoes and tomato purée. Pour on to the meat in the saucepan. Add the herbs and season to taste. Cover and simmer for 1–1½ hrs, or until the meat is tender. If greasy, skim off as much of the fat as possible.

4 While the sauce is cooking, push the spaghetti into a large saucepan of boiling salted water and stir until the water reboils. Boil uncovered for 10–12 minutes, or until just tender. Tip into a colander, then rinse under hot running water. Return to the rinsed-out pan and toss gently with 1 tablespoon oil, turning carefully with a wooden spoon.

5 Place the spaghetti onto warmed plates and pour over the Bolognese sauce. Serve with Parmesan cheese sprinkled on top of the sauce or pass separately.

wine: **LIGHT FRUITY RED**

Boiled Silverside

SERVES 6

1.35 kg | 3 lb piece of salt silverside

6 pieces of marrow bone

1 bouquet garni (1 bay leaf, 2 parsley stalks, 6 peppercorns, 1 small onion, tied in muslin)

6 medium onions

4 large carrots, quartered

2 turnips, quartered

12 dumplings (see page 458)

To garnish

chopped fresh parsley

1 Soak the beef in cold unsalted water for about 3 hours.
2 Put the bones and beef into a large saucepan of fresh unsalted water and bring slowly to the boil, skimming as the scum rises to the surface.
3 When simmering, add the bouquet garni and half-cover the pan. Simmer for about 3 hours. Remove the bouquet garni and skim off any fat.
4 Now add the vegetables and simmer for 1 hour, or until the meat and vegetables are tender.
5 Meanwhile, cook the dumplings: if there is room in the saucepan, float them in the liquid 20 minutes before the end of the cooking time. If not, take some of the stock (topping up with boiling water if necessary) and simmer them in a separate saucepan. Do not cover.
6 Place the beef on a large warmed serving dish. Surround it with the vegetables, dumplings and marrow bones. Cover and keep warm.
7 Taste the stock. Skim if necessary. If weak-flavoured, reduce by rapid boiling.
8 Ladle a cupful or so of hot liquid over the meat and vegetables, sprinkle with parsley and serve immediately. Serve more liquid separately in a warmed sauceboat.

NOTE: Dumplings are always a little soggy cooked on the stove. For a drier, fluffier version, they can be baked in the oven.

wine: **FULL RED**

Dumplings

These dumplings can be flavoured with chopped fresh herbs or grated fresh horseradish, if desired.

SERVES 4

200 g | 7 oz plain flour
3 teaspoons baking powder
½ teaspoon dry English mustard
¼ teaspoon cayenne pepper

½ teaspoon salt
55 g | 2 oz lard, suet or solid vegetable shortening
about 150 ml | ¼ pint iced water

1 Sift the flour, baking powder, mustard, cayenne and salt into a large bowl. Add the fat.
2 Using 2 table knives scissor-fashion cut the fat into the flour until each piece is no bigger than a small pea. Rub in lightly. Mix in the herbs or horseradish, if used.
3 Stir in enough water to make a soft dough, taking care not to overwork the dough.
4 Divide the dough into 8 pieces and place on the hot stew or soup, spacing them evenly. Cover and simmer for about 15 minutes. Do not lift the lid during cooking or the dumplings will be heavy.
5 When the dumplings feel firm to the touch, remove the lid and cook for a further 5 minutes to dry the surface of the dumplings. Break one open to check that it is cooked through. There should not be any uncooked, doughy mixture left in the centre.

Pot au Feu Ordinaire

This recipe has been adapted from Time Life's *The Good Cook: Beef and Veal*.

SERVES 4–6

1 kg │ 2¼ lb beef bones, sawn into 5–7.5 cm │ 2–3 in pieces	200 g │ 7 oz carrots
1 kg │ 2¼ lb silverside or topside of beef, tied in a compact shape	110 g │ 4 oz turnips
	200 g │ 7 oz leeks
2.25 litres │ 4 pints water	3 onions, 1 stuck with cloves
15 g │ ½ oz salt	30 g │ 1 oz parsnip
	30 g │ 1 oz celery

1 Put the bones into the bottom of a large saucepan with the meat on top. Add the water and the salt. Place over a very low heat, so that you can skim the liquid when it boils. It should take about 30 minutes to come to the boil – it must be skimmed constantly to make a very clear broth.

2 When the liquid boils, splash on 3 tablespoons cold water. Skim again and, once the liquid starts to boil again, add another 3 tablespoons cold water. This produces a third lot of scum, this time almost white. Skim. When the liquid starts to boil once more, add a further 3 tablespoons cold water. The little scum that rises this time should be perfectly white and clean. Skim it. Then add the vegetables and skim off any scum that rises. With a damp cloth, carefully wipe the inside edges of the saucepan so that no traces of scum remain.

3 Simmer, very slowly, for 3 hours. Keep checking and should any scum rise to the surface, remove it with a slotted spoon. It can also be cooked in a low oven or ideally in the slow oven of an Aga.

4 Traditionally the broth is served as a first course, either with noodles or with the vegetables cooked with the beef.

5 The beef is served sliced and garnished with freshly cooked vegetables. It can be accompanied by a selection of the following: pickled gherkins, coarse salt, horseradish sauce, capers, mustard and French dressing.

wine: **SPICY RED**

Family Beef Stew

SERVES 4

675 g │ 1½ lb stewing beef	salt and freshly ground black pepper
dripping or oil	1 bay leaf
2 large mild onions, sliced	2 parsely stalks
3 medium carrots, cubed	a pinch of chopped fresh thyme
1 medium turnip, cubed	30 g │ 1 oz pearl barley
570 ml │ 1 pint brown stock (see page 102)	

1 Preheat the oven to 150°C│300°F│gas mark 2.

2 Remove any gristle and excess fat from the meat and cut it into 3 cm│1½ in cubes.

3 Melt a little of the dripping or oil in a sauté pan. Brown the beef cubes on all sides, a few at a time, and transfer to a casserole. If the bottom of the pan becomes too brown and sticky, pour in a little stock and swish it about, scraping the sediment from the bottom of the pan. Pour this into the casserole, and then heat a little more dripping or oil and continue browning the meat until all is transferred to the casserole.

4 Fry the onion, carrot and turnip in the pan until golden-brown and place them in the casserole.

5 Pour the stock into the pan and bring to the boil, scraping any remaining sediment from the bottom. Stir in the seasoning, bay leaf, parsley and thyme and pour on to the meat. The meat should be covered almost competely. Bring to the boil, then simmer for 2 minutes.

6 Cover the casserole and cook in the oven for 2–2½ hours. After 1 hour stir in the barley. Skim off any excess fat.

NOTE: This stew is even better if kept for a day before eating – the barley swells up even more and the flavour improves.

wine: **FULL RED**

Beef Olives

SERVES 4

4 thin slices of lean beef buttock	**For the stuffing**
seasoned plain flour	55 g │ 2 oz streaky bacon, chopped
2 tablespoons oil	1 tablespoon oil
225 g │ 8 oz mirepoix of carrot, onion and celery	225 g │ 8 oz flat mushrooms, finely chopped
1 tablespoon flour	55 g │ 2 oz fresh white breadcrumbs
425 ml │ ¾ pint brown stock (see page 102)	2 tablespoons chopped fresh parsley
150 ml │ ¼ pint red wine	salt and freshly ground black pepper
	beaten egg to bind

1 Preheat the oven to 150°C│300°F│gas mark 2.

2 Put the slices of beef between damp greaseproof paper and flatten lightly with a rolling pin or mallet.

3 Cook the bacon in the oil until light brown then stir in the mushrooms. Cook, stirring, until all the liquid has evaporated. Stir in the breadcrumbs and the parsley. Allow to cool.

4 Season the stuffing with salt and freshly ground black pepper. Stir in the egg.

5 Divide the mixture between the slices of beef and roll up, folding in the ends to make neat parcels. Tie the beef olives with fine string and roll them in seasoned flour.

6 Heat half the oil in a frying pan and brown the beef olives on all sides. Remove them and lightly brown the mirepoix in the remaining oil. Stir in the flour and cook to a russet brown.

7 Place the beef olives on top of the mirepoix in a shallow casserole or small roasting pan. Pour over the stock and the wine bring to the boil and cover. Cook in the oven for $1\frac{1}{2}-2$ hours.

8 Dish the beef olives on a warmed serving plate. Remove the string. Skim any fat off the liquid and then strain into a saucepan. Boil until syrupy. Pour over the beef.

NOTE: If the sauce is too thin, thicken it either by reduction or by adding beurre manié (see page 109). If the sauce is too thick, thin it down with a little extra stock.

wine: **MEDIUM RED**

Boeuf Bourguignonne

SERVES 4

675 g | 1½ lb chuck steak

1 tablespoon beef dripping or oil

12 small button onions or shallots

30 g | 1 oz butter

1 clove of garlic, crushed

2 teaspoons plain flour

290 ml | ½ pint red wine

290 ml | ½ pint brown stock (see page 102)

1 bouquet garni (bay leaf, sprig of fresh thyme, a few parsley stalks and 1 stick of celery, tied up with string)

salt and freshly ground black pepper

55 g | 2 oz piece of fatty bacon, diced

110 g | 4 oz button mushrooms

To garnish

chopped fresh parsley

1 Preheat the oven to 150°C | 300°F | gas mark 2.

2 Cut the beef into 3 cm | 1½ in cubes, discarding any fat and gristle.

3 Heat half the dripping or oil in a flameproof casserole and brown the beef cubes very well, a few at a time. They must be brown on all sides. Put them into a bowl as they are done. If the bottom of the pan becomes very dark or too dry, pour in a little water, swish it about, scraping off the sediment stuck to the bottom, and pour over the meat. Heat up a little more dripping or oil and continue to brown the meat. When it is all brown repeat the déglaçage (adding water and scraping the pan).

4 Peel the shallots by immersing them in boiling water for 30 seconds and then removing the skins. Dry them and fry in half the butter until well browned.

5 Add the garlic and stir in the flour. Cook, stirring, for 1 minute.

6 Stir in the wine and stock. Boil until reduced by one third, stirring to scrape the bottom of the pan.

7 Put the meat and sauce together in the casserole and add the bouquet garni. Season with salt and pepper. Cover and cook bake for 2–3 hours, or until the meat is very tender.

8 Meanwhile, prepare the bacon and mushrooms: cut the bacon into $\frac{1}{2} \times 2$ cm $|\frac{1}{4} \times \frac{3}{4}$ in lardons and blanch in boiling water for 1 minute. Refresh and drain well. Wipe the mushrooms but do not peel or remove the stalks. Cut into quarters if large. Melt the remaining butter in a frying pan and, when foaming, add the bacon and mushrooms and cook fairly fast until delicately browned. Lift them out and add the bacon to the stew when it has been cooking for $1\frac{1}{2}$ hours. Continue for a further 30 minutes. Add the mushrooms and cook until the meat is tender (about 30 minutes).

9 When the beef is tender, use a slotted spoon to lift the meat, bacon and vegetables into a clean casserole. Remove the bouquet garni, check the seasoning and boil the sauce fast to reduce to a syrupy consistency. If the sauce is too salty do not reduce it but thicken with a little beurre manié (see page 109).

10 Pour the sauce over the beef and serve sprinkled with the parsley.

NOTES: This stew can be cooked on top of the stove, over a low heat, for 2 hours, but slow oven-cooking produces a better result, with the meat as soft as butter but not shredded or falling apart and with no danger of 'catching' on the bottom.

It can of course be made entirely with wine using no stock at all – delicious but more expensive.

wine: **MEDIUM RED**

Carbonnade de Boeuf

SERVES 4

675 g $|1\frac{1}{2}$ lb chuck steak	1 teaspoon wine vinegar
1 tablespoon beef dripping or oil	1 bay leaf
3 onions, thinly sliced	a pinch of chopped fresh thyme
1 clove of garlic, crushed	a pinch of freshly grated nutmeg
2 teaspoons soft brown sugar	salt and freshly ground black pepper
2 teaspoons plain flour	4 slices of French bread spread thickly with French
290 ml $|\frac{1}{2}$ pint brown ale	mustard
290 ml $|\frac{1}{2}$ pint brown stock (see page 102)	

1 Preheat the oven to 150°C|300°F|gas mark 2.

2 Cut the beef into small steaks, cutting across the grain of the meat. Heat half the dripping or oil in a large frying pan and fry the steaks, a few at a time, until browned all over, putting them into a flameproof casserole as they are done. If the bottom of the pan becomes very dark or too dry, pour in a little water, swish it about, scraping off the sediment stuck to the bottom, and pour over the meat. Heat up a little more dripping or oil and continue to brown the meat. When it is all brown, repeat the déglaçage (adding water and scraping the pan).

3 Fry the onions slowly and, when beginning to brown, add the garlic and sugar. Cook for a further minute or until nicely brown.

4 Stir in the flour and cook, stirring, over the heat for 1 minute. Remove from the heat and pour in the brown ale and the stock.

5 Return to the heat and bring slowly to the boil, then simmer for 2 minutes, stirring continuously. Pour into the casserole and add the vinegar, bay leaf, thyme, nutmeg, salt and pepper.

6 Cover and bring to simmering point over direct heat, then cook in the oven for $1\frac{1}{2} - 2$ hours.

7 Increase the oven temperature to 190°C|375°F|gas mark 5. Put the slices of bread, mustard-side up, on top of the stew (they are there to absorb the fat) and return the casserole, without the lid, to the oven until the bread is brown and crisp (about 15 minutes).

wine: **BEER OR FULL RED**

Gaeng Ped Nua (Spicy Red Beef)

Ingredients for this recipe are available in specialist Thai shops.

SERVES 6–8

2 tablespoons Thai red curry paste	340 g|12 oz creamed coconut
3 tablespoons oil	2 tablespoons nam pla (Thai fish sauce)
1.35 kg|3 lb braising steak, cut into strips	½ teaspoon sugar
1 stalk of lemon grass, cut into strips	2 red peppers, cored, deseeded and cut into strips
a few makrut (citrus) leaves	1 bunch of fresh basil

1 Fry the curry paste in the oil in a large wok or pan for 1 minute. Add the strips of beef and stir-fry, then, ensuring that the curry paste coats the meat, cover with water and add the lemon grass and broken-up makrut leaves.

2 Simmer until the beef is tender (about $1\frac{1}{2}$ hours).

3 Mix the creamed coconut with 570 ml|1 pint water and add it to the pan. Reduce until the sauce is thick.

4 Add the nam pla sugar and red peppers and simmer until the peppers are just cooked.

5 Finally add the basil leaves.

6 Serve with steamed or boiled rice.

NOTE: If the sauce curdles (which it often does) it can be brought back with vigorous whisking.

wine: **FULL SPICY RED**

Sauté of Beef with Green Peppercorns

SERVES 4

675 g | 1½ lb skirt of beef

1 tablespoon oil

1 tablespoon brandy

450 ml | ¾ pint demi-glace sauce (see page 116)

salt and freshly ground black pepper

4 tablespoons double cream (optional)

2 teaspoons canned green peppercorns, well rinsed and drained

1 Cut the beef into 6 cm | 2½ in cubes, discarding any fat.

2 Heat the oil in a heavy frying pan and brown the beef pieces very well on all sides, a few at a time. Transfer them to a bowl as they are done.

3 Tip off any excess fat from the pan, put back the meat, add the brandy and set alight with a match. When the flames subside, pour in the demi-glace sauce, cover and simmer very gently until the meat is tender. This will take about 2 hours, or longer, depending on the quality of the meat.

4 Add the cream, if using, and the peppercorns, and adjust the seasoning to taste.

wine: **SPICY RED**

Beef Curry with Almonds

This is an adaptation of a recipe by Josceline Dimbleby. As with many recipes using a large variety of dried spices, if you have not got them all do not worry, just use a little extra of the ones you do have. The cumin and coriander, however, are essential.

SERVES 4

675 g | 1½ lb chuck steak

2 onions, sliced

4 tablespoons sunflower oil

1 teaspoon ground cardamom

½ teaspoon ground cloves

2 teaspoons freshly ground black pepper

2 teaspoons ground cumin

1 tablespoon ground coriander

½ teaspoon ground turmeric

85 g | 3 oz blanched almonds

2.5 cm | 1 in piece of fresh root ginger, peeled and very finely chopped

2 cloves of garlic, crushed

1   400 g | 14 oz can of tomatoes

salt

2 tablespoons Greek yoghurt

To garnish

fresh coriander leaves

1 Trim the beef of as much fat and gristle as possible and cut into 3.5 cm | 1½ in cubes.

2 Preheat the oven to 170°C | 325°F | gas mark 3. Place the onions in a saucepan with 2 tablespoons oil. Cover with a piece of dampened greaseproof paper and a lid. Sweat over a low heat until soft.

3 Put 1 tablespoon of the oil into a frying pan and heat gently. Add the almonds and fry until golden-brown. Set aside. Add a little more oil to the pan, add the dry spices and cook slowly for 1 minute.

4 Put the spices and almonds into a blender and whizz to a smooth purée with 150 ml | ¼ pint water.

5 Wipe the frying pan clean. It is important to prevent the final curry having bits of burnt dried spices in it. Add 1 tablespoon oil, heat well and brown the beef cubes well on all sides, a few at a time. Transfer to a casserole. If the bottom of the pan becomes too brown and sticky pour in a little water and swish it about, scraping the sediment from the bottom of the pan. Pour this into the casserole and then add a little more oil to the frying pan and continue to brown the meat until all is transferred to the casserole.

6 Add the ginger and garlic to the onions and fry slowly until the onions are a deep golden-brown. Add the spice and almond mixture and the tomatoes. Stir well and bring to the boil, then simmer for 1 minute. Season to taste with salt and pour over the meat. Place over direct heat and bring back up to the boil. Cover and bake the oven for 2–3 hours, or until the meat is very tender.

7 Check the curry 2 or 3 times during the cooking process and if it is becoming too dry add a little water.

8 Just before serving, stir the yoghurt into the curry and reheat without boiling. Turn into a warmed serving dish and garnish with the coriander leaves.

wine: **FULL SPICY RED**

Cooking Steaks

All cooked steaks should be well browned on the surface, but the varying degrees of 'doneness' are defined as follows.

Blue: The inside is almost raw (but hot).

Rare: Red inside with plenty of red juices running freely.

Medium rare: As rare, but with fewer free-flowing juices and a paler centre.

Medium: Pink in the centre with juices set.

Well done: The centre is beige but the flesh is still juicy.

The best way to tell if meat is done is by its texture. Feel the meat by pressing firmly with a finger. Rare steak feels soft, almost raw; medium steak is firmer with some resilience to it; well-done steak feels very firm. With practice there will soon be no need to cut-and-peep.

Fried Steak

SERVES 4

4 sirloin steaks, cut 2 cm|¾ in thick or 4 fillet
  steaks, cut 2.5 cm|1 in thick
freshly ground black pepper and salt

oil or dripping
Maître d'Hôtel Butter (see page 134)

1 Season the steaks with pepper. Leave to warm to room temperature if they have been chilled. Sprinkle lightly with salt just before cooking.
2 Brush a frying pan with a little oil or dripping and place over good heat until it is beginning to smoke.
3 Brown the steaks quickly on both sides. For a blue or rare steak, keep the heat fierce for the whole cooking time. For better-done steaks, lower the temperature to medium after the initial good browning. Length of cooking time varies according to the type of steak, the degree of heat, etc. Cooking times, assuming a good hot pan, would be very approximately as below.
4 Serve each steak topped with a slice of Maître d'Hôtel Butter.

Sirloin		Fillet	
Blue steak:	1 minute per side	Blue steak:	1½ minutes per side
Rare steak:	1½ minutes per side	Rare steak:	2¼ minutes per side
Medium rare:	2 minutes per side	Medium rare:	3¼ minutes per side
Medium steak:	2¼ minutes per side	Medium steak:	4½ minutes per side

wine: **MEDIUM RED**

Green Peppercorn Steaks

SERVES 4

2 teaspoons canned or frozen green peppercorns
oil
4 × 2.5 cm|1 in thick fillet steaks

2 tablespoons brandy
2 tablespoons double cream
salt

1 Rinse the peppercorns if they are canned.
2 Brush a frying pan with oil. Heat until hot. Fry the steaks as fast as you dare on both sides, until done to your liking (see chart in previous recipe).
3 Pour in the brandy and set alight.
4 When the flames subside, remove the steaks to a warmed serving dish.
5 Add the peppercorns, cream and a pinch or two of salt to the pan. Mix well, scraping up any sediment. Boil up and pour over the steaks.

wine: **FULL RED**

Grilled Steak

SERVES 4

4 fillet steaks, cut 2 cm | ¾ in thick, or 4 sirloin
  steaks, cut 2.5 cm | 1 in thick
salt and freshly ground black pepper

butter, melted
Maître d'Hôtel Butter (see page 134)

1 Season the steaks with pepper. Leave to warm to room temperature if they have been chilled. Sprinkle lightly with salt just before cooking.

2 Preheat the grill to its highest setting. Do not start cooking until it is at maximum temperature.

3 Brush the grill rack and steak with a little melted butter.

4 Grill the steak quickly on both sides. For a blue or rare steak, keep the heat fierce for the whole cooking time. For better-done steaks, lower the temperature to medium after the initial good browning. Length of cooking time varies according to the thickness of the meat, the type of steak, the efficiency of the grill, etc. With experience it is possible to tell from the feel of the steak how well cooked it is – it feels very soft when blue, very firm when medium. But if you want to be certain, there is nothing for it but to cut a tiny slit in the fattest part of the meat and take a look. Don't do this until you are fairly sure that the steak is ready – too many cuts will mean loss of juices. Cooking times, assuming a good hot grill, will be approximately as below:

5 Serve each steak topped with a slice of maître d'hôtel butter.

Sirloin		Fillet	
Blue:	1¼ minutes per side	Blue:	2¼ minutes per side
Rare:	1¾ minutes per side	Rare:	3¼ minutes per side
Medium rare:	2¼ minutes per side	Medium rare:	4¼ minutes per side
Medium:	2¾ minutes per side	Medium:	5 minutes per side

wine: **FULL RED**

Hamburger

SERVES 4

675 g | 1½ lb minced lean beef steak
1 small onion, grated (optional)
2 tablespoons chopped fresh parsley or mixed herbs

1 teaspoon Worcestershire sauce (optional)
salt and freshly ground black pepper

1 Preheat the grill.
2 Mix all the ingredients together with a fork. Check the seasoning.
3 With wet hands, shape the meat into flattish rounds, making sure that they are equal in size. Make a slight dip in the centre. They will shrink and thicken when they cook.
4 Grill steadily, turning once. Allow 3 minutes each side for rare burgers, 5 for well done.
5 Serve on a warmed dish, or between heated soft buns sliced in half.

NOTE: See pages 802–5 for relishes.

wine: **MEDIUM RED**

Kibbeh

This recipe for stuffed cracked wheat shells has been adapted from one by Claudia Roden in her book *Middle Eastern Food*.

For the shells

225 g | 8 oz bulghur (cracked wheat)
450 g | 1 lb minced beef
1 onion, roughly chopped
salt and freshly ground black pepper

1 tablespoon chopped fresh parsley
1 tablespoon chopped fresh mint
salt and freshly ground black pepper
sunflower oil for deep-frying

For the filling

1 onion, finely chopped
2 tablespoons sunflower oil
55 g | 2 oz pinenuts
285 g | 10 oz minced beef
1 teaspoon ground cinnamon
½ teaspoon ground allspice

To serve

plain yoghurt
sesame oil

To garnish

sprigs of watercress

1 First make the shells: Prepare the cracked wheat according to the manufacturer's instructions.
2 Process the mince, onion, salt and pepper together in a food processor. Drain the cracked wheat and process, in batches, with the beef mixture, until very soft. Knead well by hand.
3 Make the filling: fry the onion in the oil until soft but not brown, add the pinenuts and fry until golden-brown. Remove the onion and pinenuts and reserve. Add the mince and fry until lightly browned all over. Add the cinnamon, allspice, parsley, mint, salt and pepper. Return the onion and pinenuts to the mince.
4 With wet hands, take a small egg-sized portion of the shell mixture and roll into a ball. Make a hole in the centre and shape into a thin-walled pot with a pointed bottom by turning and pressing it in your palm.

5 Put some stuffing inside the hole and pinch the top of the pot together to seal it. Shape the top to a point. Repeat with the rest of the mixture, wetting your hands frequently.

6 Heat the oil in a deep-fryer until a crumb sizzles and fry 4–5 kibbeh at a time until golden-brown. Drain well on absorbent kitchen paper.

7 Flavour the yoghurt with sesame oil.

8 Arrange the kibbeh on a warmed serving plate, garnish with watercress and hand the yoghurt sauce separately.

wine: **FULL RED**

Tournedos Chasseur

SERVES 4

4 slices of white bread, crusts removed

oil for frying

55 g | 2 oz butter

4 × 170 g | 6 oz fillet steaks

1 shallot, finely chopped

110 g | 4 oz field mushrooms, sliced dry

1 tablespoon dry white wine or Madeira

290 ml | ½ pint demi-glace sauce (see page 116), or
   good beef gravy, slightly thickened

1 teaspoon chopped fresh chervil

1 Trim each slice of bread into a round or octagonal croûte. Heat some oil in a frying pan and fry the bread on both sides until crisp and brown. Keep warm on a serving platter.

2 Heat 1 teaspoon of the oil in a heavy frying pan and cook the steaks on both sides until done to your liking (4–5 minutes a side for well done, 1–2 minutes a side for rare). Lift them out when ready and place on top of the croûtes. Keep warm.

3 Melt the butter in the same pan in which you fried the steaks. Add the shallot and cook over a medium heat until just turning colour. Add the remaining butter and fry the mushrooms in this, scraping the bottom of the pan to loosen any of the sediment left from the fried steaks, to add flavour to the sauce.

4 After about 2 minutes, pour in first the wine, then the demi-glace sauce. Allow to bubble rapidly to reduce and thicken to a coating consistency. Add the chervil and spoon carefully over the steaks.

wine: **FULL RED**

Beef Stroganoff

SERVES 4

450 g | 1 lb fillet of beef

55 g | 2 oz butter

1 medium onion, thinly sliced

225 g | 8 oz mushrooms, thinly sliced

100 ml | 3½ fl oz dry white wine

150 ml | ¼ pint brown stock (see page 102)

1 tablespoon oil

2 tablespoons brandy

salt and freshly ground black pepper

2 tablespoons double cream

2 tablespoons soured cream

1 Cut the beef into 5 cm | 2 in strips, the thickness of a finger.

2 Melt half the butter in a frying pan and cook the onion over a low heat until soft and transparent. Add the mushrooms and toss over the heat for 1 minute. Add the wine and stock. Boil rapidly to reduce to about 2 tablespoons. Stir well, then pour into a bowl, scraping the pan.

3 Now heat the oil and the remaining butter in the pan until very hot but not smoking. Drop in the beef strips. Fry over fast heat to brown and seal the edges without over-cooking the middle. Remove the strips to a plate as they are browned. Then reduce the heat.

4 Pour the brandy into the hot pan. Set it alight. As soon as the flames subside, pour in the mushroom and stock mixture. Return the beef strips to the pan and stir in the double cream. Season the sauce to taste with salt and pepper. If the sauce is too thin, remove the beef strips and boil rapidly to reduce to a syrupy consistency.

5 Reheat, then tip into a warmed serving dish and fork the soured cream in roughly. If the soured cream is very thick it can be diluted slightly with a little water.

NOTE: The essence of a perfect Beef Stroganoff is the speed at which the beef strips are cooked. If using tougher meat, there is nothing for it but to stew the beef gently (after adding the mushrooms and stock) until tender. This alternative can be very good.

wine: **MEDIUM RED**

Mixed Grill

Grilling times depend on the thickness of the ingredients and the temperature of the grill. The suggestions below should be regarded as guidelines only.

SERVES 1

110 g | 4 oz rump or sirloin steak
oil
freshly ground black pepper
55 g | 2 oz calves' liver
1 chipolata sausage
1 lamb's kidney
1 rasher of back bacon

1 whole tomato
2 large flat mushrooms
salt and freshly ground black pepper

To garnish
1 bunch of watercress

When preparing a mixed grill, begin by grilling the meat that will take the longest time to cook and then gradually add the other ingredients so that everything is ready at the same time.

Steak: Flatten the steak slightly, brush it with oil and season with pepper. Do not use salt as this drains out the juices and makes the meat tough and dry. It should be salted just before cooking.

Liver: Remove the membrane that surrounds the liver, cut into thin pieces, brush with oil and season with pepper.

Chipolata sausages: Prick with a fork to allow the fat to escape during cooking. Do not add any extra fat.

Kidney: Skin and halve the kidney, snipping out the core. Brush with oil and season with pepper.

Bacon: Cut off the rind. Put the bacon on a board and, using the back of a knife, stretch it. This helps to prevent shrinking and curling during grilling.

Tomato: Cut in half, brush with a little oil and season with salt and pepper.

Mushrooms: Wipe and peel the mushrooms, cut the stalk to 1 cm | $\frac{1}{2}$ in, brush with oil and season with salt and pepper.

1 Preheat the grill to its highest setting.
2 When very hot, place the chipolata sausage under it. Turn as it browns.
3 After 5 minutes, add the liver and the kidney.
4 After 1 further minute, add the steak and bacon. Grill for 1 minute.
5 Turn over all the ingredients and grill for 1 further minute.
6 Add the tomatoes and mushrooms and grill for a further 2 minutes or so, turning over the ingredients as necessary.
7 As the items are ready, put them on to a warmed serving platter, draining the fat from the sausage and bacon carefully. Just before serving, garnish with sprigs of watercress.

NOTE: Mixed grill is traditionally served with potato chips or straw potatoes.

wine: FULL RED

Steak Wellington

SERVES 4

4   170 g | 6 oz fillet steaks or tournedos
salt and freshly ground black pepper
Worcestershire sauce
30 g | 1 oz beef dripping or 1 tablespoon oil
55 g | 2 oz flat mushrooms, chopped
85 g | 3 oz chicken liver pâté (see page 213)
225 g | 8 oz flour quantity rough puff pastry (see page 565)
beaten egg

To serve
290 ml | $\frac{1}{2}$ pint wild mushroom sauce (see page 125)

To garnish
watercress

1 Preheat the oven to 230°C|450°F|gas mark 8. Trim any fat or membranes from the steaks. Season with pepper and a few drops of Worcestershire sauce.

2 Heat the dripping or oil in a frying pan and brown the steaks quickly on both sides. The outside should be brown, the middle absolutely raw. Reserve the frying pan unwashed. Leave the meat to cool on a wire rack (this is to allow the fat to drip off the steaks rather than cooling and congealing on them).

3 Cook the mushrooms in the frying pan. Tip into a bowl.

4 Beat the mushrooms into the pâté. Check the seasoning. Spread one side of each steak with the mixture. Roll out the pastry until it is about the thickness of a £1 coin. Cut into 4 × 18 cm|7 in squares.

5 Place each steak, pâté side down, on a piece of pastry. Brush the edges with water and draw them together over the steak, making a neat and well-sealed parcel. Place them on a damp baking sheet, pâté side up, and brush with beaten egg. Make a small slit in the top of each parcel so that the steam can escape. Decorate with leaves made from the pastry trimmings. Brush these with egg too. Place in the refrigerator for 30 minutes to allow the pastry to become firm.

6 Now brush the steak parcels with a little more beaten egg. Bake for 15 minutes, or until the pastry is golden-brown and the meat pink.

7 Meanwhile, reheat the sauce.

8 Arrange the steaks on a warmed serving plate. Garnish with watercress and serve the sauce separately.

wine: **MEDIUM RED**

Fillet of Beef en Croûte

SERVES 8–10

1.8 kg|4 lb piece of fillet from the thick end
freshly ground black pepper
Worcestershire sauce (optional)
30 g|1 oz beef dripping or 1 tablespoon oil
340 g|12 oz flour quantity puff pastry (see page 566)

110 g|4 oz flat mushrooms, very finely chopped
30 g|1 oz butter
110 g|4 oz chicken liver pâté (see page 213)
beaten egg

1 Preheat the oven to 230°C|450°F|gas mark 8.

2 Skin and trim the fillet and season well with pepper and Worcestershire sauce, if using. Heat the dripping or oil in a roasting pan and when hot add the meat and brown on all sides. Roast for 20 minutes.

3 Remove the fillet from the roasting pan and allow to cool.

4 Take one-third of the pastry and roll it on a floured board until it is a little more than the length and breadth of the fillet. Place it on a damp baking sheet, prick all over with a fork and bake in the oven for about 20 minutes, until golden-brown. Do not turn the oven off. Place the pastry on a wire rack and leave to cool.

5 Fry the mushrooms quickly in the butter in a frying pan. Mix with the pâté and spread

the mixture over the cooked pastry base. Place the cold fillet on top of this and, with a sharp knife, cut away any pastry that is not covered by the fillet.

6 Roll the remaining pastry on a floured board into a 'blanket' large enough to cover the fillet easily. Lift up the 'blanket' and lay it gently over the fillet. With a sharp knife, cut off the corners of the 'blanket' and reserve these trimmings.

7 Lift one length of the 'blanket' and brush the underside with beaten egg. With a palette knife, lift the base and tuck the 'blanket' neatly underneath it. Repeat with the other 3 sides. Shape the pastry trimmings into leaves. Brush the pastry-covered fillet with beaten egg. Decorate with the pastry leaves and brush again with beaten egg. Chill until the pastry feels hard.

8 Bake the fillet in the oven for 20 minutes, or until the pastry is very dark brown and shiny. This recipe assumes that rare beef is desired, but longer cooking in the first instance, without the pastry, will ensure a more well-done fillet. For medium beef, cook for a further 10 minutes and for well-done beef, a further 15 minutes.

9 Serve hot or cold. If served hot, the fillet should be carved at the table or the juices will be lost and the meat may have a grey, unappetizing look.

NOTE: The dish may be prepared in advance up to the final baking. It should be left ready for the oven on the baking sheet, loosely covered with clingfilm or kitchen foil to prevent the egg glaze from drying. If prepared in advance, it is important that the mushrooms and pâté should be completely cold before mixing together, and that the meat should be cold before covering with the pastry.

wine: MEDIUM RED

Beef en Gêlée

SERVES 4

450 g | 1 lb centre piece of beef fillet
salt and freshly ground black pepper
55 g | 2 oz butter, softened
170 g | 6 oz good-quality duck liver pâté
¼ teaspoon Dijon mustard
2 teaspoons dry sherry

4 slices of very good-quality cooked ham
850 ml | 1½ pints aspic (see page 105)

To garnish

2 tomatoes, peeled and deseeded
4 sprigs of fresh chervil

1 Fill a saucepan large enough to hold the beef with water and bring to the boil.

2 Tie the beef fillet into a neat shape. Poach for 9–10 minutes. Season with salt and pepper.

3 Remove from the water and leave to get completely cold.

4 Beat the butter into the duck pâté, a little at a time. Add the mustard and sherry and season to taste with salt and pepper. Set aside.

5 Cut the cold beef fillet into 4 even-sized steaks about 1 cm | ½ in thick. Spread a layer of pâté on top of each steak. Lay a slice of ham on top of the layer of pâté and press down lightly. Trim the edges neatly.

6 Set a thin layer of aspic in a sandwich tin large enough to hold the beef.

7 Put the steaks into the tin and carefully spoon in enough liquid, but cold, aspic just to cover them. Leave to set in the refrigerator.

8 Meanwhile, prepare the garnish: cut the tomato flesh into small diamond shapes and pick over the chervil.

9 Dip the garnish in the aspic then arrange on top of the steaks and coat again, very carefully, with a little cold aspic. Leave to set in the refrigerator.

9 Pour any remaining aspic into a shallow tray and chill until firm, then dice.

10 To serve: cut round the steaks with a warmed round or oval cutter. Place on individual plates and garnish with the diced aspic.

wine: MEDIUM RED

English Roast Beef

SERVES 10

2.3 kg | 5 lb sirloin or rib roast of beef
a little dry English mustard
salt and freshly ground black pepper

To serve

horseradish cream (see page 111)

1 Weigh the beef to calculate the cooking time (see stage 5 below).

2 Preheat the oven to 220°C | 425°F | gas mark 7.

3 Place the beef in a roasting pan and sprinkle with salt, a little mustard and plenty of pepper.

4 Roast for 20 minutes.

5 Turn the oven temperature down to 160°C | 325°F | gas mark 3 and roast for 20 minutes per 450 g | 1 lb for medium meat or 10–15 minutes for very rare. Serve with horseradish cream in a separate dish.

NOTES: If allowed to rest for 20 minutes before serving, the meat will be easier to carve, and juicer.

If thickened gravy is required in addition to 'God's gravy' – the juices that will run from the meat before and during carving – pour off the fat and juices from the roasting tin. Return 2 tablespoons of fat to the pan. Add 2 tablespoons flour to the fat and stir over the heat until the flour has browned and any sediment from the bottom of the pan is loosened. Add up to 570 ml | 1 pint of stock and stir or whisk until boiling. Season to taste with salt and pepper. Simmer for 2–3 minutes.

wine: FULL RED

Yorkshire Pudding

SERVES 4

110 g | 4 oz plain flour

a good pinch of salt

2 eggs, beaten

290 ml | ½ pint milk or milk (200 ml | 7 fl oz) and water (90 ml | 3 fl oz) mixed

4 tablespoons good beef dripping or 2 tablespoons oil

1 Sift the flour and salt into a bowl. Make a well in the centre and add the eggs.

2 Beat the eggs with a wooden spoon, gradually drawing in more flour to the centre.

3 Add the milk little by little until the batter is smooth. Chill for at least 30 minutes before use.

4 Preheat the oven to 200°C | 400°F | gas mark 6.

5 Heat the dripping or oil until very hot in a roasting pan, flameproof dish or Yorkshire pudding tin.

6 Pour in the batter. Bake for 40 minutes, or until the pudding is risen and golden. Yorkshire puddings baked in individual patty moulds take about 15 minutes and 25 minutes in muffin tins.

NOTE: If making the pudding as a sweet course, use flavourless oil instead of dripping and serve with honey, treacle or maple syrup.

Spiced Beef

This recipe takes 8 days to complete.

SERVES 8

1 clove of garlic

1.35 kg | 3 lb boneless sirloin of beef

55 g | 2 oz soft light brown sugar

30 g | 1 oz ground allspice

2–3 bay leaves, chopped

85 g | 3 oz salt

about 450 g | 1 lb plain flour

1 Peel the garlic and cut it into thin slivers. Stick these into the beef. Rub the surface of the joint with the sugar.

2 Refrigerate for 12 hours. Mix together the allspice, bay leaves and salt.

3 Take a little of the salt mixture and rub it well into the meat.

4 Keep for a week, turning and rubbing with more salt and spice each day.

5 Preheat the oven to 190°C | 375°F | gas mark 5.

6 Mix the flour with water to make enough of a fairly thick, doughy paste to completely envelop the beef.

7 Wrap the joint in the paste.

8 Put it, paste and all, into a roasting pan and pour in a small cup of water. Bake for $1\frac{1}{4}$ hours.

9 Remove from the oven and allow to cool. Snip off the crust and discard it before serving the beef.

NOTE: This is especially good eaten cold with Cumberland sauce (see page 131) or a sweet pickle.

wine: **FULL RED**

Rogan Josh

SERVES 4

675 g | 1½ lb leg of lamb, boned	150 ml | ¼ pint plain yoghurt
4 tablespoons vegetable oil	1 teaspoon fennel seeds
4 bay leaves	2 teaspoons ground cumin
6 cardamom pods	2 teaspoons ground coriander
5 cm | 2 in cinnamon stick	1 teaspoon chilli powder
6 cloves	200 ml | 7 fl oz water
1 medium onion, finely chopped	salt
4 cloves of garlic	½ teaspoon garam masala
5 cm | 2 in piece of fresh root ginger, peeled	4 teaspoons paprika

1 Cut the lamb into 2.5 cm | 1 in cubes.

2 Heat the oil in a medium saucepan and fry a few pieces of lamb at a time until browned. Reheat the oil after each addition and add more oil if necessary.

3 Add the bay leaves, cardamom, cinnamon, cloves and onion to the pan and fry until the onion is lightly browned.

4 Blend the garlic, ginger and yoghurt in a food processor. Grind the fennel to a fine powder and add to the cumin and coriander.

5 Add the ground spices to the onion in the pan and cook for 1 minute. Add the lamb and any juices and stir until well mixed. Add the yoghurt mixture, chilli powder, water and salt to taste, and bring slowly to the boil. Cover the pan, lower the heat and simmer for $1\text{-}1\frac{1}{2}$ hours.

6 Just before serving, add the garam masala and paprika and heat through.

NOTE: As Rogan Josh should be red in colour, it is best to add the paprika at the end of the cooking time to retain its redness.

wine: **SPICY RED OR BEER**

Steak Tartare

The beef in this recipe is served raw, so it is essential that it is top quality and very fresh.

SERVES 4

450 g | 1 lb fillet or rump steak
salt and freshly ground black pepper
about 4 tablespoons salad oil
3 egg yolks
Worcestershire sauce (optional)
about 3 tablespoons finely chopped onion

about 1 tablespoon finely chopped green pepper
about 1 tablespoon chopped fresh parsley

To garnish
crisp lettuce

1 Chop or mince the steak finely and mix with all the other ingredients.
2 Shape into 4 rounds and arrange on a serving dish. Garnish with the lettuce.

NOTES: To cater for varying tastes, in restaurants this dish is mixed to the customer's requirements at the table. The meat is presented in a hamburger shape on the plate, with the egg yolk in a half shell sitting on the top of it, and surrounded by the prepared chopped vegetables. The waiter then proceeds to beat the flavourings, oil and yolk into the meat with a fork.

Steak tartare is sometimes garnished with anchovy fillets or even caviar.

Steak tartare is surprisingly good with hot potatoes of some kind, rather than a salad. Chips or matchstick potatoes are best.

wine: **FULL RED**

Boeuf Philippe

SERVES 6

560 g | 1¼ lb fillet of beef (ends will do)
Worcestershire sauce
freshly ground black pepper
1 tablespoon beef dripping or oil
½ cauliflower
170 g | 6 oz French beans
3 tomatoes

½ teaspoon horseradish sauce
1 clove of garlic, crushed
3 tablespoons French dressing (see page 123)
8 black olives, pitted

To garnish
1 bunch of watercress

1 Preheat the oven to 200°C | 400°F; | gas mark 6.
2 Season the meat with Worcestershire sauce and pepper. Heat the dripping or oil in a roasting pan over direct heat and add the beef. Brown evenly on all sides. If the beef is in one thick piece, roast it in the oven for 15 minutes, less if it is thin or in smaller pieces. It should be pink inside. Remove from the oven and allow to cool.
3 Wash the cauliflower and cut into florets. Plunge these into a saucepan of boiling water and cook for 4–5 minutes. Drain. Rinse briefly under cold water. Drain again.

4 Wash and top and tail the beans. Cook in boiling salted water for 5 minutes, then rinse under cold running water and drain.

5 Plunge the tomatoes into boiling water for 10 seconds, then put into cold water. Peel and cut into quarters.

6 Add the horseradish sauce and garlic to the French dressing. The salad is now ready for assembly but this should not be done until just before serving. The beef will lose its colour if dressed too soon, and the salad will look tired if left to stand.

7 Cut the beef into thin slices and then into thin strips, cutting across the grain of the meat. Place in a bowl with the other ingredients, reserving 1 tomato and 4 olives for decoration.

8 Mix in three-quarters of the French dressing and pile into a serving dish. Place the reserved tomatoes and olives on top of the dish and brush with a little French dressing. Garnish with the watercress dipped into the remaining dressing.

wine: **FULL RED**

Sesame Beef Salad

SERVES 6

450 g | 1 lb sirloin steak, about 5 cm | 2 in thick
oil for frying
225 g | 8 oz button mushrooms, sliced
225 g | 8 oz mangetout, topped, tailed and blanched

For the marinade
2 onions, thinly sliced
5 tablespoons dry sherry
5 tablespoons light soy sauce
3 tablespoons sesame oil
plenty of freshly ground black pepper

For the dressing
6 tablespoons grapeseed or sunflower oil
3 tablespoons white wine vinegar
1 tablespoon Dijon mustard
1 teaspoon clear honey

1 Remove any fat or gristle from the steak.

2 Mix together the marinade ingredients, add the steak and leave to marinate overnight in the refrigerator. Turn the steak occasionally if not completely submerged in the marinade.

3 Place the dressing ingredients in a bowl and whisk until well emulsified.

4 Remove the beef from the marinade. Strain the marinade (reserving the onions and marinade). Heat a little oil in a frying pan and brown the steak well on both sides. Cook as desired (see page 465). Remove the steak, place on a wire rack and leave to get completely cold.

5 Add the onions from the marinade to the frying pan and cook over a medium heat until soft and golden brown. Lift out and place in the dressing.

6 Add the mushrooms and the marinade to the frying pan and cook until the marinade has become syrupy. Add to the dressing and allow to get completely cold.

7 When all the ingredients are cold, cut the steak into very thin strips and add to the dressing with the mangetout. Toss together and pile on to a serving dish.

wine: **FULL RED**

Dried-fried Shredded Beef

SERVES 4–6

450 g | 1 lb lean beef, such as rump steak, or top round

3–4 oz | 85–110 g carrots, cut into julienne strips

3–4 sticks of celery, cut into julienne strips

½ teaspoon salt

2½ cups of oil for deep-frying

1 teaspoon cornflour

2–3 dried red chillis, halved and deseeded

½ teaspoon ground roasted Sichuan peppercorns

1 teaspoon sesame oil

For the marinade

2 tablespoons light soy sauce

2 teaspoons sugar

1 tablespoon Shaoxing wine or dry sherry

1 teaspoon sesame oil

½ teaspoon ground roasted Sichuan peppercorns

For the thickening

1–1½ teaspoons cornflour

scant 1 teaspoon sugar

4 tablespoons water

1 Shred the beef across the grain into pencil-like strips 7.5 cm | 3 in long. Put into a bowl.

2 Add all the ingredients for the marinade and combine well. Allow to stand at room temperature for 45–60 minutes so that the marinade permeates every sliver of beef.

3 Put the carrots and celery into a bowl and add a pinch of salt to draw out the water. Leave for 20–30 minutes, then drain. Pat dry, if necessary.

4 Mix the ingredients for the thickening in a small bowl and set aside.

5 Heat the oil in a wok until very hot. Remove the beef from the marinade and coat evenly with the cornflour. Tip the beef gently into the oil and deep-fry for 2–3 minutes, or until crisp. Turn off the heat, remove the beef with a slotted spoon and drain on absorbent kitchen paper. Sieve the oil into a container for future use. Wash and dry the wok.

6 Reheat the wok over a medium heat until hot. Add 2 tablespoons oil and swirl it around. Tip in the chillis and fry until dark in colour. Remove and discard. Add the carrots and celery. Stir for a few minutes until dry before adding the beef. Continue to stir over a low heat for a further 1–2 minutes, or until everything is quite dry and crisp. Add the thickening and stir until the beef is coated.

7 Sprinkle with the ground Sichuan peppercorns and sesame oil before serving.

wine: **MEDIUM RED**

Lancashire Hotpot

SERVES 4

900 g | 2 lb middle neck of mutton or lamb

3 lambs' kidneys (optional)

900 g | 2 lb potatoes

salt and freshly ground black pepper

1 teaspoon chopped fresh thyme or a pinch of dried thyme

2 large onions, thinly sliced

2 carrots, sliced

1 bay leaf

570 ml | 1 pint brown stock (see page 102)

55 g | 2 oz butter

1 Preheat the oven to 180°C | 350°F | gas mark 4.
2 Cut the meat into chops, trimming away most of the fat.
3 Skin, split, core and quarter the kidneys.
4 Wash and peel the potatoes, discard any eyes and cut into slices about 5 mm | ¼ in thick.
5 Butter a casserole dish and line it with a layer of potatoes. Season well with salt, pepper and thyme.
6 Layer the chops, sliced onions, carrots and kidneys on top of the potatoes, seasoning well with salt, pepper and thyme and adding the bay leaf when the casserole is half full. Finish with a neat layer of potatoes overlapping each other.
7 Pour in enough stock to come to the bottom of the top layer of potatoes.
8 Brush the top with plenty of melted butter and season well with salt and pepper.
9 Cover the casserole and bake in the oven for about 2 hours.
10 Remove the lid and continue to cook for a further 30–40 minutes, until the potatoes are brown and crisp and the meat is completely tender.

wine: **FULL RED**

Navarin of Lamb

SERVES 4

900 g | 2 lb middle neck of lamb

salt and freshly ground black pepper

2 tablespoons dripping or oil

1 tablespoon plain flour

1 litre | 1¾ pints brown stock (see page 102)

1 clove of garlic, crushed

1 tablespoon tomato purée

1 bouquet garni (parsley, bay leaf and a stick of celery, tied together with string)

12 button onions, peeled

a pinch of caster sugar

1 turnip, cut into sticks

3 carrots, cut into sticks

3 potatoes, peeled and cut into chunks

1 Cut the lamb into pieces and season with salt and pepper.
2 Heat 1 tablespoon of the dripping or oil in a heavy saucepan and brown the meat on all sides. Pour off the fat into a frying pan. Sprinkle the meat with the flour. Cook for 1

minute, then stir in the stock, garlic and tomato purée. Add the bouquet garni. Stir until boiling, then simmer for 1 hour. Skim off any surface fat.

3 Heat a little more fat and soften and brown first the onions with the sugar, then the turnips, carrots and potatoes, adding more dripping or oil as needed.

4 Add the browned vegetables to the meat stew, cover tightly and continue cooking over a low heat, or in a moderate oven, for a further 30–40 minutes or until the meat is tender. Taste for seasoning.

5 Remove the bouquet garni. Allow the navarin to stand for 5 minutes, then skim off the surface fat. Boil to thicken if necessary. Spoon the stew into a warmed serving dish.

NOTE: Fresh peas or beans are sometimes added to the navarin after the final skimming. The stew must then be cooked until they are just tender.

wine: **FULL RED**

Noisettes of Lamb with Bacon and Sweet Onion Purée

SERVES 4

2 × 6–7 bone best end necks of lamb, chined
10 rashers of streaky rindless bacon
2 tablespoons oil

For the purée

30 g | 1 oz butter
2 large onions, very finely chopped

To garnish

1 small bunch of watercress

1 First prepare the lamb (see page 448). Surround with the bacon and tie each best end into 4–5 noisettes.

2 Make the purée: melt the butter in a frying pan, add the onions, cover with a dampened piece of greaseproof paper and a lid and cook slowly until absolutely soft (this may well take 45 minutes). Increase the heat and cook until the onions are browned but not burnt. Liquidize in a blender, then push through a sieve.

3 Fry the lamb in the oil till the bacon is cooked, then cut each into 4–5 noisettes. Brown the cut sides of the noisettes. Remove the string and arrange the noisettes on warmed serving plates. Garnish with watercress and serve the warm onion purée separately.

wine: **MEDIUM RED**

Collops of Lamb with Onion and Mint Sauce

This dish can also be made with lamb noisettes or cutlets: simply grill until tender.

SERVES 4

2 6–7 bone racks of lamb

thick onion and mint sauce (see page 128)

For the sauce

bones from the racks of lamb

1 carrot, chopped

1 onion, chopped

2 teaspoons plain flour

1 teaspoon tomato purée

570 ml|1 pint water

1 bay leaf

1 sprig of fresh mint

1 clove of garlic, crushed

1 Preheat the oven to 240°C|475°F|gas mark 8.

2 Prepare the meat: trim the fat from the rack of lamb and place in a roasting pan in the oven to render down. Reserve this dripping to brown the collops and the bones.

3 Remove the 'eye' or fillet from the best ends in one piece and trim off all the fat and gristle.

4 Prepare the sauce: cut up the remains of the rack of lamb and brown over a medium heat in a little of the dripping. Remove from the pan.

5 Add the carrots and onions and cook until well browned. Add the flour and cook, stirring until lightly coloured, then add the tomato purée and cook for 1 further minute.

6 Return the bones to the pan and add the water, herbs and garlic. Bring to the boil and leave to simmer for at least 1 hour.

7 Strain the sauce, and skim off any fat. Reduce, by boiling rapidly until syrupy, and season to taste with salt and pepper.

8 Brown the meat quickly in a little dripping and then place in the oven, still at 240°C|475°F|gas mark 8, for 10 minutes. Remove from the oven and leave for 5 minutes to allow the juices to set before carving.

9 Warm 4 dinner plates. Heat the sauce and the onion and mint purée. Place a spoonful of the purée on each plate. Slice the fillet and arrange, in overlapping slices, on top of the purée. Spoon over some of the sauce and serve the remainder separately in a warmed sauceboat.

wine: **FULL RED**

Lamb Daube

SERVES 4

900 g | 2 lb lamb (preferably from the shoulder)

For the marinade
290 ml | ½ pint red wine
1 medium onion, cut into thick slices
1 clove of garlic, bruised
4 whole allspice berries
1 tablespoon oil

110 g | 4 oz streaky bacon, diced
1 onion, chopped
150 ml | ¼ pint brown stock (see page 102)
55 g | 2 oz plain flour
1 bouquet garni (1 bay leaf, a sprig each of fresh
   thyme, rosemary and parsley, and a small strip of
   orange zest, tied together with string)

1 Trim the lamb and cut into large pieces.
2 Prepare the marinade by mixing all the ingredients together. Lay the pieces of meat in
   it and leave overnight.
3 Preheat the oven to 170°C | 325°F | gas mark 3.
4 Drain the meat from the marinade and pat the meat dry. Reserve the marinade.
5 Heat the oil in a heavy frying pan and brown the bacon and the onion. Lift out with a
   slotted spoon and place in a casserole.
6 Brown the meat in the same pan in small batches. Lay it on top of the bacon and
   onion.
7 Strain the marinade into the empty pan. Add the stock. Bring to the boil, scraping the
   bottom of the pan to loosen any sediment. Pour over the meat.
8 Immerse the bouquet garni in the liquid in the casserole.
9 Make a stiff dough by adding water to the flour. Put the lid on the casserole and press a
   band of dough around the join of the lid and the dish to seal completely.
10 Cook in the oven for 1½ hours. Remove the bouquet garni.
11 Lift the meat out and put it on a warmed serving dish. Keep warm.
12 Boil the sauce to reduce to a syrupy consistency and pour over the meat.

wine: **MEDIUM RED**

Lamb Curry

SERVES 4

30 g | 1 oz clarified butter (see page 385) or ghee
1 small onion, finely chopped
675 g | 1½ lb boneless lamb, preferably shoulder, cut
   into 4 cm | 1½ in cubes
2 teaspoons ground turmeric
½ teaspoon ground ginger
1 clove of garlic, crushed

1½ teaspoon ground coriander
¼ teaspoon salt
¼ teaspoon cayenne pepper
425 ml | ¾ pint brown stock (see page 102) or
   vegetable stock (see page 107)
1 tablespoon chopped fresh parsley
½ tablespoon chopped fresh mint

1 Melt the butter in a large saucepan and brown the onion in it. Remove to a plate.
2 Put the meat into the pan and brown all over. Add the turmeric, ginger, garlic and coriander. Return the onions to the pan and stir and cook over a low heat for 1 minute.
3 Season with salt and cayenne and add enough stock to come 1 cm | $\frac{1}{2}$ in below the top of the meat. This level should be kept constant. Bring to the boil, then cover and simmer gently for about $1\frac{1}{2}$ hours, until the meat is tender, adding more stock as necessary.
4 When the lamb is tender, remove it from the pan and keep warm. Reduce the liquid by rapid boiling. Add the parsley and mint and pour over the meat.

NOTES: More (or fewer) spices may be added according to taste.
Ghee is clarified fat sold in tins in Indian stores.

wine: LAGER OR FULL SPICY RED

Accompaniments for Curries

Banana and Coconut: Chop 2 bananas and squeeze the juice of 1 lemon over them. Mix in 2 tablespoons freshly grated coconut.

Tomato and Onion: Chop 1 large onion and 3 peeled tomatoes finely. Mix together with salt and pepper, 1 tablespoon olive oil and a squeeze of lemon juice.

Chutney and Cucumber: Mix 1 cupful chopped cucumber into the same quantity of sweet chutney (such as mango or apple).

Green Pepper, Apple and Raisin: Chop equal quantities of apple and green pepper finely, or mince them. Add 1 tablespoon raisins or sultanas and salt, pepper, lemon juice, cayenne and sugar to taste.

Poppadoms: These are large flat wafers, available in most supermarkets. They are heated in the oven or under the grill, or fried in hot fat until crisp. They can be bought spiced or plain.

Lamb Cutlets Grilled with Herbs

SERVES 4

12 French-trimmed lamb cutlets (see page 447)
30 g | 1 oz butter, melted
1 tablespoon oil

a selection of chopped fresh herbs, such as thyme, basil, mint, parsley, marjoram, rosemary
salt and freshly ground black pepper

1 Preheat the grill to its highest setting. Mix the butter and oil.
2 Brush the cutlets with melted butter and oil, sprinkle over half the herbs and season with salt and pepper.
3 Place the cutlets under the grill, about 8 cm | 3 in away from the heat, and cook for 3–4 minutes.

4 Turn them over, baste with the fat from the bottom of the pan and sprinkle over the remaining herbs.

5 Grill for 3–4 minutes (3 minutes each side should give a succulent pink cutlet, 4 minutes a well-done cutlet).

6 Arrange the cutlets on a warmed serving dish and pour over the pan juices. Serve immediately.

wine: **FULL RED**

Indonesian Mixed Meat Kebabs

SERVES 4

225 g|8 oz lean lamb, cut into 1 cm|½ in cubes

225 g|8 oz lean pork, cut into 1 cm½ in cubes

2 medium onions, blanched and quartered

1 green pepper, blanched, cored, deseeded and cut into 8

1 red pepper, blanched, cored, deseeded and cut into 8

110 g|4 oz button mushrooms

For the marinade

140 g|5 oz low-fat plain yoghurt

1 teaspoon ground ginger

1 clove of garlic, crushed

a pinch of ground cumin

a pinch of ground coriander

grated zest and juice of ½ lemon

salt and freshly ground black pepper

To garnish

1 small bunch of watercress

1 Mix the marinade ingredients in a bowl. Add the lamb and pork, then coat well. Cover and leave for several hours in a cool place, turning occasionally.

2 Preheat the grill to its highest setting.

3 Thread the ingredients on to 4 skewers alternating pieces of meat with the vegetables. Baste with any extra marinade.

4 Place under the grill and cook for 5 minutes on each side. Garnish with sprigs of watercress.

wine: **FULL SPICY RED**

Braised Lamb Shanks with Flageolet Beans

SERVES 4

4 × 450 g|1 lb lamb shanks

2 cloves of garlic, peeled and sliced

1 onion, chopped

1 bouquet garni (a baton of celery tied with a bay leaf, thyme sprig and parsley stalk)

1 bottle of Côtes du Rhône or other full-bodied red wine

250 g|9 oz dried flageolet beans

2 tablespoons vegetable oil

100 g|3½ oz smoked streaky bacon, diced

570 ml|1 pint brown stock (see page 102)

30 g|1 oz butter

2 tablespoons plain flour

salt and freshly ground black pepper

1 Remove any skin and fat from the lamb shanks. Put the lamb shanks into a large non-metallic bowl with the garlic, onion and bouquet garni. Pour over the wine. Refrigerate for 24 hours.

2 Cover the flageolet beans with water and leave to stand overnight.

3 Preheat the oven to 170°C|325°F|gas mark 3.

4 Heat the oil in a heavy sauté pan, add the onion and cook until soft. Add the bacon and cook until lightly browned. Lift out with a slotted spoon and place in a deep casserole.

5 Remove the lamb shanks, onion, and bouquet garni from the wine and pat the meat dry. Reserve the wine.

6 Brown the lamb shanks on all sides in the sauté pan and place on top of the bacon and onion. Add the wine to the pan and scrape to remove any sediment. Add the stock, bring to the boil and boil for 2 minutes.

7 Pour the wine over the lamb shanks in the casserole and add the bouquet garni. Cook in the oven for 2½ hours, or until the meat will come away from the bone easily.

8 Meanwhile, drain the flageolet beans and place in a saucepan. Cover with water and bring to the boil. Boil hard for 10 minutes, then lower the heat and simmer until tender. Drain.

9 Turn the oven temperature down to 100°C|200°F|gas mark 1.

10 Transfer the lamb, bacon and onion to a warmed serving dish. Place the beans around the meat. Cover with foil and return to the oven.

11 Discard the bouquet garni and skim off as much of the fat as possible from the sauce. Boil the sauce to reduce to approximately 570 ml|1 pint. Mix the butter and flour to a paste, then whisk it into the boiling sauce a little at a time to thicken it. Season to taste with salt and pepper and strain over the meat. Serve immediately.

wine: FULL RED

Lamb Steak Catalane with Lentils

SERVES 4

4 lamb steaks 1 cm|½ in thick, cut across the upper leg, bones removed

For the marinade
150 ml|¼ pint olive oil
6 cloves of garlic, crushed
2 tablespoons chopped fresh thyme
1 large onion, sliced
24 black peppercorns, slightly crushed
salt

For the lentils
4 onions, finely chopped
4 cloves of garlic, crushed
olive oil
225 g|8 oz (raw weight) green|brown lentils, cooked
2 tablespoons tomato purée
4 tablespoons chopped mixed fresh herbs
salt and freshly ground black pepper
sesame oil

To garnish
watercress

1 Lay the lamb steaks in a shallow dish. Pour over the oil and add all the other marinade ingredients. Leave the steaks to marinate in the refrigerator for at least 8 hours, preferably 24 hours, turning them over 2 or 3 times.

2 Sweat the onion in a little oil until completely soft and transparent. Add the garlic and cool for a further minute.

3 Add the lentils, tomato purée and herbs, season well with salt and pepper and sprinkle over sesame oil to taste. Keep warm.

4 Meanwhile, get a heavy frying pan or griddle really hot, or preheat the grill for at least 10 minutes.

5 Remove most of the oil from the steaks and put them in the hot pan or under the grill. Fry or grill, turning once, until both sides are a good brown. Like beef steaks, they can be eaten in any state from blue to well done, but if overcooked they become very tough. They are best pink in the middle. Garnish with a bouquet of watercress.

wine: MEDIUM RED

Roast Stuffed Shoulder of Lamb

SERVES 6

1.8 kg | 4 lb boned whole shoulder of lamb	½ cup cooked rice
15 g | ½ oz butter	2 tablespoons sultanas
1 large onion, finely chopped	1 small bunch of watercress
55 g | 2 oz mushrooms, sliced	
1 clove of garlic, crushed	**For the gravy**
1 tablespoon chopped mixed fresh herbs, such as	15 g | ½ oz plain flour
mint, thyme, parsley, rosemary	1 teaspoon tomato purée
a squeeze of orange juice	290 ml | ½ pint brown stock (see page 102)
salt and freshly ground black pepper	100 ml | 3½ fl oz red wine

1 Weigh the lamb and calculate its cooking time: 20 minutes to 450 g | 1 lb plus 20 minutes.

2 Preheat the oven to 220°C | 425°F | gas mark 7.

3 Melt the butter in a frying pan and add the onion. Fry over a low heat until soft.

4 Add the mushrooms, garlic, herbs and orange juice. Cook over a low heat until the mushrooms are soft. Season with salt and pepper. Cool.

5 Remove from the heat and mix with the cooked rice. Stir in the sultanas.

6 Push this stuffing into the shoulder of lamb, sewing up the edges with thin string. Place in a roasting pan.

7 Roast in the oven for 20 minutes. Then turn the temperature down to 190°C | 375°F | gas mark 5 and roast for the calculated cooking time.

8 Lift the meat from the roasting pan and keep warm on a serving platter in the turned-off oven.

9 Make the gravy: pour off most of the fat from the roasting pan, then stir in the flour to make a soft paste. Cook until brown, then add the tomato puree and cook for a further minute.

10 Add the stock and wine, and stir over the heat until the sauce boils, scraping the brown bits from the bottom of the pan as you go. Simmer for 2–3 minutes. Season to taste with salt and pepper. Strain into a warmed gravy-boat.

11 Garnish the lamb with bouquets of watercress and serve with the gravy.

wine: **MEDIUM RED**

Shoulder of Lamb Stuffed with Feta

This dish is served with a tomato and mint salsa.

SERVES 6

1.8 kg | 4 lb boned whole shoulder of lamb
85 ml | 3 fl oz red wine
15 g | ½ oz plain flour
290 ml | ½ pint brown stock (see page 102)

For the stuffing
225 g | 8 oz feta cheese, cut into 1 cm | ½ in cubes
2 teaspoons green peppercorns, rinsed
1 shallot, finely chopped
85 g | 3 oz fresh white breadcrumbs
2 tablespoons thinly sliced sun-dried tomatoes, or 2 tomatoes, peeled, deseeded and finely chopped

1 tablespoon fresh thyme leaves
1 egg, beaten
salt and freshly ground black pepper

To garnish
springs of watercress

To serve
tomato and mint salsa (see page 127)

1 Preheat the oven to 220°C | 425°F | gas mark 7.

2 Trim the lamb of any excess fat, leaving a thin layer on the outside.

3 Mix together the stuffing ingredients, beat lightly and season carefully with salt and pepper (the feta can be very salty).

4 Season the inside of the lamb and stuff it carefully. Using thin string, sew the lamb up, but not too tightly.

5 Weigh the lamb and for pink lamb allow 20 minutes per 450 g | 1 lb plus 20 minutes. For better-done lamb cook for a further 30 minutes.

6 Put the lamb into a roasting pan and roast in the oven for 20 minutes then turn the oven temperature down to 190°C | 375°F | gas mark 5 and roast for the calculated cooking time.

7 Thirty minutes before the lamb is ready, pour the wine over the joint.

8 When the lamb is cooked, remove it from the oven and place in a warm place to rest for 10 minutes.

9 Pour off all but 2 tablespoons of fat from the roasting pan, place the pan over direct heat and stir in the flour. Cook, stirring until brown. Add the stock and also any cooking juices. Bring to the boil, then simmer for 5 minutes.

10 Just before serving remove the string from the lamb. Garnish with small sprigs of watercress. Serve with the gravy and hand the tomato and mint salsa separately.

wine: FULL RED

Shoulder of Lamb 'en Ballon'

This dish is served with a sweet port gravy.

SERVES 6–8

1.8 kg | 4 lb boned shoulder of lamb
salt and freshly ground black pepper
sprigs of fresh rosemary
290 ml | ½ pint brown stock, made with lamb bones
   (see page 102) or water
150 ml | 5 fl oz port

For the seasoning in the centre of the lamb
2 tablespoons chopped fresh parsley
85 g | 3 oz smoked ham, chopped
salt and freshly ground black pepper

For the glaze
2 tablespoons redcurrant jelly

To garnish
watercress

1 Preheat the oven to 220°C | 425°F | gas mark 7.

2 Mix the seasoning ingredients together and push into the lamb, or, if the lamb has been opened out, spread it on one half and fold the other half over to cover it.

3 Using a long piece of string, tie the shoulder so that the indentations made by the string resemble the grooves in a melon or the lines between the segments of a beachball (see page 447).

4 Weigh the lamb and calculate the cooking time at 20 minutes per 450 g | 1 lb plus 20 minutes.

5 Sprinkle with salt and pepper. Scatter a few rosemary leaves on top. Pour the stock into the pan.

6 Roast in the oven for 20 minutes then turn the temperature down to 190°C | 375°F | gas mark 5 and roast for the calculated cooking time. Half an hour before the end of cooking, smear the lamb with redcurrant jelly and return to the oven.

7 Remove the string carefully and lift the lamb on to a warmed serving dish. Leave to rest for 15 minutes before serving. It will retain heat even if not placed in a warming cupboard.

8 Meanwhile, make the gravy: skim the fat from the juices in the pan. Add the port and bring to the boil. Boil vigorously until the sauce is syrupy and reduced to about 200 ml | 7 fl oz. Check the seasoning. Strain into a warmed gravy-boat. Garnish the lamb with watercress and serve with the gravy.

wine: FULL RED

Crown Roast of Lamb

SERVES 4–6

1 crown roast or 2 × 7-bone matching racks (best
  ends) of lamb, chined
55 g|2 oz butter
1 large sprig of fresh rosemary
1 bunch of watercress

To serve hot

15 g|½ oz plain flour
290 ml|½ pint brown stock, made with lamb bones
  (see page 102)
salt and freshly ground black pepper

To garnish

paper cutlet frills

1 If the butcher has not trimmed and tied the meat into a crown, follow the instructions on page 449.
2 Preheat the oven to 200°C|400°F|gas mark 6. Melt the butter in a roasting pan. Add the crumbled rosemary and put in the crown of lamb. Wrap up the ends of the bones with wet brown paper, then with kitchen foil to prevent them from burning. It is easier to cover a few bones at a time than to cover the whole crown. Brush over the melted butter.
3 Weigh the lamb and allow 20 minutes per 450 g|1 lb plus 20 minutes. Roast for the calculated cooking time. Lift out the crown.
4 Pour off the contents from the roasting pan. Skim off 2 tablespoons fat and return to the pan. Stir in the flour, scraping any sediment off the bottom of the pan. Cook over medium heat until brown. Add the stock and stir until boiling. Simmer for 2 minutes. Season to taste with salt and pepper.
5 Place a cutlet frill on each cutlet bone. Garnish with sprigs of watercress in the centre. Hand the gravy separately in a warmed gravy-boat.

wine: **FULL RED**

Rack of Lamb with Mustard and Breadcrumbs

SERVES 2

1 rack (best end) of lamb, chined, trimmed and
  skinned
4 teaspoons Dijon mustard
2 tablespoons fresh white breadcrumbs

2 tablespoons chopped mixed fresh herbs, such as
  mint, chives, parsley, thyme
¼ teaspoon salt
½ teaspoon freshly ground black pepper
1½ tablespoons unsalted butter

1 Preheat the oven to 220°C|425°F|gas mark 7.
2 Trim off as much fat as possible from the meat.
3 Mix together the mustard, breadcrumbs, herbs, salt, pepper and butter. Press a thin layer of this mixture over the rounded, skinned side of the best end. Chill in the refrigerator for 30 minutes.

4 Place, crumbed side up, in a roasting pan and roast for 25 minutes for a 7-cutlet best end, less for a smaller one. This will give pink, slightly underdone lamb.

wine: **FULL RED**

Spiced Roast Leg of Lamb with Red Onion Marmalade

SERVES 6–8

1 2–3 kg leg of lamb	110 g	4 oz raisins
4 cloves of garlic	4 sprigs of fresh thyme
1 tablespoon ground coriander	2 tablespoons olive oil
1 tablespoon ground cumin	1 bottle of fruity red wine
1 teaspoon ground cinnamon	1 tablespoon plain flour
salt and freshly ground black pepper	2–4 tablespoons soft brown sugar
4 red onions, peeled and sliced	1 tablespoon balsamic vinegar

1 Trim the lamb of any fat and membrane so that the surface of the meat is exposed.

2 Peel the garlic and cut into slivers, then make small slits in the meat with the point of a sharp knife and insert the slivers into the slits.

3 Mix together the coriander, cumin and cinnamon and rub into the lamb. Sprinkle with salt and pepper. Set aside.

4 Preheat the oven to 170°C|325°F|gas mark 3.

5 Place the onions in a casserole large enough to hold the lamb or a roasting pan. Scatter over the raisins and the thyme.

6 Heat the oil in a frying pan over a medium heat. Brown the lamb lightly on all sides, taking care not to allow the spices to burn.

7 Place the lamb on top of the onions. Pour the wine into the frying pan and bring to the boil, scraping the base of the pan to remove any sediment. Pour over the lamb.

8 Cover the lamb with a lid or a tent of kitchen foil. Cook in the oven for 4–4½ hours or until very tender, turning the lamb every 30 minutes.

9 Place the lamb on a warmed serving platter and tent with kitchen foil to keep warm.

10 Make the sauce: skim the fat from the meat juices. Mix 1½ tablespoons of the fat with the flour and reserve. Sieve the cooking juices in a saucepan reserving the onions and raisins. Bring to the boil and boil to reduce by half. Whisk in the flour paste and boil until thickened.

11 Meanwhile, place the onions and raisins in a saucepan. Stir in the sugar to taste and cook, stirring frequently, until caramelized. Stir in the vinegar and place in a warmed serving bowl.

12 When the sauce is of a light syrupy consistency, strain through a sieve, pour into a warmed sauce boat and hand separately with the lamb, accompanied by the red onion marmalade.

wine: **FULL, SPICY RED**

Roast Saddle of Lamb

A saddle of lamb is a cut consisting of both loins, left in a single piece. It can weigh anything from 2–4.5 kg | 4½ –10 lb. New Zealand lamb cuts are generally smaller than British.

1 saddle of lamb
dripping
1 clove of garlic, peeled and cut into slivers
  (optional)
salt and freshly ground black pepper
sprigs of fresh rosemary

For the gravy
425 ml | ¾ pint brown stock, made with lamb bones
  (see page 102)
15 g | ½ oz plain flour

To serve
redcurrant jelly or soubise sauce (see page 113)

1 Preheat the oven to 200°C | 400°F | gas mark 6.

2 Trim off any excess fat from underneath the saddle and remove the kidneys. Trim away all but 2.5 cm | 1 in of the 2 flaps.

3 Skin the saddle: the best way to do this is to lift the skin at one corner with a sharp knife and hold it tightly in a tea-towel to prevent it slipping out of your grip. Give a sharp tug and pull off all the skin in one piece. This sounds more difficult than it is. Score the fat in a criss-cross pattern with a sharp knife.

4 Heat 2 tablespoons dripping in a roasting pan. When it is hot, add the saddle of lamb, tucking the flaps underneath and basting well.

5 If liked, stick a few slivers of garlic into the saddle near the bone. Season with salt, pepper and a scattering of rosemary. Weigh the joint and calculate the cooking time at 15 minutes per 450 g | 1 lb plus 15 minutes for pink lamb.

6 Roast for the calculated time. If the saddle is extremely large, it should be covered with damp greaseproof paper halfway through roasting to prevent it from becoming too brown.

7 Lift the meat on to a warmed serving platter. Pour away all but 2 tablespoons fat from the pan, taking care not to lose any of the juices or sediment. Stir the flour into the pan to absorb the remaining fat. Cook, stirring, over the heat for 1 minute. Add the stock and stir until boiling, taking care to scrape up any sediment stuck to the bottom of the pan. Simmer for 2 minutes and season to taste with salt and pepper.

8 To carve the saddle: cut thin strips parallel to the backbone, down the length of the meat. The thicker, chump end may be cut across in slices if preferred but the main part is usually carved lengthways (see page 452).

wine: **FULL RED**

Roast Leg of Lamb

SERVES 4

1 1.5–2 kg leg of lamb
salt and freshly ground black pepper
3 large sprigs of fresh rosemary
200 ml | 7 fl oz red wine

For the gravy

15 g | ½ oz plain flour
290 ml | ½ pint brown stock, made with lamb bones
  (see page 102)
1 teaspoon redcurrant jelly
salt and freshly ground black pepper

1 Preheat the oven to 220°C | 425°F | gas mark 7.

2 Weigh the joint and calculate the cooking time at 20 minutes per 450 g | 1 lb plus 20 minutes.

3 Wipe the lamb. Season with salt and pepper and place in a roasting pan, with the sprigs of rosemary on top.

4 Roast in the oven for 20 minutes, then reduce the oven temperature to 190°C | 375°F | gas mark 5 and roast for the calculated time. Thirty minutes before the end of cooking, pour the wine over the lamb.

5 When the lamb is cooked, the juices that run out of the meat when pierced with a skewer will be faintly pink. Remove the joint from the oven and place it on a warmed serving dish, discarding the sprigs of rosemary. Keep warm while making the gravy.

6 Carefully pour off all but 2 tablespoons fat from the roasting pan.

7 Add the flour to the fat and, using a wire whisk or wooden spoon, stir it over a low heat until a delicate brown. Remove from the heat and stir in the stock and redcurrant jelly. Return to the heat, stirring all the time, and simmer for 2 minutes.

8 Check the seasoning and strain into a warmed gravy-boat.

NOTE: For well-done lamb allow 25 minutes per 450 g | 1 lb and 20 minutes extra. When cooked the juices that run out of the meat, when pierced with a skewer, should be clear.

wine: **FULL RED**

Gigot of Lamb with Stuffed Artichoke Hearts

SERVES 4–5

1 1.5–2 kg leg of lamb
salt and freshly ground black pepper
1 clove of garlic, peeled and cut into slivers
a large pinch of fresh rosemary leaves
2 tablespoons oil
8 globe artichokes or 8 canned artichoke bottoms
225 g | 8 oz celeriac

110 g | 4 oz mashed potato
30 g | 1 oz butter
15 g | ½ oz plain flour
290 ml | ½ pint brown stock, made with lamb bones
  (see page 102)
1 teaspoon redcurrant jelly

To garnish

1 small bunch of watercress

1 Preheat the oven to 220°C|425°F|gas mark 7.

2 Wipe the lamb. Season with salt and pepper. Spike thin slivers of garlic into the meat near the bone. Sprinkle with rosemary. Weigh the lamb and calculate the cooking time at 20 minutes per 450 g|1 lb plus 20 minutes.

3 Heat the oil in a roasting pan, add the lamb, baste well and roast in the oven for 20 minutes then turn the oven temperature down to 190°C|375°F|gas mark 5 and roast for the calculated time. When pierced with a skewer, the juices that run out of the meat should be fairly pink.

4 Prepare the fresh artichokes, if using: wash them and cook in a saucepan of boiling salted water for about 45 minutes or until the leaves will pull away easily. Peel away all the leaves, keeping them, to serve with a vinaigrette dressing as a first course. Using a teaspoon, scrape out the prickly choke of each artichoke, and trim the base with a sharp knife so that it will stand steady.

5 While the artichokes are cooking, peel the celeriac and boil in salted water until quite tender. Drain well. Mash with a fork. Beat in the mashed potato, half the butter, and salt and pepper to taste.

6 Pile this mixture into the artichoke bottoms. Brush with the remaining butter and place on a greased baking sheet.

7 When the lamb is cooked, remove from the oven. Turn the oven temperature down to 150°C|300°F|gas mark 2 and put the artichokes into the oven to heat.

8 Place the lamb on a warmed serving dish.

9 Carefully pour off all but 2 tablespoons fat from the roasting pan.

10 Add the flour to the remaining fat in the pan and, using a wire whisk or wooden spoon, stir it over a low heat until a delicate brown. Remove from the heat and stir in the stock and redcurrant jelly. Return to the heat, stirring all the time, and simmer for 2 minutes.

11 Check the seasoning and strain into a warmed gravy-boat. Surround the lamb with the artichokes and garnish with bouquets of watercress.

wine: **MEDIUM RED**

Butterfly Leg of Lamb

SERVES 6–8

1 large leg of lamb, 2–3 kg|4½–6¾ lb butterfly
  boned (see page 446)
1 tablespoon soy sauce
½ onion, sliced
4 sprigs of fresh thyme
2 bay leaves
3 cloves of garlic, peeled and sliced
2 tablespoons good-quality olive oil
salt and freshly ground black pepper

For the gravy
20 g|⅔ oz flour
425 ml|¾ pint brown stock, made with lamb bones
  (see page 102)
55 ml|2 fl oz red wine

To garnish
1 small bunch of watercress

1   Weigh the boned leg of lamb and calculate the cooking time at 8 minutes per 450 g | 1 lb plus 20 minutes.
2   Open the leg of lamb and place it skin side down on a large plate. Sprinkle over the soy sauce, onion, thyme, bay leaves, garlic, oil and pepper. Fold the 2 'butterfly' ends inwards to encase the flavourings, cover and leave to marinate overnight.
3   Preheat the oven to 220°C | 425°F | gas mark 7.
4   Open out the boned leg. Sprinkle the fatty side fairly liberally with salt. Lay it, flesh side down, in a roasting pan and roast in the oven for 20 minutes, then reduce the oven temperature to 190°C | 375°F | gas mark 5 and roast for a further 8 minutes per 450 g | 1 lb.
5   Transfer the meat to a serving plate.
6   With a large metal spoon, skim off 4 tablespoons of fat and place in the roasting pan. Stir in the flour. Cook over medium heat until brown, then stir in the wine and stock. Bring to the boil and cook until syrupy. Stir well to loosen any sediment stuck to the bottom of the pan. Simmer for 4–5 minutes. Check the seasoning and add extra salt, pepper or soy sauce as necessary, then strain into a warmed gravy boat.
7   Garnish the lamb with watercress and serve the gravy separately.

wine: **MEDIUM RED**

Armenian Lamb

This is a favourite family recipe from Eithne Neame, who used to teach at Leiths School.

SERVES 6

900 g	2 lb lamb, preferably from the shoulder	30 g	1 oz plain flour
2 tablespoons vegetable oil	1 teaspoon ground cumin
2 medium onions, sliced	½ teaspoon allspice
salt and freshly ground black pepper	1 tablespoon tomato purée
1 clove of garlic, crushed	290 ml	½ pint brown stock (see page 102)

1   Trim the lamb and cut it into 5 cm | 2 in cubes.
2   Heat half the oil in a small saucepan and stir in the onions. Cover with a piece of damp greaseproof paper and a lid. Sweat for about 10 minutes until soft.
3   Heat the remaining oil in a sauté pan. Season the lamb with salt and pepper, then brown, in small batches. Transfer to a bowl.
4   In between browning the batches of meat, pour a little water into the pan and bring to the boil, scraping the bottom of the pan to loosen any sediment. Pour over the meat.
5   Remove the lid and the greaseproof paper from the onions and add the garlic. Cook for 1 further minute. Add the flour and spices and cook for a further 2 minutes.
6   Add the tomato purée and stock to the onion mixture. Bring to the boil, stirring.
7   Return the lamb to the sauté pan and pour over the onion and stock mixture. Bring to a simmer and cook, covered, for 45–60 minutes or until the meat is cooked through and tender.

wine: **SPICY RED**

Forcemeat Balls

Forcemeat balls are traditionally made to accompany jugged hare (see page 418) or Roast Turkey (see page 416).

SERVES 20–24

450 g | 1 lb good-quality pork sausagemeat

1 medium onion, very finely chopped

1 tablespoon finely chopped fresh parsley

1 tablespoon finely chopped fresh sage or 1 teaspoon
    dried sage

grated zest of ¼ lemon

30 g | 1 oz fresh white breadcrumbs

salt and freshly ground black pepper

1 Preheat the oven to 200°C | 400°F | gas mark 6.

2 Mix together the sausagemeat, onion, parsley, sage, lemon zest and breadcrumbs. Season with salt and pepper.

3 Using wet hands, shape into balls the size of a ping-pong ball.

4 Place in a roasting pan and bake for 30 minutes.

Simple Sausages

This sausagemeat mixture can be used to fill sausage skins or simply made into skinless sausages as described below.

SERVES 4

450 g | 1 lb minced fatty pork (e.g. from the belly)

1 medium onion, very finely chopped (optional)

4 slices of white bread, crusts removed, crumbed

1 egg

3 fresh sage leaves, chopped or 1 teaspoon dried
    sage

salt and freshly ground black pepper

fat for frying

1 Mix together the pork and onion, if using.

2 Stir the breadcrumbs into the mixture with the egg and sage.

3 Add plenty of salt and pepper and mix thoroughly. Cook a spoonful of the mixture. Taste and season further if necessary.

4 Wet your hands and form the mixture into sausage shapes.

5 Fry the sausages in hot fat, turning them frequently. They should cook slowly, and will take about 12 minutes if 2.5 cm | 1 in diameter.

wine: **SPICY RED**

Pork Chops with Rosemary

SERVES 4

1 small onion, finely chopped

1 teaspoon finely chopped fresh parsley

1 teaspoon finely chopped fresh rosemary

1 egg

salt and freshly ground black pepper

4 × 170 g | 6 oz pork chops, trimmed of fat

dried white breadcrumbs

oil

1 Mix the onion, parsley, rosemary and egg together in a bowl. Season well with salt and pepper. Coat each pork chop with the egg mixture and then dip in breadcrumbs, covering them well.
2 Heat the oil in a frying pan. Add the chops and fry for 12–15 minutes, until golden brown on both sides and cooked all the way through.

wine: MEDIUM RED

Spare Ribs

SERVES 4

1.25 kg|2½ lb skinned pork belly pieces (American spare ribs)

For the marinade
4 tablespoons clear honey

2 tablespoons soy sauce
4 clove of garlic, crushed
juice of 1 lemon
salt and freshly ground black pepper

1 Mix together the ingredients for the marinade and soak the spare ribs in it for at least 1 hour or overnight in the refrigerator. The longer they marinate the better.
2 Preheat the oven to 180°C|350°F|gas mark 4.
3 Put the ribs, with the marinade, into a roasting pan and bake, covered, for 2 hours minutes. Increase the temperature to 200°C|400°F|gas mark 6. Remove the cover and cook, basting occasionally, for 45 minutes, or until glazed and sticky.

wine: MEDIUM RED

Glazed Ham or Gammon Joint

SERVES 6–8

1 ham or gammon joint
1 onion
1 carrot
1 bay leaf
fresh parsley stalks

black peppercorns
demerara sugar
dry English mustard
a handful of cloves

1 Soak the joint overnight in cold water to remove excess salt.
2 Place it in a large saucepan of cold water and add the onion, carrot, bay leaf, parsley stalks and peppercorns. Bring slowly to the boil, cover and simmer for 25 minutes per 450 g|1 lb. For large joints (i.e. 3.5 kg|8 lb upwards) allow 20 minutes per 450 g|1 lb.
3 Leave the joint to cool slightly in the stock. Then lift out and carefully pull off the skin without removing any of the fat. Reserve the cooking liquor as ham stock.
4 Preheat the oven to 220°C|424°F|gas mark 7.
5 While the ham is still warm, press a thin even layer of dry English mustard over the surface then cover completely with a layer of demerara sugar.

6 Using a sharp knife, cut a lattice pattern across the joint through the sugar and fat. Press on again any sugar that falls off. Stick a clove into each diamond segment, or into the cuts where the lines cross.

7 Bake the joint for about 20 minutes, or until brown and slightly caramelized.

NOTES: If you haven't time to soak salty ham or gammon overnight, cook it for 30 minutes in plain water and then transfer to a pan of simmering water with the vegetables and herbs.

The joint can be decorated with a ham frill: to make one, cut a piece of greaseproof paper to about 12 × 30 cm│5 × 12 in. Fold it loosely in half lengthways, without pressing down the fold. Make 5 cm│2 in cuts, 1 cm│½ in apart, parallel to the end of the paper, cutting through both thicknesses from the folded side towards the open sides. Make the cuts all along the strip. Now open out the paper and refold it lengthways in the opposite direction. Wrap the frill round the ham bone and secure with a paper clip.

wine: **FULL RED**

Roast Pork

SERVES 4

1.35 kg│3 lb loin of pork, with skin intact
oil
salt

For the gravy
2 teaspoons plain flour
290 ml│½ pint brown stock (see page 102)

To serve
1 small bunch of watercress
apple sauce (see page 130)

1 Preheat the oven to 220°C│425°F│gas mark 7.
2 Score the rind (crackling skin) with a sharp knife in cuts about 5 mm│¼ in apart, cutting through the skin but not right through the fat.
3 Brush the skin with oil and sprinkle with salt to help give a crisp crackling.
4 Place the pork in a roasting pan and roast for 25 minutes per 450 g│1 lb plus 25 minutes.
5 Once the pork is cooked, turn off the oven, put the pork on a serving dish and replace it in the oven, leaving the door ajar if it is still very hot.
6 Tip all but 2 tablespoons of the fat from the roasting pan, reserving as much of the meat juices as possible.
7 Add the flour and stir over the heat until well browned.
8 Remove from the heat, add the stock and mix well with a wire whisk or wooden spoon. Return to the heat and bring slowly to the boil, whisking all the time. Simmer for a few minutes until the gravy is shiny. Season to taste with salt and pepper. Strain into a warmed gravy-boat.
9 Garnish the pork with watercress and serve with the gravy and apple sauce.

NOTE: If the crackling is not crisp by the time the pork is done remove the crackling in one piece and return to the oven.

wine: **MEDIUM RED**

Loin of Pork with Prunes

SERVES 4

1.35 kg | 3 lb loin of pork without skin or much fat
oil for frying
15 g | ½ oz butter
1 onion, finely chopped
290 ml | ½ pint brown stock (see page 102)
100 ml | 3½ fl oz red wine
110 g | 4 oz no-need-to-soak prunes

1 bay leaf
1 tablespoon redcurrant jelly
2 sprigs of fresh thyme
150 ml | ¼ pint single cream

To garnish
1 small bunch of watercress

1 Preheat the oven to 150°C | 300°F | gas mark 2.
2 Heat the oil in a flameproof casserole. Add the butter and, when foaming, add the pork. Fry until lightly browned all over. Add the onion and fry until golden.
3 Add the stock, wine, one-third of the prunes, the redcurrant jelly, bay leaf and thyme. Bring to the boil, then cover and cook in the oven for 1½ hours.
4 Remove the pork from the casserole and slice neatly. Arrange in overlapping slices on a serving dish and keep warm in the turned-off oven while you make the sauce.
5 Strain the cooking liquor, removing any excess fat. Boil until reduced to a syrupy consistency. Add the cream and remaining prunes.
6 Spoon the sauce over the pork and garnish with watercress.

wine: **MEDIUM RED**

Pork Medallions Vallée d'Auge

SERVES 4

675 g | 1½ lb pork fillets
salt and freshly ground black pepper
2 tablespoons oil
1 medium onion, very finely chopped
1 stick of celery, chopped
2 teaspoons Calvados
30 g | 1 oz cooked ham, diced
150 ml ¼ pint dry cider
2 dessert apples

lemon juice
caster sugar
15 g | ½ oz butter
1 egg yolk
150 ml | ¼ pint double cream

To garnish
a bouquet of watercress

1 Preheat the oven to 180°C | 350°F | gas mark 4.
2 Prepare the pork fillets by trimming off any fat and membrane with a sharp, flexible knife. Season with salt and pepper.
3 Heat 1 tablespoon of the oil in a large frying pan and brown the fillets carefully on all sides. Place them in a casserole dish.

4 Lower the heat under the frying pan, add the onion and celery and fry gently until soft but not coloured. Remove from the pan with a slotted spoon and place in the casserole dish. Add the Calvados and set alight with a match. When the flames subside, add the ham and cider, and allow to simmer for 2 minutes.

5 Pour the contents of the pan over the pork fillet, cover and cook in the oven for about 20 minutes or until the fillets are completely tender.

6 Meanwhile, peel, quarter and core the apples and cut them into wedges. Brush each wedge with lemon juice and sprinkle with sugar. Melt the butter in the frying pan and fry the apple wedges until barely soft and brown on both sides. Keep them warm.

7 Remove the pork fillets from the oven and keep them warm while preparing the sauce.

8 Strain the liquor from the casserole (reserve the ham and vegetables) into a saucepan and bring to simmering point. Mix the egg yolk with the cream in a bowl and add a little of the hot stock to the mixture. Return this to the saucepan and set over a gentle heat until the sauce becomes creamy and thickens slightly, but take great care not to curdle it by boiling.

9 Arrange the reserved ham and vegetables neatly on a warmed serving dish. Slice the pork fillets into medallions and arrange on top of the ham and vegetables. Coat with the creamy sauce and garnish with the apple wedges and a bouquet of watercress.

wine: **MEDIUM RED**

Pork Fillets in Cider

SERVES 4

1 tablespoon oil	**To garnish**
15 g|½ oz butter	2 dessert apples
1 medium onion, finely chopped	butter
675 g|1½ lb pork tenderloin (fillet), trimmed	caster sugar
290 ml½ pint cider	chopped fresh parsley
salt and freshly ground black pepper	
1 bay leaf	
1 tablespoon single cream	

1 Preheat the oven to 180°C│350°F│gas mark 4.

2 Heat the oil in a frying pan. Add the butter and when hot add the pork and brown quickly all over. Remove to a plate. Reduce the heat, add the onion and cook slowly until soft and golden brown. Add the cider and bay leaf. Bring to the boil, then tip into a flameproof casserole. Return the pork to the pan. Season with salt and pepper, cover and cook in the oven for 25 minutes.

3 Peel, and core the apples and cut into wedges. Fry in butter, sprinkled with sugar, until lightly coloured.

4 Take out the pork and keep warm. Strain the cooking liquor, remove the bay leaf from the sieve, and place the onions in a serving dish. Keep warm.

5 Boil the cooking liquor rapidly until reduced to a syrupy consistency. Add the cream. Taste and adjust the seasoning if necessary.

6 Slice the pork thickly, arrange on top of the onions, pour over the sauce and sprinkle with parsley and garnish with the fried apple.

wine: CIDER OR LIGHT RED

Medallions of Pork with Prunes

This recipe has been adapted from *Cuisine à la Carte* by Anton Mosimann.

SERVES 4

8 pork medallions cut 2.5 cm|1 in thick, well trimmed	**To garnish**
8 small prunes, stones removed	50 g|2 oz turned carrots, boiled and refreshed
seasoned plain flour	50 g|2 oz turned turnips, boiled and refreshed
1 tablespoon olive oil	8 small prunes, blanched, stones removed
20 g|¾ oz butter	20 g|¾ oz butter
100 ml|3½ fl oz dry white wine	a little chopped fresh parsley
150 ml|¼ pint brown stock (see page 102)	
40 g|1¼ oz butter, diced	

1 Flatten the pork medallions lightly between 2 sheets of wet greaseproof paper to a thickness of 1 cm|⅓ in.

2 Place the prunes in cold water in a saucepan, cover and bring to the boil.

3 Remove from the heat and set aside for 30 minutes in the water.

4 Pour off the water, cut the prunes in half and dry on a cloth.

5 Make small slits in the meat then push the prunes through the pork medallions. Dust with seasoned flour.

6 Heat the oil and butter in a large frying pan.

7 Put in the pork medallions and sauté over a medium heat on both sides until firm, basting constantly.

8 Remove the medallions from the pan and keep warm. Pour off all the fat from the pan.

9 Add the wine and stock and reduce, by boiling rapidly, to about 150 ml|¼ pint. Strain through a sieve, reheat and gradually add the butter, piece by piece, whisking all the time until smooth and glossy. Season to taste and pour over the medallions.

10 Sauté the carrots, turnips and prunes for the garnish in the butter and scatter around the pork.

11 Garnish with parsley and serve immediately.

wine: MEDIUM RED

Sweet and Sour Pork

SERVES 4

675 g | 1½ lb lean boneless pork
½ teaspoon salt
1 tablespoon cornflour
oil for deep-frying
1 green pepper, cored, deseeded and sliced

2 tablespoons sugar
2 tablespoons wine vinegar
2 tablespoons tomato purée
2 tablespoons orange juice
2 tablespoons soy sauce
2 tablespoons finely chopped pineapple
½ teaspoon oil

For the sweet and sour sauce

1 teaspoon cornflour
4 tablespoons water

1 Start with the sauce: blend the cornflour with the water and mix it with the sugar, vinegar, tomato purée, orange juice and soy sauce.
2 Fry the chopped pineapple in the oil for 1 minute. Add this to the sauce.
3 Cut the pork into 2 cm | ¾ in cubes. Sprinkle with salt and toss in the cornflour.
4 Heat the oil in a deep-fryer until a cube of bread browns in 20 seconds. Deep-fry the pork for 4 minutes. Drain on absorbent kitchen paper.
5 Heat 1 tablespoon oil in a wide pan. Fry the green pepper quickly for 30 seconds. Reduce the heat, add the sauce to the pan and cook for 1 minute. If the sauce seems too thick, add a little water before serving.

wine: **BEER OR SPICY RED**

Jambon Persillé

SERVES 6

1   900 g | 2 lb piece of mild gammon or unsmoked lean bacon
1 slice of onion
1 bay leaf
½ carrot
2 parsley stalks
6 black peppercorns

1 litre | 2 pints white stock, made with veal bones (see page 203) plus 15 g | ½ oz powdered gelatine if the stock is not jellied
150 ml | ¼ pint dry white wine
1 tablespoon tarragon vinegar
2 egg shells, sterilized
2 egg whites, frothed
3 tablespoons finely chopped fresh parsley

1 Soak the gammon in cold water overnight.
2 Simmer it in fresh water to cover with the onion, bay leaf, carrot, parsley stalks and peppercorns for about 1½ hours, or until tender. Remove from the heat and leave to cool in the liquid.
3 Put the stock into a large clean saucepan. If it is not set to a solid jelly, sprinkle in the gelatine. Add the wine and vinegar. Set over a low heat to dissolve the gelatine or to melt the jelly, then allow to cool.

4 Put the crushed shells and egg whites into the stock. Place over the heat and whisk steadily with a balloon whisk until the mixture begins to steam. Stop whisking immediately and remove the pan from the heat. Allow the mixture to subside. Take care not to break the crust formed by the egg white.

5 Bring the aspic just up to the boil again, and again allow to subside. Repeat this once more; the egg-white will trap the sediment in the stock and clear the aspic. Allow to cool for 2 minutes.

6 Fix a double layer of fine muslin or absorbent kitchen paper in a sieve over a clean bowl. Place a spoonful of the crust in the sieve and carefully strain the aspic through it. Then strain the aspic again – this time through both egg-white crust and cloth. Do not try to hurry the process by squeezing the cloth, or murky aspic will result. Allow to cool.

7 Cut the gammon into thick slices and then into strips. Arrange a neat layer in the bottom of a mould or soufflé dish which has been rinsed out with cold water or very lightly oiled.

8 Pour in enough almost-cold jelly to hold the gammon in place when the jelly sets. Leave in the refrigerator to set.

9 Mix the parsley into half the just-liquid jelly and pour 1 cm/½ in into the mould. Allow to set. Arrange a second layer of ham on top and set it in place with clear jelly.

10 Continue the layers in this way, finishing with clear jelly. Chill well.

11 To turn out: dip the mould into hot water to loosen the jelly. Invert a plate over the mould and turn the plate and mould over together. Give a slight shake to dislodge the jelly and remove the mould.

NOTES: A good but less elegant jambon persillé is made with uncleared veal jelly, chopped parsley and cubes of cooked ham simply combined in a dish and allowed to set.

When clearing it is advisable to scald the saucepan, sieve, eggshells and whisk before use.

wine: MEDIUM RED

Grilled Pork Chops with Caramelized Apples

SERVES 4

4 × 170 g / 6 oz pork chops	**To garnish**
a little oil	2 dessert apples
freshly ground black pepper	butter for frying
3–4 fresh sage leaves, chopped, or a pinch of dried	1 teaspoon sugar
sage	a few sprigs of watercress

1 Preheat the grill to its highest setting.

2 Trim the rind from the chops and snip short cuts through the fat towards the meat, about 1 cm|½ in apart, to prevent curling up during grilling. Brush lightly with oil.

3 Season with pepper and sage.

4 Grill the chops for 5–7 minutes on each side, or until cooked right through. Keep warm on a serving platter.

5 Peel and core the apples and cut them into quarters.

6 Melt a small knob of butter in a frying pan and when it is foaming add the apples. Sprinkle with a little sugar and fry lightly on both sides until golden-brown but not mushy. The sugar will caramelize, giving a brown, toffee-like coating to the apples.

7 Garnish the chops with the caramelized apples and the watercress.

wine: MEDIUM RED

Stir-fried Pork

SERVES 4

450 g | 1 lb pork tenderloin (fillet), trimmed

1 tablespoon dry sherry

1 tablespoon soy sauce

1 cm | ½ in piece of fresh root ginger, peeled and grated

1 bunch of spring onions, cut into rings

110 g | 4 oz baby sweetcorn, blanched

110 g | 4 oz mangetout, topped and tailed

freshly ground black pepper

For the sauce

1 tablespoon dry sherry

1 tablespoon soy sauce

1 Cut the pork into strips the size of your little finger and marinate for at least 1 hour in the sherry, soy sauce and ginger.

2 In a non-stick frying pan or wok, stir-fry the pork with the marinade until just cooked through.

3 Add the spring onions, baby corn and mangetout. Add the sauce. Cook for a further 4 minutes.

4 Season with pepper and serve.

NOTE: If not using a non-stick frying pan or wok, the pork will have to be fried in a little oil.

wine: LIGHT RED

Pork Medallions with Ginger Sauce

SERVES 6–8

For the marinade

225 ml | 8 fl oz teriyaki sauce

110 g | 4 oz clear honey

110 ml | 4 fl oz medium-dry sherry

2 teaspoons peeled and finely chopped fresh ginger root

2 tablespoons sesame oil

3 pork fillets, cut into 2.5 cm | 1 in medallions

oil for frying

1 Whisk together the marinade ingredients and pour over the pork medallions. Cover and allow to marinate for 2 hours in the refrigerator, turning the meat occasionally.

2 Drain off the marinade. Strain into a saucepan, bring to the boil and allow to reduce a little until the sauce has thickened slightly.

3 Heat a little oil in a frying pan. Fry the medallions a few at a time until cooked through. Serve with the sauce.

NOTE: This goes very well with stir-fried batons of parsnip and carrot.

wine: **LIGHT RED**

Braised Pig's Trotters

This recipe comes from Marco Pierre White's *White Heat*. He calls it Braised Pig's Trotters 'Pierre Koffman'.

SERVES 6

6 pig's trotters, from back legs only

1 tablespoon oil

2 carrots, cubed

1 stick of celery, cubed

1 onion, diced

290 ml | ½ pint dry white wine

425 ml | ¾ pint white stock, made with veal bones (see page 103)

1 sprig of fresh thyme

½ bay leaf

salt and freshly ground black pepper

For the stuffing

40 g | 1½ oz dried morels

675 g | 1½ lb veal sweetbreads, soaked in water overnight

½ onion, diced

1 290 ml | ½ pint quantity chicken mousse (see next recipe)

olive oil for frying

For the sauce

2 chicken legs

2 tablespoons sunflower oil

110 g | 4 oz mushrooms, sliced

110 g | 4 oz shallots, chopped

½ head of garlic, sliced across to halve each clove

1 sprig of fresh thyme

½ fresh bay leaf

1½ tablespoons sherry vinegar

1½ tablespoons cognac

425 ml | ¾ pint Madeira

570 ml | 1 pint white stock, made with veal bones (see page 103)

200 ml | ⅓ pint white stock, made with chicken bones (see page 103)

150 ml | ¼ pint water

4 dried morels

lemon juice to taste

a few drops of cream

a knob of butter

olive oil for frying

To garnish

72 wild mushrooms, chopped

30 g | 1 oz butter

72 roast button onions (optional)

900 g | 2 lb mashed potato (see page 268)

1 Soak the pig's trotters in cold water for 24 hours. Drain and pat dry. Singe off any remaining hairs, particularly between the toes. Scrape off the singed stubble and any stray hairs with a knife.

2 Slit the underside of each trotter lengthways, starting at the ankle end. Using a sharp knife, cut the main tendon and then start to work off the skin by cutting around it close to the bone. (Remember that the trotter skin is effectively going to form a sausage skin, so be careful not to tear it.)

3 Pull the skin right down and cut through the knuckle joint at the first set of toes. Continue to pull the skin off as far as the last toe joint. Snap and twist off the bones and discard them.

4 Preheat the oven to 220°C | 425°F | gas mark 7.

5 Heat the oil in a flameproof casserole dish and fry the carrot, celery and onion over a medium heat for about 2 minutes. Add the trotter skins, outside down, and the wine and boil until the wine has reduced by about half.

6 Add the stock, thyme and bay leaf. Bring to the boil, then cover and cook in the oven for about 3 hours. During cooking, shake the casserole from time to time to prevent the skins from sticking to the pan. Remove the skins from the cooking liquor (they should be a wonderful oak-brown colour) and leave to cool.

To make the stuffing

7 Soak the morels in cold water for 10 minutes. Drain and rinse. Repeat this process once more.

8 Put the sweetbreads into a saucepan of clean cold water, bring to the boil and poach for 2 minutes. Drain and refresh under running cold water. Remove the membrane and sinew from the sweetbreads, saving the trimmings for the sauce. Cut the sweetbreads into cubes and fry these in very hot oil in a large frying pan over a high heat until they are golden-brown with a crunchy texture.

9 Add the soaked morels and the onion and cook for 1 minute only. (Remember that this mixture is to be cooked again in the trotters.) Season well with salt and white pepper, drain the mixture through a colander and leave to cool.

10 When the mixture is cool, stir in just enough chicken mousse to bind it together. Taste and adjust the seasoning again, if necessary.

To make the sauce

11 Fry the chicken legs and sweetbread trimmings in the oil in a large frying pan over a medium heat until they are golden brown but not cooked through.

12 Add the mushrooms, shallots, garlic, thyme and bay leaf and stir well. Deglaze the contents of the pan with the vinegar, cooking to drive off the acidity. Deglaze in the same way with the cognac.

13 Add the Madeira and reduce the mixture until it has a caramelized appearance. Add the stocks and water to cover the bones and vegetables. Add the dried morels and simmer the mixture for 20 minutes. Pass the sauce through a sieve or muslin cloth several times, reserving the morels for garnish if you wish. Keep warm.

14 Just before serving, reduce the strained stock just a little to a coating consistency. Taste and adjust the seasoning. Add a few drops of lemon juice and one or two drops of cream, then add the butter and a little pepper. Taste the sauce while adding all these to get exactly the required flavour.

To stuff the trotters

15 Cut 6 large squares of kitchen foil, each big enough to wrap and seal a trotter.

16 Butter one side of each piece of foil, then place on a trotter outside skin side down. Pick out and discard the little pieces of fat inside the skin.

17 Divide the stuffing mixture between the 6 trotters. There should be enough to give each of the trotters enough bulk to hold its original shape.

18 Roll the foil tightly around each trotter, making a sausage shape, and twist at either end to seal securely. Chill the trotter parcels in the refrigerator for about 15 minutes to allow to set.

19 Poach the trotters in a large saucepan of boiling water for about 12 minutes.

To make the garnish

20 Cook the wild mushrooms in half the butter in a large frying pan over a high heat until they produce their liquid.

21 Drain the mushrooms and cook them again in the remaining butter for 1–2 minutes. Keep warm.

To serve

22 Remove the trotter parcels from the poaching water and unwrap them.

23 Carefully place the trotters, uncut skin side up, on 6 warmed individual serving plates.

24 Place 12 onions, if using, on each plate and scatter the mushrooms over the trotter.

25 Spoon a serving of mashed potato alongside each trotter and dot it with slices of the morels reserved from the sauce.

26 Coat the trotters with the sauce and spoon more sauce around the plate.

NOTE: If you prefer a crisp skin, glaze the trotters with honey and grill briefly before serving.

wine: **FULL DRY WHITE**

Marco's Chicken Mousse

225 g | 8 oz chicken breast, skin and sinews removed, chopped
a pinch of ground mace
1 tablespoon chopped fresh tarragon

1 egg
2 teaspoons salt
200 ml | 7 fl oz double cream

1 Process the chicken flesh in a blender for 1 minute with the mace and tarragon.

2 Add the egg and salt and work the mixture for another minute in the blender.

3 Chill the resulting mixture for 10–15 minutes in the refrigerator. Force the mixture through a sieve to ensure a velvety texture.

4 Place the chicken in a cold bowl set in an ice bath. Gradually beat in the cream. Taste and adjust the seasoning. Store any excess mousse, wrapped in clingfilm, in the refrigerator.

Veal Escalopes with Rosemary

SERVES 4

4 × 140 g | 5 oz veal escalopes
salt and freshly ground black pepper
30 g | 1 oz butter

1 teaspoon chopped fresh rosemary or ½ teaspoon
  dried rosemary
4 tablespoons dry white wine
2 tablespoons double cream

1 Place the escalopes between 2 sheets of wet greaseproof paper or clingfilm and beat gently with a mallet or rolling pin until they are 5 mm | ¼ oz thick. Season with salt and pepper.
2 Melt the butter with the rosemary in a frying pan over a medium heat. When the butter is foaming, fry the escalopes (one or two at a time if they won't fit in the pan together) for 1–2 minutes on each side until a very delicate brown. Remove the veal with a slotted spoon or fish slice and keep warm in a very low oven.
3 Pour the wine into the pan and heat, scraping the surface of the pan with a wooden spoon to incorporate any sediment. Boil up well and add the cream. Check the seasoning. Pour over the veal and serve immediately.

wine: **LIGHT RED**

Veal Escalopes with Ragoût Fin

SERVES 4

110 g | 4 oz calves' sweetbreads
20 g | ¾ oz butter
1 small onion, finely chopped
30 g | 1 oz bacon, diced
55 g | 2 oz button mushrooms, sliced
1 tablespoon chopped fresh parsley
7 g | ¼ oz plain flour
150 ml | ¼ pint well-flavoured white stock, made
  with veal bones (see page 103)

4 × 140 g | 5 oz veal escalopes
extra butter for frying
a squeeze of lemon juice

To garnish
sprigs of watercress
lemon wedges

1 Soak the sweetbreads in cold water for 4 hours, changing the water every time it becoms pink; probably 4 times. There should be no blood at all when the sweetbreads are ready for cooking.
2 Place them in a saucepan of cold water and bring to boiling point, but do not allow to boil. Simmer for 2 minutes. Rinse under cold running water and dry well.
3 Pick over the sweetbreads, removing all the skin and membrane. Chop them coarsely.
4 Melt the butter and add the onion. Cook slowly until soft but not coloured. Add the bacon and sweetbreads and cook for 3 minutes. Stir in the mushrooms and parsley and leave over a low heat for 1 minute.
5 Mix in the flour and cook for 1 minute. Remove from the heat and stir in the stock.

Return to the heat and bring slowly to the boil, stirring continuously. Season with salt and pepper. Simmer for 1 minute, then set aside to cool and solidify.

6 Place the veal escalopes between 2 pieces of wet greaseproof paper or clingfilm and, with a rolling pin or mallet, beat them lightly until quite thin.

7 Divide the sweetbread mixture between the escalopes and fold them in half.

8 Melt some butter in a large frying pan and when foaming, add the escalopes. Brown lightly on both sides. Reduce the heat and cook slowly for 4–5 minutes. Lift out the escalopes on to a warmed serving plate.

9 Increase the heat under the frying pan and brown the butter, remove from the heat and add a squeeze of lemon juice. Pour over the escalopes and serve garnished with watercress and lemon wedges.

wine: **MEDIUM RED**

Veal Marsala

SERVES 4

4 × 140 g | 5 oz veal escalopes

15 g | ½ oz butter

1 tablespoon oil

salt and freshly ground black pepper

2 tablespoons Marsala

4 tablespoons double cream

lemon juice

1 Put the veal escalopes between 2 sheets of wet greaseproof paper and beat lightly with a mallet or rolling pin until thin. Season with salt and pepper.

2 Melt the butter in a frying pan and, when it is foaming, fry the escalopes briskly to brown them lightly on both sides (1–2 minutes per side).
Remove them to a warmed plate and keep warm.

3 Tip off any fat in the pan. Add 4 tablespoons water and the Marsala, swill it about and bring to the boil. Add the cream and season well with salt, pepper and a squeeze of lemon juice.

4 Return the veal to the pan to heat through gently.

wine: **LIGHT RED**

Veal Medallions with Wild Mushrooms

SERVES 4

4 × 140 g | 5 oz veal medallions

110 g | 4 oz mixed wild mushrooms, sliced

425 ml | ¾ pint brown stock (see page 102)

100 ml | 3½ fl oz dry white wine

170 g | 6 oz unsalted butter, chilled and diced

1 Melt 15 g | ½ oz of the butter in a frying pan and, when it is foaming, fry the veal medallions to brown them lightly on both sides (2–3 minutes per side). Remove them to a warmed plate.

2 Add the mushrooms to the pan and fry until tender. Remove the mushrooms with a slotted spoon and arrange on the veal medallions.

3 Add the stock and wine and boil, scraping the bottom of the pan to incorporate any sediment, for 3 minutes. Continue to boil the stock until reduced to 5 tablespoons.

4 Allow the stock to cool slightly. Using a wire whisk and plenty of vigorous continuous whisking, add the butter. The process should take about 2 minutes and the sauce should thicken. Taste, season and pour over the veal.

NOTE: Veal cutlets may be used instead of medallions.

wine: **LIGHT RED**

Veal Medallions and Grilled Vegetables with Aïoli

SERVES 8

8 × 140 g | 5 oz veal medallions
olive oil
salt and freshly ground black pepper

For the aïoli

6 cloves of garlic, peeled and crushed
3 egg yolks
3 tablespoons fresh white breadcrumbs
½ teaspoon salt
4 tablespoons white wine vinegar
290 ml | ½ pint olive oil
1 tablespoon boiling water

For the vegetables

2 aubergines, cut in slices lengthways
olive oil
3 large red peppers, halved and deseeded
6 medium courgettes, cut into thin diagonal slices
4 onions, sliced
6 tomatoes, peeled, quartered and deseeded
balsamic vinegar
finely chopped fresh mint
finely chopped fresh basil

1 Make the aïoli: put the garlic, egg yolks, breadcrumbs, salt and vinegar into a food processor. Process to a paste, then with the motor running, slowly add the oil to make a thick sauce. Add the boiling water.

2 Salt the aubergines and leave in a colander for 20 minutes to extract the bitter juices (degorge). Rinse and pat dry with absorbent kitchen paper. Paint each side of the aubergine slices lightly with oil and grill until dark brown but not burnt.

3 Preheat the grill to its highest setting.

4 Grill the peppers skin side up until they are charred and blistered. Place in a plastic bag to cool. Remove the skin and cut the flesh into strips.

5 Lightly oil the courgettes and grill until just cooked.

6 Sauté the onions in a little oil until light brown.

7 Layer the vegetables, including the tomatoes, in a bowl, sprinkling each layer with balsamic vinegar, mint and basil. Set aside to marinate at room temperature for 1 hour.

8 Brush both sides of the veal with oil and sprinkle with salt and pepper. Grill under a preheated grill for 3–4 minutes each side, depending on the thickness of the meat.

9 To serve: place the cooked veal and some of the marinated vegetables on warmed dinner plates. Serve a spoonful of aïoli beside the vegetables.

wine: **LIGHT FRUITY RED**

Osso Bucco

Osso bucco is a substantial peasant dish made brighter by a last-minute scattering of chopped parsley and grated lemon zest (gremolata). It is quite often served without sieving the sauce.

SERVES 4

4 large meaty pieces of knuckle of veal, cut crossways with the bone and marrow in the centre

3 tablespoons good-quality olive oil

1 large or 2 small onions, finely chopped

1 large carrot, finely chopped

2 cloves of garlic, crushed

2 teaspoons plain flour

2 teaspoons tomato purée

340 g | 12 oz ripe tomatoes, peeled and chopped

150 ml | ¼ pint dry white wine

290 ml | ½ pint white stock, made with veal bones (see page 103)

salt and freshly ground black pepper

1 bouquet garni (a sprig each of fresh parsley and thyme, 1 stick of celery and 1 bay leaf, tied together with string)

To garnish

1 tablespoon chopped fresh parsley

grated zest of 1 lemon

1 Put 1 tablespoon of the oil into a saucepan, add the onion and carrot cover with a well-fitting lid. Cook over a low heat without browning until soft. Add the garlic and cook for a futher minute. Remove with a slotted spoon.

2 Brown the meat on all sides, one or two pieces at a time, in the remaining oil in a large saucepan. Remove to a plate as they are browned.

3 When all are done, sprinkle the flour into the pan and stir well. Add the tomato purée, cooked vegetables, tomatoes, wine, stock, salt and pepper and bring to the boil.

4 Replace the veal, immerse the bouquet garni in the liquid and cover the pan. Simmer for 1½ hours, or until the veal is very tender but not quite falling off the bone.

5 Take the veal out and place on a warmed serving platter with a fairly deep lip. Cover with kitchen foil and keep warm while you boil the sauce rapidly until thick. Stir frequently and watch that it does not catch and burn at the bottom.

6 Remove the bouquet garni. Push the sauce through a sieve and boil until syrupy. Pour over the meat. Sprinkle with the parsley and grated lemon zest.

wine: MEDIUM RED

Blanquette de Veau

SERVES 4

900 g | 2 lb pie veal

1 slice of lemon

1 bouquet garni (4 parsley stalks, 2 bay leaves, 1
   blade of mace tied together with string)

salt and freshly ground white pepper

2 carrots, peeled and cut into sticks

2 onions, peeled and sliced

1 teaspoon cornflour

1 egg yolk, or 2 for a very rich sauce

150 ml | ¼ pint double cream

To garnish

8 fried bread triangles made from 2 slices of white
   bread, crusts removed

chopped fresh parsley

1 Trim the fat from the veal but do not worry about the gristle. Put the veal into a saucepan of cold water with the lemon slice. Bring slowly to the boil, skimming carefully. Add the bouquet garni and a little salt. Remove the lemon slice. Simmer gently for 30 minutes.

2 Add the carrots and onions and continue to simmer until the meat is really tender and the vegetables cooked (probably a further 30–40 minutes).

3 Strain the liquid into a jug. Skim off any fat. There should be 290 ml | ½ pint. If there is less, add a little water. If there is more, return the liquid to the pan and reduce, by rapidly boiling. Pick over the meat, removing any fat or gristle, and put the meat and vegetables into an ovenproof serving dish. Remove the bouquet garni.

4 Mix the cornflour in a cup with a few spoons of cold water and add some of the hot liquid from the veal. Stir the mixture into the remaining liquid in the pan and continue to stir while bringing to the boil. You should now have a sauce that is very slightly thickened: about the consistency of single cream. If it is still too thin, do not add more cornflour, but boil rapidly until reduced to the correct consistency. Season to taste with salt and pepper.

5 Mix the egg yolks and cream together in a bowl. Add some of the sauce, mix well, and return to the pan. Do not boil or the eggs will scramble. Reheat gently, stirring until the egg yolks have thickened the sauce to the consistency of double cream, then pour over the meat and vegetables.

6 Serve garnished with triangles of fried bread with their corners dipped in chopped parsley.

wine: **FULL DRY WHITE**

Veal Florentine

SERVES 4

1 clove of garlic, crushed
55 g | 2 oz butter
6 tomatoes, peeled and sliced
900 g | 2 lb spinach, cooked and chopped
salt and freshly ground black pepper

a pinch of freshly grated nutmeg
4 × 140 g | 5 oz veal escalopes
570 ml | 1 pint Mornay sauce (see page 112)
1 tablespoon grated cheese
1 tablespoon dried breadcrumbs

1 Preheat the oven to 180°C | 350°F | gas mark 4.

2 Fry the garlic lightly in a quarter of the butter. Then add the tomatoes and cook for 30 seconds. Place them in a dish big enough to hold the veal in one layer.

3 Toss the spinach in a little butter in the pan. Season with salt, pepper and nutmeg. Spread the spinach on top of the tomatoes.

4 Put the veal between 2 pieces of wet greaseproof paper and flatten by batting evenly with a rolling pin.

5 Heat the remaining butter in a large frying pan. Fry the veal in this until lightly browned all over. Cut across the grain into strips. Put them on top of the spinach and season well with salt and pepper.

6 Heat the Mornay sauce and pour evenly over the veal and spinach. Sprinkle with the grated cheese and breadcrumbs.

7 Bake for 15 minutes or until bubbly and hot, then grill to brown the top, if necessary.

NOTE: Chicken Florentine can be made in the same way using poached chicken in place of fried veal.

wine: **DRY WHITE**

Hungarian Veal Goulash

SERVES 4

900 g | 2 lb pie veal
450 g | 1 lb onions, sliced
20 g | ¾ oz butter
1 tablespoon paprika pepper
290 ml | ½ pint white stock, made with veal bones
  (see page 103)
a squeeze of lemon juice
100 ml | 3½ fl oz dry white wine

2 teaspoons tomato purée
salt and freshly ground black pepper
1 teaspoon plain flour
150 ml | ¼ pint soured cream

To garnish
fresh chopped parsley

1 Cut the veal into 5 cm | 2 in cubes. Trim off as much fat as possible but do not worry about any skin and gristle.

2 In a large saucepan, cook the onions in the butter until soft. Add the paprika and cook for 1 further minute.

3 Add the veal, stock, lemon juice, wine, tomato purée, salt and pepper, bring to the boil and simmer for 45–60 minutes, until the meat is tender.

4 Strain the stock into a jug. Skim off any fat. There should be about 290 ml | ½ pint. If there is less, add some water. If there is more, reduce by boiling rapidly. Pick off any skin or gristle from the veal and place the meat in an ovenproof dish. Return the stock to the pan, mix the flour with a little of the soured cream and add some of the hot stock to it. Mix thoroughly and return the paste to the stock in the pan. Bring slowly to the boil, stirring continuously; cook for 2 minutes.

5 Check the seasoning and pour the sauce over the veal. Streak in the remaining soured cream and sprinkle with parsley.

wine: **MEDIUM RED**

Veal and Ham Raised Pie

The pastry case should be made at least 1 hour in advance of the filling. The finished pie must be left overnight for the aspic to set.

SERVES 4

675 g	1½ lb boned shoulder of veal	450 g	1 lb flour quantity hot watercrust pastry (see page 562)
110 g	4 oz ham	
salt and freshly ground black pepper	1 egg, beaten
1 onion, chopped	290 ml	½ pint aspic, flavoured with tarragon (see page 104)
2 tablespoons chopped fresh parsley	

1 Make the pastry and mould the pastry case (see page 562).

2 Preheat the oven to 190°C | 375°F | gas mark 5.

3 Cut the veal and ham into cubes. Trim away most of the fat and all the skin and gristle. Season with salt, pepper, the onion and parsley.

4 Fill the pie with the seasoned meat, making sure that you press it firmly into the corners, then cover with the remaining pastry. Press the edges together. Make a neat hole in the middle of the lid. Secure a lightly buttered double piece of greaseproof paper around the pie with a paper clip.

5 Bake for 15 minutes. Reduce the oven temperature to 170°C | 325°F | gas mark 3. Bake for 1 further hour. Thirty minutes before the pie is due to come out of the oven, remove the paper 'collar' and brush the pastry evenly all over with beaten egg. Remove the pie from the oven and allow to get quite cold.

6 Warm the aspic enough to make it just liquid but not hot. Using a funnel, fill up the pie with jelly. Allow the liquid to set slightly and then add more liquid until you are sure that the pie is completely full. This will take some time. Leave in the refrigerator for the jelly to reset.

NOTE: A richer and, frankly, better result is achieved with a pâte à pâte crust, though the classic English pie is made as above. The recipe for pâte à pâte is found on page 565.

wine: **LIGHT RED OR ROSÉ**

Veal Fricandeau

This dish has been adapted from a recipe in the Time Life *Veal and Beef* book.

SERVES 8

200 g│7 oz long strips of pork fat
salt and freshly ground black pepper
1.35 kg│3 lb piece of rump or loin of veal, cut
  lengthways along the grain
45 g│1½ oz unsalted butter
2 onions, thinly sliced
2 carrots, thinly sliced

570 ml│1 pint white stock, made with veal bones (see
  page 103)
200 ml│7 fl oz dry white wine

To serve

1.35 kg│3 lb leaf spinach, destalked and well washed
15 g│½ oz butter
salt and freshly ground black pepper
freshly grated nutmeg

1 Season the pork fat with salt and pepper.
2 Take a strip of pork fat and press into the tunnel of a larding needle. Push the needle right through the meat. Gently turn the needle so that the fat does not come loose. When the fat is through the length of the meat, pull the needle away, leaving the fat embedded in the meat. Repeat this 10–12 times, making sure that there is an equal distance between each strip. Leave the little ends of the pork fat sticking out of the veal flesh.
3 Preheat the oven to 180°C│350°F│gas mark 4.
4 Melt the butter in a flameproof casserole. Add the onions and carrots and cook until just beginning to soften. Remove the vegetables and reserve. Add the veal and brown it lightly all over. Season with salt and pepper. Return the vegetables to the pan.
5 Add 5 tablespoons each of the stock and wine. Bring to the boil, then reduce the heat and simmer until the liquid has just evaporated. Add the remaining stock and wine. Bring to the boil, then cover with a piece of buttered greaseproof paper and a lid and cook in the oven for 1 hour.
6 Using a ladle, remove half the braising liquid and place in a saucepan. Reduce by boiling rapidly until syrupy. Use this to baste over the fricandeau as it cooks. The surface of the meat should become brown and sticky.
7 Increase the oven temperature to 190°C│375°F│gas mark 5 and remove the covering paper and lid. Baste the veal frequently with the braising juices. Cook for 1 further hour.
8 Remove the veal from the casserole pot. Leave to stand, covered, in the turned off oven while you make the sauce and prepare the spinach.
9 Strain all the meat juices into a saucepan. Bring to the boil, then add a dash of cold water. (This will help to bring the scum to the surface.) Skim off all the scum. Repeat this process if necessary.
10 Meanwhile cook the spinach. Melt the butter in a large sauté pan. Add the well washed spinach and turn in the pan until wilted. Season with salt, pepper and nutmeg.
11 Arrange the spinach on a large warmed serving dish. Place the veal on top of the spinach and hand the sauce separately.

wine: FULL RED

Roast Loin of Veal

SERVES 6

1 kg | 2¼ lb piece of boned loin of veal

30 g | 1 oz butter, softened

2 teaspoons Dijon mustard

chopped fresh mixed herbs

salt and freshly ground black pepper

1 tablespoon oil

1 tablespoon plain flour

290 ml | ½ pint veal or chicken stock (see page 103)

1 Preheat the oven to 180°C | 350°F | gas mark 4. Weigh the veal and calculate the cooking time at 20 minutes per 450 g | 1 lb.

2 Using a very sharp knife, cut away the rind and most of the fat from the loin, leaving about 1 cm | ½ in of fat on the joint.

3 Using a sharp knife, make criss-cross incisions into the outer layer of fat.

4 Spread the butter and half the mustard over the lean side of the joint. Spread mustard only on the fat side, making sure that it goes well into the incisions. Sprinkle with herbs, salt and pepper, and tie up neatly with string.

5 Put the oil into a roasting pan and melt over a low heat. When it begins to spit, put the joint into it, baste, then place in the oven. Roast for the calculated cooking time.

6 Remove the joint to a warmed serving dish. Remove all but 1 tablespoon fat from the pan. With a whisk or wooden spoon, scrape the bottom of the pan and stir in the flour. Remove from the heat. Gradually add the stock. Return to the heat. Stir until boiling, then simmer for 2 minutes.

7 Check the seasoning and pour into a warmed sauceboat. Serve with the joint.

wine: MEDIUM RED

Kidneys Turbigo

SERVES 4

8 lambs' kidneys

butter for frying

225 g | 8 oz small pork sausages

12 baby onions or shallots, peeled

225 g | 8 oz button mushrooms

2 tablespoons dry sherry

425 ml | ¾ pint brown stock (see page 102)

1 bouquet garni (1 stick of celery, 1 bay leaf, 1 sprig each of parsley and thyme, tied together with string)

salt and freshly ground black pepper

30 g | 1 oz butter

30 g | 1 oz plain flour

150 ml | ¼ pint soured cream

1 Skin the kidneys, halve them and remove the cores with kitchen scissors.

2 Heat the butter in a frying pan. Brown the kidneys quickly, a few at a time, on both sides. They should cook fast enough to go brown rather than grey. Remove them into a sieve set over a bowl as you go.

3 Now fry the sausages, then the onions, and finally the mushrooms in the same way. Put them on to a plate, not with the kidneys.

4 Put everything back into the pan, except for the kidney juice in the bowl (the blood can be very bitter). Pour over the sherry and stock and immerse the bouquet garni in the liquid. Add salt and pepper and cover with the lid.

5 Cook over a very low heat for about 1 hour, or until the kidneys and onions are tender. Make sure that the kidneys are submerged during cooking.

6 Lift the meat and vegetables on to a warmed serving dish and discard the bouquet garni. Reduce the liquid by boiling rapidly to half the original quantity.

7 Work the butter and flour together to a paste (beurre manié). Whisk about half of it bit by bit into the sauce and stir briskly while bringing slowly to the boil. If the sauce is still on the thin side, add the remaining butter and flour mixture in the same way, whisking out the lumps. Boil for 1 minute.

8 Mix half the soured cream with some of the hot liquid. Add to the pan, stir, but do not boil, and pour over the dish. Serve the remaining soured cream separately.

NOTE: Classic turbigo does not have the soured cream but the addition is delicious.

wine: FULL RED

Calves' Liver with Parsnip Crisps

SERVES 6

675 g | 1½ lb sliced calves' liver

6 tablespoons plain flour seasoned with salt and freshly ground black pepper

30 g | 1 oz unsalted butter

2 tablespoons hazelnut oil

2 tablespoons water

2.5 cm | 1 in piece of fresh root ginger, peeled and grated

55 g | 2 oz pecan nuts

1 tablespoon chopped fresh thyme

1 tablespoon soft dark brown sugar

3 tablespoons orange juice

3 tablespoons Madeira

2 tablespoons balsamic vinegar

1 teaspoon cornflour

290 ml | ½ pint brown stock (see page 102)

salt and freshly ground black pepper

For the crisps

2 large parsnips

oil for deep-frying

salt

1 Trim the liver, removing the fine outer membrane and any large tubes.

2 Dip the slices of liver into the seasoned flour and shake off any excess. Heat the butter and 1 tablespoon of the oil in a large frying pan until foaming. Add the liver slices a few at a time and fry for about 1 minute on each side until nicely browned on the outside but pale pink in the middle. Drain well and arrange in overlapping slices on an ovenproof serving dish. Keep warm while frying the remaining liver in the same way.

3 Tip off any fat in the pan. Add the water, scrape any sediment from the bottom of the pan and bring to the boil. Pour into a bowl. Taste the liquid: if it tastes burnt, throw it away and substitute 2 tablespoons extra stock.

4 Heat the remaining oil in a pan and add the ginger, pecan nuts, thyme and sugar. Stir for 1 minute, then add the orange juice, Madeira and vinegar. Cook for 1 further minute.

5 Slake the cornflour with a little of the stock and add to the pan. Add the stock gradually, then add the deglazing liquid. Boil for at least 2 minutes until syrupy. Season to taste with salt and pepper.

6 Top and tail and peel the parsnips. Cut thin strips by running a vegetable peeler along the length. Heat a saucepan half full of oil until cube of bread browns in 20 seconds. Drop the parsnip strips a few at a time into the hot oil until golden brown. Remove with slotted spoon. Drain on kitchen paper. Sprinkle with salt.

7 Pour the sauce over the liver and top with the parsnip crisps. Serve immediately.

wine: **MEDIUM RED**

Lambs' Kidneys with Mushrooms in Mustard Sauce

SERVES 2

6 lambs' kidneys

30 g | 1 oz clarified butter (see page 385)

110 g | 4 oz large flat mushrooms, chopped

4 tablespoons double cream

2 teaspoons Dijon mustard

salt and freshly ground black pepper

To garnish

chopped fresh parsley

1 Skin, halve and core the kidneys with kitchen scissors. Cut into chunks.

2 Melt the butter in a frying pan and brown the kidneys quickly all over. Remove to a sieve set over a bowl and discard the juices. Return the kidneys to the pan, add the mushrooms and cook for 1 minute.

3 Reduce the heat and stir in the cream, mustard, salt and pepper. Garnish with parsley and serve immediately.

wine: **FULL RED**

Veal Kidneys Robert

SERVES 2–3

150 ml | ¼ pint dry white wine

450 g | 1 lb veal kidneys

45 g | 1½ oz unsalted butter

1 teaspoon Dijon mustard

2 teaspoons chopped fresh parsley

a squeeze of lemon juice

salt and freshly ground black pepper

2 tablespoons double cream

1 Put the wine into a saucepan and boil until reduced by half.

2 Remove the membranes and cores from the kidneys, and cut into chunks.

3 Fry a handful of kidney pieces at a time in hot butter in a frying pan, shaking the pan until the kidneys are brown but still pale inside. Remove to a sieve set over a bowl and discard the juices.

4 Add the mustard and reduced wine to the pan. Bring to the boil, stirring continuously. Stir in the cream. Simmer until syrupy. Stir in the kidneys and add season with lemon juice, salt and pepper.

5 Turn into a warmed serving dish and sprinkle with parsley.

wine: **FULL RED**

Veal Kidney Feuilletées

If ceps, chanterelles or morels are not available, use small button mushrooms instead.

SERVES 4

225 g | 8 oz flour quantity puff pastry (see page 566)
1 beaten egg to glaze

For the filling
150 ml | ¼ pint dry white wine
340 g | 12 oz veal kidneys

55 g | 2 oz ceps, sliced
55 g | 2 oz small chanterelles
55 g | 2 oz small morels
2 teaspoons Dijon mustard
1 tablespoon chopped fresh parsley
salt and freshly ground black pepper
6 tablespoons double cream

1 Preheat the oven to 220°C | 425°F | gas mark 7.

2 Roll the pastry into a large rectangle. Cut it into 4 diamonds. Place the diamonds on a damp baking tray and brush with beaten egg. Using a sharp knife, trace a line about 1 cm | ½ in from the edge of each diamond, without cutting all the way through the pastry. A small diamond is thus traced, which will form the hat for the pastry case. Make a design inside this diamond with the knife. Flour the blades of the knife and use this to 'knock up' the sides of pastry. Chill for 15 minutes.

3 Bake for 20 minutes or until puffed up and brown. With a knife, outline and remove the 'hats' and scoop out any uncooked dough inside. Transfer the cases and hats to a wire rack to cool. Reduce the oven temperature to 180°C | 350°F | gas mark 4.

4 Meanwhile, prepare the filling: put the wine into a saucepan and boil until reduced by half.

5 Remove the membranes and cores from the kidneys and cut into chunks.

6 In a frying pan, fry the ceps, chanterelles and morels in a little of the butter over a very low heat for about 3 minutes. Set aside.

7 Fry the kidneys, a small handful at a time, in the remaining butter over a low heat. Remove to a sieve set over a bowl. Bitter juices will run out of the kidneys and these should be discarded.

8 Return the pastry cases to the oven for 4 minutes to reheat.

9 Put the wine, mustard, parsley, salt, pepper and cream into the frying pan. Bring to the boil and reduce, by boiling rapidly, for 1 minute or until syrupy. Add the kidneys and mushrooms to the sauce.

10 Divide the filling between the 4 pastry cases. Put on the hats and serve immediately.

wine: **MEDIUM RED**

Calves' Liver Lyonnaise

SERVES 4

450 g | 1 lb calves' liver, skinned and sliced
55 g | 2 oz unsalted butter
1 large onion, thinly sliced
seasoned plain flour
salt and freshly ground black pepper
290 ml | ½ pint brown stock (see page 102)

1 tablespoon orange juice
1 tablespoon finely chopped mixed fresh herbs, such
   as rosemary, sage, thyme

To garnish

chopped fresh parsley

1 Remove any large tubes from the slices of liver.
2 Heat half the butter in a frying pan and slowly cook the onion until first soft and transparent and then golden-brown. Set aside.
3 Dip the slices of liver into the seasoned flour, shaking off any excess.
4 Heat the remaining butter until foaming. Fry the liver pieces in it, a few at a time, for about 2 minutes each side. The liver should be nicely browned on the outside but pale pink in the middle. Drain well. Arrange in overlapping slices with the onions in an ovenproof dish. Keep warm.
5 Sprinkle enough of the seasoned flour (about 1 teaspoon) into the frying pan to absorb the remaining fat. Cook until light brown, stirring and scraping any sediment from the bottom of the pan. Gradually stir in the stock and the orange juice. Allow to boil. Season with pepper and salt and add the herbs. Simmer until syrupy. Pour over the liver, garnish with parsley and serve immediately.

wine: **MEDIUM RED**

Liver and Bacon

SERVES 4

450 g | 1 lb calves' or lambs' liver, skinned and sliced
seasoned plain flour
55 g | 2 oz butter
1 onion, thinly sliced
6 rashers of rindless bacon

290 ml | ½ pint brown stock (see page 102)
2 tablespoons sherry

To garnish

1 small bunch of watercress

1 Heat half the butter in a frying pan and fry the onion slowly until soft and brown. Set aside.
2 Preheat the grill. Grill the bacon until crisp and brown but not brittle. Turn off the grill and leave the bacon under it to keep warm.
3 Remove any large tubes from the liver. Dip the slices in seasoned flour and keep well separated on a plate.
4 Heat the remaining butter in the frying pan and fry the liver slices, a few at a time,

adding more butter if necessary. Note that liver is easily spoiled by overcooking. Arrange the slices on a warmed shallow platter and keep warm.

5 Put the onion, and any of its fat, back into the pan and add a sprinkling of the seasoned flour – just enough to absorb the fat. Cook for 1 minute. Pour in the stock and stir well as it comes to the boil. Add the sherry.

6 Boil the sauce rapidly to reduce in quantity and thicken it. This will also give a richer appearance and concentrate the flavour. Check the seasoning.

7 Pour the sauce over the liver, top with the bacon and garnish with watercress. Serve immediately as liver toughens on standing.

wine: **FULL RED**

Oxtail Stew

SERVES 4

2 oxtails, cut into 2.5 cm|1 in lengths, total weight about 1.35 kg|3 lb
seasoned plain flour
30 g|1 oz beef dripping or oil
340 g|12 oz carrots, thickly sliced
225 g|8 oz onions, sliced
150 ml|¼ pint red wine
570 ml|1 pint water or stock

1 teaspoon chopped fresh thyme
salt and freshly ground black pepper
½ teaspoon sugar
1 teaspoon tomato purée
juice of ½ lemon

To garnish
2 tablespoons chopped fresh parsley

1 Wash and dry the oxtails. Trim off any excess fat and toss in seasoned flour.

2 Melt the dripping in a heavy saucepan, add the oxtail, a few pieces at a time, and brown on all sides evenly and well. Remove to a plate as they are done.

3 Brown the carrots and onions in the same pan.

4 Replace the oxtail. Pour over the wine and water or stock and add the thyme, salt, pepper and sugar. Bring to the boil, then simmer for 2 hours.

5 Preheat the oven to 150°C|300°F|gas mark 2.

6 Take out the pieces of meat and vegetables and place in a casserole.

7 With a small ladle or spoon, skim off the fat which will rise to the top of the remaining liquid. Add the tomato purée and lemon juice and bring quickly to the boil.

8 Pour this over the oxtail, cover with a lid, and cook in the oven for about 3 hours, or until the meat is almost falling off the bone. Sprinkle with the parsley.

NOTES: If the sauce is too thin, remove the meat and vegetables to a warmed serving dish and boil the sauce rapidly until reduced to the desired consistency.

When buying oxtail choose short fat tails with a good proportion of meat on them. Long stringy thin tails are poor value – pale in flavour and short on meat.

Oxtail is very good served with dumplings (see page 458).

wine: **FULL RED**

Pressed Tongue

SERVES 4

1 ox tongue, fresh or salted

salt

6 black peppercorns

1 bouquet garni (1 stick of celery, 1 bay leaf, 1 sprig each of fresh parsley and thyme, tied together with string)

2 onions, sliced

2 carrots, peeled and sliced

1 stick of celery, sliced

425 ml | ¾ pint aspic made from brown stock and gelatine (see page 105)

1 If the tongue is salted, soak it in fresh water for 4 hours. If the tongue is fresh, soak it in brine (salty water) for 1–2 hours.

2 Place it in a saucepan and pour in enough water to cover completely.

3 Add salt if the tongue is fresh. Add the peppercorns, bouquet garni, onions, carrots and celery.

4 Bring gently to the boil, skimming off any scum. Cover tightly and simmer for 3–4 hours, or until tender when pierced with a skewer. Remove from the heat and leave to cool for 1 hour in the liquid.

5 Take out the tongue. Remove the bones from the root and peel off the skin.

6 Curl the warm tongue tightly and fit it into a deep round cake tin or tongue press. Cool.

7 Pour a little cool jellied stock or aspic into the tin.

8 Place a plate which just fits inside the tin on top of the tongue. Stand a heavy weight (about 4 kg | 8 lb) on the plate and leave overnight in the refrigerator.

9 To carve: slice thinly across the top of the round.

NOTE: The stock in which the tongue is cooked is suitable for use in making the jellied stock if it is not too salty.

wine: **MEDIUM RED**

Haggis

Even in Scotland haggis is seldom made at home today, mainly because a sheep's pluck, consisting of the liver, heart and lights (lungs), makes too much haggis for a modern-sized family, and cleaning the stomach of the sheep (which forms the skin of the haggis) is a tedious and messy business, requiring much washing and careful scraping. This is a simplified haggis, cooked in a pudding basin instead of a sheep's stomach.

SERVES 4

2 onions

2 sheep's hearts

450 g | 1 lb lambs' liver

55 g | 2 oz oatmeal

85 g | 3 oz chopped beef suet

1 teaspoons chopped fresh sage

a pinch of ground allspice

salt and freshly ground black pepper

butter for greasing

1 Peel the onions and put them, with the cleaned hearts and liver, into a saucepan of water. Boil for 40 minutes, then lift them out of the liquid.
2 Mince the hearts, liver and onions and mix with the oatmeal, suet, sage, allspice and plenty of salt and pepper. Add enough of the cooking liquid to give a soft dropping consistency.
3 Grease a pudding basin, fill with the mixture, cover with greaseproof paper and kitchen foil and tie down with string.
4 Steam for 2 hours. Serve hot.

NOTE: Very good haggis can be bought in reliable shops. Do not prick haggis before boiling or baking – it may burst. A haggis should be boiled for 30 minutes per 450 g│1 lb, but for a minimum of 1 hour. It can also be baked, wrapped in kitchen foil, at 180°C│350°F│gas mark 4 for 3 minutes per 450 g│1 lb, but for a minimum of 1 hour. Place the wrapped haggis in a casserole, add a little water and cover tightly.

wine: **WHISKY OR FULL RED**

Breakfasts and Brunches

Fried English Breakfast

Eggs should be fried in clean fat. Frying them in a pan in which bacon or sausages have been cooking leads to sticking and possible breaking of the yolks. If eggs are to be fried in the same pan as other items, fry the bacon, ham, sausages, potatoes, mushrooms and bread first as this will all keep in a warm oven for a few minutes. Tip the fat into a cup. Rinse the pan, removing any stuck sediment, dry it, then pour the fat back into the pan. Using enough sizzling fat to spoon over eggs speeds up the process and prevents the edges of the whites from overcooking before the thicker parts are set.

Sausages generally have skins which, as the stuffing expands in the hot pan, can burst or split open. Avoid this by cooking slowly. Shake the pan with rapid but careful side-to-side or forward-and-backward movements; this will dislodge any pieces that are stuck with less damage than a prodding utensil. Fry the sausages slowly until evenly browned all over and firm to the touch.

Bacon rashers can be fried in an almost dry pan as they readily produce their own fat. However, they cook faster and more evenly in shallow fat.

Eggs are often boiled, yet there is considerable confusion about the correct method of doing this. The easiest and most foolproof is as follows:

1 Bring a pan of water to the boil. Have the eggs at room temperature. (If chilled, add 30 seconds to cooking time.)
2 Carefully lower the eggs into the water on a perforated spoon.
3 Time the cooking from the moment of immersion, keeping the water simmering or gently boiling, and not boiling too vigorously, which tends to crack the shells and toughen the whites. Three minutes will cook a medium-sized egg until the white is barely set; indeed, the white closest to the yolk will still be slightly jelly-like. Four minutes give a runny yolk and a just-set white. Six minutes give a well-set white and moist but runny yolk (set on the rim and thick but wet inside). Eight minutes give a hardboiled egg with a set, but still moist, yolk. Ten minutes will give a yolk sufficiently cooked to be dry and crumbly when mashed. Fifteen minutes will give a yellow-green rim to the dry yolk and make the white tough and unpalatable. For hardboiling eggs, see page 162.

Poached Eggs on Toast

SERVES 4

4 very fresh cold eggs

4 slices of fresh toast, buttered

1 teaspoon white wine vinegar (optional)

salt and freshly ground black pepper

1 Fill a large saucepan with water and vinegar if using and bring to simmering point.

2 Crack an egg into a cup and tip into the pan, holding the cup as near to the water as possible.

3 Raise the temperature so that the water bubbles gently.

4 With a slotted spoon, draw the egg white close to the yolk.

5 Poach each egg for 2–3 minutes until the white is set, but the yolk is still soft.

6 Lift out with the slotted spoon, drain on absorbent kitchen paper and trim the egg whites if they are very ragged at the edges.

7 Place each egg on a piece of toast and sprinkle with salt and pepper. Serve immediately.

Baked Eggs

SERVES 4

melted butter for brushing

4 medium eggs at room temperature

salt and freshly ground black pepper

4 teaspoons single cream

15 g | ½ oz butter

1 Preheat the oven to 180°C | 350°F | gas mark 4.

2 Brush 4 cocotte dishes with butter and stand them in a roasting pan half-filled with hot water (a bain-marie).

3 Break an egg carefully into each dish and season with salt and pepper. Spoon over a little cream and place a knob of butter on top.

4 Bake uncovered in the centre of the oven for about 10 minutes, until the whites are set and the yolks runny.

NOTES: The eggs will continue cooking for a short time after removing from the oven, so be very careful not to overcook.

Tarragon eggs can be made by adding 2 fresh tarragon leaves to each egg before spooning over the cream.

wine: **LIGHT RED**

Oeufs Florentine

Eggs for poaching must be very fresh; if not, a little vinegar can be added to the water to help the white coagulate but too much vinegar will have an adverse effect on the taste.

SERVES 4

450 g | 1 lb fresh spinach, cooked and chopped

15 g | ½ oz butter, melted

salt and freshly ground black pepper

a good pinch of freshly grated nutmeg

4 eggs, chilled

290 ml | ½ pint Mornay sauce (see page 112)

a little grated cheese

browned breadcrumbs

1 Turn the spinach in the melted butter. Season with salt, pepper and nutmeg. Place in the bottom of an ovenproof dish.

2 Preheat the oven to 150°C | 300°F | gas mark 2. Preheat the grill.

3 Poach the eggs: three-quarters fill a large shallow pan with water. Bring to the boil, then lower the temperature to a simmer. Break an egg into a cup and slip it into the water. Immediately raise the temperature slightly so that the bubbles help to draw the white round the yolk. Poach for about 3 minutes, then lift out with a slotted spoon.

4 Trim the whites neatly with a pair of scissors or a stainless steel knife and drain thoroughly by shaking the slotted spoon.

5 Arrange the eggs on top of the spinach and coat with the cheese sauce. Sprinkle over the cheese and crumbs.

6 Brown the top under the hot grill.

wine: **LIGHT RED**

Scrambled Eggs on Toast

SERVES 1

2 eggs	1 slice of crustless buttered toast
salt and freshly ground black pepper	15 g ½ oz butter

1 In a bowl mix together the eggs, salt and pepper with a fork until no white streaks remain.

2 Toast the bread. Place on a heated plate and keep warm.

3 Melt the butter in a saucepan over medium-low heat. Tip in the egg mixture and using a wooden spoon keep it constantly moving until set but still moist.

4 Pile on to the prepared toast and serve immediately.

Smoked Salmon and Scrambled Eggs

Most recipes for smoked salmon and scrambled eggs suggest chopping up the smoked salmon and adding it to the eggs just before they are ready to serve. We serve the salmon cold as we feel warm smoked salmon can taste a little like smoked ham.

SERVES 4

110 g 4 oz Scotch smoked salmon	8 eggs
salt and freshly ground black pepper	55 g 2 oz butter

1 Divide the smoked salmon into 4 and arrange on one half of 4 side plates. Grind over a little pepper.

2 Mix together the eggs, salt and pepper. Beat well.

3 Melt the butter in a non-stick frying pan. Tip in the egg mixture and using a wooden spoon stir constantly until set but still creamy.

4 Pile on the plates and serve immediately.

wine: **SPICY WHITE**

Plain French Omelette

SERVES 1

3 eggs

salt and freshly ground black pepper

a pinch of freshly grated Parmesan cheese (optional)

1 tablespoon cold water

15 g | ½ oz butter

1 Break the eggs into a bowl and whisk with a fork until foamy and no longer streaky. Mix in the seasoning, Parmesan cheese and water.
2 Melt the butter in a heavy 15 cm | 6 in non-stick omelette pan and swirl it around so that the bottom and sides are coated. When foaming, pour in the egg mixture.
3 Hold the pan handle in your left hand and move it gently back and forth over the heat. At the same time, move the mixture slowly, scraping up large creamy flakes of egg mixture. As you do this some of the liquid egg from the middle of the omelette will run to the sides of the pan. Tilt the pan to help this process. Leave over the heat until the bottom has set and the top is creamy. Remove from the heat.
4 With a fork or palette knife fold the nearside edge of the omelette over to the centre and then flick the whole omelette over on to a warmed plate with the folded edges on the underside. Alternatively, fold the omelette in two and slide it on to the plate.

NOTE: Grated cheese, fresh chopped herbs, fried mushrooms or other flavourings can be added to the basic omelette mixture.

wine: **LIGHT RED**

Omelette Arnold Bennett

SERVES 4

1 slice of onion

1–2 slices of carrot

1 bay leaf

4 black peppercorns

150 ml ¼ pint milk

110 g | 4 oz smoked haddock

30 g | 1 oz butter

15 g | ½ oz plain flour

3 eggs, separated

3 tablespoons single cream

fresh ground black pepper

1 tablespoon freshly grated Parmesan cheese

1 Put the onion, carrot, bay leaf, peppercorns and milk into a saucepan and heat slowly.
2 When the milk is well infused, add the haddock skin side down. Cover with a piece of damp greaseproof paper. Poach gently for 10 minutes, or until the fish is just cooked.
3 Take out the fish and skin, bone and flake it. Strain and reserve the cooking liquor.
4 Melt 15 g | ½ oz of the butter in a small saucepan, remove from the heat and add the flour. Return to the heat and stir over the heat for 1 minute.

5 Remove from the heat. Gradually add 150 ml | ¼ pint of the strained cooking liquor. Stir until boiling. Cook for 1 minute.

6 Beat the egg yolks with 2 tablespoons of the cream. Season with pepper only (do not add salt as the haddock is salty). Stir the sauce, a little at a time, into the egg yolks.

7 Add the haddock and half the cheese. Check the seasoning.

8 Whisk the egg whites to medium peaks and fold into the sauce.

9 Preheat the grill to its highest setting.

10 Melt the remaining butter in an omelette pan over a medium-high heat, tipping the pan so that the bottom and sides are coated. When the foaming begins to subside quickly pour in the egg mixture.

11 When the omelette is beginning to set, sprinkle on the remaining cheese, pour over the remaining tablespoon of cream and brown quickly under the hot grill.

12 Slide the omelette on to a warmed dish.

wine: **SPICY WHITE**

Waffles

MAKES 8–10

2 eggs
170 g | 6 oz plain flour
a pinch of salt
1 tablespoon baking powder
30 g | 1 oz caster sugar
290 ml | ½ pint milk
55 g | 2 oz butter, melted

a few drops of vanilla essence
extra melted butter

To serve

butter
honey, maple syrup or jam

1 Separate the eggs.

2 Sift the flour, salt, baking powder and sugar together into a large bowl. Make a well in the centre and put in the egg yolks.

3 Stir the yolks, gradually drawing in the flour from the edges and adding the milk and melted butter until you have a thin batter. Add the vanilla essence.

4 Grease a waffle iron and heat it.

5 Whisk the egg whites until stiff but not dry and fold into the batter with a large metal spoon.

6 Add a little melted butter to the hot waffle iron, pour in about 4 tablespoons of the mixture, close and cook for 1 minute on each side.

7 Serve hot with butter and honey, maple syrup or jam.

NOTE: The first waffle always sticks to the iron and should be discarded.

Granola

340 g | 12 oz rolled jumbo oats
2 tablespoons sunflower seeds
2 tablespoons pumpkin seeds
85 g | 3 oz skinned hazelnuts
85 g | 3 oz flaked almonds
55 g | 2 oz demerara sugar

8 tablespoons unsweetened apple juice
2 tablespoons clear honey
30 g | 1 oz dried cherries
30 g | 1 oz dried blueberries
4 dried figs, roughly chopped

1 Preheat the oven to 175°C | 275°F | gas mark 5.

2 In a large bowl, mix together the oats, seeds, nuts and sugar.

3 Mix the apple juice and warm honey together and pour over the oat mixture. Stir well.

4 Spread the mixture over a large baking sheet and bake in the centre of the oven for 20–25 minutes, stirring occasionally, until crisp and beginning to brown. It is important to check the toasting oat mixture from time to time to prevent it from burning.

5 Remove from the oven and allow to cool.

6 When cold, stir in the dried fruit and transfer to an airtight container until required.

French Toast

MAKES 16 FINGERS

4 slices of white bread, crusts removed
2 eggs
150 ml | ¼ pint milk

a good pinch of freshly grated nutmeg
55 g | 2 oz butter
oil

1 Cut each slice of bread into 4 fingers.

2 Beat the eggs, milk and nutmeg together in a pie dish or soup plate.

3 Dip the bread fingers into this mixture, coating them well.

4 Melt half the butter with a tablespoon of oil in a heavy frying pan. When the butter is foaming, fry the bread in it until golden-brown on both sides. Drain on absorbent kitchen paper. Add the remaining butter and more oil as needed, until all the bread fingers are cooked.

NOTE: French toast is sometimes served with crisp bacon, or with marmalade, maple syrup or a mixture of sugar and cinnamon, or with strawberries sprinkled with icing sugar.

Jugged Kippers

This is a simple, labour-saving method of cooking kippers.

SERVES 4

4 kippers   freshly ground black pepper
butter

1 Place the kippers, tails up, in a tall stoneware jug. Pour over enough boiling water to cover the kippers and leave to stand for 5–10 minutes. Remove from the jug and drain.
2 Serve immediately on a warmed dish with a knob of butter and plenty of pepper.

Kedgeree

SERVES 4

55 g | 2 oz butter   3 hardboiled eggs, roughly chopped
140 g | 5 oz (raw weight) long-grain rice, boiled   salt and freshly ground black pepper
340 g | 12 oz smoked haddock or fresh salmon fillet,   cayenne pepper
   cooked, skinned and boned

1 Melt the butter in a large shallow saucepan and add all the remaining ingredients.
2 Stir gently until very hot.

NOTE: If making large quantities, heat in the oven instead of on the top of the stove. Kedgeree will not spoil in a low oven (130°C | 250°F | gas mark 1). Stir occasionally.

Porridge

SERVES 4

1.1 litres | 2 pints water   110 g | 4 oz medium oatmeal
1 teaspoon salt

1 Bring the water to the boil in a saucepan and add the salt.
2 Sprinkle in the oatmeal, keeping the water on the boil and stirring all the time.
3 Simmer for 30 minutes, stirring occasionally. If necessary add a little more water.

NOTE: Porridge keeps for an hour or so in a cool oven if covered with a lid, but should not be made too far in advance. Traditionally it is served with salt in Scotland, but in the south milk and sugar are added.

Supper Dishes and Snacks

Baked Eggs with Mushrooms

SERVES 4

45 g | 1½ oz butter

1 shallot, finely chopped

110 g | 4 oz mushrooms, finely chopped

2 teaspoons chopped fresh parsley

salt and freshly ground white pepper

4 eggs

4 tablespoons single cream or creamy milk

1 Preheat the oven to 180°C | 350°F | gas mark 4. Lightly butter 4 ramekin or cocotte dishes.

2 Melt half the remaining butter, add the shallot and cook until very soft but not coloured.

3 Add the remaining butter with the mushrooms. Cook slowly over a low heat until the mushrooms are soft. Add the parsley and season to taste with salt and pepper.

4 Divide this mixture between the 4 dishes, make a dip in each cocotte and break an egg into each. Spoon 1 tablespoon cream on to each egg and season with salt and pepper.

5 Stand the dishes in a roasting pan half-filled with hot water (a bain-marie) and bake in the oven for 10–12 minutes, until the whites are just set and the yolks still runny.

wine: **LIGHT RED**

Scotch Eggs

SERVES 4

340 g | 12 oz good-quality sausagemeat

salt and freshly ground black pepper

4 hardboiled eggs, shelled (see page 162)

seasoned plain flour

oil for frying

beaten egg

2 tablespoons dried white breadcrumbs

1 Season the sausagemeat with salt and pepper. Divide it into 4 equal pieces.

2 Roll the eggs in seasoned flour. Dip your hands in a little water and mould the sausagemeat around each egg, making sure they are completely and evenly covered.

3 Place at least 3.5 cm | 1½ in of oil in a deep-fryer and begin to heat it up slowly.

4 Dip the eggs in seasoned flour, brush with beaten egg and coat with breadcrumbs.

5 Place the prepared eggs in the deep-fryer basket when the oil is hot enough to brown a

cube of bread in 60 seconds. Put in the eggs and fry for about 12 minutes. Remove from the oil. Increase the oil temperature so that the cube of bread will brown in 30 seconds.

6 Fry the egss for a further 5 minutes to brown. Drain on absorbent kitchen paper and sprinkle with a little salt.

wine: **MEDIUM RED**

Frogs' Legs with Rosemary and Ginger

SERVES 4

45 g | 1½ oz butter, softened

a large pinch of ground ginger

a small piece of fresh root ginger, peeled and finely chopped

1 sprig of fresh rosemary, roughly chopped

½ clove of garlic, crushed

salt and freshly ground black pepper

8 frogs' legs

a little butter for frying

150 ml | ¼ pint dry white wine

1 Mix together the butter, ground and fresh ginger, rosemary, garlic, salt and pepper and beat well. Spread this mixture over the frogs' legs.

2 Fry the frogs' legs briefly on both sides in a little butter in a frying pan to just colour.

3 Pour over the wine and simmer for 7 minutes. If the wine evaporates too much, add a little water.

4 Remove the frogs' legs and keep them warm. Bring the sauce to a rolling boil and reduce, whisking all the time until slightly thickened.

5 Pour the sauce over the frogs' legs and serve immediately.

wine: **SPICY DRY WHITE**

Hot Sweet Potato Stew

SERVES 4

120 ml | 4 fl oz oil

1 tablespoon yellow mustard seeds

1 teaspoon ground mace

2 green chillies, chopped

5 cloves of garlic, crushed

30 g | 1 oz fresh root ginger, peeled and sliced

2 onions, peeled and sliced

225 g | 8 oz sweet potatoes, sliced

225 g | 8 oz parsnips, sliced

450 g | 1 lb tomatoes chopped, or 1 × 400 g | 14 oz can

1 tablespoon garam masala

lemon juice to taste

salt and freshly ground black pepper

1 Heat the oil in a large pan, add the mustard seeds and mace and cook until the seeds pop.

2 Reduce the heat, add the onion and cook until soft. Add the chilli, garlic, ginger and onion, and cook for a further minute.

3 Add the sweet potato, parsnip and tomatoes. Cover and simmer very gently until the vegetables soften. Add the garam masala. Season to taste with lemon juice, salt and pepper.

wine: **MEDIUM DRY WHITE**

Lentil 'Cassoulet'

SERVES 4

tablespoons olive oil

340 g | 12 oz lamb fillet (shoulder), sliced

1 large onion, thinly sliced

1 clove of garlic, crushed

450 g | 1 lb brown lentils

1 × 400 g | 14 oz can of tomatoes

water to moisten

100 ml | 3½ fl oz red wine

5 cloves, tied in a muslin bag or a clean 'J'-cloth

salt and freshly ground black pepper

1 tablespoon herbes de Provence

1 large spicy sausage, sliced

1 Heat the oil in a large, flameproof casserole and lightly brown the lamb on both sides. Remove to a plate. Reduce the heat and add the onion and cook until beginning to soften, then add the garlic.

2 Add the lentils, lamb, tomatoes and enough water to cover. Bring gradually to the boil and add the wine, cloves, salt and pepper and herbs.

3 Cover and simmer very slowly until the lentils are soft but not mushy (about 1 hour). Check every so often to make sure that the mixture is not getting too dry. If so, add extra water.

4 Add the sausage about 10 minutes before the lentils are cooked. Serve with a green salad.

wine: **FULL RED**

Pipérade

SERVES 4

2 tablespoons olive oil

1 gammon steak, about 170 g | 6 oz, cut into thin strips

1 Spanish onion, thinly sliced

2 red or green peppers, deseeded and thinly sliced

2 cloves of garlic, peeled and sliced

4 tomatoes, peeled and quartered

55 g | 2 oz butter

8 eggs, beaten

salt and freshly ground black pepper

1 tablespoon chopped fresh parsley

1 Heat the oil in a large sauté pan, add the gammon strips and fry until lightly browned. Remove from the pan and keep warm.

2 Add the onion to the pan and cook until beginning to soften.

3 Add the peppers and continue frying until they are softened.

4 Add the garlic and cook for 1 minute. Add the tomatoes and fry to warm through. Remove the vegetables from the pan, combine with the gammon strips and keep warm.

5 Melt the butter in the sauté pan over a low heat. Add the eggs and cook, stirring, until they are set.

6 Stir the warm vegetables and gammon mixture into the eggs. Season with salt and pepper.

7 Garnish with the parsley and serve immediately.

wine: **SPICY WHITE**

Chorizos

This recipe is from Jane Grigson's *Charcuterie and French Pork Cookery*. The sausages are lightly smoked in a food smoker before they are cooked. The smoking, which does not cook the sausages but simply adds flavour, may be omitted.

MAKES 20
For the filling

450 g | 1 lb lean pork (neck or shoulder)
225 g | 8 oz pork fat
1 small red pepper
1 small chilli
70 ml | 2½ fl oz red wine
1 tablespoon salt

¼ teaspoon granulated sugar
a good pinch of saltpetre, if available
¼ teaspoon ground mixed spice
¼ teaspoon cayenne pepper
1 large clove of garlic, crushed
sausage skins (2.5 cm | 1 in diameter), washed
    (available from good butchers)

1 Mince the pork and fat, using the coarse blade of the mincer.
2 Cut the pepper and chilli in half, remove the seeds and stalks, put through the mincer and add to the pork.
3 Add the remaining ingredients and mix well.
4 Fill the sausage skins with the mixture, but do not pack too tightly or the sausages will burst. Twist every 12.5–15 cm | 5–6 in.
5 Smoke for 20 minutes.
6 Cook as required.

wine: **MEDIUM RED**

Venison Sausages

MAKES ABOUT 80

1.8 kg | 4 lb boned venison (haunch or shoulder)
900 g | 2 lb rump steak
675 g | 1½ lb pork fat
225 g | 8 oz canned anchovy fillets
4 teaspoons juniper berries, crushed
1 clove of garlic, crushed
1 tablespoon ground ginger
1½ tablespoons salt
1 tablespoon dried sage

1 teaspoon ground mace
1 teaspoon mignonette or cracked black pepper
425 ml | ¾ pint red wine
150 ml | ¼ pint Jamaica rum
340 g | 12 oz Cox's apples, unpeeled and grated
oil for frying
sausage skins (2.5 cm | 1 in diameter), washed
    (available from good butchers)

1 Mince together the meats, fat and anchovy fillets. Mince again. Mix in all the remaining ingredients and beat well.

2 Fry a small amount of the mixture in a little oil to test for seasoning before filling the skins.

3 Fill the sausage skins with the mixture; do not pack too tightly or they will burst. Twist every 10–12.5 cm | 4–5 in.

4 Cook as required.

wine: **FULL RED**

Boudin Blanc

This recipe has been adapted from *The Observer French Cookery School*.

MAKES ABOUT 10

1 onion, chopped

15 g | ½ oz butter

150 ml | ¼ pint double cream

100 g | 3½ oz fresh white breadcrumbs

2 metres | 6 yards pork intestine

225 g | 8 oz lean veal

225 g | 8 oz fatty pork

225 g | 8 oz boned chicken breast, or a further
      225 g | 8 oz lean veal

½ teaspoon ground allspice

salt and freshly ground white pepper

3 eggs, beaten

oil for frying

For cooking

1.5 litres 2½ pints water

750 ml | 1¼ pints milk

1 Sweat the onion in the butter until very soft, then cool.

2 Scald the cream by bringing it to just below boiling point, pour it over the breadcrumbs and leave to cool.

3 Soak the pork intestine in cold water.

4 Work the veal, fat pork and chicken, if used, twice through the fine blade of a mincer, adding the onion before the second mincing. Alternatively, work the meat and onion a little at a time in a food processor. Put the mixture into a bowl and stir in the soaked breadcrumbs, allspice and plenty of salt and pepper.

5 Add enough egg to bind the mixture. Sauté a small ball of the mixture in a little oil and check the seasoning – the mixture should be quite spicy. Beat with a wooden spoon or your hand until very smooth.

6 Fill the sausages: drain the pork intestine – it should be pliable. Tie one end, insert the sausage-stuffer or funnel in the other and squeeze in the filling. Do not fill them too tightly or they will burst during cooking. Tie into 15 cm | 6 in sausages.

7 Bring the water and milk to the boil in a large pan. Lower the sausages into the pan. Cover and poach very gently until firm, about 18–20 minutes. Remove, drain and leave to cool completely. They can be cooked up to 24 hours ahead and kept covered in the refrigerator. They are very good fried and served with slices of fried apple.

wine: **LIGHT RED**

Pumpkin and Lentil Strudel

SERVES 4–6

1 tablespoon olive oil

4 shallots, sliced

1 large clove of garlic, crushed

675 g | 1½ lb pumpkin, peeled, deseeded and cut into 2.5 cm | 1 in cubes

110 g | 4 oz brown lentils, cooked

1 × 400 g | 14 oz can of tomatoes

1 teaspoon chopped fresh thyme

1 bay leaf

½ teaspoon sugar

salt and freshly ground black pepper

140 g | 5 oz flour quantity strudel pastry (see page 563) or 6 sheets of ready-made filo pastry

85 g | 3 oz butter, melted

1 tablespoon very finely chopped fresh parsley

1 egg, beaten

1 tablespoon sesame seeds

1 Heat the oil in a large saucepan. Add the shallots and cook until soft and transparent.

2 Stir in the pumpkin and lentils. Then add the garlic and cook for a further minute.

3 Add the tomatoes, thyme and bay leaf. Cook for 20 minutes or until the pumpkin and lentils are soft but still holds their shape. The mixture should be moist but not runny. Season to taste with the sugar, salt and pepper. Remove from the heat and leave to cool. Remove the bay leaf.

4 Preheat the oven to 200°C | 400°F | gas mark 6. Grease a large baking sheet.

5 If using home-made strudel pastry, stretch it on a floured tea towel. If using ready-made filo pastry, arrange overlapping sheets on the tea towel.

6 Brush the pastry with the melted butter.

7 Place the pumpkin and lentil filling in a line at one end of the pastry and scatter with parsley. Using the tea towel to help, roll up the pastry as for a Swiss roll, trying to maintain a fairly tight roll. Lift the cloth and gently tip the strudel on to the prepared baking sheet. Bend into a crescent.

8 Brush with beaten egg and sprinkle with sesame seeds.

9 Bake on the middle shelf of the preheated oven for 30 minutes or until golden-brown. Serve hot.

wine: **LIGHT RED**

Cassoulet

SERVES 12

900 g | 2 lb dried haricot beans

225 g | 8 oz salt pork or unsmoked bacon

1 onion, studded with 8 cloves

1 bouquet garni (see page 19)

2 cloves of garlic, crushed

450 g | 1 lb pork blade bone

225 g | 8 oz Toulouse sausage or Cumberland sausage

1 tablespoon tomato purée

675 g | 1½ lb boned breast of lamb

8 large tomatoes, peeled and quartered

2 tablespoons chopped fresh thyme

2 tablespoons chopped fresh parsley

salt and freshly ground black pepper

4 tablespoons fresh white breadcrumbs

1 Wash the beans well in cold water and leave to soak overnight. Blanch in clean water for 5 minutes, then drain.
2 Rinse well and place in a pan of fresh cold water, making sure the beans are covered. Add the rind of the salt pork or bacon, the onion and cloves, bouquet garni and garlic.
3 Bring to the boil, then skim and simmer for $1\frac{3}{4}$ hours, or until the beans are very soft.
4 Meanwhile, preheat the oven to 190°C│375°F│gas mark 5. Roast the lamb, salt pork, pork and sausages in the oven for 30 minutes or until the meat is cooked and the sausages brown.
5 Remove the meat from the oven, tip off and reserve the fat, slice the sausages into 2.5 cm│1 in pieces and cut the meat into 2.5 cm│1 in chunks.
6 When the beans are cooked strain them, reserving the cooking liquor. Discard the rind, onion and bouquet garni. Add the tomato purée.
7 Turn the oven temperature down to 180°C│350°F│gas mark 4.
8 Place a layer of beans in a deep ovenproof dish. Cover with a layer of meat, sausage, tomatoes and herbs. Season generously with salt and pepper. Continue to layer up, finishing with a layer of beans. Pour over the cooking liquor until it nearly reaches the top, and sprinkle the breadcrumbs on the top. Reserve any remaining cooking liquid in case the cassoulet gets dry.
9 Cook uncovered in the oven for $1\frac{1}{2}$ hours. If the breadcrumbs become dry and crusty, stir them into the cassoulet and add more liquid if necessary. Sprinkle more breadcrumbs on top. At the end of the cooking time the meat and beans should be very tender and creamy and the top crisp and brown.

wine: FULL RICH RED

Chilli con Carne with Avocado Salsa

SERVES 4–6

3 tablespoons vegetable oil
1 large onion, chopped
500 g│1 lb 2 oz minced beef
290 ml│½ pint brown stock (see page 102)
2 cloves of garlic, crushed
1–2 teaspoons mild chilli powder
½ teaspoon ground cumin
¼ teaspoon ground cinnamon
1 teaspoon dried oregano
2   400 g│14 oz cans of tomatoes in tomato juice
225 g│8 oz cooked red kidney beans (or 2 400 g│14 oz cans, rinsed and drained)

1 teaspoon salt
freshly ground black pepper
1 teaspoon caster sugar

For the salsa
1 avocado
salt and freshly ground black pepper
juice of 1 lime
1 fresh green chilli, deseeded and diced
1 red pepper, deseeded and diced
2 tablespoons chopped fresh coriander

1 Heat half the oil in a small saucepan. Stir in the onion. Cover with a piece of dampened greaseproof paper and a lid. Sweat over a low heat for about 20 minutes until soft.
2 Heat the remaining oil in a frying pan, then brown the minced beef in batches. Deglaz

the pan between batches with a little of the stock. Place the cooked beef in a sieve over a bowl to drain off the fat.

3 Turn the onion into the frying pan and cook until browned.

4 Add the garlic and cook, stirring, for 1 further minute.

5 Combine the spices and oregano in a bowl, then stir into the onions. Cook for 1 minute.

6 Place the meat, onions, stock and tomatoes in a large saucepan. Break up the tomatoes with a wooden spoon. Stir in the kidney beans, salt, pepper and sugar. Simmer, covered, for 1 hour, stirring occasionally, until the meat is tender and the juices are syrupy.

7 Make the salsa – peel the avocado and cut it into small cubes. Season with salt and pepper, then toss with the lime juice.

8 Stir in the chilli, red pepper and coriander. Serve with the chilli.

wine: **SPICY RED**

Roman-style Grilled Mozzarella Cheese

2 loaves of ciabatta (Italian bread)

2 × 110 g | 4 oz mozzarella cheeses

3 tablespoons olive oil, infused with garlic

salt and freshly ground black pepper

10 anchovy fillets in oil, drained and soaked in milk

85 g | 3 oz unsalted butter

1 Cut the bread and the mozzarella cheese into 2 cm | ¾ in thick slices.

2 Preheat the grill to its highest setting.

3 Skewer the bread alternately with the cheese on 2 long skewers, packing them tightly.

4 Place the skewers on an oiled baking sheet. Brush the slices of bread liberally with the oil and season with salt and pepper.

5 Lower the grill temperature slightly and grill the skewers for 6–8 minutes, turning occasionally, making sure that the bread doesn't burn.

6 Meanwhile, drain the anchovies from the milk. Heat the butter and, when melted, remove the pan from the heat. Add the anchovies and mash with a fork until they are well emulsified. Season to taste with pepper.

7 Remove the skewers from the grill, place on a large flat serving dish, and pour some of the sauce over both skewers.

wine: **DRY WHITE**

Pizza

MAKES 2 × 25 CM | 10 IN PIZZAS

10 g | ⅓ oz fresh yeast

110 ml | ¼ fl oz warm water

200 g | 7 oz strong flour

½ teaspoon salt

1 tablespoon olive oil

1 quantity salsa pizzaiola (see page 126)

225 g | 8 oz mozzarella cheese, diced or grated

3 tablespoons freshly grated Parmesan cheese

1 Cream the yeast with the sugar and 2 tablespoons of the lukewarm water.
2 Sift the flour with the salt and make a well in the centre. Pour in the yeast mixture, the remaining water and the oil. Mix together to make a soft but not wet dough. Add more water or flour if necessary.
3 Turn out on to a floured surface and knead well for about 5 minutes until the dough is smooth. Place in a clean bowl and cover with greased clingfilm. Leave in a warm place until the dough has doubled in bulk.
4 Preheat the oven to 230°C|450°F|gas mark 8. Divide the dough in 2. Roll each piece into a 25 cm|10 in circle. Place on greased and floured baking trays.
5 Crimp or flute the edges of the dough slightly to help keep in the filling. Spread with the pizzaiola sauce. Sprinkle with the cheese and pour over a little oil. (The pizza can be left for up to 1 hour before baking.)
6 Bake in the top third of the oven for 5 minutes, then turn down the temperature to 200°C|400°F|gas mark 6 and bake for a further 15 minutes.

wine: LIGHT/MEDIUM RED

Pizza Calzone

SERVES 2

200 g|7 oz flour quantity pizza dough (see above)
2 slices of cooked ham, cut into strips
170 g|6 oz mozzarella cheese, cut into slices
6 tomatoes, peeled and sliced

salt and freshly ground black pepper
1 tablespoon chopped fresh basil
extra virgin olive oil

1 Preheat the oven to 240°C|475°F|gas mark 8.
2 Divide the dough into 4 equal pieces and place on 4 floured baking sheets. Using the heel of your hand, push and punch the dough into 4 ovals about 20 cm|8 in in diameter.
3 Arrange the ham, mozzarella cheese and tomato slices over half of each pizza base, leaving the edge clear. Season with salt and pepper and sprinkle over the basil and a little oil.
4 Fold over the uncovered half of the pizza and press the edges firmly together.
5 Bake for 15–20 minutes.

wine: LIGHT/MEDIUM RED

Toad in the Hole

SERVES 4

450 g|1 lb pork sausages
4 tablespoons beef dripping

For the batter
110 g|4 oz plain flour

a good pinch of salt
2 eggs
150 ml|¼ pint water mixed with 150 ml|¼ pint milk

To serve
290 ml|½ pt meat gravy (see p. 474)

1 Make the batter: sift the flour with the salt into a large wide bowl. Make a well or hollow in the centre of the flour and break the eggs into it.

2 With the whisk or wooden spoon, mix the eggs to a paste and very gradually draw in the surrounding flour, adding just enough milk and water to the eggs to keep the central mixture a fairly thin paste. When all the flour is incorporated, stir in the rest of the liquid. The batter can be made more speedily by putting all the ingredients in a blender or food processor for a few seconds, but take care not to over-whisk or the mixture will be bubbly. Leave to rest in the refrigerator for 30 minutes before use. This allows the starch cells to swell, giving a lighter, less doughy final product.

3 Preheat the oven to 220°C|425°F|gas mark 7.

4 Heat 1 tablespoon of the dripping in a frying pan and fry the sausages until evenly browned all over, but do not cook them through.

5 Heat the remaining dripping in an ovenproof shallow metal dish or roasting pan until smoking hot, either in the oven or over direct heat. Add the sausages and pour in the batter.

6 Bake in the oven for 40 minutes or until the batter has risen and the sausages are brown. Serve with hot gravy.

wine: **FULL RED**

Crespelle alla Fiorentina

SERVES 4–6

30 g|1 oz butter
1 medium onion, finely chopped
55 g|2 oz prosciutto (Parma ham), chopped
290 ml|½ pint Béchamel sauce (see page 112)
225 g|8 oz ricotta cheese
450 g|1 lb spinach, cooked and chopped
55 g|2 oz Parmesan cheese, freshly grated

10 g|4 oz pinenuts, toasted
salt and freshly ground black pepper
freshly grated nutmeg
double quantity (425 ml|¾ pint) tomato sauce 2 (see page 129)
16 French pancakes (see page 569)

1 Melt the butter in a sauté pan, add the onion and cook slowly until soft but not coloured. Add the prosciutto and cook over a medium heat for 1 minute. Tip into a bowl and leave to cool.

2 Add 5 tablespoons of the Béchamel sauce, the spinach, ricotta cheese, Parmesan cheese and pinenuts to the onion and prosciutto. Mix well and season to taste with salt, pepper and nutmeg.

3 Preheat the oven to 200°C|400°F|gas mark 6.

4 Tip a little of the tomato sauce into a large ovenproof gratin dish.

5 Divide the spinach filling between the pancakes and fold into quarters. Arrange them in a single layer on top of the tomato sauce.

6 Cover with the remaining tomato sauce and bake for 30 minutes, or until the pancakes are thoroughly hot.

7 Reheat the Béchamel sauce and, just before serving, dribble it over the crespelle.

wine: **MEDIUM RED**

Pushpa's South Indian Dhal

This recipe is from a family collection belonging to Jane Nemazee, a teacher at Leiths School.

SERVES 4–6

225 g | 8 oz red lentils

1 onion, chopped

2 teaspoons garlic purée

2 teaspoons ginger purée

1 tablespoon vegetable oil

2 teaspoons ground coriander

2 teaspoons ground cumin

1 teaspoon ground turmeric

1 teaspoon ground chilli

6 tomatoes, peeled and chopped

½ teapoon salt

a handful of fresh coriander leaves, chopped

To garnish

2 tablespoons vegetable oil

1 onion, thinly sliced

6 cloves of garlic, sliced

1–2 teaspoons whole cumin seeds

1–2 teaspoons mustard seeds

about 10 curry leaves

1 Wash the lentils and place in a large saucepan with the onion. Add water to cover, then add the garlic and ginger purée and the oil.

2 Heat and when the mixture is coming up to the boil, add the ground spices, tomatoes, salt and half the coriander. Simmer for 15–20 minutes.

3 Prepare the garnish: heat the oil in a frying pan, add the onion and fry until light brown. Add the garlic and fry for 5 minutes, then add the cumin seeds, mustard seeds and curry leaves.

4 When the mixture is a rich dark brown, spoon it over the lentil mixture.

5 Serve garnished with the remaining coriander.

wine: SPICY WHITE OR BEER

Bocconcini di Parma

SERVES 4–6

900 g | 2 lb ricotta cheese

4 egg yolks

1 whole egg

170 g | 6 oz Parmesan cheese, freshly grated

55 g | 2 oz butter, softened

freshly grated nutmeg

salt and freshly ground black pepper

16 French pancakes (see page 569), made with a pinch of freshly grated nutmeg added to the batter

1 Drain the ricotta and put into a bowl. Using a wooden spoon, start to break it up, adding the egg yolks, whole egg, Parmesan cheese and butter. Mix well and season to taste with nutmeg, salt and pepper. Refrigerate for 30 minutes.

2 Place a pancake on a board and spread 3 heaped tablespoons of the filling along one side. Roll up. Place the rolled pancake, seam side down, on a baking sheet. Repeat until all the pancakes are filled. Refrigerate for 30 minutes.

3 Preheat the oven to 190°C|375°F|gas mark 5.

4 Grease a 33 × 22 cm|13½ × 8 in baking dish with butter. Using a very sharp knife, cut each pancake into thirds. Arrange them standing up in the baking dish, side by side. Bake for 20 minutes and serve hot.

wine: DRY WHITE

Baked Stuffed Aubergines

SERVES 4

2 medium aubergines	1 bay leaf
285 g|10 oz lean minced beef	2 teaspoons tomato purée
2 tablespoons olive oil	1 teaspoon chopped fresh parsley
1 onion, finely chopped	salt and freshly ground black pepper
½ green pepper, cored, deseeded and chopped	lemon juice
55 g|2 oz mushrooms, chopped	4 tablespoons, grated Gruyère or strong Cheddar
1 clove of garlic, crushed	cheese
1 teaspoon plain flour	dried breadcrumbs
290 ml|½ pint brown stock (see page 102)	290 ml|½ pint tomato sauce 2 (see page 129)

1 Cut the aubergines in half lengthways and scoop out the centre, leaving the shell with about 5 mm|¼ in of flesh attached. Sprinkle lightly with salt and leave upside down to drain.

2 Chop the aubergine flesh and sprinkle lightly with salt. Leave to drain in a sieve for 20 minutes.

3 Fry the mince in the oil until evenly brown.

4 Rinse and dry the aubergine flesh. Add to the mince with the onion, green pepper, mushroom and garlic and cook for a further 3–4 minutes.

5 Stir in the flour. Cook for 1 minute, then add the stock, bay leaf, tomato purée, parsley, pepper and lemon juice. Bring to the boil, stirring continuously, then cover and simmer for 20–25 minutes. Remove the bay leaf.

6 Preheat the oven to 200°C|400°F|gas mark 6.

7 Wash and dry the aubergine shells, fill with the mince mixture. Sprinkle over the grated cheese and crumbs.

8 Bake for 30 minutes, or until the aubergine shells are tender and the cheese well browned and crusty. Serve with the tomato sauce.

wine: MEDIUM RED

Bubble and Squeak

SERVES 4

450 g | 1 lb mashed potatoes (see page 268)

450 g | 1 lb cooked vegetables, such as cabbage, onion, leek or Brussels sprouts

salt and freshly ground black pepper

55 g | 2 oz good dripping or butter

1 Mix the potato with the other vegetables. Season to taste with salt and pepper.

2 Melt the dripping or butter in a heavy frying pan.

3 Put in the vegetable mixture, pressing it down flat on the hot dripping. Cook slowly to heat through and allow a crust to form on the bottom of the mixture.

4 Now flip the cake over on to a plate and return it to the pan to brown the second side.

5 Slide on to a warmed serving dish and serve immediately.

NOTE: Bubble and squeak is really a leftover fry-up and it does not matter if the cake is neat and even or crumbly and broken. But if you prefer it to be round and neat so that you can cut it into slices, a beaten egg added to the mixture will ensure that the ingredients hold together.

wine: **LIGHT RED**

Provençale Potato Tart

SERVES 6

225 g | 8 oz plain flour

a pinch of salt

110 g | 4 oz butter

1 egg yolk

very cold water

150 ml | ¼ pint crème fraîche

freshly grated nutmeg

For the tomato filling

3 tablespoons olive oil

1 onion, finely chopped

8 medium tomatoes, peeled, deseeded and chopped

1 tablespoon tomato purée

1 sprig of fresh thyme

a pinch of caster sugar

salt and freshly ground black pepper

For the potato filling

6 waxy potatoes, peeled and cut into even chunks

2 tablespoons olive oil

For the onion filling

85 g | 3 oz unsalted butter

5 medium onions, thinly sliced

1 Preheat the oven to 200°C | 400°F | gas mark 6.

2 Sift the flour with the salt into a large bowl. Rub in the butter until the mixture resembles breadcrumbs.

3 Mix the egg yolk with 2 tablespoons water and add to the mixture. Mix to a firm dough, first with a knife and then with one hand, adding more water if necessary.

4 Roll the pastry out and use to line a 25 cm | 10 in flan ring. Chill in the refrigerator for 20 minutes.

5 Brush the potatoes with oil and sprinkle with salt. Roast in the oven for about 1 hour, until tender. Cut into 5 mm|¼ in slices. Turn the oven temperature up to 230°C|450°F|gas mark 8.

6 Bake the pastry case blind (see page 557).

7 Make the tomato filling: heat the oil in a saucepan over a low heat and cook the onion gently for about 10 minutes. Add the tomatoes, tomato purée, thyme, sugar, salt and pepper. Increase the heat and cook until all the liquid evaporates (about 35 minutes).

8 Make the onion filling: melt the butter in a frying pan, add the onions and cover with a piece of dampened greaseproof paper and a lid. Cook over a low heat for about 30 minutes until soft and creamy.

9 Spread the onions on the pastry base and cover with the tomato filling, then arrange the sliced potatoes around the top. Cover with the crème fraîche and sprinkle with nutmeg. Bake in the oven for 15 minutes, or until brown. Serve at room temperature.

wine: **LIGHT RED**

Babotie

SERVES 4

1 slice of white bread
150 ml|¼ pint milk
1 onion, chopped
1 small dessert apple, chopped
30 g|1 oz butter
1 tablespoon curry powder
450 g|1 lb cooked lamb, minced
1 tablespoon chutney

a few raisins
1 tablespoon vinegar or lemon juice
salt and freshly ground black pepper

For the topping

2 eggs
290 ml|½ pint Greek yoghurt
salt and freshly ground black pepper
1 tablespoon flaked almonds

1 Soak the bread in the milk.

2 Grease an ovenproof dish and preheat the oven to 180°C|350°F|gas mark 4.

3 Cook the onion and apple in the butter in a saucepan over a low heat until soft but not coloured. Add the curry powder and cook for 1 further minute.

4 Mix the onion and apple with the lamb, chutney, almonds, raisins and vinegar or lemon juice. Fork the bread into the meat. Season with salt and pepper and pile into the dish.

5 Mix the eggs with the yoghurt. Season with salt and pepper.

6 Pour this over the meat mixture, place the almonds on top and bake in the oven for about 30–35 minutes, until the custard has set and browned.

wine: **LIGHT RED**

Moussaka

Moussaka is a traditional dish found in every village in Greece. There are as many different variations as there are cooks, but the ingredients of tomatoes, onions, garlic and aubergines are universal.

SERVES 4

340 g | 12 oz aubergine
salt and freshly ground black pepper
6 tablespoons olive oil
1 large onion, finely chopped
675 g | 1½ lb minced lamb or beef
150 ml | ¼ pint white wine
150 ml | ¼ pint water
1 clove of garlic, crushed
1 × 400 g | 14 oz can of tomatoes or 3 large
   tomatoes, peeled and chopped

2 tablespoons chopped fresh parsley
2 teaspoons chopped fresh oregano or 1 teaspoon
   dried oregano
a pinch of ground cinnamon
225 g | 8 oz floury potatoes, peeled

For the topping
200 ml | 7 fl oz Greek yoghurt
1 egg, beaten
4 tablespoons grated Parmesan cheese

1 Remove the stalk from the aubergine, then cut the aubergine into slices 6 mm | ¼ in thick. Salt the slices on both sides, then leave in a colander for 30 minutes to degorge.

2 Place 2 tablespoons of the oil in a small saucepan, add the onion and sweat over a low heat until soft.

3 Heat 2 tablespoons of the remaining oil in a sauté pan and brown the mince in batches, taking care not to overcrowd the pan.

4 Mix together the wine and water and use a little to deglaze the pan in between batches. Reserve the déglacage. Place the browned mince in a sieve over a bowl to drain away the excess fat.

5 Add the garlic to the onion and cook for 1 minute.

6 Combine the onion, garlic, browned meat, tomatoes, remaining wine, water, deglaçage, parsley, oregano and cinnamon in a large saucepan and simmer for 45 minutes.

7 Boil the potatoes until tender. Drain, cool and cut into slices 6 mm | ¼ in thick.

8 Preheat the grill. Rinse the aubergine slices and pat dry on absorbent kitchen paper.

9 Brush the aubergine on both sides with the remaining oil and grill until browned.

10 Preheat the oven to 180° | 350°F | gas mark 4.

11 Place a thin layer of the meat sauce in a shallow ovenproof dish. Arrange a layer of aubergine slices on the sauce, then add a thin layer of sauce and then a layer of potato slices. Continue layering, finishing with a layer of sauce.

12 Mix together the yoghurt, egg and cheese. Spread over the moussaka. (The dish can be made 1 day in advance and refrigerated at this point.)

13 Bake for 45 minutes until golden-brown on top and hot in the centre.

wine: **SPICY RED**

Aubergine Charlotte

This supper dish is made by layering aubergine and tomato. It is good served with a crisp green salad and basmati rice. It can also be made individually in small dariole moulds.

SERVES 4

4 large aubergines

salt and freshly ground black pepper

1 onion, finely chopped

olive oil

1 clove of garlic, crushed

15 tomatoes, peeled, deseeded and chopped

290 ml | ½ pint plain yoghurt

stock

1 Slice and salt the aubergines and leave to degorge in a colander for 30 minutes. Meanwhile, cook the onion in a little oil in a saucepan for 3 minutes. Add the garlic, tomatoes, salt and pepper and cook for a further 25 minutes.

2 Rinse and dry the aubergines. Fry in oil in a frying pan until soft and highly browned. Drain on absorbent kitchen paper.

3 Preheat the oven to 180°C | 350°F | gas mark 4.

4 Arrange a layer of aubergine slices along the bottom and up the sides of a loaf or charlotte tin.

5 Layer up two-thirds of the tomatoes, the yoghurt and remaining aubergines, finishing with a layer of aubergines.

6 Cover with kitchen foil and bake for 40 minutes.

7 Remove from the oven and leave to cool for 5 minutes. Tip off any excess liquid. Turn out and serve hot with the remaining tomatoes, thinned to the consistency of a sauce with a little stock.

wine: ROSÉ

Red Onion Polenta Tatin

SERVES 6–8

170 g | 6 oz flour quantity polenta pastry (see page 563)

For the topping

55 g | 2 oz butter

900 g | 2 lb red onions, thinly sliced

2 tablespoons white wine

2 cloves of garlic, crushed

1 tablespoon soft light brown sugar

¼ tablespoon chopped fresh rosemary

3 large red peppers

1 tablespoon capers, rinsed and drained

4 anchovies, slivered

1 Preheat the oven to 190°C | 375°F | gas mark 5.

2 To make the topping: melt 30 g | 1 oz of the butter in a heavy, ovenproof frying pan. Add the onions and cook, covered, for 15 minutes, until they begin to soften. Add the wine, garlic, rosemary and half the sugar and cook for 20 minutes. Turn up the heat and reduce, by boiling rapidly, until the liquid has evaporated and the onions start to fry. Turn on to a plate to cool.

3 Preheat the grill to its highest setting. Cut the peppers into quarters, then remove the

stalks, membrane and seeds. Grill the peppers, skin side uppermost, until the skin is black and blistered. Place in a plastic bag to cool. The steam will help loosen the skin.

4 Melt the remaining butter in a non-stick 20 cm | 8 in frying pan, stir in the remaining sugar and remove from the heat. Peel the peppers and arrange the red pepper pieces in the pan in a daisy pattern. Place the capers and anchovies between the peppers and cover with the cooked onions, taking care not to dislodge the peppers.

5 Place the pan over a high heat until the butter and sugar start to caramelize, which may take 5 minutes. Remove the pan from the heat and place it on a baking sheet.

6 Lay the polenta pastry on top of the onions and press down lightly. Bake for 25 minutes. Allow to cool slightly, then invert the pan over a serving plate and serve warm.

wine: LIGHT RED

Aubergine Tagine with Spiced Dumplings

If a tagine (an earthenware cooking pot with a conical lid) is not available, this recipe can just as easily be cooked in a standard casserole.

SERVES 4

4 large aubergines, cut into large chunks

salt

5 tablespoons groundnut oil

2 large onions, cut into chunks

4 wide strips of lemon zest

2 large cloves of garlic, crushed

2 tablespoons ground turmeric

1 tablespoon ground cinnamon

2 × 400 g | 14 oz cans of tomatoes

2 tablespoons chopped fresh coriander

juice of ½ lemon

110 g | 4 oz cooked chickpeas or 55 g | 2 oz raw chickpeas, soaked and cooked

200 g | 7 oz fresh dates, stoned and cut into quarters lengthways

55 g | 2 oz blanched almonds, toasted

salt and freshly ground black pepper

For the dumplings

110 g | 4 oz self-raising flour

1 tablespoon ground mixed spice

1 tablespoon cayenne pepper

a pinch of chilli powder

salt and freshly ground black pepper

30 g | 1 oz cold butter, grated

about 5 tablespoons water

1 Put the aubergine into a colander, sprinkle with salt and toss. Leave to degorge for 30 minutes. Rinse well and drain.

2 Heat half the oil in a flameproof tagine or casserole, or a large, heavy saucepan. Add the onions and lemon zest and cook over a low heat for 10 minutes or until the onions are soft and transparent. Add the garlic, turmeric and cinnamon. Turn up the heat a little and fry until the onions and spices begin to brown.

3 In a seperate frying pan, heat the remaining oil and fry the aubergine until brown. Lower the heat, add the onion mixture, the tomatoes with their juice, the coriander and lemon juice, and simmer for 20 minutes, stirring from time to time to prevent the mixture from sticking.

4 Meanwhile, make the dumplings: put all the ingredients into a bowl and mix well. Stir

in enough water to make a soft dough. Turn the dough on to a floured surface, divide into 8 equal pieces and shape into balls, using floured hands.

5 Add the chickpeas, dates and almonds to the aubergine mixture: it should not be too dry; add some water if necessary. Season to taste with salt and pepper.

6 Put the dumplings on top and spoon over some of the juices. Cover and cook for 15–20 minutes until the dumplings have doubled in size.

7 Serve straight from the casserole.

NOTE: If the tagine or casserole is more than two-thirds full, cover it loosely with kitchen foil when cooking the dumplings so they will have room to rise.

wine: **SPICY RED**

Prosciutto and Aubergine Gougère

SERVES 4

butter for greasing

55 g | 2 oz Parmesan or Gruyère cheese, coarsely grated

½ teaspoon dried mustard

2-egg quantity choux pastry (see page 563)

1 small aubergine, cut into ½ cm | ¼ in

1 tablespoon olive oil

85 g | 3 oz prosciutto, cut into shreds

1 teaspoon chopped fresh basil

4 tablespoons double cream

salt and freshly ground black pepper

1 tablespoon freshly grated Parmesan cheese

1 Lightly butter 4 ramekins.

2 Preheat the oven to 200°C | 400°F | gas mark 6.

3 Beat the 55 g | 2 oz cheese and the mustard into the choux pastry. Fit a piping bag with a 1 cm | ½ in plain nozzle and pipe the choux mixture round the sides of the ramekins, leaving a small well in the centre.

4 Fry the aubergine in the oil until soft.

5 Mix together the prosciutto, basil, aubergine and cream. Season to taste with salt and pepper.

6 Spoon the filling into the centre of the ramekins. Sprinkle with the Parmesan cheese. Bake for 15–20 minutes until well risen and brown. Serve very hot.

wine: **MEDIUM RED**

Gem Squash with Mushrooms

SERVES 4

1 tablespoon vegetable oil

2 red onions, finely chopped

2 cloves of garlic, crushed

450 g | 1 lb mushrooms, sliced

4 gem squash

2 tablespoons chopped fresh lemon thyme

4 tablespoons crème fraîche

salt and freshly ground black pepper

4 tablespoons freshly grated Parmesan cheese, to serve

1 Heat the oil in a large saucepan and stir in the onions. Cover with a dampened piece of greaseproof paper and a lid. Cook over a low heat until softened.

2 Meanwhile, bring a large saucepan of salted water to the boil. Cut the tops off the gem squash and scoop out the seeds and stringy centres. Boil the squash and their tops for 10–15 minutes or until just tender. Drain thoroughly.

3 Remove the lid and paper from the onions and add the garlic. Cook for 45 seconds, then add the mushrooms and allow to cook until they have softened and the liquid has evaporated.

4 Add the lemon thyme and crème fraîche to the mushroom mixture and stir through. Season to taste with salt and pepper, then reduce by boiling rapidly until the sauce is creamy.

5 Season the inside of the squash lightly with salt and pepper and pile the mushroom filling into them so that it comes above the tops. Sprinkle over the cheese, replace the lids and serve immediately.

wine: LIGHT RED

Flat Ham Pie

SERVES 10

450 g | 1 lb flour quantity pâte à pâte (see page 565)	2 tablespoons chopped fresh dill or chives
110 g | 4 oz Gruyère or Cheddar cheese, grated	1 large clove of garlic, crushed
55 g | 2 oz Parmesan cheese, freshly grated	150 ml | ¼ pint soured cream
85 g | 3 oz butter, melted	freshly ground black pepper
110 g | 4 oz fresh white breadcrumbs	juice of 1 lemon
450 g | 1 lb cooked ham	beaten egg

1 Roll the pastry out into rectangles, one the size of a Swiss roll tin, the other slightly larger. Chill in the refrigerator for 20 minutes.

2 Preheat the oven to 200°C│400°F│gas mark 6.

3 Lightly grease and flour the back of a Swiss roll tin or a rectangular baking sheet. Put the small rectangle of pastry on it and prick all over with a fork. Bake in the oven for 15 minutes, then leave to cool on a wire rack.

4 Mix together the cheeses, the melted butter and the breadcrumbs. Scatter half this mixture all over the baked pastry, leaving a good 1 cm │ ½ in clear all round the edge.

5 Chop the ham into small pieces and scatter it on top of the cheese mixture. Then scatter over the dill or chives.

6 Mix the garlic with the soured cream and spread all over the ham. Season well with pepper but no salt.

7 Sprinkle evenly with the lemon juice and top with the remaining cheese mixture. Wet the edge of the bottom piece of pastry with lightly beaten egg and put the top sheet of pastry in place, pressing the edges to seal it well.

8 Use any pastry trimmings to decorate the pie and brush all over with beaten egg.

9 Bake in the preheated oven until the pastry is crisp and pale brown. Serve hot or cold.

wine: LIGHT RED OR ROSÉ

Tortilla

SERVES 4

oil for frying

225 g|8 oz floury potatoes, peeled and thinly sliced

1 small onion, thinly sliced

salt and freshly ground black pepper

5 eggs, beaten

1 Heat about 1 cm|½ in of oil in a non-stick frying pan, add the potatoes and onion, season with salt and pepper and fry slowly until soft but not coloured (up to 20 minutes). Remove the onions and potatoes from the pan using a slotted spoon and place into the eggs.

2 Tip all the oil, but for a thin film, out of the pan. Pour the egg mixture into the pan.

3 Cook the omelette over a medium heat until it is set, then slip on to a plate. Turn it over and put it back into the frying pan with the uncooked side down.

4 Cook for 1 further minute, then turn out on to a serving plate. Serve warm or cold, cut into wedges.

NOTE: A non-stick pan is very helpful when making tortilla. Frying the potatoes from raw is the usual Spanish method. But if the potatoes are small and waxy it is better to boil them first, then slice and fry. Boiled potatoes give a light, soft omelette.

wine: **FULLER RED**

Savoury Stuffed Pancakes

SERVES 4

12 French pancakes (see page 569)

450 g|1 lb smoked haddock

290 ml|½ pint milk

1 bay leaf

1 slice of onion

3–4 black peppercorns

1 parsley stalk

salt and freshly ground black pepper

15 g|½ oz butter

15 g|½ oz plain flour

a pinch of dry English mustard

a pinch of cayenne pepper

55 g|2 oz Cheddar cheese, grated

1 teaspoon chopped fresh tarragon

450g|1lb spinach, cooked and chopped

30 g|1 oz melted butter

dried white breadcrumbs

1 tablespoon freshly grated Parmesan cheese

1 Place the smoked haddock skin side down in a sauté pan with the milk, bay leaf, onion, peppercorns and parsley stalk.

2 Cover the fish with greaseproof paper and poach for 15 minutes, or until the fish flakes easily with a fork.

3 Strain off and reserve the liquor and flake the fish, taking care to remove any bones and skin. Taste the liquor and if it is too salty, dilute with a little water. Make sure you have 290 ml|½ pint cooking liquor.

4 Melt the butter in a saucepan, remove from the heat and add the flour, mustard and cayenne. Return to the heat and cook for 1 minute. Remove the pan from the heat, slowly stir in the reserved liquor. Return to the heat and bring to the boil, stirring continuously.

5 Remove the sauce from the heat, stir in half the Cheddar cheese and season with salt, pepper and tarragon. Stir in the fish and the cooked spinach. Preheat the grill.

6 Divide the fish mixture between the pancakes and roll up. Lay the pancakes side by side in a buttered ovenproof dish. Brush with melted butter. Sprinkle with the remaining Cheddar cheese, the breadcrumbs and the Parmesan cheese.

8 Place under the hot grill until well browned.

wine: **LIGHT RED**

Cottage Pie

SERVES 4

1 tablespoon oil	1 tablespoon chopped fresh thyme
1 onion, chopped	1 tablespoon plain flour
340 g|12 oz cooked beef or lamb, minced	290 ml|½ pint brown stock (see page 102)
2 tomatoes, peeled and chopped	675 g|1½ lb mashed potatoes (see page 268)
2 teaspoons Worcestershire sauce	butter
2 tablespoons tomato ketchup	

1 Preheat the oven to 200°C|400°F|gas mark 6.

2 Heat the oil in a frying pan and cook the onion over a low heat until lightly browned.

3 Add the meat, tomatoes, Worcestershire sauce, ketchup and thyme. Sprinkle with the flour and stir into the meat. Cook over a low heat for 2 minutes.

4 Add the stock and bring to the boil, stirring continuously. Simmer for 20 minutes, adding more stock if necessary. Season with salt and pepper.

5 Tip into a pie dish and allow to cool slightly.

6 Spread the mashed potato on the top. Fork it up to leave the surface rough or draw the fork over the surface to mark with a pattern. Alternatively the potato can be piped using a 1 cm|½ in star nozzle. Pipe across the dish diagonally to give a rope effect.

7 Place the pie on a baking sheet and cook in the oven for 20–30 minutes, or until the potato is golden-brown and crisp.

wine: **MEDIUM RED**

Jambalaya

SERVES 4–6

450 g | 1 lb pork tenderloin (fillet)
2–3 tablespoons oil
1 onion, finely chopped
2 sticks of celery, finely chopped
55 g | 2 oz garlic sausage, diced
110 g | 4 oz rice
2 teaspoon ground ginger

½ teaspoon ground turmeric
½ teaspoon paprika pepper
290 ml | ½ pint white stock, made with chicken bones (see page 103)
lemon juice
salt and freshly ground black pepper
110 g | 4 oz peeled cooked prawns

1 Trim the pork and cut into 1 cm | ½ in cubes. Heat half the oil in a heavy saucepan and quickly fry the pork until well browned. Lift the pieces out and put them aside. Add the onion and celery to the pan, reduce the heat and fry over a low heat until soft and evenly coloured. Lift them out on to a plate.

2 Now fry the garlic sausage, adding more oil if necessary and turning them until evenly browned. Lift them out and add to the pork. Heat the remaining oil, stir in the rice and fry, stirring constantly, until opaque. Add the ginger, turmeric and paprika and fry for 30 seconds.

3 Add the stock and put all the fried food back into the pan. Bring to the boil and season with a dash of lemon juice, salt and pepper. Reduce the heat, cover and simmer until all the stock has been absorbed and the rice is cooked (about 20 minutes). Add the prawns and warm them in the rice for a minute or two before serving.

wine: **SPICY RED**

Cornish Pasties

MAKES 8 LARGE OR 20 CANAPÉ SIZE

For the cheese pastry
110 g | 4 oz plain flour
55 g | 2 oz butter
15 g | ½ oz Parmesan cheese, freshly grated
a pinch of cayenne pepper
a pinch of dry English mustard
½ egg, beaten
cold water

For the filling
225 g | 8 oz lean minced beef
1 small onion, finely chopped
1 small potato, diced
1 small carrot, diced
1 teaspoon plain flour
stock to moisten
salt and freshly ground black pepper
a few drops of Worcestershire sauce
1 egg, beaten, to glaze

1 Make the pastry: sift the flour into a mixing bowl and rub in the butter. Add the Parmesan, cayenne and mustard. Bind to a firm dough with the beaten egg and a little water. Chill in the refrigerator.

2 Make the filling: brown the mince and vegetables in a non-stick saucepan. Add the flour and cook over a low heat for 1 minute. Add the stock, salt, pepper and Worcestershire sauce and cook until the vegetables are just soft. Remove from the heat and allow to cool.

3 Preheat the oven to 200°C|400°F|gas mark 6.

4 Roll out the pastry thinly, and stamp out rounds with a pastry cutter.

5 Divide the filling between the pastry rounds. Brush the edges of the pastry with beaten egg and fold over into tiny Cornish pasties. Seal the edges well. Brush the pastry with beaten egg and place the pasties on a greased baking sheet. Bake for 10–15 minutes until golden brown.

Croque Monsieur

SERVES 4

85 g|3 oz butter for spreading

8 thin slices of white bread

4 slices of cooked ham

4 slices of Edam or Gruyère cheese

freshly ground black pepper

1 Butter the bread.

2 Make 4 sandwiches, each with a slice of ham and a slice of cheese inside, seasoned with pepper but not salt. Press well together.

3 Toast under the grill until golden-brown on both sides. Cut in half and serve immediately.

NOTE: The sandwiches are best toasted in a sandwich maker. They can also be fried in 5 mm|¼ in hot fat or oil, turning over as necessary and draining well on absorbent kitchen paper before serving.

Pain Bagna

1 French stick or ciabatta

1 clove of garlic, peeled and halved

2 tablespoons extra virgin olive oil

sliced mozzarella cheese

sliced avocado pear

sliced peeled tomatoes

pitted black olives

chopped anchovy fillets

sliced artichoke hearts

1 Cut the bread in half horizontally, remove a little of the soft bread in the centre, rub each side with a cut clove of garlic and sprinkle liberally with extra virgin olive oil.

2 Scatter the other ingredients over the base.

3 Season with salt and freshly ground black pepper. Sandwich together.

4 Wrap tightly in clingfilm or foil and weight with a chopping board for at last 30 minutes to compress slightly.

5 Slice into 5 cm|2 in pieces on the diagonal to serve.

Mozzarella in Carrozza

SERVES 4

8 thin slices of sandwich bread, crusts removed

4 large slices of mozzarella cheese

2 eggs, beaten with a little salt

oil for frying

1 Make 4 rounds of cheese sandwiches. Cut each round into 4.
2 Leave the sandwiches to soak in the beaten egg for 30 minutes. Turn them over once so that both sides are saturated with the egg.
3 Press the edges of the sandwiches firmly together and fry in hot oil in a frying pan until golden-brown. Drain well on absorbent kitchen paper.

wine: **LIGHT RED**

Baked Bread with Garlic and Oil

1 large French stick

5 cloves of garlic, peeled

coarse salt

extra virgin olive oil

1 Preheat the oven to 200°C|400°F|gas mark 6.
2 Cut the bread into diagonal slices 2 cm|¾ in thick. Place on a baking sheet and bake for about 15 minutes, or until golden-brown.
3 Cut the garlic in half and, when the bread is golden-brown, rub each side with the cut surface of the garlic.
4 Arrange the bread on a warmed serving dish and sprinkle with the salt. Then drizzle over the oil. Serve immediately.

NOTE: The baked bread may be served with the oil poured over it and the salt and garlic handed separately.

Pastry and Batters

Pastry comes in many forms. All of them are made from a mixture of flour and liquid, and usually contain fat. Variations in quantities and the ingredients themselves give each type its distinctive texture and taste. The three most common types of pastry are short, flaky and choux, all of which have variations. The degree of shortness (or crisp crumbliness) depends on the amount and type of fat (the shortening factor) incorporated into the flour and the way in which the uncooked pastry, or paste, is handled.

The Ingredients

Fats

Butter gives a crisp, rich shortcrust pastry with excellent flavour. Solid margarine gives a similar result that is slightly less rich and flavourful. Lard gives flaky, but rather tasteless pastry. It gives excellent results when used in combination with butter. Solid cooking fat and vegetable shortening give a crust similar to that produced by lard. Suet is used only in suet crust, which is soft and rather heavy.

Flour

The flour in shortcrust pastry is usually plain, all-purpose flour. Weak, or cake, flour is excellent for pastry-making. Wholemeal flour produces a delicious nutty-flavoured crust but is more absorbent than white flour and needs more liquid. This makes it harder and heavier. For this reason, a mixture for wholemeal and white flour, usually half and half, is generally used to make 'wholemeal' pastry. Self-rising flour is occasionally used in pastry-making. It produces a softer, thicker, more cake-y crust. It is also sometimes used to lighten cheese dough and other heavy pastes like suet crust. Whatever the flour, it should be sifted, even if it has no lumps, to incorporate air and give the pastry lightness.

Liquid

The less liquid used in pastry-making the better. Some very rich doughs, such as almond pastry which contains a high proportion of butter and eggs, can be brought together without any water or milk at all. Others need a little liquid to bind them. Water gives the pastry crispness and firmness. Too much makes a pastry that is easy to handle but results in a hard crust that shrinks in the oven. The addition of egg or egg white instead of water will give a firm but not a hard crust. Egg yolk on its own helps to produce a rich, soft and crumbly crust.

Making Pastry

Rubbing in

Shortcrust pastry is made by rubbing fat into sifted flour and other dry ingredients with the fingertips or food processor, then adding other ingredients such as egg yolks or any liquid. Everything should be kept as cool as possible. If the fat melts the finished pastry may be tough and greasy.

Cut the fat, which should be firm and cold but not hard, into pea-sized pieces using a small knife and floured fingers. The flour prevents the fat from sticking to the fingers. Mix the fat into the flour then chop through the fat and flour using two table knives scissor fashion. When the fat pieces are reduced to about half their original size pick the pieces of fat and flour up between your thumbs and fingers, about 10 cm | 4 in above the bowl. Gently and quickly rub the little pieces of fat into the flour, squashing the fat lightly as you go, until the mixture resembles fresh breadcrumbs. Drop the mixture from a height; this cools the fat and aerates the flour, making the finished pastry lighter. A food processor can be used to rub in the fat. Take care not to over-process. Turn the mixture into a bowl and rub in by hand for about 10 seconds before adding any liquid by hand.

Adding liquid

Shortcrust pastry needs a little water to make it easier to work with and to prevent it from becoming too crumbly. Although over-moist pastry is easy to handle and roll out, the baked crust will be tough and may well shrink in the oven as the water evaporates in the heat. The drier and more difficult to handle the pastry is the more tender the result. Add only as much water as needed to get the pastry to hold together, and sprinkle it, 1 teaspoonful at a time, over as large a surface as possible.

Mixing should be kept to a minimum. Mix the pastry with a fork or knife so you handle it as little as possible. As soon as it holds together in lumps, stop mixing. Use your fingertips to pull the dough together into a ball.

Relaxing

Pastry needs to rest or relax before baking to help avoid shrinkage. This can be done either immediately after making, or if the dough is too sticky to use immediately, after rolling out. Flatten the dough to 1 cm | ½ in thick and wrap in clingfilm. Chill until firm enough to roll out.

Relaxing is less important, though is still a good idea, for pastries used to cover pies. To prevent the surface of the pastry from drying out and cracking in the refrigerator, wrap it with clingfilm or greaseproof paper.

Rolling out

Lightly dust the work surface with flour. Do not use too much as it could make the pastry dry. Roll the pastry with a lightly floured rolling pin. Roll gently away from you. Use a palette knife to loosen the pastry from the work surface. Give the pastry frequent turns to keep the shape round.

Lining a flan ring

Use a pastry brush to brush any excess flour from the pastry. Place the flan ring on a baking sheet. Drape the pastry over the rolling pin and carefully lift the pastry over the flan ring, placing the uppermost side down. Ease the pastry into the corners using the side of your finger or a piece of excess pastry. Take care not to stretch the pastry. Roll the rolling pin across the top edge of the flan ring to remove any excess pastry. Gently ease the pastry away from the edge of the flan ring. If it overhangs the edge it will be impossible to remove the flan ring when the pastry is baked. Chill the pastry until it is firm before baking.

Baking blind

Line the pastry case with a piece of greaseproof paper and fill it with dried beans, rice or ceramic baking beans. This is to support the sides of the pastry until they are cooked and to prevent the base from bubbling up. Bake the pastry in the top third of the oven, pre-heated to 200°C|400°F|gas mark 6. When the sides of the pastry case are cooked, remove the beans and paper, then continue baking the pastry until the base is done.

Types of Pastry

Shortcrust: See recipe on page 559.

Rich Shortcrust: See recipe on page 559.

Suet crust pastry

This is made like shortcrust pastry except that the suet is chopped or shredded before use. Because self-raising flour (or plain flour and baking powder) is used in order to produce a less heavy dough pastry, it is important to cook the pastry soon after making it, while the raising agent is at its most active. During cooking the raising agent causes the dough to puff up and rise slightly and as it hardens, air is trapped. This makes the suet crust lighter and more bread-like (see page 462).

Pâte sucrée, almond pastry and pâte à pâte

These and other very rich pastries are extreme forms of rich shortcrust, with all the liquid replaced by fat or eggs. Traditionally they are made by working together the egg yolks and fat, and sometimes sugar, with the fingertips until soft and creamy (see page 466). The flour is then gradually incorporated until a soft, very rich paste is achieved. To mix the paste, use only the fingertips of one hand. The warmth of the fingertips is important for softening the fat, but once that is done, mixing and kneading should be as light and quick as possible. The pastry can be brought together very quickly by using a palette knife. Because of the high proportion of fat, no water is added.

Modern food processors enable these pastries to be made in seconds, although the air incorporated by the machine will produce a less crisp result. Simply put all the ingredients (the fat in smallish pieces) into the machine and pulse until the mixture comes together.

These pastries are baked blind as for shortcrust, above. Chill the pastries before baking at 190°C|375°F|gas mark 5 until pale biscuit-coloured. Remove from the tin and/or loosen the pastry from the baking sheet while it is still warm or it will stick then break when cool.

Hot watercrust

This is made by heating water and fat together and mixing them into the flour. Because of the high proportion of water, this pastry is inclined to be hard. Its strength and firmness allow it to encase heavy mixtures, such as an English pork pie, without collapsing. Also, as the fat used is generally lard, the pastry can lack flavour, so add plenty of salt. Many old recipes recommend throwing the pastry away uneaten once it has done its duty as container. Our recipe for veal and ham pie (see page 514) is a better-tasting modification of hot watercrust, containing butter and egg.

Do not allow the water to boil before the fat has melted. If the water reduces by boiling, the proportion of water to flour will not be correct. Quickly mix the water and melted fat into the flour in a bowl, then keep it covered with a damp cloth. This prevents the fat from becoming set and the pastry from flaking and drying out.

Choux pastry

Like Yorkshire pudding batter, this pastry contains water and eggs and depends on the rising of the steam within it to produce a puffy, hollow pastry case. It is used most often for profiteroles, and èclairs but it can also be used in savoury dishes, such as chicken and mushroom gougere. Choux pastry is also used to make deep-fried morsels called Beignets. It is easy to make if the ingredients are measured accurately and the recipe is followed closely.

Flaky pastry and puff pastry

These are begun in rather the same way as the first stage for preparing shortcrust pastry, though the consistency is initially softer and less short, as they contain a high proportion of water. Then fat, either in a solid block or in small pieces, is incorporated into the paste, which is rolled and folded several times. This process creates layers of pastry which, in the heat of the oven, will rise into light thin leaves. For instance, puff pastry, which is folded in three and rolled out six times, will have 729 layers.

As the whole aim is to create the layers without allowing the incorporated fat to melt, start with everything cool, including the bowl, the ingredients, and the worktop if possible. Short, quick strokes (rather than long steady ones) allow the bubbles of air so carefully incorporated into the pastry to move about while the fat is gradually and evenly distributed in the paste. Work lightly and do not stretch the paste, or the layers you have built up will tear and allow the air and fat to escape. Chill the pastry between rollings or at any point if there is a danger of the fat breaking through the pastry, or if the pastry becomes sticky and warm. It sounds like a complicated business, but it is a lot easier done than said: follow the instructions on puff pastry (page 566), rough puff pastry (page 565) and flaky pastry (page 566).

The layered pastries are baked with the oven temperature set at 200°C|400°F|gas mark 6 to cause rapid expansion of the trapped layers of air and quick cooking of the dough before the fat has time to melt and run out.

This differs from most other pastries in that it actually benefits from heavy handling. It is beaten and stretched, thumped and kneaded. This treatment promotes elasticity in the dough. The paste is rolled and stretched on a floured cloth (the bigger the better) until it is so thin that you should be able to read fine print through it. Keep the paste covered when not in use so it does not dry out. When the pastry is pulled out, brush it with butter or oil to prevent it cracking and drying. Strudel pastry can be bought in ready-rolled leaves from specialist food shops, especially Greek-owned ones. Sometimes called phyllo or filo pastry, it is used to make the Middle Eastern baklava. Detailed instructions for strudel pastry appear on page 563.

Shortcrust Pastry (Pâte Brisée)

170 g|6 oz plain flour
a pinch of salt
30 g|1 oz lard

55 g|2 oz butter
very cold water to mix

1 Sift the flour with the salt into a large bowl.
2 Rub in the fats until the mixture resembles coarse breadcrumbs.
3 Add 1–2 tablespoons water to the mixture. Mix to a firm dough, first with a knife, and finally with one hand. It may be necessary to add more water, but the pastry should not be too damp. (Though crumbly pastry is more difficult to handle, it produces a shorter, lighter result.)
4 Chill, wrapped, in the refrigerator for 30 minutes before using. Or line the flan ring then allow to relax in the refrigerator before baking. Chill until firm before baking.

Rich Shortcrust Pastry

170 g|6 oz plain flour
a pinch of salt
100 g|3½ oz butter

1 egg yolk
very cold water to mix

1 Sift the flour with the salt into a large bowl.
2 Rub in the butter until the mixture resembles breadcrumbs.
3 Mix the egg yolk with 2 tablespoons water and sprinkle half over the flour. It may be necessary to add more liquid, but the pastry should not be too damp.
4 Mix to a firm dough, first with a knife, and finally with one hand. It may be necessary to add more water, but the pastry should not be too damp. (Though crumbly pastry is more difficult to handle, it produces a shorter, lighter result.)
5 Chill, wrapped, in the refrigerator for 30 minutes before using. Or line the flan ring then allow to relax in the refrigerator before baking.

NOTE: To make sweet rich shortcrust pastry, mix in 2 tablespoons caster sugar once the fat has been rubbed into the flour.

Lemon Pastry

170 g | 6 oz plain flour
a pinch of salt
1 teaspoon grated lemon zest

30 g | 1 oz solid vegetable shortening
55 g | 2 oz butter
very cold water to mix

1 Sift the flour with the salt into a large bowl. Add the lemon zest.
2 Rub in the fats until the mixture resembles breadcrumbs.
3 Add 2 tablespoons water to the mixture. Mix to a firm dough – first with a knife, and finally with one hand. It may be necessary to add more water, but the pastry should not be damp. (Although crumbly pastry is more difficult to handle, it produces a shorter, less tough result.)
4 Wrap in clingfilm and chill in the refrigerator for 30 minutes before using, or allow to relax in the refrigerator after rolling out but before baking.

Wholemeal Pastry

110 g | 4 oz wholemeal flour
110 g | 4 oz plain flour
a pinch of salt

140 g | 5 oz butter
very cold water to mix

1 Sift the flours with the salt into a large bowl and add the bran from the sieve. Rub in the butter until the mixture looks like coarse breadcrumbs.
2 Add 2 tablespoons water and mix to a firm dough, first with a knife and then with one hand. It may be necessary to add more water, but the pastry should not be too damp. (Although crumbly pastry is more difficult to handle, it produces a shorter, lighter result.)
3 Chill, wrapped, in the refrigerator for at least 30 minutes before using, or line the flan ring then allow the pastry to relax in the refrigerator before baking.

NOTES: To make sweet wholemeal pastry, mix in 2 tablespoons sugar once the fat has been rubbed into the flour.
    All wholemeal flour may be used if preferred.

Herb Wholemeal Pastry

110 g | 4 oz plain flour
110 g | 4 oz wholemeal flour
a pinch of salt

110 g | 4 oz butter, chopped
1 tablespoon chopped fresh thyme
very cold water to mix

1 Sift the flours with the salt into a large bowl and add the bran from the sieve.
2 Rub in the butter until the mixture resembles coarse breadcrumbs. Add the thyme.

3 Add 2–3 tablespoons water to the mixture and mix first with a knife and then with one hand to a firm dough adding more water if required.

4 Use as required.

NOTES: Any herb can be used in this recipe. Rosemary should be chopped finely.

The pastry can also be made in a food processor (see page 557).

Walnut Pastry

225 g | 8 oz plain flour

a pinch of salt

110 g | 4 oz butter, chopped

140 g | 5 oz ground walnuts

45 g | ½ oz sugar

beaten egg

1 Sift the flour and salt into a large bowl. Rub in the butter with the fingertips until the mixture resembles coarse breadcrumbs.

2 Stir in the walnuts and sugar and add enough beaten egg (probably half an egg) just to bind the mixture together. Pull together with your fingertips.

3 Press into a 25 cm | 10 in flan ring. Chill in the refrigerator for 30 minutes before baking.

Suet Pastry

As suet pastry is most often used for steamed puddings, instructions for lining a pudding basin are included here. Make the filling before making the pastry so you can use the pastry as soon as it is made.

butter for greasing

340 g | 12 oz self-raising flour

salt

170 g | 6 oz shredded beef or vegetarian suet

very cold water to mix

1 Grease a 1.1 litre | 2 pint pudding basin.

2 Sift the flour with a good pinch of salt into a large bowl. Stir in the suet and rub in lightly with your fingertips. Add enough water, first with a knife, and then with one hand, to mix up a soft dough.

3 On a floured surface, roll out two-thirds of the pastry into a round about 1 cm | ½ in thick. Sprinkle the pastry evenly with flour.

4 Fold the round in half and place the open curved sides towards you.

5 Shape the pastry by rolling the straight edge away from you and gently pushing the middle and pulling the sides to form a bag that, when spread out, will fit the pudding basin.

6 With a dry pastry brush, remove all excess flour and place the bag in the well-greased basin.

7 Fill the pastry with the desired mixture.

8 Roll out the remaining piece of pastry and use it as a lid, damping the edges and pressing them firmly together.

9 Cover the basin with buttered greaseproof paper, pleated in the centre, and a layer of pleated kitchen foil. (Pleating the paper and foil allows the pastry to expand slightly without bursting the wrappings.) Tie down firmly to prevent water or steam getting in during cooking.

NOTE: Occasionally suet pastry is used for other purposes than steamed puddings, in which case it should be mixed as above and then handled like any other pastry, except that it does not need to relax before cooking.

Hot Watercrust Pastry

This pastry is used for raised pies, such as pork pie and game pie.

225 g|8 oz plain flour	100 ml|3½ fl oz water
½ teaspoon salt	40 g|1¼ oz butter
1 egg, beaten	40 g|1¼ oz lard

1 Wrapt the outside of a wide jar or soufflé dish with clingfilm, then wrap a double piece of backing parchment around the outside. Secure with a paper clip.
2 Sift the flour with the salt into a large bowl. Make a dip in the middle, break the egg into it and toss a liberal covering of flour over the egg.
3 Put the water, butter and lard into a saucepan and bring slowly to the boil.
4 Once the liquid is boiling, pour it on to the flour, mixing with a knife as you do so. Knead until all the egg streaks have gone and the pastry is smooth.
5 Chill, wrapped, in the refrigerator for 10 minutes.
6 Reserve about a third of the paste for the pie lid, keeping it wrapped. Roll out the remaining paste to a circle and drape it over the jar or saucepan. Working fast, shape the pastry to cover the jar or saucepan to a depth of about ½ cm\|¼ in (see below). Leave to chill uncovered in the refrigerator.
7 As the pastry cools it will harden. When hard, turn the jar or saucepan over and remove it carefully, leaving the paper inside the pastry case. Remove the clingfilm and the paper. Stand the pastry case on a baking sheet and fill as required. Wrap the doubled baking parchment around the outside and secure with string. Use the reserved third of the pastry to make the lid, wetting the rim of the pie case to make it stick down firmly. Bake as required.

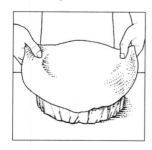  

To shape a raised pie, drape pastry over prepared jar; when set, remove jar and carefully draw out the paper. Fill, crimp the edges together and bake.

Polenta Pastry

170 g | 6 oz plain flour
a pinch of salt
85 g | 3 oz polenta (coarse cornmeal)

140 g | 5 oz butter
30 g | 1 oz Parmesan or Gruyère cheese, grated
1 egg, beaten

1 Sift the flour, salt and polenta into a large bowl. Rub in the butter until the mixture resembles breadcrumbs.
2 Add the cheese and enough of the egg to bind to a dough.
3 Roll into a circle 1 cm | ½ in thick to fit the top of a 25 cm | 10 in frying pan. Chill in the refrigerator.

Choux Pastry

85 g | 3 oz butter
220 ml | 7½ fl oz water
105 g | 3¾ oz plain flour, well sifted

a pinch of salt
3 eggs, beaten

1 Put the butter and water into a heavy saucepan. Heat slowly to melt the butter then turn up the heat and bring to a rolling boil. Sieve the flour and salt 3 times.
2 When the mixture is boiling really fast, tip in all the flour with the salt and remove the pan from the heat.
3 Working as fast as you can, beat the mixture hard with the wooden spoon: it will soon become thick and smooth and leave the sides of the pan. This mixture is called the panade.
4 Spread the paste on a plate to cool to room temperature.
5 When the mixture is no longer hot, return it to the saucepan and beat in the eggs, a little at a time, until it is soft, shiny and smooth. If the eggs are large, it may not be necessary to add all of them. The mixture should be of a dropping consistency – not too runny. ('Dropping consistency' means that the mixture will fall off a spoon rather reluctantly and all in a blob; if it runs off, it is too wet, and if it will not fall even when the spoon is jerked slightly, it is too thick).
6 Use as required.

Filo or Strudel Pastry

285 g | 10 oz plain flour
a pinch of salt
1 egg

150 ml | ¼ pint water
1 teaspoon oil

1 Sift the flour with the salt into a large bowl.
2 Beat the egg and add the water and oil. First with a knife and then with one hand, mix the water and egg into the flour, adding more water if necessary to make a soft dough.

3 The dough has now to be beaten: lift the whole mixture up in one hand and then, with a flick of the wrist, slap it on to a lightly floured board. Continue doing this until the dough no longer sticks to your fingers, and the whole mixture is smooth and very elastic. Wrap in clingfilm. Cover and leave to relax for at least 15 minutes.

4 The pastry is now ready for rolling and pulling. To do this, flour a tea-towel or large cloth on a work top and roll out the pastry as thinly as possible. Now put your hand (well floured) under the pastry and, keeping your hand fairly flat, gently stretch and pull the pastry, gradually and carefully working your way round until the paste is paper-thin. You should be able to see through it easily. Trim off the thick edges.

5 Use immediately, as strudel pastry dries out and cracks very quickly. Brushing with melted butter or oil helps to prevent this. Or the pastry sheets may be kept covered with a clingfilm.

NOTE: If the paste is not for immediate use wrap it well and keep refrigerated (for up to 3 days) or frozen. Flour the pastry surfaces before folding up. This will prevent sticking.

Pâte Sucrée

170 g|6 oz plain flour
a pinch of salt
85 g|3 oz unsalted butter, softened

3 egg yolks
85 g|3 oz sugar
2 drops of vanilla essence

1 Sift the flour with the salt on to a board. Make a large well in the centre and put the butter in it. Place the egg yolks and sugar on the butter with the vanilla essence.

2 Using the fingertips of one hand, mix the butter, yolks and sugar together. When mixed to a soft paste, draw in the flour and knead just until the pastry is smooth.

3 If the pastry is very soft, wrap and chill, before rolling or pressing out to the required shape. In any event the pastry must be allowed to relax for 30 minutes either before or after rolling out, but before baking. Chill until firm before baking.

Pâte Sablée

285 g|10 oz plain flour
a pinch of salt
225 g|8 oz unsalted butter, softened

2 egg yolks
110 g|4 oz icing sugar, sifted
2 drops of vanilla essence

1 Sift the flour with the salt on to a board. Make a large well in the centre and put the butter in it. Place the egg yolks and sugar on the butter with the vanilla essence.

2 Using the fingertips of the one hand, 'peck' the butter, yolks and sugar together.

3 Wrap and chill before rolling or pressing out to the required shape. Then chill again.

Almond Pastry (Pâte Frollée)

Care must be taken when making this because if it is over-kneaded the oil will run from the almonds, resulting in an oily paste.

110 g | 4 oz plain flour
a pinch of salt
45 g | 1½ oz ground almonds
85 g | 3 oz unsalted butter, softened

45 g | 1½ oz caster sugar
1 egg yolk
2 drops of vanilla essence

1 Sift the flour with the salt on to a board or work top. Scatter over the ground almonds. Make a large well in the centre and put in the butter, sugar, yolk and vanilla essence.
2 Using one hand only, mix with your fingertips. When creamy, gradually draw in the flour and almonds.
3 Knead gently to a paste. Chill, wrapped, in the refrigerator for 30 minutes before baking.

Pâte à Pâte

225 g | 8 oz plain flour
½ teaspoon salt
165 g | 5½ oz unsalted butter, softened

2 small egg yolks
2–3 tablespoons water

1 Sift the flour with the salt on a work top. Make a large well in the centre and put the butter and yolks in it. Work the yolks and butter together with the fingers on one hand and draw in the surrounding flour, adding the water to give a soft, malleable, but not sticky paste.
2 Chill, wrapped in the refrigerator for 30 minutes. Use as required.

Rough Puff Pastry

225 g | 8 oz plain flour
a pinch of salt

140 g | 5 oz butter
85–135 ml | 3–4 fl oz very cold water to mix

1 Sift the flour with the salt into a chilled bowl. Cut the butter into knobs about the size of a sugar lump and add to the flour. Do not rub in but add enough water to just bind the paste together. Mix first with a knife, then with one hand. Knead very lightly.
2 Chill, wrapped, in the refrigerator for 10 minutes.
3 On a floured board, roll the pastry into a strip about 30 × 10 cm | 12 × 4 in long. This must be done carefully: with a heavy rolling pin, press firmly on the pastry and give short, sharp rolls until the pastry has reached the required size. Take care not to over-stretch and break the surface of the pastry.

4 Fold the strip into 3 like a letter and turn so that the folded edge is to your left, like a closed book.

5 Again roll out into a strip 1 cm|½ in thick. Fold in 3 again and chill, wrapped, in the refrigerator for 15 minutes.

6 Roll and fold twice again, by which time the pastry should be ready for use, with no signs of streakiness. If it is still streaky, roll and fold once more.

7 Roll into the required shape.

8 Chill again in the refrigerator before baking.

Flaky Pastry

225 g|8 oz plain flour　　　　　　　　　85–135 ml|3–4 fl oz cold water
a pinch of salt　　　　　　　　　　　　85 g|3 oz lard
85 g|3 oz butter, slightly soft

1 Sift the flour with a pinch of salt into a large bowl. Rub in half the butter. Add enough water to mix with a knife to a doughy consistency. Turn on to a floured board and knead until just smooth. Chill for 10 minutes.

2 Roll into a rectangle about 30 × 10 cm|12 × 4 in. Cut half the lard into tiny pieces and dot them evenly all over the top two-thirds of the pastry, leaving a 1 cm|½ in margin.

3 Fold the pastry in 3, folding first the unlarded third up, then the larded top third down and pressing the edges to seal them. Give a 90-degree anti-clockwise turn so that the folded closed edge is to your left.

4 Repeat the rolling and folding process (without adding any fat) once more so that the folded, closed edge is on your left. Chill for 10 minutes.

5 Roll out again, dot with the remaining butter as before, and fold and seal as before.

6 Roll out again, dot with the remaining lard, fold, seal and roll once more.

7 Fold, wrap the pastry and chill in the refrigerator for 10–15 minutes.

8 Roll and fold once again (without adding any fat) and then use as required. If the pastry is still streaky, roll and fold once again.

Puff Pastry

225 g|8 oz plain flour　　　　　　　　　85–135 ml|3–4 fl oz iced water
a pinch of salt　　　　　　　　　　　　140–200 g|5–7 oz unsalted butter
30 g|1 oz lard

1 If you have never made puff pastry before, use the smaller amount of butter: it is easier. If you have some experience, more butter will produce a lighter, very rich pastry.

2 Sift the flour with the salt into a large bowl. Rub in the lard. Add 6 tablespoons of water to mix with a knife to a doughy consistency, adding more water if too dry. Turn on to a floured board and knead quickly until just smooth. Chill, wrapped, in the refrigerator for 30 minutes.

Summerberry Soufflé

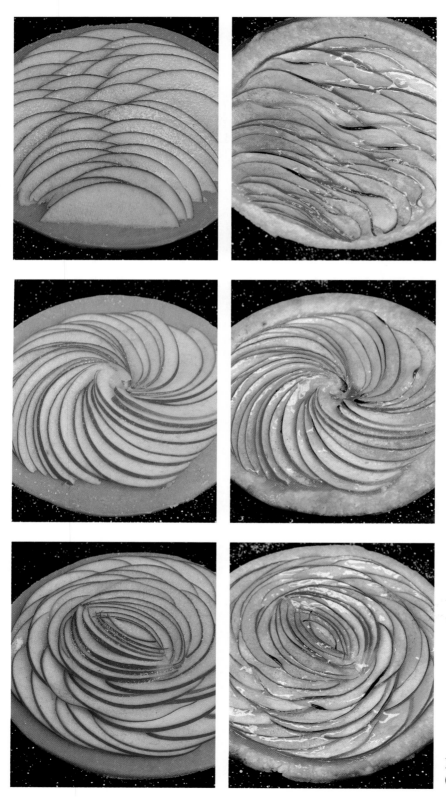

Individual Apple Tarts
(three ways)

Pâte Sucré Technique
(clockwise from top left)

Gâteau Pithiviers

Tarte Tatin

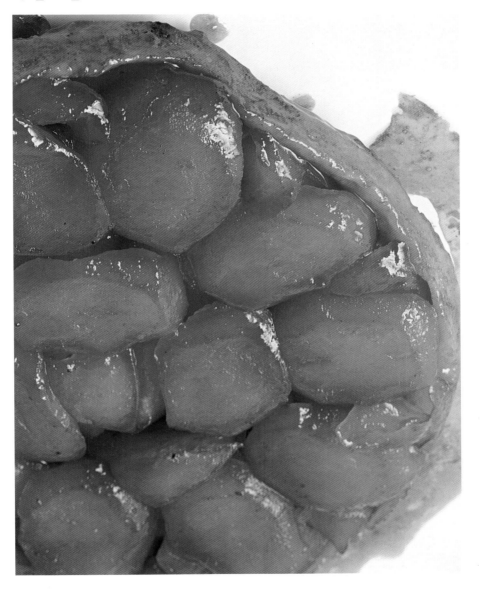

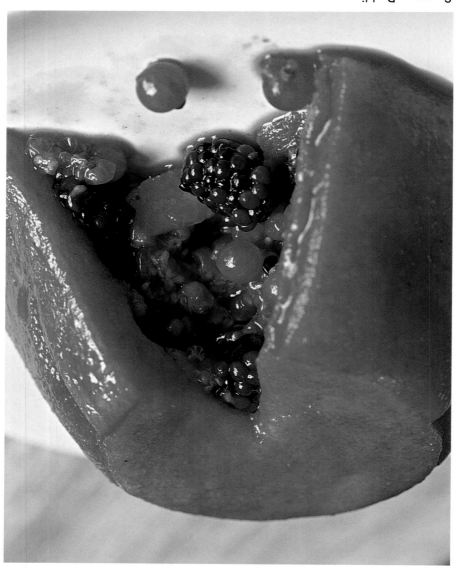

Summer Fruit Feuilletée

Chocolate Profiteroles

Stretching Strudel Pastry

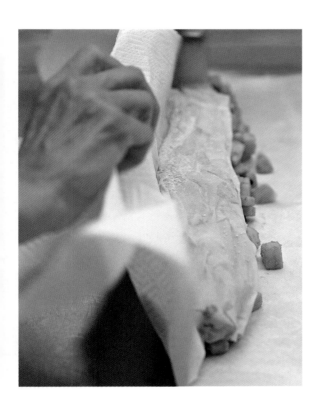
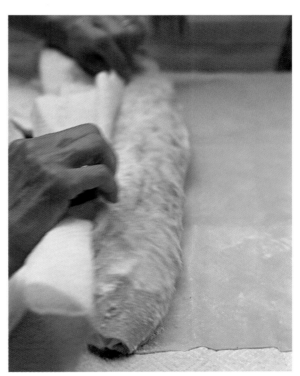

Rolling the Strudel

Apple Strudel

3 Lightly flour the worksurface and roll the dough into a rectangle about 15 × 28 cm|
6 × 12 in.

4 Tap the butter lightly with a floured rolling pin to shape it into a flattened block a little smaller than half the pastry. Put the butter on the lower half of the rectangle of pastry and fold the edges over to enclose it. Fold over the top half of the pastry,

5 Tap the pastry parcel with the rolling pin to flatten the butter a little; then roll out, quickly and lightly, until the pastry is 3 times as long as it is wide. Fold it very evenly in 3, first folding the third closest to you over, then bringing the top third down. Give it a 90-degree anti-clockwise turn so that the folded, closed edge is on your left. Again press the edges firmly with the rolling pin. Then roll out again to form a rectangle as before.

6 Now the pastry has had 2 rolls and folds. It should be put to rest in a cool place for 10–20 minutes. The rolling and folding must be repeated twice more, the pastry again rested, and then again given 2 more turns. This makes a total of 6 turns. If the pastry is still very streaky with butter, roll and fold it once more.

Bouchée Cases

MAKES ABOUT 20

225 g|8 oz flour quantity puff pastry (see page 566)
beaten egg to glaze

1 Preheat the oven to 200°C|400°F|gas mark 6.

2 Roll out the pastry 5 mm|¼ in thick. With a 4 cm|1½ in round pastry cutter, stamp it out in rounds. With a slightly smaller cutter, cut a circle in the centre of each round, but be careful not to stamp the pastry more than halfway through.

3 Brush the tops with beaten egg, taking care not to get egg on the sides, which would prevent the pastry layers from separating and rising.

4 Bake in the oven for about 12 minutes, until brown and crisp.

5 Take off the pastry 'lids' and scrape out any raw pastry left inside. Return the bouchée cases to the oven for 4 minutes to dry out. Cool on a wire rack.

NOTE: Bouchée cases, if they are to be eaten hot, should either be filled while they are still very hot with a cooked hot filling, or (if they are cooked and cold) with a cooked cold filling. Hot fillings will tend to make the pastry soggy during the reheating process. If both filling and pastry go into the oven cold, the pastry will have time to become crisp again before the filling is hot.

Vol-au-Vents

MAKES 2

225 g|8 oz flour quantity puff pastry (see page 566)   beaten egg to glaze
a pinch of salt

1 Preheat the oven to 200°C|400°F|gas mark 6.

2 Roll out the pastry to 1 cm|½ in thickness and cut into a round about the size of a dessert plate. Place on a baking sheet. Using a cutter half the size of the pastry round, cut into the centre of the pastry, but take care not to cut right through to the baking sheet.

3 Flour the blade of a knife and use this to knock up the sides of the pastry: try to slightly separate the leaves of the pastry horizontally; this enables the edge to flake readily when baking: it counteracts the squashing effect of the cutter used to cut out the round, which may have pressed the edges together, making it more difficult for the pastry to rise in even layers.

4 Mix the salt into the beaten egg. Brush the top of the pastry carefully with this egg wash, avoiding the knocked-up sides (if they are covered with egg, the pastry will not rise).

5 With the back of the knife blade, make a star pattern on the borders of the vol-au-vent case and mark a lattice pattern on the inner circle. (The back rather than the sharp edge of the blade is used as this will not cut into the pastry; the idea is to make a pattern without cutting through the surface of the pastry.)

6 Bake for 30 minutes, then carefully lift off the top of the inner circle. Keep this for the lid of the case when filled. Pull out and scrape out discard any partially cooked pastry from the centre of the case.

7 Return the case to the oven for 5 minutes to dry out. The vol-au-vent is now ready for filling. Ideally the heated pastry case is filled with hot filling, and then served.

NOTE: Flaky or rough puff pastry is also suitable. But the method of cutting is different: cut the pastry into 2 rounds the size of a side plate. Stamp a circle right out of the centre of one of them. Brush the uncut round with egg and place the ring of pastry on top. Bake the middle small round of pastry too, and use it for the vol-au-vent lid.

Palmiers

Palmiers are usually made from leftover trimmings of puff pastry.

1 Preheat the oven to 200°C|400°F|gas mark 6.

2 Do not roll the trimmings up into a ball as you would with shortcrust pastry – this would spoil the carefully created layers in the paste. Lay the strips or pieces flat on top of each other, folding them if necessary.

3 Using caster sugar instead of flour, on a work top or board, roll the pastry out into a rectangle 5 mm|¼ in thick. Sprinkle well with caster sugar. Fold each end of the pastry to the centre, then fold the pastry in half. Cut the roll across into slices 1 cm|½ in wide.

4 Lay the slices flat on a damp baking sheet, set well apart, and flatten well with a rolling pin or your hand. Bake for 10 minutes or until pale brown, with the underside caramelized. Turn over and bake for a further 10 minutes.

5 Leave to cool on a wire rack.

NOTE: These are delicious sandwiched together with strawberry jam and whipped cream.

Reasons for Failure in Pastry-making

Shortcrust, Rich Shortcrust, etc.

Shrinkage	Too much water added, stretched too much during rolling, not chilled sufficiently, oven temperature too low
Tough texture	Too much water, over-handled
Greasy appearance	Over-worked, over-baked
Grey appearance	Not baked blind for long enough, or not covered well in the refrigerator

Rough puff, flaky, puff pastry

Tough pastry	Too much water, over-handling, fat not cold enough, insufficient resting
Fat escaping	Fat has not been incorporated correctly, pastry not chilled enough, oven too cool
Poor rising	Butter broke through, final pastry rolled too thin, not chilled sufficiently.
Uneven rise	Uneven pressure when rolling, oven temperature uneven

Choux pastry

Flat, cracked appearance	Panade beaten too much when the flour was added
Badly risen	Undercooked, too little egg added
	Egg added to hot panade

Suet pastry

Grey, oily, unrisen	Water was not boiling before mixing.
Tough, heavy texture	Over-handling, too much liquid, allowed to stand before steaming

French Pancakes (Crêpes)

MAKES ABOUT 12

110 g | 4 oz plain flour
a pinch of salt
1 egg, beaten
1 egg yolk

290 ml | ½ pint milk, or milk and water mixed
1 tablespoon oil
oil for cooking

1 Sift the flour with the salt into a bowl and make a well in the centre, exposing the bottom of the bowl.
2 Put the egg and egg yolk with a little of the milk into this well.

3 Using a wooden spoon or whisk, mix the egg and milk and then gradually draw in the flour from the sides as you mix.

4 When the mixture reaches the consistency of thick cream add the remaining milk and stir in the oil.

5 The consistency should now be that of thin cream. (Batter can also be made by placing all the ingredients together in a blender for a few seconds, but take care not to over–whizz or the mixture will be bubbly.)

6 Cover the bowl and refrigerate for about 30 minutes. This is done so that the starch cells will swell, giving a lighter result.

7 Prepare a pancake pan or frying pan by heating well and wiping with oil. Pancakes are not fried in fat – the purpose of the oil is simply to prevent sticking.

8 Heat the pan, pour in enough batter to thinly coat the bottom of the pan. Swirl the pan to help the batter spread across the bottom.

9 Place over medium heat and, when the pancake is pale brown on the underside, using a palette knife and your fingers, turn the pancake over and cook the other side until brown. (Pancakes should be extremely thin, so if the first one is too thick, add a little extra milk to the batter. The first pancake is unlikely to be perfect, and is often discarded.)

10 Make up all the pancakes, turning them out on to a tea-towel or plate.

NOTES: Pancakes can be kept warm in a folded tea-towel on a plate over a saucepan of simmering water, in the oven, or in a warmer. If allowed to cool, they may be reheated by being returned to the frying pan or by warming in the oven.

Pancakes freeze well, but should be separated by pieces of greaseproof paper. They may also be refrigerated for a day or two.

Fritter Batter

125 g | 4½ oz plain flour
a pinch of salt
2 eggs

290 ml | ½ pint milk
1 tablespoon oil

1 Sift the flour with the salt into a bowl.

2 Make a well in the centre, exposing the bottom of the bowl.

3 Put 1 whole egg and 1 yolk into the well and mix with a wooden spoon or whisk until smooth, gradually incorporating the surrounding flour and the milk; the consistency should be thick and creamy.

4 Add the oil. Cover with clingfilm and refrigerate for 30 minutes.

5 When ready to use the batter, whisk the egg white until just stiff. Fold it into the batter with a large metal spoon. Use the batter to coat the food and fry immediately.

Scotch Pancakes or Drop Scones

MAKES 30

225 g | 8 oz plain flour

½ teaspoon salt

4 teaspoons baking powder

2 eggs, separated

290 ml | ½ pint milk

2 tablespoons butter, melted and cooled

To serve

butter

jam

1 Sift the flour with the salt into a large bowl.
2 Make a well in the centre of the mixture and add the egg yolks and a quarter of the milk.
3 Mix with a wooden spoon and gradually draw in the flour from the sides of the bowl making a smooth batter. Add the remaining milk gradually until the batter is the consistency of thick cream.
4 Fold in the melted butter.
5 Whisk the egg whites until stiff but not dry and fold into the batter.
6 Meanwhile, lightly grease a heavy frying pan or griddle iron and heat it. When really hot, drop spoonfuls of batter on to the surface, keeping them well separated.
7 Cook for 2–3 minutes. When the undersides of the pancakes are brown and bubbles rise to the surface, lift the pancakes with a fish slice, turn over and brown the other side.
8 Keep warm, covered with a clean tea-towel.

Puddings

Orange Fool

SERVES 4

2 small oranges

150 ml | ¼ pint sugar syrup (see page 665)

290 ml | ½ pint double cream

2 tablespoons icing sugar, sifted

1 Using a potato peeler, pare about half the zest off 1 orange. The strips should have no white pith on the underside. Using a very sharp fruit knife, cut into tiny thin strips about 2.5 cm | 1 in long.

2 Bring the sugar syrup to the boil. Place the needleshreds in the syrup. Rinse in cold water until completely cool. Drain.

3 Grate the remaining orange zest and squeeze the juice.

4 Whip the cream. When stiff, stir in the orange juice, grated zest and icing sugar.

5 Spoon into small glasses or little china pots or coffee cups. Scatter over the needleshreds of orange zest to decorate.

wine: SWEET WHITE

Gooseberry Fool

SERVES 4

250 g | 9 oz gooseberries

2 tablespoons water

110 g | 4 oz caster sugar

For the custard

290 ml | ½ pint milk

3 egg yolks

1 tablespoon cornflour

1 Wash the gooseberries and top and tail them.

2 Place the water and sugar in a saucepan and add the gooseberries.

3 Cover and cook over a low heat for about 5 minutes, stirring occasionally, until the gooseberries have softened.

4 Remove the lid, then cook the fruit over a medium heat, stirring, until it is thick enough not to run when a spoon is drawn across the bottom of the saucepan. This will take about 5 minutes. Remove from the heat and allow to cool.

5 Make the custard: place the milk in a saucepan and heat until steaming.

6 Combine the egg yolks and cornflour in a bowl, then gradually stir in the hot milk.

7 Return the custard mixture to the rinsed-out pan and cook over a medium-low heat,

stirring constantly, until the mixture is thick enough to coat the back of the spoon. Do not allow to boil.

8 Strain through a sieve into a cold bowl. Place a piece of dampened greaseproof paper directly on the surface of the custard to prevent a skin from forming.

9 When the custard is cold, fold together with the gooseberry purée.

10 Turn into a serving bowl or individual ramekins and refrigerate. Serve chilled.

wine: SWEET WHITE

Lemon Syllabub

SERVES 4

290 ml | ½ pint double cream
finely grated zest of ½ lemon
juice of 2 lemons
2 tablespoons sweet white wine

icing sugar to taste, sifted
thinly pared zest of ½ lemon

1 Place the cream in a bowl with the grated lemon zest. Whip, adding the lemon juice, wine and icing sugar at intervals. Spoon into individual glasses.

2 Cut the lemon zest into very thin needleshreds. Drop them into boiling water and cook for 2 minutes. Drain and dry them. Scatter on top of the syllabub.

wine: SWEET WHITE

Ginger Syllabub

SERVES 4

4–5 tablespoons Advocaat liqueur
2 tablespoons ginger marmalade

290 ml | ½ pint double cream
1–2 pieces of preserved stem ginger

1 Mix together the Advocaat and ginger marmalade.

2 Whip the cream lightly and stir in the ginger marmalade mixture.

3 Spoon into small glasses, little china pots or coffee cups.

4 Put 2–3 thin slivers of preserved ginger on top of each syllabub. Chill in the refrigerator before serving.

NOTES: For a smoother texture the ginger marmalade and the Advocaat can be liquidized or sieved together.

In the absence of ginger marmalade use orange marmalade well flavoured with finely chopped preserved ginger and its syrup.

wine: RICH SWEET WHITE

Chocolate Mousse

SERVES 4

110 g|4 oz plain chocolate   4 eggs

1 Chop the chocolate into small even-sized pieces. Put into a heatproof bowl set over, not in, a saucepan of simmering water. Allow it to melt.
2 Separate the eggs.
3 Whisk the egg whites to medium peak. Stir the melted chocolate into the egg yolks. Mix well. Fold the whites into the chocolate mixture.
4 Turn immediately into a soufflé dish or individual pots or glasses.
5 Chill until set, preferably overnight, but for at least 4 hours.

wine: **FORTIFIED SWEET WHITE**

Rich Chocolate Mousse

SERVES 4

70 g|2½ oz granulated sugar   170 g|6 oz plain chocolate, chopped
110 ml|4 fl oz water   340 ml|12 fl oz double cream, lightly whipped
3 egg yolks

1 Put the sugar and water into a small heavy saucepan and heat gently until the sugar has completely dissolved, then bring to the boil.
2 Boil to the short thread stage (when a little syrup is placed between a wet finger and thumb and the fingers are opened it should form a thread about 1 cm|½ in long).
3 Allow to cool slightly.
4 Pour the sugar syrup over the egg yolks, whisking all the time. Carry on whisking until the mixture is thick and mousse-like.
5 Carefully melt the chocolate in a heatproof bowl set over, not in, a saucepan of simmering water. Fold the chocolate into the egg mixture.
6 Immediately and carefully fold in the lightly whipped cream. Chill until set.

wine: **LIQUEUR MUSCAT**

White Chocolate Mousse

This mousse is firm when it is cold so it can be cut with a warm knife or biscuit cutter into shapes for using in a plated dessert. When it nears room temperature it becomes soft and creamy. The mousse is also delicious served with fresh fruit.

SERVES 8–10

For the Crème Pâtissière

200 ml | 7 fl oz milk

3 egg yolks

45 g | 1½ oz caster sugar

30 g | 1 oz plain flour

½ vanilla pod, split

For the mousse

400 g | 14 oz white chocolate, broken into pieces

200 g | 7 oz crème patissiere

400 ml | 14 fl oz double cream, lightly whipped

2 tablespoons brandy

1 Line a 20 cm | 8 in square baking tin with baking parchment.
2 Make the crème pâtissière: place the milk in a saucepan and bring to steaming point.
3 In a bowl, cream the egg yolks and sugar together well, then mix in the flour.
4 Scrape the seeds from the vanilla pod and add to the milk.
5 Pour the milk in a thin stream on to the egg mixture, stirring to remove any lumps.
6 Cook over a low heat, stirring to make a smooth cream, until the mixture boils. Place in a bowl and press a piece of dampened greaseproof paper on to the surface to prevent a skin from forming.
7 Melt the white chocolate in a bowl set over, but not in, a pan of steaming water. Do not let it get too hot. Add the melted chocolate to the warm crème pâtissière. Leave to cool.
8 Fold the whipped cream and the brandy into the chocolate mixture and spoon into the prepared tin. Refrigerate until set.
9 To serve, cut into neat diamonds, circles or squares.

wine: **SWEET WHITE**

Chocolate and Chestnut Mousse Cake

SERVES 4–6

140 g | 5 oz plain chocolate

45 g | 1½ oz unsalted butter

225 g | 8 oz canned unsweetened chestnut purée

4 eggs

55 g | 2 oz caster sugar

1 egg white

icing sugar, sifted

To serve

double cream, lightly whipped

1 Line the base and sides of a 20 cm | 8 in diameter, 5 cm | 2 in deep, cake tin with greaseproof paper. Lightly oil the paper and dust it with flour.
2 Melt the chocolate and butter in a small heavy saucepan over, but not touching, a pan of steaming water.

3 Preheat the oven to 180°C|350°F|gas mark 4.

4 Sieve the chestnut purée into the chocolate and butter mixture. Stir to combine.

5 Separate the eggs. Whisk the egg yolks with the sugar until thick, pale and mousse-like. Fold this into the chocolate and chestnut mixture.

6 Whisk the egg whites until stiff but not dry. Fold into the chocolate mixture. Pour into the prepared cake tin.

7 Bake for 50 minutes. Remove from the oven and leave in the tin to set and cool for 5 minutes. Turn out and dust lightly with the icing sugar. Serve the cream separately.

wine: **LIQUEUR MUSCAT**

Chocolate Mousse and Ginger Syllabub in Chocolate Cases

SERVES 6

chocolate mousse (see page 574)

ginger syllabub (see page 573)

To decorate

chocolate shapes (see page 737)

For the chocolate cases

225 g|8 oz best-quality plain chocolate

1 First make the chocolate cases: break up the chocolate and place it in a heatproof bowl. Set it over, not in, a saucepan of steaming water. Stir until the chocolate is smooth and melted. Do not overheat.

2 Brush the melted chocolate thinly over the insides of 8 small paper cases. (It is easier if you make double paper cases by slipping one case inside another.) Chill between layers. Repeat the process until you have a reasonably thick but even layer. Leave to harden, then carefully peel away the paper.

3 Make up the chocolate mousse and ginger syllabub according to the recipes but do not dish them up.

4 Divide the chocolate mixture between the 8 chocolate cases. Spread flat and leave to set slightly. Spoon over the ginger syllabub. Decorate each case with a chocolate shape.

wine: **FORTIFIED SWEET WHITE**

Caramel Mousse

SERVES 4

170 g|6 oz granulated sugar

2 level teaspoons powdered gelatine

1 tablespoon of lemon juice

3 eggs

45 g|1½ oz caster sugar

150 ml|¼ pint double cream

To decorate

55 g|2 oz caster sugar

double cream, whipped

1 Melt the granulated sugar in a heavy saucepan with 3 tablespoons water and boil until it turns to a brown caramel. Pour in 5 tablespoons water very carefully – it will hiss alarmingly. Cook over a low heat until the caramel is dissolved. Cool slightly.

2 Sprinkle the gelatine over the lemon juice with 2 tablespoons water in a small saucepan. Leave for 5 minutes to become spongy.

3 When the caramel is cool whisk the eggs with the caster sugar in a heatproof bowl set over, not in, a saucepan of simmering water until mousse-like and thick. Remove from the heat and whisk until beginning to cool.

4 Dissolve the soaked gelatine over a low heat without boiling until liquid. Fold into the mousse mixture with the caramel sauce. Stir gently over a bowl of ice until beginning to thicken and set.

5 Lightly whip the cream and fold into the mixture.

6 Pour into a serving dish and refrigerate until set.

7 Meanwhile, make the caramel chips for the decoration: lightly oil a flat dish or baking sheet. Put the sugar into a small heavy saucepan and heat gently, without any water, until it first melts, then turns to caramel. When it is evenly brown, pour immediately on to the oiled dish or baking sheet. Allow to cool until hard as glass, then immediately break into small chips with the end of a rolling pin. Keep dry and cool until needed.

8 Decorate the mousse with rosettes of whipped cream and caramel chips.

NOTE: For details and instructions on gelatine see page 201.

wine: **FORTIFIED SWEET WHITE**

Charlotte Russe

SERVES 4–6

150 ml | ¼ pint clear lemon jelly (see page 601)
15 sponge fingers (see page 781)

For the custard

1 vanilla pod or ½ teaspoon vanilla essence
425 ml | ¾ pint milk
45 g | 1½ oz caster sugar
5 egg yolks

3 tablespoons sweet sherry
3 level 5 ml teaspoons powdered gelatine
4 tablespoons water
235 ml | 8 fl oz double cream, lightly whipped

To decorate (optional)

4 glacé cherries, cut in half
a few pieces of angelica

1 Make the lemon jelly. When it is cool but not set, wet a charlotte mould and pour in a thin layer (about 5 mm | ¼ in) of jelly. Decorate the base with cherries and angelica and leave to set in the refrigerator. Pour in the remaining jelly and refrigerate again until nearly set. Arrange the sponge fingers, sugared side outside, standing up around the sides of the mould with their ends in the jelly.

2 Make the custard: put the vanilla and milk in a saucepan and heat gently.

3 In a heatproof bowl, mix the sugar and egg yolks well together. When the milk is almost boiling, remove the vanilla pod, if using, and pour on to the yolks, stirring vigorously. Set the bowl over, not in, a saucepan of simmering water and stir until thick enough to coat the back of the spoon. Strain and allow to cool. Add the sherry.

4 Sprinkle the gelatine over the water in a small saucepan and leave for 5 minutes to become spongy. Dissolve over a low heat, without boiling, until liquid and clear, then stir into the cooling custard. When the custard is almost set, fold in the partially whipped cream and turn the mixture into the mould, spreading it flat. Leave in the refrigerator to set.

5 Trim off any biscuits sticking up above the level of the filling. Run a knife between the biscuits and the mould to make sure they are not stuck. Dip the bottom of the mould briefly into hot water to dislodge the jelly. Invert a plate over the mould, turn both over together and carefully lift off the mould.

NOTE: For details and instructions on gelatine, see page 201.

wine: **SWEET WHITE**

Armagnac and Prune Mousse

SERVES 4

110 g|4 oz prunes, stoned
30 ml|1 fl oz Armagnac or brandy
1½ level 5 ml teaspoon powdered gelatine
110 g|4 oz granulated sugar

150 ml|¼ pint water
2 egg whites
150 ml|¼ pint double cream, lightly whipped

1 Soak the prunes in the Armagnac for a day, then purée them in a food processor or liquidizer.

2 Sprinkle the gelatine over 3 tablespoons water in a small saucepan.

3 Put the sugar and water into a small saucepan and heat gently until the sugar has completely dissolved, then bring to the boil. Allow it to boil to the short thread stage (when a little syrup is placed between a wet finger and thumb and the fingers are opened it should form a thread about 1 cm|½ in long). Leave to cool for 30 seconds.

4 Whisk the egg whites until stiff and pour on the cooked sugar syrup, whisking all the time until they have formed a thick, shiny meringue.

5 Dissolve the gelatine over a low heat without boiling until liquid and clear, then add it to the prune purée.

6 Gradually whisk the purée into the meringue mixture. Fold in the cream. Pour into a serving dish and leave in the refrigerator to set.

NOTE: For details and instructions on gelatine, see page 201.

wine: **SWEET WHITE**

Le Gasçon

This is a very complicated recipe but the end result justifies all the effort.

SERVES 8–10

3 egg quantity sponge fingers (see page 781)

3 egg quantity chocolate génoise (see page 716)

2 tablespoons Armagnac or brandy

150 ml | ¼ pint sugar syrup (see page 665)

3 egg quantity Rich Chocolate Mousse (see page 574)

2 egg white quantity Armagnac and Prune Mousse (see page 578)

110 g | 4 oz chocolate quantity Glaçage Koba (see below)

1 Trim one end of the sponge fingers and use to line the sides of a 20 cm | 8 in spring-clip tin, making sure all the fingers are the same height.

2 Cut the chocolate génoise in half horizontally and place one half cut side up in the bottom.

3 Add the Armagnac to the sugar syrup.

4 Brush both cakes with the sugar syrup.

5 Pour the chocolate mousse into the centre until it comes halfway up the sponge fingers. Allow it to set.

6 Place the other half of the génoise cut-side up on top of the set chocolate mousse.

7 Pour the prune mousse on top, leaving a space of 5 mm | ¼ in at the top. Allow to set.

8 Pour the glaçage koba over the top and level with a palette knife if necessary. Leave to set.

wine: FORTIFIED SWEET RED

Glaçage Koba (Chocolate Icing)

70 ml | 2½ fl oz milk

225 g | 8 oz plain chocolate, chopped

30 ml | 1 fl oz double cream

55 g | 2 oz butter

15 g | ½ oz powdered glucose

4 tablespoons sugar syrup (see page 665)

1 Bring the milk to the boil in a saucepan and add the chocolate, cream, butter and glucose. Stir over a low heat until well mixed and all the chocolate has melted.

2 Add the sugar syrup.

3 Allow the icing to cool to a coating consistency. If it gets too thick, place over a pan of simmering water and stir until the correct consistency is obtained.

NOTE: Use couverture chocolate if available.

Cassis Cream Pie

SERVES 6

For the base

2 eggs, separated

55 g│2 oz caster sugar

30 g│1 oz plain flour, sifted

1 tablespoon blackcurrant jelly or sieved jam

For the mousse and glaze

340 g│12 oz blackcurrants

5 tablespoons crème de cassis liqueur

3 eggs, separated

110 g│4 oz caster sugar

3 level 5 ml powdered gelatine

150 ml│¼ pint double cream

2 tablespoons blackcurrant jelly or sieved jam

1 Preheat the oven to 220°C│425°F│gas mark 7.

2 Grease and flour a 20 in│8 in diameter loose-bottomed cake tin.

3 Make the base: whisk the egg yolks and half the sugar in a heatproof bowl set over, not in, a saucepan of simmering water with an electric or balloon whisk until pale, mousse-like and very thick. Remove from the heat.

4 Whisk the egg whites until stiff and fold in the remaining sugar.

5 Fold the yolk and white mixtures together, then fold in the flour.

6 Turn into the cake tin and bake in the oven for 15 minutes until evenly brown and slightly shrunk from the tin sides.

7 Remove the cake from the tin and cool, upside down, on a wire rack.

8 When cold, spread evenly with the blackcurrant jelly or jam.

9 Wash the cake tin and oil its sides.

10 Make the blackcurrant purée by simmering the fruit with 2 tablespoons water. Keep stirring and boiling until the juice has evaporated without the fruit catching and burning on the bottom of the pan.

11 Push the fruit through a nylon sieve to extract the seeds, scraping the paste-like purée from the back of the sieve with a clean spoon. Take one-third of the purée and reserve it for the top. Mix the remainder with 2 tablespoons of the crème de cassis.

12 Make the mousse: whisk the egg yolks, 2 tablespoons of the crème de cassis and 75 g│3 oz of the sugar in a heatproof bowl set over, not in, a saucepan of simmering water. It will be more liquid than the first mixture and the whisking will take longer; it should thicken sufficiently to leave a ribbon-like trail when the whisk is lifted. Remove from the heat and leave to cool, whisking occasionally.

13 Put 3 tablespoons water into a small saucepan and sprinkle over the gelatine. Leave for 5 minutes to become spongy.

14 Stir the blackcurrant purée into the egg-yolk mixture.

15 Dissolve the gelatine over a low heat without boiling until liquid and clear, then stir into the blackcurrant mixture.

16 When the blackcurrant mixture is just starting to set, whip the cream until it will just hold its shape, and fold into the mousse.

17 Whisk the egg whites until stiff and fold in the remaining sugar.

18 Fold the blackcurrant mousse and the meringue mixtures together lightly and without overmixing – a few air pockets are preferable to a mixture with all the air stirred out of it.

19 Fit the cooled and jam-spread cake back into the cake tin, and pour the mousse into it. Level the top and freeze until very solid.

20 To remove the mousse from the tin: loosen the sides by wrapping the cake tin in a cloth dipped in very hot water. Push the nearly or completely frozen mousse out of the tin on the base. Using a fish slice, ease the pie on to a serving plate. Allow to thaw in the refrigerator. (The only reason the pie is frozen is to make getting it out of the tin easier. But if a deep flan ring on a baking sheet is used instead of the tin, or a spring-form cake pan – with sides that unclip – then freezing is not necessary.)

21 Make the glazed top: gently heat together the reserved blackcurrant purée, the blackcurrant jelly or sieved jam and the remaining crème de cassis. Stir until melted, then boil hard for a few seconds to get a shiny clear syrup.

22 Cool the glaze until just liquid, pour over the set mousse, and ease to the edges with a palette knife. Prick any air bubbles with the knife.

wine: **SWEET WHITE**

Cold Lemon Soufflé

SERVES 4

3 tablespoons of water
1½ level 5 ml teaspoons powdered gelatine
3 eggs
grated zest and juice of 2 large lemons
140 g | 5 oz caster sugar
150 ml | ¼ pint double cream, lightly whipped
icing sugar (optional)

To decorate
150 ml | ¼ pint double cream, whipped
nibbed almonds, toasted

1 Put the water into a small saucepan, sprinkle over the gelatine and leave for 5 minutes to become spongy.

2 Separate the eggs. Place the yolks, lemon juice and sugar in a mixing bowl and whisk together with an electric motor (or with a balloon whisk or rotary beater with the bowl set over a saucepan of simmering water). Whisk until very thick. Remove from heat and whisk for a few minutes longer, until the mixture is lukewarm. Add the lemon zest.

3 Dissolve the gelatine over a low heat without boiling until liquid and clear, then add to the mousse mixture. Stir gently until the mixture is on the point of setting, then fold in the cream. Taste and if too tart, sift in a little icing sugar; if too bland, add a little more lemon juice.

4 Whisk the egg whites until just stiff but not dry and fold them into the soufflé with a large metal spoon.

5 Pour the mixture into a soufflé dish and leave to set in the refrigerator for 2–3 hours. Decorate with rosettes of cream and almonds.

NOTES: This dish can be given a more soufflé-like appearance by tying a double band of oiled paper round the top of the dish so that it projects about 2.5 cm | 1 in above the rim, before pouring in the mixture. (The dish must be of a size that would not quite contain the mixture without the added depth given by the paper band.) Pour in the soufflé mixture to come about 2.5 cm | 1 in up the paper, above the rim of the dish. When the soufflé is set, carefully remove the paper and spread a thin layer of lightly whipped cream round the exposed sides then press on the almonds.

For details and instructions on gelatine, see page 201.

wine: **SWEET WHITE**

Cold Raspberry Soufflé

SERVES 4

3 eggs
110 g | 4 oz caster sugar
3 tablespoons water
15 g | ½ oz powdered gelatine
340 g | 12 oz raspberries
150 ml | ¼ pint double cream
icing sugar (optional)

To decorate
chopped or nibbed almonds, toasted
150 ml | ¼ pint double cream, whipped
whole raspberries

1 To prepare the soufflé dish (which should be 15 cm | 6 in diameter), tie a double piece of greaseproof paper around the outside and secure the ends with a paper clip or pin. The paper should stick up about 2.5 cm | 1 in above the rim. Brush the inside of the projecting paper with oil.

2 Separate the eggs. Whisk the yolks with the sugar either over a low heat (with the bowl set over a saucepan of simmering water), or in an electric mixer, until light and fluffy, and thick enough for the whisk to leave a 'ribbon trail' when lifted.

3 Remove from the heat and whisk again until the mixture is almost cold.

4 Put the water into a small pan and sprinkle over the gelatine. Leave for 5 minutes until spongy.

5 Purée the raspberries in a food processor and sieve the purée into the egg-yolk mixture. Stir to combine.

6 Dissolve the gelatine over a low heat without boiling until liquid and clear, then stir into the raspberry mixture. Stir gently until on the point of setting. Fold in the whipped cream. Taste and sift in a little icing sugar if too tart.

7 Whisk the egg whites until just stiff and fold them into the soufflé mixture with a large metal spoon. Pile into the prepared dish and flatten the top neatly. The soufflé mixture should come at least 2 cm|¾ in above the rim of the dish. Refrigerate for at least 4 hours until set.

8 Remove the oiled paper carefully. Spread the exposed sides thinly with cream. Press almonds gently on to the cream. Pipe rosettes of whipped cream round the top and garnish each with a whole raspberry.

wine: SWEET WHITE

Cold Passionfruit Soufflé

SERVES 4

8 passionfruits
grated zest and juice of 1 lemon
1 tablespoon water
1½ level 5 ml powdered gelatine
3 eggs
110 g|4 oz caster sugar

150 ml|¼ pint double cream
icing sugar (optional)

To decorate
1 passionfruit

1 Cut the passionfruits in half. Scoop out and sieve all the flesh. Discard the seeds.
2 Put the lemon juice and water into a small saucepan and sprinkle over the gelatine. Leave for 5 minutes to become spongy.
3 Separate the eggs. Place the yolks, lemon zest and sugar into a mixing bowl and whisk together with an electric mixer (or with a balloon whisk or rotary beater with the bowl set over a saucepan of simmering water). Whisk until very thick. Remove from the heat and whisk for a few minutes longer, until the mixture is lukewarm. Gradually add the passionfruit pulp.
4 Dissolve the gelatine over a low heat without boiling until liquid and clear, then add to the mousse mixture. Stir gently until the mixture is on the point of setting, then fold in the cream. Taste and if too tart sift in a little icing sugar; if too bland add a little more lemon juice.
5 Whisk the egg whites until stiff but not dry and fold them into the soufflé with a large metal spoon.
6 Pour the mixture into a soufflé dish and leave to set in the refrigerator for 2–3 hours. When set decorate with the seeds of 1 passionfruit.

wine: SWEET WHITE

Seville Orange Soufflé

This is a recipe of Sophie Grigson's, published in the London *Evening Standard*.

SERVES 4

softened butter for the soufflé dish

110 g | 4 oz caster sugar

30 g | 1 oz plain flour

150–200 ml | 5–7 fl oz milk

1 vanilla pod, split

15 g | ½ oz butter

finely grated zest and juice of 2 Seville oranges

4 egg yolks

5 egg whites

icing sugar, to dust

1 Spread a layer of butter 1 cm deep and 1 mm thick inside the rim of a soufflé dish or dishes.

2 Preheat the oven to 200°C | 400°F | gas mark 6. Preheat a baking sheet.

3 Mix half the sugar with the flour in a saucepan. Pour in a little of the milk, warm gently over a low heat, then gradually stir in the remaining milk, making sure there are no lumps. Add the vanilla pod, bring to the boil and simmer, stirring all the time, for 1 minute. Remove from the heat. Scrape the seeds from the vanilla pod and add to the milk. Discard the vanilla pod.

4 Beat in the butter and stir in the orange zest and juice and finally the egg yolks. Transfer to a large mixing bowl.

5 Whisk the egg whites until stiff, then gradually whisk in the remaining sugar, continuing to whisk until the mixture is stiff and shiny. Fold gently but thoroughly into the orange mixture. Pour into the prepared soufflé dish – do not fill more than two-thirds full. Run the blade of a knife around the top edge of the soufflé mixture. This gives a 'top hat' appearance to the cooked soufflé. Bake the soufflé on the preheated baking sheet for 20–25 minutes.

6 Test by giving the dish a slight shake or push. If the soufflé wobbles alarmingly, it needs further cooking; if it wobbles only slightly, it is ready. Dust with icing sugar and serve immediately.

wine: **RICH SWEET WHITE**

Summerberry Soufflés

SERVES 4

softened butter for greasing

250 g | 9 oz frozen mixed berries, defrosted and drained

55 g | 2 oz caster sugar

15 g | ½ oz plain flour

85 ml | 3 fl oz milk

2 egg yolks

3 egg whites

icing sugar for dusting

1 Thickly butter the top 1 cm|½ in of the rims of 4 ramekins.
2 Preheat the oven to 200°C|400°F|gas mark 6. Place a baking sheet on the shelf in the top third of the oven (the hottest part).
3 Purée the fruit in a food processor, then pass through a sieve to remove the seeds. Set aside.
4 Mix half the sugar with the flour in a saucepan. Pour in a little of the milk to form a smooth paste. Add the remaining milk.
5 Heat the mixture over a medium heat, stirring until the mixture boils. Boil for 1 minute.
6 Place the egg yolks in a small bowl and slowly stir in the hot, thickened milk mixture. Stir in the fruit purée.
7 Whisk the egg whites in a clean bowl until just stiff, then whisk in the remaining sugar.
8 Fold a spoonful of the whisked egg whites into the fruit mixture to loosen it, then carefully fold in the remaining whites.
9 Spoon the mixture into the prepared ramekins. Run a small knife around the edge of the rim of the soufflés to release the mixture from the rim.
10 Place the ranekins on the hot baking sheet and bake in the oven for about 12 minutes. The soufflés should wobble gently when ready.
11 Remove from the oven, dust with icing sugar and serve immediately.

wine: SWEET WINE

Hot Chocolate Soufflé

To make a successful chocolate soufflé you must have everything organized before you start to cook and work as quickly as possible. It is quite difficult to do.

SERVES 4

butter, softened	4 egg yolks
55 g|2 oz caster sugar plus 1 teaspoon	5 egg whites
110 g|4 oz plain chocolate	icing sugar

1 Preheat the oven to 200°C|400°F|gas mark 6. Preheat a baking sheet. Prepare a soufflé dish by buttering the inside rim 1 cm deep and 1 mm thick.
2 Chop the chocolate into small pieces and put it into a heatproof bowl set over, not in, a saucepan of gently steaming water, stirring until the chocolate has completely melted.
3 Beat the remaining sugar and the egg yolks together for 1 minute with a wooden spoon until thick. Add the chocolate to the egg-yolk mixture, mixing well – it will thicken slightly.
4 Whisk the whites until they will stand in soft peaks when the whisk is withdrawn from the bowl. Whisk in 1 teaspoon caster sugar, until stiff and shiny. Gently but thoroughly fold into the chocolate mixture.
5 Turn into the soufflé dish but do not fill more than two-thirds full. Run the end of a

knife around the edge of the soufflé mixture. This gives a 'top hat' appearance to the cooked soufflé.

6 Bake on the hot baking sheet for 20–25 minutes. Test by giving the dish a slight shake or push. If the soufflé wobbles alarmingly, it needs further cooking; if it wobbles slightly, it is ready. Dust lightly with icing sugar and serve immediately.

wine: **FORTIFIED SWEET WINE**

Sweet Soufflé Omelette

SERVES 2

2 eggs	30 g│1 oz caster sugar
1 tablespoon apricot jam	15 g│½ oz butter
1 tablespoon lemon juice	icing sugar to finish

1 Separate the eggs. Use a 15 cm│6 in nonstick frying pan.
2 Preheat the oven to 180°C│350°F│gas mark 4.
3 Warm the jam with the lemon juice.
4 Beat the yolks with the sugar until light.
5 Whisk the egg whites until just stiff.
6 Heat the frying pan and melt the butter in it.
7 Fold the egg whites into the yolks and when the butter is foaming, but not coloured, pour in the egg mixture.
8 Lower the heat and cook for 1 minute until the underside has just set.
9 Place in the oven for 5 minutes, or until the omelette top is just set – do not overcook.
10 Get 2 long skewers red-hot in a gas flame. Leave them there while baking the omelette.
11 Spread the warmed jam over half the omelette and fold in 2 with a spatula – you may need to cut the omelette a little in the middle.
12 Slip on to a warmed flat serving dish. Sprinkle the surface with icing sugar.
13 Brand a criss-cross pattern in the sugar with the red-hot skewers. Serve immediately.

NOTES: It is not strictly necessary to finish the cooking in the oven, but it avoids the risk of burning the bottom of the omelette before the top is set.

The branding with the hot skewer is not essential either, but the omelette should be sprinkled with icing sugar before serving.

wine: **SWEET WHITE**

Hot Apricot Soufflé

SERVES 4

softened butter for greasing

20 g | ¾ oz butter

30 g | 1 oz caster sugar, plus extra for dusting

110 g | 4 oz good-quality dried apricots, soaked overnight in 200 ml | 7 fl oz water

20 g | ¾ oz plain flour

200 ml | 7 fl oz orange juice

grated zest of 1 orange

5 egg whites

1 Butter the inside rim, 1 cm deep and 1 mm thick, of a 15 cm | 6 in soufflé dish. Preheat the oven to 200°C | 400°F | gas mark 6.

2 Poach the apricots in the water until very tender and then liquidize in a food processor or blender with the cooking liquor.

3 Melt the butter in a small saucepan, add the flour and cook for 1 minute. Remove from the heat and add the orange juice and zest. Return the pan to the heat and bring to the boil, stirring continually. Simmer for 2 minutes. Remove from the heat and add the apricot purée.

4 Whisk the egg whites until just stiff, add the sugar and whisk again until stiff.

5 Add 1 tablespoon of egg white to loosen the soufflé base and then gently fold in the remaining egg whites. Pour into the prepared soufflé dish.

6 Run the blade of a knife around the edge of the soufflé mixture. This gives a 'top hat' appearance to the cooked soufflé.

7 Bake in the oven for 12–15 minutes. Test by giving the dish a slight shake or push. If the soufflé wobbles alarmingly, it needs further cooking; if it wobbles slightly, it is ready. Serve immediately.

wine: **SWEET SPARKLING**

Junket

SERVES 4

570 ml | 1 pint fresh milk

2 teaspoons sugar

1 teaspoon rennet

1 Heat the milk with the sugar to blood temperature (lukewarm).

2 Stir well and pour into a serving bowl.

3 Stir in the rennet and leave to set at room temperature. Once set, the dish may be refrigerated.

NOTE: To vary the flavour of plain junket, spoon over a little whipped cream and sprinkle with crumbed ratafia biscuits; sprinkle the surface with freshly grated nutmeg; or flavour with coffee essence, grated orange zest or grated chocolate.

Baked Custard

SERVES 4

3 eggs

1 egg yolk

3 drops of vanilla essence

55 g│2 oz caster sugar

425 ml│¾ pint very creamy milk, or milk plus single cream, scalded

1 bay leaf

freshly grated nutmeg

1 Preheat the oven to 150°C│300°F│gas mark 2.

2 Lightly beat the eggs, egg yolk, vanilla essence and sugar together with a wooden spoon; don't make them frothy.

3 Pour the milk and the cream, if using, on to the eggs, stirring all the time with a wooden spoon, not a whisk, to avoid creating bubbles.

4 Strain the mixture into an ovenproof dish. Straining removes any egg 'threads' which would spoil the smooth texture of the finished custard. Add the bay leaf and sprinkle with nutmeg.

5 Stand the custard dish in a roasting pan half-filled with hot water (a bain-marie) and bake for 40 minutes. The custard is set when there is a definite skin on the top and the centre is no longer liquid (although it will wobble).

6 Serve hot, warm or chilled.

Rice Pudding

SERVES 4

a nut of butter

1 tablespoon caster sugar

55 g│2 oz round (pudding) rice

570 ml│1 pint milk

vanilla essence

freshly grated nutmeg

1 Preheat the oven to 150°C│300°F│gas mark 2.

2 Rub the butter round a pie dish. Put the sugar, rice, milk and vanilla essence into the dish. Sprinkle with nutmeg.

3 Stir, and bake in the oven for 3–4 hours, by which time it should be soft and creamy with an evenly coloured brown skin.

Bread and Butter Pudding

SERVES 4

3 slices of white bread

30 g│1 oz butter, softened

2 tablespoons currants and sultanas, mixed

2 teaspoons chopped mixed peel

2 eggs

1 egg yolk

1 rounded tablespoon sugar

290 ml│½ pint creamy milk

vanilla essence

ground cinnamon

demerara sugar

1 Remove the crusts then spread the bread with the butter. Cut into quarters. Arrange half of the bread in a shallow buttered ovenproof dish, buttered side up, and sprinkle with currants, sultanas and peel. Cover with the remaining bread.
2 Mix the eggs and egg yolk with the sugar and stir in the milk and vanilla essence.
3 Strain the custard carefully over the bread. Place in the refrigerator and leave to soak for 30 minutes. Sprinkle with cinnamon and demerara sugar.
4 Preheat the oven to 170°C|325°F|gas mark 3.
5 Place the pudding in a roasting pan half-filled with hot water (a bain-marie) and cook in the middle of the oven for about 45 minutes, or until the custard is set and the top is brown and crusty.

NOTE: The pudding may be baked quite successfully without the bain-marie, but if used it will ensure a smooth, not bubbly custard.

wine: SWEET WHITE

Brioche Bread and Butter Pudding

SERVES 4–6

1 brioche (see page 761), weighing 225 g|8 oz	3 egg yolks
55 g|2 oz butter	55 g|2 oz sugar
85 g|3 oz dried apricots, chopped	860 ml|1½ pints creamy milk
30 g|1 oz raisins	2 teaspoons vanilla essence
2 teaspoons chopped mixed peel	1 teaspoon ground cinnamon
6 eggs	5 tablespoons apricot jam

1 Slice the brioche into 1 cm|½ in slices, leaving the crusts on. Spread the slices with butter and cut them in half diagonally.
2 Grease a large shallow oval dish (1.75 litres|3 pints capacity) and scatter the apricots, the raisins and the mixed peel. Arrange the brioche slices buttered side up, slightly overlapping, in the dish.
3 Mix together the eggs, yolks, sugar, milk, vanilla essence and cinnamon, using a wooden spoon. Strain the mixture over the brioche and leave to stand in the refrigerator for 30 minutes.
4 Preheat the oven to 170°C|325°F|gas mark 3.
5 Heat up a bain-marie (a roasting pan half-filled with hot water) and put the dish in it. Bake in the centre of the oven for about 1 hour, or until the custard is set.
6 Meanwhile, heat the apricot jam in a saucepan with 1 tablespoon water. Push through a sieve and keep warm.
7 When the pudding is cooked, remove it from the bain-marie and using a pastry brush, brush the surface with the apricot glaze. Serve warm.

Crème Caramel

SERVES 4–5

110 g | 4 oz granulated sugar

4 tablespoons water

4 eggs

2 tablespoons caster sugar

570 ml | 1 pint milk

vanilla essence

1 Preheat the oven to 150°C | 300°F | gas mark 2. Warm a soufflé or other ovenproof dish in it.

2 Place the granulated sugar in a heavy saucepan with the water and allow it to melt slowly. When melted, boil rapidly until it has turned to a good brown caramel. Pour into the hot soufflé dish and coat all over by carefully tipping the dish. Leave until cold.

3 Beat the eggs and caster sugar together with a wooden spoon.

4 Scald the milk by bringing it to just below boiling point and stir it into the egg mixture. Add the vanilla essence. Strain into the prepared dish.

5 Stand the dish in a roasting pan half-filled with hot water (a bain-marie) and cover with a piece of foil. Do not let the foil touch the custard. Cook in the oven for 1 hour, or until the custard has set.

6 Allow to cool until tepid or stone-cold, then turn out on to a dish with a good lip.

NOTE: The caramel can be made in the microwave. Put the sugar and water into a shallow dish. Cover with clingfilm and pierce. Microwave on HIGH for 2 minutes. Stir, then microwave for a further 6 minutes. Swirl it carefully around the dish.

wine: FORTIFIED SWEET WHITE

Queen's Pudding

SERVES 4

290 ml | ½ pint milk

15 g | ½ oz butter

140 g | 5 oz caster sugar

55 g | 2 oz fresh white breadcrumbs, sieved

grated zest of 1 lemon

2 eggs

2 tablespoons raspberry jam, warmed

1 Heat the milk and add the butter and 30 g | 1 oz of the sugar. Stir until the sugar dissolves, then add the breadcrumbs and lemon zest. Allow to cool.

2 Preheat the oven to 150°C | 300°F | gas mark 2.

3 Separate the eggs. Mix the egg yolks into the breadcrumb mixture. Pour into a pie dish and leave to stand for 30 minutes in the refrigerator.

4 Place the pudding in a roasting pan half-filled with hot water (a bain-marie) and bake in the oven for 45 minutes, or until the custard mixture is set. Remove from the oven and allow to cool slightly.

5 Increase the oven temperature to 180°C | 350°F | gas mark 4.

6 Carefully spread the jam over the top of the custard.

7 Whisk the egg whites until stiff. Whisk in 2 teaspoons of the remaining sugar. Whisk again until very stiff and shiny and fold in all but half a teaspoon of the remaining sugar.

8 Pile the meringue on top of the custard and dust the top lightly with the reserved sugar.

9 Bake in the oven until the meringue is set and straw-coloured, about 10 minutes.

NOTES: This is particularly good served hot with cold whipped cream.

See 'Whisking egg whites', page 669.

wine: SWEET WHITE

Semolina Pudding

SERVES 4

570 ml|1 pint milk	85 g|3 oz caster sugar
a few drops of oil	juice of 1 lemon
85 g|3 oz semolina	a few drops of vanilla essence
2 eggs	4–5 tablespoons double cream

1 Heat the milk with the oil in a heavy saucepan and when boiling, gradually stir in the semolina.

2 Reduce the heat and simmer for 10 minutes, or until the semolina is cooked, stirring from time to time. Remove from the heat and allow to cool slightly.

3 Separate the eggs. Whisk the yolks with the sugar until light and fluffy, then stir into the semolina mixture.

4 Beat in the lemon juice, vanilla essence and cream.

5 Whisk the egg whites until stiff and fold into the semolina mixture with a large metal spoon.

6 Serve immediately or chill up to 24 hours.

Petits Pots de Crème

SERVES 6

290 ml\|½ pint milk

just over 290 ml\|½ pint single cream

30 g\|1 oz caster sugar

1 vanilla pod or 2 drops of vanilla essence

4 egg yolks

1 large egg

1 Preheat the oven to 150°C|300°F|gas mark 2.

2 Place the milk and cream with the sugar and vanilla pod, if using, in a saucepan and scald by bringing to just below boiling point. Allow to infuse for 10 minutes, then remove the vanilla pod. (If using vanilla essence, add it once the milk is scalded.)

3 Beat the egg yolks with the whole egg and pour on the scalded milk. Strain.

4 Pour into the ramekins. Stand the 6 ramekins in a roasting pan half-filled with hot water (a bain-marie).

5 Bake in the oven, covered with a sheet of greaseproof paper or kitchen foil, for 35–40 minutes. Remove the covering, being careful not to let any condensed water drop on to the crèmes. Lift out of the water and allow to cool.

NOTE: Chocolate-flavoured custards may take longer to cook (about 45 minutes).

Crème Brûlée

Crème brûlée is best started a day in advance.

SERVES 4

290 ml | ½ pint double cream
1 vanilla pod or 1 teaspoon vanilla essence
4 egg yolks
1 tablespoon caster sugar

For the topping
caster sugar

1 Put the cream with the vanilla pod, if using, into a saucepan and heat to scalding point (just below boiling point), making sure it does not boil. Allow to infuse for 10 minutes. Remove the vanilla pod. Scrape out the seeds and add to the cream.

2 Preheat the oven to 170°C | 325°F | gas mark 3.

3 Beat the egg yolks with the sugar and when light and fluffy, stir in the warm cream. If using vanilla essence, add it now. Pass through a sieve.

4 Pour the custard into an ovenproof serving dish, place in a roasting pan half-filled with hot water (a bain-marie) and bake in the oven for 20 minutes to create a good skin on top. Refrigerate overnight. On no account break the top skin.

5 The next day preheat the grill to its highest setting.

6 Sprinkle the top of the custard with a 5 mm | ¼ in even layer of caster sugar. To do this, stand the dish on a tray or a large sheet of greaseproof paper and sift the sugar over the dish and the tray or paper. In this way you will get an even layer of sugar. Collect the sugar falling wide for re-use. Mist the sugar with water, using a plant sprayer, to help it dissolve. Wipe clean the rims of the dishes.

7 Put the custard under the very hot grill, as close as you can get it to the heat. The sugar will melt and caramelize before the custard underneath it boils. Watch carefully, turning the custard if the sugar is browning unevenly.

8 Allow to cool completely before serving. The top should be hard.

9 To serve: crack the top with the serving spoon. Crème brûlée is also good made in individual ramekins. In this case, bake the custard for only 10 minutes.

NOTE: If making crème brûlée for more than 4 or 5 people, either make in individual ramekin dishes or in more than one large dish.

wine: **FORTIFIED SWEET WHITE**

Almond Bavarois with Apricot Sauce

SERVES 8

110 g | 4 oz ground almonds

1 vanilla pod

290 ml | ½ pint milk

2 eggs, separated

55 g | 2 oz caster sugar

3 tablespoons water

15 g | ½ oz powdered gelatine

grated zest of 1 orange

3 drops of almond essence

150 ml | ¼ pint double cream, lightly whipped

TO SERVE

apricot sauce (see page 666)

1 Preheat the oven to 180°C | 350°F | gas mark 4.

2 Put the almonds in a thin layer on a baking sheet and place in the oven for 10 minutes or until lightly browned. Remove from the oven and allow to cool.

3 Put the vanilla pod into a saucepan with the milk and bring to scalding point (just below boiling point), making sure it does not boil. Infuse for 10 minutes.

4 Whisk the egg yolks and sugar together.

5 Remove the vanilla pod from the milk and stir the milk into the egg yolk and sugar mixture. Return to the pan and reheat, stirring continuously with a wooden spoon until the custard is thick enough to coat the back of the spoon. It will curdle if allowed to boil. Strain.

6 Put the water into a small saucepan and sprinkle over the gelatine. Leave for 5 minutes until spongy.

7 Dissolve the gelatine over a low heat without boiling until liquid and clear, then pour into the custard mixture. Stir occasionally until on the point of setting.

8 Stir in the ground almonds, the orange zest and the almond essence.

9 Fold in the cream.

10 Whisk the egg whites until just stiff but not dry and fold into the bavarois mixture. Tip into 8 very lightly oiled ramekins. Cover and leave to set.

11 To serve: Turn an almond bavarois out on to individual plates and decorate with the sauce.

wine: SWEET WHITE

Iles Flottantes

(Floating Islands)

SERVE 4–6

For the meringue islands

3 tablespoons water

1½ teaspoons cornflour

3 egg whites

85 g | 3 oz caster sugar

For poaching

290 ml | ½ pint milk

water

For the custard

290 ml | ½ pint full-fat milk

½ vanilla pod or ½ teaspoon vanilla extract

2 tablespoons caster sugar

3 egg yolks

For the caramel

85 g | 3 oz caster sugar

1 Make the meringue islands: mix the water and cornflour to a paste in a small saucepan. Heat over a medium heat, stirring, until thick and translucent. Allow to cool.

2 Place the milk for poaching in a sauté pan, then half fill with water. Place over a medium heat until the liquid steams.

3 Whisk the egg whites to stiff peaks, then whisk in the sugar a tablespoon at a time.

4 Quickly whisk in the cooled cornflour paste.

5 Using 2 dessertspoons, shape the meringue mixture into egg-sized quenelles, dropping 3–4 into the steaming sauté pan as they are formed.

6 Poach the meringues for 2 minutes on each side. If possible, use a thermometer to check the temperature of the poaching liquid: it should remain at 80°C | 28°F. The liquid will be steaming heavily but the surface will not be moving or bubbling.

7 Remove the meringues from the poaching liquid with a slotted spoon and place them on a plate lined with absorbent kitchen paper to drain. Continue poaching the meringues, 3–4 at a time, until all the mixture has been used up.

8 Make the custard: heat the milk with the vanilla pod or extract until it steams. Remove from the heat and allow to stand for 10 minutes to infuse.

9 Mix the sugar with the egg yolks in a small saucepan. Remove the vanilla pod, if using, from the milk, then slowly pour the infused milk on to the egg yolk mixture.

10 Place the mixture over a medium heat and cook, stirring, until it is thick enough to coat the back of the spoon. Do not allow to boil.

11 Strain through a sieve into a bowl to remove any eggy threads. Scrape the vanilla seeds from the inside of the pod and add to the custard. Press a piece of dampened greaseproof paper on to the surface to prevent a skin from forming. Allow to cool.

12 Pour the cooled custard into a shallow serving bowl. Float the meringue islands on the custard.

13 Make the caramel: heat the sugar in a small saucepan until it melts and then turns to a golden caramel. Drizzle the caramel over the islands with a teaspoon. Be careful not to touch the caramel because it will be very hot.

wine: SWEET WHITE

Coffee Cream Bavarois

SERVES 4

2 tablespoons water
1½ level teaspoons powdered gelatine
225 ml | 8 fl oz milk
1 tablespoon instant coffee powder
20 g | ¾ oz plain chocolate, broken up
3 egg yolks

85 g | 3 oz caster sugar
150 ml | ¼ pint double cream

To decorate
grated chocolate
double cream, whipped

1 Place the water in a small saucepan and sprinkle over the gelatine. Leave for 5 minutes to become spongy.

2 Place the milk, coffee powder and chocolate in a heavy saucepan and heat gently until the chocolate has completely melted.

3 Mix the egg yolks and sugar together. Stir in the warm milk and chocolate mixture. Return to the rinsed out saucepan.

4 Stir continuously with a wooden spoon for 3–5 minutes until the custard will coat the back of the spoon. Be careful not to overheat or the mixture will curdle. Strain into a bowl and leave to cool to room temperature covered with a piece of greaseproof paper.

5 Dissolve the gelatine over a low heat without boiling until liquid and clear, then stir into the cooling custard. Stir occasionally until on the point of setting. Whip the cream lightly and fold it into the coffee mixture.

6 Turn into a large dish or individual pots and leave in the refrigerator to set. Decorate with grated chocolate and whipped cream. If you want to unmould the bavarois, oil the mould before filling.

NOTE: An attractive way to present this bavarois is to serve individual moulds on a plate flooded with crème anglaise (see page 663) and decorated with tiny chocolate shapes (see page 737).

wine: **FORTIFIED SWEET WHITE**

Three Chocolate Bavarois

6 tablespoons water
3 leaves of gelatine
375 ml | 13 fl oz milk
8 egg yolks, beaten
45 g | 1½ oz caster sugar
140 g | 5 oz white chocolate, grated
140 g | 5 oz milk chocolate, grated

140 g | 5 oz plain chocolate, grated
720 ml | 1¼ pints double cream, lightly whipped

To decorate
290 ml | ½ pint crème anglaise, flavoured with grated orange zest and/or 1 tablespoon Grand Marnier (see page 663)

1 Line a 900 g | 2 lb loaf tin with a piece of greaseproof paper cut to fit the bottom of the tin. Lightly oil the tin. Line with clingfilm.

2 Scald the milk in a saucepan. Beat the eggs and sugar together with a wooden spoon and pour over the milk. Return the mixture to the saucepan and heat gently, stirring constantly with a wooden spoon until the custard will coat the back of the spoon. Pass through a sieve.

3 Place each variety of chocolate in a separate bowl and divide the custard equally between them. Stir well to melt the chocolate.

4 Soak one and a half leaves of the gelatine for 5 minutes in cold water, then add the squeezed leaves to the white chocolate custard. Stir gently and when the mixture is on the point of setting, fold in one-third of the cream. Pour into the base of the loaf tin. Refrigerate until set.

5 Once the white chocolate bavarois has set, soak one leaf of gelatine for 5 minutes in cold water, squeeze, then add it to the milk chocolate custard. When it is on the point of setting, fold in another third of the cream. Pour over the set white chocolate bavarois, very carefully. Refrigerate until set.

6 Once the milk chocolate bavarois has set, soak the remaining half leaf of gelatine, squeeze and add it to the plain chocolate custard. When it is on the point of setting, fold in the remaining cream. Pour very carefully over the set milk chocolate bavarois and refrigerate until set.

7 To serve: turn the bavarois out carefully, using a knife to loosen it, or dip the tin very quickly in boiling water. Remove the greaseproof paper from the top. Slice the bavarois with a hot knife and serve with the flavoured crème anglaise.

wine: **FORTIFIED SWEET WHITE**

Striped Chocolate and Grand Marnier Bavarois

This recipe had been adapted from *The Roux Brothers on Pâtisserie*.

SERVES 8

3 egg quantity sponge fingers mixture (see page 781)

3 egg quantity sponge fingers mixture (see page 781) made with 30 g | 1 oz sifted cocoa powder instead of arrowroot

55 ml | 2 fl oz sugar syrup (see page 665)

30 ml | 1 fl oz Grand Marnier

30 g | 1 oz plain chocolate, grated

For the Grand Marnier bavarois

150 ml | ¼ pint milk

2 egg yolks

45 g | 1½ oz caster sugar

2 tablespoons water

1½ teaspoons or 1½ leaves powdered gelatine

30 ml | 1 fl oz Grand Marnier

150 ml | ¼ pint double cream, lightly whipped

For the chocolate bavarois

2 tablespoons water

1 teaspoon powdered gelatine or 1 leaf

55 g | 2 oz plain chocolate

150 ml | ¼ pint milk

55 g | 2 oz caster sugar

2 egg yolks

10 g | ⅓ oz plain flour

150 ml | ¼ pint double cream, lightly whipped

1 Preheat the oven to 200°C | 400°F | gas mark 6. Line 2 baking sheets, one measuring 22.5 cm × 37.5 cm | 9 × 15 in, the other 27.5 square cm | 9 in square, with non-stick baking paper.

2 Using 2 separate piping bags fitted with 5 mm | ¼ in plain nozzles, pipe out the plain and chocolate sponge mixtures alternately in diagonal lines on the baking sheets. The lines should just touch each other

3 Bake for 10–15 minutes.

4 Invert the sponges on to a clean tea-towel. Place them on to a wire rack. Leave to cool. Peel away the lining paper.

5 When the sponge is cold, trim the edges with a serrated knife. Cut 2 bands the depth of a 20 cm | 8 in spring clip tin (i.e. 7.5 cm | 3 in) from the rectangular sponge. From the square sponge, cut out a circle slightly smaller than the diameter of the tin.

6 Line the sides of the tin with the bands of sponge, and place the circle of sponge in the bottom of the tin.

7 Mix the sugar syrup with the Grand Marnier and brush the sponge with the mixture.

The Grand Marnier Bavarois

8 Bring the milk slowly to the boil in a saucepan.

9 Beat in the yolks with the sugar in a bowl. Pour the milk on to the egg yolks, stirring steadily. Return to the pan.

10 Stir over a low heat, stirring continuously with a wooden spoon, until the mixture thickens enough to cover the back of the spoon. Pass through a sieve.

11 Place the water in a small saucepan and sprinkle over the gelatine. Leave for 5 minutes to become spongy. Dissolve the gelatine over a low heat without boiling until liquid and clear, then add to the custard with the Grand Marnier. Allow to stand until starting to thicken.

12 Fold in the cream.

The Chocolate Bavarois

13 Place the water in a small saucepan and sprinkle over the gelatine. Leave for 5 minutes until spongy.

14 Cut the chocolate into small, even-sized pieces. Heat the milk with half the sugar and the chocolate.

15 Cream the egg yolks and remaining sugar and stir in the flour.

16 Pour the milk on to the egg-yolk mixture, stirring well. Return the custard to the pan and cook over low heat, stirring all the time until thick enough to coat the back of a spoon. Pass through a sieve.

17 Dissolve the gelatine over a low heat without boiling until liquid and clear, then add to the chocolate mixture. Allow to stand until starting to thicken.

18 Fold in the cream.

To Assemble

19 Pour the chocolate bavarois into the prepared sponge case. Ladle over the Grand Marnier bavarois to make an irregular marbled effect. (If necessary stir both mixtures together quickly.)

20 Allow to set for 4 hours in the refrigerator.

21 To serve: unclip the tin and remove the sides. Trim off any excess sponge with kitchen scissors. Scatter grated chocolate around the edges of the pudding.

wine: **FORTIFIED SWEET WHITE**

Coeurs à la Crème

These are best started 4 days in advance.

SERVES 4

340 g | 12 oz cottage cheese, drained
55 g | 2 oz icing sugar
290 ml | ½ pint double cream

2 egg whites
290 ml | ½ pint single cream

1 On the first day: push the cheese through a sieve. Stir the icing sugar and double cream into it and mix thoroughly.

2 Whisk the egg whites until stiff. Fold into the cheese mixture.

3 Line a small sieve with a clean piece of muslin and place over a bowl. Turn the cheese mixture into the muslin and leave to drain in a cool place for 3–4 days.

4 To serve: turn the cheese out on to an attractive serving dish. Pour over the single cream and serve with fresh summer fruits.

NOTES: Classically, coeurs à la crème are made in small heart-shaped moulds (hence the name). If you do not have these moulds, individual sweet cheeses can be made by securing muslin with rubber bands over small ramekin dishes filled with the cheese mixture, and then inverting the ramekins on to a wire rack to drain.

For a less rich cream, substitute Greek yoghurt or yoghurt for the single cream.

wine: **SWEET WHITE**

Vanilla Panna Cotta with Rhubarb and Strawberries

SERVES 6

570 ml | 1 pint double cream
45 g | 1½ oz caster sugar
1 vanilla pod
1 strip of lemon zest
oil for greasing
55 ml | 2 fl oz milk
2 teaspoons powdered gelatine
55 ml | 2 fl oz white rum

To serve

170 g | 6 oz rhubarb, cut into 2 cm | ¾ in lengths
55 g | 2 oz caster sugar
55 ml | 2 fl oz water
250 g | 9 oz strawberries, hulled

1 Heat half the cream with the sugar, vanilla pod and lemon zest in a heavy saucepan over a medium heat, until small bubbles appear around the edge of the pan. Remove from the heat and set aside to infuse for 20 minutes.

2 Meanwhile, oil 6 dariole moulds or ramekin dishes.

3 Place the milk in a small saucepan and sprinkle over the gelatine.

4   Remove the lemon zest from the cream and discard. Remove the vanilla pod and scrape out the seeds. Add the seeds to the cream.

5   Heat the gelatine over a low heat until it is liquid (do not boil), then stir into the warm cream.

6   Stir in the rum. Place the saucepan in a bowl of iced water to help it cool. Stir occasionally.

7   When the vanilla cream has reached setting point, whip the remaining cream until it just holds its shape.

8   Fold together the whipped cream and vanilla cream, adding whichever is thinner to the thicker mixture. Pour into the prepared moulds. Tap them on a work surface to release any air bubbles and refrigerate for about 4 hours until set.

9   Make the sauce: preheat the oven to 190°C|375°F|gas mark 5. Place the rhubarb in a ceramic dish and bake for 15 minutes or until tender when pierced with a knife but not collapsing.

10 Heat the sugar and the water over a low heat until the sugar is dissolved. Bring to the boil and boil for 1 minute. Stir in the rhubarb and strawberries and allow to cool.

11 To serve, dip the moulds quickly into very hot water and unmould on to individual dishes. Serve immediately with the rhubarb and strawberries.

wine: FORTIFIED SWEET WINE

Iced Sabayon

SERVES 4

4 egg yolks

4 tablespoons caster sugar

150 ml|¼ pint sweet white wine

2 tablespoons Marsala

150 ml|¼ pint double cream, lightly whipped

1   Put the egg yolks, sugar and wine into a heatproof bowl. Set over, not in, a saucepan of simmering water. Whisk for 15–20 minutes until thick and creamy. Remove from the heat and continue to whisk until cool. Add the Marsala and fold in the cream.

2   Serve well chilled.

NOTE: Sabayon can only be left to stand for about an hour before separating.

wine: FORTIFIED SWEET WHITE

Zabaglione

SERVES 4

4 egg yolks

85 g | 3 oz caster sugar

8 tablespoons Marsala

1 Put the egg yolks and sugar into a heatproof bowl. Whisk well and set the bowl over, not in, a saucepan of simmering water. Continue whisking until frothy and pale.

2 Gradually whisk in the Marsala until the mixture is very thick. Take care that the bowl does not touch the simmering water as if it does, the eggs will scramble.

3 Pour into individual glasses and serve immediately.

wine: **FORTIFIED SWEET WHITE**

Jellies

These are fruit juices or syrups set with gelatine. Some are clarified in a similar manner to aspic and clear soups.

You will need:

1 Jelly bag, usually made of flannel, or a large double muslin cloth.

2 Balloon whisk.

3 Large saucepan.

Points to remember

1 All equipment must be spotlessly clean and grease-free. Scalding in boiling water will ensure this.

2 Weigh all ingredients carefully.

3 Follow the whisking and clearing methods very carefully. Short cuts will only lead to murky jelly.

4 When turning out jellies, it is a good idea to wet the serving plate. If the unmoulded jelly is not in the right place you can then slide it gently to the correct position. If the plate is dry, the jelly will cling to it and be difficult to budge.

5 Recipes often say to wet a jelly mould – if using a china mould, it may be necessary to grease it with a flavourless oil to ensure that it turns out.

Clear Lemon Jelly

See notes on jelly-making, page 600.

SERVES 6

860 ml | 1½ pints water	290 ml | ½ pint lemon juice
200 g | 7 oz granulated sugar	1 2.5 cm | 1 in piece cinnamon stick
thinly pared zest of 4 unwaxed lemons	45 g | 1½ oz powdered gelatine
	whites and crushed shells of 3 eggs

1 Infuse the syrup. Put half of the water into a very clean saucepan with all the ingredients except the gelatine, egg whites and egg shells. Place over a medium heat and stir, without boiling, until the sugar has dissolved. Sprinkle over the gelatine.

2 Leave to infuse for at least 30 minutes. Strain the syrup and add the remaining water to cool the mixture down. Taste, adding more lemon or sugar, as required. Remove the cinnamon stick.

3 Put the egg whites and crushed shells into the jelly mixture. Place over a medium heat and whisk steadily with a balloon whisk until the mixture begins to steam. Stop whisking immediately and bring to the boil. Remove the pan from the heat. Allow the crust to subside. Take care not to break the crust formed by the egg whites.

4 Bring just up to the boil again, and allow to subside (the egg white will trap the sediment in the liquid and clear the jelly). Remove from the heat.

5 Fix a sieve lined with a layer of fine muslin or kitchen paper over a large clean bowl. Put a large spoonful of the egg white crust into the muslin and carefully strain the jelly through it. Do not try to hurry the process by squeezing the cloth, or murky jelly will result. If the jelly begins to set before it is completely strained, warm it up again to melt it just enough to filter through the muslin.

6 Pour into a wet jelly mould. Refrigerate until set (at least 4 hours, but preferably overnight).

7 Turn out the jelly: loosen the top edge all around with your finger. Dip the mould briefly into hot water. Place a damp serving plate over the mould and invert the 2 together. Give a good sharp shake and remove the mould.

Claret Jelly

SERVES 4

570 ml | 1 pint claret or other red wine	2 bay leaves
570 ml | 1 pint water	2 tablespoons redcurrant jelly
thinly pared zest of 2 lemons	45 g | 1½ oz powdered gelatine
170 g | 6 oz granulated sugar	whites and crushed shells of 2 eggs
2 small cinnamon sticks	

1 Put all the ingredients except the gelatine, egg whites and shells into a very clean saucepan, sprinkle over the gelatine and place over a medium heat. Stir until the gelatine and sugar have dissolved. Taste, adding more sugar if necessary, and cool. Remove the bay leaves, cinnamon sticks and lemon zest.

2 Put the egg whites and crushed shells into the jelly mixture. Place over a medium heat and whisk steadily with a balloon whisk until the mixture begins to boil. Stop whisking immediately and bring to the boil. Remove the pan from the heat. Allow the mixture to subside. Take care not to break the crust formed by the egg whites.

3 Bring just to the boil again, and again allow to subside (the egg whites will trap the sediment in the liquid and clear the jelly). Allow to cool for 2 minutes.

4 Fix a double layer of fine muslin over a clean bowl and carefully strain the jelly through it. Do not try to hurry the process by squeezing the cloth, or murky jelly will result.

5 Pour into a wet jelly mould and refrigerate for 3–4 hours, or until set.

6 Invert a damp serving plate over the mould and turn the 2 over together. Give a sharp shake and remove the mould.

Orange Jelly

SERVES 4

For the orange jelly
3 tablespoons water
4 level teaspoons powdered gelatine

570 ml | 1 pint freshly squeezed orange juice

1 Put the water into a small saucepan. Sprinkle over the gelatine and leave for 5 minutes to become spongy. Dissolve over a very low heat without boiling or stirring until liquid and clear.

2 Warm 150 ml | $\frac{1}{4}$ pint of the orange juice and mix it into the gelatine. Add the remaining orange juice and pour into a wet plain jelly mould or pudding basin.

3 Chill in the refrigerator for 2–4 hours, or until set.

4 Loosen the jelly round the edges with a finger. Invert a damp serving plate over the jelly mould, turn the mould and plate over together, give a sharp shake and remove the mould. If the jelly won't budge, dip the outside of the mould briefly into hot water to loosen it.

Black Jelly with Port

SERVES 4

450 g | 1 lb blackcurrants
225 g | 8 oz granulated sugar
190 ml | $\frac{1}{3}$ pint ruby port

3 tablespoons water
20 g | $\frac{3}{4}$ oz powdered gelatine
whipped cream or crème anglaise (see page 663)

1 Put the blackcurrants and sugar into a saucepan and cook over a low heat until the fruit is soft. Push through a nylon sieve.

2 Add the port to the blackcurrant purée and enough water to bring the liquid up to 570 ml | 1 pint.

3 Put the water into a small saucepan and sprinkle over the gelatine. Leave for 5 minutes to become spongy. Dissolve over a low heat without boiling until liquid and clear. Pour into the blackcurrant mixture and mix well. Pour into a wet jelly mould or dish. Refrigerate for 3–4 hours until set.

4 To turn out, briefly dip the mould into hot water – just enough to loosen it without melting the jelly. Put a damp serving plate over the mould and invert it so that the jelly falls on to the plate. Serve with whipped cream or crème anglaise.

Ballymaloe's Jelly of Fresh Raspberries with a Mint Cream

SERVES 6

560 g | 1¼ lb fresh raspberries
225 g | 8 oz caster sugar
290 ml | ½ pint water
4 sprigs of fresh mint
2 teaspoons Framboise liqueur
1 tablespoon lemon juice
3 tablespoons water
1 tablespoon powdered gelatine

For the mint cream

15 fresh mint leaves
1 tablespoon lemon juice
200 ml | 7 fl oz double cream

To decorate

fresh mint leaves

1 Pick over the raspberries and reserve about 110 g | 4 oz of the best ones for decoration.

2 Put the sugar, water and mint sprigs into a small, heavy saucepan. Bring slowly to the boil. Simmer for a few minutes, then remove from the heat and allow to cool. Add the Framboise and lemon juice.

3 Put the 3 tablespoons water into a small saucepan and sprinkle over the gelatine. Leave for 5 minutes to become spongy.

4 Oil 6 ramekins very lightly.

5 Strain the flavoured syrup into a bowl. Dissolve the gelatine over a low heat without boiling until liquid and clear, then add it to the strained syrup. Add the raspberries.

6 Pour three-quarters of the jelly into the ramekins, making sure that all the raspberries are used up. Refrigerate until beginning to set, then spoon over the remaining jelly. (This is to ensure that the jellies have flat bottoms when turned out.)

7 Meanwhile, make the mint cream: crush the mint leaves in a pestle and mortar with the lemon juice. Add the cream and stir. The lemon juice will thicken the cream. If the cream becomes too thick, add a little water.

8 Turn out a raspberry jelly on the plates. Decorate with the reserved raspberries, extra mint leaves and the mint cream.

wine: **LIGHT SWEET WHITE**

Apple Charlotte

SERVES 4

1 kg | 2¼ lb cooking apples

85 g | 3 oz sugar

2 tablespoons apricot jam

15 g | ½ oz butter

8 slices of stale, medium-sliced bread, crusts
  removed

110 g | 4 oz butter, melted

For the apricot glaze

3 tablespoons apricot jam

4 tablespoons water

TO SERVE

cream or custard

1 Core and slice the apples and put them into a heavy saucepan. Add the sugar and cook, without water, until very soft. Boil away any extra liquid, whisk in the apricot jam and push through a sieve.

2 Butter a charlotte mould or deep cake tin.

3 Using a pastry cutter, stamp one piece of bread into a circle to fit the bottom of the mould or tin and cut it into 6 equal triangles. Cut the remaining bread into strips.

4 Preheat the oven to 200°C | 400°F | gas mark 6.

5 Dip the pieces of bread into the melted butter. Arrange the triangles over the bottom of the mould then arrange overlapping strips around the sides. The strips of bread should extend over the rim of the tin.

6 Spoon in the apple purée and fold over the buttery bread.

7 Bake in the oven for 40 minutes. Remove from the oven and allow to cool for 10 minutes.

8 Meanwhile, make the apricot glaze: put the jam and water into a small, heavy saucepan, and heat, stirring occasionally, until warm and completely melted.

9 Turn out the pudding: invert a plate over the mould and turn the mould and plate over together. Give a sharp shake and remove the mould.

10 Brush the charlotte with the apricot glaze and serve with cream or custard.

wine: **SWEET WHITE**

Individual Apple Charlottes

SERVES 4

55 g | 2 oz granulated sugar

5 dessert apples, such as Cox's, peeled, cored and
  sliced

2 tablespoons Calvados

juice of 1 orange

a pinch of ground cinnamon

70 g | 2½ oz butter

8 slices of white bread, crusts removed

For the sauce

55 g | 2 oz granulated sugar

grated zest of 1 orange

1 tablespoon Calvados

1 Put the sugar into a heavy saucepan with 2 tablespoons water and place over a low heat. Allow the sugar to dissolve slowly and become lightly caramelized.
2 Add the apples to the caramel, stir and then add the Calvados, orange juice, cinnamon and 15 g | ½ oz of the butter. Simmer together for 2 minutes.
3 Preheat the oven to 225°C | 425°F | gas mark 7.
4 Melt the remaining butter. Flatten the bread slightly with a rolling pin. Cut out 8 rounds and dip them in the melted butter on both sides. Reserve 4 of the rounds and use the remaining 4 to line the base of 4 dariole moulds. Use the remaining bread to line the sides.
5 Drain the apple filling (but reserve the strained liquor) and pile the apple slices into the lined moulds. Cover with the remaining rounds of bread.
6 Put the moulds on to a baking sheet and bake for 15–20 minutes.
7 Meanwhile, prepare the sauce: put the sugar with 2 tablespoons of water into a heavy saucepan and place over a low heat. Allow the sugar to dissolve and then caramelize. When lightly browned add the apple liquor, the orange zest and Calvados. Simmer until syrupy.
8 To serve: turn the apple charlottes out on to individual plates and serve with the caramel sauce.

wine: **SWEET WHITE**

Chocolate Roulade

SERVES 6

225 g | 8 oz plain chocolate, roughly chopped
85 ml | 3 fl oz water
1 teaspoon strong instant coffee powder
5 eggs

140 g | 5 oz caster sugar
200 ml | ⅓ pint double cream
icing sugar

1 Take a large roasting pan and cut a double layer of non-stick baking parchment slightly bigger than it. Lay the parchment in the pan; don't worry if the edges stick up untidily round the sides. Preheat the oven to 200°C | 400°F | gas mark 6.
2 Put the chocolate, water and coffee into a heavy saucepan and melt over a low heat.
3 Separate the eggs and beat the yolks and all but 1 tablespoon of the caster sugar until pale and mousse-like. Fold in the melted chocolate.
4 Whisk the whites until just stiff but not dry. Whisk in the reserved tablespoon of sugar. With a large metal spoon, stir a small amount thoroughly into the chocolate mixture, to loosen it. Fold the remaining whites in gently. Spread the mixture evenly on the baking parchment.
5 Bake in the oven for about 15 minutes until the top is well-risen and just set.
6 Slide the cake and parchment out of the roasting pan on to a wire rack. Cover immediately with a damp tea-towel (to prevent the cake from cracking) and leave to cool.

7 Place a piece of greaseproof paper just larger than the cake on the work surface. Sieve over an even layer of icing sugar. Quickly turn the cake on to the paper then peel away the baking parchment. Trim the edges.

8 Whip the cream and spread it evenly over the cake. Roll up like a Swiss roll, removing the parchment as you go. Put the roll on to a serving dish and, just before serving, sift a little icing sugar over the top, if necessary.

wine: **FORTIFIED SWEET WHITE**

Hazelnut Roulade

SERVES 4–6

oil for greasing	¼ teaspoons baking powder
3 eggs	55 g│2 oz ground hazelnuts, toasted
55 g│2 oz caster sugar	icing sugar
1 tablespoon plain flour	150 ml│¼ pint double cream, whipped

1 Preheat the oven to 180°C│350°F│gas mark 4.

2 Prepare a paper case as for a Swiss roll (see page 713). It should be the size of a piece of A4 paper. Brush lightly with oil.

3 Separate the eggs and beat the yolks and caster sugar together until pale and mousse-like.

4 Sift the flour with the baking powder and fold it into the egg-yolk mixture along with the nuts.

5 Whisk the egg whites until stiff but not dry and fold into the mixture.

6 Spread the mixture into the prepared paper case.

7 Bake for about 20 minutes until the top is slightly browned and firm to touch.

8 Remove the roulade from the oven and allow to cool, covered with a sheet of absorbent kitchen paper.

9 Sprinkle icing sugar on to a piece of greaseproof paper and turn the roulade on to it. Remove the lining paper.

10 Spread the whipped cream evenly over the roulade and roll it up like a Swiss roll.

NOTE: Serve the hazelnut roulade with a raspberry coulis, or add fresh fruit to the cream before rolling up the roulade.

wine: **RICH SWEET WHITE**

Spiced Ginger Cake

SERVES 4

For the cake

caster sugar

110 g | 4 oz plain flour

1 teaspoon ground mixed spice

1 teaspoon ground ginger

70 g | 2½ oz butter

2 tablespoons black treacle

2 tablespoons golden syrup

1 egg

150 ml | ¼ pint water

1 teaspoon bicarbonate of soda

For the filling

450 g | 1 lb cooking apples

30 g | 1 oz butter

1 teaspoon ground cinnamon

55 g | 2 oz caster sugar

To serve

double cream, whipped

icing sugar

1 First make the filling: peel and core the apples. Slice them roughly.
2 Melt the butter in a saucepan and add the cinnamon, sugar and apples. Cover and cook over a very low heat, stirring occasionally, until the apples become pulpy. Beat until smooth, adding more sugar if the apples are still tart.
3 Preheat the oven to 180°C | 350°F | gas mark 4. Prepare a Swiss roll tin by greasing the inside, then covering the base with greaseproof paper, and greasing again. Dust with caster sugar.
4 Sift together the flour, mixed spice and ginger. Melt the butter in a saucepan with the treacle and syrup. Whisk the egg with the water and soda. Allow to cool. Remove the syrup mixture from the heat and pour in the egg and water. Mix well.
5 Now pour this into the flour and whisk together for 30 seconds. Pour into the prepared tin and bake for 12–15 minutes, or until firm to the touch.
6 Turn out on to a sheet of greaseproof paper dusted with caster sugar. Allow to cool. Remove the lining paper. Spread the cake with the apple purée and roll up like a Swiss roll. Serve with whipped cream. Dust with sifted icing sugar.

wine: RICH SWEET WHITE

Baked Cheesecake

SERVES 6

For the crust

12 digestive biscuits (200 g | 7 oz), crushed
85 g | 3 oz butter, melted

For the filling

225 g | 8 oz best-quality cream cheese
5 tablespoons double cream
1 egg

1 egg yolk
1 teaspoon vanilla essence
about 1 tablespoon sugar

For the topping

70 ml | 2½ fl oz soured cream
ground cinnamon

1 Preheat the oven to 150°C | 300°F | gas mark 2.
2 Mix together the crust ingredients and line the base of a shallow 20 cm | 8 in pie dish or flan ring with the mixture.
3 Bake for 10 minutes, or until lightly browned. Remove from the oven and allow to cool.
4 Beat the cream cheese to soften and then add the remaining filling ingredients. Beat well until smooth and pour into the crust.
5 Return to the middle of the oven and bake until the filling has set (about 30–40 minutes).
6 Remove from the oven and allow to cool.
7 Spread with the soured cream and dust with the cinnamon.

wine: **LIGHT SWEET WHITE**

Treacle Sponge

SERVES 4–6

a knob of butter for greasing
4 tablespoons golden syrup
2 teaspoons fine fresh white breadcrumbs
110 g | 4 oz butter, softened
110 g | 4 oz caster sugar
grated zest of 1 lemon

2 eggs, beaten
110 g | 4 oz self-raising flour
a pinch of salt
1 teaspoon ground ginger

To serve

custard or cream

1 Grease a pudding basin with the knob of butter.
2 Place the syrup in the basin and sprinkle over the breadcrumbs.
3 In a mixing bowl, cream the butter until very soft, then add the sugar. Beat until light and fluffy. Add the lemon zest.
4 Gradually add the eggs, beating very well after each addition.
5 Sift the flour with the salt and ginger and fold in.
6 Turn into the pudding basin, cover (see page 609) and steam for 1½ hours.
7 Turn out and serve with custard or cream.

wine: **RICH SWEET WHITE**

Preparing a Pudding Basin for Steaming

Cover with pleated double greaseproof paper

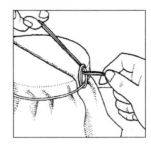

Tie down and make a string handle for easy removal

Simpson's Treacle Roll

SERVES 4

225 g | 8 oz self-raising flour
a pinch of salt
110 g | 4 oz shredded suet
225 g | 8 oz golden syrup

To serve

whipped cream or custard

1 Sift the flour with the salt into a bowl. Stir in the suet and add enough water to mix first with a knife, and then with one hand, to a soft dough.
2 Roll it on a floured surface to a large rectangle.
3 Spread the surface with the golden syrup.
4 Roll up and fold the sides underneath.
5 Wrap first in greaseproof paper, then in a cloth.
6 Place in the top half of a steamer and steam for $1\frac{1}{2}$ hours. Serve with whipped cream or custard.

wine: RICH SWEET WHITE

Sussex Pond Pudding

This recipe has been taken from Jane Grigson's *English Food*.

SERVES 6

225 g | 8 oz self-raising flour

110 g | 4 oz shredded suet

150 ml | ¼ pint milk and water, half and half

110 g | 4 oz slightly salted butter

110 g | 4 oz demerara sugar

2 large lemon or 2 limes, very well washed

1 Mix the flour and suet together in a bowl. Make into a dough with milk and water. The dough should be soft, but not too soft to roll out into a large circle. Cut a quarter out of this circle, to be used later as the lid of the pudding.

2 Butter a 1.4 litre | 2½ pint pudding basin liberally. Drop the three-quarter circle of pastry into it and press the cut sides together to make a perfect join. Put half the remaining butter, cut up, into the pastry, with half the sugar.

3 Prick the lemon or limes all over with a larding needle, so that the juices will be able to escape, then put the fruit on to the butter and sugar. Add the remaining butter, again cut into pieces, and sugar.

4 Roll out the pastry set aside to make the lid. Lay it on top of the filling, and press the edges together so that the pudding is sealed completely. Cover the basin with pleated kitchen foil. Tie it in place with string, and make a string handle over the top so that the pudding can be lifted easily (see page 609).

5 Put a large saucepan of water on to boil, and lower the pudding into it; the water must be boiling, and it should come halfway or a little further up the basin. Cover and leave to steam for 3–4 hours. If the water gets too low, replenish with boiling water.

6 To serve: put a deep dish over the basin after removing the foil lid, and quickly turn the whole thing upside down: it is a good idea to ease the pudding from the sides of the basin with a knife first. Serve immediately. The buttery juices will flow out of the pudding to form a 'pond'.

wine: **RICH SWEET WHITE**

Christmas Pudding

MAKES 2 × 900 G | 2 LB PUDDINGS

170 g | 6 oz raisins

110 g | 4 oz currants

200 g | 7 oz sultanas

85 g | 3 oz chopped mixed peel

225 g | 8 oz mixed dried apricots and figs, chopped

290 ml | ½ pint brown ale

2 tablespoons rum

grated zest and juice of 1 orange

grated zest and juice of 1 lemon

110 g | 4 oz prunes, stoned and soaked overnight in cold tea, then drained and chopped

1 dessert apple

225 g | 8 oz butter, softened

340 | 12 oz soft dark brown sugar

2 tablespoons treacle

3 eggs

110 g | 4 oz self-raising flour, sifted

1 teaspoon ground mixed spice

½ teaspoon ground cinnamon

a pinch of freshly grated nutmeg

a pinch of ground ginger

a pinch of salt

225 g | 8 oz fresh white breadcrumbs

55 g | 2 oz chopped hazelnuts, toasted

1 Soak all the dried fruit except the prunes overnight in the beer, rum, orange juice and lemon juice. Mix with the prunes.

2 Grate the unpeeled apple.

3 Beat the butter with the sugar until light. Add the orange and lemon zest and treacle.

4 Whisk the eggs together and gradually add them to the mixture, beating well after each addition.

5 Fold in the flour, spices, salt and breadcrumbs and stir in the nuts, dried fruit and soaking liquor.

6 Divide the mixture between 2 greased pudding basins and cover with 2 layers of pleated greaseproof paper and one piece of pleated kitchen foil (see page 609). Tie with string and steam for 10–12 hours.

wine: LIQUEUR MUSCAT

Light Christmas Pudding

This pudding is made with no added fat or sugar and therefore is less rich and more moist and tangy than traditional Christmas pudding (see previous recipe). The fruit should be soaked for 1–7 days in advance.

MAKES 2 PUDDINGS

110 g | 4 oz dried apple, chopped
110 g | 4 oz dried apricots, chopped
110 g | 4 oz dried figs, chopped
110 g | 4 oz dried pitted prunes, chopped
225 g | 8 oz raisins
225 g | 8 oz sultanas
110 g | 4 oz currants
55 g | 2 oz candied orange peel
290 ml | ½ pint cold tea
4 tablespoons brandy or rum
4 tablespoons medium sherry
1 large banana, mashed

225 g | 8 oz carrots, grated
30 g | 1 oz hazelnuts, chopped
30 g | 1 oz ground almonds
3 eggs
1 tablespoon clear honey
1 teaspoon ground cinnamon
1 teaspoon ground mixed spice
1 teaspoon ground ginger
a pinch of freshly grated nutmeg
85 g | 3 oz plain flour
170 g | 6 oz fresh wholemeal breadcrumbs

1 Put all the dried fruit and candied peel into a bowl, and pour in the tea, brandy and sherry. Mix well and leave to soak in a cool place for at least 1 day or up to 7 days.

2 When the fruit has soaked, add the banana, carrot, hazelnuts and ground almonds to the mixture.

3 Beat the eggs with the honey and stir into the fruit mixture.

4 Sift the spices with the flour and add with the breadcrumbs to the pudding mixture. Stir well.

5 Place in 2 × 1.1 litre | 2 pint greased pudding basins and cover with 2 layers of pleated greaseproof paper and 1 of pleated kitchen foil (see page 609). Tie with string and steam for 6 hours in the usual way.

NOTE: Christmas puddings can be kept for up to 1 year – after this period they begin to dry out. They can be frozen very successfully. Ideally a pudding should be made about 3–4 months before Christmas. To store a pudding re-cover it and keep in a cool dark place. To reheat steam for about 2 hours.

wine: **FORTIFIED DESSERT WINE**

Eve's Pudding

SERVES 4

butter for greasing
675 g | 1½ lb cooking apples
150 ml | ¼ pint water
160 g | 5½ oz caster sugar
grated zest of 1 lemon

30 g | 1 oz butter
1 small egg, beaten
55 g | 2 oz self-raising flour
a pinch of salt
1 tablespoon milk

1 Preheat the oven to 200°C | 400°F | gas mark 6. Butter a pie dish.
2 Peel, core and slice the apples and place them in a heavy saucepan with the water, 110 g | 4 oz of the sugar and half the lemon zest. Stew gently until just soft, then tip into the pie dish.
3 Cream the butter until soft and beat in the remaining sugar. When light and fluffy, gradually add the beaten egg and mix until completely incorporated.
4 Sift the flour with the salt and fold it into the butter and egg mixture.
5 Add the remaining lemon zest and enough milk to bring the mixture to a soft dropping consistency. Spread over the apple.
6 Bake for about 25 minutes, or until the sponge mixture is firm to the touch and has slightly shrunk at the edges.

wine: SWEET WHITE

Black Cherry Clafoutis

SERVES 4

4 tablespoons Kirsch
450 g | 1 lb canned black cherries, drained
100 ml | 3½ fl oz milk
150 ml | ¼ pint whipping cream
½ vanilla pod

4 eggs
140 g | 5 oz caster sugar
20 g | ¾ oz plain flour
a pinch of salt
butter and caster sugar for greasing and sprinkling

1 Preheat the oven to 180°C | 350°F | gas mark 4.
2 Sprinkle the Kirsch over the cherries. Leave to macrerate.
3 Put the milk, cream and vanilla pod into a small saucepan. Bring to the boil, then turn off the heat and leave to infuse.
4 Place the eggs and sugar in a mixing bowl. Whisk until creamy. Add the flour and salt and whisk until smooth.
5 Remove the vanilla pod from the milk. Scrape out the seeds and add to the milk. Strain the infused milk and cream into the egg mixture, and beat until well mixed.
6 Generously butter an ovenproof dish about 25 × 23 × 5 cm | 10 × 9 × 2 in and sprinkle with caster sugar.

7 Place the cherries in the dish and pour over the batter.

8 Bake for 25 minutes. Remove and allow to cool slightly before serving sprinkled with a little extra caster sugar.

wine: **FORTIFIED SWEET WINE**

Steamed Valencia Pudding

SERVES 4

15 g | ½ oz butter for greasing
a handful of large seedless raisins
110 g | 4 oz butter, softened
grated zest of 1 lemon
110 g | 4 oz caster sugar
2 eggs

110 g | 4 oz self-raising flour
a pinch of salt

To serve
Crème Anglaise (see page 663)

1 Grease a pudding basin. Line the sides of the basin with split raisins (split side against the basin), arranging them in a pattern if you like.

2 Cream the butter and when very soft add the lemon zest and the sugar. Beat until light, pale and fluffy.

3 Gradually add the eggs, beating well after each addition.

4 Fold in the flour, sifted with the salt, and turn into the pudding basin.

5 Cover with a pleated piece of double greaseproof paper or kitchen foil and tie down.

6 Steam for 2 hours. Turn out and serve with the custard handed separately.

wine: **FORTIFIED SWEET WINE**

Warm Chocolate Puddle Cakes

These little cakes are served warm and slightly undercooked so that the runny centre becomes a chocolate sauce for the cake. Serve with vanilla ice cream.

SERVES 4

softened butter for greasing
2 tablespoons cocoa powder for dusting
85 g | 3 oz plain dark chocolate, chopped
85 g | 3 oz unsalted butter
1 medium egg

1 egg yolk
30 g | 1 oz caster sugar
½ teaspoon vanilla extract
1 tablespoon plain flour, sifted
vanilla ice cream (see page 684), to serve

1 Preheat the oven to 190°C | 400°F | gas mark 6.

2 Butter 4 × 150 ml | ¼ pint timbale moulds and dust with cocoa powder

3 Put the chocolate into a bowl set over, not in, a saucepan of simmering water. When melted, stir in the butter. Remove from the heat when the butter has just melted.

4 Put the egg, egg yolk, sugar and vanilla into a large bowl and whisk until thick and mousse-like.

5 Fold in the chocolate mixture and then the flour.

6 Divide between the timbale moulds (the mixture will only fill them about half full), then place on a baking sheet and bake in the centre of the oven for 8–10 minutes. The surface should look cooked but should have a slight wobble.

7 Turn on to individual plates and serve immediately with vanilla ice cream.

wine: **RICH SWEET WINE**

Sticky Toffee Pudding

SERVES 4–6

225 g | 8 oz dates, chopped
290 ml | ½ pint tea
110 g | 4 oz butter
170 g | 6 oz caster sugar
3 eggs
225 g | 8 oz self-raising flour, sifted

1 teaspoon bicarbonate of soda
1 teaspoon vanilla essence
1 teaspoon strong coffee

To serve
toffee sauce (see page 666)

1 Preheat the oven to 180°C | 350°F | gas mark 4.

2 Soak the dates in the hot tea for 15 minutes.

3 Oil a 22 cm | 8½ in deep cake tin and line the base with a circle of oiled greaseproof paper.

4 Cream together the butter and sugar until pale.

5 Beat in the eggs gradually, and then fold in the sifted flour.

6 Add the soda, vanilla essence and coffee to the date | tea water and then fold into the cake mixture.

7 Turn into the prepared tin and bake in the middle of the oven for 1–1½ hours, or until a skewer inserted into the centre of the cake comes out clean.

8 Pour the warm toffee sauce over the hot pudding and serve immediately.

wine: **RICH SWEET WHITE**

Apple and Orange Crumble

SERVES 4

3 oranges
900 g | 2 lb cooking apples
3 tablespoons demerara sugar
a pinch of ground cinnamon

For the crumble
170 g | 6 oz plain flour
a pinch of salt
110 g | 4 oz butter
55 g | 2 oz granulated sugar

1 Peel the oranges as you would an apple, with a sharp knife, removing all the pith. Cut out the orange segments over a bowl, leaving behind the membranes but reserving the juice.
2 Peel and core the apples. Cut into chunks. Mix with the orange segments and their juice. Add the sugar and cinnamon. Tip into an ovenproof dish.
3 Preheat the oven to 200°C|400°F|gas mark 6.
4 Sift the flour with the salt into a bowl. Rub in the butter and when the mixture resembles coarse breadcrumbs mix in the sugar. Sprinkle the mixture over the fruit.
5 Place on a baking sheet and bake for 35–45 minutes or until hot and slightly browned on top.

NOTE: If using wholemeal flour for the crumble topping, use 140 g|5 oz melted butter. Instead of rubbing it into the flour, mix briskly with a knife.

wine: **SWEET WHITE**

Plum Pie

This recipe leaves the stones in the plums – if preferred, the plums can be cut in half and stoned. If the plums are large or not very ripe they should be cooked in a little sugar syrup before they are baked.

SERVES 6

225 g|8 oz plain or wholemeal flour
a pinch of salt
55 g|2 oz lard
85 g|3 oz butter
2–3 tablespoons cold water
caster sugar for dredging

For the filling
675 g|1½ lb small plums
½ teaspoon ground cinnamon
3 tablespoons demerara sugar

1 Preheat the oven to 200°C|400°F|gas mark 6.
2 Sift the flour with the salt into a bowl. Rub in the fats until the mixture resembles coarse breadcrumbs.
3 Stir in enough water to bind together. Pat into a flat disc, wrap and chill in the refrigerator while you prepare the filling.
4 Wash the plums and place them in a pie dish with the cinnamon and sugar.
5 Roll out the pastry on a floured work surface. Cut a band of pastry wider than the rim of the pie dish. Wet the rim and press the band on all the way round. Brush with water and lay over the rolled-out pastry. Trim the edges, press them down firmly and mark with a fork or press into a frilly edge with fingers and thumb.
6 Roll out the pastry trimmings and shape into leaves. Brush the top of the pie with water and decorate with the leaves. Chill until the pastry is firm.
7 Brush with water and dredge the whole pie with sugar. Cut 1 or 2 small slits in the pastry top to allow the steam to escape. Bake on the top shelf of the oven for 25–35 minutes.

wine: **RICH SWEET WHITE**

Treacle Tart

SERVES 4

110 g | 4 oz plain flour
a pinch of salt
55 g | 2 oz butter
2 teaspoons caster sugar
1 egg yolk
very cold water

For the filling

10 tablespoons golden syrup
grated zest of ½ lemon and 2 teaspoons lemon juice
a pinch of ground ginger (optional)
5–7 tablespoons fresh white breadcrumbs

1 Preheat the oven to 190°C | 375°F | gas mark 5. Place a baking sheet in the oven.
2 Sift the flour with the salt into a bowl. Rub in the butter until the mixture resembles breadcrumbs. Add the sugar.
3 Mix the egg yolk with 1 tablespoon water, and add enough to the mixture to make a dough.
4 Roll out the pastry and use to line a 20 cm | 8 in pie plate.
6 Heat the golden syrup with the lemon zest and juice to make it a little runny. Add the ginger, if using.
7 Pour half the syrup into the pastry case.
8 Sprinkle with breadcrumbs until they are soaked. Pour in the remaining syrup and sprinkle in the remaining breadcrumbs.
9 Bake on the hot baking sheet for about 30 minutes, or until the filling is almost set and the edge of the pastry is brown. The filling should be a little on the soft side if the tart is to be eaten cold because it hardens as it cools. Ideally, serve warm.

wine: **SWEET SPARKLING**

Lemon Meringue Pie

SERVES 8

170 g | 6 oz flour quantity sweet rich shortcrust
  pastry (see page 559)

For the filling

4 tablespoons cornflour
225 g | 8 oz caster sugar
290 ml | ½ pint water
4 egg yolks
grated zest and juice of 2½ large unwaxed lemons

For the meringue topping

3 tablespoons water
2 teaspoons cornflour
4 egg whites
110 g | 4 oz caster sugar
a little extra caster sugar

1 Preheat the oven to 200°C | 400°F | gas mark 6. Roll out the pastry and use to line a 20 cm | 8 in flan ring. Chill until firm, then bake blind (see page 557). Turn the oven temperature down to 180°C | 350°F | gas mark 4.
2 Make the filling: place the cornflour and sugar in a saucepan. Stir in the water.

3 Cook over a medium heat, stirring, until the mixture boils. It will become thick and translucent.

4 Whisk the egg yolks into the hot mixture, then pass through a sieve to remove any eggy threads.

5 Whisk in the lemon zest and juice.

6 Pour the hot filling into the warm pastry case and place in the centre of the preheated oven for 5 minutes.

7 Make the meringue topping: place the water and cornflour in a small saucepan and whisk over a medium heat until the mixture is thick and translucent. Remove from the heat.

8 Whisk the egg whites to stiff peaks, then gradually whisk in the caster sugar. Whisk in the warm cornflour mixture.

9 Pile the meringue on top of the filling, starting at the edge next to the pastry case then moving towards the centre. Mound the filling slightly in the centre.

10 Use a fork to makes peaks on the meringue, then sprinkle with a little extra sugar.

11 Bake in the oven for 15 minutes until the topping is light brown.

12 Allow to cool before serving or refrigerate if keeping overnight.

NOTES: Lemon curd (see page 799) makes a good alternative to the lemon custard filling.

When making a meringue mixture with a powerful electric mixer, add half the sugar when the whites are stiff. Whisk again until very shiny, then add the remaining sugar and whisk until just incorporated. If using a hand-held electric blender, add half the sugar gradually then fold in the remaining sugar once the whites are stiff.

If making a 15cm|6 in tart a topping of 2 egg white quantity Swiss meringue can be used (page 670)

Custard Tart

SERVES 6

140 g|6 oz flour quantity rich shortcrust pastry
  (see page 559)

For the filling
4 eggs

55 g|2 oz caster sugar
290 ml|½ pint milk
290 ml|½ pint single cream
a few drops of vanilla essence
freshly grated nutmeg

1 Preheat the oven to 200°C|400°F|gas mark 6. Roll out the pastry and use to line a 20 cm|8 in flan ring or dish. Bake blind (see page 557).

2 Turn the oven temperature down to 170°C|325°F|gas mark 3.

3 Lightly beat the eggs with the sugar. Pour on the milk and cream and add the vanilla essence. Strain into the prepared flan case and sprinkle a little grated nutmeg over the top. Place on a baking tray.

4 Bake for 1 hour, or until the custard has set.

wine: FORTIFIED SWEET WHITE

Mincemeat Flan

SERVES 8

225 g | 8 oz flour quantity rich shortcrust pastry (see page 559) or pâte sucrée (see page 564)

caster sugar for sprinkling

For the filling

1 small cooking apple
55 g | 2 oz butter
85 g | 3 oz sultanas

85 g | 3 oz raisins
85 g | 3 oz currants
45 g | 1½ oz chopped mixed peel
45 g | 1½ oz almonds, chopped
grated zest of 1 large lemon
½ teaspoon ground mixed spice
1 tablespoon brandy
85 g | 3 oz soft light brown sugar
1 banana, coarsely mashed

1 Preheat the oven to 200°C | 400°F | gas mark 6.

2 Roll out the pastry and use to line a 25 cm | 10 in flan ring, keeping the pastry trimmings for the lattice decoration. Bake blind (see page 557). Remove the lining paper and beans.

3 Prepare the mincemeat: grate the unpeeled apple. Melt the butter and add it, with all the remaining filling ingredients, to the apple. Mix well.

4 Fill the flan with the mincemeat. Cut the pastry trimmings into thin strips and lattice the top of the flan with them, sticking the ends down with a little water. Brush the lattice with water and sprinkle with caster sugar. Return to the oven for 10–12 minutes, removing the flan ring after 5 minutes to allow the sides of the pastry to bake to a pale brown.

wine: **FORTIFIED SWEET WHITE**

Pecan Pie

SERVES 8–10

For the pastry

225 g | 8 oz plain flour
a pinch of salt
55 g | 2 oz lard
85 g | 3 oz butter
2 teaspoons caster sugar
2–3 tablespoons cold water

For the filling

450 g | 1 lb pecan nuts
4 eggs
225 g | 8 oz soft light brown sugar
170 g | 6 oz golden syrup
½ teaspoon salt
55 g | 2 oz unsalted butter, melted
teaspoon vanilla essence
2 tablespoons plain flour, sifted

1 Preheat the oven to 200°C | 400°F | gas mark 6. Preheat a baking sheet.

2 Sift the flour with the salt into a bowl. Rub in the fats until the mixture resembles breadcrumbs.

3 Add the sugar and stir in enough water to bind the pastry together.

4 Roll out the pastry and use to line a 28 cm | 11 in flan case. Leave it in the refrigerator for about 30 minutes to relax. (This prevents shrinkage during baking.)

5 Bake the pastry case blind (see page 557).

6 Meanwhile, make the filling: chop half the pecan nuts. The remaining nuts will be used for the topping, so chop any that are broken, keeping back the best-looking ones. Whisk the eggs in a large bowl. Stir in the sugar, golden syrup, salt, melted butter and vanilla essence. Stir in the flour, making sure there are no lumps of flour in the mixture.

7 Stir in the chopped pecan nuts and pour into the pastry case. Arrange the remaining halved pecan nuts on top.

8 Bake on the hot baking sheet in the oven for 10 minutes, then turn the oven temperature down to 170°C | 325°F | gas mark 3 and bake for a further 30–40 minutes, or until the centre is just set. Serve warm or cold.

wine: **FORTIFIED SWEET WHITE**

Individual Apple Tarts

MAKES 6

170 g	6 oz flour quantity rich sweet shortcrust pastry (see page 559)	2 tablespoons caster sugar
3 dessert apples	6 teaspoons Calvados
	warm apricot glaze (see page 727)

1 Preheat the oven to 200°C | 400°F | gas mark 6.

2 Roll out the pastry and divide into 6 equal pieces.

3 On a floured work surface, roll out each piece of pastry as thinly as possible. Cut each into a 12.5 cm | 5 in circle, place on a baking sheet and refrigerate for 20 minutes.

4 Peel the apples, if liked. Cut in quarters and carefully remove the cores.

5 Slice the apples very thinly and arrange the slices of half an apple on each circle of chilled pastry. Take care to pack the apples tightly to allow for shrinkage during cooking.

6 Sprinkle each tart evenly with 1 teaspoon caster sugar.

7 Bake on the top shelf for 20 minutes, or until the pastry is golden-brown. If the apples are not quite brown, place them under a hot grill for 1–2 minutes.

8 Sprinkle with a little Calvados and brush with warm apricot glaze.

wine: **SWEET WHITE**

Redcurrant and Blackcurrant Flan

SERVES 6

170 g|6 oz flour quantity sweet rich shortcrust pastry (see page 559)

For the sponge lining

2 eggs
55 g|2 oz caster sugar
55 g|2 oz plain flour, sifted

For the filling

170 g|6 oz redcurrants, fresh or frozen
170 g|6 oz blackcurrants, fresh or frozen
85 g|3 oz caster sugar

For the glaze

3 tablespoons redcurrant jelly

To serve

double cream, whipped

1 Strip the redcurrants and blackcurrants off the stalks by holding each sprig of berries by the stalk and using a fork to dislodge the berries. (If they are frozen, thaw and drain them.)

2 Put the black- and redcurrants in separate bowls and add half the sugar to each bowl, shaking to distribute the sugar without crushing the fruit. Leave for 4 hours. (Alternatively, simmer the fruits very gently with the sugar and a few spoons of water for 3–4 minutes to soften and cook them.)

3 Roll out the pastry and use to line a deep 18 cm|7 in flan ring. Refrigerate for 20 minutes.

4 Preheat the oven to 200°C|400°F|gas mark 6.

5 Bake the pastry case blind (see page 557).

6 Meanwhile, make the sponge lining: put the eggs and sugar into a heatproof bowl and set it over, not in, a saucepan of simmering water. Whisk steadily until the mixture is thick and mousse-like and the whisk will leave a ribbon-like trail when lifted. Remove from the heat and fold in the flour. Remove the lining paper and beans from the half-cooked flan case and pour in the mixture.

7 Bake in the oven for a further 10 minutes, then remove the flan ring. Turn down the oven temperature to 190°C|375°F|gas mark 5. Continue baking until the outside of the pastry case is crisp and pale biscuit-coloured, then remove from the oven and allow to cool.

8 Strain the fruit well, tipping both juices into a small saucepan, and arrange the black- and redcurrants in alternate quarters of the flan.

9 Add the redcurrant jelly to the juice and boil rapidly until syrupy and smooth. Cool until near setting, then spoon over the tart to give it a good clear glaze.

10 Serve with whipped cream.

wine: **SWEET WHITE**

Rhubarb Tart

SERVES 4–6

For the filling

675 g | 1½ lb trimmed rhubarb

1 tablespoon caster sugar

55 g | 2 oz lard

1 teaspoon caster sugar

For the pastry

225 g | 8 oz plain flour

a pinch of salt

55 g | 2 oz butter

For the flan mixture

2 eggs

125 g | 4½ oz caster sugar

150 ml | ¼ pint crème fraîche or single cream

1 Cut the rhubarb into 2.5 cm | 1 in lengths and sprinkle with the sugar.

2 Preheat the oven to 190°C | 375°F | gas mark 5.

3 Sift the flour with the salt into a medium bowl. Rub in the fats until the mixture resembles breadcrumbs. Stir in the sugar. Add enough cold water to bind the pastry together.

4 Roll out the pastry and use to line a 25 cm | 10 in flan ring. Refrigerate for 30 minutes.

5 Place the rhubarb and sugar in a shallow saucepan and cook over a low heat until the rhubarb softens slightly but still holds its shape. Remove from the heat and allow to cool.

6 Bake the pastry case blind (see page 557). Turn the oven temperature down to 150°C | 300°F | gas mark 2.

7 Mix the flan mixture ingredients together with a wooden spoon.

8 Arrange the rhubarb, without its juice, carefully in the baked flan case. Pour over the flan mixture and bake in the oven for 20–30 minutes until just set. This tart is best served cold but not chilled.

wine: SWEET WHITE

Charlotte's Higgledy Piggledy Tart

SERVES 8–10

225 g | 8 oz flour quantity walnut pastry (see page 561)

1 recipe crème pâtissière (see page 663)

soft seasonal fruit, such as apricots, oranges, plums, kiwis, bananas and strawberries

warm apricot glaze (see page 727)

1 Line a 25 cm | 10 in flan ring with the pastry, pressing it in. Refrigerate for 30 minutes.

2 Preheat the oven to 375°C | 190°F | gas mark 5.

3 Bake the flan case blind (see page 557). Leave to cool.

4 Pile the crème pâtissière into the flan case. Spread out evenly.

5 Prepare the fruit as for fruit salad and arrange in a higgledy piggledy fashion in the flan case.

6 Brush or spoon the warm apricot glaze over the top.

wine: SWEET WHITE

Apple Flan Ménagère

SERVES 4

170 g | 6 oz flour quantity rich shortcrust pastry or
  pâte sucrée (see pages 559, 564)

For the filling and topping

1kg | 2 lb 4oz medium dessert apples

caster sugar

6 tablespoons warm apricot glaze

1 Preheat the oven to 190°C | 375°F | gas mark 5.
2 Roll out the pastry and use to line a 20 cm | 8 in flan ring. Refrigerate until firm. Bake blind (see page 557).
3 Peel, quarter and core the apples. Using a stainless steel knife, thinly slice them into the flan ring (the apples will shrink considerably during cooking, so make sure that the flan is well filled). When the flan is nearly full, arrange the uppermost apple slices very neatly in overlapping circles.
4 Dust the apples well with caster sugar and bake for about 25 minutes.
5 When the flan is cooked, brush with warm apricot glaze and slide on to a wire rack to cool.

wine: SWEET WHITE

Danish Strawberry Shortcake

SERVES 4

85 g | 3 oz plain flour

a pinch of salt

55 g | 2 oz butter

30 g | 1 oz caster sugar

30 g | 1 oz ground hazelnuts, browned

450 g | 1 lb strawberries

For the redcurrant glaze

4 tablespoons redcurrant jelly

1 tablespoon lemon juice

1 Preheat the oven to 190°C | 375°F | gas mark 5.
2 Sift the flour with the salt into a bowl. Rub in the butter until the mixture resembles breadcrumbs. Stir in the sugar and ground hazelnuts. Knead together to form a stiff dough.
3 On a lightly greased baking sheet, roll or press the pastry into a flat 20 cm | 8 in cake-sized round. Prick with a fork through to the baking sheet. Refrigerate until firm.
4 Bake for 10–15 minutes until pale brown all over. Loosen and leave to cool and harden on the tray.
5 Make the glaze: melt the redcurrant jelly with the lemon juice, but do not allow it to boil. Keep warm.
6 Place the baked shortcake on a serving dish, arrange the strawberries neatly over the top and brush thickly with the redcurrant glaze.

wine: SWEET WHITE

Tarte Tatin

SERVES 6

For the pastry
170 g | 6 oz plain flour
55 g | 2 oz ground rice
140 g | 5 oz butter
55 g | 2 oz caster sugar
1 egg, beaten

For the topping
85 g | 3 oz butter
85 g | 3 oz granulated sugar
1.4 kg | 3 lb dessert apples
grated zest of 1 lemon

1 Preheat the oven to 190°C | 375°F | gas mark 5.
2 Make the pastry: sift the flour and ground rice into a large bowl. Rub in the butter until the mixture resembles breadcrumbs. Stir in the sugar. Add enough of the egg to bind the dough together. Roll between 2 sheets of greaseproof paper into a round to fit the top of the frying pan. Refrigerate while you prepare the topping.
3 Melt the butter in a 25 cm | 10 in frying pan with a metal handle. Add the sugar and when the mixture just starts to brown, remove from the heat.
4 Peel, core and quarter the apples. Arrange the apples rounded side down over the melted butter and sugar in the base of the frying pan. Sprinkle on the lemon zest. Cut the remaining apples into smaller pieces and fill in the gaps in the bottom layer. Then heap the remaining apple pieces to make a second layer.
5 Return the frying pan to a medium heat and cook until the sugar is a deep caramel and the apples have started to brown. It may take 15–20 minutes and you will be able to smell the change – it is essential that the apples get dark. Remove from the heat.
6 Lay the pastry on top of the apples and press down lightly. Bake for 25–30 minutes.
7 Remove from the oven and allow to cool for no more than 5 minutes, then turn out on to a serving plate and serve warm.

NOTE: If you do not have a frying pan with a metal handle, cook the apples in an ordinary frying pan. Let the butter and sugar mixture become well caramelized and tip into an ovenproof dish. Cover with the pastry and then bake in the oven on a hot baking sheet.

wine: **SWEET WHITE**

Upside-down Apricot Tart

SERVES 6

For the pastry
170 g | 6 oz plain flour, plus extra for rolling
85 g | 3 oz caster sugar
a pinch of salt
85 g | 3 oz butter
1 egg, beaten

For the filling
340 g | 12 oz dried apricots
55 g | 2 oz butter
85 g | 3 oz caster sugar

1 Soak the apricots in a bowl of water for 2 hours.

2 Make the pastry: sift the flour, sugar and salt into a bowl. Gently melt the butter in a saucepan and stir into the flour mixture with a wooden spoon. Then thoroughly mix in the egg until the dough is smooth. Press the mixture together in a flat disc, cover with clingfilm and refrigerate for at least 1 hour.

3 Make the filling: drain the apricots and pat dry with absorbent kitchen paper. Grease the base and sides of a 25 cm | 10 in flan dish or tin (not one with a loose base) with the butter. Sprinkle all over with the sugar and arrange the apricots neatly in circles on top of the sugar, rounded side down.

4 Preheat the oven to 190°C | 375°F | gas mark 5. Now take the pastry from the refrigerator and roll out on a floured surface to a circle slightly larger than the flan dish. (If the pastry breaks, just press it together again and don't worry if it looks messy as it won't show.) Press the edges of the pastry firmly down within the flan dish.

5 Bake the tart in the centre of the oven for 30–35 minutes. Remove from the oven and allow to cool slightly. Then turn out the tart upside down on to a serving plate and serve while warm.

wine: SWEET WHITE

Martha Stewart's Fudge Tart

This tart is served with Crème Anglaise and orange sauce.

SERVES 6

a deep 20 cm | 8 in shortcrust pastry (see page 559) tart case, baked and cooled

For the filling

140 g | 5 oz plain chocolate, finely chopped
170 g | 6 oz unsalted butter, cut into small pieces
340 g | 12 oz granulated sugar
95 g | 3½ oz plain flour
6 eggs, lightly beaten

For the Crème Anglaise

570 ml | 1 pint milk
1 vanilla pod
170 g | 6 oz granulated sugar
6 egg yolks
2 teaspoons cornflour
2 tablespoons brandy

For the orange sauce

170 ml | 6 fl oz freshly squeezed orange juice
2 tablespoons Grand Marnier
225 g | 8 oz granulated sugar
1 tablespoon grated orange zest

1 Preheat the oven to 180°C | 350°F | gas mark 4.

2 Make the filling: melt the chocolate and butter together in a heatproof bowl set over, not in, a saucepan of steaming water. When melted, remove from the heat and stir well to mix. Set aside to cool.

3 Mix together the sugar, flour and eggs in a bowl and whisk until well blended. Stir in the chocolate and butter mixture. Pour the filling into the tart case and bake for about 50 minutes, until the filling is just set. Remove to a wire rack and leave to cool completely.

4 Make the crème anglaise: put the milk and vanilla pod into a saucepan. Bring to the boil. Turn off the heat under the pan and leave the milk to infuse for 6 minutes. Remove the vanilla pod. Using an electric mixer, beat the sugar and egg yolks together until thick and fluffy. Add the cornflour. Mixing on low speed, gradually add the infused milk. When thoroughly incorporated, transfer the mixture to a heavy saucepan. Cook over a low heat, stirring constantly, until the sauce thickens to a light, creamy consistency. (Do not let the mixture boil or the egg yolks will curdle.) Remove the mixture from the heat and whisk in the brandy. Strain the mixture through a fine sieve and cool. Refrigerate until ready to use.

5 Make the orange sauce: mix together the orange juice, Grand Marnier and sugar in a heavy saucepan and cook over a low heat, stirring constantly, until thick and syrupy and reduced by half. Remove from the heat, stir in the grated orange zest and leave to cool.

6 To serve: place a slice of the tart on a plate and spoon some Crème Anglaise around it. Drizzle a small amount of orange sauce into the crème anglaise in swirls.

wine: **FORTIFIED SWEET WHITE**

Poached Pear and Polenta Tart with Soft Cream

SERVES 8

425 ml | ¾ pint red wine
55 g | 2 oz sugar
6 whole cloves
3 strips of thinly pared lemon zest
½ teaspoon ground cinnamon
8 pears

For the pastry
140 g | 5 oz butter at room temperature
140 g | 5 oz sugar

3 egg yolks
200 g | 7 oz plain flour
85 g | 3 oz polenta, plus 1 tablespoon
½ teaspoon salt

For the soft cream
150 ml | ¼ pint double cream
pear poaching liquid (see recipe)
brandy to taste
a few drops of vanilla essence

1 Bring the wine, sugar, cloves, lemon zest and cinnamon to the boil in a medium saucepan and simmer until reduced by about one-fifth.

2 Peel the pears and cut them in half. Remove the cores carefully with an apple corer. Cut the pears into 1 cm | ½ in slices. Put the pear slices into the wine mixture and cook over a low heat for about 40 minutes, or until the pears are tender. Lift them out with a slotted spoon and allow them to cool to room temperature.

3 Strain the wine to remove the lemon zest and cloves. Put the syrup back on the heat, bring to the boil and reduce by half. Some of this will be used to flavour the cream. Preheat the oven to 200°C | 400°F | gas mark 6.

4 Make the pastry: cream the butter and sugar together until well blended. Add the egg yolks one at a time, beating well after each addition. Sift the flour, 85 g | 3 oz polenta and salt together and mix into the creamed mixture. Beat until the dough comes together, then knead lightly on a floured surface, adding more flour if necessary, until the pastry is no longer sticky. Refrigerate for 20 minutes.

5 Cut the dough in half. Press one half of the dough on to the base and sides of a 22 cm | 9 in flan ring. Sprinkle the base with the tablespoon of polenta. Spoon the drained pears into the pastry case.

6 Roll out the remaining dough 1 cm | ½ in thick. Using a fluted biscuit cutter, cut out as many circles as possible from the dough. Place them on top of the pears, starting on the outside. Overlap the shapes and continue to cover the top.

7 Bake the tart for about 30 minutes, covering with greaseproof paper after 20 minutes if the tart shows signs of becoming too dark.

8 Make the soft cream: whip the double cream until soft peaks are formed. Flavour with some of the poaching liquid, the brandy and the vanilla essence to taste. Serve with the warm tart.

wine: SWEET WHITE

Tarte Normande

SERVES 8–10
For the rich shortcrust pastry
225 g | 8 oz plain flour

110 g | 4 oz butter

1 egg yolk

¾ level teaspoon salt

2–3 tablespoons cold water

2 eggs, beaten

2 egg yolks

4 teaspoons Calvados or Kirsch

200 g | 7 oz blanched almonds, ground

4 tablespoons plain flour

For the frangipane
200 g | 7 oz butter

200 g | 7 oz caster sugar

3–4 ripe dessert apples

To finish
150 ml | ¼ pint warm apricot glaze (see page 727)

1 Make the pastry as described on page 461 and wrap and chill for at least 30 minutes.

2 Preheat the oven to 200°C | 400°F | gas mark 6. Preheat a baking sheet.

3 Roll out the pastry and use to line a 30 cm | 12 in tart tin. Refrigerate again until firm. Bake blind (see page 557) then allow the pastry case to cool.

4 Make the frangipane: cream the butter in a bowl, gradually beat in the sugar and continue beating until the mixture is light and soft. Gradually add the eggs and egg yolks, beating well after each addition. Add the Calvados or Kirsch, then stir in the ground almonds and the flour. Spread the frangipane into the pastry case.

5 Peel the apples, halve them and scoop out the cores. Cut the apples crosswise into very thin slices and arrange them on the frangipane like the spokes of a wheel, keeping the slices of each half apple together. Press them down gently until they touch the pastry base.

6 Bake the flan on the hot baking sheet near the top of the oven for 10–15 minutes until the pastry dough is beginning to brown. Turn down the oven temperature to 180°C|350°F|gas mark 4 and bake for a further 30–35 minutes, or until the apples are tender and the frangipane is set.

7 Transfer to a wire rack to cool. Brush the tart with the apricot glaze and serve at room temperature.

NOTES: This tart is best eaten the day it is baked, but it can also be frozen. Just before serving, reheat in a low oven.

If using red apples, they need not be peeled.

wine: **SWEET WHITE**

Millefeuilles

SERVES 4–6

225 g|8 oz flour quantity rough puff pastry (see page 565) or puff pastry (see page 565)

225 g|8 oz strawberries, hulled and sliced

290 ml|½ pint double cream, whipped

225 g|8 oz icing sugar, sifted

1 Preheat the oven to 220°C|425°F|gas mark 7.

2 On a floured board, roll the pastry into a thin rectangle about 30 × 20 cm|12 × 8 in. Place on a baking sheet. Prick all over with a fork. Refrigerate until firm.

3 Bake in the oven until brown, about 20 minutes. Remove from the oven and allow to cool.

4 Cut the pastry into 3 neat strips, each 10 × 20 cm|4 × 8 in. (Keep the trimmings for decoration.) Choose the piece of pastry with the smoothest base, and reserve. Spread the other 2 strips with cream, top with strawberries and sandwich together. Cover with the third, reserved, piece of pastry, smooth side uppermost. Press down gently but firmly.

5 Mix the icing sugar with boiling water until it is thick, smooth and creamy. Be careful not to add too much water. Coat the top of the pastry with the icing and, while still warm, sprinkle crushed cooked pastry trimmings along the edges of the icing. Allow to cool before serving.

NOTES: To 'feather' the icing, put 1 tablespoon warmed, sieved liquid jam in a piping bag fitted with a 'writing' nozzle. Pipe parallel lines of jam down the length of the newly iced millefeuilles, about 2 cm|¾ in apart. Before the icing or jam is set, drag the back of a knife across the lines of jam. This will pull the lines into points where the knife crosses them. Repeat this every 5 cm|2 in in the same direction, then drag the back of the knife in the opposite direction between the drag-lines already made.

Millefeuilles are also delicious covered with fresh strawberries and glazed with warm melted redcurrant jelly instead of icing the top.

wine: **SWEET SPARKLING WHITE**

Jalousie

SERVES 4

225 g | 8 oz flour quantity rough puff pastry (see
  page 565)
225 g | 8 oz apple marmalade (see page 667)

milk
caster sugar

1 Preheat the oven to 220°C | 425°F | gas mark 7.
2 Roll the pastry into 2 thin rectangles, one about 2.5 cm | 1 in bigger all round than the other. The smaller one should measure around 13 × 20 cm | 5 × 8 in, and the larger 18 × 25 cm | 7 × 10 in. Refrigerate until firm.
3 Prick the smaller rectangle all over with a fork and bake until crisp and brown. Remove from the oven and turn over on to a baking sheet. Allow to cool. Spread the apple marmelade all over the cooked piece of pastry.
4 Lay the larger pastry rectangle on a board, dust it lightly with flour and fold it, gently so that nothing sticks, in half lengthways. Using a sharp knife, cut through the folded side of the pastry, at right angles to the edge, in parallel lines, as though you were cutting between the teeth of a comb. Leave an uncut margin about 2.5 cm | 1 in wide, all round the other edges, so that when you open up the pastry you will have a solid border.
5 Now lay the cut pastry on top of the pastry covered with apple marmalade and tuck the edges underneath. Brush the top layer carefully all over with milk. Sprinkle well with sugar.
6 Bake for about 20 minutes, until well browned. Serve cold or warm.

NOTE: Jalousie is French for a shutter, which the pie resembles.

wine: RICH SWEET WHITE

Individual Apple Tarts with Calvados Crème Anglaise

SERVES 4

225 g | 8 oz flour quantity puff pastry (see page 565)
4 dessert apples
caster sugar
beaten egg, to glaze
warm apricot glaze (see page 727)

To serve
1 tablespoon Calvados
290 ml | ½ pint Crème Anglaise (see page 663),
  chilled

1 Preheat the oven to 200°C | 400°F | gas mark 6.
2 Roll out the pastry 2 mm | ⅛ in thick and cut into 4 circles 12.5 cm | 5 in in diameter. Place on a baking sheet. Using a sharp knife, trace an inner circle about 1 cm | ½ in from the edge of each pastry circle. Do not cut all the way through the pastry.
3 Peel, core and thinly slice the apples and arrange in concentric circles within the border of each pastry tart.
4 Sprinkle lightly with caster sugar. Brush the rim of each pastry circle with beaten egg, taking care not to let it drip down the sides of the pastry.

5 Flour the blade of a knife and use this to knock up the sides of the pastry. Refrigerate until firm.

6 Bake for 20 minutes. Remove from the oven and leave to cool slightly, then brush liberally with warm apricot glaze.

7 Add the Calvados to the Crème Anglaise. Serve the tarts warm with the cold custard.

wine: SWEET WHITE

Feuilletée de Poires Tiède

SERVES 4

2 William pears

340 g | 12 oz flour quantity puff pastry (see page 565)

290 ml | ½ pint double cream, lightly whipped

55 ml | 2 fl oz Poire William liqueur

icing sugar, sifted, for dusting

1 Peel the pears, cut in quarters and remove the cores. Poach carefully in the sugar syrup until translucent.

2 Preheat the oven to 220°C|425°F|gas mark 7.

3 On a lightly floured board, roll the pastry into 4 neat rectangles, each 10 × 6 | cm|4 × 2½ in. Refrigerate for 20 minutes.

4 Bake for 15 minutes until brown. Split in half horizontally, remove any uncooked dough and return to the turned-off oven to dry out. Remove from the oven.

5 Flavour the cream with the liqueur.

6 Sandwich the pastry slices together with the cream mixture and slices of warm poached pear. Dust the pastry lightly with icing sugar.

wine: SWEET WHITE

Summer Fruit Feuilletées

SERVES 4

225 g | 8 oz flour quantity puff pastry (see page 565)

1 egg, beaten, to glaze

8 tablespoons Greek yoghurt, sweetened with 2 teaspoons sugar

a selection of summer fruits, such as 110 g | 4 oz raspberries, 110 g | 4 oz strawberries, hulled, 110 g | 4 oz blueberries

icing sugar, sifted, for dusting

For the coulis

250 g | 9 oz blackcurrants

110 g | 4 oz redcurrants

110 g | 4 oz caster sugar

45 ml | 3 tablespoons crème de cassis

1 Roll the pastry to a 1 cm | ½ in thickness. Trim off the edges then cut out 4 diamonds. Chill in the refrigerator for 30 minutes.

2 Preheat the oven to 220°C|425°F|gas mark 7.

3 Place the pastry on a baking sheet. Brush the tops with beaten egg and bake for 15–20 minutes until risen and golden-brown. Split in half horizontally, remove any uncooked dough and return to the turned-off oven to dry out. Remove from the oven. Leave to cool on a wire rack.

4 Prepare the coulis: destalk the blackcurrants and redcurrants and place in a saucepan with the sugar. Cook over a low heat for 15 minutes or until the fruit is pulpy.

5 Press the pulp and juice through a sieve. Taste for sweetness and add more sugar if necessary. Stir in the crème de cassis.

6 Spoon 2 tablespoons of yoghurt on to each of the 4 pastry bases.

7 Arrange the summer fruits of your choice on top. Spoon 2 teaspoons of coulis on to the fruit and cover with the pastry lids. Dust the top of the lids with icing sugar.

8 Spoon the layer of coulis on to 4 individual plates and place a feuilletée on each plate.

wine: **SPARKLING ROSÉ**

Gâteau Pithiviers

SERVES 6–8

225 g | 8 oz flour quantity puff pastry (see page 565)
1 egg, beaten with ½ teaspoon salt
icing sugar

For the almond filling
125 g | 4½ oz butter, softened
125 g | 4½ oz sugar

1 egg
1 egg yolk
125 g | 4½ oz whole blanched almonds
15 g | ½ oz plain flour
2 tablespoons rum

1 Refrigerate the puff pastry.

2 Make the almond filling: cream the butter in a bowl, add the sugar and beat thoroughly. Beat in the egg and the egg yolk; then stir in the ground almonds, flour and rum.

3 Roll out half the puff pastry to a circle about 27 cm | 11 in in diameter. Using a pan lid as a guide, cut out a 25 cm | 10 in circle from this with a sharp knife, angling the knife slightly. Roll out the remaining pastry slightly thicker than for the first round and cut out another 25 cm | 10 in circle. Set the thinner circle on a baking sheet, mound the filling in the centre, leaving a 2.5 cm | 1 in border, and brush the border with beaten egg. Set the second circle on top and press the edges together firmly.

4 Scallop the edge of the gâteau by pulling it in at intervals with the back of a knife. Brush the gâteau with beaten egg and working from the centre, score the top in curves like the petals of a flower. Do not cut through to the filling. Refrigerate the gâteau until firm. Preheat the oven to 220°C | 425°F | gas mark 7.

5 Bake the gâteau in the oven for 30–35 minutes, or until firm, puffed and brown.

6 Preheat the grill to its highest setting.

7 Dust the gâteau with icing sugar. Place under the grill until lightly glazed.

wine: **SWEET SPARKLING WHITE**

Tarte Française

SERVES 4

225 g | 8 oz flour quantity puff pastry (see page 565)
beaten egg
3 tablespoons warm apricot glaze (see page 727)
a squeeze of lemon juice

fruit as for fruit salad, such as 2 oranges, a small bunch of black grapes, a small bunch of white grapes, a small punnet of strawberries, 1 banana

1 Roll out the pastry into a rectangle the size of an A4 sheet of paper.
2 Cut out a 'picture frame' 2.5 cm | 1 in wide. Dust liberally with flour and fold into 4. Carefully set aside.
3 Roll out the remaining pastry until it is a little larger than A4 size.
4 Preheat the oven to 220°C | 425°F | gas mark 7.
5 Transfer the pastry to a baking sheet and prick it well all over with a fork. Using a pastry brush, dampen the edges with water. Place the 'picture frame', still folded, on to the pastry and unfold. Trim the edges neatly. Brush off any excess flour. Knock up the pastry and brush the frame with beaten egg (take care not to dribble the glaze down the sides or the layers will stick together). Refrigerate until firm.
6 Bake for 15–20 minutes or until crisp and brown.
7 Remove from the oven and leave to cool on a wire rack.
8 Use a little of the apricot glaze to brush the surface of the pastry.
9 Cut up the fruit as you would for a fruit salad and lay the pieces in rows on the pastry as neatly and closely together as possible. Be careful about colour (do not put 2 rows of white fruit next to each other, or tangerine segments next to orange segments, for example). When complete, paint liberally with the warm apricot glaze.

wine: SWEET WHITE

Chocolate Profiteroles

MAKES 30

For the profiteroles
1 quantity choux pastry (see page 563)

For the filling and topping
570 ml | 1 pint double cream, whipped and sweetened with 1 tablespoon sifted icing sugar

225 g | 8 oz plain chocolate, chopped
15 g | ½ oz butter
2 tablespoons water

1 Preheat the oven to 200°C | 400°F | gas mark 6.
2 Put teaspoons of the choux mixture on a lightly greased baking sheet, about 4 cm | 1 ½ in apart. Pat down any spikes with a dampened finger.
3 Bake for 20–30 minutes. The profiteroles will puff up and become fairly brown and firm when squeezed. If they are taken out when only slightly brown, they will be soggy when cool.

4 Using a skewer, make a hole the size of a pea in the base of each profiterole and return to the oven placed upside down on the baking sheet for 5 minutes to allow the insides to dry out. Leave to cool completely on a wire rack.

5 When cold, put the sweetened cream into a piping bag fitted with a small plain nozzle. Pipe the cream into the profiteroles through the holes made by the skewer, until well filled.

6 Put the chocolate, butter and water in a heatproof bowl set over, not in, a saucepan of steaming water and leave until melted.

7 Dip the tops of the profiteroles in the melted chocolate, then allow to cool.

NOTE: If no piping bag is available for filling the profiteroles, they can be split, allowed to dry out, and filled with cream or crème pâtissière when cold, and the icing can be spooned over the top. However, made this way they are messier to eat in the fingers.

wine: FORTIFIED SWEET WHITE

Coffee Éclairs

MAKES 20–25

1 quantity choux pastry (see page 563)

225 g | 8 oz icing sugar
2 tablespoons very strong hot black coffee

For the filling and topping

570 ml | 1 pint double cream, lightly whipped and
  sweetened with 2 tablespoons sifted icing sugar,
  or crème pâtissière (see page 663)

1 Preheat the oven to 200°C | 400°F | gas mark 6.

2 Using a piping bag fitted with a 1 cm | ½ in plain nozzle, pipe 7.5 cm | 3 in lengths of choux pastry on to the lightly greased baking sheets (keep them well separated as choux pastry puffs up during baking). Bake for 25–30 minutes until crisp and pale brown.

3 Using a skewer, make a hole the size of a pea in each éclair and return to the oven for 5 minutes to allow the insides to dry out. Leave to cool completely on a wire rack.

4 Put the sweetened cream or the crème pâtissière into a piping bag fitted with a medium plain nozzle. Pipe the cream into the éclairs through the holes made by the skewer until well filled.

5 Mix the icing sugar and very hot coffee together and beat with a wooden spoon until smooth. The mixture should be just runny.

6 Dip each éclair upside down into the icing so that the top becomes neatly coated.

7 Set aside to dry. Alternatively, the icing can be carefully spooned along the top ridge of each éclair.

NOTE: The éclairs may be split lengthways when cooked, allowed to dry out, and filled with cream or crème pâtissière when cold. The tops are then replaced and the icing spooned over but they are then messier to eat with the fingers.

wine: FORTIFIED SWEET WHITE

Beignets Soufflés

When dropping the choux into the hot oil, grease the teaspoon to prevent sticking.

MAKES ABOUT 30

oil for deep-frying
1 quantity choux pastry (see page 563)

290 ml|½ pint Crème Pâtissière (see page 663)
 (optional)
caster sugar and ground cinnamon for dusting

1 Heat the oil in the deep-fryer until a crumb will sizzle gently in it. Drop teaspoonfuls of the choux pastry into the hot oil, one at a time, so that they do not stick together. Tap them lightly with a spoon to puff them up. Deep-fry for about 5 minutes or until brown and crisp. Drain well on absorbent kitchen paper. Sprinkle with caster sugar and cinnamon.

2 The beignets can be split open and filled with warm Crème Pâtissière, if wished.

NOTE: Apricot sauce (see page 666) is delicious served hot with these.

wine: **SWEET SPARKLING WHITE**

Gâteau St Honoré

SERVES 6

170 g|6 oz flour quantity Pâte Sucrée (see page 564)
1 quantity choux pastry (see page 563)

double quantity crème pâtissière (see page 663)
170 g|6 oz granulated sugar

1 Preheat the oven to 190°C|375°F|gas mark 5. Line an 20 cm|8 in flan ring with the pâte sucrée. Bake blind until biscuit coloured (see page 557).

2 Make the profiteroles: increase the oven temperature to 200°C|400°F|gas mark 6.

3 Put teaspoonfuls of the choux pastry on to 2 lightly greased baking sheets and bake for 25 minutes until firm and pale brown.

4 Using a skewer, make a hole the size of a pea in the base of each choux bun and return to the oven for 5 minutes to allow the insides to dry out. Leave on a wire rack to cool completely.

5 Put the Crème Pâtissière into a piping bag fitted with a plain nozzle and pipe into the profiteroles through the holes made by the skewer. Spread the remaining Crème Pâtissière in the bottom of the pastry case. Pile the profiteroles into a pyramid on top of the filling.

6 Heat the sugar in a heavy saucepan over a low heat until it caramelizes. Remove from the heat and dip the base of the saucepan into cold water.

7 Pour the caramel over the profiteroles.

wine: **SWEET SPARKLING WHITE**

Apricot Ring

SERVES 6

225 g | 8 oz fresh apricots
150 ml | ¼ pint sugar syrup (see page 665)
1 quantity choux pastry (see page 563)
2 tablespoons apricot jam

140 g | 5 oz icing sugar, sifted
290 ml | ½ pint double cream, whipped
30 g | 1 oz almonds, toasted

1 Preheat the oven to 200°C | 400°F | gas mark 6.
2 Wash and halve the apricots and remove the stones. Poach in the sugar syrup until just tender (about 15 minutes). Drain well and leave to cool.
3 Spoon the pastry into a circle about 20 cm | 8 in in diameter on a lightly grease baking tray. Bake for about 30 minutes until brown and crisp. Allow to cool.
4 Split horizontally with a bread knife. Scoop out any uncooked pastry and discard. Leave the choux ring on a wire rack to cool completely.
5 Heat the jam and spread it on the base of the choux ring.
6 Mix 30 g | 1 oz of the icing sugar with the cream and layer the cream and apricots on the base of the ring.
7 Mix the remaining icing sugar with a little boiling water until just runny. Coat the top of the choux ring with the icing and, while still wet, sprinkle with browned almonds.

wine: **SWEET WHITE**

Apple Strudel

SERVES 6

285 g | 10 oz flour quantity strudel pastry (see page 563), rolled to a rectangle at least 40 × 60 cm | 16 × 24 in

For the filling
900 g | 2 lb cooking apples
a handful of currants, sultanas and raisins

55 g | 2 oz soft light brown sugar
½ teaspoon ground cinnamon
a pinch of ground cloves
3 tablespoons browned breadcrumbs
grated zest and juice of ½ lemon
85 g | 3 oz butter, melted
icing sugar, sifted, for dusting

1 Preheat the oven to 200°C | 400°F | gas mark 6. Grease a baking sheet.
2 Prepare the filling: peel, core and cut the apples into chunks and mix together with the dried fruit, sugar, spices, breadcrumbs, lemon zest and juice. Taste apples and add more sugar if required.
3 Flour a large tea-towel. Lay the pastry on this.
4 Brush with melted butter. Place the filling at one end of the pastry. Using the tea-towel

to help, roll up as for a Swiss roll, trying to maintain a fairly close roll. Lift the cloth and gently tip the strudel on to the baking sheet. Brush with melted butter.

5 Bake for 30–40 minutes until golden-brown and the apples are tender. Dust with icing sugar while still warm. Trim the ends neatly.

NOTE: In delicatessens, strudels are generally sold in one-portion sizes. To make these you will need leaves of pastry about 22 cm | 9 in square. As they are easier to handle, they can be lifted without the aid of the cloth – just flour the table top to prevent sticking. Bake for 20 minutes.

wine: **SWEET WHITE**

Baklava

This recipe has been taken from Claudia Roden's *A New Book of Middle Eastern Food*. It is fascinating to read and an excellent book from which to cook.

SERVES 6

170 g | 6 oz unsalted butter, melted
450 g | 1 lb filo pastry (24 sheets)
340 g | 12 oz pistachios, walnuts or almonds, ground or finely chopped

For the syrup

450 g | 1 lb granulated sugar
290 ml | ½ pint water
2 tablespoons lemon juice
2 tablespoons orange-blossom water

1 Make the syrup: put the sugar, water and lemon juice into a saucepan, dissolve over a low heat and then simmer until thick enough to coat the back of a wooden spoon. Add the orange-blossom water and simmer for a further 2 minutes. Remove from the heat and leave to cool, then refrigerate.

2 Preheat the oven to 160°C | 325°F | gas mark 3.

3 Brush melted butter on the base and sides of a deep baking tray. Put half the filo sheets into the tray, brushing each sheet with melted butter and overlapping or folding the sides over where necessary.

4 Spread the nuts evenly over the pastry, spoon over 4 tablespoons of the sugar syrup and then cover with the remaining sheets of filo, brushing each one as you layer it up. Brush the top layer with butter. Cut diagonally into lozenge shapes with a sharp, serrated knife.

5 Bake for 45 minutes, then turn the oven temperature up to 220°C | 425°F | gas mark 7 and bake for a further 15 minutes or until well risen and golden brown.

6 Remove from the oven and pour the chilled syrup over the hot baklava. Leave to cool.

7 When cold, cut into lozenge shapes as before and place on a serving dish.

wine: **RICH SWEET WHITE OR SPARKLING**

Konafa

SERVES 8
450 g | 1 lb konafa pastry (available in delicatessens)

225 g | 8 oz unsalted butter, melted

For the syrup

450 g | 1 lb granulated sugar

290 ml | ½ pint water

2 tablespoons lemon juice

2 tablespoons orange-blossom water

For the filling

6 tablespoons ground rice

4 tablespoons caster sugar

1 litre | 1¾ pints milk

150 ml | ¼ pint double cream

1 Make the syrup: put the sugar, water and lemon juice into a saucepan, dissolve over a low heat and then simmer until thick enough to coat the back of a wooden spoon. Add the orange-blossom water and simmer for a further 2 minutes. Remove from the heat and leave to cool, then refrigerate.

2 Mix the ground rice and sugar to a smooth paste with 150 ml | ¼ pint of the milk. Bring the remaining milk to the boil and gradually add the ground rice paste, stirring vigorously. Simmer, stirring to prevent the mixture catching on the bottom of the pan, until very thick. Remove from the heat and allow to cool, then add the cream and mix well.

3 Preheat the oven to 170°C | 325°F | gas mark 3.

4 Put the konafa pastry into a large bowl. Pull out and separate the strands as much as possible with your fingers so that they do not stick together too much. Pour in the melted butter and work it in very well. Put half the pastry into a large, deep ovenproof dish. Spread the filling evenly over and cover with the remaining pastry. Flatten it with the palm of your hand.

5 Bake for 1 hour. Then turn the oven temperature up to 220°C | 425°F | gas mark 7 and bake for a further 10–15 minutes or until golden-brown.

6 Remove from the oven and pour the cold syrup over the hot konafa.

NOTE: Konafa can be made with a variety of fillings, such as curd cheese, nuts and cinnamon or sliced bananas. They can also be made as individually rolled pastries instead of one large pastry.

wine: RICH SWEET WHITE OR SPARKLING

Almond Pastry Fruit Flan

SERVES 6–8
110 g | 4 oz flour quantity almond pastry (see page 565)

a selection of fruit, such as oranges, pears, grapes, cherries, strawberries, bananas, apples, plums, depending on the season

4 tablespoons apricot glaze (see page 727)

1 Preheat the oven to 190°C|375°F|gas mark 5.

2 On a baking sheet roll or press the pastry into a 22 cm|9 in circle. Decorate the edges with a fork or by pinching between fingers and thumb. Prick lightly all over with a fork. Refrigerate until firm.

3 Bake for about 15–20 minutes until a pale biscuit colour. Loosen from the baking sheet with a palette knife and allow to cool slightly and harden on the baking sheet. Slip on to a wire rack and leave to cool completely.

4 Prepare the fruits leaving any that discolour (such as apples or pears) until you assemble the flan.

5 Brush the pastry with some of the apricot glaze (this helps to stick the fruit in place and prevents the pastry from becoming too soggy).

6 Arrange the fruit in neat overlapping circles, taking care to get contrasting colours next to each other. Brush with apricot glaze as you go, especially on apples, pears or bananas. When all the fruit is in place, brush with the remaining glaze.

NOTE: This flan should not be assembled too far in advance as the pastry will become soggy in about 2 hours.

wine: SWEET WHITE

Tarte au Citron

SERVES 6

170 g|6 oz flour quantity Pâte Sucrée (see page 564)

4 eggs

1 egg yolk

200 g|7 oz caster sugar

150 ml|¼ pint double cream

grated zest and juice of 2 lemons

icing sugar, sifted, for dusting

1 Preheat the oven to 190°C|375°F|gas mark 5.

2 Line a 20 cm|8 in flan ring with the pâte sucrée. Refrigerate until firm, then bake blind (see page 557). Remove the lining paper and beans. Turn the oven temperature down to 150°C|300°F|gas mark 2.

3 Make the filling: mix the eggs and egg yolk with the sugar until smooth. Pass through a sieve. Stir in the cream. Add the lemon zest and juice. The mixture will thicken considerably.

4 Pour the lemon filling in the pastry case. Bake in the oven for 50 minutes until almost set.

5 When the tart is cooked, remove the flan ring and leave to cool. To serve dust thickly and evenly with sifted icing sugar.

wine: SWEET WHITE

Strawberry Tartlets

MAKES 20

170 g│6 oz flour quantity Pâte Sucrée (see page 564)

55 g│2 oz caster sugar
450 g│1 lb strawberries, hulled
4 tablespoons redcurrant jelly, melted

For the filling

225 g│8 oz Mascarpone cheese

1 Preheat the oven to 190°C│375°F│gas mark 5.
2 Roll out the pastry thinly and use to line 20 tartlet tins. Bake blind (see page 557) until a pale biscuit colour. Remove the lining papers and beans. If the pastry is not quite cooked, return to the oven for 5 minutes. Carefully remove the pastry cases from the tins and leave to cool on a wire rack.
3 Cream the cheese with the sugar and place a teaspoonful of the mixture at the bottom of each case. Arrange the strawberries, cut in half if necessary, on top of the cheese and brush lightly with warm melted redcurrant jelly.

wine: **SWEET WHITE**

Sablés aux Fraises

This recipe has been adapted from *The Roux Brothers on Pâtisserie*.

SERVES 6

280 g│10 oz flour quantity pâte sablée (see page 564)
675 g│1½ lb strawberries, hulled and sliced

425 ml│¾ pint raspberry coulis (see page 667)
55 g│2 oz icing sugar, sifted, for dusting

1 Preheat the oven to 190°C│375°F│gas mark 5.
2 Divide the chilled dough into 2 pieces to make rolling easier.
3 Roll out the doughs to the thickness of a 20p coin and cut into a total of 18 × 7.5 cm│3 in circles. Refrigerate to relax for 10 minutes. Bake for 8 minutes or until pale golden. Transfer to a wire rack and leave to cool.
4 Save a few whole strawberries for garnish then thickly slice the remainder. Mix the sliced strawberries with enough raspberry coulis to coat them. Leave to macerate.
5 Place a pastry base on each of 6 plates. Arrange a few macerated strawberries on top. Cover with a second pastry base and more strawberries. Cover with a third piece of pastry and dust generously with icing sugar.
6 Serve the remaining raspberry coulis separately or poured around the sablés.

NOTE: Do not assemble this pudding in advance as the pastry will become soggy.

wine: **SWEET WHITE**

Peach Pastry Cake

SERVES 6

70 g | 2½ oz hazelnuts
55 g | 2 oz caster sugar
85 g | 3 oz butter, softened
110 g | 4 oz plain flour

a pinch of salt
3 fresh peaches
200 ml | 7 fl oz cream, whipped
icing sugar, sifted, for dusting

1 Preheat the oven to 200°C | 400°F | gas mark 6. Toast the nuts in the hot oven. When brown, rub in a dry cloth to remove the skins. Cool. Grind the nuts with 1 tablespoon of the sugar taking care not to overgrind them or they will become oily.

2 Beat the butter until soft, add the remaining sugar.

3 Sift the flour with the salt and stir into the mixture with the nuts.

4 Turn the oven temperature down to 190°C | 375°F | gas mark 5.

5 Divide the nut mixture into 3 and press out into thin flat 15 cm | 6 in rounds. Refrigerate for 30 minutes or until firm.

6 Place on baking sheets and bake in the oven for 10–12 minutes. Loosen from the baking sheet with a palette knife. Cut 1 biscuit round into sixths before it cools. Allow to cool on a wire rack. The pastry will become crisp as it cools.

7 Skin and slice the peaches. Mix the peach slices with the cream. Using half this mixture as a filling, sandwich the 2 whole biscuit rounds together. Spread the remaining filling on the top.

8 Set the cut portions of biscuit into the cream mixture, placing each at a slight angle. Dust with icing sugar before serving.

wine: **SWEET WHITE**

Brioche Tart with Grapes and Mascarpone

SERVES 8–10

450 g | 1 lb flour quantity brioche dough (see page 761)
170 g | 6 oz raisins (optional)

200 g | 7 oz Mascarpone
225 g | 8 oz seedless grapes
110 g | 4 oz soft dark brown sugar

1 Preheat the oven to 190°C | 375°F | gas mark 5.

2 Knock back the risen brioche dough and roll out to a circle about 28 cm | 11 in in diameter. Place on a baking sheet.

3 If using raisins, sprinkle them over the surface of the dough and press in lightly.

4 Spread the Mascarpone over the surface, leaving a 2.5 cm | 1 in border all the way around the edge.

5 Scatter the grapes on top and press firmly into the Mascarpone. Sprinkle over the sugar.

6 Bake the tart in the centre of the oven for 30–40 minutes until golden brown. Reduce oven temperature if the tart shows signs of becoming too dark.

7 Serve the tart warm.

NOTE: Other soft fruits can be used in place of the grapes, for example pitted cherries, peaches or plums.

Rum Baba

SERVES 4

For the sugar syrup

170 g | 6 oz granulated sugar

225 ml | 8 fl oz water

2 tablespoons rum

For the yeast mixture

110 g | 4 oz plain flour

15 g | ½ oz fresh yeast

15 g | ½ oz caster sugar

100 ml | 3½ fl oz warm milk

2 egg yolks

grated zest of ½ lemon

55 g | 2 oz clarified butter (see page 385)

To decorate

fresh fruits, such as grapes and raspberries

150 ml | ¼ pint double or whipping cream, lightly
   whipped

1 First make the sugar syrup: dissolve the sugar in the water in a heavy saucepan and boil rapidly to the short thread stage (see page 665). Add the rum.

2 Now make the yeast mixture: sift the flour into a bowl.

3 Mix the yeast with ½ teaspoon of the sugar, 1 teaspoon of the flour and enough milk to make a batter-like consistency.

4 Whisk the egg yolks, remaining sugar and lemon zest until fluffy.

5 Make a well in the centre of the flour and add the yeast and egg-yolk mixtures. With your fingers, mix together and gradually draw in the flour from the sides, adding more milk as you take in more flour. When all the flour has been incorporated, beat with your hand until smooth.

6 Gradually add the clarified butter, kneading and slapping the dough until it looks like a very thick batter and no longer sticks to the palm of your hand.

7 Cover and leave to rise in a warm place, for about 45 minutes, until doubled in size.

8 Preheat the oven to 190°C | 375°F | gas mark 5. Grease a 1 litre | 1¾ pint savarin (ring) mould with plenty of butter.

9 When the dough has risen, beat it down again and place in the mould, which it should half-fill.

10 Cover and leave to prove (rise again) for 10–15 minutes in a warm place.

11 Bake for 30–35 minutes.

12 Turn out on to a wire rack and place on a serving dish. While still hot, prick all over with a cocktail stick and brush with plenty of rum syrup until the baba is really soaked and shiny.

13 Serve plain or surround with fresh fruit and pile the whipped cream in the centre.

NOTE: If using dried yeast, use half the amount called for. Mix it with 3 tablespoons of the liquid, warmed to blood temperature, and 1 teaspoon sugar. Leave until frothy (about 15 minutes), then proceed. If the yeast does not go frothy, it is dead and unusable. If using easy-blend yeast, use half the quantity called for and add it to the dry ingredients.

wine: SWEET WHITE

Orange and Grand Marnier Pancakes

SERVES 4

grated zest of 1 large orange

290 ml | ½ pint Crème Pâtissière (see page 663)

2 tablespoons Grand Marnier

8 French pancakes (see page 569)

icing sugar, sifted, for dusting

1 Preheat the grill to its highest setting.
2 Mix the orange zest with the crème pâtissière and the Grand Marnier.
3 Divide the mixture between the pancakes.
4 Fold each pancake in half and dust heavily with icing sugar.
5 Place under the hot grill until the icing sugar begins to caramelize.

Crêpes Suzette

SERVES 4–6

12 French pancakes (see page 569)

For the orange butter

85 g | 3 oz unsalted butter

30 g | 1 oz caster sugar

grated zest of 1 orange

2 tablespoons orange juice

2 tablespoons orange Curaçao or Grand Marnier

To flame

caster sugar

2 tablespoons orange Curaçao or Grand Marnier

1 tablespoon brandy

1 Put the butter, sugar, orange zest, juice and Curaçao or Grand Marnier into a large frying pan and simmer gently for 2 minutes.
2 Put a pancake into the frying pan and, using a spoon and fork, fold it in half and then in half again. Add a second pancake and repeat the process until the pan has been filled. If the pan begins to look a little dry, add a little water.
3 Sprinkle the pancakes with caster sugar. Heat the Curaçao or Grand Marnier and brandy in a laddle over a flame or in a small saucepan. Light the alcohol. Pour it over the pancakes and shake the pan until the flames have subsided. Serve immediately.

Baked Apples

1 smallish cooking apple per person

soft light brown sugar

sultanas

1 Preheat the oven to 180°C | 350°F | gas mark 4.
2 Wash the apples and remove the cores with an apple corer. With a sharp knife cut a ring just through the apple skin about two-thirds of the way up each apple.
3 Put the apples into an ovenproof dish and stuff the centres with a mixture of sugar and sultanas.

4 Sprinkle 2 teaspoons sugar over each apple. Then pour 5 mm | ½ in of water into the dish over the apples.

5 Bake for about 45 minutes, or until the apples are soft right through when tested with a skewer.

wine: SWEET WHITE

Poached Apples

SERVES 4

170 g | 6 oz granulated sugar
570 ml | 1 pint water
450 g | 1 lb dessert apples

1 cinnamon stick
a squeeze of lemon juice

To serve
cream (optional)

1 Dissolve the sugar in the water in a heavy saucepan. When completely dissolved, boil rapidly until you have a thin syrup (3–4 minutes).

2 Peel, core and quarter the apples. Place them in the sugar syrup with the cinnamon.

3 Bring slowly to the boil, then reduce the heat and poach gently for 20 minutes, or until the apples are tender.

4 Remove the apples with a slotted spoon and arrange in a shallow dish.

5 Reduce the syrup a little by further boiling, then add the lemon juice. Allow to cool to room temperature and pour over the fruit.

6 Serve hot with cream, or chilled with or without cream.

wine: LIGHT SWEET WHITE

Apples and Blackberries in Cassis Syrup

SERVES 4

4 Granny Smith apples, with stalks if possible

For the poaching liquid
225 g | 8 oz blackberries
juice and 2 strips of zest from ½ lemon
½ cinnamon stick
2 strips of orange zest

110 g | 4 oz sugar
150 ml | ¼ pint crème de cassis
150 ml | ¼ pint dry white wine

To serve
2 tablespoons of the poaching juices (see above)
plain yoghurt
225 g | 8 oz blackberries

1 Put the poaching ingredients into a large shallow pan and simmer over a low heat until the sugar has dissolved.

2 Peel the apples, cut in half leaving the stalk on one half, and remove the cores with a melon baller or small spoon.

3 Add to the poaching liquid, cut side up, and cover with a lid.

4 Poach the apples over a low heat for about 15 minutes, or until just tender. Baste frequently, using a wooden spoon to avoid damaging the fruit. Remove the pan from the heat. Leave the fruit to cool in the liquid. The longer the apples are left in the poaching liquid the more coloured they will become.

5 Remove the apples with two wooden spoons and place, cut side down, on a plate. Strain the cooking liquid through a plastic or nylon sieve, return to a clean saucepan and simmer over a medium heat until reduced to a coating consistency. Leave to cool.

6 To serve: put 2 apple halves on each of 4 pudding bowls and spoon the syrup over and around. Add a spoonful of yoghurt if wished or serve it separately.

7 Decorate with blackberries.

NOTE: This recipe also works well with pears; cook them for 20 minutes.

Alain Senderens' Soupe aux Fruits Exotiques

SERVES 4

1 small papaya
16 lychees
20 strawberries
2 kiwi fruits
8 passionfruits

For the syrup

6 tablespoons sugar
1 sprig of fresh mint
1 clove
¼ teaspoon Chinese 5-spice (from good food stores and Chinese specialist shops)

thinly pared zest of 1 lime
thinly pared zest of ¼ lemon
1 vanilla pod, split lengthways
½ teaspoon peeled and finely chopped fresh root ginger
2 coriander seeds
425 ml | ¾ pint water

To decorate

1 tablespoon finely chopped fresh mint

1 Make the syrup: put the sugar, mint sprig, clove, Chinese 5-spice, lime and lemon zest, vanilla pod, ginger, coriander seeds and water into a heavy saucepan and bring slowly to the boil, stirring to dissolve the sugar. Reduce, by boiling rapidly, for 1 minute. Remove the pan from the heat and leave to infuse until cool.

2 Meanwhile, peel the papaya and cut the flesh into even-sized pieces. Skin the lychees and remove the stones. Wash and hull the strawberries. Peel the kiwi fruits and slice thinly.

3 When the syrup is cool, strain through a fine sieve into a bowl. Add the prepared fruits. Cut the passionfruits in half and spoon out the seeds and juice into the bowl of syrup. Chill for 2–3 hours.

4 To serve: divide the prepared fruits into 4 shallow bowls; spoon over the syrup and sprinkle with mint.

wine: LIGHT SWEET WHITE

Gratin de Fruits

SERVES 6

4 ripe peaches	2 egg yolks
4 ripe plums	85 g $\vert$ 3 oz caster sugar
4 ripe apricots	a dash of Kirsch (optional)
2 eggs	55 g $\vert$ 2 oz flaked almonds

1 Skin, stone and slice the peaches. Halve and stone the plums and apricots. Arrange on 6 small gratin dishes.
2 Preheat the grill to its highest setting.
3 Put the eggs, egg yolks and sugar into a heatproof bowl set over, not in, a saucepan of simmering water. Whisk for 10–15 minutes until thick and creamy. It is important that the eggs should thicken, not scramble. Add the Kirsch, if using.
4 Spoon the sauce over the fruits. Sprinkle with the almonds and grill until evenly browned. Serve immediately.

wine: **SWEET WHITE**

Green Fruit Salad

SERVES 4

3 kiwi fruits	1 small ripe melon with green flesh
225 g $\vert$ 8 oz greengages	1 green dessert apple
225 g $\vert$ 8 oz white grapes	apple juice or ginger cordial

1 Peel and slice the kiwi fruits. Stone and quarter the greengages and halve and seed the grapes.
2 Using a melon baller, scrape the melon flesh into balls, or simply cut into even-sized cubes. Core the unpeeled apple and cut it into chunks.
3 Mix the fruits together, moisten with the apple juice or ginger cordial and chill well before serving.

wine: **LIGHT SWEET WHITE**

Red Fruit Salad

SERVES 4

675 g | 1½ lb assorted red fruit, such as raspberries, strawberries, redcurrants, watermelon, plums

fresh orange juice (optional)

1 Wash the fruit.
2 Check the raspberries, discarding any bad ones.
3 Hull and halve the strawberries.
4 Wash, top and tail the redcurrants with the prongs of a fork.
5 Cut the melon flesh into cubes, discarding the seeds, but reserving the juice.
6 Halve and stone the plums.
7 Put the fruit into a glass dish and moisten with orange juice, if required. Chill well.

NOTE: Red fruit salad is also very good if sprinkled with a little triple-distilled rosewater in place of the orange juice. A teaspoonful will be plenty.

wine: **LIGHT SWEET WHITE**

Blackcurrant Kissel

SERVES 4

450 g | 1 lb blackcurrants
grated zest and juice of 1 orange
1 cinnamon stick

caster sugar to taste (about 170 g | 6 oz)
2 teaspoons arrowroot

1 Wash the blackcurrants and remove the stalks.
2 Barely cover with water and add the orange zest and juice, the cinnamon and sugar. Stew gently for about 20 minutes. Remove the cinnamon stick, then push through a sieve. Return to the saucepan and bring back to the boil.
3 Mix the arrowroot to a smooth paste with a little cold water.
4 Add a cupful of the boiling purée to the arrowroot paste and mix thoroughly. Add the arrowroot mixture to the fruit, stirring, and allow to thicken. Simmer for 1 minute. Pour into a serving bowl. Sprinkle evenly with caster sugar to prevent a skin from forming.

wine: **LIGHT SWEET WHITE**

Fresh Papaya with Limes

Simply serve halved papayas, with the seeds removed, with a wedge of fresh lime. Allow one half of a papaya per head.

Turned Mangoes with Limes

½ mango and 2 lime wedges per person

1 Cut a thick slice off the mango as close to the flat stone as possible.
2 Repeat on the other side. (Use the remaining mango flesh for another dish.)
3 With a small, sharp knife, make diagonal cuts through the flesh right down to the skin, taking care not to pierce the skin.
4 Push the skin so that the mango is domed and can be eaten with a spoon. Serve with lime wedges.

 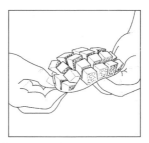

Cut the flesh to give a lattice finish. Turn mango inside out

Summer Fruit Compote

SERVES 6–8

110 g | 4 oz black cherries, pitted	225 g | 8 oz raspberries
225 g | 8 oz strawberries	110 g | 4 oz red cherries, pitted
juice of 1 orange	110 g | 4 oz blueberries
juice of 1 lemon	225 g | 8 oz blackberries
2 tablespoons caster sugar	225 g | 8 oz loganberries
2 tablespoons Kirsch	

1 Process together half the black cherries, half the strawberries, the orange and lemon juice, the sugar and Kirsch. Taste and add more sugar if necessary.
2 Mix the remaining fruit together and pour the purée over it. Mix gently and pile into a serving bowl.
3 Keep the compote covered and refrigerated if not using immediately, but serve at room temperature.

wine: **LIGHT SWEET WHITE**

Arranged Fruit Salad

SERVES 4

2 ripe passionfruits

1 large ripe mango

3 tablespoons fresh orange juice

seasonal fruit, chilled, such as 4 kiwi fruits, peeled and sliced, 110 g|4 oz strawberries, hulled, 110 g|4 oz black grapes, halved and deseeded

4 sprigs of fresh mint

1 Process (but do not liquidize) the passionfruit pulp, mango flesh and orange juice together for 2 minutes.

2 Sieve the purée on to the base of 4 pudding plates so that each one is well flooded.

3 Arrange the prepared fruit in an attractive pattern on each plate. Decorate each with a sprig of mint.

NOTE: If you do not have a food processor, the sauce can be made in a blender if the passionfruit are sieved before 'whizzing'.

wine: **SWEET WHITE**

Hot Winter Fruit Salad

SERVES 4

450 g|1 lb good-quality mixed dried fruits, such as prunes, apricots, figs and apples

1 tablespoon Calvados

cold tea

4 tablespoons fresh orange juice

3–4 cloves

1 × 5 cm|2 in cinnamon stick

¼ teaspoon ground mixed spice

thinly pared zest of 1 lemon

1 star anise

1 Soak the mixed dried fruits in the Calvados and enough tea to just cover. Leave overnight.

2 Pour into a saucepan and add the orange juice, cloves, cinnamon, mixed spice, lemon zest and star anise. Bring to the boil, then simmer slowly until the fruits are soft (about 20 minutes).

3 Remove the cloves, cinnamon, lemon zest and star anise. Serve hot or cold.

wine: **RICH, SWEET WHITE**

Oranges in Caramel

1 large orange per person

caramel sauce (see page 665)

1 With a potato peeler, pare the zest of 1 or 2 oranges very thinly, making sure that there is no pith on the back of the strips. Cut into fine shreds.

2 Simmer the needleshreds in caramel sauce until soft and almost candied. They should be very sticky and quite dark.

3 Peel the remaining oranges with a knife, making sure that all the pith is removed.

4 Remove the segments from the oranges and place in a bowl with the juice. Discard the membrane and pips.

5 Pour over the cold caramel sauce. Chill well.

6 Scatter with the needleshreds before serving.

wine: **FORTIFIED SWEET WHITE**

Butterscotch Figs

SERVES 4

8 ripe figs
140 g | 5 oz caster sugar
55 g | 2 oz unsalted butter
a pinch of ground cinnamon
4 tablespoons Grand Marnier

To serve
150 ml | ¼ pint double cream, lightly whipped

1 Preheat the oven to 150°C | 300°F | gas mark 2.

2 Prick the figs with a fork. Place them in a casserole dish and sprinkle over 30 g | 1 oz of the sugar. Add a little water and bake for 30 minutes. Baste the figs occasionally.

3 Meanwhile, melt the butter in a large sauté pan, add 4 tablespoons water and the sugar and boil until lightly browned. Add the figs, sprinkle with a little cinnamon and toss gently with 2 wooden spoons so that they become lightly caramelized all over.

4 Heat the Grand Marnier in a small saucepan and then pour it over the figs to flame.

5 Serve the figs with the cream handed separately.

wine: **FORTIFIED SWEET WHITE**

Apricot Cheesecake

SERVES 4

For the crust

170 g | 6 oz digestive biscuits, crushed
85 g | 3 oz butter, melted
a pinch of ground cinnamon

For the filling

3 tablespoons water
3 teaspoons powdered gelatine
200 g | 7 oz can of good-quality apricots

225 g | 8 oz soft cheese
150 ml | ¼ pint double cream, whipped
70 ml | 2½ fl oz soured cream
grated zest and juice of ½ lemon
sugar to taste (about 45 g | 1½ oz)

To decorate

150 ml | ¼ pint double cream, whipped
flaked almonds, toasted

1 Place an oiled flan ring on a flat, lipless baking sheet. Mix together the crust ingredients and put the mixture into the flan ring, pressing down firmly. Refrigerate for 20 minutes to harden.

2 Put the water into a small saucepan, sprinkle over the gelatine and leave for 5 minutes until spongy.

3 Reserve 3 apricot halves for decoration. Process the remaining apricots with enough syrup to make a coating consistency purée. Beat the cheese until creamy, then mix with the apricot purée, creams, lemon zest, juice and sugar.

4 Dissolve the gelatine over a low heat, without boiling, until liquid and clear. Pour this into the cheesecake mixture, stirring well. Pile the filling into the flan ring and spread it flat with a palette knife. Refrigerate for 2–3 hours or until set.

5 To serve: with a sharp knife, loosen the flan ring from the cheesecake and remove gently, being careful not to knock the edges. Using 2 palette knives, or fish slices, carefully lift or slide the cake on to a serving dish. If this proves difficult, the biscuit base can be loosened by placing the baking sheet over a low heat for 30 seconds. Decorate the edges with rosettes of whipped cream and the reserved apricot halves, each halved again. Sprinkle the almonds over the cream and serve.

NOTE: In the absence of a lipless baking sheet, use the back of a baking tray or roasting pan. The cake is easier to slide off a flat surface.

wine: RICH SWEET WHITE

Bristol Apples

SERVES 4

170 g|6 oz granulated sugar
290 ml|½ pint water
4 dessert apples

2 oranges
oil

1 Make the syrup: place 110 g|4 oz of the sugar and the water in a heavy saucepan and set over a low heat until the sugar dissolves. Once dissolved, boil rapidly for 3 minutes.

2 Peel, quarter and core the apples and place in the sugar syrup. Simmer very gently until just tender (about 20 minutes). Remove the apples and allow them to cool.

3 With a sharp knife or potato peeler, thinly pare the zest from 1 orange, taking care to leave behind the bitter pith. Cut the zest into very fine even-sized needleshreds. Put these into the syrup and boil until a thick syrup.

4 Peel the oranges with a sharp knife as you would an apple, making sure that all the pith is removed. Cut into neat segments, discarding any pips and membrane.

5 Put the remaining sugar into a heavy saucepan and let it dissolve over heat, without stirring.

6 Meanwhile, oil a baking sheet.

7 As the sugar bubbles, it will become a dark-golden colour. Pour this on to the oiled baking sheet and leave it to set into a thin layer like brown glass. When cold, break into chips, and set aside in a cool, dry place.

8 Arrange the apples and oranges in a glass serving bowl, pour over the sugar syrup and chill in the refrigerator. When ready to serve, scatter over the broken caramel chips and the needleshreds.

wine: RICH SWEET WHITE

Raspberry and Almond Malakoff

SERVES 6

170 g | 6 oz caster sugar
170 g | 6 oz unsalted butter
290 ml | ½ pint double cream
170 g | 6 oz ground almonds

3 tablespoons Kirsch
225 g | 8 oz raspberries
1 large packet of boudoir biscuits (sponge fingers)

1 Beat the sugar and butter together until very fluffy, soft and white.
2 Whip the cream and fold with the ground almonds, Kirsch and finally the raspberries into the butter and sugar mixture.
3 Put an oiled circle of greaseproof paper (oiled side up) into the bottom of a 15 cm | 6 in straight-sided cake tin or soufflé dish.
4 Line the sides with the biscuits, standing them up round the edge. Spoon the mixture into the middle, pressing down gently and smoothing the top level.
5 Chill in the refrigerator for 4 hours.
6 With a bread knife, trim the tops of the biscuits to the level of the mixture. Turn the Malakoff out on to a serving plate. Remove the lining paper.

NOTE: The top can be decorated with rosettes of whipped cream and a few fresh raspberries, but the pudding also looks very pretty without further adornment.

wine: SWEET WHITE

Peach Melba

SERVES 4

4 large ripe peaches
290 ml | ½ pint Melba sauce (see page 667)

425 ml | ¾ pint vanilla ice cream
about 30 g | 1 oz flaked almonds, toasted

1 Place the peaches in a saucepan of boiling water for 10 seconds, then remove the skins. Stone the peaches and cut into segments.
2 Flood the base of 4 pudding bowls with the Melba sauce. Arrange a peach attractively on each plate, top with ice cream and scatter over the almonds.

wine: LIGHT SWEET WHITE

Summer Fruit Parcels

SERVES 6

For the fruit purée

¼ melon

4 peaches

2 apricots

150 ml|¼ pint water

a dash of bitter almond essence

2 vanilla pods, split lengthways

For the parcels

2 bananas

1 orange

8 greengages

8 Victoria plums

24 raspberries

1 pear

3 vanilla pods, split lengthways

fresh mint leaves

55 ml|2 fl oz Grand Marnier

1 Preheat the oven to 230°C|450°F|gas mark 8.

2 First make the fruit purée: cube the melon flesh, halve and stone the peaches and apricots and cut the flesh into cubes. Put the fruit into a small saucepan with the water, almond essence and vanilla pods. Cover and simmer for about 10 minutes or until reduced to a light purée. Remove the vanilla pods. Liquidize the purée in a food processor or blender, then sieve it. You should have about 290 ml|½ pint purée.

3 Pre-heat the oven to 190°C|375°|p|gas mark 5.

4 Prepare the remaining fruit: cut the bananas in half lengthways, then cut each piece in half. Peel the orange with a knife as you would an apple, making sure that all the pith is removed, then cut the orange into segments. Halve and stone the greengages and plums. Pick over the raspberries. Peel, core and quarter the pear and cut each quarter into 3 pieces.

5 Cut 6 × 35 cm|14 in squares of kitchen foil. Place 3 tablespoons purée on each square. Arrange the fruit on top. Add half a vanilla pod to each parcel, 2 or 3 mint leaves and a dash of Grand Marnier. Fold up the edges of the foil to form sealed parcels and place on a baking sheet.

6 Bake for 7 minutes. Serve immediately on individual plates.

wine: LIGHT SWEET WHITE

Sweet Fritter Batter

110 g|4 oz plain flour

a pinch of salt

2 eggs

150 ml|¼ pint milk

1 tablespoon oil

55 g|2 oz caster sugar

1 Sift the flour with the salt into a bowl.

2 Make a well in the centre, exposing the bottom of the bowl.

3 Put one whole egg and one yolk into the well and mix with a wooden spoon or whisk until smooth, gradually incorporating the surrounding flour and the milk. The consistency of thick cream should be reached.

4 Add the oil and sugar. Refrigerate for 30 minutes.

5 Whisk the remaining egg white and fold into the batter with a metal spoon just before using.

NOTE: This batter can be made speedily in a blender. Simply put all the ingredients, except the egg white, into the machine and whizz briefly, then fold in the whisked egg whites just before serving.

Banana Fritters

SERVES 6

4 bananas	oil for shallow-frying
150 ml|¼ pint fritter batter (see page 652)	icing sugar to finish

1 Peel the bananas and cut into 5 cm|2 in chunks.

2 Dip immediately into the prepared batter.

3 Heat 5 mm|¼ in of oil in a frying pan and when hot, fry the fritters for about 2 minutes on each side until golden-brown. Drain well and dust with icing sugar.

wine: RICH SWEET WHITE

Chinese Apple Fritters

SERVES 6

450 g|1 lb granulated sugar	85 g|3 oz cornflour
150 ml|¼ pint water	oil for deep-frying
3 dessert apples	2 tablespoons sesame seeds
lemon juice	1 teaspoon white wine vinegar

1 Have ready a bowl of iced water.

2 Place the sugar and water in a heavy pan and set over a low heat to dissolve without boiling. When the sugar has dissolved, boil rapidly until the mixture caramelizes (becomes toffee-brown), then add the vinegar, taking care as the mixture will splutter and sizzle.

3 Meanwhile, toast the sesame seeds in a small, heavy, dry frying pan.

4 Add the sesame seeds and stand the saucepan in a roasting pan of warm water. (This will prevent the caramel from becoming too hard.)

5 Heat the oil in a deep-fryer.

6 Peel, core and quarter the apples. Cut into chunks. Sprinkle with lemon juice and roll in the cornflour.

7 Deep-fry the apples in the hot oil for about 4 minutes until golden-brown. Drain well on absorbent kitchen paper.

8 Turn a few apples at a time in the caramel and sesame seeds.

9 Dip each fritter into cold water to rapidly cool and harden the caramel, then drain and serve immediately.

wine: **FORTIFIED SWEET WHITE**

Melon with Ginger Wine

small melons, such as Ogen   ginger wine

1 Halve the melons, scoop out the seeds and pour 1 tablespoon ginger wine into each.

2 Chill well in the refrigerator before serving.

NOTE: Buy tiny individual melons or slightly bigger ones that can be split between 2 people.

wine: **GINGER WINE**

Pears in Red Wine

SERVES 4

150 ml | ¼ pint water   thinly pared zest of 1 lemon
290 ml | ½ pint red wine   a pinch of ground cinnamon or 1 cinnamon stick
110 g | 4 oz granulated sugar   4 firm pears
1 tablespoon redcurrant jelly

1 Place the water, wine, sugar and jelly in a heavy saucepan and heat gently until the sugar has dissolved. Add the lemon zest and cinnamon.

2 Peel the pears very neatly without removing the stalks. Place upright in the pan and cover with a lid. The pears should be completely covered by the wine and water mixture, so choose a tall, narrow pan. If this is not possible, wet the pears thoroughly with the mixture and turn them during cooking.

3 Bring the mixture to the boil, then simmer slowly for about 40 minutes. The pears should be a deep crimson colour and very tender. The longer and slower the pears cook the better. (They can even be cooked overnight in an extremely low oven.)

4 Remove the pears from the pan and place in a glass serving bowl. Reduce the wine liquid by rapid boiling to a syrupy consistency, then strain it over the pears. Allow to cool, then chill in the refrigerator.

wine: **RICH SWEET WHITE**

Pear Sabayon with Pear Sorbet

SERVES 4

4 Conference pears
570 ml|1 pint sugar syrup (see page 665)
pear sorbet (see page 696)

3 tablespoons caster sugar
55 ml|2 fl oz Poire William liqueur
150 ml|¼ pint double cream, lightly whipped

For the sabayon sauce
4 egg yolks

To decorate
a few sprigs of mint

1 Peel the pears very neatly, without removing the stalks. Place upright in a pan with the sugar syrup, which should completely cover the pears. Choose a tall, narrow pan. If this is not possible, wet the pears thoroughly in the syrup and turn them during cooking.
2 Cover the pan and bring to the boil, then simmer slowly for about 40 minutes, until the pears are glassy and very tender. Remove from the syrup, allow to cool and then refrigerate until cold.
3 While the pears are poaching, prepare the sabayon sauce: put the egg yolks, 1 tablespoon Poire William and sugar into a heatproof bowl set over, not in, a saucepan of simmering water. Whisk for at least 10 minutes until thick and creamy. Remove from the heat and continue to whisk until cool. Add the liqueur and cream. Chill in the refrigerator.
4 To serve: flood the base of 4 pudding plates with the sabayon sauce. Slice the pears in such a way that they can be rearranged on the sabayon as a whole, fanned-out pear. Place a large scoop of pear sorbet on each plate and decorate with a sprig of mint.

wine: **SWEET WHITE**

Raspberries and Fromage Blanc with Fresh Figs

This is a low-fat, sugar-free pudding.

SERVES 4

225 g|8 oz fresh raspberries
concentrated apple juice (optional)
4 tablespoons low-fat fromage blanc
4 ripe figs, cut into quarters

To decorate
sprigs of fresh mint

1 Liquidize the raspberries in a food processor or blender with enough water to make a smooth purée. Taste and add a little apple juice to sweeten, if required. Strain and pour on to one side of 4 pudding plates.
2 Mix the fromage blanc with a little water and pour on to the other half of the pudding plates.
3 Marble the fromage blanc and raspberry purée together with a large fork and arrange the figs on top of the sauces. Decorate with the sprigs of mint.

wine: **LIGHT SWEET WHITE**

Raspberry Plate

SERVES 4

225 g | 8 oz cooked blackcurrants

140 g | 5 oz icing sugar

4 tablespoons crème de cassis liqueur

150 ml | ¼ pint double cream

450 g | 1 lb fresh fruit, such as raspberries, figs, blackberries, blueberries

To decorate

sprigs of fresh mint

1 Liquidize the blackcurrants, icing sugar and cassis in a food processor or blender. Strain.
2 Pour this sauce on to one side of 4 pudding plates and pour the cream on the other side. Squiggle with a fork where they join to marble slightly.
3 Pile fresh raspberries or a mixture of sliced figs, blackberries and blueberries in the centre of each plate and top each with a sprig of mint.

wine: LIGHT, SWEET WHITE

Creamed Cheese with Fresh Fruit

This dessert is simple to prepare and particularly suitable for a buffet party.

SERVES 4–6

225 g | 8 oz cottage cheese

290 ml | ½ pint double cream, lightly whipped

55 g | 2 oz icing sugar, sifted

2 drops of vanilla essence

squeeze of lemon juice

3 figs, quartered

3 kiwi fruits, peeled and sliced

4 oranges, peeled and sliced

1 Put the cottage cheese into a sieve and drain very well. Discard the liquid.
2 Push the cheese through the sieve (or process briefly in a food processor or blender) and fold in the cream. Sweeten with the icing sugar and flavour with the vanilla essence and lemon juice.
3 Pile the mixture on to a large oval serving dish and shape into a shallow mound. Arrange the fruit attractively on top of the cheese.

wine: LIGHT SWEET WHITE

Summer Pudding

SERVES 4–6

900 g | 2 lb mixed redcurrants, blackcurrants,
    blackberries, raspberries and strawberries, or a
    mixture of just some of these
150 ml | ¼ pint water

170 g | 6 oz caster sugar
6–9 slices of stale white bread, crusts removed

To serve
290 ml | ½ pint double cream, lightly whipped

1 Cook the redcurrants, blackcurrants and blackberries with the water and sugar in a saucepan for 5 minutes, or until just soft but still bright in colour. Add the raspberries and strawberries. Place the fruit in a sieve over a bowl to catch the juice.

2 Dip slices of the bread into the reserved fruit juice and use to line a pudding basin.

3 While the fruit is still just warm, spoon it into the bread-lined basin. Cover with a round piece of bread dipped in the fruit juice. Tip the remaining juice into a saucepan and reduce, by boiling rapidly, to a syrupy consistency. Leave to cool.

4 Stand the pudding basin on a dish. Press a saucer or plate on top of the pudding and put a 450 g | 1 lb weight on top. Leave in a cool place overnight. Remove the saucer and weight.

5 Invert a serving dish over the bowl and turn both over together. Give a sharp shake and remove the bowl. Spoon over the reserved fruit juice. Serve the cream separately.

wine: SWEET WHITE

Pashka

A rich, creamy cheese mixture, this is traditionally moulded in a tall wooden container, like a cut-off metronome. You can use a tall flowerpot or plastic pot instead. Whatever container you use, make sure it has a hole in the bottom for draining.

SERVES 8

125 ml | 4 fl oz double cream
10 cm | 4 in piece of vanilla pod, split lengthways
2 large egg yolks
85 g | 3 oz caster sugar
110 g | 4 oz unsalted butter, creamed
675 g | 1½ lb curd cheese or ricotta cheese

55–85 g | 2–3 oz candied fruit and peel, chopped
55–85 g | 2–3 oz blanched almonds, chopped

To decorate
blanched almonds
candied fruit and peel
glacé fruits or raisins

1 Bring the cream, with the vanilla pod, to the boil in a small saucepan.

2 Beat the egg yolks with the sugar until creamy, then whisk in the hot cream.

3 Return the pan to the heat and cook, without boiling, until thick. Sieve into a bowl and remove the vanilla pod. Allow the custard to cool. Mix it with the remaining ingredients.

4 Spoon the mixture into your chosen mould, lined with muslin – this helps you to turn it out, and gives a good surface pattern to the cream cheese.

5 Chill in the refrigerator for at least 10 hours or up to 3 days. Stand the pot in a dish so that the whey can drain (some may ooze out, depending on the type of cheese that is used). Turn out and decorate. Serve with Kulich (see page 768), or any brioche (see page 761).

NOTE: Chopped chocolate is a delicious addition to pashka.

wine: **FORTIFIED SWEET WHITE**

Trifle

SERVES 6

1 Victoria sandwich cake (see page 703), preferably stale	5 egg yolks
very good-quality raspberry jam	2 tablespoons caster sugar
4 tablespoons sherry	2 drops of vanilla essence
2 tablespoons brandy	290 ml | ½ pint double cream
290 ml | ½ pint milk	30 g | 1 oz split blanched almonds, toasted
	a few ratafia biscuits (optional)

1 Cut the sponge cake into thick pieces. Sandwich the pieces together sparingly with jam. Pile them into a large glass serving dish.

2 Pour over the sherry and brandy and leave to soak while you prepare the custard.

3 Put the milk into a saucepan and scald by bringing to just below boiling point.

4 In a large bowl, lightly beat the yolks and sugar with a wooden spoon. Pour the scalding milk on to them, stirring.

5 Return the mixture to the rinsed-out pan and heat carefully, stirring all the time, until the mixture is thick enough to coat the back of the spoon. Care must be taken not to boil the custard, or it will curdle. Add the vanilla essence.

6 Strain on to the cake and leave to get completely cold.

7 Whip the cream until fairly stiff and spread or pipe over the trifle.

8 Decorate with the almonds and the ratafia biscuits, if using.

wine: **SWEET SPARKLING**

Zuccotto

SERVES 8

2 Madeira cakes (see page 704)

3 tablespoons brandy

2 tablespoons Maraschino

2 tablespoons Cointreau

170 g | 6 oz plain chocolate

55 g | 2 oz split almonds, roasted

55 g | 2 oz hazelnuts, roasted and skinned

110 g | 4 oz icing sugar

290 ml | ½ pint double cream, whipped

290 ml | ½ pint mocha custard (see page 664)

1 Line a 1.5 litre | 2½ pint round-bottomed pudding basin with damp muslin or a clean damp 'J'-cloth.

2 Cut the Madeira cakes into slices 9 mm | ¾ in thick. Mix the brandy, Maraschino and Cointreau together and use to moisten each slice of cake. Line the pudding bowl as neatly as possible with these slices. Reserve 2 slices for the top.

3 Chop the chocolate into tiny, even-sized pieces. Mix half the chocolate with the nuts. Fold the sugar into the cream. Mix the chocolate and nuts with half the sweetened cream. Pile into the pudding basin and spread evenly over the sliced Madeira cake.

4 Melt the remaining chocolate in a bowl over steaming water and mix with the remaining cream. Pile into the pudding basin and spread flat.

5 Cover the chocolate filling with the remaining slices of Madeira cake. Cover and refrigerate overnight.

6 The next day turn the zuccotto out on to a serving dish and coat with the cold mocha custard. Serve the remaining custard in a sauceboat.

wine: **FORTIFIED SWEET WHITE**

Nice Biscuit Refrigerator Cake

SERVES 4

200 ml | 7 fl oz double cream

3 tablespoons milk

2 tablespoons sweet sherry

15 Nice or 'morning coffee' biscuits

225 g | 8 oz canned sweetened chestnut purée

110 g | 4 oz plain chocolate

30 g | 1 oz butter

a few walnut halves

1 Whip the cream until thick.

2 Mix the milk and sherry together.

3 Soak 3 biscuits in the milk and sherry and place them side by side on a serving dish.

4 Spread half the cream over this.

5 Soak the next 3 biscuits and place them on top of the cream.

6 Spread this with half the chestnut purée.

7 Repeat these 2 layers.

8 Top with 3 biscuits.
   9 Place the chocolate in a heavy saucepan with 2 tablespoons water and heat gently until smooth and thick. Beat in the butter.
   10 Pour over the biscuits and, when nearly set, decorate with the walnuts. Refrigerate.

wine: LIQUEUR MUSCAT

Atholl Brose

The Duke of Atholl's original recipe for Atholl Brose involved steeping oatmeal in boiling water and then draining off the milky liquid and mixing it with whisky and heather honey to make a warming drink. This recipe for a pudding has been adapted from the original.

SERVES 4–6

55 g | 2 oz medium oatmeal
290 ml | ½ pint double cream

2 tablespoons clear honey, or more to taste
85 ml | 3 fl oz whisky

1 Toast the oatmeal under the grill and allow to cool.
2 Whip the cream until it just holds its shape and stir in the toasted oatmeal and the honey. Add the whisky and transfer to a glass serving dish.
3 Cover and chill in the refrigerator for at least 1 hour before serving.

NOTE: This also freezes well. Because of the amount of alcohol it remains soft but it is very powerful and goes well with mince pies or Christmas pudding instead of brandy butter.

Carrot Halva

This recipe for a typical Indian pudding has been adapted from one by Madhur Jaffrey.

SERVES 6

450 g | 1 lb carrots, peeled and finely grated
6 cardamom pods
720 ml | 1¼ pints milk

85 g | 3 oz clarified butter or ghee (see page 385)
140 g | 5 oz caster sugar
55 g | 2 oz unsalted pistachio nuts, skinned and chopped

1 Put the carrots, cardamom pods and milk into a pan. Bring to the boil, then simmer for 1–1½ hours, or until most of the liquid has evaporated. Remove the cardamom pods.
2 Melt the butter in another saucepan. Stir the carrot mixture into the melted butter and cook for 5–7 minutes. Add the sugar and nuts. Cook for a further 5 minutes.
3 Pile the mixture into a serving dish and serve at room temperature.

wine: FORTIFIED SWEET WHITE

Tiramisù

SERVES 8

6 egg yolks

scant 150 ml | ¼ pint Marsala

5 tablespoons dry white wine

85 g | 3 oz icing sugar, or more to taste

500 g | 1 lb 2 oz Mascarpone or cream cheese

10 amaretti biscuits

24 Savoy biscuits ('ladies' fingers')

5 tablespoons strong black coffee

unsweetened cocoa powder, for sprinkling

1 Mix the egg yolks, half the Marsala, the white wine, icing sugar and Mascarpone together to make a cream.

2 Dip the biscuits in the remaining Marsala mixed with the coffee (once again, leave out the Marsala if so desired), taking care not to make the biscuits so soggy that they break. Line a dish about 25 cm | 10 in square with a layer of biscuits and a layer of the cream.

3 Repeat, until all the ingredients have been used, ending with a layer of cream. Sprinkle a thin layer of cocoa powder on top and refrigerate for a few hours before serving.

wine: **RICH SWEET WHITE**

Chocolate Biscuit Cake

SERVES 4

85 g | 3 oz plain chocolate

85 g | 3 oz butter

45 g | 1½ oz caster sugar

4 tablespoons golden syrup

340 g | 12 oz plain biscuits, crushed

85 g | 3 oz glacé cherries

85 g | 3 oz flaked almonds

1 Chop the chocolate and melt it slowly with the butter, sugar and syrup in a heavy saucepan, stirring all the time.

2 Add the crushed biscuits, cherries and almonds.

3 Grease a sheet of greaseproof paper and the inside of a 20 cm | 8 in flan ring.

4 Press the mixture on to the paper and flatten it, using the flan ring to get a round shape.

5 Allow to cool until set hard.

6 Cut into small wedges.

wine: **LIQUEUR MUSCAT**

French Toast with Apples

SERVES 4

For the soaking liquid

30 ml | 1 fl oz single cream

2 eggs

2 tablespoons cognac

45 g | 1½ oz caster sugar

For the vanilla Crème Anglaise

290ml | ½ pint milk

3 vanilla pod, split lengthways

3 egg yolks

45 g | 1½ oz caster sugar

For the French toast

8 slices of baguette, 2.5 cm | 1 in thick

55 g | 2 oz unsalted butter

2 cooking apples, peeled, quartered, cored and each
   quarter cut into 3

For the butterscotch sauce

150 g | 4 oz caster sugar

4 tablespoons water

150 ml | ¼ pint double cream

30g | 1 oz unsalted butter

1 Whisk together the cream, eggs, cognac and sugar. Strain into a shallow dish. Add the baguette slices and set aside.

2 Make the Crème Anglaise: scald the milk with the vanilla pod by bringing it to just below boiling point.

3 Beat the egg yolks and sugar together, pour in the milk and mix well. Return to the rinsed out pan and stir over a low heat with a wooden spoon, until the custard is thick enough to coat the back of the spoon. Do not allow to boil. Strain into a bowl and cover closely with a disc of greaseproof paper to prevent a skin from forming.

4 Make the butterscotch sauce: put the sugar and water into a heavy saucepan over a medium heat. Allow the sugar to dissolve completely, then bring to the boil. Cook to a golden-brown and remove from the heat. Immediately add the cream and return to the heat. Stir to dissolve any lumps of sugar. Add the butter.

5 Put the apple pieces in the butterscotch sauce and cook very gently until they are soft. Take great care as cooking apples fall apart very easily. Set them aside.

6 Drain the baguette slices. Heat the butter in a frying pan. Cook the slices on both sides until golden-brown.

7 To assemble: ladle the vanilla crème anglaise on to 4 pudding plates. Set a slice of toast on each plate and arrange the apples on top. Strain over the caramel sauce and serve.

Sweet Sauces

Crème Chantilly

150 ml | ¼ pint double cream
1 teaspoon icing sugar

2 drops vanilla essence

1 Put all the ingredients into a chilled bowl and whisk with a balloon whisk, steadily but not too fast, for about 2 minutes or until the cream has thickened and doubled in volume.
2 Whisk faster for 30–40 seconds until the mixture is very fluffy and will form soft peaks.

NOTE: Chilling the ingredients and the bowl gives a lighter, whiter result.

Crème Pâtissière

290 ml | ½ pint milk
2 egg yolks
55 g | 2 oz caster sugar
20 g | ¾ oz plain flour

20 g | ¾ oz cornflour
vanilla essence
150 ml | ¼ pint double cream

1 Scald the milk by bringing it to just below boiling point in a saucepan.
2 Cream the egg yolks with the sugar and a little of the milk and when pale, mix in the flours. Pour on the milk and mix well.
3 Return the mixture to the pan and bring slowly to the boil, stirring continuously. (It will go alarmingly lumpy, but don't worry, keep stirring vigorously and it will become smooth.) Allow to cool slightly, then add the vanilla essence.
4 Cover with greaseproof paper to prevent a skin from forming. Refrigerate.
5 Place the Crème Patissière in a food processor and whizz until smooth. Turn into a bowl.
6 Whip the cream to the soft peak stage then fold into the crème pâtissière.

Crème Anglaise (English Egg Custard)

290 ml | ½ pint milk
1 vanilla pod or a few drops of vanilla essence

2 large egg yolks
1–2 tablespoons caster sugar

1 Heat the milk and vanilla pod, if using, and bring slowly to the boil. Leave to infuse for 10 minutes. Remove the vanilla pod.

2 Beat the yolks in a bowl with the sugar. Pour the milk on to the egg yolks, stirring steadily. Mix well and return to the pan.

3 Stir over a low heat until the mixture thickens sufficiently to coat the back of a spoon (about 5 minutes). Do not boil.

4 Strain into a bowl, place a piece of greaseproof paper directly on the surface to prevent a skin from forming. Allow to cool.

5 Add the vanilla essence, if using.

Orange Crème Anglaise

290 ml | ½ pint milk

finely grated zest of 1 small orange

1 vanilla pod

2 tablespoons caster sugar

2 egg yolks

1 tablespoon Grand Marnier

1 drop of orange essence

1 Heat the milk with the orange zest and vanilla pod and bring slowly to the boil.

2 Beat the sugar with the egg yolks until pale. Pour the milk on to the egg yolks, stirring steadily. Remove the vanilla pod.

3 Return the milk to the pan and cook over a low heat, stirring well until the custard will coat the back of a spoon (about 5 minutes).

4 Strain into a cold bowl and add the Grand Marnier and orange essence. Allow to cool before using.

Mocha Custard

290 ml | ½ pint milk

8 coffee beans

55 g | 2 oz plain chocolate

2 egg yolks

15 g | ½ oz caster sugar

1 Put the milk into a small saucepan with the coffee beans. Place over a low heat and bring to the boil. Turn off the heat and leave to infuse for 10 minutes.

2 Break the chocolate into small, even-sized pieces and add to the warm milk. Allow to melt completely.

3 Whisk the egg yolks with the sugar until pale and creamy.

4 Strain the milk to remove the coffee beans. Add the milk to the egg-yolk mixture.

5 Pour this mixture into a rinsed-out saucepan and place over a medium heat, stirring until the mixture thickens so that it will coat the back of a spoon (3–4 minutes), but do not boil. Strain into a bowl.

Sugar Syrup

285 g | 10 oz granulated sugar
570 ml | 1 pint water

thinly pared zest of 1 lemon

1 Put the sugar, water and lemon zest into a saucepan and heat slowly until the sugar has completely dissolved.
2 Bring to the boil and cook to the required consistency (see below). Allow to cool.
3 Strain. Keep covered in a cool place until needed.

NOTE: Sugar syrup will keep unrefrigerated for about 5 days, and for several weeks if kept chilled.

Caramel Sauce

225 g | 8 oz granulated sugar

290 ml | ½ pint water

1 Place the sugar in a heavy saucepan with half the water.
2 Dissolve the sugar slowly without stirring it or allowing the water to boil.
3 Once all the sugar has dissolved, turn up the heat and boil until it is a good caramel colour.
4 Immediately tip in the remaining water (it will fizz dangerously, so stand back).
5 Stir until any lumps have dissolved, then remove from the heat and allow to cool.

Stages in Sugar Syrup Concentration

Type of Sugar Syrup	Boiling Point	Uses
Vaseline	107°C	225°F	Syrup and sorbets
Short thread	108°C	227°F	Syrup and sorbet
Long thread	110°C	230°F	Syrup
Soft ball	115°C	239°F	Fondant, fudge
Firm ball	120°C	248°F	Italian meringue, mousse-based ice creams
Hard ball	124°C	255°F	Marshmallows
Soft crack	138°C	280°F	Soft toffee
Hard crack	155°C	310°F	Hard toffee and some nougat
	160°C	320°F	Nougat
Spun sugar	152°C	305°F	Spun sugar
Caramel	194°C	382°F	Sauces and flavourings

Toffee Sauce

2 tablespoons brandy
110 g | 4 oz butter

55 g | 2 oz demerara sugar
2 tablespoons double cream

1 Place all the ingredients in a saucepan and heat until melted. Bring to the boil and allow to thicken slightly.

Apricot Sauce

170 g | 6 oz dried apricots, soaked overnight

570 ml | 1 pint water

1 Drain the dried apricots and put them into a saucepan with the water. Bring to the boil, then simmer until tender.
2 Liquidize in a blender, then push through a sieve. If the sauce is too thin, reduce it by rapid boiling to the required consistency. If it is too thick, add a little water.

Fresh Apricot Sauce

85 g | 3 oz granulated sugar
290 ml | ½ pint water

225 g | 8 oz apricots, halved
juice of ½ lemon

1 Dissolve the sugar in the water in a heavy saucepan over a low heat. Do not allow to boil until the sugar has completely dissolved (this will prevent the syrup from crystallizing).
2 Add the apricots to the pan with the stones and lemon juice.
3 Bring to the boil and cook until the apricots are soft (about 15 minutes).
4 Remove and reserve the stones.
5 Boil the apricots rapidly for a further 5–10 minutes, or until the pulp is reduced to a syrupy consistency. Push the apricot sauce through a nylon or stainless steel sieve. Taste and add extra sugar if necessary.

Hot Chocolate Sauce

170 g | 6 oz plain chocolate, chopped
4 tablespoons water
1 tablespoon golden syrup

1 teaspoon instant coffee powder, dissolved in 1 tablespoon boiling water
15 g | ½ oz butter

1 Put the chocolate into a heatproof bowl set over, not in, a saucepan of simmering water. When melted, add all the remaining ingredients and stir until smooth and shiny.

Apple Marmalade

3 cooking apples
a little butter

a strip of thinly pared lemon zest
about 85 g | 3 oz soft light brown sugar

1 Wash the unpeeled apples, quarter and core them. Rub the bottom and sides of a heavy saucepan with butter.
2 Slice the apples thickly into the pan and add the lemon zest. Cover and cook over a low heat, stirring occasionally, until completely soft.
3 Push through a sieve. Rinse out the pan and return the purée to it. Add at least 55 g | 2 oz sugar to 570 ml | 1 pint purée. Cook rapidly until the mixture is of dropping consistency (about 4 minutes). Allow to cool. Add more sugar if necessary.

Brandy Butter

Cream equal quantities of softened unsalted butter and caster sugar together until very light. Add finely grated orange zest and brandy to flavour fairly strongly.

Melba Sauce

225 g | 8 oz fresh or frozen (not canned)
    raspberries

icing sugar

1 Defrost the raspberries if frozen.
2 Place in a small saucepan. If using fresh raspberries add 2 tablespoons water. Bring to the boil. Push them through a nylon or stainless sieve to remove all the seeds.
3 Sift in icing sugar to taste. If too thick, add a few additional spoonfuls of water.

Raspberry Coulis

This coulis is made with sugar syrup.

250 g | 9 oz fresh or defrosted frozen raspberries
55 g | 2 oz granulated sugar

5 tablespoons water
lemon juice, to taste

1 Place the raspberries in the bowl of a food processor.
2 Place the sugar and water in a small pan over a medium heat until dissolved, then bring to the boil.
3 Boil the syrup for 2 minutes and pour over the raspberries.
4 Purée the raspberries in the machine, then pass them through a fine sieve to remove the seeds.
5 Adjust the seasoning with lemon juice or additional sugar, if required.

Any soft fruit is suitable for making a coulis. Water, fruit juice, or sugar syrup can be used to thin the sauce.

Sweet Gooseberry Sauce

225 g | 8 oz ripe gooseberries   110 g | 4 oz caster sugar
150 ml | ¼ pint water   a pinch of ground ginger

1 Put all the ingredients into a heavy saucepan. Bring gradually to the boil, then simmer until the gooseberries pop open and change to a yellowish colour.
2 Push through a nylon sieve and reheat.

Mango and Passionfruit Sauce

2 ripe passionfruits   3 tablespoons fresh orange juice
1 large ripe mango

1 Purée (but do not liquidize) the passionfruit pulp, mango flesh and orange juice together for 2 minutes in a food processor. Sieve.

Meringues

Meringues have been made since at least 1700. Some cookery historians believe that they were invented by a Swiss pastry cook called Gasperlini, who practised his art in the small town of Meringen.

There are 3 main types of meringue: Italian (see page 677); cuite, or cooked (see page 678); Swiss (see page 670). Meringues are not that easy to make, as it is possible to whisk the albumen in the egg white either too much or too little, with resulting poor volume, premature collapse, and in the case of overwhisking, some curdling.

Whisking Egg Whites

The points below should be followed when whisking egg whites
- An electric mixer, hand-held electric beater or balloon whisk may be used.
- Both bowl and whisk (ideally balloon) must be scrupulously clean, dry and free from grease.
- Do not use a plastic bowl as plastic tends to retain traces of fatty material on the surface.
- When the egg yolks are separated from the whites, try to avoid any specks of yolk in the whites: the fat in the yolk can reduce the whisked volume.
- When making Swiss meringues, once the whites are stiff, gradually whisk in half the total sugar quantity, whisking until very shiny, then fold in the remainder. If using a hand-held electric beater, once the whites are stiff whisk in half the sugar a tablespoon at a time, then fold in the remainder.
- When egg whites are whisked by hand with a balloon whisk in a clean copper bowl (see note) a chemical reaction takes place between the egg whites and the copper. This stabilizes the egg whites and they hold for several minutes without separating. Egg whites whisked in a copper bowl also give a greater volume. The foam is easy to fold into soufflé bases and makes for excellent meringues. It is difficult to overwhisk whites in a copper bowl.
- Acid, usually in the form of cream of tartar, is sometimes added to stabilize the foam. Although it has no effect on the volume of foam produced, it makes it less prone to overwhisking and resulting lumpiness, draining and collapse. Only a minute amount of acid is necessary to make a significant difference – about $1/16$ teaspoon per egg white.

NOTE: A copper bowl must be cleaned before use. Rub the inside with half a lemon dipped in a generous quantity of salt. Wipe thoroughly and use immediately. The clean bowl is essential; once the copper becomes oxidized the chemical reaction between the egg whites and copper bowl is weakened. The acid in the lemon also helps to increase the volume of egg white.

Cooking Meringues

Paper for cooking meringues: The best is silicone-coated, non-stick baking parchment. Meringues may be left to cool completely on it and can then be easily removed without sticking or breaking.

Hard meringues are baked at 110°C|225°F|gas mark ½ for an hour or two, or put into a hot oven with the heat turned off, and allowed to dry for several hours.

Soft meringues are typically baked at 180°C|350°F|gas mark 4 for 15 minutes. This browns the surface but leaves the centre moist and chewy.

Meringues (Swiss Meringues)

This quantity makes 50 miniature or 12 large meringues.

4 egg whites
225 g|8 oz caster sugar

For the filling
570 ml|1 pint double cream, whipped

1 Preheat the oven to 110°C|225°F|gas mark ½.
2 Line 2 baking sheets with non-stick baking parchment.
3 Whisk in the egg whites until stiff but not dry.
4 Whisk in half of the sugar gradually until very stiff and shiny.
5 Fold in the remaining sugar with a large metal spoon.
6 Drop the meringue mixture on to the lined baking sheets in spoonfuls set fairly far apart. Use a teaspoon for tiny meringues; a dessertspoon for larger ones.
7 Bake for about 1½ – 2 hours until the meringues are dry right through and will lift easily off the paper.
8 When cold, sandwich the meringues together in pairs with whipped cream.

NOTE: See 'Whisking Egg Whites', page 669.

Meringue Baskets

MAKES 4
2 egg whites
110 g|4 oz caster sugar

For the filling
150 ml|¼ pint double cream, lightly whipped
250 g|9 oz strawberries or raspberries

1 Preheat the oven to 110°C|225°F|gas mark ½. Line 2 baking sheets with non-stick baking parchment.
2 Whisk the egg whites to stiff peaks. Gradually whisk in half of the sugar until the mixture is stiff and shiny. Fold in the remaining sugar with a large metal spoon.

3 Put the mixture into a piping bag fitted with a star nozzle and pipe on to the lined baking sheets to form little baskets.

4 Place in the oven to dry out for 2 hours. Remove from the oven, and allow to cool on a wire rack.

5 Place a little cream in each basket and fill with strawberries or raspberries.

NOTE: Meringue baskets are also often made with meringue cuite (see page 678), which is very solid and does not rise out of shape in the oven.

Pavlova

SERVES 6–8

4 egg whites
225 g | 8 oz caster sugar
1 teaspoon cornflour
1 teaspoon vanilla essence

1 teaspoon white wine vinegar or lemon juice
290 ml | ½ pint double cream, lightly whipped
450 g | 1 lb soft fruits

1 Preheat the oven to 140°C | 275°F | gas mark 1.

2 Line a baking sheet with non-stick baking parchment.

3 Whisk the egg whites until stiff. Gradually add half of the sugar, then fold in the remainder with a large metal spoon.

4 Fold in the cornflour, vanilla and vinegar or lemon juice.

5 Pile half of the mixture on to the prepared baking sheet, shaping to a 20 cm | 8 in circle. Pile the remaining meringue around the edges to form walls. Bake for about 1 hour. The meringue is cooked when the outer shell is pale biscuit-coloured and hard to the touch. Remove from the oven and leave to cool completely on a wire rack.

6 When cold, place on a serving dish, layer the whipped cream and fruit in the centre.

NOTE: See 'Whisking Egg Whites', page 669.

wine: **SWEET WHITE**

Banana and Grape Vacherin

SERVES 6

4 egg whites
225 g | 8 oz caster sugar
1 banana
lemon juice

85 g | 3 oz black grapes
85 g | 3 oz green grapes
290 ml | ½ pint double cream, lightly whipped

1 Preheat the oven to 110°C | 225°F | gas mark ½. Line 2 baking sheets with non-stick baking parchment. Trace a 20 cm | 8 in circle on the underside of each piece of paper.

2 Whisk the egg whites until stiff but not dry, then gradually whisk in half of the sugar until very stiff and shiny. Fold in the remaining sugar with a large metal spoon.

3 Fill a piping bag fitted with a medium plain nozzle with the meringue. Pipe into a round on each prepared baking sheet.

4 Place in the oven to dry out for 2 hours. The meringue is ready when light and dry and the paper will peel off the underside easily.

5 Cut the banana into chunks and toss in the lemon juice. Halve and deseed the grapes.

6 Spread three-quarters of the cream over one of the meringue bases and scatter over the banana and all but 4 each of the black and green grapes. Place the second meringue on top of this. Using the remaining cream, pipe rosettes around the top. Decorate the rosettes alternately with the grape halves.

NOTE: See 'Whisking Egg Whites', page 669.

wine: SWEET WHITE

Walnut and Lemon Meringue Cake

SERVES 6

4 egg whites
225 g | 8 oz caster sugar
140 g | 5 oz walnuts, roughly chopped

290 ml | ½ pint double cream
4 tablespoons lemon curd (see page 799)
2 tablespoons icing sugar

1 Preheat the oven to 190°C | 375°F | gas mark 5.

2 Line 2 × 20 cm | 8 in cake tins with lightly oiled kitchen foil or simply line the base with non-stick baking parchment and oil the sides of the tin.

3 Whisk the egg whites until stiff, then gradually whisk in half of the sugar. Whisk again until very stiff and shiny.

4 Fold the remaining sugar with the walnuts. Then fold into the meringue.

5 Divide the mixture between the 2 tins, smoothing the tops slightly.

6 Bake for 40 minutes. Turn the cakes out on to a wire rack, peel off the lining paper and leave to cool completely.

7 Whip the cream and mix with the lemon curd. Sandwich the cakes with this mixture.

8 Sift the icing sugar over the top to decorate.

NOTE: See 'Whisking Egg Whites', page 669.

wine: SWEET WHITE

Hazelnut Meringue Cake with Raspberry Sauce

SERVES 6

110 g | 4 oz hazelnuts

225 g | 8 oz caster sugar

4 egg whites

a drop of vanilla essence

½ teaspoon white wine vinegar

225 g | 8 oz raspberries

icing sugar, sifted

a squeeze of lemon juice

290 ml | ½ pint double cream

1 Preheat the oven to 190°C | 375°F | gas mark 5. Line 2 × 20 cm | 8 in cake tins with lightly oiled kitchen foil.

2 Place the hazelnuts on a baking sheet and roast in the oven until brown. Remove the skins by rubbing the nuts in a tea-towel. Leave to get completely cold. Set aside 6 nuts and grind the remainder with 1 tablespoon of the caster sugar. Do not overgrind or they will become greasy and make the meringue heavy. Add half the remaining caster sugar.

3 Whisk the egg whites until stiff, then gradually whisk in the remaining caster sugar a tablespoon at a time, with the vanilla and vinegar, whisking until very stiff. Fold in the nuts and sugar very gently with a large metal spoon. Pile the mixture into the prepared tins, spreading evenly with a spatula.

4 Bake in the oven for 40 minutes. Remove from the oven and allow to cool for 5 minutes. Lift out the meringues in the foil, then carefully peel away the foil. Leave the meringues to cool completely on a wire rack.

5 Meanwhile, liquidize the raspberries in a blender with icing sugar and lemon juice to taste. Push through a nylon sieve and taste for sweetness. If very thick, add a little water.

6 To decorate: whip the cream and sandwich two meringues together with two-thirds of it. Dust the top with icing sugar. Pipe 6 large rosettes of cream round the edge of the top of the meringue and decorate each rosette with a reserved hazelnut. Serve the raspberry sauce separately.

NOTE: See 'Whisking Egg Whites', page 669.

wine: RICH SWEET WHITE

Meringue Mont Blanc

SERVES 6

For the meringue

3 egg whites

170 g | 6 oz caster sugar

icing sugar, sifted

For the filling

1 × 440 g | 15 oz can of sweetened chestnut purée

150 ml | ¼ pint double cream, lightly whipped

To decorate

chocolate caraque (see page 715) or coarsely grated chocolate

1 Preheat the oven to 110°C | 225°F | gas mark ½. Line a baking sheet with non-stick baking parchment.

2 Whisk the egg whites until stiff but not dry. Gradually add half of the caster sugar and whisk again until very stiff and shiny. Fold in the remaining sugar.

3 Place the meringue in a piping bag with a fitted 1 cm | ½ in plain nozzle. Pipe the mixture into an 18 cm | 7 in circle on the prepared baking sheet, starting from the centre and spiralling outwards. Pipe a rim 3 cm | 1½ in deep. Dust lightly with icing sugar.

4 Bake in the oven for 2 hours, until the meringue is dry and crisp. When cooked, remove from the oven, and leave to cool completely on a wire rack. Carefully peel off the lining paper.

5 Beat the chestnut purée until soft. Pile into the meringue case, cover with the cream and sprinkle the chocolate on top.

NOTE: See 'Whisking Egg Whites', page 669.

wine: **SWEET SPARKLING WHITE**

Almond Dacquoise with Apricot Purée

This meringue is best made using an electric whisk.

SERVES 6

5 egg whites

a large pinch of cream of tartar

285 g | 10 oz caster sugar

110 g | 4 oz ground almonds

290 ml | ½ pint double cream

For the purée

225 g | 8 oz fresh apricots, halved and stoned

2 tablespoons caster sugar

1 Preheat the oven to 140°C | 275°F | gas mark 1.

2 Line 2 baking sheets with non-stick baking parchment and mark a 22.5 cm | 9 in diameter circle on each. Turn the paper over.

3 Whisk the egg whites with the cream of tartar until stiff, then whisk in half of the sugar, a tablespoonful at a time. Continue to whisk until very stiff and shiny.

4 Fold in the remaining sugar with the ground almonds and fold into the meringue.

5 Divide the mixture between the 2 baking sheets and spread the meringue evenly all over the marked circles.

6 Bake in the oven for 1 hour. Remove from the oven and cool slightly, then remove the lining paper and leave to become completely cold.

7 While the meringues are baking, make the apricot purée. Put the apricots into a saucepan with 2 tablespoons sugar and enough water to come halfway up the apricots. Cook over a low heat, stirring occasionally, until the apricots are tender.

8 Cut 4 apricots in half and reserve for the garnish. Process the poached apricots in a blender or food processor with enough of the liquid to make a thick purée. Taste and add extra sugar if required. Cool.

9 Whip the cream. Sandwich the cake together with half the cream mixed with the apricot purée. Decorate the top of the dacquoise with rosettes of cream and the reserved apricots.

NOTE: See 'Whisking Egg Whites', page 669.

wine: **SWEET WHITE**

Galette au Chocolat Cordon Bleu

SERVES 6

5 egg whites
285 g | 10 oz caster sugar
45 g | 1½ cocoa powder

For the filling

1   400 g | 14 oz can of pitted black cherries
3 tablespoons of Kirsch
110 g | 4 oz plain chocolate
70 ml | 2½ fl oz water
570 ml | 1 pint double cream

To decorate

icing sugar to dust
150 ml | ¼ pint double cream
chocolate caraque (see page 715)

For the cherry sauce

the cherries not used in the cake
1 teaspoon arrowroot
the drained cherry juice

1 Preheat the oven to 140°C | 275°F | gas mark 1. Line 3 baking sheets with non-stick baking parchment and mark a 18 cm | 7 in circle on each.

2 Whisk the egg whites until stiff, gradually whisk in half of the caster sugar and continue whisking for about 30 seconds. Sift the cocoa with the remaining sugar and quickly fold into the whites. Spread or pipe the mixture into 3 rounds on the baking parchment. Bake for 1–1¼ hours, or until dry and crisp. Remove from the oven and cool completely, then remove the lining paper.

3 Drain the cherries, reserving the juice, and leave to macerate in the Kirsch.

4 Break the chocolate into small pieces, put into a heavy pan with the water and stir continuously over a low heat until melted. Remove from the heat and allow to cool slightly.

5 Start whisking the cream and, as it thickens, add the chocolate, and then continue whisking until the cream holds its shape.

6 Sandwich the meringue rounds together with chocolate cream, each topped with a quarter of the cherries. Dust the top with icing sugar. Decorate with rosettes of plain cream and chocolate caraque.

7 Make the cherry sauce: mix the arrowroot with 1 tablespoon cold water. Heat up the reserved cherry juice in a small saucepan. Add a little of the hot cherry juice to the arrowroot. Return to the pan and boil, stirring continuously, for 45 seconds until slightly thickened and shiny. Add the remaining macerated cherries. Serve hot or cold with the galette.

NOTE: See 'Whisking Egg Whites', page 669.

wine: FORTIFIED SWEET WINE

Meringue Croquembouche

MAKES 30 MERINGUE SHELLS
For the white sugar meringue
4 egg whites
225 g | 8 oz caster sugar

For the brown sugar meringue
4 egg whites

30 g | 1 oz caster sugar
200 g | 7 oz soft light brown sugar, sifted

To serve
450 ml | ¾ pint double cream, whipped
icing sugar, sifted

1 Preheat the oven to 110°C | 225°F | gas mark ½.
2 Line 4 baking sheets with non-stick baking parchment.
3 Make the white sugar meringue: whisk the egg whites until very stiff but not dry. Gradually whisk in half of the sugar and whisk again until very stiff and shiny. Carefully fold in the remaining sugar.
4 Put the meringue mixture into a piping bag fitted with a 1 cm | ½ in plain nozzle. Squeeze gently to get rid of any pockets of air. Pipe the meringue into 5 cm | 2 in shells set fairly far apart on 2 baking sheets. Place in the oven to bake.
5 Make the brown sugar meringue: whisk the egg whites until very stiff but not dry. Gradually whisk in the caster sugar and whisk again until very stiff and shiny. Carefully fold in the brown sugar.
6 Pipe the mixture in the same way as for the white sugar meringues.
7 Bake all the meringues in the oven for 1 hour, or until they will lift cleanly from the paper. Using your thumb, make an indentation in the base of each meringue (this helps to pile them up neatly). Put back on the baking sheet on their sides and continue to cook for a further 15 minutes.
8 Lift the meringues from the paper, transfer to a wire rack and leave to cool completely.
9 Sandwich the white sugar meringues then the brown sugar meringues together in pairs with the cream. Pile them into a pyramid on a serving dish and dredge with icing sugar.

NOTE: See 'Whisking Egg Whites', page 669.

wine: SWEET WHITE

Flaming Baked Alaska

1 × 18 cm | 7 in Victoria sandwich (see page 703)
150 ml | ¼ pint sugar syrup (see page 665)
choice of 340 g | 12 oz fresh fruits, such as peaches,
    strawberries, etc.

1.14 litres | 2 pints vanilla, chocolate or strawberry
    ice cream
4 egg whites
225 g | 8 oz caster sugar
3 tablespoons brandy

1 Put the sponge cake on a plate with a good lip and sprinkle with a little of the sugar syrup.
2 Arrange the fruit on top of the cake and cover with ice cream.
3 Preheat the oven to 230°C | 450°F | gas mark 8.
4 Meanwhile, make the meringue: whisk the egg whites to stiff peaks. Gradually whisk in half the sugar. Fold in the remaining sugar with a large metal spoon.
5 Place the meringue in a piping bag fitted with a star nozzle and pipe it over the cake and ice cream.
6 Place the pudding in the oven for about 10 minutes until it has turned golden-brown.
7 Meanwhile, heat the brandy. When the meringue is browned, light the brandy and pour it flaming over the meringue. Serve immediately.

NOTE: See 'Whisking Egg Whites', page 669.

wine: **RICH SWEET WHITE**

Italian Meringue

This meringue is much more laborious to make than Swiss meringue (see page 670), but it has the advantage that once mixed it is extremely stable. Provided it is covered with clingfilm or a damp cloth to prevent drying out, the cook can leave it for hours before using it without risk of disintegration. It hardly swells at all in the oven so is ideal for piped meringue baskets, vacherins, etc. It cooks rather faster than Swiss meringue, is chalkier and more powdery, and stays a brilliant white. Although it is not quite as nice to eat as Swiss meringue, it is useful if catering for large numbers, and delicious if filled with strawberries and cream.

225 g | 8 oz granulated sugar
6 tablespoons water

4 egg whites

1 Put the sugar and water into a heavy saucepan.
2 Bring slowly to the boil, stirring occasionally. If any sugar crystals get stuck to the side of the pan, brush them down into the syrup with a clean wet brush. Use a sugar thermometer if available.
3 The syrup is ready when it reaches 120°C | 248°F. Alternatively, test for the firm ball stage (see note).
4 While the syrup is boiling to the correct stage, whisk the egg whites to stiff peaks.
5 If using an electric mixer, pour the bubbling hot syrup on to the whites in a steady stream while whisking, taking care not to pour the syrup on to the wires of the whisk – it cools fast against the cold metal and can harden and stick to the whisk. If whisking the

whites by hand, and in the absence of anyone to pour as you whisk, pour the syrup on to the whites in stages, about one-third at a time, whisking hard after each addition and working as fast as possible. The syrup must be bubbling hot as it hits the egg white to partially cook it.

6 Once the syrup is all in, whisk hard until the mixture is stiff, shiny and cool. If the whisk is lifted, the meringue should not flow at all.

7 Keep covered with clingfilm or a damp cloth if not using immediately.

8 Bake as for Swiss meringue.

NOTE: To test the syrup, drop a teaspoonful into a cup of cold water. If the syrup has reached the right temperature, it will set into a firm ball which can be squashed between the fingers. If the syrup forms a hard ball, like a hard-boiled sweet, it has reached too high a temperature to make Italian meringue.

See 'Whisking Egg Whites', page 669.

Meringue Cuite

'Cuite', or 'cooked', meringue is a professional chef's meringue used largely for frosting petits fours, for fruit pie tops and as unbaked frosting for cakes. This meringue requries a lot of whisking so use an electric whisk. It produces an even chalkier and finer-textured meringue than Italian meringue and, if used on baked confections, comes out of the oven shiny, smooth and pale biscuit-coloured.

Like Italian meringue, meringue cuite is very stable in the oven, hardly swelling at all and unlikely to cook out of shape. For this reason it is often used for intricate work such as the meringue basket on page 679. When baked at very low temperatures, it emerges smooth and shiny white.

The proportions of egg white to sugar are the same as for most meringues, but the sugar used is icing (confectioner's) sugar, rather than caster. Sometimes a 50–50 mixture of caster and icing sugar is used and occasionally, when the meringue is for a fine cake frosting that will not be baked, the sugar content can be increased above the normal 55 g|2 oz per egg white to 85 g|3 oz.

4 egg whites   3 drops of vanilla essence
225 g|8 oz icing sugar, sifted

1 Use a heatproof bowl that will fit snugly over a saucepan of simmering water without being in direct contact with the water. Whisk the egg whites until foamy, then add the icing sugar. It flies about in sugar-dust clouds, so take care. Set over the water.

2 Whisk until thick and absolutely stable – there should be no movement at all when the whisk is lifted. Add the vanilla essence.

3 Keep covered with clingfilm or a damp cloth if not using immediately.

NOTE: If the mixture is whisked in an electric mixer, a good result can be achieved without beating over heat. But it takes a good 15 minutes to get a perfect 'cuite' consistency.

See 'Whisking Egg Whites', page 669.

Noix au Café

SERVES 4–6

225 g|8 oz granulated sugar
6–7 tablespoons water

2 teaspoons coffee essence
4 egg whites

1 Preheat the oven to 140°C|275°F|gas mark 1. Line 2 baking sheets with non-stick baking parchment (it can be held in place with a few dots of the uncooked meringue).
2 Put the sugar, and water and coffee essence into a heavy saucepan. Dissolve over a low heat and then cook quickly, without stirring, to 120°C|248°F. Use a sugar thermometer for this, or wait until the sugar syrup reaches the firm ball stage (see note, page 678).
3 Whisk the egg whites until stiff. Pour the sugar syrup steadily on to the egg whites, whisking all the time, but taking care that the syrup does not strike the whisk wires (where it would cool and solidify). Continue whisking until the meringue is completely cool.
4 Reserve a small quantity of the meringue for the filling. Place the remaining mixture in a piping bag fitted with a medium plain nozzle. Pipe cherry-sized mounds on to the prepared baking sheets. Bake for 1–1½ hours. They lift easily off the lining paper.
5 Allow to become completely cold, then sandwich together with the reserved coffee meringue mixture.

NOTES: The meringues feel sticky when warm but will crisp and dry in 1–2 minutes.
   See 'Whisking Egg Whites', page 669.

Strawberry Meringue Basket

This is a classic meringue cuite recipe. You will need to make this quantity of meringue in 2 batches. It is best made using an electric whisk.

SERVES 8

For the meringue cuite
8 egg whites
450 g|1 lb icing sugar, sifted
6 drops of vanilla essence

For the filling
425 ml|¾ pint double cream, lightly whipped
450 g|1 lb fresh strawberries, hulled

1 Preheat the oven to 140°C|275°F|gas mark 1. Line 3 large baking sheets with non-stick baking parchment. Mark 18 cm|7 in diameter circles on each piece of paper.
2 Make up the first batch of meringue cuite. Put half the egg whites into a heatproof mixing bowl. Whisk until frothy then add half the sugar. Set the bowl over, not in, a saucepan of simmering water. Whisk until the meringue is thick and will hold its shape. This may well take up to 10 minutes of vigorous beating. (A very good imitation meringue cuite can also be made by whisking the egg whites and sugar together in a powerful electric mixer without needing to heat the meringue.)

3 Add half the vanilla essence. Remove from the pan and whisk for a further 2 minutes.

4 Put the meringue into a piping bag fitted with a 1 cm | ½ in plain nozzle. Squeeze gently to get rid of any pockets of air. Hold the bag upright in your right hand and, using your left hand to guide the nozzle, pipe a circular base on the first baking sheet, using one of the marked circles as a guide. Pipe 2 × 18 cm | 7 in empty hoops around the edges of the 2 remaining pencilled circles.

5 Bake the meringue base and hoops in the oven for 45–60 minutes until dry and crisp. Cool on a wire rack.

6 Make up the second batch of meringue cuite using the remaining ingredients. Return the baked meringue base to the baking sheet. Use a little uncooked mixture to fit the hoops on the base, one on top of the other. Return to the oven for 20 minutes to set the meringue.

7 Put the remaining mixture into a piping bag fitted with a rose nozzle. Cover the hoops with the meringue.

8 Bake in the oven at the same temperature for 45–60 minutes until set and crisp. Cool on a wire rack, then carefully remove the paper.

9 Fill with the cream and strawberries just before serving.

wine: LIGHT SWEET WHITE

Ice Creams and Sorbets

Ice cream is a foam stabilized by freezing much of the liquid (even in frozen ice cream some of the liquid is left unfrozen). Ice cream contains tiny ice crystals composed of pure water, solid globules of milk fat and tiny air bubbles. The liquid in ice cream prevents the formation of a solid block. The ice crystals stabilize the foam by trapping air and fat in its structure and if ice creams contain a good proportion of fat they freeze to a smooth creaminess without too much trouble. If they consist of mostly sugar and water or milk they need frequent beating during the freezing process to prevent too large ice crystals from forming. In any event the more a mixture is beaten and churned during freezing the more air will be incorporated and the creamier in texture it will be. The tiny air bubbles are very important as they break up the solid liquid to make a lighter, softer texture. Ice cream without air would be difficult to serve, scoop or eat.

Making Ice Cream

Churning

Ice-Cream maker: The best modern method of churning ice cream is with an ice-cream maker with a built-in chiller and electric motor. These machines are expensive, scaled-down versions of the commercial machines used by caterers. Their chief advantages are that they operate independently of the freezer, and are powerful and large enough to churn even a thick mixture to smoothness. The main disadvantages are the expense and the fact that they are bulky to store.

Electric sorbetière: This is useful if making small quantities of ice cream from a fairly thin mixture, such as a custard or syrup. But few are powerful enough to churn a mixture containing solid pieces (meringue or raisins, for example) or thick mixtures from, say, mashed bananas. Also, sorbetières must be put into a freezer as they have no built-in chilling equipment, and care must be taken when setting up the machine that the lead that connects the churn placed in the freezer to the plug on the wall will not be damaged by closing the freezer door, or prevent the door from closing tight.

Food processor: This will not chill the mixture, of course, but it is powerful enough to churn it to smoothness in a few minutes. Freeze the mixture in a shallow tray until solid, then break it up and process the frozen pieces again, using the chopping blade, to pale creaminess. Return to the tray and refreeze.

Bucket churns: can be bought with electric motors or with a handle for manual operation. Most have a good large capacity and are reliable and powerful, but they require a supply of ice and of salt. Coarsely crushed ice is packed in layers, sprinkled with coarse salt, between the metal ice-cream container and the outer bucket. The ice cream in the container is churned steadily by a strong paddle for 25 minutes or so, until the ice cream is thick. It can be left, without fear of melting, in the churn for an hour or so after making.

Mixing ice creams by hand: Finally, ice cream can be made without any special equipment. All that is needed is a shallow ice-cube tray or roasting pan, a bowl, and a strong whisk. The ice cream is half-frozen in the tray, then tipped into the bowl (which is chilled) and whisked until smooth. This is repeated until the icy shards are eliminated.

Sugar and flavourings: Extreme cold inhibits our sense of taste, the tastebuds being too cold to operate effectively. For this reason ice creams must be sweetened or flavoured more than seems right when tasting the mixture at room temperature.

Storage

Theoretically, ice cream can be stored for very long periods, but, certainly in a domestic freezer, there is some deterioration. Ice crystals may form on the surface of the ice cream after a week or so, meringue-based ices or ices containing gelatine may become rubbery, and if raw fruit (such as puréed peach) has been used, the colour will change for the worse. For total perfection, ice cream should be eaten the day it is made, but a few days' freezing is acceptable. If fruit ices are to be stored for longer than a few days, the fruit should be cooked to preserve the colour.

Thawing

Unless the mixture is very soft, it is wise to transfer it to the refrigerator for 30 minutes before serving to allow the ice to soften slightly. Or the ice cream may be softened sufficiently to scoop into balls, then put into a chilled serving dish and returned to the freezer until needed.

Types of Ice Cream

There are four basic types of ice cream.

Custard-based: These ice creams are made by freezing very rich, flavoured custards consisting of eggs, sugar, cream and/or milk and the required flavouring.

Mousse-based parfaits: In a mousse-based parfait the air that will give the creaminess to the frozen mixture is beaten into the egg base over heat before cooling and freezing. This means that there is no need to churn or beat once the mixture is in the freezer, and it can be poured into a china soufflé dish with a paper collar tied round (see page 689) it so that it looks deceptively like a risen soufflé or an ice soufflé.

Meringue-based ice creams: These are similar to the mousse-based parfaits, but the air is incorporated into the egg whites, as for meringue, before the flavouring fruit purée is added. The method is suitable for fruit ice creams, where the acidity of the fruit nicely cuts the sweet meringue.

Yoghurt-based: Ice creams made with a yoghurt base are often made by the all-in-one method. It is not easy to freeze smoothly without the aid of a machine that beats or stirs constantly during freezing because it is so low in fat. Yoghurt-based ice cream thaws and melts too fast to be churned in the processor. Frozen yoghurt is often served as a healthy alternative to a fattening dessert.

Frozen Ices

Sorbets and Granita: Sorbets (sherberts or water ices) are made by freezing flavoured syrups or purées. The essential thing is to get the proportions right. Too much sugar and the sorbet will be oversweet, syrupy and too soft to hold its shape. Too little and it will be icy, crystalline and hard. Chefs use a sacchrometer to measure the amount of sugar in a syrup (or a 'pèse-syrop' to get the desired 37 per cent sugar), but good results can be obtained if the mixture contains about one-third sugar and two-thirds other ingredients. Bearing this figure in mind, the cook can make almost any sorbet with two-parts liquid (unsweetened) and one-part sugar, bringing the syrup slowly to the boil, cooling it, and freezing it, whisking as necessary.

There is no question that a machine gives the best results. If no machine is available the addition of powdered gelatine (1 tablespoon for every 300 ml | ½ pint of liquid) or the addition of whisked egg whites does help prevent the formation of large ice crystals and slows melting.

If slightly less sugar is used, and the mixture is forked rather than beaten while freezing, a granita results – a granular, fast-melting sorbet.

The recipes for ice creams assume that you do not have an ice-cream maker – if you do, however, simply follow the manufacturer's instructions. Light, sweet wines go with most ice creams, particularly Italian Muscato with fruit ices. Also, try sweet sparkling wine or champagne.

Plum or Apricot Ice Cream

This ice cream is made with a mousse base.

SERVES 6

900 g | 2 lb plums or apricots, washed and halved
290 ml | ½ pint water
110 g | 4 oz granulated sugar

3 egg yolks
150 ml | ¼ pint double cream

1 Stew the fruit with 2 tablespoons of the water and 55 g | 2 oz of the sugar in a saucepan. When tender, push the fruit and the juice through a nylon or stainless steel sieve. You should have 290 ml | ½ pint purée. Check for sweetness.

2 Dissolve the remaining sugar in the remaining water without boiling. Then boil rapidly to 120°C | 248°F.

3 Remove from the heat. Beat the egg yolks with a whisk. Pour on the sugar syrup, whisking all the time, until the mixture is thick, pale and mousse-like, and quite cold.

4 Add the cream to the fruit purée with the yolk mixture. Turn into a freezerproof dish.

5 Freeze for about 45 minutes or until beginning to freeze around the edges. Remove the ice cream, stir thoroughly, then return to the freezer to freeze completely.

6 If the ice cream is not perfectly smooth, tip it into a chilled bowl, beat until smooth and creamy and freeze again.

Ginger Ice Cream

This ice cream is made with a mousse base.

SERVES 6

85 g | 3 oz granulated sugar
150 ml | ¼ pint water
4 egg yolks

2 teaspoons ground ginger
570 ml | 1 pint double cream, lightly whipped
4 pieces of preserved stem ginger, cut into slivers

1 Put the sugar and water into a small heavy saucepan. Dissolve over a low heat. Then boil until 120°C | 248°F.

2 Put the egg yolks into a large bowl with the ground ginger, whisk lightly and pour on to the warm sugar syrup. Do not allow the syrup to touch the whisk if doing this in a machine as it cools fast against the cold metal and can harden and stick to the whisk.

3 Fold in the cream and pour into an ice tray.

4 Freeze until half-frozen, then fold in the stem ginger. Freeze again.

5 Remove from the freezer 30 minutes before it is to be eaten and scoop into a glass bowl.

Rich Vanilla Ice Cream

This ice cream is made with a mousse base.

SERVES 4

70 g | 2½ oz granulated sugar
8 tablespoons water
1 vanilla pod, split lengthways

3 egg yolks
425 ml | ¾ pint double cream

1 Put the sugar, water and vanilla pod into a heavy saucepan and dissolve the sugar over a low heat, stirring.

2 Beat the egg yolks well. Half whip the cream.

3 When the sugar has dissolved completely, boil rapidly to 120°C|248°F. Remove the vanilla pod. Scrape out the seeds and add to the syrup.

4 Whisk the egg yolks and gradually pour in the sugar syrup. Whisk until the mixture is very thick and will leave a trail when the whisk is lifted.

5 Cool, whisking occasionally. Fold in the cream, pour into a freezer container and freeze.

6 When the ice cream is half-frozen, whisk again and return to the freezer.

Damson Ice Cream

This is a meringue-based ice cream.

SERVES 6–8

450 g|1 lb damsons
340 g|12 oz caster sugar
150 ml|¼ pint water

2 large egg whites
finely grated zest and juice of 1 small orange
290 ml|½ pint double cream

1 Wash the damsons and put them, still wet, into a heavy saucepan with 110 g|4 oz of the sugar. Stew gently, covered, over a very low heat or bake in a medium oven until soft and pulpy.

2 Push through a sieve, removing the stones.

3 Dissolve the remaining sugar in the water in a heavy pan, then bring to the boil.

4 Boil steadily for 5 minutes to 120°C|248°F.

5 Meanwhile, whisk the egg whites until stiff. Pour the boiling syrup on to the egg whites, whisking as you do so. The mixture will go rather liquid at this stage, but keep whisking until you have a thick meringue.

6 Stir in the orange zest and juice and the damson purée.

7 Whip the cream until thick but not stiff, and fold into the mixture.

8 Turn into an ice tray and freeze. It is not necessary to rewhisk the ice cream during freezing.

NOTE: The damson purée can be replaced by a purée of cooked plums, greengages, rhubarb, dried apricots or prunes, or a raw purée of soft fruit, such as fresh apricots or peaches.

Coffee Ice Cream

This ice cream is made with a custard base.

SERVES 2–3

4 egg yolks
85 g|3 oz caster sugar
a pinch of salt

425 ml|¾ pint single cream
5 teaspoons instant coffee powder

1 Mix the egg yolks with the sugar and salt.
2 Place the cream and coffee in a saucepan and heat gently until the coffee dissolves.
3 Add the cream to the egg yolk mixture, stirring all the time.
4 Pour the mixture into the top of a double saucepan or into a heatproof bowl set over, not in, a saucepan of simmering water.
5 Stir continuously until thick and creamy.
6 Strain into a bowl and allow to cool, whisking occasionally.
7 Chill, then pour into an ice tray and freeze.
8 When the ice cream is half-frozen, whisk again and return to the freezer.

Raspberry Ice Cream

This ice cream is made with a mousse base.

SERVES 4–6

450 g | 1 lb raspberries	a little vanilla essence
85 g | 3 oz icing sugar, sifted	3 egg yolks
70 g | 2½ oz granulated sugar	290 ml | ½ pint single or double cream
110 ml | 4 fl oz water	a squeeze of lemon juice

1 Liquidize or crush the raspberries and push through a nylon or stainless steel sieve.
2 Sweeten with the icing sugar.
3 Place the sugar and water in a heavy saucepan and dissolve over a low heat.
4 When completely dissolved, boil to 120°C | 248°F.
5 Remove from the heat. Add the vanilla essence.
6 Pour the sugar syrup on to the egg yolks and whisk until the mixture is thick and mousse-like.
7 Cool and add the cream, raspberry purée and lemon juice.
8 Check for sweetness and add more icing sugar if necessary.
9 Chill, then pour into an ice tray and freeze.
10 If the ice cream is not quite smooth when half-frozen, whisk it once more and return to the freezer.

Raspberry Ripple Ice Cream

This ice cream is made with a meringue base.

450 g | 1 lb frozen raspberries, defrosted	2 egg whites
110 g | 4 oz granulated sugar	290 ml | ½ pint double cream, lightly whipped
3 tablespoons water	

1 Push the raspberries through a sieve to make a purée. Freeze the purée overnight.
2 Put the sugar and water into a heavy saucepan and bring slowly to the boil without stirring. If any sugar crystals get stuck to the side of the pan, brush them down into the syrup with a clean wet brush.
3 Boil the syrup until it reaches a temperature of 120°C|248°F.
4 While the syrup is boiling, whisk the egg whites to stiff peaks.
5 If using an electric mixer, pour the bubbling hot syrup on to the whisked egg whites in a steady stream while whisking, taking care not to pour the syrup on to the beaters – it cools fast against the cold metal and can harden and stick. If whisking the egg whites by hand, and in the absence of anyone to pour as you whisk, pour the syrup on to the whites in stages, about one-third at a time, whisking hard after each addition and working as fast as possible. The syrup must be bubbling hot as it hits the egg whites, to partially cook them.
6 Once all the syrup has been added, whisk until the mixture is stiff and shiny and absolutely stable if the whisk is lifted, the meringue should not flow at all.
7 Remove the raspberry pureé from the freezer and leave to defrost into large crystals.
8 Fold the cream into the meringue and then swirl in the semi-frozen raspberry pureé, to create a marbled effect. Freeze until firm.
9 Spoon into individual glass dishes and decorate with the sprigs of mint.

Chocolate Ice Cream

This ice cream is made with a custard base.

SERVES 6–8

340 g|12 oz plain chocolate, cut up into small pieces	55 g|2 oz caster sugar
570 ml|1 pint milk	570 ml|1 pint whipping cream
1 egg	1 teaspoon vanilla essence
1 egg yolk	

1 Dissolve the chocolate in the milk in a heavy saucepan over a low heat.
2 Whisk the egg and egg yolk with the sugar in a heatproof bowl set over, not in, a saucepan of simmering water. Whisk until light and fluffy.
3 When the chocolate has melted and the milk nearly boiled, pour on to the egg mixture and whisk well. Strain and allow to cool.
4 Whip the cream lightly and fold it into the chocolate mixture with the vanilla essence. Pour into a freezer container and freeze.
5 When half-frozen, whisk again and return to the freezer.

NOTE: Chocolate mint crisps or mint cracknel, crumbled up and added to the mixture at the time of the final whisking, give a delicious flavour and crunchy texture.

Lemon Curd Ice Cream

This ice cream is made by the all-in one method.

SERVES 6

3 eggs, beaten
grated zest and juice of 2 lemons
225 g|8 oz caster sugar

85g|3 oz unsalted butter, at room temperature, cut
into small pieces
570 ml|1 pint plain yoghurt

1 Put the eggs, lemon juice, sugar and butter into a small saucepan. Set over a low heat and stir with a wooden spoon until the butter has melted and the curd is thick enough to coat the back of the spoon. Allow one or two bubbles to come to the surface.

2 Remove from the heat and stir in the lemon zest. Allow the curd to cool, then stir in the yoghurt. Cover closely and freeze.

3 Transfer the ice cream to the refrigerator about an hour before serving.

NOTE: This ice cream is also delicious made with good-quality shop-bought lemon curd.

Pistachio Parfait

This ice cream is made with a meringue base.

SERVES 6

170 g|6 oz caster sugar
60 ml|2½ fl oz water
3 egg whites
570 ml|1 pint double cream

1 drop of green colouring (optional)
1 tablespoon vanilla essence
1 drop of almond essence
75 g|2½ oz unsalted pistachio nuts, skinned and
chopped

1 Put the sugar and water into a heavy saucepan. Bring slowly to the boil, without stirring, then boil the syrup to 120°C|248°F.

2 Meanwhile, whisk the egg whites to stiff peaks.

3 If the whites are in a machine, pour the bubbling hot syrup on to them in a steady stream while whisking, taking care not to pour the syrup on to the wires of the whisk – it cools fast against the cold metal and can harden and stick to the whisk. If whisking the whites by hand, and in the absence of anyone to pour while you whisk, pour the syrup on to the whites in stages, about one-third at a time, whisking hard between each addition, and working as fast as possible. The syrup must be bubbling hot as it hits the egg white, to partially cook it.

4 When all the syrup has been added, whisk hard until the mixture is stiff and shiny and absolutely stable. When the whisk is lifted, the meringue should not flow at all.

5 Lightly whip the cream and colour it a delicate green.

6 Fold the cream into the meringue mixture. Add the essences and chopped pistachio nuts.

7 Pour into an ice tray and freeze. Remove from the freezer 30 minutes before serving.

Individual Mango Parfaits with Passionfruit Sauce

SERVES 8

2 ripe mangoes

3 egg yolks

110 g | 4 oz icing sugar, sifted

200 ml | 7 fl oz double cream

lemon juice

For the sauce

4 passionfruits

fresh orange juice

sugar syrup (see page 665)

To decorate

8 springs of fresh mint

1 Lightly oil 8 ramekins.

2 Process the mango flesh until smooth.

3 Whisk the egg yolks with the icing sugar until very thick and light.

4 Lightly whip the double cream.

5 Fold the mango purée and cream into the egg-yolk mixture.

6 Add lemon juice to taste; it may also be necessary to add extra icing sugar.

7 Pour the mixture into the prepared ramekins, cover with clingfilm and freeze for at least 4 hours.

8 Make the sauce: scoop the flesh and seeds from the passionfruit and mix with a little orange juice and sugar syrup to taste.

9 To serve: turn the parfaits out on to individual plates, spoon over a little passionfruit sauce and decorate each with a sprig of mint.

Hazelnut Ice Cream

This is a meringue-based ice cream.

SERVES 8

For the hazelnut praline

150 g | 5 oz granulated sugar

3 tablespoons water

150 g | 5 oz hazelnuts, toasted and skinned

For the Italian meringue

150 g | 5 oz granulated sugar

4 tablespoons water

8 egg whites

290 ml | ½ pint double cream, lightly whipped

To serve

raspberry coulis (see page 667)

1 Prepare a 15 cm | 6 in soufflé dish: tie a double piece of greaseproof paper around the outside of the dish. The paper should stand about 5 cm | 2 in above the rim. Lightly brush the inside of the 'paper collar' with oil.

2 Lightly oil a baking sheet.

3 Make the hazelnut praline: melt the sugar in a heavy saucepan with the water. When the sugar has dissolved, boil until it turns to a pale caramel. Add 130 g | 4½ oz of the still-warm hazelnuts and cook for a further 2 minutes until a rich brown. Pour on to the oiled baking sheet.

4 Cool, until hardened, then pound or liquidize.

5 Make the Italian meringue: dissolve the sugar in the water in a heavy saucepan over a low heat, then boil until the syrup reaches 120°C | 248°F. In a large bowl, whisk the egg whites until stiff, then gradually add the sugar syrup, whisking all the time. Continue to whisk until thick and shiny.

6 Fold the cream into the meringue.

7 Pour into the prepared soufflé dish. When half-frozen, fold in the praline. Freeze until firm.

8 To serve: remove the greaseproof paper. Roughly chop the remaining hazelnuts and scatter on top of the soufflé. Serve the raspberry coulis separately.

Coconut Ice Cream

This is a custard-based ice cream.

SERVES 4

290 ml	½ pint milk	85 g	3 oz caster sugar
1 vanilla pod, split lengthways	8 tablespoons coconut milk powder
3 egg yolks	290 ml	½ pint whipping cream

1 Place the milk in a saucepan with the vanilla pod and heat until steaming. Remove from the heat and leave to infuse for 10 minutes, then scrape the seeds out of the vanilla pod and stir into the milk.

2 Mix the egg yolks and sugar together in a bowl, then slowly stir in the hot milk. Stir in the coconut milk powder.

3 Pour the mixture into the rinsed-out milk pan. Heat over a medium-low heat, stirring, until the mixture thickens enough to coat the back of the spoon. Strain into a cold bowl to remove any eggy threads.

4 Stir in the cream. Allow to cool to room temperature, then freeze in an ice-cream machine according to the manufacturer's directions or place in a shallow container in the freezer. When half frozen, beat thoroughly with a fork, then return to the container to continue freezing. Beat once or twice again until the mixture is frozen solid.

Vanilla and Prune Ice Cream

This is a custard-based ice cream.

SERVES 4

290 ml | ½ pint milk
290 ml | ½ pint double cream
2 vanilla pods, split lengthways
6 egg yolks
100 g | 3½ oz caster sugar

8 prunes, stoned, cut in half and marinated in brandy
  for 24 hours

To serve
2 ripe peaches, halved

1 Scald the milk and cream with the vanilla pods in a heavy saucepan by bringing to just below boiling point.
2 In a bowl, beat the egg yolks with the sugar until creamy, add the milk mixture gradually and whisk together.
3 Return it to the pan and cook over a low heat, stirring constantly with a wooden spoon, until the custard is thick enough to coat the back of the spoon. Strain through a sieve into a bowl and allow to cool.
4 Pour the mixture into an ice tray and freeze.
5 Once frozen, take the ice cream out of the freezer and allow to soften at room temperature. Either place in a food processor and whizz to remove the ice crystals or use an electric beater. Fold in the prunes and brandy.
6 Return the ice cream to the container and freeze again.
7 Serve with the peaches.

Brown Bread Ice Cream

SERVES 4

110 g | 4 oz wholemeal breadcrumbs
110 g | 4 oz soft dark brown sugar
2 eggs

290 ml | ½ pint double cream
150 ml | ¼ pint single cream
2 drops of vanilla essence

1 Preheat the oven to 200°C | 400°F | gas mark 6.
2 Place the breadcrumbs in the oven for 15 minutes or until dry.
3 Mix the sugar and breadcrumbs and return to the oven for a further 15 minutes or until the sugar caramelizes. Remove, allow to cool and crush lightly.
4 Separate the eggs. Beat the yolks, add the creams and fold in the caramelized crumbs. Add the vanilla essence.
5 Whisk the egg whites to soft peaks and fold into the mixture. Freeze until required.

Morello Cherry Bombe

This is a cheat's bombe – simple to make and delicious to eat.

SERVES 8

400 g | 14 oz can of morello cherries, pitted
110 g | 4 oz meringue shells (see page 670)
570 ml | 1 pint double cream, or 675 g | 1½ lb rich
    vanilla ice cream (see page 684)
1 tablespoon brandy or Kirsch (optional)

icing sugar to taste
110 g | 4 oz raspberries

For the sauce

2 teaspoons arrowroot
1 tablespoon brandy or Kirsch

1 Drain the cherries well, reserving the juice. Break the meringues up roughly.
2 Whip the cream until stiff, add the brandy or Kirsch if using, and sweeten to taste with icing sugar. (If using ice cream, allow it to soften but not to melt.) Mix in the cherries, raspberries and meringue. Check for sweetness.
3 Spoon the mixture into a bombe mould or freezerproof bowl and put immediately into the freezer. It will take at least 2 hours, and probably 4, to harden. It can then be turned out on to a plate and put back in the freezer until needed.
4 Make the sauce: mix the arrowroot with a little water. Heat the reserved cherry juice in a saucepan. Pour some of the hot juice on to the arrowroot, stirring to a paste, then stir the paste into the saucepan. Bring to the boil, stirring. Allow to simmer for 1 minute after boiling. Add the brandy or Kirsch and serve hot with the bombe.

NOTE: This dessert can also be made with fresh or frozen strawberries, pineapple or peaches, but the fruits should be chopped rather than left whole or in large pieces.

Rum Bombe with Mincemeat Sauce

SERVES 8

290 ml | ½ pint double cream
3 tablespoons rum
225 ml | 8 fl oz plain yoghurt
110 g | 4 oz meringue shells (see page 670), crushed
1 teaspoon freshly grated nutmeg

For the mincemeat sauce

1 large dessert apple

55 g | 2 oz raisins
55 g | 2 oz sultanas
55 g | 2 oz hazelnuts, chopped and lightly toasted
55 g | 2 oz soft dark brown sugar
½ teaspoon ground mixed spice
grated zest and juice of ½ lemon
grated zest and juice of 1 orange
4 tablespoons rum

1 Lightly oil 8 ramekins and line them with discs of greaseproof paper.
2 Whip the cream until it holds its shape. Whisk in the rum and fold in the yoghurt, meringues and nutmeg. Turn into the ramekin dishes and freeze until firm.

3 Make the sauce: peel, core and chop the apple and add the remaining ingredients for the sauce, with more orange juice or rum to taste.

4 To serve: run a knife around the ramekins and turn out on to individual plates. Place in the refrigerator for 10 minutes before serving.

5 Heat the sauce until very hot, but not boiling, and hand it separately.

Chocolate Christmas Bombes

SERVES 6

85 g | 3 oz plain chocolate, chopped

2 tablespoons rum

1 tablespoon water

170 g | 6 oz unsweetened chestnut purée

30 g | 1 oz raisins

30 g | 1 oz sultanas

30 g | 1 oz chopped mixed peel

55 g | 2 oz glacé cherries

290 ml | ½ pint double cream

2 egg whites

45 g | 1½ oz caster sugar

To decorate

chocolate holly leaves (see page 737)

1 Line 6 individual ramekins or large dariole moulds with clingfilm.

2 Put the chocolate, 1 tablespoon of the rum and the water into a heatproof bowl set over, not in, a saucepan of simmering water until the chocolate has just melted. Remove from the heat and stir into the chestnut purée. Set aside.

3 Sprinkle the remaining rum over the dried fruits, peel and cherries and leave to stand for 5 minutes.

4 Whip the cream lightly. Whisk the egg whites until stiff and then gradually add the sugar, a teaspoon at a time, whisking well after each addition.

5 Carefully fold the fruit into the chocolate and chestnut mixture, then add the cream and finally the whisked egg whites.

6 Divide the mixture between the ramekins, cover and freeze for at least 3 hours.

7 To serve: remove the moulds from the freezer 10 minutes before serving. Turn on to a plate, remove the clingfilm and decorate with the holly leaves.

Brandy Snap Tortes

SERVES 6

110 g | 4 oz flour quantity brandy snap mixture (see page 778)

450 g | 1 lb damson ice cream, slightly softened (see page 685)

raspberry coulis (see page 667)

100 g | 4 oz mixed raspberries and blueberries

To decorate

sprigs of fresh mint

icing sugar, sifted, for dusting

1 Preheat the oven to 190°C|375°F|gas mark 5. Line a baking sheet with non-stick baking parchment. Grease a palette knife.
2 Make the brandy snap mixture. Bake 18 brandy snaps on the baking sheet as in the recipe on page 630 but lift them, flat, on to a wire rack and leave them to cool and harden.
3 Put a flat brandy snap on to each of 6 pudding plates. Cover with some of the damson ice cream and flatten slightly. Cover with a second flat brandy snap. Arrange some more ice cream on top of the brandy snaps and cover with a third brandy snap.
4 Pour the raspberry coulis around the tortes.
5 Arrange the raspberries and blueberries on the coulis and decorate with a small sprig of mint.
6 Dust lightly with icing sugar.

Frozen Chocolate Torte

SERVES 6

For the chocolate biscuit base

170 g|6 oz butter

85 g|3 oz caster sugar

170 g|6 oz self-raising flour

45 g|1½ oz cocoa powder

85 ml|3 fl oz black coffee or water

4 eggs, separated

140 g|5 oz caster sugar

290 ml|½ pint double cream

For the chocolate mousse

170 g|6 oz plain chocolate, chopped

30 g|1 oz bitter chocolate, chopped

To finish

2 teaspoons each sifted icing sugar and cocoa powder, mixed

1 Preheat the oven to 190°C|375°F|gas mark 5.
2 Make the base: cream the butter until soft. Add the sugar and beat until light and fluffy. Sift the flour and cocoa powder together and stir into the mixture.
3 Press into the bottom of a 25 cm|10 in spring form tin or deep-sided cake tin lined with kitchen foil.
4 Bake in the oven for 10 minutes. Do not allow to colour. Remove from the oven and leave to cool.
5 Make the mousse mixture: place the chocolates and coffee or water in a bowl set over, not in, a saucepan of simmering water. Allow to melt.
6 Whisk the egg yolks with half the sugar until light and mousse-like. Stir in the melted chocolate.
7 Whip the cream until it just holds its shape.
8 Whisk the egg whites until stiff, then gradually add the remaining sugar, a spoonful at a time, whisking well after each addition.
9 Fold the cream into the chocolate mixture, followed by the egg whites. Pour on to the cooked biscuit base, cover and freeze for at least 4 hours.
10 To serve: remove the torte from the freezer. Remove from the tin. Dust with the icing sugar and cocoa. Allow to stand for 20 minutes before serving.

Melon and Champagne Granita

SERVES 4–6

1 large Ogen melon or cantaloupe

340 g | 12 oz granulated sugar

10 tablespoons water

juice of 1 lemon

290 ml | ½ pint champagne

1 Cut the melon into quarters. Remove the skin and seeds and purée the flesh in a food processor or blender.

2 Put the sugar and water into a heavy saucepan. Dissolve slowly over a low heat.

3 When the sugar has completely dissolved, increase the heat and boil rapidly to the short thread stage (see page 665).

4 Mix together the melon purée, lemon juice, champagne and warm sugar syrup. Allow to cool, then pour into a freezer container. Stir with a fork every few hours.

5 Freeze overnight. Serve in well-chilled goblets.

NOTE: If you have an ice-cream machine, it makes short work of this sorbet. It is a soft sorbet because of the high alcoholic content.

Tomato Sorbet

SERVES 4–6

110 g | 4 oz granulated sugar

290 ml | ½ pint water

500 ml | 18 fl oz tomato juice

juice of ½ lemon

fresh mint or basil leaves, roughly chopped

1 tablespoon Worcestershire sauce

Tabasco sauce

salt and freshly ground black pepper

1 egg white

1 Put the sugar and water into a heavy saucepan. Dissolve slowly over a low heat. When the sugar has completely dissolved, increase the heat and boil to the short thread stage (see page 665). Remove from the heat and allow to cool for 1 minute.

2 Meanwhile, mix together the tomato juice, lemon juice and herbs. Season to taste with Worcestershire sauce, Tabasco, salt and pepper. Add the cooling sugar syrup. Transfer to a freezer container and freeze.

3 Once large crystals have formed and the sorbet is almost set, remove from the container and break up with a fork.

4 Whisk the egg white until just stiff and fold into the tomato mixture. Return to the container and freeze again. Remove from the freezer 10–15 minutes before serving.

NOTE: If using a food processor, when the sorbet is partially frozen remove from the container, roughly chop and then quickly process. Add the unwhipped egg white through the lid funnel as the blade is moving. Process until frothy for 30 seconds. Return the mixture to the container and freeze again.

Apple Sorbet with Caramelized Apples

SERVES 4

110 g | 4 oz granulated sugar
200 ml | 7 fl oz water
500 g | 12 lb oz (about 4) Granny Smith apples
juice of ½ lemon
½ egg white (optional)

To garnish

30 g | 1 oz butter
55 g | 2 oz caster sugar
2 Granny Smith apples, peeled, cored and cut into
   eighths

1 Heat the sugar and water in a saucepan over a low heat to dissolve the sugar. Boil for 1 minute.
2 Peel, core and slice the apples and toss with the lemon juice. Tip into the sugar syrup.
3 Cover and simmer for about 10 minutes until the apples are translucent.
4 Allow the apples to cool, then liquidize with the syrup.
5 Freeze in a machine according to the manufacturer's directions or freeze until solid, then purée briefly in a food processor and refreeze until firm.
6 If desired, the egg white can be beaten with a fork until frothy and added to the sorbet at the end of churning or when puréed in the food processor. The mixture will fluff up tremendously. Return to the container and freeze until firm.
7 Make the garnish: melt the butter and sugar in a small frying pan until starting to colour. Turn the apple pieces in the mixture until lightly caramelized and softened but not mushy. Remove from the pan and use immediately to garnish individual portions of the sorbet. Serve immediately.

Pear Sorbet

SERVES 4

4 ripe William pears
160 g | 5½ oz caster or icing sugar

juice of 2 lemons
1 egg white, lightly whisked

1 Peel, core and quarter the pears.
2 Put the pears into a saucepan with the sugar and enough water to just cover the pears. Poach gently for 20 minutes or until glassy.
3 Remove the pears and reduce the cooking liquor by boiling rapidly to the short thread stage (see page 665). Purée the pears, syrup and lemon juice together in a food processor or blender.
4 Allow to cool, then pour into a freezer container and freeze.
5 When nearly frozen, fold in the egg white and freeze until firm.

NOTE: If you have a food processor, allow the sorbet to freeze and then defrost until half-frozen. Whizz in the food processor and add the egg white. It will fluff up tremendously. Return to the container and freeze until firm.

Lemon Sorbet

SERVES 4

thinly pared zest and juice of 3 lemons
140 g | 5 oz granulated sugar

570 ml | 1 pint water
½ egg white

1 Place the lemon zest, sugar and water in a heavy saucepan. Dissolve the sugar over a low heat and, when completely dissolved, boil rapidly to the short thread stage (see page 665, sugar syrups).
2 Remove from the heat and allow to cool completely. When the syrup is cold, add the lemon juice and strain.
3 Freeze for 30 minutes, or until beginning to solidify.
4 Whisk the egg white until stiff and fold into the mixture.
5 Return to the freezer until firm.

NOTE: If you have a food processor, allow the lemon syrup to freeze and then process until soft. Pour in the egg white through the funnel, with the motor running. Freeze until firm.

Strawberry Sorbet

SERVES 4

170 g | 6 oz caster sugar
570 ml | 1 pint water
juice of ½ lemon or small orange

340 g | 12 oz fresh or frozen strawberries
1 egg white

1 Place the sugar and water in a heavy saucepan. Dissolve the sugar over a low heat. When completely dissolved, boil gently for 5 minutes. Add the lemon or orange juice and cool.
2 Liquidize or mash the strawberries to a pulp and add the syrup. Place in a bowl in the freezer for 30 minutes or until beginning to solidify.
3 Whisk the egg whites until stiff and fold into the mixture.
4 Return to the freezer until firm.

NOTE: If you have a food processor, allow the strawberry syrup to freeze, then process until soft. Pour in the egg white through the funnel, with the motor running. Freeze until solid.

Passionfruit Sorbet

SERVES 6

140 g | 5 oz granulated sugar
425 ml | ¾ pint water
thinly pared zest and juice of 1 lemon

450 g | 1 lb passionfruit pulp (from about 32 passionfruits)
½ egg white

1 Dissolve the sugar in the water in a heavy saucepan. When completely dissolved, add the lemon zest and boil rapidly for 5 minutes, or until the syrup is tacky.

2 Sieve the passionfruit pulp and add to the syrup with the lemon juice. Cool.

3 Place in a bowl in the freezer until half-frozen.

4 Tip into a chilled bowl and whisk well. Refreeze until almost solid.

5 Tip the sorbet into another chilled bowl and break up. Whisk until smooth and whisk in the egg white.

6 Freeze again until firm.

NOTE: If you have a food processor, allow the passionfruit, syrup and lemon juice to freeze. Defrost slightly, then process until soft. Pour the egg white in through the funnel, with the motor running. Freeze until firm.

Cakes

Successful cake-making is a most satisfying activity for the cook. It is also most demanding on account of the accuracy needed in measuring the ingredients and the skill necessary in preparing certain cakes. Confidence is best built by beginning with the easier cakes, such as gingerbread or fruit cake. First attempts at making more difficult cakes such as a génoise sponge are often disappointing. Happily, practice, with good ingredients, proper utensils, careful weighing and measuring, precise oven temperatures and exact timing – in short, careful attention to detail – makes perfect.

Most cakes are made by combining fat, sugar, flour, eggs and liquid. Air and/or other raising agents are incorporated to make the mixture rise during baking. As it bakes, the proteins in the eggs and flour are stretched by the expansion of gas until the heat finally sets the cake. It is the rising that gives a cake a light, sponge-like texture.

Ingredients

Fats

Butter makes the best-flavoured cakes. Margarine, particularly the soft or tub variety, is useful for speed but has less flavour than butter. Vegetable shortenings are flavourless but give light cakes. Lard cakes have a distinctive 'lard' flavour and are often heavy, and for this reason lard is little used in cake-making. Oils are not much used as they do not easily hold air when they are creamed or beaten, and the resulting cakes therefore can be heavy.

Sugars

The finer texture of caster sugar makes it most suitable for cake-making. Coarse granulated sugar can give a speckled appearance to a finished cake unless the sugar is ground down first in a blender or food processor. Soft brown sugars give colour and flavour to dark cakes like gingerbread, but they give sponge cakes a drab look and too much caramel flavour.

Golden syrup, honey, treacle and molasses are used in cakes made by the melting method. Such cakes are cooked relatively slowly, as these thick liquid sugars tend to caramelize and burn at higher temperatures.

Eggs

Unless specified, most recipes assume a medium egg weighing 55 g | 2 oz. The eggs should be used at room temperature – cold eggs tend to curdle the mixture and this results in the cake having a tough, coarse, too open texture.

Flours

Plain white flour is used in cake-making unless otherwise specified. The high proportion of 'soft' or low-gluten wheat in European plain flour makes it particularly suitable for cake-making. In North America, plain or 'all-purpose' flour is made with more 'hard' than soft wheat, so cornflour, which is also weak (low in gluten), is sometimes substituted for some of the all-purpose flour, or special soft 'cake flour' is used. Although a little gluten is needed to allow the mixture to stretch and expand as it rises, too much would given a tough, chewy cake.

Self-raising flour has a raising agent (baking powder) added to it and should be used only if specified in the recipe. All flours, even if labelled 'ready-sifted', should be sifted before use to eliminate any lumps and to incorporate air.

Raising Agents

Air is incorporated into cake mixtures by agitating the ingredients. Methods include sifting the flour, beating the butter and beating or creaming it again with the sugar to a fluffy, mousse-like consistency, and whisking the eggs. The heat of the oven causes the air trapped in the mixture to rise and leaven or lighten the cake, either by itself or in conjunction with other raising agents. Steam raises wet cake mixtures such as gingerbread even when air has not been beaten into them.

Bicarbonate of soda, or baking soda, is a powder which, when mixed with liquid, quickly gives off half its substance as carbon dioxide. In a cake the trapped gas causes the mixture to puff up. Heat sets the mixture once it has risen. By the time the cake cools, the gas will have escaped and will have been replaced by air. Unfortunately, the bicarbonate of soda remaining in the cake can give it a slightly unpleasant smell and taste, and a yellowish colour. For this reason, bicarbonate of soda is most often used in strong-tasting cakes such as gingerbread and those flavoured with chocolate, treacle or molasses. The carbon dioxide reaction is enhanced by acidic substances, so bicarbonate of soda is usually used in cake mixtures with ingredients such as sour milk, vinegar, buttermilk, soured cream, cream of tartar and yoghurt. It gives them a soft texture and firm crust with a deep colour. Unfortunately the process destroys some of the vitamins present in the flour.

Baking powder in commercial forms consists of bicarbonate of soda and an acid powder that varies according to the brand, plus a starch filler, usually cornflour, arrowroot or ground rice. The starch keeps the mixture dry by absorbing any dampness in the air, which might cause the soda and the acid in the powder to react. For most cakes, use 4 level teaspoons baking powder per 250 g│9 oz flour. A 'double action' baking powder is sold in the USA that reacts when moistened then again when heated. It is more reliable and can be substituted for single action baking powder. It is not widely known in Europe.

Yeast cakes that rise by the growth of yeast cells are really sweetened enriched breads. They are traditional in Eastern European cookery. The kulich on page 768 is a classic example.

Preparing a Cake Tin

All tins should be greased before use to prevent the cake mixture from sticking. Melted butter or oil are the most suitable fats. Always turn the tin upside down after greasing to allow any excess fat to drain away. Use a pastry brush to get a thin layer. Non-stick sandwich tins need no preparation other than lining. Tins for cakes made by the melting or creaming methods should be greased, then the base lined with greaseproof paper, cut exactly to size and the paper brushed out with more melted butter or oil. To cut the paper accurately place the tin on top of the paper then draw round the outside of the tin. Cut just inside the line. For cakes made by the whisking method, a dusting of caster sugar and flour should be given after lining and greasing.

For fruit cakes, grease the tin, then line the sides and base with greaseproof paper as follows:

1 Cut 2 pieces of greaseproof paper to fit the base of the cake tin.
2 Cut another piece long enough to go right round the sides of the tin and to overlap slightly. It should be 2.5 cm|1 in deeper than the height of the cake tin.
3 Fold one long edge of this strip over 2.5 cm|1 in all along its length.
4 Cut snips at right angles to the edge and about 1 cm|½ in apart, all along the folded side. The snips should just reach the fold.
5 Grease the tin, place one paper base in the bottom and grease again.
6 Fit the long strip inside the tin with the folded cut edge on the bottom (the flanges will overlap slightly) and the main uncut part lining the sides of the tin. Press them well into the corners.
7 Grease the paper and lay the second base on top of the first.
8 Brush the base again with more oil.
9 After making the cake mixture and placing in the tin, wrap the outside of the tin in newspaper and place a triple thickness of newspaper in the oven to place the cake on during baking.

Methods Used in Cake-Making

Rubbing in

The rubbing-in method gives a fairly heavy cake with a crumbly, moist texture. The raising agent is always bicarbonate of soda. In rock cakes the agent is in the self-raising flour. These cakes are delicious served sliced and spread with butter, or eaten as a warm pudding with custard.

Melting

The melting method is used for very moist cakes like gingerbread. The fat, sugar, and syrup are heated together to melt, then cooled to room temperature. The eggs and any other liquid ingredients are added. The flour and other dry ingredients are sifted together. The wet ingredients are then stirred, not beaten, into the dry ingredients. The raising agent is always bicarbonate of soda. These cakes are perfect for the beginner – easy, reliable and delicious.

Creaming

Creaming or beating fat and sugar to a mousse-like consistency, and thereby incorporating air, is the secret of lightness in cakes like Victoria sponge, although a little chemical raising agent is usually added to supplement rising. The fat is never allowed to melt. If it did the carefully incorporated air beaten into it would escape.

The eggs are lightly beaten and added, by degrees, to the creamed mixture. The mixture is beaten after each addition to incorporate it thoroughly. At this point the batter can curdle, especially if the eggs are too cold, but a spoonful of sifted flour taken from the recipe can correct this. Cakes made from curdled mixtures are acceptable, but they have a less delicate, more open and coarse texture than those made from uncurdled mixture.

Plain flour, if used, should be sifted with the baking powder and salt. Self-raising flour should be sifted with salt. The flour mixture is then folded carefully into the creamed mixture with a metal spoon and with as little mixing as possible to ensure minimum air loss in the batter. A little warm water or milk is added, if necessary, to bring the mixture to a soft dropping consistency.

All-in-one creaming

The all-in-one method is an easy version of the creaming method, because all the ingredients are beaten together at the same time, but a strong electric mixer is necessary to make these cakes successfully. Soft tub margarine gives a lighter result than butter.

Creaming for fruit cakes

The creaming method, above, is used for fruitcakes, but the flour is added with the last few additions of egg to reduce the risk of curdling. After the mixture is well combined, the dry fruit is folded in well to distribute it throughout the cake. The mixture should have a soft, dropping consistency (it should fall reluctantly off a spoon given a slight shake, neither sticking obstinately nor running off) and be spread evenly in the prepared tin, with a dip in the centre of the mixture to counteract the cake 'peaking'.

Because fruit cakes are generally large and dense and contain a high proportion of fruit, which burns easily, they are cooked extremely slowly.

Whisking

In the whisking method, the only raising agent is air that has been trapped in the cake batter during mixing. As the air expands in the heat of the oven, the cake rises. Cakes like Swiss roll (page 713) and génoise commune (page 714) are made by this method.

The simplest whisked sponge contains no fat. Sugar and eggs are whisked together in a bowl set over a pan of barely simmering water until they are thick and light, then flour is folded in gently to keep in as much air as possible.

Make sure that the bowl does not touch the water or the heat could scramble the eggs. The gentle heat from the steam speeds up the dissolving of the sugar and slightly cooks and thickens the eggs, so encouraging the mixture to hold the maximum number of air bubbles. The mixture should change colour from yellow to almost white and increase to four times its original volume. The mixture is ready when a lifted whisk will leave a ribbon-like trail.

A hand-held electric whisk is recommended as whisking can take about 10 minutes. If a powerful food mixer is used, the heat can be dispensed with, though the process is speeded up if the mixture is put into a warmed bowl.

When the flour is folded in, great care should be taken to fold rather than stir or beat, as the aim is to incorporate the flour without losing any of the beaten-in air, which alone will raise the cake. The correct movement is more of lifting the mixture and cutting into it, rather than stirring it.

Although they are light and springy, a drawback of these cakes is that they go stale quickly. Always plan to make fatless sponge on the day of serving, or freeze the cake once it is cool.

In a lighter but more complicated whisked sponge, the eggs are separated and the yolks are whisked with the sugar followed by the flour. The whites are whisked in another bowl, then folded into the yolks Sometimes half the sugar is whisked with the yolks, and half with the whites to give a meringue.

The génoise is a whisked sponge that has cool, melted butter folded into it with the flour. Butter gives it flavour and richness and makes it keep a day or two longer than fatless sponges. The butter should be poured in a stream around the edge of the bowl and then folded in. If the butter is poured heavily on top of the whisked mixture, it forces out some of the air, and needs excessive mixing, with the danger of more air loss.

Whisked cakes are cooked when the surface will spring back when pressed with a finger. The cakes should be cooled for 10 minutes in the tin placed upside down on a wire rack and then turned out on to the rack. The baking paper should be carefully peeled off to allow the escape of steam.

Victoria Sandwich

oil for greasing
110 g | 4 oz butter
110 g | 4 oz caster sugar
2 eggs

110 g | 4 oz self-raising flour, sifted
water
2 tablespoons raspberry jam
caster sugar for dusting

1 Preheat the oven to 180°C | 350°F | gas mark 4.
2 Prepare 2 × 15 cm | 6 in sandwich tins by lightly brushing with oil then lining the bottom of each with a disc of greaseproof paper and brushing again with oil.
3 Cream the butter and sugar together until light and fluffy.
4 Beat the eggs in a separate bowl, and gradually beat into the creamed mixture a little at a time, adding 1 tablespoon of the flour if the mixture begins to curdle.
5 Fold in the flour, adding enough water to bring the mixture to a dropping consistency.
6 Divide the mixture between the prepared tins and smooth the tops with a spatula. Bake in the middle of the oven for about 20 minutes, or until the cakes are well risen, golden and feel spongy to the fingertips.
7 Allow the cakes to cool for a few minutes in the tins, then turn out on to a wire rack. Peel off the lining paper. Invert the cakes so they cool right-side up. Cool completely.

8 Sandwich the cakes together with the jam.

9 Dust the top of the cake with caster sugar.

Lemon Victoria Sponge

oil for greasing

170 g | 6 oz butter

170 g | 6 oz caster sugar

grated zest of 1 lemon

3 eggs

170 g | 6 oz self-raising flour

For the filling and topping

recipe lemon curd (see page 799)

feather icing (see page 628)

1 Preheat the oven to 180°C | 350°F | gas mark 4.

2 Prepare 2 × 20 cm | 8 in sandwich tins (see page 701).

3 Cream the butter and when soft add the sugar and the lemon zest. Beat until light and fluffy.

4 Beat the eggs in a separate bowl then beat gradually in to the butter mixture.

5 Fold in the flour. Add a little water to bring the mixture to a dropping consistency.

6 Divide the mixture between the prepared tins and smooth the tops with a spatula. Bake in the middle of the oven for 20–25 minutes, or until the cakes are well risen, golden and feel spongy to the fingertips.

7 Allow the cakes to cool for a few minutes in the tins, then turn out on to a wire rack. Peel off the lining paper. Invert the cakes so that they cool right-side up.

8 Sandwich the cakes with lemon curd.

9 Ice the top and 'feather' it as described in the icing recipe.

Madeira Cake

oil for greasing

170 g | 6 oz unsalted butter

170 g | 6 oz caster sugar

grated zest and juice of 1 lemon

a pinch of ground cinnamon

3 eggs

110 g | 4 oz self-raising flour

55 g | 2 oz ground almonds

milk (optional)

1 slice of candied citrus peel

1 Preheat the oven to 170°C | 325°F | gas mark 3.

2 Prepare a deep 18 cm | 7 in cake tin (see page 701).

3 Cream the butter and when soft add the sugar and lemon zest. Beat until light and fluffy. Add the cinnamon.

4 Beat in the eggs together in a separate bowl then beat gradually into the butter mixture. Add a little flour to prevent the mixture from curdling if necessary. Add the lemon juice.

5 Fold in the flour and the ground almonds.

6 Add enough milk to bring the mixture to a dropping consistency.

7 Spoon the mixture into the prepared tin and smooth the top with a palette knife or spatula.

8 Bake for 45 minutes. Place the citrus peel on top of the cake, then bake for a further 30 minutes. A skewer inserted in the centre should come out clean.

9 Cool the cake for 10 minutes in the tin before gently easing out on to a wire rack.

Marbled Chocolate Cake

oil for greasing

4 egg quantity Victoria sandwich cake mixture (see page 703)

1 tablespoon cocoa powder

1 tablespoon warm milk

110 g | 4 oz plain chocolate

15 g | ½ oz butter

1 Preheat the oven to 180°C | 350°F | gas mark 4.

2 Lightly oil a 20 cm | 8 in ring mould.

3 Divide the Victoria sandwich mixture equally between 2 bowls.

4 Mix the cocoa powder with the milk and add it to one bowl.

5 Place spoonfuls of the mixture, alternating the colours, in the ring mould. Use a skewer in a figure-of-eight motion to swirl the colours together.

6 Bake for 20–25 minutes, or until the cake is well risen and feels spongy. Allow to cool for a few minutes in the tin, then turn out on to a wire rack to cool completely.

7 Break up the chocolate into small even pieces. Put into a heatproof bowl, add the butter and place over, not in, a saucepan of steaming water. Stir until completely melted.

8 Pour the chocolate over the cake, making sure that it is completely covered. Leave to cool and harden.

Chocolate Fudge Cake

This cake, using the all-in-one method, is straightforward to make. It keeps well for up to 3 days.

MAKES A 20 CM | 8 IN CAKE

oil for greasing

4 medium eggs, beaten

110 g | 4 oz soft tub margarine

110 g | 4 oz caster sugar

110 g | 4 oz soft light brown sugar

6 tablespoons crème fraiche or soured cream

1 teaspoon vanilla extract

170 g | 6 oz self-raising flour

55 g | 2 oz good-quality cocoa powder

1½ teaspoons bicarbonate of soda

a pinch of salt

To ice

1 quantity soured cream chocolate icing (see page 728)

1 Preheat the oven to 180°C | 350°F | gas mark 4.

2 Brush a 20 cm | 8 in deep cake tin with vegetable oil, then line the base with baking parchment.

3 Place the eggs, margarine, sugars, cream and vanilla in a large bowl and beat with an electric hand whisk for 2 minutes or until smooth.

4 Sift the flour, cocoa, bicarbonate of soda and salt on to a piece of greaseproof paper to combine, then tip into the egg mixture.

5 Beat for 30 seconds to combine.

6 Turn the mixture into the prepared tin and bake in the centre of the oven for 40–45 minutes. A skewer inserted into the centre should come out clean.

7 Leave to cool for 10 minutes in the tin, then release the cake from the edge of the tin with a spatula. Invert the cake on to a wire rack to cool top-side up.

8 Remove the lining paper and cut the cake in half when cool. Use the soured cream icing to fill the middle and ice the top and sides.

Christmas Cake

110 g | 4 oz glacé cherries
55 g | 2 oz chopped mixed peel
450 g | 1 lb raisins
285 g | 10 oz sultanas
110 g | 4 oz currants
grated zest of ½ lemon
2 tablespoons black treacle

200 ml | 7 fl oz beer or sweet sherry
225 g | 8 oz butter
225 | 8 oz soft dark brown sugar
5 eggs, beaten
285 g | 10 oz plain flour
2 teaspoons ground mixed spice
110 g | 4 oz ground almonds

1 Preheat the oven to 170°C | 325°F | gas mark 3.

2 Prepare a 22 cm | 9 in round cake tin with a double thickness of greased greaseproof paper (see page 701). Tie a double thickness of brown paper or newspaper around the outside of the tin.

3 Cut up the cherries and mix with the remaining fruit. Place in a bowl or plastic bag.

4 Add the lemon zest, treacle and beer to the fruit and stir the mix well. Leave in a cool place overnight

5 Cream the butter until soft. Add the sugar and beat until light and fluffy.

6 Add the eggs slowly, beating well after each addition. If the mixture curdles, beat in 1 tablespoon of the flour.

7 Fold in the flour, mixed spice, and ground almonds alternately with the fruit mixture.

8 Place the mixture in the prepared tin and make a deep hollow in the middle.

9 Bake for 2½ hours, or until a skewer emerges clean when inserted into the middle of the cake.

10 Allow to cool for 10 minutes then turn out of the tin on to a wire rack.

Old-fashioned Boiled Fruit Cake

This cake is not, as its name suggests, boiled instead of baked, but the fruit is boiled in water and orange juice and allowed to stand for 3 days before completing. This makes the cake particularly moist. Instead of being decorated with marzipan and icing, the cake is finished with a glazed fruit and nut topping and a pretty ribbon.

225 g | 8 oz butter
225 g | 8 oz sultanas
225 g | 8 oz raisins
110 g | 4 oz currants
55 g | 2 oz chopped mixed peel
55 g | 2 oz glacé cherries, halved
170 g | 6 oz dried apricots, chopped
55 g | 2 oz dried apples, chopped
110 g | 4 oz dried dates, chopped
110 g | 4 oz dried peaches, chopped
110 g | 4 oz dried pears, chopped
225 g | 8 oz soft dark brown sugar
grated zest and juice of 1 lemon
grated zest and juice of 1 orange
110 ml | 4 fl oz water
110 ml | 4 fl oz orange juice

110 ml | 4 fl oz brandy
½ teaspoon freshly grated nutmeg
1 teaspoon ground cinnamon
1 teaspoon ground allspice
½ teaspoon ground ginger
¼ teaspoon ground cardamom
1 tablespoon black treacle
5 eggs, beaten
310 g | 11 oz plain flour
1 teaspoon baking powder

For the fruit topping

340 g | 12 oz apricot jam
340 g | 12 oz mixed dried fruit and nuts, such as pecans, brazils, almonds, apricots, red and green cherries, prunes, peaches, pears, etc.

1 Put the butter, sultanas, raisins, currants, mixed peel, cherries, apricots, apples, dates, peaches, pears, sugar, lemon and orange zest and juice, water and orange juice into a large pan. Bring slowly up to the boil. Stir with a wooden spoon, cover with a lid, and simmer for 10 minutes.

2 Remove from the heat and allow to cool slightly. Add the brandy and spices and transfer to a large bowl. When the mixture is completely cold, cover and put in a cool place (not the refrigerator) for 3 days, stirring daily.

3 Preheat the oven to 170°C | 325°F | gas mark 3. Line the base and sides of a 25 cm | 10 in round cake tin with a double thickness of greased greaseproof paper.

4 Stir the treacle into the boiled fruit mixture and beat in the eggs. Sift together the flour and baking powder and stir into the cake mixture, which will be slightly sloppy. Turn it into the prepared cake tin and bake for about 3½ hours, or until a skewer inserted into the centre of the cake comes out clean.

5 Leave the cake to cool in the tin.

6 When completely cold, wrap up in kitchen foil until ready to decorate. It will mature well for 2–3 months.

7 To decorate the cake: put the apricot jam into a saucepan with 1 tablespoon water. Heat until boiling and then push through a sieve. Allow to cool slightly, then brush the top of the cake with the apricot glaze. Arrange the fruit and nuts all over the top of

the cake in a haphazard fashion and then, using a pastry brush, glaze carefully with the apricot glaze.

8 Before serving, tie a decorative ribbon round the cake.

NOTES: The glaze will remain shiny on the cake for a few days but after a week it will begin to lose its gloss so it is better not to decorate the cake too early.

  If the cake top becomes very dark during baking cover it with a double layer of damp greaseproof paper.

Simnel Cake

On this festive Easter cake the 11 balls of marzipan are said to represent the apostles (without Judas). Sometimes they are made into egg shapes, the symbol of spring and rebirth.

oil for greasing
225 g | 8 oz plain flour
55 g | 2 oz rice flour
a large pinch each of salt and baking powder
110 g | 4 oz glacé cherries
225 g | 8 oz butter, softened
225 g | 8 oz caster sugar

grated zest of 1 lemon
4 eggs, separated
225 g | 8 oz sultanas
110 g | 4 oz currants
30 g | 1 oz chopped mixed peel
675 g | 1½ lb marzipan (see page 734)
beaten egg

1 Preheat the oven to 180°C | 350°F | gas mark 4.

2 Prepare a 20 cm | 8 in cake tin with a double lining of greased greaseproof paper. Wrap the outside of the cake tin with a double thickness of brown paper or newspaper to insulate the cake from direct heat.

3 Sift the flours with the salt and baking powder. Cut the cherries in half.

4 Cream the butter until soft. Add the sugar and lemon zest. Beat until light and fluffy.

5 Beat in the egg yolks. Whisk the whites until stiff.

6 Fold one-third of the sifted flour into the mixture. Fold in the egg whites, alternately with the remaining flour and the fruit and peel.

7 Put half the mixture into the prepared tin, spreading a little up the sides.

8 Take just over one-third of the marzipan paste. Roll it into a smooth round just smaller than the size of the cake tin. Place in the tin. Cover with the remaining cake mixture.

9 Using a palette knife, make a dip in the centre of the cake to counteract any tendency to rise in the middle.

10 Bake for 2 hours, then turn the oven temperature down to 150°C | 300°F | gas mark 2. Bake for a further 30 minutes.

11 Roll the remaining marzipan into a circle the same size as the top of the cake. Cut a piece from the centre about 12.5 cm | 5 in in diameter and shape into 11 small even-sized balls.

12 Preheat the grill to its highest setting. Lay the ring of marzipan on top of the cake and brush with beaten egg. Arrange the marzipan balls on top of the ring and brush again with beaten egg. Grill until golden-brown.

Coffee Almond Layer Cake

oil for greasing
110 g | 4 oz butter, softened
110 g | 4 oz caster sugar
85 g | 3 oz plain flour
a pinch of salt
1 teaspoon baking powder
2 eggs
2 teaspoons instant coffee powder, dissolved in 2
    tablespoons hot water
55 g | 2 oz ground almonds

For the filling

170 g | 6 oz unsalted butter, softened
340 g | 12 oz icing sugar
2 teaspoons instant coffee powder, dissolved in 1
    tablespoon hot water

To decorate

55 g | 2 oz flaked almonds, toasted

1 Preheat the oven to 180°C | 350°F | gas mark 4.
2 Prepare 2 × 18 cm | 7 in sandwich tins (see page 701).
3 Cream the butter until soft. Add the sugar and beat until light and fluffy.
4 Sift the flour with the salt and baking powder. Beat the eggs together in a separate bowl.
5 Gradually add the eggs to the butter and sugar mixture. Fold in the flour and the ground almonds. Stir in the coffee. Divide the mixture between the prepared tins and smooth the tops with a spatula.
6 Bake for 20–25 minutes, or until the cakes are firm and golden-brown. Allow to cool in the tins for 5 minutes, then turn out on to wire racks to cool completely. Peel off the lining paper.
7 Meanwhile, make the filling: beat the butter and sugar until light and fluffy and stir in the coffee.
8 Sandwich the cake layers with half the butter icing and spread the remainder around the sides and top of the cake. Decorate with flaked almonds.

Chocolate Almond Cake

oil for greasing
110 g | 4 oz butter
110 g | 4 oz caster sugar
2 eggs
2 tablespoons golden syrup
30 g | 1 oz ground almonds
110 g | 4 oz self-raising flour
a pinch of salt
30 g | 1 oz cocoa powder

For the icing

110 g | 4 oz granulated sugar
110 ml | 4 fl oz milk
140 g | 5 oz plain chocolate, chopped
55 g | 2 oz butter
2 tablespoons double cream
vanilla essence

1 Preheat the oven to 180°C | 350°F | gas mark 4.
2 Prepare an 18 cm | 7 in deep cake tin (see page 701).

3 Cream the butter until soft. Add the sugar and beat until light and fluffy.

4 Whisk the eggs together and add a little at a time to the butter and sugar mixture, beating well after each addition. If the mixture curdles, beat in 1 tablespoon flour.

5 Stir in the golden syrup and ground almonds.

6 Sift the flour with the salt and cocoa powder and fold into the mixture, which should have a reluctant dropping consistency; if it is too thick add a little water or milk.

7 Pile the mixture into the prepared tin and smooth the top with a palette knife. Bake for 40 minutes, or until the cake is well risen and feels spongy.

8 Allow to cool in the tin for 10 minutes then turn out and cool on a wire rack. Peel off the lining paper.

9 Meanwhile, make the icing: put the sugar and milk into a saucepan. Allow the sugar to dissolve over a low heat then bring to the boil.

10 Remove the pan from the heat and stir in the chocolate; add the butter, cream and vanilla essence. Stir until completely melted.

11 Put into a bowl, cover and chill for 2 hours until the icing is spreadable.

12 When the cake is cool, split it in half horizontally and sandwich together again using a quarter of the icing. Spread the remaining icing on the top and sides of the cake.

Rice Cake

oil for greasing
110 g | 4 oz butter, softened
225 g | 8 oz caster sugar

finely grated zest of ½ lemon
4 eggs
225 g | 8 oz ground rice

1 Preheat the oven to 180°C | 350°F | gas mark 4.

2 Line an 18 cm | 7 in cake tin with a double layer of greased and floured greaseproof paper.

3 Cream the butter until soft. Add sugar and beat until light and fluffy. Add the lemon zest and mix well.

4 Separate the eggs. Add the yolks to the mixture one at a time, beating hard all the time.

5 Whisk the egg whites until fairly stiff but not dry. Fold in the egg whites in two additions alternately with the ground rice.

6 Pour the mixture into the prepared tin. Make a slight hollow in the centre of the mixture to counteract any tendency to rise in the middle.

7 Bake for 45 minutes, or until firm to the touch and slightly shrunken at the edges.

8 Allow to cool in the tin for 10 minutes, then turn out on to a wire rack to cool completely. Peel off the lining paper.

Individual Coffee Walnut Cakes

MAKES 12

110 g|4 oz butter, softened

110 g|4 oz caster sugar

2 eggs

110 g|4 oz self-raising flour

2 teaspoons instant coffee powder

¼ teaspoon vanilla essence

55 g|2 oz chopped walnuts

55 g|2 oz plain chocolate, grated

1 Preheat the oven to 180°C|350°F|gas mark 4. Grease and flour 12 bun tins or paper cases.
2 Cream the butter and sugar until light and fluffy.
3 Beat in the eggs, a little at a time.
4 Fold in the flour, coffee, vanilla essence and walnuts. Add a little water if necessary to make a soft dropping consistency.
5 Fill the tins or paper cases two-thirds full and bake for 15–20 minutes. Leave to cool on a wire rack.
6 Melt the chocolate in a heatproof bowl over but not touching a saucepan of steaming water.
7 Spread each bun with a little melted chocolate and leave to cool and harden.

Squashy Rhubarb Cake

For the crumble topping

55 g|2 oz butter

85 g|3 oz plain flour

30 g|1 oz sugar

For the filling

675 g|1½ lb rhubarb, cut into 2.5 cm|1 in pieces

2 tablespoons sugar

For the cake

85 g|3 oz butter, softened

85 g|3 oz sugar

2 small eggs

85 g|3 oz self-raising flour, sifted with a pinch of salt

milk

To finish

icing sugar

1 Preheat the oven to 180°C|350°F|gas mark 4.
2 Prepare a deep 20 cm|8 in cake tin (see page 701).
3 First make the crumble topping: rub the butter into the flour and add the sugar. Set aside.
4 Now make the cake: cream the butter until soft. Add the sugar and beat until very pale, light and fluffy.
5 Lightly beat the eggs and add them to the sugar mixture, beating in a little at a time, and folding in a spoonful of flour if the mixture curdles.

6 Fold in the remaining flour and add a little milk if the mixture is too stiff; it should be of a dropping consistency.

7 Turn the mixture into the tin and smooth the top with a spatula.

8 Cover carefully with the raw rhubarb pieces and the sugar. Sprinkle with the crumble mixture.

9 Bake for about 45 minutes, or until the cake feels firm on top. Leave to cool in the tin.

10 Just before serving, remove from the tin and sift a thin layer of icing sugar over the top.

Pain de Gênes (Rich Almond Cake)

This is a difficult cake to make. If the oven door is opened too early it will sink.

melted butter for greasing	a good pinch of salt
110 g|4 oz blanched almonds	85 g|3 oz butter, melted and cooled
3 eggs	1 tablespoon Amaretto or Kirsch
140 g|5 oz caster sugar	
55 g|2 oz potato starch or plain flour	**To finish**
½ teaspoon baking powder	icing sugar

1 Preheat the oven to 180°C|350°F|gas mark 4.

2 Brush a moule-à-manqué or 20 cm|8 in cake tin with melted butter, line the bottom with a circle of greaseproof paper and brush it again with butter.

3 Grind the almonds finely with 1 tablespoon of the sugar.

4 Whisk the eggs and remaining sugar together until light and fluffy.

5 Sift the potato starch or flour with the baking powder and salt into a bowl. Stir in the nuts. Half fold this mixture into the egg and sugar mixture.

6 Carefully fold the butter into the cake mixture with the minimum of stirring. Add the Amaretto or Kirsch. Pour the mixture into the prepared tin.

7 Bake for 35–40 minutes, or until the cake is brown on top and springs back when lightly pressed with a finger.

8 Allow the cake to cool in the tin for 10 minutes, then loosen the sides with a knife and turn out on to a wire rack to cool. Peel off the lining paper. When cold, sift a thin layer of icing sugar over the top.

Whisked Sponge

oil for greasing	1½ tablespoons warm water
3 eggs	85 g|3 oz plain flour, sifted
85 g|3 oz caster sugar	a pinch of salt

1 Preheat the oven to 180°C|350°F|gas mark 4. Prepare a 20 cm|8 in cake tin (see page 701).

2 Place the eggs and sugar in a heatproof bowl set over, not in, a saucepan of simmering water. Whisk the mixture until light, thick and fluffy. (If using an electric mixer no heat is required.)

3 Remove the bowl from the heat and continue whisking until slightly cooled. Add the water.

4 Sift the flour with the salt and, using a large metal spoon, fold into the mixture, being careful not to beat out any of the air.

5 Turn the mixture into the prepared tin and bake in the middle of the oven for about 30 minutes. When the cake is ready, it will shrink slightly and the edges will look crinkled. When pressed gently it will feel firm but spongy and will sound 'creaky'.

6 Turn out on to a wire rack to cool.

Swiss Roll

oil for greasing	1½ tablespoons warm water
85 g⎟3 oz plain flour, sifted	2–3 drops of vanilla essence
a pinch of salt	caster sugar
3 eggs	3 tablespoons warmed jam
85 g⎟3 oz caster sugar	

1 Preheat the oven to 180°C⎟350°F⎟gas mark 4.

2 Prepare a Swiss roll tin. Place in it a piece of greaseproof paper cut to fit the bottom of the tin exactly and brush with oil. Dust with sugar and flour.

3 Sift the flour with the salt.

4 Put the eggs and sugar into a heatproof bowl set over, not in, a saucepan of simmering water. Whisk the mixture until light, thick and fluffy. (If using an electric mixer, no heat is required.) Continue whisking until slightly cooled.

5 Using a large metal spoon, fold the water, essence and flour into the egg mixture.

6 Pour the mixture into the prepared tin.

7 Bake for 12–15 minutes, or until no imprints remains when the sponge is lightly pressed with a finger, and the edges look very slightly shrunken.

8 Lay a piece of greaseproof paper on a work top and sprinkle it evenly with caster sugar. Using a knife, loosen the edges of the baked sponge, then turn it over on to the sugared greaseproof paper. Remove the lining paper.

9 While the cake is still warm, spread it with the jam.

10 Using the paper under the cake to help you, roll the cake up firmly from one end. Making a little cut across the width of the cake just where you begin to roll helps to get a good tight Swiss roll.

11 Dredge the cake with caster sugar.

NOTE: If the cake is to be filled with cream, this cannot be done while it is hot. Roll the cake up, unfilled, and keep it wrapped in greaseproof paper until cool. Unroll carefully, spread with whipped cream, and roll up again.

Normandy Apple and Nut Cake

For the apple filling

3 cooking apples (about 450 g | 1 lb)

a little butter for greasing

1 strip of thinly pared lemon zest

about 85 g | 3 oz soft light brown sugar

4 egg yolks

50 g | 1¾ oz plain flour, sifted

40 g | 1½ oz ground hazelnuts, toasted

50 g | 1¾ oz arrowroot

3 egg whites

For the cake

butter for greasing

125 g | 4½ oz caster sugar

To finish

icing sugar

150 ml | ¼ pint double cream, whipped

1 Wash, peel, quarter and core the apples. Grease the bottom and sides of a heavy saucepan with butter. Slice the apples thickly into the pan and add the lemon zest and 4 tablespoons water. Cover and cook over a low heat, stirring occasionally, until completely soft.

2 Push through a sieve. Rinse out the pan and return the purée to it. Add at least 55 g | 2 oz sugar to 570 ml | 1 pint purée. Cook rapidly until the mixture is of a dropping consistency (about 4 minutes). Leave to cool.

3 Preheat the oven to 180°C | 350°F | gas mark 4. Butter a 20 cm | 8 in moule-à-manqué or sandwich tin and dust it out with flour.

4 Beat the sugar and egg yolks together until creamy and white, then fold in the flour, hazelnuts and arrowroot.

5 Whisk the egg whites until stiff but not dry and fold them into the cake mixture. Turn into the prepared tin and smooth the top with a spatula.

6 Bake for 40 minutes, until firm to the touch. Turn on to a wire rack to cool.

7 Split the cake and sandwich it with the apple filling. Dredge the top with icing sugar.

8 Serve with whipped cream.

Génoise Commune

oil for greasing

4 eggs

125 g | 4½ oz caster sugar

55 g | 2 oz butter, melted and cooled

125 g | 4½ oz plain flour

1 Preheat the oven to 180°C | 350° | gas mark 4.

2 Prepare a 20 cm | 8 in moule-à-manqué or deep sandwich tin (see page 701).

3 Break the eggs into a large heatproof bowl and add the sugar. Set the bowl over, not in, a saucepan of simmering water and whisk until the mixture has doubled in bulk, and will leave a ribbon trail on the surface when the whisk is lifted. Lift the bowl off the heat and continue to whisk until cooled. (If using an electric mixer, whisking need not be done over heat.) Pour the butter around the edges of the mixture and give a couple of folds.

4 Sift the flour over the cake mixture and fold it in with the butter, using a large metal spoon.

5 Pour the mixture into the prepared tin. Bake in the oven – the edges should look slightly shrunken and the top should spring back when pressed lightly with a fingertip – for 30–35 minutes. Allow to cool slightly in the tin placed upside-down before turning out on to a wire rack to cool completely. Peel off the lining paper.

Génoise Fine

oil for greasing
4 eggs
125 g | 4½ oz caster sugar

100 g | 3½ oz butter, melted and cooled
100 g | 3½ oz plain flour

1 Preheat the oven to 180°C | 350°F | gas mark 4.

2 Prepare a 20 cm | 8 in moule-à-manqué or deep sandwich tin.

3 Break the eggs into a large bowl and add the sugar. Set the bowl over, not in, a saucepan of simmering water and whisk until light, fluffy and doubled in bulk. Remove from the heat and continue whisking until cooled (if using an electric mixer, whisking need not be done over heat). Pour the butter around the edge of the mixture and give a couple of folds.

4 Sift the flour over the cake mixture and fold it in with the butter with a large metal spoon.

5 Turn the mixture into the prepared tin and bake for 30–35 minutes – the edges should look slightly shrunken and the top should spring back when pressed lightly with a fingertip. Allow the cake to cool in the tin upside down for a few minutes on a wire rack, then remove from the tin to cool completely. Peel off the lining paper.

NOTE: This is sometimes called a 'butter sponge'. However, this description is not culinarily correct, as a true sponge contains no fat.

Coffee Génoise with Chocolate Caraque

For the cake
oil for greasing
4 eggs
125 g | 4½ oz caster sugar
55 g | 2 oz butter, melted and cooled
100 g | 3½ oz plain flour
2 teaspoons instant coffee powder

110 g | 4 oz unsalted butter
110 g | 4 oz salted butter
coffee essence

For the chocolate caraque
55 g | 2 oz plain chocolate

For the coffee buttercream
110 g | 4 oz sugar
150 ml | ¼ pint milk
2 egg yolks

To decorate
toasted chopped almonds
icing sugar

1 Preheat the oven to 180°C|350°F|gas mark 4.

2 Prepare a 20 cm|8 in moule-à-manqué or deep sandwich tin (see page 701).

3 Break the eggs into a large heatproof bowl and add the sugar. Set the bowl over, not in, a saucepan of simmering water. Whisk until the mixture leaves a ribbon when the beaters are lifted. Remove from the heat and continue whisking until slightly cooled. (If using an electric mixer, whisking need not be done over heat.) Pour in the butter around the edge of the mixture. Give a couple of folds.

4 Sift the flour and coffee powder over the cake mixture and fold in thoroughly but gently with the butter using a large metal spoon. Turn the mixture into the prepared tin.

5 Bake for about 35 minutes or until cooked – the edges should look slightly shrunken and the top should spring back when pressed lightly with a fingertip. Allow the cake to cool upside-down in the tin, then turn out on to a wire rack to cool completely. Peel off the paper lining.

6 Make the buttercream: put half the sugar and the milk into a saucepan and bring to the boil. Beat the egg yolks with the remaining sugar, pour on the milk, mix well and return the mixture to the saucepan. Stir over a low heat without boiling until slightly thickened. Strain and leave to cool.

7 Beat the butter until creamy and gradually whisk in the custard mixture. Flavour with coffee essence.

8 Make the chocolate caraque: melt the chocolate on a heatproof plate over a saucepan of boiling water. Spread thinly on a marble slab or other hard cold surface. When just set, use a thin, flexible knife to shave off curls of chocolate: hold the knife with one hand on the handle and one hand on the tip of the blade. Hold it horizontally and scrape the chocolate surface by pulling the knife towards you. Chill the curls to harden them.

9 To decorate: split the cake in half and sandwich with one-third of the buttercream. Spread the tops and sides with the remainder. Press almonds on to the sides of the cake. Cover the top with a pile of caraque chocolate and sift over a very fine dusting of icing sugar.

Chocolate Génoise

oil or melted lard for greasing	55 g|2 oz unsalted butter, melted and cooled
4 eggs	85 g|3 oz plain flour, sifted
125|4½ oz caster sugar	30 g|1 oz cocoa powder, sifted

1 Preheat the oven to 180°C|350°F|gas mark 4.

2 Prepare a 20 cm|8 in moule-à-manqué tin (see page 701).

3 Whisk the eggs and sugar together until very light and fluffy. If you have an electric mixer, this should take 5 minutes. If not, the whisking has to be done with a hand-held electric whisk in a bowl set over, not in, a saucepan of simmering water and it can take up to 10 minutes. Be careful not to allow the base of the bowl to become too hot.

4 Remove from the heat and continue whisking. The mixture should then be whisked until cooled. It is ready when it leaves a ribbon trail when the whisk is lifted. Do not over-whisk and stop if it begins to lose bulk. Pour the butter around the edge of the bowl and fold in with two strokes.

5 Sift the flour and cocoa powder over the mixture and fold in using a large metal spoon.

6 Tip the mixture into the prepared tin and give a light tap on the work top to get rid of any large air pockets. Bake for 25–35 minutes – the edges should look slightly shrunken and the top should spring back when pressed lightly with a fingertip. Allow the cake to cool in the tin placed upside-down for 10 minutes, then turn out on to a wire rack to cool completely. Peel off the lining paper.

Very Rich Chocolate Cake

This is an adaptation of a Martha Stewart recipe.

For the cake

55 g | 2 oz sultanas, chopped

55 ml | 2 fl oz brandy

oil for greasing

200 g | 7 oz plain chocolate, chopped evenly

2 tablespoons water

110 g | 4 oz unsalted butter

3 eggs, separated

140 g | 5 oz caster sugar

55 g | 2 oz plain flour, sifted

85 g | 3 oz ground almonds

For the icing

140 g | 5 oz dark chocolate, cut into small pieces

150 ml | ¼ pint double cream

1 Soak the sultanas in the brandy overnight.

2 Preheat the oven to 180°C | 350°F | gas mark 4.

3 Prepare a 20 cm | 8 in moule-à-manqué or cake tin (see page 701).

4 Put the chocolate and water into a heatproof bowl set over, not in, a saucepan of steaming water. Stir until melted, then stir in the butter piece by piece until the mixture is smooth.

5 Beat the egg yolks and sugar until pale and mousse-like. Stir the chocolate into the egg-yolk mixture.

6 Very carefully fold the flour into the egg yolk and chocolate mixture with the ground almonds, sultanas and brandy.

7 Whisk the egg whites until stiff but not dry and fold into the chocolate mixture.

8 Turn the mixture into the prepared tin and bake for 35–40 minutes (the centre should still be moist). Leave to get completely cold in the tin.

9 Remove the cake from the tin and place it on a wire rack. Peel off the lining paper.

10 Make the icing: heat together the chocolate and cream. Stir until all the chocolate has melted and the mixture is smooth. Allow to cool and thicken to a coating consistency before pouring it over the cake.

11 Leave for at least 2 hours to allow the icing to harden.

Chocolate and Orange Cake

For the cake
oil for greasing
85 g | 3 oz plain chocolate
1 teaspoon vanilla essence
340 g | 12 oz soft light brown sugar
290mlg | ½ pint milk
grated zest of ½ orange
110g | 4 oz butter
2 eggs
225g | 8 oz plain flour
1 teaspoon bicarbonate of soda

For the icing
110 g | 4 oz plain chocolate
4 tablespoons milk

For the orange filling
grated zest of ½ orange
290ml | ½ pint double cream, whipped
caster sugar to taste

1 Preheat the ove to 190°C | 375°F | gas mark 5.
2 Prepare 2 × 8 cm sandwich tins (see page 701).
3 Put the chocolate, vanilla, half the sugar and half the milk into a heavy saucepan. Cook, stirring, until quite smooth. Add the orange zest.
4 Beat the butter with the remaining sugar until very light and creamy. Beat in the eggs, then add the melted chocolate mixture and beat again. Sift in the flour and soda and beat well to get rid of all lumps. Stir in the remaining milk. The mixture should now have the consistency of pancake batter.
5 Divide the mixture between the prepared tins and bake in the middle of the preheated over for about 30 minutes, or until the cakes have a very slightly shrunken look around the edges. Do not worry if they do not feel very firm – they should be very moist and rather sticky. Allow the cakes to cool in the tins for 3 minutes before turning out on to a wire rack to cool. Peel off the lining paper.

Orange filing
Mix the orange zest into the whipped cream and sweeten to taste with caster sugar. Sandwich the 3 layers of cake together with the cream filing.

Icing
Put the chocolate and milk into a small, heavy saucepan. Heat gently, stirring, until smooth and thick. Cool slightly, then pour or spread over the top of the cake.

Gâteau Nougatine

For the cake

oil for greasing

110 g | 4 oz hazelnuts

4 eggs

1 egg white

110 g | 4 oz caster sugar

55 g | 2 oz butter, melted and cooled

100 g | 3½ oz plain flour

For the royal icing

1 small egg white

170 g | 6 oz icing sugar

a squeeze of lemon juice

For the nougat

45 g | 1½ oz finely chopped almonds

85 g | 3 oz caster sugar

½ teaspoon powdered glucose or a pinch of cream of tartar

1 lemon

a little oil

For the crème au beurre mousseline

85 g | 3 oz lump or granulated sugar

3 tablespoons water

2 egg yolks

110–140 g | 4–5 oz unsalted butter, softened

For the chocolate fondant icing

225 g | 8 oz loaf sugar

½ teaspoon liquid glucose or a pinch of cream of tartar

115 ml | 4 fl oz water

30 g | 1 oz plain chocolate

1 drop of vanilla essence

1 Preheat the oven to 180°C | 350°F | gas mark 4.

2 Prepare a 20 cm | 8 in moule-à-manqué tin (see page 701).

3 Make the cake: brown the hazelnuts in the oven. Remove the skins. Cool and grind with 1 tablespoon of the sugar.

4 Separate the eggs. Beat the yolks and 1 egg white with all but 1 tablespoon of the remaining sugar, until white and creamy.

5 Whisk the remaining egg whites until stiff. Whisk in the reserved sugar.

6 Pour the butter around the edge of the egg-yolk mixture. Add the dry ingredients and the meringue and fold swiftly together.

7 Pile into the prepared tin and smooth the top with a spatula. Bake for 40–50 minutes, or until the cake is firm to the touch and just shrinking away from the sides of the tin. Cool on a wire rack. Peel off the lining paper.

The royal icing

8 Whisk the egg white until frothy. Beat the icing sugar into it with the lemon juice until very smooth, white and stiff. Cover with a damp cloth until ready for use.

9 Oil a baking sheet.

10 Bake the chopped almonds until pale brown. Keep warm. Put the sugar and glucose into a heavy saucepan and place over a medium heat. When golden, add the warm almonds and continue to cook for 1 minute.

11 Turn the mixture on to the oiled baking sheet. Turn it over with an oiled palette knife, using a half-mixing, half-kneading motion. While still warm and pliable, roll as thinly as possible with an oiled lemon.

The crème au beurre mousseline

12 dissolve the sugar in the water. Boil to the short thread stage (a little syrup stretched between a wet finger and thumb will form a short thread). Whisk the yolks as you pour on the sugar syrup in a steady stream. Whisk until thick and mousse-like. Cream the butter and, when soft, add the mousse mixture to the butter.

The chocolate fondant icing

13 Dissolve the sugar and liquid glucose in the water in a heavy saucepan over a low heat without boiling. Cover and bring to the boil. Boil to the soft ball stage (see page 665). Meanwhile, scrub a stainless steel work top and sprinkle with water. Stop the sugar syrup from cooking further by dipping the bottom of the pan into a bowl of very cold water. Cool slightly.

14 Chop the chocolate and melt it in a heatproof bowl set over, not in, a saucepan of steaming water. Pour the sugar syrup slowly on to the moistened stainless steel top. With a wet palette knife, fold the outsides of the mixture into the centre. When opaque but still fairly soft, add the melted chocolate and vanilla essence and continue to turn with a spatula and work until the fondant becomes fairly stiff. Put in a bowl and stand over a saucepan of simmering water to soften.

To assemble

15 Split the cake into 3 layers. Crush the nougat with a rolling pin and mix half of it with half the crème au beurre mousseline. Sandwich the cake together with this. Pour the melted chocolate fondant icing over the top. Spread crème au beurre around the sides and press on the remaining crushed nougat.

16 When the chocolate has set, fill a piping bag fitted with a writing nozzle with the royal icing and pipe the word 'nougatine' across the top.

Black Cherry Cake

1   400 g|14 oz can of black cherries, pitted
Kirsch
290 ml|½ pint double cream
1 chocolate génoise cake (see page 716)
85 g|3 oz plain chocolate, grated

3 tablespoons water
110 g|4 oz icing sugar
about 55 g|2 oz split almonds, toasted
icing sugar for dusting

1 Sprinkle the cherries with a little Kirsch.

2 Whip the cream until it just holds its shape.

3 Split the cake into 3 thin rounds. On the bottom layer spread about one-third of the cream and sprinkle with half the cherries. Place the next layer of cake on top. Spread on another third of cream and the rest of the cherries. Place the top round on and flatten gently with your hands.

4 Place the chocolate in a small, heavy saucepan with the water and stir over a low heat until smooth, taking care not to boil.

5 Sift the icing sugar into a bowl and blend in the chocolate, adding a little extra water if necessary. Do this drop by drop to make a thick, pouring consistency. Pour over the top of the cake and allow to set.

6 Spread the remaining cream around the sides of the cake and press the almonds against it.

7 Cut 3 strips of paper about 25 cm|10 in long and about 2.5 cm|1 in wide. Place them over the cake about 2.5 cm|1 in apart and sift over a heavy dusting of icing sugar.

8 Remove the paper strips carefully to reveal a striped brown and white top.

Dobez Torte

This is a cake with 5 layers. The mixture will not deteriorate if all the layers cannot be baked at the same time because of a lack of baking sheets or space in the oven.

For the cake
4 eggs
170 g|6 oz caster sugar
140 g|5 oz plain flour
a pinch of salt

For the buttercream
85 g|3 oz granulated sugar
4–5 tablespoons water
3 egg yolks

225 g|8 oz unsalted butter, softened
coffee essence
55 g|2 oz hazelnuts, toasted, skinned and ground

To decorate
140 g|5 oz caster sugar
2 tablespoons toasted chopped almonds or toasted
    ground hazelnuts
6 whole toasted, skinned hazelnuts

1 Preheat the oven to 180°C|350°F|gas mark 4. Grease and flour 5 baking sheets and mark a 20 cm|8 in circle on each sheet with a flan ring or saucepan lid.

2 Make the cake: whisk the eggs in a large heatproof bowl, adding the sugar gradually. Set the bowl over, not in, a saucepan of simmering water and whisk until the mixture is thick and mousse-like. Remove from the heat and whisk until slightly cooled. Sift the flour and salt and fold into the egg mixture with a metal spoon. Divide the mixture between the 5 baking sheets and spread into the circles as marked.

3 Bake for 8 minutes. Trim the edges and leave to cool on a wire rack.

4 Make the buttercream: dissolve the sugar in the water and, when clear, boil rapidly to the short thread stage. (see page 665, Sugar Syrup.) Allow the syrup to cool slightly for about 1 minute.

5 Whisk the egg yolks in a bowl and then pour the syrup slowly on to them, whisking all the time. Keep whisking until you have a thick mousse-like mixture. Cream the butter well and beat in the egg and sugar mixture. Cool. Flavour 2 tablespoons of the buttercream with coffee essence and reserve for decoration. Mix the ground hazelnuts and the remaining coffee essence into the remaining mixture.

6 Lay one round of cake on a wire rack over an oiled tray. Melt the sugar for the caramel in a little water and, when dissolved, boil fiercely until a good caramel colour, then pour immediately over the piece of cake, covering it completely.

7 Allow to harden slightly and mark into 6 portions with an oiled knife, cutting through the setting caramel but not through the cake. Trim the edges of excess caramel.

8 Sandwich the cake layers together with the coffee and hazelnut buttercream, placing the one with caramel on top. Spread the coffee and hazelnut buttercream thinly around the sides and press on the nuts.

9 Put the remaining plain buttercream into a piping bag fitted with a large star nozzle, and pipe a rosette on top of each portion of cake. Decorate each rosette with a whole hazelnut.

Black Sticky Gingerbread

butter for greasing
225 g|8 oz butter
225 g|8 oz soft dark brown sugar
225 g|8 oz black treacle
290 ml|½ pint milk

340 g|12 oz plain flour
2 teaspoons ground ginger
1 tablespoon ground cinnamon
2 teaspoons bicarbonate of soda
2 eggs, beaten

1 Preheat the oven to 150°C|300°F|gas mark 2.

2 Grease a 30 × 20 cm|12 × 8 in roasting pan with butter and line the base and sides with greaseproof paper.

3 Melt the butter, sugar and treacle in a saucepan. Add the milk and allow to cool.

4 Sift the flour with the ginger, cinnamon and bicarbonate of soda, then stir in the melted mixture with the beaten eggs. Stir well and pour the mixture into the prepared tin.

5 Bake for about 45 minutes – 1 hour. It is cooked when a skewer inserted into the centre comes out clean.

6 When the gingerbread is cold, cut it into fingers. This gingerbread keeps very well: in fact, it improves with keeping.

American Carrot Cake

MAKES A 20 CM | 8 IN CAKE

250 ml | 9 fl oz vegetable oil, plus extra for greasing

4 medium eggs, beaten

225 g | 8 oz soft light brown sugar

140 g | 5 oz carrots, peeled and finely grated

225 g | 8 oz self-raising flour

½ teaspoon bicarbonate of soda

1½ teaspoon ground cinnamon

½ teaspoon ground ginger

140 g | 5 oz walnuts, coarsely chopped

For the icing

45 g | 1½ oz unsalted butter, softened

170 g | 6 oz good-quality full-fat cream cheese

300 g | 10 oz icing sugar

1 teaspoon vanilla extract

lemon juice to taste

To decorate

8 walnut halves (optional)

1 Preheat the oven to 180°C | 350°F | gas mark 4. Lightly oil 2 × 20 cm | 8 in sandwich tins and line the bases with discs of baking parchment.

2 In a large bowl, stir together the oil, eggs, and sugar.

3 Stir in the carrots.

4 Sift the flour, bicarbonate of soda, cinnamon and ginger on to a large piece of greaseproof paper and tip into the egg and sugar mixture. Fold together, using a large metal spoon.

5 Fold in the walnuts, then turn the mixture into the prepared tins.

6 Bake in the centre of the oven for 25 minutes or until the cakes spring back when pressed lightly in the centre and a wooden cocktail stick inserted in to the centre comes out clean.

7 Release the cakes from the tins and turn out on to a wire rack. Leave to cool, then remove the lining paper.

8 Make the icing: beat the butter and cream cheese together until smooth. Sift the icing sugar over the top and stir in.

9 Stir in the vanilla, then flavour with the lemon juice. Use the icing to fill the cake and ice the top. Garnish with the walnut halves, if desired.

Quick Carrot Cake

MAKES A 27 20 CM|11 8 SHEET CAKE

170 ml|6 fl oz vegetable oil

225 g|8 oz caster sugar

2 large eggs, beaten

225 g|8 oz plain flour

1 teaspoon bicarbonate of soda

½ teaspoon salt

1½ teaspoon ground cinnamon

1 teaspoon vanilla extract

170 g|6 oz carrots, peeled and finely grated

For the icing

55 g|2 oz butter, softened

110 g|4 oz cream cheese

finely grated zest of ½ orange

225 g|8 oz icing sugar, sifted

1 Preheat the oven to 170°C|325°F|gas mark 3. Grease a 27 × 20 cm|11 × 8 in cake sheet tin with a little of the oil.

2 Combine the oil and sugar, then mix in the eggs.

3 Sift the flour, bicarbonate of soda, salt and cinnamon together and add to the egg and sugar mixture. Mix thoroughly.

4 Add the vanilla and the carrots. Pour the mixture into the prepared tin.

5 Bake the cake in the oven for 1 hour until a wooden skewer inserted into the centre comes out clean.

6 Turn the cake out on to a wire rack and leave to cool.

7 Make the icing: beat together the butter, cream cheese and orange zest. Stir in the icing sugar. Spread over the top of the cake.

Reasons for Failure in Cake-making

Creamed Cakes

Close texture	Eggs added too quickly, making the mixture curdle
Flat, dense cake	Wrong flour used or no raising agent added
Flattish cake with large bubbles on surface	Long delay before cake put in oven
	Oven temperature too low
Base and sides of cake wet and soggy	Cake not turned on to a wire rack to cool

Fruit cakes

Cake risen to a peak	No dip put in the cake mixture prior to baking
Hard, dark crust round base and sides	Cake tin not lined
	Oven too hot
	Cake overcooked
Fruit, e.g. cherries, sunk to bottom of cake	Cake mixture too liquid
	Too little flour

Whisked sponges

Unrisen sponge	Not whisked enough before flour added
Unrisen génoise with large bubbles on the top	Mixture overfolded
Flat sponge with very hard crust	Egg and sugar mixture too hot when flour folded in
Pockets of flour in cake	Flour underfolded into cake

Melted method cakes, e.g. gingerbreads

Slightly fizzy taste	Too much bicarbonate of soda
Greeny, orange colour	Too much bicarbonate of soda
Cake sunk in the middle	Open door opened during cooking
	Cake not put in oven soon enough
	Cake removed from the oven too soon

General mistakes

Cake risen to high peak with the surface cracked	Too much raising agent
	Oven temperature too high
	Cake tin too small
Thick crust all around cake	Overcooked
Thick, crunchy crust round base and sides	Too much oil, butter or lard used to grease the tin
Cake sunk in middle	Not cooked for long enough
	Oven door opened before cake has set, causing cake to collapse

Reasons for Failure in Cake-making–*contd*

General mistakes

Hard, shiny crust	Too much sugar
Cake overflowed over sides of tin	Cake tin too small
Cake good texture but very thin and overcooked	Cake tin too big
Cake leaked out of the bottom of loose-bottomed tin	Tin not lined
	Wrong type of tin for particular cake
Dense, heavy texture	Cake mixed too quickly, e.g. not enough air beaten in
Cake stuck to tin	Tin not greased
	Tin not lined
	Silicone non-stick baking parchment not used when specified in recipe

Melon and Champagne Sorbet

Mango Parfait with
Passionfruit Sauce

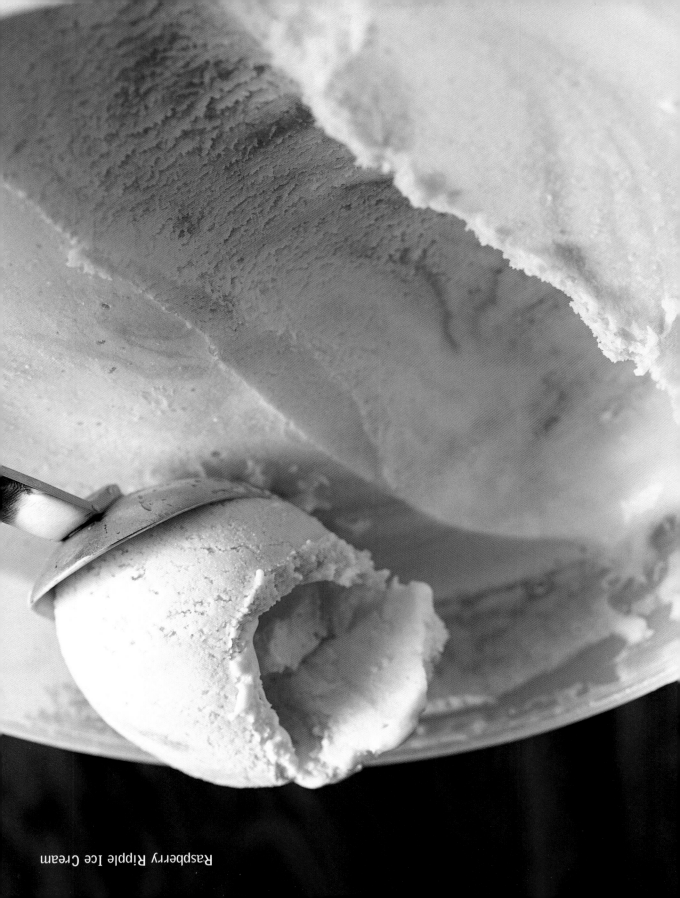

Raspberry Ripple Ice Cream

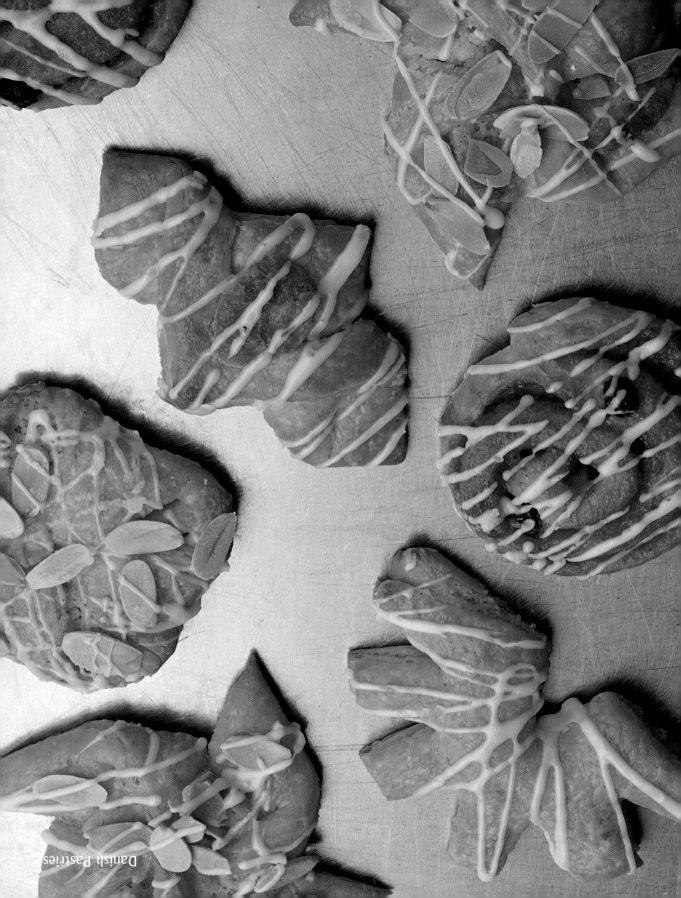

Danish Pastries

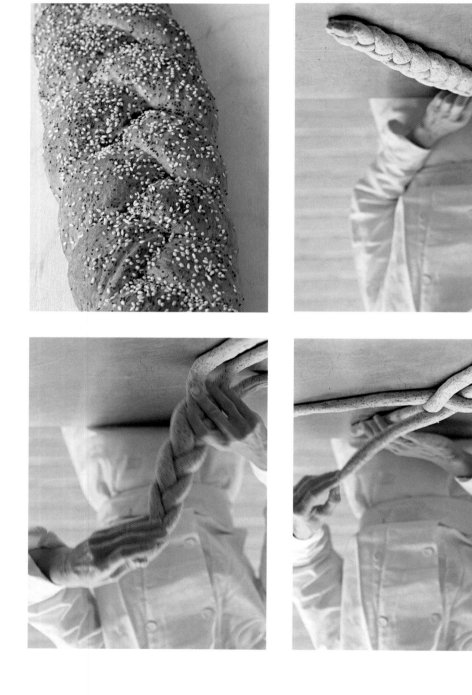

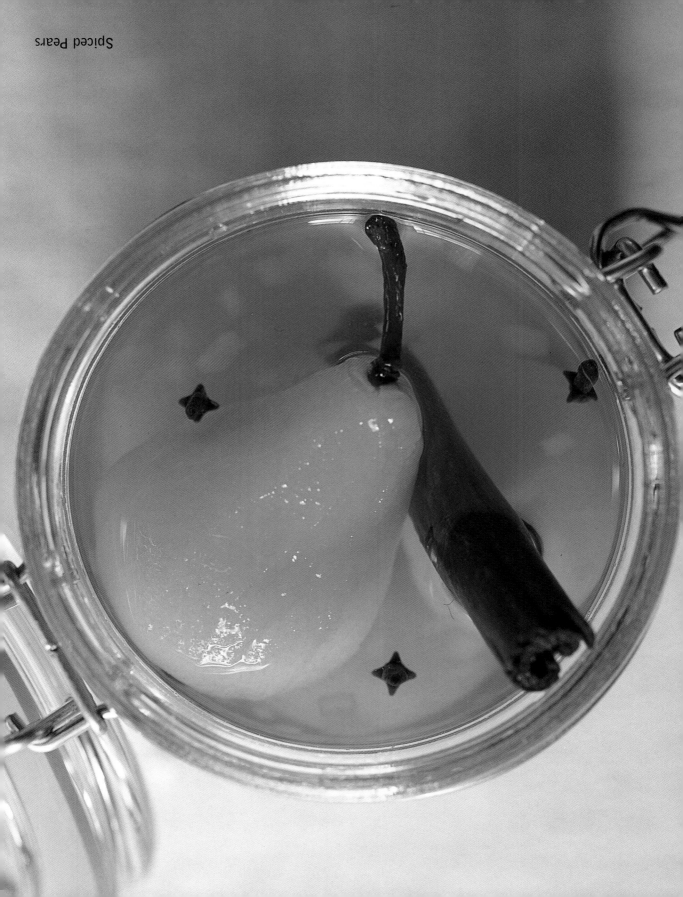

Italian Bread

Brandy Snap Tortes with Damson Icecream

Individual Fruit Tartlettes

Cheese Gannat

Guacamole with Crudités

Spiced Fruit Pickle, Three Fruit Marmalade and Lemon Curd
(from left to right)

Icings and Fillings

Apricot Glaze

3 tablespoons apricot jam
1 tablespoon water

juice of ½ lemon

1 Place all the ingredients in a heavy saucepan.
2 Bring slowly to the boil, stirring gently (avoid beating in bubbles) until syrupy in consistency. Strain.

NOTE: Use when still warm, as the glaze becomes too stiff to manage when cold. It will keep warm standing over a saucepan of very hot water.

Chocolate Butter Icing

225 g | 8 oz plain chocolate, chopped
2 tablespoons water
110 g | 4 oz unsalted butter

625 g | 8 oz icing sugar, sifted
2 egg yolks

1 Melt the chocolate in a heavy saucepan with the water, stirring continuously.
2 Beat together the butter and icing sugar until light and fluffy.
3 Beat in the egg yolks followed by the melted chocolate.

Crème au Beurre Meringue

This is a light, soft cake frosting.

For the meringue
3 egg whites
170 g | 6 oz icing sugar
140 g | 5 oz unsalted butter, softened
140 g | 5 oz salted butter, softened

Suggested flavourings
grated lemon or orange zest
melted plain chocolate
coffee essence

1 Put the egg whites with the icing sugar into a heatproof bowl and set over a saucepan of simmering water. Whisk until the meringue is thick and will hold its shape. Remove from the heat and continue to whisk until slightly cooled.
2 Beat the butter until soft and gradually beat in the meringue mixture.
3 Flavour to taste as required.

Soured Cream and Chocolate Icing

225 g|8 oz plain chocolate   1 tablespoon caster sugar
200 ml|7 fl oz soured cream

1 Break up the chocolate and place in a double saucepan.
2 Add the soured cream and sugar. Melt together over a low heat. Leave to cool and thicken.

Crème au Beurre Mousseline

This is a rich, creamy cake filling.

170 g|6 oz granulated sugar   grated zest of 1 lemon and 1 orange
170 ml|6 fl oz citrus juice or water   110 g|4 oz unsalted butter, softened
6 egg yolks   110 g|4 oz salted butter, softened

1 Dissolve the sugar in the water and when completely dissolved boil rapidly to the short thread stage, about 108°C|227°F on a sugar thermometer. At this point a little sugar syrup, pulled between finger and thumb, will form a thread. Remove from the heat immediately.
2 Whisk the yolks and the zests and pour on the syrup. Keep whisking until thick.
3 Beat the butter and whisk gradually into the mixture. Allow to cool.

NOTE: This makes quite a small quantity of icing. However, it is very rich.

Glacé Icing

FOR AN 18 CM|7 IN SPONGE
225 g|8 oz icing sugar   boiling water to mix

1 Sift the icing sugar into a bowl.
2 Add enough boiling water to mix to a fairly stiff coating consistency. The icing should hold a trail when dropped from a spoon but gradually find its own level. It needs surprisingly little water.

NOTE: Hot water produces a shinier icing than cold. Also, the icing, on drying, is less likely to craze, crack or become watery if made with boiling water.

Feather Icing

225 g | 8 oz icing sugar   food colouring or melted chocolate
boiling water to mix

1 Sift the icing sugar into a bowl.
2 Add enough boiling water to mix to a fairly stiff coating consistency. The icing should hold a trail when dropped from a spoon but gradually find its own level.
3 Take 2 tablespoons of the icing and colour it with food colouring or melted chocolate.
4 Place in a piping bag fitted with a fine writing nozzle.
5 Spread the remaining icing smoothly and evenly over the top of the cake, using a warm palette knife.
6 While it is still wet, quickly pipe lines, about 2.5 cm | 1 in apart, across the top of the cake.
7 Now draw lines at right angles to the coloured lines with a pin or sharp knife, dragging the tip through the coloured lines to pull them into points. If the pin is dragged in one direction through the coloured icing lines, Pattern A will result: if the pin is dragged alternately in opposite directions through the coloured icing lines, Pattern B will result.

NOTE: Smooth melted jam can be used instead of coloured icing for the feathering.

Pattern A

Pattern B

Sugar Paste

Sugar paste is a simple mock fondant icing and is easy to mould and shape; it is very useful for decorating children's party cakes.

1 tablespoon liquid glucose   450 g | 1 lb icing sugar, sifted
1 egg white

1 Warm the liquid glucose in the bottle in a saucepan of hot water.
2 Beat together the glucose, egg white and icing sugar. Shape into a ball.
3 Knead on a surface dusted with icing sugar until pliable. This will take 5 minutes.

NOTES: Store in a polythene bag in the refrigerator for up to 3 months.
   Sugar paste can be coloured as required. Simply add food colouring and knead until thoroughly incorporated.

Fondant Icing

225 g | 8 oz loaf sugar
115 ml | 4 fl oz water

½ teaspoon liquid glucose, or a pinch of cream of tartar plus 1 teaspoon water

1 Dissolve the sugar in the water over a low heat without boiling.

2 Mix in the glucose or the cream of tartar and the water. Cover and bring to the boil. Boil to the soft ball stage (115°C | 235–240°F on a sugar thermometer). At this point, a spoonful of the sugar syrup dropped into a bowl of cold water will form a soft ball when rolled between the fingers. Stop the sugar syrup from cooking any further by dipping the bottom of the pan into a bowl of cold water. Let it cool slightly.

3 Moisten a cold hard surface and pour the sugar syrup on to it in a steady stream. With a metal spatula, fold the outsides of the mixture into the centre.

4 Continue to turn with a spatula and work until the fondant becomes fairly stiff. Knead into balls. Place in a bowl and cover with a damp cloth for 1–2 hours.

5 If the fondant is to be stored, place in a screw-top jar. When required, put it into a heatproof bowl and set it over a saucepan of simmering water to melt.

NOTES: A sugar thermometer is almost essential to get the syrup exactly the right consistency: not too liquid, nor too hard.

To make coffee fondant icing, proceed as above but add 2 teaspoons coffee essence to the sugar syrup before pouring on to the work surface.

Royal Icing

Icing a cake with royal icing is an advanced skill, and these notes are intended as a reminder for those who have already iced a cake or two. Royal icing is traditionally used (over a layer of marzipan) for the coating and decoration of special-occasion fruit cakes. It keeps very well.

- More than with any other cooking, it is vital to clean up as you go along. It is almost impossible to produce delicate and neat work from a cluttered work surface. Get all the nozzles and piping bags lined up before you begin icing.
- Never overfill the piping bag. This leads to the sticky icing oozing out of the top.
- Keep all full piping bags under a damp cloth or in a polythene bag to prevent the icing in the nozzle from drying out.
- Always keep the icing covered with a damp cloth when not in use to prevent it from drying out.
- Always clean the nozzles immediately after use, using a pin to ensure that no icing is left in the tip.
- Practise the required pattern on the work surface before tackling the cake. Don't try complicated things like roses and scrolls before you have mastered the easier decorations like trellis, shells, stars and dots.

- Follow the instructions slavishly.
- 450 g|1 lb sugar makes enough for a 20 cm|8 in cake; 900 g|2 lb sugar makes enough for a 25 cm|10 in cake.

For 1 coat of icing for a 20 cm|8 in cake

1–2 egg whites   450 g|1 lb icing sugar

Mix the egg white with 3 tablespoons of the icing sugar, and add lemon juice or glycerine if required (see below). Gradually add the remaining sugar and mix very well until the icing is soft, very white, fluffy and will hold its shape. More sugar can be added if the mixture is too sloppy. Blue colouring, if used (see below), is added last.

Flavourings and Colourings

- 1 drop of blue food colouring makes white icing a very bright white.
- 1 teaspoon lemon juice to 225 g|8 oz sugar makes the icing a little sharper and less sickly.
- $\frac{1}{2}$ teaspoon glycerine to 225 g|8 oz sugar produces a softer icing which will not splinter when cut. Without glycerine, royal icing eventually hardens to an unbreakable cement. More glycerine can be added, but this will give a softer icing unsuitable for a tiered cake. None need be used if the cake is to be eaten within 24 hours of icing.

Consistency

A cake is normally covered with 2–3 coats of icing and decorated with either piping or 'run-in' work. The consistency varies for each coat.

First coating: very thick – the icing should stand up in points if the beating spoon is lifted from the bowl.

Second coating: a little thinner (the points should flop over at the tips, like rabbit ears).

Third coating: the icing should be of thick pouring consistency.

For piping: consistency as for the first coating.

For run-in work: as for the third coating.

Bubbles
Royal icing should be beaten as little as possible: if making it by hand or in an electric mixer, stop as soon as it is smooth and glossy. If there are any bubbles, leave the icing, covered with a damp cloth, in the refrigerator overnight.

Applying the first coat
It is easier to apply the first layer of royal icing in two (for a round cake) or three (for a square cake) stages rather than all at once. The top is iced first and allowed to dry for 24

hours before icing the sides. On a square cake two of the opposite sides are iced and allowed to dry before the second two sides are iced.

Place a small spoonful of icing on a cake board about 5 cm|2 in larger in diameter than the cake, and put the cake on top. It will now stick to the board. Spoon half the icing on to the top of the cake with a palette knife and spread to the edge, using a paddling action to remove any air bubbles. Then, using a clean metal ruler, a 'straight edge' or large palette knife placed in the centre of the cake, draw the icing forwards and backwards across the cake until it is completely smooth and level and can be drawn off the cake.

Carefully remove any icing that has fallen down the sides of the cake. Leave to dry for 24 hours. Put the cake and board on an icing turntable or upturned bowl and spread the icing evenly around the sides, using a special icing scraper or a palette knife held at an angle of 45 degrees to the cake. Try to turn the cake around in one movement as you ice in order to ensure a smooth finish. For a square cake, ice two of the opposite sides.

Store the cake for at least 24 hours in a clean, cool, dry place to dry before you ice the other two sides. If the storage place is damp, it will prevent the icing from hardening and it will slowly slip down the sides of the cake. If it is too warm, the cake will 'sweat' and oil from the marzipan will be drawn into the icing.

Applying the second coat

This may not be necessary if the first layer is very smooth. Brush the surface well with a grease-free brush to remove any loose icing. Ice the cake as for the first coating, but use a slightly thinner icing.

Applying the third coat or float

A three-tier wedding cake or a less than perfectly iced cake may need a third layer of icing. If this is necessary, proceed when the second coating is dry. Prepare the surface as previously instructed.

Before converting the icing into the desired pouring consistency, pile a little thick icing into a piping bag fitted with a no. 1 or 2 writing nozzle and cover it with a damp cloth. Add a little egg white to the remaining icing and beat until smooth and of a pouring consistency. Leave in a tightly covered container for 30 minutes. (Stretching a piece of clingfilm over the bowl will do.) This is to make the air bubbles rise to the surface. If you do not do this, air bubbles will break all over the surface of the cake, making little holes in the icing.

With the writing nozzle, pipe an unbroken line of icing around the top edge of the cake. Now pour the runny icing into a piping bag, remove the nozzle and guide it over the top of the cake, flooding the surface and carefully avoiding the piped line. With the handle of a teaspoon, work the flooding to edge of the cake. The piped line will prevent the icing running off.

Decorating with Royal Icing

You must have a clear idea of the design before you begin. If it is a geometric pattern, draw it on a piece of tracing paper and place this on the cake. Using a large pin, prick where the lines meet. Remove the paper and you will be left with guidelines made by the pinpoints. Join these up with more pricked holes so that the design is visible. Half-fill the piping bags, fitted with the chosen nozzles, with the icing mixed to the correct consistency. Put them under a wet cloth until needed. Get everything you will need ready on or near your work surface (such as more bags and extra nozzles, a large spoon, a palette knife, a small bowl of hot water for washing the nozzles).

Direct Piping

Star piping: Fit the bag with a star nozzle. Hold the nozzle upright, immediately above and almost touching the top of the cake, and squeeze gently from the top of the bag. Stop pressing and lift the bag away. Always stop pressing before lifting the bag away.

Dot or pearl piping: Use a plain nozzle, and pipe as for stars. If the dots are too small, do not try to increase their size by squeezing out more icing; use a larger nozzle.

Straight lines: with a plain nozzle, press the bag as for making a dot but leave the icing attached to the cake surface – do not draw away by lifting the bag. Hold the point of the nozzle about 4 cm | 1½ in above the surface of the cake and, pressing gently as you go, guide rather than drag the icing into place. The icing can be directed more easily into place if it is allowed to hang from the tube.

Trellis work: with a plain nozzle, pipe parallel lines 5 mm | ¼ in apart. Pipe a second layer over the top at right angles or at an angle of 45 degrees to the first. Then pipe another layer as closely as possible over the first set of lines, then another set over the second layer, and so on until you have the desired height of trellis. Six layers (three in each direction) is useful for an elaborate cake.

Shells: Use a star nozzle. Hold the bag at an angle of about 45 degrees. Pipe a shell, release the pressure on the bag and begin a new shell one-eighth of the way up the first shell, so that each new shell overlaps its predecessor.

Scrolls: Use a star nozzle. Hold the bag at an angle of about 45 degrees. Pipe a scroll first from left to right and then from right to left.

Run-in work: Using a writing nozzle, pipe the outline of a design (e.g. leaf, Father Christmas, etc.) on to oiled kitchen foil or greaseproof, waxed paper or non-stick baking parchment. 'Float' runny icing in the centre, and leave to set. Lift off and stick on to the cake with wet icing.

NOTE: Variations of pressure when piping both shells and scrolls make the icing emerge in the required thickness. Shells and scrolls can be made into very attractive borders when combined with trellis work and edged with pearls.

Causes of Failure

- Icing too stiff.
- Pulling rather than easing into place.
- Making the icing with a mixer set at too high a speed, causing air bubbles.

Wobbly lines
- Squeezing the icing out too quickly.
- Icing too liquid.

Flattened lines
- Icing too liquid.
- Bag held too near the surface.

Indirect Piping

Indirect piping is done on to oiled moulds or waxed paper and, when dry, the piped shapes are stuck to the cake with a little wet icing.

Trellised shapes: Pipe as for direct piping on to waxed paper or oiled moulds (the backs of teaspoons, patty tins, cups or glasses). Leave for 24 hours, then warm over a very low heat to dislodge them. Slide off the mould and fix to the cake with a little wet icing.

Flowers: you need confectioner's flower nails and petal nozzles. The icing should be thick. The petals are piped individually on to the oiled surface of the flower nail, the biggest petals first and then the smaller ones. If the lower nail is covered with oiled kitchen foil, the flower can be removed carefully after piping and the nail used for the next flower. When dry, green icing leaves (piped and dried separately) can be attached to the back of the flowers with a little wet icing.

When making coloured flowers, it is helpful to tint the icing to a pale colour first. After they have dried, they can be touched up with a paint brush to give the flowers a more natural appearance. By varying the angle at which the piping bags are held, flatter petals (for daisies, violets and primroses) or thicker, more rounded petals (for roses) can be made. Sweet peas are made with 2–3 flat petals slightly overlapping each other with a smaller upright rounded petal piped on top of each flat one.

Marzipan or Almond Paste (Uncooked)

225 g | 8 oz caster sugar
225 g | 8 oz icing sugar
450 | 1 lb ground almonds
2 egg yolks

2 eggs
2 teaspoons lemon juice
6 drops of vanilla essence

1 Sift the sugars together into a bowl and mix with the ground almonds.
2 Mix together the egg yolks, whole eggs, lemon juice and vanilla essence. Add to the sugar mixture and beat briefly with a wooden spoon.

3 Lightly dust the working surface with icing sugar. Knead the paste until just smooth (overworking will draw the oil out of the almonds, giving a too greasy paste).

4 Wrap well and store in a cool place.

To cover a round cake with uncooked marzipan

For a 22 cm | 9 in cake you will need:

uncooked marzipan made with 450 g | 1 lb ground almonds

apricot glaze (see page 727)
icing sugar for dusting

1 If the cake is not level, carefully shave off some of the top and turn it upside down.

2 Measure around the side with a piece of string.

3 Lightly dust a very clean work top with icing sugar and roll out two-thirds of the marzipan to a strip the length of the piece of string and the depth of the cake. Trim it neatly.

4 Roll out the remaining marzipan to a circle the size of the cake top.

5 Brush the sides of the cake with apricot glaze and, holding the cake firmly between both hands, turn it on to its side and roll it along the prepared strip of marzipan. Turn the cake right side up again. Use a round-bladed knife to smooth the join. Take a jam jar or straight-sided tin and roll it around the side of the cake.

6 Brush the top with apricot glaze and, using a rolling pin, lift the circle of marzipan on to the cake. Seal the edges with the knife and smooth the top with a rolling pin.

7 Leave to dry on a cake board 5 cm | 2 in larger in diameter than the cake.

To cover a square cake with uncooked marzipan

For a 20 cm | 8 in square cake you will need:

uncooked marzipan made with 450 g | 1 lb ground almonds

apricot glaze (see page 727)
icing sugar for dusting

1 If the cake is not level, shave off a little of the top. Turn it upside down.

2 Measure one side of the cake with a piece of string.

3 Lightly dust a very clean work top with icing sugar and roll out two-thirds of the marzipan into 4 strips the length of the piece of string and the depth of the cake. Trim neatly.

4 Roll the remaining marzipan, with any trimmings, to a square to fit the top of the cake.

5 Brush one side of the cake with apricot glaze. Turn the cake on to its side and, holding it firmly between both hands, place the glazed edge on one strip of marzipan. Trim the edges and repeat with the other 3 sides. Smooth the joins with a round-bladed knife. Take a jam jar or straight-sided tin and roll it around the sides of the cake, keeping the corners square.

6 Brush the top of the cake with apricot glaze and, using a rolling pin, lift the square of marzipan on to the cake. Seal the edges with the knife and smooth the top with a rolling pin. Leave to dry on a cake board about 5 cm | 2 in wider, all round, than the cake.

NOTE: Square cakes are normally covered with uncooked marzipan. The cooked paste is too pliable and it is therefore difficult to get square corners.

Cooked Marzipan

This recipe gives a softer, easier-to-handle paste than the more usual uncooked marzipan.

2 eggs	4 drops of vanilla essence
170 g	6 oz caster sugar	1 teaspoon lemon juice
170 g	6 oz icing sugar	icing sugar for kneading
340 g	12 oz ground almonds	

1 Beat the eggs lightly in a heatproof bowl.
2 Sift the sugars together and mix with the eggs.
3 Place the bowl over a saucepan of boiling water and whisk until light and creamy or until the mixture just leaves a trail when the whisk is lifted. Remove from the heat and whisk until the bowl is cold.
4 Add the ground almonds, vanilla and lemon juice.
5 Lightly dust a very clean work top with icing sugar. Carefully knead the paste until just smooth. (Overworking will draw out the oil from the almonds giving a too greasy paste.) Wrap well and store in a cool place.

To cover a round cake with cooked marzipan

For a 20 cm | 8 in cake you will need:

cooked marzipan made with 340 g	12 oz ground almonds	apricot glaze (see page 727)
	icing sugar

1 If the cake is not level, shave off a little of the top. Turn it upside down. Brush lightly with apricot glaze.
2 Lightly dust a very clean work top with icing sugar and roll out the marzipan to a circle 20 cm | 8 in larger in diameter than the cake.
3 Place the glazed cake upside down in the centre of the marzipan and, using your hands, carefully work the marzipan up the sides of the cake.
4 Take a jam jar or straight-sided tin and roll it around the sides of the cake to make sure that the sides are quite straight, and the edges square.
5 Turn it the right way up and place on a cake board 5 cm | 2 in larger in diameter than the cake.

NOTE: Once a cake has been covered with marzipan, it should be left for a minimum of 2 days before icing, otherwise the oil from the marzipan can stain the icing.

Chocolate Shapes

170 g│6 oz best-quality plain chocolate

1 First make a paper piping bag. Cut a 38 cm│15 in square of greaseproof paper and fold diagonally in half.
2 Hold the paper down with a finger on the middle of the long folded edge. Then bring one corner up to the apex opposite your steadying finger, and hold it with the apex corners together.
3 Wrap the other side corner right round the cone to join the other 2 corners. You should now be holding all 3 corners together.
4 Fold the corners over together.
5 Cut a tear in them so that you have a lug or flange. Fold down this flange to prevent the bag from unravelling.
6 Meanwhile, break up the chocolate and place it in a heatproof bowl. Set it over, not in, a saucepan of simmering water. Stir until the chocolate is smooth and melted. Do not overheat or the chocolate will lose its gloss.
7 Fill the piping bag with some of the chocolate and snip the tip of the cone to make a small hole.
8 Use the chocolate-filled bag to pipe small elegant shapes on a piece of greaseproof paper. Leave to cool and harden.
9 Tip the remaining chocolate on to a second piece of greaseproof paper. Leave to cool and, when almost hard, cut into shapes.
10 Use as required.

Chocolate Leaves

MAKES 20–30
110 g│4 oz best-quality plain chocolate, melted

Choose clean, dry, non-poisonous leaves such as bay or rose leaves. Using a pastry brush, brush the melted chocolate on to each leaf. Continue to brush layers of chocolate until the desired thickness is reached. Leave to harden, then peel the leaf to reveal a perfect chocolate replica. These are useful for decorating cakes and puddings and will keep well in an airtight container in a cool, dry place for up to a week.

Breads, Buns and Pastries

Bread-making

With the advent of factory-made bread, bread-making became, for a while, almost a lost art amongst home cooks. It has recently been rediscovered and many people make the time to produce their own bread. Bread-making can be improved by understanding what is happening to the dough as it rises and bakes and what factors affect it. Once the process is understood, the cook can branch out from plain white bread to breads that contain nuts, herbs, fruits, vegetables, cheeses and different seeds and grains.

Yeast

Baker's yeast, the most usual leavening agent for bread, is a single-celled organism that belongs to the fungus family. For yeast to reproduce it needs warmth, moisture and food. Given the right conditions it can reproduce very quickly, giving off carbon dioxide as it does so. This is trapped in the dough or batter and so aerates it. The optimum temperature for yeast to reproduce is $27°C|80°F$. Too much heat can kill it so care must be taken to ensure that the liquid used in making bread is lukewarm. A high concentration of sugar, fat or salt can slow down its rates of reproduction. If a dough is high in these ingredients then rising times will be longer. There are three types of yeast available: fresh, dried and fast-action dried yeast.

Fresh yeast should be beige, crumbly-soft and sweet-smelling. It is usually thought of as the most satisfactory form of baker's yeast as it is less likely to produce 'beery' bread. Fresh yeast keeps for five days or so wrapped in clingfilm in the refrigerator, and can be frozen for short periods, though results after freezing are less predictable. If it is difficult to obtain, use dried yeast, or buy fresh yeast, divide it into $30g|1$ oz pieces, wrap them individually, then overwrap and freeze. Use as soon as the yeast thaws, as it liquefies upon defrosting. Do not keep frozen for more than a month.

Dried yeast is bought in granular form. It will remain active for about 6 months in a cool, dry place. If substituting dried for fresh yeast when following a recipe, halve the weight of yeast called for. Dried yeast takes slightly longer to work than fresh yeast, and must first be 'sponged' in liquid, partly to reconstitute it, partly to check that it is still active.

Fast-action dried yeast can be mixed directly with the flour, not reconstituted in liquid first. Sold in small airtight packages, it is also included in bought bread mixtures. One 7 g | ¼ oz package usually equals 15 g | ½ oz conventional dried yeast or 30 g | 1 oz fresh yeast.

Flour

Flour is the main ingredient in bread and gives it its individual character. Wheat flour is the most common because it contains a large amount of a form of protein that absorbs liquid to produce elastic strands, gluten, in the dough. As the yeast works, it gives off carbon dioxide, which is trapped in the expanding dough, making it rise and puff up. When the loaf is baked and set rigidly, the gas leaks out and is replaced by air.

Rye, maize, millet and other flours contain less gluten than wheat flour. Because these flours lack the essential elasticity of wheat gluten, some wheat flour is usually added to the dough.

Plain flour is general, all-purpose flour suitable for sauces and cakes. It has a lower protein content than strong flour.

White flour is ground from wheat with the outer bran and inner germ removed, leaving 70–75 per cent of the original wheat. Removing the wheatgerm means the flour keeps longer, while removing the bran makes the flour lighter and finer. On the other hand, it will have fewer vitamins. For this reason white flours, whether bleached or unbleached, have B vitamins and other nutrients added to them in most countries. With or without such additions, bread made from white flour will have less flavour and less fibre than that made from wholegrain flour.

Strong flour is flour made from varieties of wheat known as 'hard' wheat, which contain a particularly high proportion of protein. Also called bread flour, the best comes from North America and is usually known as durum wheat. It is highly suitable for bread-making, giving the dough a remarkable capacity to expand and rise and produce a light, well-risen, springy loaf.

Self-raising flour is usually made from soft wheat. A raising agent – usually a mixture of bicarbonate of soda and cream of tartar – is mixed with the flour. It is not used in yeast cookery, though some 'breads', such as wholemeal soda bread, can be made with it.

Wholemeal or wholewheat flour is milled from the whole grain so that it contains the germ and the bran. Most of the B vitamins are in the wheatgerm, while bran provides roughage necessary for the digestive system. Bread made from wholemeal flour is undoubtedly healthier, but regardless of its natural gluten, it produces a heavier loaf. A mixture of wholemeal and white flour is a good compromise.

Stoneground flour is usually wholemeal flour that has been milled between stone rollers rather than by modern milling methods. It is a coarser and heavier flour, even in its white version, than factory-milled flour, so more yeast or a longer rising time is needed to make it rise. It is claimed that more of the wheat's nutrients are retained as the grain is kept cooler during stone-grinding.

Wheatmeal flour judging by its name, should refer to any wheat flour. However, the term is used by commercial bakers to describe brown bread flour that is not wholemeal. The colour may simply come from dye. Containing little or no bran or wheatgerm, it makes a lighter loaf. It is usually no more nutritious or 'healthy' than refined white flour.

Other Bread Ingredients

Liquids: For plain everyday bread the only liquid needed is water. It gives a crisp crust and a fairly hard or chewy bread. Milk produces a softer bread and a golden crust and increases the keeping quality of bread. Beer gives the bread a malty taste.

Salt is very important in bread. It affects not only the flavour but also the rising action of the yeast, the texture of the loaf and the crust. Without salt the flavour of the loaf can be bland. If a quick rising time is required, more yeast and less salt are needed, as in a pizza dough for example. If a dough does not seem to be rising very fast it is worth tasting it. If it tastes noticeably salty, the dough will produce a tough, badly risen loaf.

Sugar is often included in savoury recipes for bread as a food for the yeast. White, demerara and brown sugars are used in doughs as well as molasses, black treacle and golden syrup. Honey can be substituted for golden syrup. A large amount of sugar slows the yeast activity and softens the gluten.

Fats added to a yeast dough include butter, lard, oil and vegetable fats. Butter gives a very good flavour and a good-looking crust. A large amount of fat can impede the action of the yeast and so a dough that is heavily enriched, such as brioche dough, may not rise as much as an ordinary dough. Fat softens the gluten so the bread will have a tender, cake-like texture. Oil makes bread wonderfully easy to knead even when added in small quantities, for example 2 tablespoons to $675\,\mathrm{g}\,|\,1\frac{1}{2}$ lb flour. Olive oil is the best oil to use, but alternatives are sunflower, peanut or sesame oil.

Stages in Bread-making

Mixing: If the yeast is fresh, first cream it with about 1 teaspoonful caster sugar and a spoonful of lukewarm water. Dried yeast should be mixed with a little sweetened lukewarm water and left in a warm place for about 15 minutes. Once the yeast liquid is frothy, or 'sponges', add it to the flour, and mix in any remaining ingredients specified. If it does not froth, the yeast is dead and should not be used. Some recipes, usually those enriched with fat and sugar, require the yeast mixture and all the liquid to be beaten with a small proportion of the flour to a yeasty batter, called the starter, and left in a warm place until it 'sponges'. Then the remaining flour is added and the mixing completed. This method used to be common to all breads. The process takes longer but is said by old-fashioned bakers to produce the lightest, most even-textured bread.

Kneading the dough, is the next stage. It is necessary in order to distribute the yeast cells evenly and develop the gluten. The length of time for kneading varies according to the type of flour and the skill of the kneader, but the dough must lose its stickiness and become smooth, elastic and shiny – this usually takes about 10 minutes. Techniques vary, but the most common is to push the lump of dough down and away with the heel of the hand, then to pull it back with the fingers, slap it on the work top and repeat the process, turning the dough slightly with each movement. Table-top electric mixers with dough hooks can also be used for kneading. Kneading in a machine takes less time than kneading by hand, but follow the manufacturer's instructions closely.

Rising: Once kneaded, the dough is formed into a ball, put into a lightly oiled bowl, and turned to coat it evenly with oil to prevent drying out. The bowl is covered with a piece of clingfilm or a damp cloth, put in a warm (24°C│75°F) draught-free place and left until about twice its original size. The dough should remain indented when pressed lightly with a finger. The longer the rising takes the better. Too rapidly risen or over-risen bread has a coarse texture and a beery smell.

Knocking back/shaping is the next process. The risen dough is knocked down, or punched with the knuckles to re-distribute the yeast and to knock out air bubbles to create an even texture. It is then kneaded briefly to make it pliable. Fruit or nuts are usually added at this point, before the dough is shaped and put into a loaf tin or on to a baking sheet.

Proving is the last rising of the dough before it is baked. When this is completed, the loaf will have nearly doubled in bulk and should look the size and shape you hope the finished bread will be. Proving can be done in a slightly warmer place, about 28°C│80°F, for a shorter time, about 30 minutes, because the previous rising and further kneading will have made the dough even more elastic and it will rise more easily. With a second rising, the bread will be lighter when baked.

Baking: The bread will continue to rise in the oven for a short time partly because of the rising steam in the loaf and partly because the yeast keeps working until the dough reaches 60°C│140°F. Then the heat of the oven will cook the dough into a rigid shape. This final rising may push the top crust away from the body of the loaf. This is called oven spring. To avoid too much oven spring, bread is baked at a fairly high temperature to kill the yeast quickly or it is slashed before baking.

The baked bread should be golden-brown and have shrunk slightly from the sides of the tin. To make sure that the bread is done, it should be turned out on to a cloth and tapped on the underside. If it sounds hollow, it is done. If not, it should be returned to the oven, on its side, without the tin. Bread is cooled on a wire rack. After 2 hours, it will slice easily. Once stone-cold it may be stored in a bread tin or a plastic bag. A lukewarm loaf stored in an airtight container will become soggy, if not mouldy.

Soda Bread

Soda bread has bicarbonate of soda as a raising agent. However, in order to activate the soda an acid must be included in the ingredients. This is usually cream of tartar, which must be sifted with the bicarbonate of soda and the other dry ingredients to incorporate it thoroughly. In some recipes cream of tartar is replaced by sour milk or buttermilk. These doughs are the exact opposite of yeast doughs. High-speed mixing and quick light handling are required, rather than careful mixing and vigorous kneading.

Shapes for Rolls

These shapes are made using approximately 40 g | 1½ oz made-up bread dough each. Once the dough has had its first rising, knock it back and divide into equal-sized pieces of dough. A 450 g | 1 lb flour quantity of bread dough will make about 16 rolls. Rolls have to be made and shaped quickly or the first rolls will have overproved before the last rolls have been shaped.

Plain rolls: Roll the dough into a ball on the work top, pinching with the fingers to create a smooth surface on the underside. Turn the roll over, place on a baking sheet and press down slightly.

Plain roll

Bap

Knot

Baps: As above except that when they are placed on the baking sheet press down firmly to make them round and flattish.

Knots: Shape the dough, with your hands, into a sausage about 10 cm | 4 in long. Carefully, without stretching, tie into a knot.

Plaits: Divide the dough into 3 equal pieces and shape each piece into a sausage about 40cm | 16 in long. Put 2 pieces parallel to each other 2.5 cm | 1 in apart, and put the third one across them, threading it under the left-hand piece and over the right-hand piece. Starting from the middle, take the left-hand piece and place it over the right-hand piece and proceed as for a plait (see diagrams). When one end is completed turn the plait over so that the unplaited pieces are towards you and proceed as before.

Preparing to plait

Turning the plait over

The completed plait

Twists or wreaths: Divide the dough into 2 equal pieces and shape each into a sausage about 12 cm | 5 in long. Twist each piece around the other to look like a rope, then draw round into a circle pressing the ends together.

Twist

Bloomer

Crown

Bloomers: Make as for plain rolls, except oval and not round. Make 3 diagonal slashes into the surface before proving.

Crowns: Shape as for plain rolls, and cut a cross into the surface before proving.

Cottage loaves: Divide the dough into 2 pieces, one three-quarters larger than the other. Shape both into balls as for plain rolls. Make a small indentation in the centre of the top of the larger one and place the smaller roll on it. Using a floured finger or a wooden spoon handle, press a hole through both rolls to the baking sheet below, thus fixing the top to the bottom.

Catherine wheel: Shape the dough into a sausage about 15 cm | 6 in long. Coil the dough round from the centre, forming a Catherine wheel.

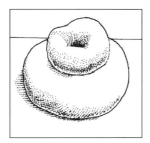

Cottage loaf

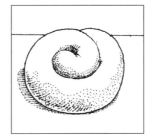

Catherine wheel

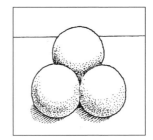

Pawnbroker

Pawnbroker: Divide the dough into 3 equal pieces. Form each into a neat ball and place next to each other on the baking sheet to make a triangle.

Propeller: Shape the dough as for plain rolls and with a pair of scissors make 1 cm | ½ in snips at an angle of 45 degrees all round the edge. Prove.

Maltese cross: Shape the dough as for plain rolls and with a pair of scissors snip into the dough in 4 places as illustrated. Prove.

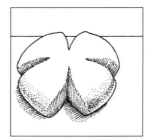

Propeller   Maltese cross

Hedgehogs: Shape the dough into an elongated plain roll. Pinch with finger and thumb at one end to form the nose and eyes. With a pair of scissors make tiny snips into the dough to form the prickles. Use peppercorns or currants for the eyes.

Basic White Bread

MAKES 1 LOAF OR 12 DINNER ROLLS

225 g｜8 oz strong white flour

1 teaspoon salt

170 ml｜6 fl oz water

10 g｜⅓ oz fresh yeast or 1 teaspoon fast-action yeast or 2 teaspoons dried yeast

1 teaspoon caster sugar

30 g｜1 oz butter, melted and cooled

extra flour for kneading

oil for greasing

1 egg, beaten with a pinch of salt, to glaze

1 Sift the flour with the salt into a large bowl and make a well in the centre.

2 Warm the water to 37°C｜100°F (blood temperature) if using fresh yeast, or to 40°C｜110°F if using fast-action or dried yeast.

3 If using fast-action yeast, mix the yeast and sugar with the flour and continue with step 5. Otherwise, place the fresh or dried yeast in a small bowl and add the sugar. Stir in enough water to dissolve the yeast and make a smooth cream.

4 Tip the yeast mixture into the well. Rinse the yeast bowl with a little of the water, then tip all of the water and the butter into the well.

5 Stir the mixture in the bowl with a wooden spoon to make a soft dough, adding more water or flour as necessary.

6 Turn the dough out on to a floured work surface. Knead for 10–15 minutes by hand or for 5–7 minutes in an electric mixer, adding extra flour if the dough is too sticky, until the dough is smooth and elastic.

7 Place the dough in an oiled bowl, turning it over to coat the surface with the oil. Cover the bowl with oiled clingfilm and place in a warm place to rise, about 22°C｜75°F. A good place to put a dough for rising is on a wire rack near a warm cooker. Airing cupboards are usually too warm.

8 When the dough has doubled in bulk, punch your fist into the centre of the dough to deflate it. Turn it on to the work surface and knead for 1 minute to knock it back. Let the dough rest for 5 minutes before shaping as required. For a plain loaf, lightly oil a small loaf tin.

9 Preheat the oven to 200°C｜400°F｜gas mark 6.

10 Cover the dough loosely with oiled clingfilm and leave to prove (rise again) until nearly doubled in size.

11 Glaze the dough with the beaten egg, taking care not to let the glaze drip into the tin. (This would seal the bread into the tin, making it difficult to remove after baking.)

13 Place the dough in the top third of the preheated oven (the hottest part). Bake for 30 minutes or until the loaf is golden-brown and sounds hollow when tapped on the underside. Cool on a wire rack before slicing.

Variations: To make a wholemeal loaf or rolls, replace 110 g | 4 oz of the white flour with wholemeal flour. Increase the quantity of water by 2 tablespoons.

Enriched White Bread

oil for greasing
15 g | ½ oz fresh yeast
scant 290 ml | ½ pint scalded lukewarm milk
1 teaspoon caster sugar
450 g | 1 lb strong plain flour

2 teaspoons salt
30 g | 1 oz butter
1 egg, lightly beaten
beaten egg to glaze

1 Dissolve the yeast with a little of the milk and the sugar in a small bowl.

2 Sift the flour with the salt into a large mixing bowl and rub in the butter as you would for pastry.

3 Pour in the yeast mixture, the remaining milk and the beaten egg and mix to a softish dough.

4 Add a small amount of flour if the dough is too sticky. When the dough will leave the sides of the bowl, press it into a ball and tip it out on to a work surface.

5 Knead until it is elastic, smooth and shiny (about 10 minutes).

6 Put the dough back into the bowl and cover it with a piece of lightly greased clingfilm.

7 Put it in a warm, draught-free place and leave it to rise until it has doubled in size (at least 1 hour). Bread that rises too quickly has a yeasty, unpleasant taste; the slower the rising the better – overnight in a cool larder is better than 30 minutes over the boiler!

8 Knock down and knead for a further minute. Pre-heat the oven to 200°C | 400°F | gas mark 6.

9 Shape the dough into an oblong and put it into a 1 kg | 2¼ lb loaf tin.

10 Cover again with oiled clingfilm and prove (allow to rise again) until it has nearly doubled. Brush with beaten egg.

11 Bake the loaf for 30 minutes, or until it is golden and firm.

12 Turn the loaf out on to a wire rack to cool. It should sound hollow when tapped on the underside. If it does not, or feels squashy and heavy, return it to the oven, without the tin, for a further 5 minutes.

NOTE: If using dried or fast-action yeast, see page 738.

Soda Bread

MAKES 1 LOAF

oil for greasing
225 g | 8 oz wholemeal flour
225 g | 8 oz plain white flour
1½ teaspoons salt

2 teaspoons bicarbonate of soda
45 g | 1½ oz butter
1 tablespoon caster sugar
290–425 ml | ½– ¾ pint buttermilk

1 Preheat the oven to 190°C | 375°F | gas mark 5. Oil a baking sheet.
2 Stir the flours, salt and bicarbonate of soda together 3 times. Reserve any bran left in the sieve.
3 Cut the butter into small pieces, then rub into the flour using the fingertips.
4 Stir in the sugar.
5 Make a well in the centre. Stir in enough buttermilk to make a soft dough.
6 Knead lightly to bring together into a round.
7 Place on the baking sheet and sprinkle with the reserved bran.
8 Using a wooden spoon handle, make a deep cross in the centre of the bread nearly all the way to the baking sheet.
9 Bake in the preheated oven for about 40 minutes or until well-risen and browned. The cross in the centre of the bread should not seem damp.
10 Transfer to a wire rack and leave to cool.

NOTE: If you are unable to obtain buttermilk, use regular milk and add 2 teaspoons cream of tartar to the flour in step 2.

Wholemeal Baps

MAKES 12 BAPS

20 g | ¾ oz fresh yeast
290 ml | ½ pint lukewarm milk
1 teaspoon caster sugar
225 g | 8 oz wholemeal flour
225 g | 8 oz strong plain white flour

2 teaspoons salt
55 g | 2 oz butter
1 egg, lightly beaten
sesame seeds

1 Dissolve the yeast with a little of the milk and the sugar in a teacup.
2 Sift the flours with the salt into a bowl. Rub in the butter as you would for pastry.
3 Pour in the yeast mixture, the remaining milk and nearly all the beaten egg and mix to a fairly soft dough.
4 When the dough will leave the sides of the bowl, press it into a ball and tip it out on to a work surface. Knead it until elastic and smooth (about 10 minutes).
5 Put the dough back into the bowl and cover it with a piece of lightly greased clingfilm. Put it into a warm place. Leave until the dough has doubled in size (at least 1 hour).

6 Take the dough out of the bowl, knock down and knead again for 1 minute.

7 Preheat the oven to 200°C|400°F|gas mark 6.

8 Divide the dough into 12 equal pieces and shape them into flattish ovals. Place on a floured baking sheet and prove until nearly doubled in size (allow to rise again). Brush with the remaining beaten egg. Sprinkle with the sesame seeds.

9 Bake for 20 minutes, or until brown. Leave to cool on a wire rack. Covering the baps with a tea-towel will ensure a very soft crust.

NOTE: If using dried or fast-action yeast, see page 738.

Wholemeal Bread

This wholemeal bread is simple to make as it has only one rising. As with all bread made from purely 100% wholemeal flour it will be heavier than bread made from a mixture including white flour. The flour and water quantities are approximations as wholemeal flours vary enormously. The dough should be moist but not sticky. Use the smaller quantity called for and then add extra flour or water as necessary.

MAKES 2 LOAVES

550 g–600 g|1 lb 4 oz–1 lb 6 oz stoneground 100% wholemeal flour

2 teaspoons salt

3 tablespoons buttermilk

290–340 ml|10–12 fl oz warm water

15 g|½ oz fresh yeast

1 tablespoon black treacle

1 Warm the flour with the salt in a large mixing bowl in the bottom of a low oven for about 5 minutes. Oil 2 × 675 g|1½ lb loaf tins.

2 Mix the buttermilk with the warm water. Add a little of the liquid to the yeast with a pinch of flour and the treacle.

3 Make a well in the centre of the flour, pour in the yeast mixture and nearly all the water and buttermilk. Mix to a dough. Add extra flour or liquid as required. Knead well.

4 Fill the tins three-quarters full of dough. Smooth the tops and cover with a piece of lightly oiled clingfilm. Leave in a warm place for 45 minutes, or until the dough has risen to the top of the tins.

5 Meanwhile, preheat the oven to 220°C|425°F|gas mark 7.

6 Bake the bread for 15 minutes. Turn down the oven temperature to 190°C|375°F|gas mark 5 and bake for a further 25 minutes.

7 The bread should sound hollow when it is tapped on the underside. If it does not or feels squashy and heavy, then return to the oven, without the tin, for a further 5–10 minutes. Leave to cool on a wire rack.

NOTE: If using dried or fast action- yeast, see page 738.

Ballymaloe Brown Bread

MAKES 1 LOAF

30 g | 1 oz yeast

1 teaspoon black treacle

350–425 ml | 12–15 fl oz water at blood heat

450 g | 1 lb wholemeal flour

1 teaspoon salt

1 tablespoon sesame seeds

1 Grease a 13 × 20 cm | 5 × 8 in loaf tin.

2 Mix the yeast with the treacle and 150 ml | 1/4 pint of the water, and leave in a warm place for about 5 minutes, by which time it should look creamy and slightly frothy on top.

3 Sift the flour with the salt into a warmed large mixing bowl. Make a well in the centre and add the yeast mixture and enough of the remaining liquid to make a wettish dough that would be just too wet to knead.

4 Put the dough into the loaf tin and smooth down the surface. Sprinkle with the sesame seeds and pat down. Place the tin in a warm place and cover with a dry tea-towel. Leave to rise for 15–30 minutes.

5 Preheat the oven to 220°C | 425°F | gas mark 7.

6 Bake the bread in the preheated oven for 30 minutes, then remove the bread from the tin and return it to the oven to bake for a further 15–25 minutes. When cooked, the bread should sound hollow when tapped on the underside.

NOTE: If using dried or fast-action yeast, see page 738.

Beer Bread

MAKES 1 LOAF

55 g | 2 oz butter

2 teaspoons soft light brown sugar

290 ml | 1/2 pint brown ale

30 g | 1 oz fresh yeast

2 teaspoons salt

1 egg

225 g | 8 oz wholemeal flour

225 g | 8 oz strong plain white flour

1 Grease a 900 g | 2 lb loaf tin.

2 Bring the sugar, beer and the remaining butter to boiling point, then allow to cool until lukewarm.

3 Use 1–2 spoonfuls of this liquid to cream the yeast. Add the creamed yeast and lightly beaten egg to the beer mixture.

4 Sift the flours and salt into a warmed large mixing bowl. Make a well in the centre and pour in the liquid. Mix, first with a knife, and then with your fingers, to a soft but not sloppy dough. Knead for 10 minutes or until smooth, a little shiny and very elastic.

5 Put the dough back into the bowl and cover with a piece of oiled clingfilm. Leave in a warm place until it has doubled in bulk.

6 Take the dough out of the bowl, knock it down and knead until smooth again. Shape the dough into a loaf shape and put into the tin. Cover again with oiled clingfilm and return in the warm place to prove (rise again) until doubled in size and the shape of the finished loaf.

7 Meanwhile, preheat the oven to 200°C | 400°F | gas mark 6. Bake the loaf in the top third of the oven for 35 minutes, or until it is brown on top and sounds hollow when tapped on the underside. Cool on a wire rack.

NOTE: If using dried or fast-action yeast, see page 738.

Hazelnut and Raisin Bread

MAKES 1 LOAF
225 g | 8 oz strong plain flour
225 g | 8 oz wholemeal flour
1 teaspoon salt
15 g | ½ oz fresh yeast
290 ml | ½ pint warm milk

1 tablespoon oil
55 g | 2 oz raisins
55 g | 2 oz hazelnuts, toasted
extra flour for dusting

1 Sift the flours and salt into a large mixing bowl and make a well in the centre.

2 Mix the yeast with 1 tablespoon of the milk. Pour into the well with the remaining milk and the oil.

3 Mix with a knife and then draw together with the fingers of one hand to make a soft but not sticky dough.

4 Knead until smooth and elastic (about 10 minutes), using more flour if necessary.

5 Put the dough into a large, clean bowl and cover with a piece of lightly greased clingfilm. Put in a warm place to rise until doubled in bulk (about 1 hour).

6 Preheat the oven to 190°C | 375°F | gas mark 5.

7 Knock back the dough and knead the raisins and hazelnuts carefully into it. Shape into a round loaf and place on a baking sheet.

8 Cover the loaf with lightly greased clingfilm and leave in a warm place until it is 1½ times its original size. Dust the top with a little flour.

9 Bake the loaf in the oven for 30 minutes, or until it sounds hollow when tapped on the underside.

10 Place the loaf on a wire rack and leave to cool.

NOTE: If using dried or fast-action yeast, see page 738.

Three-Seed Bread

MAKES 1 LOAF OR 14 ROLLS

15 g | ½ oz fresh yeast or 1½ teaspoons fast-action yeast

1 teaspoon caster sugar

225 g | 8 oz strong white flour

225 g | 8 oz strong wholemeal flour

2 teaspoons salt

2 tablespoons olive oil

290 ml | ½ pint warm water

oil for greasing

6 tablespoons mixed seeds, such as poppy, sesame, millet, sunflower beaten egg, to glaze

1 Cream the fresh yeast with the sugar and a little warm water. If using fast-action yeast, mix the yeast and the sugar with the flour in step 2 after sifting.

2 Sift the flours and salt into a large bowl and make a well in the centre. Add the yeast mixture to the well.

3 Add the oil and about 290 ml | ½ pint warm water to the flour and stir to make a soft dough. Knead the dough for about 8–10 minutes or until smooth and elastic.

4 Place the dough in a large oiled bowl, turning it so it is coated with a thin film of oil. Cover with clingfilm and leave in a warm place to rise for about 1 hour, or until doubled in size.

5 Preheat the oven to 200°C | 400°F | gas mark 6.

6 Knock back the dough by pushing it down and pulling the edges into the centre. Knead for 30 seconds, then roll out on a floured work surface about 2.5 cm | 1 in thick. Reserve 2 tablespoons of the seeds and sprinkle the remainder over the dough. Fold the dough over itself to encase the seeds and continue to knead for 10 seconds.

7 Shape the dough into a plait or 14 equal rounds and place on oiled clingfilm. Leave in a warm place to prove (rise again) until one and a half times the original size.

8 Glaze with the beaten egg, sprinkle with the reserved seeds and bake in the preheated oven for 20 minutes for rolls and 30–35 minutes for a loaf. When done, the bread will feel light and sound hollow when tapped on the underside. Transfer to a wire rack and leave to cool.

Italian Bread

This is a basic olive oil bread which can be easily adapted by adding a variety of herbs such as rosemary or sage or grated cheese.

MAKES 1 LARGE OR 2 SMALL LOAVES

30 g | 1 oz fresh yeast

225 ml | 8 fl oz warm water

450 g | 1 lb strong plain flour

2 teaspoons salt

4 tablespoons olive oil

coarse sea salt (optional)

1 Dissolve the yeast in the warm water.

2 Sift the flour with the salt into a large bowl and make a well in the centre. Pour in the dissolved yeast and 2 tablespoons of oil. Quickly mix the ingredients to form a dough, then knead the dough for 8 minutes.

3 Oil a baking sheet. Roll the dough with a rolling pin into 1 or 2 ovals about 2 cm|¾ in thick. Cover with oiled clingfilm and leave in a warm place to rise.

4 Preheat the oven to 200°C|400°F|gas mark 6.

5 When the dough feels soft and pillowy, make about 8 indentations in the dough with your finger. Drizzle with the remaining olive oil and sprinkle with the sea salt if using.

6 Bake for 20 minutes. Remove the loaf from the baking sheet and place directly on the oven shelf. Bake for a further 10 minutes. Transfer to a wire rack and leave to get completely cold.

NOTE: If using dried or last-action yeast, see page 738.

Potato Bread

MAKES 3 LOAVES
450 g|1 lb potatoes, peeled
30 g|1 oz fresh yeast
1 tablespoon malt extract
extra flour for dusting

425 ml|¾ pint warm water
675 g|1½ lb strong plain flour
4 teaspoons salt

1 Cut the potatoes into 5 cm|2 in chunks. Cover with water then boil until tender. Drain, saving the water for the bread. Mash the potatoes and cool until lukewarm.

2 Dissolve the yeast in a little of the warm water. Stir in the malt extract. Mix it with the mashed potatoes.

3 Sift the flour with the salt into a large mixing bowl. Add the potato mixture and enough water to mix to a soft dough. Mix well. When the mixture will leave the sides of the bowl, press it into a ball and tip it out on to a floured surface.

4 Knead until elastic, smooth and shiny (about 15 minutes).

5 Put the dough back into the bowl and cover with lightly oiled clingfilm.

6 Put it into a warm place and leave to rise until doubled in size (at least 1 hour).

7 Knock down and knead for a further minute. Preheat the oven to 220°C|425°F|gas mark 7.

8 Shape into 3 loaves, cover again with oiled clingfilm and leave to prove (rise again) until 1½ times its original size. Dust lightly with flour. Slash the top of the loaves.

9 Bake the loaves in the oven for 10 minutes. Turn the oven temperature down to 190°C|375°F|gas mark 5 and bake for a further 25 minutes, or until golden-brown and firm.

10 Turn out on to a wire rack to cool. The bread should sound hollow when tapped on the underside.

NOTES: This recipe can be used for making attractive bread rolls. For details of making these see pages 742–4.

If using dried or fast-action yeast, see page 738.

Sourdough Bread

A natural yeast starter for sourdough bread will take about a week to get started. Feed it every 3 days with an addition of 50 per cent of its weight in organic flour and mineral water. A loaf will take approximately 24 hours to produce from an active starter.

Whole wheat grain can be found in health food stores.

MAKES 1 LOAF

For the starter

225 g|8 oz organic wheat grain or strong organic flour

225 ml|8 fl oz warm natural mineral water

225 g|8 oz strong organic flour

1 teaspoon golden caster sugar

150 ml|¼ pint warm natural mineral water

For the loaf

170 g|6 oz starter (see above)

55 ml|2 fl oz warm natural mineral water

1 tablespoon clear honey or barley malt syrup

170 g|6 oz strong plain organic flour

55 g|2 oz organic rye flour or wholemeal flour

1 slightly rounded teaspoon sea salt

1 Make the starter: grind the wheat grain in a clean coffee grinder. Place in a bowl and stir in 225 ml|8 fl oz water to make a paste. Leave to stand uncovered for 3 days at room temperature. A few whole unwashed grapes can be added to the mixture, which should start to bubble and smell sweetly yeasty. If it smells unpleasant, throw it away and start again.

2 On the third day stir in the flour, the sugar and the 150 ml|¼ pint water. Let stand, uncovered, for a further 3 days. Remove 170 g|6 oz of the starter to make the bread. Feed the remaining starter, as described above, then place in the refrigerator.

3 Make the bread: place 170 g|6 oz of the starter in a large bowl and stir in the water and honey or malt syrup. Sift the flours together, then add enough flour to make a soft but not sticky dough.

4 Knead for 10 minutes by hand or for 5 minutes by machine. Place in an oiled bowl, cover with oiled clingfilm and let stand at room temperature to rise until doubled in size. This will take 12–24 hours.

5 Knock down the dough and knead for 1 minute. Return to the oiled bowl, cover with oiled clingfilm and let rise until doubled in size, about 3–8 hours.

6 Sprinkle the salt over the dough, then knead to knock back for 2 minutes. Cover the dough with clingfilm and let the dough rest for 10 minutes. Line a 20 cm|8 in diameter basket or bowl with a heavily floured linen tea towel.

7 Shape the dough into a smooth round and place in the basket or bowl. Cover with oiled clingfilm and let prove (rise again) until nearly doubled in size.

8 Meanwhile, preheat the oven to 225°C|425°F|gas mark 7. Place a pizza stone in the centre of the oven.

9 When the dough is ready to bake, remove the stone from the oven and sprinkle it liberally with flour. Carefully turn the dough on to the stone, then slash it with a razor or serrated knife in a 'noughts and crosses' pattern.

10 Place the dough in the oven, then pour a cup of cold water on to the floor of the oven to create a steamy environment. Bake for 35–40 minutes or until the loaf is well browned and sounds hollow when tapped on the underside. Transfer to a wire rack and leave to cool for 1 hour before slicing.

Pumpernickel Bread

The dough is very heavy and sticky so it is a good idea to use a machine to knead it.

MAKES 2 LOAVES

For the starter

290 ml | ½ pint water

1 teaspoon instant espresso coffee powder

30 g | 1 oz bitter chocolate, chopped

1 tablespoon treacle or molasses

150 ml | ¼ pint plain organic yoghurt

10 g | ⅓ oz fresh yeast or 1 teaspoon fast-action yeast

225 g | 8 oz rye flour

For the dough

340 g | 12 oz strong bread flour, preferably organic

110 g | 4 oz rye flour

1 tablespoon sea salt

1 teaspoon caraway seeds, ground

55 g | 2 oz unsalted butter, melted and cooled

20 g | ⅔ oz fresh yeast or 2 teaspoons fast-action yeast

150 ml | ¼ pint warm water

oil for greasing

2 tablespoons polenta (optional)

For the glaze

1 egg white, beaten lightly with a fork

1 tablespoon caraway or sesame seeds

1 Make the starter: place the water, espresso powder, chocolate and treacle in a small saucepan and heat, stirring, to melt the chocolate and combine the ingredients.

2 Stir in the yoghurt. When the mixture has reached 37°C | 100°F (blood temperature), stir in the yeast. Turn into a large bowl.

3 Stir in the flour and allow to stand at a cool room temperature overnight.

4 Make the dough: sift the flours, salt and caraway seeds into a large bowl. Make a well in the centre and tip in the cooled melted butter and the starter.

5 Mix the yeast with 2 tablespoons of the warm water and pour into the well.

6 Stir to make a sticky dough, adding warm water or flour as necessary.

7 Knead for 10 minutes until smooth and elastic. Place in an oiled bowl and cover with oiled clingfilm. Rise at normal room temperature until doubled in size. This can take 2–3 hours.

8 Knock the dough back by kneading for 30 seconds, then cover with oiled clingfilm and allow to rise again.

9 Preheat the oven to 200°C | 400°F | gas mark 6.

10 Divide the dough in half and shape each piece to fit into a large greased loaf tin, or shape into ovals and place on a greased baking sheet sprinkled with polenta, if using. Cover with oiled clingfilm and allow to prove (rise again) until nearly doubled in size.

11 Brush with the egg white and sprinkle with the seeds. Slash if desired.

12 Place in the top third of the oven (the hottest part) and bake for 10 minutes. Turn the oven temperature down to 170°C | 350°F | gas mark 4 and bake for a further 30–40 minutes. The loaves should sound hollow when tapped on the underside. Turn out on to a wire rack and leave to cool before slicing or freezing.

NOTE: If using fast-action yeast, mix directly with the flour. It is not necessary to mix the yeast with the liquid.

Cheese Gannat

This recipe is based on a cheese brioche originally from Gannat, a small town in Auvergne.

105 ml | 3½ fl oz milk
15 g | ½ oz fresh yeast
⅓ teaspoon sugar
225 g | 8 oz wholemeal flour
1 teaspoon salt
a pinch of cayenne pepper
a pinch of dry English mustard

freshly ground black pepper
55 g | 2 oz butter
2 eggs, beaten
110 g | 4 oz cheese, preferably strong Cheddar or Gruyère, grated
a little milk to glaze

1 Scald the milk, then allow to cool until lukewarm.

2 Cream the yeast with the sugar.

3 Sift the flour with the salt, cayenne, mustard and pepper into a warmed mixing bowl and make a well in the centre.

4 Melt the butter, remove from the heat and add the milk. Mix with the eggs and the creamed yeast. Pour this liquid into the flour and mix to a soft dough. Knead until just smooth.

5 Cover and leave to rise in a warm place (do not worry if it does not rise very much – it will during baking).

6 Preheat the oven to 200°C | 400°F | gas mark 6.

7 Mix most of the cheese into the dough.

8 Pile into a well-greased 20 cm | 8 in sandwich tin and flatten so that the mixture is about 2.5 cm | 1 in deep. Put back in the warm place to prove (rise again) for 10–15 minutes.

9 Bake in the oven for 25–30 minutes.

10 Brush lightly with the milk and sprinkle with the remaining cheese, and return to the oven for a further 5 minutes.

NOTES: The mixture can be divided into 8 round rolls: put 7 around the edge of a Victoria sandwich tin and one in the middle. Leave to prove and then bake. It will look like a crown loaf.

If using dried or fast-action yeast, see page 738.

Grissini

This recipe has been taken from Arabella Boxer's *Mediterranean Cookbook*.

7 g|¼ oz fresh yeast
2 teaspoons sugar
3 tablespoons warm water
1 teaspoon sea salt
150 ml|¼ pint boiling water

225 g|8 oz strong flour
1 tablespoon olive oil
1 egg, beaten
55 g|2 oz sesame seeds

1 Preheat the oven to 150°C|300°F|gas mark 2.
2 Dissolve the yeast and sugar in the lukewarm water.
3 Dissolve the sea salt in the boiling water, allow to cool to blood temperature.
4 Sift the flour into a large bowl, make a well in the centre, pour in the yeast mixture, the salted water and the oil. Mix to a soft dough.
5 Tip the dough on to a floured board and knead for 3–4 minutes, until smooth and elastic. Cover with a damp cloth and leave for 5 minutes. Knead for 3 minutes and then divide into 20 equal pieces.
6 Roll each piece of dough out until it is finger thickness. Place on oiled baking sheets and prove (allow to rise again) for 10–15 minutes.
7 Brush with beaten egg, sprinkle with sesame seeds and bake in the oven for about 45 minutes until crisp and golden brown.

Herb Fougasse

Fougasse is traditional French hearth bread from the Provence region, shaped like a fern or leaf, hence the name.

MAKES 1 LARGE OR 2 SMALL LOAVES

For the starter
10 g|⅓ oz fresh yeast or 1 teaspoon fast-action
   yeast
150 ml|¼ pint warm water
½ teaspoon caster sugar
140 g|5 oz strong bread flour

For the dough
10 g|⅓ oz fresh yeast or 1 teaspoon fast-action
   yeast
150 ml|¼ pint warm water
340 g|12 oz strong bread flour
2 level teaspoons salt
4 tablespoons olive oil
2 tablespoons rice flour

To finish
1 tablespoon olive oil
1 tablespoon dried herbes de Provence or dried
   mixed herbs
coarse sea salt

1 Make the starter: whisk the yeast into the water, then stir in the sugar and the flour. Cover with clingfilm and leave in a cool place overnight.

2 Make the dough: whisk the yeast into the water. Sift the flour into a large bowl with the salt and make a well in the centre.

3 Tip the starter into the well along with the new yeast mixture and half the oil.

4 Stir to make a soft dough, adding a little more water or more flour if required.

5 Knead the dough for 10 minutes by hand or for 5 minutes by machine to make a smooth, elastic dough.

6 Place the dough in an oiled bowl and cover with oiled clingfilm. Allow to rise in a warm place until doubled in size, about 1 hour.

7 Preheat the oven to 200°F|400°C|gas mark 6. Place a roasting pan on the lower shelf of the oven.

8 Sprinkle the rice flour on to a baking sheet. Carefully lift the risen dough out of the bowl and place on the baking sheet, stretching it into one or two ovals. Cut slits in the dough where the veins in a leaf would be found.

9 Brush the dough with half the remaining oil. Cover with clingfilm and leave to prove (rise again) until it is pillowy and springs back only a little when prodded.

10 Sprinkle the dough with the dried herbs and a little salt. Splash a little cold water into the roasting pan to create a steamy environment. Bake in the top third of the oven (the hottest part) for 20–30 minutes.

11 After 20 minutes remove the bread from the baking sheet and place it directly on the oven shelf so that the base can brown. Bake for a further 5–10 minutes. The bread is done when it is golden-brown, feels light and sounds hollow when tapped on the underside.

12 Transfer to a wire rack and drizzle with the remaining oil. Allow to cool.

NOTE: If using fast-action yeast, mix the dry yeast directly with the flour. It is not necessary to mix the yeast with the liquid.

Naan

450 g|1 lb strong plain flour

1 tablespoon salt

15 g|½ oz fresh yeast

1 teaspoon sugar

90–150 ml|3–5 fl oz warm milk

2 tablespoons sesame oil

150 ml|¼ pint plain yoghurt

1 egg, beaten

1 tablespoon black onion seeds

1 Sift the flour and salt into a bowl.

2 Cream the yeast with the sugar, then mix with the milk, oil, yoghurt and the egg.

3 Mix the yeast mixture into the flour to form a soft but not sticky dough. Knead for 5 minutes or until smooth.

4 Put the dough into an oiled bowl. Cover with greased clingfilm and leave to rise in a warm place until doubled in size.

5 Turn the dough on to a floured board and knead for a further 5 minutes. Knead the seeds into the bread.

6 Divide the dough into 8 equal pieces and roll each piece into an oval measuring about 12.5 × 20 cm | 5 × 8 in. Place on a greased baking sheet, cover with clingfilm and leave to rise for about 15 minutes or until 1½ times the original size.

7 Preheat the grill.

8 Brush the bread with water and grill on each side for 3 minutes or until well browned. Serve warm.

NOTE: If using dried or fast-action yeast, see page 738.

Walnut Loaf

This bread is particularly delicious when served with apple marmalade (see p. 667) and Roquefort cheese.

MAKES 2 LOAVES

225 g | 8 oz strong plain flour
225 g | 8 oz malted brown flour
1 teaspoon salt
15 g | ½ oz fresh yeast

290 ml | ½ pint warm milk
1 tablespoon walnut or olive oil
170 g | 6 oz walnuts, roughly chopped
1 tablespoon clear honey

1 Sift the flours and salt into a large mixing bowl and make a well in the centre.

2 Mix the yeast with 1 tablespoon of the milk. Pour into the well with the remaining milk and the oil.

3 Mix with a knife and then draw together with the fingers of one hand to make a soft but not sticky dough.

4 Knead until smooth, about 10 minutes by hand, using more flour if necessary.

5 Put the dough into a lightly oiled bowl and cover with a piece of lightly greased clingfilm. Put in a warm place to rise until the dough has doubled in bulk (about 1 hour).

6 Preheat the oven to 190°C | 375°F | gas mark 5.

7 Knock back the dough and knead the walnuts into it. Divide the dough into 2 equal pieces and shape into ovals. Place on a baking sheet. Slash the tops with a sharp knife.

8 Cover the loaves with lightly greased clingfilm and leave in a warm place until they are 1½ times their original size.

9 Bake in the oven for 30 minutes, or until they sound hollow when tapped on the underside. Brush the honey evenly over the loaves. Return to the oven for 5 minutes.

10 Place on a wire rack and leave to cool.

NOTE: If using dried or fast-action yeast, see page 738.

Doughnuts

MAKES 8

225 g│8 oz plain flour
a pinch of salt
7 g│¼ oz fresh yeast
45 g│1½ oz sugar

30 g│1 oz butter
2 egg yolks
150 ml│¼ pint warm milk
oil for deep-frying
caster sugar flavoured with ground cinnamon

1 Sift the flour with the salt into a bowl.

2 Cream the yeast with 1 teaspoon of the sugar.

3 Rub the butter into the flour. Make a well in the centre.

4 Mix together the egg yolks, yeast mixture, remaining sugar and milk. Pour this into the well in the flour.

5 Using the fingertips of one hand, mix the central ingredients together, gradually drawing in the surrounding flour. Mix to a smooth soft dough.

6 Cover the bowl with a piece of greased clingfilm and leave to rise in a warm place for 45 minutes.

7 Knead the dough well for at least 10 minutes. Roll out on a floured board to 1 cm│½ in thick. With a plain cutter, press into small rounds. Place on a greased tray and leave to prove (rise again) until doubled in size.

8 Heat the oil in a deep-fryer until a crumb will sizzle vigorously in it. Put the doughnuts into the fryer basket and lower into the fat. Fry until golden-brown, then drain on absorbent kitchen paper.

9 Toss in caster sugar and cinnamon.

Chelsea Buns

MAKES 12

225 ml│7½ fl oz milk
15 g│½ oz fresh yeast
85 g│3 oz caster sugar
450 g│1 lb strong plain flour
½ teaspoon ground cinnamon
1 teaspoon salt
85 g│3 oz butter
1 egg

½ teaspoon ground mixed spice
55 g│2 oz sultanas
55 g│2 oz currants
sugar for sprinkling
apricot glaze (see page 727)

1 Scald the milk. Cool until lukewarm.

2 Cream the yeast with 1 teaspoon of the sugar and 1 tablespoon warm milk.

3 Sift the flour with the salt and cinnamon into a mixing bowl. Rub in half the butter and stir in half the sugar.

4 Beat the egg and add to the flour with the lukewarm milk and yeast mixture.

5 Cover the bowl with lightly oiled clingfilm and leave to rise in a warm place until doubled in size (about 1 hour).

6 Knock the dough down and knead again on a floured board. Roll into a 30 cm│12 in square.

7 Mix the remaining butter with the remaining sugar and the mixed spice and spread over the dough. Sprinkle with the fruit.

8 Preheat the oven to 200°C│400°F│gas mark 6.

9 Roll the dough up like a Swiss roll and cut into 2 cm│1 in slices.

10 Arrange the buns cut side up on the baking sheet and leave in a warm place to prove (rise again) for 15 minutes.

11 Sprinkle with sugar. Bake in the oven for 20–25 minutes. Brush with apricot glaze.

12 Leave the buns to cool on a wire rack before separating.

NOTE: If using dried or fast-action yeast, see page 738.

Hot Cross Buns

MAKES 16

20 g│¾ oz fresh yeast	½ teaspoon salt
55 g│2 oz caster sugar	4 teaspoons ground mixed spice
200 ml│7 fl oz milk	85 g│3 oz butter
2 eggs, beaten	110 g│4 oz currants
450 g│1 lb strong plain flour	30 g│1 oz finely chopped mixed peel
	a little sweetened milk to glaze

1 Cream the yeast with 1 teaspoon of the sugar.

2 Scald the milk and allow to cool to blood temperature. Mix about two-thirds of the milk with the eggs and yeast.

3 Sift the flour with the salt and spice into a large mixing bowl. Rub in the butter. Add the remaining sugar. Make a well in the centre of the flour. Tip in the warm milk mixture and beat until smooth, adding more milk if necessary to produce a soft, sticky dough.

4 Turn the dough on to a floured board. Knead until the dough is smooth, about 10 minutes.

5 Place in a lightly oiled bowl. Cover with oiled clingfilm. Leave to rise in a warm place until doubled in size (about 1½ hours).

6 Preheat the oven to 200°C│400°F│gas mark 6.

7 Turn out on to a floured board, knock down and knead again for a few minutes. Then work in the currants and peel, making sure that they are distributed evenly.

8 Shape into small round buns. Mark a cross on top of each bun with a knife. Place on baking trays and leave to prove (rise again) until doubled in bulk (about 15 minutes). Brush the tops with sweetened milk.

9 Bake in the oven for about 15 minutes. Brush again with sweetened milk, bake for a further 5 minutes, then cool on a wire rack.

NOTES: The crosses can be made by laying strips of shortcrust pastry or by piping a cross of flour and water paste on top of the buns just before baking. To make the paste, combine 110 g | 4 oz plain flour with a pinch of baking powder and 1 tablespoon oil and mix with cold water.

If using dried or fast-action yeast, see page 738.

Stollen

225 ml	8 fl oz warm milk	110 g	4 oz sultanas
450 g	1 lb strong plain white flour	30 g	1 oz chopped mixed peel
1 teaspoon caster sugar	30 g	1 oz walnuts or almonds, chopped
15 g	½ oz fresh yeast	2 teaspoons granted orange or lemon zest
1 teaspoon salt	1 egg
85 g	3 oz butter	55 g	2 oz glacé cherries
110 g	4 oz currants	icing sugar for dusting

1 Scald the milk and allow to cool to blood temperature.
2 Prepare the yeast batter: mix together 110 g | 4 oz of the flour, the sugar, yeast and warm milk. Set aside in a warm place until bubbly (about 20 minutes).
3 Mix the remaining flour with the salt in a mixing bowl. Rub in 55 g | 2 oz of the butter. Add the currants, sultanas, mixed peel, nuts and citrus zest.
4 Beat the egg and add it to the yeast batter with the flour, fruit and nuts. Mix well to a soft but not too sticky dough.
5 Knead until smooth and elastic (about 10 minutes). Shape into a ball, place in a clean bowl cover with lightly oiled clingfilm and leave in a warm place until doubled in size (at least 1 hour).
6 Knock down, knead again for 2 minutes and shape into a 30 × 20 cm | 12 × 8 in oval.
7 Melt the remaining butter and brush half of it over the dough. Spread the glacé cherries over half the dough. Fold over the other half of the dough and press down lightly. Cover with lightly oiled clingfilm and leave to prove (rise again) until 1½ times the original size.
8 Preheat the oven to 190°C | 375°F | gas mark 5.
9 Brush the remaining butter over the proved loaf and bake on a baking sheet in the oven for 20–25 minutes. Leave to cool on a wire rack. Dust with icing sugar.

NOTES: An alternative version of this traditional German Christmas cake is to use 225 g | 8 oz made-up marzipan to stuff the Stollen. Roll the marzipan into a sausage and place in the middle of the dough. Roll up and seal the ends by pinching them together. Bake as before.

If using dried or fast-action yeast, see page 738.

Brioche (1)

Brioche can be sweetened or not, depending on how the finished product is to be used. Plain flour produces a brioche with a fine, cake-like texture, whilst strong flour produces a brioche with a more open, bread-like texture.

MAKES 1 LARGE OR 12 SMALL BRIOCHE

85 ml | 3 fl oz milk

15 g | ½ oz fresh yeast

30 g | 1 oz caster sugar

500 g | 1 lb 2 oz flour (see above for type)

1½ teaspoons salt

6 eggs, beaten

340 g | 12 oz unsalted butter, softened

extra butter melted and flour for the tins

1 egg yolk, beaten with 1 tablespoon milk, to glaze

1 Scald the milk, then allow to cool to blood temperature.
2 Cream the yeast with the milk and a pinch of the sugar.
3 Sift the flour with the salt into a large bowl and make a well in the centre.
4 Place the milk and yeast mixture and the eggs in the well, then stir to make a soft, very sticky dough.
5 Beat the dough in an electric mixer or by hand. If kneading by hand, take a lump of the dough and pull it up vertically, then push it back down and away from you. Continue this process until the dough becomes smooth and elastic and forms a cohesive ball.
6 Cover the dough with lightly oiled clingfilm and place in a warm place to rise until doubled in size.
7 Beat the butter and sugar together to dissolve the sugar and bring the mixture to the same texture as the dough.
8 To add the butter to the dough using a mixer, beat a tablespoon of the butter at a time into the dough, only adding more butter when the previous addition has been incorporated. To add the butter by hand, turn the dough on to a work surface. Bury the butter a tablespoon at a time in the centre of the dough, then knead the dough as above until it becomes a smooth, silky mass. Continue adding butter in this way until it has all been added.
9 Place the dough in a bowl and cover with oiled clingfilm. Allow to rise until doubled in size. It should not be risen in a very warm place, i.e. no more than 21°C | 70°F, or the butter could become too soft which would result in a greasy brioche.
10 When the dough has risen, gently knock it back by folding the edges of the dough over the centre and patting it down lightly.
11 Cover the dough with oiled clingfilm and refrigerate for at least 8 hours or overnight.
12 Generously grease the brioche tins with 2 coatings of butter and dust with flour, tapping any excess flour on to the work surface.
13 Half fill the prepared tins with the cold brioche dough. For brioche *à tête*, make a hole in the centre of the dough all the way to the bottom, using the floured handle of a wooden spoon. Place an elongated 'head' of dough into the hole and secure it by pressing through the centre of the 'head' with the spoon handle.

14 Preheat the oven to 190°C|375°F|gas mark 5. Cover the brioche tins with oiled clingfilm and leave to rise until the dough is mounding slightly over the top of the tins.

15 Brush the dough with the egg yolk glaze, taking care not to let any of the glaze drip between the edge of the dough and the tin or the glaze could 'glue' the dough to the tin, making the brioche difficult to remove.

16 Bake in the top third of the oven (the hottest part) for 8–10 minutes for individual brioches or 30–40 minutes for a large mould. Larger brioches will need to be covered with greaseproof paper after about 15 minutes' baking to prevent then from overbrowning. The brioche is done when it is deep brown on the top and pale golden brown and firm where it was covered by the tin. It should feel light for its size.

17 Allow to cool on a wire rack. Eat within 1 day or freeze for up to 1 month.

Brioche (2)

This is a less rich, slightly sweeter brioche than the previous recipe and is best for cooking as a large loaf.

MAKES 1 LARGE OR 12 SMALL BRIOCHES

7 g|¼ oz fresh yeast

5 teaspoons caster sugar

2 tablespoons warm water

225 g|8 oz plain white flour

½ teaspoon salt

2 eggs, beaten

55 g|2 oz melted butter, cool

For the glaze

1 egg, mixed with 1 tablespoon water and 1 teaspoon
    sugar

1 Butter and flour a large brioche mould or 12 small brioche tins.

2 Mix the yeast with 1 teaspoon of the sugar and the water. Leave to dissolve.

3 Sift the flour with the salt into a mixing bowl. Sprinkle over the sugar. Make a well in the centre. Drop in the eggs, yeast mixture and melted butter and mix with the fingers of one hand to a soft but not sloppy paste. Knead on an unfloured board for 5 minutes or until smooth. Put into a clean bowl, cover with a damp cloth or lightly oiled clingfilm and leave to rise in a warm place until doubled in bulk (about 1 hour).

4 Turn out and knead again on an unfloured board for 2 minutes.

5 Place the dough in the brioche mould (it should not come more than halfway up the mould). If making individual brioches, divide the dough into 12 pieces. Using three-quarters of each piece, roll them into small balls and put them in the brioche tins. Make a dip on top of each brioche. Roll the remaining paste into 12 tiny balls and press them into the prepared holes. Push a pencil, or thin spoon handle, right through each small ball into the brioche base as this will anchor the balls in place when baking.

6 Cover with lightly oiled clingfilm and leave in a warm place to prove (rise again) until risen to the top of the mould or tin (about 30 minutes for the large brioche, 15 minutes for individual ones).

7 Preheat the oven to 200°C│400°F│gas mark 6.

8 Brush the brioches with the egg glaze. Bake the large one in the preheated oven for 20–25 minutes, the small ones for 10 minutes.

NOTE: If using dried or fast-action yeast, see page 738.

Croissants

The détrempe should be made 12–24 hours in advance to allow the flavours to develop.

MAKES 10 CROISSANTS AND 4 PAIN AU CHOCOLAT

15 g│½ oz fresh yeast
300 ml│½ pint cold milk
500 g│1 lb 2 oz strong white flour
45 g│1½ oz caster sugar
1 teaspoon salt
285 g│10 oz pliable unsalted butter

For the glaze
1 egg yolk, beaten with 1 Tablespoon milk

For the pain au chocolat
30 g│1 oz plain chocolat

1 Whisk the yeast into the milk.
2 Sift the flour and salt into a large bowl and stir in the sugars. Mix to a smooth, soft dough with the yeast mixture but do not knead.
3 Cover the dough with lightly oiled clingfilm and leave in a warm place until doubled in size, about 1 hour.
4 Knock back the dough by patting it firmly. Do not work the dough. Place it in a lightly oiled plastic bag and refrigerate for 4 hours or overnight.
5 Shape the dough into a ball and cut a cross into the top halfway through the centre of the dough. Pull each quarter lobe away from the dough ball and roll into a thin flap.
6 Place the butter in the centre, then fold over the flaps to encase the butter.
7 Lightly flour a work surface, then ridge the dough to form a 40 × 70 cm│16 × 30 in rectangle. Brush off the excess flour and fold the dough into 3 like a business letter.
8 Give the dough a quarter turn so that the folded edge of the dough is on your left. Repeat step 7.
9 Wrap the dough in clingfilm and refrigerate for 20 minutes.
10 Repeat steps 7 and 8 until the dough has had 4 rolls and folds and is no longer streaky.
11 Roll the dough out into a 40 × 75 cm│16 × 30 in rectangle. Place on a baking sheet covered with greaseproof paper, then cover the dough with lightly oiled clingfilm. Refrigerate until firm or overnight.
12 Using a large knife, trim the edges, then cut the dough lengthways into 2 equal strips. Using a triangular template 15 × 17.5 cm│6 × 7 in, cut the dough into triangles. Save the trimmings for the Pain au Chocolat.
13 Place the triangles one at a time on the work surface with the longer point towards

you. Stretch out the 2 shorter points, then roll the triangle up loosely. The tip should fold over the top of the croissant and touch the baking sheet but it should not be underneath the croissant.

14 Place the shaped croissants on a baking sheet, curving them into a crescent shape and leaving enough space for them to double in size without touching. The points should be facing towards the middle of the baking sheet to help prevent them from burning.

15 Cover the croissants with lightly oiled clingfilm and prove at room temperature, 20°C|70°F, until they are very puffy. Refrigerate for 20 minutes to set the shape.

16 Meanwhile, preheat the oven to 250°C|450°F|gas mark 8.

17 Glaze the croissants with the egg yolk and milk and bake in the hottest part of the oven for 15 minutes, then turn the oven down to 190°C|375°F|gas mark 5 and bake for a further 20 minutes or until the croissants are a deep brown. If they are becoming too brown, cover with greaseproof paper. Cool on a wire rack.

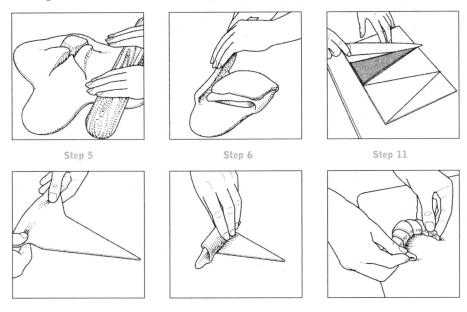

Step 5   Step 6   Step 11

Step 13

Pain au Chocolat

1 Layer the trimmings on top of one another, and give the pile a roll and fold.

2 Roll pastry out to ½ cm | ¼ in thick. Cut into 4 rectangles.

3 Divide the chocolate between the rectangles and fold the pastry in three over the chocolate, like a letter.

4 Place on the baking sheet seam side down.

5 Proceed as for step 15.

Danish Pastries

Most Danish pastries require almond filling and icing as well as the basic paste. Instructions for these are given first, followed by individual instructions for Almond Squares, Pinwheels, etc.

When rolling out Danish pastry, care should be taken to prevent the butter breaking through the paste and making the resulting pastry heavy. Use a heavy rolling pin, bring it fairly firmly down on to the paste and roll with short, quick, firm movements. Do not push it. Avoid using too much flour. If the paste is becoming warm and unmanageable, wrap it up and chill well in the refrigerator before proceeding.

The icing should not be made until the pastries are baked. Danish pastries are frequently scattered with toasted flaked almonds while the icing is still wet. Sometimes sultanas, small pieces of canned pineapple or apple purée are included in the filling.

MAKES 6

For the pastry

15 g | ½ oz fresh yeast
1 tablespoon caster sugar
110 ml | 4 fl oz warm milk
110 g | 4 oz strong flour
110 g | 4 oz plain flour
a pinch of salt
1 egg, beaten
110 g | 4 oz unsalted butter, softened
1 egg, beaten, to glaze

For the almond paste filling

45 g | 1½ oz butter, softened
45 g | 1½ oz icing sugar
30 g | 1 oz ground almonds
2 drops of vanilla essence

For the glacé icing

boiling water to mix
110 g | 4 oz icing sugar
55g | 2 oz toasted flake almonds to finish

1 Dissolve the yeast with 1 teaspoon of the sugar and the milk.
2 Sift the flour with a pinch of salt into a bowl. Add the remaining sugar. Make a well in the centre and drop into it the egg and the yeast mixture.
3 Using a round-bladed knife, quickly mix the liquids into the surrounding flour to make a soft dough. If extra liquid is required, add a little more milk.
4 When the dough leaves the sides of the bowl, turn it on to a floured work top and bring together gently until smooth. Roll into a long rectangle 5 mm | ¼ in thick three times as long as it is wide. Place in an oiled plastic bag and chill for 30 minutes.
5 Divide the butter into hazelnut-sized pieces and dot it over the top two-thirds of the dough, leaving a 1 cm | ½ in clear margin round the edge. Fold the pastry in 3, folding the unbuttered third up over the centre section first, and then the buttered top third down over it. You now have a thick 'parcel' of pastry. Give it a 90-degree turn so that the folded edge of the dough is on your left, like a book. Press the edges together.
6 Roll again into a long rectangle. Fold in 3 as before. Chill in the refrigerator for 10 minutes.
7 Roll and fold the pastry twice again, turning it in the same direction as before, until the butter is worked in well and the paste does not look streaky. Chill in the refrigerator for at least 30 minutes, or overnight, before shaping as described in one of the recipes below.
8 To make the almond paste, cream the butter with the sugar. Mix in the ground almonds and flavour with vanilla essence. Do not overbeat or the oil will run from the almonds, making the paste greasy.

9 When ready to use, make the glacé icing: mix enough boiling water a spoonful at a time into the sugar to give an icing that will run fairly easily – about the consistency of cream.

NOTE: If using dried or fast action yeast, see page 738.

Almond Squares

1 Follow the instructions on page 765.
2 Preheat the oven to 200°C|400°F|gas mark 6.
3 Roll the pastry on a floured work surface into a 25 × 20 cm|10 × 7 in rectangle. Cut into 5 cm|2 in squares.
4 Put a spoonful of the filling into the centre of each piece of pastry. Fold each corner into the middle and press it down lightly into the almond paste to stick it in position.
5 Place the pastries on a greased baking sheet. Allow the pastries to rise at room temperature until puffy.
6 Chill until firm. Brush with beaten egg and bake for 15–20 minutes.
7 Leave to cool completely on a wire rack, then drizzle over freshly made glacé icing.

Crosses

1 Follow the instructions on page 765.
2 Preheat the oven to 200°C|400°F|gas mark 6.
3 Roll the pastry out thinly on a floured work surface and cut it into 10 cm|4 in squares.
4 Cut through each square and then overlap the 2 opposite corners.
5 Fill the central hole with almond paste filling or apple purée.
6 Allow the pastries to rise at room temperature until puffy.
7 Chill until firm. Brush with beaten egg and bake for 15–20 minutes.
8 Leave to cool on a wire rack, then dust with icing sugar or spoon over freshly made glacé icing.

Pinwheels

1 Follow the instructions on page 765.
2 Preheat the oven to 200°C|400°F|gas mark 6.
3 Roll the pastry out thinly on a floured work surface and cut it into 10 cm|4 in squares. From each corner, towards the centre of each square, make a cut about 3 cm|1½ in long. Put a blob of almond filling in the uncut centre of each square.
4 Fold alternate points of pastry (one from each corner) into the middle and press on to the filling to secure. This leaves one unfolded point at each corner, and the pastry should now resemble a child's pinwheel.
5 Place the pastries on a greased baking sheet. Allow the pastries to rise at room temperature until puffy.
6 Chill until firm. Brush with beaten egg and bake for 15–20 minutes.
7 Leave to cool on a wire rack, then drizzle over freshly made glacé icing.

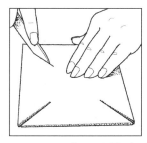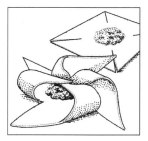

Cut and fill pinwheels as in recipes

Cinnamon Wheels

In this recipe the almond paste is replaced with a cinnamon filling.

For the cinnamon filling

55 g | 2 oz butter

55 g | 2 oz sugar

2 teaspoons ground cinnamon

small handful of dried fruit and chopped mixed peel

1 Follow the instructions on page 765, omitting the almond filling.
2 Make the cinnamon filling: cream the butter with the sugar. Add the cinnamon and mix well.
3 Preheat the oven to 200°C|400°F|gas mark 6.
4 Roll the pastry out to a 25 × 20 cm|12 × 8 in rectangle.
5 Spread the filling over the dough, leaving a narrow margin clear all around. Scatter over the dried fruit and peel.
6 Roll the pastry, from one end, into a thick roll. Cut into 2.5 cm|1 in slices. Place on a greased baking sheet. With lightly floured hand, flatten each slice to the size of the palm of your hand. Leave to prove (rise) at room temperature.
7 Chill until firm. Brush with egg glaze and bake for 15 minutes.
8 Allow to cool slightly on a wire rack, then drizzle over freshly made glacé icing.

Crescents

1 Follow the instructions on page 765.
2 Preheat the oven to 200°C|400°F|gas mark 6. Roll out the pastry on a floured work surface into a 30 × 15 cm|12 × 6 in rectangle. Cut into 7.5 cm|3 in squares and cut each square diagonally in half.
3 Place a small piece of almond paste at the base (long side) of each triangle. Roll it up from the base to the tip and curve into a crescent shape.
4 Leave to prove (rise) for 15 minutes at room temperature.
5 Chill until firm. Bake for 15–20 minutes or until a good brown.
6 Leave to cool on a wire rack, then drizzle over freshly made glacé icing.

Kulich

570 g | 1¼ lb plain flour, sifted

2 teaspoons fast-action yeast

180 ml | 6 fl oz warm milk

¼ teaspoon salt

3 egg yolks

140 g | 5 oz caster sugar

3 cardamom pods, seeded and crushed

140 g | 5 oz butter, softened

3 egg whites

75 g | 2½ oz raisins

30 g | 1 oz each candied fruit and blanched almonds, chopped

To decorate (optional):

blanched almonds, chopped, candied fruit and peel or white glacé icing

1 Mix 225 g | 8 oz of the flour with the yeast in a mixing bowl, then stir in the milk. Put the mixture into a polythene bag and leave in a warm place until spongy and doubled in size (about 1 hour).

2 Mix in the salt, 2½ egg yolks (reserve about half a yolk for glazing the kulich later), sugar, cardamom and butter. Whisk the egg whites until stiff and fold in with 225 g | 8 oz more flour. The dough will be on the wet and sticky side. Add the remaining flour gradually until the dough leaves the sides of the bowl. If it is a little sticky, do not worry too much. Put in a warm place and leave to rise again (about 2–3 hours).

3 Knock down the dough and add the fruits and almonds. Divide between 2 buttered and floured tall round moulds, such as large brioche tins. If you have no suitable moulds, use coffee tins. The dough should come half or two-thirds of the way up the tins. Leave in a warm place to prove for about 1 hour.

4 Preheat the oven to 180°C | 350°F | gas mark 4. Bake the kulichs for about 45 minutes. Check after 35 minutes by inserting a cocktail stick or thin skewer, which should come out clean. When the dough is cooked, the cake should have the appearance of a chef's hat.

5 When ready, turn out and brush with the remaining egg yolk and decorate, if you like, with chopped fruit and nuts, or icing, pouring it on so that it dribbles down the sides. At Easter time, stick a candle in the top of each cake.

Eccles Cakes

MAKES 6

225 g | 8 oz flour quantity rough puff pastry (see page 565)

For the filling

15 g | ½ oz butter

55 g | 2 oz soft light brown sugar

110 g | 4 oz currants

30 g | 1 oz chopped mixed peel

½ teaspoon ground cinnamon

¼ teaspoon freshly grated nutmeg

¼ teaspoon ground ginger

grated zest of ½ lemon

1 teaspoon lemon juice

For the glaze

1 egg white

caster sugar

1 Preheat the oven to 220°C|425°F|gas mark 7.

2 Roll out the pastry to the thickness of a £1 coin. Cut out 12.5 cm|5 in rounds. Refrigerate.

3 Melt the butter in a saucepan and stir in all the other filling ingredients. Cool.

4 Place a good teaspoon of filling in the centre of each pastry round.

5 Dampen the edges of the pastry and press together in the centre, forming a small ball. Trim away any excess pastry with a small sharp knife. Place on a baking sheet. Turn the balls over and flatten them lightly with a rolling pin until the fruit begins to show through the pastry.

6 Beat the egg white lightly with a fork, until frothy. Brush the top of the Eccles cakes with this and sprinkle with caster sugar.

7 With a sharp knife, make 3 small parallel cuts on the top.

8 Bake for 20 minutes, or until lightly browned.

Reasons for Failure in Bread-Making

Close texture

- Stale yeast
- Insufficient yeast
- Too much salt or sugar
- Insufficient kneading
- Too much/too little liquid
- Second rising too short
- Overproved dough collapsed

Poor rising of dough

- Stale yeast
- Too much salt or sugar
- Mixture too dry
- Rising time too short
- Too little yeast

Uneven texture and holes

- Too much liquid
- Too much salt
- Too long rising
- Not knocked back enough

Coarse texture

- Too much|too little salt
- Too much liquid
- Overproved

Wrinkled top crust
- Bread cooked too quickly
- Poor shaping.
- Overproved.

Sour or yeasty flavour
- Stale yeast
- Too much yeast
- Risen at too high a temperature
- Overproved

Cracked crust (oven spring)
- Underproved
- Tin too small for mixture
- Oven too cool
- Dough not covered during proving

If the oven is too cool the bread will be pale, dry and hard, with an uneven texture. If the oven is too hot the crust will be too dark or burnt.

Scones and Biscuits

Scones

MAKES 6

225 g | 8 oz self-raising flour

½ teaspoon salt

55 g | 2 oz butter

30 g | 1 oz caster sugar (optional)

150 ml | ¼ pint milk

1 egg, beaten, to glaze

1 Preheat the oven to 220°C | 425°F | gas mark 7. Flour a baking sheet.
2 Sift the flour with the salt into a large bowl.
3 Rub in the butter until the mixture resembles breadcrumbs. Stir in the sugar, if using.
4 Make a deep well in the flour, pour in the milk and mix to a soft, spongy dough with a knife.
5 On a floured surface, knead the dough very lightly until it is just smooth. Roll or press out about 2.5 cm | 1 in thick and stamp into rounds with a small pastry cutter.
6 Brush the scones with beaten egg for a glossy crust, sprinkle with flour for a soft one or brush with milk for a light gloss and soft crust.
7 Bake the scones at the top of the oven for 20–25 minutes, or until well risen and brown. Leave to cool on a wire rack, or serve hot from the oven.

NOTE: 30 g | 1 oz sultanas or other dried fruit may be added to the flour. For cheese scones, substitute 30 g | 1 oz grated strong cheese for half the butter, and omit the sugar.

Shortbread

MAKES 6–8

110 g | 4 oz unsalted butter, softened

55 g | 2 oz caster sugar

110 g | 4 oz plain flour

55 g | 2 oz ground rice

1 Preheat the oven to 170°C | 325°F | gas mark 3.
2 Stir together the butter and sugar.
3 Sift in the flours and work to a smooth paste.
4 Place a 15 cm | 6 in flan ring on a baking sheet and press half the shortbread paste into a neat circle. Repeat with the other half. Remove the flan ring and flatten the paste slightly with a rolling pin. Crimp the edges. Mark the shortbread into 6–8 wedges. Prick with a fork through to the baking sheet. Chill until firm.

5 Sprinkle the shortbread lightly with a little extra caster sugar and bake for 40 minutes, until a pale biscuit colour.

6 Run a palette knife underneath the shortbread to release it from the baking sheet. Leave to cool for 5 minutes, then transfer to a wire rack to cool completely.

Flavoured shortbreads

Shortbread can be stamped into biscuits or made into petticoat tails and put into attractive tins. Many variations can be created by adding different ingredients to the basic recipe (see above).

Almond shortbread

Replace half of the flour with the equivalent weight of ground almonds.

Hazelnut shortbread

Add 30 g | 1 oz roughly chopped, browned and skinned hazelnuts with the flour to the creamed butter and sugar.

Ginger shortbread

Add 1 teaspoon ground ginger and 55 g | 2 oz chopped crystallized stem ginger with the flour.

Orange shortbread

Add the finely grated zest of 2 oranges to the creamed butter and sugar before adding the flour.

Chocolate Fork Biscuits

MAKES ABOUT 20

225 g | 8 oz butter
110 g | 4 oz caster sugar
1 teaspoon vanilla essence
225 g | 8 oz self-raising flour
55 g | 2 oz cocoa powder
extra butter for greasing

For the filling

7 tablespoons strong coffee
55 g | 2 oz cocoa powder
55 g | 2 oz butter, softened
icing sugar, sifted, to taste
vanilla extract or rum to taste

1 Preheat the oven to 180°C | 350°F | gas mark 4.
2 Cream the butter until soft, add the sugar and vanilla, and beat until light and fluffy.
3 Sift the flour and cocoa powder together and work into the butter mixture.
4 Roll teaspoons of the mixture into walnut-sized pieces and arrange well spaced on a greased baking sheet. Flatten each piece with a fork dipped in water.
5 Bake for about 12 minutes.
6 Transfer the biscuits to a wire rack and leave to cool completely.

7 Meanwhile, make the filling: heat the coffee in a small saucepan and stir in the cocoa powder. Cook for 1 minute, then remove from the heat, when it should be the consistency of a paste. If too thick, add a little water and leave to cool.

8 Gradually beat in the butter and add icing sugar and vanilla or rum to taste.

9 Sandwich the biscuits together with the filling.

NOTE: If preferred, the biscuits may be served without the filling, simply dusted with sifted icing sugar.

Iced Biscuits

MAKES 20

110 g│4 oz unsalted butter	**For the glacé icing**
110 g│4 oz caster sugar	225 g│8 oz icing sugar
1 egg, beaten	boiling water
a few drops of vanilla essence	food colouring
285 g│10 oz plain flour	
a pinch of salt	

1 Preheat the oven to 190°C│375°F│gas mark 5.

2 Beat the butter until soft, add the sugar and beat until light and fluffy. Gradually beat in the egg. Add the vanilla essence.

3 Sift the flour with the salt and mix it into the butter, sugar and egg mixture.

4 Roll the paste out to the thickness of a £1 coin and stamp into rounds with a small pastry cutter. Place on an ungreased baking sheet.

5 Bake for 8–10 minutes until just beginning to brown at the edges. Leave to cool on a wire rack.

6 Make the glacé icing: sift the icing sugar into a bowl. Add enough boiling water to mix to a fairly stiff consistency.

7 Colour the icing as required.

8 Spoon the icing smoothly and evenly over the top of the biscuits. Leave to dry and harden.

Peanut Butter Cookies

MAKES ABOUT 40

140 g | 5 oz butter

110 g | 4 oz caster sugar

110 g | 4 oz soft light brown sugar

1 large egg, beaten

110 g | 4 oz crunchy peanut butter

½ teaspoon vanilla essence

200 g | 7 oz plain flour

½ teaspoon salt

1 teaspoon baking powder

1 Preheat the oven to 180°C | 350°F | gas mark 4.
2 Cream the butter and both sugars together until smooth and soft. Beat in the egg, then the peanut butter, and add the vanilla essence.
3 Sift the flour with the salt and the baking powder into the mixture and stir until smooth. Do not overbeat or the dough will be oily.
4 Roll the mixture into small balls with the fingers and place well apart on 3 ungreased baking sheets. Flatten with the prongs of a fork.
5 Bake for 10–15 minutes to an even, not too dark, brown.
6 While hot, ease off the baking sheets with a palette knife or fish slice and cool on a wire rack. Once completely cold and crisp, store in an airtight container.

Flapjacks

MAKES 16

170 g | 6 oz butter

110 g | 4 oz soft light brown sugar

55 g | 2 oz golden syrup

225 g | 8 oz rolled oats

1 Preheat the oven to 190°C | 375°F | gas mark 5.
2 Melt the butter.
3 Weigh out the sugar, then weigh the syrup by spooning it on top of the sugar (thus preventing it sticking to the scale pan) and add to the warm melted butter to heat through.
4 Remove the pan from the heat and stir in the oats.
5 Spread the mixture into a well-greased shallow tin.
6 Bake for about 30 minutes until golden-brown.
7 Remove from the oven, mark immediately into bars and leave to cool in the tin.

Brownies

The brownies should be fudgy when cooked but not at all runny.

MAKES 16

5 oz | 140 g unsalted butter

7 oz | 200 g dark chocolate, chopped

8 oz | 225 g sugar

2 teaspoons vanilla extract

a pinch of salt

2 large eggs, at room temperature, beaten

1 large egg yolk, at room temperature

3 oz | 85 g plain flour

1 Preheat the oven to 180°C | 350°F | gas mark 4. Line a 20 cm | 8 in square tin with baking parchment.

2 In a bowl set over, not in, a pan of simmering water, melt the butter with the chocolate. Remove the pan from the heat and allow to cool slightly.

3 Stir in the sugar, vanilla and salt. The mixture will be somewhat grainy.

4 Whisk in the beaten eggs and egg yolk until well mixed. Sift in the flour, beating for about 1 minute until thick and smooth.

5 Pour the mixture into the prepared tin and bake for 35–45 minutes or until a knife inserted into the middle comes out with moist crumbs (not wet batter) clinging to it.

6 Allow to cool in the tin, then cut into squares with a sharp knife.

Easter Biscuits

MAKES 8

55 g | 2 oz butter

55 g | 2 oz caster sugar

grated zest of ½ lemon

½ egg or 1 egg yolk

110 g | 4 oz plain flour

½ teaspoon caraway seeds

55 g | 2 oz currants

30 g | 1 oz granulated sugar

1 Preheat the oven to 180°C | 350°F | gas mark 4. Line a baking sheet with greaseproof paper.

2 Cream together the butter, caster sugar and lemon zest. Beat in the egg.

3 Stir in the flour, caraway seeds and currants.

4 Roll out the dough 5 mm | ¼ in thick on a floured board. Cut into large rounds and carefully lift them on to the baking sheet. Prick with a fork and sprinkle with granulated sugar.

5 Bake for 10–15 minutes until set and pale golden.

6 Leave on a wire rack to crisp and cool.

NOTE: If the dough becomes soft and difficult to handle, wrap it up and chill for 15 minutes before proceeding.

Old-fashioned Gingerbread Biscuits

These can be cut into different shaped biscuits and used as Christmas tree decorations. To do this, cut a hole in the baked biscuits while they are still hot. Leave to cool on a wire rack. When cool, thread through green and red ribbons and tie on to the Christmas tree.

MAKES ABOUT 120 SMALL BISCUITS

340 g | 12 oz plain flour

1 teaspoon baking powder

½ teaspoon salt

1 teaspoon freshly grated nutmeg

1 teaspoon ground cloves

2 teaspoons ground cinnamon

2 teaspoons ground ginger

225 g | 8 oz butter, softened

170 g | 6 oz caster sugar

170 g | 6 oz soft dark brown sugar

1 egg, beaten

1 Sift the flour, baking powder, salt and spices into a large bowl.

2 Beat the butter with the sugars. Gradually beat in the egg.

3 Stir in the dry ingredients. Roll to the thickness of a £1 coin between 2 sheets of greaseproof paper. Place in the refrigerator until completely cold.

4 Preheat the oven to 180°C|350°F|gas mark 4.

5 Stamp into different shapes, such as stars, balls, angels, Christmas trees. Place on a greased baking sheet and bake in batches for about 10 minutes.

Almond and Apricot Cookies

MAKES 18

85 g | 3 oz butter

85 g | 3 oz granulated sugar

110 g | 4 oz ground almonds

To decorate

apricot jam

toasted flaked almonds

1 Preheat the oven to 180°C|350°F|gas mark 4.

2 Beat the butter and when soft, add the sugar and beat until light and fluffy. Stir in the ground almonds and roll the paste into balls the size of a marble. Refrigerate for 10 minutes.

3 Place each ball in a paper case and put the cases into tartlet tins. Bake for 15–20 minutes. Remove from the oven and allow to cool in the cases.

4 Remove from the cases, spread with a little apricot jam and decorate each cookie with a toasted flaked almond.

Hazelnut Sablés

MAKES ABOUT 24

225 g | 8 oz butter

110 g | 4 oz icing sugar, sifted

2 egg yolks

340 g | 12 oz plain flour

55 g | 2 oz ground hazelnuts

1 Preheat the oven to 180°C | 350°F | gas mark 4.
2 Cream the butter and icing sugar together until light and fluffy. Beat in the egg yolks.
3 Sift the flour and mix with the ground hazelnuts. Stir into the butter mixture and bring together to form a dough.
4 Roll out the dough to the thickness of a 50 p coin and stamp out biscuits with a small round pastry cutter. Place on a baking sheet and refrigerate for 10 minutes.
5 Bake the biscuits for 20 minutes, or until golden-brown.

Pine Nut Sablés

Literally meaning 'covered in sand', these dry, crumbly biscuits make a delicious accompaniment to sorbets and ice creams.

MAKES ABOUT 30

oil for greasing

85 g | 3 oz pine nuts

55 g | 2 oz unsalted butter

30 g | 1 oz vegetable shortening

30 g | 1 oz icing sugar, sifted

30 g | 1 oz caster sugar, plus a little extra for sprinkling

125 g | 4½ oz plain flour

½ teaspoon baking powder

a pinch of salt

1 Preheat the oven to 170°C | 325°F | gas mark 3.
2 Spread the pine nuts on an ungreased baking sheet and place in the preheated oven for about 8 minutes or until lightly browned (pine nuts burn very easily, so check after 5 minutes). Remove from the oven and transfer the nuts to a plate to cool.
3 Reserve a few nuts for decorating the sablés, then chop the remainder finely.
4 Cream the butter and shortening in a bowl until soft. Add the sugars and beat until well combined.
5 Sift the flour, baking powder and salt together with the chopped nuts and mix thoroughly to form a soft dough.
6 Roll teaspoonfuls of the mixture into balls and place on a lightly oiled baking sheet. Press them lightly with the palm of the hand to form rounds about 1 cm | ½ in thick.
7 Press a few whole pine nuts on top of each sablé and sprinkle lightly with caster sugar.
8 Bake the sablés in the centre of the oven for about 30 minutes or until they are light golden. Transfer to a wire rack and leave to cool. Store in an airtight container.

Gingernuts

MAKES 20–25

30 g | 1 oz demerara sugar
55 g | 2 oz butter
85 g | 3 oz golden syrup

110 g | 4 oz plain flour
½ teaspoon bicarbonate of soda
1 heaped teaspoon ground ginger

1 Preheat the oven to 180°C | 350°F | gas mark 4. Grease a baking sheet.

2 Melt the sugar, butter and syrup together slowly, without boiling. Make sure the sugar has dissolved, then remove from the heat and allow to cool.

3 Sift the flour with the soda and ginger into a bowl. Make a well in the centre.

4 Pour the melted mixture into the well and knead until smooth. Roll into balls and flatten, on the prepared baking sheet, into biscuits about 3.5 cm | 1½ in in diameter.

5 Bake for 20–25 minutes, or until golden-brown. Leave on a wire rack to crisp and cool.

Brandy Snap Cups

MAKES 8

110 g | 4 oz caster sugar
110 g | 4 oz butter
4 tablespoons golden syrup
110 g | 4 oz plain flour

juice of ½ lemon
a large pinch of ground ginger

To serve
whipped cream or ice cream

1 Preheat the oven to 190°C | 375°F | gas mark 5. Grease a baking sheet, a palette knife and one end of a wide rolling pin or a narrow jam jar or bottle.

2 Melt the sugar, butter and syrup together in a saucepan. Remove from the heat and allow to cool to room temperature.

3 Sift in the flour, stirring well. Add the lemon juice and ginger.

4 Place teaspoonfuls of the mixture on the prepared baking sheet about 15 cm | 6 in apart. Bake for 5–7 minutes until golden-brown and still soft. Watch carefully as they burn easily. Remove from the oven.

5 When cool enough to handle, lever each biscuit off the baking sheet with a greased palette knife.

6 Working quickly, shape around the end of the rolling pin or greased jam jar to form a cup-shaped mould.

7 When the biscuits have been shaped, remove them and leave to cool on a wire rack.

8 Serve filled with whipped cream or ice cream.

NOTES: If the brandy snaps are not to be served immediately, once cool they must be put into an airtight container for storage, or they will become soggy. Similarly, brandy snaps should not be filled with moist mixtures like whipped cream or ice cream until shortly before serving, or they will quickly lose their crispness. Do not bake too many snaps at one time as once they become cold, they are too brittle to shape. They can be made pliable again if returned to the oven.

Brandy Snaps

The mixture for these is exactly the same as for brandy snap cups (above) but the biscuits are shaped round a thick wooden spoon handle and not over the end of a rolling pin or jam jar. They are filled with whipped cream from a piping bag fitted with a medium nozzle.

Miniature brandy snaps (served as petits fours after dinner) are shaped over a skewer. They are not filled.

Filigree Baskets

These make excellent 'cups' or baskets in which to serve ice cream and sorbets.

MAKES 6

2 egg whites

110 g | 4 oz caster sugar

125 g | 4½ oz plain flour

½ teaspoon vanilla essence

1 Cut a template out of cardboard. For a basket big enough to hold a ball of sorbet, the stencil should be about 5 cm | 2 in wide and 20 cm | 8 in long.
2 Line a baking sheet with greaseproof paper and grease and flour it. Mark the shape of the template in the flour coating.
3 Preheat the oven to 200°C | 400°F | gas mark 6.
4 Whisk the egg whites and sugar together in a bowl until the whisk will leave a ribbon-like trail when lifted.
5 Sift in the flour, add the vanilla essence and beat until smooth.
6 Put the mixture into a piping bag fitted with a plain 2 mm | ⅛ in nozzle, or into a paper piping bag with the point snipped to provide the small nozzle mouth.
7 Pipe the mixture into the shapes on to the prepared baking sheet.
8 Bake for 4–6 minutes or until just pale brown.
9 Remove from the oven and ease the biscuits off the tray. Have ready 6 timbale moulds.
10 Return the biscuits to the hot oven for 30 seconds or just long enough for them to become very pliable again. While hot, curl them round and drop them into the moulds. Leave on a wire rack to cool completely.
11 Once cold, store in an airtight container.

Langues de Chat

MAKES 30–40

100 g | 3½ oz butter

100 g | 3½ oz caster sugar

3 egg whites

100 g | 3½ oz plain flour

1 Preheat the oven to 200°C | 400°F | gas mark 6. Grease a baking sheet or line it with non-stick baking parchment.

2 Soften the butter with a wooden spoon and add the sugar gradually. Beat until pale and fluffy.

3 Whisk the egg whites slightly and add gradually to the mixture, beating thoroughly after each addition.

4 Sift the flour and fold into the mixture with a metal spoon. Put into a piping bag fitted with a medium plain nozzle. Pipe into fingers the thickness of a pencil and about 5 cm|2 in long on the prepared baking sheet.

5 Tap the baking sheet on the table to release any over-large air bubbles. Bake for 5–7 minutes or until biscuit-coloured in the middle and brown at the edges. Cool slightly, then lift off the baking sheet with a palette knife. Leave on a wire rack to cool completely.

6 Once cold, store in an airtight container.

Macaroons

Macaroons are particularly good made with freshly ground blanched almonds.

MAKES 25

110 g|4 oz ground almonds
170 g|6 oz caster sugar
1 teaspoon plain flour
2 egg whites

2 drops of vanilla essence
rice paper for baking

To decorate
split blanched almonds

1 Preheat the oven to 180°C|350°F|gas mark 4.

2 Mix together the ground almonds, sugar and flour.

3 Add the egg whites and vanilla essence. Beat very well. Leave to stand for 5 minutes. Beat again for 1 minute.

4 Line a baking sheet with rice paper or non-stick baking parchment and with a teaspoon put on small heaps of the mixture, well apart.

5 Place a split almond on each macaroon and bake for 20 minutes. Leave on a wire rack to cool completely.

NOTES: To use this recipe for petits fours the mixture must be put out in very tiny blobs on the rice paper. Two macaroons can then be sandwiched together with a little thick apricot jam and served in petits fours paper cases.

Ratafia biscuits are tiny macaroons with almond essence added.

Sponge Fingers

MAKES 30

6 eggs

140 g | 5 oz caster sugar

110 g | 4 oz self-raising flour

30 g | 1 oz arrowroot

1 Preheat the oven to 200°C | 400°F | gas mark 6. Line 2 large baking sheets with non-stick baking parchment. Draw parallel lines 12.5 cm | 5 in apart on the parchment.

2 Separate 5 of the eggs. Beat the yolks with the whole egg and 110 g | 4 oz of the sugar in a large bowl until nearly white.

3 Whisk the egg whites until stiff and gradually whisk in the remaining sugar. Fold the egg whites into the egg-yolk and sugar mixture. Carefully fold in the flour sifted with the arrowroot.

4 Fill a piping bag fitted with a 5 mm | ¼ in plain nozzle with the mixture. Pipe 12.5 cm | 5 in fingers between the parallel lines on the baking parchment. The fingers should be just touching.

5 Bake in the top of the oven for about 10 minutes, or until the sponge has risen and is biscuit-coloured.

6 Remove from the oven, invert on to a clean tea-towel and immediately and carefully peel off the lining paper. Turn the sponge fingers on to a wire rack to cool.

Tuiles à l'Orange

MAKES 25

2 egg whites

110 g | 4 oz caster sugar

55 g | 2 oz butter, melted and cooled

55 g | 2 oz plain flour, sifted

grated zest of 1 orange

1 Preheat the oven to 190°C | 375°F | gas mark 5 and line a baking sheet with non-stick baking parchment.

2 Whisk the egg whites until just frothy. Stir in the sugar.

3 Fold in the butter and orange zest.

4 Spread out teaspoonfuls of the mixture very thinly on the baking parchment, keeping them well apart to allow for spreading during cooking. Bake for 5–6 minutes until golden-brown.

5 Oil a rolling pin or the handle of a large wooden spoon. Loosen the tuiles from the baking sheet while still hot. While they are still warm and pliable curl them over the rolling pin or round the wooden spoon handle. When they are firm slip them off. Leave to cool completely on a wire rack.

6 When cold, store in an airtight container.

Tuiles Amandines

MAKES 25

2 egg whites

110 g | 4 oz caster sugar

55 g | 2 oz plain flour

½ teaspoon vanilla essence

55 g | 2 oz butter, melted and cooled

30 g | 1 oz flaked almonds

1 Preheat the oven to 190°C | 375°F | gas mark 5. Line a baking sheet with non-stick baking parchment.

2 Place the egg whites in a bowl. Beat in the sugar with a fork. The egg white should be frothy. Sift in the flour and add the vanilla essence. Mix with the fork.

3 Add the melted butter to the mixture. Stir well.

4 Place teaspoonfuls of the mixture at least 13 cm | 5 in apart on the prepared baking sheets and spread thinly into circles. Sprinkle with the flaked almond.

5 Bake in the oven for about 6 minutes until pale biscuit-coloured in the middle and a good brown at the edges. Remove from the oven and cool for a few seconds.

6 Lift the biscuits off carefully with a palette knife. Lay them, while still warm and pliable, over the rolling pin to form them into a slightly curved shape. Leave on a wire rack to cool completely.

7 When cold, store in an airtight tin.

Chocolate Chip Muffins

MAKES 12

oil for greasing

110 g | 4 oz butter

110 g | 4 oz soft light brown sugar

30 g | 1 oz caster sugar

150 ml | ¼ pint milk

2 medium eggs, beaten

½ teaspoon vanilla extract

250 g | 9 oz self-raising flour

½ teaspoon bicarbonate of soda

110 g | 4 oz chocolate drops

1 Preheat the oven to 170°C | 350°F | gas mark 4. Line 12 muffin tins with paper cases or greaseproof paper discs brushed lightly with oil.

2 Melt the butter in a saucepan with the sugars. Allow to cool slightly.

3 Stir the milk into the butter and sugar mixture, then add the eggs and vanilla.

4 Sift the flour with the bicarbonate of soda into a large bowl. Make a well in the centre.

5 Quickly stir the milk, butter and sugar mixture into the flour to combine, using no more than 12 strokes, then fold in the chocolate drops.

6 Using a teacup, quickly ladle the mixture into the muffin cups. They should be nearly full.

7 Bake the muffins for 25–30 minutes in the centre of the oven until a wooden cocktail stick inserted into the centre comes out clean. Transfer to a wire rack and leave to cool. For soft tops, cover the muffins with a tea towel while they cool.

Orange Muffins

MAKES 12

oil for greasing
340 g | 12 oz plain flour
1 teaspoon bicarbonate of soda
finely grated zest of 2 oranges
225 g | 8 oz caster sugar

2 eggs, beaten
110 g | 4 oz butter, melted and cooled
290 ml | 10 fl oz plain yoghurt
110 g | 4 oz raisins

1 Preheat the oven to 200°C | 400°F | gas mark 6. Grease 12 muffin tins or line them with paper cases.
2 Sift the flour with the bicarbonate of soda into a large mixing bowl. Add the orange zest and sugar. Make a well in the centre.
3 Put the eggs, butter and yoghurt into the well and gradually incorporate all the flour, mixing to a smooth batter.
4 Stir in the raisins and spoon the mixture into the muffin tins, filling each two-thirds full.
5 Bake the muffins in the centre of the preheated oven for 20–25 minutes or until they spring back when pressed lightly with a fingertip.
6 Transfer to a wire rack and leave to cool.

Cinnamon Raisin Muffins

MAKES 12

oil for greasing
110 g | 4 oz butter
150 ml | ¼ pint milk
2 medium eggs, beaten
110 g | 4 oz soft light brown sugar
2 tablespoons caster sugar
125 g | 4½ oz self-raising white flour

125 g | 4½ oz wholemeal flour
2 teaspoons baking powder
½ teaspoon bicarbonate of soda
1 teaspoon ground cinnamon
30 g | 1 oz oat flakes
170 g | 6 oz raisins
1 tablespoon oat flakes, to finish

1 Preheat the oven to 190°C | 375°F | gas mark 5. Line 12 muffins tins with paper cases or greaseproof paper discs brushed lightly with oil.
2 Melt the butter in a saucepan, then stir in the milk. Beat in the eggs and sugars.
3 Sift the flours with the baking powder, bicarbonate of soda and the cinnamon into a large bowl. Stir in the oat flakes and make a well in the centre.
4 Tip the milk, egg and sugar mixture into the well and stir to combine, using no more than 12 strokes.
5 Fold in the raisins, then turn the mixture into the muffin tins. Sprinkle over the oat flakes.
6 Bake the muffins in the centre of the oven for 15–20 minutes until well risen and brown and a wooden cocktail stick inserted into the centre comes out clean.

Banana Bread

MAKES 1 LOAF

oil for greasing

85 g | 3 oz butter

225 g | 8 oz plain flour

3 teaspoons baking powder

¼ teaspoon bicarbonate of soda

¼ teaspoon salt

¼ teaspoon grated nutmeg

2 large bananas (225 g | 8 oz peeled weight)

110 g | 4 oz caster sugar

2 eggs, beaten

100 g | 3½ oz walnuts, roughly broken

1 Grease a 20 × 10 cm | 8 × 4 in loaf tin and line the base with baking parchment.

2 Preheat the oven to 190°C | 375°F | gas mark 5.

3 Melt the butter in a small saucepan and allow to cool.

4 Sift together the flour, baking powder, bicarbonate of soda, salt and nutmeg.

5 Mash the bananas with a potato masher or fork in a mixing bowl and stir in the sugar, eggs and melted butter.

6 Sift the flour mixture over the top and fold in. Stir in the walnuts.

7 Turn the mixture into the prepared tin. Smooth the top and bake in the oven for 45–60 minutes or until a skewer inserted into the centre comes out clean.

8 Leave to cool for 10 minutes in the tin, then remove from the tin and transfer to a wire rack. Leave to cool completely. To store, wrap in foil.

Fruit and Nut Biscotti

This recipe is from Peter Gordon.

MAKES ABOUT 48

500 g | 1 lb 2 oz plain flour

500 g | 1 lb 2 oz unrefined caster sugar

1 tablespoon baking powder

5 eggs, lightly beaten

100 g | 3½ oz plump sultanas

100 g | 3½ oz dried apricots

100 g | 3½ oz pitted dates, chopped

100 g | 3½ oz shelled pistachio nuts

100 g | 3½ oz whole blanched almonds

100 g | 3½ oz shelled hazelnuts

grated zest of 2 lemons

1 Preheat the oven to 180°C | 350°F | gas mark 4.

2 Mix the flour, sugar and baking powder in a large bowl. Add three-quarters of the eggs and mix well. Add the remaining egg a little at a time until the dough takes shape but is not too wet (you may not need to use all the eggs).

3 Add the fruit, nuts and lemon zest and mix well.

4 Divide the dough into 6 equal pieces. With wet hands, roll each into a sausage shape with a diameter of 2.5 cm | 1 in. Place the rolls at least 5 cm | 2 in apart on baking trays lined with baking parchment.

5 Lightly flatten the rolls and bake in the oven for about 20–30 minutes until golden-brown. Remove from the oven and leave for 10 minutes to cool and firm up.

6 Turn the oven down to 140°C|275°F|gas mark 1. Using a serrated knife, cut the biscotti on the diagonal into 6 mm|¼ in slices and lay these, cut side up, on the baking trays. Return to the oven and cook for 12 minutes, then turn the biscotti over and bake for a further 10–15 minutes until they are a pale golden colour.

7 Remove from the oven and cool on wire racks. Store in an airtight jar.

Chocolate Chip Biscotti

MAKES ABOUT 48

110 g|4 oz blanched almonds
450 g|1 lb plain flour
a pinch of salt
1 teaspoon baking powder

140 g|5 oz granulated sugar
85 g|3 oz plain chocolate, chopped into small pieces
4 large eggs, lightly beaten
1 egg white to glaze

1 Preheat the oven to 190°C|375°F|gas mark 5. Grease a baking sheet.

2 Place the almonds on the baking sheet and bake in the oven until golden-brown for about 8 minutes. Remove from the oven and cool. Chop two-thirds of the almonds and grind the remainder finely.

3 Sift the flour with the salt and baking powder into a large bowl. Add the sugar, chocolate and chopped and ground almonds. Mix well.

4 Make a well in the centre and add the eggs. Gradually incorporate the dry ingredients with the eggs to make a firm dough.

5 Divide the dough into 4 equal pieces and roll each piece into a long thin sausage shape about 2 cm|¾ in in diameter and 20 cm|8 in long.

6 Place the rolls at least 5 cm|2 in apart on the baking sheet. Lightly whisk the egg white until just frothy and brush over the tops of the rolls.

7 Bake for 20 minutes.

8 Remove the rolls from the oven and turn the temperature down to 80°C|175°F|gas mark ¼. Cut the rolls at a 45-degree angle into 1 cm|½ in slices and place on the baking sheet. Turn the biscuits over after 30 minute. Bake for a further hour. Leave on a wire rack to cool completely.

NOTE: Raisins or glacé fruit can be used in place of the chocolate. The biscuits are meant to be very dry and crisp and to be eaten after being dipped in a liqueur, such as Amaretto or Grappa.

Florentine Biscuits

MAKES 20

55 g | 2 oz butter

55 g | 2 oz caster sugar

2 teaspoons clear honey

55 g | 2 oz plain flour

45 g | 1½ oz chopped mixed peel

45 g | 1½ oz glacé cherries, chopped

45 g | 1½ oz blanched almonds, chopped

85 g | 3 oz plain chocolate, melted

1 Preheat the oven to 180°C | 350°F | gas mark 4. Line 2 baking sheets with non-stick baking parchment.

2 Melt the butter, sugar and honey together in a heavy saucepan. Allow to cool to room temperature. Remove from the heat and stir in the flour, peel, cherries and almonds.

3 Drop teaspoonfuls of the mixture on to baking sheets lined with non-stick baking parchment, leaving plenty of space for them to spread during baking. Spread slightly with the spoon.

4 Bake for 8–10 minutes until golden. Remove from the oven and leave on the sheets for 2 minutes, then transfer to a wire rack to cool completely.

5 When cold spread the flat sides of the biscuits with melted chocolate. Allow to set. Spread a second layer of chocolate on to the biscuits, then mark it with wavy lines with the prongs of a fork. Leave until the chocolate hardens.

Preserving

The term 'preserves' covers all food that has been treated to keep for longer than it would if fresh. Frozen food, dried food, salted food and smoked food are all preserves. But in household language, the word means jams, jellies, marmalades, pickles and sometimes bottled food.

Jellies are clear preserves, made from strained fruit juice. They should be neither runny nor too solid. Jams are made from crushed fruit. They should almost hold their shape, but be more liquid than jelly. Conserves are traditionally made from a mixture of fruit, but the term has come to mean a slightly softer set containing whole or large chunks of fruit. Marmalade is jam made exclusively from citrus fruit. Fruit butters are made from smooth fruit purées, cooked with sugar to the consistency of thick cream. Fruit cheeses, are made in the same way but cooked until very thick. Butters and cheeses, because they are not set solidly and generally contain less sugar than jams, should be potted in sterilized jars. Curds generally contain butter and eggs, are best kept refrigerated, and will not keep for more than a week.

Jams, Jellies and Marmalades

These preserves depend on four main factors to make them long-lasting:

1 **The presence of pectin:** This is a substance, converted from the gum-like pectose found to some degree in all fruit, which reacts with the acids of the fruit and with the sugar to form a jelly-like set. Slightly under-ripe fruit is higher in pectin than over-ripe fruit, and some types of fruit are higher in pectin than others, notably apples, quinces, damsons, sour plums, lemons and redcurrants. Jam made from these will set easily. Jam from low-pectin fruit such as strawberries, rhubarb, mulberries and pears may need added commercial pectin or lemon juice (or a little high-pectin fruit) to obtain a good set.

   To test for pectin: before you add the sugar, take 1 teaspoon of the simmered fruit juice and put it into a glass. When it is cold add 1 tablespoon methylated spirit. After a minute a jelly will have formed. If it is in 1 or 2 firm clots there is adequate pectin in the fruit. If the jelly clots are numerous and soft the jam will not set without the addition of more pectin.

2 **A high concentration of sugar:** Sugar is itself a preservative, and without sufficient sugar the pectin will not act to form the set.

3 **The presence of acid** which, like sugar, acts with the pectin to form a gel or set. Acid also prevents the growth of bacteria, and it helps to prevent the crystallization of the sugar in

the jam during storage. If the fruit is low in acid, then tartaric acid, ascorbic acid or lemon juice may be added.

4 **The elimination and exclusion of micro-organisms:** The jam itself is sterilized by rapid boiling. Jam jars should be sterilized. Harmless moulds sometimes form around the rim and on the surface of jams potted in this way, and sterilizing the jars helps to prevent this. The jam funnel should be sterilized with the jars. It is not necessary to sterilize ladles or spoons except by leaving them in the bubbling jam for a minute or two. Jelly cloths or bags need not be sterilized as the juice is dripped through them before being boiled.

Once put into the clean, dry jars, the jam is sealed to prevent the infiltration of mildew spores etc. Melted paraffin wax (melted white candles will do) poured over the surface of the jam makes a good old-fashioned and most effective seal, but most cooks rely on ordinary paper jam covers.

Ideally, the jam should be sealed while boiling hot, i.e. before any fresh mildew spores can enter. However, if liquid wax is used on hot jam, it may disturb the flat surface, so the slightly cooled but still clear wax is poured on once the jam is set. Two applications of wax are necessary if the first covering shrinks away from the sides of the jar, leaving a gap.

Perhaps the best method of sealing is to use metal screw-tops. They should be sterilized and checked for a tight fit. The jam should be poured up to the shoulder of the jars, leaving a good 1 cm | $\frac{1}{2}$ in space. The caps are screwed on tightly as soon as the jars are filled. The cooling jar will form a partial vacuum in the neck, tightly sealing the jar. Plastic lids do not give a reliable seal.

Jam that has gone mouldy should be discarded. Scraping off visible mould will not prevent the invisible spores from multiplying. Jam that is fizzy or fermented should be thrown away.

Yield

The amount of finished jam obtained from a given quantity of fruit varies according to type, jellies giving comparatively little, marmalades and whole fruit jams much more. As a general rule, the mixture will yield between 1$\frac{1}{2}$ times and double the weight of sugar used. It is wise to over-estimate the amount of jars needed, rather than to have to prepare more at the last minute.

Equipment

Making jam is easy enough, but it requires a little organization. First the equipment should be assembled. You will need:

Accurate scales
Preserving pan or a large, heavy saucepan with a solid base
Sharp knives
Grater
Mincer
Long-handled wooden spoons
Slotted spoon
Metal jug with a large lip or a jam funnel

Jam jars

Jam covers, labels and rubber bands (available from chemists and stationers) or metal screw-top lids

Sugar thermometer (not essential but useful)

Perforated skimmer (not essential but useful)

Points to remember

1 Make sure all equipment is absolutely clean.

2 Use dry, unblemished, just-ripe fruit.

3 Use preserving, lump, caster sugar or granulated. Modern white sugars are highly refined and therefore suitable. They need little skimming and give a clear preserve. Using preserving sugar has a slight advantage because the crystals are larger and the boiling liquid circulates freely round them, dissolving them rapidly. Caster sugar is inclined to set in a solid mass at the bottom of the pan and takes longer to dissolve. Brown sugar gives an unattractive colour to preserves.

4 Covering lukewarm jam could lead to mildew. If the jam is covered immediately, any bacteria or mildew spores present in the atmosphere are trapped between jam and seal and will be killed by the heat. If the atmosphere is lukewarm and steamy, perfect incubating conditions are created.

Basic procedure

1 Wash and dry the jam jars and warm them in the oven.

2 Pick over the fruit, wash or wipe and cut up if necessary.

3 Put the fruit and water into the pan and set to simmer until the fruit has softened sufficiently.

4 Warm the sugar in a cool oven for 20 minutes. When it is added to the fruit it will not lower the temperature too much, necessitating prolonged cooking which could impair the colour of the jam.

5 Bring the fruit to a good boil. Tip in the sugar and stir, without reboiling, until the sugar has dissolved.

6 Once the sugar has dissolved, boil rapidly, stirring gently but frequently.

7 When the mixture begins to look like jam – usually after about 10 minutes – test for setting. It is important not to overboil since this can make the colour too dark and the texture too solid. It will also ruin the flavour. Overboiling can sometimes even prevent a set by destroying the pectin. If you are using a thermometer, you can check the setting point: 105°C│220°F for jam and 106°C│222°F for marmalade. To test for setting, put a teaspoon of the jam on to an ice-cold saucer and return it to the ice compartment or freezer to cool rapidly. When cold, push it gently with a finger. The jam should have a slight skin, which will wrinkle if setting point is reached. If a finger is drawn through the jam, it should remain separated, not run together. Also, clear jam or jelly should fall from a spatula not in a single stream, but forming a wavy curtain and dripping reluctantly from more than one point. Remove the pan from the heat whilst testing or it may over cook.

8 As soon as a setting test proves positive, remove the jam from the heat. Skim carefully and then, if the jam contains whole fruit or large pieces of fruit, allow to cool for 15 minutes. This will prevent the fruit rising to the top of the jam jars.

9 Put the hot jars close together on a wooden board or tray. Fill them with hot jam with the aid of a jug or jam funnel.

10 Seal at once with screw-tops or put waxed paper discs, waxed side down, on the surface of the jam, and cover the tops of the jars with cellophane covers, securing them with a rubber band. Brush the cellophane tops with water to stretch them slightly. Carefully pull them tight. As they dry they will shrink tightly around the jars.

11 Wipe the sides of the jars with a hot, clean, damp cloth to remove any drips of jam.

12 Label each jar with the type of jam and the date.

13 Leave undisturbed overnight.

14 Store in a cool, airy, dark place.

Mildew on the surface of the jam is probably caused by one of the following:
- Using wet jars.
- Covering the jam when lukewarm.
- Imperfect sealing.
- Damp or warm storage place.
- Equipment that is less than spotless.

The jam should be discarded.

Crystallization of the sugar in jam is caused by:
- Insufficient acid in the fruit.
- Boiling the jam before the sugar has dissolved.
- Adding too much sugar.
- Leaving jam uncovered.
- Storing in too cold an atmosphere, such as a refrigerator.

Fermentation of jam is caused by:
- Insufficient boiling leading to non-setting.
- Insufficient acid leading to non-setting.
- Insufficient pectin leading to non-setting.
- Insufficient sugar leading to non-setting.
- A storage place that is too warm.
- Jars that are less than spotless.

Pickles

Pickles are foods, usually vegetables or fruit, preserved in vinegar. Fruit for pickles is generally cooked in sugared vinegar, and stored in this sweetened vinegar syrup. Vegetables are usually, but not always, pickled raw, and are generally salted in dry salt, or steeped in brine, before being immersed in the vinegar. Salting draws moisture out of the food. If salting is omitted, the juices from the vegetables leak into the vinegar during storage, diluting it and impairing its keeping quality. Salt also has preservative powers, and its penetration into the food helps to prevent it going bad, but the main preservative in pickles is vinegar, which prevents the growth of bacteria.

The best salt is pure rock salt or crushed block salt. Pure sea salt is good too, but very expensive. Table salt has additives to make it conveniently free-flowing, but these may cause the pickle to go cloudy.

NOTE: Brass, old-fashioned iron or copper preserving pans or saucepans should not be used in the preparation of foods containing vinegar. The acid reacts with the metal, spoiling both colour and flavour.

Brining

Brine is a solution of salt in water, and is suitable for the steeping of vegetables for pickling. Firm vegetables such as shallots should be pierced with a needle to allow the brine to penetrate.

225 g | 8 oz pure salt (not table salt)   2.8 litres | 4 pints water

1 Heat the salt and water slowly together until the salt has dissolved.
2 Allow to cool.
3 Prepare (peel, cut up, prick, etc.) the vegetables to be picked, put them into a bowl and pour over the cold brine. Put a plate on top to keep the food submerged.
4 After 24 hours (usually, but check individual recipes) drain well, pat dry and pack into clean jars ready for pickling.

Dry-Salting

This is particularly suitable for 'wet' vegetables such as marrow and cucumber.

110 g | 4 oz dry pure salt (not table salt) per 1 kg | 2¼ lb prepared vegetables

1 Prepare (peel, cut up, etc.) the vegetables. If they are tough (like onions or shallots) pierce them deeply with a needle.
2 Put them in a bowl, sprinkling each layer liberally with salt. Cover and keep cool for 24 hours.
3 Drain off all the liquid, rinse the vegetables in cold water and pat dry in a clean cloth.
4 Pack into clean jars ready for pickling.

The Vinegar

Pickling vinegar should be strong, containing at least 5 per cent acetic acid. Most brand vinegars contain sufficient acid, but homemade vinegars or draught vinegars are not suitable. Brown malt vinegar is the best for flavour, especially if the pickle is to be highly spiced or is made with strong-tasting foods. White vinegar has less flavour, but obviously gives a clearer pickle. Wine vinegar is suitable for delicate mild-tasting foods. Commercial cider vinegar is good too. The vinegar may be spiced and flavoured according to taste by the addition of cayenne pepper, ginger or chillies, or aromatic spices such as cardamom seeds, cloves or nutmeg. Whole spices are best as they can be removed easily, and will not leave the vinegar murky. Ready-spiced pickling vinegar may also be purchased.

Chutneys

Chutneys are the easiest preserves to make. They are mixtures, always sweet and sour, somewhere between a pickle and a jam. They are generally made of fruit, or sometimes soft vegetables such as tomato or marrow, with vinegar, onion and spices.

Both sugar and salt, themselves preservatives, are present in chutneys, but they are there for flavour more than for their keeping powers. As with jams, boiling the ingredients destroys micro-organisms, but with chutneys obtaining a set is not necessary – like pickles, they depend on vinegar for their keeping qualities.

Fruit and vegetables for chutneys should be sliced or cut small enough to be lifted with a teaspoon, but not so small as to be unidentifiable in the chutney. As the ingredients are seldom used whole, you can use damaged or bruised fruit, with the imperfect bits removed.

Chutneys improve with keeping. They can generally be eaten after 2 months (before this their taste is harsh) but are at their best between 6 months and 2 years. If the chutney is to be kept for more than 6 months a more secure seal than a jam cover is advisable. See the notes for jars and lids on page 788.

Basic procedure for chutney

1 Prepare the ingredients: wash fruit and vegetables, peel where necessary, cut up, etc. Wash dried fruit if bought loose. Chop or mince onions. Use a stainless steel fruit knife for fruit or vegetables liable to discolour.
2 Put all the ingredients, except the sugar and vinegar, into a saucepan (not an unlined copper, brass or old-fashioned iron one: see note on page 791). The spices should be tied in a muslin bag if they are to be removed later.
3 Add enough of the vinegar to easily cover the other ingredients.
4 Cook slowly, covered or not, until the fruit or vegetables are soft, and most of the liquid has evaporated.
5 Add the sugar and the rest of the vinegar and stir until the sugar has dissolved.
6 Boil to the consistency of thick and syrupy jam.
7 Put into clean, hot jars. Cover as for jam if to be eaten within 6 months. Use non-metal lids or stoppers if the chutney is to be kept longer.

NOTE: In recipes for chutneys that do not require prolonged cooking to soften the ingredients (e.g. apricot and orange chutney, page 804) the sugar and vinegar may be added with the other ingredients, the whole being boiled together.

Bottling Fruit

The preservation of food by bottling works on the principle of destruction by heat of all micro-organisms present in the fruit or syrup. Because a partial vacuum is created in the jar, by expelling air during processing, a tight seal is formed between the lid and jar, keeping the sterilized contents uncontaminated.

The procedure described here applies to the bottling of fruit only. Because vegetables and meat contain little or no acid, and are therefore likely to harbour bacteria, they need considerably longer processing at higher temperatures to become safe. This lengthy heating tends to spoil the texture and flavour of the food. In general, bottling meat and vegetables is not worth the effort, time and risks involved. But fruit and tomatoes, because they are fairly acid, do not contain bacteria; and the relatively harmless yeasts and moulds are more easily destroyed.

Jars

Kilner jars come with a glass lid and a rubber ring. The lid is kept in place by a metal screw-band. The rubber ring must not be re-used as it is perishable and will not give a good seal twice. Kilner jars are closed loosely before processing, and only tightened fully when they come out of the sterilizer or saucepan, while still hot. As the hot air inside cools it will contract, pulling the lid on tightly as it does so.

Parfait jars are similar to Kilner jars but the lid is held in place by a metal gimp or clip. It is clipped shut before processing. There is sufficient spring in the gimp to allow the escape of steam during heating. The lid tightens automatically as the jar cools after processing.

Preparing the fruit

Fruit can be bottled raw or cooked. If the fruit is cooked the processing time need only be long enough for sterilization, not for tenderizing the fruit. If raw, the fruit is cooked and sterilized at the same time, and may need longer processing. Fruits that cook to a pulp easily, such as berries and cooking apples, are generally processed from raw as the minimum time at great heat is the objective. Other fruits, such as pears and peaches, which require an uncertain time to soften, are frequently precooked as it is then possible to tell if they are tender. Precooking has a further advantage. Once the fruit is cooked and softened, more of it can be packed into the jars. Also, it will not rise up in the jar when sterilized. Fruit bottled from raw frequently rises.

Points to remember

1 Make sure the bottling jars are not cracked and that the tops are in good condition. Jars must have new rubber rings fitted each year. Screw bands or metal clips should work properly and jars should be clean.
2 Make the sugar syrup before peeling the fruit.
3 Choose perfect, not over-ripe fruit.
4 If fruit needs cutting or peeling, use a stainless steel knife.
5 If it is likely to discolour (apples or pears), toss with lemon juice or drop the pieces into cold water containing a teaspoonful of ascorbic acid (vitamin C powder or a fizzy Redoxon tablet will do) until you are ready to process them.
6 Pack the fruit (cooked or raw) up to the necks of the jars.

Processing the fruit

The fruit can be processed (or sterilized) in the following ways:

1 In a sterilizer (sometimes called a pressure canner). This is a purpose-made machine like a large pressure cooker. It is reliable and easy to use, but by no means essential. Follow the manufacturer's instructions.

2 In a pressure cooker, which works like a sterilizer but holds fewer jars and will not hold tall ones. About 2.5 cm | 1 in of water in the bottom is sufficient, as no evaporation will take place. The process is very quick, and the jars and fruit sterilize in the steam. Wedge the jars with cloths to stop them rattling. Allow the pressure to fall before opening the cooker. Consult the manufacturer's manual.

3 In a deep saucepan or bath of boiling water. Stand the jars in the container and wedge them with cloths to stop them rattling or cracking. Fill with hot water right over the tops of the jars, or at least up to their necks. Cover as best you can with a lid or foil.

NOTES: Processing in the oven is not recommended. The temperatures cannot be reliably checked and the jars sometimes crack or explode, or boil over.

If the fruit has been cooked in an open pan with its syrup, it is possible to get a good seal by closing the jar as soon as the hot fruit and boiling syrup are in it, without further sterilization, but the method is not reliable and processing according to the instructions on page 793 is recommended.

Testing for sealing

After processing, the jars should be lifted on to a board. Kilner jars should be screwed up tight. Jars should be left undisturbed for 24 hours. They must then be tested for sealing. Remove the bands on the Kilner jars, or loosen the clips on the Parfait jars. It should be possible to lift the jars by the lids, without breaking the seal. If the lid of a jar comes off, the jar must be reprocessed with a new rubber ring or the contents must be eaten within a day or two.

Storing

Wipe the jars with a damp clean cloth, label them with the date of bottling, and store in a dark place. They will keep for at least 18 months, probably for many years.

Gooseberry and Orange Jam

MAKES 675 G | 1½ LB

450 g | 1 lb gooseberries
grated zest and juice of 2 oranges

150 ml | ¼ pint water
450 g | 1 lb warmed preserving sugar

1 Top and tail the gooseberries.
2 Put them into a preserving pan or large saucepan with the orange zest and juice and the water. Simmer until soft and yellowish.
3 Add the sugar, allow it to dissolve, then boil rapidly until setting point is reached. Allow to stand for 10 minutes
4 Pour into warmed dry jars.
5 Cover and label the jars.
6 Leave undisturbed overnight. Store in a cool, dark, airy place.

Blackcurrant Jam

MAKES 1.3 KG|3 LB

900 g|2 lb blackcurrants

150 ml|¼ pint water

900 g|2 lb warmed preserving sugar

1 Wash the blackcurrants and, using the prongs of a fork, remove the stalks.
2 Put the blackcurrants and water into a preserving pan or large saucepan and boil for 30 minutes.
3 Add the sugar to the pan and heat slowly until the sugar has dissolved. Then boil rapidly until the jam reaches setting point (about 10–15 minutes). Allow to stand for 10 minutes.
4 Pour into warmed, dry and sterilized jars.
5 Cover and label the jars.
6 Leave undisturbed overnight. Store in a cool, dark, airy place.

Plum or Damson Jam

MAKES 675 G|1½ LB

900 g|2 lb barely ripe plums or damsons

900 g|2 lb preserving sugar

1 Halve and stone the plums. Crack half the stones and remove the kernels.
2 Put the fruit and sugar together in a bowl and leave to stand overnight. (Do not use a metal container.)
3 Next day, transfer to a preserving pan or a large saucepan and heat slowly until the sugar has dissolved. Then boil rapidly until the jam reaches setting point (about 7–10 minutes). Add the kernels while the jam is still bubbling. Allow to stand for 10 minutes.
4 Pour into warmed, dry and sterilized jars.
5 Cover and label the jars.
6 Leave undisturbed overnight. Store in a cool, dark, airy place.

NOTES: If the plums are difficult to stone, or damsons or greengages are used, simply slit the flesh of each fruit before mixing with the sugar. During boiling, the stones will float to the top and can be removed with a slotted spoon.

Macerating the fruit with the sugar helps to soften the fruit before cooking and allows the cook to dispense with added water. Cooking is quicker as less liquid must be driven off.

Strawberry and Redcurrant Jam

MAKES 1.5 KG|3½ LB

900 g|2 lb strawberries

450 g|1 lb redcurrants

900 g|2 lb warmed preserving sugar

1 Hull the strawberries and, using the prongs of a fork, remove the stalks of the redcurrants.
2 Put the redcurrants into a preserving pan or large saucepan with 1 tablespoon water. Cook to a pulp (about 5 minutes).

3 Add the whole strawberries and bring to the boil.

4 Add the sugar and, when dissolved, boil rapidly for 10–12 minutes until the jam reaches setting point. Remove from the heat and allow to cool for 15 minutes. This will prevent the berries from rising in the jars. Allow to stand for 10 minutes.

5 Pour into warmed, dry and sterilized jars.

6 Cover and label the jars. Leave undisturbed overnight.

7 Store in a cool, dark, airy place.

Orange Marmalade

MAKES 1.5 KG | 3½ LB

900 g | 2 lb Seville oranges

2 lemons

2.8 litres | 5 pints water

1.5 kg | 3 lb warmed preserving sugar

1 Cut the oranges and lemons in half and roughly squeeze them into a large bowl. (Do not bother to extract all the juice: squeezing is done simply to make removing the pips easier.)

2 Remove the pips and tie them up in a piece of muslin or a clean 'J' cloth.

3 Slice the skins of the oranges and lemons, finely or in chunks as required, and add them to the juice with the bag of pips and the water. Leave to soak for 24 hours if time.

4 Transfer to a preserving pan or large saucepan and simmer gently until the orange rind is soft and transparent-looking (about 2 hours).

5 Tip the sugar into the orange pulp. Stir well while bringing the mixture slowly to the boil.

6 Once the sugar has dissolved, boil rapidly until setting point is reached (106°C | 222°F). This may take as long as 20 minutes, but usually less. Test after 5 minutes and then again at 3-minute intervals.

7 Allow to cool for 10 minutes, then pour into warmed, dry and sterilized jars. Cover with jam covers and leave for 24 hours.

8 Label and store in a cool, dark, airy place.

NOTE: Soaking overnight helps to soften the fruit. It may be dispensed with, but longer simmering will then be necessary.

Clear Grapefruit Marmalade

MAKES 675 G | 1½ LB

2 grapefruit

4 lemons

2.2 litres | 4 pints water

900 g | 2 lb warmed preserving sugar

1 Wash the grapefruit and lemons. Cut in half and squeeze out the juice.

2 Strain the juice into a bowl with the water.

3 Shred or chop the skins of the lemons and grapefruit. Put them into a loose muslin bag with the pips of the lemons only.

4 Put the bag into the pan of juice and water. Allow to soak overnight.

5 Transfer the juice and muslin bag to a preserving pan or large saucepan and simmer until the skins in the bag are tender (1–2 hours) and the liquid in the pan has reduced by half.

6 Remove the muslin bag, squeezing it to extract all the juice before discarding.

7 Add the warmed sugar, stir and bring to the boil.

8 Boil rapidly for 8–10 minutes and test for setting.

9 Pour the marmalade into warmed, dry and sterilized jars and cover. Leave undisturbed for 24 hours. Store in a cool, dark place.

NOTE: If shreds of rind are wanted in the jelly, pare the zest from the pith and shred it separately. Add to the boiling liquid.

Three-fruit Marmalade

MAKES 2.7 KG | 6 LB

900 g | 2 lb oranges

3 lemons

1 grapefruit

2.7 kg | 6 lb warmed preserving sugar

1 Scrub the fruit well and put into a preserving pan or large saucepan with 3.3 litres | 6 pints of water. Bring to the boil, then simmer until the fruit is tender. Test by piercing the skin with the handle of a wooden spoon. This will take about 1½ hours and the water will have reduced in quantity.

2 Leave the water in the pan and remove the fruit, allow to cool and cut in half. Scoop out the pips and tie them in a piece of muslin, leaving a long piece of string that can be tied to the pan handle.

3 Cut the fruit halves into strips or alternatively chop them, in batches, in a blender. Put back into the pan of water and add the sugar. Warm gently and stir until the sugar dissolves.

4 Bring to the boil and boil rapidly until setting point is reached.

5 Leave for 15 minutes until the peel has settled. Stir the marmalade and discard the pips.

6 Fill the warmed sterilized jars and seal. Leave for 24 hours. Label and store in a cool, dark, dry place.

Redcurrant Jelly

redcurrants

450 g | 1 lb warmed preserving sugar to each
570 ml | 1 pint of juice extracted

1 Place the washed redcurrants in a stone or earthenware pot, cover and place in the oven preheated to 180°C | 350°F | gas mark 4. If the jar or pot used is glass rather than pottery, stand it in a bain-marie (a roasting pan half-filled with hot water) before placing in the oven. Cook until the redcurrants are tender and the juice has run from them (about 1 hour). Mash the redcurrants with a fork 3 or 4 times during cooking.

2 Alternatively, cook the redcurrants until soft in a microwave oven, or in a saucepan with a little water, stirring frequently.

3 Turn into a scalded muslin or jelly bag and allow to drain overnight.

4 Measure the juice and pour into a preserving pan or large saucepan and add 450 g|1 lb sugar to each 570 ml|1 pint of juice.

5 Dissolve over a low heat, then boil rapidly until setting point is reached (about 5 minutes).

6 Pour into warmed, dry and sterilized jars.

7 Cover with jam covers and leave for 24 hours.

8 Label and store in a cool, dark, dry place.

Hedgerow Jelly

Pick rosehips, haws (hawthorn berries), blackberries, crab apples, sloes, wild bullaces or plums, rowanberries and elderberries in any proportions you like, making sure, however, that there is a good proportion of high-pectin fruit among them.

If the rosehips are very hard, simmer them in water until soft, then add everything else, roughly cut up if large (e.g. crab apples) but not peeled or pitted. Add enough water to cover three-quarters of the fruit. Simmer slowly, stirring occasionally, until mushy.

Drip overnight through a jelly bag or several layers of cloth, without stirring. Measure the juice and return to a clean pan, with 450 g|1 lb warmed preserving or granulated sugar for every 570 ml|1 pint of juice. Boil to 105°C|220°F for a set. Cover while hot if using screw-top jars; while cold if using paper or wax covers.

Apple and Sage Jelly

MAKES 1.8 KG|4 LB

2 kg|4½ lb cooking apples	450 g|1 lb warmed preserving sugar to each
1.1 litre|2 pints water	570 ml|1 pint juice
150 ml|¼ pint cider vinegar	55 g|2 oz fresh sage leaves, finely chopped

1 Wash the apples and cut them into thick pieces without peeling or coring.

2 Put the apples and water into a saucepan, bring to the boil, cover and simmer for about 1 hour. Add the vinegar and boil for a further 5 minutes.

3 Meanwhile, scald a jelly bag twice with boiling water.

4 Hang the jelly bag from the legs of an upturned stool and place a bowl underneath it.

5 Pour the apple pulp and juice into the jelly bag and allow to drip steadily for about 1 hour or until the bag has stopped dripping. Do not squeeze the bag.

6 Measure the juice and pour into the preserving pan. Add 450 g|1 lb sugar to every 570 ml|1 pint of juice.

7 Bring to the boil slowly, ensuring that the sugar has dissolved before the juice has boiled, and stirring constantly.

8 Boil briskly, uncovered, for about 10 minutes, skimming frequently. Test for setting point. When this has been reached, allow the jelly to cool slightly and stir in the sage.

9 Pour into the warmed, dry and sterilized jam jars and cover.

Lemon Curd

MAKES 450 G | 1 LB

2 large lemons
85 g | 3 oz butter

225 g | 8 oz granulated sugar
3 eggs, lightly beaten

1 Grate the zest of the lemons on the finest gauge on the grater, taking care to grate the zest only, not the pith.

2 Squeeze the juice from the lemons.

3 Put the lemon juice, butter, sugar and eggs into a heavy saucepan or double boiler and heat gently, stirring all the time until the mixture is thick.

4 Pass through a sieve then stir in the lemon zest.

5 Spoon into warmed jam jars and cover.

NOTES: This curd will keep in the refrigerator for about 3 weeks.

If the curd is boiled, no great harm is done, as the acid and sugar will help prevent the eggs from scrambling.

Orange Curd

MAKES 450 G | 1 LB

juice of 1 lemon
grated zest of 2 oranges
juice of 1 orange

85 g | 3 oz butter
225 g | 8 oz granulated sugar
3 eggs, lightly beaten

1 Put all the ingredients except the zest into a heavy saucepan or double boiler and heat gently, stirring all the time until the mixture is thick.

2 Sieve into a bowl, stir in the zest and allow to cool. Spoon into warmed jam jars and cover.

Damson Cheese

MAKES ABOUT 900 G | 2 LB

1 kg | 2¼ lb damsons
150 ml | ¼ pint water

450 g | 1 lb granulated sugar to each 570 ml | 1 pint purée

1 Wash the damsons and remove the stalks. Put them into a saucepan with the water. Cook slowly until the fruit is very soft.

2 Sieve the fruit and discard the stones.

3 Measure the pulp and use 450 g | 1 lb granulated sugar for every 570 ml | 1 pint of purée.

4 Put the pulp and sugar together in a large, heavy saucepan. Heat gently until the sugar has completely dissolved, then bring to the boil.

5 Boil steadily until you can make a clear track through the purée with a wooden spoon, showing the base of the pan. Keep stirring, otherwise the cheese will burn on the bottom of the pan.

6 Pour into warmed jars and cover with waxed discs and cellophane circles.

NOTE: Traditionally, this cheese is served as an accompaniment to lamb or game. It therefore needs to be put into a straight-sided jar or bowl so that it can be turned out and sliced. It is also delicious spread on bread.

Spiced Pears

560 g | 1¼ lb preserving sugar

425 ml | ¾ pint white malt vinegar or white wine vinegar

6 small whole pears, peeled

15 g | ½ oz cinnamon stick

5 cloves

2 dried chillies (optional)

2 pieces of preserved stem ginger, diced

1 Dissolve the sugar with the vinegar over a low heat. When completely dissolved, bring to the boil.

2 Add the prepared pears, the spices and the ginger.

3 Simmer gently until the pears are tender but not broken (about 35 minutes).

4 Remove the pears with a slotted spoon and pack into a preserving jar.

5 If the syrup is rather thin, boil it rapidly until fairly thick and tacky.

6 Pour over the pears, and add the spices and ginger.

7 Put on the lid (if using a Kilner jar do not tighten). Place in a deep saucepan and cover with boiling water.

8 Boil steadily for 10 minutes.

9 Remove the jars and (if Kilner jars) seal firmly.

10 Leave for 24 hours, then test for sealing.

Bottled Raspberries

900 g | 2 lb raspberries

340 g | 12 oz granulated sugar

1 Pick over the fruit but do not wash it.

2 Pack into 1 kg | 2¼ lb jars, sprinkling with sugar between the layers. Shake the jars to settle the fruit. Leave overnight.

3 Top up with more fruit and sugar so that the jars are absolutely full.

4 Cover with the lids (not screwed too tightly if Kilner jars). Place in a deep saucepan and cover with boiling water.

5 Boil steadily for 10 minutes.

6 Remove the jars and (if Kilner jars) seal firmly.

7 Leave for 24 hours, then test for sealing.

Bottled Plums

450 g|1 lb preserving sugar

570 ml|1 pint water

thinly pared zest of 1 orange

1 cinnamon stick

1 kg|2¼ lb barely ripe plums

1 Make a sugar syrup by dissolving the sugar in half the water over a low heat. When the sugar has dissolved completely, add the orange zest and cinnamon stick and boil rapidly for 2–3 minutes. Add the remaining water and allow to cool.

2 Halve the plums and remove the stones. Pack the fruit tightly into 1 kg|2¼ lb jars, using the handle of a wooden spoon to press it in firmly, but taking care not to bruise it.

3 Strain the sugar syrup and reheat until hot but not boiling. Pour the syrup over the plums. Cover with lids (not screwed tight if using Kilner jars with screw-top lids) and place in a deep saucepan. Pour in boiling water to cover the jars completely if possible, but to come at least up to their necks.

4 Slowly bring the water to simmering point (ideally this should take 20–25 minutes), then continue to simmer for 15 minutes.

5 Remove the jars from the pan, and if using screw-top Kilner jars, seal firmly.

6 Leave to cool, then test for sealing.

Pickling Vinegar

1.1 litres|2 pints malt vinegar

7 g|¼ oz blades of mace

7 g|¼ oz cinnamon stick

7 g|¼ oz allspice berries

7 g|¼ oz black peppercorns

7 g|¼ oz mustard seeds

4 cloves

1 chilli

15 g|½ oz fresh root ginger, sliced

1 Put everything into a large saucepan (not an unlined copper or brass or iron one), cover tightly and heat gently, until on the point of simmering. Remove from the heat.

2 Leave for 3 hours, then strain through muslin or a jelly bag. The vinegar is now ready for use.

Pickled Shallots or Small Onions

An example of a raw pickle, salted in brine.

small, even-sized pickling onions or shallots

brine (see page 791)

pickling vinegar (see above)

1 Scald the onions or shallots to make peeling them easier. Peel them. Prick deeply all over with a needle or skewer.

2 Put the onions or shallots into a bowl and cover with brine. Leave for 48 hours.

3 Drain thoroughly and pat dry with a clean cloth.

4 Pack tightly, but without bruising, into clean jars.

5 Cover well with the cold pickling vinegar.

6 Seal and store for 6 months before eating.

Pickled Beetroot

An example of a cooked pickle not given preliminary salting.

small, even-sized beetroots, unpeeled
pure salt

pickling vinegar (see page 801)

1 Cook the beetroots in boiling, heavily salted water (1 tablespoon to 1.1 litres|2 pints) until tender (1–2 hours).

2 Drain and allow to cool, then peel.

3 Pack, without bruising, into jars.

4 Cover well with cold pickling vinegar.

5 Add 1 teaspoon pure salt to each 1 kg|2¼ lb jar.

6 Seal and store.

NOTE: If a milder pickle is wanted, the vinegar may be diluted by an equal amount of water. But if this is done the beetroot must be packed in a preserving (Kilner or Parfait) jar, and must be given a sterilization treatment in a boiling water bath for 30 minutes, or in a pressure cooker or canner for 2 minutes.

Dill Cucumber Pickle

An example of a pickle dry-salted and packed in sweet spiced vinegar.

MAKES 900 G|2 LB

900 g|2 lb cucumbers
pure salt
pickling vinegar (see page 801)
1 head of fresh dill, or 1 tablespoon dill seeds

2 teaspoons mustard seeds
2 cloves of garlic, sliced
170 g|6 oz granulated or preserving sugar

1 If the cucumbers are small enough to leave whole, prick them all over with a needle. If large, cut them into chunks, without peeling. Put into a bowl, sprinkling each layer liberally with salt. Leave for 24 hours.

2 Put the spiced vinegar (about 1 litre|1¾ pints) into a saucepan and add the dill, mustard seed, garlic and sugar. Bring slowly to the boil, then cool.

3 Rinse the cucumber well and pat dry with a clean cloth.

4 Pack the cucumber into jars. Leave ½ cm|¼ in space at top. Cover with the cooled vinegar, adding the flavourings.

5 Seal and store.

Angela's Italian Pickles

225 g | 8 oz shallots or pickling onions
1 head of garlic
450 g | 1 lb small pickling cucumbers
6 fresh red chillies
110 g | 4 oz pickling salt

For the pickling vinegar

1.1 litres | 2 pints distilled white vinegar
7 g | ¼ oz blade of mace
7 g | ¼ oz cinnamon stick
7 g | ¼ oz black peppercorns
7 g | ¼ oz mustard seeds
55 g | 2 oz caster sugar

1 Place the shallots or pickling onions in a bowl and cover with boiling water. Let stand for 1 minute, then drain and peel.
2 Break the garlic into cloves and peel.
3 Using a thin skewer, pierce the shallots, garlic, cucumbers and chillies all over.
4 Place in a colander over a bowl. Toss the vegetables with the salt and leave to stand for 24 hours.
5 Place the ingredients for the pickling vinegar in a large saucepan and bring to the boil. Allow to infuse for 3 hours, then strain and cool.
6 The following day, rinse the salt from the vegetables. Bring the spiced vinegar to the boil and add the vegetables. Return to the boil, then pack the hot vegetables into warm preserving jars, leaving ½ cm | ¼ in space from the rim of the jar. Wipe the rims.
7 Seal the jars, then place in a large saucepan. Cover with water and bring to the boil for 10 minutes. Allow to cool, then store in a cool, dark place for up to 6 months.

Green Tomato and Apple Chutney

MAKES 2.25 KG | 5 LB
1.35 kg | 3 lb green tomatoes
900 g | 2 lb apples (any kind)
2 large onions, chopped
110 g | 4 oz sultanas
1 teaspoon salt

1 teaspoon ground ginger
½ teaspoon freshly grated nutmeg
½ teaspoon freshly ground white pepper
a pinch of ground allspice
340 g | 12 oz granulated or preserving sugar
860 ml | 1½ pints vinegar

1 Chop the tomatoes. Peel, core and chop the apples.
2 Put all the ingredients except the sugar and a cupful of vinegar into a saucepan and simmer gently, giving an occasional stir, or 1½ hours, or until the ingredients are soft and the liquid almost evaporated.
3 Add the sugar and the remaining vinegar and stir over a low heat until the sugar has dissolved.
4 Bring to the boil and boil rapidly, stirring, until thick.
5 Pour into warmed dry jars. If the chutney is to be eaten within 6 months, cover as for jam. If it is to be kept longer, use non-metal lids or stoppers.

Apricot and Orange Chutney

MAKES 675 G | 1½ LB

4 oranges

450 g | 1 lb dried apricots, soaked overnight

1 onion, thinly sliced

225 g | 8 oz sultanas

400 g | 14 oz demerara sugar

2 teaspoons rock salt

570 ml | 1 pint cider vinegar

1 tablespoon mustard seeds

1 teaspoon ground turmeric

1 Boil the whole oranges for 5 minutes. Pare off the zest with a sharp knife, removing all pith left on the back.

2 Shred the zest into thin needleshreds.

3 Peel the oranges and discard all the pith. Chop up the flesh.

4 Place the orange zest and flesh together with all the remaining ingredients, except for 150 ml | ¼ pint of the vinegar, into a large saucepan and simmer until the fruit is soft and pulpy and the mixture very thick. Add the remaining vinegar. Boil briefly.

5 Pour immediately into warmed dry jars and cover with jam covers if to be eaten within a few months, or more securely with non-metal lids or stoppers if to be kept longer.

Plum and Orange Chutney

MAKES 1.5 KG | 3½ LB

450 g | 1 lb cooking apples, peeled, cored and chopped

450 g | 1 lb onions, finely chopped

450 g | 1 lb plums, stoned and chopped

1 clove of garlic, peeled and finely chopped

2 teaspoons yellow mustard seeds

1 stick of cinnamon

1 star anise

290 ml | ½ pint cider vinegar

85 g | 3 oz soft light brown sugar

85 g | 3 oz soft dark brown sugar

grated zest and juice of 1 orange

1 Put all the ingredients except the sugars and the orange zest and juice into a large heavy saucepan and simmer gently, stirring occasionally, for 1 hour or until the mixture is soft and the liquid has almost evaporated.

2 Add the sugars and orange zest and juice and stir over a low heat until the sugar has dissolved.

3 Bring to the boil and boil rapidly, stirring, until thick.

4 Pour into sterilized dry jars and cover as for jam. Store in a cool, dark place.

Date Chutney

SERVES 8

170 ml | 6 fl oz malt vinegar

3 tablespoons soft dark brown sugar

140 g | 5 oz chopped dried dates

2 cloves of garlic, finely chopped

2.5 cm | 1 in piece of fresh root ginger, peeled and finely chopped

30 g | 1 oz sultanas

1 teaspoon paprika

salt

1 Put the vinegar and sugar into a saucepan and bring slowly to the boil. Stir until the sugar has dissolved. Lower the heat and add the dates, garlic and ginger. Cook over a low heat for 15 minutes, stirring all the time. Add the sultanas, paprika and salt to taste and cook for a further 5 minutes.

2 Put into sterilized dry jars and cover as for jam. Store in a cool, dark place. Once opened, store in the refrigerator for up to 1 month.

Spiced Fruit Pickle

MAKES 1.3 KG | 3 LB

900 g | 2 lb mixed fresh fruit, such as plums, apricots, peaches, rhubarb

455 g | 1 lb granulated sugar

425 ml | ¾ pint cider vinegar

grated zest and juice of 1 orange

1 teaspoon ground ginger

4 teaspoons mustard seeds

6 cloves

1 cinnamon stick

1 Prepare the fruit by removing the stones and cutting the flesh into 1 cm | ½ in pieces. Do not peel.

2 Dissolve the sugar in the vinegar and add the orange zest and juice, ginger, mustard seeds, cloves and cinnamon stick.

3 Add the fruit and bring to the boil. Simmer carefully for 15 minutes.

4 Strain the fruit and reduce the liquid by boiling until syrupy. Mix it with the fruit.

5 Pour the pickle into sterilized jam jars and seal with jam seals.

NOTE: This can be used straight away but is better if left to mature for at least a month. Store in a cool, dry, dark place.

Hot Piccalilli

MAKES 2.7 KG | 6 LB

450 g | 1 lb salt

4.6 litres | 8 pints boiling water

675 g | 1½ lb cauliflower, broken into small florets

450 g | 1 lb cucumber, unpeeled and diced

675 g | 1½ lb pickling onions, peeled

450 g | 1 lb green beans, topped and tailed and cut into 2.5 cm | 1 in lengths

450 g | 1 lb marrow, unpeeled and diced

45 g | 1½ oz dry English mustard

15 g | ½ oz ground turmeric

45 g | 1½ oz ground ginger

1½ tablespoons plain flour

170 g | 6 oz caster sugar

1.1 litres | 2 pints distilled vinegar

1 Mix together the salt and boiling water. Leave to cool.

2 Prepare the vegetables and cover with the brine (salt and water). Leave for 24 hours.

3 Drain and rinse the vegetables.

4 Mix the mustard, turmeric, ginger, flour and sugar together and mix to a smooth liquid with 570 ml | 1 pint vinegar.

5 Pour the remaining vinegar into a large saucepan. Add the prepared vegetables, and simmer until tender but still crisp. Stir in the spiced flour mixture. Cook, stirring continuously, until the pickles come to the boil and the sauce thickens. Simmer for 3 minutes.

6 Pack into jars and cover when cold.

Membrillo

This is delicious eaten with cheese, or with cream cheese as a pudding or just as sweets.

1.8 kg | 4 lb quinces	granulated sugar
290 ml | ½ pint water	icing sugar, sifted, to finish

1 Chop the quinces and stew in the water until soft.

2 Sieve and weigh the pulp.

3 Mix the pulp with an equal quantity of sugar. Put into a saucepan, bring to the boil and stir until the paste leaves the side of the pan. It will spit and splutter furiously so cover your hand with a cloth and stir the paste continuously.

4 Pile into flat trays lined with greaseproof paper and leave in an airing cupboard or other warm place for 3–4 days.

5 When it is completely firm, cut into small pieces and roll in icing sugar. Store between greaseproof paper in airtight tins.

Marinated Goat's Cheese

SERVES 6–12

6 crottin goat's cheeses	2 fresh basil leaves
2 cloves of garlic, cut in half	10 black peppercorns
4 sprigs of fresh rosemary	10 coriander seeds
4 sprigs of fresh thyme	380 ml | 13 fl oz good-quality olive oil
4 sprigs of fresh oregano	

1 Cut the goat's cheeses in half horizontally.

2 Arrange the cheese, garlic, herbs, peppercorns and coriander seeds in a preserving jar in alternate layers. Pour in enough oil to cover the cheeses.

3 Seal the jar and store in a cool place for at least a week but no longer than a month. (If you leave it longer, the oil will turn rancid and the cheese will become too soft.)

4 Serve the marinated cheese sprinkled with the oil from the jar, with piping hot slices of toasted French bread.

Canapés, Savouries and Dips

Smoked Salmon Triangles

MAKES 40 SMALL TRIANGLES

5 slices of wholemeal bread

soft butter for spreading

freshly ground black pepper

110 g | 4 oz smoked salmon

lemon juice

1 Butter the bread, sprinkle with black pepper and lay the smoked salmon slices carefully on top.

2 Sprinkle with lemon juice, then cut off the crusts and cut each slice into 8 triangles.

Smoked Salmon on Rye with Horseradish

MAKES 50

12–14 slices of rye bread

225 g | 8 oz cream cheese

horseradish cream

salt and freshly ground black pepper

225 g | 8 oz smoked salmon

sprigs of fresh dill

1 Remove the crusts from the bread. Cut each slice into 4 even-sized rectangles $4 \times 3 \, \text{cm} \mid 1\frac{1}{2} \times 1\frac{1}{4}$ in.

2 Season the cream cheese with the horseradish, salt and pepper. Spread it on to the bread rectangles, mounding it neatly.

3 Cut the smoked salmon into long thin strips and coil it neatly on top of the cream cheese mixture.

4 Decorate each rectangle with a sprig of dill.

Smoked Oyster Tartlets

MAKES 20

1 carrot

white part of 1 leek

salt and freshly ground black pepper

20 smoked oysters

20 boat or oblong tartlet cases, warmed

55 g│2 oz beurre blanc (see page 121)

1 Cut the carrots and leeks into very fine julienne strips. Place in a steamer, season with salt and pepper and cook until tender.

2 Reheat the smoked oysters in their own juice. Drain well.

3 Place a little of the cooked vegetables in the base of each tartlet case, cover with a smoked oyster and coat with the beurre blanc. Serve immediately.

Spinach Roulade with Smoked Salmon and Soured Cream

MAKES 36 SLICES

450 g│1 lb fresh spinach or 170 g│6 oz frozen leaf spinach

7 g│¼ oz butter

2 eggs, separated

salt and freshly ground black pepper

a pinch of freshly grated nutmeg

For the filling

150 ml│¼ pint soured cream

110 g│4 oz smoked salmon, chopped

1 teaspoon chopped fresh dill

1 Preheat the oven to 190°C│375°F│gas mark 5.

2 Line a 26 × 19 cm│10½ × 7½ in Swiss roll tin with non-stick baking parchment.

3 Cook the spinach and drain it thoroughly. Push through a sieve and beat in the butter.

4 Gradually beat the egg yolks into the spinach and season with salt, pepper and nutmeg. Whisk the egg whites until stiff but not dry, and fold them into the spinach. Pour the mixture into the prepared Swiss roll tin and spread it flat. Bake for 10–12 minutes, or until dry to the touch.

5 Mix all the filling ingredients together.

6 Turn the roulade out on to a piece of greaseproof paper and remove the lining paper.

7 Cut the roulade in half lengthways. Spread each rectangle with the filling and, starting with the longer edge, roll each up as you would a Swiss roll. Wrap in damp greaseproof paper and return to the oven for 5 minutes. Remove and allow to cool.

8 Remove from the greaseproof paper and slice each roll into about 18 pieces.

Smoked Salmon and Dill Parcels

MAKES ABOUT 16

250 g|9 oz smoked trout

150 ml|¼ pint double cream, lightly whipped

a squeeze of lemon juice

½ teaspoon horseradish cream

freshly ground black pepper

8 slices of smoked salmon

sprigs of fresh dill

1 Cut off the heads and tails of the trout. Skin them and remove the bones. Mince or pound the flesh and mix with the cream, lemon juice, horseradish and pepper to taste. It should be a firm pâté.

2 Cut the smoked salmon into 6 cm|2½ in squares. Trim off the corners. Place a teaspoon of the pâté on the centre of the smoked salmon square and fold the ends together. Turn over and place a small sprig of dill on each.

Anchovy Puff Pastry Fingers

MAKES 40

225 g|8 oz flour quantity rough puff pastry (see page 565)

40 anchovy fillets

6 tablespoons milk

beaten egg to glaze

1 Divide the pastry in half and roll each piece thinly to a 30 × 10 cm|12 × 4 in rectangle. Place on 2 baking sheets and chill in the refrigerator to relax.

2 Meanwhile, soak the anchovies in the milk for 15 minutes to remove any oil and excess salt. Drain and trim the fillets neatly.

3 Preheat the oven to 200°C|400°F|gas mark 6.

4 Brush one piece of pastry with beaten egg, prick with a fork and place the anchovy fillets neatly on it. You should be able to lay out 2 neat rows of 20 fillets each.

5 Cover with the second piece of pastry and brush again with beaten egg. Press well together and prick all over with a fork.

6 Bake for 10–12 minutes until golden-brown. Leave to cool on a wire rack.

7 When cold, cut the pastry into neat 5 × 1 cm|2 × ½ in fingers so that each finger has an anchovy fillet sandwiched inside it.

8 Warm through before serving.

Twisted Cheese Straws

MAKES 50

170 g | 6 oz plain flour

a pinch of salt

100 g | 3½ oz butter

45 g | 1½ oz freshly grated Parmesan cheese or
  mixed Parmesan and Gruyère or Cheddar cheese

a pinch of freshly ground black pepper

a pinch of cayenne pepper

a pinch of dry English mustard

beaten egg

1 Preheat the oven to 190°C | 375°F | gas mark 5.
2 Sift the flour with the salt into a bowl. Rub the butter into the flour with your fingertips until the mixture resembles fine breadcrumbs. Add the cheese, pepper, cayenne and mustard.
3 Bind the mixture together with enough egg to make a stiff dough. Refrigerate for 10 minutes.
4 Line 2 baking sheets with greaseproof paper. Roll the dough into a rectangle and cut into 9 × 2 cm | 3½ × ¾ in strips. Twist each strip 2–3 times like a barley sugar stick.
5 Bake for 8–10 minutes until biscuit-brown.

Poppy and Sesame Seed Straws

MAKES 40

110 g | 4 oz flour quantity puff pastry (see page 565)

1 egg, beaten

2 tablespoons poppy seeds

½ tablespoons sesame seeds

1 Preheat the oven to 200°C | 400°F | gas mark 6.
2 Roll out the pastry quite thinly, brush with beaten egg and cut in half.
3 Sprinkle one half with poppy seeds and the other half with sesame seeds.
4 Line 2 baking sheets with greaseproof paper. Roll each piece of pastry out very thinly. Cut into long strips and twist like barley sugar strips. Place on the prepared baking sheets.
5 Bake for 10–12 minutes until golden-brown.

Cheese Sablés

MAKES 24

225 g | 8 oz plain flour

salt and freshly ground black pepper

225 g | 8 oz butter

225 g | 8 oz Gruyère or strong Cheddar cheese, grated

a pinch of dry English mustard

a pinch of cayenne pepper

beaten egg

1 Preheat the oven to 190°C | 375°F | gas mark 5. Line 2 baking sheets with greaseproof paper.
2 Sift the flour with a pinch of salt into a bowl. Rub in the butter until the mixture resembles breadcrumbs.

3 Add the cheese, salt, pepper, mustard, cayenne and enough egg just to bind. Work into a paste but do not over-handle or the pastry will become greasy and tough.

4 Roll out on a floured board to a 5 mm|¼ in thickness. Cut into rounds or triangles and brush with the remaining beaten egg.

5 Bake for about 10 minutes until golden-brown. Leave to cool on a wire rack.

Parmesan and Chive Crisps

Use these to garnish soups and salads.

butter for greasing
110 g|4 oz fresh Parmesan cheese, finely grated

1 tablespoon very finely chopped chives

1 Preheat the oven to 200°C|400°F|gas mark 6. Grease a baking sheet lightly with melted butter. Heat it in the oven until really hot.

2 Sprinkle the cheese into 4 × 7.5 cm|3 in rounds on the baking sheet. Flatten them slightly.

4 Bake oven for 2½ minutes, sprinkle with the chives and bake for 30 seconds.

5 Remove from the oven and allow to crisp and harden for 2 minutes. Remove to a wire rack and leave to cool.

Stilton Grapes

110 g|4 oz Stilton cheese
110 g|4 oz cream cheese

110 g|4 oz seedless grapes
110 g|4 oz walnuts, finely chopped

1 Beat the cheeses together. Press a little of the mixture around each grape and roll in the nuts.

Tiger Prawns with Chinese Dipping Sauce

20 large Mediterranean prawns
sesame oil

For the marinade

3 tablespoons soy sauce
1 tablespoon sesame oil
2 tablespoons dry sherry
1 cm|½ in piece of fresh root ginger, peeled and finely chopped
1 clove of garlic, cut into slivers

For the dipping sauce

1 tablespoon sesame oil
2 tablespoons soy sauce
1 tablespoon clear honey
3–4 tablespoons ginger syrup (from a jar of preserved ginger)
1 tablespoon red wine vinegar
4 spring onions, chopped

1 Peel the prawns and remove the black vein down the back of each prawn.

2 Mix together the marinade ingredients and add the prawns. Chill for 3–4 hours.

3 Make the dipping sauce: mix together all the ingredients except the spring onions.

4 Fry the prawns fairly briskly in the sesame oil. They are cooked when they turn pink and begin to butterfly out.

5 Tip the prawns on to a serving platter. Put the dipping sauce in a bowl, add the spring onions and serve immediately.

NOTE: Serve cocktail sticks with the prawns.

Dill Pancakes with Smoked Trout Mousse

MAKES 16

1 tablespoon chopped fresh dill

150 ml | ¼ pint French pancake batter (see page 569)

For the smoked trout mousse

140 g | 5 oz smoked trout

70 ml | 2½ fl oz double cream, lightly whipped

a squeeze of lemon juice

½ teaspoon horseradish cream

freshly ground black pepper

To garnish

sprigs of fresh dill

1 Mix the chopped dill into the pancake batter.

2 Make the pancakes as described on page 569, then stamp out into rounds, using a small fluted cutter.

3 Make the mousse: remove the skin and bones from the trout. Mince or pound the flesh and mix with the cream, lemon juice, horseradish and pepper to taste.

4 Place a teaspoon of the mousse on each pancake and pinch the edges together to form a cone.

5 Garnish each pancake with a sprig of dill.

Gravad Lax on Rye

MAKES 24

1 packet of rye bread

mustard and dill mayonnaise

lollo rosso lettuce

55 g | 2 oz gravad lax (see page 183)

1 Stamp out rounds of rye bread, using a small round cutter.

2 Spread a little mustard and dill mayonnaise on each round.

3 Place a little lollo rosso on top, spread with a little more mustard and dill mayonnaise and arrange a piece of gravad lax on top.

Toastie Cases

MAKES 20

5 thin slices of bread   butter, melted

1 Preheat the oven to 180°C|350°F|gas mark 4. Stamp out rounds of bread, using a small fluted cutter.
2 Brush with the melted butter and mould into tiny patty tins. Press an empty patty tin on top and bake in the oven until golden-brown and crisp.

Toasties with Salmon Roe

MAKES 20

20 toastie cases (see above)   small jar of salmon roe
70 ml|2½ fl oz soured cream

1 Fill the toasties with soured cream and top with a little salmon roe.

Toasties with Tuna Pâté

MAKES 20

110 g|4 oz cream cheese   20 toastie cases (see above)
110 g|4 oz tuna fish
lemon juice   **To garnish**
freshly ground black pepper   sprigs of fresh chervil or dill

1 Beat the cream cheese and tuna fish together until very smooth. Season to taste with lemon juice and black pepper.
2 Pipe into the toastie cases and garnish each with a sprig of chervil or dill.

Mascarpone Tartlets with Salmon Roe

225 g|8 oz Mascarpone cream cheese
30 tartlet cases (see page 814)   **To garnish**
1 small jar of salmon roe   sprigs of fresh dill

1 Beat the Mascarpone cheese lightly and place in a piping bag fitted with a fluted nozzle.
2 Pipe the cheese into the tartlet cases and top with a little salmon roe.
3 Garnish each tartlet with a small sprig of dill.

Tartlet Cases

MAKES ABOUT 60

225 g | 8 oz quantity rich shortcrust pastry (see page 559)

1 Preheat the oven to 190°C | 375°F | gas mark 5.
2 Roll out the pastry 2 mm | ⅛ in thick. Stamp out circles, using a small fluted cutter.
3 Press the circles into tiny patty tins or barquette (boat-shapes) moulds. Chill in the refrigerator for 20 minutes.
4 Bake the tartlet cases blind for about 10 minutes (see page 557), removing the lining paper and beans after 5 minutes.
5 Cool on a wire rack and use as required.

Drop Scones with Caviar

MAKES 20

150 ml | ¼ pint drop scone batter (see page 571) or blinis (see page 157)

70 ml | 2½ fl oz soured cream
1 small jar of black lumpfish roe

1 Make up small drop scones 3 cm | 1¼ in in diameter. Spread each drop cone with a little soured cream and top with lumpfish roe.

Stuffed Mangetout

MAKES 20

20 mangetout
110 g | 4 oz cream cheese
a little milk

1 tablespoon mixed finely chopped fresh chives and parsley
salt and freshly ground black pepper

1 Blanch and refresh the mangetout, then top and tail and split them open. Soften the cream cheese with a little milk, add the herbs and season to taste with salt and pepper.
2 Open the mangetout along one side. Put the cheese mixture into a piping bag fitted with a small plain nozzle and pipe into the mangetout.

Tartlets with Quail's Eggs and Smoked Salmon

MAKES 20

70 ml | 2½ fl oz mayonnaise (see page 117)
20 tartlet cases (see above)
10 quail's eggs, hardboiled (see page 159)
55 g | 2 oz smoked salmon, cut into julienne strips

To garnish
sprigs of fresh chervil or dill

1 Spoon or pipe a little mayonnaise into each pastry case.
2 Halve the quail's eggs and place a half, cut side up, on top of the mayonnaise.
3 Place a little smoked salmon on the quail's egg and garnish with a sprig of chervil or dill.

Tartlets with Smoked Salmon and Caviar

MAKES 20

70 ml | 2½ fl oz Greek yoghurt

20 tartlet cases (see page 814)

85 g | 3 oz smoked salmon, cut into julienne strips

½ small jar of black lumpfish roe

1 Spoon or pipe a little Greek yoghurt into each tartlet case.

2 Fill the tartlet case with the smoked salmon and top with a little black lumpfish roe.

Cherry Tomato, Avocado and Mozzarella Kebabs

MAKES 20

20 cherry tomatoes

1 avocado, cut into cubes

1 mozzarella cheese, cut into cubes

8 fresh basil leaves, shredded

3 tablespoons French dressing (see page 123)

1 Using 20 bamboo sticks, thread a cherry tomato, a cube of avocado and a cube of mozzarella on to each stick.

2 Mix the basil with the French dressing and spoon a little over the avocado and mozzarella.

Cherry Tomatoes with Cream Cheese and Mint

MAKES 20

20 cherry tomatoes

110 g | 4 oz cream cheese

1½ teaspoons chopped fresh mint

a squeeze of lemon juice

salt and freshly ground black pepper

1 Slice a quarter of each tomato off at the rounded end. Scoop out the flesh and reserve.

2 Mix a little of the tomato flesh with the cream cheese, mint, lemon, salt and pepper. Cut a very thin slice from the bottom of each tomato so that it can stand upright. Fill the tomatoes with the cream cheese mixture and stick the tops back at a jaunty angle.

Mini Yorkshire Puddings with Rare Roast Beef

MAKES 30

beef dripping or oil

290 ml | ½ pint Yorkshire pudding batter (see page 475)

170 g | 6 oz fillet or sirloin steak

horseradish cream (see page 111)

To garnish

1 bunch watercress

1 Preheat the oven to 220°C | 425°F | gas mark 7.

2 Heat the dripping or oil in small patty tins.

3 Pour in the batter and bake for 10–15 minutes, or until risen and golden.

4 Meanwhile, grill or fry the steak and cut into thin slices.

5 Spoon or pipe a little horseradish cream into each Yorkshire pudding. Arrange a slice of beef on top and garnish with a tiny sprig of watercress.

Mini Baked Potatoes with Cheese and Bacon

MAKES 20

20 small new potatoes

55 g|2 oz streaky bacon, grilled and diced

55 g|2 oz Cheddar cheese, grated

a little melted butter

salt and freshly ground black pepper

1 Preheat the oven to 200°C|400°F|gas mark 6.

2 Scrub the potatoes and bake in the oven for about 45 minutes, or until cooked.

3 Cut a slice from the top of each potato. Scoop out the centre and mix with the remaining ingredients.

4 Pile the filling back into the potatoes.

5 Heat through in the oven for about 8 minutes.

Mushrooms Stuffed with Spinach, Bacon and Garlic

MAKES 20

20 even-sized button mushrooms

55 g|2 oz butter

225 g|8 oz fresh spinach, washed, destalked, cooked and finely chopped

55 g|2 oz streaky bacon, grilled and cut into tiny dice

2 cloves of garlic, crushed

salt and freshly ground black pepper

plain flour

1 egg, beaten

dried white breadcrumbs

oil for deep-frying

1 Wipe the mushrooms and remove the stalks.

2 Melt the butter, add the spinach, bacon, garlic, salt and pepper.

3 Pile the stuffing into the mushrooms.

4 Dip the mushrooms first into the flour, then into the beaten egg and finally into the breadcrumbs, to coat thoroughly.

5 Heat the oil in a deep-fryer and fry the mushrooms until golden-brown.

6 Drain on absorbent kitchen paper, sprinkle with salt and serve immediately.

Tandoori Chicken with Cucumber and Yoghurt Dip

MAKES 12

225 g | 8 oz boneless chicken meat

150 ml | ¼ pint plain yoghurt

a pinch of chilli powder

a pinch each of ground cumin and coriander

1 teaspoon garam masala

1 teaspoon tomato purée

grated zest and juice of ½ lemon

1 clove of garlic, crushed

1 teaspoon peeled and chopped fresh root ginger

salt and freshly ground black pepper

For the cucumber and yoghurt dip

¼ cucumber

150 ml | ¼ pint plain yoghurt

1 tablespoon double cream

1 tablespoon finely chopped fresh mint

salt and freshly ground black pepper

1 Cut the chicken into bite-sized chunks.

2 Place all the remaining tandoori ingredients together in a food processor or blender and process until smooth.

3 Lay the pieces of chicken in a shallow dish, pour over the marinade, cover and refrigerate overnight.

4 The following day, just before serving, lift the chicken out of the marinade and place in a roasting pan. Preheat the grill or oven to its highest setting. Cook the chicken for about 10 minutes, or until reddish-brown and tender.

5 Make the cucumber and yoghurt dip: chop the cucumber finely and pat dry with absorbent kitchen paper. Mix all the ingredients together and season with salt and pepper. Place in a bowl.

6 Spear the chicken pieces with cocktail sticks and serve on a round dish surrounding the cucumber and yoghurt dip.

Chicken Saté with Peanut Sambal

MAKES 60 COCKTAIL PIECES

5 chicken breasts, skinned

For the marinade

1 medium onion, grated

1 clove of garlic, crushed

1 teaspoon ground coriander

1 teaspoon ground ginger

3 tablespoons dark soy sauce

juice of 1 small lemon

2 teaspoons soft dark brown sugar

freshly ground black pepper

For the peanut sambal

1 small onion, finely chopped

1 tablespoon oil

½ teaspoon chilli powder

110 g | 4 oz crunchy peanut butter

2 tablespoons dark soy sauce

2 tablespoons lemon juice

200 ml | 7 fl oz cold water

soft dark brown sugar and salt to taste

1 Cut each chicken breast into 12 cubes.

2 Mix together the ingredients for the marinade and add the chicken pieces. Refrigerate for at least 1 hour.

3 Make the sambal: cook the onion in the oil in a saucepan over a very low heat. Add the chilli powder and cook for 10 seconds.

4 Remove from the heat and add the peanut butter, soy sauce, lemon juice and water.

5 Return to the heat and stir until the sauce is thick and smooth. Season to taste with sugar and salt.

6 Preheat the grill to its highest setting.

7 Skewer the chicken pieces on long wet bamboo sticks and grill for about 3 minutes each side.

8 Serve the peanut sambal as a dip.

NOTE: Soak the bamboo sticks for 30 minutes to prevent them from burning.

Chicken Livers Wrapped in Bacon

MAKES ABOUT 60

450 g | 1 lb chicken livers   60 small slices of streaky bacon

1 Preheat the oven to 220°C | 425°F | gas mark 7.

2 Trim the livers, discarding the discoloured parts.

3 Cut the livers into small pieces. Roll each piece in a slice of bacon and lay the rolls side by side in a roasting pan, fairly tightly packed to prevent unravelling.

4 Bake for about 15 minutes or until they are just beginning to brown on top. Drain well.

5 Spear each roll with a cocktail stick. They are now ready to serve, but if they are to be reheated, remove them from the roasting pan and keep in a cool place until needed.

NOTE: If the cocktail sticks are stuck in before reheating, make sure that they are wooden, not plastic.

Roquefort Toasts

MAKES 16

2 rashers of rindless streaky bacon	1 teaspoon Worcestershire sauce
110 g	4 oz Roquefort cheese	1 teaspoon grated onion
1 tablespoon tomato chutney	4 slices of bread, each cut into 4 squares

1 Preheat the oven to 200°C | 400°F | gas mark 6.

2 Dice the bacon. Fry in a heavy frying pan until crisp but not brittle. Drain well on absorbent kitchen paper and break up into small pieces. Keep warm.

3 Mix the Roquefort, chutney, Worcestershire sauce and onion to a smooth paste.

4 Divide the mixture between the squares of bread and spread it evenly, being sure to cover all the edges. Place on a greased baking sheet.

5 Bake for 5 minutes until crisp and brown.

6 Sprinkle with the fried bacon and serve immediately.

Sausage Rolls

MAKES 12

15 g | ½ oz butter

30 g | 1 oz very finely chopped onion

400 g | 14 oz sausagemeat

30 g | 1 oz very finely chopped fresh parsley

salt and freshly ground black pepper

225 g | 8 oz flour quantity shortcrust pastry (see page 559)

1 egg, beaten, to glaze

1 Melt the butter, add the onion and sweat for 20 minutes.

2 Preheat the oven to 200°C | 400°F | gas mark 6.

3 Mix together the sausagemeat, parsley, onion, salt and pepper.

4 Roll out the pastry to a large rectangle about 2 mm | ⅛ in thick and cut in half lengthways.

5 With wet hands, roll the sausagemeat mixture into 2 long sausages the same length as the pastry and place one down the centre of each piece.

6 Damp one edge of each strip and bring the pastry over the sausagemeat, pressing the edges together and making sure that the join is underneath the roll. Chill for 10 minutes.

7 Brush with beaten egg. Cut into 5 cm | 2 in lengths. Using a pair of kitchen scissors, snip a small 'V' in the top of each sausage roll. (This is to allow steam to escape during cooking. A couple of small diagonal slashes made with a sharp knife will do as well.)

8 Place on a baking sheet and bake for 25–30 minutes until the pastry is golden-brown.

Cheese Aigrettes

MAKES ABOUT 30

105 g | 3¾ oz plain flour

salt and freshly ground black pepper

½ teaspoon dry English mustard

cayenne pepper

85 g | 3 oz butter

225 ml | 8 fl oz water

3 eggs, lightly beaten

55 g | 2 oz strong Cheddar cheese, finely diced

oil or fat for deep-frying

freshly grated Parmesan cheese

1 Sift the flour with the salt, pepper, mustard and cayenne.

2 Slowly heat the butter and water together in a large saucepan. As soon as the butter is completely melted, bring to a full rolling boil and tip in the flour. Remove from the heat at once and beat with a wooden spoon until the mixture leaves the side of the pan. Allow to cool for 10 minutes.

3 Gradually beat in the eggs until the mixture is smooth and shiny and of a dropping consistency (you may not need all the egg). Add the Cheddar cheese.

4 Heat oil or fat in a deep-fryer until a crumb will sizzle vigorously in it.

5 Shape the mixture into even-sized balls, using 2 teaspoons, and deep-fry a few at a time, leaving plenty of room for them to rise, for about 7 minutes, or until they are puffed and golden.

6 Lift out and drain on absorbent kitchen paper. Dust with Parmesan cheese and serve immediately.

Angels on Horseback

SERVES 3

12 oysters
6 rashers of rindless streaky bacon
6 small slices of bread
butter for spreading

To garnish
1 bunch of watercress

1 Preheat the oven to 200°C|400°F|gas mark 6. Preheat the grill.

2 Prepare the oysters: wrap a tea-towel round your left hand. Place an oyster on your left palm with the flat side upwards. Slip a short, wide-bladed kitchen or oyster knife under the hinge and push it into the oyster. Press the middle fingers of your left hand on to the shell and, with your right hand, jerk up the knife and prise the 2 shells apart. Free the oyster from its base.

3 On a board, stretch the bacon with the back of a knife (this helps to prevent shrinking, during cooking). Wrap half a rasher around each oyster. Place the rolls on a baking sheet, tightly packed side by side to prevent them unravelling. Bake in the preheated oven for about 8 minutes.

4 Meanwhile, cut the bread into rounds and toast them under the grill. Butter the toast and set 2 'angels' on each round. Arrange on a serving dish and garnish with watercress.

Devils on Horseback

SERVES 3

12 prunes
mango chutney
6 rashers of rindless streaky bacon
6 small slices of bread
butter for spreading

To garnish
1 bunch of watercress

1 Pour boiling water over the prunes and leave to soak for 30 minutes. Preheat the oven to 200°C|400°F|gas mark 6. Preheat the grill.

2 Remove the stones from the prunes and stuff each cavity with half a teaspoon of mango chutney.

3 On a board, stretch the bacon with the back of a knife (this helps to prevent shrinking during cooking). Wrap half a rasher around each prune.

4 Place on a baking sheet, packed tightly side by side to prevent them unravelling. Bake for about 8 minutes.

5 Meanwhile, cut the bread into rounds and toast them under the grill. Butter the toast and set 2 'devils' on each round. Arrange on a serving dish and garnish with watercress.

Scotch Woodcock

SERVES 4

8 anchovy fillets

30 g | 1 oz butter

freshly ground black pepper

4 slices of bread, crusts removed

4 egg yolks

290 ml | ½ pint single cream

1 tablespoon chopped fresh parsley

a pinch of cayenne pepper

1 Preheat the grill.

2 Pound the anchovy fillets into the butter and add pepper to taste.

3 Toast the bread under the grill and spread thinly with the anchovy paste. Put on a warmed serving plate and keep warm.

4 Put the egg yolks, cream, parsley and cayenne together in a saucepan. Stir or whisk over a medium heat until thick and creamy.

5 Pour over the toasts and serve immediately.

wine: SPICY DRY WHITE

Mushroom Strudel

MAKES 16

225 g | 8 oz rashers of rindless streaky bacon

30 g | 1 oz butter

2 small onions, finely chopped

450 g | 1 lb button mushrooms, sliced

salt and freshly ground black pepper

1 tablespoon chopped fresh parsley

140 g | 5 oz flour quantity strudel pastry (see page 563)

melted butter for brushing

beaten egg, to glaze

1 Preheat the oven to 200°C | 400°F | gas mark 6.

2 Dice the bacon and fry in its own fat in a frying pan until cooked and slightly browned. Remove to a plate. Add the butter to the pan.

3 Reduce the heat, add the onions and cook until soft but not coloured. Add the mushrooms and cook briskly for 5 minutes or until dry.

4 Season with salt and pepper and add the parsley. Boil rapidly until the liquid has evaporated. Remove from the heat and allow to cool. Add the bacon.

5 Cut the strudel sheets into 5 cm | 2 in squares. Brush each square with melted butter.

6 With a slotted spoon, place some mushroom mixture in the centre of each square.

7 Using both hands, draw the edges of the pastry together so that the strudel looks like a pouch. Pinch the neck of the pouch with your fingers to secure it tightly. Alternatively, roll each strudel up into a sausage shape. Brush the pastry with beaten egg. Place on a greased baking sheet and bake for 25 minutes, or until the pastry is golden-brown.

NOTE: When working with strudel pastry it is vital to prevent the thin sheets from drying out and cracking. Keep the pastry covered with clingfilm or a damp cloth, and when the sheets are exposed to the air, work fast. Brush the strudels with butter as quickly as you can.

wine: SPICY DRY WHITE

Barquettes of Puff Pastry with a Julienne of Vegetables

Use as a garnish for fish, poultry and veal dishes.

MAKES 14–16

170 g | 6 oz flour quantity puff pastry (see page 565)

2 carrots, peeled and cut into fine julienne strips

white part only of 2 leeks, washed and cut into fine julienne strips

salt and freshly ground black pepper

1 teaspoon chopped fresh thyme leaves

110 g | 4 oz beurre blanc (see page 121)

1 Preheat the oven 220°C | 425°F | gas mark 7.

2 Roll the pastry out thinly and use it to line 14–16 small pastry boats. Prick well with a fork and bake blind (see page 557).

3 Steam the carrots and leeks together with the salt, pepper and fresh thyme leaves.

4 Arrange the vegetables in the warm pastry boats and spoon over the beurre blanc.

Filo Pastry Baskets Filled with Tomatoes and Dill

These pretty baskets can be used to garnish chicken, lamb and fish dishes.

MAKES 20

1½ sheets of filo pastry

45 g | 1½ oz unsalted butter, melted

2 ripe tomatoes

2 large sprigs of fresh dill, roughly chopped

salt and freshly ground black pepper

1 Preheat the oven to 200°C | 400°F | gas mark 6.

2 Brush each sheet of filo pastry with melted butter to prevent it from drying out and cracking.

3 Using a small pastry cutter, press out rounds of filo pastry and use to line 20 × 2.5 cm | in tartlet tins, placing 3 layers of pastry in each tin.

4 Bake for 5–7 minutes, or until golden-brown.

5 Meanwhile, prepare the tomato filling: plunge the tomatoes into boiling water and leave for 10 seconds. Transfer to a bowl of cold water to prevent any further cooking. When cool, peel them. Cut them into quarters and remove the seeds. Chop the tomato flesh neatly into tiny dice.

6 Heat 1 tablespoon of the remaining butter in a frying pan and quickly fry the tomatoes for about 30 seconds, taking care that they do not cook to a purée. Add the chopped dill and season to taste with salt and pepper.

7 Place a spoonful of the tomato mixture in each pastry basket and serve immediately to prevent them going soggy.

Deep-fried Parsley

Pick sprigs of fresh but dry parsley and place in a frying basket. Heat oil in the deep-fryer until a crumb will sizzle in it, then lower in the basket. It will hiss furiously. When the noise stops, the parsley is cooked. It should be bright green and brittle, with a very good concentrated flavour.

NOTE: To avoid splashing any hot oil, tie the parsley on to the end of a piece of string and lower into the oil from a height.

Parmesan-chive Scones with Red Onion Marmalade

MAKES ABOUT 30

225 g│8 oz plain flour

½ teaspoon salt

½ teaspoon bicarbonate of soda

½ teaspoon cream of tartar

55 g│2 oz butter

30 g│1 oz finely grated Parmesan cheese

1 tablespoon finely chopped fresh chives

150 ml│¼ pint milk

1 egg, beaten, to glaze

TO SERVE

red onion marmalade (see recipe below)

2 tablespoons finely chopped fresh parsley to garnish

1 Preheat the oven to 220°C│425°F│gas mark 7. Flour a baking sheet.

2 Sift the flour, salt, bicarbonate of soda and cream of tartar into a large bowl.

3 Cut the butter into small pieces, then rub in with your fingertips until the mixture resembles breadcrumbs. Stir in the cheese and chives.

4 Make a deep well in the flour, then pour in the milk and mix to a soft dough using a table knife.

5 On a floured surface, knead the dough lightly until it is just smooth.

6 Roll out 2.5 cm│1 in thick and cut into rounds using a floured 2.5 cm│1 in cutter.

7 Place the scones on the baking sheet, brush the tops with the beaten egg and bake on the top shelf of the oven for 10 minutes or until well risen and lightly browned. Transfer to a wire rack and leave to cool.

8 Cut the scones in half and top each half with red onion marmalade to serve. Garnish with the parsley.

Red Onion Marmalade

4 tablespoons olive oil

450 g│1 lb red onions, finely chopped

250 g│9 oz red peppers, deseeded and finely diced

150 ml│¼ pint red wine

2 tablespoons soft dark brown sugar

2 tablespoons finely chopped fresh thyme

1 tablespoon balsamic vinegar

1 Place the olive oil in a large sauté pan and stir in the onions. Place a piece of dampened greaseproof paper over the top of the onions and cover with a lid. Sweat the onions over a low heat until very soft.

2 Remove the greaseproof paper and stir in the red peppers. Continue to cook until the peppers begin to soften and the onions are beginning to brown.

3 Add the wine and the sugar and cook until the wine has become syrupy and the vegetables are lightly caramelized. Stir in the thyme and vinegar. Allow to cool.

Sesame Prawn Toasts

MAKES 20

140 g|5 oz raw tiger prawns, peeled and deveined

1 tablespoon egg white

1 heaped teaspoon cornflour

a squeeze of lemon juice

a large pinch of salt

5 slices of white bread

2–3 tablespoons sesame seeds

oil for deep-frying

1 Put the prawns, egg white, cornflour, lemon juice and salt into a food processor. Whizz to a paste.

2 Cut the crusts off the bread. Spread the prawn paste evenly over the slices of bread and press a generous quantity of sesame seeds on top. Cut the slices of bread in half, then cut each half into 4 triangles or short fingers.

3 Heat the oil in a deep-fryer or heavy saucepan until a crumb will brown in 15 seconds.

4 Fry a few sesame seed toasts at a time, prawn side down, in the hot oil for 10–15 seconds, then flip them over and fry for a further 10–15 seconds until golden-brown. Drain on absorbent kitchen paper and serve immediately.

Stuffed Vine Leaves (Dolmades)

SERVES 8

about 30 small young vine leaves

1 onion, finely chopped

2 tablespoons olive oil

225 g|8 oz cooked rice

a pinch of ground allspice

½ teaspoon chopped fresh mint

salt and freshly ground black pepper

white stock (see page 103)

1 tablespoon lemon juice

plain yoghurt or tomato sauce 2 (see page 129)

1 Plunge the vine leaves into a saucepan of boiling salted water for 10 seconds. Rinse under cold running water and drain well. Lay the leaves, smooth side up, side by side on a worktop or board.

2 Fry the onion in the oil until soft but not coloured. Mix the onion (with its oil) together with the rice, allspice and mint. Season to taste with salt and pepper.

3 Lay a teaspoon of rice mixture on each vine leaf and roll up the leaf, tucking in the ends to make a small parcel. Squeeze the rolls in the palm of your hand – this will ensure that the dolmades hold their shape and will not need tying up. Pack all the dolmades into a wide saucepan and add enough stock to half-cover them. Sprinkle over the lemon juice.

Cover tightly, preferably with a small plate that fits inside the pan (this will prevent the dolmades moving during cooking) and a lid. Simmer for 1 hour.

4 Lift out the dolmades with a slotted spoon and arrange on a serving dish. Chill. Coat with yoghurt or tomato sauce.

NOTE: Dolmades may be served hot, with the yoghurt or sauce handed separately.

Tzatziki

Recipes for this are legion: some include mint; some do not call for garlic.

SERVES 6

1 medium cucumber, grated	1 clove of garlic, crushed
salt	freshly ground black pepper
570 ml│1 pint low-fat plain yoghurt	

1 Place the cucumber in a sieve, sprinkle lightly with salt and leave to degorge for 30 minutes. Drain and pat dry.

2 Mix the cucumber with the yoghurt, garlic and plenty of pepper.

NOTE: The yoghurt can be thickened by draining it in a muslin-lined sieve; this will make for a creamier finish.

Crudités

A selection of:	young asparagus
celery	tiny mangetout
red and yellow pepper	baby sweetcorn
cauliflower	
radishes	**For the dressing**
spring onions	1 clove of garlic, crushed (optional)
carrots	150 ml│¼ pint mayonnaise (see page 117)

1 Prepare the vegetables, making sure they are perfectly clean, and as far as possible evenly sized.
Celery: wash and cut into sticks.
Pepper: wipe and cut into strips, discarding the inner membrane and seeds.
Cauliflower: wash and break into florets. Peel the stalks if tough, blanch and refresh if required.
Radishes: wash and trim off the root and long leaves, but leave a little of the green stalk.
Spring onions: wash. Cut off most of the green part, and the beard (roots). Leave whole, or cut in half lengthways if large.
Carrots: peel and cut into sticks the same shape and size as the celery.
Asparagus: peel the tough outer stalk and trim away the hard root ends.

2 Mix the garlic, if using, with the mayonnaise. Spoon it into a small serving bowl.

3 Arrange the raw prepared vegetables in neat clumps on a tray or flat platter with the bowl of mayonnaise dip in the centre.

Taramasalata

SERVES 6

1 slice of white bread, crusts removed
225 g | 8 oz fresh smoked cod's roe, skinned
1 large clove of garlic, crushed

about 150 ml | ¼ pint each sunflower oil and olive oil
freshly ground black pepper
juice of ½ lemon

1 Hold the bread slice under the tap to wet it. Squeeze dry and put it into a bowl with the cod roe and the garlic. Using a wooden spoon or electric whisk, beat very well.
2 Now add the oils very slowly, almost drop by drop (as with mayonnaise), beating all the time. The idea is to form a smooth emulsion, and adding the oil too fast will result in a rather oily, curdled mixture.
3 The amount of oil added is a matter of personal taste: the more you add, the paler and creamier the mixture becomes and the more delicate the flavour. Stop when you think the right balance is achieved.
4 Add pepper and lemon juice to taste. If the mixture seems too thick or bitter add a little hot water.

NOTE: Taramasalata can be served as a spread for cocktail snacks, or with toast or fresh rolls, but it is best served as a first course with hot Greek bread (pitta).
   If it begins to separate, add a little boiling water.

Hummus

This is a spicy hummus and has been adapted from a recipe by one of Leiths' most popular authors, Claudia Roden.

SERVES 4

225 g | 8 oz chickpeas
salt and freshly ground black pepper
2 teaspoons ground cumin
2 cloves of garlic, crushed
juice of 1 lemon

4 tablespoons olive oil
a pinch of cayenne pepper

To garnish
flat-leaf parsley

To serve
pitta bread

1 Soak the chickpeas overnight in cold water.
2 Drain the chickpeas and cook slowly in fresh water for 1–1½ hours. Add the salt towards the end of cooking. Drain and reserve the cooking liquor.
3 Cool for a few minutes, then tip into a food processor. Whizz and add the remaining ingredients. Add enough of the cooking liquor to produce a soft cream.
4 Serve on a flat plate garnished with the parsley. Hand hot pitta bread separately.

Tuna Fish Pâté

SERVES 4

1 × 200 g | 7 oz can of tuna fish steak in olive oil
55 g | 2 oz unsalted butter, softened
grated zest and juice of ½ lemon

1 teaspoon grated onion
salt and freshly ground black pepper

To serve
crudités or Melba toast (see pages 825, 225)

1 Place the tuna with its oil in the bowl of a food processor.
2 Add the butter, lemon zest and juice and onion. Process until smooth.
3 Season with salt and pepper, then turn into a serving dish.
4 Serve at room temperature with crudités or Melba toast.

Guacamole

This authentic Mexican recipe calls for 3 chillies. We found this too hot and think one is enough, but use according to taste.

SERVES 4

1–3 fresh green chillies
1 large clove of garlic, crushed
1 teaspoon salt
3 tablespoons fresh coriander leaves
juice of 1 lime
2 ripe avocados

1 large tomato, concassed
1–2 spring onions, thinly sliced on the diagonal
  (optional)

To serve
crudités or tortilla chips

1 Wearing rubber gloves, quarter the chillies, remove the seeds and roughly chop the flesh. Place in a food processor or blender with the garlic, salt and coriander and process to a fine pulp. Scrape down the sides of the bowl or goblet with a spatula as often as necessary. Use a little lime juice to help the mixture move, if necessary.
2 Peel and stone the avocados; reserve the stones. Place the avocado flesh in a mixing bowl and mash to a rough-textured purée with a fork.
3 Spoon in the chilli mixture to taste and combine well. Add lime juice to taste. Stir in the tomato and the spring onions.
4 Serve with crudités or tortilla chips.

NOTE: Guacamole cannot be made too far in advance or it will discolour. To help prevent discoloration keep the reserved stones in the mixture until it is served.

Babaganoush (Aubergine Caviar)

SERVES 8

2 medium aubergines

4 tablespoons good-quality olive oil

2 cloves of garlic

salt and freshly ground black pepper

2 tablespoons chopped fresh parsley

lemon juice to taste

1 Preheat the oven to 190°C|375°F|gas mark 5.

2 Brush the aubergines with a little oil and bake in the oven for 40–60 minutes, until they collapse. After 20 minutes add the whole cloves of garlic.

3 Allow the aubergines and garlic to cool. Peel.

4 Put the garlic into a food processor with the aubergine flesh, salt and pepper. Whizz to a smooth purée. Stir in the chopped parsley.

5 Gradually beat in the remaining oil and when the mixture is stiff stir in the lemon juice and season to taste with salt and pepper.

6 Refrigerate for 2 hours before serving.

Thai Noodle Balls

MAKES 22

200 g|7 oz egg noodles or fine spaghetti

salt and freshly ground black pepper

400 g|14 oz crabmeat

4 large eggs

4 tablespoons chopped fresh coriander leaves

55 g|2 oz Parmesan cheese, freshly grated

70 g|2½ oz plain flour

1 onion, finely chopped

3 cloves of garlic, crushed

oil for deep-frying

For the sauce

125 ml|4½ fl oz Thai sweet chilli sauce

½ cucumber, peeled, deseeded and finely diced

55 ml|2 fl oz rice vinegar

1 Cook the egg noodles in plenty of salted boiling water until just cooked. Drain well, then cut into small lengths. Place in a large bowl.

2 Add all the remaining ingredients except the oil to the bowl and mix to a firm, slightly sticky mixture.

3 Mould the mixture into balls about the size of golf balls. Chill well in the refrigerator.

4 Preheat the oil in a deep-fryer to 160°C|300°F. Fry about 4 balls at a time until golden-brown, being careful not to overload the fryer as this will reduce the temperature of the oil. Drain well on absorbent kitchen paper.

5 Meanwhile, make the sauce by mixing the ingredients together in a small bowl.

6 To serve: arrange on a serving plate with a small dish of sauce.

Chinese Spring Rolls

MAKES 16

16 spring roll wrappers

For the filling

55 g | 2 oz beansprouts

55 g | 2 oz French beans

55 g | 2 oz carrots, peeled and cut into julienne strips

1 stick of celery, trimmed and cut into julienne strips

1 courgette, cut into julienne strips

110 g | 4 oz lean veal or pork, cut into fine julienne strips

1 tablespoon oil

1 × 1 cm | ½ in piece of fresh root ginger, peeled and sliced

1 clove of garlic, peeled and sliced

1 tablespoon soy sauce

salt and freshly ground black pepper

To cook

lightly beaten egg white

oil for deep-frying

1 First make the filling: blanch the beansprouts in boiling water for 15 seconds. Drain and refresh under cold running water. Top and tail the French beans and cut them in half lengthways. Mix the sprouts and beans with the carrots, celery and courgette.

2 Mix in the veal or pork.

3 Heat the oil in a wok or frying pan, add the ginger and garlic and cook over a low heat for 2 minutes. Remove the ginger and garlic – the oil should by now be well infused with their flavour.

4 Turn up the heat and quickly stir-fry the meat and vegetables. Season with the soy sauce, salt and pepper. Remove from the heat and leave to cool.

5 Divide the filling between the spring roll wrappers. Put the filling in the centre of each wrapper and fold 2 opposite corners on top of it. Then roll up from one of the exposed corners to the other to form rolls.

6 Brush the rolls with the beaten egg white.

7 Heat oil in a deep-fryer until a crumb will sizzle vigorously in it and add the spring rolls. Fry until golden-brown, then drain well on absorbent kitchen paper. Sprinkle with salt, and serve.

Chicken and Spring Onion Wontons

MAKES 12

For the stuffing

140 g | 5 oz boneless, skinned chicken meat

5 spring onions, thinly sliced

2 teaspoons soy sauce

a few drops of sesame oil

salt and freshly ground black pepper

110 g | 4 oz packet wonton skins

oil for frying

peanut oil

To garnish

2 tablespoons peanut oil

2 tablespoons sesame seeds

1 teaspoon peeled and grated fresh ginger root

10 spring onions, thinly sliced

1 Make the stuffing: finely chop or process the chicken flesh. Place in a bowl and add the spring onions, soy sauce, sesame oil, salt and pepper. Mix well.
2 Place a teaspoon of the stuffing mixture in the centre of a wonton skin. Brush the edges of the skin with water and place a second skin on top, then press the edges together to seal. Repeat until all the filling and wonton skins are used.
3 Cook the stuffed wonton skins in boiling salted water for 2 minutes. Drain, then refresh under cold running water. When cold, drain well and toss in a little peanut oil.
4 When ready to serve, fry the wontons. Heat 3 tablespoons oil in a frying pan and cook the wontons until golden-brown on both sides. You may well need to add extra oil for each batch of wontons.
5 Prepare the garnish: heat the oil in a frying pan, add the sesame seeds and cook, stirring, until just turning brown. Add the ginger and spring onions and cook for a further minute.
6 Arrange the stuffed wonton skins on a serving dish and scatter the garnish over the top.

Pork and Chinese Leaf Wonton Stuffing

This is an alternative filling for the chicken and spring onion wontons (in the previous recipe).

MAKES 12

225 g | 8 oz Chinese leaves

1 teaspoon salt

freshly ground black pepper

110 g | 4 oz pork, finely chopped

3 spring onions, finely chopped

1 tablespoon sesame oil

1 tablespoon corn oil

1 teaspoon Shaoxing wine or medium-dry sherry

1 Chop the Chinese leaves very finely, discarding any tough stalks, and put into a bowl. Cover with water and add half the salt. Leave for 30 minutes.
2 Mix together the remaining salt, the pepper, pork, spring onions, sesame and corn oil and wine. Beat well.
3 Drain the Chinese leaves, squeeze dry and add to the pork mixture. Mix thoroughly.
4 Follow the recipe above to stuff and cook the wontons.

Peking Duck Pancakes

To save time, try ready-made pancakes from a Chinese supermarket. They can be frozen successfully.

SERVES 6

For the Peking pancakes

450 | 1 lb plain flour

290 ml | ½ pint very hot water

2 tablespoons sesame oil

For the Peking duck

1 oven-ready duckling

1 lemon

1 litre | 1¾ pints water

3 tablespoons clear honey

3 tablespoons soy sauce

150 ml | ¼ pint dry sherry

To serve

hoisin sauce

2 bunches of spring onions, cleaned and cut into thin strips

½ cucumber, cut into thin sticks

1 Prepare the duck the day before cooking. Wash and dry it well with absorbent kitchen paper. Slice the lemon thickly and put it into a saucepan with the water, honey, soy sauce and sherry. Bring to the boil, then simmer for about 30 minutes.

2 Ladle the honey and lemon syrup over the duck several times, until it is completely coated with the mixture. Hang the duck in a cool, well-ventilated place and leave to dry overnight. Place a roasting pan underneath it to catch any drips.

3 The following day, prepare the pancakes: sift the flour into a large bowl. Gradually add enough of the hot water to form a soft but not sticky dough. Knead the dough for 10 minutes until it is soft and smooth, cover it with a damp cloth and leave for 30 minutes.

4 After the dough has rested, knead it again for 5 minutes. Shape it into 2 sausages, each about 30 cm | 12 in long, and cut each roll into 2 cm | 1 in pieces. Shape each piece into a ball.

5 Take 2 balls at a time and dip one side of one ball in the sesame oil, put the oiled side on top of the other ball and roll the 2 together into a 15 cm | 6 in circle.

6 Heat a heavy frying pan or griddle and cook the pancake until it has dried on one side, then cook the other side. Remove from the pan and peel the 2 sides apart. Continue to roll and cook the pancakes. Cover tightly in clingfilm until you are ready to use them.

7 To finish the duck: preheat the oven to 250°C | 500°F | gas mark 9. Place the duck breast-side up on a wire rack. Stand the rack over a roasting pan containing 150 ml | ¼ pint water. Cook the duck for 15 minutes, then reduce the oven temperature to 180°C | 350°F | gas mark 4 and cook for 1 further hour, or until the juices from the cavity are no longer pink. Allow the duck to stand for 10 minutes, then remove the meat from the bone and cut both meat and skin into neat slices. Keep warm.

8 To serve the pancakes: give each guest a tiny dish of hoisin sauce. Dry the spring onion and cucumber well and put into serving dishes. Steam the pancakes to reheat them and serve immediately with the filling. The guests help themselves to duck, spring onions and cucumber (dipped into hoisin sauce if they like) wrap them in the pancakes.

Welsh Rarebit

SERVES 2

55 g	2 oz Gruyère cheese, grated	½ egg, beaten
55 g	2 oz Cheddar cheese, grated	1 tablespoon beer
2 teaspoons French mustard	2 slices of bread
salt and freshly ground black pepper	butter for spreading
cayenne pepper	

1 Preheat the grill.

2 Combine the cheese and mix all but 1 tablespoon with the mustard, salt, pepper, cayenne, egg and beer.

3 Toast the bread and spread with butter.

4 Spoon the cheese mixture on to the toast and spread it neatly, making sure that all the edges are covered.

5 Sprinkle over the remaining cheese and grill until nicely browned.

Sweets and Petits Fours

Chocolate Cherries

These chocolates should be made a week in advance to allow the full flavour of the brandy to be infused into the cherries. You will need 24 small foil cups to make these sweets.

MAKES 24

24 black cherries, pitted	225 g|8 oz good quality plain chocolate
5 tablespoons brandy	170 g|6 oz fondant icing (see page 730)

1 Put the cherries into a bowl. Heat up the brandy and pour it over the cherries. Leave to stand for as long as possible.
2 Break up the chocolate into even pieces and place in a heatproof bowl set over, not in, a saucepan of simmering water. When the chocolate has melted, use a teaspoon to line the little foil cups with it. Pour out any excess chocolate. Leave to dry.
3 Melt the fondant with 2 teaspoons of the brandy from the cherries in a heatproof bowl set over, not in, a saucepan of simmering water.
4 Pour in enough fondant to come a third of the way up each foil cup.
5 Drain the cherries very well. Add one to each cup. Fill almost to the top with more fondant. Leave to harden for 5–10 minutes.
6 Spoon over enough chocolate, swirling it to seal the edges, to cover the fondant icing completely. Leave to cool and harden. Serve in the foil cups.

Marrons Glacés

These chestnuts are time-consuming to prepare, but nicer than the commercially prepared ones.

900 g|2 lb large chestnuts in their skins	570 ml|1 pint water
570 ml|1 pint milk	450 g|1 lb granulated sugar
1 vanilla pod, split	225 ml|8 fl oz liquid glucose

1 Put the chestnuts into a large saucepan and cover with water. Bring to the boil, then simmer gently for 5 minutes. Remove from the heat.
2 Remove the chestnuts one by one and peel, taking care to remove the inner membrane of the chestnut as well as the skin. It is easier to peel the chestnuts while they are still hot.
3 Put the peeled chestnuts into a clean saucepan, pour over the milk and add the vanilla pod. Bring to the boil, then cook the chestnuts over a low heat for 5 minutes, or until completely soft, but not breaking up. Lift the chestnuts out of the milk with a slotted spoon and leave to dry on kitchen paper. Rinse and reserve the vanilla pod.

4 Meanwhile, make the syrup: put the water, sugar and liquid glucose into a saucepan. Dissolve the sugar over a low heat, then bring to the boil. Simmer for 5 minutes. Add the chestnuts to the pan with the vanilla pod and bring back to the boil. Simmer for 1 further minute. Pour the chestnuts and syrup into a bowl and leave to cool overnight.

5 The following day, put the chestnuts back into the saucepan, bring back to the boil and simmer for 1 minute. Cool overnight. Repeat this process once more the following day.

6 Lift the chestnuts out of the syrup with a slotted spoon and leave to drain on a wire rack overnight.

7 Place each chestnut in a petit four case and store in a sealed container in a cool, dry place.

Marzipan Dates

MAKES ABOUT 20

about 20 fresh or dried dates   225 g | 8 oz marzipan (see page 734)

1 Slit the dates lengthways almost in half. Take out the stones carefully, making sure that the dates stay whole.

2 Form the marzipan into a long sausage about 5 mm | 1/4 in in diameter. Cut it into lengths about the size of the dates.

3 Place a piece of marzipan in each date and half-close the opening. Place in tiny paper cases.

NOTE: The marzipan can be coloured pale green by the addition of a few drops of green colouring. Work the colour into the marzipan by kneading with one hand.

Tommies

MAKES ABOUT 20

70 g | 2½ oz caster sugar   140 g | 5 oz plain flour
110 g | 4 oz butter   clear honey
85 g | 3 oz ground hazelnuts   225 g | 8 oz plain chocolate, chopped

1 Preheat the oven to 180°C | 350°F | gas mark 4.

2 Cream the sugar and butter together until white.

3 Stir in the hazelnuts and flour.

4 As soon as the mixture becomes a paste, wrap it and refrigerate for 30 minutes.

5 Roll out thinly and cut into 2.5 cm | 1 in rounds with a biscuit cutter.

6 Place on a baking sheet and bake for 12 minutes. Transfer to a wire rack to cool.

7 Spread honey on half the biscuits, then sandwich them with the others. Return to the cooling rack.

8 Place the chocolate into a bowl over a saucepan of steaming water until it is melted and smooth.

9 Spoon the chocolate over to cover the biscuits completely.

10 Leave until set. If there is enough melted chocolate left, place in a small piping bag fitted with a writing nozzle and pipe a design over the set chocolate. Store in an airtight container.

Nougat

This recipe has been adapted from one by Mary B. Bockmeyer in *Candy and Candy Making*. You need rice paper to make nougat.

MAKES 850 G | 1¾ LB

rice paper

225 g | 8 oz granulated sugar

140 g | 5 oz clear honey

1½ tablespoons liquid glucose

110 ml | 4 fl oz water

2 egg whites

1 teaspoon vanilla essence

285 g | 10 oz blanched almonds, toasted, chopped and warmed

110 g | 4 oz skinned pistachio nuts, chopped and warmed

1 Line a 20 cm | 8 in square tin with rice paper.
2 Put the sugar, honey, liquid glucose and water into a heavy saucepan and stir over a very low heat until the sugar dissolves. Then boil rapidly to the hard crack stage (160°C | 318°F on a sugar thermometer).
3 Whisk the egg whites lightly, and gradually pour on the hot syrup, whisking continuously. Whisk until stiff, then add the vanilla essence and chopped nuts. The mixture must be stiff; if not, place in the top of a double boiler and stir until it dries out a little.
4 Turn into the prepared tin. Cover with a second piece of rice paper. Place a board on top, weight lightly and leave for 1 hour.
5 Cut into diamond shapes to serve.

NOTE: We take the sugar syrup to a very high temperature. This gives the finished sweet a good texture and a very slightly caramelized flavour. For a softer nougat, take the sugar syrup to 155°C | 310°F.

Fudge

oil for greasing

310 g | 11 oz sugar

1 tablespoon liquid glucose

290 ml | ½ pint double cream

110 g | 4 oz butter

1 tablespoon icing sugar, sifted

To flavour

1 vanilla pod, split, or 110 g | 4 oz chocolate couverture, melted

1 Prepare 2 trays with a raised edge 2 cm | ¾ in high all the way round by greasing lightly with oil.
2 Place the sugar, glucose, cream and butter in a large clean, heavy saucepan. (If a vanilla flavour is required, add the pod with other ingredients.) Bring slowly to the boil, stirring frequently.
3 When boiling, allow to cook to 117°C | 243°F.

4 Remove from the heat and very carefully pour into a machine bowl. Allow to stand for 10 minutes. Place on a machine with a balloon whisk and turn on to the lowest speed (remember this mixture is very hot, so be careful to check the speed of machine before switching on).

5 Very carefully add the icing sugar and continue whisking until well mixed in. (If a chocolate flavour is required, add the melted couverture after the icing sugar while still on the machine, and mix well).

6 Now very carefully pour the mixture into the oiled trays, ensuring that they are filled to the top.

7 Allow to cool and set, preferably overnight. Cut the fudge into petit four-sized pieces and serve in paper sweet cases.

Chocolate Truffles

MAKES 24

255 g│9 oz chocolate couverture, roughly chopped   20 g│¾ oz unsalted butter
100 ml│3½ fl oz double cream   cocoa powder, sifted, to finish
1 vanilla pod, split lengthways

1 Melt the chocolate in a heatproof bowl set over, not in, a saucepan of steaming water. Remove from the heat and leave to cool.

2 Put the cream into a saucepan, add the vanilla pod and bring to scalding point (just below boiling). Remove from the heat and leave to cool. Remove the vanilla pod.

3 Beat the butter until very soft. Mix it into the chocolate, add the vanilla cream and refrigerate until firm.

4 Shape into small balls and roll lightly in cocoa powder.

Amaretti Truffles

MAKES ABOUT 40

250 g│9 oz good-quality dark plain chocolate   1 tablespoon golden syrup or liquid glucose
110 ml│4 fl oz double cream   2 tablespoons Amaretto liqueur
55 g│2 oz unsalted butter   110 g│4 oz Amaretti biscuits, finely crushed

1 Chop the chocolate into pea-sized pieces and place in a bowl.

2 Bring the cream to the boil, then pour over the chocolate. Stir to combine. Place over, but not in, a saucepan half-filled with steaming hot water to melt the chocolate completely.

3 Stir in the butter, golden syrup or glucose and Amaretto.

4 Refrigerate for about 10 minutes until starting to thicken.

5 With an electric whisk, beat the mixture for 2 minutes until it lightens in colour, then immediately, stop whisking. Refrigerate for about 10 minutes until firm.

6 Line a baking sheet with baking parchment. Use a piping bag fitted with a plain nozzle to pipe small moulds of the mixture on to the paper, or use a teaspoon to mound the mixture into rounded teaspoonfuls. Do not worry if they are not perfectly round.

7 To crush the Amaretti biscuits, place them in a plastic bag and bash with a rolling pin. Place the crushed biscuits on a dinner plate. Use a fork to roll the truffles in the crushed biscuits. Store in a tightly covered container in a cool place.

Whisky Truffles

MAKES 24

225 g | 8 oz milk chocolate

4 tablespoons double cream

3 tablespoons whisky

30 g | 1 oz unsalted butter

sifted cocoa powder, to finish

1 Break the chocolate into even pieces and melt in a heatproof bowl set over, not in, a saucepan of simmering water.

2 In another saucepan, bring the cream to the boil, then remove from the heat and mix with the melted chocolate.

3 When well mixed, add the whisky and beat in the butter.

4 Refrigerate until firm.

5 Roll the mixture into a sausage shape, slice crossways and roll into balls the size of a walnut. Toss in the cocoa powder.

Coffee and Orange Mini Meringues

MAKES 20

For the meringues

3 egg whites

170 g | 6 oz soft light brown sugar

1 teaspoon instant coffee powder

For the filling

425 ml | $\frac{3}{4}$ pint double cream

1 tablespoon Grand Marnier

grated zest of 1 orange

1 Preheat the oven to 110°C | 225°F | gas mark $\frac{1}{2}$.

2 Line 4 baking sheets with non-stick baking parchment.

3 Whisk the egg whites until stiff but not dry.

4 Gradually add $1\frac{1}{2}$ tablespoons of the sugar and whisk again until stiff and very shiny.

5 Whisk in the remaining sugar gradually, with the instant coffee powder.

6 Put the meringue into a piping bag fitted with 1 cm | $\frac{1}{2}$ in plain nozzle. Pipe the meringue into small whirls.

7 Bake in the preheated oven for about 2 hours until the meringues are dry and will lift easily off the paper. Leave to cool.

8 Whip the cream and fold in the Grand Marnier and orange zest. Sandwich the meringues together in pairs.

NOTE: See 'Whisking egg whites', page 669.

Bâtons Maréchaux

MAKES 25–30

5 egg whites

110 g | 4 oz caster sugar

30 g | 1 oz plain flour

110 g | 4 oz ground almonds

55 g | 2 oz nibbed almonds

apricot jam, for filling

1 Preheat the oven to 190°C | 375°F | gas mark 5.

2 Whisk the egg whites until stiff but not dry. Gradually whisk in half the sugar and whisk again until very stiff and shiny.

3 Mix together the remaining sugar, the flour and ground almonds, and fold into the meringue.

4 Place the meringue in a piping bag fitted with a ½ cm | ¼ in plain nozzle and pipe 5 cm | 2 in lengths on to baking sheets lined with non-stick baking parchment.

5 Sprinkle with nibbed almonds. Shake the trays to make the almonds stick to the meringues.

6 Bake for 45 minutes until crisp.

7 Sandwich the biscuits together in pairs with apricot jam.

NOTE: Instead of sandwiching together with jam, the back of each biscuit may be coated with melted chocolate and decorated by marking with a comb scraper or the tines of a fork. (Two coats of chocolate may have to be applied to obtain a good finish.)

Orange Tartlets

MAKES 24

170 g | 6 oz flour quantity rich shortcrust pastry (see page 559)

For the candied orange zest

1 medium orange

340 g | 12 oz granulated sugar

3 tablespoons liquid glucose

6 tablespoons water

For the orange curd

1 large orange

1 medium lemon

55 g | 2 oz unsalted butter

110 g | 4 oz caster sugar

4 egg yolks, lightly beaten

1 First make the candied orange zest: remove the zest from the orange with a potato peeler or small sharp knife and cut into 5 mm | ¼ in strips. Put into a small saucepan with enough water to cover and boil for 5 minutes to remove the bitter taste. Drain and refresh under running cold water.

2 Bring 225 g | 8 oz of the sugar, the liquid glucose and water to the boil in the saucepan. Remove from the heat and stir in the zest. Allow to stand for 30 minutes. Bring the liquid back to the boil and allow to stand for a further 30 minutes. Remove the zest with a fork and transfer to a wire rack to cool.

3 Put the remaining sugar on a plate and roll the orange strips in it. Once they are dry they can be stored in an airtight container at room temperature for up to a week.

4 Preheat the oven to 180°C|350°F|gas mark 4.

5 Line small tartlet tins or petit four tins with the pastry. Prick with a fork and chill in the refrigerator to relax.

6 Bake the tartlet cases blind for 10 minutes (see page 557). Remove the lining paper and beans and bake until the pastry is dry and light brown. Cool.

7 Next make the curd: grate the zest of the orange and half the lemon on the finest gauge of the grater, taking care to grate only the zest, not the pith.

8 Squeeze the juice from the orange and lemon.

9 Put the zest, juice, butter, sugar and egg yolks into a heavy saucepan or double boiler and heat gently, stirring all the time, until the mixture is thick.

10 Strain into a bowl and allow to cool.

11 To assemble: using a piping bag fitted with a very small plain nozzle, pipe a round of curd into each shell. Cut the orange zest into small diamonds and use to decorate the tartlets.

Tiny Bakewell Tarts

MAKES 36

225 g|8 oz flour quantity rich shortcrust pastry (see page 559)

For the raspberry purée
225 g|8 oz raspberries
2 tablespoons Framboise liqueur

For the frangipane
100 g|3½ oz butter
100 g|3½ oz caster sugar

1 egg, beaten
1 egg yolk
100 g|3½ blanched almonds, ground
2 tablespoons plain flour
2 drops of almond essence

For the feather icing
200 g|7 oz icing sugar
boiling water
red food colouring

1 Line 6 × 8 cm|3½ in tartlet tins with the rich shortcrust pastry. Chill thoroughly.

2 Preheat the oven to 200°C|400°F|gas mark 6.

3 Make the raspberry purée: put the raspberries into a small saucepan and bring to the boil. Add the Framboise and boil to reduce to a thick purée. Push through a nylon sieve and leave to cool.

4 Make the frangipane: cream the butter and when soft add the sugar and beat again until the mixture is light and fluffy.

5 Gradually add the egg and the egg yolk, beating well after each addition. Stir in the ground almonds and the flour. Set aside.

6 Spread a little of the raspberry purée on to the base of each pastry case. Pile in the frangipane mixture and spread evenly with a palette knife.

7 Place the tartlets on a baking sheet and bake in the preheated oven for 20–25 minutes, or until the filling is set and the pastry crisp.

8 Allow the tartlets to cool completely, then remove from the tins.

9 Make the icing: sift the icing sugar into a bowl and add enough boiling water to mix to a soft coating consistency. The icing should hold a trail when dropped from a spoon, but gradually find its own level.

10 Take 2 tablespoons of the icing and colour it with the food colouring. Place in a piping bag fitted with a fine writing nozzle.

11 Spread the remaining icing smoothly and evenly over the top of each tartlet, using a warm palette knife.

12 While the icing is still wet, quickly pipe lines of coloured icing about 5 mm | ½ in apart across the top of each tartlet.

13 Now draw lines at right angles to the coloured lines with a cocktail stick, dragging the tip through the coloured lines to pull them to points.

14 Allow the icing to set very slightly and cut each tartlet into 6 pieces. Arrange on a serving plate.

Chocolate Mint Crisps

450 g | 1 lb good-quality dark chocolate   225 g | 8 oz demerara sugar
2 teaspoons peppermint essence

1 Place the chocolate and the peppermint essence in a bowl set over, but not in, a saucepan of steaming water. Stir occasionally so that the chocolate melts evenly.

2 Allow the mixture to cool so that it is no longer warm to the touch, but still fluid.

3 Stir in the sugar. Spread the mixture thinly over a large piece of baking parchment. Place another piece of parchment over the top and roll with a rolling pin to an even thinness.

4 Refrigerate until set.

5 When the chocolate is firm but not brittle, cut into individual pieces.

Drinks

Mulled Wine

The important ingredient in mulled wine is, rather surprisingly, the water. Without it it can be far too rich and sickly. This recipe is just a guideline and can be altered according to individual tastes.

4 × 75 cl bottles of full-bodied red wine
1.7 litres|3 pints water
20 cloves, wrapped up in muslin or a 'J' cloth
3 oranges, sliced

3 lemons, sliced
225 g|8 oz granulated sugar, or more according to taste
2 cinnamon sticks

Put all the ingredients into a large saucepan and dissolve the sugar over a low heat. Bring up to simmering point and keep warm for at least 15 minutes. Do not boil or the alcohol will evaporate.

Champagne Cocktail

sugar lumps
Angostura bitters
brandy

champagne or sparkling white wine such as Saumur or an Australian, chilled

1 Put a sugar lump in each glass and add a couple of drops of Angostura bitters and 1 teaspoon brandy.
2 Just before serving, pour on the chilled champagne to fill the glasses.

Bellini

The most cheerful drink of all – the classic of Harry's Bar.

Simply mix peach juice and champagne in equal quantities. If you add the champagne to the juice, the bubbles will last considerably longer.

NOTE: It is possible to buy cartons or cans of peach juice.

Apple Punch

1 litre | 1¾ pints apple juice
5 cm | 2 in piece of fresh root ginger, peeled
2 red dessert apples

1 litre | 1¾ pints dry ginger ale
ice

1 Put the apple juice into a large bowl. Bruise the ginger with a rolling pin. Quarter, core and thinly slice the apples and add with the ginger to the apple juice. Leave to marinate overnight or for at least 2 hours.

2 Remove the ginger and add the dry ginger ale just before serving. Chill with ice cubes.

NOTE: If a clear punch is wanted, use clear apple juice. English apple juice is cloudy but is less sweet.

Cider Punch

This is deceptively alcoholic.

150 ml | ¼ pint brandy, chilled
1.1 litres | 2 pints dry sparkling cider, well chilled
2 dessert apples, cored and sliced

1 orange, sliced
a few sprigs of fresh mint

Pour the brandy into a jug. Add the cider, fruit and mint.

NOTE: This should be served really well chilled. If a sweeter punch is preferred, use a medium-dry cider.

Wassail Cup

This warming brew is traditionally served around Christmas time as a welcome drink. It looks wonderful presented in a large china bowl with lightly baked apples floating on the top.

1.7 litres | 3 pints brown ale
225 g | 8 oz soft light brown sugar
1 cinnamon stick
½ teaspoon freshly grated nutmeg

½ teaspoon ground ginger
1 lemon, thinly sliced
350 ml | 12 fl oz medium-dry sherry

1 Place 570 ml | 1 pint of the ale in a large pan. Add the sugar and cinnamon stick and bring to the boil, stirring all the time to dissolve the sugar.

2 Add the spices, lemon, sherry and the remaining ale. Warm through but do not boil. Allow 150 ml | ¼ pint per person.

A Note on the Authors

Prue Leith was the founder of the prestigious Leiths Restaurant, Leiths School of Food and Wine and Leiths Ltd, a catering company founded in 1961. She has been a prolific contributor to the press, TV and radio and is the author of many cookbooks. In 1989 she was awarded the OBE for services to good food, and in 1991 she won the Veuve Clicquot Award for Businesswoman of the Year. Prue was married to the author Rayne Kruger and is now writing novels.

Caroline Waldegrave joined Prue's catering company in 1971 and helped set up the school in 1975. Caroline was the Principal and Managing Director until 1993 when she became the co-owner with Christopher Bland. In 2002 Jenny Stringer became the school's principal. Caroline has written numerous cookery books. Formerly a member of the Health Education Authority (1983–7), and ex-Chair of the Guild of Food Writers, she is also a qualified instructor in wine. In June 2000 she was awarded the OBE for services to the catering industry. She lives in London and Somerset with her husband and their four children.

Susan Spaull trained as a chef at Cordon Bleu and Leiths School of Food and Wine. After running her own catering and cooking demonstration business for 10 years, Susan returned to Leiths as teacher and demonstrator.

Leiths School of Food and Wine was established to provide professional training for career cooks and short courses for amateurs. The school offers comprehensive theoretical and practical teaching, qualifying students to enter the highly competitive food and wine business and begin a rewarding career. There is a commitment to classical techniques and methods but with a fresh and modern approach. The guiding principle of the teaching at Leiths School is to impart enthusiasm for the trade and instil a lasting love of good food and wine in the students.

If you would like details of any of the courses at the school, you may get in touch with Jenny Stringer at Leiths School of Food and Wine, 21 St Alban's Grove, London, W8 5BP, tel. 020 7229 0177 or 020 7937 3366 or look at our website www.leiths.com.

Index

The handbook of psychotherapy

Psycho... ...ok of
Psycho... ...many
aspects ...practi-
tioners ...roach
or opi... Each
brings ...ension
of the ...rmed
picture
Pres... ...y and
its rese... ...ffers a
rich so
The ...uding
nurses ...apists
in trai... ...eking
psycho ...e who
need o

Petrūs... ...al and
counse... ...rative
psycho ...aining
Institu... ...erapy.
She is ...sycho-
therap ...air of
the Br... ...erapy
Integra... ...rd of
Examiners for the Diploma in Counselling Psychology.

Michael Pokorny, MB, ChB, DPM, FRCPsych., Member Brit. Psi.-An.
Soc., is a psychoanalyst and psychoanalytic psychotherapist. He is a
member of the Council of the London Centre for Psychotherapy and is
current Chair of the Registration Board of the United Kingdom Council
for Psychotherapy. He is past Chair of the United Kingdom Standing
Conference for Psychotherapy. 141952

The handbook of psychotherapy

Edited by
Petrūska Clarkson
and
Michael Pokorny

London and New York

First published 1994
by Routledge
11 New Fetter Lane, London EC4P 4EE

Simultaneously published in the USA and Canada
by Routledge
29 West 35th Street, New York, NY 10001

Reprinted 1995

Typeset in Times by J&L Composition Ltd, Filey, North Yorkshire
Printed and bound in Great Britain by
Biddles Ltd, Guildford and King's Lynn

British Library Cataloguing in Publication Data
A catalogue record for this book is available from the British Library

Library of Congress Cataloguing in Publication Data
A catalogue record for this book is available from the Library of Congress

ISBN 0–415–07722–2 (hbk)
ISBN 0–415–07723–0 (pbk)

Contents

Illustrations

The dying and the bereaved

Appendix A

TABLES

Nature and range

Family

Communities

Sexual contact

Contributors

Nachman Alon, MA, is a Clinical Psychologist in private practice in Tel Aviv, Israel. His main therapeutic interest is the integration of several modes of psychotherapy, including hypnosis. He gained experience of PTSD patients during several years of military service both as a commander and as a psychologist.

Talia Levine Bar-Yoseph, MA (Hons Clin. Psych.) is a Clinical Psychologist and Psychotherapist and is currently Director of the Gestalt Programme at **metanoia** Psychotherapy Training Institute. She trained at the Gestalt Training Centre in San Diego and at the Gestalt Institute of Los Angeles, and is a consultant in Organisational Behaviour.

Michael Barkham, MA, MSc, PhD, is a Research Clinical Psychologist at the MRC/ESRC Social and Applied Psychology Unit, University of Sheffield, and has published scientific papers in the areas of psychotherapy, clinical psychology and counselling psychology. He is currently engaged in several major psychotherapy studies and has particular interests in the areas of research design and methodology, brief psychotherapies and service evaluation. He was the recipient of the British Psychological Society's May Davidson Award for 1991 in recognition of his contribution to clinical psychology, and is currently UK Vice-President of the International Society for Psychotherapy Research.

Arnon Bentovim, MB, BS, FRCPsych., DPM, is Consultant Psychiatrist in Child and Adolescent Psychiatry at the Hospital for Sick Children, Great Ormond Street, and the Tavistock Clinic, London, having trained in psychiatry and psychotherapy at the Maudsley Hospital. He trained as a psychoanalyst and has been interested in the development of family therapy approaches since the early 1970s. He was a founder and chair of both the Association and Institute of Family Therapy and was closely associated with the Group Analytic Society and Institute of Group Analysis where he helped found the first Family Therapy course with Dr Robin Skynner. He has been concerned with child protection matters for some years and helped to set up the first sexual abuse treatment project in the United Kingdom in 1980; he has written extensively in this field, most recently *Trauma-Organized Systems: Systemic Understanding of Family Violence* (Karnac, 1992).

Janet Bungener, MEd, MACP, is a Psychoanalytic Child Psychotherapist working in Wood Green Child and Family Consultation Centre and Haringey Child Development Centre. She has a special interest in psychodynamic work with children and families with learning and physical disabilities as well as autism. She is a visiting teacher at the Tavistock Clinic for various courses concerning learning disability.

Gillian Butler, PhD, CPsychol., after qualifying as a clinical psychologist, worked as a therapist in the NHS offering short-term psychological treatment to patients referred to a busy out-patient department. She then held a research post in Oxford University Department of Psychiatry for nine years, and specialised in the development and evaluation of treatments for the more complex and long-standing anxiety disorders. In addition, she has trained as a cognitive therapist and has always been interested in developing a wide range of clinical skills. She now works for the NHS again, and divides her time between therapy, supervision, training, teaching and writing.

Petrūska Clarkson, MA, PhD, is a Chartered Clinical Psychologist and practising psychotherapist, supervisor and organisational consultant. She is Principal Clinical Psychologist of the **metanoia** Psychotherapy Training Institute in London. She was Chair for the British Institute of Integrative Psychotherapy (BIIP), which is affiliated with the Society for Exploration of Psychotherapy Integration (SEPI International). She has written numerous papers in the field of psychotherapy, supervision, counselling and organisations, and several books, amongst which are *Transactional Analysis Psychotherapy: An Integrated Approach* (Routledge, 1992), *Gestalt Counselling in Action* (Sage, 1989), *On Psychotherapy* (Whurr, 1993) and *The Therapeutic Relationship* (Wiley, in press).

Alan Cooklin, MB, ChB, FRCPsych., DPM, is Consultant in Family Psychiatry at the Marlborough Family Service and University College and the Middlesex Hospitals, and Honorary Senior Lecturer at University College London, and Birkbeck College, London. He was Chairman of the MSc degree course in Family Therapy between the Institute of Family Therapy and Birkbeck College. He is currently Chair of the Institute of Family Therapy and Clinical Director in the North-west London Mental Health NHS Trust.

Louise Embleton Tudor, Adv. Cert. Biodynamic Massage, Dip. Dram. Art, Dip. Ed., Dip. Psychotherapy, ITHP, is an Integrative Psychotherapist. She worked in further education and in the mental health field before training at the Minster Centre for Analytic and Humanistic Psychotherapy, and is a member of the Institute for Traditional and Humanistic Psychotherapy.

She has undertaken further training in Biodynamic Massage at the Chiron Centre for Holistic Psychotherapy and in the Supervision of Counsellors and Psychotherapists at **metanoia** Psychotherapy Training Institute, and has recently established herself in Sheffield as a freelance psychotherapist, supervisor, trainer and consultant.

Sheila Ernst, BA, CertEd, Member Inst. Group Analysis, has worked at the Women's Therapy Centre in London for many years. She is in private practice as a member of the Group Analytic Network and trains counsellors and psychotherapists. She is co-author (with Lucy Goodison) of *In Our Own Hands* (Women's Press, 1981) and co-editor (with Marie Maguire) of *Living with the Sphinx: Papers from the Women's Therapy Centre* (Women's Press, 1987).

Alexandra Fanning trained as a psychoanalytic psychotherapist with the Arbours Association and has held a number of posts within it. She founded and was first Chair of the Arbours Association of Psychotherapists. Having been for many years on the Arbours Training Committee, she is currently the Director of Training. She is also a delegate to the UKCP, having been delegate to the prior organisations, the UKSCP and the original Rugby Psychotherapy Conference, where she was a member of the Working Party and the first treasurer in the period leading up to the inauguration of the UK Standing Conference for Psychotherapy. She is in full-time private practice as a psychoanalytic psychotherapist with a special interest in conjoint marital psychotherapy.

Tanya Garrett, BA, MSc, CPsychol., AFBPsS, is a Chartered Clinical Psychologist and Associate Fellow of the British Psychological Society. She works as a Clinical Psychologist with Walsall Community Health Trust where she manages the Clinical Psychology Service to children, young people and families and provides a psychotherapy resource for the Clinical Psychology Department. She is currently undertaking PhD research at the University of Warwick in the field of sexual contact between psychotherapists and their patients.

Gill Gorell Barnes, MA, MSc, is Senior Clinical Lecturer in the Child and Family Department of the Tavistock Clinic, Consultant to the Training Department at the Institute of Family Therapy, and was previously Director of Training at the Institute for many years.

David Gowling, Dip. Soc. Stud. (Oxford), CQSW, initially worked in industry for twelve years. After qualifying as a social worker, he specialised in work with adolescents, with child abuse and in mental health. During this period he trained and qualified as a psychotherapist. Currently he has a private psychotherapy practice and is involved in both the training and supervision of counsellors and psychotherapists. He is a qualified

Transactional Analysis Clinician and a Provisional Teaching and Supervising Transactional Analyst (with Clinical Speciality).

Pat Grant, MSc (Counselling Psychology), BEd (Hons), RNT, DN, RMN, SCM, RGN, is a Senior Lecturer at the University of Greenwich, London, where she lectures in education and counselling psychology. She is a Counselling Psychologist involved in counselling and supervision. She is a black woman who has done a lot of work with black clients and black supervisees in England. One of her many interests in the field of counselling is working with bereaved clients.

Helena Hargaden, BA (Hons), PGCE, CTA, CIP, BAC Accredited Counsellor, has a psychotherapy and supervision practice in South-east London and is a Primary Tutor on the Diploma in Counselling course at **metanoia** Psychotherapy Training Institute. Previously she was a lecturer in communication studies.

Peter Harper, BSocSc, BA (Hons), MSc (Clinical Psychology), AFBPsS, is a Consultant Clinical Psychologist working in the Child Health Directorate, Northampton. He has a wide range of experience as a clinician, psychotherapist, trainer and supervisor, both in the United Kingdom and abroad. He is a member of several professional organisations and is on the Editorial Board of *The Child Care Worker*, a journal to which he has made a number of contributions on working therapeutically with children.

Judith Hassan, BSc (Hons), CQSW, Dip. App. Soc. Stud., began work at the Jewish Welfare Board in 1969. Since 1977 she has specialised in working with survivors of the Nazi Holocaust, and has chaired the Survivor Centre Steering Group. In 1990 she became Director of Shalvata (Jewish Care), a therapy centre for adults with emotional difficulties, and in 1992 Chair of the Management Committee of the new Centre for Holocaust Survivors in Hendon, and she maintains management responsibility for both centres. In 1992 she organised the European Conference for Professionals Working with Survivors. She has published numerous papers on survivors, presented work on radio and television, and teaches rabbis, hospital staff, social services and Jewish organisations.

Peter Hawkins, BA(Hons), MAHPP, PhD, is Organisational Consultant and founding Partner of Bath Consultancy Group, through whom he works with a wide variety of organisations. He is also a psychotherapist and founder of the Bath Centre for Psychotherapy and Counselling. He is co-author with Robin Shohet of *Supervision in the Helping Professions* (Open University Press, 1989).

Paul Hitchings, MSc, BSc, PGCE, Chartered Psychologist, Accredited Counsellor (BAC), is a practising counselling psychologist with over ten years' experience of working with clients individually, in couples and in group settings. His practice also includes training and supervision of counsellors, teaching counselling psychology in academic settings on undergraduate and postgraduate programs and consultancy work for staff teams in the helping professions.

Robert Jezzard, MA, MRCP, FRCPsych., is a Consultant Child and Adolescent Psychiatrist based at the Bloomfield Clinic, Guy's Hospital. He works in the context of a multidisciplinary team of mental health professionals, primarily with young people and their families from Southeast London. Although he is based in a hospital, he sees many of the young people in community settings in addition to the clinic.

Adele Kosviner, MSc, AFBPsS, CPsychol., is a Consultant Clinical Psychologist working within the National Health Service in Riverside Mental Health Trust, London. She is at present Chair of the British Psychological Society's Psychotherapy Section and representative of the Society to its Joint Standing Committee with the Royal College of Psychiatrists and to the United Kingdom Council for Psychotherapy.

Tom Leary is a priest in the Church of England. He trained in couples work with the National Marriage Guidance Council, St George's Hospital, and at the Tavistock Institute of Marital Studies. At present he is co-ordinator of family and marital work at Westminster Pastoral Foundation, and also works in private practice.

Christine Lister-Ford, BEd, Dip. Hum. Psych., Training and Supervising Transactional Analyst (ITAA), Recognised Supervisor (BAC), is a director of Stockton Psychotherapy Training Institute where she co-ordinates the four-year psychotherapy training in Transactional Analysis. She is Chairperson of the Training Standards Committee of the Institute of Transactional Analysis. She has maintained a private practice for thirteen years.

Sara Llewellin, BA (Hons), PGCE, is currently the Director of St Giles Trust – a voluntary sector agency providing services for homeless people in South London. She has been active in women's, lesbian and anti-racist politics. She is studying TA at **metanoia** Psychotherapy Training Institute.

James Low, PhD, works as a psychotherapist, supervisor and trainer at the Monroe Clinic, Guy's Hospital and in private practice.

Brendan McCormack, MB, BCh, LRCP & SI, MSc Clinical Psychotherapy, MRC Psych., trained in psychiatry at St Thomas and Guy's Hospitals in London. He is Clinical Director and Consultant Psychiatrist at Cheeverstown House, Templeogue in Dublin. He has worked as Consultant Psychiatrist (Mental Handicap) at the Harperbury Hospital and for Haringey Health Authority's Services for People with Learning Difficulties, at St Anne's Hospital in London, and was also a visiting teacher and member of the Mental Handicap Workshop at the Tavistock Clinic.

Oded Manor, BA, PhD, PGDip. App. Soc. Studies and CQSW Dip. Counselling Skills, is Principal Lecturer in Social Work at Middlesex University, London. Previously a Senior Practitioner for group and family work, he continues to supervise group workers and has published numerous papers on the subject. For over twenty years he has been engaged in lecturing and consultancy in various other countries as well.

David Millard, MA, MB, ChB, FRCPsych., is honorary Consultant Psychiatrist to Oxfordshire Health Authority and Emeritus Fellow of Green College, Oxford. He recently retired after twenty years as Lecturer in Applied Social Studies, University of Oxford and consultant at Warneford Hospital. He was previously editor of the *International Journal of Therapeutic Communities*.

Eric Miller, MA, PhD (Cantab), carried out anthropological fieldwork in India and Thailand and was an internal consultant to textile companies in the United States and India before joining the Tavistock Institute in 1958. His main field is organisational research and consultancy, combining systemic and psychodynamic perspectives, and he has worked with a wide variety of organisations in the United Kingdom and internationally. He has also been director of the Institute's Group Relations Programme since 1969. His published output includes numerous papers and six books.

Colin Murray Parkes, MD, FRCPsych., is Honorary Consultant Psychiatrist to the Royal London Hospital and to St Christopher's Hospice, Sydenham. He is author of *Bereavement: Studies of Grief in Adult Life* (Pelican/IUP, 1986), and of numerous papers on the psychological aspects of bereavement, crisis, amputation of a limb and terminal cancer care. He is President of Cruse (Bereavement Care), Scientific Editor of *Bereavement Care* and editorial advisor on numerous journals concerned with hospices and bereavement.

Haya Oakley, BA, PSW, UKCP Reg. Psy. Psychotherapist, was born and educated in Israel, where she graduated as a psychiatric social worker from the Hebrew University of Jerusalem. She is a training committee member of the Philadelphia Association and Chair of the Guild of Psychotherapists. She works as a Psychoanalytic Psychotherapist in private practice and has worked as a community therapist in PA Houses. She appeared on the Channel 4 series *A Change of Mind*, and BBC Radio 4's 'Room to Listen, Room to Talk', and has contributed to 'Thresholds between Philosophy and Psychoanalysis', FAB, London 1989. She was honorary secretary of the UKCP.

Miranda Passey, BA, CQSW, MACP, is Principal Clinical Psychotherapist on the Isle of Wight. She trained at the Tavistock Clinic and has a particular interest in developing awareness of the work of Child Psychotherapists in order to reach a greater number of children in difficulties than is at present possible. As well as her work in the Health Service, she works in a school for children with speech and language difficulties.

Michael Pokorny, MB, ChB, DPM, FRCPsych., Member Brit. Psi.-An. Soc., trained in medicine and psychiatry before training in psychoanalysis and psychoanalytic psychotherapy with adults: individual, group and marital. He was Chair of the Rugby Psychotherapy Conference Working Party from 1982 until the inauguration of the United Kingdom Standing Conference for Psychotherapy in 1989. He was elected Chair of UKSCP annually from 1989 until 1993, when he was appointed to be the first Chair of the Registration Board of the United Kingdom Council for Psychotherapy. He is in full-time private practice as a Psychoanalyst and Psychotherapist with a special interest in conjoint marital psychotherapy.

Charlotte Sills, MA, DipIntegrative Psychotherapy, TSTA (ITAA), is a UKCP registered psychotherapist in private practice and works as a trainer and consultant in a variety of settings, including the National Institute of Social Work and various counselling organisations. Her particular interest has been in bereavement and loss, and for four years she ran the Hounslow Social Services' Bereavement Project. She is also committed to the psychotherapeutic use of groups. She is a qualified Transactional Analysis clinician and a Teaching and Supervising Transactional Analyst (with Clinical Speciality). She is Director of the T.A. Psychotherapy Training Programme at **metanoia** Psychotherapy Training Institute.

Jonathan Smith, LLB, CQSW, Dip. App. Soc. Stud., Dip. Psychotherapy, studied law at Warwick University, then trained as a social worker and obtained a CQSW from Sheffield University. He worked for five years as a social worker for the London Borough of Hounslow, before training as a psychotherapist at the Institute of Psychotherapy and Social Studies. For a further five years he worked on a project to develop counselling and psychotherapy for social services clients in Hounslow, and now works full-time as a psychotherapist and supervisor, and as a tutor on a counselling course at Birkbeck College, University of London.

Kenneth Kirk Smith, MA (Oxon), Dip. App. Soc. Stud. (London), read law at Brasenose College, Oxford, and after two years Voluntary Service Overseas in India, trained to be a social worker at Bedford College, London. In 1967, he began to work with the London Probation Service at the Old Street Magistrates Court in Hackney. In 1970, he became a child-care worker in Barnet. After the local government re-organisation following the Seebohm Report, he spent a year at the Tavistock Clinic on the full-time social work course. After this, he worked for the Family Welfare Association for ten years, and for Wandsworth Social Services for a further eight. Facing another reorganisation, he took early retirement, and spent a year at the LSE as a social worker with a group of people researching new religious movements. He now works with the Church Army as a social worker, at the Marylebone Project which is in the forefront of the problem of homelessness. He is a member of BASW, and was chair of GAPS for six years. He is treasurer of the United Kingdom Council for Psychotherapy.

Keith Tudor, MA, CQSW, is a qualified social worker and has worked in the mental health field for a number of years. He has completed four years of clinical training as a Transactional Analysis psychotherapist and is studying on the Gestalt in Organisations programme; both at **metanoia** Psychotherapy Training Institute, where for the last three years he has been a primary tutor on the BAC-recognised Person-Centred Counselling Course, and is a BAC Accredited Counsellor. He is an Honorary Research Fellow at King's College, University of London. He has a private practice in Sheffield, offering counselling and psychotherapy as well as training, consultancy and research.

Marianne Tranter, BSc, CQSW, Psychiatric Social Worker, Family Therapist, trained in social work at the London School of Economics and had placements at the Maudsley Hospital, where she trained in family therapy initially with Dr Robin Skynner. She has worked in community mental health and child protection teams and was concerned with the founding of family therapy workshops in the community. She has worked at the Hospital for Sick Children for twelve years and has worked in a variety of teams, co-founding the Child Sexual Abuse Team with Arnon Bentovim. She is concerned with integrating individual and family approaches, and she and Arnon Bentovim have been involved with training throughout the United Kingdom and internationally. She also works in private practice.

Gillian Walton, MA, Dip. Ed., after careers in social work and teaching, trained as a marital therapist with the National Marriage Guidance Council and the Tavistock Institute for Marital Studies. She is Head of Training and Supervision at London Marriage Guidance, and works in private practice as a therapist and consultant.

Estela V. Welldon, MD, FRCPsych., is President of the International Association for Forensic Psychotherapy; Consultant Psychotherapist at the Portman Clinic; founding Director of the Forensic Psychotherapy Diploma Course; and an Honorary Lecturer in Forensic Psychotherapy at the British Postgraduate Medical Federation (University of London). She is the author of *Mother, Madonna, Whore: The Idealisation and Denigration of Motherhood* (1988). She has specialised in the application of group analysis to social and sexual deviancy and has written several papers on these subjects. She is a member of the Board of Directors of the International Association of Group Psychotherapy. She also works in private practice and is Consultant to professional women's groups.

Jenifer Elton Wilson, BA, MSc, is a Chartered Psychologist whose work as a psychotherapist has been focused on the recent establishment and provision of counselling psychology within the UK. Having both studied and taught counselling psychology at Master's level, she is currently Head of an expanded counselling service at the new University of the West of England, Bristol. She is Chair of the British Psychological Society Special Group in Counselling Psychology. Her main interest is in the interface between personal meanings and the impossible struggle for excellence in the practice of psychological therapy.

Preface

Petrūska Clarkson and Michael Pokorny

THE BACKGROUND

From our differing but complementary backgrounds, we have shared the idea of a *Handbook of Psychotherapy* for some time. As far back as 1990, Bob Hinshelwood was prescient by linking our two names together in working to push forward the frontiers of psychotherapy in our respective ways. In an editorial of the *British Journal of Psychotherapy*, he wrote:

> If the Standing Conference (UKSCP) shows signs of cohering into a proper professional organisation at last it is because of years of cool (though sometimes impatient) debate. The Conference has become a forum where those who would never normally feel inclined to speak to each other have sat down and shared passionate hopes together. Michael Pokorny's letter, as chairman of the Conference, marks steady progress in the political organisation of psychotherapy in this country and in Europe.
>
> Politics is one thing: perhaps, however, we are still a long way from a similar engagement over differences of theory and practice. However Petrūska Clarkson's careful analysis of the various levels of the psychotherapeutic relationship is an attempt to find a perspective from which an overview might become possible. She contends that all therapeutic relationships have five levels even though the different psychotherapies prioritise different levels. This offers a way of circumventing the inherent contradictions and incompatibilities that exist between different psychotherapies; instead of compatibilities we have different priorities and emphasis. And this leaves a way open for the beginnings of a possible integration of the psychotherapies.
>
> (Hinshelwood 1990: 119)

Although the idea for this book was first mooted by Routledge to Petrūska in 1989, it has taken several years to come to maturity. It was when Michael Pokorny joined as co-editor that a dialogic relationship was formed which provided the necessary impetus for carrying it to completion.

The original idea for the *Handbook* was to provide a reasonably comprehensive overview of the field of psychotherapy which was accessible enough to the intelligent lay person; as well as useful enough for people who may wish to use or refer in terms of these services (such as general practitioners, social workers and employers), and serious enough to be interesting to practitioners, trainers and supervisors in the field of psychotherapy.

THE *HANDBOOK*: BACKGROUND

The *Handbook* is divided into five parts: Introductions, Culture, Modalities, Settings and Issues. The three chapters in the introductions series constitute a scene-setting: first comes 'The nature and range of psychotherapy', which surveys (1) the different professions involved in this field such as counsellors, psychotherapists and counselling psychologists (differentiating them from adjacent disciplines), (2) the three different ideological traditions or 'schools' in psychotherapy, and (3) presents a map for conceptualising the different modalities of psychotherapy. The second chapter is a version of the paper 'The multiplicity of psychotherapeutic relationships'. It is this paper which first appeared in the *British Journal of Psychotherapy*, and which Hinshelwood introduced above as having 'the potential for the beginnings of a possible integration', or at the very least a framework within which to begin to communicate across the inevitable schisms, suspicions and territorial disputes of different schools. Even at the end of this book it became clear that, throughout most of the chapters, there was a constant implicit, if not explicit, awareness and exploration of the importance of the therapeutic relationship.

Contrary to the usual procedure of putting the research chapter last, or towards the end, we acceded to the request of Wilson and Barker to position the research paper near the beginning as the third chapter. This chapter could, in addition to the relationship paper, act as an initial prism to highlight a perspective through which to view all the chapters that follow, rather than being an afterthought.

We believe that cultural issues in psychotherapy have been significantly neglected compared to theoretical disputations, and that the influence of such factors is vastly underrated in many of the approaches to psychotherapy that tend to be Eurocentric, patriarchal and limiting. That is why cultural issues are separately grouped in Part II of the book. Here, from her vast experience, Grant explores some of the issues of psychotherapy and race. Ernst and Gowling, from their different perspectives, address the influence of gender on psychotherapy – the counter-transference issues which are so enormous that none of us, however conscious, can consider ourselves free from the pernicious influences of the sexism that has pervaded the theory, practice and management of psychotherapy. In

Chapter 6, Hassan discusses her work – the result of another of our culture's most penetrating abuses. This is particularly relevant at the time of writing as we read reports, for example, about ethnic cleansing in Bosnia. Hitchings then offers a view of the issue of sexual orientation as it affects psychotherapy.

In Part III, Modalities, Pokorny and Lister-Ford survey the field of individual adult psychotherapy in Chapter 8, with a brief glance at some of the therapeutic orientations. It must be said that this book, contrary to some excellent others, has attempted to underplay the emphasis on difference between schools and to emphasise common themes and concerns across schools. Harper gives an overview of the spectrum of psychological therapies with children, and Passey surveys the field of analytical psychotherapy with children, while Jezzard gives another perspective on psychotherapy with adolescents culled from his own rich experience. Butler and Low give, jointly and severally, two of the many perspectives on short-term psychotherapy; Leary and Walton briefly but effectively discuss marital psychotherapy. Gorell Barnes and Cooklin skilfully review family psychotherapy, followed by Manor's contribution of a perspective on group psychotherapy of different orientations.

Part IV concerns settings. Psychotherapy in and with organisations brings together the work of Hawkins and Miller, whereas Kosviner expertly reviews the state of psychotherapy within the NHS, with additional material from Knowles. The two Smiths look at the place of psychotherapy in the social services, whereas Oakley and Millard contribute a wide-ranging theoretical perspective on psychotherapeutic communities. Llewellin uses the contributions of several colleagues to bring together her chapter on psychotherapy in the voluntary sector, while Pokorny and Fanning discuss some of the issues of psychotherapy in private practice, with additional material from Hargaden.

Part V concerns recurring and significant current issues in psychotherapy. Bungener and McCormack explore the relatively neglected area of psychotherapy and learning difficulties; Embleton and Tudor, some aspects of the roles of power and influence in psychotherapy – the subject of a number of current conferences. Bentovim and Tranter describe the very important sector of psychotherapy with adult survivors of sexual abuse. This is followed by a chapter on its professional corollary – sexual contact between psychotherapists and their patients, in which Garrett gives a preview of her research. Alon and Levine Bar-Yoseph draw on their experience of post-traumatic stress disorder, and Welldon surveys the less well-known but significant field of forensic psychotherapy. Finally, and fittingly, the book ends with the chapter by Parkes and Sills on psychotherapy with the dying and the bereaved. Two appendices follow – the structure of the United Kingdom Council for Psychotherapy and its member organisations, and the UKCP Code of Ethics.

It is definitely not expected that this book will be read from start to finish, but rather that it will become a useful resource for professionals and lay people alike, beginners and experts, in opening or re-opening doors to areas of interest, learning and professional growth.

With many of the chapters, the authors and/or editors have adduced sources, contact addresses and further reading lists in addition to the usual references. We apologise for no doubt numerous omissions, but wanted to indicate some rather than be exhaustive. For the interested inquirer just beginning a search into a particular area, contacting or reading a couple of sources can often act as a key to unlock the riches which are available but sometimes difficult to access. Information on training is also available from any one of the UKCP member organisations.

The authors in this *Handbook* are an unrepresentative cross-section of the field as it exists today, based on the response we elicited from practitioners able and willing to write within the time limits at our disposal. Each chapter should therefore not be seen as a definitive statement: the diversity of styles and approaches illustrates a sampling of the wide diversity of the voices in the field. Our aim was to have more than one author speak on each subject where possible; this way, the reader benefits not only from two expert perspectives, but from the creative tension that can emerge from all such dialogue. The final collection is not intended to be representative of all themes, modalities, settings and forms of psychotherapy. In many cases we did ask colleagues to contribute and they could not join the project in time. The authors finally represented here are the outcome of a long and frequently fraught process of contacting authors who promised and did not deliver, who backed out at the last minute, who stepped into the breach, who delivered promptly and with good humour, who forgave our occasional mistakes with good grace, and those who showed some care and concern for our responsibilities and for us as people.

Diversity is an integral and important element of psychotherapy in the United Kingdom and we are proud to carry this flag into Europe and the wider world. It is an integral phenomenon of the English-speaking world to tolerate idiosyncrasy, celebrate difference *and* maintain professional standards. The diversity in this book, we hope, reflects and respects the multitudinous differences that exist among the human beings who come to us for help.

Where clinical material is used for illustration by any author, details have been changed to ensure anonymity. The responsibility for clinical material belongs to the author(s) who have written it, as does the responsibility for permission to reproduce material in the form of extended quotations or diagrams. Despite research showing that no single school has 'all the answers', as mentioned in several chapters (such as 2 and 3), most psychotherapists adhere to a particular orientation, even if it is their one version of the integrative psychotherapies. Authors will therefore refer to people who seek help from psychotherapists, sometimes as patients and sometimes as clients.

The views expressed in these chapters are the view of the authors and not necessarily of the editors. We have also used the terms 'he' and 'she' interchangeably for both the psychotherapist and client in order to try to maintain a balance.

We wish you *bon voyage*.

REFERENCE

Hinshelwood, R. D. (1990) 'Editorial', *British Journal of Psychotherapy* 7(2): 119–20.

Acknowledgements

Our gratitude is due to the many people who have collaborated on this project: in particular Bob Hinshelwood and Windy Dryden; also Ann Kearns for her sterling editorial help and valuable advice, Helena Hargaden for her material, and Camilla Sim, Rita Cremona and Barbara Kulesza. Our thanks go also to all other people who may not be named here but have assisted in various ways. The physical and administrative construction of this book is almost wholly thanks to the dedicated, encouraging and careful ministrations of Katherine Pierpoint, who navigated with patience, fortitude and imagination a task of enormous complexity, involving many authors who did or did not eventually participate and two editors, whose professional lives made constant counter-claims on their time and attention. Particular gratitude is due to our families, the local curry house and all those who have helped late at night, at the end of the project, and when times were difficult.

Edwina Welham, our editor, is especially thanked for her patience and foresight in waiting for the most propitious timing for this book to appear; and it is hoped that the support which has been given to the project by **metanoia** Education for Living Ltd (while Petrüska Clarkson was principal) will continue to bear fruit.

The editors gratefully acknowledge permission to reproduce material previously published elsewhere. Penguin Books granted permission to reproduce Figure 8.1 (Berne's original ego state model) from *Games People Play*. Whurr Publishers granted permission to reproduce Table 13.1 (Comparison between family group therapy, 'stranger' group therapy and individual therapy) from *An Outline for Trainee Psychiatrists, Medical Students and Practitioners*. Every effort has been made to obtain permission to reproduce copyright material throughout this book. If any acknowledgement has not yet been made, the copyright holder should contact the publisher.

Part I

Introduction

Chapter 1

The nature and range of psychotherapy*

Petrūska Clarkson

A chapter of this length cannot fully do justice to the ongoing debate about the nature and range of psychotherapy. It is a subject which continues to exercise some of the finest minds active in psychotherapy today, as witness both the mainstay texts in any training course in counselling and psychotherapy, and the current debate in specialist journals.

In the first instance, definitions of psychotherapy will be briefly reviewed. This will be followed by an attempted differentiation between the major professions engaged in counselling and psychotherapy, following closely the conventions of the main professional bodies involved. The third section will concern a review of the major traditions in psychology which have given rise to different approaches, and briefly review the significance of research in this field. Lastly, there is a diagram for differentiating between different modalities or arenas for counselling and for psychotherapy.

DEFINITIONS

Definitions of psychotherapy are legion, and none is entirely comprehensive nor entirely satisfactory.

> Legislators and courts of law have found it almost impossible to define 'psychotherapy' in such a way as to include, by universal agreement among therapists, that which *is* psychotherapy and to exclude that which *is not* psychotherapy.
>
> (Watkins 1965: 1142)

In their textbook of psychiatry, Henderson and Gillespie (1956) regard psychotherapy as any therapy of the mind, appearing to include talking treatment alongside insulin coma in their fifth edition of 1940 but, by their

* The author wishes to thank Michael Carroll for his valuable editorial input, and for providing the definition of counselling psychology; also Michael Pokorny for his additional material. A portion of this chapter is from 'Counselling, psychotherapy, psychology and applied psychology: the same and different', by P. Clarkson with M. Carroll, in P. Clarkson (1993) *On Psychotherapy*, London: Whurr.

eighth edition of 1956, psychotherapy has become specific to psycho-analysis and its derivatives. Mayer-Gross *et al.* (1954) do not offer a general definition of psychotherapy but use the term to cover a variety of talking treatments. They seem to distinguish it from psychoanalysis as well as from behaviour therapy. They regard all forms of physical treatments as quite separate and different. Merskey and Tonge (1965) clearly regard psychotherapy as talking treatment.

Holmes and Lindley offer a definition: 'The systematic use of a relation-ship between therapist and patient – as opposed to pharmacological or social methods – to produce changes in cognition, feelings and behaviour' (1989: 3). Notice that the use has to be systematic. Holmes and Lindley go on to consider forms of psychotherapy under the headings of structure, space and relationship. Another idea is that psychotherapy is the treatment of psychological conflicts no matter what the presenting symptoms are.

All these definitions rely on the idea of bringing about changes in the personality and manner of a person's relating by the use of essentially psychological techniques. If we are to cover all forms of psychotherapy, that seems to be about as definite as we can get. As soon as we try to be more specific, we begin to exclude some therapies. Of course we may wish to exclude some therapies. There is no agreement on the exact boundaries of psychotherapy. One result of this is that the political definition of psychotherapy has given rise to great argument and considerable tensions within the profession. I refer to the process by which the United Kingdom Council for Psychotherapy (UKCP) has come into being from the original Rugby Psychotherapy Conferences, via the intermediate stage of the UK Standing Conference for Psychotherapy. It is possible to define psycho-therapy as all those therapies that are recognised by the UKCP. That is a simple way of reaching some sort of agreement. The trouble is that there are always some who claim that some psychotherapy is excluded from the Council. This is merely another way of having the argument of what is, and what is not, psychotherapy. On the other hand we can recognise that other professions also have ill-defined borders, and we can stop worrying so much about our general definition or our political solution by recognising that the borders of psychotherapy are not fixed.

The time-span within which psychotherapy operates ranges from one interview to many years of treatment. The rise of brief psychotherapy (as discussed in Chapter 11) has shown that not only can important changes be made very quickly, such as in ten or fifteen sessions, but can also occur within just one interview. The time boundaries of group psychotherapy have proved to be very varied. From a start of once-weekly group meetings lasting one-and-a-half or one-and-a-quarter hours, groups have become marathon, intermittent, more than once a week; the variations that have been tried out seem endless. Once the psychotherapy is exported to the home setting, as can happen in some family therapy clinics, the time frame changes altogether, lasting until something is achieved, or the team has to leave. Even in the psychoanalytic sphere there has been change. In some places analysis takes place five times per week, in others four or three times weekly. Even more radical, the revolutionary French psychoanalyst Lacan would end the session when some significant moment had been experienced. Thus sessions could last for ten minutes or two hours.

In many psychotherapies a contract for time and fees is made at the start, although it may have to be modified later. Even where the contract appears not to have been made overtly, as in psychoanalysis, in reality the contract is for as long as it takes, even if that is many years. Of course in a therapeutic community the time involved is twenty-four hours a day for many weeks, months or years.

The range of clients that are offered psychotherapy has varied from time to time and from place to place. There seems to be general agreement that neurotic symptoms are amenable to psychotherapy, and there is so far no clear evidence that the form of the psychotherapy makes a material difference to the outcome. Other diagnostic categories, or the psychotherapy from which they draw, produce very different reactions from different psychotherapists. There are therapeutic communities that specialise in treating psychosis, such as the Arbours Association and the Philadelphia Association, both being descendants of the original work of Laing. Some psychotherapy schools seem to specialise in certain types of client, so that, for instance, specific phobias have become largely the province of behaviour therapy, especially the implosion treatment for phobia of spiders (arachnophobia). Others have specialised in the treatment of psychopathy, especially the Henderson Hospital, and yet others in the treatment of offenders, such as the Portman Clinic for sexual offenders and Grendon Underwood prison which has an excellent record in the rehabilitation of recidivist criminals using a combination of community and group methods, including psychodrama. The validation of results, psychotherapy studies or outcome (as discussed in Chapter 3) is another matter of great concern to us all. It is hoped that the new moves towards psychotherapy audit will help on this front.

ALLIED DISCIPLINES

This section considers some of the factors involved in differentiating counselling, psychotherapy, psychology, psychiatry and several allied fields. It is written for several reasons. One is to help establish for counsellors, psychotherapists and counselling psychologists separate and valuable professional identities which have a place and domain of their own. Such an attempt can provide helpful guidelines for referral agencies, professionals and members of the public to distinguish between different kinds of service provision, so that needs and resources can be more

accurately aligned. Ignorance and confusion in themselves further perpetuate difficulties endemic to the most complex task of providing the best
and most cost-effective help for individuals in emotional trouble, with the
least long-term detrimental effects, and hopefully of most benefit in terms
of improved psychological health. Secondly, the ability to know where
helping modalities overlap and where they differ can be a tremendous help
to professionals themselves. It can establish boundaries, acknowledge
strengths and limitations and afford a working relationship between them
that fosters mutual respect rather than distrust. Professionalisation, accreditation and ethical sanctions can go some way towards reducing potential
damage: they can also provide the first step towards professional identity
and the ability to relate to other professionals from similar and different
helping backgrounds.

According to Carroll (1991, 1992b), there are three main approaches to
considering the relationship between counselling, psychotherapy, psychology
and psychiatry.

First, there are those who 'lump them together' and refuse to acknowledge any differences. They point dramatically to the client groups dealt
with by each profession and hail the fact that counsellors see clients,
psychotherapists see clients (but they may call them patients) and counselling psychologists see clients (they call them both clients and patients)
and that these clients do not differ substantially from one another.
Domains held sacred by one profession are invaded without apology by
another. Psychotherapists see clients in long-term therapy, some of whom
are very disturbed and difficult people who may even have psychiatric
histories and they may work with transference and the unconscious. Such
very disturbed clients traditionally have been the work of the psychiatrist,
the clinical psychologist, or the psychotherapist. The counsellor, on the
other hand, sometimes works in a college of higher education, can average
six sessions a client and deals with crisis and developmental issues. The
counselling psychologist (a new breed on the British scene) works in
hospitals, organisations, mental health centres and all those areas once
claimed by counsellors, psychotherapists and clinical psychologists. Why
try to fabricate differences if all three approaches do much the same thing?

According to Carroll, a second group 'split' the groups and refuse to
acknowledge many similarities. Counsellors, they claim, are low on theory,
have no requirement for personal therapy in their training, work in the
short term and with developmental issues. Counselling psychologists are
psychologists who use counselling in their work, are high on theory and
research and as yet seem unsure about where they will end up or in what
client groups they will specialise. Psychotherapists concentrate on personal
psychotherapy, use supervised client work, spend a long time as appren-
tices, and have deeply disturbed and long-term clients. However you view
it, these are three different approaches to helping people and proponents

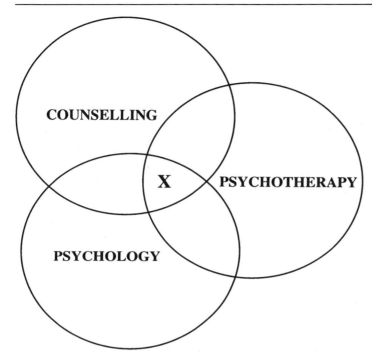

Figure 1.1 Venn diagram representing the three primary arenas of counselling, psychology and psychotherapy

of this view believe they must be kept separate. Some view the differences in terms of specialisation, others in terms of training. It is also true that issues of power, ideology, money, status, employability and snobbery play a significant part in such territorial anxieties.

A third group talk about 'overlap' between the three: areas of similarity and areas of difference. Duffy (1990: 11) recognises the areas in common and sees differences coming from 'intentionality'; that is, not what is done but how practitioners think of their work. This contribution of Carroll is supplemented here by a diagram (Figure 1.1), which I developed to illustrate the discussion. Figure 1.1 is offered as a potentially helpful tool in guiding and demarcating the discussion areas between the overlapping fields of counselling, psychology and psychotherapy and will form the basis for the discussion in the rest of this section.

Figure 1.1 shows each area as distinct in itself, but relating to each of the other two areas, and indicates the interrelationship between all three. The overlap area between counselling and psychotherapy represents the work of counselling professionals with advanced practice qualifications or the psychotherapist using counselling skills. The overlap area between psycho-therapy and psychology represents psychotherapists with a psychology qualification or psychologists trained as psychotherapists. The overlap area between counselling and psychology represents counselling psychologists – that is, psychology graduates with counselling qualifications, but no special training in psychotherapy. 'X' marks the area of work which involves the work of psychology graduates who have training and experience in both counselling and psychotherapy. This may be the appropriate area for the profession of counselling psychology.

We will look in detail at each of the above – namely, the counsellor, the psychotherapist and the counselling psychologist – and then note four areas where dialogue can take place between the three approaches. For each profession, people can be self-referred, or come via their general practitioners, friends or contacts.

Counsellor

The British Association for Counselling, founded in 1977, defines counselling as follows:

> Counselling is the skilled and principled use of relationship to facilitate self-knowledge, emotional acceptance and growth, and the optimal development of personal resources. The overall aim is to provide an opportunity to work towards living more satisfyingly and resourcefully. Counselling relationships will vary according to need but may be concerned with developmental issues, addressing and resolving specific problems, making decisions, coping with crisis, developing personal insights and knowledge, working through feelings of inner conflict or improving relationships with others.
>
> The counsellor's role is to facilitate the client's work in ways that respect the client's values, personal resources and capacity for self determination.
>
> (BAC 1989: 1)

Counsellors may bring special training, experience and expertise to the counselling relationship, to enable people to further their own growth and enhance their personal functioning. In this way, counsellors are enablers and facilitators, helping a client with a specific problem and focusing on evolutionary change. Counselling is largely a general field, but it can also be quite specific; for example, redundancy counselling, marital or sexual counselling, debt counselling, HIV, retirement and health counselling, or bereavement counselling.

The British Association of Counselling publishes a directory of counsellors throughout the United Kingdom. This body also has a Code of Ethics and Practice for Counsellors, whose aim 'is to establish and maintain standards for counsellors and to inform and protect members of the public seeking their services'. Also under this code, 'counsellors subscribe to principles in the areas of (1) the nature of counselling, (2) issues of responsibility, and (3) issues of competence' (BAC 1984: 1).

Counsellors may be eligible for accreditation through the BAC, which has a Counselling at Work Division as well as a Personal, Family, Sexual and Marital division, a Division for Pastoral Counselling, Counselling in Education and one for Counselling in Medical Settings. Training in counselling is usually one to three years, although some people who become counsellors have no other qualifications than experience and expertise. Counsellors often argue, sometimes with good reason, that they do psychotherapy, as there is much overlap between the two areas. A well-trained counsellor may do work of equal value to that of people in other fields. Their focus, however, is *likely* to remain with more short-term work, with the less seriously disturbed members of the population, and with areas of life adjustment such as bereavement or career counselling or crisis support, guidance and problem-solving rather than in-depth work on a person's childhood. The task of counselling is to give the client an opportunity to explore, discover and clarify ways of living more satisfyingly and resourcefully. Counselling is thus not a destructuring and restructuring of personality, but aims to create the conditions through the counselling relationship wherein a person can connect with their basic drive towards health, and be enabled in adjusting to changes of role situations and developmental states in life. Counsellors usually do not have psychology degrees and thus do not consciously use psychology as an academic discipline as a basis for their practice. Pastoral counselling centres (for example, the Westminster Pastoral Foundation) more usually train counsellors in psychodynamic theory and practice.

It seems at this stage best to serve the two areas, counselling and psychotherapy, by concentrating on where they are most different; that is, highlighting the polar opposites, rather than getting stuck in a quagmire of overlap. Counselling can be seen to focus on evolutionary change, whereas psychotherapy focuses on revolutionary change. Proctor (1989) writes about person-centred problem solving in the here-and-now. Difficulties in distinguishing between counselling and psychotherapy do not absolve us from responsibility to look at the poles. Issues become clearer when we look at the two poles; and just because the task is difficult does not mean it shouldn't be done. Doing this, we can establish whether an issue is closer to one 'end' or the other. This is easier and more effective than trying to make a boundary, because clearly there is considerable overlap.

Counsellors help to oil the wheels of someone's experience so that they manage to function better. It is meant to alleviate suffering. It is for those whose life position is comfortable enough so that they could get through life very well without a 'metanoia' or a turnabout. Counselling seems most suited to a model of human growth in human beings, and indeed many counselling courses are predicated on the work of Rogers, who emphasised that, through the creation of the necessary conditions of respect, empathy and genuineness, the human being will naturally learn

> to *be* more of his experience – to be the feelings of which he has been frightened as well as the feelings he has regarded as more acceptable. He becomes a more fluid, changing, learning person . . . the motivation for learning and change springs from the self-actualising tendency of life . . . to flow into all the differentiated channels of potential development, insofar as these are experienced as enhancing.
>
> (Rogers 1961: 285)

A characteristic of revolutionary change is that the starting conditions and basic components of the system have to be changed, and may even appear out of the regions of probable predictions. Evolutionary change, in contrast, suggests that the same starting conditions and basic components can conceivably lead to the accomplished outcomes; that is, one could predict the range of probable outcomes. The juxtaposition of evolutionary and revolutionary change emphasises different sets of skills, different goals and different methodologies. An individual's defensive structures can be left intact or strengthened in counselling, by using existing personality resources and the individual's potential for growth and self-healing.

Psychotherapy, on the other hand, focuses on discontinuous, revolutionary change. The justification for psychotherapy often needs to be that such an expensive and time-consuming intervention is necessitated because, unless discontinuous change is implemented, serious tragedy may result. In this case, the medical model may be appropriate in terms of diagnosis (or at least assessment) leading to treatment implementing or seeking for a 'cure'. A medical model may be more effective when there is actual structural damage to the organism which has to be reversed before the organism can start reconnecting with its own innate healing process. Psychotherapy, whether psychodynamic, behavioural or humanistic/existential, concerns the destructuring and restructuring of the personality, whether it is conceived of as belief-and-behaviour systems, ego states, or super-ego and self structures.

Sometimes counsellors lack the training and the facilities in screening, assessing and monitoring risks of suicide, homicide or psychosis which may only become apparent in the later stages of a helping relationship. Of course, this is not to suggest that all screening or assessment procedures, even when done by extremely experienced psychotherapists or psychiatrists, are always either effective or helpful. On the other hand, there are many reports of well-functioning individuals who set out to find someone to help them with a circumscribed problem such as a lack of interest in sex with a marital partner, and then end up several years later, having entered (for example) three-times-weekly psychoanalysis, with a sense of having been misled or misinformed. The point here is not to suggest that there are absolute dividing lines between the work of the different professions, but to engage others (in and outside these professions) to continue to question and articulate what differences there may be; not so much in the overlap areas, but in the areas which are more distinctly differentiated.

Loughley (1985), during a conference on training in counselling and psychotherapy, put it this way:

> Counselling and psychotherapy are not the same process, although I know there are some of you who would disagree with that statement. For me the difference between them is one of history. Counselling focuses on that which belongs to the now-here. It can be achieved through care and cognition, it is possible to think about it. Psychotherapy on the other hand, is to take the now as a living history: that the things learnt then are happening now but in a different context.

Counselling therefore can be seen to focus on *enabling* and *facilitating*, whereas psychotherapy can be seen to emphasise *intervention*, *treatment* and *reconstruction*. Given that in evolutionary change the organism is striving, naturally and probably successfully, towards its fulfilment, the helper needs to be supportive, enabling and facilitating of this self-generated and self-directed process. In revolutionary change the focus is on interpretation, confrontation, destructuring and reconstruction. The risk of systemic disintegration is naturally lesser in evolutionary change than in revolutionary change, and therefore the skills and experience involved in the latter are naturally of a different order; but not necessarily better or worse than the skills of enabling or facilitation. Goal-setting and the educational task will therefore be more important in counselling training, and diagnosis of pathology more important in the training of psychotherapists.

It is less differentiating but, practically, still the case that counselling assists people in finding the solution to a particular problem, or dealing with a particular crisis, whereas psychotherapy helps people to develop new ways of solving problems which can become generalised to new situations. There is also sometimes, as with Loughly above, a differentiation drawn between counselling as dealing with a current situation contrasted with psychotherapy as dealing with a past situation.

Psychotherapist

Psychotherapy can also be defined as:

> a form of treatment for mental illness and behavioural disturbances in which a trained person establishes a professional contact with the

patient and through definite therapeutic communication, both verbal and non-verbal, attempts to alleviate the emotional disturbance, reverse or change maladaptive patterns of behaviour, and encourage personality growth and development. Psychotherapy is distinguished from such other forms of psychiatric treatment as the use of drugs, surgery, electric shock treatment and insulin coma treatment.

(Freedman et al. 1975: 2601)

Psychotherapy is the treatment by psychological means of problems of an emotional nature in which a trained person deliberately establishes a professional relationship with a patient with the object of removing, modifying or retarding existing symptoms, of mediating disturbed patterns of behavior and of promoting positive personal growth and development.

(Wolberg 1954: 118)

Previously, anybody could set up as a psychotherapist: that is, prior to the formation of the UKCP, whose aim is to create a profession and a register so that the public can identify appropriately trained practitioners who are subject to an enforceable Code of Ethics. It was founded as the UKSCP in 1989, is now the UKCP and has seventy-three member organisations grouped into eight sections, each containing a distinct kind of psychotherapy (see Appendix A for details). The voluntary Register, which appeared in May 1993, will form the foundation of a Statutory Register of psychotherapists. A national audit of psychotherapy is in preparation and a variety of initiatives are under way, including co-operation with the development of national vocational qualifications at the higher levels, research into and management of the overlap between psychotherapy, counselling and counselling psychology.

There is now usually a minimum of three years' training, and most psychotherapy training institutions involved in the UKCP require most of their trainees to be in extended personal psychotherapy so that professionals who graduate from these training programmes have personal experience of the process and uses of psychotherapy themselves. Thus, personal psychotherapy is considered to be a vital part of most training. The personal psychotherapy of trainees usually is of a similar duration, type and frequency as that which they would be offering their clients.

Psychotherapists would expect to deal with more serious problems, such as clinical aspects; clients are seen frequently, in regular sessions at least once a week, perhaps more frequently. Clients (or patients) may want to go deep and far back into their past; repetitive patterns of behaviour are identified, worked on and cleared if they are having a negative effect upon the client's present life. Psychotherapists will usually have a wider range and greater flexibility in their working methods than counsellors or psychoanalysts. Psychotherapists may or may not be psychoanalysts.

Psychoanalyst

Freud gave several definitions of psychoanalysis. One of the most explicit is to be found at the beginning of an encyclopaedia article written in 1922:

Psycho-analysis is the name (i) of a procedure for the investigation of mental processes which are almost inaccessible in any other way, (ii) of a method (based on that investigation) for the treatment of neurotic disorders and (iii) of a collection of psychological information obtained along those lines, which is gradually being accumulated into a new scientific discipline.

(Laplanche and Pontalis 1988: 367)

The word 'psychoanalysis' refers to a theoretical viewpoint concerning personality structure and function, in the application of this theory to other branches of knowledge and also to a specific psycho-therapeutic technique. Although much developed since his time this body of knowledge is based upon the discoveries of Sigmund Freud.

(British Psycho-Analytical Society 1990: 37)

Psychoanalysts may or may not be medical doctors; but all psychiatrists are medically qualified. Psychoanalysts have recently organised themselves into a body called the British Confederation of Psychotherapists.

Psychiatrist

The Shorter Oxford Dictionary defines psychiatry as 'healing, medical treatment. . . . The medical treatment of diseases of the mind' (Onions 1968: 1700). The relevant professional body is the Royal College of Psychiatrists. Psychiatrists have a medical degree, then undergo further specialist training in psychiatry. Many psychiatrists are not trained in psychotherapy, but they can prescribe drugs. There is a clear difference between child and adult psychiatry. Psychiatrists are specialists in the treatment and management of serious disturbances such as psychosis, schizophrenia, manic-depressive disorders and so on. They tend to work in hospital or psychiatric settings, unless they work in private practice settings.

Psychologist and applied psychologist

Psychologists and applied psychologists are another category to be distinguished. Psychologists are professionals with at least one degree in psychology. Many move on to further postgraduate studies in applied psychology, one of which, these days, is counselling psychology.

The dictionary definition of 'psychology' as 'the science of the nature, functions and phenomena of the human soul or mind' (Onions 1968: 1700) is somewhat restrictive in its view. Psychology is not only the 'science of the mind' but also the science of human behaviour in all its aspects. Psychology interprets the person (Carroll and Pickard 1993) and results in a number of theories of personality and research methods for understanding the person. Its questions are person-related: why do people behave the way they do? What motivates the individual? How do people grow and begin to think and use language? Can we isolate stages of life as individuals progress towards old age? From its academic base, psychology is divided into a number of subsections, such as development psychology, cognitive, personality theory, biological basis of behaviour, abnormal psychology psychological assessment. From this academic basis, psychologists move to apply their subject to the world.

The British Psychological Society is an amalgamation of the various applied psychologies. There are approximately thirteen Divisions, Sections and Special Interest Groups within the Society, ranging through developmental psychology, educational, occupational, clinical, counselling, clinical neuropsychology and so on. It can be difficult at times to differentiate between the three: the occupational psychologist, the clinical psychologist and the counselling psychologist.

Occupational psychologist

An occupational psychologist will have knowledge in relation to the following eight areas: 'Human-machine interaction, design of environments and of work, personnel selection and assessment, performance appraisal and career development, training (including identification of needs and evaluation), employee relations and motivation and organization development' (Fitzgibbon 1990).

Not many occupational psychologists train to do psychotherapy. Occupational psychologists are usually better paid than clinical psychologists, since they usually work in industry (as opposed to the NHS), and they may, for example, work on computers to make software programs.

Clinical psychologist

'The key tasks of clinical psychologists are: Assessment, Treatment, Training/teaching and Research (both patient and service related) as well as Management' (BPS 1988b: 4).

All clinical psychologists must belong to their professional body, the British Psychological Society, and they will then be on the Register of Chartered Psychologists. This document is available from the BPS, and it contains the names, qualifications and contact addresses of all the chartered psychologists in the United Kingdom. The BPS distinguishes between members who are prohibited from using MBPsS on publicity (BPS

1991: 26–27), and chartered psychologists who have done additional training in psychology in addition to holding a psychology degree.

A clinical psychologist will have studied psychology for a long time (usually a bachelor's and often a master's degree in psychology), and will have trained in clinical settings; for example hospitals, with clinical focus, or made special study of mental retardation, or management of phobias or behaviour disorders. Not all chartered clinical psychologists are trained in psychotherapy; many have not been in psychotherapy themselves. They do not prescribe drugs, but they are usually trained to do psychodiagnostics, such as the use of tests such as the Rorschach, Myers Briggs, MMPI or Wechsler.

> The range of treatment techniques has grown considerably during the last twenty years, from the previously limited range of essentially educational or psychodynamic techniques. . . . Examples are the treatment of elimination disorders in children, phobic conditions in adults and the remediation of cognitive difficulties following different types of brain injury. Some of these treatments now offer positive alternatives to drug treatments (such as anxiety-management procedures), and supplement medical treatments in people with long-term-disabling conditions.
>
> Behavioural methods (such as desensitisation), methods based on social learning principles (such as social skills training) and cognitive methods, used especially for altered mood states, are now widely used. In addition, a wider range of psychotherapeutic approaches has been developed, based on theories that are not essentially psychodynamic (such as personal construct theory). It has become apparent that there are a number of non-specific factors which are relevant to many apparently different techniques. A number of these approaches are used by counsellors and other non-psychologists to help people with less serious conditions.
>
> (BPS 1988a: 5)

As said before, 'the boundaries between clinical psychology as a discipline and other academic and health-care disciplines, are not fixed' (BPS 1988a: 1), and the development of the profession of counselling psychology demonstrates this further.

Counselling psychologist

Training as a Counselling Psychologist is already an avenue to chartered psychologist status and the group may soon become an independent Division of the BPS. At the time of writing it is a Special Group of the BPS, as Carroll makes clear:

counselling psychology moved from being a 'Section' in 1982 to becoming a 'Special Group' in 1988 with increasing aspirations to becoming a Division within BPS. Its membership . . . is still probably the fastest-growing section of the BPS. . . . Becoming a Division with BPS would bring with it major implications for training, training courses, career structure and pay levels, status, and supervision. A proposed new Diploma in Counselling has been outlined as the next step on the journey to Division status.

(1991: 74)

One important, if not the most important, difference between counsellors and counselling psychologists is the conscious use of academic psychology alongside practical counselling skills. Counselling psychologists have a basic degree in psychology, and then further training in counselling psychology (MSc). Counselling psychology is here conceptualised as the overlapping area between counselling and psychotherapy in the Venn diagram (see Figure 1.1 above) representing the three primary arenas of counselling, psychology and psychotherapy.

Counselling psychology is not considered identical with counselling (even when it is carried out by psychology graduates). In counselling psychology, there is an emphasis on the systemic application of distinctively psychological understanding, based on empirical research of the client and the counselling process, to the practice of counselling. The relevant psychological knowledge is partly concerned with the problems of presenting clients, and partly with the procedures and processes involved in counselling. It would be remembered that counselling psychology involves work in an organisational context as well as with individual clients, and synthesises elements of better-developed areas of professional work such as clinical and occupational psychology. Life-span developmental psychologies, and the social psychology of interpersonal processes are among the areas that supply the academic foundations of counselling psychology. Of central scientific relevance, of course, are empirical investigations of the processes and outcomes of counselling and of related methods of psychotherapy.

The psychological understanding of counselling derives not only from formal psychological enquiry but also from the *interpersonal relationships* between practitioners and their clients. The essence of such relationships is one of personal exploration and clarification in which psychological knowledge is utilized and shared in ways which enable clients to deal more effectively with their inter- and intra-personal concerns. The capacity to establish and maintain such relationships ultimately rests upon the personal qualities and maturity of the individual counselling psychologist. Personal qualities such as non-defensiveness and a capacity to experience and communicate empathic resonance, constitute essential resources which the counselling psychologist draws upon. Whilst these characteristics may be enhanced by skills training they derive primarily from a foundation of personal experience and integrative maturity.

(BPS 1989: 1; author's italics added)

Emerging issues

From the above, a number of interesting areas emerge as crucial to the ongoing dialogue of exploring, differentiating or ignoring professional disciplinary boundaries.

First, the concept of change and what it means. There are different kinds of change possible within therapeutic settings: problem-solving, environmental change, adjustment, renegotiation (as in a relationship), developmental change (evolutionary) and revolutionary change (personality restructuring). Is it possible to look at the professional approaches above to see if certain approaches are more appropriate for certain kinds of change within the person and his/her environment?

A second area of interest is the area of relationship within therapeutic settings. Clarkson (1991) and Gelso and Carter (1985) have outlined different kinds of relationships appropriate to different therapeutic approaches or more applicable to different client groups. It may well be that such relationships are also in keeping with the professions above.

The third area is that of training. Carroll (1991) has outlined ways of connecting training and education in counselling, psychotherapy and counselling psychology that connects rather than diversifies them. He suggests a three-stage model depicting pathways in which counselling is (1) integrated in an already existing profession, such as nursing or social work, (2) seen as the primary work of the practitioner, (3) a specialisation in a given area or field, like employee counselling, student counselling, working with eating disorders, marital counselling (psychotherapy training and practice would enter here). Further theory, practice and research that connects counselling and psychotherapy with psychology (or indeed another profession – counselling could be connected to sociology or education or politics) would add postgraduate qualifications to the above, leading to Advanced Diplomas, MA or MSc degrees. Carroll (1991) has also pointed out the problems emerging if the three main organisations to whom counsellors, psychotherapists, and counselling psychologists are affiliated (the BAC, UKCP and BPS) become too isolated and ally themselves to rigid training that refuses to recognise other expertise.

DIFFERENT APPROACHES

For lay persons, as well as helping professionals, it is not exactly easy to find one's way (in addition to disciplinary confusion) around the theories and psychotherapy prevalent at this time of the late twentieth century. In the professional literature, some 250 different schools or approaches to counselling and psychotherapy have been identified (Corsini 1986); Holmes and Lindley (1989) refer to the existence of over 300 types of psychotherapy. In addition to the difficulties attendant on differentiating professional boundaries, this task can be bedevilled by the incredible range of approaches, theories and schools which are all part of the vast ocean of work conducted by the different professionals in these fields. Karasu (1986) has talked of polling 450 models of counselling/psychotherapy nationwide in the United States alone.

It can be both difficult to identify where particular approaches come from historically, or where they share characteristics or belong *vis-à-vis* other approaches in terms of family resemblances. Dryden's book *Individual Therapy in Britain* (1984) can be extremely useful to help understand the differences between the approaches. Any attempt to map out psychotherapy is fraught with ambiguity and argument, because deep psychological as well as social, ideological and economic factors influence this profession as much as any other. However, many people have found it helpful to have some kind of overall location diagram of major thinkers in psychotherapy, at least to give them some initial starting points (see Table 1.1 below). It is thus not suggested that this table is the only way to do it, or that it does any more than provide the starting point for several debates. However, its usefulness over two decades with psychology students and interested lay people has acted as an encouragement to make it more available. Inevitably, where space and time is restricted, some important names have been omitted. It is hoped that the general notion is clear enough for readers to continue to fill in from their own reading, their inquiries and their own experience.

A brief overview follows of the underlying traditions of counselling and psychotherapy, with a look to the future and the goals of integrative psychotherapy as one of the ways forward.

THE THREE MAJOR TRADITIONS IN TWENTIETH-CENTURY PSYCHOTHERAPY

Three major streams of psychotherapy all originated around the turn of the twentieth century. Freud's (1915/1973) theory of psychoanalysis came to represent one major stream of psychological thinking and psychotherapy. His first major work, *The Interpretation of Dreams*, was published in 1900. Freudian and Kleinian psychoanalytic thinking tended to view human beings as biologically determined, and motivated primarily by sexual and aggressive drives. For Freud, the purpose of psychoanalysis was exploration and understanding or analysis, not necessarily change (1915/1973).

The second major stream derives its theoretical lineage from Pavlov (1927), the Russian psychophysiologist who studied conditioned reflexes and other learning behaviours. Theoreticians following in this tradition are usually referred to as learning theorists, behaviour modification specialists, or latterly, cognitive-behaviour therapists.

In 1968 Abraham Maslow coined the term 'third-force psychology' (1968: iii) to distinguish the third grouping shown below. This tradition did *not* originate from Freud or from Pavlovian ideas. The intellectual and ideological grandfather of this humanistic/existential tradition is Jacob Moreno. Moreno was arguably the first psychiatrist to put 'the patient' in a centrally responsible role in his own life drama. He worked with people to empower them to do their own healing. Moreno was applying group psychotherapy with children based on humanistic existential principles, and writing about it by 1908 (Greenberg 1975: 201).

Professionals and lay people familiar with the inter- and intra-disciplinary squabbles of different traditions will be able to use their own knowledge to augment or modify this presentation in Table 1.1 considerably for themselves. Such attempts at distinguishing between different kinds of service provision can provide basic guidelines for members of the public and trainees, so that needs and resources can be more accurately aligned. The task of providing the best and most cost-effective help for individuals in emotional trouble is complex in itself, and ignorance of the field can intensify the complexity for people already in trouble. For someone who may already be confused and simply in need of emotional help, it may not be easy to find that appropriate help (that holds the least long-term detrimental effects, and the most benefit in terms of improved psychological health). The person may need emergency help and may not have the leisure and rationality to sift through the huge variety of approaches available. Secondly, the ability to know where helping modalities overlap and where they differ can be a tremendous help to professionals themselves. It can establish boundaries, acknowledge strengths and limitations and afford a working relationship between them that fosters mutual respect rather than distrust.

There are some psychotherapists who are quite hard to place in Table 1.1 because they cross over in terms of values or according to their interpreters, or because they have become fundamentally integrated with others. For example, Reich (1945) was primarily from a psychoanalytic lineage, but his influence today is most clearly manifested in the humanistic/existential grouping through the presence of the bio-energetic therapy of Lowen (1969). Further examples are Alice Miller (1979/83), originally a psychoanalyst who sounds very humanistic, and Geoffrey Kelly (1955), who developed a constructivist view. Whereas Masterson (1976) is clearly in the first group, despite his early protestations, Kohut's (1977) actual

Table 1.1 Map of major traditions of psychotherapy

School of therapy	Psychoanalytic	Behavioural	Humanistic/ existential
Founder	Freud	Pavlov	Moreno
Date when active	1893	1902	1908
Comments about philosophy, orientation and practice	Bio-psychological determinism. Analysand lying on couch. Psychotherapist is abstinent/opaque, makes interpretations from position of greater understanding. Centrality of unconscious process and transference relationship.	Behaviours seen as a result of learning and conditioning. Emphasis on experimental research and measurable variables. Stimulus/response chains. Cognitive processes. Working alliance essential.	Centrality of responsibility. Non-interpretative concern with here-and-now. Psychotherapist as person, plus transference in some approaches. Occasionally includes transpersonal. Dialogue and relationship. Real relationship emphasised.
Application	Used particularly for neurotic illness, usually modified approach for other disorders. Select client group.	Used particularly for phobias and obsessive behaviours, also depression. Wide client group.	Used for psychoses, personality disorders and neuroses, but also for growth and development. Self-motivated client group.
Aetiology	Sexual and aggressive drives. Early childhood experience.	Conditioned reflexes. Biology. Contingencies of reinforcement.	Biological, social and creative needs from child to adult.
Techniques	Analysis, free association, dream interpretation, parapraxes, etc. Resistance and transference. Interpretation. Catharsis.	Learning and conditioning. Flooding. Modelling. Desensitisation. Thought-stopping. Role rehearsal. Creation of reinforcement schedules. Other cognitive/behavioural techniques (Hawton *et al.* 1989).	Meaning and change. Feelings expressed. Wide and diverse. Active. Interventionist. Invitation to take responsibility. Creative.
Goal	Resignation to the depressive position (Hinshelwood, 1989: 153). Insight.	Adjustment or elimination.	Self-realisation. Self-responsibility.

Table 1.1 Continued

School of therapy	Psychoanalytic	Behavioural	Humanistic/ existential
Other workers	Bion (1962/84)	Beck *et al.* (1990)	Berne (1972/75)
	Bowlby (1952)	Dryden (1984)	Binswanger (1958)
	Anna Freud (1968)	Ellis (1962)	Boss (1979)
	Fairbairn (1952)	Eysenck (1968)	Egan (1975/1982)
	Federn (1977)	Hawton *et al.* (1989)	Frankl (1969)
	Jung (1953)	Lazarus (1981)	Laing (1960)
	Klein (1949)	Skinner (1953)	Maslow (1968)
	Lacan (Benvenuto 1986)		May (1969)
	Malan (1979)		Perls *et al.* (1969)
	Samuels (1985; 1989)		Rogers (1986)
	Symington (1986)		Rowan (1990)
	Winnicott (1958)		Yalom (1970)
Focus	Why?	What?	How?
	The past.	The present, including the immediate past.	The present, including past and future.

position can be ambiguous. Some of Berne's TA followers have remained linked to psychoanalytical developmental theory. Some approaches do not easily fit into this map at all. Hypnotherapy is originally Pavlovian, and systems theorists may be psychodynamic, cognitive-behavioural, humanistic, existential, or all of these in combination or integration (Beutler and Clarkin 1990).

Jung (1953), particularly when thoroughly infused with Kleinian developmental principles, is clearly within the psychoanalytic tradition; for example, in the work of Fordham (1958). However, when the focus is on the positive role of the unconscious, the interactive humanity of the psychotherapist and the person's self-realisation, his theories and approaches are very much more at home with the humanistic/existentialist group. Samuels (1985), in *Jung and the Post-Jungians*, explores some of the important issues of such a debate, and provides an excellent example of how, within the Jungian tradition, different schools have emerged. Also, the humanistic/existentialist traditions have, more explicitly than the others, emphasised the importance of values, self-chosen meaning and the spiritual dimensions of human life and psychotherapy. This has led to the close liaison with approaches to psychotherapy like psychosynthesis, which emphasise a transpersonal view of the person. I believe this transpersonal relationship (however defined) forms an important dimension in all healing encounters. It has been suggested (Rowan 1990) that these transpersonal approaches may even constitute a fourth force in psychotherapy. The wider use of all three therapeutic approaches by counsellors has also blurred differences.

Of course, individual psychotherapists rarely fit into categories, particularly the more experienced they become. It has been found (Heine 1953) that it was not possible, from client descriptions of psychotherapist activity, to determine to which theoretical school a psychotherapist belongs. What differentiates between therapists appears to be, in fact, the names and labels clients attach to the 'fundamental causes' of their troubles. Ever since Fiedler's studies in the 1950s, it has become more accepted that differences in actual practice between more experienced people are considerably smaller than between beginners of different schools and their more senior colleagues. That is, it appears that which theory guides practice is much less important than experience gained in the field.

Internationally, there is now a discernible trend towards integrative or pluralistic psychotherapy which draws on many traditions and does not adhere to only one 'truth'. In the United States, most psychologists say they are integrative; and it is likely that this trend will become more established in the next few years in the United Kingdom (Dryden 1984). Psychotherapy 'after schoolism' is in view (Clarkson 1995a).

In this book we have brought together experienced psychotherapists from a large variety of approaches, ranging from the purist to the eclectic, from hypnotherapeutic approaches to behavioural, from group analysis to cultural perspectives, from orthodox psychoanalytic to humanistic and existential – with all shades in between – to exemplify the richness and diversity of the field.

THE FUTURE

Whatever the nature of psychotherapy in the future, we believe that certain issues will be crucial to the ongoing debate as to its core concerns. First, the concept of change and what it means. As discussed, there are different kinds of change possible within therapeutic settings: problem-solving, environmental change, adjustment, renegotiation (as in a relationship), developmental change (evolutionary) and personality restructuring (revolutionary change). Certain professional approaches may well be more appropriate than others for certain kinds of change within the person and his/her environment. A second area of great interest is that of relationship within therapeutic settings. Research (Norcross 1986) shows that theoretical differences between 'schools or approaches' is far less important in terms of successful outcome of counselling or psychotherapy, than the quality of the *relationship* between counsellor and client and certain client characteristics, including motivation for change and the willingness to take responsibility for their part in the process. Clarkson (1991, 1995b) and Gelso and Carter (1985) have outlined different relationships appropriate to different therapeutic approaches or client groups (also see Chapters 2 and 8 in this *Handbook*).

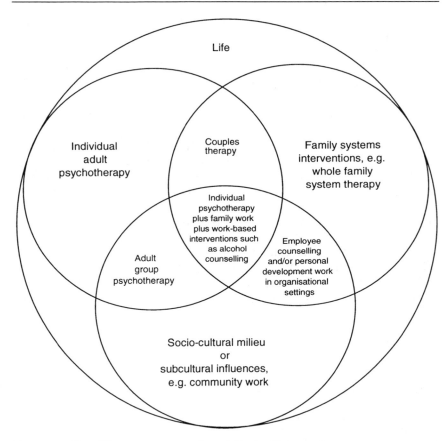

Life

Individual adult psychotherapy

Couples therapy

Family systems interventions, e.g. whole family system therapy

Individual psychotherapy plus family work plus work-based interventions such as alcohol counselling

Adult group psychotherapy

Employee counselling and/or personal development work in organisational settings

Socio-cultural milieu or subcultural influences, e.g. community work

Figure 1.2 The different arenas and modalities of intervention

The third area is that of training. It has now been agreed by all the organisations of UKCP that entry to psychotherapy training must be at postgraduate level and have an academic content roughly equivalent to a master's degree, in addition to supervised clinical practice. It has also been agreed that each psychotherapy training must show that it has adequate arrangements for the trainee to become aware of and manage appropriately their own personal contribution to the kind of psychotherapy being practised. For the psychoanalytically based and humanistic/existential or integrative psychotherapies, these arrangements will continue to be the personal training psychotherapy or psychoanalysis. All require ongoing professional supervision. Further requirements of training courses are evolving gradually and will affect not only the form and content of the courses but are likely to introduce requirements for good educational practice and to establish the universality of external assessment. Moves are being made to link private psychotherapy trainings with academic units offering psychotherapy diplomas and degrees.

Finally, the question of different arenas and modalities of interventions emerges. Figure 1.2 maps out some of the possibilities. The indication or contra-indication for working with different modalities will be addressed in different chapters as the book progresses. The reader is invited to refer back to this diagram whenever it would prove useful to clarify options, complementary modalities and conceptualisations. Are there clients who could be designated as more appropriately the domain of one approach rather than another? This could be done in terms of the 'change' envisaged (or the degree of disturbance); it could be seen in terms of the training of the helper; it could be viewed from the assessed problem of the client. Or indeed, it might well be a combination of all three. *Systematic Treatment Selection* (Beutler and Clarkin 1990) is a good text with which to explore this.

As all these professions continue to develop as fully articulated disciplines, it is hoped that there would be a rich representation of both specialist and integrative approaches to the field, so that this endeavour of alleviating human distress and increasing human happiness can benefit from the uniqueness of classical exclusivity and purity, as well as from the complexity of pluralism, synthesis or even, occasionally, integration.

REFERENCES

Beck, A. T., Freeman, A. and associates (1990) *Cognitive Therapy of Personality Disorders*, New York: Guilford Press.

Benvenuto, B. and Kennedy, R. (1986) *The Works of Jacques Lacan: An Introduction*, London: Free Association Books.

Berne, E. (1975) *What Do You Say After You Say Hello?* London: Corgi (first published 1972).

Beutler, L. E. and Clarkin, J. F. (1990) *Systematic Treatment Selection: Toward Targeted Therapeutic Interventions*, New York: Brunner/Mazel.

Binswanger, L. (1958) 'The existential analysis school of thought' (E. Angel, trans.), pp. 191–213 in R. May, E. Angel and H. F. Ellenberger (eds), *Existence: A New Dimension in Psychiatry and Psychology*, New York: Clarion Books.

Bion, W. R. (1984) *Learning from Experience*, London: Karnac (first published 1962).

Boss, M. (1979) *Existential Foundations of Medicine and Psychology*, New York: Jason Aronson.

Bowlby, J. (1952) *Maternal Care and Mental Health*, Geneva: World Health Organisation.

British Association for Counselling (1984) *Code of Ethics and Practice for Counsellors* (Form no. 20, Sept.), BAC: Rugby.

—— (1989) *Invitation to Membership* (Form no. 1, Oct.), BAC: Rugby.

British Psycho-Analytical Society (1990) *UKSCP Member Organisations' General Information and Training Courses (Sept.)*, London: UKCP.

British Psychological Society, Division of Clinical Psychology (1988a) *MPAG*

Project on Clinical Psychology Services, Manpower and Training Issues: Key Tasks of Clinical Psychology Services (19 July), Leicester: BPS.

—— Division of Clinical Psychology (1988b) *The Representation of Clinical Psychologists: Interim Briefing Paper (Aug.)*, Leicester: BPS.

—— Membership and Qualifications Board (1989) *Report of the Working Party on the Diploma in Counselling Psychology (20 Nov.)*, Leicester: BPS.

—— (1991) *Code of Conduct, Ethical Principles and Guidelines (March)*, Leicester: BPS.

Carroll, M. (1991) 'Counsellor training or counsellor education? A response', *Counselling* 2(3) 104–5.

—— (1992a) *The Generic Tasks of Supervision*, private publication.

—— (1992b) Personal communication.

Carroll, M. and Pickard, E. (1993) 'Psychology and counselling', in B. Thorne and W. Dryden (eds) *Counselling: Interdisciplinary Perspectives*, Milton Keynes: Open University Press.

Clarkson, P. (1991) 'A multiplicity of psychotherapeutic relationships', *British Journal of Psychotherapy* 7(2) 148–63.

—— (1995a) 'After schoolism'. Unpublished paper.

—— (1995b) *The Therapeutic Relationship*, London: Whurr.

Corsini, R. (ed.) (1986) *Current Psychotherapies*, Itasca, IL: F. E. Peacock Publishers.

Dryden, W. (ed.) (1984) *Individual Therapy in Britain*, London: Harper & Row.

Duffy, M. (1990) 'Counselling psychology USA: patterns of continuity and change', *Counselling Psychology Review* 5(3) 9–18.

Egan, G. (1982) *The Skilled Helper: Models, Skills and Methods for Effective Helping*, Belmont, CA: Brooks/Cole (first published 1975).

Ellis, A. (1962) *Reason and Emotion in Psychotherapy*, Secaucus, NJ: Citadel Press.

Eysenck, H. J. (1968) *Handbook of Abnormal Psychology*, London: Pitman Medical.

Fairbairn, W. R. D. (1952) *Psycho-analytic Studies of the Personality*, London: Tavistock.

Federn, P. (1977) *Ego Psychology and the Psychoses*, London: Maresfield Reprints.

Fiedler, F. E. (1950) 'A comparison of therapeutic relationships in psychoanalytic, nondirective and Adlerian therapy', *Journal of Consulting Psychology* 14: 436–45.

Fitzgibbon, G. (1990) Personal communication.

Fordham, M. (1958) *The Objective Psyche*, London: Routledge & Kegan Paul.

Frankl, V. (1969) *Man's Search for Meaning*, London: Hodder & Stoughton.

Freedman, A. M., Kaplan, H. I. and Sadock, B. J. (1975) *Comprehensive Textbook of Psychiatry*, vol. 2, Baltimore: Williams & Wilkins Co.

Freud, A. (1968) 'The widening scope of indications for psychoanalysis: discussion', in *Indications for Child Analysis and Other Papers 1945–1956, the Writings of Anna Freud*, vol. 4, New York: International Universities Press.

Freud, S. (1915/1973) 'Introductory lectures on psychoanalysis', in A. Richards (ed.), J. Strachey (trans.), *The Pelican Freud Library*, vol. 1, Harmondsworth: Pelican (first published 1915–17).

Gelso, C. J. and Carter, J. A. (1985) 'The relationship in counselling and psychotherapy: components, consequences, and theoretical antecedents', *The Counselling Psychologist* 13(2) 155–243.

Greenberg, I. A. (ed.) (1975) *Psychodrama: Theory and Therapy*, London: Souvenir Press.

Hawton, K., Salkovskis, P. M., Kirk, J. and Clark, D. M. (eds). (1989) *Cognitive Behaviour Therapy for Psychiatric Problems: A Practical Guide*, Oxford: Oxford Medical Publications.

Heine, R. W. (1953) 'A comparison of patients' reports on psychotherapeutic experience with psychoanalytic, nondirective and Adlerian therapists', *American Journal of Psychotherapy* 7: 16–23.

Henderson, D. and Gillespie, R. D. (1956) *A Text-Book of Psychiatry*, Oxford: Oxford University Press (first published 1940).

Hinshelwood, R. D. (1989) *A Dictionary of Kleinian Thought*, London: Free Association Books.

Holmes, J. and Lindley, R. (1989) *The Values of Psychotherapy*, Oxford: Oxford University Press.

Jung, C. G. (1953) *Psychological Types*, London: Routledge & Kegan Paul; New York: Trench Trubner.

Karasu, T. B. (1986) 'The psychotherapies: benefits and limitations', *American Journal of Psychotherapy* 40(3) 324–43.

Kelly, G. (1955) *The Psychology of Personal Constructs*, vols 1 and 2: 75, 595, 600–1, New York: Norton.

Klein, M. (1949) *The Psychoanalysis of Children*, London: Hogarth Press.

Kohut, H. (1977) *The Restoration of the Self*, New York: International Universities Press.

Laing, R. D. (1960) *The Divided Self*, Harmondsworth: Penguin Books.

Laplanche, J. and Pontalis, J. B. (1988) *The Language of Psychoanalysis*, London: Karnac (first published 1973).

Lazarus, A. A. (1981) *The Practice of Multi-modal Therapy*, New York: McGraw-Hill.

Loughley, J. (1985) Personal communication at BPS Counselling Psychology Conference, London.

Lowen, A. (1969) *The Betrayal of the Body*, New York: Collier-Macmillan.

Malan, D. H. (1979) *Individual Psychotherapy and the Science of Psychodynamics*, London: Butterworth.

Maslow, A. H. (1968) *Toward a Psychology of Being* (2nd ed.), New York: D. Van Nostrand.

Masterson, J. F. (1976) *Psychotherapy of the Borderline Adult: A Developmental Approach*, New York: Brunner/Mazel.

May, R. (1969) *Love and Will*, New York: W. W. Norton.

Mayer-Gross, W., Slater, E. and Roth, M. (1954) *Clinical Psychiatry*, London: Cassell.

Merskey, H. and Tonge, W. L. (1965) *Psychiatric Illness*, London: Baillière, Tindall & Cox.

Miller, A. (1983) *The Drama of the Gifted Child and the Search for the True Self* (R. Ward, trans.), London: Faber & Faber (first published 1979).

Moreno, J. (1965) 'Therapeutic vehicles and the concept of surplus reality', *Group Psychotherapy* 18(4): 213.

Norcross, J. (ed.) (1986) *Handbook of Eclectic Psychotherapy*, New York: Brunner/Mazel.

Onions, C. T. (1968) *The Shorter Oxford English Dictionary*, Oxford: Clarendon/ Oxford University Press.

Pavlov, I. P. (1927) *Conditioned Reflexes*, New York: Oxford University Press (first published 1908).

Perls, F. S., Hefferline, R. F. and Goodman, P. (1969) *Gestalt Therapy: Excitement and Growth in the Human Personality*, New York: Julian Press.

Proctor, B. (1989) Personal communication.

Reich, W. (1945) *Character Analysis*, New York: Simon & Schuster.

Roget, P. M. (1947) *Thesaurus of Words and Phrases*, New York: Grosset & Dunlap.

Rogers, C. R. (1961) *On Becoming a Person: A Therapist's View of Psychotherapy*, London: Constable.
—— (1986) *Client-centred Therapy*, London: Constable.
Rowan, J. (1990) *What is Humanistic Psychotherapy?* London, Routledge.
Samuels, A. (1985) *Jung and the Post-Jungians*, London: Routledge & Kegan Paul.
—— (1989) *The Plural Psyche*, London: Routledge.
Skinner, B. F. (1953) *Science and Human Behaviour*, New York: Macmillan.
Symington, N. (1986) *The Analytic Experience*, London: Free Association Books.
Watkins, J. G. (1965) 'Psychotherapeutic Methods', pp. 1143–67 in B. B. Wolman (ed.) *Handbook of Clinical Psychology*, New York: McGraw-Hill.
Winnicott, D. W. (1958) *Collected Papers*, London: Tavistock Publications.
Wolberg, L. R. (1954) *The Technique of Psychotherapy*, New York: Grune & Stratton.
Wolman, B. B. (ed.) (1965) *Handbook of Clinical Psychology*, New York: McGraw-Hill.
Yalom, I. D. (1970) *The Theory and Practice of Group Psychotherapy*, New York: Basic Books.

Chapter 2

The psychotherapeutic relationship*

Petrūska Clarkson

In this chapter I want to present a theoretical and conceptual lens through which to view the many and varied contributions which follow in the rest of this book. Not every reader may find themselves in agreement with this, nor is it necessary to accept this perspective in its entirety in order to derive benefit from what follows. However, it is meant to provide a complete contribution in and of itself – a review of five different kinds of psychotherapeutic relationship which may be potentially available for constructive use in psychotherapy. It is also an invitation to engage in, reflect on and view the contributions which follow. Most of the approaches discussed in the previous chapter can be considered in terms of which, or how many, of the five relationships I have identified, are foregrounded or emphasised in the work of the practitioners from that discipline or from that approach. As you read the following chapters, you may be aware of how implicitly or explicitly the relationship is dealt with, and how aspects of it are treated more fully. It is nevertheless my contention that all of these five relationships are available in every psychotherapeutic encounter, available for attention or not, according to the nature of the people involved, the context, the approach and the setting. For example, it may be more difficult to acknowledge transpersonal influences on the psychotherapeutic endeavour in a highly rationalist, experimentally orientated, cognitive-behavioural clinic. Similarly, the ideologies and cultural constraints of some forms of psychoanalysis may impede and inhibit the therapeutic use of, say, the provision of an educationally needed, enacted rehearsal for a job interview, or a longed-for touch on the shoulder when in deep distress. It is my belief that these five modalities of relationship exist in every psychotherapeutic relationship (whether it be with individuals, groups, families or larger systems). Like the keys on a piano, some of them may be played more frequently or more loudly than others, depending on the

* This chapter forms the basis of Petrūska Clarkson's *The Therapeutic Relationship* (London: Whurr).

nature of the music. But they are always potentially there in every therapeutic encounter whether or not the pianist uses them, whether or not the composer acknowledges their existence in the written score.

In this way, I think that the variety and nature of psychotherapeutic relationships is present implicitly or explicitly throughout the psychotherapeutic canon. In working with this material, experienced clinicians tend to recognise that in their own practices some aspects of these relationships are indeed more or less present. Novice psychotherapists have found it very helpful as a matrix from which to learn from many different traditions in psychotherapy and as a framework for integrating what they may still learn; helping them to order, categorise and prioritise the literature while developing precision and purpose in practice.

Relationship or the interconnectedness between two people has been significant in all healing since the time of Hippocrates and Galen. Relationship can be defined as 'the state of being related; a condition or character based upon this; kinship' (Onions 1973: 1786). Relationship is the first condition of being human. It circumscribes two or more individuals and creates a bond in the space between them which is more than the sum of the parts. It is so obvious that it is frequently taken for granted, and so mysterious that many of the world's greatest psychologists, novelists and philosophers have made it a lifetime's preoccupying passion. According to the received wisdom of the late twentieth century, of all the forces of nature it is our familial relationships which often serve to cause the most damage. Statistically you are more likely to be killed by a relation than by a stranger. According to Boss, the great existentialist, all illness and treatment develop out of the patient's disturbed human relationships: 'In focusing on the physician–patient relationship, Freud called attention to the true locus of all therapeutic efforts, whether they were surgical, internal or psychotherapeutic' (1979: 257).

It is the intention of this chapter to make explicit what is often implicit in psychotherapy literature regarding the variety and nature of psychotherapeutic relationships. This chapter reaches for an elucidation of relationship, the *betweenness* of people. It is common knowledge that ordinary human relationships can have therapeutic value. The old structures of religion, accepted moral order and extended family networks used to provide supportive relationships and healing matrices for many people. These appear to have started to crumble in the twentieth century. Indeed, it is possible that psychotherapy as an institutionalized profession became necessary as a consequence of such a decline in the society and quality of healing relationships which were available in previous centuries.

As discussed in Chapter 3 regarding research, one of the most important factors to emerge is the significance of the therapeutic relationship, which is thought to be common to all psychotherapies. 'A constant focus has been on what it is that therapists do which leads to client change' (Barkham and

Elton Wilson, p. 58 in this volume). As discussed in the previous chapter and as emerges from the research, it is very difficult if not impossible to establish with anything more than partisan preferences that any one psychotherapy is more effective than any other: 'All have won and all must have prizes' (Luborsky *et al.* 1975). However, there is a consensus of agreement of the crucial importance of the therapeutic relationship. This has led to a development of integrative psychotherapy on the one hand, and on the other to the broadening and deepening of the understanding of interventions, and to theoretical explorations of many of the unimodal approaches to psychotherapy.

Research, empirical studies and reviews have failed to demonstrate clear advantages differentially attributable to different psychotherapy systems. Research has focused on the identification of the common factor or common ingredients. It seems that success in psychotherapy can best be predicted by the properties of the psychotherapist, the client and their particular relationship. Frank (1979) and Hynan (1981) are two of the many researchers who have found that the client, the psychotherapist and the therapeutic relationship between them are repeatedly more closely related to outcome than whatever technique has been used.

> Most beginning clinicians understand that it is important to live by the basic ground rules of therapy. Confidentiality must be honored, and the boundaries of the therapeutic relationship must be respected, which means remembering every moment that our clients are neither friends nor lovers. Most therapists know these rules, but until one has grasped just how subtle and complex the relationship can be, and how important the therapist becomes to the client, one is likely to seriously under-estimate how easy it is to damage the therapy. The slightest breach of confidentiality can be magnified by the client into a major betrayal; a chance encounter with a client outside the consulting room can evolve into a problematic social situation and have serious repercussions. An off-hand remark or thoughtless joke can cause pain or confusion the client may not be able to acknowledge. . . . The second reason for attending to the relationship is that it gives one a major therapeutic advantage. This book will take the position that awareness of the subtleties and changes in the relationship provides the therapist with a powerful tool, perhaps the most powerful therapeutic tool of all. It will try to show why that is true and how that tool might be used in our work with clients.
>
> (Kahn 1991: 2–3)

It was after the publication of my paper that I came across Kahn's book, in which he introduces a perspective on using the relationship as a central factor in all of psychotherapy. Kahn's teacher said, 'The relationship *is* the therapy' (Kahn 1991: 1).

If indeed the therapeutic relationship is one of the most, if not *the* most, important factor in successful psychotherapy, one would expect much of the training in psychotherapy to be training in the intentional use of relationship. Some psychotherapists claim that psychotherapy requires use of only one kind of relationship, or at most two. Some specifically exclude the use of certain kinds of relationship. For example, Goulding and Goulding (1979), transactional analysts, minimise the use of transference, whereas Moiso (1985), also in transactional analysis, sees it as a central focal point of classical Bernian psychotherapy. Gestaltists Polster and Polster (1973) and the existentialist May (1969) focus on the existential nature of the therapeutic relationship. Some psychotherapeutic approaches pay hardly any theoretical attention to the nature of the relationship and they may attempt to be entirely free of content. For example, in some approaches to hypnotherapy or Neuro-Linguistic Programming (NLP), therapeutic changes are claimed to be made by the patient without the practitioner necessarily knowing what these changes may be.

Psychoanalysts, whether most influenced by Freud or Klein or Bion, consider the transference relationship to be the most important, if not the only, defining characteristic of the approach.

THE WORKING ALLIANCE

The working alliance is probably the most essential relationship modality operative in psychotherapy. Without such a working alliance psychotherapy is certainly limited in its goals and restricted in scope. This working alliance is represented by the client's or patient's willingness to engage in the psychotherapeutic relationship even when they at some archaic level may no longer wish to do so (see also Chapter 8 regarding individual adult psychotherapy).

In transactional analysis, the working alliance is conceptualised as a contract or agreement between the adult of the psychotherapist and adult of the client. In psychoanalysis it is 'the relatively non-neurotic, rational, and realistic attitudes of the patient toward the analyst. . . . It is this part of the patient–analyst relationship that enables the patient to identify with the analyst's point of view and to work with the analyst despite the neurotic transference reactions' (Greenson 1967: 29). The attitudes and character traits which further the development of the transference neurosis are basically antithetical to those which further the working alliance (Stone 1961; Greenson 1965, 1967). So it is unlikely that both can become operative at the same moment. Which one is allowed to become figure, or focus, must depend on the nature of the psychotherapeutic task at a particular time with each unique patient. Other modes of therapeutic relationship may also be present but may be more in the background at a particular time.

For many psychotherapists the working alliance is the crucial and necessary relationship for effective therapy (Dryden 1984). It certainly is the necessary co-operation that even the general practitioner requires in order to work effectively with patients, be it simply at the level that the patient takes the medication as prescribed. Anecdotal evidence and research have shown that this working alliance is frequently missing in general practice (Griffith 1990). 'The therapeutic alliance is the powerful joining of forces which energizes and supports the long, difficult, and frequently painful work of life-changing psychotherapy' (Bugental 1987: 49). Bordin (1979) differentiated goals, bonds and tasks – three aspects of the working alliance which seem to be required for any form of therapy to be successful. Several studies emphasise the importance of further common factors:

> Among the common factors most frequently studied have been those identified by the client-centred school as 'necessary and sufficient conditions' for patient personality to change; accurate empathy, positive regard, nonpossessive warmth, and congruence or genuineness. Virtually all schools of psychotherapy accept the notion that these or related therapist relationship variables are important for significant progress in psychotherapy and, in fact, fundamental in the formation of a working alliance.
>
> (Lambert 1986: 444–5)

Most forms of psychotherapy use this state of voluntary kinship or relationship more or less consciously and more or less in awareness. The Jungian Samuels states that 'the psychology of the soul turns out to be about people in relationship' (Samuels 1985: 21).

THE TRANSFERENTIAL/COUNTER-TRANSFERENTIAL RELATIONSHIP

This mode of therapeutic relationship is the one most extensively written about, for it is extremely well developed, articulated and effectively used within the theoretically rich psychoanalytic tradition and other approaches (Racker 1982; Heimann, 1950; Cashdan 1988; Langs 1976; Clarkson 1992). It is important to remember that Freud did not intend psychoanalysis to be a cure but rather a search for understanding, and he frowned upon people who wished to 'change' instead of analyse. So the transference relationship is an essential part of the analytic procedure since the analysis consists in inviting the transference and gradually dissolving it by means of interpretation (Greenson 1967).

Laplanche and Pontalis describe transference as follows:

> For psycho-analysis, a process of actualization of unconscious wishes. Transference uses specific objects and operates in the framework of a

specific relationship established with these objects. Its context *par excellence* is the analytic situation. In the transference, infantile prototypes re-emerge and are experienced with a strong sensation of immediacy. As a rule what psycho-analysts mean by the unqualified use of the term 'transference' is *transference during treatment*. Classically, the transference is acknowledged to be the terrain on which all the basic problems of a given analysis play themselves out: the establishment, modalities, interpretation and resolution of the transference are in fact what define the cure.

(1988: 455)

Freud (1912b) went so far at one point as to suggest that the analyst model himself on the surgeon, put aside his human sympathy and adopt an attitude of emotional coldness. 'This means that the analyst must have the ability to restrain his therapeutic intentions, must control his urge for closeness and must "blanket" his usual personality' (Stone 1961: 20). Freud advocated that the analyst should refrain from intruding his personality into the treatment, and he introduced the simile of the analyst being a 'mirror' for the analysand (Freud 1912b: 118). This may not in fact be an accurate picture of what Freud had in mind. Perhaps he emphasised certain 'unnatural' aspects of psychoanalytic technique because they were so foreign and artificial to the usual doctor–patient relationship and the customary psychotherapy of his day.

For example, in a paper written in the same year (1912) as the one in which he cites the recommendations for emotional coldness and the mirror-like attitude, Freud stated:

Thus the solution of the puzzle is that transference to the doctor is suitable for resistance to the treatment only in so far as it is a negative transference or a positive transference of repressed erotic impulses. If we 'remove' the transference by making it conscious, we are detaching only these two components of the emotional act from the person of the doctor; the other component, which is admissible to consciousness and unobjectionable, persists and is the vehicle of success in psycho-analysis exactly as it is in other methods of treatment.

(1912a: 105)

Alexander and French expressed the psychoanalytic principle as follows:

The old pattern was an attempt at adaptation on the part of the child to parental behavior . . . the analyst's objective and understanding attitudes allows the patient . . . to make a new settlement of the old problem. . . . While the patient continues to act according to outdated patterns, the analyst's reaction conforms strictly to the actual therapeutic situation.

(1946: 66–7)

Berne wrote:

> Transactionally, this means that when the patient's Child attempts to provoke the therapist's Parent, it is confronted instead with the therapist's Adult. The therapeutic effect arises from the disconcertion caused by this crossed transaction.
>
> (1961: 174)

The patient's question 'How are you?' may often be met with analytic silence. Alternatively the analyst may reply: 'I wonder what prompts your concern for me? It may be that you are anxious again, like you were with your mother, that I will not be able to withstand your envy towards me.'

This transferential psychotherapeutic relationship can be compared to that of stepparent or godparent. Negative transference connects with the former (the witch of many traditional fairy tales – for example, Hansel and Gretel) and idealising positive transference resonates with the godparent or fairy godmother relationship in that a putative family connection exists, but it lacks the immediacy of a real parent. Whether or not the psychotherapist identifies with such projections, and how he or she handles them, may destroy or facilitate the psychotherapy. Clearly, the nature and vicissitudes of the counter-transference are inextricably interwoven with the management of the transference relationship, and efficacy of the psychotherapy may well be determined by it.

A narcissistic, apparently generous but dynamically retentive patient whose mother over-fed him physically while never responding to his real feelings of isolation, abandonment or rage reports the following dream: 'I am at a sumptuous banquet which is presided over by you [the psychotherapist]. I take the food from the table, but I don't eat it. I put it in a plastic bag so that you won't see and I throw it in a wastepaper basket. I want to continue to be invited, but not to have to eat the food.'

> The great importance of the transference has often led to the mistaken idea that it is absolutely indispensable for a cure, that it must be demanded from the patient, so to speak. But a thing like that can no more be demanded than faith, which is only valuable when it is spontaneous. Enforced faith is nothing but spiritual cramp. Anyone who thinks that he must 'demand' a transference is forgetting that this is only one of the therapeutic factors.
>
> (Jung 1966: 172)

THE REPARATIVE/DEVELOPMENTALLY NEEDED RELATIONSHIP

The reparative/developmentally needed relationship is another relationship mode which can occasionally be differentiated from the others. This is the intentional provision by the psychotherapist of a corrective/reparative or replenishing parental relationship (or action) where the original parenting was deficient, abusive or over-protective. The following dream shows a client separating out a developmentally needed relationship (for the client's future) from the transferential relationship (based on the client's past).

He dreams about two psychotherapists, both with the same name as his psychotherapist. One psychotherapist says to him in the dream: 'How could you make such mistakes, this is terrible, you ought to be punished!'. In the dream the other psychotherapist says, 'Look, I myself received a D in this subject. I wasn't very interested in it, and you can see that you don't have to be perfect in all things.' The first psychotherapist responds with anger and accusations of unethical conduct, saying, 'How could you say such things, you are just encouraging him to make mistakes and setting a very bad example!' The client himself then steps in to arbitrate and explains to the first psychotherapist: 'Actually she is right. You have to understand what she is saying *in the right spirit.*' This is what the client needed to hear.

Dreams often act as unconscious communication about the progress of the psychotherapy from the unconscious of the client. In this dream the client is clearly telling the psychotherapist what he needs developmentally – what was absent in the original relationship where he veered between being the saintly, clean little boy who has to play without getting dirty and the disgusting child who causes embarrassment and shame to his family if he as much as gets his hands dirty. (In his adult life he veers between saintly self-sacrifice and secret addictions.) The client is also communicating a most significant fact – not only has he internalised the psychotherapist and distinguishes the two personifications of the person of the same name, but happily he is siding with the psychotherapist who has his best interests at heart, and least resembles the transferential parent who would 'write him off' for the smallest misdemeanour, or shame him for not getting the best marks in every subject regardless of his true interests (even the D is still a passing mark!).

The developmentally needed relationship as indicated in the cited dream refers to those aspects of relationship which may have been absent or traumatic for the client at particular periods of his or her childhood and which are supplied or repaired by the psychotherapist, usually in a contracted form (on request by or with agreement from the patient) during the psychotherapy. Ferenczi (1926/1980), one of Freud's early followers, attempted this early in the history of psychoanalysis. He departed from neutrality and impassivity in favour of giving nursery care, friendly hugs or management of regression to very sick patients, including one whom he saw any time, day or night, and took with him on his holidays. Ferenczi held that there needed to be a contrast between the original trauma in infancy and the analytic situation so that remembering can be facilitative instead of a renewed trauma for the patient.

The advocacy relationship proposed by Alice Miller (1983, 1985) can be seen to be the provision of the developmentally needed force in a child's life which should have been provided by a parent or other significant caretakers but which the psychotherapist ultimately has to provide. The holding environment of Winnicott (1958) is another example of such provision, as are the reparenting techniques of Schiff *et al.* (1975) in transactional analysis.

Freud (1912b) prescribed a mirror-like impassivity on the part of the analyst, who should him- or herself be analysed, who should not reciprocate the patient's confidences, nor try to educate, morally influence, or 'improve' the patient, and who should be tolerant of the patient's weakness. In practice, however, Freud conducted psychotherapy as no classical Freudian analyst would conduct it nowadays (Malcolm 1981); shouting at the patient, praising him, arguing, accepting flowers from him on his birthday, lending him money, visiting him at home and even gossiping with him about other patients!

The psychoanalyst Sechehaye (1951) was able to break through the unreal wall that hemmed in her patient Renée and bring her into some contact with life. In order to do this, Sechehaye not only took her on holiday to the seashore, as Ferenczi had done with one of his patients, but also took Renée into her home for extended periods. She allowed her to regress to the point where she felt she was re-entering her mother's body, thus becoming one of the first of those psychotherapists who have actually undertaken to 'reparent' schizophrenic clients. She allowed her to lean on her bosom and pretended to give milk from her breasts to the doll with whom Renée identified.

> That Sechehaye was far more involved personally than even the most humanistic of therapists usually are we can infer from the accounts of how she gave instructions for her meals, saw to her baths, and in general played for Renée the nourishing mother that she had been denied as an infant. That this took an emotional toll far beyond the ordinary is evident from Renée's own account that 'Mama was extremely upset' or that she regained consciousness and found Mama weeping over her.
>
> (Friedman, 1985: 188)

The psychotherapist's reply to a client who asks: 'How are you?' in this kind of relationship will be determined by the specific needs that were not appropriately responded to by their caretakers in childhood. In response to the adult who as a child was never allowed to show her care or love for the parent the therapist may reply: 'I'm fine, thank you, and I appreciate your caring.' Alternatively, in response to the adult who as a child was burdened with parental intimacies, a therapist may reply, 'It is not necessary for you to worry about me, right now I am here to take care of you and I am ready to do that.'

In the developmentally needed relationship, the metaphoric kinship relationship being established is clearly closer to a real parent-and-child relationship than any of the other forms of bonding in psychotherapy. In the words of J. Schiff:

> I am as much part of the symbiosis and as vulnerable as any parent. While my attachments don't occur at the same kind of depth with each youngster, they have not been selective in favor of those kids who were successful, and several times I have experienced tremendous loss and grief.
>
> (1977: 63)

In view of the regressive nature of this kind of work and the likely length of time involved, the professional and ethical responsibilities of the psychotherapists are also concomitantly greater and perhaps so awesome that many psychotherapists try to avoid them. It is certainly true that this depth of long-standing psychotherapeutic relationship as the primary therapeutic relationship modality is more frequently reported between psychotherapists and more severely damaged patients.

THE I–YOU RELATIONSHIP

Particularly within the humanistic/existential tradition, there is appreciation of the *person-to-person relationship* or *real relationship*. This therapeutic relationship modality shows most continuity with the healing relationships of ordinary life. Buber (1970) called this the I–Thou, or I–You relationship to differentiate it from the I–It relationship. The I–You relationship is referred to elsewhere in psychotherapeutic literature as the real relationship or the core relationship (Barr 1987). It is very likely that those ordinary relationships which human beings have experienced as particularly healing over the ages have been characterised by the qualities of the I–You relationship (Buber 1970). This has been retrieved and valued for its transformative potential in the psychotherapeutic arena *if* used skilfully and ethically (Rogers 1961; Laing 1965; Polster and Polster 1973). However, there has always been, and there is again, growing recognition within psychoanalytic practice that the real relationship between analyst and analysand – following Freud's own example – is a deeply significant, unavoidable and potentially profoundly healing force also within the psychoanalytic paradigm (Malcolm 1981; Klauber 1986; Archambeau 1979).

With Freud's discovery of the importance of the transference relationship came deep suspicion of the real relationship – the therapeutic relationship most similar to ordinary human relationships. Certainly for some decades psychoanalysts' emotional reactions to their patients were usually understood to be a manifestation of the analysts' unresolved conflicts. It is only comparatively recently that analyst feelings or counter-transference reactions have been seen as valid and important sources of information to be used effectively in the psychotherapy (Heimann 1950).

Object relations theorists have offered psychotherapy profoundly useful concepts and theoretical understandings, but the I–You therapeutic relationship is the opposite of an object relationship. For Buber, the other is a person, not an object.

> Whoever says You does not have something for his object. For wherever there is something there is also another something; every It borders on other Its; It is only by virtue of bordering on others. But where You is said, there is no something. You has no borders. Whoever says You does not have something; he has nothing. But he stands in relation.
>
> (Buber 1970: 55)

The emotional involvement in this relationship between psychotherapist and patient is that between *person and person* in the existential dilemma where both stand in a kind of mutuality to each other. Indeed, as Friedman (1985) points out, it is a kind of mutuality because the psychotherapist is also *in* role. However, in the immediacy of the existential encounter, the mutuality is almost complete and the Self of the therapist becomes the instrument through which the healing evolves.

An intuitive, introverted type of patient sadly remembers difficulty with differentiating right from left, along with physical discomfort in the real world and incomprehension when required to learn kinaesthetically. The psychotherapist bends down to show the scar on her leg which she used as a little girl to help her decide which side was left. The moment is unforgettable; the bonding, person to person. Yet it is enacted by a professional person who, at that very moment, has taken responsibility for that self-disclosure in the psychotherapy, judging it appropriate and timely to trust or delight the patient with a sense of shared personhood. The two then become siblings in incomprehension, siblings in discovery, and siblings in the quest for wholeness.

Such self-disclosure needs, of course, to be done with extreme care and, in its worst, abusive form, has been an excuse for inauthentic acting out of the psychotherapist's own need for display, hostility or seductiveness. Genuine, well-judged use of the I–You relationship is probably one of the most difficult forms of therapeutic relating. Doubtless this was the very good reason behind the early analysts' regarding it with extreme suspicion. It probably requires the most skill, the most self-knowledge and the greatest care, because its potential for careless or destructive use is so great. Yet there are only a few trainings – for example, in Gestalt – which specifically address this experientially and theoretically. Sometimes lip-service is paid to the I–You, person-to-person concept as if we know what it's about, or it is 'outlawed' in the analysis – as if this were possible.

'There can be no psychoanalysis without an existential bond between the analyst and the analysand', writes Boss (1963: 118). The I–You relationship is characterised by the *here-and-now existential encounter* between the two people. It involves mutual participation in the process and the recognition that each is changed by the other. Its field is not object relations, but subject relations. The real person of the psychotherapist can never be totally excluded from an interactional matrix of therapy. Existential psychotherapy (Boss 1963; Binswanger 1968; May 1969), specifically includes the I–You genuine encounter as a major therapeutic modality, but analysts are also addressing the issue.

> It is good for analyst and patient to have to admit some of the analyst's weaknesses as they are revealed in the interchange in the consulting room. The admission of deficiencies may help patient and analyst to let go of one another more easily when they have had enough. In other words, the somewhat freer admission of realities – but not too free – facilitates the process of mourning which enables an analysis to end satisfactorily. The end of analysis is in this way prepared from the beginning.
>
> (Klauber 1986: 213)

To Fromm-Reichmann (1950/1974), Sullivan's (1940) concept of the psychotherapist as 'participant observer' included spontaneous and genuine responses on the part of the psychotherapist and even, in some cases, reassuring touch and gestures of affection. This does *not* include transforming the professional relationship into a social one, nor seeking extraneous personal gratification from the dialogue with the patient. But it does include confirmation of patients as worthy of respect, and meeting them on the basis of mutual human equality.

Guntrip (1961) also rejected the traditional restriction of the functions of the psychotherapist to the dual one of a screen upon which the patient projects his fantasies and a colourless instrument of interpretative technique. Instead, he saw the real personal relationship between patient and analyst as the truly psychotherapeutic factor on which all others depend. For him, true psychotherapy only happens when the therapist and patient find the person behind each other's defences.

Deep insight, as Fairbairn (1952) points out, only develops inside a good therapeutic relationship. What is therapeutic, when it is achieved, is 'the moment of real meeting'. This experience is transforming for both psychotherapist and patient because it is not what happened before (that is transference) but what has never happened before, a genuine experience of relationship centred in the here-and-now.

What Freud calls 'transference' Boss (1979) describes as 'always a genuine relationship between the analysand and the analyst'. Despite the difference in their positions the partners disclose themselves to each other as human beings. It seems that Freud and Boss are describing different therapeutic relationship modalities which are intrinsically different in intent, in execution, and in effect; not merely a semantic blurring.

Of course, the humanistically orientated psychotherapies (such as Gestalt which emphasises here-and-now *contact* as a valid form of therapeutic relating) have greatly amplified the value and use of the person-to-person encounter in psychotherapy.

> The details of technique vary, but the strategy is always to keep a steady, gentle pressure toward the direct and responsible I–thou orientation, keeping the focus of awareness on the difficulties the patients experience in doing this, and helping them find their own ways through these difficulties.
>
> (Fagan and Shepherd 1971: 116)

For Rogers and Stevens (1967), too, the establishment of a relationship of genuineness, respect and empathy became the cornerstone conditions for facilitating human growth and development. In psychoanalysis, even Anna Freud called for the recognition that in analysis two real people of equal adult status stand in a real personal relationship to each other: 'There are differences in the ways in which we receive and send off patients, and in the degree to which we permit a real relationship to the patient to coexist with the transferred, fantasied one' (1968: 360). It is the neglect of this side of the relationship, and not just 'transference' that may cause the hostile reactions analysts get from their patients, according to Stone (1961). Stone expressed concern lest the analyst's unrelentingly analytic behaviour subvert the process by shaking the patient's faith in the analyst's benignity. He declared that a failure to show reasonable human response at a critical juncture can invalidate years of patient, skilful work.

According to Malcolm (1981), honesty and spontaneity can correct the patient's transference misperceptions, making the psychotherapist's responses unpredictable and therefore less likely to be manipulated by the patient. The patient's distrust may be relieved when the psychotherapist provides a model of authentic being with which he can identify. Such authenticity on the psychotherapist's part may mean that the therapeutic relationship changes the therapist as much as the patient. Both Jourard (1971) and Jung (1966) held this as a central truth in all healing endeavour. Searles (1975) also believed that the patient has a powerful innate striving to heal the analyst (as he or she may have desired to heal the parents), which can and does contribute to greater individuation and growth for the psychotherapist as they are *both* transformed in the therapeutic dialogue. 'What is confirmed most of all is the personal "realness" of the therapist that has arisen from and been brought into the therapeutic relationship'

(Archambeau 1979: 141–58). I also quote Greenson directly: 'A certain amount of compassion, friendliness, warmth, and respect for the patient's rights is indispensable. The analyst's office is a treatment room and not a research laboratory' (1967: 391).

Greenacre (1959) and Stone (1961) are clear that the analyst must be able to become emotionally involved with and committed to the patient. He must like the patient; prolonged dislike or disinterest as well as too strong a love will interfere with therapy. He must have a wish to help and cure the patient, and he must be concerned with the patient's welfare without losing sight of his long-range goals.

In all cases the person-to-person relationship will be honoured by truthfulness or authenticity – not at the expense of the client but in the spirit of mutuality. According to Buber, the genuine psychotherapist can only accomplish the true task of regenerating the stunted growth of a personal centre by entering as 'a partner into a person-to-person relationship, but never through the observation and investigation of an object' (1970: 179). Significantly, though, this does not mean injudicious honesty. Buber further acknowledges the limited nature of the psychotherapeutic person-to-person relationship: 'Every I–You relationship in a situation defined by the attempt of one partner to act on the other one so as to accomplish some goal depends on a mutuality that is condemned never to become complete' (1970: 179).

THE TRANSPERSONAL RELATIONSHIP

This refers to the spiritual dimension of relationship in psychotherapy. Within the Jungian tradition (Jung 1969) and also within the humanistic/ existential perspective (Rowan 1983), there is acknowledgement of the influence of the qualities which presently transcend the limits of our understanding (as expressed by Hamlet with 'There are more things on heaven and earth, Horatio, than are dreamt of in your philosophy' (Shakespeare, in Alexander 1951: 166). However defined, some implicit or explicit recognition of the possibility, if not the existence, of a *transpersonal relationship* between healer and healed as it unfolds within the psychotherapeutic *vas* (container) is gradually beginning to gain more acceptance (Clarkson 1990).

'If the analyst has been moved by his patient, then the patient is more aware of the analyst as a healing presence' (Samuels 1985: 189). The transpersonal relationship in psychotherapy is characterised by its timelessness, and in Jungian thought is conceived of as the relationship between the unconscious of the analyst and the unconscious of the patient not mediated by consciousness (Guggenbuhl-Craig 1971).

The psychotherapist and the client find themselves in a relationship built on mutual unconsciousness. The psychotherapist is led to a direct

confrontation of the unreconciled part of himself. The activated unconsciousness of both the client and the therapist causes both to become
involved in a transformation of the 'third'. Hence, the relationship itself
becomes transformed in the process.

(Archambeau 1979: 162)

There is surprisingly little documented about the transpersonal relationship in psychotherapy. Peck (1978) mentions the concept of 'grace', as has
Buber before him, as the ultimate factor which operates in the person-to-
person encounter and which may make the difference between whether a
patient gets better or not. Berne, too, was aware of it in 1966 when he
quoted: '"Je le pensay, et Dieu le guarit" . . . I treat him, but it is God
who cures him' (Agnew 1963: 75).

The nature of this transpersonal dimension is therefore quite difficult to
describe, because it is both rare and not easily accessible to the kind of
descriptions which can easily be used in discussing the other forms of
therapeutic relationships. 'The *numinosum* is either a quality belonging to
a visible object or the influence of an invisible presence that causes a
peculiar alternation of consciousness' (Jung 1969: 7). It is also possible that
there may be a certain amount of embarrassment in psychotherapists who
have to admit that after all the years of training and personal analysis and
supervision, ultimately we still don't know precisely what it is that we are
doing or whether it makes any difference at all. This is the kind of statement one can only be sure of being understood correctly by experienced
psychotherapists who have been faced repeatedly with incomprehensible
and unpredictable outcomes – the person of whom you despaired, suddenly
and sometimes apparently inexplicably, gets well, thrives and actualises
beyond all expectation. At the other polarity, the client for whom the
analyst had made an optimistic prognosis reaches plateaux from which in
effect they never move, and the analysis is abandoned with a lingering
sense of potential glimpsed but never to be reached.

The transpersonal relationship is also characterised paradoxically by a
kind of intimacy and by an 'emptying of the ego' at the same time. It is
rather as if the ego of even the personal unconscious of the psychotherapist
is 'emptied out' of the therapeutic space, leaving space for something
numinous to be created in the 'between' of the relationship. This space
can then become the 'temenos' or 'the *vas bene clausum* inside which the
transmutation takes place' (Adler 1979: 21). It implies a letting-go of
skills, of knowledge, of experience, of preconceptions, even of the desire
to heal, to be present. It is essentially allowing 'passivity' and receptiveness
for which preparation is always inadequate. But paradoxically you have
to be full in order to be empty. It cannot be made to happen, it can only
be encouraged in the same way that the inspirational muse of creativity
cannot be forced, but needs to have the ground prepared or seized in

the serendipitous moment of readiness. What can be prepared are the conditions conducive to the spontaneous or spiritual act.

A trainee reports:

When I first started learning psychotherapy it was like trying to learn a new language, say French, but when I saw a very experienced psychotherapist working it appeared to me that she was speaking an entirely different language, such as Chinese. The more I have learnt the more I have come to realize that she does indeed speak French, she just speaks it very well. And sometimes she speaks Chinese.

This comment arose from the context of how he has perceived the supervisor at times intuitively to know facts, feelings or intentions of patients without there being any prior evidence to lead to the conclusions. It is these intuitive illuminations which seem to flourish the more the psychotherapist dissolves the individual ego from the therapeutic container, allowing wisdom and insight and transformation to occur as a self-manifesting process. The essence of the communication is in the heart of the shared silence of being-together in a dimension impossible to articulate exactly, too delicate to analyse and yet too pervasively present in psychotherapy to ignore.

Another trainee in supervision brought the following ethical problem. He had seen a particular client for several years, who was seriously disturbed and showed no sign of improvement. He had utilised all the major interpretations and strategies for such cases to no avail. Indeed, the client refused to form any working alliance in the shape of an agreed goal for her psychotherapy. It was exceedingly uncertain what benefit there could be for her, yet she continued coming because (we speculated) this was the only human relationship which was alive for her in a physically and emotionally impoverished life.

The psychotherapist responsibly questioned whether she should be referred to another treatment facility. Yet he feared that she would experience this as abandonment. In our supervision we explored the possibility that he let go of expectations that she should be different from the way she was. The psychotherapist was even willing and able to let go of the healer archetype, allowing himself to become an empty vessel, a container wherein healing could have space to manifest, or beingness could be validated without any expectation even of the acceptance. This needs to be truly done in good faith and not based on the trickery of paradoxical interventions where expectations are removed *in order* for the patient to change. The atmosphere is more a trance-like meditation, the quality of which is conveyed by the being-with of highly evolved psychotherapists with patients who are in acute psychosis, such as Gendlin (1967), who affirm the spiritual dimension in psychotherapy. (It is quite possible that psychotherapists may be deluding themselves in ways which may be dangerous for themselves and their clients if they mistakenly, prematurely or naïvely focus on the transpersonal and, for example, overlook or minimise transferential or personal phenomena.)

James and Savary contributed the notion of a third self created in such a dimension of betweenness when the inner core energies of the dialoguing partners merge. 'Third-self sharing, perhaps the most complete form of sharing, involves not only *self-awareness* (of the individual self) and *other-awareness* (of the relating self), but *together-awareness* (of the third self)' (1977: 325). Psychosynthesis also recognises the notion of a higher self (Hardy 1989).

This resembles the archetype of the Self which Jung refers to as the person's inherent and psychic disposition to experience centredness and meaning in life, sometimes conceived of as the God within ourselves. Buber was essentially concerned with the close association of the relation to God with the relation to one's fellow men, with the I–Thou which issues from the encounter with the *other in relationship*. This dimension in the psychotherapeutic relationship cannot be proved and can hardly be described, and Buber concludes: 'Nothing remains to me in the end but an appeal to the testimony of your own mysteries' (1970: 174).

CONCLUSION

This chapter has briefly described five kinds of psychotherapeutic relationship available as potential avenues for constructive use, and each will be expanded in following chapters. It has indicated some characteristics of each and begun an effort to clarify, specify and differentiate more acutely in theory and practice the nature and intentions of the multiplicity of psychotherapeutic relationships available in the consulting room. Different psychotherapies stress different relationships for different reasons. Whatever the orientation, the psychotherapeutic relationship is therefore a continuing theme throughout all the chapters in this *Handbook*.

It is perhaps time that psychotherapists acknowledged explicitly that these five forms of relationship are intentionally or unintentionally present in most approaches to psychotherapy. Which of these modes of psychotherapeutic relationships are used, and how explicitly and purposefully, may be one of the major ways in which some approaches resemble one another more and differ most from others.

It may need to be recognised in most psychotherapy trainings that experience and supervision are required in distinguishing between such different forms of psychotherapeutic relationship and assessing and evaluating the usefulness of each at different stages of psychotherapy. Equally, different modes may be indicated for individuals with different characteristic ways of relating so that there is not a slipshod vacillation due to error or neurotic counter-transference, nor a denial of the obvious.

Confusion and lack of clarity abound when types of psychotherapeutic relationship are confused with one other, or the validity of one is used as necessarily substituting for the other. It is possible that humans need all of these forms of relating, and that psychotherapists with flexibility and range can become skilful in the appropriate use of all of them, although not all are required in all psychotherapies or for all patients.

The far-ranging implications of this perspective for psychotherapy research, assessment and treatment need to be developed further. Integration of a multiplicity of therapeutic relationship modalities does not mean eclectic or unconscious use. Indeed, if such is the declared field, the responsibility is awesome. Freedom does not mean that we forgo discipline. Courage in actively embracing the fullest range of potentials of the self, theory or the *numinosum* needs to be accompanied by the severest form of testing, and forged anew with each client from moment to moment, no matter what the prescriptions or proscriptions of theoretical orthodoxy.

REFERENCES

Adler, G. (1979) *Dynamics of the Self*, London: Coventure (first published 1951).

Agnew, L. R. C. (1963) 'Notes and events: Paré's apophthegm', *Journal of the History of Medicine* 18: 75–7.

Alexander, F. and French, T. (1946) *Psychoanalytic Therapy*, New York: Ronald Press.

Archambeau, E. (1979) 'Beyond countertransference: the psychotherapist's experience of healing in the therapeutic relationship', Doctoral dissertation, San Diego: California School of Professional Psychology.

Barr, J. (1987) 'Therapeutic relationship model', *Transactional Analysis Journal* 17(4): 141.

Berne, E. (1961) *Transactional Analysis in Psychotherapy: A Systematic Individual and Social Psychiatry*, New York: Grove Press.

—— (1966) *Principles of Group Treatment*, New York: Grove Press.

Binswanger, L. (1968) *Being-in-the-World*, New York: Harper Torchbooks.

Bordin, E. S. (1979) 'The generalizability of the psychoanalytical concept of the working alliance', *Psychotherapy: Theory, Research and Practice* 16(3): 252–60.

Boss, M. (1963) *Psychoanalysis and Daseinanalysis* (L. B. Lefebre, trans.), New York: Basic Books.

—— (1979) *Existential Foundations of Medicine and Psychology*, New York: Jason Aronson.

Buber, M. (1970) *I and Thou* (W. Kaufmann, trans.), Edinburgh: T. & T. Clark (first published 1923).

Bugental, J. F. T. (1987) *The Art of the Psychotherapist*, New York: W. W. Norton.

Cashdan, S. (1988) *Interactional Psychotherapy: Stages and Strategies in Behavioural Change*, New York: Grune & Stratton.

Clarkson, P. (1990) 'A multiplicity of psychotherapeutic relationships', *British Journal of Psychotherapy* 7(2) 148–63.

—— (1992) *TA Psychotherapy: An Integrated Approach*, London: Routledge.

—— (1995) *The Therapeutic Relationship*, London: Whurr.

Dryden, W. (ed.) (1984) *Individual Therapy in Britain*, London: Harper & Row.

Fagan, J. and Shepherd, I. L. (eds) (1971) *Gestalt Therapy Now: Theory, Techniques, Applications*, New York: Harper & Row.

Fairbairn, W. R. D. (1952) *Psychoanalytic Studies of the Personality*, London: Tavistock Publications.

Ferenczi, S. (1980) *Further Contributions to the Theory and Technique of Psychoanalysis*, London: Maresfield Reprints/Karnac Books (first published 1926).

Frank, J. D. (1979) 'The present status of outcome studies', *Journal of Consulting and Clinical Psychology* 47: 310–16.

Freud, A. (1968) *Indications for Child Analysis and Other Papers 1945 to 1956: The Writings of Anna Freud*, vol. 4, New York: International Universities Press.

Freud, S. (1912a) 'The dynamics of transference', pp. 97–108 in J. Strachey (ed.), *The Standard Edition of the Complete Psychological Works of Sigmund Freud*, vol. 12, London: Hogarth Press.

—— (1912b) 'Recommendations to physicians practising psycho-analysis', pp. 109–20 in J. Strachey (ed.) *The Standard Edition of the Complete Psychological Works of Sigmund Freud*, vol. 12, London: Hogarth Press.

Friedman, M. (1985) *The Healing Dialogue in Psychotherapy*, New York: Jason Aronson.

Fromm-Reichmann, F. (1974) *Principles of Intensive Psychotherapy*, Chicago: University of Chicago Press (first published 1950).

Gendlin, E. (1967) 'Subverbal communication and therapist expressivity: trends in client-centred therapy with schizophrenics', pp. 119–49 in C. R. Rogers and B. Stevens (eds) *Person to Person – the Problem of Being a Human: A New Trend in Psychology*, Lafayette, CA: Real People Press.

Goulding, M. M. and Goulding, R. L. (1979) *Changing Lives through Redecision Therapy*, New York: Grove Press.

Greenacre, P. (1959) 'Certain technical problems in the transference relationship', *Journal of the American Psychoanalysis Association* 7: 484–502.

Greenson, R. R. (1965) 'The working alliance and the transference neurosis', *Psychoanalysis Quarterly* 34: 155–81.

—— (1967) *The Technique and Practice of Psychoanalysis*, vol. 1, New York: International Universities Press.

Griffith, S. (1990) 'A review of the factors associated with patient compliance and the taking of prescribed medicines', *British Journal of General Practice* 40: 114–16.

Guggenbuhl-Craig, A. (1971) *Power in the Helping Professions*, Dallas, TX: Spring Publications.

Guntrip, H. (1961) 'Personality structure and human interaction: the developing synthesis of psychodynamic theory', No. 56 in J. D. Sutherland (ed.) *The International Psycho-analytical Library*, London: Hogarth Press and the Institute of Psycho-Analysis.

Hardy, J. (1989) *A Psychology with a Soul*, London: Arkana.

Heimann, P. (1950) 'On countertransference', *International Journal of Psycho-Analysis* 31: 81–4.

Hynan, M. T. (1981) 'On the advantages of assuming that the techniques of psychotherapy are ineffective', *Psychotherapy: Theory, Research and Practice* 18: 11–3.

James, M. and Savary, L. (1977) *A New Self: Self-therapy with Transactional Analysis*, Reading, MA: Addison-Wesley.

Jourard, S. M. (1971) *The Transparent Self*, New York: Van Nostrand Reinhold.

Jung, C. G. (1966) 'The psychology of the transference', pp. 162–323 in *The*

Collected Works, vol. 16 (R. F. C. Hull, trans.), London: Routledge & Kegan Paul (first published 1946).

—— (1969) 'Psychology and religion', pp. 3–105 in *The Collected Works*, vol. 11 (R. F. C. Hull, trans.), London: Routledge & Kegan Paul (first published 1938).

Kahn, M. D. (1991) *Between the Therapist and Client: The New Relationship*, New York: W. H. Freeman.

Kidd, C. (1988) Personal communication.

Klauber, J. (1986) 'Elements of the psychoanalytic relationship and their therapeutic implications', pp. 200–13 in G. Kohon (ed.) *The British School of Psychoanalysis: The Independent Tradition*, London: Free Association Books.

Laing, R. D. (1965) *The Divided Self*, Harmondsworth: Penguin.

Lambert, M. J. (1983) 'Introduction to assessment of psychotherapy outcome: historical perspective and current issues', in M. J. Lambert, E. R. Christiansen and S. S. DeJulio (eds) *The Assessment of Psychotherapy Outcome*, New York: Wiley & Sons.

—— (1986) 'Implications of psychotherapy outcome research for eclectic psychotherapy', pp. 436–62 in J. C. Norcross (ed.) *Handbook of Eclectic Psychotherapy*, New York: Brunner/Mazel.

Langs, R. (1976) *The Bipersonal Field*, New York: Jason Aronson.

Laplanche, J. and Pontalis, J-B. (1988) *The Language of Psycho-analysis*, London: Karnac (first published 1973).

Luborsky, L., Singer, B. and Luborsky, L. (1975) 'Comparative studies of psychotherapies: is it true that "Everybody has won and all must have prizes"?', *Archives of General Psychiatry* 32: 995–1008.

Malcolm, J. (1981) *Psychoanalysis: The Impossible Profession*, New York: Knopf.

May, R. (1969) *Love and Will*, London: Collins.

Miller, A. (1983) *The Drama of the Gifted Child and the Search for the True Self* (R. Ward, trans.), London: Faber & Faber (first published 1979).

—— (1985) *Thou Shalt Not be Aware: Society's Betrayal of the Child* (H. and H. Hannum, trans.), London: Pluto (first published 1981).

Moiso, C. (1985) 'Ego states and transference', *Transactional Analysis Journal* 15(3) 194–201.

Norcross, J. C. (1986) *Handbook of Eclectic Psychotherapy*, New York: Brunner/ Mazel.

Onions, C. T. (1973) *The Shorter Oxford English Dictionary: On Historical Principles*, vol. 2, Oxford: Clarendon Press.

Peck, S. (1978) *The Road Less Traveled: A New Psychology of Love, Traditional Values and Spiritual Growth*, New York: Simon & Schuster.

Polster, E. and Polster, M. (1973) *Gestalt Therapy Integrated*, New York: Random House.

Racker, H. (1982) *Transference and Countertransference*, London: Maresfield Reprints (first published 1968).

Rogers, C. R. (1967) *On Becoming a Person: A Therapist's View of Psychotherapy*, London: Constable (first published 1961).

Rogers, C. R. and Stevens, B. (1967) *Person to Person – the Problem of Being Human: A New Trend in Psychology*, Lafayette, CA: Real People Press.

Rowan, J. (1983) *The Reality Game: A Guide to Humanistic Counselling and Therapy*, London: Routledge & Kegan Paul.

Samuels, A. (1985) *Jung and the Post-Jungians*, London: Routledge & Kegan Paul.

Schiff, J. L., with Schiff, A. W., Mellor, K., Schiff, E., Schiff, S., Richman, D., Fishman, J., Wolz, L., Fishman, C. and Momb, D. (1975) *Transactional Analysis Treatment of Psychosis*, New York: Harper & Row.

Schiff, J. L. (1977) 'One hundred children generate a lot of TA', pp. 54–7 in
  G. Barnes (ed.) *Transactional Analysis after Eric Berne*, New York: Harper's
  College Press.
Searles, H. (1975) 'The patient as therapist to his analyst', pp. 95–151 in R. Langs
  (ed.) *Classics in Psycho-analytic Technique*, New York: Jason Aronson.
Sechehaye, M. (1951) *Reality Lost and Regained: Autobiography of a Schizophrenic
  Girl* (G. Urbin-Rabson, trans.), New York: Grune & Stratton.
Shakespeare, W. *The Complete Works* (P. Alexander, ed.), London: Collins
  (1951).
Stone, L. (1961) *The Psychoanalytic Situation*, New York: International Universities
  Press.
Sullivan, H. S. (1940) *Conception of Modern Psychiatry*, New York: Norton.
Winnicott, D. W. (1958) *Collected Papers: Through Paediatrics to Psycho-analysis*,
  London: Tavistock Publications.

Chapter 3

A practitioner-scientist approach to psychotherapy process and outcome research

Jenifer Elton Wilson and Michael Barkham

Several recent lines of thinking . . . strongly suggest . . . the need for a science of human action that intensively studies individual life courses as a means of appropriately understanding (and intervening) with human beings.

(Howard 1986: 73)

Psychotherapy practitioners are pragmatists, interested in the theory and research which 'fits' with their current belief system and with their observations of their own practice. It is commonplace to bemoan the lack of interest shown by most practitioners in reading or using research findings (Howarth 1988; Morrow-Bradley and Elliott 1986). Volumes purporting to be 'complete guides' of psychotherapy contain only cursory mention of research or evaluation (Corey 1986; Kovel 1976). This dismissive reaction usually stems from some previous encounter with the historical struggle to argue for and against the effectiveness of psychotherapy in general and any one therapeutic approach in particular.

Eysenck's (1952, 1966) relegation of the curative claims of psychotherapy, with the exception of behaviour therapy, to the results of spontaneous remission is remembered as hostile and partisan. The resulting claims and counter-claims (Lambert *et al.* 1986; Rachman and Wilson 1980), together with an over-reliance on the logic of the randomised clinical trial, seem distant and alien to the rich experience of psychotherapy. Many practitioners finally lost interest after the review of Luborsky *et al.* (1975) – 'Everyone has won and all must have prizes' – showing the positive but broadly equivalent outcomes of diverse psychotherapies, findings which were substantiated in later meta-analytic studies (Shapiro and Shapiro 1982; Smith and Glass 1977). The researchers could continue with their critiques as long as practitioners could continue with their own practices, supported by the literature of interesting case studies, novel approaches and theoretical propositions which engaged and challenged the imagination. Doubts remain about the absolute necessity for structured research as a 'means to test the accuracy and meaningfulness of our theories' (Ivey *et al.*, 1987: 380). However, the climate of increasing accountability has heightened the need for individual practitioners to monitor and evaluate the outcome of their own clinical work, a situation which is likely to become more urgent if renewable licences to practice are introduced. In addition, the development of innovative procedures for tapping the process of psychotherapy has rekindled interest in investigating within-session change.

In response to this developing situation, we aim in this chapter to provide a 'practitioner-scientist' perspective on research into the processes and outcomes of psychotherapy. Rather than provide a purely academic perspective on research findings, of which there are many accessible volumes (for example, Barkham 1990; Goldfried *et al.* 1990; Lambert *et al.* 1986), we have adopted the position that psychotherapy 'practitioners' are continuously employing, monitoring, evaluating and testing hypotheses at the moment-to-moment level with individual clients. From this position, we wish to extend and place this information within a 'research' or scientific paradigm such that the individual practitioner, as well as the discipline itself, is able to be reflexive and apply this knowledge base to increase our understanding about what is therapeutic about psychotherapy. To facilitate this procedure, we have made explicit reference to potential measures at both process and outcomes levels. However, to convert research 'fantasies' into action – see Waskow (1975b) for an account of this process – practitioners need to understand some of the basic assumptions of research and also be able to apply these assumptions in a practical setting. We therefore begin by setting out a range of choices in research approach and then address questions of research application and evidence in a sequential manner through three stages of psychotherapy: first, the precursors to psychotherapy – namely, what the client and psychotherapist bring to the psychotherapy; second, the process of psychotherapy itself – namely, what happens during psychotherapy; and third, the outcomes of psychotherapy – that is, the effectiveness or otherwise of these processes. Finally, we consider a number of guidelines for evaluating psychotherapy process and outcome.

SELECTING A RESEARCH DESIGN

Most practitioners can describe their own methods of evaluating their work. Some rely on purely subjective observation of their clients' progress and their own feelings of interest and satisfaction. Others use feedback from supervisors, consultants and the clients themselves. Those with a more structured strategy keep careful records of each client's initial aims, and the practitioner's planned approach, in order to check these against actual progress made. Almost all psychotherapy consists of an inquiry into the client's experience, although the focus and the application of this information varies between psychotherapists. Psychotherapists make notes and/or listen to audio-tapes of their work. They share their observations with colleagues, supervisors and consultants. Psychotherapists read about psychotherapeutic approaches, attend conferences and undertake retraining. From these activities, hypotheses are generated, theoretical constructs modified and clinical interventions planned. All these activities are potentially research enterprises. The data are already available and the necessary attitude of curiosity and investigation is not far distant. To make the shift from conscientious practice maintenance to a structured research project involves some consideration of the issues which influence any form of data collection. It is the aim of this section to outline and summarise four inter-linking issues: (1) purpose, (2) design and methodology, (3) values, and (4) resources.

1 Purpose – *what* does the practitioner wish to know?

To a large extent this will depend on the interests and views of the practitioner as inquirer. It has been suggested that there are distinct psychological styles that have created alternative forms of scientific inquiry (Mitroff and Kilmann 1978; Southgate and Randall 1981). It may be helpful to consult Reason and Rowan's (1981) review of Mitroff and Kilmann's (1978) scientific-style typology which is aligned with Jung's (1971) four psychological types as follows: (1) the 'Analytical Scientist' (that is, sensing-thinking); (2) the 'Conceptual Theorist' (that is, intuitive-thinking); (3) the 'Conceptual Humanist' (that is, intuitive-feeling); and (4) the 'Particular Humanist' (that is, sensing-feeling). Identifying and accepting one's own approach, and level of subjectivity, encourages the birth of a need to know. From this base, research questions are likely to arise which fit the prospective investigator's own field of talent and competence. The practitioner-scientist to whom we address this chapter is likely to be the 'Conceptual Theorist' or 'Conceptual Humanist' type. The more detached 'Theorist' may seek to find widely applicable answers to precisely defined questions in a nomothetic search for general laws. In this case a structured survey or the introduction of specific experimental interventions could be used by practitioners in collaboration with their clients. The more personally involved 'Humanist' may seek to arrive at a more precise ideographic understanding of extensive clinical experience which can be made relevant to individual experience. Process research, with its detailed observation of variables, and action research through which a series of experientially based hypotheses are explored with the client as co-researcher, are both suitable research designs for this type of practitioner.

2 Design and methodology – *how* will the practitioner find out?

The decisions made when arriving at a design are complex, and the requirements for a 'good' study as well as the possible criticisms which can be levelled at any 'well-designed' study are numerous (Barkham and Shapiro 1992; Kazdin 1986; Kline 1992). For the practitioner-scientist, as for the researcher, both psychological style and the nature of the research question are likely to influence choices made at this stage. Practitioners of psychotherapy are particularly encouraged to consider qualitative research as a complement to the quantitative experimental model. Reason and Rowan argue that much qualitative research is not 'new paradigm' research, retaining too strong an allegiance to the old ideal of an objective search to find answers to 'efficiency questions' (1981: xx). We suggest that the 'new paradigm' principle of objective subjectivity (Reason and Rowan 1981) is likely to inform most qualitative research undertaken by practitioner-scientists, especially those which emphasise the collaborative and the experiential. However, we do not wish to set up a contest between qualitative and quantitative methodologists. Our view is that the greatest gains will result from employing the most appropriate methodology for the research question being asked. To do so, practitioner-scientists need to adopt a position of methodological pluralism such that they can utilise the relative strengths of each approach rather than claim the superiority of a single method.

An ideographic approach, mentioned above, has considerable appeal to practitioners because of its being rooted in the client's experience. This approach, exemplified in the use of the Personal Questionnaire method (see Phillips 1986) and developed by M. B. Shapiro, utilises items chosen by clients as having personal significance for them. Clients compile statements (such as 'My difficulty in dealing with my dementing mother') which are personally meaningful to them in a way that items in standard measures are sometimes not. Whereas items may be unique to clients, the scale on which they are evaluated is standardised, thereby enabling comparisons both within and between clients. Such an approach has been further developed in the concept of 'moving targets' whereby new statements are introduced throughout psychotherapy as new or repressed issues surface, thereby reflecting the developmental nature of the therapeutic process.

In adopting a quantitative approach, the practitioner-scientist is selecting a paradigm in which the phenomenon under investigation is deemed to be amenable to summary in numerical format. In order to secure a sufficient degree of confidence that the phenomenon is being tapped, researchers employ a wide range of items and/or measures in order that sufficient data are collected such that the accumulated evidence will provide a reasonable approximation to the phenomenon under investigation. The aim of quantification has been to standardise the measurement procedure, and has been adopted in the comparative outcome trial which is based on the logic of the randomised clinical trial (Elkin *et al.* 1989; Shapiro *et al.* in press) where questions concerning the relative efficacy of one treatment compared with another are central. Nomothetic measures – that is, those which set an individual's score against some normative context – are important in making comparisons between any individual and a particular population. However, comparative outcome trials are rarely suited to individual practice unless carried out in collaboration with colleagues and a well-resourced research centre.

The adoption of a qualitative approach is sometimes taken as a reaction against the use of 'numbers' to summarise the therapeutic process. The danger is that it becomes anecdotal and, as a result, under-estimates the potency of the qualitative tradition. What is important is to appreciate that qualitative methods are no less rigorous than those employed in quantitative methodology. For example, there is a growing body of research espousing the use of task analytic procedures (Greenberg 1991, 1992; Safran *et al.* 1988). Task analysis is a research strategy in which the focus is on the individuals actually engaged in performing some therapeutic task rather than relating dependent and independent variables within an experimental design. The procedure involves testing a theoretical model of a 'perform-ance' (for instance, the resolution of an interpersonal conflict) against an experimental verification of that model, which in turn feeds back and adjusts the original assumption.

In addition, the single-case design, utilising a time-series methodology (that is, the collection of a series of measures on the same individual over a period of time), offers the practitioner-scientist a potentially powerful but manageable approach to carrying out process and outcome research. This methodology allows the practitioner to set up and test specific hypotheses for specific clients but also to replicate any component of the design with subsequent clients. Accordingly, it provides considerable flexibility and is a user-friendly way of introducing oneself to carrying out psychotherapy research. In this respect, McCullough (1984) has summarised some important principles for carrying out single-case 'investigatory' research based on the pioneering work of M. B. Shapiro. In addition, the single-case approach can be used as an initial step in a progressive strategy for carrying out further research with many individuals. However, single-case designs need not be confined to research where the number of clients is small. As Barlow *et al.* (1984) point out, this reflects a misunderstanding about single-case studies in that such strategies are applicable to the analysis of the *individual* and are not intended to *restrict* the numbers of individuals analysed.

In terms of adopting a research strategy, Horowitz (1982) has suggested that any psychotherapy research should progress through three distinct stages. First, descriptive studies in which much naturalistic information can be obtained about the phenomenon under investigation. Second, cor-relational studies in which associations between relevant variables are investigated through the literature. And third, only after the previous two stages have been employed, is the group contrast design employed. In response to this suggestion as well as what is seen as a disappointing yield from the traditional group contrast design, there is currently a strong move within psychotherapy research towards description and explanation (Greenberg 1986), in which the emphasis is upon understanding the therapeutic process: we need rigorous description and explanation to illuminate prediction – to define what it is that leads to positive out-comes in psychotherapy (Greenberg 1986: 708). In particular, there are increasing examples in the literature of researchers adopting a 'case formulation' approach to evaluate the process of outcome (for example Persons *et al.* 1991; Silberschatz *et al.* 1989). The case formulation approach proposes that treatment outcome is more related to the accuracy of the formulation than to the intervention strategies used. From a research perspective, this approach clearly has considerable utility for individual practitioner-scientists for whom the significance of the clinical material is paramount and who are willing to work collaboratively with colleagues.

3 Values – *which* approach is acceptable to the practitioner?

Whereas the direction of the research question may be dependent on the psychological style of the researcher, the choices made regarding method-ology will depend on the researcher's own personal convictions. In the same way in which the role of psychotherapists' values are increasingly recognised as an important variable in psychotherapy (Kelly 1990), so the values of the practitioner-scientist are similarly important. All recorded observations are data, and reflect the values and beliefs of the observer. For example, the use of audio- or video-tapes of psychotherapy sessions is still debated. Many psychoanalytic practitioners contend that recording devices are *always* invasive, exploitative of the client, and damaging to the analytic endeavour (Casement 1991). Other psychotherapy practitioners argue that, without tapes, a dangerously subjective view of the therapeutic process is maintained and many eminent psychotherapists have strongly espoused their use both for clinical as well as research purposes (for example, Hobson 1985: 208). The range of issues arising from audio- and video-taping of psychotherapy sessions has been well documented (see Aveline 1992). This issue is only one illustration of a potential ethical dilemma in respect of methodological choices, which demonstrates the limitations likely to be imposed on any research design by the cultural and individual values of the scientist-practitioner.

4 Resources – *how much* time, money and support is available?

A defining constraint upon any research is that of resources, be it human, financial, space and so on. The guiding rule is to design the research within the limits of the resources available. Considerable effort can be expended on the logistics of implementation and equal consideration to practicalities is a hallmark of the proficient practitioner-scientist.

PRECURSORS TO PSYCHOTHERAPY – CLIENT AND PSYCHOTHERAPIST FACTORS

Having considered issues central to the research endeavour, we turn now to the content of the therapeutic enterprise first by addressing factors which are brought to the psychotherapy session (precursors) and then, in the following two sections, addressing issues of therapeutic process and outcome respectively. Addressing the first of these, there is general agreement between psychotherapists that the *person* of the practitioner has a major influence on the progress of psychotherapy. However, it has been stated that '[N]one of the professional, demographic or personal characteristics of psychotherapists studied have been consistently associated with therapeutic outcome' (Orlinsky 1989: 427). In general, psychotherapist activity and skilfulness appear possible candidates for enhancing therapeutic outcomes (Orlinsky and Howard 1986a) and these appear to be more prominent characteristics than the traditional demographic features. In summary, Orlinsky concludes: 'How much and how skilfully psychotherapists do what they do seems to be more important than who they are, or which of many possible techniques they use' (1989: 427). Tangentially, it is likely that future research into psychotherapist effectiveness (that is, skilfulness) may show considerably more differentiation of outcomes than have comparisons between theoretical orientations.

A consideration which has been the subject of some controversy and research is the need for psychotherapy practitioners to have engaged in personal psychotherapy before commencing a professional practice. Norcross, who has explored this area exhaustively with colleagues (Norcross and Prochaska 1986; Norcross *et al.* 1988), concludes that the person of the psychotherapist is 'inextricably entwined' (Dryden 1991: 35) with the success or failure of any psychotherapeutic intervention. He argues that all practitioners should prioritise psychological health and recommends personal psychotherapy as the most efficacious means of ensuring this, although he stops short of making personal psychotherapy a requirement, even for the psychotherapist in training (Dryden 1991: 59). The requirement for personal psychotherapy as the foundation for psychotherapeutic training and practice is grounded in the Freudian tradition and has been adopted by many other models of psychotherapy. The marked exception to this legacy is the cognitive-behavioural paradigm, which has dominated clinical and academic psychology and been actively influential in psychotherapy research.

Most of the findings which question or oppose the need for the practitioners to engage in personal psychotherapy are linked to outcome research, with all the associated methodological difficulties of measurement and definition. Even the most usually quoted studies (for example, Grunebaum 1986) fail to show a clear relationship between professional ability and the use, misuse or absence of personal psychotherapy. Two major reviews of this debate, Clark (1986) and Herron (1988), comment on the difficulty in designing effective studies and find the evidence ambiguous. Herron (1988) concludes that there is some logic in the notion that psychotherapy is likely, at the very least, to provide a useful personal learning experience for most psychotherapy practitioners. More recent research (Guy *et al.* 1988; Liaboe *et al.* 1989; Norcross *et al.* 1988) has surveyed the taboo topic of the amount and type of psychotherapy actually used by psychotherapists in practice. The largest of these studies (Liaboe *et al.* 1989) found their predictions confounded. The majority of the psychotherapists interviewed *had* experienced psychotherapy since qualification and the most frequent reason given for this re-engagement was not professional stress but difficulties with intimate personal relationship.

The other primary factor to consider in practice-based research is the influence of the client's qualities and characteristics. The client's level of motivation and preparation for psychotherapy has been cited by Garfield (1986) as a major predictor of the level of engagement in psychotherapy. Lambert and Asay (1981) take account of a variety of client characteristics, including motivation, symptoms, expectations and intelligence. Orlinsky (1989) identified client 'openness' (that is, lack of defensiveness) and initial level of functioning to be client characteristics which have been consistently related to differential outcome. He concludes: 'The net impression is that patients who initially are psychologically stronger, less disturbed, and better prepared for psychotherapy derive more benefit from it' (1989: 427). In addition, cultural, demographic and environmental factors should be considered, since all of the client's experience is likely to affect the psychotherapy process. The practitioner-scientist, engaging in collaborative research, will need to consider all these variables for *both* psychotherapist and client.

There has been an ongoing interest in the match between client, psychotherapist and setting. Paul's (1967) difficult question as to '*What* treatment, by *whom*, is most effective for *this* individual with *that* specific problem, and under *which* set of circumstances?' still haunts psychotherapy research, and disturbs the practitioner. It seems likely that the ideal of close client–psychotherapist matching on demographic and experiential variables is unlikely to be achieved by the majority of practitioners. The practitioner brings a set of theoretical expectations, a complex training in human relations and a relevant range of skills and experience. All but the most sophisticated clients are likely to have different expectations of the therapeutic encounter. Both parties bring along their own personal and demographic characteristics. Issues arising from attempts to progress client–therapy matching have been addressed by Beutler (for example, 1989). In particular, he advances the role of 'dispositional' assessment (that is, treatment response) rather than 'diagnostic' assessment (namely, syndromes) for matching clients to psychotherapy. Accordingly, directive interventions might match with external locus-of-control clients while more insight-orientated approaches might better suit more psychologically minded clients. In addition, practitioners bring to the research endeavour their own personal and demographic characteristics. A keen awareness of these variables is needed, perhaps leading to their use in creating a more meaningful dialogic interpretation of the process of psychotherapy within a research model.

For practitioners seeking to carry out research into their own practice, it may be imperative to select clients not only with respect to their suitability for the research envisaged, but also with regard to the likely effect of such involvement on their well-being and on the therapeutic alliance. Most often this selection is made by the psychotherapists themselves (Oldfield 1983), although the risk of their collusion, defensiveness and bias needs to be guarded against. Full participatory involvement in most practice-based research can be an empowering experience for clients and their resilience should not be under-estimated. The open disclosures of therapeutic and research intention, recommended here, are in contrast with the tradition of clinical observation and case-history write-up which has been widely used by psychotherapists from a variety of orientations.

Both Heron (1981) and Harré (1981) have been influential social scientists encouraging the shift towards participatory psychological engagement. Exemplars of an investigative approach can be seen in Malan's (1963) meticulous studies of brief psychotherapy, which provide a congenial model for client selection and psychotherapist matching. These studies take full account of situational variables and limitations but do not attempt to include the patients studied as full participants in the research project.

THE PROCESS OF PSYCHOTHERAPY AND HOW TO EVALUATE IT

Process research has traditionally been viewed as the analysis of what actually takes place *within* the psychotherapy session. Historically, process research has developed as a distinct area of inquiry when interest moved away from discovering *whether* psychotherapy was effective and towards discovering *what* was effective about the psychotherapeutic encounter. The central components of psychotherapy 'process' have been encapsulated within Orlinsky and Howard's (1987) generic model of psychotherapy: therapeutic contract, therapeutic intervention, therapeutic bond, patient self-relatedness and therapeutic realisation. Research findings pertaining to these particular areas have been well documented (Orlinsky and Howard 1986a), as have a range of areas central to carrying out research in the area of psychotherapy process (Greenberg and Pinsof 1986). These all relate to a central question asked by practitioners: what are the necessary *components* of effective psychotherapy? In a similar vein, psychotherapy process researchers are seeking to understand the mechanisms by which change is achieved.

In this respect, research interest focuses on two domains. One is termed 'specific' effects, which comprise behaviours such as psychotherapist interpretations, the role of which is theoretically identified with a therapeutic modality. The other is termed 'common' factors, and comprises process such as the *therapeutic relationship*, the importance of which is deemed to be common to all psychotherapies. The debate between the role of specific and common factors has continued unabated, with Lambert (1986) estimating that approximately 15 per cent of outcome variance is accounted for by specific factors while common factors account for twice that amount. As stated above, a constant focus has been on what it is that psychotherapists do which leads to client change. Fiedler's (1950) much-quoted observation that experienced psychotherapists have similar clinical behaviours, whatever their theoretical orientation, pointed the way to a continuing investigation and classification of these behaviours. Examples of instruments developed to code particular psychotherapist (and client) behaviours have been taxonomies of verbal response modes (VRMs: see Elliott *et al.* 1987), and core conflictual relationship themes (CCRTs) with a high correlation having been reported between the accuracy of interpretations (as derived from CCRTs) and outcome (Crits-Christoph *et al.* 1988).

The careful specifications of psychotherapist qualities made by Rogers (1957) have become part of the essential world view of psychotherapists and counsellors. Almost all would argue that the qualities of warmth, personal congruence, empathy, contact and positive regard are necessary if not sufficient components of any effective psychotherapeutic alliance. However, empirical research on these constructs has not resulted in a clear endorsement. For example, Orlinsky and Howard (1986a) report that 45 of 86 findings drawn from 40 studies showed no positive relationship between psychotherapist empathy and outcome. Indeed, the literature remains somewhat equivocal as to the specific role of, for example, empathy in psychotherapy outcome. More recently, the Rogerian components have become enshrined in work on the quality and nature of the client–psychotherapist relationship which has itself emerged as the crucial variable linked with outcome (Gaston 1990). Psychotherapists have an interest and a responsibility to explore this particular domain of their practice.

The function of the *therapeutic relationship* varies between the major orientations. Behaviour therapists seek to establish a positive reality-oriented working alliance so as to facilitate the client's experiments with behaviour change. Cognitive therapists are concerned to model authenticity, and offer personal warmth so as to enable clients to accept challenges to their established constructions of reality. Psychodynamic therapists seek to explore beyond the working alliance and to engage with the transferential elements of the relationship. Existential humanists, in addition, work towards a more genuine real relationship. All these are different theoretical concepts which reflect the expectations of the psychotherapist, and may or may not match the client's expectations and motivations. This potential is gaining research interest through the use of measures such as the California Psychotherapy Alliance Scales (CALPAS; for example, Gaston 1991) and the Working Alliance Inventory (WAI; for instance, Horvath and Greenberg 1989) with the latter identifying the distinct domains of tasks, goals and bonds, thereby providing the logic for investigating the development of different bonds as a function of differing therapeutic tasks and goals.

The consensus of agreement about the crucial importance of the *therapeutic relationship* has encouraged a more integrative approach to psychotherapy research. Seeking links between process and outcome has been a constant task for researchers. Kiesler (1981) argued that the comparison of different 'treatment packages', typical of conventional outcome research, was meaningless without some understanding of what goes on within the treatment. Research sought to verify the link between the psychotherapist's interventions and actual change, or lack of change, on the part of the client. Process analysis clarifies the correlation between client change within psychotherapy and client change external to psychotherapy. Kiesler (1981) concluded that 'scientific outcome research requires process analysis of both psychotherapists' and patients' interview behaviors'. However, the scientific yield from investigations into links between process and outcome (namely, the establishment of process–outcome correlations) has been disappointing. Indeed, attempts to establish direct links between process and outcome variables have been roundly criticised as being conceptually flawed (Stiles 1988; Stiles and Shapiro 1990).

Disquiet with this approach has provided support for the adoption of a more phenomenologically based approach termed the 'events paradigm' in which data are collected on specific classes of phenomenon which occur in psychotherapy (such as insight events, perceived-empathy and so on) and which are purported to be crucial to understanding the process of change. Elliott (1983) has elaborated the search for 'significant events' in the psychotherapy process and has developed a methodology producing highly detailed transcripts of taped sessions, which are subjected to multiple revisions, through the use of Interpersonal Process Recall (IPR: Elliott 1986; Kagan 1980) and a range of rating scales to produce a comprehensive qualitative analysis. Building upon these procedures, Elliott and Shapiro (1992) provide an account of the use of the Comprehensive Process Analysis method (CPA: Elliott 1989) in understanding a single event during psychotherapy. The aim of such work is to develop general models of particular kinds of significant events which can then be used to improve the practice of psychotherapy (Elliott and Shapiro 1992: 165). Such an approach, rather than relying upon a pool of independent raters, depends upon the collaboration between client and psychotherapist in these analytic procedures.

A different, but complementary, approach to evaluating the process of psychotherapy can be seen in work evaluating models of stages of change (Prochaska and DiClemente 1986) and the assimilation of problematic experiences (Stiles *et al.* 1990). The Stages of Change model identifies four stages which categorise the level at which *clients* are ready to work thera-peutically: pre-contemplation, contemplation, action and maintenance. The Assimilation model articulates eight stages through which a particular *problematic experience* may be progressively resolved: warded off, un-wanted thoughts, vague awareness, problem clarification, insight, applica-tion of understanding, problem solution and mastery. Clearly, not all problems originate from the same stage nor do they progress to the same point of resolution. However, both models provide the practitioner-scientist with frameworks for describing their therapeutic work and contri-buting to our understanding about the factors which bring about effective client change.

For the novice practitioner-scientist, these developments in the field of psychotherapy research are exciting and accessible. Focus on process is part of the psychotherapist's repertoire. The research task is to structure and systematise this focus. Modern technology has made possible minutely detailed observation of the psychotherapy session through frame-by-frame video analysis. Recall procedures, for example using brief structured recall (a variant of IPR), would enable psychotherapists to work as co-researchers in which one would act as the observer for the other. Once again, this methodology may be uncongenial to psychoanalytic practitioners for the reasons given above. One possible solution to this quandary is the use of structured case notes in combination with post-session rating scales for practitioner and client. Another opportunity to observe process is the use of the one-way screen, which has been accepted by many psychoanalytically trained psychotherapists and is widely used in family psychotherapy. All these methods provide access to the therapeutic arena to a wider range of observers, although needing to be balanced with concerns for professional containment and confidentiality.

Howard (1986) argues cogently and extensively for the integration of practice and research. He takes a broad view of process research, encouraging practitioners to use the model of historical research to explore personal patterns with their clients in conjunction with carefully structured phenomenological interventions. His view is that a highly individualised experimental approach, which takes account of each client's role as active agent in their own life course, can still yield information about the 'lawlike regularities' (Howard 1986: 72) of the human situation which condition human endeavours. This type of mini-research project will be familiar to many psychotherapists whose approach is existential humanist, with Gestalt psychotherapy being particularly accessible to this research application. We give below a suggested research design for the type of individualised study which practitioners might carry out within their own practice, following Howard's (1986) model of the single case study which includes experiments carried out with client as co-researcher.

Research question

What has been the client's chosen strategy for survival in the past and how is this maintained by problematic behaviours and distressed feelings in the present?

Research design

We suggest using specific experimental interventions within the psychotherapy session, planned in advance with the client's co-operation, and using 'experimental' and 'control' recorded sessions to monitor the responses of client and psychotherapist. These constructed 'significant events' (Elliott 1983) can then be submitted to multiple revisions through the use of IPR (Interpersonal Process Recall) by the two participants as well as external analysis by observers.

Kagan's (1980) IPR technique represents a phenomenological approach to process research with its structured attempt to elicit from memory the moment-by-moment details of experience. McLeod (1990a; 1990b), in his reviews of the literature regarding client and practitioner experience of the therapeutic encounter, comments on the reliance on external observations demonstrated by the majority of process studies in contrast with the comparatively sparse research which utilises the experience of clients and practitioners, as actually *reported*.

When asked to give an account of their own experiences of psychotherapy, clients emphasise *the importance of positive relationship* factors and clear contractual agreements as to the structure and aims of psychotherapy (Maluccio 1979; Rennie 1987). Some of these findings make uncomfortable reading for most psychotherapists. Clients describe feelings of confused ambivalence between the need to be fully understood and the wish to avoid conflict and discomfort (Orlinsky and Howard 1986b). In particular, clients are shown as highly motivated to defer to and please their psychotherapists (Rennie 1987), and preferring advice and reassurance (Llewelyn 1988; Murphy *et al.* 1984).

Orlinsky and Howard's (1977: 585) post-session questionnaires also explored the practitioners' experiences of psychotherapy and arrived at a categorisation of sessions as *'smooth sailing, coasting, heavy going or foundering'*. 'Heavy going' sessions, during which the client was perceived to be in distress and the psychotherapist highly effective, seemed to be the experience most highly prized by practitioners. Studies in this area have utilised the Session Evaluation Questionnaire (SEQ: Stiles 1980), and have replicated psychotherapists' preference for 'deep and rough' sessions (Stiles and Snow 1984) and contrasts with most clients' endorsement of safe, warm and encouraging sessions. However, it is important to grasp that people having different roles will undoubtedly have differing perspectives on the psychotherapeutic process. For example, Stiles *et al.* (1988) found psychotherapists, in line with theoretical predictions, to rate sessions in which a *relationship-orientated psychotherapy* was utilised as significantly 'deeper' than sessions of cognitive-behavioural psychotherapy. In contrast, clients rated neither orientation as significantly deeper than the other. For clients, psychotherapy sessions *per se* were deep (as compared with their experiences of other everyday interactions during their period of depression). What is both obvious but at the same time important to appreciate, is that many of the concepts which researchers investigate, although having theoretical salience for them, simply do not have 'psychological significance' for clients. This mismatch of values and objectives between client and psychotherapist is one of the interesting issues uncovered by research into the experiences of psychotherapy which are not usually disclosed within the *therapeutic relationship*.

The literature reflects several developing interests which appear to have potential implications for our understanding of psychotherapy. The study of 'therapists' dilemmas' (Dryden 1985) and difficulties (Davis *et al.* 1987) is likely to engage the interest of many practitioners with the courage to explore their own experience of impasse. Similarly, there is a slow but increasing recognition of clients', and indeed psychotherapists', inter-session experiences and the need to take account of them in understanding the change process (Tarragona and Orlinsky 1988). A striking feature of both these areas is their amenability to investigation at the clinically descriptive level.

These studies all accept, celebrate and employ subjectivity within a research format. The methodology used offers a choice or combination of the following: rating scales, IPR interviews, journals, structured questionnaires, open-ended questionnaires (rich in material but difficult to analyse). More recently, there has been a conceptual *rapprochement* between process and outcome research in that it is recognised that within sessions there are mini-outcomes (small o's) which influence processes within subsequent sessions, all of which ultimately lead, at the end of psychotherapy, to a final outcome (the big O). Accordingly, within-session events comprise both process and mini-outcomes which have implications for carrying out research.

OUTCOMES OF PSYCHOTHERAPY AND HOW TO EVALUATE THEM

Outcome research attempts to examine the validity of any theory of change. Research into outcomes of psychotherapy has been shadowed by arguments regarding the effectiveness of psychotherapy in general or of one psychotherapeutic approach over another. Practitioners, critical of this research, complain about the lack of agreement as to *what* constitutes a satisfactory outcome. There are philosophical and moral differences between social adjustment and self-realisation goals. There are questions of *whose* judgement is sought, *how* the outcome is measured, and for *how long* after termination of the psychotherapy contract. Even more complex are the arguments for and against the plausibility of assigning a causal effect to any psychotherapeutic intervention. Bohart and Todd (1988) point out the dangers of over-reliance on the psychotherapist's own experience as sufficient validation for any theory of change. They state that therapy sessions are an important source of ideas but do not provide empirically validated *truth* (1988: 292). It is our view that practitioners remain very interested in *appropriate* research into effectiveness, particularly findings which compare different theoretical approaches and which comment on the results obtained by approaches similar to their own.

The flood of outcome studies generated by Eysenck's (1952) challenge have been extensively reviewed, summarised and meta-analysed (Glass and Kliegl 1983; Meltzoff and Kornreich 1970; Nietzel *et al.* 1987; Robinson *et al.* 1990; Smith and Glass 1977; Shapiro and Shapiro 1982). In general, they uphold the effectiveness of psychotherapy such that the average client receiving psychotherapy is better off than 80 per cent of a control population, and comment on the possibility of an average 8 per cent of clients being 'harmed' by psychotherapy (Lambert *et al.* 1986). Most interestingly, they fail to identify any one therapeutic approach as significantly more effective than any other (Luborsky *et al.* 1975; Sloane *et al.* 1975). This 'outcome' has been termed the 'equivalence paradox', in which psychotherapies which are technically diverse in their content have been shown to be *broadly* equivalent in their outcomes (Stiles *et al.* 1986).

However, the desirability of matching particular problem areas to specific treatment approaches is not well supported (Parloff 1979). For example, systematic desensitisation is acknowledged as effective with simple phobias, cognitive-behavioural techniques with anxiety and depression, and the verbal psychotherapies with self-esteem difficulties (Smith *et al.* 1980). Matching clients' presenting problems with specific therapeutic orientations has not produced the clinical yield which was once expected, but it has provided some basis for the move towards eclecticism among some psychotherapists. Although the risks of hasty and inappropriate incorporation of techniques is recognised by most practitioners, a more considered integration might be achieved by means of the practice-based mini-research projects we have recommended in this chapter.

Practitioner-scientists, in researching the effectiveness of their own interventions, are encouraged to shift from a limited range of explanations, based on the practitioner's current belief system, to an open-minded search to understand the multiplicity of variables and processes which contribute to client change. The tendency for psychotherapy practitioners to over-emphasise the influence of the psychotherapy session can be curbed by taking account of situational and environmental factors, as well as the healthy human drive towards 'spontaneous recovery' (Eysenck 1952). In addition, a focus on inter-session change is much needed in order to further our understanding of how clients work on issues and problematic experiences between sessions. Outcome research should be broad enough to include these data, and outcome measures designed accordingly.

The issue of the cost-effectiveness of psychotherapy is a major one which has implications for any psychotherapeutic service delivery system. Howard *et al.* (1986) established that the relationship between the number of weekly psychotherapy sessions administered to clients and the percentage of clients showing measurable improvement was portrayed as a negatively accelerating curve. That is, while more clients improved the longer psychotherapy continued (that is, an accelerating function), the increase showed diminishing returns (namely, a negative function) with, for example, 53 per cent of clients meeting the criterion of measurable improvement after eight sessions but only 62 per cent after thirteen sessions. Indeed, many studies have reported the major impact of psychotherapy to occur within the initial ten sessions. Another way of phrasing this issue is in terms of 'How much psychotherapy is enough?' Operationalising change in terms of reliable and clinically significant change (see below), Kopta *et al.* (1992) have estimated that there is a 0.66 probability of a client improving after 20 sessions and rises to a 0.82 probability after 52 sessions (that is, one year). However, such estimates are functions of the measures employed and the criterion of improvement used.

In terms of evaluating psychotherapy outcomes, some general approaches have been described in an earlier section. In addition, a range of measures for use in psychotherapy is outlined elsewhere (Lambert *et al.* 1983). However, there are a range of readily available client self-report measures which can be easily acquired and implemented. Two complementary measures are the Symptom Checklist-90R (SCL-90R: Derogatis 1983), which is a 90–item measure tapping nine dimensions (such as depression, anxiety, somatisation and so on), and the Inventory of Interpersonal Problems (IIP: Barkham *et al.* in press; Horowitz *et al.* 1988), which comprises 127 items and taps a range of interpersonal dimensions (for example, assertiveness, intimacy and so forth). In terms of making comparisons, general agreement among researchers to adopt one core outcome battery would have distinct advantages for evaluating individual change as well as being able to make comparisons with clients in other practices or disciplines. However, although the notion of a core outcome battery has long existed in the literature (Waskow 1975a), there is currently no general agreement between professions about such a protocol.

In addition to considering change measures, there is also the issue of how best to manipulate data in order to reflect the change process. For example, how much change has to occur before a client can be said to have 'improved'? Recently, operational definitions of reliable and clinically significant change have been devised (Jacobson and Truax 1991) which provide a viable and meaningful criterion for determining change. In brief, these procedures establish 'how much' change is required to be reliable and 'at what level' the client needs to be functioning after psychotherapy in order for the change to be clinically significant (that is, is more likely to belong to the normal than to the dysfunctional population). What is important for the practitioner is that these procedures only require a pocket calculator and enable a database to be built up from a few clients which can be added to in order that any single client's progress can be set in the context of all clients seen within the practice. Ultimately, such data are both informative for the practitioner and can also be used as feedback for clients. In this way, evaluation becomes an important part of the therapeutic process rather than an adjunct. These features of cost-effectiveness, measures and the presentation of data are all central to current concerns with evaluating psychotherapy service delivery systems, and there is a growing body of literature in this area (such as Fonagy and Higgitt 1989; Parry 1992).

GENERAL GUIDELINES AND PITFALLS IN EVALUATING PSYCHOTHERAPY PROCESS AND OUTCOME

In this final section, we conclude with a number of practical hints which we believe will lead to better research or evaluation as well as more cost-efficient learning. As change is multifaceted, it is undesirable to rely on any single measure of change. To obtain an understanding of a particular phenomenon, it is generally best to employ more than one measure. For example, a phenomenon which is tapped only by a single measure will be extremely vulnerable to the specific 'noise', and unreliability carried by that one measure and findings may be an artefact of that one measure. Without the availability of a parallel measure, it is sometimes difficult to unravel this problem. Another issue concerns the frequency with which any phenomenon is tapped. A simple rule is to measure as often as possible. Two reasons underlie this rationale. First, how a particular measure performs can be better understood the more often it is used. Secondly, in line with current psychotherapy research, practitioner-scientists should be tapping the *process* of change. By implication, a measure used only once or twice (that is, pre- and post-psychotherapy) is unlikely to summarise adequately any process of change. A simple rule of mathematics is that only a linear relationship (namely, a straight line) can be deduced from two data points. Given that all practitioners know that change is not always linear, it is only when a minimum of three data points exist that a more accurate or clinically representative profile of the change process can be deduced.

Thirdly, we would recommend the adoption of multiple methodologies (that is, methodological pluralism). Psychotherapy research is unlikely to be sufficiently informed by practitioner-scientists selecting on principle one approach rather than another. Differing psychotherapeutic approaches are tools employed towards enabling clients to achieve improved well-being. The issue is being able to select a method or approach which is most appropriate to the phenomenon under investigation. And fourthly, we would encourage piloting of any procedures: implementing what may seem a very simple and straightforward evaluation procedure can throw up unforeseen obstacles. Often, the introduction of smaller components of a study in stages enables the evaluation of whichever aspect of the study is causing difficulties in implementation.

In designing any research or evaluation, it is best to be focused and arrive at findings which have a sense of clarity. Too many researchers spread themselves too thinly such that, while they take account of many possible moderating variables, they can say very little of substance which is clear and which has implications for other practitioners. In contrast, being able to state clearly a relationship between *two* variables does provide a scientific advance. The relationship between either of these two variables and a third variable can be investigated in a separate study. In designing and, in particular, reporting any study, however small-scale, it is important to remember a central component of science: replication. This is true whether the methodological approach is qualitative, quantitative, ideographic or descriptive. What is of interest is building upon single results and obtaining general theories of how psychotherapy works and under what conditions specific clients respond differentially. As argued elsewhere, this will not be obtained in any single study (Barkham and Shapiro 1992). However, to replicate the work of others, practitioner-scientists are required to record all characteristics of their sample and the procedures used.

ETHICAL ISSUES

When carrying out research, experience suggests that most clients appreciate the need for evaluation, both in terms of their own progress (similar to the medical profession taking readings of body temperature and blood pressure) and in order to enhance the quality of service for future clients. However, adherence to certain ethical procedures is required. General information about any evaluation should be passed to the client before starting psychotherapy. If data, be it questionnaire or audio-tapes, is to be used afterwards and worked on by other people, then the client's consent needs to be obtained. This is referred to as 'informed consent'.

To ensure that the client's rights are not infringed, agreement for the client to release material for research purposes can only be obtained *after* psychotherapy has finished, particularly in the case of audio-taped material. That is, only when the client knows what is on the audio-tapes can they make an informed decision whether or not to release them for research purposes. This procedure both empowers clients and saves clients guarding against speaking freely in the presence of a tape-recorder. Finally, any research which takes place in a public arena and which is beyond standard working practice should have ethical approval from the appropriate local body.

REFERENCES

Aveline, M. (1992) 'The use of audio and videotape recordings of therapy sessions in the supervision and practice of dynamic psychotherapy', *British Journal of Psychotherapy* 8: 347–58.

Barkham, M. (1990) 'Research in individual therapy', pp. 282–312 in W. Dryden (ed.) *Individual Therapy: A Handbook*, Milton Keynes: Open University Press.

—— (1992) 'Research on integrative and eclectic therapy', pp. 239–68 in W. Dryden (ed.) *Integrative and Eclectic Therapy: A Handbook*, Milton Keynes: Open University Press.

Barkham, M., Hardy, G. E. and Startup, M. (in press) 'The structure, validity and clinical relevance of the Inventory of Interpersonal Problems (IIP)', *British Journal of Medical Psychology*.

Barkham, M. and Shapiro, D. A. (1992) 'Response', pp. 86–96 in W. Dryden and C. Feltham (eds) *Psychotherapy and its Discontents*, Milton Keynes: Open University Press.

Barlow, D. H., Hayes, S. C. and Nelson, R. O. (1984) *The Scientist Practitioner: Research and Accountability in Clinical and Educational Settings*, New York: Pergamon.

Beutler, L. E. (1989) 'Differential treatment selection: the role of diagnosis in psychotherapy', *Psychotherapy* 26: 271–81.

Bohart, A. C. and Todd, J. (1988) *Foundations of Clinical and Counseling Psychology*, New York: Harper & Row.

Casement, P. (1991) Personal communication.

Clark, M. (1986) 'Personal therapy: a review of empirical research', *Professional Psychology: Research and Practice* 17: 541–3.

Corey, G. (1986) *Theory and Practice of Counselling and Psychotherapy*, Pacific Grove, CA: Brooks Cole.

Crits-Christoph, P., Cooper, A. and Luborsky, L. (1988) 'The accuracy of therapists' interpretations and the outcome of dynamic psychotherapy', *Journal of Consulting and Clinical Psychology* 56: 490–5.

Davis, J. D., Elliott, R., Davis, M. L., Binns, M., Francis, V. M., Kelman, J. E. and Schroder, T. A. (1987) 'Development of a taxonomy of therapist difficulties: initial report', *British Journal of Medical Psychology* 60: 109–19.

Derogatis, L. R. (1983) *The SCL-90R Administration, Scoring and Procedures Manual-II*, Towson, MD: Clinical Psychometric Research.

Dryden, W. (1985) *Therapists' Dilemmas*, London: Harper & Row.

—— (1991) *A Dialogue with John Norcross: Toward Integration*, Milton Keynes: Open University Press.

Elkin, I. E., Shea, M. T., Watkins, J. T., Imber, S. D., Sotsky, S. M., Collins, J. F., Glass, D. R., Pilkonis, P. A., Leber, W. R., Docherty, J. P., Fiester, S. J. and Parloff, M. B. (1989) 'NIMH Treatment of Depression Collaborative Research Program: general effectiveness of treatments', *Archives of General Psychiatry* 46: 971–82.

Elliott, R. (1983) '"That in your hands . . .": a comprehensive process analysis of a significant event in psychotherapy', *Psychiatry* 46: 113–27.

—— (1986) 'Interpersonal process recall (IPR) as a psychotherapy process research method', pp. 503–27 in L. S. Greenberg and W. M. Pinsoff (eds) *The Psychotherapeutic Process: A Research Handbook*, New York: Guilford Press.

—— (1989) 'Comprehensive process analysis: understanding the change process in significant change events', pp. 165–84 in M. Packer and R. B. Addison (eds) *Entering the Circle: Hermeneutic Investigation in Psychology*, Albany, NY: SUNY Press.

Elliott, R., Hill, C. E., Stiles, W. B., Friedlander, M. L., Mahrer, A. R. and Margison, F. R. (1987) 'Primary therapist response modes: comparison of six rating systems', *Journal of Consulting and Clinical Psychology* 55: 218–23.

Elliott, R. and Shapiro, D. A. (1992) 'Client and therapist as analysts of significant events', pp. 163–86 in S. G. Toukmanian and D. L. Rennie (eds) *Psychotherapy Process Research: Paradigmatic and Narrative Approaches*, Newbury Park, CA: Sage.

Eysenck, H. J. (1952) 'The effects of psychotherapy: an evaluation', *Journal of Consulting Psychology* 16: 319–21.

—— (1966) *The Effects of Psychotherapy*, New York: International Sciences.

—— (1992) 'The outcome problem in psychotherapy', pp. 100–24 in W. Dryden and C. Feltham (eds) *Psychotherapy and its Discontents*, Milton Keynes: Open University Press.

Fiedler, F. E. (1950) 'A comparison of therapeutic relationships in psychoanalytic, non-directive and Adlerian therapy', *Journal of Consulting Psychology* 14: 121–53.

Fonagy, P. and Higgitt, A. (1989) 'Evaluating the performance of departments of psychotherapy', *Psychoanalytic Psychotherapy* 4: 121–53.

Garfield, S. L. (1986) 'Research on client variables', pp. 213–56 in S. L. Garfield and A. E. Bergin (eds) *Handbook of Psychotherapy and Behavior Change*, 3rd edn., New York: John Wiley.

Gaston, L. (1990) 'The concept of the alliance and its role in psychotherapy: theoretical and empirical considerations', *Psychotherapy* 27: 143–53.

—— (1991) 'Reliability and criterion-related validity of the California Psychotherapy Alliance Scales – patient version', *Psychological Assessment: A Journal of Consulting and Clinical Psychology* 3: 68–74.

Glass, G. and Kliegl, R. M. (1983) 'An apology for research integration in the study of psychotherapy', *Journal of Consulting and Clinical Psychology* 51: 28–41.

Goldfried, M. R., Greenberg, L. S. and Marmar, C. R. (1990) 'Individual psychotherapy: process and outcome', *Annual Review of Psychotherapy* 41: 659–88.

Greenberg, L. S. (1986) 'Research strategies', pp. 707–34 in L. S. Greenberg and W. M. Pinsof (eds) *The Psychotherapeutic Process: A Research Handbook*, New York: Guilford Press.

—— (1991) 'Research on the process of change', *Psychotherapy Research* 1: 3–16.

—— (1992) 'Task analysis: identifying components of intrapersonal conflict resolution', pp. 22–50 in S. G. Toukmanian and D. L. Rennie (eds) *Psychotherapy Process Research: Paradigmatic and Narrative Approaches*, Newbury Park, CA: Sage.

Greenberg, L. S. and Pinsof, W. M. (eds) (1986) *The Psychotherapeutic Process: A Research Handbook*, New York: Guilford Press.

Grunebaum, H. (1986) 'Harmful psychotherapy experiences', *American Journal of Psychotherapy* 40: 165–76.

Guy, D. G., Stark, M. J. and Polestra, P. L. (1988) 'Personal therapy for psychotherapists before and after entering professional practice', *Professional Psychology* 19: 474–6.

Harré, R. (1981) 'The positivist-empiricist approach and its alternatives', pp. 3–17 in P. Reason and J. Rowan (eds), *Human Enquiry: A Sourcebook of New Paradigm Research*, Chichester: John Wiley.

Heron, J. (1981) 'Philosophical basis for a new paradigm', pp. 19–36 in P. Reason and J. Rowan (eds) *Human Enquiry: A Sourcebook of New Paradigm Research*, Chichester: John Wiley.

Herron, W. G. (1988) 'The value of personal psychotherapy for psychotherapists', *Psychological Reports* 62: 175–84.

Hobson, R. F. (1985) *Forms of Feeling: The Heart of Psychotherapy*, London: Tavistock Publications.

Horowitz, L. M., Rosenberg, S. E., Baer, B. A., Ureno, G. and Villasenor, V. S. (1988) 'Inventory of Interpersonal Problems: psychometric properties and clinical applications', *Journal of Consulting and Clinical Psychology* 56: 885–92.

Horowitz, M. (1982) 'Strategic dilemmas and the socialization of psychotherapy researchers', *British Journal of Clinical Psychology* 21: 119–27.

Horvath, A. O. and Greenberg, L. S. (1989) 'The development and validation of the Working Alliance Inventory', *Journal of Counseling Psychology* 36: 223–33.

Howard, G. S. (1986) 'The scientist-practitioner in counseling psychology: toward a deeper integration of theory, research and practice', *The Counseling Psychologist* 14: 61–105.

Howard, K. I., Kopta, S. M., Krause, M. S. and Orlinsky, D. E. (1986) 'The dose-effect relationship in psychotherapy', *American Psychologist* 41: 159–64.

Howarth, I. (1988) 'Psychotherapy: who benefits?' *The Psychologist* 2: 150–2.

Ivey, A. E., Ivey, M. B. and Simek-Downing, L. (1987) *Counselling and Psychotherapy*, London: Prentice-Hall International.

Jacobson, N. S. and Truax, P. (1991) 'Clinical significance: a statistical approach to defining meaningful change in psychotherapy research', *Journal of Consulting and Clinical Psychology* 59: 12–19.

Jung, C. G. (1971) *Collected Works*, vol 6, *Psychological Types* (R. F. C. Hull, revised trans.), Princeton, NJ: Princeton University Press.

Kagan, N. (1980) 'Influencing human interaction: eighteen years with IRP', in A. K. Hess (ed.) *Psychotherapy Supervision: Theory, Research, Practice*, New York: John Wiley.

Kazdin, A. E. (1986) 'The evaluation of psychotherapy: research design and methodology', pp. 23–68 in S. L. Garfield and A. E. Bergin (eds) *Handbook of Psychotherapy and Behavior Change*, 3rd edn., New York: John Wiley.

Kelly, T. A. (1990) 'The role of values in psychotherapy: a critical review of process and outcome effects', *Clinical Psychology Review* 10: 171–86.

Kiesler, D. J. (1981) 'Process analysis: a necessary ingredient of psychotherapy outcome research', Paper presented at the Annual Conference of the Society for Psychotherapy Research, Aspen, CO, June.

Kline, P. (1992) 'Problems of methodology in studies of psychotherapy', pp. 64–86 in W. Dryden and C. Feltham (eds) *Psychotherapy and its Discontents*, Milton Keynes: Open University Press.

Kopta, S. M., Howard, K. I., Lowry, J. L. and Beutler, L. E. (1992) 'The psychotherapy dosage model and clinical significance: estimating how much is enough for psychological symptoms', Paper presented at the Annual Meeting of the Society for Psychotherapy Research, Berkeley, CA, June.

Kovel, J. (1976) *A Complete Guide to Therapy*, New York: Pantheon.

Lambert, M. J. (1986) 'Implications of psychotherapy outcome for eclectic psychotherapy', in J. C. Norcross (ed.) *Handbook of Eclectic Psychotherapy*, New York: Brunner/Mazel.

Lambert, M. J. and Asay, T. P. (1981) *Patient Characteristics and Psychotherapy Outcome*, New York: Pergamon Press.

Lambert, M. J., Christensen, E. R. and DeJulio, S. S. (1983) *The Assessment of Psychotherapy*, New York: John Wiley.

Lambert, M. J., Shapiro, D. A. and Bergin, A. E. (1986) 'The effectiveness of psychotherapy', pp. 157–211 in S. L. Garfield and A. E. Bergin (eds) *Handbook of Psychotherapy and Behavior Change*, 3rd edn., New York: John Wiley.

Liaboe, G. P., Guy, J. D., Wong, T. and Deahnert, J. R. (1989) 'The use of personal therapy by psychotherapists', *Psychotherapy in Private Practice* 7: 115–34.

Llewelyn, S. P. (1988) 'Psychological therapy as viewed by clients and therapists', *British Journal of Clinical Psychology* 27: 223–37.

Luborsky, L., Singer, B. and Luborsky, L. (1975) 'Comparative studies of psychotherapies: is it true that everybody has won and all must have prizes?' *Archives of General Psychiatry* 32: 995–1008.

McCullough, J. P. (1984) 'Single-case investigative research and its relevance for the nonoperant clinician', *Psychotherapy* 21: 382–8.

McLeod, J. (1990a) 'The client's experience of counselling and psychotherapy: a review of the research literature', pp. 1–19 in D. Mearns and W. Dryden (eds) *Experiences of Counselling in Action*, London: Sage.

—— (1990b) 'The practitioner's experience of counselling and psychotherapy: a review of the research literature', pp. 66–79 in D. Mearns and W. Dryden (eds) *Experiences of Counselling in Action*, London: Sage.

Malan, D. H. (1963) *A Study of Brief Psychotherapy*, London: Tavistock.

Maluccio, A. (1979) *Learning from Clients: Interpersonal Helping as Viewed by Clients and Social Workers*, New York: Free Press.

Meltzoff, J. and Kornreich, M. (1970) *Research in Psychotherapy*, New York: Atherton Press.

Mitroff, I. and Kilmann, R. H. (1978) *Methodological Approaches to Social Science: Integrating Divergent Concepts and Theories*, San Francisco: Jossey Bass.

Morrow-Bradley, C. and Elliott, R. (1986) 'Utilization of psychotherapy research by practicing psychotherapists', *American Psychologist* 41: 188–97.

Murphy, P. H., Cramer, D. and Lillie, F. J. (1984) 'The relationship between curative factors perceived by patients in psychotherapy and treatment outcome: an exploratory study', *British Journal of Medical Psychology* 57: 187–92.

Nietzel, M. T., Russell, R. L., Hemmings, K. A. and Gretter, M. L. (1987) 'Clinical significance of psychotherapy for unipolar depression: a meta-analytic approach to social comparison', *Journal of Consulting and Clinical Psychology* 55: 156–61.

Norcross, J. C. and Prochaska, J. O. (1986) 'Psychotherapist heal thyself – II: the self-initiated and therapy facilitated change of psychological distress', *Psychotherapy* 23: 345–56.

Norcross, J. C., Strausser-Kirtland, D. and Missar, C. D. (1988) 'The processes and outcomes of psychotherapists' personal treatment experiences', *Psychotherapy* 25: 36–43.

Oldfield, S. (1983) *The Counselling Relationship*, London: Routledge & Kegan Paul.

Orlinsky, D. E. (1989) 'Researchers' images of psychotherapy: their origins and influence on research', *Clinical Psychology Review* 9: 413–41.

Orlinsky, D. E. and Howard, K. I. (1977) 'The therapist's experience of psychotherapy', pp. 566–689 in A. Gurman and A. Razin (eds) *Effective Psychotherapy: A Handbook of Research*, Oxford, Pergamon.

—— (1986a) 'Process and outcome in psychotherapy', pp. 311–81 in S. L. Garfield and A. E. Bergin (eds) *Handbook of Psychotherapy and Behavior Change*, 3rd edn., New York: John Wiley.

—— (1986b) 'The psychological interior of psychotherapy: explorations with therapy session reports', pp. 477–501 in L. S. Greenberg and W. M. Pinsof (eds) *The Psychotherapeutic Process: A Research Handbook*, New York: Guilford Press.

—— (1987) 'A generic model of psychotherapy', *Journal of Integrative and Eclectic Psychotherapy* 6: 6–27.

Parloff, M. B. (1979) 'Can psychotherapy research guide the policymaker? A little knowledge may be dangerous', *American Psychologist* 34: 296–306.

Parry, G. (1992) 'Improving psychotherapy services: applications of research, audit and evaluation', *British Journal of Clinical Psychology* 31: 3–19.

Paul, G. L. (1967) 'Strategy of outcome research in psychotherapy', *Journal of Consulting Psychology* 31: 109–18.

Persons, J. B., Curtis, J. T. and Silberschatz, G. (1991) 'Psychodynamic and cognitive-behavioral formulations of a single case', *Psychotherapy* 28: 608–17.

Phillips, J. P. N. (1986) 'Shapiro personal questionnaire and generalized personal questionnaire techniques: a repeated measures individualized outcome measurement', pp. 557–89 in L. S. Greenberg and W. M. Pinsof (eds) *The Psychotherapeutic Process: A Research Handbook*, New York: Guilford Press.

Prochaska, J. O. and DiClemente, C. C. (1986) 'The transtheoretical approach', pp. 163–200 in J. C. Norcross (ed.) *Handbook of Eclectic Psychotherapy*, New York: Guilford Press.

Rachman, S. and Wilson, G. (1980) *The Effects of Psychological Therapy*, New York: Wiley.

Reason, P. and Rowan, J. (1981) 'Foreword', pp. xi–xxiv in P. Reason and J. Rowan (eds) *Human Inquiry: A Sourcebook of New Paradigm Research*, Chichester: John Wiley.

Rennie, D. L. (1987) 'A model of the client's experience of psychotherapy', Paper presented at the Sixth Annual International Human Science Conference, Ottawa.

Robinson, L. A., Berman, J. S. and Neimeyer, R. A. (1990) 'Psychotherapy for the treatment of depression: a comprehensive review of controlled outcome research', *Psychological Bulletin* 108: 30–49.

Rogers, C. R. (1957) 'The necessary and sufficient conditions of therapeutic personality change', *Journal of Consulting Psychology* 21: 95–103.

Safran, J. D., Greenberg, L. S. and Rice, L. N. (1988) 'Integrating psychotherapy research and practice: modeling the change process', *Psychotherapy* 25: 1–17.

Shapiro, D. A., Barkham, M., Hardy, G. E., Rees, A., Reynolds, S. and Startup, M. J. (in press) 'Effects of treatment duration and severity of depression on the effectiveness of cognitive/behavioral and psychodynamic/interpersonal psychotherapy', *Journal of Consulting and Clinical Psychology*.

Shapiro, D. A. and Shapiro, D. (1982) 'Meta-analysis of comparative psychotherapy outcome studies: a replication and refinement', *Psychological Bulletin* 92: 581–604.

Silberschatz, G., Curtis, J. T. and Nathans, S. (1989) 'Using the patient's plan to assess progress in psychotherapy', *Psychotherapy* 26: 40–6.

Sloane, R. B., Staples, F. R., Cristol, A. H., Yorkston, N. J. and Whipple, K. (1975) *Psychotherapy versus Behavior Therapy*, Cambridge, MA: Harvard University Press.

Smith, M. L. and Glass, G. V. (1977) 'Meta-analysis of psychotherapy outcome studies', *American Psychologist* 32: 752–60.

Smith, M. L., Glass, G. V. and Miller, T. I. (1980) *The Benefits of Psychotherapy*, Baltimore, MD: Johns Hopkins University Press.

Southgate, J. and Randall, R. (1981) 'The troubled fish: barriers to dialogue', pp. 53–62 in P. Reason and J. Rowan (eds) *Human Inquiry: A Sourcebook of New Paradigm Research*, Chichester: John Wiley.

Stiles, W. B. (1980) 'Measurement of the impact of psychotherapy sessions', *Journal of Consulting and Clinical Psychology* 48: 176–85.

—— (1988) 'Psychotherapy process–outcome correlations may be misleading', *Psychotherapy* 25: 27–35.

Stiles, W. B., Elliott, R., Llewelyn, S. P., Firth-Cozens, J. A., Margison, F. R., Shapiro, D. A. and Hardy, G. (1990) 'Assimilation of problematic experiences by clients in psychotherapy', *Psychotherapy* 27: 411–420.

Stiles, W. B. and Shapiro, D. A. (1990) 'Abuse of the drug metaphor in psychotherapy process–outcome research', *Clinical Psychology Review* 9: 521–43.

Stiles, W. B., Shapiro, D. A. and Elliott, R. (1986) 'Are all psychotherapies equivalent?', *American Psychologist* 41: 165–80.

Stiles, W. B., Shapiro, D. A. and Firth-Cozens, J. A. (1988) 'Do sessions of different treatments have different impacts?', *Journal of Counseling Psychology* 35(4): 391–6.

Stiles, W. B. and Snow, J. (1984) 'Dimensions of psychotherapy session impact across sessions and across clients', *British Journal of Clinical Psychology* 23: 59–63.

Tarragona, M. and Orlinsky, D. E. (1988) 'During and beyond the therapeutic hour: an exploration of the relationship between patients' experiences of therapy in-sessions and between sessions', Paper presented at the Annual Meeting for the Society for Psychotherapy Research, Santa Fe, NM, June.

Waskow, I. E. (1975a) 'Selection of a core battery', pp. 245–69 in I. E. Waskow and M. B. Parloff (eds) *Psychotherapy Change Measures*, Rockville, MD: National Institute of Mental Health.

—— (1975b) 'Fantasied dialogue with a researcher', pp. 274–327 in I. E. Waskow and M. B. Parloff (eds) *Psychotherapy Change Measures*, Rockville, MD: National Institute of Mental Health.

Part II

Culture

Chapter 4

Psychotherapy and race

Pat Grant

'Race' is a term frequently used but not easily defined. Haralambos wrote that race is simply a group of people who see themselves, or are seen by others as a race (1983: 97). Black people do see themselves as a race and are seen by others as a race. Race plays a big part in group identity and it affects the belief systems of that group. Culture is also another factor influencing group identity and this is closely bound up with race. Marsella and Pedersen (1981) suggested that culture has to do with the passing on of a way of life from one generation to another – a way of life that becomes so ingrained within people that they become unaware of assumptions they make about themselves and others. As d'Ardenne and Mahtani (1989) suggested, it is very difficult to separate race from culture, and no attempt will be made to do so in this chapter. Fernando is correct in suggesting that 'In a multi-cultural society where racism is prevalent cultural issues are not easily differentiated from racial ones' (1988: 155).

Two races will be referred to in the chapter – black and white. Black is used in reference to all non-whites. 'Black had a highly pejorative connotation in England in and before the sixteenth century. White had a corresponding pure connotation' (Milner 1983: 7). Today there are still negative images attached to being black. The Moynihan (1965) report about black families in the United States, but which was also influential in Britain, painted a very negative picture of black people, seeing the black family as 'a tangle of pathology'. Generally the image of black people that is put across in society is quite poor, and does not in any way help to enhance the self-esteem of blacks. Fortunately that is now changing, and black people themselves are presenting a more positive view of black. Movements such as the Black Power movement have helped black people to see themselves as people of worth and beauty. There is, however, still a long way to go in getting society as a whole to see black in a more positive light.

The black race is not a homogeneous group (neither is the white race, of course). Black people come to Britain from different geographical regions, lifestyles, religious backgrounds, socio-economic status and so on.

There are, however, certain social and political realities attached to being black in British society. Black people stand out because of their colour. All of them to a greater or lesser extent are faced with the reality of combating discrimination on the basis of their colour, and they all develop ways of coping with racism. Throughout history, black people have found different ways of coping with racism – these strategies of coping have been passed on from generation to generation. A given individual may use a whole range of these strategies, some of these consciously and others unconsciously. One of the tasks of psychotherapy may be to help clients to become conscious of the strategies they use and to compare those strategies with other available options, in order that they might make a more active and conscious choice regarding the options they use.

This chapter will cover issues such as the black client finding a psychotherapist, expectations of psychotherapy and working effectively with the black client, particularly in cases where the psychotherapist is white.

FINDING A PSYCHOTHERAPIST

The choice of psychotherapist is governed by a number of factors, such as availability, cost, sex, race, psychotherapeutic orientation of the psychotherapist and so on. For many black clients, race may be a very important factor in their choice of a psychotherapist. Many black clients will actively choose black psychotherapists because they feel better understood by them, and are able to engage in greater self-disclosure with someone of their own race. Sue and Sue (1990) argue that, because of their past experience of racism and prejudice, black clients often find it difficult to trust a white psychotherapist, and so find self-disclosure difficult. They are wary of self-disclosure as it may lead to misunderstanding, hurt and vulnerability to racism. The author has had black clients who have actively sought out black psychotherapists because they did not want to discuss certain family issues with a white psychotherapist, whom they perceived might use the information to judge black people negatively.

The degree of importance that a black person might attach to having a black psychotherapist may say something about that person's view of themselves, and how they cope with living in a predominantly white society. There are those black people who cope with the 'white world' by acting like white people – that is, mimicking their mannerisms, speech patterns, way of life and so on. These people tend to see themselves as different from other black people, and as far as they are concerned, white is the way to be – it is 'correct'. These black people might actively choose a white psychotherapist because they believe white therapists are better than black ones.

There are also those black people who are very anti-white; they are angry with white people and they do not trust them. This group of black people would resist having a white therapist, and even if they appear to accept one they find ways to sabotage the therapy. They may also resist having a black psychotherapist, as they may see the black psychotherapist as 'selling out', adopting white middle-class values of counselling and psychotherapy, and giving up on their own people. Basically, they may see the black psychotherapist as a 'white man in black clothing'. There are those black people who are more interested in their own group, who, while not rejecting white people, see them as somewhat irrelevant. These black people might prefer a black psychotherapist. Finally, there are those black people who are more interested in the expertise of the psychotherapist, and the ability of the psychotherapist to share and accept their world views, rather than in the race of the psychotherapist (Jackson 1975; Sue and Sue 1990).

Marsella and Pedersen (1981) reported that a majority of the studies on the effects of race and treatment have concluded that black people responded more favourably to black therapists. This was backed up by Atkinson and Schein (1986), who indicated that certain similarities between psychotherapist and client may actually enhance therapy. They suggested that racial similarities between psychotherapist and client may indeed influence the client's willingness to return for therapy. In the light of the preceding information it would seem understandable that black clients would seek out a black psychotherapist. There are not many black therapists, however, and therefore many black clients are left with a choice of white psychotherapists.

In choosing a white psychotherapist there are certain factors to which black clients will pay particular attention. They will be concerned about the racial reaction of the psychotherapist. Marsella and Pedersen (1981) identified three types of racial reaction that the psychotherapist might exhibit – the illusion of colour-blindness, the 'great white father' syndrome, and the assumption that all black people's problems revolve around the issues of being black. Let us return to the issue of colour-blindness. Black clients do not want to be treated as just another white client, as this is only another denial of many of the factors unique to them. Psychotherapists who are colour-blind are not ready to work with black people, as they may still be resisting having to confront and deal with colour differences. While they are in that state, they cannot help the black clients to confront and develop ways of dealing with the reality of being a black person in this society. Often, psychotherapists who come across as colour-blind also have a fear of finding racism in themselves, and unless they face this, they will be unable to work effectively with black clients.

Some white psychotherapists take the view that they know exactly what the black client needs, and they understand the intimate working of the black person's mind. Their only wish is to do good to the black person – all the black client has to do is to put their trust in this 'great white father'.

This sort of response is offensive to many black people and they reject white psychotherapists who have this racial reaction. Similarly, they also reject psychotherapists who act as if all the problems of the black client revolve around their colour – they do not. Although it is true that black people are faced with the problem of combating discrimination on the basis of their colour, it is untrue to suggest or imply that all problems of black people are centred around their colour. It is good for white psychotherapists to have some understanding of black people as a group, but they should not stereotype them; they cannot afford to lose sight of blacks as individuals. Black clients will not truly engage in psychotherapy with psychotherapists who stereotype them.

Black clients, like white clients, are interested in finding psychotherapists who are experts. They prefer psychotherapists who are experts in a variety of theories and skills, because such a psychotherapist can choose the skills and theory appropriate for working with them, rather than clinging to a particular orientation which might not suit the client. Many black clients may not necessarily articulate this, but they will act it out by not returning for the therapy if the therapy is not meeting their needs. Black clients also prefer psychotherapists who have some knowledge and understanding of the socio-political forces affecting them.

So far there has been an implication that black clients are always active in the choice of their psychotherapist. Unfortunately this is not the case. Many black clients cannot afford to pay for psychotherapy and so have to take whatever psychotherapist they are offered by those doing the paying, such as social services, the NHS and so on. Often the people involved in allocating black clients to psychotherapists feel they are doing their black clients favours by referring them to black psychotherapists. A black psychotherapist might not necessarily be the best person to work with a black client, and indeed the black client might not want to work with a black psychotherapist. When referring a black client to a black psycho-therapist, a good question to ask oneself is 'Why am I doing this?'

EXPECTATIONS

One's expectation of psychotherapy is influenced by one's view of the world and issues such as abnormality and health. Different racial groups have differing perceptions of health and normality. For example, a white middle-class psychotherapist with a British background may see the family relations of the nuclear family as normal, and view the black West Indian who was brought up by a family friend in a different home, a few streets away from the mother's home, as abnormal and an 'issue' for psycho-therapy. What this psychotherapist fails to understand is the importance of the modified extended family which have ties that are just as important as blood ties. In fact, these people are chosen to be part of the family even though there are no blood ties. The other issue that the psychotherapist may fail to understand is that, even though streets may separate the home, in the family's minds it is like one home, with family members seeing one another just as often as if they were living in the same house.

Relationships with authority figures are often influenced by one's racial heritage. Psychotherapists are often seen as authority figures, and clients will expect to relate to them as they would to authority figures from their own culture. An example of this is the author inviting a middle-aged black client to address her by her first name and the client choosing to put 'Miss' before the first name as a sign of respect for the psychotherapist's position. According to Marsella *et al.* (1979), if a client comes from a background where they relate to authority in an autocratic way, then the tendency will be for them to do so in the psychotherapeutic setting. They also expect the psychotherapist to be active, instructive and assertive. It is the author's experience that some clients may even begin to doubt the credibility of the psychotherapist if expectations are not met. On the other hand, clients from a background of relating to authority figures in a democratic way will prefer a more equal relationship.

Many psychotherapists attach high status to goals such as self-exploration and personal growth. These goals may need to be examined when working with some racial groups.

Barbarin (1984) pointed out that, for lower-class black clients, goals such as these might be insufficient since the tendency for this group is to focus on external conditions rather than intrapsychic concerns. This is not surprising, as it is difficult to imagine how to concentrate on those issues when they may have immediate problems of survival such as housing, food, employment and other socio-economic issues. If the psychotherapists are expecting to pursue personal growth and self-exploration and the clients are expecting to find ways of meeting their needs as related to their external condition, then there will be a mismatch of expectations. This could lead to frustration and anxiety for both the client and the psychotherapist.

Sue (1981) indicated that many Puerto Ricans who came for therapy expected information, advice and direct suggestions. Asian Americans also sought advice and suggestions, and they preferred a structured, more practically orientated type of psychotherapy. The author's own experience of working with black clients of West Indian origin suggests that they too tend to prefer psychotherapy that is structured and practically orientated. Different racial groups experience the environment differently, and it is from their perception of the social/cultural environment that they draw their conclusions about how the world works and how they need to relate to it. As mentioned earlier, many black people experience racial prejudice or discrimination of one sort or another. This has led Jones to write, 'One of the tasks facing all Black Americans is the development of ways to cope with experiences of racial prejudice and discrimination' (1985: 364). Some might argue that this is a task facing black people in general. This may therefore be an issue that many black clients would expect to tackle in psychotherapy.

WORKING WITH THE BLACK CLIENT

To work with any client you first have to engage that client. Engagement begins with the psychotherapist's first contact with the client; it could take a few minutes or several sessions, or it might never happen. The initial contact that is made with the client is vital, whether this is by phone, letter or in person. A lot can be read into one's use of language or tone of voice. A client once told me that it was my voice which was the deciding factor in coming along to the session. Clients going for psychotherapy often feel vulnerable, and they need to feel the warmth of the psychotherapist if they are to open themselves up. The initial interview, which may also be the assessment interview or part of it, is also important; and the psychotherapist should remember that this is a two-way process. While the psychotherapist is assessing whether or not the client is someone he or she could work with, the client is making the same decision. If the psycho-therapist fails to make this a meeting of persons and hides behind the role of psychotherapist, this could make the black client suspicious of the white psychotherapist.

Many black clients have little experience of psychotherapy, and so it is always helpful to discuss with them how the session will be structured, and how one will work with them. Failure to structure early may lead to clients not returning for psychotherapy. During the assessment interview it is necessary to find out what the concerns of the client are. Also useful is to explore 'the personal meanings that presenting concerns have for the client' (Nelson-Jones 1982: 281). For example, a black client had concerns about returning to his country. On exploration it emerged that the concern was related to the client's perceived failure – failure to live up to his village's expectation of him as a bright boy who had gone to England to become a doctor but who had not achieved this. Another kind of information that one would need to collect in the assessment interview is related to the client's personal and social history, as this will give some indication of their personal identity. Where the client is, in terms of their own black identity, may be significant for working with that client.

At the end of the assessment the psychotherapist has to make the decision whether to work with the client, or indeed whether he or she is the best person to work with that client. Psychotherapists may choose not to work with black clients because of their own personal biases or limitations in cross-racial psychotherapy. In cases such as these the psychotherapist may choose to make a referral to another psychotherapist;

maybe a black psychotherapist. This should not be seen as a failure on the part of the psychotherapist; it is best to refer rather than struggle to work with clients they are not yet ready to work with. Psychotherapists are human and they too can have a racist attitude, which may be conscious or unconscious. This attitude could come across as a feeling of superiority, or the psychotherapist viewing cultural differences involving lifestyle as negative and indicative of pathology (Sue and Sue 1990). A white psychotherapist who would never consider herself as someone who makes racist comments and who strives for racial harmony once said, 'Anyone who is decent would know that female circumcision is wrong.' The implication here was that the black group she was referring to was not decent. I suppose this is an indication of the biases we all carry around with us. Greene (1985) aptly stated that psychotherapists of all backgrounds must confront their own biases when dealing with any culturally diverse group. What is maladaptive in one situation maybe quite adaptive in another.

In working with black clients psychotherapists need to understand that there may be barriers to communication which arise from cultural differences, such as the psychotherapist's personal prejudices (mentioned earlier). There are also other problems such as lack of knowledge of the culture, which could result in the client and psychotherapist misunderstanding each other. As McGoldrick wrote, 'Often it is very difficult to understand the meaning of behaviour without knowing something of the value orientation of the group. The same behaviour may have a different meaning in families of a different background' (1982: 23). For example, in some black cultures it is disrespectful to make eye contact with one's elders or people in authority when they are speaking to one. The reverse is true in Britain, where one would be expected to make eye contact with the individual addressing one.

Language can be a problem in cross-racial psychotherapy. Black clients might use words and phrases not understandable to the psychotherapist. Sometimes they may even use words that are familiar to the psychotherapist but they do not use the words to mean the same thing as the psychotherapist would. For example, some black West Indians may use the term 'What's happening?' as a form of greeting. The psychotherapist might not see this as a greeting and begin to wonder what the client meant by 'What's happening?'. Vontress (1981) argued that differences in language pattern on the part of the psychotherapist and client can lead to rapport problems in the psychotherapeutic relationship. Although it is not always easy to pinpoint these rapport problems, one can always feel them. Lack of rapport between psychotherapist and client will often lead to premature termination of psychotherapy. One of the mistakes white psychotherapists sometimes make is to continue a dialogue with the black client when they are unable to understand. They often do this with the hope of catching on as the conversation progresses. Unfortunately, they often find out that the more they allow the client to talk without clarification, the more confused they become (Vontress 1981).

One of the important factors in the client–psychotherapist relationship is the power-authority dimension (which is discussed further in Chapter 22 of this book). This hierarchical dimension takes on an added significance when one of the participants in the relationship is a 'majority person' (in this case, the white psychotherapist) and the other a 'minority person' (in this case, the black client) primarily because it is a microcosm of the larger social context (Jewelle 1985). Many black clients find it difficult to disclose as they do not 'initially perceive Whites as persons of good will' (Vontress 1981: 97). Self-disclosure is dependent on trust, and this is in turn affected by the degree to which psychotherapists and clients perceive themselves as similar and acceptable to each other. A black client and a white psychotherapist are obviously dissimilar in appearance but there are a number of other ways in which the psychotherapist might seek to develop a trusting relationship in which the client feels accepted. This certainly is one of the tasks of psychotherapy.

Transference is important in any therapeutic relationship but it has a special slant in cross-racial psychotherapy, particularly when the psychotherapist is from the 'majority group' (Vontress 1981). It is therefore necessary for white psychotherapists working with black clients to have an awareness of their own and their client's feelings about blackness and whiteness and the possible effect of these on transference and counter-transference (Gurman and Razin 1977). For example, the client may transfer onto the psychotherapist negative feelings about a white teacher who treated him or her as stupid. Psychotherapists may also engage in their own counter-transference by becoming excessively sympathetic to the black client; so sympathetic that they set a lower standard for black clients than for white clients. Psychotherapists may also demonstrate a counter-transference reaction by overcompensating when they work with black clients. For example, out of fear of hurting the black client they suppress any negative feelings they might have and become all positive and over-accommodating.

An area that psychotherapists frequently neglect when working with black clients is the strengths of the black family. Black families often have strong family ties and family roles are quite flexible. They also tend to place high value on religion. For example, aunts or grandmother may take responsibility for child care. Here psychotherapists must not be too quick in making assumptions that this is a negative practice leading to rejection of the child. In fact, this might be a very positive experience for the child. Finding out about the family and who helps whom within the family is therefore a necessary part of working with the black client.

Finally, it is sometimes useful to examine issues to do with racial identity, as this might influence how you work with the client. For example, if the black client is at the conformity stage of black identity where they believe in the superiority of white ways and inferiority of black ways, they might find exploration of cultural identity difficult. Any psychotherapist working with a client at this stage will need to help the client sort out conflicts related to racial identity. Black clients at this stage are often eager to identify with the white psychotherapist, but this process could be used in a positive way as the white psychotherapist helps the clients work through their need to over-identify. It will also be important for the white psychotherapist to model positive attitudes toward blacks. Unlike the clients at the conformity stage, the clients at the resistance and immersion stage do not view white psychotherapists positively. White psychotherapists are often seen as belonging to the 'oppressors' and as such are often challenged by these clients. If challenged, it is important not to be defensive, as a non-defensive approach is best if one wants to help the clients to explore these racial feelings or beliefs. Sue and Sue (1990) give a number of ways in which a psychotherapist might work with clients at different stages of black identity.

SUMMARY

In this chapter the relationship between race and culture was examined and it was decided that a separation of the two concepts was difficult. While race was divided between black and white, the point was made that 'blacks' were not a homogeneous group. It was acknowledged that one thing all black clients had in common was having to combat discrimination at one level or another. The difficulty of finding black psychotherapists was highlighted; also some of the things black clients look for when they choose a white psychotherapist. The exceptions of black clients in relation to psychotherapy were explored, as well as how the white psychotherapist might work with a black client.

The chapter concentrated on white psychotherapists working with black clients, but there are, of course, cases of black psychotherapists working with white clients and black psychotherapists working with black clients. The concentration on the first is not a denial of the importance of the others but rather a statement of what is more common in Britain.

ACKNOWLEDGEMENT

The editors would like to acknowledge the life and work of the late Jafar Kareem in raising awareness of intercultural issues.

REFERENCES

Atkinson, D. R. and Schein, S. (1986) 'Similarity in counselling', *The Counselling Psychologist* 4: 319–54.

Barbarin, O. (1984) 'Racial themes in psychotherapy with blacks: effect of training on the attitudes of black and white psychiatrists', *American Journal of Social Psychology* 4: 13–20.

d'Ardenne, P. and Mahtani, A. (1989) *Transcultural Counselling in Action*, London: Sage.

Fernando, W. (1988) *Race and Culture in Psychiatry*, London: Croom Helm.

Greene, B. (1985) 'Consideration in the treatment of black patients by white therapists', *Psychotherapy* 22(2): 389–93.

Gurman, A. and Razin, A. (1977) *Effective Psychotherapy*, New York: Pergamon.

Haralambos, M. (ed.) (1983) *Sociology*, London: Causeway Press.

Hines, P. and Boyd-Franklyn, N. (1982) 'Black families', pp. 84–107 in M. McGoldrick, J. Pearce and J. Giordando (eds) *Ethnicity and Family Therapy*, New York: Guilford Press.

Jackson, B. (1975) 'Black identity development', *Journal of Educational Diversity* 2: 19–25.

Jewelle, T. G. (1985) 'Can we continue to be colour-blind and class bound?', *The Counselling Psychologist* 13(3): 426–35.

Jones, A. (1985) 'Psychological functioning in black Americans: a conceptual guide for use in psychotherapy', *Psychotherapy* 22(3): 363–9.

McGoldrick, M. (1982) 'Ethnicity and family therapy – an overview', pp. 84–107 in M. McGoldrick, J. Pearce and J. Giordano (eds) *Ethnicity and Family Therapy*, New York: Guilford Press.

Marsella, A. and Pedersen, P. (eds) (1981) *Cross Cultural Counselling and Psychotherapy*, New York: Pergamon Press.

Marsella, A., Tharp, R. and Ciborowski, T. (1979) *Perspective in Cross Cultural Psychology*, New York: Academic Press.

Milner, D. (1983) *Children and Race*, London: Ward Lock Educational.

Moynihan, D. (1965) *The Negro Family in the US: The Case for National Action*, Washington, DC: US Government Report.

Nelson-Jones, R. (1982) *The Theory and Practice of Counselling Psychology*, London: Holt, Rinehart & Winston.

Sue, D. W. (1981) 'Evaluating process variables in cross-cultural counselling and psychotherapy', pp. 181–4 in A. Marsella and P. Pedersen (eds) *Cross Cultural Counselling and Psychotherapy*, New York: Pergamon Press.

Sue, D. W. and Sue, D. (1990) *Counselling the Culturally Different*, New York: John Wiley.

Vontress, C. (1981) 'Racial and ethnic barriers in counselling', pp. 87–107 in P. Pedersen, J. Dragus, W. Lonner and J. Trimble (eds) *Counselling Across Cultures*, Honolulu: University of Hawaii Press.

SOME USEFUL ADDRESSES

Asian Family Counselling Service
2nd Floor Rooms
40 Equity Chambers
Piccadilly
Bradford
West Yorkshire BO1 3NN
Tel.: 0274 720486

Black and Asian Trainees Support Group
metanoia Psychotherapy Training Institute
13 North Common Road
Ealing
London W5 2QB
Tel.: 081 579 2505

Black and Ethnic Minority Health Development Team
MIND South-east Regional Office
24–32 Stephenson Way
London NW1 2HD
Tel.: 071 387 9070

Black HIV and AIDS Network (BHAN)
111 Devonport Road
London W12 8BP
Tel.: 081 749 2828

British Refugee Council
Bondway House
3–9 Bondway
London SW8 1SJ
Tel.: 071 582 6922

Chinese Information and Advice Centre
68 Shaftesbury Avenue
London W1
Tel.: 071 836 8291

NAFSIYAT Intercultural Therapy Centre
278 Seven Sisters Road
London N4 2HY
Tel.: 071 263 4130

Newham Alcohol Advisory Service
7 Sebart Road
Forest Gate
London E7 ONG
Tel.: 081 519 3354

RACE Race and Cultural Education in Counselling
c/o British Association for Counselling
1 Regent Place
Rugby CV21 2PJ
Tel.: 0788 550899

The BAC's Training Directory lists cross-cultural courses and also those which raise multicultural awareness. It also publishes a Counselling and Psychotherapy Resources Directory. *Details of these directories and other publications, from the BAC above.*

Transcultural Psychiatry Unit
Lynfield Mount Hospital
Heights Lane
Bradford BD9 6DP
Tel.: 0274 494194

Chapter 5

Psychotherapy and gender

Sheila Ernst and David Gowling

'Common sense' tells us that to know who I am is to know that I am a man or a woman, a boy or a girl. When a baby is born, the first question is 'What is it?' We know that does not mean is it a frog or a lobster, but 'Is it a boy or a girl?' When my third child was born the midwife said, 'It's a lovely boy. Oh . . . no.' She looked again: 'I mean a girl'. In those few seconds my mental image of my baby had to shift rapidly. The midwife was looking at the presence or absence of labia and a vagina or penis but for me, even in those brief moments, I had begun to think of my baby as a boy and in my head I had to reconstruct her as a girl. The journey towards establishing a gendered identity starts in those first few moments of life; that vivid moment of first realisation, 'It's a girl'; 'It's a boy'.

If gender is so much a part of who a person is, it is not surprising to find that when someone is in distress and seeking psychotherapeutic help, gender and gender-related complaints are often experienced as key issues.

For a man this might be expressed as: 'I don't feel like a man. I can neither live up to my own expectations of a man, nor other people's.' 'How can I be a father?' 'My girlfriends always complain that I am too remote and unaffectionate and in the end it ruins the relationship. I don't know how to be different. I think I'm just an ordinary bloke, but I can't be.' Even when the problem is not explicitly about masculinity it is often gender-related; difficulties at work, obsessive jealousy, fear of one's own violence, being preoccupied with pornography or feeling nagged or henpecked.

Women may come to psychotherapy because they feel disturbed about their femininity or because they fear that they cannot live up to their own or society's images of what a woman should be. Women may seek psychotherapy because in their struggle to survive and to resolve unbearable internal conflicts they find they are abusing themselves, for instance through anorexia, or because of the distress they suffer through being abused by others. Women also often need help in working out the conflicts that arise for them related to their reproductive cycle; pregnancy, childbirth, abortion or the menopause.

Often a woman will express her anxieties and fears about herself in terms of her capacity to develop satisfying, intimate relationships. Whereas with men, stereotypically, problems are to do with an experienced incapacity to be intimate and feelings of claustrophobia in a relationship, with women the difficulties may be expressed in terms of longings for closeness and intimacy which are never fulfilled. Popular books like Robin Norwood's *Women Who Love Too Much* (1986) reflect this aspect of women's experience, but unfortunately do not provide a sufficiently critical stance of social norms alongside the psychological account.

There follows an example of the kinds of difficulties which a couple may bring to psychotherapy. A young couple came to 'sort out their relationship'. She had been in individual psychotherapy for two years and had begun to acknowledge her dissatisfaction with her relationship.

Their phrases were poignant: 'I feel that I'm a chattel just like my mother. A child carer and a shopper.' 'But I'm a worker, always have been. I'm proud of that; my father brought me up to earn good money. You can't expect me to care for the children as well.' Her response is, 'I want more of you.' And his, 'You're too demanding. I don't have energy at the end of the day.' 'All I want is for you to share more.' 'You're always going on and on.'

The dynamic is familiar. The young woman wanting contact, intimacy and sensitivity while the young man is feeling threatened, tense and put-upon; one partner defining sharing as natural, the other experiencing the idea as inherently alien and unmasculine.

These subjective expressions of distress as being gender-related are backed up by statistics which suggest that seeking help with your mental health is something women are far more likely to do than men, whether this means going to the GP, using the psychiatric services or having psychotherapy (Barnes and Maple 1992: 11). In other words, there does seem to be a significant relationship between gender and emotional distress, although, we suggest, it is important for psychotherapists and their patients that we take a careful look at how this is understood. What have we learned about men and women's psychological formation and the way it is structured within society which can help us to understand why it is that far more women than men seek psychotherapy? Is it simply that women are more 'sick' or more troubled than men? Or is it that men simply refuse to go for help when they need it, and opt out? Is this something that could be affected by will-power or does it run deeper? How these questions are answered will affect the understanding of men and women's psychology which, in turn, determines the kind of psychotherapeutic understanding offered to our men and women patients.

CHOOSING A PSYCHOTHERAPIST: DO I WANT A MAN OR A WOMAN, AND WHY?

Men and women seeking help with their emotional difficulties may have many anxieties about how the psychotherapist tackles 'gender issues' even though they may not have formulated it in quite this way. A man may feel that he won't be able to talk freely about his feelings or that the psychotherapist will disapprove of his fantasies. He may also fear that dwelling on painful or distressing feelings in psychotherapy will incapacitate him; will turn him into a cissie. A heterosexual man may fear that his sexual habits with women will be criticised while a homosexual man may fear that a psychotherapist will want to 'cure him' of a disease rather than enable him to discuss freely the difficulties he is encountering in his sexual partnership. A woman may fear that her feelings about the conflicting demands of children and work will be pathologised and she will be deemed an 'unnatural mother', or that as a lesbian she will not be seen as womanly with womanly feelings.

THE PSYCHOTHERAPIST'S ANXIETIES

The psychotherapist may find himself or herself identifying with the young couple who were seeking help. Perhaps the psychotherapist has grown up in a similar environment, white and working-class where there was a firm, if unwritten, agreement, that men work and women stay at home. Lucy Goodwin expressed this vision succinctly: 'We see women as nourishment . . . embodied in the symbol of the ideal mother who is paraded before us in so many commercials, cooking, washing, caring, touching immaculate babies, loving and radiantly happy' (1990: 7).

Coming from this background the psychotherapist's early experience provided little challenge to this view. Few alternative dystonic values were ever presented. Growing men were asked to see women as sexual adventures or as potential wives and mothers but not as individuals separate from their roles. This strictly heterosexual value system influenced the psychotherapist's experience of themselves; how they formed an opinion of their self-worth and ultimately a sense of their existential place in society.

Inevitably, whatever background the psychotherapist comes from will affect how they see patients/clients, and they have a responsibility to understand fully the implications of these influences. We can then potentially meet the significant challenge of both the ego-syntonic restrictions described above and the ego-dystonic possibilities.

THE IDEAS BEHIND THE PRACTICE

We have looked at the thoughts and feelings of the client/patient and the psychotherapist as they approach working together. We will now look at the ideas which influence psychotherapeutic practice and theory on this topic, taking both a humanistic and psychoanalytical perspective.

Humanistic perspective on gender

From a humanistic perspective everyone, irrespective of gender, is born with as full a potentiality for self-actualising growth as they can have within the parameters of physical and mental health.

Berne, the founder of Transactional Analysis, named Physis as 'the growth force of nature, which makes organisms evolve into higher forms, embryos develop into adults, sick people get better and healthy people strive to attain their ideals . . . it may be a more basic force than libido itself' (1981: 369–70). Clarkson supports this view that Physis is 'nature, coming from the deepest biological roots of the human being and striving towards the greatest realisation of the good' (1992: 12).

Therefore, in considering gender as a very significant factor in life and psychotherapy, what are the influences, other than Physis, which we have to take into account?

Clarkson, in further quoting Berne, states that,

> the autonomous aspiration of individual human beings rises from the depths of the somatic Child (the oldest ego state) and transcends the limit-inducing downward pressures of the script which is shaped in the matrix of love and death in our earliest relationships.
>
> (1992: 12)

What is meant by the oldest child ego state and the limit-inducing downward pressures of the script?

Weiss said, 'Every ego state is the actually experienced reality of one's mental and bodily ego with the contents of the lived-through period. Some ego states are easily remembered, some are difficult to recall, some are strictly repressed!' (1950: 141). Specifically, our child ego state is archaic, from the past, and we can re-experience and relive fully those past experiences in the here-and-now, and the crucial emphasis here is that we are not just remembering, but reliving.

Applied to gender, the oldest child ego state is that moment in psychic and physical time when we are born, either as a boy or girl. In the fullest sense this oldest ego state is laid down at the moment of conception.

How does this concept relate to scripting theory? Our script is a life plan made in childhood, enforced by parents, justified by subsequent events and culminating in a chosen alternative: each child decides in childhood how they will live.

As the adults lean over the cot, the baby is clothed in many attributions such as big, bouncy, strong, beautiful, handsome, pretty, gentle, smiley and intelligent. These statements begin to attribute a socially acceptable identity to that newly arrived bundle of flesh and feelings. Although the grown-up cannot know if many of these attributions are true, they constitute the earliest projected wish from the influencing environment that the child grows in a certain way.

So in scripting theory the two essential influencing elements are the environment the child is born into and the sense he or she makes from a place of primitive understanding. From this he will lay down his personality and expectations of self relationships and life. So an accident of birth will determine my sex but, from that moment of birth, determining script influences on my gender identity are legion.* As above, determining descriptive language gives us an initial identity and as we grow the gender split becomes increasingly pronounced. 'He's just like his father/brother/ Uncle George/the Prime Minister.' 'She's going to be a beautiful girl, just like her aunt/Madonna/her mother.' Although the child may have some primitive aspirations to be a politician or a pop star, can she be allowed, and allow herself to be herself? This is a crucial question, because we can already experience the client being objectified, becoming a function of a prescribed set of gender-specific rules.

As a consequence, on many occasions in the therapy room individuals, having exposed and understood these prescriptions, begin to ask the question 'Who am I?' (as man/woman). There is often a profound sense of internal emptiness. A young, high-achieving man had 'all of a sudden' plunged into 'depression'. Over time he began to understand that he did not know who he was if he wasn't a worker. As he traced this further he realised that his father had been described by the family as a failure because he only held down seasonal or occasional work and he drank. His mother had often said to him, 'You won't be like your father, will you?' 'You're going to do all the things he never did!' and 'You're going to be Mummy's little success!'

Therefore our identity continues to be formed within the matrix of parental influence, class, money, cultural background, race, school and friendships. Take two of the above; the interrelation between gender and culture. How may these influences bear directly on the psychotherapy relationship?

For example: first, a young Jewish woman carrying the full weight of post-Holocaust survivor's trauma. Her identity as an autonomous woman is seriously impaired by her responsibilities to take into the next generation the episcript tragedy of her father's family (who were concentration camp victims). Her experience and life task was to find and take care of tragic, wounded men (her brother was not expected to care in this way).

Secondly, a young man from an aristocratic background, having authority

---

* It is important to note here the distinction between sex (physiological) and gender (socially formed).

vested in him by birth, class and status, not through personal qualities. He had presenting arrogance and belief in obedience to his word, and there was a tragic internal conflict between his wish to be his 'own man' and his profound sense of duty to the family tradition.

Thirdly, a middle-aged woman who read a book for the first time, and said she felt 'as if I fell to bits inside'. The book was *Women Who Love Too Much* (Norwood 1986). She had never seen her life portrayed so vividly and the consequent sense of profound personal loss precipitated a breakdown.

These are a few examples of the above scripting process, which, it is hoped, emphasise aspects of gender-splitting. They pose significant challenges to us as therapists which we discuss later in the chapter.

Psychoanalytic theory and gender

Gender has been a hotly debated subject within psychoanalytic theory. It is easy for us now to pick holes in Freud's theories from a modern feminist perspective, and indeed many feminists did do precisely that in the seventies; Freud was criticised for the sexism of his concept of 'penis envy', and his ideas of so-called normal sexual development culminating in genital sexuality which privileges the existing forms of heterosexual relationships and pathologises both alternative forms of heterosexuality and homo-sexuality. Yet gradually feminists, including myself (Sheila Ernst), found themselves returning to read Freud, for he was a great initiator of a new way of perceiving human beings. He himself compared the discovery of the unconscious to the discovery that the earth is not the centre of the universe, and that human beings are descended from animals rather than being the unique creation of God. He recognised that 'to prove to the ego that it is not master in its own house' but merely the recipient of 'scanty information' from the unconscious (Freud 1922: 241) would be a truly shocking notion which would in time transform people's understanding of human behaviour.

Recognising the immensity of this work, it is then fascinating to see what can be learned from the gaps and silences within his work; not only because of what it tells us about Freud, but more significantly because it can help us to understand subsequent psychoanalytic thinking and indicate the work that needs to be done to introduce a gendered or gender-aware psycho-analytic psychotherapy. For Freud was concerned with some of the most fundamental questions: What is gender? How and why do gender reactions have their current forms? Can these forms be changed and what would be the benefits of doing so? How are the relations of domination established, maintained and replicated? To what extent are such relations a necessary and unalterable aspect of human life? A re-reading of Freud reveals that he did not simply lay out a naïve theory which discriminated against women but rather that he was profoundly ambiguous in, I would argue, a good sense. He was prepared to allow himself to acknowledge that some of his theories were not consistent with others and that he could not simply pull them into shape. (I think that this can also be reassuring for prospective patients who fear that any psychoanalytic psychotherapy will 'tell' them what to think in a dominating way.) On the one hand, he maintained his belief that the natural state of the child is 'polymorphous perversity', which led him on to thinking that 'the exclusive sexual interest felt by men for women is also a problem that needs elucidating and is not a self-evident fact' (Freud 1962). On the other hand, he maintains his developmental model of sexuality which unfolds until the person reaches the 'normal' adult stage of genitally orientated, heterosexual sexual intercourse. Thus Freud opened up some questions which we might want any psychological theory to be addressing, but at the same time he did not question the division between men and women in his society but rather assumed them to be natural. It followed from this that he accepted the way in which to become a man was to define yourself as separated from the devalued world of mother and women.

Some of the subsequent development of psychoanalytic theory has laid a foundation for feminist theorists and practitioners to look at new ways of working which could challenge this conservative aspect of Freud's work.* This has important consequences for both men and women wanting help from psychotherapy. There were two crucial ways in which the British object relations school paved the way for contemporary thinking on gender. They began by questioning the centrality of the Oedipal conflict and suggested that the focus of the analyst's attention needed to go much further back into the child's earliest infancy. Klein's (1949) work as a child analyst provided controversial theories about the inner unconscious phantasy life of the child. Fairbairn (1952) and Winnicott (1960) took this work into a slightly different direction by stating much more clearly than Klein had done that the early psychic development of the child was a result of the interaction between the infant and the environment. Winnicott conceptualised this as the need for the mother and family to provide a 'holding' environment within which the child could develop; he saw the work of a psychoanalyst (and of others in the 'caring' professions) as being as much about providing a similar sort of 'holding' environment for the client/patient as it was about offering the 'correct' interpretations.

What was new and important about these psychoanalysts' work was that they were focusing on the importance of the environment and the early mother–infant relationship; what they were not doing was acknowledging fully what implications the different roles and power of men and women

* There has been a steady stream of psychoanalytic writing which has criticised Freud's views on women and gender, such as Jones (1927) and Horney (1967).

might have on boy and girl infants being reared by mothers; nor what this might mean from the mother's point of view. In the past fifteen years much work has been done on developing a theory and practice drawing on a psychoanalytic history but seeing how the social reality of gender relations is incorporated into the psychology of each individual man or woman. Inevitably, once social relations are seen as having such significance other differences between men and women have to be incorporated into the psychotherapy relationship (hence the fact that this book has a whole section entitled 'Structural Themes'). What feminism brings to psychoanalysis is the understanding that we can only grasp the different development of men and women if we understand that femininity and therefore mothering have been devalued in our society. We shall see how this affects the practice of psychotherapy with men and women.

Feminist psychoanalytic writers (drawing on the object relations tradition) recognise the importance of the mother–infant relationship, but they see it within the framework of a society in which mothers are responsible for mothering, may be idealised or denigrated and yet get little recognition or real status for the task they perform. Meanwhile they have little role in the external world, or where they do, this is either markedly inferior to men or they are expected to somehow maintain their family responsibilities without letting them interfere. (A good example of the latter is the MP Harriet Harman's complaint that the way that Parliament's sittings are organised makes it impossible for her to get home to see her children at tea-time. Clearly, Parliament does not relate to after-school child-care concerns, but it is interesting that no male MP seems to have made similar complaints.) Thus the early period of extreme dependency and all the often frightening and chaotic feelings and fantasies associated with this period are inextricably connected to the mother. For boys this means that to become a man means escaping from the dependency and intimacy that are associated with mother and identifying with father who is not seen as being part of mother's world. Thus masculinity becomes associated with independence and detachment, while femininity is associated with connection and dependency. The girl forms her identity through her awareness of the mother's role and position; she tries to get closer to mother by being like her or, sensitive to mother's deprivation, she feels that she has to care for mother.

Olivier (1990) gives some examples of the contrasting ways in which men and women typically relate to a psychotherapist. 'I don't know what I'm doing here. I haven't anything to tell you. There's nothing I feel like sharing with you,' and 'Got to keep quiet so as to keep a distance. I hate talking when we make love. I don't want to bring any feeling into it.' Here the man is expressing his fears of communicating with his psychotherapist, and this is connected to his attempt to prevent intimacy with his sexual partner by not talking when they make love.

'If I stop talking I'm afraid you will see that I don't amount to anything.'
'If I let the silence take over again, I won't be able to bridge the distance
between us. It frightens me.' In these two statements women are talking
about their low self-esteem and the need to be constantly reassured by
contact with the psychotherapist.

Within the relationship between patient and psychotherapist what
matters is that the roots of these two positions are understood. A
psychotherapist unaware of the gender issues may find themselves reacting
unconsciously in a way that reproduces these positions instead of analysing
them. The psychotherapist may unwittingly respond to the man's distancing
without recognising the fear that underlies it, or may feel distaste for the
woman's cloying demands rather than helping her to see how unrecognised
she feels.

Gender-awareness in practice

A session of a mixed psychotherapy group (a group analytic group) is in
progress. Alison is talking about how difficult she finds the weekends. She
explains that she doesn't know what to do with herself because everyone
else seems to have partners, husbands, wives or lovers to spend time with
and she feels she is always taking the initiative to ring up friends and try
to arrange to go out together. She thinks she always needs other people
more than they need her. This theme is taken up by Helga, who says that
having a partner doesn't really make any difference; she wants more from
her boyfriend than he seems to want from her. She finds herself starting
conversations, suggesting outings or inviting friends round and even, to
her surprise, having to initiate sex. Alison and Helga wonder what is wrong
with them; why do they always want so much; why do they always feel so
needy? The three men in the group listen attentively but do not say
anything, which suggests that they might identify with what is being said.
Mark seems particularly interested, and asks Alison and Helga some
searching questions about their previous relationships and then about their
family backgrounds. The woman psychotherapist is beginning to feel
uncomfortable. She doesn't like this image of poor needy Alison and Helga
and three solicitous and helpful men. While the conversation continues she
is examining her own reaction.

She thinks, 'What is it I don't like? Is it that I identify with Alison and
Helga and can't bear to acknowledge my/their neediness? Do I feel that,
as group conductor, I should be playing the good mother and helping them
to feel nurtured and cared for? Is what they are really talking about – my
lack of concern and attention; are they wanting to ask me for more
attention? Do I feel competitive with Mark, who is being the second
psychotherapist in the group?'

The psychotherapist is exploring some of the difficult feelings which she might be having because of her own personal reactions to the situation; in technical terms she is looking at the aspect of her counter-transference which may be to do with her own unresolved difficulties. She is particularly aware of the way in which a woman's neediness may be unacceptable to another woman because it puts her in touch with her own unmet needs. She is also aware that she may be ambivalent about her nurturing role; on the one hand, resenting it because she feels inadequately nurtured, but, on the other hand, threatened because this nurturing maternal role may be her way of defending herself against her own neediness.

She then feels ready to acknowledge to herself that some of her discomfort is to do with the painful way in which Alison and Helga are exposing themselves, but something else comes to mind. She feels that the attentiveness of Mark, Henry and Bill may be because they too feel many of the things which Helga and Alison are talking about but they cannot allow them to come to consciousness. Alison and Helga are working on their behalf to express the whole group's neediness. In gender terms, the women are expressing the emotions and making themselves vulnerable while the men are apparently concerned observers. The psychotherapist is now ready to make a comment or interpretation which will enable the three men to see how they are defending themselves against their own needy feelings and thus missing out on the opportunity to understand more about this aspect of themselves, while Alison and Helga are carrying the split-off parts of the men's vulnerability and in this way losing touch with their own capacity to begin to understand how and why it is that they have such difficulty in finding ways of getting some of their needs addressed.

Implications for users and psychotherapists, male and female, psychoanalytic and humanist

Patients and psychotherapists may be frustrated with traditional psycho-analytic theory which both offers a way of understanding the deepest roots of gender identity and at the same time can often to the modern reader appear to be sexist, patriarchal and pathologising of the experience of women and men, particularly if they are homosexual. As a psychoanalytic psychotherapist who has been very influenced by the 'second wave' of feminist thinking I (Sheila Ernst) have tried to give an account of how work has been done in the last twenty years, initially on women's psychology and more recently also about men too, which has revised and developed psychoanalytic thought and practice to encompass new thinking about gender and homosexuality. What this means in clinical practice is that there are a growing number of psychoanalytic psychotherapists who have begun to address these questions in their practice and have at least some awareness of the issues involved. For the patient who is concerned that within treatment their gender identity or sexual preferences will not be pathologised, as opposed to explored and analysed, it is important to search for a psychotherapist who is open to thinking in this way. (For the particularly problematic relationship of lesbians and gay men to psycho-analytic psychotherapy, see Chapter 8 on Psychotherapy and Sexual Orientation.)

For me (Dave Gowling), writing as a man from a humanist perspective, it is here as client and as psychotherapist that we are confronted by the interplay of gender-motivated forces. For instance, a male psychotherapist could be seen as Santa Claus, white knight, punisher, saviour, abuser or sought-after lover. We can see this as projection within the transferential relationship; that this is not necessarily me; this is an introjected and projected other, and we (the psychotherapists) have a responsibility to stay adult; empathic, confrontative, supportive, whatever is clinically appropriate in that time of our relationship. This does assume, however, that we have freed ourselves sufficiently from our counter-transferential influences. Can we assume that our emotional response is based on a 'correct interpretation' of our client's true intentions and meaning? There-fore, for instance, can the male psychotherapist see his client as distinct from his demanding or engulfing or marshmallow mother in the intensity of the moment-to-moment relationship?

If we store in our child ego state all experiences of our primary parenting, may the above intensity not press on a lesion (sore spot) in our child, such as a belief or decision that, say, we are not quite good enough to meet up to our parents' standards, their expectations of maleness? The effort to stay in 'integrated adult' in the intensity of that moment could be significantly costly to the quality of the ongoing relationship, and both psychotherapist and client's sense of self may be affected. The psycho-therapist may trigger old felt incompetence and the client may experience that they have met another inept or incompetent male. So we are faced with ongoing, intense challenges to our sense of self, our sense of wholeness and intrapsychic integrity. This, I believe, makes essential a commitment to continue in personal therapy for our duration as a psychotherapist.

Can I as a man identify with issues of female sexual abuse, menstruation and sexual attraction, and stay non-threateningly, non-sexually involved without giving up on my essential maleness? I am challenged by the contrast between my archaic syntonic belief, about the 'place' women should have in society, and a wish to stay unbiased (or to use my bias constructively), a wish to see the wholeness of the person as they struggle to find their own unique path in psychotherapy and in life.

Furthermore, do we as men have an immutable problem, as Jung states:

> woman with her very dissimilar psychology is, and always has been a source of information about things for which a man has no eyes. She can be his inspiration, her intuitive capacity, often superior to man's,

can give him timely warning, and her feelings, always directed towards the personal, can show him ways which his own less personally accented feelings would never have discerned.

(Jung 1986)

This does seem to indicate an inherent problem which the male brings to psychotherapy: this separation, seemingly immutable, and only to be attained via a woman's intuitive capacity. Jung seems to speak of the very challenge and conflict manifested in the relationship of the young couple mentioned above.

Now I don't hold this as a truth, but perhaps in pursuit of this feminine 'source of information' Bly met his soft man: 'Men welcoming their own "feminine consciousness" and nurturing it'. He went on to say though, 'this is important, and yet I have the sense that there is something wrong. The male in the past twenty years has become more thoughtful, more gentle. But by this process he has not become more free. He's a nice boy who pleases not only his mother but also the young woman he is living with' (1990: 2).

Perhaps the challenge therefore is that as men we have to embrace what Bly calls 'the beast'. Embrace more fully those 'male values' of strength, anger, determination, hard work and comradeship, and integrate them with, not separate from, the seemingly feminine virtues of sensitivity, emotional awareness and expression of feelings. In this sense we could remove ourselves from fixed ego syntonic expectations and embrace them at the same time.

From the patient's viewpoint it is important to find psychotherapists and institutions which share an awareness of the importance of looking at the issue of gender. There are already organisations like the Women's Therapy Centre in London (see address below) which, as well as providing psychoanalytic psychotherapy, will help prospective patients to find a psychotherapist who concerns themselves with these issues. A patient seeking a psychotherapist can also feel entitled to ask his or her own questions, although we must recognise how difficult this can feel when one is in a state of distress.

It is important that the question of gender is continually raised in discussion amongst professionals and that pressure is put on training organisations to include and integrate a gendered way of thinking into their curriculum for trainees and for their members as part of their own postgraduate ongoing study. This is happening slowly, but requires constant attention because there is a tendency towards conservatism in this most deeply personal area; there is also a tendency towards an anti-feminist backlash (Faludi 1992). There is also a way in which psychotherapists, like other professionals, may find it more pressing to address other forms of discrimination, such as racial discrimination, believing them to have a stronger moral or political imperative. The competition within a hierarchy of discriminated groups is dangerous and, we would argue, unprofitable territory. I do not think that we can place gender above or below other forms of discrimination which need to be addressed, but rather would point out that gender is a fundamental part of any theory of personality development and therefore to discuss it in a new way could threaten existing theory and practice profoundly. This might be why it so easily slips out of consciousness.

SUMMARY

Another way of expressing this would be to say that addressing the issue of gender in psychoanalytic and humanistic psychotherapy means helping the patient to find the repressed masculine and feminine parts of themselves. To do this the psychotherapist must be aware of the ways in which social forces influence the girl's and the boy's psychological development. Psychotherapists themselves are also part of this society and will need to work on their own often unconscious adaptation to gender stereotypes; this needs to be as much a part of any psychotherapist's training as uncovering the other aspects of the life of the unconscious.

REFERENCES

Barnes, M. and Maple, N. (1992) *Women and Mental Health*, London: Venture.
Berne, E. (1981) *A Layman's Guide to Psychiatry and Psychoanalysis*, Harmondsworth: Penguin (first published 1947).
Bly, R. (1990) *Iron John*, London: Element.
Clarkson, P. (1992) 'Physis in Transactional Analysis', *ITA News* 33: 14–19; also published in *Transactional Analysis Journal* 22(4): 202–209.
Fairbairn, W. R. D. (1952) *Psycho-analytic Studies of the Personality*, London: Tavistock.
Faludi, S. (1992) *Backlash*, London: Chatto.
Freud, S. (1922) *Introductory Lectures in Psychoanalysis*, London: Allen & Unwin.
—— (1962) *Three Essays on the Theory of Sexuality*, New York: Basic Books.
Goodwin, L. (1990) *Moving Heaven and Earth*, London: Women's Press.
Horney, K. (1967) *Feminine Psychology*, New York: Norton.
Jones, E. (1927) *Papers on Psychoanalysis*, Boston: Beacon Press.
Jung, C. G. (1986) *Aspects of the Feminine*, London: Ark (first published 1982) (selection from *Collected Works* between 1954 and 1971).
Klein, M. (1949) *The Psychoanalysis of Children*, London: Hogarth Press.
Norwood, R. (1986) *Women Who Love Too Much*, London: Arrow.
Olivier, C. (1990) *Jocasta's Children*, London: Routledge.
Weiss, E. (1950) *Principles of Psychodynamics*, New York: Grune & Stratton.
Winnicott, D. W. (1960) *The Maturational Process and the Facilitating Environment*, London: Hogarth Press.

FURTHER READING

Chodorow, N. (1978) *Reproduction of Mothering: Psychoanalysis and the Sociology of Gender*, Berkeley, CA: University of California Press.

Eichenbaum, L. and Orbach, S. (1982) *Understanding Women*, Harmondsworth: Penguin.

Ernst, S. and Maguire, M. (eds) (1987) *Living with the Sphinx: Papers from the Women's Therapy Centre*, London: The Women's Press.

Estés, C. P. (1992) *Women Who Run with the Wolves: Contacting the Power of the Wild Woman*, London: Rider.

Jukes, A. (1993) *Why Men Hate Women*, London: Free Association Books.

O'Connor, N. and Ryan, J. (1993) *Wild Desires and Mistaken Identities*, London: Virago.

Pines, D. (1993) *A Woman's Unconscious Use of Her Body*, London: Virago.

Tannen, D. (1991) *You Just Don't Understand: Women and Men in Conversation*, London: Virago.

FURTHER INFORMATION

Albany Trust
Sunra Centre
26 Balham Hill
Clapham South
London SW12 9EB
Tel.: 081 675 6669

London Lighthouse
111–117 Lancaster Road
London W11 1QT
Tel.: 071 792 1200

Red Admiral Project
51a Philbeach Gardens
London SW5 9EV
Tel.: 071 835 1495

The Men's Therapy Centre
Tel.: 071 267 8713

The Women's Therapy Centre
6–9 Manor Gardens
London N7 6OA
Tel.: 071 263 6200

Chapter 6

Therapy with survivors of the Nazi Holocaust

Judith Hassan

I have chosen to write about my work with the survivors of the Nazi Holocaust, set in the voluntary sector of Jewish Care – formerly the Jewish Welfare Board (JWB) – because it is a subject I feel passionately about, both personally and professionally. Looking at it in the context of the agency is a new angle for me. It makes me reflect on the years of development in both my work and in myself within the agency and how the two have become intertwined. I write because I want to show the process I have been through in this special area of work; to spare others some of the pitfalls that have inevitably happened and also to pass on what I have learned.

Though the terminology I will use will be familiar to the therapeutically trained, the social work context of the agency as well as my training as a social worker will broaden the meaning of therapy. This may not only differentiate me from the more traditional therapist, but even alienate me in some circles. The world of the survivor is a unique one; not comparable, they would feel, to any other event in history. Obviously comparisons are made to other disasters and genocides, but the Nazi Holocaust remains on its own. Interestingly, I am writing this chapter on my own. Though various logistical reasons could explain why this happened, it is perhaps no coincidence that I have no co-author. Yet I have an important and urgent task, which is to make the work with survivors come alive, and engage other therapists whilst the need is still there. In ten years' time it may be too late.

This chapter is therefore not an academic exercise but a plea for those who can open themselves up to this work, both personally and professionally, to become involved. I have divided the chapter into three parts. The first part will concentrate on how, on the one hand, my training and theoretical framework gave me the foundation to work with elderly refugees from Nazi persecution using psychodynamic approaches. I will also look at how the organisational setting enabled this work to begin. I will examine how I became aware of the restrictions in what I could offer survivors from the concentration camps and those who had been in hiding, because I had become imprisoned by my professional boundaries as well as the organisational walls – I was at that stage mirroring the incarceration of the survivor in the camp.

Few survivors of the camps could or wished to penetrate the fortress. In the context of working therapeutically with Holocaust survivors, organisations take on a different perspective. In terms of the death camp experience the 'production of death became bureaucratised', wrote Kren (1989); death camps were literally death factories. With efficiency and care to meticulous detail, the genocide went on. Within this order, chaos ruled. The death camp was a mad world, a world turned upside down in which human dignity and humanity had no meaning. With this in mind, how could any organisation offer services to Holocaust survivors? Entering an office building and being greeted by a security guard could flash back to another place and another time.

In this first stage, I will concentrate on looking at contributing factors to this wasteland between the survivor and the professional. Factors such as the over-emphasis on pathology; survivors' feelings towards Anglo-Jewish organisations; the authority issues related to the helper and the resultant inequality and vulnerability of the relationship; the lack of understanding of the nature of extreme experience in making sense of the survivor and his world – these are but a few of the reasons why the organisation and professional framework kept death-camp survivors away.

The second stage of this chapter will look at how the organisation's fortifications were broken down by reaching out to survivors through an understanding of self-help support groups, social bonding, human reciprocity, power shifting from the therapist authority figure, the emergence of the coping, adapting survivor. The emphasis is on the meaningfulness of the therapy to the survivor – a question of being understood rather than diagnosed. New approaches then began to emerge such as the power of the testimony as a therapeutic tool and the relevance of ritual prayer and mourning. This stage was also mirroring the opening up of the camp gates, with the prisoners being set free. I have linked it to my experience of passing through the organisational doors to a world unknown. For me the 'prison' gates had opened up, but I did not know what I would find. As the survivors have reported, they faced a world that did not want to hear the atrocities they had been through. I, similarly at that stage, found many professionals unwilling or unable to hear and share the world of massive trauma I was uncovering forty years on.

The last stage of the chapter focuses on how a true sense of liberation is reached, contrasted with the disappointment of the 'setting-free' stage. The liberation is away from the psychopathology and victim role of the survivor to an image of strength and health. Through the empowerment of the survivor the possibility of meaning and healing can begin to happen. The development will be put in the context of the shift in setting to a new community-based location, as well as looking at my own professional metamorphosis.

The development of these stages can be seen metaphorically as a journey. It forms a link between the past, the present and the future. There is a beginning, a setting-out on the journey, a middle and an end or final part of the journey. The constant reflection between the camp experience, the 'therapy' and the setting and how these three component parts fit together will be focused on as an essential ingredient for this work to happen. It is in a sense my testimony, my story of a long and difficult journey which I have undertaken with survivors, but which ends with hope and optimism.

THE FIRST STAGE – THE BEGINNING OF A JOURNEY

The story began when I returned to the JWB, having been seconded to my social work training. This training had given me an excellent foundation in psychodynamic work which I hoped to put into practice. At that time I was in an area-based team in Swiss Cottage. The setting was a beautiful old house in an area in which a very high number of survivors/refugees had settled. There was a day centre for the elderly beneath our offices, and so it was not unusual for elderly people to walk in and ask for help. This was mostly of a practical nature, because that was how the agency was perceived. However, I gradually began to notice patterns emerging related to unresolved issues that refugees were experiencing forty or fifty years on. There appeared to be a current loss such as the death of someone close, retirement, loss of health – all of which reactivated earlier losses which had not been worked through. Secondly, I knew from my work with the elderly that it is a natural process of ageing that short-term memories tend to grow weaker, whilst long-term memories become stronger, allowing events from the past to return to consciousness much more vividly.

Case study 1

An example from practice: Mrs H was a refugee in her eighties. Most of her family had perished in the war. She came to the JWB asking for a volunteer to help her to move. On first contact it seemed to me that her level of anxiety was excessive for the request she was making. This was conveyed to her, and we agreed to meet over a period of time to try and understand what had brought her to me at that moment. After all, she said she had managed for over eighty years. Before our meeting, however, she had a road accident and was admitted to hospital. I continued to see her there. Mrs H refused to be operated on for a fractured leg and, indeed, refused all treatment for infection. The staff in desperation called in a psychiatrist who diagnosed her as a paranoid schizophrenic, without taking into account her background. During her time in hospital, as she lay helpless and vulnerable, unable to move, she began to talk about her past, particularly her persecution under the Nazis. Her current helplessness seemed to reactivate similar feelings she had about being unable to save her mother, whom she left behind, from being killed.

She began to mourn for her mother, which she said she had never done before. Though she displayed considerable hostility with paranoid features towards the staff, she allowed me to continue to see her regularly. Our relationship was not without difficulty, and I felt I was always walking a fine line between colluding with her paranoid feelings, and becoming yet another persecuting 'Nazi' in her eyes by differentiating myself from her. However, I seemed to convey to her a sense that she was heard and understood, and some feeling of trust developed. I continued to see her weekly over one-and-a-half years. The move which had brought her to me initially turned out to be an eviction – a traumatic enough event at any time, but for her it was also a reminder of her enforced 'eviction' from Germany as a refugee. Mrs H was able to share with me her real fear of breaking down mentally and being admitted to psychiatric hospital. This did not happen, though she came very close to it. She made a successful move to new accommodation, thereby avoiding the trauma of eviction.

However, once the crisis was over, Mrs H's defences re-emerged. What she found so difficult to acknowledge was that through our relationship I had become significant to her. Once more in control of events, she defended herself against the feelings of vulnerability and helplessness, first by trying to use my sessions with her to do practical tasks which the local authority worker was already doing, and secondly by rejecting me altogether. Klein has noted that this 'fear of getting to love someone is not uncommon in survivors of the Holocaust' (1968: 73).

Understanding the reality base of her paranoia rather than labelling her as psychiatrically ill allowed us an opportunity to struggle with the fears and anxieties I had initially felt at our first meeting. Mrs H was a highly intelligent, articulate woman who internalised something from what transpired in our sessions. Despite a great deal of denial concerning the connections made between current and past trauma, we were able to work through some of the 'unfinished business' which had contributed to her vulnerability and sense of aloneness. Entering into Mrs H's world gave me a unique opportunity to learn how to relate to someone who, in another setting, would be labelled as paranoid, and consequently seen as having impaired ability to relate.

Mrs H had been touched by a 'mad' environment under the Nazis. She may have had some disturbance prior to this period, but there is no doubt that the reality of what she experienced affected her ability to trust. Despite her 'paranoia' she had amazing support from neighbours and friends as well as social services. There was a warmth that emanated from her, and it was these strengths on which I tended to build. I could so easily just have seen Mrs H as yet another victim of Nazi persecution, perhaps feeling that her state was unsurprising, considering what she had been through. Consequently, I might have tried to make reparation to her through practical provision and giving as much emotional comfort as possible. However, it was the struggle and fight which constituted our work together that I believe helped Mrs H to break out from the 'victim' category. It may have helped her to experience again a feeling of being in control of events so that her current trauma did not overwhelm her. Mrs H's other agenda was to tell her 'story' so that someone would know what really happened.

Interestingly, during the course of our meetings, Mrs H's son came from the United States to visit his mother for the first time in many years. He had written to her that he had wanted to know more about what happened to her and her family, and wanted to help her to write it down. The survivor who feels they can tell their story because they believe that it will be heard and thereby transmitted can sometimes unburden themselves dramatically. This may make great demands on the social worker, who often becomes the sole means for passing this on – it demands availability by the social worker to the survivor to an extent possibly not encountered with other clients.

The agency's specialisation of working with the elderly, plus my own psychodynamic training, encouraged me to undertake this work with the elderly refugees whom many would agree were beyond the age at which emotional growth or change was possible. My experience had shown me that chronological age was not the main factor in ability to grow emotionally. In addition, the flexibility to see her in hospital as well as at home allowed me to engage her in a therapeutic process so that she could subsequently live more comfortably with herself and die more peacefully. My increasing tendency to pick up on the underlying issues which brought these elderly refugees to the organisation allowed me to begin my involvement. It is very easy to miss the opportunities to confront these painful events from the past, especially as those who have been traumatised or persecuted do not easily verbalise them, as was seen in the hospital setting in which the client found herself. In addition, it may be the therapist who finds it difficult to face these painful areas. Survivors and therapists have become locked in to what has come to be known as a 'conspiracy of silence'. Consequently we must also focus on the therapists – on the counter-transference factors, as these too can imprison us in our defences in a similar way to the organisational walls which become impenetrable to the pain the survivor experiences.

I have often asked myself why I became involved in the work with survivors. Why did I start to see the patterns emerging in my work rather than another worker? Admittedly, at that time I did not even know what I was beginning to touch – my naïvety was in a sense a good thing. I felt that I could apply my psychodynamic training in any setting. I saw myself as a professionally qualified worker who just happened to be working in a Jewish organisation. As I entered the world of these persecuted refugees, so I started to look at my own Jewish identity. I began to think about issues of assimilation and how this has led to the persecution and in its extreme form to genocide. I began to appreciate how the organisation's separate identity in meeting the needs of the Jewish community *vis-à-vis* social/health services seemed to fit with this theme of confronting my own separate Jewish identity.

I was also addressing this issue in my work with people who had been persecuted for being Jews, whether they adhered religiously or not. Just as their Jewishness could not be avoided, nor could mine. Now I knew why I had chosen to work in a Jewish setting – the work began to take on meaning for me on a level it had not done before. I also became more aware about my personal connection to the Holocaust, which had not been spoken about previously. My mother had come to England as a refugee from Nazi Germany in 1939, and my grandparents were interned in a camp in France. The memories of what happened to them returned to me vividly recently when I was preparing for our most recent conference in January 1992, called 'Creative Approaches to Working with Holocaust Survivors'. Looking at artwork from the camp at Gurs brought home to me in images the link between my work and my own family.

In the self-exploration which needed to be done for me to engage in this work, I had asked myself whether I was making reparation for the suffering my family had been through, but which I had been spared. Wishing to make reparation also brought with it the corollary that survivors who had been through such terrible happenings should be spared any more suffering. How then could I address the rage that was underlying the massive losses that the survivors had been through? In one sense the survivor would be treated as the victim who had suffered so much, and it would be anathema to confront the rage. Having worked this through, however, I was then able to use my personal experience as a bridge between myself and the survivor, and this ultimately led to my acceptance as a non-survivor. In turn this allowed the therapeutic work to take place.

Though my training has encouraged the boundary between the personal and the professional sides of myself, this had to be looked at again in terms of reaching out and encouraging survivors to look at their unfinished business from the past. This work depends on trust, but for people whose trust has been shattered, as many survivors had experienced, how does such a relationship come about? Krell, himself a survivor as well as a therapist, points out that 'in the psychotherapy with holocaust survivors/and or their children, the therapist may be sought out for precisely those reasons that make them feel that some degree of intimacy is possible' (1989a: 224). The adaptation process had started to happen in myself. Survivors in their incarceration or under persecution had to find new ways of coping with the extremely adverse environment they found themselves in. Similarly, if I worked in this world, I had to find new therapeutic ways of doing this.

In the world of the survivor, theory develops from contact with survivors – listening very closely to what they say helps them. However, much of the early work with Holocaust survivors tried to deal with the chaos they presented by trying to fit them into syndromes and theories. Steinberg wrote: 'The early investigations seem to struggle with understanding the survivor via pre-existing theories. Survivors were in a sense fit into the theories, but the fit, as critics have pointed out, was not quite right' (1989: 31). Much of the early work with survivors was based on compensation claims from Germany. Reparation claims looked for causal connections between current emotional difficulties and the experience in the Holocaust. The professionals were looking for 'damage' to justify the claim rather than looking for the survivors' ability to cope. Under these particular circumstances one can understand how the pathological aspects came to be accentuated. However, the model of survivor syndrome which was the medical model for understanding the survivor then transferred itself into different settings with which survivors came into contact; for example, treatment settings. Yet 'the limited power of this model to explain the behaviour of Holocaust survivors in treatment did not appear to inhibit its use' (Steinberg 1989: 27).

The implication of this has been that very little hope could be offered by psychoanalytic therapy for survivors, as their personalities were considered irreversibly damaged by their Holocaust experience. Certainly, survivors would agree that their experiences had scarred them, but in turn, survivor syndrome tended to incarcerate them further in the psychopathology with which they have been labelled. The setting again became of paramount importance in breaking away from this model of understanding survivors. The non-clinical setting of the JWB encouraged me to see the healthy, coping, adaptive side of the survivor. If we look again at the concentration camp setting we see, as Frankl (1987) has concluded, that it was the environment under persecution and in the camps which was abnormal; the survivor reaction to it was normal. We are talking about life in extremity, which cannot be understood within our normal framework.

When we do start to understand this dehumanised, degrading world of the camp, we can then re-examine such issues as the survivors' need to go over and over again what happened. Some therapists have interpreted this need as neurotic behaviour and an inability to complete the mourning process. Krystal (1984), for example, saw the survivor as locked into his anger, unable to accept his past. The answer, he writes, is that 'it must be accepted or we must keep waging an internal war against the ghosts of our past. This does not acknowledge the survivors' need to bear witness' (p. 113). As des Pres points out, psychiatric treatment is directed towards processes of 'adjustment, acceptance, forgetting' (1976: 39). However, these goals are at variance with the survivors' goal to remember so others will not forget. To assume that the need to bear witness is rooted in neurosis is to ignore entirely the nature of extreme experience. This view is supported by Davidson (1981), Baron (1977), Ornstein (1985) and many others. Baron concludes that bearing witness for the survivors is a duty, not a disease.

The pessimistic, pathological approach coloured much of the thinking on survivors at that time. With relatively little known about the long-term effect of massive trauma, the structure it offered was appealing. I was at the Survivor Syndrome Conference in London in 1980, attended by therapists from all over the world. It put survivors on the map as far as therapy was concerned. Interestingly, however, very few of the therapists remained involved in the work in Britain. This again may be linked to the overwhelming nature of the syndromes portrayed. The deskilling process experienced at the conference is something often felt in working with severely traumatised people, and there is a reluctance by many therapists to get involved. In a survey carried out at about that time concerning possible services needed by survivors, the results received were very negative. The questionnaire was sent to GPs in areas in which survivors were living. The response was either that we should not bring up the trauma again, or that anything we could offer would be too late.

Just as a survivor was trying to be fitted into a pre-existing framework, so my own work was not being understood. The excellent consultation I had been receiving for years at the Tavistock Centre could not help me deal with these issues that were emerging from the work. The JWB encouraged me to find an alternative consultant, which I did in Professor Shamai Davidson, who had many years' experience in this work. Without this intervention I might not have survived this stage of the work. The organisation's sensitivity and awareness of the need to invest in this support was crucial.

THE MIDDLE STAGE – OPENING THE ORGANISATIONAL DOORS

I began to realise that those who had been most traumatised in the concentration camps or in hiding rarely came forward to ask for help. One would have expected their emotional needs to be greater. This was a grave misunderstanding on my part. I have since learned through my contact with concentration camp survivors why they kept their distance from our professional organisation – anger towards our Jewish community for not having done enough to help them when they needed it after liberation; the indifference of Jews towards their suffering; their feelings towards authority and institutions; their fears of weakness and vulnerability which asking for help would imply. The office setting was therefore potentially an obstacle to reaching survivors of the death camps. The therapist as well as the organisation were seen as authority figures, which in terms of the camp experience could be equated with the Nazis. Vulnerability in the camps meant certain death, and hence the survivors tended to cope on their own. It should be stressed that most survivors coped extremely well without any professional support. They achieved well at work and raised families despite extreme difficulty. This was in some sense their victory over the Nazis.

The evidence of pathology and sickness among survivors which many professionals, as well as the media, wanted to emphasise, would have implied that Hitler had done the job extremely well. However, in reality this was not the case. The coping continued for many years and these years came to be known as the 'symptom-free interval'. The needs of the survivors changed as they grew older. However, it was difficult for the needs to find meaningful expression within the confines of the therapeutic office setting.

A turning point in my work with survivors came when a camp survivor (not a client) came to see me, having heard my name through an organisation in Israel that specialised in working with Holocaust survivors. The JWB had sent me to a conference in Israel to give a paper on my work, having recognised the importance of these links. This survivor asked me to help her set up a self-help group for some camp survivors whom she knew wanted to come together. They did not want therapy, but to help one another mutually. They would not need to explain why they were there. In this self-help group I was an honorary member (a non-survivor). Instead of the comfort of my usual professional role, I had to face role conflicts and paradoxes in enabling the group to get off the ground – being there as a catalyst but leaving space for the survivors to find their own way; hearing the hidden agendas but using the survivors to draw these out rather than interpreting them, acknowledging my own identity as a professional, but allowing the survivors to use my presence in a way acceptable to them – often in an informal social role.

To the survivor, the meaningfulness of the self-help group was in its mirroring of the camp experience. The non-clinical informal atmosphere of the group which met in premises of their own choice (non-institutional) was a far more acceptable environment for the therapeutic work to take place. The group created a sense of belonging, a sense of family and community which many survivors had been deprived of for a very long time. They celebrated the Jewish festivals together, they phoned one another outside of group meetings. In that sense of belonging and sharing they also fought with one another – as one survivor told me, 'This is the only place that we can bring our bestiality – in all other groups we have to behave'. Despite the hierarchies of suffering which developed, their experience was also in a sense normalised. From this experience of a self-help group, I learned about the power of a group as a therapeutic medium, particularly for camp survivors. Instead of trying to fit the survivor into the boundaries of my professional expertise, I began to develop my theoretical framework from the position that I saw working in practice.

I then turned to the literature and read that mutual aid constituted the key to survival in the camps. After overcoming the initial shock of being tossed into such debilitating circumstances, the prisoner gradually realised the struggle was a collective one (Baron 1977: 27). This mutual aid which had helped during the incarceration could then be translated into therapy in the self-help group. Des Pres refers to the teamwork aspect in the camp when talking about the importance of 'organising' – for example, sharing out clothes and food, or propping one another up during roll call to prevent being selected for death. 'In extremity life depends on solidarity for collective action is more effective than individual efforts' (Frankl 1987: 121). Through this understanding I was able to progress on from Krystal's (1984) account of the influence of the impact of massive psychic trauma with its emphasis on how the traumatic process relates to intrapsychic events, to a recognition of the importance of the interpersonal dimension – what Davidson calls 'social bonding' (1984: 556).

Such social support was not only important during the incarceration, but was also an important variable in preventing or modifying long-term effects of massive psychic trauma. It was in the interpersonal bonding that human dignity was in some way sustained and survivors continued with their struggle to live. It is recognition of this essential yet understated dynamic which gives credence to view Frankl's quotation from Nietzsche that 'he who has a why to live for can bear almost any how' (Allport 1987: iii). The social work context of this therapeutic work with survivors seems to fit comfortably with the shift from the individual surviving for himself, as proposed by Bettelheim (1986), to the wider context of the group, as proposed by des Pres (1976) and Davidson (1981). To see the survivor without a context is to misinterpret the experience.

In addition, it was in this agency context that the need for professionals to come together in groups as well as the survivors was realised. To be able to undertake this work takes courage as well as skill. The JWB recognised this through the consultancy arrangements they made for me with Sonny Herman, a therapist working with survivors in Holland. Together we run monthly groups for professionals working with survivors, where they can share their work in a supportive environment. Being a voluntary agency gives the space to address these difficult issues.

Prioritising this work and with the agency giving it its full backing has made my task infinitely easier than it would otherwise have been. Both in the groups and at the conferences we have organised on working with survivors, I have often heard counsellors/therapists declaring their sense of isolation in their organisations when they take on this work with Holocaust survivors. I spend considerable amounts of time visiting hospitals and other organisations, or receiving phone calls from professionals who have begun to work with survivors. The sense of not being alone with the trauma seems to bring relief, as well as the exchange of information on the services which have been developing.

Through the experience of the self-help groups the walls of the setting had become more elastic. My role of listener and facilitator overcame the authority issue and also the sense of vulnerability and dependency that the therapeutic relationship often brings. The importance of not knowing because I was not there (in the camp) was a humbling but essential part of my acceptance in the group. As Wiesel has written, 'Listen to survivors, listen to them very carefully. They have more to teach you than you them' (1982: i). There can be no assumptions, no sense of knowing. Listening and learning from survivors as witnesses of the unimaginable rebalances the relationship in such a way that therapy can then begin. With the survivor teaching us, we start to search with them for meaning in their survival, but the methods we use are varied. They are not patients or even clients but individuals whom we engage in a process which may lead to healing. They take us on a journey with them. Krell (1989b) has, for example, found the use of a map an excellent tool for encouraging the process of communication. Looking at the map conveys interest and involves both parties in a joint venture.

Some of these survivors from the self-help group were then able to come forward and ask for counselling. The office setting then became a safe place in which to conduct therapy. Just as they had become individualised to me, so had I to them. The myth of the 'pathetic victim' was fast disappearing and the strength of the survivor emerging. I became more aware of the variables which affected the coping – issues such as early childhood experiences; the age of the survivor on entering the camp; whether they remained with members of their family in the camp; what happened to them after liberation; whether they adhered to their religious beliefs. The myth of the professional was also broken down through personalising the experience and loosening the constrictions of my professional role. At the same time, when the location shifted to the office, there was no sense of undermining my professional status. The preparatory work of the self-help group enables the survivor's ego to be strengthened, so that, when the trauma is re-experienced, which it may be in the therapy, this is not so overwhelming. Ornstein emphasises the importance of the survivor being understood rather than diagnosed, and this seems to open up a possibility of survivors sharing some of their most painful memories. 'Feeling understood by the psychotherapist fosters the development of one of the self-object transferences. . . . Only when such a rehabilitation of the self has occurred can the process of mourning begin' (Ornstein 1985: 99).

Case study 2

A way of dealing with the process of mourning can be illustrated by reference to a particular survivor. This work contrasts a traditional psychodynamic approach with one which is more meaningful to the survivor. Mrs L came to the JWB at the point when her husband had died. She was seen at the office by a social worker, who assessed her need for bereavement counselling. The social worker was sympathetic of her need to mourn, but Mrs L could not make use of the counselling and so terminated. I met Mrs L six years later in the self-help group just described.

After I had got to know her in that setting, she asked if she could come and see me. She told me her command of English was not good, and she would like me to help her record what had happened to her before, during and after the Holocaust. She had never been able to tell her children what had really happened and she wanted them to know. We met regularly over several months. She would talk to me about her life before Auschwitz-Birkenau during the incarceration and what happened to her at liberation and later. Her imagery was vivid and we recorded vignettes about her experience.

> The summer was very hot inside the overcrowded barracks – the air smelled fetid and rotten, the atmosphere was suffocating – it was a nightmare. I looked at these well-fed Germans who externally looked prime examples of the human race and yet inside were mere empty shells, devoid of those values which make them human. I looked at myself, whose outer shell was a pathetic specimen of life, yet inside I kept the values which my parents had given to me and which no one could take away. If I survived, I thought the world would be a better place because this would never be allowed to happen again.
>
> (Survivor's testimony)

Mrs L would talk to me and I would record, writing it up after the session in the first person. She told me she found the process acceptable and helpful because she was also giving something to me – she was helping me to understand the incomprehensible. My recording seemed to demonstrate the success of her teaching. We shared the painfulness of what was recalled, and for the first time she felt heard.

One day I was ordered to search through some clothing and chanced to find a diamond hidden away in a shoulder pad. Yet I could so easily discard it – it had no usefulness to me – it could not get me what I needed – the food that would sustain me. The diamond had no value in that world. The beauty of the diamond only reflected me as I really was; dirty and full of lice.

(Survivor's testimony)

In that world beyond metaphor, this survivor's creativity and imagination are put to full use to convey her testimony.

Having completed our task, Mrs L arranged to go on an organised trip back to Auschwitz. She took her daughter with her. In this group of young people, she was the only survivor – this is how she described it:

As we passed through to Birkenau, the horror of the place struck me once more. I went up into the watchtower from which the Germans had looked down on me. The emptiness of the place struck me and the absolute silence. It appeared like a timeless place – time does not exist. I had expected the earth to be red with the blood of those murdered there, but only greyness could be seen – the greyness of ashes. It seemed so quiet and still. I tried to visualise again the seething bodies in that hell of forty years ago. I could see nothing, yet the smell of death still hangs in the air.

(Survivor's testimony)

We, as therapists, need to be looking at what helps the individual to survive and cope, both during the incarceration and after liberation. Our task is to help find meaning in their survival. Survivors cannot forget what happened, but we should try and help them find the means to have a present as well as a future. By helping them to record their testimony we help them to bear witness to what happened. With no graves to help in expressing the loss, the testimonies became the tombstones and the 'paper monuments' (Rosenbloom 1983).

In addition to the testimonies, the mourning process can also be helped through the survivors' participation in the ritual prayers for the dead. Many survivors have come to me and said that they felt so helpless in not being able to save their families, and some feel they should have died with them in the Holocaust. Many do not even know where their families were murdered. Finding out what really happened to them through the tracing service, saying kaddish (the mourners' prayer) for the family who died, setting up a memorial stone for those who died are all practical ways in which survivors can feel there is still something positive they can do, and that they have not survived in vain. I have been assisted in this spiritual task through the help of Rabbi Rodney Mariner, a rabbi whose congregation is largely made up of survivors. Rabbi Mariner chose to spend a three-month sabbatical with me in the team to learn about working with survivors. This link formed an essential part in a chain in developing approaches appropriate to survivors. He also conducted a memorial service for the child survivors whose families had perished, and this took place in our premises. The partnership between the spiritual and the therapeutic seems to happen naturally with the Jewish setting I work in. While I was writing this chapter, one of the survivors I had been seeing over some time said that she wanted me to know that she had started to believe in God, having previously wanted to take her own life. The ritualistic mourning had reconnected her to her spirituality which comforted her as she grew older.

THE FINAL STAGE – THE END OF THE JOURNEY

In January 1990 the work shifted out of the JWB office to a new location at a centre in Hendon called Shalvata. By this time my work with survivors had become well established, and hence the work came over with me. Though the work of Shalvata is for anyone over the age of 18 who is experiencing an emotional problem, the name also links with a centre in Israel that works with Holocaust survivors. Shamai Davidson had been director of that Centre but died some years ago. Shalvata is a memorial to his work.

The strength of Shalvata's work is firmly linked to what I have learned from survivors – the non-clinical approach; the Jewish dimension; the importance of groups; the balance of creative approaches with the therapeutic; finding the healthy, coping, adaptive side of those seeking help. Overall, the approach is to adapt the services we offer to the individual needs of those who come to us for help rather than asking them to fit into pre-existing frameworks. Our need to be creative is challenged constantly by survivors. The multidisciplinary nature of the team at Shalvata opened up opportunities to widen the scope of possible services.

For example, some survivors do not wish to return to the traumatic memories of their past, and yet nevertheless carry with them emotions that at times can be overwhelming. In my view, many survivors need their defences to cope. Some professionals have argued that those who do not wish to look at their past are resistant to help. It is my view that it is not the survivor who is resistant, so much as our inability to find the suitable channel or medium. A theatre workshop for survivors was started by the creative therapist at Shalvata. Again this idea was rooted firmly in the survivor experience, not conjured up from nowhere. We listened to what had helped survivors cope in the camps. When we talk to survivors we hear ample evidence of the use of creative imagination in helping to pass, minute by minute, the extent of their adversity. As one survivor told me, when she was hungry she imagined eating a slice of bread; another, who was so tired, imagined being asleep.

As an example from my work, I had been seeing a survivor weekly over a long period of time. Her divorce had been the trigger for bringing back the memories of what had happened to her when she was 'abandoned' at the age of five when her parents were taken away to the camp. She was left hidden in a cupboard and remained in hiding during the war suffering other tragedy during that time. The trauma returned in the present with such ferocity that she felt the only course open to her was to commit suicide – she felt she should have died with her family. She had also met me in a self-help group, and the trust which had developed allowed her to come and see me in my office. Gradually she came to feel that she could not reverse what had happened but she would have to find some way of making her life more bearable. She had told me how during her life she had enjoyed being the life and soul of the party and had a great sense of fun and laughter. She had now lost touch with this emotion, and would dearly love to find it again, but felt she had no right to enjoy herself.

I wondered whether, if she were able to take the part of someone else who did laugh, such as that role in a play, maybe she would reconnect with that emotion without experiencing any guilt. This survivor, who had thought suicide was the only option, now participates not only in the theatre workshop, but also the self-help group for child survivors (those who were children in the camps and in hiding during the Holocaust). She attends a weekly therapy group for child survivors run by a group analyst, as well as individual sessions with myself. Shalvata is the focal point for all those inputs. We as therapists meet together regularly and create in a sense the lost family. We acknowledge the 'missing years' for those child survivors – their childhood and the adolescence of which they were deprived. Our ability to come together as professionals has resulted in Shalvata being seen as their 'home' and not only a place for treatment. They tend to go around together, almost like an adolescent peer group or gang. They go on theatre outings, they meet socially in one another's homes – all factors which would traditionally not be acceptable in treatment situations. Again, in my view the only good therapy is the one that works, and the success of what we do is more dependent on our professional adaptability.

At this stage we are still breaking new ground, but it is our openness to look again at the traditional approaches which is crucial. The family model is one which is central in terms of the Jewish dimension of the work with Holocaust survivors. The client above commented in a recent meeting with me that her knowledge of my always being there for her at Shalvata reassured her at times when the absence and loss of her own mother could have overwhelmed her. I was her 'lifeline' as she called it, whether she was actually seeing me or not. Her ongoing need to do this is accepted by me, and perhaps more important than the in-depth work I could do with her.

The focus of much of the developments included in this chapter in working with survivors has to do with the concept of empowerment. Many saw survivors as pathetically going like sheep to the slaughter. Some ask, why did more people not resist? Some did, of course, but in the death camps, starvation ruled out the possibility of much physical force, apart from a lack of weapons. However, the survivors resolved that it should never happen again. Much of this positive energy was channelled into the creation of the state of Israel. Survivors are often passionate in their support of Israel. At the same time, however, their fears are growing rapidly concerning the rise of fascism again in Europe. The reunification of Germany and the Nazi war crimes trials bring back anxieties and remembrances of what they have been through in the Holocaust.

A sense of helplessness concerning these events could reactivate their fears of persecution and victimisation. How, then, do we offer alternative approaches which can liberate the survivor from their victim role to fight the rise of fascism? The remembrance of what happened can be translated positively into survivors becoming educators in schools. Survivors are the living witnesses: they are not out of history books, they were actually there. They can convey to children, for example, what it meant to be a child similar to them, but in very different circumstances. They can talk about the Holocaust through the eyes of a child. This can be digested and have meaning – a very different meaning from the media's portrayal of the survivor. The survivor who looks no different from you or me is a far more powerful messenger about the past, and can warn those they speak to about where fascism leads.

The survivor as teacher was also used by me at Jewish Care to train professionals in working with survivors. Six survivors spoke about what it meant to survive and how professionals could have helped but did not and how they now have a second opportunity. We worked with these six survivors for some weeks preparing them for the event. They feared they might break down as they recounted what had happened. In the event, it was the professionals who were in tears. The survivors were strengthened by the experience and have continued this role of teacher in various settings. 'Education as remembrance brought relief no sleeping pill or insightful analysis could match' (Krell 1989b: 222). There is still something the survivor can do, and make a contribution to the community they are living in. This political stance which the survivor can take fits into the notion of a voluntary agency's brief as a pressure group. We are concerned not just for the individual but in social change. The identification of the agency with this political role can be seen in their choice of speaker at the next annual public meeting; namely, Martin Gilbert. Fascism is brought into our consciousness and how we engage survivors in this task of speaking out is the therapy. It also unites the organisation with the survivor in a common cause, whereas before I had described the survivors' alienation from this Anglo-Jewish edifice.

Taking this notion of empowerment even further, Jewish Care and the Central British Fund for World Jewish Relief have created a new setting in which survivors will take responsibility for the development of the first Survivor Centre in the United Kingdom. This was opened in 1993 next door to Shalvata. It is a centre for survivors run by survivors. The co-ordinator's role as facilitator is to ensure that all the survivors who wish to can participate in the Centre. The focus of the Centre will be a café, and there will be a social programme which the survivors will help in organising. They will not be dependent recipients of services, but will be creating services which meet their needs. It is not a therapy centre in the same sense as Shalvata, and will have a separate entrance. The self-help groups which currently run both for the older survivors and the child survivors will transfer to the Centre, as well as the theatre workshop. The Spouses of Survivors Group, and the Second-Generation Group, will continue at Shalvata, as will the individual therapeutic work.

Recording the testimonies, the educational programme, advice on reparation claims, a library on Holocaust work and issues related to medical or legal matters as experienced by survivors will be on offer. Involvement of the second generation through participation in some of the activities may also have a therapeutic effect. This centre will in a sense re-create the lost community which survivors often perceive as the greatest loss they have experienced. As they grow older, so their need to be together in a 'home of their own' increases. With vastly diminished families, they need to support one another. Their collective voice is far louder and more significant than any individual effort and is thereby the most powerful tool towards empowerment and strength. The foundation for this ultimate goal had been laid during my years of struggle to find the most suitable approach with survivors. The Centre is both the end of a journey and a new beginning. When people are near to death their greatest fear is that they will not be remembered – that it will be as though they had never existed. This is even more so for the survivor who may have few people in whom they will live on. So the new Centre is there not only for them to enjoy but also to be able to let go of their lives – in the knowledge that their struggle will not have been in vain. For myself as well, the Centre represents the end of one piece of work but also unburdens me of the weight I have carried around in ensuring that the survivors' important message is heard and passed on. I am now free to go forward with them. The central role of the organisation in supporting me in my task, and the financial as well as emotional backing received for the projects I have undertaken need to be emphasised. The encouragement to innovate and to take risks in what some therapists may see as untraditional ways can perhaps only be done in the enlightened setting I have been working in.

CONCLUSION

Aspects of the organisation and setting have been crucial in the development of this work with Holocaust survivors: the Jewish dimension; the social work context; the non-statutory nature of the work; the role of the voluntary sector; the concept of a therapeutic community in a non-clinical environment. A personal conviction on my part towards the need to develop new ways of working with survivors seems to be an essential ingredient in transforming what could have been an intransigent setting into one which opened its doors outwards. It let me pass through to a world unknown which in turn had a profound influence on the organisation.

REFERENCES

Allport, G. W. (1987) 'Preface', pp. i–iv in V. E. Frankl, *Man's Search for Meaning: An Introduction to Logotherapy* (I. Lasch, trans.), London: Hodder & Stoughton.

Baron, L. (1977) 'Surviving the Holocaust', *Journal of Psychology and Judaism* 1(2): 27.

Bettelheim, B. (1986) *The Informed Heart*, Harmondsworth: Penguin (first published 1960).

Davidson, S. (1981) *On Relating to Traumatised Persecuted People*, Israel/Netherlands: Symposium on the Impact of Persecution II, 14–18 April, Dalfern, Amsterdam: Rijsvijk.

—— (1984) 'Human Reciprocity among Jewish Prisoners in the Nazi Concentration Camps', Proceedings of the 4th Yad Vashem International Conference, 1980, Jerusalem: Yad Vashem.

Frankl, V. E. (1987) *Man's Search for Meaning: An Introduction to Logotherapy* (I. Lasch, trans.,), London: Hodder & Stoughton.

Klein, H. (1968) 'On problems in the psychotherapeutic treatment of Israeli survivors of the Holocaust', in H. Krystal (ed.) *Massive Psychic Trauma*, New York: International Universities Press, p. 233.

Krell, R. (1989a) 'Alternative therapeutic approaches to holocaust survivors', in P. Marcus and A. Rosenberg (eds) *Healing their Wounds: Psychotherapy with Holocaust Survivors and their Families*, London and New York: Praeger.

—— (1989b) 'Psychotherapy with Holocaust survivors and their families', in P. Marcus and A. Rosenberg (eds) *Healing their Wounds: Psychotherapy with Holocaust Survivors and their Families*, London and New York: Praeger.

Kren, I. G. M. (1989) 'The Holocaust survivor and psychoanalysis', in P. Marcus and A. Rosenberg (eds) *Healing their Wounds: Psychotherapy with Holocaust Survivors and their Families*, London and New York: Praeger.

Krystal, H. (1968) *Massive Psychic Trauma*, New York: International Universities Press.

—— (1984) 'Integration and self healing in post traumatic states', pp. 113–34 in S. A. Luel and P. Marcus (eds) *Psychoanalytic Reflections on the Holocaust: Selected Essays*, New York: Ktav Publishing House.

Ornstein, A. (1985) 'Survival and recovery', p. 99–130 in D. Lewis and N. Averhahn (eds) *Psychoanalytic Inquiry 5*, Hillsdale, NJ: Analytic Press.

—— (1989) 'Treatment issues with survivors and their offspring: an interview with Anna Ornstein, Paul Marcus and Alan Rosenberg', pp. 16–106 in P. Marcus and

A. Rosenberg (eds) *Healing their Wounds: Psychotherapy with Holocaust Survivors and their Families*, London and New York: Praeger.

Pres, T. des (1976) *The Survivor – an Anatomy of Life in the Death Camps*, Oxford and New York: Oxford University Press.

Rosenberg, A. (1989) 'A joint interview', in P. Marcus and A. Rosenberg (eds) *Healing their Wounds: Psychotherapy with Holocaust Survivors and their Families*, London and New York: Praeger.

Rosenbloom, M. (1983) 'Implications of the Holocaust to social work', *Casework: The Journal of Contemporary Social Work* (April), Family Services Association of America.

Steinberg, A. (1989) 'Holocaust survivors and their children: a review of the clinical literature', pp. 27–31 in P. Marcus and A. Rosenberg (eds) *Healing their Wounds: Psychotherapy with Holocaust Survivors and their Families*, London and New York: Praeger.

Wiesel, E. (1982) 'The Holocaust Patient', Address to Cedars-Sinai Medical Staff, Los Angeles.

FURTHER INFORMATION ABOUT WORK WITH HOLOCAUST SURVIVORS

Jewish Care
221 Golders Green Road
London NW11
Tel.: 0181 458 3282

Shalvata
Parson Street
Hendon
London NW4
Tel.: 0181 203 9033

Chapter 7

Psychotherapy and sexual orientation

Paul Hitchings

Despite attempts to 'cure' homosexuality being reported in the scientific literature, even comparatively recently by methods such as psychosurgery on two gay men (Schmidt and Schorsch 1981) and by hypnotherapy on a young lesbian (Roden 1983), these are now exceptions and the last two decades have witnessed a shift in the attitudes of psychotherapists towards an affirmative view of homosexuality. In part, this shift reflects the failure of the medical model as a result of its simplicity (Gonsoriek 1977; 1985), the lack of success in attempts at 'cure' (Coleman 1978) and the questionable ethics involved (Symposium on Homosexuality and the Ethics of Behavioural Intervention 1977). This shift also reflects the modest changes in legislation, social attitudes and awareness over this time.

In moving away from a pathological model toward gay/lesbian affirmative models of psychotherapy a gap has been left that needs to be filled. This requires that practitioners share their clinical experience and develop and refine such alternative models. It is to these aims that this chapter intends to address itself.

The following discussion has, for the sake of clarity, made the oversimplified assumption of a discrete division between heterosexuality and homosexuality. The situation is clearly more complex. Kinsey *et al.* (1948) have suggested a seven-point scale to reflect that people could rate at any point of gradation between exclusive homosexual and heterosexual behaviour. In an effort to refine categories, Bell and Weinberg (1978) have suggested categories that reflect types of homosexual expression and lifestyle, and in a similar vein Coleman (1985) has suggested categories that reflect not only behaviour but also fantasy and emotional attachments. This measurement problem of course reflects the diversity of meaning that the term 'homosexual' can have for any particular individual. Consequently, the clinician and the reader need to bear in mind that we are always referring to individuals who are unique in their own sexuality, even if for the sake of clarity and simplicity we continue to refer to the abstraction of homosexuality.

THERAPIST ISSUES

Sexual orientation of the psychotherapist

Are lesbian/gay clients more likely to be helped by working with a psychotherapist of the same sex and orientation? The answer to this question is complex, and to a considerable extent depends on what the client hopes to gain from psychotherapy. There is very little direct research in this area; however, two studies (Beutler *et al.* 1978; Hart 1981) found that where there is mutual acceptance between client and psychotherapist of each other's sexual viewpoints, such acceptance is associated with facilitating global improvement within the client.

In summarising the effects of psychotherapist variables of sex and gender on outcomes, Beutler *et al.* (1986: 265) state that 'research is needed to explore the possibility that egalitarianism rather than sexual attitudes or gender roles themselves provoke change'. The above suggestion, which is in keeping with the author's experience, implies that the crucial variable is the ability of the psychotherapist to recognise fully and believe in the equal validity of a homosexual lifestyle and not so much the sexual orientation of the psychotherapist *per se*. This of course also applies to psychotherapists who have chosen a homosexual lifestyle since they are equally vulnerable to harbouring and communicating anti-homosexual prejudice.

There is a particular potential advantage for gay men and lesbian women in working with a heterosexual psychotherapist since it is less likely that particular prejudices, that perhaps could be fostered by the gay/lesbian subculture, would go unnoticed or be actively colluded with.

There are, however, arguments that a gay psychotherapist can provide a client with certain dimensions that a non-homophobic heterosexual psychotherapist would be unable to offer. Rochlin (1982) argues that three particular dimensions are of significance: first, the enhanced degree of empathy that can be communicated from having personally shared the experiences of growing up gay in a heterosexual culture; secondly, the provision of a role model for clients who are unlikely to have been exposed to any positive role models in their childhood or their adult life; thirdly, the personal knowledge and experience of gay culture and lifestyles, which allows the client to further their work without having to educate the psychotherapist along the way.

Therapist self-disclosure

Discussion in the preceding paragraphs might imply to the reader that the author believes that psychotherapists should automatically disclose to the client in a routine way their sexual orientation. Almost all schools of psychotherapy caution on the use of self-disclosure by the psychotherapist, from those that prohibit any information being proffered, to those which believe that appropriate self-disclosure is essential in maintaining the relationship as an authentic encounter. The question then becomes, when is it appropriate and when inappropriate for the psychotherapist in working with gay and lesbian clients to withhold information regarding their sexuality?

Malyon argues as follows: 'If the clinician is gay, it is often of therapeutic value to reveal this early in the treatment process in order to help assure the client that the details of his homosexual feelings will be understood and accepted by the therapist' (1985: 63–4).

In practice, where the psychotherapist is gay the client has often contacted them because they specifically want a gay psychotherapist and have gained this information from one of the various gay referral sources or via word of mouth within the gay community. Where the psychotherapist is not gay and the client clearly identifies as being gay, there is a value in the psychotherapist sharing explicitly with the client their value system with respect to a homosexual lifestyle.

Malyon follows his position on self-disclosure with a caution:

There are instances where early therapist disclosure would be counter-therapeutic, particularly where the client has not yet come out and is deeply conflicted over his homo-erotic promptings. In this instance therapist disclosure might be too threatening to the client and result in a premature termination of treatment.

(1985: 64)

Those clients who have not yet come out and might find such a psychotherapist disclosure too threatening are less likely to have been referred by such sources.

Homophobia in psychotherapists

In the same way that it has taken and continues to take considerable effort and self-awareness to recognise and eradicate sexism within ourselves, even for those who at a conscious level affirm anti-sexist values, so too does it take this effort with our own homophobia and heterosexism irrespective of an individual's sexual orientation.

When working with gay men or lesbians, irrespective of whether or not the psychotherapist is gay or lesbian themselves, a therapist needs to have explored their own sexuality and at least to some degree have transcended the sex-role stereotypes offered to us in our society. For gay or lesbian clinicians this probably means we have achieved the latter stages in the 'coming out' models which are discussed later in this chapter.

TREATMENT MODALITIES

In choosing between individual or group formats for psychotherapy, particularly where the presenting problem involves the acceptance and development of a gay/lesbian identity, there are considerable potential benefits to be gained from group psychotherapy, which are not as easily available in individual work. Working in a group provides a gay/lesbian client with an opportunity to be with others in an intimate but non-sexual way, and to own their homosexuality in a comparatively safe setting. The latter two points are worthy of amplification. Providing a comparatively safe place to own and explore their homosexuality can provide sufficient confidence for lesbian women and gay men to own their sexuality in other less safe groupings, such as with straight friends, colleagues and family. Additionally, a group that provides non-sexual intimacy is of particular value since frequently the main social groupings available to homosexual men and women are the sexualised meeting places of bars and clubs. Although such venues have an important place in the culture, they do not easily provide for a nurturing environment conducive to co-operation and intimacy. Such groups can be particularly effective in facilitating the homosexual client through the phases of the 'coming out' process.

Is a gay/lesbian client better placed in an all-gay or a mixed group? Yalom (1975), in advocating mixed groups, was among the first authors to describe the potential benefits to the homosexual client and the benefits that could accrue to the other heterosexual group members of being included in a mixed group. He defines success for the gay client when they no longer consider their homosexuality to be a particular problem and the benefits to the other members of being confronted with their own homophobia, which requires that they accept the homosexual part of themselves.

In contrast, Conlin and Smith (1985: 109) describe the psychotherapeutic value of homogeneous groups for gay and lesbian clients.

> The group provides community sanction and support for minority sexual orientation status as a valid lifestyle. Also, by reducing internal conflict over sexual orientation, it decreases maladaptive reactions, such as depressions, suicidal gestures, and dependence on alcohol and other drugs.

In determining which type of group is likely to be of most value to a gay person, Conlin and Smith (1985: 109) further conclude:

> We have found that mixed groups can be useful to the homosexual patient who is already functioning at a high level of self acceptance and adaptation as a gay person, and presents with problems unrelated to sexual orientation. . . . On the other hand when internalised homophobia is the major issue for the homosexual patient, all gay groups are better suited to facilitating homosexual adjustment.

My own clinical experience and that of numerous colleagues who run both types of group generally support Conlin and Smith's arguments. However, if the homosexual client is placed into a mixed group, then, as Yalom (1975) suggests, the psychotherapist needs to be alert to subtle attempts on the part of the group to convert the member to heterosexuality. With this provision, provided the client has sufficient ego strength to accept being different, there is no reason why a gay/lesbian client should not benefit from membership in a group of heterogeneous composition.

There are particular boundary issues that are worthy of mention at this point concerning the facilitating of all-gay groups. Because the gay/lesbian subculture even in a large city is essentially comparatively small, the psychotherapist does need to stress the importance of the group's maintaining confidentiality. Such an all-gay/lesbian group approximates to a group run in a rural area where the importance of confidentiality needs to be underlined due to the obvious increase in probability of known or unknown friendship/acquaintanceship connections between members. Another major boundary issue that needs to be made explicit by the group psychotherapist is that of clients not having sexual relationships with one another. The provision of this boundary allows the group to become and remain a safe place where the more significant intrapsychic issues can surface unclouded by the potential complications of sexual liaisons.

There are, of course, gay/lesbian clients whose ego boundaries are too fragile to benefit from group membership at all. A format of initial individual psychotherapy might be indicated as a preparation for group psychotherapy and later can be used concurrently with it.

Models of the coming out process

In my work with homosexual clients I have found it helpful to use a developmental model as a framework to inform my treatment planning. A developmental model is appropriate since adult identity development, a task that Erikson (1946) defines as belonging to adolescence, is unlikely to have been properly resolved, since this task includes the integration of sexuality including sexual orientation. This is likely to have been prevented since identity formation is an interactive process between the adolescent, their family and the wider society (Erikson 1946). Clearly, in Western societies the development of the homosexual person's identity is hindered by anti-homosexual norms and values which thwart the appropriate completion of developmental tasks at least from adolescence onwards and probably have had an impact on earlier experiences.

There are a number of such models in the literature (Cass 1979; Coleman 1985; Dank 1971; Henken and O'Dowd 1977; Lee 1977; Grace 1979) which all have broadly comparable tasks. For a brief account of these models, see Hanley-Hackenbruck (1989). The particular model I prefer to use is that of Coleman (1985), and in proposing this model he suggests that individuals who are homosexual need to negotiate certain stages in the formation of their identity development. However, the use of such a model does not assume that a person follows through each stage in a progressive, linear manner. A person may work at a number of stages concurrently and may need to recycle previous stages at particular points in their development.

The entire process of developing an identity has been referred to in the gay and lesbian community as 'coming out'. Cohen and Stein (1986), quoted by Hanley-Hackenbruck, define the term as follows:

> Coming out refers to a complicated developmental process which involves at a psychological level a person's awareness and acknowledgement of homosexual thoughts and feelings. For some persons, coming out ultimately leads to public identification as a gay man or lesbian.
>
> (1989: 21)

The five stages of Coleman's (1985) model are described below, together with some of the associated relevant psychotherapeutic considerations:

1 Pre-coming out

Of this stage Coleman states:

> Because individuals at the pre-coming out stage are not consciously aware of same sex feelings, they cannot describe what is wrong. They can only communicate their conflict through behavioural problems, psychosomatic illnesses, suicidal attempts, or various other symptoms. It is conceivable that some suicidal attempts by children and adolescents are due to this conflict.
>
> (1985: 33)

At this stage a person is aware that there is something different about themselves but cannot conceptualise this difference and/or admit this difference to themselves. This task is filled with confusion, and Cass (1979) refers to it as the stage of 'identity confusion'. This task is completed when an individual acknowledges to themselves their same-sex feelings.

Psychotherapeutic considerations

In the early part of this stage the client is not aware of homosexual impulses as being the conflict that underlies the presenting problem. This possibility is then a psychotherapeutic hypothesis. In both the early and latter part of this stage the client is likely to be experiencing a high degree of conflict. The significant psychotherapeutic task at this stage is to allow the client to explore their sexuality without any prejudice on the part of the psychotherapist as to which orientation they should further explore and develop. This will eventually allow the client to make a genuine choice, at a pace that is in keeping with their own readiness. Whilst the psychotherapist needs to guard against pushing the client in one direction or another the psychotherapist needs nevertheless to provide accurate information including correcting common misconceptions about homosexuality. This requires a fine balance of judgement on the part of the psychotherapist, since too frequent correction of misconceptions or, on the other hand, ignoring misconceptions, could be misinterpreted by the client as pushing towards one or other orientation. Of particular value at the latter part of this stage is suggested reading, such as Hart's (1984) text.

Coleman (1985) states that a healthy resolution to this stage is to face the existential crisis of being different.

2 Coming out

Coleman writes of this task,

> Once their same sex feelings have been identified and acknowledged, individuals face the next developmental task of the coming out stage: telling others. The function of this task is to begin self acceptance.
>
> (1985: 34)

At the beginning of this task it is important that the person chooses to tell people who are relatively 'safe', that is, those who almost certainly will be validating of their sexuality. The counsellor/psychotherapist is obviously within this category. When sufficient positive experiences have been accrued by the person, they are in a better position to tell people whose response is less predictable. On this point Coleman comments:

> This is a very critical point, for the confidants' reaction can have a powerful impact. If negative, it can confirm all the old negative impressions and can put a seal on a previous low self-concept. If positive, the reaction can start to counteract some of the old perceived negative feelings, permitting individuals to begin to accept their sexual feelings and increase their self esteem. The existential crisis begins to resolve in a positive direction.
>
> (1985: 34)

At this stage it is of particular value for the client to begin to develop a friendship circle that can offer support and guidance, since social isolation can be especially damaging. Many gay organisations run social groups either specifically for people engaged in the process of coming out or that would provide a supportive social environment.

In the latter stages of this task, telling significant people in their lives who are heterosexual is an important step, since homosexual people may still be perceived as of lower status. Particularly painful can be negative responses from family members, and the person might find it helpful to remind themselves how long the process has taken them and to appreciate the grieving process that their parents and other family members are likely to be involved in. 'It is important that they persevere with their parents and family through a grieving process. Parents will often grieve the loss of the image of their son or daughter as married and having children' (Coleman 1985: 35).

Psychotherapeutic considerations

Here the psychotherapist needs to praise new behaviour, from the initial statements the client makes that they are gay/lesbian, to finding information about homosexuality and to telling significant others. Sketchley (1989) notes the importance of helping the client distinguish between the first, possibly negative reactions of others and their later second reaction, which is more likely to be positive when they have had more time to respond.

The issue of telling significant others such as family members needs to be carefully dealt with by the psychotherapist. The client could possibly at this stage either approach the situation in a provocative manner or in an ill-thought-through way, motivated by euphoria at embracing their new-found self concept. The possibility of delaying this self-disclosure until the client is more psychologically ready needs to be explored.

3 Exploration

This period is the equivalent of the adolescent period of learning through exploring and experimenting with relationships. A particular cluster of issues is often of relevance at this stage. These are: development of interpersonal skills for meeting others, the development of skills of sexual competence, setting appropriate boundaries for self, recognising internalised self-oppression, awareness of the potential use of intoxicants to anaesthetise the pain and shore up a weak self concept. For gay men there is also the issue of the separation of self-esteem from sexual 'conquest'. Additionally, they must be aware of the danger of obtaining casual sex apparently for pleasure but in effect to reinforce a negative view of the self.

Cass (1979) describes this phase as the time when identity tolerance can lead to identity acceptance. This is a particularly intense phase of learning since the social rules and norms of gay culture need to be learned. In addition, this is a phase like adolescence but without the usual parental and economic constraints which would normally operate to provide safe boundaries for the person. Grace (1979) has suggested the concept of 'developmental lag' to describe the process.

Psychotherapeutic considerations

In relation to the cluster of issues discussed above there are a large number of potential psychotherapeutic tasks involved. Many of the tasks of the psychotherapist will be more clearly educative than at other periods in the coming out process. Frequently, the psychotherapist will need to teach certain social skills and/or encourage the client in order to overcome possible shyness and awkwardness. Additionally, the psychotherapist is well placed to help the client acquire the relevant information about health issues.

The possibility of the client being stuck at this stage needs to be borne in mind by the psychotherapist. In the author's experience clients often present for psychotherapy as a result of having been stuck at this stage for many years. This may well be indicative of internalised homophobia expressed in beliefs such as 'homosexual relationships will never last', which is then lived out as a self-fulfilling prophecy. The psychotherapist needs to be alert to subtle as well as more obvious manifestations of such belief systems.

Towards the end of this phase clients frequently need to experience and express their feelings of anger and sadness at not having had permission from their parents and the wider culture to live their sexuality properly. There is often a period of mourning for the decades of their life that cannot now be lived in a way that would have been healthy and satisfying.

4 First relationships

First relationships, irrespective of sexual orientation, are frequently over-romanticised and essentially function as learning grounds for relationship skill-building. However, for homosexual clients who are chronologically older than is usual for this task, first relationships can often take on an intensity and optimism that is unrelated to the reality of the two people involved. Also such relationships are often entered into before the previous tasks have been completed and consolidated. Frequently the individual attempts to use the relationship as a protection against dealing with a still delicate self concept. A further factor here is the lack of homosexual role models or cultural support offered. When such a relationship ends there is the possibility that it will not be used as a learning experience but that the ending is bitter or traumatic. Such a situation can lead to depression, recreational drug abuse and, particularly for gay men, the use of casual sex to feel guilty and reinforce negative beliefs about homosexuality. In this way, then, the individual may return to the previous developmental phase and become stuck in it.

Psychotherapeutic considerations

The psychotherapist needs to help the client think through the expectations made of the relationship and explore internalised homophobia which often is given expression in very subtle forms. When such a relationship ends the psychotherapist needs to encourage the client to appreciate what they have learned and to encourage the ending in as healthy a way as possible.

5 *Integration*

Cass (1979) refers to individuals at this stage as having moved from 'identity confusion' through 'identity comparison, tolerance, acceptance, and pride, to identity synthesis'.

Here, then, is the task of fully 'choosing' to be gay in an existential sense. Being gay at this stage becomes at one and the same time central to the individual's identity and paradoxically totally irrelevant. Against such a background the individual is then free to negotiate the tasks of the various stages of adult life that we all face irrespective of our sexual orientation.

During this stage, which is essentially an ongoing process of growth, the client is likely to be involved with choosing a lifestyle that fits with their own temperament and with the phase they are in, in their life journey. Frequently, clients will put some energy into the creation of 'families' of their own making and choice, which may or may not include their biological family. For some gay clients this may involve lifestyles that are not modelled on the heterosexual norms and might involve more than one ongoing committed relationship, none at all or an exploration of the variety of relationships that are possible.

Psychotherapeutic considerations

This is essentially the phase of existential psychotherapy when homosexual clients, who are less likely to be distracted by the prescribed meanings offered by the majority heterosexual culture, engage with the existential task of choosing a meaning for their lives. Typically this is an issue that comes to the fore in the forties and fifties, and can be all the more clearly highlighted as a result of living a life that does not conform to the usual traditions.

Discussion of stages

In outlining the above stages together with the associated psychotherapeutic considerations, the reader may well have questioned whether counselling/ psychotherapy is necessary to move through this process of coming out. Clearly the majority of homosexual people do negotiate these stages using the support of other homosexual friends as guides. What factors would seem to suggest that psychotherapeutic help should be sought? Hanley-Hackenbruck (1989) suggests five particular indicators:

1 The family environment was particularly rigid, especially if there was a religious emphasis.
2 The person experienced negative experiences relating to sex-role behaviour or body type.
3 Having experienced anti-homosexual prejudice.
4 There is serious underlying pathology.
5 Sexual abuse, especially same-sex, was experienced as a child or as an adolescent.

However, whilst such indicators are valuable to the clinician, it is also likely that an individual attempting to negotiate these stages does experience some stuck points in the process for which counselling/psychotherapeutic help would not be invaluable.

DIFFERENTIAL DIAGNOSES AND THE COMING OUT PROCESS

Each client negotiates the coming out process against their own particular psychological make-up. The complexity of the interaction between possible underlying pathology and that of the stress of the coming out process is one that every clinician needs to be aware of. This issue has been discussed succinctly by Gonsoriek, who states,

> There are a number of clinical conditions in which individuals at times manifest homosexual behaviour or concerns, and the client may there-fore appear to be coming out or having a sexual identity crisis when, in reality, these behaviours or concerns are part of a serious pathology. On the other hand the coming out process in itself can produce in some individuals considerable psychiatric symptomatology reminiscent of serious underlying psychopathology; but, in fact, such pathology does not exist and the individual is having a particularly difficult time coming to terms with his or her sexuality. Finally, the coming out process may serve as a precipitating event for some individuals who do have severe underlying problems; that is, both may be present.
>
> (1985: 100)

In particular, here the clinician needs to be cautious in ascribing to the homosexual individual diagnoses of which paranoia is a prominent part. To have lived in a society with a strong anti-homosexual prejudice, to pass as straight and to have managed to make contact with other homosexuals often without the benefit of homosexual meeting places has required that the person develop a powerful sensitivity or heightened awareness. This at times may manifest in what appears to be paranoid thoughts and behaviour. In addition, given the real nature of prejudice that continues to exist, sometimes hiding behind liberal façades, some paranoia, if held in awareness, is healthy and adaptive.

THE IMPACT OF AIDS

Working with gay men, it is inevitable that the subject of AIDS will come up. If not worried about themselves, most gay men will have known other men who have died of AIDS or men who currently have AIDS or who are HIV positive. Eventually, fears and anxieties about AIDS are highly likely to emerge. The psychotherapist will often be asked to help the client decide whether or not to test for HIV. The question then arises as to whether the individual is better off not knowing his HIV status, or knowing and making life decisions accordingly. A frequent fear is that the client will not be able to cope if it turns out they are HIV positive. If there is a partner involved, this agonising decision becomes twice as difficult. Should they both test? What if one is HIV positive and the other HIV negative? Sometimes the decision to test is based on the premise that 'I'm so scared and worried now, that it could not be worse'.

Psychotherapists working with a large number of gay men are likely to have clients who are HIV positive or who have AIDS. The task for the psychotherapist and client is to work through the issues around illness and death, so that the client can get on with his life. Frequently, a client with HIV or AIDS will exhibit the stages of mourning set out by Kübler-Ross (1969). At first, there is often a massive denial. Then the client will go into the angry or bargaining phase. If the psychotherapist has been successful, eventually the client will move into the acceptance phase, although regression to earlier phases is frequently seen. In working with these issues, the work of the existential psychotherapists can be very helpful (Yalom 1975).

Together with the subject of AIDS goes the issue of safer sex. A psychotherapist working with gay men may be asked for specific information about safe sex practices, and should be well informed on the subject. The thorny question then arises about what to do in relation to a client who tells you that he is practising unsafe sex? The issue is similar to other kinds of destructive and self-destructive behaviour such as driving whilst intoxicated. During the period when psychotherapist and client are exploring the dynamics and aetiology of such other and self-destructive behaviour, it is often possible to use the power of the therapeutic alliance to contract with the client to cease this harmful behaviour. If the client refuses, the psychotherapist has the option of refusing to work with the individual.

Within this area it is obviously important that the psychotherapist validates the tragedy that this disease has brought, through bereavement work, and also is aware of the existential issues that are in terms of life stages prematurely brought to the fore. The psychotherapist needs also to validate the way in which the gay community has also transformed the experience of this tragedy to build a community based on genuine intimacy.

SUMMARY

Gay and lesbian clients deserve to work with psychotherapists who have resolved to as great extent as they can their own homophobia so that gay and lesbian affirmative models of psychotherapy can be most effectively utilised. The lives of homosexual clients, in having the courage to break with social norms and create healthy lifestyles and communities for themselves, offer us all the encouragement that oppressive social norms can be changed.

ACKNOWLEDGEMENTS

The author wishes to acknowledge the help of Nina Miller for suggestions and corrections, in the context of a lesbian perspective, to the initial drafts of this chapter.

REFERENCES

Bell, A. and Weinberg, M. (1978) *Homosexualities: A Study of Diversity Among Men and Women*, New York: Simon & Schuster.

Beutler, L. E., Crago, M. and Arizmendi, T. G. (1986) 'Research on therapist variables in psychotherapy', pp. 257–310 in S. L. Garfield and A. E. Bergin (eds) *Handbook of Psychotherapy and Behaviour Change*, New York: Wiley.

Beutler, L. E., Pollack, S. and Jobe, A. M. (1978) ' "Acceptance" values and therapeutic change', *Journal of Consulting and Clinical Psychology* 46: 198–9.

Cass, V. C. (1979) 'Homosexual identity formation: a theoretical model', *Journal of Homosexuality* 4: 219–35.

Cohen, C. and Stein, T. (1986) 'Reconceptualising individual psychotherapy with gay men and lesbians', *Psychotherapy with Lesbians and Gay Men*, New York: Plenum.

Coleman, E. (1978) 'Towards a new treatment model of homosexuality: a review', *Journal of Homosexuality* 3(4): 345–59.

—— (1985) 'Developmental stages of the coming out process', pp. 31–43 in J. C. Gonsoriek (ed.) *A Guide to Psychotherapy with Gay and Lesbian Clients*, New York/London: Harrington Park (first published 1982).

Conlin, D. and Smith, J. (1985) 'Group psychotherapy for gay men', pp. 105–12 in J. C. Gonsoriek (ed.) *A Guide to Psychotherapy with Gay and Lesbian Clients*, New York/London: Harrington Park (first published 1982).

Dank, B. M. (1971) 'Coming out in the gay world', *Psychiatry* 34: 180–97.

Erikson, E. (1946) 'Ego development and historical change', *The Psychoanalytic Study of the Child* 2: 356–9.

Gonsoriek, J. C. (1977) 'Psychological adjustment and homosexuality', *JSAS Catalogue of Selected Documents in Psychology* 7(45): MS no. 1478.

—— (ed.) (1985) 'Introduction to mental health issues and homosexuality', pp. 18–22 in *A Guide to Psychotherapy with Gay and Lesbian Clients*, New York/London: Harrington Park (first published 1982).

Grace, J. (1979) 'Coming out alive', Paper presented at the Sixth Biennial Professional Symposium of the National Association of Social Workers, San Antonio, quoted by E. Coleman in J. C. Gonsoriek (ed.) (1985) *A Guide to*

Psychotherapy with Gay and Lesbian Clients, New York/London: Harrington Park (first published 1982).

Hanley-Hackenbruck, P. (1989) 'Psychotherapy and the "Coming out process"', *Journal of Gay and Lesbian Psychotherapy* 1: 1.

Hart, J. (1984) *So You Think You're Attracted to the Same Sex?* Harmondsworth: Penguin.

Hart, L. E. (1981) 'An investigation of male therapists' views of women on the process and outcome of therapy with women', *Dissertation Abstracts International* 42: 2529B.

Henken, J. D. and O'Dowd, W. T. (1977) 'Coming out as an aspect of identity formation', *Gai Saber*: 18–22.

Kinsey, A., Pomeroy, W. and Martin, C. (1948) *Sexual Behaviour in the Human Male*, Philadelphia: Saunders.

Kübler-Ross, E. (1969) *On Death and Dying*, New York: Macmillan.

Lee, J. D. (1977) 'Going public: a study in the sociology of homosexual liberation', *Journal of Homosexuality* 7(2/3): 59–70.

Malyon, A. K. (1985) 'Psychotherapeutic implications of internalised homophobia in gay men', pp. 59–69 in J. C. Gonsoriek (ed.) *A Guide to Psychotherapy with Gay and Lesbian Clients*, New York/London: Harrington Park (first published 1982).

Rochlin, M. (1982) 'Sexual orientation of the therapist and therapeutic effectiveness with gay clients', pp. 21–9 in J. C. Gonsoriek (ed.) *A Guide to Psychotherapy with Gay and Lesbian Clients*, New York: Hawarth Press.

Roden, R. G. (1983) 'Threatening homosexuality: a case study treated by hypnosis', *Medical Hypnoanalysis* 4: 166–9.

Schmidt, G. and Schorsch, E. (1981) 'Psychosurgery of sexually deviant patients', *Archives of Sexual Behaviour* 10: 301–21.

Sketchley, J. (1989) 'Counselling and sexual orientation', pp. 237–51 in W. Dryden, D. Charles-Edwards and R. Woolfe (eds) *Handbook of Counselling in Britain*, London: Tavistock/Routledge.

Symposium on Homosexuality and the Ethics of Behavioural Intervention (1977) *Journal of Homosexuality* 2(3): 195–259.

Yalom, I. D. (1975) *The Theory and Practice of Group Psychotherapy*, New York: Basic Books.

FURTHER READING

Kitzinger, C. (1987) *The Social Construction of Lesbianism*, London: Sage.

—— (1992) 'The regulation of lesbian identities: liberal humanism as an ideology of social control', pp. 82–98 in J. Shotter and K. J. Gergen (eds) *Texts of Identity*, London: Sage.

Part III

Modalities

Chapter 8

Individual adult psychotherapy

Christine Lister-Ford and Michael Pokorny

Although psychotherapy with individuals is commonly thought to have begun with Breuer and Freud (1893/1955) in Vienna around the turn of the century, and group psychotherapy with Moreno (1972), the problem of the meaning of life and human existence is as old as mankind itself. Forms of what we might now call psychotherapy have been in existence far longer than 100 years. Freud started with the analysis of hysteria, and with Breuer he gave meaning to the symptoms. At last the enigma of psychological symptoms had been solved by finding an interpretation of the hidden meaning to questions that had eluded thinkers for centuries. This was the great achievement from which the entire psychodynamic movement began, and which formed the basis of many of the psychotherapy methods that are in use today. Learning theory originated from different roots in the study of observed behaviour. As long ago as 1693 Locke was recommending a form of graduated exposure to the feared situation as a method of treatment. Interestingly, the development of all forms of psychotherapy is essentially a phenomenon of the twentieth century.

Even as the discovery of the known or unconscious mind was being made known to the world, Moreno (1965) was starting to work with children in the park, then later with prostitutes. Thus alongside the beginnings of individual adult psychotherapy, a start was being made on group psychotherapy with children and with other specific client groupings. Both these developments are now very widely practised from a variety of orientations. In this sense Moreno is also the ideological father (see Chapter 2) of all subsequent humanistic/existential approaches where group psychotherapy has always flourished alongside individual psychotherapy; including psychodrama, of which Moreno was the founder (1972).

We shall discuss the rationale and indications for individual psychotherapy as well as giving an idea of the range of psychotherapies that are available. A more detailed view of definitions and the nature and range of psychotherapy is available in Chapter 1 of this *Handbook*.

Why would an adult in our society choose to go for help to a psychotherapist? Socially and culturally, our society has evolved in such a way that we expect to go to a 'specialist' with our problems. When we are experiencing emotional difficulties, be they internal or in our interpersonal communications, or both, we can use the option of consulting someone who specialises in treating emotional problems. In the past this has been the role of the priest or the doctor, who offered reparative emotional relationships. Many people still consult their priest or their doctor as their specialist or first choice, as shown in the *Report of the Psychotherapy Working Party* (1989) of the South Tees District Health Authority. Today spiritual, medical and emotional help have evolved into separate specialisms, with the psychotherapist being trained as our modern-day emotional healer, offering a culturally congruent response to the emotional watersheds that daily life inevitably brings.

In general terms, a psychotherapist will help the client to face and work through emotional problems. Usually, this involves finding the past personal experiences that have contributed to present-day problems and re-experiencing these, to the point at which they become a phenomenological reality. At the point of impasse, where the old dilemmas and ways of solving them interfere with current needs by preventing an appropriate response to the here-and-now, the psychotherapist helps the client find new options for dealing with the old pain. Freed from the tyranny of his personal past, an individual is able to respond differently to present circumstances. Psychotherapeutic effectiveness depends upon the client having built a strong trusting relationship with the psychotherapist, such that the new choices uncovered during the psychotherapy can be accepted as more viable options than the old choices. Old relationship patterns which encouraged and supported these historical choices can be relinquished in favour of new ones discovered through the therapeutic relationship.

Individual psychotherapy offers the client the experience of an intense concentration by another human being on concerns of importance to him. He and he alone is the focus of interest and attention for at least fifty minutes every week. For most people this is an extremely rare, and therefore precious, opportunity. The need to be listened to with unswerving attention, for another actively and committedly to seek to enter into and understand life from 'my' perspective, to offer explanations and assist with the formulation of new choices, is something most of us crave at times of tension and difficulty in our lives. It is precisely to this that the psychotherapist commits herself.

With his psychotherapist as companion to the journey of self-discovery, the client, like the hero of yore, restructures both his internal psychological make-up and his relationship patterns to claim the holy grail of the full restoration of himself to himself.

TYPES OF ADULT INDIVIDUAL PSYCHOTHERAPY

It is extremely difficult to be specific about types of psychotherapy and remain brief. The United Kingdom Council for Psychotherapy has eight sections; each is meant to represent a different kind of psychotherapy, yet some clearly represent a client group, such as children or marriages. Others represent particular problems such as sexual problems, whilst the two largest sections contain quite a wide variety. So these sections will not serve as a working model for our purpose. If we turn to the *Handbook of Individual Psychotherapy* (Dryden 1990), we find eleven psychotherapies listed, although three of these are essentially psychodynamic in their foundation. Holmes and Lindley (1989) refer to the existence of over 300 types of psychotherapy. In this chapter we shall confine ourselves to a broad general classification (see also Chapter 2 of this book). The major schools we are able to identify are: psychodynamic, humanistic, integrative, behavioural, cognitive and experiential constructivist. Within these major schools there are great variations. Broadly speaking, the psychodynamic school is based on the idea of the dynamic unconscious, and there are very many derivatives of this school in existence. The best-known are those of Jung, Reich, Adler, Sullivan and Horney. The list could be very long. It is a moot point whether to include Klein with Freud or to list her work separately, as Dryden (1990) does. As well as individual adult work, this school has spread into child, group, organisational, marital and self-help modalities.

The basic root of the psychodynamic psychotherapies is the idea of psychic determinism, which is that all behaviour and thinking are influenced by our unconscious mind, which Breuer and Freud (1895/1955) originally called the 'Unbewusst' (literally translated as 'unknown'). That is not to say that the unconscious rules us, but that its influence will be greater in some ways than others. Fathoming out which is which is the essence of psychoanalytically based psychotherapy. This is done through the elucidation of the transference in the interaction between the psychotherapist and the client. By interpreting the underlying unconscious activity, the psychotherapist helps the client to understand and to feel the force of the way that the client's personal past is intruding into present-day reality. Any of the manifestations of the activities of the unconscious may be used in this process, from dreams to the common observation that actions speak louder than words. When Freud first came upon the fact of unconscious resistance he saw it as an obstacle to analysis. Soon, however, he became aware that the resistance was actually a feature of unconscious activity which repeats patterns of behaviour dressed up in modern clothing as a way of maintaining the repressions of the past. Thus Freud became aware that what the unconscious does is to produce in disguise what is hidden. So the elucidation of the new edition of the past became the central activity of the psychoanalyst. This is described as the analysis of the transference, meaning that the new edition appears as a version of the relationship to the psychoanalyst, and analysis of that new relationship uncovers the dynamic past in a meaningful way so that new reality-testing may take place. What may have been appropriate at an early age can be re-examined to see if it is still the best way of coping. Equally, emotions that could not be coped with when young may be reworked differently when the client is adult. Very often the reworking has to be done several times over because of the way that human beings use their existing defences as they progress through life. Any new situation will be dealt with by the defences that already exist. When these defences come under scrutiny, it is usual for some items to be taken over by other defences that already exist.

When in turn these defences are analysed, yet another way of dealing with all the items under their protection must be found. Far from being just a nuisance, the defence mechanisms serve an essential function, that of preventing the primary process of the unconscious from invading the conscious part of the mind. The unconscious parts of the mind work on what is called the pleasure principle. This means that gratification must be sought at once, that the passage of time is not appreciated, that opposites exist together without clashing and that a thing and its symbol are treated as the same. These features of the unconscious mean that repetition in the present can occur and that substitute gratifications can be just as satisfying as the original version. By contrast, the conscious mind works on the reality principle and has to manage conflict and ambivalence, and learn to wait for gratifications. The theory of the defence mechanisms is that they maintain the division of the mind into reality, or secondary process, on the one hand, and the pleasure principle or primary process on the other. When the defences break down the conscious mind is invaded by the fragmentary elements of the primary process which gives rise to phenomena that we regard as psychotic, such as delusions and hallucinations. The developing child utilises those defences that are available to it. As it grows and its defensive capacity expands, new experiences can be managed better and some old ones can be reworked with new techniques. Much of the upheaval of adolescence can be accounted for by the need to rework the past relationship to the parents in the light of the new situation of puberty. The Oedipus complex has to undergo a re-edition in the presence of physical sexual maturity, which was not the situation in the original version (Laufer and Laufer 1984). Thus, in the analysis of the personal history there has to be some repeat of this pattern of reworking, done retrospectively.

It is this need to re-edit several times that largely accounts for the longwindedness of psychoanalytic psychotherapy. Once the analysis of the transference became the central activity of the psychoanalyst, it was only a matter of time before analysts became aware that they also had unconscious reactions to the unconscious communications of their clients. Many of these reactions in the psychoanalyst become manifest through feelings that are derived from the unconscious response of the psychoanalyst. Learning to read their own unconscious responses became recognised as a reliable route to understanding the transference, and indeed eventually came to be seen as an excellent way to understand very obscure or very silent clients. Thus the capacity to understand became enlarged and gradually ceased to be dependent upon the client's being very articulate. Thus it has become possible to apply psychoanalytic understanding to an ever-increasing range of clients. Today it is commonplace for psycho-analytic psychotherapists to have clients who are deeply disturbed in all their relationships, who may have suffered severe deficit in their upbring-ing, leading to impairment of the capacity for relatedness in all directions. The actual severity of the pathology that is the usual psychoanalytic caseload has increased enormously over the years. As this process has gone on, less severe problems have been treated by shorter methods or group methods. This phenomenon of the shift in the content of the caseload is only a reflection of the shift that has also gone on in the severity of illness treated in hospital these days compared to thirty or forty years ago. It is the inevitable accompaniment to any increase in knowledge and skills.

Naturally, as knowledge of the transference and counter-transference increased, ways of shortening the period of treatment were sought. Psychotherapy based in psychoanalytic theory grew and in many senses reached its apogee in the use of knowledge of how the transference is formed to conduct short-term psychotherapy. If the theory is basically sound, then the deductions made from it should bring results. One can test psychodynamic theory by using it to predict the response to specific interpretations. However, it is also true that only some selected cases are suitable for brief psychotherapy, although the indications for this method are also widening.

An example of brief focal psychotherapy in practice is the story of the angry executive, which has been published in full (Pokorny 1984). An executive sought help because of frequent loss of temper to a serious degree, which was invading every area of his life. The diagnosis was displacement of affect with some reaction formation. His family had moved house twice early in his life and the rages had begun after the second move, and had worsened since that time whenever he had moved house. Thus the starting hypothesis was of loss at the first move which could not be coped with at the time and re-emerged at the second move as a symptom of displaced affect (in this case, rage). The question was: whom had he lost at the first move, why was nothing done about it at the time, and why had nothing been done till now? When the client reported that he had a recurrent nightmare starting after the second move of house in which he was trapped in a corner about to be crushed by a huge ball, the psychotherapist took the bull by the horns and interpreted the dream as representing his fear of being crushed by his feelings of grief and rage because he had lost someone important in the first house move. The response to this interpretation was dramatic, both in terms of the client's feelings and history. In a state of great emotional upheaval he began to pour out a story that he had 'forgotten' which not only explained a lot of his behaviour over the years, but also his present predicament. The outcome was that his relationships improved all round. His children and wife were no longer afraid of him and at work he coped more easily as well as more effectively. Finally, he moved house with his family with no hint of a recurrence in his symptoms.

One of the salient features of the treatment was the anger that the executive felt towards the psychotherapist during much of the treatment. He rationalised this as his distress that a stranger could so quickly understand and give expression to problems with which his own family had been unable to cope. However, it was in his anger with the psychotherapist that his displaced rage towards his parents first made its appearance. On several occasions the treatment almost broke down because of an unconscious pressure to re-enact the anger in the present, rather than understand its roots and origins.

The question of how such treatment works is of central importance. At first Freud thought that to repeat the experience by connecting the feelings with the fantasy brought about an abreaction which undid the repression. At that time the term 'repression' was used as a word for making something unconscious. Later, a variety of defence mechanisms were described, for instance by Anna Freud (1936/1966). Subsequently it was realised that simple abreaction was only reliable for very recent traumatic experiences and that the workings of the human mind are more complex. The discovery of the extent to which we are the author of our own misfortunes was enshrined in the theory of the repetition compulsion (S. Freud 1920/1961). This states that all human beings tend to stick with learned patterns of expectations and behaviour. It is in reality very difficult to get people to give up the habits of a lifetime, even when those habits are causing them frustration or harm. The determined clinging to old ways is another reason why psychoanalysis takes a long time and never has a perfect result. There is always something that a person will absolutely refuse to give up from their own personal past. It is also very hard to restructure the mind in the new ways that become available through an understanding of the past and its influence in the present. At least there is a comforting side to these difficulties. Many people seem to be afraid that psychoanalysis and its derivatives can unduly persuade people to change their beliefs. This is far from true. People may be fairly gullible over things that they wish to believe, but they are generally fairly obstinate about those things they regard or feel to be inconvenient to their outlook on life. To persuade someone into something that they would in any case be likely to favour is no achievement at all. To help someone see themselves in an entirely new light is very difficult indeed. The influence of the psychotherapist is thus very profound and very limited.

Humanistic and existential schools

Humanistic and existential schools have developed in many different ways from a rich variety of sources, including philosophy (Spinelli 1989). For an excellent account of existential counselling in practice, see van Deurzen-Smith 1988). Moreno (1965; 1972), initially working in Vienna and later in the United States, is widely recognised as one of the earliest, if not the first, exponent of the humanistic/existential school. Moreno gives 1921 as the date from which psychodrama may be considered a specific and discrete form of psychotherapy.

From his observations of and work with children and later with adults, Moreno came to recognise how enactment can provide a creative and spontaneous release of tension for an individual, known for the purposes of the enactment as the 'protagonist'. When this enactment is therapeutically directed by a competent psychotherapist, the protagonist can be helped to personal insights which facilitate the resolution of internal and interpersonal conflicts.

Enactment offers the client a satisfying vehicle for re-experiencing past moments that goes beyond merely recalling or recounting. The protagonist is able to relive moments from his own life, knowing them in their full emotional, physical and cognitive richness. The catharsis that comes from such phenomenological experience leads to release from old traumas and an increased openness to responding spontaneously and creatively to one's own living.

Philosophically, Moreno believed that enacting one's 'immortal primordial nature' (1946: 3) offers catharsis to a degree which releases the individual from the kind of self-constraint that is not merely necessary personal and social containment, but an unhelpful form of self-imprisonment. The therapeutic dialogue is opened up and enacted as part of the process of the psychotherapy, interpretation by the psychotherapist diminishes and the client creates new self-definitions.

Transactional Analysis

Transactional Analysis developed and grew from Berne's (1961/1980) interest in his patients' phenomenological experience of their personal past. Qualified as a psychiatrist, and having himself been in analysis with the ego psychologist Federn and later Erikson, Berne was well aware of the current trends in psychiatric and analytic thinking and practice. He integrated his knowledge in these areas with neurosurgeon Penfield's discoveries that during certain neurosurgical procedures people re-experience past situations with full emotional intensity. Berne created a tripartite system of the person, his ego state model (see Figure 8.1).

Emphasising that ego states are phenomenological realities and not

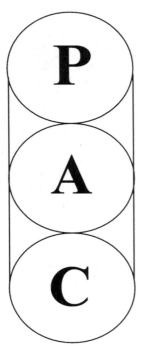

Feelings, attitudes and behaviours
introjected from parental figures
and significant others

Feelings, attitudes and behaviours
related to the current
here-and-now reality

Archaic feelings, attitudes
and behaviours which are
remnants of the person's past

Figure 8.1 Berne's original ego-state model (reproduced with permission from Berne 1964/1985)

merely abstract concepts, Berne writes: 'Parent, Adult and Child represent real people who now exist, or who once existed, who have legal names and civic identities' (1961/1980: 32).

Using the ego state model, a client can be helped phenomenologically to re-experience aspects of himself that are contributing to his immediate personal difficulties. By gaining insight into his inner world and the influences that are affecting and distorting his perceptions, relationships and behaviour, he is able to highlight sources of internal conflict. Once these conflicts are identified, a working-through process can commence.

One approach that can be useful in facilitating phenomenological awareness is the ego state dialogue. Three chairs are used, one to represent each ego state, and the client verbalises in a dialogue the internal conflicts which are contributing to his difficulties and the differing ego states within himself which generate these conflicts. The client moves between chairs as he speaks from each ego state. Normally, of course, he would contain this dialogue within his private world, but with the psychotherapist as guide he is able to externalise this, seeing and hearing himself in new ways.

Garth sought help for his lack of self-confidence which he saw as the source of his inability to achieve promotion successfully at work. It was clear from the way in which Garth spoke about himself that his difficulties arose from the harsh self-criticisms he made in his Parent ego state and the resulting despair and loss of self-esteem experienced in his Child ego state. Through a process of ego state dialogue Garth was able to experience the power of this internal dynamic. Protected and supported by the skill and care of his psychotherapist, he wept freely from his Child ego state, expressing his pent-up pain and despair. Garth was able to free himself from some of the effects of his internal tyranny. In the weeks that followed, he experienced a new sense of self-worth and, supported by further psychotherapeutic work, he eventually successfully secured the promotion he sought.

Philosophically, Berne stressed the importance of mutual respect between people which is expressed in his shorthand phrase, 'I'm OK – You're OK'. He translated this into practice in a number of ways. First, whatever occurs in the therapeutic relationship must be by explicit agreement between client and psychotherapist; contracting is, therefore, given high focus as a vital part of the psychotherapy. Contracts are open to review, renewal and change. Secondly, as a matter of professional practice, Berne taught that the only comments worth making about a client are those that the psychotherapist could make face to face to him. Anything else is immaterial. Thirdly, clients are encouraged to discover as much about the process and theoretical bases of the psychotherapy as is of interest to them. For example, those who wish may choose to attend a short introductory course in Transactional Analysis that offers opportunities for didactic and experiential understanding of the major aspects of the model.

Using the concept of Freud's repetition compulsion as his starting point, Berne emphasised the predictability of behaviour. This has become a major philosophical precept of Transactional Analysis. In practice this principle underpins the theory of psychological games which Berne defines in his book *Games People Play* as follows: 'A Game is an ongoing series of complementary ulterior transactions progressing to a well-defined, predictable outcome' (1964/1985: 44); in other words, engaging with others in predictable patterns of communicating whereby, without initially realising it, we either issue or respond to an unspoken message that is, nevertheless, fully apparent through voice tone, facial expression, physical posture or some other meta-communication. This leads to a familiar, unpleasant outcome, because we are involved in a psychological game. The long-term outcome of such patterns of transacting is to confirm and complete our script outcome; that is, to ensure that the life dramas, the scripts we have decided upon for ourselves, are played out to the last scene. The goal of TA psychotherapy is to help the client prevent these outcomes and recover his full capacity for spontaneity, intimacy and awareness.

The third major philosophical principle is that emotional problems can be resolved and changes made where the right approach and adequate knowledge are available. Berne writes of three major forces within the human psyche: Eros – the power of sexual drives; Mortido – the drive to self-harm; and Physis – the urge to transformation. The TA psychotherapist works with the client to help him harness his own Physis in the service of the metamorphosis. Physis has been defined by Clarkson as 'nature . . . coming from the deepest biological roots of the human being and striving towards its greatest realisation' (1992: 15).

Gestalt psychotherapy

Perls, the father of Gestalt psychotherapy, shared with Berne and Moreno a belief in the innate instinctual drive to health of the human being. He described this as organismic flow. He writes:

> The view here taken of the human organism is that it is *active*, not *passive*. For instance, inhibition of certain behaviors is not merely absence of these behaviors . . . [it is] an active holding in. If the inhibition is lifted, what was held in does not then passively emerge. Rather, the person actively, eagerly brings it forth.
>
> (in Perls *et al.* 1951/1989: 22)

Perls conceived of neurosis as a growth disorder. One's natural organismic flow is interrupted and the cycle of experience, which begins at the moment of sensing, is artificially arrested before it can reach completion or satisfaction. The natural drive to growth and satisfaction becomes stunted. Such interruptions lead to the unfinished business of an incomplete Gestalt (a German word with no exact English translation, meaning 'whole'). The individual holds and stores these incomplete fragments inside. The tension of holding what is incomplete is in direct opposition to the flow to healthy completion. This tension manifests through several dysfunctional ways of being which are known as interruptions to contact. Perls (in Perls *et al.* 1951/1989) makes reference to five interruptions; later Gestalt practitioners have added others. It is not our intention to discuss these in detail, but rather to give the reader a sense of Perls's understanding.

Desensitisation, numbing oneself to stimuli that are painful or evoke great fear, is a common method of interrupting contact with others and the environment. This interruption is found frequently in adults who as young children were subjected to persistent physical or sexual abuse. Clients report having used a variety of strategies to achieve desensitisation: 'By imagining myself sailing on a pink cloud I could pretend I was far away'; 'I would count backwards from one hundred, over and over until he had stopped'. As adults these individuals experienced difficulty in making full pleasurable contact during times of intimacy, usually

desensitising instead, and were haunted by unexpressed pain ,
their unfinished business. They needed to release this and ,
resolution of their trauma before meaningful intimacy was possible
current relationships.

Other interruptions include introjection – swallowing whole anoth
feelings or attitude – such as 'Never rest until your work is done
Projection means imbuing the environment with a disowned aspect of the
self. A client starts the session by saying to the psychotherapist, 'You look
angry today', when in fact it is she who is experiencing unacknowledged
anger towards the psychotherapist. Retroflection is the holding back of
energy that is about to be expressed. A female client who had been
brought up to hide her feelings was involved in a road accident in which
another driver received serious injuries. Instead of expressing her horror
she held it in, appearing calm and unmoved to rescue workers. Confluence
is where there is neither a sense of boundary between two people, nor an
awareness of their differences. Occasionally a client may request psychotherapy, and what emerges during the initial discussion is that the client is
there because his partner has sent him. He has not paused to consider
whether or not he has a need for psychotherapy.

When our organismic flow is interrupted, physical and emotional problems
occur. The Gestalt psychotherapist helps the client to become aware of his
interruptions and to restore his natural organismic rhythm.

Claire had returned to full-time education as a mature student. She was
excited by the opportunities she saw opening before her. Within two weeks
her excitement had turned to anxiety. Every time she entered the building
where most of her lectures were held she felt nauseous. Her symptoms
persisted and she began to experience panic attacks. She was concerned
that she might not be able to enjoy her learning or fulfil her academic
potential. Assisted by a friend, she referred herself to a Gestalt psychotherapist. What Claire discovered surprised her. Without her having been
aware of it, Claire's senses had been restimulated by a combination of the
smell of furniture polish used in the building and the high Victorian
windows of the lecture hall. These were similar to those of the boarding
school she had attended as a child of seven. Claire had loathed boarding
school, feeling abandoned by her parents and homesick for familiar
surroundings and routines. Here was her unfinished business, the unresolved
grief and pain of her 'banishment'.

Claire's psychotherapist helped her fully to express these long-pent-up
feelings. Through this Claire gained a new understanding of her past
experiences at boarding school and her current difficulties at university.
With her new awareness she was able to enter her university lecture hall
free of the shadows of the past.

Philosophically, Gestalt is rooted in both existentialism and phenomenology. Influenced by thinkers like Buber (1937/1987) and Tillich (1973),

Perls placed great emphasis on 'response-ability', his belief in the ability of individuals actively to respond to themselves and their environment. Each of us must take responsibility for our own thoughts, feelings and behaviours, and thereby for our own existence. In the meeting between client and psychotherapist this is initially made explicit and continues to be assumed throughout the psychotherapy as the client is supported to discover and become fully aware of her subjective experience. Buber's influence is further discernible in Perls's model of the therapeutic relationship, which is based on Buber's 'I–Thou' relationship. The two partners to the therapeutic relationship are both present with the full range of their human resources, and the personhood of each is to be respected.

As a final point, it is interesting to note the importance of paradox in Gestalt psychotherapy. Based on the belief that people grow best by becoming more fully who they are already, striving to become the opposite of one's qualities is seen as unproductive and a barrier to growth. A client who wishes to become less timid is encouraged to express her timidity to its full in the therapeutic setting until she can go no further with it, at which point she is likely to be surprised to find herself having shifted her energy into a more outgoing mode.

Overall, the goals of the humanistic/existential psychotherapies can be summarised as assisting the client to learn to express himself at the boundaries of himself; at his heights, depths and breadth; to be fully himself, with all the richness that is implied. The diversity of methodologies within this school used in the service of these aims indicates the complexities and richness of the journeying. There are, of course, many other forms of humanistic psychotherapy which it has not been possible to include.

Integrative psychotherapy

Integrative psychotherapy is a new genre which is now widely accepted in the United States and is gaining a strong foothold in Britain. The integrative school uses those features that are common across the psychotherapies to create a meta-model of the therapeutic relationship. There are a number of these models, which are derived according to the philosophy and working practice of the integrative psychotherapist. Mahrer (1989: 2), using the work of Orlinsky and Howard (1987), identifies six basic components that constitute psychotherapy: a therapeutic contract; intervention strategies; a therapeutic bond; the nature of self-relatedness in client and psychotherapist; assessment of therapeutic realisation; and the interrelationships of these five components.

An integrative approach provides a way of understanding the therapeutic process and intervening with the client that extends beyond the bounds of any of the particular schools. Storr comments, 'research discloses the common factors which lead to a successful outcome in psychotherapy, which, to my mind, is largely independent of the school to which the psychotherapist belongs' (1979: viii). These themes are expanded by Norcross and Goldfried (1992), who offer an up-to-date view of the developments in integrative psychotherapy in their handbook. In Chapter 2, Clarkson's integrative model based on five kinds of therapeutic relationship is more fully discussed. This framework has been quite widely adopted and used in training and research in the group field and in integrative psychotherapy.

Behaviour therapy

Behaviour therapy is well described in detail in Dryden (1990) by Geraldine Sullivan, who goes into its background and historical roots. The actual term was first used by Skinner (1953). Behaviour therapy is based on applying learning theory to the treatment of psychological symptoms in a variety of ways. The main ingredient is the identification of methods of unlearning in which the client can work with the behaviour therapist to correct an unwanted pattern or symptom. There are fairly specific indications for this form of treatment: the problem should be defined in terms of observable behaviour, be current and predictable and have consistently identifiable triggers. Anxiety should be situational as opposed to free-floating, and clearly defined goals should be identified by client and psychotherapist. Lastly, client co-operation is essential. The most notable limitation is the degree of discomfort that the client must endure during the treatment in order to make worthwhile gains. As with all forms of psychotherapy, many clients do not have the will to undergo the required degree of difficulty.

Cognitive therapy

Cognitive therapy started with the observation that, whilst the behavioural school were concerned with external factors and the psychodynamic school with internal unconscious factors, nobody was paying any attention to the value and meaning of the thoughts that clients were aware of having and which they felt were central to their experience of life.

In 1955 Kelly put the emphasis on how people give meaning to their world, and the foundation stone of cognitive therapy was laid. Now there are about seventeen cognitive therapies, of which three are the most influential. These are the rational-emotive therapy of Ellis (1958), the cognitive-behaviour modification of Meichenbaum (1969) and the cognitive therapy of Beck *et al.* (1979). It is the latter, or a derivative, which is probably the most widely used form in Britain. In the cognitive model psychological disturbance is seen as one result of malfunction in the process of evaluating and interpreting the personal experience of the subject. Thus information is processed in a way that is biased, usually negatively biased, so that the experience of the world is distorted by the way the input is processed. This also tends to produce thinking which is more global, more absolute and more judgemental than normal. This primitive thinking leads to what are called 'logical errors', which characterise the thinking in emotional disturbance. Thus the basic assumptions that underlie cognitive therapy are that the person is an active agent who interacts with their own world through interpretations, inference and evaluation of stimuli. The results of these cognitive processes are conceptualised as accessible to consciousness in the form of thoughts and images. Thus each person has the potential to change what goes on in their mind. In other words, both emotions and behaviour are seen as being mediated by cognitive processes that are amenable to change. This is different from behavioural and psychoanalytic theory, the first paying little attention to the internal world, and the second regarding the internal world as all-important, but obscure, except to the professional guide.

So far, cognitive theory has remained focused on emotional disturbance and has not yet tried to offer a general theory of development that includes normal cognitive processes. The indications for cognitive therapy are expanding. So far it has been used in depression, generalised anxiety, panic disorders, eating disorders and hypochondriasis – a fairly large range of emotional problems. Selection is by clinical judgement, as the criteria have not yet been fully worked out. However, as with other forms of psychotherapy, motivation plays a key role in success. The client must be able to engage in the self-help programme, do the homework tasks and accept the underlying beliefs of the theoretical orientation. Clients with personality problems which are expressed as difficulties in relating will bring these difficulties into the therapeutic arena where they will interfere with the treatment. Work is currently being done on this problem area. The choice between individual or group cognitive therapy is under review. Generally, the more severe disturbances tend to be treated individually, but opinion is moving with experience, just as it seems to have moved in the choice between individual or group psychotherapy by the analytic method. Using more than one psychotherapist in a group setting can be helpful both as a training model for the psychotherapist and to help with difficult or stuck situations with clients. There is a developing tendency to use group therapy also as a follow-on from individual, to provide a type of laboratory setting in which to test the newly learned beliefs and behaviours. The method is limited in its application to those who can cope with its demands. People with severe mental disturbance are not suitable, particularly if they suffer from hallucinations or delusions. Severe obsessional behaviour can interfere too much with the homework programme. Depressives who prefer ideas of self-control do better than those who do not. Equally, where the symptoms are vague or generalised, such as global problems in relating, it can prove difficult to find a focus. An excellent account of cognitive therapy is given by Moorey (1990).

Personal construct therapy

Personal construct therapy is another derivative of the original work of Kelly (1955). It postulates that people construe the world according to what are known as personal constructs. If these constructs are rigid then that person will have difficulties in coping with everyday life. Those difficulties will appear in many different forms. One of the distinguishing features of personal construct theory is its emphatic rejection of the medical model. Thus it is in some contrast to the cognitive and behavioural schools, which are rooted in clinical psychology and appear to follow the medical model quite closely. The theoretical framework is expressed in the form of postulates, corollaries and other theoretical constructs. The fundamental postulate states that 'a person's processes are psychologically channelized by the ways in which he anticipates events' (1955). Three of the corollaries which elaborate this postulate are experience, choice and modulation.

The experience corollary states that 'a person's construction system varies as he successively construes the replication of events' (1955). This means that experience is only gained by having had to reconstrue a situation or some aspect of it, in a way that is different from previous constructions.

The choice corollary states that 'a person chooses for himself that alternative in a dichotomized construct through which he anticipates the greater possibility for extension and definition of his system' (1955).

The modulation corollary states that any variation within a construing system 'is limited by the permeability of the constructs within whose range of convenience the variants lie' (1955). New events, or new versions of events, are difficult to construe if many of the person's constructs are not open enough to receive them.

Change is conceptualised as cycles of movement which may, or may not, occur. The cycle of experience is about the process of reconstruing. The whole of psychotherapy is thus thought of in terms of human experience rather than in terms of treatment. Indeed, Kelly himself regarded the whole idea of treatment in relation to psychotherapy as misleading; a view that may well be shared by many psychotherapists of diverse schools.

The personal construct view of psychological problems is that the problem represents being stuck in a particular way of construing experience which keeps it always the same. As the person is seen as a form of motion, enabling the person to get on the move is in itself a goal of psychotherapy.

As everything is seen in terms of construing, there are no limitations of the client in terms of selection for personal construct therapy. The limiting factors are of time and place, and the personal limitations of any particular personal construct psychotherapist. Of course it is recognised that clients who already have the construct that it is possible to change, and that they themselves might change, will have a more favourable prognosis than those who have no such constructs. As in all forms of psychotherapy, the client must be able and willing to do his or her fair share of the hard work that is involved in psychological change. The most widely known tool is the Repertory Grid. There are, of course, many tools used in Personal Construct Therapy. For a clear account and references to the relevant literature, see Fay Fransella's chapter on the subject in Dryden (1990).

Neuro-Linguistic Programming

Neuro-Linguistic Programming began as an attempt to find out what were the factors in psychotherapy that made the difference to the client. It became a whole model of psychotherapy by the process of reframing. This means that any experience can be felt and seen as quite different if the context in which it occurs can be changed. The names that are particularly associated with Neuro-Linguistic Programming are Richard Bandler and John Grinder, and their book *Reframing* (1982) sets out their views very clearly. As a simple example, Bandler and Grinder (1982) describe a woman who spent all her time cleaning her house. The family were nagged remorselessly to take off their shoes, to enter by the back door and, in particular, not to walk on the living-room carpet as it showed dents from their footprints. Outside the house the family got on fine and there was no problem. The woman was asked to visualise her living-room carpet in its most pristine state – no footprints at all. She did so and felt happy. Then she was told that this image meant that none of her loved ones were in the home. She was entirely alone and, as long as the carpet remained perfect, not one of her family were at home with her. This made her unhappy. Then she was asked to imagine that the family had come home – she felt better – and finally that the footprints on the carpet meant that those she loved most in the world were with her. This kind of clinical example raises all the problems of small snapshots. Although in itself quite clear, it leaves us with the problem of what is being compared to what. The woman in this example is clearly not a true sufferer from obsessive compulsive neurosis, because if she were, she would not have been so happy and carefree outside the home. Whether that is a fair critique of the example is not clear, as there is no claim made to treat very severe pathology by Neuro-Linguistic Programming, as far as we know. It would be essential to study the whole matter much more thoroughly to arrive at a clearer understanding and to be able to envisage a set of indications and contra-indications for NLP. The systematisation of the techniques of reframing is currently the central concern for NLP.

It is perhaps a moot point whether personal construct therapy belongs to the cognitive therapies, as one of the variations that have arisen from the work of Kelly. Is it really any more than another version of the use of his work to provide a different framework for changing behaviour? The answer to this question is very complex, and no doubt it would be answered differently according to people's frames of reference. This raises the whole problem of the classification of the psychotherapies, which is not yet entirely satisfactory (see Chapter 1 of this *Handbook*). In this chapter we have followed the usual conventions as they exist today and, hopefully, they will be classified satisfactorily.

INDICATIONS FOR INDIVIDUAL PSYCHOTHERAPY

There are endless contradictions in the area of indications for different modalities of psychotherapy. It is helpful to remember that today's indications can easily become tomorrow's contra-indications.

Norcross and Goldfried suggest that individual psychotherapy is indicated in

> Problems of dyadic intimacy . . . require the development of a relationship with a therapist for some resolution to occur. Patients whose character or symptoms are based on firmly structured intrapsychic conflict, which causes repetitive life patterns that, more or less, transcend the particulars of the current interpersonal situation (e.g., family, job relationships). Adolescents or young people who are striving for autonomy. Symptoms or problems that are of such private and/or embarrassing nature that secrecy of individual treatments is required at least for the beginning phase.
>
> (1992: 466)

They continue by adding that relative contra-indications include patients who meet clear indications for family or marital treatment or patients who regress in individual therapeutic relationships.

This last caveat is something of a puzzle. It is difficult to imagine how problems of dyadic intimacy, their first indication, can be managed in individual psychotherapy without regression. Indeed, in the psychoanalytically based psychotherapies, regression is one of the major elements in the elucidation of the transference. It is possible that Norcross and Goldfried are thinking of uncontrolled regression, and not of regression that is confined to the psychotherapy sessions. Alternatively, what we are seeing is the difficulty inherent in any attempt to arrange a set of indications that are comprehensive enough to cover all forms of psychotherapy. For indications in the area of group psychotherapy, see Chapter 14 of this *Handbook*.

Dryden (1990) follows much the same pattern as Norcross and Goldfried, beginning with a quotation from Ellis, the founder of rational-emotive therapy, in which Ellis says that he usually lets the client pick the treatment modality. Dryden asked a number of psychotherapists to describe what they saw as the indications and advantages of individual psychotherapy as well as the contra-indications and disadvantages. The resulting list shows that the psychotherapists are generally in agreement:

Indications

Providing there is a situation of complete confidentiality it is suitable for clients to disclose 'secret' material. Thus greater openness is possible and the dyadic nature provides more opportunity for a close relationship between client and psychotherapist. It is indicated for more disturbed clients whose lives are chaotic and, where the development and resolution of a transference relationship is deemed curative, it is the treatment of choice. It can proceed at the clients pace, with the full attention of the psychotherapist and free from interruption from other clients. This is specially important for clients who are confused and who are struggling with value dilemmas, as well as those whose constructions of the world are loose and require tightening. It is indicated where the client's major problem is in relation to themselves or where others are not centrally implicated. It may be indicated for clients who wish to differentiate self from others or who have decided to leave a relationship and want to deal with the individual problems that this may involve. Individual sessions also allow the psychotherapist greater freedom to vary their own style of interaction free from concern about how this might affect other clients. In the dyad, a wider range of goals can be set than in other formats, and it is particularly appropriate where a major reconstruction of the self is called for. There are also a number of indications that are essentially negative, such as with clients who are deemed not likely to benefit from any other mode of treatment. The examples given are of clients who would monopolise a group or who would be too withdrawn to participate or are too vulnerable for group or family work. Other indications are extreme anxiety or depression.

Contra-indications for individual psychotherapy

To set against the criteria for individual psychotherapy, Dryden's psychotherapists offer a list of criteria which they consider as contra-indications: clients who are likely to become too dependent and who are threatened by the intimacy of the close encounter of the dyad. As a group is less likely to be manipulated than an individual, manipulative clients or those diagnosed as 'borderline' are deemed to be better treated in a group. Individual psychotherapy may not be appropriate for those who use intellectualisation as a major defensive form, as well as for those who have a sexual problem that is maintained by their partner's response. Many of Dryden's psychotherapists are agreed that individual psychotherapy is contra-indicated when the client finds it too comfortable. This is based on the idea that change is facilitated by arousal. As a follow-on from this it is also suggested that it may be unhelpful to offer individual psychotherapy to clients who have had a lot of individual work in the past, except where the previous work has been ineffectively conducted.

Discussion of indications

In setting out fairly fully the indications for and against individual psychotherapy from two different textbooks, we hope to illustrate the difficulties in making general statements about which format to recommend in different circumstances. We did not want to give a picture of greater clarity than exists in reality. What we have to deal with is a situation where almost every indication and every contra-indication has a caveat that renders it fairly useless. The need for intimacy and structural change requires individual attention, but dependency can become a contra-indication even though it is an essential component of some psychotherapies. Secrecy is better dealt with in private, but manipulative clients should be offered a group format. Symptoms that are embarrassing or private are better not dealt with in a group, but if a partner is involved, group psychotherapy is indicated.

The problems of this attempt to create indications can be looked at as a secondary problem. The primary problem could be one of diagnosis, or classification (what is known in psychiatry by the Greek derivative, taxonomy). As we do not have a reliable means of identifying and classifying emotional problems, we cannot even begin to make sense of indications. Where we cannot categorise a condition, we are also not able to describe its history. In medicine this exercise is called the 'natural history of the disease', meaning that it is possible to describe the course of an illness if it is untreated. Only then can we say whether a treatment has been effective. Even then we have to be very careful that we do not confuse remission with cure. Quite a lot of work has been done, and is being done, in this area, but it is clear from what we have reported of psychotherapists' views on indications, as reported in the literature, that we still do not know enough about recognising and classifying emotional illnesses to have a comprehensive set of treatment criteria. Perhaps in this context it is more honest to let the client choose, as Ellis (1958) said he did, or to renounce the whole idea of illness and treatment in the context of psychotherapy. Either way does not actually solve anything, but it does provide a reframe that can illuminate the difficulties. Perhaps we should regard every form of psychotherapy as different from every other form. The problem here is that research suggests that no form of psychotherapy is demonstrably better than any other (Holmes and Lindley 1989). If we are to continue to use the term 'psychotherapy' in our title, we must find out more about how to recommend the most appropriate form of psychotherapy, or admit that it makes no difference which form is applied. This last option is probably not a realistic one for psychotherapists to adopt.

AVAILABILITY OF PSYCHOTHERAPY

As most of the psychotherapy in the United Kingdom takes place in the private sector, it is quite difficult to be clear about the availability. There is some provision in the NHS, mainly by psychiatrists and clinical psychologists. Some of the NHS Health Authorities have no, or only one or two, consultant psychotherapists, but although psychotherapy is provided by consultant psychiatrists and their teams it is 'invisible' because it is part of a general provision of services to a particular area. Departments of clinical psychology have offered a variety of psychotherapy services for many years; traditionally these have been mainly of the behavioural and cognitive schools, but by no means exclusively so. In addition, a number of other adjacent professionals have been pursuing psychotherapeutic activities within the NHS; most obviously, of course, in the Child Guidance Clinics within the interdisciplinary teams. Also social workers have at times and in different places become interested and active in providing psychotherapy either directly in relation to their social work activities, or instead of it. Occupational therapists have also developed some interest. For some years there has been a move to train suitably qualified nurses as psychotherapists, as part of their specialist psychiatric training, in the techniques of behaviour therapy, as well as in dynamic psychotherapy. In a recent article, Duggan et al. (1993) describe a clinical audit of behaviour therapy training of nurses from 1978 to 1991 at the Maudsley Hospital.

Reading through the list of the seventy organisations which are members of the United Kingdom Council for Psychotherapy, it is easy to see that the vast majority of psychotherapists are based in or near London. This is gradually changing as psychotherapists continue to spread. There are now groups of psychotherapists in several locations. Once the Register of psychotherapists is published it will be much easier to get an idea of the spread, and it will also be possible to buy, at a very reasonable fee, a list of psychotherapists in any named postal district. The Directory of Training of UKCP gives an overview of the availability of trainings in different locations. However, all of this does not catch those Health Service psychotherapists who are listed under their general professional title, nor does it indicate the whereabouts of those psychotherapists who do not belong to a professional organisation, or whose organisation does not belong to the UKCP. The only way that a comprehensive view of the availability of psychotherapy will be achieved, as well as the modality that is offered, will be the formation of a statutory register. Until then a certain amount of guesswork will be unavoidable.

CONFIDENTIALITY

This is a complex and thorny subject that applies to all forms and modalities of psychotherapy. In theory, confidentiality between client and psychotherapist is absolute. In reality, there are circumstances in which a court can demand that the psychotherapist, like the medical practitioner, must reveal the content of the psychotherapy sessions. This is very rare, and the only recorded instance of this was when a psychoanalyst was subpoenaed to appear in the High Court to give evidence about an alleged former patient. The psychoanalyst attended court and pleaded that it was essential to maintain confidentiality as an essential part of psychoanalysis. It was improbable that the material of sessions would provide the kind of objective evidence that the court was seeking, and that to divulge anything would amount to malpractice. The court accepted this plea. It was as though the practitioner had been treated like a priest with regard to the content of the confessional. The events were reported anonymously in *The Lancet* in 1965.

A new problem about confidentiality arose when the Access to Health Records Act (1990) came into force on 1 November 1991. This Act is an extension of the Data Protection Act and is part of the whole campaign for freedom of information. The first Act was to enable ordinary people to have a legal right of access to records held on a computer. Those rights have now been extended to handwritten records that had escaped the original legislation, so that the same rights now exist to any handwritten as well as computerised or typewritten records. There is an excellent summary in *Which?* magazine (1991).

Clients have the right to see their records from 1 November 1991 onwards if they make a written request. There is a time limit within which the records must be produced and there are some restrictions on who can make the request on behalf of minors. As there are no test cases so far, it is impossible to give definite advice. It is possible that if there are informal notes that do not carry the name of the client and are used only for supervision, that they might escape the Act, but it is not certain. The promoters of the Act take the view that if a client in any form of analytic treatment were to make a written request instead of trying the understand the meaning of the wish to see their notes, then the treatment would have already broken down and access to the records would not have a harmful effect on the psychotherapy (Frankel 1991). Included in the Act is the condition that technical terms must be explained. If the client asks for a change to the record, this must either be agreed to and carried out, or the wish of the client for a specific change must be noted in the record. Whether there will ever be a case that tests the Act remains to be seen. To whom does the Act apply? To professionals who hold records about health in the private sector as well as the NHS, except in Northern Ireland which will be covered by a separate law. Who is recognised as a professional? For practical purposes it boils down to registered professionals. That means psychotherapists will be included once they have a register. Whether this applies equally to a voluntary register as it will to a statutory register is not yet clear, but it is most likely that it will.

CONCLUSION

Psychotherapy for adults in the dyad is common to all schools of psychotherapy and there is something of a confusion about when to refer to dyadic or group psychotherapy. This confusion spreads right across all the forms of psychotherapy. It could be that the problem of coherent indications is secondary to a problem of definition and classification. Not enough is known about how much and what kind of psychotherapy is available in the United Kingdom, but that will change with the Register of Psychotherapists launched on 20 May 1993. It is to be hoped that the need for psychotherapy will gain ground and that the provision of services right across the United Kingdom will soon begin to be a reality.

REFERENCES

Access to Health Records Act (1990) London: HMSO.
Anonymous (1965) 'Psychoanalyst subpoenaed', *The Lancet* 16 Oct.: 785–6.
Bandler, R. and Grinder, J. (1982) *Reframing: Neurolinguistic Programming and the Transformation of Meaning*, Moab, UT: Real People Press.
Beck, A. T., Rush, A. J., Shaw, B. E. and Emery, G. (1979) *The Cognitive Therapy of Depression*, New York: Guilford.
Berne, E. (1985) *Games People Play*, Harmondsworth: Penguin (first published 1964).
—— (1980) *Transactional Analysis in Psychotherapy: A Systematic Individual and Social Psychiatry*, London: Souvenir Press (first published 1961).
Breuer, J. and Freud, S. (1955) 'Studies on hysteria', in J. Strachey (ed.) *The Standard Edition of the Complete Psychological Works of Sigmund Freud*, vol. 2, London: Hogarth Press (first published 1895).
Buber, M. (1987) (R. Gregor Smith, trans.) *I and Thou*, Edinburgh: T. & T. Clark (first published 1937).
Clarkson, P. (1992) 'Physis in Transactional Analysis', *ITA News* 33: 14–19. Also published in *Transactional Analysis Journal* 22(4): 202–9.

Deurzen-Smith, E. van (1988) *Existential Counselling in Practice*, London: Sage.

Dryden, W. (ed.) (1990) *Individual Therapy: A Handbook*, Milton Keynes: Open University Press.

Duggan, C., Marks, I. and Richards, D. (1993) 'Health trends', *Journal of the Department of Health* 25(1): 25–30.

Ellis, A. (1958) 'Rational psychotherapy', *Journal of General Psychology* 59: 35–49.

Frankel, M. (1991) Personal communication.

Fransella, F. (1990) 'Personal construct therapy', pp. 127–48 in W. Dryden (ed.) *Individual Therapy: A Handbook*, Milton Keynes: Open University Press.

Freud, A. (1966) *The Ego and the Mechanisms of Defence* (rev. edn.) London: Hogarth and the Institute of Psycho-Analysis (first published 1936).

Freud, S. (1920/1961) *Beyond the Pleasure Principle*, London: Hogarth Press.

—— (1958) 'Remembering, repeating and working through', pp. 145–156 in A. Richards (ed.), J. Strachey (trans.), The Pelican Freud Library, vol. 12, Harmondsworth: Pelican (first published 1915–17).

Holmes, J. and Lindley, R. (1989) *The Values of Psychotherapy*, Oxford: Oxford University Press.

Kelly, G. (1955) *The Psychology of Personal Constructs*, vols 1 and 2, New York: Norton.

Laufer, M. and Laufer, M. E. (1984) *Adolescence and Developmental Breakdown*, New Haven and London: Yale University Press.

Locke, G. (1693) *Some Thoughts Concerning Education*, London: Ward Lock.

Mahrer, A. R. (1989) *The Integration of Psychotherapies: A Guide for Practicing Therapists*, Ottawa: Human Sciences Press.

Meichenbaum, D. H. (1969) 'The effects of instructions and reinforcement on thinking and language behavior of schizophrenics', *Behaviour Research and Therapy* 7: 101–14.

Moorey, S. (1990) 'Cognitive therapy', pp. 226–51 in W. Dryden (ed.) *Individual Therapy: A Handbook*, Milton Keynes: Open University Press.

Moreno, J. L. (1946) *Psychodrama*, vol. 1, New York: Beacon House.

—— (1965) 'Therapeutic vehicles and the concept of surplus reality', *Group Psychotherapy* 18(4): 213.

—— (1972) *Psychodrama*, New York: Boston House.

Norcross, J. C. and Goldfried, M. R. (eds) (1992) *Handbook of Psychotherapy Integration*, New York: Basic Books.

Orlinsky, D. E. and Howard, K. I. (1987) 'A generic model of psychotherapy', *Journal of Integrative and Eclectic Psychotherapy* 6: 6–27.

Perls, F. S., Heffenline, R. F. and Goodman, P. (1989) *Gestalt Therapy: Excitement and Growth in the Human Personality*, New York: Julian Press (first published 1951).

Pokorny, M. R. (1984) 'Brief psychotherapy and the validation of psychodynamic theories', *British Journal of Psychotherapy* 1(1): 68–76.

Skinner, B. F. (1953) *Science and Human Behavior*, New York: Macmillan.

South Tees District Health Authority (1989) *Report of the Psychotherapy Working Party*, South Tees District Health Authority (March).

Spinelli, W. (1989) *The Interpreted World: An Introduction to Phenomenological Psychology*, London: Sage.

Storr, A. (1979) *The Art of Psychotherapy*, London: Secker & Warburg.

Tillich, H. (1973) *From Time to Time*, New York: Stein & Day.

Which? (1991) 'Your right to know', *Which? Magazine* (Oct.), London: Consumers' Association.

A spectrum of psychological therapies for children

Peter Harper

> In childhood, with its rapid development of new modes of function, the therapeutic context of safety permits not only exploration and risks of change but also the emergence of more benign, healthy, adaptive modes at each developmental stage.
>
> (Pine 1985: 34)

This chapter presents an overview of several therapeutic schools, styles and structures used in therapeutic endeavours with children and young people. It highlights the universal and integrating factors of therapeutic frameworks from a meta-perspective. The setting and other contexts of working with children are discussed. Psychological literature is permeated with models of child development, and it is acknowledged that a knowledge of child development is useful in finalising treatment plans. However, developmental perspectives are not a focus in this review.

Common to therapeutic endeavours with children is the facilitation of particular forms of relationship in which the therapist will exhibit behaviours which consistently communicate acceptance, understanding and respect. Specific therapist behaviours will derive from the diagnostic acumen of the therapist, and the theoretical framework underpinning the therapy. However, influenced by a systemic awareness, many current therapeutic endeavours with children now place considerable importance on an assessment of the ecology of the child's life before intervention is planned. Accordingly, a broader range of interventions is made possible. Clarkson and Fish (1988) provided a categorisation of children's difficulties frequently encountered in therapy and summarised the advantages and disadvantages of individual, family and group work with children. In integrating children's difficulties in their model of overlapping subsystems, and in their promotion of an awareness of child, family and societal development and change, therapists working with children and young people are offered a robust model from which treatment choice, prioritisation and sequencing is made possible.

Although therapeutic endeavours with children have their origins in

Freudian analytic psychology, a wide spectrum of therapies from a variety of philosophical roots now prevails. The theoretical boundaries delineated for the purposes of this discussion may appear superficial, incomplete and even contradictory; however, they have been used in an attempt to summarise what is a broad and complex body of literature and knowledge.

THE PSYCHOANALYTIC SCHOOL

Although Freud himself did not work directly with children, his pioneering and classical analysis of 'Little Hans' (1909) exhibited that psychoanalytic concepts could be applied to work with the emotional disturbances of children. In this specific case, Freud directed his work through the father. The therapeutic goal was the reliving, during the therapeutic hour, of the affect associated with repressed experiences. In this process the ego was restored to control, co-ordinate and integrate the impulses which were previously repressed by neurotic defences. For adults in analysis the technique of free association was used to bring these repressed experiences to consciousness. However, the method was not practicable in the case of children undergoing analysis, and changes in technique were necessary.

From observations of children's play, Hug-Hellmuth (1921) noted the expressive quality of play and its potential, when used with verbal comments, to establish effective therapeutic alliances with children. Anna Freud (1946) noted the natural resistance of children to the use of free association, and modified the classical psychoanalytic technique to include the use of play. She used play too as a way of producing a positive emotional attachment to the analyst, and thereby to facilitate the analysis.

Klein (1932) maintained that her efforts extended the psychoanalytic understanding of the individual to early childhood, and thereby to deeper levels of the unconscious. Klein treated her first patient, Fritz, in his home in 1919, and noted the manner in which he used his toys symbolically to represent his experiences, fantasies and anxieties. 'Klein assumed that the child's play activities, including his accompanying verbalisations, were quite as motivationally determined as the free associations of the adult. Hence they could be interpreted to the child, in lieu of interpretations based on adult-style free associations' (Dorfman 1955: 236). In the Kleinian frame, the child is considered able to distinguish between play and reality, and to have the capacity to re-create real world objects and situations in play. Thus it is possible for the child to experiment with mastering life's predicaments using play. Adhering to two core tenets of psychoanalysis (namely, that psychoanalysis is based upon insight and exploration of the unconscious, and that insight is gained by an analysis of the transference relationship), Klein used the play of children as a *via regia* to the unconscious in the same manner that dreams were used by the adult analysts. She commented that 'we soon find that the child brings as many associations to separate elements of its play as do adults to the separate elements of their dreams. These separate play elements are indications to the trained observer; and as it plays, the child talks as well, and says all sorts of things which have the value of genuine associations' (1932: 30).

Klein's child play analyses were largely child-directed, with the analyst providing non-judgemental interpretations which were intended neither to encourage nor suggest courses of action to the child. The child is allowed to experience their fantasies as they occur, and to present them in whatever way they choose: using toys, drawing or dramatisation. The psychotherapist gives clear, succinct psychoanalytic interpretations geared to the child's level of understanding. The past is thereby uncovered, and the ego is strengthened to be better able to cope with the demands of the id and the super-ego.

PSYCHOANALYTIC VARIANTS

Child psychoanalysis in its pure form (in which children were seen in analysis several times a week) was unable to meet the increased public and clinical demand that treatment of childhood psychological disorders be made available to all children presenting with problems. Gradually, psychodynamic psychotherapies and techniques, as variants of child psychoanalysis, began to emerge. Horney, Fromm, Sullivan, Fromm-Reichmann and others began to practise more goal-directed treatments, incorporating into their theories a psychoanalytic understanding of pathology and its development.

For these theorists the primary focus of the child's psychotherapy is the strengthening of ego defences and the amelioration of specific symptoms or problem areas. The child is allowed to exercise free choice in play, and a positive transference relationship is encouraged. The containment offered by the transferential relationship enhances the ventilation of conflicts and the overcoming of resistance. Interpretations are used, but these are delivered with caution, at less depth and less systematically than is the case in classical psychoanalysis. The attainment of insight is seen to be a precursor of therapeutic change with constructive action being in place by the termination of therapy.

Concurrent with individual therapy for the child, the parents may be engaged in psychotherapy. Close attention is paid to contextual/environmental issues and their active modification.

Expressive or release psychotherapy

Building on the early psychoanalytic concepts of catharsis and abreaction, Levy (1939) carefully structured and directed his play therapy with children to facilitate the reliving of previously traumatic experiences which the history suggests may have contributed to the child's disturbance. Levy's 'release therapy' does not focus on the development of a transference relationship and he made no attempt to point out the feelings implicit in the child's play, or to promote changes in behaviour. Instead the child's own imaginative play was considered to be the medium by which anxiety was released. The therapeutic purpose then is the expression of blocked emotion in the security of the relationship with the therapist in the working through of traumatic experiences.

Clearly, this is a therapeutic method which is sufficiently flexible to accommodate a wide range of specific situations in which the child may have experienced trauma. The purpose is to provide the child with the opportunity to express emotional material without having it interpreted and without having to verbalise the nature of the specific trauma and the child's associated emotions. The method demands careful diagnosis of the specific trauma and is contra-indicated in situations in which serious parental pathology exists.

Relationship child therapy

Rankian (1945) theory, elaborated by Taft (1933) and Allen (1942), highlighted the curative potential intrinsic in the healing dynamic of the therapist–child relationship, and it viewed the analytic effort to recover the past as superfluous. Rogers (1957) later encapsulated the essence of the 'Rankian therapeutic relationship' in his work 'The necessary and sufficient conditions for therapeutic personality change'. The therapist–child relationship, with its focus on the present, does not dwell on the patient's earlier trauma and emotion. Relationship therapy is concerned with emotional problems as they exist in the present and the provision of a friendly and supportive relationship with an accepting adult, and a therapeutic environment in which the child's inherent capacity for growth and self-help can develop and flourish. This notion is conceptually similar to that of 'Physis' (Berne 1971; Clarkson 1992).

The core purpose of the therapeutic hour was to provide the child with the opportunity to define themselves in relation to the therapist, to differentiate and re-evaluate their conceptualisation of themselves in the therapeutic process. The therapy hour was seen to belong truly to the child, who was guaranteed acceptance and was given the freedom to feel, say and do whatever they chose, within clearly defined limits of time, and rules against damage to the property, the self and the therapist. In using therapeutic reassurance, active encouragement and the clarification of reality as primary therapeutic techniques, the use of interpretation was relegated to a role of lesser importance. The need for the patient to retrace developmental steps and to relive earlier relationships was therefore minimised. The therapeutic focus was on healing, and the restoration of the child's capacity for growth and self-help resulted in a considerable reduction in the time-span of therapy.

Non-directive or client-centred therapy

Client-centred play therapy has not extended or made use of the psycho-analytic premise that it is necessary for the patient to relive earlier emotional relationships and to retrace any developmental lines within the therapeutic hour. Instead, Rogers (1951), Axline (1947), Moustakas (1953) and others incorporated the notion of the Rankian (1945) theory that it is the therapeutic relationship that is curative in its own right. The previous history of the child's emotional problems is unimportant. The manifestation of the problem in the moment, and a focus on present feelings was considered the most important focus for therapy. With its fundamental postulate that play is the child's natural medium of expression, play therapy offers the child the opportunity to 'play out' their feelings, problems and difficulties, and thereby to develop an image of self rather than to 'reality' as others see it.

The child's free expression of themselves is facilitated by communicating three basic therapist attitudes: faith, acceptance and respect. It is in the context of these attitudes that 'children may achieve feelings of security, adequacy and worthiness through emotional insight' (Moustakas 1953: 2). It is by the constant recognition and clarification of the emotions in the non-directive play therapy relationship that the child's insight into the feelings that motivate behaviour and self-definition can emerge.

With its roots in Rankian relationship theory, the central philosophy of client-centred play therapy holds that the individual has the potential for growth and the capacity for self-direction. A primary therapeutic objective is to provide the child with the maximum opportunity to express their feelings so that these can be recognised and clarified, and that the child is eventually enabled to identify their own feelings and thereby to become master of them. The child

> needs good growing ground to develop a well balanced structure – the individual needs the permissiveness to be himself by himself, as well as by others . . . the right to be an individual entitled to the dignity that is the birthright of every human being, in order to achieve a direct satisfaction of this growth impulse.
>
> (Axline 1947: 10)

Diagnosis is not an endeavour undertaken by the non-directive play therapist. Meeting children where they are does not necessitate knowledge of symptomatic behaviour. Equally, with its focus on the present, the techniques of interpretation and probing have no place in the therapeutic hour. The individual will select the issues most relevant to them and their lives when they are ready to do so. Instead, recognition and clarification of the expressed emotional attitudes using reflection constitutes the essence of the therapist's activity.

Play therapy is a unique experience for any child. The relationship offered has wider boundaries than the child is ever likely to have experienced. In the play-room children are given the opportunity to be completely themselves. Emotions across the spectrum from anger and hate through to love and affection can be expressed in the confidence of complete acceptance. 'The therapeutic relationship does not set up standards or social values for them – it honours every impulse, need or projection as it is expressed' (Moustakas 1953: 19). Play therapy challenges the child to 'be', to take responsibility for themselves, to make their own decisions and ultimately to be masters of their own emotional destiny.

The Lowenfeld method

A therapeutic method which gave credence to both individual biography and socio-historical processes, and one which was strongly influential in establishing child psychology as a separate endeavour, was that developed by Margaret Lowenfeld (1935) and her founding of the Institute of Child Psychology in 1928. Lowenfeld believed that disturbances in children emerged not only from emotional conflicts but also from the conceptualising and experience of the infant or young child in their development of an understanding of the world in which they live. Thus it was that Lowenfeld developed her ideas on the importance of the 'non-verbal thinking' of children. She contested the analytic supposition that the meaning of children's play, and therefore the interpretations given in the course of analysis, could be derived from adults. Instead, as a result of her observational studies, she based her psychotherapeutic method on the conclusion that play was not only a mechanism for the release of tension, but also a medium through which children could access their feelings and fantasies, and 'think' about the world. She postulated that children 'cluster' inner experiences in making sense of their worlds, and considered this process to be primary in the development of personality. Where such conceptualisations were incorrect and disturbing, the mental work the child undertakes is aberrant and emotionally painful.

Lowenfeld's psychotherapeutic method was facilitated through the careful design and selection of play materials which, when presented by various projective methods, allowed the child to externalise thoughts and feelings and to clarify and come to an understanding of the experiences which were causing conflict. Play and action gave therapeutic access to the child's 'natural idiom', and in work with the child 'connections were observed and the attention of children was drawn to them, but comparatively few interpretations were offered' (Trail and Rowles 1964: 21). Lowenfeld was predominantly 'non-interventionist' in style, and by making constant reference to observational studies she guarded against getting her client material to fit a theoretical perspective.

Psychodrama

This systematised method of role playing is essentially a group therapy method in which enactment rather than play or verbalisation is the primary means by which a patient explores and achieves varying degrees of resolution in problem situations.

Psychodrama as a therapeutic method was initiated and developed by Moreno (1972). Classically, the method is now applied in a wide variety of settings which range from mental health facilities through the military to education resources and even professional training. However, psychodrama has its roots in Moreno's informal work with children's play in the parks of Vienna, during his years as a student. Moreno established himself as a story- or tale-teller, and noticed how the children who gathered around him spontaneously acted out themes from their histories or from their fantasies. He observed that these children were able to express their feelings powerfully through role play, and noticed that the children's improvisations followed an observable process in which hostility diminished in favour of a blossoming of creativity.

These early observations formed the basis of Moreno's (1974) spontaneity-creativity theory and influenced the development of his therapy located philosophically in existentialism and based on an action method. In favouring active expression over repression, Moreno's ideas are in stark contrast to Freud's prohibition against the acting out of neurotic defences. Moreno moved on from his work with children to develop meetings with prostitutes, and further developed the ideas which formed the beginnings of group work as a psychotherapeutic method. Like many therapies, psychodrama offers the individual an opportunity for catharsis and relief, insight and self-understanding, making modifications of behaviour possible.

Unlike the Freudian preoccupations with the past and the client-centred focus on the present, 'Psychodrama is concerned with an individual's personal life, past, present or future; his interpersonal relationships, his feelings, his fears, his concerns, and his fantasies, and even his delusions and hallucinations' (Rabson-Hare 1975: 3).

Group therapy

Group therapy for children had its origins in the 1930s work of Slavson (1943), who facilitated activity groups for pre-pubertal children with behaviour problems. Although derived from psychoanalytic theory, Slavson's groups were non-interpretative and experiential. A desire for group acceptance was seen to serve the same function in the group as transference serves in individual therapy. The expression of conflicting feelings while sustaining a relationship with a permissive therapist was seen as the therapeutic means by which egocentricity could be eradicated.

Slavson was one of the first to stress the role of the conductor and the importance of the relationship as the foundation of therapy. From Slavson's early work a variety of group therapies utilising play as a therapeutic medium were developed in the psychoanalytic school. Later developments in the analytic tradition, based on the natural inclination of children and adolescents to form peer relationships, were to include Bion's (1984) analysis of the group, and Foulkes's (1948) introduction of talk to facilitate analysis through and by the group.

In Axline's (1947) original formulation of non-directive, client-centred play therapy she placed little emphasis on group therapy. Her acceptance of group therapy as an adjunct for the child in individual therapy was limited, and only in the case of children who were poorly socially adjusted did she acknowledge the merits of group therapy.

However, Ginott (1961) dealt more fully with therapy in a group context. In accordance with Slavson's formulation, Ginott considered the group setting to provide a corrective emotional experience. Through the group and the therapeutic relationship children are provided with an opportunity to experience a sense of belonging and understanding, to experience support, and to have opportunities for vicarious catharsis. In group therapy the child is forced to re-evaluate behaviour in terms of peer relationships. The group provides a more tangible setting in which the child can discover and experiment with different styles of relating to peers by externalising aspects of themselves onto other members and onto the group therapist. Finally, in the case of younger children, separation from mother was considered less problematic when other children were around.

Group analytic drama

Willis (1988) developed group analytic drama, a therapeutic method, used in the treatment of disturbed adolescents, in which the principles of group analysis in the Foulkes (1948; Foulkes and Anthony 1965) tradition is applied, and use is made of a dramatic method which lies between classical psychodrama and sociodrama.

The interaction in group analytic drama with adolescents is entirely verbal. This is based on the notion that adolescents use activity as a defence against change. The conductor assumes a low profile in the group analytic drama session, and the therapist facilitates the group members becoming therapists in their own right.

Action groups in therapy with adolescents

Loftus (1988) documented his use of action group methods in his work with adolescents presenting with a wide range of emotional and behavioural problems. Social skills groups are based on the assumption that social behaviour is learned and should therefore be facilitated and taught by structured methods. By contrast, action groups, with their origins in the Gestalt philosophy, focus primarily on emotions, and maintain that young people have both the responsibility for themselves and the resources and skills to deal with their problems.

The therapeutic task in action group therapy is to put young people in touch with their own resources by encouraging them to experience their feelings. Based on the Reichian assumption that feelings are held in the body, the group members are encouraged to experience their feelings by physically moving themselves. Action groups occur within a therapeutic environment in which clear boundaries and limits exist, and the leadership function is made overt. The locus of decision-making is a key therapeutic issue, with the decision to attend being located as a parental function. Decisions to make the personal changes which are necessary to facilitate a decision for discharge from the group rests squarely with the young person. The pace of action groups is fast, and the major focus is on facilitating the experience of feelings. Interpretations are not made, but an atmosphere of intimacy and closeness is facilitated and enhanced by the shared experience and feedback which occurs during the course of the group.

COMMONALITIES IN THE SPECTRUM OF THERAPIES WITH CHILDREN AND YOUNG PEOPLE

The therapeutic relationship

A common theme running through all therapies is the delineation, with various degrees of importance, of the role of the therapist and the nature of the therapeutic relationship. The therapeutic relationship is the primary tool of the therapist's 'trade'. Research indicates that therapist qualities (rather than the gender, age or physical appearance of the therapist), and the nature of the relationship developed in the course of therapy will have a powerful impact on the efficacy of therapy (Norcross 1986).

In the psychoanalytic tradition, the analyst classically assumed a role of emotional distance in order to promote the transference relationship, the primary vehicle of the analysis. In her work with children Anna Freud (1965) made reference to the role of the analyst in the child's pursuit of a new relationship. Such a relationship was seen to not only have a corrective emotional capacity, but was also considered to be the springboard from which deeper interpretations were made.

Rogers (1957) listed the ingredients of empathy, genuineness and unconditional positive regard as therapist prerequisites for bringing about therapeutic change. The therapeutic relationship is one characterised by faith, acceptance and respect. Commitment to the Transactional Analysis concept of 'Physis', a creative force aspiring to growth and perfection (Berne 1971) is an act of faith and a belief in the potential of the individual. A 'consumer response' to such a demonstration of faith is reflected in the following statement: 'You were the first person who believed in me – who didn't think I was all bad' (Moustakas 1953: 3). Stability and consistency in the therapeutic relationship are also important in facilitating change. Unconditional acceptance too is an important therapeutic ingredient in the journey to mental health. Clarkson (1990) illustrated five different kinds of psychotherapeutic relationship potentially available to the therapist (see Chapter 2 of this *Handbook*). These distinct treatment modalities are useful as an integrating meta-perspective on the essence of all therapeutic endeavours, therapy with children and adolescents being no exception. As a very minimum a 'working alliance' between therapist and client has to be forged. In the case of children and adolescents, this contractual agreement to embark on a course of therapy frequently involves a 'three-cornered' commitment to the therapeutic endeavour. The literal dependence of children on their caretakers is an important consideration in treatment planning, and regarding 'customership' as being located in those persons who separately or jointly have the authority, the need and the means is an important consideration in therapy with children and young people.

The therapist

The therapist's role is a demanding one. The therapist must continually be sensitive to, aware of and alert to the child, their issues, actions, verbalisations and therapeutic needs. In spite of the child or young person being the chief architect of their own therapy, it is incumbent on the therapist to facilitate the provision of an environment in which the child is permitted free expression, in the context of protection from a therapist prepared to exercise potency in the therapeutic endeavour. An examination by therapists of their therapeutic role and the skills and personal qualities which they bring to bear in the therapeutic relationship should be undertaken, both in the context of regular case review and of supervision. Training analyses have long been a prerequisite for those working in an analytic frame, and increasingly an emphasis is being placed on the importance of therapists' knowledge of their 'inner maps', and the nurturing and replenishing potential of personal psychotherapy. This is particularly pertinent in work with children and young people, which has the potential to reverberate powerfully with unresolved issues in the therapist's own life.

The child or young person

The child or young person entering therapy is, in most cases, in serious personal trouble. The distress of the child may be exhibited in the behavioural or emotional symptoms precipitating referral, and a careful dynamic diagnosis of the problems and the systems in which they are located is required. Therapy is not, however, reserved for those in 'serious personal trouble'. It has been used successfully with children with physical handicap (Cruickshank and Cowan 1948), for children suffering situational disturbances, and the categories delineated by Clarkson and Fish (1988).

The session

The therapy hour belongs to the child and to the child alone. It is the prerogative of the child or young person to determine the pace and direction of their therapy. However, it is the role of the therapist to ensure that the psychologically pertinent issues are addressed in a client-relevant manner.

The wider context

Consent to treatment and the way in which therapeutic content will be communicated to parents and others (teachers or care-workers where relevant) should be clarified in the process of negotiating the therapy contract. Respecting the ethic of confidentiality, whilst also taking account of the implications of the Children Act (1989) and the Access to Health Records Act (1990), often raises difficult issues for the therapist. Unless these issues are clarified during the initial contractual negotiations, they may interfere with the therapeutic process. In practice, many therapists negotiate permission to communicate the themes and general issues arising from the therapy rather than communicating exact therapeutic content. Issues involving the disclosure of child abuse always override the ethic of confidentiality.

Some therapists insist that if a child is accepted into treatment, one or both parents should also enter therapy. It is acknowledged that there are occasions on which children are presented as a 'foil' for difficulties in an associated system (Clarkson and Fish 1988). However, some propound that unless the core and background issues are addressed, anti-therapeutic forces are likely to overwhelm the child and negate any change achieved in therapy. Others question this notion, believing that having undergone personal change, the child will change in relation to the environment in which they live and, in so doing, acquire a stimulus value of their own, drawing changed perceptions and reactions. Generally, an awareness of the implications of the interaction between the child and the various systems which are relevant will require consideration when deciding on treatment direction and goals.

The treatment setting

Psychological therapies with children and young people are undertaken in a variety of settings. These may range from specially equipped consulting rooms to sparsely furnished offices. Wherever therapy is undertaken it is important that time, space and boundaries are safeguarded. Attention to the detail of safety is an important consideration in finalising the setting in which children and young people are seen.

The therapist must be sure that the issues highlighted in the diagnostic formulation will be appropriately addressed during the course of therapy. Clearly this necessitates therapist knowledge of the developmental relevance of the materials provided, and an ability to respond in ways which take account of both the cognitive capacity of the child and their level of developmental maturity.

CONCLUSION

Therapeutic endeavours with children and young people are wide and varied, requiring specialist training and expertise. Further scientific research into the efficacy of the psychological therapies with this target population is required before their undisputed validity is established. None the less, the anecdotal evidence of large numbers of children and young people who have undertaken a therapeutic journey continues to bear testimony to the creative capacity of these endeavours.

Early concepts developed in therapy continue to influence the field, though latterly increasing service demands have led to their modification, revision and replacement with new theory and enhanced therapeutic techniques and styles.

REFERENCES

Access to Health Records Act (1990) London: HMSO.
Allen, F. H. (1942) *Psychotherapy with Children*, New York: W. W. Norton.
Axline, V. M. (1947) *Play Therapy*, New York: Ballantine Books.
—— (1950) 'Play therapy experiences as described by child participants', *Journal of Consulting Psychology* 14: 53–63.
—— (1964) *Dibs: In Search of Self*, London: Gollancz.
Berne, E. (1971) *A Layman's Guide to Psychiatry and Psychoanalysis*, Harmondsworth: Penguin.
Bion, W. R. (1984) *Elements of Psychoanalysis*, London: Karnac.
Children Act (1989) London: HMSO.
Clarkson, P. (1990) 'A multiplicity of psychotherapeutic relationships', *British Journal of Psychotherapy* 7: 148–63.

—— (1992) 'Physis in transactional analysis', *Transactional Analysis Journal* 22(4): 202–09.

Clarkson, P. and Fish, S. (1988) 'Systemic assessment and treatment considerations in TA child psychotherapy', *Transactional Analysis Journal* 18(2): 123–32.

Cruickshank, W. M. and Cowan, E. L. (1948) 'Group therapy with physically handicapped children', *Journal of Educational Research* 39(4): 193–215.

Dorfman, E. (1955) 'Personality outcomes of client centred therapy', *Psychological Monographs, General and Applied* 72(3): 1–22.

Foulkes, S. H. (1948) *Introduction to Group-Analytic Psychotherapy: Studies in the Social Integration of Individuals and Groups*, London: Maresfield Reprints.

Foulkes, S. H. and Anthony, E. J. (1965) *Group Psychotherapy: The Psychoanalytic Approach*, Harmondsworth: Penguin Books.

Freud, A. (1946) *The Psychoanalytic Treatment of Children*, New York: International Universities Press.

—— (1965) *Normality and Pathology in Childhood*, New York: International Universities Press.

Freud, S. (1909) 'Analysis of a phobia in a five-year-old boy' ('Little Hans'), *Standard Edition*, vol. 10, London: Hogarth Press.

Ginott, H. G. (1961) *Group Psychotherapy with Children*, New York: McGraw-Hill.

Hug-Hellmuth, H. (1921) 'Zur Technik der Kinderanalyse', *Internationale Zeitschrift der Psychoanalyse* 7: 179–97.

Klein, M. (1932) *The Psychoanalysis of Children*, London: Hogarth Press.

—— (1975) *Envy and Gratitude and Other Works*, London: Hogarth Press.

Klein, M., Heimann, P. and Money-Kyrle, R. E. (1955) *New Directions in Psychoanalysis*, London: Tavistock.

Levy, D. (1939) 'Release therapy', *American Journal of Orthopsychiatry* 9: 731–6.

Loftus, M. L. (1988) 'Moving to change: action groups in an out-patient setting', *Journal of Adolescence* 11: 217–29

Lowenfeld, M. (1935) *Play in Childhood*, London: Gollancz.

Moreno, J. L. (1972) *Psychodrama*, New York: Boston House.

—— (1974) 'The creativity theory of personality: spontaneity, creativity and human potentialities,' pp. 73–84 in I. A. Greenberg (ed.) *Psychodrama: Theory and Therapy*, vol. 33, London: Condor/Souvenir Press.

Moustakas, C. (1953) *Children in Play Therapy*, New York: Ballantine.

—— (1967) *Creativity and Conformity*, New York: Van Nostrand.

Norcross, J. C. (ed.) (1986) *Handbook of Eclectic Psychotherapy*, New York: Brunner/Mazel.

Pine, F. (1985) *Developmental Theory and Clinical Process*, London: Yale University Press.

Rabson-Hare, J. (1975) Psychodrama, Unpublished paper.

Rank, O. (1945) *Will Therapy and Truth and Reality*, New York: Knopf.

Rogers, C. R. (1951) *Client Centred Therapy*, Boston: Houghton Mifflin.

—— (1957) 'The necessary and sufficient conditions of therapeutic personality change', *Journal of Consulting Psychology* 21(2): 95–103.

Slavson, S. R. (1943) *An Introduction to Group Therapy*, New York: International Universities Press.

Taft, J. (1933) *The Dynamics of Therapy in a Controlled Relationship*, New York: Macmillan.

Trail, P. M. and Rowles, F. H. (1964) 'Nonverbal "thinking" in child psychotherapy', in M. Lowenfeld, P. M. Trail and F. H. Rowles (eds) *The Nonverbal 'Thinking' of Children and its Place in Psychotherapy*, London: Institute of Child Psychology.

Willis, S. (1988) 'Group analytic drama: a therapy for disturbed adolescents', *Group Analysis* 21: 153–68.

FURTHER INFORMATION

Association of Play Therapists
11 Hanover Street
Brighton
East Sussex BN2 2ST
Tel.: 0273 691166

The Institute for Arts and Therapy in Education
70 Cranwich Road
London N16 5JD
Tel.: 081 809 5866

Chapter 9B

Analytical psychotherapy with children

Miranda Passey

This chapter describes the work of child psychotherapists. It discusses what sorts of disorders can be treated by child psychotherapy, the settings in which child psychotherapists work, and the historical development and theoretical framework which underlie the work. There is a brief description of the training undertaken and some clinical examples to give a flavour of the child psychotherapist's approach. The wide range of consultative and supportive work offered to other professionals working with children is described.

A great variety of standpoints coexist within the general framework of present-day child psychotherapy. These are unified, however, by a fundamental belief that 'the immediate causes of psychological stress arise from internal conflict' (Reeves 1981: 271), whatever theoretical description may be given as the source of this conflict.

CHILDREN IN NEED

Children are especially vulnerable to disturbance; their emotional immaturity makes it difficult for them to discriminate between fantasy and reality. Events in childhood or within their families can either strengthen their capacity for healthy development or lead to self-destructive behaviour and a damaged capacity to make healthy relationships.

Up to 10 per cent of British children and young people (1.2 million) have some psychiatric or psychological problem which handicaps them for a year or more, and this percentage rises to 25 per cent in inner city areas. Of this 1.2 million at least 2 per cent (240,000) need psychiatric help.

There is increasing evidence that early effective intervention can be important in preventing adult mental ill health (Department of Health 1992). While many forms of intervention are available (family therapy, casework and so on), a high proportion (30 per cent) of those children referred to child psychotherapists (Beedell and Payne 1988) have failed to respond satisfactorily to other forms of treatment. Even when external changes have taken place, some children and young people are still unable to gain relief from their emotional disturbance because it is very deeply rooted.

THE CHILD PSYCHOTHERAPIST'S ORIENTATION

The chief concern of the child psychotherapist is the child's inner world. That is the subjective picture of people and things we all carry around within us, sometimes without being aware of it, and which may or may not sufficiently correspond to outward reality. The child psychotherapist attempts to help the patient understand his or her own situation and, in particular, any unconscious factors which may be contributing to the current difficulties. The aim is to help the patient come to terms with their past experience, their response to it, and their own present personality characteristics. This is achieved through the relationship the patient makes with their child psychotherapist, onto whom they transfer the attitudes and feelings that determine their relationships outside the psychotherapy. The psychotherapist endeavours to identify these attitudes and feelings and to put them to the child in such a way that they can see and feel them and, in the experience of them, make changes in the way they behave. Such changes do not imply that the child is enabled to put up with ill-treatment or abuse. Indeed, the child may become angry for the first time about what has happened or is happening, or become able to perceive correctly a situation of cruelty or abuse, however painful this may be.

External events may prove incomprehensible to children and be misinterpreted in terms of existing fears or worries. Divorce, family breakdown, the death of a parent or sibling are all experiences which may feed the child's picture of a baffling or hostile world where mistrust and hatred thrive.

WHO CAN BE TREATED?

Child psychotherapists treat children with a wide variety of difficulties and disorders. These range from symptoms arising from family breakdown, bereavement, child abuse, difficulties related to mental and physical handicap, developmental failure, behavioural problems, bed-wetting, soiling, eating or sleeping difficulties, school refusal, to severe conditions such as autism and anorexia.

In addressing the child's difficulties, child psychotherapists work closely with others to enable other aspects of the problem to be understood. This might involve arranging for help for the child's parents, for foster parents or others caring for the child, or addressing the needs of the family as a whole.

WHERE ARE CHILDREN SEEN?

Child psychotherapists work in a range of Health Service establishments, usually as part of inter-disciplinary teams, which may include child psychiatrists, clinical psychologists, family therapists, educational psychologists, social workers and others. These teams may be in Child and Family Treatment Centres (Child Guidance Clinics), Departments of Child and Family Psychiatry or Psychological Medicine, in hospitals, in special schools, in consultation centres for young people and in student health centres. Some also work in private practice.

WHO REFERS?

Referrals can come from GPs, teachers, social workers, paediatricians, from parents directly and from adolescents in their own right. These self-referrals often have the best outcome.

HISTORICAL DEVELOPMENT

A variety of developmental perspectives underpin theories and methods of psychotherapy with children; all are rooted in Freud's theories. Although the different trainings have particular orientations, in practice individual child psychotherapists tend to find a broad measure of agreement in their common aim of understanding children's communications and working together to bring to light the unconscious aspects of experience.

I propose to give a brief description of the development of two child psychotherapy perspectives, to indicate both how these methods of working sprang from adult analytic work and how they differ from them, so as to be able to reach children directly. Early child psychoanalysis contributed vitally to our understanding of children's emotional lives and to present-day practice.

Little Hans

Though Freud never treated a child directly himself, in the case of Little Hans (1909) he had the opportunity to study in depth a phobia in a five-year-old boy, through the boy's father. In common with other 'close adherents' of Freud, Hans's father had already been sending Freud observation of the child's sexual development before the onset of symptoms, and these enriched Freud's understanding of the way in which the difficulties developed. Freud enabled Hans's father to treat his son, by encouraging him to confide his fantasies, act out his hostility and describe his dreams. Together, Freud and Hans's father found a way of understanding this material and of talking to little Hans about it. Freud stresses that the father's position of trust and intimacy with his son is a crucial factor in making the treatment possible. As a result of this work of understanding and bringing to light the meaning of Hans's fears and anxieties, Hans seemed to have recovered from his symptoms. The treatment Freud supervised was essentially 'reconstructive' (Meltzer 1978); that is, aimed at an understanding of the pathology looking backwards at the internal meaning of significant events in the child's life.

The Oedipus complex

His work with adults, coupled with his researches into the sexual develop-ment of children, led Freud to the discovery of the crucial stage of emotional development known as the Oedipus complex. In simple terms, this is a normal stage of development when the young child desires the parent of the opposite sex, in rivalry with his father or mother, but at the same time loves and fears the retaliation of his rival in love. Freud emphasised how crucial it was for this conflict between desire, love and fear to be negotiated and resolved. If all proceeded well, the child's 'ego', the organising, reality-based part of the personality, would have mastered the instinctual 'I want it now' desires of the 'id'. The child would give up his immediate desire for his mother or father and postpone the satisfaction of his genital longings for the prospect of future rewards: 'When I'm grown up, I'll marry someone just like Daddy!' The healthy negotiation of this stage, he believed, would lay the foundation for future growth and personality development.

The infantile neurosis

Freud coined the term 'the infantile neurosis' to describe the conflicts engendered by the Oedipus complex. He believed that an unresolved infantile neurosis would be forgotten and repressed, but would form the basis for a reappearance in adult life of neurotic symptoms (Meltzer 1978).

In her pioneering work with children, which began in 1927, Freud's daughter Anna challenged critics' assumptions that the 'infantile neurosis', if it existed at all, was just a stage of development, and not to be interfered with. She took the view that disturbance in children which she could identify as stemming from unsuccessfully negotiating the Oedipus complex constituted neuroses in the proper sense – a source of intrapsychic conflict. At the start of her work, she saw the child analyst's primary task as that of helping to resolve the conflicts which arose directly as a result of the child's Oedipal longings (A. Freud 1986). In formulating the nature of the child's difficulties, Anna Freud and her followers would attempt to determine the stage of development which the child had reached (which she conceived of in terms of the oral, anal and genital stages) and to describe the earlier levels where the child might have retreated or become stuck because of the conflicts which this stage aroused.

Adapting the technique

In order to make psychotherapy with children effective, Anna Freud believed children would need a preparatory phase of analysis in order to build a trusting and positive relationship with the psychotherapist (this was later abandoned). She did not, at first, see the transference as equally important to child analysis because she believed it was precluded by the child's primary involvement with their parents, and felt the negative transference would be actively unhelpful, preventing the child from co-operating with treatment. Anna Freud also saw the child psychotherapist as having an implicitly educational role towards the child; for example, inherently influencing the child's attitudes or their conscience. These early views have been developed and altered in the light of experience, as have those of Melanie Klein.

Melanie Klein

For Melanie Klein, the child developed a sense of self as part of their earliest relationship with their mother, first experienced in the feeding situation. The taking in of food, comfort and good experiences were seen alongside the expulsion of urine and faeces, and of painful or fearful feelings. The baby could begin to organise a sense of themselves as a result of being responded to both physically and emotionally in a way which gave their experiences meaning, based on the mother's attempts to understand their different states of mind, and think about them.

The paranoid-schizoid position

As Klein described it, at the onset of life, the baby splits its good and bad feelings and experiences, as they cannot be tolerated or contained together by the immature ego. The good feelings maintain the baby's sense of being part of a mother who is wholly good. The bad, aggressive or destructive feelings which arise out of hunger or frustration are got rid of, projected, and are therefore experienced initially by the infant not as belonging to them but as coming from outside, thereby giving rise to terrifying persecutory experiences. For example, night terrors, anxieties about separation and difficulties about eating may all indicate feelings of persecution coming from projected hostile feelings. Her observations led Klein to describe this early 'position' (predominant mode of mental functioning) as the paranoid-schizoid position. As she conceived them, these positions overlap and are not superseded, as they continue to characterise our basic attitudes towards ourselves and others throughout life.

The depressive position

Gradually, the baby realises that the good mother who comforts and feeds them is the same mother whom they hate when angry and frustrated. This realisation brings feelings of guilt and concern at the aggression and phantasied attacks that they carried out on those they love. The struggle to maintain concern for others' welfare over predominant self-interest continues throughout life. The integration of these opposing feelings leads to a strengthening of the personality.

Theory to practice

Melanie Klein differed from Anna Freud in undertaking analytic therapy with extremely young children, as young as two years old. As she believed that anxiety, guilt and conflict were all present in the young child, and could be coherently expressed, they should be able to be addressed and described directly. This, she believed, would be a relief to the child.

Anna Freud believed that unconscious impulses and phantasies were at first unorganised and unavailable as raw data for conscious thought. Consequently she suggested that these impulses could only be reached by means of analysing the 'resistances' or defence mechanisms the child had erected against knowing about its feelings, thus allowing for the subsequent emergence of the unconscious content.

Play as communication

It was Klein's genius to see that play, as a way of communicating for a child, could replace adults' free association to words; also that the development of a direct and expressive way of talking was required, that could have meaning to the child, and would include using the child's own special words for such things as bodily functions and parts of the body (1932a and b).

> We soon find that the child brings as many associations to separate elements of play as adults do to the separate elements of their dreams. These separate play elements are indications to the trained observer, and as it plays the child talks as well and says all sorts of things that have the value of genuine associations.
>
> (Klein 1932a: 8)

Here is a vivid illustration of Klein's direct and expressive communication with a child. She describes her first session with Peter, aged three years and nine months:

At the beginning of his first session, Peter took the toy carriage and cars and put them first one behind the other and then side by side, and alternated this arrangement several times. In between he took two horse-drawn carriages and bumped one into another so that the horses' feet knocked together and said, 'I've got a new little brother called Fritz.' I asked him what the carriages were doing. He answered, 'That's not nice' and stopped bumping them together at once, but started again quite soon. Then he knocked the toy horses together in the same way. Upon which I said, 'Look here, the horses are two people bumping together.' At first he said, 'No, that's not nice', but then 'Yes, that's two people bumping together'. The material develops from here as Mrs Klein links his statement about Fritz's birth with his curiosity about how Fritz came, which he thinks is because of two people bumping together: 'You thought to yourself that Daddy and Mummy bumped their thingummies together and that is how your little brother Fritz came.' Peter's play continues to describe his phantasies of his parents' intercourse, and what it led to.

(Klein 1932a: 17)

As this passage indicates, Klein carefully gathers evidence before she suggests to Peter that the two carriages bumping together represent Mummy and Daddy. Child psychotherapists do not jump to conclusions, but carefully gather clues to help them understand the child's communications.

Developments and modifications

Klein's direct experience and observations opened up the study of some of the more primitive states of mind. This enlarged the scope and range of both adult and child psychotherapists' work to allow for the treatment of psychotic and 'borderline' children (Tustin 1969) as well as neurotic ones, although with some important modifications of technique. Tustin (1990, 1993) has been a pioneer in this field. Alvarez's (1992) book *Live Company: Psycho-analytic Psychotherapy with Autistic, Borderline, Deprived and Abused Children* is a brilliant example of the development and achievements of this sort of work.

Differences between child analysis and child psychotherapy

As work developed, psychoanalytic child psychotherapy became distinguished from child analysis. The main differences were that, while child analysis aimed at the transformation of the personality, child psychotherapy focused on the removal of symptoms.

Practical developments

The impact of the Second World War led to fundamental developments in the understanding of the meaning of separation and bereavement for children. The films made by James and Joyce Robertson (1972) showing the effects of separation from parents are still compelling today. They showed the crucial difference that might be made by the provision of good substitute care for a child faced with a separation, and the disastrous effect of such separation in a context where there was a constant change of caretaker for the child. Bowlby's research (1951, 1969) brought into vital focus the importance of a continuous, loving relationship between mother and baby; although this was later misused to suggest that mothers should never leave their children. Linked in with this work, it became possible to see how much the whole emotional context of the family could contribute to a child's difficulties. The establishment of multidisciplinary teams in Child Guidance Clinics which became more widespread after the war allowed for the concurrent treatment or support of a child's parents.

TRAINING IN CHILD PSYCHOTHERAPY

In 1928, Margaret Lowenfeld, one of the pioneers in child psychotherapy, established a children's centre in London where play was observed and studied. In 1933 she set up a training here for a small number of child psychotherapists. In 1935 her department became the Institute of Child Psychology, and this training continued until the close of the ICP in 1978 (Lowenfeld 1935).

The Anna Freud training dates from 1948, and the Tavistock (Kleinian) training from 1948, when it was set up to address the need for an analytical training for non-medical personnel practising psychotherapy in clinics.

The application of Jungian ideas to child psychotherapy arose from the work of Dr Michael Fordham at the London Child Guidance Clinic before the war (Astor 1988). Fordham's writings (1957, 1977, 1985) explain the development of his ideas about the treatment of children. A Jungian training was established in 1973.

The British Association of Psychotherapy child training course was started in the early eighties in association with a body well established in training adult psychotherapists. This training represents the 'middle' or 'independent' school of thought whose theoretical position embraces some of both Anna Freudian and Kleinian viewpoints, and whose stance is perhaps most fully represented by the work of Winnicott (1981).

Child psychotherapy in the United Kingdom has been organised since 1949 under the Association of Child Psychotherapists, which has members from four recognised training schools and two new provisionally recognised training schools. These are listed on page 191. The trainings are recognised by the Department of Health. The ACP is also the designated authority for the European Community.

Prerequisites for training

The basic prerequisites for training are an honours degree and professional experience in a relevant field such as education, social work, medicine and psychology. Following this, the training lasts a minimum of four years. The trainee undergoes a personal psychoanalysis, preferably five times weekly.

Pre-clinical training

The training falls into two parts, pre-clinical and clinical. During the pre-clinical years, along with the study of psychoanalytic theory and developmental research, the trainee will probably be involved in work in some other related field of work with children. During this time the trainee will undertake detailed observations of infants and young children and their families. In practice, each trainee follows an infant for the first two years of its life, and a young child for a year – making weekly visits for an hour at a time and writing up observations in depth. Each student's observations are then discussed in seminars. The work in these baby observation seminars can have a profound impact on the trainees, and deepens their conviction about the power of unconscious processes and the rich meanings inherent in non-verbal communication. This work develops in the trainee the capacity to observe and think about initially confusing or incomprehensible states of being encountered in the infant. The observations also provide a model for understanding the process of emotional growth and development in depth. As well as studying the unique impact of each child's personality on its family and environment, the observer is also introduced to the powerful experience of the counter-transference, as they discover that their own feelings are a useful source of information about what they are observing. This work has been described in *Closely Observed Infants* (Miller *et al.* 1989), and wider interest in infant observation is spreading due to the work done by child psychotherapists.

Work discussion

Trainees also bring their current work for discussion in work experience seminars. Here students are introduced to the application of psychoanalytic ideas to the different kinds of work with children they may be undertaking; for example, work in children's homes, individual casework with children in care, or work in a day nursery.

Trainees are able to explore different aspects of communication with children, and can study the meaning of behaviour and interaction, and the significant impact that working with particular children has on the worker, which can become a vital ingredient in understanding the communications of the child.

Clinical training

The second part of the training involves intensive (three times weekly) psychotherapeutic work with three children of different ages and developmental stages – a young child, a latency child and an adolescent. Trainees also see a number of non-intensive cases weekly. They also gain experience of working with parents and families, of doing assessments for psychotherapy and in offering brief counselling to adolescents and young people. All clinical work is carried out under the supervision of a senior child psychotherapist. When the training requirements have been satisfactorily carried out, the candidate is eligible for membership of the Association of Child Psychotherapists.

WHAT CHILD PSYCHOTHERAPISTS ACTUALLY DO

Setting up treatment

Child psychotherapists see children once weekly; or more frequently, where appropriate to the child's needs and to clinical resources. A child psychotherapist will usually carry out an assessment of perhaps three sessions. This is in order to gain some first-hand picture of the child and their difficulties and, by giving the child a direct experience of what psychotherapy is like, to give them a flavour of what is involved and to establish whether they can make use of this form of treatment.

The child psychotherapist first meets with the parents to hear their description of symptoms and events, to gather a valuable early history of the child, and of course to give them a chance to meet the person who will be treating their child. In this meeting the psychotherapist will also be able to explain the boundaries of treatment, and address the anxieties and doubts the parents may have.

In this meeting the child psychotherapist also explains that the content of the child's sessions are generally confidential, which will allow the child to explore painful or hostile feelings without the fear that these will be disclosed to their parents, whom they also love and on whom they depend.

Parental support

With our increasing awareness of the power of the family system to affect its members and sometimes to work against the improvement of an individual member, in the treatment of children consideration of the needs of the child's parents and the rest of the family is vital. Where possible, another worker will offer the parents or family regular appointments to help them with their own difficulties.

The setting

The child psychotherapist aims to provide a consistent and reliable setting for the child. This comprises the same, simply furnished room, available at the same regular time, for the same length of time; and the regular presence of the psychotherapist without interruptions and without avoidable alteration to the regular pattern of sessions. Holiday breaks are carefully prepared for and much advance notice is given.

The room should have simple furniture, if possible, access to water, and should be safe for the child to explore. It should not contain intimate or personal items belonging to the psychotherapist or drawings or materials belonging to other children, which would affect the nature of the child's transference. The aim of this consistency is to create conditions of reliability and predictability, which will allow the child to communicate and explore ideas in a context where they can feel reasonably sure that they will be contained both physically and emotionally.

These boundaries can, of course, also constitute frustrations which the child resents and seeks to destroy, thus also giving useful indication of the child's response to other boundaries or restrictions in the outside world.

The materials

Depending on the child's age, the child psychotherapist provides simple play materials for each child's exclusive use, contained within a separate box or drawer, which can be locked away or otherwise kept safe for the child between sessions. These materials are designed to facilitate expressive play, and as far as possible are simple and neutral. It is the understanding of the communication made by the play rather than simply the opportunity for free play which is therapeutically important. The materials might include small figures and animals, wild and domestic, fences, paper, crayons, scissors, glue, Sellotape, Plasticine, string, some small cars or trucks and bricks or building materials. For adolescents who find talking difficult, the provision of paper and crayons can provide a means of beginning communication.

Of course, some children cannot 'play' in any organised way, and the child psychotherapist's task is then to work with the states of mind, often of terror or confusion, which the child conveys (Hoxter 1988) in order to develop the capacity for symbolisation.

The technique

While adults use the capacity for words to express and communicate thoughts and feelings to others, children need to do this by playing. The young child may communicate by creating a three-dimensional play situation into which they can put themselves, or at least toys representing themselves or aspects of themselves. In this way, the child can describe or enact unbearable emotions or painful situations.

> Easing the impact of the child's anxieties by reassurance, guiding his instinctual drives along educational or creative lines, stimulating him with our own ideas, attempting to civilise his hostile impulses by control or by presenting him with our own values, and providing safe outlets for 'letting off steam' – all these aims can be undertaken by adults in sensitive rapprochement with a child. But these have no part in the Kleinian Child Psychotherapy technique, which aims to open the doors to the unconscious and scrutinize what can seem unacceptable or even unthinkable.
>
> (Hoxter 1988: 209)

Working from what the child says and does, and from the way the child is in the room, the psychotherapist attempts to understand the child's state of mind. This may be gathered from small, apparently insignificant details, or from powerful feelings stirred up in the child psychotherapist in relation to what is happening (or not happening) in the session.

The child psychotherapist has first to make sure that these feelings do not come from their own life and relationships. Of course, their own analysis is intended to enable them to separate the two. Given this, the feelings a child is able to evoke in their child psychotherapist can be an intense form of communication of otherwise unreachable states of mind in the child (Brenman-Pick 1988).

The child psychotherapist has to be receptive, to allow for the impact of the child's communications, both verbal and non-verbal. It can be very difficult to maintain this receptivity, perhaps under a barrage of violent speech or destructive behaviour in the room or of attempts to drown out the child psychotherapist's interpretations. An open state of mind relies most profoundly of all on the psychotherapist's self-knowledge, gained through their own analysis. This awareness allows for receptivity to their patients' more painful or unacceptable communications about parts of themselves.

Interpretations

Interpretations have to be based on the living evidence unfolding in the experience of each session. The timing of the interpretation is important, as what the psychotherapist says will have the most impact if it is most emotionally immediate for the child. There may be many aspects of the child's behaviour worthy of note, but what is actually said must correspond to the here-and-now of the session to enable the child to feel understood and to illuminate the meaning of their actions as they are engaged in them.

I want to give an example of a session with a ten-year-old boy, 'Eric'. I am not aiming to describe his treatment in any depth but to give a flavour of the work and the way in which he communicated his feelings before a holiday break, the second in the treatment. What a child makes of holidays or breaks in treatment is one very useful way of seeing how the child perceives themselves in relation to others. Do they feel rejected, or do they fear that they have damaged the psychotherapist, making them unable to continue?

Eric is in once-weekly treatment. He was referred for aggression at school, poor relationships at home and at school, failure to learn despite high intelligence, and a challenging of all authority. For large parts of his early life his mother was clinically depressed. He seems to have reacted to this by becoming 'impossible to manage', having tantrums which frightened and overwhelmed his mother, and spending much of his time pretending he was 'Superman'. His parents' relationship is a deeply dissatisfied one, with father feeling equally powerless to help Eric or to help his wife. There is a 'much easier' younger sister.

In Eric's sessions there is much evidence of his contempt which wrecks things for him, including an opportunity to use the helpful aspects of his parents, and often the potential usefulness of my interpretations. He finds it very hard to acknowledge any loving feelings, distancing them in himself – for example, by making a Valentine's Day card as a trick for another boy at school to give to someone he knew the boy liked, but without the boy's knowledge.

In this last session before a holiday break, Eric had been ill during the preceding week. He came into the room listlessly and sat slumped in his chair. He flashed open his jacket to reveal a glimpse of the T-shirt of his favourite football team, and muttered something, but wouldn't repeat it. I said something about his T-shirt and his giving me a glimpse of it and yet not letting me hear what he had said. Again, I could not hear his muttered words. I said that I couldn't hear him properly, and that I wondered if he was showing me something about a feeling of slipping out of touch with me because of the holiday, perhaps he was testing me out to see if I was really watching, listening or interested? In his cryptic, baffling communications perhaps he was both tantalising me and wondering if it was worth the effort in the last session before a break, as perhaps he felt *I* was tantalising *him* with my holiday absence.

Eric responded to this by moving from his chair to a chair at the table where his box is. He then spent some time carefully constructing a paper 'fortune teller', using a ruler I had got for him to make accurate measurements of paper. He abandoned his first one in distress, as he had made one black mark on it in a place clearly not intended. To him the 'mistake' seemed irreparable. I linked his upset at the one black mark's spoiling the fortune teller to his worries about damaging me, perhaps making me weary or depressed or needing a holiday, and how he had to abandon it completely as if it felt too awful.

In his second attempt (although he had made several in previous sessions), he couldn't seem to remember how to make the pockets into which the child inserts his fingers to make the fortune teller open like a mouth. I watched his struggles, finding myself thinking how closed up the paper construction seemed, how impossible to imagine how one could fold it so as to make the pockets. I felt he was showing me his sense that I was closed off to him in the holiday, there would be no way in. He responded by asking me if I had seen a *Streetfighter* film. When I asked him to tell me about it, he commented that I didn't watch much television, and I suggested that he was wondering what I did do when I wasn't there with him, and what I would be doing over the holiday. Was there anything we could share (a 'way in' to me)? He then began to construct the pockets and write the 'fortunes'. These were 'You will meet a tall dark man' (he is small and blond), and 'A dog will bite your trousers'. He said they were meant to be 'secret' but also asked for more ideas as he couldn't think of any. I suggested that 'fortunes' indicated his thoughts and mixed feelings about what would be happening for both of us in the holidays. Part of him wanted to hurt me or bite me for going away, part of him hoped for good things for me, part of him was very curious about who else there was in my life, the 'tall dark man' who might take his place or absorb my interest. These thoughts seemed to amuse and interest him without his having to be contemptuous of them, and I felt he was able to face the holiday in a more positive frame of mind.

The development I can see in him will, I hope, lead to his being able to form better relationships with his family and at school, and prevent him from discouraging their best efforts on his behalf.

Interpretations may have several functions. They may begin a sorting out of powerful, frightening or confusing feelings the child has depicted – naming the confusion and making it available for thought. They may describe in simple terms the way in which the child seems to be experiencing the psychotherapist. When a psychotherapist can gather impressions together, they may make an interpretation which can link the here-and-now way in which the relationship between psychotherapist and patient is proceeding to significant experiences in the child's past which may be colouring what is seen to be happening now. Understanding the impact of past experience which can come alive in this way through repeated interpretations in different but related situations can enable the child to become more aware of the difference between the past and reality, to think about the fantasies which may have distorted his perception of reality, and to come to terms with both.

Much of the time, unfolding themes or the meaning of a particular piece of play may need to be held in mind by the psychotherapist for some time, until the most appropriate moment comes to put them together for the child. Often the psychotherapist may not know what is 'going on' and may have to bear states of confusion or fear with and on a child's behalf until some understanding can be gained and expressed. This process also provides a model for the processing of emotional experience for the child, of 'containing' it (Bion 1962), which may in time become part of the child's own mental capacities to contain and understand.

THE AIMS OF PSYCHOTHERAPY

By means of an attentive presence, the psychotherapist aims to provide an 'internal mental space' for the patient in which he and his communications can be thought about. Her interpretations make links between his behaviour, feelings and anxieties, and also describe the nature of the here-and-now relationship he is making with her. Gradually, if all goes well, the child will integrate an understanding, thinking capacity for themselves. Their ability to sort out and come to terms with different, previously unthinkable aspects of their personality and experience will in turn diminish their fears of external persecutors and strengthen their sense of self. The child becomes capable of a greater capacity for concern for others, and as their internal world changes, they are enabled to make more positive relationships in the outside world. To illustrate some of these issues, I want to describe the effect of psychotherapy on Kay.

Difficulties related to mourning

Kay was referred to me by her GP at the age of five. Her own mother had died of leukaemia on Christmas Eve when Kay was three-and-a-half. She had seemed unaffected by the death (according to her father), and he thought she was too young to have made much of it. Within a year the father remarried, and it was her developing relationship with this new stepmother, who really made enormous efforts to reach Kay, that made her feel sufficiently safe for her difficulties to emerge. She was clingy and had bouts of uncontrollable weeping. She seemed cut off at school and was terrified of rain, of baths, showers and any running water, and seemed to become frozen with fear especially when going to the lavatory.

In our early sessions (I saw her three times a week), Kay showed me by her frightened looks and her miserable attempts to alter drawings to cover up anything I had referred to, how persecuting she felt my presence to be. Gradually this began to shift and she began to look at me for reassurance as she drew something frightening, as if beginning to trust that there might be something helpful about my attempts to understand. She drew frightening things. Bodies in coffin-shaped boats surrounded by fire, scenes with a dangerous witch in them who, she said, wanted to kill her and cook her for her husband's dinner, children being spirited away by this same witch with no chance of escape. Gradually we could understand that she felt me to be a potentially persecuting witch, and that this was connected to fears that her dead mother would come back to attack and murder her with 'black rain', as she called it.

Kay feared that her mother had died because Kay had damaged her in some way, or at least failed to keep her alive. Perhaps she also confused in her mind her normal, infantile demands, seeing these as being too much for her mother. She drew a picture of a lady having a shower and, as I watched, drew in the 'black rain'. She and I together worked out that this hail was like the 'pooh' she didn't feel mother had been able to manage. Mother's loss had in fact occurred at Kay's developmental stage of being preoccupied with toilet training. This material threw some light on her fear of water, which she felt became contaminated with wee and pooh, and her fear of her real waste products when she went to the toilet, as if they were potentially extremely dangerous and unmanageable. The fantasy was at times inseparable from reality.

Gradually Kay became able to play with the farm and wild animals, using drawing less. At first the scenes she created showed the animals all muddled up and uncertainly protected by a male caretaker who was often asleep or absent, leaving the animals in great danger. It seemed that this caretaker vividly represented the father who she felt had 'allowed' mother to die. However, she was gradually able to allow for the possibility of something more hopeful. The part of a session I describe shows how vividly she responded to my interpretation. This was a Monday session following a weekend break.

Kay arranged the animals in a long procession with the families all muddled up, saying, 'It doesn't matter because they're all friends'. She said they were all going somewhere because of the man; he always wanted them to do things or go out to places when they didn't want to, and they didn't like it. I suggested that perhaps she was seeing me as the 'man' who made her come for her session when she didn't want to, especially with a weekend to get through, and that this made her not want to come again, at least with a part of herself.

She responded to this by getting out some fences. She said there were people in the house who put food out for the animals because they knew they were coming, and the animals had thought there was nothing there but houses and people asleep in them.

It seems that, in response to my interpretation, she is able to modify her expectation that there will be nothing there for her when she comes and that I will be like the people asleep, unthinking and unprepared. She then feels that I can 'feed' her and think about her needs.

Gradually her sense of persecution lessened. In her play she was able to protect the vulnerable animals and allow important food supplies to be shared out fairly between the animals. It seemed that this indicated her feeling that there could be 'enough' for her in the sessions, and that there could be enough for others, the beginning of a capacity for concern. As she began to tackle an awareness of the power of her destructive rage and her fear that it was dangerous to take the good things she might be offered, she explained to me (indicating the crocodile), 'When he's hungry, he's not nice, he'll eat anyone, even his best friend'. Gradually this crocodile part of herself became more manageable. She began to experience a delight in 'putting things right', which I think indicated a renewed hope that the fantasied damage and destruction which she felt had been confirmed in her inner world by the real death of her mother could be repaired, and her inner world began to be restored.

Work with adolescents

Work with adolescents poses particular challenges and may make extra demands on the psychotherapist's capacity to sustain a therapeutic role (also see Chapter 10 of this *Handbook* regarding adolescents). Adolescents are often in turmoil, with conflicting states of mind, as they struggle to establish their sexual and personal identity. They often seem to need to set themselves up in opposition to parents and figures in authority, and this can colour the transference relationship to the psychotherapist.

Adolescents are particularly prone to acting out their intense emotions rather than being able to think about them, and this can lead to threats of suicide and sexual experimentation which brings the risk of unwanted pregnancy and disease. In the adolescent's conflict between identification with their parents and separation from them, and their anxieties about entering the wider world, they may bring very highly charged material to sessions, or attend spasmodically or not at all, leaving the psychotherapist worried.

Issues relating to the adolescent patient's uncertainties about being able to manage all the different tasks of adulthood can also produce wishes to retreat and regress. Intense and unresolved feelings belonging to infancy can be re-evoked. This work can also provoke correspondingly intense anxieties in the psychotherapist about their capacity to contain the adolescent patient. The fears stirred up by such work are also an indication of what a frightening process adolescence can be. Because of these difficulties, it may be especially hard to sustain long-term treatment with adolescents. Although this work involves a different focus, sometimes brief work can address a particular moment of crisis with good results, because repressed experiences and unconscious fears may be more available for understanding and working through (Wittenberg 1988).

How long does treatment last?

The length of a child's treatment will often depend on external circumstances and available supports for psychotherapy, as well as on ideal therapeutic goals. Although, of course, there are wide individual variations, in a study of child psychotherapists' working practices (Beedell and Payne 1988) it was found that 59 per cent of individual psychotherapy treatments were closed within eighteen months, and 76 per cent within two years. The preliminary study (Beedell and Payne 1988) suggested that there is a satisfactory outcome in 74 per cent of cases.

Short-term psychotherapy

This might range from three to ten sessions.

> Sometimes very short-term psychotherapy can be a great help. This holds true when the child is aware of the problem, the difficulty is actually near conscious level, and there is good co-operation. If a child or adolescent is seen at a time of crisis when he very much wishes to focus and work on his problem, it may be that long-term psychotherapy is unnecessary.
>
> (Lush 1988: 84)

This kind of work has been described by Wittenberg (1988).

DEVELOPING FIELDS OF WORK

Child psychotherapists have made pioneering developments in working with mentally handicapped children (Sinason 1992) and with children with severe emotional deprivation (Boston and Szur 1983). In addition to the work already described, child psychotherapists work with severely ill and dying children and their families (Judd 1989), in departments of oncology, paediatric endocrinology and orthopaedics, and in a regional burns unit. Recent extensions of fields of work include those with refugee children, children who have been the victims of torture or religious persecution, and children who have been involved in natural disasters. There is also a growing field of work with parents and infants in which child psychotherapists apply the knowledge gained from intensive work to address the difficulties that parents may experience with infants, for example with feeding and sleeping. Such difficulties can often be resolved in a few sessions and interventions of this kind may well forestall problems, which, unaddressed, might lead to more serious ongoing symptoms. An example of this is the Under-Fives Counselling Service with Infant–Parent Couples at the Tavistock Clinic, where parents and infants may be seen for up to five sessions at short notice.

Another means of extending fields of work is through teaching or supervisory and consultative work with other professional groups or institutions. For example, a child psychotherapist working alongside nurses and paediatricians in a neonatal intensive care unit can support the staff and parents in thinking about the experiences of very ill babies, often in incubators (Earnshaw 1981; Bender and Swan-Parente 1983). This work enables staff to suggest alterations in nursing or management practices which have direct benefit for the babies, or help parents feel they can make more contact with babies from whom they may feel both actually and emotionally cut off, and to whom they may also feel useless.

Professionals who use child psychotherapists in a consultative capacity may include residential care workers, social workers, health visitors, day nursery staff, neonatal intensive care nurses, midwives and teachers in special schools. Such work may also be carried out with GPs, paediatricians, occupational therapists and play therapists.

People working with disturbed children in a variety of settings often find it helpful to be able to describe the impact that these children have on them, and to explore the ways in which the child's behaviour affects their capacity to respond in a consistently helpful way.

Publications

Another significant aspect of far-reaching work being carried out by child psychotherapists is in writing for parents and others about children's normal development and their special difficulties. An example of this is the series of books *Understanding Your Baby* by Lisa Miller (1992) and *Your One-Year-Old* by Deborah Steiner (1991). Another book with broad application is *Through the Night: Helping Parents and Sleepless Infants* by Dilys Daws (1989), which tackles the enormously widespread problems of sleeping difficulties in children.

Research

Psychotherapy with children is still developing, and research into its methods and outcome is being undertaken – for example, the current (1993) Anna Freud Centre project, examining nearly 800 completed psychoanalytic treatment cases. This project aims to examine variables predictive of outcome and to generate hypotheses and measures to be used in a prospective study of treatment processes and outcomes. It also aims to identify particular groups for further study of their treatment, such as children with specific learning difficulties or with physical handicaps. Other projects aim to examine individual psychotherapy with sexually abused children.

Research has been done into the evaluation of psychotherapy with particular groups of children; for example, those fostered and adopted (Lush, Boston and Grainger 1991). Other fields of research with mentally handicapped children (Sinason 1992) are being developed. As another example, the study by Beedell and Payne (1988) retrospectively rated outcome in terminated cases, and there are further projects in progress.

SUMMARY

In this chapter, I have tried to describe the historical and theoretical development of psychotherapy with children, the training and orientation of child psychotherapists, and have given some examples showing how psychotherapy with children is carried out. I have discussed some of the wider applications of the work of child psychotherapists, which reaches parents and children through publications and brief work, and explained how consultation can contribute to the thinking of other professionals working with children in many settings. Finally, I have mentioned recent developments in the research and evaluation of practice and methodology.

APPENDIX

Child psychotherapy training:

The Tavistock Clinic
120 Belsize Lane
London NW3 5BA
Orientation: Kleinian and Post-Kleinian
Status: NHS

The Anna Freud Centre for Psycho-Analytical Study and Treatment of Children
21 Maresfield Gardens
London NW3 5SH
Orientation: Freudian and Contemporary Freudian
Status: Registered charity

Society of Analytical Psychology
1 Daleham Gardens
London NW3 5BV
Orientation: Jungian
Status: Private

British Association of Psychotherapists
37 Mapesbury Road
London NW2 4HJ
Orientation: Independent
Status: Registered charity

Scottish Institute of Human Relations
56 Albany Street
Edinburgh EH1 3QR
Orientation: Psychoanalytic, but non-specific
Status: Registered charity

Birmingham Trust for Psychoanalytic Psychotherapy
96 Park Hill
Moseley
Birmingham B13 8DS
Orientation: Kleinian and Post-Kleinian
Status: Registered Charity

REFERENCES

Alvarez, A. (1992) *Live Company: Psycho-analytic Psychotherapy with Autistic, Borderline, Deprived and Abused Children*, London: Routledge.
Astor, J. (1988) 'A conversation with Dr Michael Fordham', *Journal of Child Psychotherapy* 14(1): 3–11.
Beedell, C. and Payne, S. (1988) 'Making the case for child psychotherapy: a survey of the membership and activity of the Association of Child Psychotherapists', commissioned by the ACP, Unpublished manuscript.
Bender, H. and Swan-Parente, A. (1983) 'Psychological and psychotherapeutic support of staff and parents in an intensive care baby unit', in J. A. Davis, M. P. M. Richards and M. R. C. Robinson (eds) *Parent–Baby Attachment in Premature Infants*, London: Croom Helm, pp. 165–76.
Bion, W. R. (1962) *Learning from Experience*, London: Heinemann.
Boston, M. and Szur, R. (1983) *Psychotherapy with Severely Deprived Children*, London: Routledge.
Bowlby, J. (1951) *Maternal Care and Mental Health*, Geneva: World Health Organization.
—— (1969) *Attachment*, London: Hogarth Press.
Brenman-Pick, I. (1988) 'Working through in the counter-transference', pp. 34–47 in *Melanie Klein Today*, vol. 2, London: Tavistock/Routledge.
Daws, D. (1989) *Through the Night: Helping Parents and Sleepless Infants*, London: Free Association Books.
Department of Health (1992) *The Health of the Nation* (Green Paper), London: HMSO.
Earnshaw, A. (1981) 'Action consultancy', *Journal of Child Psychotherapy* 7(2): 149–51.
Fordham, M. (1957) *New Developments in Analytical Psychology*, London: Routledge & Kegan Paul.

—— (1977) 'Maturation of a child within a family', *Journal of Analytic Psychology* 22(2): 57–77.

—— (1985) 'Explorations into the self', *Library of Analytic Psychology*, vol. 7, London: London Academic Press.

Freud, A. (1986) *The Ego and the Mechanisms of Defence* (C. Baines, trans.), London: Hogarth Press (first published 1936).

Freud, S. (1909) 'Analysis of a phobia in a five-year-old boy' ('Little Hans'), pp. 167–305 in J. Strachey (ed.) (A. Strachey and J. Strachey, trans.), *The Standard Edition of the Complete Works of Sigmund Freud, vol. 8: Case Histories I*, London: Hogarth Press.

Hoxter, S. (1988) 'Play and communication', pp. 202–31 in M. Boston and D. Daws (eds) *The Child Psychotherapist*, London: Karnac.

Judd, D. (1989) *Give Sorrow Words: Working with a Dying Child*, London: Free Association Books.

Klein, M. (1932a) *The Psychoanalysis of Children*, London: Hogarth Press.

—— (1932b) *The Technique of Early Analysis*, vol. 2, London: Hogarth Press.

Lowenfeld, M. L. (1935) *Play in Childhood*, London: Gollancz.

Lush, D. (1988) 'The child guidance clinic', pp. 63–85 in M. Boston and D. Daws (eds) *The Child Psychotherapist*, London: Karnac.

Lush, D., Boston, M. and Grainger, E. (1991) 'Evaluation of psychoanalytic psychotherapy with children: therapist assessments and predictions', *Journal of Psychoanalytical Psychotherapy* 5(3): 191–234.

Meltzer, D. (1978) 'The case history of Little Hans', p. 52 in *The Kleinian Development*, part 1, London: Clunie Press.

Miller, L. (1992) *Understanding Your Baby*, London: Rosendale Press.

Miller, L., Rustin, M., Rustin, M. and Shuttleworth, J. (1989) *Closely Observed Infants*, London: Duckworth.

Reeves, A. C. (1981) 'Freud and child psychotherapy', pp. 251–71 in D. Daws and M. Boston (eds) *The Child Psychotherapist*, London: Wildwood House.

Robertson, J. and Robertson, J. (1972) 'Young children in brief separation: a fresh look', in A. J. Solnit, P. D. Neubauer, S. Abrams and A. S. Dowling (eds) *The Psycho-analytic Study of the Child*, vol. 26, London and New Haven: Yale University Press.

Sinason, V. (1992) *Mental Handicap and the Human Condition: New Approaches from the Tavistock*, London: Free Association Books.

Steiner, D. (1991) *Your One-Year-Old*, London: Rosendale Press.

Tustin, F. (1969) 'Autistic processes', *Journal of Child Psychotherapy* 2(3).

—— (1990) *The Protective Shell in Children and Adults*, London: Karnac.

—— (1993) *Autistic States in Children* (rev. edn), London: Routledge.

Winnicott, D. W. (1981) *The Child, the Family and the Outside World*, Harmondsworth: Penguin (first published 1964).

Wittenberg, I. (1988) 'Counselling young people', pp. 136–59 in M. Boston and D. Daws (eds) *The Child Psychotherapist*, London: Karnac.

RECENT PUBLICATIONS BY CHILD PSYCHOTHERAPISTS

Alvarez, A. (1992) *Live Company: Psycho-analytic Psychotherapy with Autistic, Borderline, Deprived and Abused Children*, London: Routledge.

Boston, M. and Daws, D. (eds) (1988) *The Child Psychotherapist*, London: Karnac.

Daws, D. (1989) *Through the Night: Helping Parents and Sleepless Infants*, London: Free Association Books.

Fonagy, P., Moran, G. and Higgett, A. (1989) 'Psychological factors in the self-management of insulin dependent diabetes mellitus in children and adolescents', in J. Wardle and S. Pearce (eds) *The Practice of Behavioural Medicine*, Oxford: Oxford University Press.

Judd, D. (1989) *Give Sorrow Words: Working with a Dying Child*, London: Free Association Books.

Miller, L., Rustin, M., Rustin, M. and Shuttleworth, J. (1989) *Closely Observed Infants*, London: Duckworth.

Sinason, V. (1992) *Mental Handicap and the Human Condition: New Approaches from the Tavistock*, London: Free Association Books.

Szur, R. and Miller, S. (eds) (1991) *Extending Horizons: Psychoanalytic Psychotherapy with Children, Adolescents and Families*, London: Karnac.

FURTHER INFORMATION

The Association of Child Psychotherapists
Burgh House
New End Square
London NW3

The Child Psychotherapy Trust
21 Maresfield Gardens
London NW3 5SH

Chapter 10

Adolescent psychotherapy

Robert Jezzard

It is not difficult to find young people during the adolescent phase of development who seem to 'need' psychotherapy or counselling. The need is usually defined by a concerned adult, but the young person may have different views! Perhaps less frequently a young person may themselves declare a wish for help but find that the relevant adults, whether they be parents, other carers or professionals, are either unsupportive or even actively against the idea. Therefore, the mutually agreed decision between all concerned that psychotherapy is 'a good idea' cannot be assumed, however obvious the 'need' appears to be.

There are a number of prerequisites that need to be satisfied before psychotherapy with young people can start. Once it has been established and agreed that psychotherapy is both desirable and acceptable then it can begin. But it is then that the psychotherapist's real difficulties may start! There are further hurdles to be crossed before the useful components of theory and technique can be utilised. Some understanding of the adolescent's way of dealing with the world is required, but of even greater importance is a capacity on the psychotherapist's part to be resilient, flexible without being unprofessional, and, at the most basic level, being able to 'survive' in a therapeutic context with the young person without being totally humiliated and de-skilled. The 'rules' of therapy are not well understood by many young people, and they do not readily take for granted that those put forward by even the most benevolent of psychotherapists are necessary or appropriate.

WORKING WITH TROUBLED ADOLESCENTS

Anyone who has attempted to understand what is troubling a distressed but inarticulate adolescent will be able to describe the feelings of helplessness that can arise. To offer advice and an understanding ear and to have them summarily rejected or ignored leaves the 'helpful' adult bemused, humiliated and frequently angry. Many of us can still hear the phrase 'You just don't fucking understand!' ringing in our ears. The desire on adults' part may then be to just let them get on with it. However, it must be remembered that it is often the failure on the part of adults that has contributed to the development of the problem in the first place. In these circumstances, the psychotherapist may feel that he is having to bear the total burden of guilt of all those adults who have somehow failed to meet the hopes and expectations of the young person. It is easy to feel angry on behalf of your client, even to the point of giving voice to views about the shortcomings of their parent(s). This may lead to an extraordinary display of loyalty by the young person to even the most apparently abusive of adults. It is rare to come across a parent who has not tried to do their best to bring up their child. They may have been misguided or brought their own unresolved issues into their child's life, but none the less they will have wanted to be a good parent. At present, more than ever, parents are exhorted to take greater responsibility for the behaviour of their children, but we all know that is easier said than done. It is incumbent upon the professionals to retain some humility in their dealings with the parents or carers. In the face of turbulent or painful emotions, the task is one of 'survival', for parent and psychotherapist alike. There may be few tangible rewards for the effort or indications that either has got anywhere near 'getting it right'.

Theoretical models of adolescent development and therapy rarely offer much in the way of practical advice about how to cope with a first interview, let alone continue a constructive long-term professional relationship with a young person. Whether it be trying to elicit psychotic phenomenology from a bemused or frustrated teenager thought to be suffering from schizophrenia or whether it be trying to understand why an overdose has been taken by a young person who hides her face and remains mute, some practical tips are required to help the adult remain in contact with the young person with some confidence. Psychodynamic theories, however well understood, may seem totally irrelevant if the client is hostile or uncooperative; practical ways of working have to be found. A firm, secure anchor with a rope that offers some flexibility and leeway is required for a teenager who is being tossed around in a sea of turbulent emotions. Too rigid or restricting a hold may pull the young person under. Too insecure and changeable a base may allow the young person to drift too far away or drown.

PREREQUISITES FOR PSYCHOTHERAPY

An understanding of developmental issues and a knowledge of the law are first required. Adolescence is often described as a time of identity acquisition (Erikson 1968). A secure identity is not an ideal that is acquired exclusively in adolescence, but during a process that occurs throughout life, and which happens to present crucial tasks in adolescence. It is the time when 'given' values from family and school are re-evaluated. It is the time when alternative beliefs are more obviously on offer, and these must be explored in the struggle to individuate from parents. It is a time of considerable change. Not only is it a time of physical and sexual development or a time in which social relationships are explored, but also a time in which there are cognitive changes. The capacity to reason, to think ahead and gain a perspective of the future, and to make connections between present and past events may develop during this period; but for each young person the process is slightly different and the stage of development may not match the chronological age. This must be borne in mind during the psychotherapy sessions; an immature seventeen-year-old may require a more structured method of working, while a more mature fourteen-year-old may be able to tolerate a more open-ended, reflective approach.

Legislation, as far as it is relevant to children, has changed a great deal over the last few years. The Children Act now encompasses most of that which is relevant for a therapist to know. However, there are areas which are still being clarified, such as consent to treatment *vis-à-vis* the rights of children as opposed to the rights of parents to give or withhold consent. There is not the scope in this chapter to address these issues, but it needs to be said that it is incumbent upon all therapists to have sufficient understanding of the legal framework in which they have to operate.

Who is requesting the help? If it is the client, they may have unrealistic expectations of what therapy can mean. They may not want to be there at all, perhaps from a profound ambivalence about authority figures, and therefore not maintain contact. If it is the parents, they may be asking the psychotherapist to change the young person, but their views on what needs changing may be very different from the young person's or the psychotherapist's. If it is private work, the parent(s) may be paying, therefore the contract is with them rather than with the young person. For example, if the young person's attitude is a product of how the family functions, it may be necessary to negotiate with the family about what is and what is not possible, and what part they may play.

The mere existence of a 'need' for help is an insufficient guide to the appropriateness for therapy. In assessing a young person for psychotherapy the therapist must have a clear understanding of the origins of a young person's problems, the extent of the need and the time-scale required. It is not uncommon for the wish to 'rescue' a person from their plight to lead to unrealistic hopes being encouraged. There is also a danger of the psychotherapist becoming a surrogate parent, if the child is living in an awful world. No matter what the time period, the therapy will usually end before the child in this situation is ready. The form of the therapy must be taken into account; for example, whether individual, group or family therapy would be the more appropriate.

Not all adolescents are in a position comfortably to explore new values and ideas. If they have grown up in an environment riddled with inconsistency and lack of clarity, this task is made especially difficult for them. Exploratory behaviour in toddlers occurs safely when there is a secure base from which to operate. Similarly, in adolescence exploration of ideas and beliefs can only really occur if childhood experience has offered some clarity about the child's place in the world. They cannot face painful feelings without a support system. If the adolescent is in 'limbo' (e.g. awaiting placement with a foster family) psychotherapy cannot take place. Equally it can be extraordinarily difficult for re-evaluation of beliefs and values to occur when the adults 'hold on' tightly and restrict the process of exploration and discovery too rigidly. The impending loss for them of their child may be unbearably painful. These restrictions may be associated with parental rigidity or unwitting over-protection, and nearly always imply some lack of understanding about the developmental needs of the young person. The therapist needs to check which adults are prepared to support the intervention. The psychotherapist's views may differ from those of parents and teachers. If there is the possibility of work being undermined by an unsupportive adult, then an additional worker may be required to work with them.

FIRST STEPS

So how do we cope with these young people? How do we ensure that they do take advantage of helpful adults? How do we listen to them and understand them? In what context do we see them – alone, with their family, or in groups? Whatever the context, whatever the theoretical model, and whatever the problem, the first aim is to ensure that no interview with a young person makes it less likely in the future that a young person will go for help or talk to an adult. A short meeting which elicits little information but which makes the young person feel that there is some prospect of being understood *may* be more helpful than a long interview with a laborious dissection of problems. The latter type of interview will feel persecutory at worst, and irrelevant at best, and may put them off seeking help for ever. If a 'need' of a fourteen-year-old cannot be met when first noted, we must ensure that we do not compound the problem by making this young person less amenable to help at a later stage.

To achieve these minimal aims a young person's view must be respected, even if an alternative adult view is presented. For example: 'I appreciate that you feel the only way to make teachers hear is to shout at them and that at present this is what you may have to do, but it is possible that this makes the problem worse and may make them less likely to listen than before. Maybe we need to look for another way of helping them to understand you.'

In addition, there is the issue of trust and the effect of past experiences. An adolescent who has been let down, perhaps by the abuse of power in the context of child abuse, who has been denied a good experience of parenting, perhaps by an alcoholic parent or who has suffered many losses, may just not feel able to trust even the most well-intentioned adult. It is no wonder that young people in this position are uncommunicative, surly and avoiding. Rekindling trust can take a long time and the process may have many genuine ups and downs.

A further issue to tackle early are the rules of the basic psychotherapy session itself. Don't be afraid of explaining the strange ways of the professional world, because it is probably new to them. After working for a while with teenagers it can seem by contrast that adults are surprisingly compliant about the basics of the session: that it starts at, say, 10 a.m. and ends at 10.50, that if they arrive late the session is shortened, that they give notice of not attending, and that it is their role to 'do the telling' about their particular difficulties. Adolescents can find this structure extremely difficult, so it may be necessary to be flexible, to negotiate a fairly formal way of seeing the young person, and to give explanations if necessary.

What information goes where, and to whom? Negotiating issues around confidentiality is a big issue in working with adolescents. For example, in working with under-sixteens a contract may need to be negotiated allowing contact with or work with parents. Under-sixteens may disclose experience of sexual or general abuse. If the contract is 100 per cent confidential, the psychotherapist may feel unable to take appropriate action to protect the child. If the contract is to work with another agency then it is less likely to be 100 per cent confidential. A typical example of this issue is the fourteen-year-old who says he feels like committing suicide: if you have told him, 'Our session is just between us and these four walls', then he states he is suicidal with 'Don't tell Mum and Dad, I want to kill myself', you are left with the dilemma of whether to go to the parents or the social services.

Finally, the various expectations that the therapist may have of the young person or vice versa can sometimes be helpfully written down in the form of a contract. If there are rules – for instance, about lateness or cancelled sessions – they must be specified. Too often young people are assumed to appreciate what is required of them or how they are meant to behave. The flexibility that may be built into such negotiations will depend upon many factors and, above all, must bear some relation to the capacity of the young person to abide by them.

SOME PRACTICAL PROBLEMS

Whether it is your first interview with a young person or your fiftieth, you can still find yourself beset with a practical communication problem which makes the task of being 'helpful' very difficult indeed. Often you will want to be finding out information, establishing trust, negotiating a problem, giving a view, reinforcing parental authority and understanding the young person all at the same time. You may find the young person walking out after ten minutes or difficult to persuade to leave after ninety minutes. It matters very little whether your task is 'in depth' psychotherapy, persuading them to take unpleasant medication, taking a medical history or advising them about their smoking habit – you still have to feel comfortable in their presence for them to feel comfortable in yours. You still have to respect them even if they give the impression of not respecting you, and you have to find a way of coping with the barriers to easy and open communication; that is, *if you wish to have a positive influence and be helpful*. Be prepared to feel incompetent and humiliated sometimes, and be prepared to learn from others about ways of communicating and listening effectively. Above all, learn from your own experiences, both positive and negative.

The young person may not want to tell you anything at all – why should they? – especially if they did not want to see you in the first place. If you manage to negotiate this first issue, it may become clear that the young person does not trust adults, for very good reasons; whether consciously or unconsciously. They may be frightened, anxious and depressed; such overwhelming feelings make it hard for many adults to talk easily, let alone teenagers.

The young person may feel they will be rejected, disliked or disbelieved if they tell you what is wrong. It may be concretely expressed, in terms of 'If you really knew, you'd never want to see me again'. Underlying this may be fear, conflicts of loyalty or belief systems, or a fragile self-esteem. The young person may feel that they will appear stupid or silly if they put their feelings and problems into words. Equally, they may just simply want to please you and collude with the psychotherapist's hope that things are getting better. These very basic doubts in the young person's mind can also contribute to the feelings of persecution that are engendered by even the most benevolent and well-intentioned question.

Denial that a problem exists presents a very real challenge – for example, 'There's nothing wrong' or 'The teachers are lying' – and this makes it very hard to solve. Equally the projection of the problem onto others, such as 'Teachers pick on me' or 'My brother keeps destroying my clothes', may deflect the psychotherapist from the task. There may some truth in their views about the problem, but equally they may be reluctant to own their part of it. If they only see themselves as 'victims' it is hard to get them to address the part they play in the process. Another version of denial to be aware of is the protest of recovery; for example, 'It's all right now! It won't happen again! I'm going back to school on Monday!' It is so easy to accept such statements against your better judgement, as it is always a relief to think a problem has been solved. However, always check the real likelihood from past experience and history.

The young person may also understate the problem, acknowledging the problem but in such a casual and/or dismissive fashion that it is hard to pursue. It is easy to collude with the expressed view that the problem is insignificant. Psychotherapists wish to believe what they hear, need to respect a young person's perception, but may be fooled in the process. A thirteen-year-old charged with the attempted rape of an adult woman commented, 'I only touched her bum.' This understatement rendered it very difficult for the psychotherapist to address the serious nature of the problem. At times it will be necessary to seek confirmation from others – school, parents, perhaps – if you are going to address the problem at all. This always requires negotiation if trust is to be preserved and does not necessarily mean that you are going to break confidentiality. To deny yourself necessary knowledge about a child's behaviour or experiences may mean you simply collude with that child's unrealistic hopes and views of the world around them.

Some young people adopt a pseudo-sophisticated manner, such as the twelve-year-old who could not play with his peers and refused to go to school, who told me, 'The child inside me has been kidnapped'. Much of his conversation and most of the explanations for his difficulties were intellectually challenging, fascinating to listen to and fertile ground for endless intriguing discussion. It is easy to be hoodwinked by apparently sophisticated discussions which, if looked at more closely, are masterpieces of illogicality, 'second-hand', or simply mechanisms to avoid painful realities.

Some young persons are very adept at avoiding serious discussions by their witty repartee. It can be very seductive and it is easy to join in if it is mutually advantageous not to deal with painful issues – especially when you are busy. Equally the 'butter-wouldn't-melt-in-my-mouth' look of angelic innocence can produce a similar response, for it misses the point and can mask despair.

Racist or sexist remarks which offend can make it very difficult to work with a young person. They nevertheless have to be dealt with in a way which does not deny the young person's right to receive help. A typical retort was 'Women should do all the housework' as a response from a male who refused to help with the washing-up at home. It can be quite difficult to address such assertively held views which are contrary to what you or others believe.

Occasionally a young person will refuse to see you. Once a fourteen-year-old travelled across London by bus and arrived for his appointment on time to tell me that he did not want to see me. After a period of much verbal abuse, running away and then returning, he eventually burst into tears and told me that he had been beaten by his father that day. Be ready to consider that the surface statement may mask real distress and overwhelming need. Equally, a request to see you less often *may* be a test of your interest in them and capacity to take them seriously and to care about them.

One of the most incapacitating modes of communication is silence. A fifteen-year-old girl attended regularly, sat down with her hair hanging in front of her face, head down, biting her nails, and if she said anything it was in an inaudible whisper. At times she would curl up into a tight, silent ball. It can leave you feeling truly helpless, hopeless and incompetent. In fact, this girl rang the clinic years later, now able to talk; and during the discussion, I asked her why she had been so quiet then. She said: 'I had so much to say I just didn't know where to begin.' This leads naturally to the next point: take care with silence, as it is often, but not always, threatening. Be sensitive to this. However, be careful not to fill up silence with conversation if it is your discomfort that you are dealing with rather than the young person's.

Another practical problem sometimes arises when verbal expression is impoverished and in its place come frequent shrugs, frequent replies such as 'I dunno!', 'I don't care', ''Cos it's boring' or 'I can't remember'. The capacity to express a viewpoint or to engage in debate requires ease with the use of language. The child brought up in a family with limited verbal stimulation or a family where feelings are rarely expressed finds themselves handicapped in adolescence when struggling to account for themselves or make themselves heard. The young person's shorthand for painful emotions can so easily not be interpreted by the psychotherapist. Taking these phrases at face value may prevent any understanding from taking place. These responses frequently stop the discussion by simply blocking it, or diverting attention away from important areas, and a way around them needs to be found. For example, 'bored' is a word that can be used to sum up almost any negative emotion, such as angry, depressed, worried, muddled and so forth. Equally, 'I don't care' almost never means what it says. I have never yet come across a young person who does not care. Finally, 'Dunno' or 'Can't remember' may simply mean they can't face telling you.

It may simply not be possible for an adolescent to name the feelings they are experiencing, for they are often diffuse and mixed emotions which are not easily differentiated; or the feelings may simply be new to the young person. This is one reason why the young person may not feel confident about, or even know, the best word for their experiences. 'I've got the hump' may be their best phrase for 'depressed', and this slang expression may mask the true despair which the psychotherapist is none the less expected to understand. To some extent, this problem may be one of cognition, so assessment of the stage of development of the young person is always an essential part of the process.

A very common problem encountered in day-to-day practice is the secret trap, such as: 'My step-father is sexually abusing me, but I don't want you to tell anyone'. The attempt to establish confidence, confidentiality and trust can lead you into the trap of not being able to take necessary action to protect a young person who is seriously at risk. Never promise what you can't deliver.

Some young people make disrespectful comments, such as 'You're a goat!' I have been called many things in my time, from the above to the misuse of my name, from 'Dr Jedi' to Bob to Sir, and it is not a matter which I waste time over. It is also easy to be totally thrown by very personal questions coming out of the blue: 'Have you ever been to dirty movies?' Often these are more genuine and innocent than they appear. They challenge your boundaries very effectively, however!

Hostile remarks such as 'Stop being so nosy' or 'You don't bloody well understand' or even a physical threat, particularly if said in a venomous tone, can render the interviewer powerless and defensive. At times they may make you angry and/or frightened – not exactly the most fertile ground for a sensitive and understanding discussion.

The 'yawn' or the sudden trip to the loo are things to look out for. Take note of when these imposed breaks in interviews take place, for you may well find that you are approaching the important issue. It may be a time to respect the young person's need to stop there, or the opposite. Maybe they simply need extra time to think. Sometimes it can be a difficult judgement to make.

SOME USEFUL PRINCIPLES

Behaviour tends to be the main communicative modality rather than words, but its interpretation is frequently misunderstood by adults. A search for meaning becomes replaced by insensitive management. Unexpected difficult behaviour usually has a 'meaning'. You may not need to interpret it directly, but the young person needs to know that you've picked up the meaning or, at the very least, that it *has meaning* even if at the time you do not understand what it is all about. This does not stop the adult from responding to the behaviour if this is required, but a search for meaning may make the management of the behaviour fairer and more consistent. For example, an attack on another child by a teenager brandishing a billiard cue may have to be managed without words in order to prevent harm. The behaviour must be stopped and contained before any attempt at understanding is achieved. This does not even preclude the use of appropriate sanctions. However, whether the young person wishes to talk about the event afterwards or not, the adult should share their bemusement as to why it happened and what was trying to be communicated. No compromise should be adopted over defining the acceptability or otherwise of such extreme behaviour, but this does not preclude understanding. A brisk, firm, authoritative response to control a situation will ultimately be more acceptable if the young person perceives the benevolent intent of the adult and the adult's interest in the background to the event. If the behaviour has no meaning, then no harm has been done; but if the behaviour is indeed meaningful and is a maladaptive communication, then much may have been lost by failing to address it.

In order to build a good relationship you need to treat the views of young people with respect. You do not have to agree with a young person to have respect for their right to hold their own opinion. They are unlikely to listen to you or reflect on their views if they feel you have not listened to them, heard what they are saying and respected their right to have a view different from your own. Make a clear distinction between hearing them and offering them your own alternative viewpoint. The latter cannot be imposed upon a young person but it can be offered to them to consider. At times they may take your opinion very seriously and value it *but* nevertheless appear to reject it; they absorb it privately and the last thing they may want to admit is that they have valued you. Self-respect and pride can very often be eroded by the clever guy imposing his own viewpoint.

Always assume the young person's interest in being helped. Many young people will make considerable efforts to give the impression that they think that you are useless and are not valued. If they have come to see you, that may say much more than the attitude presented to you. Many mistakes are made by too readily accepting the surface statements and demeanour.

In working with young people, it is important to avoid fruitless battles; and to try not to win. There are some issues which it is right to be firm about, and those require no discussion, as this often leads to deadlock or futile battles which you are likely to lose. On the other hand, many 'disagreements' are fairly minor, and it may be important to allow teenagers some sense of autonomy and independence by judiciously conceding to their view. If you are 'right', your view may then ultimately be more readily accepted.

Don't be put off if discussion seems superficial and irrelevant. Many issues are worked out 'in the metaphor' and may never require explicit clarification. The need for clarification is often the professional's need rather than that of the young person. For example, the psychotherapist may feel at times that the discussion is about trivialities, e.g. about last weekend's camping trip, but often a surprising amount of 'private' work is being done within the adolescent's mind at the same time, or after the session, which may or may not ever be acknowledged or expressed.

If possible balance the discussion, as a totally 'heavy' discussion may become unbearable. Do not avoid painful issues that can be discussed if they need to be discussed. But periods of more neutral inquiry or even light-hearted discussion may make the addressing of difficult material more bearable.

It is important to be adult. The young person won't necessarily thank you for your teenage reminiscences. They may need you to be adult and different. A frequent cry in adolescence is 'I am different', expressed through clothes, tastes, rebellion: all sorts of means. If you reply, 'Yes, I am the same', a barrier is immediately built and the young person's identity development is thwarted. Your job as an adult psychotherapist is not to join in with younger people or to 'share' their experience with, say, a reminiscence of the music of your day – although the obvious irony is that they *do* need to be understood – but to remain adult, and above all to be tolerant. Understanding can grow through the very fact of being different. 'The best thing to do is to behave in a manner befitting one's age. If you are sixteen or under try not to go bald' (Woody Allen).

You need to find a common language, which does not mean talking to them like a teenager. However, there may be words and phrases which they find comfortable in using that have more meaning to them than your own. A manifestly severely depressed young person may prefer to talk about being 'fed up' rather than depressed. Do not talk down to them and do not try and use phoney or age-inappropriate language, but 'tune in' to their key words and use them judiciously if it helps you to communicate more effectively. Develop a language common and useful to you both.

When 'stuck', asking a teenager for their three wishes can sometimes be very revealing. It can also be useful to have activity bridges. These are a shared activity which may facilitate a useful discussion. How often in residential settings have 'breakthroughs' occurred while doing the washing-up? Clearly, the activity has to be appropriate to the context.

Feedback is often better than interpretation. This is not a universal rule, but, for many, an interpretation can feel persecutory, or like an imposition of your views. Don't assume anything until you can be sure that they have heard you at face value; remember that they are giving their construction, their view. There is a tremendous temptation for adults to impose their sophisticated understanding and beliefs about 'meaning' before listening and acknowledging the communication first. For example, a psychotherapist working with an individual in a group said, 'What you're really trying to tell me is you're angry with your father' and received the angry retort, 'Stop fucking twisting everything I say!' The psychotherapist had not negotiated early with the adolescent, or respected him, but turned his statement into the therapist's own idea, own language. Later in the group session, the psychotherapist understood enough to say, 'Do you mind if I twist it around . . . ?' and got a grunt of half-acknowledgement. Later the young person said, 'I suppose you want to twist that around?' – but at least offering an opportunity for this 'twisting' or interpretation to happen. Unless the process of interpretation is both 'negotiated' and also presented with benevolence and humility (as opposed to arrogant dogmatism!), personal feedback is preferable. 'What you have just said makes me feel very sad for you' may be better than 'You are depressed about the loss of your mother'. The idea about the issue – sadness, depression – is offered in a way which respects the young person's right not to acknowledge that you are correct. It also clarifies the mood of the interaction and it does not impose an idea or a word upon the young person which does not feel right for them.

Views and comments offered as choices, for the adolescent to reject or disregard if they wish, may lead to greater use being made of helpful and clarifying remarks from the interviewer. If an adolescent is having trouble labelling an emotional state, then 'multiple choices' of feeling states offered on a series of cards can be of help; see if one card carries a better word. Don't allow the stuckness with words, for feelings block further discussion. It may be helpful to offer the choices verbally in terms of 'What I'd feel/think if I were in your shoes'. Maybe describe the choices as being like a tray of hors d'oeuvres for you to take what you like the look of best.

For the sensitive young person, eye contact also may be threatening at points in an interview. Sometimes even averting your gaze may make a young person feel less vulnerable. However, it may be useful to regain eye contact when making an important positive point, particularly if it relates to your attempt to confirm that you have heard and are sensitive to their view or their problem.

Do not leave a young person exposed, vulnerable and traumatised at the end of an interview. Some attempt to check out how they are feeling and efforts to rebuild necessary defences before they leave may be essential.

CONCLUSION

We are often unaware of when we are being at our most helpful. You will be disappointed if you expect acknowledgement or thanks; but there may be some quite unexpected and indirect thanks if you look hard. Remember, adults may often feel irritated by not hearing 'Sorry' or 'Thank you', but it gets said by teenagers in other ways.

It is important to be flexible and not restrict therapeutic opportunities by sticking rigidly to the rules of therapy; *but* don't give up those rules which have evidently some value. The main job of the adult is to survive and 'stick with it' in the face of adolescent murder, to paraphrase Winnicott (1958), but not to become punitive or impatient in response to attack or passivity. Remain tolerant and a way will be found to provide that securing anchor.

REFERENCES

Erikson, E. H. (1968) *Identity, Youth and Crisis*, New York: Norton.
Winnicott, D. W. (1958) *Collected Papers*, London: Tavistock.

FURTHER READING

Bazalgette, J. (1971) *Freedom, Authority and the Young Adult*, London: Pitman.
Klein, J. (1987) *Our Need for Others and Its Roots in Infancy*, London: Tavistock Publications.
Rutter, M. and Hersov, L. (eds) (1985) *Child and Adolescent Psychiatry: Modern Approaches*, Oxford: Blackwell.
Steinberg, D. (1983) *The Clinical Psychiatry of Adolescence: Clinical Work from a Social and Developmental Perspective*, New York: Wiley.
—— (ed.) (1986) *The Adolescent Unit: Work and Teamwork in Adolescent Psychiatry*, New York: Wiley.
York, P., York, D. and Wachtel, T. (1982) *Toughlove*, New York: Bantam/Doubleday.

Chapter 11

Short-term psychotherapy

Gillian Butler and James Low

> That there is no simple correlation between therapeutic results and the length and intensity of treatment has been recognised, tacitly or explicitly by most experienced psychoanalysts and is an old source of dissatisfaction among them. Among psychoanalysts there arise two types of reaction to this dissatisfaction. One was constructive like Ferenczi's relentless experimenting with technique in an effort to isolate the factors responsible for therapeutic results. The other was a self-deceptive defence in the form of an almost superstitious belief that quick therapeutic results cannot be genuine, that they are either those transitory results due to suggestion or an escape into 'pseudo-healthy' patients who prefer to give up their symptoms rather than obtain real insight into their difficulties.
>
> (Alexander, in Alexander and French 1946: v)

Alexander's words are as true today as they were in 1946. This chapter is concerned with psychotherapy that is intentionally carried out over a short period of time. Many psychotherapies that might become long-term are cut short due to crises, the non-establishment or collapse of the psycho-therapeutic alliance, staff changes and so forth. Although NHS psycho-therapy departments tend to allocate resources in favour of patients receiving long-term therapy, there is little evidence to suggest that most continue treatment beyond six months. Howard *et al.* (1987) provide clinical evidence from the United States that suggests that this may be a common experience.

However, there are many forms of psychotherapy that are intentionally short-term. Such psychotherapy is done with individuals, couples, families, groups and organisations. Many different theoretical perspectives are made use of, including behavioural, cognitive-behavioural, cognitive-analytic, analytic, systemic and solution-focused. Sledge *et al.* (1990) made a distinction between time-limited psychotherapy, brief therapy and long-term psychotherapy. They see time-limited psychotherapy as one where the psychotherapist offers a pre-arranged, non-negotiable number of sessions and the client agrees to this at the beginning of psychotherapy, whereas brief psychotherapy lasts for three to four months but with no pre-fixed ending date. The end occurs when the particular topic that has been the focus of psychotherapy is satisfactorily addressed. In their research they found that the drop-out rate for time-limited psychotherapy was half that for each of the other types of psychotherapy. It would seem that when patients know how long the psychotherapy will last they are able to feel more in control, and are able to work in a focused way towards the goal set. Their conscious understanding of the contract may limit the exploration and help to reduce fears of engulfment and/or abandonment (see Ryle 1990).

DIFFERENT MODELS OF SHORT-TERM PSYCHOTHERAPY

The various models of short-term psychotherapy are united in the desire to provide an effective psychotherapy in as short a time as possible, and they share a belief in the possibility of significant change occurring in months rather than years. But they have very different ways of conceptualising the problem and the processes of change. In a short chapter like this we cannot spell out all the significant differences. What we will do is present some general features of short-term psychotherapy, look at suitability and contra-indications and the process of assessment with examples from a range of short-term psychotherapists. We will then provide an account of two psychotherapies, one cognitive-analytic and the other cognitive-behavioural, to give a sense of the issues as they arise in practice.

We are using the term 'short-term psychotherapy' to indicate a therapy of up to twenty sessions, each lasting an hour, spaced at weekly intervals. Malan (1976) refers to cases of brief analytic psychotherapy ranging from four to fifty sessions. Mahrer (1989) described two-hour sessions, Ryle (1990) sixteen- or eight-session therapies, and many other permutations have been written about.

The approaches to short-term psychotherapy can be usefully classed into four 'families': dynamic or analytic, cognitive-behavioural, systemic and integrative. Existing literature seems to show little interest in short-term psychotherapy amongst humanistic practitioners. This may be due to the fact that most of the developments have occurred in public service institutions where cost-effectiveness and reduction of waiting lists have always been pressing concerns. The history of analytic brief psychotherapy is well documented, for example by Malan (1976), and Flegenheimer (1982) has provided useful summaries of the theories and techniques of the main approaches. Crits-Christoph and Barber (1991) describe recent advances highlighting the important role given to research, both process and outcome, in the development of specific applications of short-term dynamic psychotherapy. Ashurst (1991) provides a very clear, brief and comprehensive introduction to the key issues in dynamic brief psychotherapy.

Cognitive psychotherapy was developed as a short-term method of treatment, and included both cognitive and behavioural techniques.* So cognitive behaviour therapy (CBT) is based on a theoretical model of emotional disorder which explains how the relationships between thoughts and feelings can provoke and maintain distress. Theoretically, long-term improvement can be achieved in a short time by working to identify, examine and test out different ways of thinking. Precise techniques were first developed for working with depressed patients (Beck 1976; Beck *et al.* 1979), and have been elaborated for work with many other emotional disorders (for example, Beck *et al.* 1985; Hawton *et al.* 1989; Scott *et al.* 1989). A large body of research now documents the clinical effectiveness of short-term cognitive behaviour therapy and continues to contribute to the development and elaboration of the theoretical model. In contrast to more dynamic psychotherapies, longer-term treatments are being developed after the short-term ones have become established (for example, Beck *et al.*, 1990; Young 1990), and new theoretical developments continue to broaden the potential scope of this approach (for instance, Safran and Segal 1991).

From the beginning family psychotherapy, informed by a systems theory, operated with a sharp awareness of the importance of short-term interventions. When the prime concern of psychotherapists is to promote change in the system, their own position *vis-à-vis* the system should not be one that promotes stabilising dependence. Out of this basic notion a wide range of interventions have developed and with them a permission for the psychotherapist to be active and creative. This finds its most radical development in solution-focused psychotherapy where the focus of attention is consistently on difference, on what is new. The psychotherapy affects a shift in interest in the client away from problems and their convolutions and origins towards any and every event that is different. The psychotherapy has no contracted time limit but tends to be short-term (Shazer 1991).

The integrative approach to psychotherapy has opened up new ways of combining effective features of different models in order to optimise sustainable change within short-term psychotherapy. Norcross (1986), Marteau (1986) and Ryle (1990) each offer a skeletal structure which can

---

* The terms 'cognitive therapy' and 'cognitive behaviour therapy' are confusing as they have often been used interchangeably. It is fair to say that the main types of cognitive therapy make use of some behavioural strategies. These strategies play a crucial part in the treatment, as they involve carrying out 'behavioural experiments' which help to determine whether certain ways of thinking are unrealistic or unhelpful. The term 'cognitive behaviour therapy' (CBT) will be used in this chapter to make clear the distinction from cognitive analytic therapy.

be fleshed out with different emphases and techniques according to the precise needs of the individual client. Indeed, short-term models often have a predetermined feel about them, an 'off-the-peg' quality which requires a skilful adaptation by the psychotherapist so that the psychotherapy is tailored to suit the client rather than vice versa.

GENERAL FEATURES

Although there are many models of brief psychotherapy, certain general features can be identified. These are both a consequence of the brief focus and significant determining factors in its efficacy.

First, the psychotherapist is active, taking on a variety of functions including teaching, modelling, encouraging and structuring the work. This activity is designed to stimulate and support a matching activity in the patient. If it promotes dependence, something has gone wrong. The psychotherapist needs to be explicit about what is on offer at the beginning of psychotherapy so that the patient can make an informed choice. The psychotherapist needs to believe in the value of short-term work since their confidence, empathy and availability are key factors.

Secondly, the psychotherapeutic alliance is a central feature. In most forms of brief psychotherapy the alliance is strengthened by the conscious agreement to focus on an explicit problem that has been identified together. Psychotherapist and patient find themselves working together with a shared goal but different tasks. This shared belief in the possibility of solving the problem promotes negotiation and the creative channelling of difference into the further development of self-confidence and self-esteem.

Thirdly, the patient's motivation is affirmed, responded to and developed. The desire for change must be linked to the implementation of strategies that will make change a reality. These strategies may be implemented through communication or by means of tasks that shift cognition, affect or behaviour. This may include interpretation within the psychotherapeutic relationship, behaviour monitoring, set homework and so on.

Fourthly, the focus is on supporting patients in their ordinary lives. Whatever is learned during the session needs to be generalised through application in the wider social environment. Particular ways of understanding are linked to patterns and procedures in such a way as to lead the patient towards a resolution of the present difficulties.

Fifthly, the containment and structure provided by the temporal focal issue and active development of the psychotherapeutic alliance provide a context within which patients can try out new ways of thinking, feeling and behaving. Negative expectations of the patient are explored or interpreted and also confronted through reality-based feedback – for instance, about efforts and achievements in psychotherapy. The clearer the focus, the easier it is for patients to evaluate their own progress and to use the support of the psychotherapist to avoid self-sabotage or the tendency to discount their own success.

Obviously, a great deal more could be said about these points, and of course many of the factors mentioned are shared with long-term psychotherapy. Weakland *et al.*, writing of their focused problem resolution model of brief psychotherapy, make a point that short-term psychotherapists of many persuasions would agree with that.

> Our fundamental premise is that regardless of their basic origins and aetiology – if, indeed, these can ever be reliably determined – the kind of problems people bring to psychotherapists persist only if they are maintained by ongoing current behaviour of the patient and others with whom he interacts. Correspondingly, if such problem-maintaining behaviour is appropriately changed or eliminated, the problem will be resolved or vanish, regardless of its nature, origin or duration.
>
> (1974: 144–5)

Different models will give different accounts of the ongoing current behaviour that maintains problems. In short-term psychotherapy the relevant behaviours have to be readily identifiable and easily recognised by the patient.

SELECTION OF PATIENTS

The short-term psychotherapies that have an analytic approach often include selection criteria that are difficult to assess accurately or objectively. These tend to become qualities that psychotherapists learn to identify intuitively through the distillation of experience rather than being able to tick off on a checklist. This is one of the reasons why some writers believe that short-term psychotherapy is best performed by very experienced psychotherapists (Marteau 1986).

Lists of selection criteria have been provided by many writers (for example, Ashurst 1991; Malan 1976, 1979; Crits-Christoph and Barber 1991). Crits-Christoph and Barber (1991) have very usefully compared the selection criteria and disqualifiers of a range of short-term dynamic psychotherapies. Although there are wide variations, typical exclusion criteria are addictions, psychosis, severe personality disorders and suicidal acting out. In contrast, Ryle (1990, 1992) has described the successful use of cognitive-analytic psychotherapy with very disturbed borderline patients. In all cases the basic concern must be whether a short-term psychotherapy is likely to make the patient worse – a judgement that is necessarily based on accumulated wisdom and experience in the absence of an accepted body of relevant research and information.

Nielsen and Barth (1991) suggest that the patient's ability to define a circumscribed chief complaint is indicative of ego strength, reality testing, tolerance of frustration, and capacity for delaying gratification. Thus the ability of the patient to identify a focal problem in the first few sessions is an indication of their having the resources to make effective use of this psychotherapy. Of course, the patient's capacity to participate in this way is influenced by the psychotherapist's ability to respond in a flexible way in order to promote dialogue and the development of a psychotherapeutic alliance.

When psychotherapy is short-term it is important for patients to be able to engage quickly in treatment, and to make a commitment to it. The degree to which they can do this, and opt positively for the treatment offered, has therefore to be weighed up during assessment. Some patients may select themselves, or their behaviour may provide important clues. Those who can ask questions about what is on offer, and think about what they want to get out of it, may be better able to set achievable goals, less likely to be troubled by disruptive avoidance or fantasy, and more likely to develop realistic expectations about psychotherapy.

We now offer two examples of short-term psychotherapy which illustrate some of the points made above.

COGNITIVE-ANALYTIC THERAPY (CAT) WITH A BORDERLINE PATIENT

Ryle (1990) provides a clear account of the theory, structure and practice of this model. The intention here is to give an account of a case highlighting the particular concerns of a time-limited psychotherapy approach.

Mary was thirty-eight when she was referred for CAT from a sexual problems clinic where she had presented with vaginismus. Mary has had several psychiatric admissions over the last fifteen years stemming from suicide attempts, alcohol and drug problems, anxiety and depression. She met all eight of the DSM-111-R criteria for Borderline Personality Disorder. Angry and withdrawn at the beginning of psychotherapy, she treated every comment by the psychotherapist as an invasive attack and replied with disparaging remarks regarding the quality and efficacy of the psychotherapy. Once this pattern was identified the psychotherapist outlined the structure of the psychotherapy, going over what would be required of psychotherapist and patient, repeating the details until anxiety diminished and the work could begin.

Mary's mother had died shortly after her birth and she was taken care of by an aunt and uncle whom she took to be her real parents. When she was five they told her that her mother was dead and that her 'uncle' was in fact her father. She went with him to Australia for several years and then back with him to England to be passed from one set of unwilling relatives to another. Her father was drunk and violent and she often felt unsafe in his company. He was also sexually provocative with her, and she is haunted by the thought that he may have done more than she can remember.

By her late teens she was taking a lot of amphetamines and living in a chaotic manner. Her life since then had been marked by violent relationships, severe alcohol abuse and an absence of supportive relationships. Her father had died six years previously by falling into the River Thames. She was never sure if it was a drunken accident, suicide or murder, and was terrified that her own life might end in a similar way.

There were obvious specific problems that could have become the focus for the sixteen-week psychotherapy that was on offer, but through the discussion of the first two meetings, Mary came up with an existential question: 'How can I be in life when death, abandonment and confusion are so woven into my story?'

The open-endedness of this question could easily lead to wide-ranging exploration that might have become a way of avoiding distressing issues. However, the psychotherapist felt that the structure of the psychotherapy was precise enough to provide momentum and direction to the inquiry. As she said several times, 'If I know how to live, how to be alive, if I know that in myself, then I will be able to control myself. But I don't exist.' Having been deprived of so much, it seemed very important that she be allowed to stay with her question. Developmentally, the absence of consistent and reliable parenting and especially the confusion of identity of key figures in her early years had led to all her object relations being permeated by uncertainty and suspicion. She was convinced that her birth had caused her mother's death and so she was a monster whom no one could bear to be close to. 'I deserve nothing.'

This uncertainty and suspicious hostility was very evident in the transference, with each attack being followed by apologies and remorse. At the end of the first session, Mary had been given a psychotherapy file to fill in. This file gives brief descriptions of common procedures, and the patient is invited to identify the ones that they recognise some involvement with – see Ryle (1990) for a detailed description. This self-identification of the procedures facilitates the elaboration of more precisely customised procedural descriptions since it bypasses the resistance that interpretation can evoke. By the fourth session two procedures were identified as maintaining her problematic being in the world.

1 *The dilemma*: either I keep feelings bottled up, strive to be perfect and feel angry and depressed, or I let things out, risk not being perfect, hurting others, being rejected, making a mess, feeling guilty, angry and dissatisfied.
2 *The trap*: feeling depressed and uncertain about myself, I try to please others and do what they want. I have no time to meet my own needs

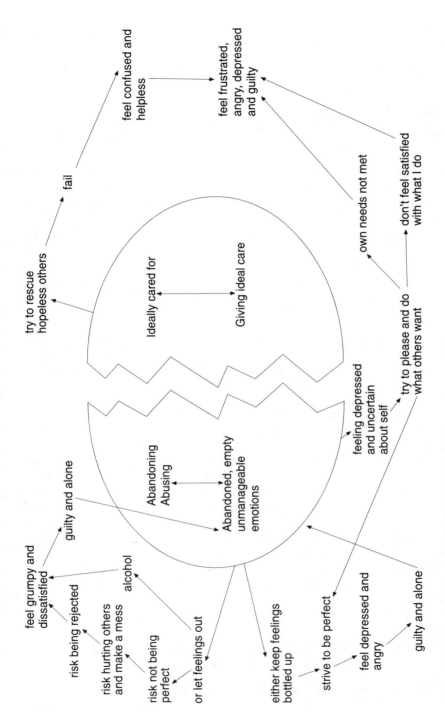

Figure 11.1 Mary's procedures in diagrammatic form

and so I feel frustrated and angry. I then get drunk, out of control, and feel guilty, depressed and confused, back where I started.

For Mary these procedures were a revelation, especially when presented in diagrammatic form (see Figure 11.1).

The split core of the diagram highlights the gap across which Mary flipped in her mood swings. The arrows indicate the way in which the procedures arise from a core state, either as a direct expression of it or as an attempt to gain distance from it. The procedural movement always returns to the core, illustrating the way the system is self-perpetuating.

Mary's intelligence, which she had never really utilised, blossomed, and she was able to make connection after connection, each week bringing new accounts of how she had recognised herself being pulled into a familiar response and being able to try something new. It was as if the diagram, apart from its cognitive heuristic value, was acting as a symbolic representation of the containing maternal mirroring that she was expecting through her relationship with the psychotherapist. The fact that the diagram was acting in some way as a Winnicottian transitional object helped to lessen regressive dependence on the psychotherapist and to encourage a movement towards seeking more reliable objects in her social life. The tasks of observing her behaviour in the light of the identified procedure and reporting back to the psychotherapist optimised the nurturing potential of setting and attaining achievable goals under the supportive and watchful eye of the psychotherapist.

Half-way through the psychotherapy Mary got a job in the canteen of the psychiatric section of another hospital. She was able to use this situation to explore her own belief that she was mad. 'They're trapped, they're mad – I'm just crazy and I'm getting better.' As her sense of herself and her identity in the world of others developed she was able to make sharper distinctions of both her own internal states and the qualities displayed by others.

As the end of the psychotherapy approached she said she felt she would be able to cope now because she was on her own side, not divided against herself. 'It is as if all of me is pointing in the same direction and I'm moving along in my own life finding out more and more about who I am.'

At three-months follow-up she reported promotion at work, minimal alcohol consumption with no episodes of drunkenness, and had taken a week's holiday for the first time in her life. Her score on the SCL94 dropped from a pre-therapy 101 to 55 at follow-up.

COGNITIVE BEHAVIOUR THERAPY (CBT) FOR MIXED AFFECTIVE DISORDER IN A DEPENDENT PERSONALITY

Karen was twenty-six when she was referred by her general practitioner for help with long-standing, intractable depression and anxiety, and she was described as 'rather a dependent personality'. At this time both her anxiety and depression were moderate to severe (Beck Depression Inventory score = 36: Beck *et al.* 1961; Beck Anxiety Inventory score = 28: Beck *et al.* 1988). She had taken an impulsive overdose two months previously after a row with her mother and had been given two courses of anti-depressants and one of counselling in the last four years without obvious benefit. She worked as a clerical assistant for the local council, and her fiancé, Robert, was a telephone engineer.

At assessment Karen was tearful and appeared flustered. She described high levels of tension, panic attacks two or three times a month, moodiness and irritability when at home in the flat she and Robert shared, feeling overwhelmed by difficulties and unable to control her feelings. She failed to go to work because of high levels of anxiety at least twice a month, frequently telephoned her mother asking to be brought home from work because she felt panicky, met Robert for support every lunch hour, and regularly demanded time and reassurance from her boss.

She was easily able to explain what she wanted from psychotherapy: to feel less anxious and panicky, especially before leaving for work every morning, and to feel less miserable and fed up, which was more of a problem in the evenings and at weekends. She also made it clear that she hoped the psychotherapist 'would make her better' – an expectation that was discussed during the first meeting when explaining the rationale for CBT. This made the point that psychotherapy requires joint, collaborative work, that patients are expected to carry out assignments between psychotherapy sessions, and that these assignments are designed as tests of different ways of thinking and behaving. Karen was willing to play an active part in treatment provided she was clearly directed. But she was frightened by the thought that 'others can make suggestions but ultimately I've got to do it myself'. For her first homework assignment Karen read a booklet describing CBT for anxiety.

Sessions 1–3

Information about the development and background to Karen's difficulties was collected over this time but will be described later, as the main work of this stage focused on her numerous worries and present symptoms. A number of 'vicious circles', or maintaining factors, were unravelled and illustrated using diagrams. One of these concerned anxiety: for example, worrying about work tasks → feeling tense and tearful → inability to concentrate → more worry about work. Another concerned her need for support from others: for example, when she felt anxious, worried or miserable → she thought 'I can't handle this' → then sought someone (Robert, her mother, her boss) on whom to 'unload' → felt better → and concluded 'I was right. I can't handle things alone.' Various behavioural strategies were introduced to start testing the idea that she was helplessly trapped in these vicious circles: relaxation and breathing exercises, graded task-setting to build up her independent work skills, and problem-solving to use before going to others for help. Karen learned these methods assiduously, and gradually came to terms with the idea of 'self-help'. But progress was slow and she continued to bring numerous different, and in her view, urgent problems to each session. These included anxieties about her performance at work, avoiding social engagements, the possibility that PMT could account for her symptoms and her irritability and lack of sexual interest in Robert.

Session 4

When Karen introduced yet another urgent problem for discussion the psychotherapist asked her to think about what was happening in psycho-therapy, and about the effects of this ever-changing focus. She said that it reflected exactly the way she felt: overwhelmed, confused and never sure what the next problem might be. This provided the opportunity to focus together on formulating the information she had so far brought to psychotherapy, looking for patterns and themes, and working out how they might fit together. At the end of this session she concluded, 'It's not that everything is a worry. It's that one problem spreads, and that's not being confident.' This conclusion, or hypothesis, provided the basis for the formulation which guided the rest of the work.

Two comments are pertinent at this stage. First, much weight is placed in this form of short-term psychotherapy on helping patients draw their own conclusions and formulate thoughts and beliefs in their own words. The aim is to engage them in sharing the work of psychotherapy at an affective as well as at a cognitive level. Secondly, it is possible that Karen's insistence, in psychotherapy also, that other people fix her problems for her, made it hard to come to such a conclusion and difficult to focus on issues other than the urgent ones she brought to each session until this pattern became obvious in psychotherapy also.

The development of Karen's problem

Karen's father left home when she was four. She was a shy child and had been bullied at school. One of her mother's boyfriends was physically violent towards both Karen and her mother, and they fled from him together, moving from house to house for three to four years. When Karen was seventeen and had just started work, they were living with an aunt. She was asked to leave the aunt's house as it was overcrowded, and did so briefly, but insisted on returning when she missed her mother. They moved into temporary accommodation with her mother's new friend John, and stayed there until Karen and Robert found their own flat about two years ago. Putting all the information together as simply as possible produced the following formulation:

Early experience
Father left home (age four)
Bullied at school (age eleven to twelve)
Violence at home: both witnessed and received
'There was nowhere that was home'

Dysfunctional assumptions: i.e., underlying, initially unrecognised beliefs such as
'I need people to look after me'
'I am not safe on my own'
'I can never be confident'
'I am not as good as others are'

Critical incidents: i.e., events that trigger the assumptions, such as
Making mistakes, especially at work
Disagreements, in particular with those in close relationships
Living away from mother, and dislike of her mother's new friend John
Threats to stability of all kinds

These activated the assumptions, for example:
'They will think I'm no good, and I'll lose my job'
'They will leave me, and I won't be able to cope alone'
'Mum doesn't need me now she's got John'
'I'm all alone in the world'

Present symptoms, for example:
Feelings: mostly anxiety, but also sadness, frustration, anger, resentment, feeling helpless and hopeless
Physical symptoms: tension, panic, headaches, agitation, apprehension
Behaviours: avoiding social contact, writing endless lists of things to do but procrastinating, disrupted sleep, 'making muddles'
Thoughts: 'I can't cope', 'There's nothing I can do', 'I need to talk to someone', and so on
Vicious circles (e.g. of anxiety and reassurance-seeking) keep the problem going in the present, reinforce the assumptions and make it hard to build confidence

Subsequent sessions

Karen said that the formulation, which had been sketched out using both diagrams and written material, enabled her to fit the problems together and make sense of what was happening in the present. Two main strategies were helpful to her subsequently. First, when she felt anxious she asked herself: 'How does this fit with not being confident?' Working this out made her feel less at the mercy of a host of unpredictable problems and better able to think what to do next. Secondly, she carried out a typical CBT homework assignment, the purpose of which was to help her think again about how confidence develops. This involved asking others how they became confident. Her findings led her, with some help, to the following main conclusions: many people who appear confident are not so underneath; you can be confident about some things but not others; confidence can be learned – it comes with practice.

In order to test out whether these conclusions applied in her own case she carried out a number of behavioural assignments, and made better use of the strategies introduced in the first sessions (problem-solving, and so on). By the end of treatment (sixteen weeks) she had joined an evening class (entitled 'Speaking with Confidence'), ate lunch without Robert on work days, and made fewer 'unreasonable' demands on her mother, Robert and her boss. She was much less depressed (BDI = 14) and somewhat less anxious (BAI = 18). During the next six months she had a couple of 'booster' sessions, and at follow-up had maintained these gains, attended work daily, had made more friends at work and now understood that her mother 'needed John as well as, and not instead of, me'. She had at one stage broken off her engagement to Robert, but returned to him a few weeks later having decided that the relationship was valuable to her, and not just rooted in her former dependence.

CONCLUDING COMMENTS

The two case examples given here outline approaches that are clearly structured and systematic, and we would suggest that the early development of a focus for the work, and a theory-backed treatment plan, help both patient and psychotherapist to optimise the potential of their brief encounter. Where the nature of the institution or the structure of the model determine the number of sessions available, the psychotherapist is freed from having to consider the duration boundary. Where that is not the case, more questions about the task of psychotherapy are often raised, and this is an area of some complexity (Frank 1961). The patient may well arrive with a difficulty that has recently been troubling, the 'presenting problem', which the psychotherapist sees as being an aspect or symptom of some longer or deeper malaise. And so a difference of desire makes itself apparent. The patient wants care while the psychotherapist seeks to promote exploration, change and development. But the route to the relief of suffering and the promotion of satisfaction and well-being may be either long or short. So perhaps it is the clinician's duty to ensure that the client is helped on a journey determined by each client's precise situation and not by the psychotherapist's curiosity or the dictates of a theoretical model.

As we have tried to illustrate in the case examples provided above, an awareness of, and competence in, the skills of short-term psychotherapy can help to keep psychotherapist and patient on course. When the course runs smoothly any conflict between focusing on presenting problems and on a 'deeper malaise' may disappear.

These two cases were obviously selected to illustrate how similar but strikingly different types of short-term psychotherapy were successfully used to help with relatively long-standing difficulties. We are well aware that psychotherapy does not always proceed smoothly but, instead of concentrating on the problems and difficulties of working in this way, and on ways of overcoming them, we have chosen instead to illustrate how complexity and the long-standing nature of difficulties need not impede progress.

It is tempting in this context to speculate a bit more about the processes that help to facilitate change, especially with two such different kinds of psychotherapy in mind. The following ideas are put forward purely in that spirit. As yet not enough is known either about process or outcome for anyone to be certain about exactly which methods and strategies used with which problems are most likely to be most beneficial.

First, the ability to specify limited goals in each case focused the work, especially at the start of psychotherapy. Discussion of goals may also have helped define appropriate expectations for psychotherapy, and to build trust between patient and psychotherapist. At the same time, this focused work enabled the psychotherapists to develop hypotheses about how to formulate the cases in terms of the theoretical frameworks they were using. Significantly, the first patient decided to focus not on her symptoms or presenting problem but on the meaning of her life. Her profound existential inquiry was then opened out and sharpened by the structure provided by cognitive-analytic therapy. The second patient initially wished to focus on symptoms and presenting problems. When doing so within the framework of cognitive-behaviour therapy she came to recognise recurring patterns and used the method to broaden and generalise the field of inquiry.

Next, the process of coming to a shared understanding, not only of the problem in the present but of the problem placed in a wider historical and developmental context, played a central part in both psychotherapies. In neither case was this achieved immediately, and in both cases it was achieved only after the psychotherapists had had the opportunity to observe the patients' different ways of engaging, and of having difficulty in engaging, in psychotherapy. Once arrived at, coincidentally by the fourth session in both cases, the formulations encompassed more issues than were raised by the specific goals. They incorporated 'critical' information about each patient's developmental history and ideas about the factors supposedly maintaining the distress. The formulation may thus have served many functions, but three of these seem to be particularly useful: explanation, understanding of the past and about why patterns repeat themselves, and specification of how to deal with these in ways relevant to specific problems arising in daily life. Using Persons' (1989) terminology, the formulation helped in both cases to relate overt difficulties to underlying mechanisms.

Sharing the formulation in an open, explicit way seemed to help the patients to define and then recognise these patterns, so as later to become free of their constraints. It is assumed that these patterns have generality; that is, they are exemplified in many different ways in the patients' lives. If the formulation offered makes sense then it can help the patient make the move from the particular to the general. A particular incident of behaviour can be seen as an instance of the general pattern, so that whatever has been learned on one occasion can more easily be generalised to other contexts and occasions. Thus, starting from a limited goal, and working with specific difficulties as they emerge in the here-and-now, provides the context for developing a good working hypothesis, or formulation. Recognising this – presuming it is accurate, of course – then enables people to become free of previous restrictions and repetitions, increases their options for adaptation, and frees up more adaptive processes of change and development. The approach of CAT, by incorporating an understanding of transference and counter-transference, makes use of what happens between patient and psychotherapist to deepen and intensify the living experience of the reality of the self-managing and reciprocal role procedures identified in the reformulation.

An important aspect of the relationship that facilitates this kind of work is that it is built up on the (often undeclared) assumption that patients have resources that they are able, or can become able, to use to their advantage. Growing independence is thus a sign of the successful use of short-term psychotherapy, and dependence will inevitably inhibit progress.

This speculation about some of the processes that may facilitate change in short-term psychotherapy assumes that there are specific reasons why psychotherapy is effective when it works, and why it is not effective when it fails. This is an important assumption underlying the different approaches to short-term psychotherapy, and one that motivates continued search and research. However, the speculation also illustrates how difficult it is to be certain about which of the aspects of short-term psychotherapy account for its effectiveness. Given the present state of our knowledge, it could therefore be tempting to conclude that there is nothing to choose between one form of short-term psychotherapy and another. In practice, the choice of method is indeed made by psychotherapists on the basis of their particular training, theoretical orientation and working context, and by patients on bases that we are not at all clear about and which are probably determined as much by chance factors and local availability as by rational matching of patient to treatment. It is important, if this somewhat unsatisfactory state of affairs is to change, that psychotherapists continue to communicate and to speculate about their methods. There are two developments which will help to support short-term psychotherapy: patients need to be supported in making informed choices about the kind of psychotherapy they enter into; and psychotherapists would benefit from an emphasis on flexibility and responsiveness in their training rather than on induction into the pseudo-safety of a system.

As short-term psychotherapy is likely to continue to develop fast, the demands on psychotherapists today are large. Perhaps their main tasks, in addition to clinical practice, should include constant appraisal of new ideas in their own as well as in related fields, and a willingness openly to examine their own practice. The more we know about one another's ways of working the more likely it is that we shall in the end be better able to select the right approach for the right person.

REFERENCES

Alexander, F. and French, T. (1946) *Psychoanalytic Therapy*, New York: Ronald Press.

Ashurst, P. (1991) 'Brief psychotherapy', pp. 187–212 in J. Homes (ed.) *Textbook of Psychotherapy in Psychiatric Practice*, London: Churchill Livingstone.

Beck, A. T. (1976) *Cognitive Therapy and the Emotional Disorders*, New York: International Universities Press.

Beck, A. T., Brown, G., Epstein, N. and Steer, R. A. (1988) 'An inventory for measuring clinical anxiety: psychometric properties', *Journal of Consulting and Clinical Psychology* 56: 893–7.

Beck, A. T., Emery, G. and Greenberg, R. (1985) *Anxiety Disorder and Phobias: A Cognitive Perspective*, New York: Guilford Press.

Beck, A. T., Freeman, A. and associates (1990) *Cognitive Therapy of Personality Disorders*, New York: Guilford Press.

Beck, A. T., Rush, A. J., Shaw, B. I. and Emery, G. (1979) *Cognitive Therapy of Depression*, New York: Guilford Press.

Beck, A. T., Ward, C., Mendelson, M., Mock, J. and Erbaugh, J. (1961) 'An inventory for measuring depression', *Archives of General Psychiatry* 4: 561–71.

Crits-Christoph, P. and Barber, J. (eds) (1991) *Handbook of Short-term Dynamic Therapies*, New York: Basic Books.

Flegenheimer, W. V. (1982) *Techniques of Brief Psychotherapy*, New York: Aronson.

Frank, J. D. (1961) *Persuasion and Healing*, Baltimore, MD: Johns Hopkins University Press.

Hawton, K., Salkovskis, P., Kirk, J. and Clark, D. (1989) *Cognitive Behaviour Therapy for Psychiatric Problems: A Practical Guide*, Oxford: Oxford University Press.

Howard, G. S., Nance, D. W. and Myers, P. (1987) *Adaptive Counselling and Therapy*, San Francisco: Jossey Bass.

Mahrer, A. R. (1989) *Experiential Psychotherapy: Basic Practices*, Ottawa: Ottawa University Press.

Malan, D. H. (1976) *The Frontier of Brief Psychotherapy*, New York: Plenum.

—— (1979) *Individual Psychotherapy and the Science of Psychodynamics*, London: Butterworths.

Marteau, L. (1986) *Existential Short Term Therapy*, London: The Dympna Centre.

Nielsen, G. and Barth, K. (1991) 'Short-term anxiety provoking psychotherapy', pp. 45–79 in P. Crits-Christoph and J. Barber (eds) *Handbook of Short-term Dynamic Therapies*, New York: Basic Books.

Norcross, J. C. (ed.) (1986) *Handbook of Eclectic Psychotherapy*, New York: Brunner/Mazel.

Persons, J. B. (1989) *Cognitive Therapy in Practice: A Case Formulation Approach*, New York: W. W. Norton.

Ryle, A. (1990) *Cognitive-Analytic Therapy: Active Participation in Change*, Chichester: Wiley.

—— (1992) 'Critique of a Kleinian case of presentation', *British Journal of Medical Psychology* 65: 309–17.

Safran, J. D. and Segal, Z. V. (1991) *Interpersonal Processes in Cognitive Therapy*, New York: Basic Books.

Scott, J., Williams, J. M. G. and Beck, A. T. (1989) *Cognitive Therapy in Clinical Practice: An Illustrative Casebook*, London: Routledge.

Shazer, S. de (1991) *Putting Difference to Work*, New York: W. W. Norton.

Sledge, W. H., Moras, K., Hartley, D. and Levine, M. A. (1990) 'Effects of time-limited psychotherapy on patient drop-out rates', *American Journal of Psychiatry* 147(10): 1342–7.

Weakland, J. H., Fisch, R., Watzlawick, P. and Bodin, A. (1974) 'Brief therapy: focused problem resolution', *Family Process* 13: 141–68.

Young, J. E. (1990) *Cognitive Therapy for Personality Disorders: A Schema-focused Approach*, Sarasota, FL: Professional Resource Exchange.

Chapter 12

Marital psychotherapy

Tom Leary and Gillian Walton

Marital therapy in the United Kingdom as a separate discipline came to birth pragmatically to address the concerns which arose in the earlier twentieth century about perceived changes in marriage and family life. There was an increase in divorce. Families were easier to limit in size, and the changing social status of women, which began in the nineteenth century with the Married Women's Property Act and continued in the twentieth century with female emancipation (not fully implemented until 1928), had a growing effect on the national consciousness.

Naturally, it is never possible to be simplistic about cause and effect, but the phenomenon of the idea of 'companionate marriage' written about as early as 1909 began to gain ground and take root as the century progressed, and we would suggest that this had an important effect on the way marriages were treated therapeutically. Marie Stopes and some of the earlier radical feminist writers were concerned about the male/female power issues. The pioneers in the field of marital work in the 1930s had a concern about the place of birth control and personal choice in marriage. Relationships other than marital relationships were barely addressed. Even as late as 1952 the Marriage Guidance Council was writing officially that its work in the field of family planning and sexuality was to be explored only within a marital relationship.

Nevertheless, in the late 1940s the Family Discussion Bureau, which was closely connected to the psychoanalytic work of the Tavistock Clinic, was beginning to formulate some of the thinking which came to underpin the work of marital counselling and psychotherapy in the United Kingdom. Notable amongst this writing was Dicks's famous book, *Marital Tensions* (1967), which took some of the thinking further and introduced the concept of the marital relationship being a place where people could, within a safe container, explore some of the unconscious issues which preoccupied them. Perhaps the nursery rhyme 'Jack Sprat' provides a simple illustration of this basic theory of projection within marriage. Jack Sprat ate only 'lean'. Mrs Sprat ate only 'fat'. Together they were content, each doing something of value for the other. Only when tastes changed would there be any difficulty, and at this stage possibly some help might be acquired.

The work of Jung was also seminal, especially to the work of the early Marriage Guidance Council workers, since it was he who first described marriage as a 'psychological relationship' and wrote of marriage as a container within which individuation could happen (1931/1981: 195). He also pointed out the impact of the unconscious lives of parents on their children, a belief which has continued to inform family and marital workers. Important too was the work of John Bowlby (1969), whose study of attachment and loss and whose belief in the possibility of repair during the course of subsequent attachment experiences inspired workers in the field with faith in the value of work in this area.

From the psychoanalytic field came the belief in and exploration of the relationship between the worker and the client as a way of understanding better the relationship between the couple. Some of the technical basis for this has come from the field of object relations with its description of projection and projective identification.

There are now many agencies working in the field of marital counselling. Although there will be variations in their orientation, from the psycho-analytical on the one hand to the pure behavioural on the other, they will have a common belief in the value of committed couple relationships both inside and outside marriage. London Marriage Guidance, for example, saw an almost equal number of married and unmarried people in 1992. For the purposes of this chapter we shall be describing a mainly psycho-dynamic approach, by which we mean that attention is paid to both the unconscious and conscious processes in the relationship and in the work, and to the way in which this is experienced through the transference and counter-transference and reflection processes. In work with couples we take the view that it is preferable to interpret the transference sparingly, concentrating rather on the dynamics of the relationship between the couple themselves.

The first task for the worker is to engage the couple to work in the psychotherapy. Couples present for psychotherapy in a variety of ways. There is often ambivalence about asking for help either on the part of one or both partners. Sometimes there is an immediate crisis such as an affair or a bereavement. At other times the search for psychotherapy is a secret and an approach is made by only one partner, the other partner not being informed. The way in which the approach is made is important and gives valuable information about the clients' feelings about psychotherapy and their feelings about themselves. An example of this would be a young couple both engaged in the caring professions who came to a first appointment saying that their problem was not grave and that they were happy to go on a waiting list. It transpired on further exploration that the problem was in fact quite urgent and pressing. That the clients found it difficult to ask for their needs to be met immediately was indicative of their difficulty in their lives in general to express their feelings and therefore to get their needs met. Another young couple came with the wife saying rather humorously, 'I've dragged him along'. Had the worker not addressed the husband's feelings of ambivalence about being present, then the work would have been jeopardised from the start. It is a cardinal rule that any ambivalence should be addressed openly and fully at the beginning of the work in order for both partners to be engaged. At this time more women than men present initially for couple therapy, but it is becoming increasingly acceptable for men to make the first move.

A mixture of warmth, firmness and confidence is required from the psychotherapist at this stage, since bringing a relationship to psychotherapy is a courageous and potentially risky thing to do, for it can expose clients more than when a partner's views are reported at second hand. It is rather like allowing another person into the most intimate part of one's life.

Psychotherapists come to the initial session with some information concerning the clients before they are met, and, as with any therapeutic encounter, the fantasies are checked out against the reality so that the psychotherapy begins with this very first contact. Attention is given to which of the parties made the approach, and why. The process of making the arrangements for the first meeting is taken seriously, and significance is given to whether the couple come together or singly at the beginning. Most marital psychotherapists have some sort of structured intake model, the aim of which is to explore whether the clients are willing to make a therapeutic alliance with the psychotherapists. Even if a partner comes alone to the first session the psychotherapist will always be keeping the other partner in mind. It can often be useful to think of intake in three stages. The first of these is the presenting problem; the second, the history of the relationship linked with a brief history of the two partners; and the third the establishing of a contract which is mutually acceptable to the client and to the worker. Equal time and attention would be given to all these three stages.

The exploration of the presenting problems relates to the question of why the couple have come now. At this stage the psychotherapist will try to find specific examples of the problem; for example, if there is a communication problem, the psychotherapist would encourage the clients to give actual and specific instances. At this stage no interpretations will be given but attention will be paid to the details of what the clients say, how they say it and how they relate with each other as they are saying it in order to get some understanding of the interaction between the clients and to discover what hurts enough for them to ask for help. The psychotherapists will be looking for the place where the pain and dysfunction are to be found. They will be trying to get some understanding of how the clients heard about marital therapy and of why they have chosen the particular agency they have at the particular time they have. When exploring the history of the relationship attention will be given to how the couple first met and what initially attracted them to each other. It will be useful and important at this stage to have some detail about the courtship and about the form of marriage ceremony chosen if it is a married couple. Couples usually have quite a clear view of when things first began to go wrong and for whom, and they would usually at this stage be encouraged to talk about the good times and the bad times, about any specific life events that they had to face such as bereavements, and the place of children in the relationship.

The physical relationship of the couple is a very important area. This clearly needs to be handled sensitively, but it is essential that it is addressed since it is so very often an indicator of the other areas of communication between the couple and of the life experience they bring to the relationship. When brief personal histories are taken, the couple will be asked to outline details of the family of origin and their place within it and, metaphorically speaking, to introduce the psychotherapist to their parents. At this stage it is useful to know about previous close relationships and whether there is any previous history of therapeutic help or any medical or psychiatric treatment which would be of significance in the work. In order to offer the clients something of value at this introductory point, the psychotherapist would gather the session together in a form which the clients might find meaningful. This would require an analysis of the convergence of knowledge – that is, the clients' impact on the worker and the worker's impact on the clients, in the light of the presenting problem. At this stage, it may be possible to suggest a time-span within which the work might take place, but this might also equally often be left open-ended for the time being. The way in which the financial arrangements are negotiated is also of great significance, and can offer insight into how the couple value each other and their relationship, and potentially the therapeutic endeavour.

The majority of marital work is carried out in a triangular situation; that is, one psychotherapist with two clients. Both clients and psychotherapists can experience this as a challenging and sometimes problematic configuration since it often reflects and re-creates some of the clients' original dilemmas; for example, if there has been a difficulty about adequate resources, then being in a situation where both parties have to share the same hour and the same psychotherapist can revive some of the pain and panic of an earlier time. There is then the opportunity to explore and rework some of the issues involved. An example would be Peter and Joan, each of whom had for different reasons felt uncertain of their value in their lives when younger. Peter's younger siblings were born soon after him and he was then sent abroad to preparatory school, whereas Joan was one of a large family in which the mother's emotional life took up much of the available energy. Whilst young and travelling the world Peter and Joan coped quite well, but marriage and the arrival of children were unexpectedly very difficult for them. They were once again having to share the available resources with others and deeply resented this, using different coping mechanisms. In psychotherapy they found using the same therapeutic space difficult also, and for perfectly good, conscious reasons for a while took to coming separately. It was as a result of allowing this to happen and being influenced by it that the central issue of whether there was enough of the worker to go round could be raised and the couple work could begin with both parties in the room at the same time.

The triangular configuration is of course of enormous significance to everybody. Classical psychoanalytic theory stresses that the original Oedipal experience stays with human beings throughout life. It is therefore important that a couple worker who works alone is very conscious of his or her own attitude to this, since arguably what is experienced by the worker is to be in the omnipotent position of being able to see another marriage from the inside and to share its secrets, rather than to have the experience of the parental relationship of being on the outside. The threat presented to marriages from third parties is often what brings couples to psychotherapy. If the therapeutic session also involves three people, then, although it inevitably mirrors the problem, it can also be used creatively to work with it. Simon and Sarah came to seek help because Simon had been expressing doubts about their ten-year-old relationship which had begun when they were at university. It very soon emerged that this doubt had been triggered off by a recent affair and, on more exploration, that there had almost always been a third party present in the relationship both in reality and certainly in their fantasy since each carried inside them an image of a damaging and intrusive parent, fathers in both cases. In neither case was the mother experienced as either powerful or protective. In the therapeutic relationship with the female psychotherapist the couple explored a different experience of being in a three-person relationship, one which eventually allowed them to be the couple and the psychotherapist the outsider.

Inevitably, one psychotherapist must be either male or female, and this can impose limitations since it is more difficult for some things such as gender issues to be addressed so effectively. Nevertheless, it is by no means ruled out, but it does demand that the psychotherapist is able to draw on both his or her masculine and feminine qualities. The gender of the psychotherapist can indeed be an important factor in constellating important themes in the work. For George and Ruth, a powerful, shared inner object was a parental couple where the father was controlling and dominating and where value was measured by external markers of success, usually examination results. Both George and Ruth were high achievers and successful professional people. However, now that they had small children Ruth was increasingly torn between her career and her maternal instincts and wish to be intimate with her children; George, although a tender father and outwardly supportive of his wife's wishes, was nevertheless torn between sharing with her this change of direction and holding on to the well-known means of valuing her. The female worker for some time was also aware of being measured and evaluated, and indeed the couple would often give feedback on the failures and successes of the previous session. It was only after some time of holding and containing this couple that it was possible to demonstrate the value of the more feminine qualities, and both George and Ruth were able to speak longingly of their mothers and to be less hard on the psychotherapist and each other. Jung's (1981) concept of a psychotherapeutic relationship as a crucible within which things can be explored and in time perhaps re-arrange themselves in a more creative form is as applicable to couples therapy as it is to one-to-one psychotherapy. In both cases the psychotherapist approaches the work open to experience what the clients bring, and open to working with them on the search for their own values and meaning.

REFERENCES

Bowlby, J. (1969) *Attachment and Loss: I – Attachment*, London: Hogarth Press.
Dicks, H. V. (1967) *Marital Tensions: Clinical Studies Towards a Psychological Theory of Interaction*, London: Routledge & Kegan Paul.
Jung, C. G. (1981) 'Marriage as a psychological relationship', pp. 187–201 in H. Read, M. Fordham, and G. Adler (eds) R. F. C. Hull (trans.) *The Development of Personality: The Collected Works*, vol. 17, London: Routledge & Kegan Paul (first published 1931).

Further information

London Marriage Guidance Council
76a New Cavendish Street
Harley Street
London W1M 7RG
Tel.: 071 580 1087

Westminster Pastoral Foundation
23 Kensington Square
London W8 5HN
Tel.: 071 376 2404

Some couples courses are run by:
metanoia Psychotherapy Training Institute
13 North Common Road
Ealing
London W5 2QB
Tel.: 081 579 2505

Chapter 13

Family therapy

Gill Gorell Barnes and Alan Cooklin

THE NATURE OF PSYCHOLOGICAL CHANGES

The nature of psychological change has always been controversial, both within groups of psychologists, sociologists and anthropologists, and between them. Disputes have often been framed in terms of causality – what causes psychological development and its defects? An alternative framework, which will be the focus of this chapter, is to consider where psychological change occurs. Is psychological development to be described, for example, in terms of changes in a young person's observable behaviour, or in terms of the unconscious processes or 'dramas' imputed to be associated with these behaviours? Alternatively, is development to be viewed as a family event in which all generations participate and all actually change, or is it to be seen as a socio-cultural event in which the changes differ markedly depending on the cultural context?

Individual psychotherapies, whether based on a model of learning theory or on psychodynamic understanding, have one thing in common. They view the patient from the standpoint that he or she is an integrated, discrete organism. Family and other 'systems' therapies view the patient as one component in a system or 'organism' (for example, the family) which can manifest malfunction through the behaviour of that component – the patient. That is the major difference.

WHAT IS FAMILY THERAPY?

Family therapy refers, on the one hand, to a 'treatment' – an activity whereby a therapist sits down for one or more sessions with various members of a family to help them change something – and, on the other hand, to a framework for conceptualisation, a way of understanding and thinking about human behaviour which may then be used in a variety of ways. This thinking can then be applied to the family or to other contexts in which human beings live in proximity and may develop intimate relationships.

THE PRINCIPLES

Two important components of the thinking are as follows. First, people are not islands, and their behaviour can only be understood in the context in which it occurs. This is an interpersonal description, which sees behaviour as principally responsive to the context of a person's relationships. This differs from most psychodynamic views in which the individual's 'internal world' is seen as the principal organiser of behaviour. In the latter framework this term 'internal' is frequently used as a synonym for 'psychic' or 'mental', on the assumption that psychic processes are located in an inner space (Rycroft 1968). Thus, 'internal reality' and 'internal conflict' are defined in contrast to the external equivalents, or actual 'external' relationships in which people are currently engaged.

Thus, while the internal world may be seen as a relatively 'closed shop', viewed principally through dreams, associations and play, or manifested by one's behaviour in aspects of relations, in this chapter the individual's internal world is also seen as accessible through the day-to-day interactions with others. These interactions themselves, and the meaning individuals attribute to them, are dependent on the context in which they occur. The meanings are co-constructed within the belief systems of the family over time, or may have been previously attributed to such interactions in former contexts of a similar kind. Such contexts might include families of origin, former marriages or cohabitations, or family interactions from a first family, highlighted for potential action replay in the context of a step family or foster family. The mental representation of sets of relationships and their 'carry-forward' into other contexts is an important contribution to family systems thinking from the field of child development research (Sroufe and Fleeson 1988).

The second major component of family systems thinking therefore is that people in close emotional proximity readily set up stable patterns of interaction. These patterns are made up from a whole series of sequences; repetitive short events involving two or more people. The sum of all these possible sequences can be called the family pattern. This is illustrated later under 'Family patterns and the "family dance"'.

This way of thinking assumes that the actions of all participants in a sequence – the players in a drama – affect one another and, inasmuch as each is reacting to the behaviour of others, the sequence becomes self-regulatory, within boundaries of time, place and role. This in turn assumes that there are no protagonists or victims but that both enter into an interaction and complement one another's behaviour. For this to happen, however, each participant must be bound by the ground rules of the group, and to some extent share similar sets of beliefs and habit responses. This concept has been problematic at times, particularly if one weaker member in a family is seen to be abused by the power – sexual, physical or economic – of another. In any interaction people may not be equal in the degree to which they choose to be bound by a particular set of beliefs. Each person's degree of choice may be dependent on their relative power related to age. Whereas each adult participant to some extent chooses to continue to participate in the drama, the cost of trying to give up that participation may be dramatically different for different family members. The child cannot leave home, and this is frequently also true of the abused wife.

If the family presents a problem, either through an individual's symptom or behaviour, or through showing a set of 'problem' relationships, it is assumed in a family system framework that the problem is in some way connected with the wider organisation of the family. It is not necessarily the case that the family 'causes' the problem, but rather that the problem, as it develops, becomes part of the life and context of the family, and over time may become part of what is familiar and comforting. A practitioner who does 'family therapy' will, therefore, be concerned with the relevant wider family organisation and how this relates to the problem, rather than with any one individual in isolation.

PATTERN AS A CONCEPT IN FAMILY STUDIES

From a research perspective, the idea of systemic properties in family pattern has been built up over the last fifteen years. The interactions between two people, the way aspects of this interaction continue to affect individuals when they are apart and the way the qualities of that interaction are affected by the introduction of a third person have been studied in a variety of family situations. Whereas some studies have focused on behaviour, others have looked at less tangible aspects of mutual influence such as changes in perception and expressed emotion. A summary of these studies can be found in Gorell Barnes (1985, 1993). How much the individual's freedom is actually curtailed by family pattern can of course only remain at the level of hypothesis (both in relation to constraints on the freedom of a client as well as constraints on any therapist who works with that client).

Family therapists address 'pattern' at different levels; some work primarily at the level of observable behaviour, and generally assume the principle that change in behaviour will be followed by changes in beliefs. Others address patterns of belief on the principle that unless beliefs change, what is permitted in the way of behavioural change will remain constrained. Some of these differences in approach will described below.

SYSTEMIC PATTERNING AND INDIVIDUAL FUNCTIONING

The common core of the systemic approach to family life is the belief that family members, engaged in the task of rearing dependent and developing beings, are necessarily interconnected. They both contribute to the formation of patterns between them and are organised in their individual behaviour by their ongoing participation in patterns of mutual influence. Over time, patterns may retain the capacity for change and adaptation or, in situations of threat or fear, may become rigidified and unamenable to adaptive change. The idea of rigidity will be discussed further below.

THE THERAPY

A practitioner who does 'family therapy' will, therefore, be concerned with the total family organisation and how this relates to the problem, rather than to any one individual. In order to do this the practitioner may use various methods, may work through individuals, but keeping their sights on the whole organism of the family. They may work with parts of the family, with the whole nuclear family or with the nuclear and extended family of three generations or more, or even include other members of the community (especially where the family is an ethnic minority in the host culture). The therapy may last for one, two or many sessions of one or more hours. The most common is for the therapist to work for a fairly small number of sessions, averaging about ten.

DISTINCTIONS FROM OTHER THERAPIES

The differences in practice and underlying model of thinking between family (or 'natural group') therapy, group ('stranger group') therapy and individual psychodynamic therapies are summarised in Table 13.1. This summarises differences in the goals of change, the locus of change (that is, between family members rather than between patient and therapist in the first instance), and the process of change, including the role of the therapist in this process.

To summarise, the family systems perspective assumes that

1 people are intimately connected, and those connections can be as valid a way to both understand and promote change in behaviour as can any individual responses;
2 people living in close proximity set up patterns of interaction made up from relatively stable sequences of interaction;
3 therefore the patterns that therapists engage with must, to some degree, and at the same time, act as cause and effect of the problem that they are presented with;
4 problems within patterns in families are related to incongruous adaptation to some environmental influence or change.

Family therapy then addresses itself to changes in patterns of relationships: to those which are lived and witnessed on a daily basis; and to those

Table 13.1 Comparison between family group therapy, 'stranger' group therapy and individual therapy

Individual therapy	'Stranger' group therapy	Natural (family) group therapy
The patient/therapist relationship exists only as a context for psychotherapy.	The group exists only as a context for psychotherapy.	The family has a life of its own, with a history and an anticipated future.
Psychotherapy occurs in the context of the intensity of relationship between therapist and patient.	Psychotherapy occurs in the context of the intensity of relationships between the therapist and group members, and between group members.	Psychotherapy occurs in context of a change in relationship pattern in the context of the current intense family relationships.
Thus the therapist is central.	Thus at different times the therapist or some part of the group may be central.	Thus the therapist is principally an agent of change rather than a central actor.
The therapist *allows* the intensity of affect from the patient to him/her to develop (although the setting may provoke it).	The therapist facilitates the 'integration' or 'gelling' of the group in the service of psychotherapy.	The therapist is more likely to be concerned to develop the differentiation of the group.
Therapist and patient maintain a non-social relationship (to varying degrees, depending on the model).	The members are discouraged from meeting between sessions.	The members remain in an intense relationship between sessions.
The therapist does not try to develop a structure in the therapeutic relationship, and interpretations may be used to highlight inappropriate structural patterns sought by the patient. In child psychotherapy the therapist *may* be forced to be a parental adult.	There is no permanent structural organisation of the group. That which evolves is transient and often seen by the therapist as a re-creation of past or 'inner' families of the members. The members are usually of similar age, as may be the psychotherapist. The psychotherapist aims to be 'meta' to the group.	The family has an inherent and necessary hierarchical organisation, relating to the different ages, developmental positions and responsibilities of the members. As the therapist is an adult, this will affect how he or she is used by the family. The therapist aims to *think* from a meta-position, but may *act* in a partisan manner.
Change occurs through understanding the meaning of an old pattern in a new context. This change has then to be generalised to other contexts. The pattern in the original context may or *may not* change.	Change occurs through understanding of the meaning of an old pattern in a new context. This change has then to be generalised to other contexts. The pattern in the original context may or *may not* change.	Change occurs through changing the pattern in an 'old' context, so that the context itself is changed.

Source: reproduced with permission from Cooklin (1990).

which are carried in people's minds. These can usefully be conceptualised as 'mental representations of sets of relationships' (Main 1991), a development of the idea of 'inner working models' of relationship, originally postulated by Bowlby (see Byng-Hall 1991).

RESISTANCE, HOMEOSTASIS, RIGIDITY AND INCONGRUENT ADAPTATION

A key concept in individual psychodynamic therapies is that of resistance. This assumes that change, particularly in terms of the acquisition of new insights, is avoided or 'resisted' in the service of preserving some aspect or fantasy of the self. In the family systems literature there is no equivalent to this notion, although two concepts are to some degrees analogous. These are the concepts of homeostasis and rigidity. The former (Jackson 1957) assumed that interactions in the family tended towards the maintenance of a steady state, rather as the biological organism uses feedback of biochemical processes to maintain a sufficiently steady internal environment. Such an idea would be in conflict with the changes inherent in growth and development and would therefore postulate possible sources of conflict at such developmental transitions as adolescence. Many writers have pointed out the potential flaws in such a concept; particularly that change is happening all the time in family life and not only at critical transitions. Furthermore, the concept assumes an almost pernicious holding-back against change. A wider sensitivity to issues of power, particularly in relation to gender, race and poverty, suggests a less 'obstructive' framework for such processes (see 'Incongruent adaptation' below).

A concept related to homeostasis was that of 'rigidity' of family pattern, meaning that roles (who dominates, who submits, who leads and who is led) and responses are rigidly organised, and that roles and responses do not adapt to changes in context. For example, if a particular adult is accustomed to making decisions about issues in which they have competence, in a 'rigid' system that person would be unlikely to defer to someone with greater competence in a context in which they may have no expertise.

The concept of rigidity has been similarly criticised as giving no recognition to the possible underlying forces that may have played a part in the failure of a family to adapt to a new context, whether this be of place – in cases of migration; of lifestyle – in response to economic changes or illness; or resulting from the changes inherent in development.

Thus, throughout all families, there is a constant tension between these contradictory forces for change and stability. Many problems can be understood in terms of the failure to resolve this conflict in the family, or, put another way, in terms of the adaptation becoming incongruent to the current focus of development in the family, although it may have been quite congruent to an earlier set of circumstances. Within this chapter this will be referred to as 'incongruent adaptation'.

The term 'incongruent adaptation' has been chosen in order to stress

1 that many problems are based on genuine attempts at adaptation to a problem or new situation, rather than on any inherent 'resistance' or pathology;
2 that the form of adaptation to a problem may have fitted well with some early situation, or some different context – but is ineffective in, or aggravates, this situation.
3 that the use of earlier and inappropriate (or incongruous) ways of adapting to a problem is often provoked or intensified in situations of fear or threat. These could include severe illness, various forms of persecution (such as ethnic or racial persecution) or disasters.

MODELS OF FAMILY THERAPY

No attempt will be made here to describe the many different models of psychotherapy used within the field over the last thirty years. These may be followed up through texts referenced at the end of this chapter. Key approaches have included strategic work, structural work, psychodynamic approaches, multigenerational approaches, the study of family myths and scripts, the 'Milan' approach, and a number of approaches which have been included under the heading of 'constructivism' (Jones 1993).

All the models include at least the premise that the connections between people are as valid a way in which both to understand and promote change in the behaviour of those individuals as any individual responses. In general, in all approaches the therapist is less concerned with pathology and with dysfunction, and more concerned with the promotion of both latent and actual strengths in the family; with encouraging the discovery of latent and new repertoires of behaviour, whilst in some way blocking those which promote dysfunction.

Gurman *et al.* have further defined family therapy as

> any psychotherapeutic endeavour that explicitly focuses on altering the interactions between or among family members, and seeks to improve the functioning of the family as a unit, or its subsystems and/or the functioning of individual members of the family. This is the goal regardless of whether or not an individual is identified as the patient.
> (1986: 565)

Three main groups of models have had a major influence on work in Britain and Europe. These are the structural approach, strategic approaches, and the Milan (and 'Post-Milan') approaches.

In structural work the therapist attempts to achieve small changes in sequence and pattern as they occur in a session. Such small changes are themselves unlikely to be lasting, unless they are repeated with sufficient intensity and frequency that they become part of a new folklore in the family. In these situations, a small shift in current behaviour becomes the focal point for the initiation of a new set of perspectives between family members about one another. Thus there can be some mutual revision of the perceptions of one another, and ultimately of their views of such relationships.

Structural family therapy addresses itself to the developmental context of the problem, the family itself; and works directly with the interactions as they occur, whereas a group of psychotherapies known collectively as 'strategic' look at the problem in a variety of social contexts. Therapists address themselves to the meaning attributed to the symptom, in the context in which it had a lived existence. Practitioners differ in their view as to whether the symptom is primarily a failed solution to another problem; or whether it carried an important meaning in relation to some other aspect of the successful functioning of the family. Strategic therapists tend to divide into those concerned with problems as a manifestation of failed solutions, and those interested almost exclusively in the 'exceptional' solutions which 'worked', and which are then amplified as the focus of psychotherapy.

Therapists who follow the solution-focused brief therapy model take as their premise the essential resilience of people which becomes depleted at times of critical life transitions, or stressful life events. At such times options for solving problems may diminish, and small problems may assume greater significance. As energy becomes increasingly directed into trying to solve a particular problem, so the attempted failed solution becomes the problem. Time in psychotherapy is therefore spent looking at the solutions that family members have used and particularly those that have 'worked' – that is, are exceptional – however rarely. It is assumed that people will have attempted more than one solution and that some of these may have had a glimmer of success. The exception to the rule of failure is therefore sought and amplified. Since people usually apply what seem to them to be common-sense solutions, uncommon solutions may be proposed, thus interrupting the usual pattern of behaviour.

A second group of strategic therapists understand the symptom primarily as part of the mechanism by which particular families regulate themselves. To lose the symptom would be to face a change in the overall organisation of the family, and a change in the beliefs by which the family regulate their collective identity. Many families would seek change for one member without wishing for change in their own living patterns. Working this way, therefore, the therapist links the symptom to the system in a number of ways, expressing curiosity and interest in the part it played in wider family life, and the maintenance of the stability and coherence of the system as it became organised over time. The goal of working this way is to create a perceptual redefinition of the problem and its 'lived existence'. However, the meanings attached to the problem may have been developed through a number of differing time-spans (Cooklin 1982). Sometimes they have come from one generation only, and sometimes they have been handed down over a number of generations without re-examination as to their usefulness.

In recent years this way of working has been developed alongside ideas of 're-authoring', or 'restorying', and narrative. The impact of the more openly politicised voices of women, of groups of different cultures, of victims of racism and of survivors of abuse, as well as work with victims of political oppression and torture, has increased awareness of the distinction between the 'dominant' and 'marginalised' discourse in different societies. It has also highlighted the way in which people only have access to part of their own history through the impact of larger systemic forces such as gender, race, class, economic status and age.

The Milan approach, developed in many settings within Britain, extended strategic thinking to address the complex mesh of meaning systems that families develop around problems; both of everyday life, and inherited from former generations. Campbell *et al.* have lucidly distinguished the value of this approach in the following way:

> We would apply this approach to any family in which the alternative solution to the problem has over time become entwined with the family's meaning system so that the alternative solutions are constrained by belief and relationships at one remove from the problem behaviour. . . . We assume that some feedback will create conflict about people's beliefs and relationships. When this happens an individual becomes preoccupied with the context of the message and the relationship to the giver of the message and the content of the message is lost. The result of this loss is that the conflict is incorporated into the family's meaning system.
>
> (1991: 325–62)

FAMILY SYSTEMS AND SOCIAL CHANGE

As family life and its structures have themselves changed in the United Kingdom, the integration of a systems perspective that pays attention to wider systems affecting family life has become more urgent. Early family therapy theory and training was largely based on the theory of the family as a stable, two-parent system. With one-third of first marriages and nearly two-thirds of subsequent marriages ending in divorce, stability can no longer be assumed. In addition, awareness of the many other disruptions and transitions experienced by families through economic pressures, such as unemployment and migration, challenged a theory based on ideas of a regulated society functionally organised at different levels with similarities of patterns between the different levels. Within Britain, attention was additionally paid to families formed by fostering and late adoption, and to the multiple serial transitions experienced by many children as a result of changes in marriage, cohabitation and separation experiences.

The diversity of race and culture within British society has led to wider recognition of many functional structures for bringing up children that differ greatly from the former norms of a family theory based on Western ethnocentric life-cycle traditions. Awareness of their own ignorance among family therapists has therefore led to the development of a more constructivist or exploratory approach in clinical settings, alongside a sensitivity to the need to understand the strengths inherent in cultural patterning that may be radically different from the therapist's own. These require changes within family therapy theory, as with other psychotherapy theory, at the levels of individual development, family and kinship structures, assumptions about health and normality within widely differing cultures, and new understandings of religion and spiritual meaning systems and their impact on culture and custom. In addition, assumptions based on the idea of stability of family life and the internal coherence of systems patterned over time, which developed in the 1950s and 1960s, have to be reconsidered in the light of the transitions and disruptions experienced by many families seen in clinical settings in the 1990s.

The degree to which social issues and psychotherapy connect within the domain of the family therapist varies widely within the field, but within a feminist perspective these are seen as part of the essential process of change. The discussion of the personal in the political, and the recognition of both client and female therapist as subject to the same socio-political forces within a patriarchal society, lead to a more open and even-handed discussion of the problem in context (Jones 1989). Women's thinking about the commonality of structured oppression within society has been amplified by the development of black commentaries on transracial and transcultural psychotherapy. The need for white professionals to develop a structural pluralist view of society, to recognise and acknowledge that there are many perspectives of equal validity, rather than one predominant homogeneous view with others marginalised or discounted, has amplified the awareness of family therapists that the way in which they think about the task of psychotherapy plays a part in a number of wider political debates.

FAMILY PATTERNS AND THE 'FAMILY DANCE': PATTERN IN ACTION

Imagine an event where you are sitting at dinner with some members of your family – say, your parents if they are alive, or perhaps your children.

Maybe there are others: grandparents, siblings, aunts, uncles or cousins. Imagine that a small and common or familiar conflict develops. Perhaps it starts with the question of who is to visit whom at the weekend, or some comment on your dress or diet. If you can imagine such a scene, you may be able to predict more or less accurately who would say what, roughly in what order, and the sort of tone in which each would speak. You may be able to go further. You may be able to predict to what degree of tension or passion the conflict will develop and two or three ways in which it will 'end'. What you will have remembered is an interactional sequence and one which is likely to be repeated with a similar shape and similar attitudes taken by the various members, despite the fact that the subject of conflict might differ markedly. We put the 'end' in inverted commas because, of course, it is not really the end. It is only the punctuation of a sequence which, together with other sequences, makes up the interactional pattern of the family. This sequence could 'end' with a senior member of the household perhaps looking stern, raising his voice, perhaps shouting, banging the table, perhaps threatening violence or perhaps carrying out violence. The amount of feeling and the level of conflict tolerated in different families will be idiosyncratic to that family. However, the ending of a sequence with one member taking a strong and challenging position is one pattern which will occur in many families in a predominantly patriarchal culture. In cultures with a different orientation to gender and power this may be different.

There are many alternative punctuations (or ways of 'slicing up' a circular event into an apparently 'linear' causal series of events) to such a sequence. It could end with somebody becoming upset, bursting into tears, leaving the room or the house, or with another member placating and 'calming things down'. It could end with a diversion: someone making a joke, an external intrusion such as the telephone or perhaps a child becoming excited or misbehaving. Diversion by a child is a common ending to such a sequence of conflict in many families. In some families, however, the child's overreaction to increasing tension is in somatic form. If the child has a predisposition to asthma, for example, the child is likely to have an asthma attack at times of high tension, particularly if this concerns the parents. Such an attack will often then divert attention from the conflict in the family, as members of the family co-operate to assist the afflicted member (Minuchin *et al.* 1978). At this point, the problem of considering causality can be seen. It could be said that the tension in the family precipitates the asthmatic attacks; alternatively, it could be said that the asthmatic attacks control tension in the family. The important point is that these patterns do not occur because somebody 'makes' them happen. Rather, they are a function of the organisation of relationships which has become set up in the family. We could postulate unconscious motives for each member which propagate such patterns, but an important aspect of these patterns is their provision of some stability to the family. Inasmuch as maintaining stability is often experienced by the members as a way of protecting the family and those in it, therefore one function of such behaviour is to achieve a degree of mutual protectiveness.

THEORIES OF ORGANISATION AND INTERACTION IN FAMILIES

Two related sets of ideas have provided frameworks for considering the family as a system rather than just a set of individuals. These are general systems theory and cybernetics (Ashby 1956; Von Bertalanffy 1950; Hoffman 1981).

General systems theory

General systems theory is not a theory of causality, but a theory of organisation. It is a way of categorising systems throughout nature both living and inanimate. It considers the family as a living system and considers its capacity to adapt in terms of the following:

1 The boundary around the family and around the subsystems in the family. This relates to the degree to which family members maintain a close unity within the family, or engage actively with the outside world. This, in turn, controls the input and output of information to and from the family. Information includes people. Thus a family with a very impermeable boundary will be likely to adapt poorly to the arrival of new members – babies, grandparents, boyfriends or girlfriends – and will be intolerant of members moving out (such as around the time of adolescence).
2 The theory also considers the differentiation of the subsystems within the family and the degree to which the boundary around these is clear. For example, the marital relationship is a separate subsystem from, say, the parental subsystem. In a family in which the members say 'We always do everything together', the differentiation of the parents having a separate relationship may be poorly recognised. This, in turn, may militate against the development of any other set of separate relationships.

In addition to the degree to which the family is differentiated into subsystems, it will also form part of other subsystems to varying degrees. For example, the family may be part of an extended family network and the different members may be part of other suprasystems within the community, such as work, school, and/or social groups.

Cybernetics

Cybernetics is a set of principles adapted from electronic control systems. The thermostat in a central heating system is the simplest example.

Cybernetic principles are used to consider ways in which the family has developed habits that tend to neutralise or stabilise any change. In an example of Susan, an anorexic girl of seventeen, the father became depressed after she was admitted to hospital, began to eat and to make relationships with boys in the same unit. Strains in the marriage appeared and her mother developed a number of hypochondriacal symptoms. Susan's younger brother, Ben, began to steal. Susan eventually became so worried about them all that she discharged herself from hospital, soon after which she resumed her fasting behaviour. The others then improved.

Thus, the behaviour of the members of the family could be seen as responding to a change (the young girl leaving home), whilst the effect of their behaviour was ultimately to maintain stability, albeit an inappropriate stability and at a high cost. It was from observations such as these that the term 'family homeostasis' was coined (Jackson 1957).

DEVELOPMENT AS MULTI-PERSON EVENT

Most child development literature considers the development of thoughts, traits or attachments as 'inside' the child (Kessen 1979), and most studies provide more information about *what* happens in large samples than about *how* it happens. As Radke-Yarrow *et al.* (1989) point out, the research data of developmental psychology do not seem to be capturing what appears obvious to the naïve observer of society: namely, the degree to which children and their environments are connected.

If we take adolescence as an example, it is not only an individual, but also a family stage of development. 'Adolescent' parents are different from the parents of young children. They are likely to be reciprocally ambiguous in their responses, may even be preoccupied with questions about separation and individuation for themselves, may have disturbing sexual fantasies precipitated by the young person's emergent sexuality or sexual behaviour, and so on.

EXAMPLE

An example of the way in which individual development and behaviour can be seen as functionally related to or 'fitting' the wider organisation of relationships in the family is given below.

Joanna, her husband Billy and baby Jemima had been referred to us during Jemima's first year of life. When Jemima was five months old Joanna's grandmother, who had been the 'good grandmother' in her family, died. She had acted as a support to Joanna when her own mother had become severely incapacitated, after suffering brain damage in a car accident. This had left Joanna as the eldest responsible female in her family of origin, in which she had been responsible for the upbringing of her three siblings. The grandmother's death recreated for Joanna a pattern in which she felt left alone to take care of others, and also posed a new challenge about how she was to do this. Was she to do it in the style of her family of origin which had made many unusual adaptations to give the handicapped mother the 'illusion' that she was still in charge, or was she to adapt to a carefully cultivated norm of health and well-being that her husband's family consciously paraded? She became acutely depressed, started drinking heavily and experienced three admissions to psychiatric hospitals, subsequently discharging herself and refusing to take medication. She and her husband both came to see us with baby Jemima throughout most of the first two years of Jemima's life. Joanna retained a hostile view of the whole process of these 'conversations'. These often consisted of her long monologues about her precarious attempts to maintain a daily structure by driving around London with her dog and her baby in a small car, and dropping in unexpectedly on friends who became less sympathetic as the time went by. She described her home as a 'trap', talked obsessively of 'being inside a concrete box' and 'a tiny dirty window' through which she would peer at a hostile world from which she felt excluded. She would often respond to any attempt at contact by the therapists or by her husband by repeating *ad nauseam*, 'I only see four walls'. None the less Jemima continued to thrive, the house was kept at a reasonable standard, and Joanna remained outside the hospital. Joanna clearly enjoyed aspects of the therapeutic conversation, in which much teasing and humour would go on, introducing a number of other frames through which her dilemmas might be considered. However, her continued obsessive preoccupation with 'the four walls' suggested to us that the choices she saw herself facing needed to be contextualised in a wider family arena for her to believe that her position could ever change.

We called together both sets of grandparents and all the living siblings. One brother had hanged himself the previous year, and the reasons for his suicide remained obscure. However, it was clear that in Joanna's mind his death was associated with staying within the domain of his parents' family home, a farm in a remote part of England. Joanna herself used to visit this farm, where her father and mother still lived, nearly every weekend. She also expressed a longing to be free of the compulsion to visit. The rationale we gave to the family for this 'clan' gathering was that together we would explore the way in which people carry into marriage the traditions, cultures and influences of the families they come from, and the way in which these cultures may form part of the difficulties any couple are having. As the whole family were very concerned about the well-being of the joint grandchild, as well as the couple, all four grandparents and the adult siblings on both sides of the family attended.

The definition of the couple as part of the wider family system was well received by Joanna's father, who had been described to us previously as highly eccentric. Throughout the meeting he remained highly self-referential, continuing an uninterrupted stream of talk which seemed at first unrelated to the concurrent family discussion. However, he also interjected messages that suggested he had a better understanding of his daughter's dilemma than anyone else. Observing that he and his wife also had problems, and that while the focus might be on the young couple today, it might more appropriately be on the senior generation tomorrow, he commented, 'Joanna has had to evolve by herself over the last twenty-five years since her mother's accident.' He described how he saw himself and his wife as actors, playing the part of normality. He constructed this for the two of them, with himself acting as his wife's memory (the young adults confirmed that her memory was lost). He contrasted the positive qualities of the grandmother Joanna had lost (his own mother) with the more eccentric and formally disturbed qualities of his wife's family: 'Everyone used to go to psychiatrists in Jane's family.' He represented a world in which all figures who were 'parental' were perceived by society as psychiatrically disturbed and in need of treatment. This presented a marked contrast to Billy's parents. They busied themselves with trying to pin down the many ways in which Joanna's 'mad' behaviour was an annoyance to the rest of the family, and ways in which this might be changed, making many practical suggestions about what would constitute good child care for Jemima.

During the course of the conversation Joanna revealed that she thought she would never make the transition from being a Brown, her family of origin which she visited each weekend, to being a Drewitt, the family name of her husband. This became a metaphor for the two different worlds of experience she was contending with, the world of her brain-damaged mother and illogical, eccentric father; a domain within which her elder brother had recently killed himself, and a world of healthy child development which she saw herself as having lost following the loss of an active participant 'mother' in her own childhood. This world was now represented by the Drewitt family, as her husband's sisters had many healthy, bright small children, and Joanna did not always feel that her own child was welcome there. To join the 'normal' world was experienced by her as an active betrayal of the world of her childhood and the current world of her family of origin. To be 'normal' was taboo. Confronted by the power of her father's rambling and random stream of interruptions, her husband challenged her more directly with the dilemma.

'Your father's world is more real to you than my world.' She denied it, but went on to show how compelling the reality of the world of her family of origin was for her: 'Every weekend when I visit, I feel I am going back into a Brown world. I have this hammering in my head to become a Brown again.' Her husband engaged her in an intense conversation about his family's readiness to have her 'enter' their family, although he was unaware of all the connotations of disloyalty outlined above. In the middle of this her father began to talk at the same time in a compelling, low-key voice on the other side of her. Gradually her head turned as her attention was drawn back to her father, who was saying without any logical sequence 'I don't worship any family . . . Jo and Billy have got to find their own way somehow . . . they got married in the Western Isles . . . where do you want to be on Friday, Saturday and Sunday?' At the point where her head turned, both therapists, her husband and her father engaged in a lively and direct critique of the very brief and intensely highly packed sequence that had just taken place. The taboo against discussing the interconnection of Joanna's behaviour with that of her father, the Brown world; and the pain of transition from her father's domain of logic (in which as the keeper of his wife's memory he held the power for two parents) to that of a more everyday reality, was vigorously debated. Her father, accepting both his power and the necessity of its overthrow, cheerfully said, 'I'm older you see . . . some weeks I accomplish nothing, other weeks I write to Washington, I write to Moscow.' His inability to achieve much in the 'everyday' world and Joanna's competence in surviving in it were highlighted.

The dangers of parenthood in this family were discussed in the context of Joanna's mother's injury. Many constuctions could be made from this dense text, but those which overtly showed themselves as freeing Joanna began with the open highlighting of the power of her father's voice in a context where other voices, her husband's and her own, could be heard in a new way by the whole family. This allowed the beginning of new constructions of how she herself could be a parent; differences both of generation and gender. These could develop because her husband, far from 'holding' her memory during her 'mad' episodes, as her father had done for her mother had always held out for them having their own validity, although their meaning was not yet revealed. Joanna and Billy needed much further support as their family grew in size, but the intervals between our meetings became longer and longer as they gained in confidence.

WHAT WERE THE FUNCTIONS OF THERAPY FOR THIS FAMILY WITH THESE PROBLEMS?

This case illustrated the vonvening of the family to face the highly complex forces (many of which could be defined as unconscious) mutually acting on the different members of the two sets of families, and which were destructively manifested in the form of Joanna's restricted life and perspective, as well as in the risks to her children. The therapists worked at three main levels:

1 challenging Joanna and Billy to accept the control of their own definitions of good and bad, close and distant, and so on;

2 Thus encouraging Joanna and Billy to view Joanna's complaints as relevant if falling in the framework of a need for new definitions of how a family should be;

3 challenging the absolute definitions of 'truth' expounded by Billy's family, while connecting to, and redefining the apparently 'crazy' world of Joanna's family.

CONCLUSION

In this chapter we have aimed to illustrate both the different and complemtary frames of thinking implicit in the family systems framework in relation to individual psychodynamic thinking. We have been at pains to stress the framework of thinking as a useful field within which other forms of thinking can easily be connected, rather than prescribing a 'therapy' as a 'cure-all'. We hope the reader will find ways to use the ideas in his or her day-to-day work, whatever the orientation.

REFERENCES

Ashby, W. R. (1956)*Introduction to Cybernetics*, New York: Wiley.

Byung-Hall, J. (1991) 'The application of attachment theory to understanding and treatment in family therapy', pp. 199-215 in C.M. Parkes, J. Stevenson-Hinde and P. Marris (eds) *Attachment Across the life Cycle*, London: Routledge.

Campbell, D., Draper, R. and Crutchly, E. (1991) 'The Milan systematic approach to family therapy', pp. 325–62 in A. S. Gurman and D. P. Kniskern (eds) *Handbook of Family Therapy*, vol. 2, New York: Brunner/Mazel.

Cooklin, A. (1987) 'Change in here and now systems vs. systems overture', pp. 37– 74 in A. Bentovim, G. Gorell Barnes and A. Cooklin (eds) *Family Therapy: Complementary Frameworks of Theory and Practice*, London: Academic Press.

——(1990) 'Therapy, the family and others', pp. 73–90 in H. Maxwell (ed.) *Psychotherapy: An Ouline for Trainee Psychiatrists, Medical Students and Practitioners*, London: Whurr.

Gorell Barnes, G. (1985) 'Systems theory and family therapy', pp. 216–32 in M. Rutter and L. Hersov (eds.) *Modern Child Psychiatry*, vol. 2, Oxford: Blackwell.

——(1993) 'Family therapy', pp. 944–65 in M. Rutter, L. Hersov and E. Taylor (eds), *Modern Child Psychiatry*, vol. 3, London: Blackwell.

Gurman, A. S., Kniskern, D. P. and Pinsof, W. M. (1986) 'Research on the process and outcome of marital and family therapy', in S. L. Garfield and A. E. Bergin (eds) *Handbook of Psychotherapy and Behaviour Change: An Emperical Analysis*, 3rd edn, New York: John Wiley.

Hoffman, L. (1981) *Foundations of Family Therapy*, New York: Basic Books.

Jackson, D. D. (1957) 'The question of family homestasis', *psychiatric Quarterly Supplement* 31: 79–80.

Jones, E. (1989) 'Feminism and family therapy: can mixed marriages work?', pp. 63–81 in R. J. Perelberg and A. C. Miller (eds) *Gender and Power in Families*, London and New York: Routledge.

——(1993) *Family Systems Therapy: Developments in the Milan Systematic Therapies*, Chichester: John Wiley.

Kessen, W. (1979) 'The American child and other cultural inventions', *American Psychologist* 34: 815–20.

Main, M. (1991) 'Metacognitive knowledge, metacognitive monitoring and single (coherent) vs multiple (incoherent) models of attachment: findings and directions for future research', in C. M. Parkes, J. Stevenson Hinde and P. Marris (eds) *Attachment across the Life Cycle*, London: Routledge.

Minuchin, S., Rosman, B. and Baker, L. (1978) *Psychosomatic Families*, Cambridge, Mass.: Harvard University Press.

Radke-Yarrow, M., Richards, J. and Wilson, W. E. (1989) 'Child development in a network of relationships', pp. 48–63 in R. A. Hinde and J. Stevenson-Hinde (eds) *Relationships within Families: Mutual Influence*, Oxford: Oxford Scientific Publications.

Rycroft, C. (1968) *A Critical Dictionary of Psychoanalysis*, Harmondsworth: Penguin.

Sroufe, L. A. and Fleeson, J. (1988) 'The coherence of family relationships', in R. A. Hinde and J. Stevenson-Hinde (eds) *Relationships within Families: Mutual Influence*, Oxford: Oxford Scientific Publications.

Von Bertalanffy, L. (1950) 'The theory of open systems in physics and biology', *Science* 3: 25–9.

INFORMATION ON TRAINING

The Institute of Family Therapy
43 New Cavendish Street
London W1M 7RD
Tel.: 071 935 1651

or

The Association for Family Therapy
5 Heol Seddon
Cardiff
Wales

A learning video/computer pack, 'Family Therapy Basics', is available from

Marlborough Family Service
38 Marlborough Place
London NW8 OPJ
Tel.: 071 624 8605

Chapter 14

Group psychotherapy

Oded Manor

Group psychotherapy usually refers to situations in which between seven and twelve people meet together with one or two specially trained psychotherapists for between one and three hours, usually once or twice a week. Sometimes the number of these meetings is agreed in advance – for example, six sessions at the minimum – but a year's duration is more common. The membership of the group may be closed or open. So-called slow open groups may continue for many years. Yet, even when membership is open – that is, new members can join whenever a vacancy is available – usually there is a core membership of people who have participated long enough to sustain the therapeutic momentum while others find their way in what is, after all, a rather unusual group situation.

Most groups meet in the same middle-sized room, where they sit in a circle so that each person can see all the others. Usually the culture is rather informal. However, in the more strict psychoanalytic groups surnames are still used, particularly in relation to the psychotherapist. Equally, the more psychoanalytically orientated the psychotherapist, the more she or he is likely to say nothing at the beginning of the session. Instead, the group members themselves are expected to say whatever comes into their minds so that free association emerges. Other psychotherapists may begin in this way or they may begin by expressing their own feelings first. Some would add to these also a theme, or a query which is on their minds. Still a third style may involve giving members a topic or even suggesting and conducting an exercise related to interpersonal relationships. Whatever the therapeutic style, full and reasonably even participation of all the members is usually considered desirable.

I would suggest that group psychotherapy is utilising experiences which are unique to group situations in offering individuals psychotherapeutic help in their personal, interpersonal and social relationships. Broad as it is, this definition marks out group psychotherapy from other uses of small groups as a way of helping people. For example, the term 'psychotherapeutic' is there to suggest that whatever else is experienced, in group psychotherapy attention is deliberately focused on processes which may be out of awareness. This is not necessarily the case in behavioural group therapy, in group counselling and in social group work.

Another difference is the focus on 'individuals'. Group psychotherapy is there first and foremost for each of its individual members. The major experiences of group psychotherapy have to be helpful to its individual members; not necessarily to the group as a whole, nor to other people involved with those individuals. This emphasis on the needs of the individual members marks out group psychotherapy as different from small-group training for managers, the T-group approach, and from social action groups.

The emphasis on relationship is included in the definition in order to acknowledge that in group psychotherapy practical help is usually not provided to members directly. Whereas some group psychotherapists encourage members to explore what they themselves can do to obtain or earn money, to secure their accommodation, or to receive legal protection, others do not do even that. Seldom would a group psychotherapist act directly for or on behalf of any of the members. This type of involvement is more typical of group counsellors and social group workers.

Before pointing to the reasons for all this and to some of the advantages of group psychotherapy, I would like to emphasise strongly that this method is only one among others, and will not always be effective.

WHEN GROUP PSYCHOTHERAPY MAY NOT BE SUITABLE

Individual situations

It is my experience that group psychotherapy is not likely to be suitable for a minority of one. People who present conditions that are likely to be recognised by other group members as totally different from those presented by the rest of the group, and cannot be changed, seem to suffer in group psychotherapy rather than benefit from it. Examples could include particularly low intelligence, psychotic difficulties in a person joining a group where everybody else presents neurotic ones, marked hearing and vision impairment, or vastly different characteristics such as age or race. However, some remarkable exceptions exist – for example, one person with very short-term memory has benefited a group and from a group in unexpected ways.

Total confidentiality is another constraint. If the person is struggling with issues that require total professional confidentiality, that person may feel too anxious to participate in a group even when the members commit themselves to such a level of confidentiality (Norcross and Goldfried 1992). For example, a bisexual married man holding a secret relationship with a man while raising his family may find a group of heterosexually involved adults not only too different, but also too threatening to his family constellation.

Disabling past experiences can also be counter-indications. Some people were so badly bullied at school that they would not entertain joining any other group for the rest of their lives. Others were so badly and continuously scapegoated that they became paralysed in group situations and no group psychotherapist can change that. Such people may well begin psychotherapy with one individual psychotherapist.

Couple situations

Not all couples should be offered group psychotherapy either. For example, couples who are struggling with immediate issues in their sexual relationship may need the detailed attention of a psychotherapist, and the privacy of couples therapy for themselves.

Family situations

When a family is concerned, some situations call for family therapy instead of group psychotherapy. It is clearly recognised now that children can influence the dynamics of their own families over and above their parents' influence (Boer and Dunn 1992). When difficulties are presented in which children are involved, and the parents show sufficient concern accompanied with the potential to change the situation, group psychotherapy may miss the point. Only family therapy can address the immediate relationships between parents and children and among the siblings themselves.

GENERAL ADVANTAGES

Detailed research findings can be found in Garfield and Bergin (1986). For this brief chapter, six general features can be mentioned in relation to all types of group psychotherapy.

1 *Strength in numbers*: If the group becomes supportive of its members, each is then appreciated by quite a number of others. The mere expression of approval, appreciation and encouragement while a group member is remembering painful past experiences or trying to change certain behaviours seems a great help to many.

2 *The anonymity of the crowd*: Almost the reverse of strength in numbers, the group also offers members escape from attention. As some talk, others can temporarily withdraw their attention. It is noteworthy that some people find the continuous attention offered in individual psychotherapy too demanding. Group psychotherapy offers them a safe haven where they can participate in their own time. Other people tend to enter such intense conflicts, particularly with authority figures, that no individual psychotherapist can contain them for long enough to effect change.

Such people can diffuse their anger by letting others take over for a while, and still benefit.

3 *The advantage of being weak*: Group situations offer their members a distinct power balance. Since each individual is to some extent unique, no two people are totally alike. Therefore, at a certain level each member is pitched against the whole group and is unable to change the group culture alone. Groups do generate the experience of helplessness as much as they raise self-esteem. When people feel helpless they easily feel as if they were children, and with those child-like experiences can come the warm acceptance of being held unconditionally, as a child is held by an accepting parent. Being so 'contained' seems to provide strong emotional encouragement to members.

4 *Going back to go forward*: Feeling helpless in the group has another consequence. As each member realises their weakness in relation to the whole group, each feels like a child. With these child-like feelings aroused, memories of earlier years surface rather easily and quite spontaneously. Such surfacing is called 'regression' and seems helpful in re-evaluating earlier experiences and altering patterns of feelings, behaviour and thoughts in the present. By being forced to go back to their childhood, members are offered the opportunity to go forward into a different adulthood.

5 *The group as a psychosocial microcosm*: If the group is properly constituted, the members have enough in common so they identify with one another while, at the same time, they also differ sufficiently to receive a wide range of responses to their feelings, thoughts and behaviour. Such diversity within commonality creates ambiguity in relationships, and ambiguity leads people to make guesses. When people begin to guess how to behave they fall back on their habits; they re-enact central patterns of their other relationships. It is assumed that these patterns – dominating others, clowning, reasoning, and so on – sustain the problems for which people come for help. At some point or another during the development of the group, each member is likely to reconstruct their prevailing pattern. So the group becomes an intense miniature of the members' relationships in the outside world. When such re-enactment occurs, each member's pattern is amenable to exploration, to change and to generalisation outside of the group.

6 *Free experimentation*: The group is usually composed of members of equal formal status, joining the group on the same basis. Therefore, during the group's development each has potentially the chance of entering many different roles: assertive, receptive, humorous, supportive and so on. Because the members are not bound to one another in any way outside the group, each can experiment with new behaviour without immediate consequences in their daily life. This freedom to experiment without consequences seems to enable the testing out of

feelings, thoughts and behaviours that have been out of bounds for the members before they have joined the group.

SPECIFIC FACTORS

Yalom (1970) was probably the first to distil the more specifically unique therapeutic experiences. Yalom identified ten 'curative factors' of group psychotherapy:

1 Imparting information
2 Instillation of hope
3 Universality
4 Altruism
5 The corrective recapitulation of the primary family group
6 Development of socialising techniques
7 Imitative behaviour
8 Interpersonal learning
9 Group cohesiveness
10 Catharsis.

Rather than merely summarising Yalom's discussion, I would like to reflect on the possible relevance of these curative factors to three major ways of offering group psychotherapy. In doing so, I shall not attempt to review all the existing approaches to group psychotherapy (for examples, see Long 1988; MacKenzie 1992; Dryden and Aveline 1988). Clearly, such a variety cannot be conveyed within one chapter. Instead, I shall highlight examples that illustrate what I, as a systems-orientated practitioner, believe to be the crucial differences. As noted by Roberts (1982) among others, these differences are among:

psychotherapy   OF   the group
psychotherapy   IN   the group
psychotherapy   THROUGH   the group.

For a useful comparative evaluation of therapeutic factors, also see Bloch (1988: 297).

Psychotherapy OF the group

Although it is rare by now, some group psychotherapists address only the group as a whole. They do not refer to individual members, nor to pairs or sub-groups. Instead, their interventions usually begin with 'the group is . . . ', and follow with what the psychotherapist feels group members want from her or him. For example, the group psychotherapist may say: 'The group is trying to force its will on me.'

This was the main contribution of Bion (1961), who began work in the late 1940s. For Bion, the major therapeutic achievement was the rational clarification of relationships, particularly relationships with authority figures. He focused on authority figures since, so he thought, they always stood for early relationships with parental figures.

Bion believed in enhancing people's ability to pursue their goals rationally. Other modes which developed in the group were seen by Bion as defences against the rational one, which he called 'work'. When the group was not able to work, it regressed to what Bion called 'basic assumption', and he identified three of these: pairing, dependency and flight–fight. The psychotherapist is concerned mainly with maintaining her or his position as a 'projection screen'; sustaining an impersonal presence to which group members can attribute feelings, thoughts and behaviour they find intolerable in themselves. This rather impersonal presence of the psychotherapist seems to lead members to focus on their experiences of the psychotherapist.

It must be said that not everybody at the Tavistock Institute in London shared Bion's purity. For example, Ezriel (1950, 1956) developed a different model. Like Bion, Ezriel too maintained a relatively impersonal, analytic stance and always began with an interpretation of the group as a whole. Yet, he would then go on to articulate how each individual member contributed to the pattern presented by the whole group. These individual contributions he saw as three types.

Ezriel saw group psychotherapy as a process through which the 'required relationships', which led to problems and symptoms, were given up. Giving up these disabling relationships was possible only once certain 'calamitous relationships' were experienced as not leading to the expected disaster. Only then can the 'avoided relationships' develop. Having pointed out the situation as a whole, Ezriel would then spell out the fears; that is, the calamitous relationships each individual harboured so that each could venture certain avoided relationships. By doing so, Ezriel involved group members with one another more than Bion did. Very specific anxieties, such as favouritism, loyalty to both parents or sexual attraction to one of the parents, could probably be explored in such groups.

Psychotherapy OF the group was further extended into peer relations by Whitaker and Lieberman (1964). As Yalom (1970: 141) points out, their approach had parallels with that of Ezriel. Ezriel's 'required relationships' could probably be seen as equivalent to Whitaker and Lieberman's 'group solution': the manifest behaviour pattern which group members adopted.

Ezriel's 'avoided relationships' seem to serve a function similar to Whitaker and Lieberman's 'disturbing motive': behaviours that group members found too disturbing to attempt. This motive was seen as too disturbing because of a fear which Whitaker and Lieberman called the 'reactive motive': for example, a negative reaction from the psychotherapist or other group members which was too risky to contemplate. The reactive motive seems rather similar to Ezriel's 'calamitous relationship'.

Similar to Ezriel, the dynamics among the solution, the disturbing motive and the reactive motive were seen as largely unconscious. The interpretation of these dynamics always revolved around a 'focal conflict': some tension between a wish (the disturbing motive) and the fear of pursuing it (the reactive motive). The focal conflict always referred to the here-and-now situation of that particular group.

However (and this is where Whitaker and Lieberman differed from Ezriel), the focal conflict was not always between the psychotherapist and the group members. Such conflict could also arise among the members themselves. This active response to peer relationships and their possible conflicts seems to have led Whitaker and Lieberman towards a wider range of responses to their groups. Although they did offer interpretations of the group as a whole, they also showed members alternatives to their restrictive solutions by modelling them, and so would express their own feelings, ask direct questions, and at times respond also to an individual rather than the whole group.

This wider version of psychotherapy OF the group seems to allude to the recapitulation of the primary family group (Yalom's factor no. 5). It can contribute towards developing socialisation techniques (Yalom's factor no. 6) in relation to impersonal authority figures, and to group cohesiveness (Yalom's factor no. 9). The combination of having to cope with the impersonal authority of the therapist and the increased cohesion often gives rise to altruism among the members (Yalom's factor no. 4).

Psychotherapy IN the group

From a systems point of view the opposite of psychotherapy OF the group is probably psychotherapy IN the group. In psychotherapy OF the group, the psychotherapist always begins with their view of the group as a whole: what pattern of behaviour is evident in the session which is different from the various contributions made by individual members of that group. Psychotherapy IN the group begins from the other end: the pattern each member shows as a unique individual in relation to the group as a whole. So, in these methods the group psychotherapist is likely to begin by asking each member, 'What do you want now?' It should be said that, like the former, pure psychotherapy IN the group is rare by now. Its original forms could probably be found in the pioneering work of Moreno's psychodrama (1972), in Rogers' encounter (1957), Perls' Gestalt therapy (Perls *et al.* 1951), and Berne's Transactional Analysis (1977). Modern practitioners of these approaches have considerably developed and/or modified these founders' theories and practices.

Transactional Analysis as developed by Eric Berne (1961/1980), being more of an integrative model than the other three, includes their central emphases on the one hand, while extending their range and ability to the interpersonal level on the other. Transactional Analysis made its unique contribution in studying the transactions between individual group members. The method offered a way of working with these to extrapolate, understand and resolve the group members' intrapsychic conflicts, outdated decisions and harmful or ineffective life scripts. TA's unique contribution is in relating past or borrowed ego states to present ways of relating to other people. Ego states are conceived to be the basic phenomenological structure of the human personality: 'An ego state may be described phenomenologically as a coherent system of feelings, and operationally as a set of coherent behaviour patterns, or pragmatically as a system of feelings which motivates a related set of behaviour patterns' (Berne 1977: 123).

Most methods of psychotherapy IN the group include the detailed enactment of earlier relationships. Therefore, Yalom's factor no. 5, the corrective recapitulation of the primary family group, is powerfully activated. Because of their active mobilisation of bodily processes, Gestalt therapy and psychodrama share an emphasis on deep release of feelings. The members intensify the expression of their feelings through bodily gestures, through direct beating of soft objects, and through acting various parts of themselves. So, it is likely that Yalom's factor no. 10, catharsis, is extremely deep in such groups. Also, in such methods the members rally round each individual as sources of support. At one point or another, each member has the opportunity of being physically held by others as well as supportively holding them. Each person experiences the ability to give and receive unconditionally and very directly. Therefore, Yalom's factor no. 4, altruism, becomes very important. The intense mutual support that comes from such physical closeness seems to generate Yalom's factor no. 9, group cohesion, to an unusual degree. At times such groups can become the most important association for their members. Coupled with the experiences of altruism and group cohesion is Yalom's factor no. 2, instillation of hope. These methods are anchored in humanistic psychology which rests on the assumption of self-actualisation rather than cure. The emphasis on self-actualisation implies an unlimited belief in the potential of each individual person to evolve further and reach a richer life. So instillation of hope can be most powerfully evoked. There is another aspect to these body methods. The psychotherapist works in detail with each individual on their very idiosyncratic patterns of physical, emotional and cognitive behaviours and on the relationships among these three levels. So, after a while, each member develops very intimate knowledge of these processes and should be able to prevent the establishment of disabling ones without any help from the psychotherapist. Yalom's factor no. 1, imparting information, is not only central but is extended to become a form of psycho-education in intimacy.

Psychotherapy THROUGH the group

Psychotherapy OF the group can be seen to begin from the top: the group as a whole. If so, then psychotherapy IN the group begins from the bottom: each individual. In this sense, psychotherapy THROUGH the group focuses on the middle: the relationships among group members and the ways in which they try to involve the psychotherapist in them. Again, the psychotherapist OF the group is likely to begin with the phrase 'The group is . . . '. The psychotherapist IN the group would begin by asking each member, 'What do you want now?' However, the group analyst is likely to wait until a member speaks and then ask, 'What do other members feel?' A great deal is turned back to the group, and only when group members are clearly stuck in their attempts to resolve issues on their own does the group therapist become involved in suggesting group phenomena that stand in the way.

Foulkes's (1948, 1964) group analysis began not long after Bion proposed his model, but took a markedly different direction. Foulkes's attention was focused on what he called 'the matrix': the intricate web of relationship, fantasies and fears that group members were developing towards one another. The individuality of each group member was seen as emerging within this overall context of the matrix. Therefore, the members' relationships with him seemed to Foulkes of secondary importance. Due to their orientation towards peer relationships, group analysts have not restricted their view of the causes of difficulties to early family influences alone. Most group analysts consider early experiences in play groups and at school important too. Furthermore, many group analysts are usually socially minded; they may express their own feelings during the session, and they may encourage members to explore practical solutions to their problems.

However, as noted by Roberts, 'Foulkes did not leave us with a clear and coherent presentation of the underlying theories . . . from which group analysis was developed . . . . Each concept is developed differently with each appearance' (1982: 112). Quite a number of group analysts are very aware of this, and would privately express the view that very little would be lost if group analytic ideas were couched in systems terms. Indeed, Roberts himself discusses the relationship between the parts and the whole and the paradox involved in ways which raises the question why the connection had not been made explicit long ago.

In fact, in the United States psychotherapy THROUGH the group seems to have progressed mainly by drawing upon general systems theory. By now, one can find psychotherapists who have come from an object relations perspective (Ashbach and Schermer 1987), a Jungian approach (Boyd 1991), psychodrama (Williams 1989), or Transactional Analysis (Peck 1981), all expanding their perceptions by resorting to various aspects of the systems approach. The most thorough work was probably done by the 'Task Force' led by James Durkin (1981). The advantages of the systems approach to group psychotherapy are almost obvious. This approach enables us to relate the parts (the members) to the whole (the group). It also accounts for step-by-step changes as much as it focuses on transformation. Systems group psychotherapists do not invent their own theory. Some link it with a vast body of knowledge developed in other disciplines (Manor 1992). Others see their theory as an over-arching model providing a framework within which different approaches can be coherently integrated (Clarkson 1990; Clarkson and Lapworth 1992).

Insight is emphasised by them as much as it was by psychotherapists OF the group. Disequilibrium and the deep release of feelings are intensified as much as was done by psychotherapists IN the group. Interaction among group members is as important to systems therapists as it was for group analysts working THROUGH the group. In addition, no group member is seen as isolated from their present network, be it marital partner, children, friends, colleagues or other affiliates. Seen as part of the member's system, all are included when change is considered. Change itself is understood in rather wide terms: from intrapsychic transformation, through interpersonal clarification, to step-by-step modification of behaviour.

Sluzki (1983) encapsulated the systems approach in his seminal paper 'Process, structure and world views: towards an integrated view of systemic models in family therapy'. This integration can be achieved by concentrating on those influences that constitute feedback. James Durkin explains that feedback arises when 'part of the output . . . is returned as input' (1981: 343). Group psychotherapists who concentrate on the processes express this somewhat more simply. They usually say that the group psychotherapist should use mainly that which the group gives her.

Feedback can be offered in various ways. Simple to understand is the communication of empathy: the facilitator captures the essence of the contents expressed by the members in relation to the most emotionally charged utterances. By focusing only on this segment, the practitioner responds to part of the group's output. She then rephrases it and communicates it back to the group as an empathic input. Repeating the process of offering a certain input gives rise to a structure. Let us see how a structure emerges.

Emerging structures

For example, let us take a situation where one member, John, dominates the interactions. The group psychotherapist can say, 'John is raising an important issue. I wonder what other members feel about this.' In such a situation, the psychotherapist has effected a certain judgement. She acted on the assumption that equal participation by group members is more desirable than being dominated by one of them. A desired level, that of equal participation, was in the psychotherapist's mind, and she was trying to steer the group towards it. This level is called 'homeostasis'. In that situation the behaviour of the dominating member disrupted and deviated from the homeostasis. The psychotherapist's intervention used part of the output ('John is raising an important issue'), and then returned it to the group as input, but that input 'negated' John's domination; it focused on 'what the other members feel'. Such 'negative feedback' counteracts the impact of the deviation and restores the homeostasis by steering the system back to a desired level of activity. If the group continues to allow John to dominate its interactions and rely on the psychotherapist to offer such negative feedback when they want to speak too, a pattern will be established. This pattern will set up a structure whereby the psychotherapist will act as a buffer between John and the group members. Although not necessarily desirable, such a structure provides the group with continuity. Other, more enabling structures can be enhanced in the same way: that is, by resorting to negative feedback. Enabling such structures requires a good understanding of the process.

Facilitating processes

Through the process of negative feedback, other step-by-step, linear changes can be introduced. Offering tasks during the session as well as homework tasks, not unlike those offered in cognitive-behavioural group psychotherapy (Alladin 1988), is a good example. These highly planned programmes aim at specific levels of interaction, and can therefore be seen as another form of negative feedback. Within the systems approach all these planned step-by-step changes are called 'first order changes'. I prefer the more humanistically meaningful expression 'incremental changes'. Incremental changes are often part of learning new interpersonal skills, and so give rise to a great deal of interpersonal and social learning (Yalom's factors nos. 8 and 6) and to imitative behaviour (Yalom's factor no. 7).

Incremental changes facilitate the often-needed continuity of patterns in relationships. We do need the continuity involved in turning up on time, in learning to say 'hello' as well as 'goodbye', or in taking care to sustain eye contact while talking with certain people. Continuity of patterns is very helpful for living. Yet, when patterns of behaviour are repeated so rigidly that they reinforce too closed a structure, they do not enable people to cope with unexpected exceptions, such as the need to change a subject or just to be in silence in the group. In such situations instability is positively needed. Imagine John, in our example, continuing to dominate the group for four or five sessions. What will happen then? Quite likely, at some point someone will shout 'For God's sake, John, stop this!' When that member protests, John's initial deviation will be temporarily intensified: someone else will assume power in the group too. The pattern comprised of John's domination, the members' passivity, and the psychotherapist as a buffer, will be destabilised. From then on, it will not be possible to predict the results; these will depend on the reactions of other members, of the psychotherapist, and John. In some instances the protest may turn out to be merely another deviation which the group will suppress again. If so, the group will soon revert to the same buffering pattern, perhaps with someone else dominating it instead of John. In systemic terms, negative feedback may be affected to return the group to its uneven pattern. In more fortunate circumstances, other members will join in, saying that they too had had enough of John's 'Sermon on the mount'. In such a case, the deviation produced by the protesting member will be further amplified. If allowed to run its course, the protest is likely to enable the group to revise its way of working together. The members are likely to question the value of allowing one of them to dominate – while trusting their psychotherapist to rescue them from the consequences. Instead, a more participative pattern may then be developed.

Instability can also be facilitated deliberately through the persistent intensification of a deviation from a too-stable structure. Helen Durkin was probably one of the first group analysts to describe how 'seemingly accidental and very fleeting emotions, thoughts and actions' were given 'conscious expression' (1981: 188). Further along these lines, the use of growth games, as initially developed by Schutz (1966), and the 'hot seat technique' used in Gestalt psychotherapy (Perls *et al.* 1951) can also be incorporated as offering such forms of feedback. Such an intensification is called 'positive feedback'. Whenever a deviation from the homeostasis is persistently intensified and the system is not directed towards a specific level of activity in advance, positive feedback is applied. Such feedback often leads to a great deal of upheaval as roles, rules and norms are fundamentally revised. The course of change cannot be planned in advance in these circumstances, exactly because it leads to some transformation of previous structures. Transformation often involves catharsis (Yalom factor no. 10). Such a deep release is often of feelings related to earlier relationships, particularly with parents and other earlier carers. The result is often the re-evaluation of the meaning of previous relationships, and the rules of future ones. So the corrective recapitulation of the primary family group (Yalom's factor no. 5) is very much part of this. This ability of psychotherapy to lead to transformation of relationships tends to charge it with hope (addressing Yalom's factor no. 2, instillation of hope) quite dramatically.

As can be seen, the processes lead to both incremental changes as advocated by behavioural psychotherapists, as well as transformational change, pursued by humanistic and existential psychotherapists. Indeed, the systems approach goes even further. This is where the 'world views' mentioned above come to bear on practice.

Reflecting a world view

Let us go back to John's behaviour in our example. The psychotherapist could have responded in other ways to John's domination. For example, the psychotherapist could have expressed how the situation affected her: contributing self-disclosure. This would be characteristic of the psychotherapist IN the group. Alternatively, she could have described the pattern of domination and submission between John and the members. She could also have suggested an unconscious dynamic underlying that pattern. Both would have suited psychotherapists OF the group. The systems approach does not exclude any of the others. Instead, this approach broadens the spectrum of responses by referring to our ability to reflect upon our own experiences and communicate their meaning to others. This ability to offer connections among various messages is called 'meta-communication' (Simon *et al.* 1985: 223).

Yet we do not simply communicate. Whenever we offer a connection we affect human judgement about the relevance of certain elements and, by implication, the irrelevance of others. In our example, the psychotherapist referred to the dominance–submission pattern. This was her choice. She could have talked about other experiences which were no doubt available to her, but she chose to focus on the theme of power in the group. Systems thinkers have been intensely interested in unearthing the moral bases of such choices. They call it 'punctuation': the ways in which each participant 'subjectively perceives different patterns of cause and effect' (Simon *et al.* 1985: 284). When Wilden explored the processes involved in punctuation, he showed that they always evolved out of certain moral values, which were often suppressed (1980: 50–6). These moral values can be related to what Sluzki called 'world views'. The uniqueness of the systems approach is in its insistence that each practitioner must make explicit the world views underlying their work. For example, I hold humanistic world views. These direct us to punctuate experiences in groups which promote such human values as pluralism, genuineness and mutuality in relationships. The freedom of the psychotherapist is considerable within the systems approach, but the burden of responsibility is quite heavy. No ready-made ideological recipes are offered. Instead, every time each practitioner is with clients they are expected to articulate the world views guiding their practice.

Through such comments, as well as those offered by the group members, the universality (Yalom's factor no. 3) of problems as well as possible solutions can be highlighted. Both psychotherapist and members impart a great deal of information (Yalom's factor no. 1), and group cohesiveness (Yalom's factor no. 9) is likely to increase.

Two beneficial aspects are particular to the systems approach. Both relate to Yalom's factor no. 8: interpersonal learning. One is the group as a 'rehearsal stage'. Sufficient evidence exists by now (Goldstein and Kanfer 1979) to accept that changes achieved during the session do not necessarily transfer to situations outside it. Special procedures have to be developed to ensure that group members actually translate their group psychotherapy experiences to real life. Therefore it is vital that the group psychotherapist offers exercises to each member during the session, rehearsing with him or her how to cope with specific external situations differently now. The systems approach would lead to such work being done by virtue of its understanding of structural inequalities in every society, such as between women and men or black and white people in Britain. Structural inequalities mean that members have actively to alter the power balance outside the group. Also, each group splits itself from the world to some extent: 'we' are different from 'them'. In view of this universal tendency for closure, group members then have to explain the change to people outside the group. Awareness of closure leads to 'linking'. The systems approach suggests that, whether consciously or not, everything which happens to one part of the system is likely to affect all the other parts. Therefore, everything that happens to a group member in psychotherapy is likely to affect their relationship in all the subsystems to which that member is committed: first and foremost those involving intimacy, such as parent or child, or any partnership between adults (marriage, cohabitation or an open relationship). The systems approach would see the member as a person-in-relationships, and would strive to involve those outside the group as each plays their part in the member's relationships.

SUMMARY

Even a single chapter already conveys the richness and diversity offered by group psychotherapy, and many approaches are not included here for lack of space. The discussion was confined to highlighting three major pointers to the differences among the approaches: psychotherapy OF the group, psychotherapy IN the group, and psychotherapy THROUGH the group. Each includes quite a number of different styles, yet some of Yalom's curative factors seem to be particularly relevant to one of them more than others.

It was suggested that, by alluding to recapitulation of primary family relationships, psychotherapy OF the group is likely to give particular prominence to coping with authority figures, and so contribute to socialisation techniques related to this level. The emphasis on the group as a whole seems to lead to increased group cohesiveness, and the combination often encourages members to help one another; that is, altruism.

Psychotherapy IN the group also promotes group cohesion and altruism. In addition, it is particularly conducive to enhancing deep catharsis, and to enabling the corrective recapitulation of the primary family group. The emphasis on self-actualisation embedded in deep cartharsis often contributes to a great deal of optimism, that is, to the instillation of hope. This strand is also an effective forum for imparting information, particularly about intimate relationships.

Psychotherapy THROUGH the group, especially when drawing on the systems approach, can address all the former curative factors, and then go further to enable a great deal of interpersonal and social learning as well.

Much more research is needed to validate these observations. If supported, this line of thinking might help us see the wood for the trees. It may suggest that the systems approach has the potential to integrate many of the others, and so link group psychotherapy more clearly to other forms of therapeutic help, notably those concerned with the family, but also couples and individual psychotherapy.

REFERENCES

Alladin, W. (1988) 'Cognitive-behavioural group therapy', pp. 115–39 in M. Aveline and W. Dryden (eds) *Group Therapy in Britain*, Milton Keynes: Open University Press.

Ashbach, C. and Schermer, V. L. (1987) *Object Relations, the Self, and the Group: A Conceptual Paradigm*, London: Routledge & Kegan Paul.

Berne, E. (1977) *Intuition and Ego States*, San Francisco: Harper & Row.

—— (1980) *Transactional Analysis in Psychotherapy: A Systematic Individual and Social Psychiatry*, London: Souvenir Press (first published 1961).

Bion, W. (1961) *Experience in Groups and Other Papers*, London: Tavistock.

Bloch, S. (1988) 'Research in group psychotherapy', pp. 283–316 in W. Dryden and M. Aveline (eds) *Group Therapy in Britain*, Milton Keynes: Open University Press.

Boer, F. and Dunn, J. (eds) (1992) *Children's Sibling Relationships: Developmental and Clinical Issues*, Hillsdale, NJ: Lawrence Erlbaum Associates.

Boyd, R. D. (1991) *Personal Transformation in Small Groups: A Jungian Perspective*, London: Tavistock/Routledge.

Clarkson, P. (1990) 'A multiplicity of psychotherapeutic relationships', *British Journal of Psychotherapy* 7(2): 148–63.

Clarkson, P. and Lapworth, P. (1992) 'Systemic integrative psychotherapy', pp. 41–83 in W. Dryden (ed.) *Integrative and Eclectic Therapy: A Handbook*, Milton Keynes: Open University Press.

Dryden, W. and Aveline, M. (eds) (1988) *Group Therapy in Britain*, Milton Keynes: Open University Press.

Durkin, H. E. (1981) 'The technical implication of general systems theory for group psychotherapy', pp. 172–98 in J. E. Durkin (ed.) *Living Groups: Group Psychotherapy and General Systems Theory*, New York: Brunner/Mazel.

Durkin, J. E. (ed.) (1981) *Living Groups: Group Psychotherapy and General Systems Theory*, New York: Brunner/Mazel.

Ezriel, H. (1950) 'A psycho-analytic approach to group treatment', *British Journal of Medical Psychology* 23: 59–74.

—— (1956) 'The first session in psychoanalytic group treatment', *Nederlands Tydskrift voor Geneeskunde* 111: 711–16.

Foulkes, S. H. (1948) *Introduction to Group-Analytic Psychotherapy*, London: Heinemann Medical Books.

—— (1964) *Therapeutic Group Analysis*, London: Allen & Unwin.

Garfield, S. and Bergin, A. E. (eds) (1986) *Handbook of Psychotherapy and Behaviour Change* (3rd edn), New York: Wiley.

Goldstein, A. P. and Kanfer, F. H. (eds) (1979) *Maximising Treatment Gains: Transfer Enhancement in Psychotherapy*, London: Academic Press.

Long, S. (ed.) (1988) *Six Group Therapies*, New York: Plenum Press.

MacKenzie, K. R. (ed.) (1992) *Classics in Group Psychotherapy*, London and New York: Guilford Press.

Manor, O. (1992) 'Transactional analysis, object relations, and the systems approach: finding the counterparts', *Transactional Analysis Journal* 22(1): 4–15.

Moreno, J. L. (1972) *Psychodrama*, New York: Boston House.

Norcross, J. C. and Goldfried, M. R. (1992) *Handbook of Psychotherapy Integration*, New York: Basic Books.

Peck, H. (1981) 'Some applications of transactional analysis in groups to general systems theory', pp. 158–71 in J. E. Durkin (ed.), *Living Groups: Group Psychotherapy and General Systems Theory*, New York: Brunner/Mazel.

Perls, F. S., Hefferline, R. F. and Goodman, P. (1951) *Gestalt Therapy: Excitement and Growth in the Human Personality*, New York: Julian Press.

Roberts, J. P. (1982) 'Foulkes' concept of the matrix', *Group Analysis* 15(2): 111–26.

Rogers, C. R. (1957) 'The necessary and sufficient conditions of therapeutic personality change', *Journal of Consulting Psychology* 21(2): 95–103.

Schutz, W. (1966) *The Interpersonal Underworld*, Palo Alto, CA: Science and Behavior Books.

Simon, C. B., Stieling, H. and Wynne, L. C. (1985) *The Language of Family Therapy*, New York: Process Press.

Sluzki, C. E. (1983) 'Process, structure and world views: towards an integrated view of systemic models in family therapy', *Family Process* 22(4): 469–576.

Whitaker, D. S. and Lieberman, M. (1964) *Psychotherapy through the Group Process*, New York: Atherton Press.

Wilden, A. (1980) *System and Structure* (2nd edn), London: Tavistock Publications.

Williams, D. (1989) *The Passionate Technique*, London: Tavistock/Routledge.

Yalom, I. D. (1970) *The Theory and Practice of Group Psychotherapy*, New York: Basic Books.

Part IV

Settings

Chapter 15

Psychotherapy in and with organisations

Peter Hawkins and Eric Miller

Freud said the whole business of therapy was to bring a person to love and to work. It seems to me we have forgotten half of what he said. Work. We have been talking of what goes wrong with love for eighty years. But what about what goes wrong with work, where has that been discussed?

(Hillman 1983)

Most people entering psychotherapy training already have another professional identity – as social workers, teachers, psychologists and so on. Many, when they have finished their training, develop a part-time practice as psychotherapists while continuing with their previous occupations, more often than not as full- or part-time employees of organisations. The training may in some cases lead to changes in the context of their jobs and will invariably have some influence on their working practices and relationships; but they carry on wearing their original professional hats.

The alternative is to start explicitly from one's professional identity as a psychotherapist and to apply in wider settings the skills and insights gained from working with individual patients. This is happening increasingly. Some training institutions are beginning to include consultancy to groups (as distinct from group psychotherapy) as an element in the final year of training. In doing so they are enlarging the professional definition of 'psychotherapist'.

This chapter is aimed mainly at this second category – psychotherapists who are thinking of using their training and experience to take up roles as counsellors, trainers or consultants in organisational settings, or who are already doing some work of this kind and want to reflect on the roles they have now or might want to take up in the future. However, it may be also relevant to the first category – the 'employees' – by offering them different perspectives from which to look back on their own situations. Some of the ideas in the chapter may also be useful to therapists in private practice who have only second-hand, consulting-room knowledge of organisations. A growing proportion of individuals seeking psychotherapy come not for treatment of an 'illness' but to enhance their lives and self-understanding. Many are successfully working in organisations. Indeed, they may have been referred on to psychotherapy by their work-based counsellor, or management consultant. The psychotherapist working with such patients/ clients needs to be attentive to the constant interplay of the psychodynamics of the individual and those of the organisation. This is sometimes like working with a relationship difficulty, such as a marital problem, where only one side of the relationship is present. The psychotherapist has to be able to distinguish when patients are projecting their own disturbance onto the organisations they work for, and when they are carrying some of the distress and disturbance that is a symptom of the organisational dynamics. Organisations play a significant part in most people's lives, starting with childhood experience in schools. Adults may spend more time in and relating to their work organisation than to any single individual, and often their self-image and self-esteem are greatly determined by the setting in which they work, and the amount of work satisfaction and positive feedback they receive. All psychotherapists therefore need to understand the complex interplay between individuals, the groups they belong to and the organisations of which they are a part.

In this chapter we suggest that psychotherapy in and with organisations has to keep a constant balance in understanding the interrelatedness of three key factors; *task*, *process* and *environment*. These can be seen as a triangle with each element affecting both the others (see Figure 15.1). We give a series of typical examples, progressively more complex; first involving work with the individual and proceeding through the levels of group, inter-group and the organisation as a whole. Working with individual

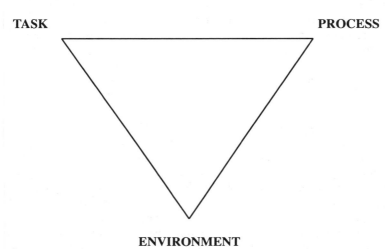

Figure 15.1 Task, process and environment

members of an organisation, the task of the psychotherapist is to help them to achieve a healthy alignment between self, work and the environment of the work organisation. Likewise, when we come on to look at the level of team development, the task of the team consultant is to help the team find a healthy alignment between their group process, their collective task and the organisational context, including customers and stakeholders who create the environment in which that team exists. The same triangle and task can also be taken one level higher, when the consultant works with the alignment of task, process and environment for the whole organisational system. Each successive level, in our view, involves more complex issues and consequently more training, and at some point in this progression the identity of 'psychotherapist' has to be discarded – or, rather, subsumed in a broader identity, such as 'organisational consultant'.

First, however, we need to say something about what psychotherapists bring to an organisation and to offer some perspectives on the nature of organisations themselves: a simple but perhaps useful framework.

WHAT PSYCHOTHERAPISTS BRING

Two great assets that a psychotherapist brings to the organisation are as follows:

1 A capacity to work at the *transaction* between patient and psychotherapist; using the transference and counter-transference as data for understanding the dynamics of the patient. Consultants drawn from other disciplines tend to see their clients as 'out there' and deny themselves the insights that could be yielded by looking at their subjective experience.
2 Related to this is an alertness to unconscious processes.

Not unconnected with these is the readiness and capacity to listen and to wait. Listening to the music as well as to the words is clearly also important; but simply to be able to listen non-judgementally and refrain from premature interpretation is an asset missing in many consultants and most managers.

The main liability is a predisposition to see problems in terms of individual pathology and interpersonal difficulties. With rare exceptions, such as combinations of individual and family therapy, the psychotherapist is accustomed to working with problems as residing in individual patients. Work, family and partner relationships are contextual. When one shifts to the organisational setting it is useful to turn this on its head and to approach the situation as if the organisation itself were the client/ patient. One might then take as a working hypothesis that the apparent pathology of the individual is a symptom of organisational illness. If the organisational problem is identified and tackled, the individual's symptoms will evaporate.

That represents, in slightly exaggerated form, the shift in perspective that is appropriate. Much the same applies to so-called 'personality clashes'. These presenting problems all too frequently turn out to spring from ambiguity and confusion in definition of roles. If one colludes in accepting that the problem lies in the individual or in interpersonal relations, then the pathogenic factors in the organisation will go on producing more and more casualties.

Another potential liability is the actual label of 'psychotherapist'. This mobilises fantasies and projections even before one arrives. One of the co-authors, not a psychotherapist, has run into similar fantasies about his associations with 'Tavistock'. Arriving by car at a Lancashire factory, he was greeted with the not entirely jocular question: 'Do you carry your couch in the boot?' Although the image of psychotherapy is shifting, stereotypes remain, such as: 'They must think we're nutcases'; 'They can read our minds'. It will be prudent to be aware of such likely transferences and to avoid compounding them by also introducing our own jargon. We need to learn and respect the language of the organisation.

THE NATURE OF ORGANISATIONS

Most psychotherapists have the experience of being an employee in an organisation. Valuable though this is, it has its disadvantages. First, there may be a tendency to extrapolate from these experiences and to assume similarities – and indeed differences – that may not be valid. Secondly, one may be tempted, without recognising it, to identify with those members of the client organisation – perhaps front-line workers or middle managers – whose position and dilemmas resonate most closely with one's own past experience. If recognised, this can be informative; unrecognised, it will mean getting caught in projections that are a threat to one's professionalism.

Learning the language of the organisation includes gaining an understanding of its technology, of its relations with its environment, and of the kinds of responsibilities attached to various functions and roles. Psychotherapists coming from health and social service institutions, as many do, may well feel lost at first when they enter, for example, an industrial company. They have to devote some serious effort to discovering how it works and who does what. Acknowledging one's ignorance and asking questions does more for one's credibility than operating from ill-informed assumptions. If you acknowledge the competence of others in areas where you are ignorant, they may be readier to accept that you have professional competence that they lack.

Beyond this acquisition of practical knowledge about the specific organisation, the incoming psychotherapist needs conceptual frameworks or models that offer a perspective on the functioning of organisations as wholes – analogous to the models of individual functioning that one has learned during training. There is no shortage of these: Gareth Morgan (1986) has devoted a substantial book to the subject, while writers such as Pugh and Hickson (1989) and Handy (1976) offer accessible introductions.

Some of these models or metaphors are less helpful than others in contributing to our understanding. Unhelpful, for example, is the traditional mechanistic metaphor – a managerialist perspective – in which the organisation is a machine and good management seen in terms of a well-designed engine: 'oiling the wheels', 'changing gears' and driving the machine. We confine ourselves here to offering four perspectives which we find illuminating and of practical use.

1 *Organisation as a socio-technical system*   Originating at the Tavistock Institute in the 1950s, this framework sprang from a pioneering study in coal-mines (Trist and Bamforth 1951) and was further developed by Trist himself, Rice, Emery and others (e.g., Rice 1958, 1963; Trist *et al.* 1963; Emery and Trist 1969). It views the organisation as an interplay between a system of technical activities necessary for task performance and a social system of relationships which meet the psychological and social needs of the work-force. Technology does not determine organisation: there are choices; and some forms of organisation are more effective than others in optimising the functioning of these systems.

2 *Organisation as an open system*   A systemic perspective alerts us to the interconnectedness of the parts of an organisation to one another and to the whole: a change in one part will have repercussions in others. The notion of the organisation as an open system (also developed at the Tavistock Institute: cf. Rice 1963; Miller and Rice 1967) draws on the analogy with the biological organism. It depends for its existence and survival on a process of interchange with its environment. A manufacturing company imports raw materials, converts them into widgets, sells them, and uses the proceeds to buy more raw materials, maintain the system and pay a dividend to shareholders. In an educational institution, the intakes are students, the outputs are graduates (and drop-outs), and through its perceived success in doing this it generates more inputs and the resources to 'process' them. These import-conversion-export processes are the *primary tasks* of these institutions – the task they must perform in order to survive; but they will also be engaged in ancillary input-output processes related to supplies, personnel and so on. The organisation as organism seeks to maintain a 'quasi-stationary equilibrium' through making internal and external changes to match shifts in its environment. There is also another type of interchange with the environment. Organisations are shaped by external perceptions, expectations

and projections; for example, societal projections onto health systems, the police, prisons, social work and so on – and they themselves project onto their environment. Similar processes pervade the interaction of subsystems: for these, the organisation as a whole is a significant feature of their environments.

Another aspect of looking at organisations as organisms is the recognition that organisations have their own stages of human growth and development (Lessom 1990; Lievegoed 1991). As with working with individuals, it is important to see the problems of the organisation in the context of its 'life history' and the 'life transition' it is currently facing.

3 *The political dimension*   An organisation is a political system, engaged in negotiating and allocating power between groups and individuals. Maintenance of this system depends much less on the actual exercise of coercive power – the manager firing a subordinate, the union going on strike – than on the shared belief that it *may* be used. The experience of the authoritarian regimes in the communist bloc is relevant. For forty years or so they had seemed invulnerable. The year 1989 showed that in maintenance of the order the secret police were much less significant than people's collusive assumptions. When they discovered that these assumptions could be questioned, the regimes collapsed like houses of cards. The key point is that shared assumptions about the distribution of power are a significant factor in holding an organisation together. Psychotherapists working in organisations, in whatever role, need to be alert to the power structure for another reason: whether they want to or not, they become part of it: simply by relating to this person or group and not to that one they will be perceived as exercising power and therefore will be exercising it. They therefore need to be aware of the consequences of the alignments they make.

4 *Organisational culture*   The culture perspective (Peters and Waterman 1982; Schein 1985; McLean and Marshall 1989) likens work organisations to tribal cultures, with their own rituals, codes of behaviour and belief systems, which derive from the ecological context in which the tribe lives and evolves over time in relation to the changing environment. The definitions of organisational culture are extremely varied: how things are done around here (Ouchi and Johnson 1978), values and expectations which organisation members come to share (van Maanen and Schein 1979), and the collection of traditions, values, policies, beliefs and attitudes that constitute a pervasive context for everything we do and think in an organisation (McLean and Marshall 1989).

As the variety illustrates, this approach does not provide an exact science but a rich multiple-level perspective for viewing and influencing organisations. Bath Associates (1989) have created an integrative model that views organisational culture as residing at four distinct but linked levels:

Artefacts – the rituals, symbols/logos, mission statements of the organisation, buildings, organisational structure.

Behaviour – the unwritten rules which constrain how people behave, what is and what is not talked about and how people relate to one another.

Mind sets – the spectacles through which members of the organisational culture view themselves, the environment with which they interact and problems that arise.

Emotional ground – the collective feelings that underlie and influence the other three levels of culture; the emotional mood and feeling within the business.

It is important to recognise that only the top level of the culture is fully visible and conscious. The behavioural norms may operate without people being aware of the conventions they are acting within. The mind sets may be subconscious, for we see not the spectacles that we see through. The emotional ground may be fully unconscious. When you first join an organisation there are many things that you notice about the culture, that three or four months later you stop noticing because you have been socialised and enculturated. You have begun to wear the collective spectacles that occlude the cultural norms that are taken for granted. As the Chinese proverb says, the last one to know about the sea is the fish.

Unconscious processes within groups and organisations contribute to and are shaped by the organisational culture. There have been many seminal studies on the unconscious dynamics of the emotional ground of organisations (Bion 1961; Jaques 1953; Menzies 1959; Merry and Brown 1987; Miller 1993). Jaques (1953) believed that the defence against psychotic anxiety was one of the primary cohesive elements binding individuals into institutionalised human associations. Menzies (1959) showed in her seminal paper on social systems as a defence against anxiety, that many of the cultural norms of nursing could be seen as designed to keep the nurses from becoming too involved with the patients, so as to avoid, for example, the anxiety that attends emotional attachment to those who are seriously ill. The culture also has a norm that the emotional ground of distress about the patients is not discussed and the system then has a deep cultural split between the feelings and the institutionalised behaviour. Thus an organisation designed for performance of a task is both used for, and to some extent subverted by, the defensive functions that it serves for its members. Although these phenomena are most prominent in hospitals and other service institutions, where staff are working with sick and dependent patients or clients, they are part of all human organisations; and indeed Jaques (1953) illustrated his paper with a case study from industry.

That, as we have said, is by no means an exhaustive set of perspectives. What they have in common is that they focus attention on the organisation as a whole – its structures, political processes, culture and unconscious dynamics. This, we argue, is the appropriate focus for psychotherapists taking up roles in relation to organisations. Their work will be informed by their therapeutic training and experience, but that is background: as a rule of thumb, if you find yourself looking at people through your psychotherapist's spectacles, you are out of role.

We go on now to consider the range of more common roles.

The individual level

More and more organisations are setting up employee assistance programmes. These come in various forms. Some are generalised counselling and welfare services, which may be contracted from outside or provided internally. Clients bring a wide range of problems – for example, housing, debt, alcoholism, divorce, bereavement – not all of which psychotherapists will be equipped to deal with: divorce may raise legal and financial as well as emotional issues; for bereavement counselling some specialised training is desirable. Much the same applies to post-trauma counselling, now routinely provided by, for example, most police forces and by British Rail. Some organisations provide stress counselling services and some out-placement counselling for redundant personnel and assistance for people approaching retirement. These, again, call for a mix of practical and therapeutic help.

What an organisation 'buys' when it hires someone is a set of skills, mental or manual (factory-floor workers, in some companies, are still called 'hands'). It is, perhaps rightly, not interested in the whole person, except when something goes wrong that interferes with the work. That is regarded as best dealt with off the job, by someone else. Now, it may well be that the 'something wrong' presents itself in another part of the individual's life-space – the marital problem or the bereavement. But, as psychotherapists well know, people's internal worlds are not so neatly compartmentalised (or, if they are, that is indeed pathological). For many years, pursuing this holistic way of thinking, some industrial medical officers have paid attention to individual illness as a symptom of organisational illness, and seen their job as promoting the health of the enterprise (Bridger *et al.* 1964). Some departments or units may generate more than their share of illnesses, absences, turnover and so on. (One industrial medical officer even used expense claims as an indicator: inflated expense claims in one section would be a sign of low morale.) Attention can then be given to the pathogenic parts of the organisation. However, note that these in turn may be a manifestation of a malaise in the system as a whole: organisations are adept at localising and concentrating their pathology into 'problem departments' and casualty roles.

This by no means implies that, say, the stress counsellor should march into the chief executive's office to protest. What is most appropriate is for the organisation providing the employee assistance programme to give feedback to the host organisation on the spread of problems emerging and what part the organisational dynamics may be contributing to the emerging personal issues. In order to preserve confidentiality, this feedback needs to be based on data that are not attributable or recognisable to the individuals on whom it is based. But even if the psychotherapist takes no action at all, merely the recognition that organisational malfunctioning is a contributory factor will make it possible to reframe the individual's problem – and perhaps prevent the client from becoming a patient.

Another type of activity in which such issues can be addressed more directly is what we call here 'role consultancy'. Here the client is typically a person having difficulty in the organisational setting (for example, a marketing manager who is seen as too abrasive; a health service manager who feels trapped between conflicting demands; a medical consultant who keeps getting scapegoated; or a manager introducing a major change and looking for help in predicting and coping with the consequences). The client may be self-referring or referred and paid for by the employing organisation. In the latter case, the issue of 'Who is the client?' is pertinent: accountability and confidentiality have to be explicitly negotiated. The focus is on the person/role boundary; the task is to help the client to clarify the issues. The role consultant can be mainly a sounding board but usually needs to do more than that – and provide a form of non-managerial consultancy supervision (Hawkins and Shohet 1989) which explores the complex interplay of the dynamics of the individual and the work setting. Sometimes the client may seem to be the victim of an impossible organisational situation; sometimes the problem seems to lie in the individual's psychopathology. Both factors will be present, in varying proportions. Clients can be helped to consider what actions they might take to influence the organisational factors and how far they are unconsciously colluding. The boundary is difficult to manage, though the consultant's experience of the difficulty offers valuable data. If the consultant is convinced that psychotherapy would be useful, this should be referred to someone else, enabling work on the role to continue.

The group level

A mental health day centre is looking for someone to run a weekly staff support group. A small voluntary welfare agency is asking for a facilitator for monthly meetings. A board of directors of a commercial company want help in being a more effective team. Requests of this kind are becoming increasingly common, and often they are directed to psychotherapists. Sometimes the proposed contract is for a limited period, while the group is managing a transition; sometimes they are open-ended: the time and the budget are built in as an inherent part of the weekly work.

The groups are usually by no means clear about what it is they are asking for: one sign of this is the fluid terminology in which 'consultant', 'facilitator', 'supervisor', or even 'leader', become interchangeable. Regrettably, psychotherapists who accept such assignments may be equally imprecise about what they are undertaking. A vague request for 'staff support' is met by an equally vague quasi-therapy group.

We argue for a much more professional response in which a number of questions have to be asked and dealt with, for example:

- What is the work-task of this group?
- What is its relatedness to the task of the wider organisation?
- What is the problem that the group seeks to address in these sessions?
- Are weekly meetings the most appropriate format for working on this problem? (For a psychotherapist with a fixed weekly time-schedule it may be very convenient to slot a group into a vacant Tuesday afternoon, but is the convenient solution actually the most appropriate to the client's needs?)
- What is the task of the meetings? What is the output to be achieved?
- What is the task of the consultant in relation to this? What kind of role is appropriate?
- If the contract is to be open-ended, what arrangements are to be built in for review? This allows both parties to consider whether the method of working matches the original intentions and either party to terminate the contract.

The answers to such questions tend to be taken for granted in individual psychotherapy – perhaps too much so: arguments about that belong elsewhere. Here we want simply to emphasise that in professional work with groups they cannot be taken for granted: they have to be discussed, negotiated and periodically re-examined (see chapter 9 of Hawkins and Shohet 1989).

Very often such a group is working with severely damaged and deprived people. This disturbance is imported into staff; staff in turn export disturbance into clients. Care and treatment suffer. Thus an appropriate task for the consultant may be to collaborate with the group in examining the specifics of this import/export process; the desired output of a session would then be a set of staff restored to effective working roles and relationships, in which they can again distinguish what belongs to them and what to the clients. If what belongs to them includes, say, differences over approaches to treatment, then these have to be identified and explored. The consultant's role is both to provide some containment and to intervene in ways that will further the task of the group. Containment alone is insufficient. Too often we have seen so-called 'sensitivity groups' which are spittoons or worse: staff merely evacuate their negative feelings and return to roles and relationships that are at best unchanged and may even be exacerbated by unbridled exchanges of abuse. In the late sixties and early seventies there was a popular trend to introduce sensitivity groups into many work settings. The research evidence shows that this had very mixed results. Some managers clearly benefited, some became worse and the benefits for the organisation as a whole were very dubious (Cooper 1972; Mangham 1975).

There are other traps for the unwary psychotherapist embarking on work with groups. One, already mentioned, is to become preoccupied with the psychopathology of an individual. Groups are adept at projecting disturbance or distress onto the most suited recipient. To treat this individual as 'the problem' is counter-productive: if that person is extruded, another potential casualty will readily be found. 'The problem' belongs to the group and has to be addressed as such.

Another trap is where the group projects its difficulties onto the wider organisation – for example, a children's home in a local authority social services department. The group may well see itself as the victim of uncaring management and there may well be an element of reality in this. The trap is identification with the oppressed: the consultant who colludes with this projection is inhibiting the group from using its own capacities to tackle those problems that actually do belong to it. The group then becomes the impotent victim; and the effect on the people in its care is, to say the least, unlikely to be beneficial.

Another group-level activity that a psychotherapist may become drawn into is 'team-building'. Outside expertise is sought because perhaps they are 'not pulling together' or there are 'interpersonal rivalries'. The client team may be a working group at any level; or an organisation may embark on a team-building exercise for, say, all levels of management (the latter is best seen as a version of organisational consultancy: see below). Writers on organisation development offer a number of useful exercises and approaches (Hastings *et al.* 1986; Woodcock 1979). However, they do not always mention the pitfalls. Identification with the oppressed is one of them: it is not difficult to mobilise cohesion against top management as a common enemy: the mobilisation of what Bion (1961) called 'basic assumption fight/flight'. Another pitfall is that warm, positive interpersonal relations are not necessarily a recipe for effectiveness. Some task-related conflict is necessary and constructive: for example, if the production director and the marketing director are in each other's pockets, both functions are likely to be less effective than they could be. Hence the intervention should not be simply people-centred: the shared work-task is also a critical element.

The inter-group level

In a large university social science department two research units are at loggerheads with each other. Each is highly critical of the other's approach, not only privately but also publicly in conferences. They are often competing for grants from the same funding bodies. One or two less senior members from each unit are so disturbed by the situation that they ask a psychotherapist for help.

Two large companies have been merged. Their cultures are very different. A regional sales manager from one company has been put in charge of a merged department and finds that so much energy is being expended on in-fighting that sales are way below target. He wants a professional to help bring the two factions together.

Requests for intervention at the inter-group level almost invariably involve conflictual situations like this. How can one respond? There is no one system for resolving such conflicts, but we can point to some pitfalls and to possible building-blocks.

The first and obvious pitfall for a psychotherapist is to attribute the problem to powerful and possibly pathological leaders. Pathological they may be, but as we suggested when we looked at organisations as political systems, they are held in position with the collusion of the followers, who, if one leader is removed, may well produce another with similar character- istics. So it is more prudent to focus on the pathology of the relationship. Here the psychotherapist is well placed to identify projective processes – the tendency to split off and project onto the other group aspects of one's own group that are to be disowned. But, as in work with individuals, if those projections are structured into defence mechanisms, there remains the problem of getting one's interpretations heard and used. Parties to a conflict are volatile: ambivalent about any resolution – perversely, each needs the other – they are quick to find excuses to withdraw. So there is the issue of containment to be considered; and to convey security it may be useful to work with a colleague.

There remain some difficult choices about methods of working. In the university example, how far does the conflict belong to these two units and what is being projected onto them by the wider organisation? Should other departmental representatives be drawn into the process? Then there are questions of how to structure meetings: with the parties separately; joint meetings with all protagonists; meetings of representatives? This last approach could well be a good starting point in the university case, but it could also misfire if members of the small negotiating group committed to conciliation become split off from their constituents, who then carry more of the fight.

The literature on conflict resolution is substantial and some of it is useful. Marital therapy offers one paradigm: nearly thirty years ago Burton (1967) began to apply a version of marital casework to settlement of international disputes. Game theory and Transactional Analysis also have their place (see Hawkins and Shohet 1989: chapter 10). A psychotherapist may sometimes need reminding that conflicts of interests are not entirely fantasy. Then there are various practical techniques, such as role reversal, which can be used in the course of a conciliation process. (In the case of the merged sales department, this revealed that each side was both envious and contemptuous of different aspects of the other's culture.) Although a combination of psychotherapeutic experience, political nous and luck may sometimes work, it will be prudent to familiarise oneself with some of these other ideas and approaches, and/or start by attaching oneself to a practitioner with more experience in these arenas.

The organisational level

At the still more complex level of consultancy to organisations – at least to those organisations that are larger than face-to-face groups and that are internally differentiated by function – some training or apprenticeship is required. Psychotherapeutic skills are nevertheless very relevant. We have noted a growing trend, not only for psychotherapists to train in the world of organisational consulting, but also for some organisational consultants from other disciplines to embark on psychotherapy training. This is leading to useful dialogue and cross-fertilisation.

Requests for consultancy at this level come in many guises. A chief executive is tired of mutual back-biting and recrimination among her heads of departments. The board of a holding company is dissatisfied with the performance of one of its subsidiaries. A production director is worried about a non-committed work-force: quality is declining and the scrap-rate is going up. There is a corresponding array of possible responses that may be made by a traditional management consultant. In the first example, it may be that definition of responsibilities is fuzzy and that the problem could be alleviated by a structural change – re-drawing the boundaries between the subsystems. In the second, one needs to discover how far the deficiency lies in the subsidiary and how far in problems of power and authority in the relationship with headquarters. The third example may point to re-examination and possibly re-design of the socio-technical system to produce a form of work organisation that is both more effective and more satisfying to the workers. In problems such as these, therefore, the perspectives outlined earlier may all be relevant and then the organisational consultant may have some practical ideas to contribute. What they have in common is that they involve management of change, particularly change in culture – a factor often neglected by management consultants using mechanistic models but central to the task of the organisational consultant.

For the organisational consultant involved in change, therefore, all four of the perspectives outlined earlier are useful, but supplementing them is the fifth perspective of the organisation as a learning organism. This sees learning as the most central task of all organisations. The approach has been developed by Argyris and Schon (1978); Senge (1990); Pedler *et al.*

(1991); Hawkins (in press). It builds on the earlier work by Revans (1972) who coincidentally, like Trist and his Tavistock colleagues, also worked for the British Coal Board in the late 1940s. Revans argued that an organisation must learn at an equal or a greater rate than that of the environmental changes around it or the organism will die. Since that time environmental changes have grown exponentially and the need for organisations to learn at a faster speed has thus also dramatically increased.

Organisational learning is clearly dependent on the continuous learning of all its members, and in particular those in senior and influential positions. However, the organisation's learning cannot be reduced to the sum of the learning of those within it, for:

> The learning organisation approach has explored ways of creating continuous learning for individuals within organisations, and how this is built into effective team learning and development. Then, how learning, feedback and communication between teams and departments is fostered and how this in turn is harvested into organisational learning. At the same time as there is this upward spiral of learning within the organisation, the system has to be helped to learn in relation to its environment, with the fostering of dialogical learning between the organisation and its key customers and stakeholders.
>
> (Hawkins, in press)

What each of these approaches does is to link the complexities of the task with a psychological understanding of individuals, groups, inter-groups and whole systems. The consultant in such traditions can be seen as functioning as a corporate psychotherapist, or what an earlier Tavistock writer termed as a 'sociotherapist' (Sofer 1961), who helps the organisation to carry out its task better by attending to the collective dynamics of the whole system, including those that are unconscious to the system itself.

If we return to our triangular model, we can see how the model can be expanded to include the hidden and unconscious elements of the organisational world, at both the team and whole organisation levels (see Figures 15.2 and 15.3). Only by reconnecting the behaviour to the emotional ground in which it has grown can the culture become conscious and the organisation learn new ways of managing its internal and external tensions.

The consultant does not focus just on the task, or just on the process, or just on the external environment, but on the relationship between these three key elements. Also the consultant needs to be more an educational facilitator than an expert surgeon, for it is important that in learning more about the relationship between the three elements of task, process and environment at one particular time the organisation also 'learns how to learn', and increases its own ability continuously to attend to the interfaces and relationships that are key to its successful development (see Figure 15.4). Humanistic psychotherapy and co-operative research methodology have provided useful and wide-ranging techniques for working with

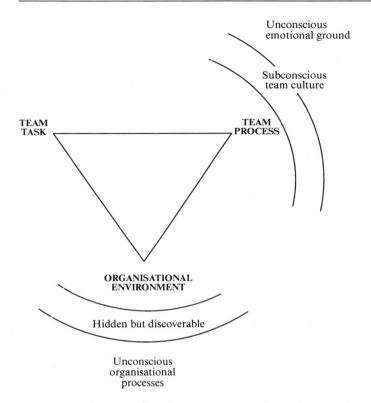

Figure 15.2 Team task, team process and organisational environment

organisations to help them get some distance on their own culture and gain fresh insight into their unwritten rules and mind sets (Bath Associates 1989; Reason 1988; Hawkins and Shohet 1989; McLean and Marshall 1989). This provides the organisation with an expanded awareness from which to make choices about future direction.

Gestalt psychotherapy has also made a major contribution to understanding the emotional learning blocks within organisations as well as approaches to help organisations overcome their stuckness (Merry and Brown 1987; Critchley and Casey 1989).

THE CONSULTING PROCESS

Psychotherapy has also informed the world of organisational consulting on how to manage the complexities of supporting a system through the processes of change.

The consultant may go through similar stages to the individual psychotherapist: building a relationship, helping the organisation tell its story;

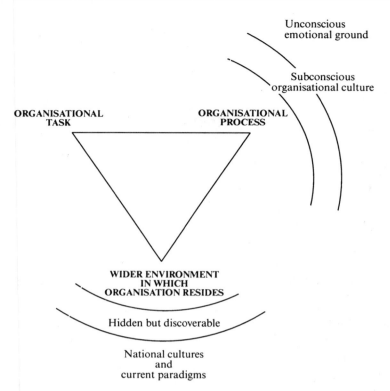

Figure 15.3 Organisational task, organisational process and the wider environment

initial formulation of the dynamics within the system; helping the client focus on the key areas of difficulty; creating new forms of dialogue within the client system; helping the client system to reframe its problems, seeing them in a new perspective; supporting experimentation with new forms of behaviour and learning from these; supporting the consolidation of new ways of being; and finally reflecting on the change process and managing the separation from the consultant and the internalisation of the consultant's contribution.

Consultants have traditionally paid less attention to their own process than have psychotherapists. For some this has been costly and the consultant team have ended up paralleling the dynamics of the client organisation rather than recognising that they can use themselves as instruments for registering those dynamics. Psychotherapy has some useful concepts and approaches for helping consultants to understand their involvement with the host organisation. These include projective splitting; supervision

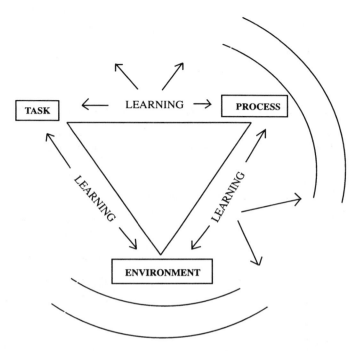

Figure 15.4 Task, process, environment and the learning organisation

processes for the consultant(s); the use of psychodrama re-enactment (Hawkins 1988) and parallel process (Hawkins and Shohet 1989).

CONCLUSION

To sum up, psychotherapists can take up valuable and effective roles in organisations as counsellors, trainers and consultants at various levels. To do this they have to be prepared for some unlearning and some new learning. They have to be alert to a number of dangerous temptations: pathologising individuals or systems; reducing collective processes to individual dynamics; inability to understand the technical, commercial or operational realities of the organisation; inability to switch levels appropriately and understand the interconnections between the individual, the team, the inter-departmental, the organisational and the environmental; and over-focusing on process while under-focusing on task. In order to be effective they need to acquire a 'good enough' knowledge of the task and technologies of the client system that impact upon the people they are working with, and also to find a language through which they can communicate. Depending on their orientation – psychodynamic, humanistic and systemic – they will bring with them some variations in perspectives, metaphors and language, but, in our view, once they take up their roles in the organisational setting the differences will be much less significant than the commonalities – in particular, attention to unconscious dynamics.

REFERENCES

Argyris, C. and Schon, D. (1978) *Organisational Learning*, Reading, MA: Jossey Bass.
Bath Associates (1989) *Organisational Culture Manual*, Bath: Bath Associates.
Bion, W. R. (1961) *Experiences in Groups*, London: Tavistock Publications.
Bridger, H., Miller, E. J. and O'Dwyer, J. J. (1964) *The Doctor and Sister in Industry: A Study of Change*, London: Macmillan (Journals) Ltd; reprinted from *Occupational Health* (1963) 15.
Burton, J. W. (1967) 'The analysis of conflict by casework', *Year Book of World Affairs*, XXI, London: Stevens.
Carlisle, J. A. and Parker, R. C. (1989) *Beyond Negotiation*, Chichester: Wiley.
Cooper, C. L. (1972) 'An attempt to assess the psychologically disturbing effect of "T" group training', *British Journal of Social and Clinical Psychology*, pp. 342–5.
Critchley, B. and Casey, D. (1989) 'Organisations get stuck too', *Leadership and Organisation Development Journal* 10(4): 3–12.
Emery, F. E. and Trist, E. L. (1969) *Systems Thinking*, Harmondsworth: Penguin.
Handy, C. (1976) *Understanding Organisations*, Harmondsworth: Penguin.
Hastings, C., Bixby, P. and Chaudhry-Lawton, R. (1986) *The Superteam Solution*, Aldershot: Gower.
Hawkins, P. (1988) 'A phenomenological psychodrama workshop', pp. 60–78 in P. Reason (ed.) *Human Inquiry in Action*, London: Sage.
—— (in press) *The Heart of the Learning Organisation*, London: Sage.
Hawkins, P. and Shohet, R. (1989) *Supervision in the Helping Professions*, Milton Keynes: Open University Press.
Hillman, J. (1983) *Interviews*, New York: Harper & Row.
Jaques, E. (1953) 'On the dynamics of social structure', *Human Relations* 6: 3–24.
Lessom, R. (1990) *Development Management*, Oxford: Blackwell.
Lievegoed, B. (1991) *Managing the Developing Organisation*, Oxford: Blackwell.
McLean, A. and Marshall, J. (1989) *Cultures at Work: How to Identify and Understand Them*, Luton: Local Government Training Board.
Mangham, I. (1975) *Some Assumptions, Objectives, Methods and Results of Team Development Activities*, CSOCD Working Paper, University of Bath.
Menzies, I. E. P. (1959) *The Functioning of Social Systems as a Defence Against Anxiety*, London: Tavistock Institute of Human Relations.
Merry, V. and Brown, G. I. (1987) *The Behaviour of the Neurotic Organisation*, Cleveland, OH: Gestalt Institute of Cleveland Press.
Miller, E. J. (1993) *From Dependency to Autonomy: Studies in Organization and Change*, London: Free Association Books.
Miller, E. J. and Rice, A. K. (1967) *Systems of Organisation: Task and Sentient Systems and their Boundary Control*, London: Tavistock Publications.
Morgan, G. (1986) *Images of Organisation*, Beverly Hills, CA: Sage.
Ouchi, W. G. and Johnson, J. B. (1978) 'Types of organisation control and their relationship to emotional well-being', *Administrative Science Quarterly* 23: 292–317.
Pedler, M., Burgoyne, J. and Boydell, T. (1991) *The Learning Company*, Maidenhead, Berks: McGraw-Hill.
Peters, T. and Waterman, R. (1982) *In Search of Excellence*, New York: Harper & Row.
Pugh, D. S. and Hickson, D. J. (1989) *Writers on Organisations* (4th edn), Harmondsworth: Penguin.

Reason, P. (1988) *Human Inquiry in Action*, London: Sage.
Revans, R. (1972) *The Origins and Growth of Action Learning*, Bromley, Kent: Chartwell Bratt.
Rice, A. K. (1958) *Productivity and Social Organisation: The Ahmedabad Experiment*, London: Tavistock Publications.
—— (1963) *The Enterprise and its Environment*, London: Tavistock Publications.
Schein, E. M. (1985) *Organisational Culture and Leadership*, San Francisco: Jossey Bass.
Senge, P. (1990) *The Fifth Discipline: The Art and Practice of the Learning Organisation*, New York: Doubleday.
Sofer, C. (1961) *The Organisation from Within: A Comparative Study of Social Institutions Based on a Sociotherapeutic Approach*, London: Tavistock Publications.
Trist, E. L. and Bamforth, K. W. (1951) 'Some social and psychological consequences of the longwall method of coal-getting', *Human Relations* 4: 3–38.
Trist, E. L., Higgin, G. W., Murray, H. and Pollock, A. B. (1963) *Organisational Choice: Capabilities of Groups at the Coal Face under Changing Technologies*, London: Tavistock Publications.
van Maanen, J. and Schein, E. M. (1979) 'Towards a theory of organisational socialisation', in B. M. Straw and L. L. Cummings (eds) *Research in Organisational Behaviour*, vol. 1, Greenwich, CT: JAI Press.
Woodcock, M. (1979) *Team Development Manual*, Aldershot: Gower.

FURTHER READING

Clarkson, P. (1990) 'The scope of "stress" counselling in organisations', *Employee Counselling Today* 2(4): 3–6.
Clarkson, P. and Shaw, P. (1992) 'Human relationships at work – the place of counselling skills and consulting skills and services in organisations', *MEAD, the Journal of the Association of Management Education and Development* 23(1): 18–29.

USEFUL ORGANISATIONS AND TRAINING COURSES

Bath Consultancy Group
(formerly Bath Associates)
Consulting Service for
Organisations and Managers
24 Gay Street
Bath
Avon BA1 2PD
Tel.: 01225 333737
Fax: 01225 333738

The Tavistock Institute
Advanced Organisational
Consultation Programme
Tavistock Centre
Belsize Lane
London NW3 5BA
Tel.: 0171 435 7111

PHYSIS
12 North Common Road
Ealing
London W5 2QB
Tel. and fax: 0181 567 0388

Chapter 16

Psychotherapies within the NHS

Adele Kosviner

A BIRD'S EYE VIEW

The psychotherapies, by their very nature, evolve and change. The National Health Service, too, is evolving and changing, as are the professions within it. Psychotherapeutic services within the NHS are therefore hard to capture as a given static picture at any one moment. Looking at things positively, there have been considerable improvements in the quality of provision of the psychotherapies in the NHS over recent years, and these continue: services aim to offer a broader range of psychotherapies and so be responsive and flexible to individual needs; collaboration between providers of the psychotherapies is improving, so more efficient and effective use can be made of all resources in the field; and standards for training and accreditation are being made more explicit, which is leading to improved standards of care. On the more negative side, service provision is still inadequate and patchy; even where it exists, it is hard to find one's way to the service one may need and there is room for further improvement in collaboration between those providing the services.

Casting an eye to the future we may envisage, in response to market forces, perhaps a greater efficiency and quality of service, or perhaps a greater fragmentation of services and emphasis on advertising our wares, rather than providing them. Improved monitoring and audit of psychotherapy services should ensure that only the best survive. We shall, I think, have to fight hard to ensure that it is the best in the psychotherapies that survives, not the best in the packaging, or the cheapest.

WHAT WE DO AND WHAT WE SAY WE DO

The professions providing the psychotherapies in the NHS can no longer rest on their laurels. Apart from the very important developments in the psychotherapies in the independent sector, the whole climate towards the professions in the NHS is increasingly one of 'demonstrate what you do', and of decreasing interest in what we merely say we do. This emphasis on actual skills and competencies rather than professional training alone is spearheaded by the Department of Employment's National Council of Vocational Qualifications (NCVQ), and is likely to be attractive to NHS Trusts and Directly Managed Units, which need to be increasingly vigilant on questions of cost-effectiveness, especially in the short term. We need to be able to demonstrate, through the effectiveness of our work, the importance of the breadth and depth of understanding that comes from years of professional training. It will no longer be taken for granted.

One of the aspects of 'what we say we do' is entangled in the very use of the word 'psychotherapy'. Within the history of the NHS the word has been used as much to demarcate territory as to describe services. Used ambiguously, it has sometimes confused the issue of whether the psychotherapeutic services being referred to are primarily psychoanalytic or are those covering the full range of psychotherapies. It has also led to confusion when services in psychotherapies in the NHS have been assumed to be coterminous with the relatively few posts specifically *labelled* 'psychotherapy' (as with some medical posts), rather than referring to the full range of psychotherapy services, both generalist and specialist, that are available within the NHS.

THE STATUS QUO

That broad psychotherapy services do exist within the NHS is not under question. It is their quality, coherence, cohesion and accessibility that has been the main concern of those involved in their practice. Different professions and, within them, different professionals, differ in the proportion of time and expertise they contribute to the provision of formal psychological therapies, in the type and range of psychotherapy they offer, and in the breadth and level of specialist training in different therapeutic approaches that they have received. Specialised psychological therapies are provided mainly by clinical psychologists and medical psychotherapists; with nurse specialists, social workers, occupational therapists and related professions (such as drama, music and art therapists) playing an increasing role. However, in many areas, services in formal psychotherapies are often uncoordinated, unevenly distributed, and poorly integrated with other psychiatric and psychological services. Some are inadequately resourced to meet even minimal public demand. Further, they are often fragmented and subject to inter-professional tensions, themselves fed by anxieties about professional roles and by anxieties that conceptual differences between psychological therapies may contaminate rather than enrich a psychotherapy service. The current changes and uncertainties in the NHS are perhaps exacerbating these tensions, but they should also provide some pressure to resolve them. The present situation is not conducive to good patient care, is incomprehensible to most referrers and will undoubtedly become an anathema to purchasers.

For this reason a Joint Statement addressing these issues has recently been prepared by the British Psychological Society (BPS) and the Royal College of Psychiatrists (1993), the two professional bodies whose members at present constitute the major source of expertise in the psychotherapies within the NHS. This statement is concerned with issues of good practice and principles underlying working arrangements within NHS psychological therapy services. It stresses that the range of psychotherapies offered should be broad and balanced, with the contribution of each approach integrated within a co-ordinated service. It suggests that co-operation between professional groups providing psychological therapies at general and specialist levels is in the best interests of service users. It emphasises the need for high standards to be ensured through specialist assessment, treatment and training resources, having at least one specialist in each of the major psychotherapies provided, and for such resources to be co-ordinated by those with a broad appreciation and understanding of all aspects of services in the psychotherapies, not just one model of psychotherapy.

We are not yet there. This chapter will now cast an eye at history before going on to look at existing needs and services, and finally look again to the future. It will ask why we need psychological therapy services in the NHS; explore existing provision and how to gain access to it; and in doing so consider some features of particular relevance to NHS provision of the psychotherapies, such as the need to prioritise demand, the need for comprehensive assessment and therapy services, implications for training and supervision of staff, and evaluation of services provided (including the effectiveness and efficiency of the psychotherapies available). In the course of this it will identify areas that, one hopes, will be the targets for improvement and development.

THE HISTORY OF THE PSYCHOTHERAPIES IN THE NHS

Psychiatry and psychotherapy

In the mid-1970s psychotherapy became a separate medical speciality within psychiatry. An original intent behind the appointment of consultant psychotherapists was to enable medical staff to think about the role of psychological factors in their treatment of and their interaction with their patients. Guidelines for staffing levels were published in 1975, with a long-term goal set at 250 whole-time equivalent (WTE) consultant psychotherapists in England and Wales, an equivalent of 1 WTE for a population of 200,000. In 1984 there were 84 consultant posts established, in 1990 there were 127 (of which thirteen were vacant). Almost half of these posts are part time and the majority of them (61) are in the London area (Royal College of Psychiatrists 1991a).

The Royal College began to establish requirements for training in the psychotherapies for General Professional training (as a general psychiatrist), for training in General Psychiatry with a Special Interest in Psychotherapy, and for specialist training in Psychotherapy (leading to eligibility for consultant psychotherapist posts). Included in the latter were accredited Senior Registrar 'in-service' training schemes, as well as accommodation for those who had received their specialist psychotherapy training in private training institutions, independent of the NHS. In-service training approaches tended to develop away from established centres of psychotherapy training, which themselves were mainly in London. Standards of training between in-service training and external centres were different, resulting in some unevenness. There was an initial preponderance of psychoanalytic interest amongst medical consultant psychotherapists but this is now being redressed, with greater numbers becoming interested in other therapeutic orientations, including cognitive and behavioural approaches. In addition the General Psychiatry section of the Royal College of Psychiatrists is becoming more interested in the integration of psychological therapies in general psychiatric practice, rather than leaving its provision and development to the separate specialty alone.

Psychology and psychotherapy

The professional Division of Clinical Psychology was established by the BPS in 1968. At that time the psychotherapeutic orientation within the Division was largely behavioural, but with vigorous, if smaller, enclaves in psychoanalytic and humanistic approaches. Over the years this has balanced out so that the core curriculum for Clinical Psychology training now covers all major psychotherapeutic approaches (Kosviner 1992).

Post-qualification further training in the psychotherapies began to be recognised by the BPS in the late 1970s. The Department of Health Manpower Advisory Group commissioned an independent review in 1989 (Management Advisory Services to the NHS 1989) which concluded that the ability to combine or change psychological approaches as appropriate, while remaining rigorous in their application, was what distinguished clinical psychologists from other practitioners of formal psychological therapies. There are now approximately 2,500 Clinical Psychologists in the United Kingdom, most of whom consider their primary responsibility to include the provision of psychological therapies. Others have specialised in specific approaches such as neuropsychology, or are working in a more educational capacity with both clients and their carers. Career structures within Clinical Psychology have now developed to include continuing professional development in specialist areas (including the psychotherapies) after professional qualification, and permit progression to the higher consultant grades within the profession on the basis of clinical expertise as well as managerial responsibilities. This is encouraging more clinical psychologists to embark on further specialist trainings in the psychotherapies. The Society has now established the necessary internal structures to enable it to address the task of formally demarcating criteria for training and accreditation of its members within the psychotherapies at general and specialist levels.

Other NHS professions

The Royal College of Nursing revised its basic mental health course for psychiatric nurses in 1982, introducing a significant emphasis on 'counselling' and on acquiring some psychological therapy skills. The establishment of posts for clinical nurse specialists within mental health is likely to increase interest amongst nurses in gaining further expertise in counselling or the psychotherapies. Occupational therapy within mental health services has for some time fostered the development of skills in some of the psychotherapies, especially perhaps the therapies based on creative activity (art, music, drama) as well as skills-based approaches; for example, anxiety management, social skills and problem-solving.

Independent psychotherapists

A few posts have been established in the NHS in response to service demand, for psychotherapists – usually of a psychoanalytic orientation – for whom a career path in the psychotherapies is not possible within their core NHS profession, or who indeed have no such 'core profession' prior to their training in a particular psychotherapeutic model.

WHY WE NEED THE PSYCHOTHERAPIES WITHIN THE NHS

A high proportion of GP consultations and referrals for specialist hospital treatments, from headaches to heart attacks, involve psychological factors. The over-prescription of psychotropic medication such as the benzodiazepines has lead to public and professional awareness of the need to provide psychological treatments as an alternative or adjunct to medication, both for the conditions which have led people to seek help in the first place, and for those who have become dependent on such medication to cope with their original problems. It is increasingly recognised, too, that psychological therapies are the treatment of choice for a wide range of psychological and psychiatric presentations, including severe personality difficulties, acute and chronic neuroses, and adjustment to the aftermath of life crises, traumatic events and disasters. There is increasing demand for psychological treatments in the prevention as well as the amelioration of major psychiatric and physical illnesses, substance misuse, and other major habit disorders such as anorexia and bulimia, sexual deviations and some criminal behaviour.

INFINITE DEMAND, FINITE RESOURCES

No National Health Service can ever meet all the demands placed upon it, and providing psychotherapies is obviously no exception. Choices have to be made at every level, from those involving individual patients to those involving government strategies. There is a need for guiding principles to inform these choices, and currently there is some concern that market forces should not be the only ones. The goal of offering the highest quality service to the greatest number who need it most should clearly guide us, but matters are not so simple. Who decides who is most in need? Increasing awareness of the need for cost-efficiency may lead to the NHS becoming a specialist service of last resort for those who are unable to obtain help elsewhere, or because they cannot afford it. It is possible that NHS resources will become more focused either on the more seriously disturbed, or on those groups which demonstrably respond well to psychological interventions, and which thereby raise any given NHS Trust's reputation for making a contribution to the 'Health of the Nation' (Department of Health 1992), not just its ill health.

MAKING BEST USE OF ALL RESOURCES

Just as medicine is not only practised at consultant level within the NHS, so formal psychological therapies are carried out both by specialists in particular orientations and by professionals with less training and experience, under their supervision, in order to make fullest use of existing resources. This has implications for standards in supervision and training within the National Health Service (BPS 1990; Royal College of Psychiatrists 1990, 1991b).

SHORT-TERM AND GROUP APPROACHES

Services in the psychotherapies are under pressure to focus increasingly on shorter-, rather than longer-term treatment approaches, and on group rather than individual work, whenever appropriate, in order to treat greater numbers of people more efficiently. This undoubtedly makes sense where such approaches can be shown to be effective, and some research is encouraging in this field. The Joint Statement from the BPS and the Royal College of Psychiatrists (1993), while recognising the need to maximise efficiency and effectiveness, has also stressed the need to ensure that an appropriate range and choice of treatments are available. It is as cost-inefficient, they have argued, to give short-term treatments which are not effective as it is to provide long-term treatments where short-term treatments would be just as effective. The choice of treatment is a matter of clinical judgement, which should none the less be influenced by issues of cost-effectiveness. This has implications for the essential skills in differential assessment for the psychotherapies, required in National Health Service provision (Fonagy and Higgitt 1989, 1992; Menzies *et al.* 1993).

WHO RECEIVES HELP?

Services in the psychotherapies within the NHS have either to prioritise the more seriously 'dis-eased' or to use resources only where they are maximally effective. These demands on the service are sometimes contradictory, since many practitioners wish to help to alleviate the distress of those with more severe or chronic psychiatric or psychological conditions, where results may not be achieved quickly nor be easy to register clearly on any gauge of 'success'. Those in need of psychological therapies presenting to the NHS are not the 'worried well', nor do they usually represent the 'YAVIS' end of the spectrum (young, attractive, verbal, intelligent and successful). In a recent patient population audit in West Berkshire, for example, 45 per cent were aged forty and over, 20 per cent had never worked, only 8 per cent had higher education or professional status and 35 per cent had had psychiatric hospital admissions in the past two years. In addition, 25 per cent acknowledged sexual abuse, 35 per cent physical abuse (often both as children and adults) and 15 per cent had at least one conviction (Jane Knowles, personal communication 1994).

THE RANGE OF PSYCHOTHERAPEUTIC SERVICES AVAILABLE WITHIN THE NHS

Any one district or unit may possess anything between a comprehensive, well-organised provision to very little in the way of range or quality of services. At best there will be the possibility of a full and comprehensive consultation followed by the treatment of choice from well-trained and experienced professionals. At worst a patient will at least be guided to the best locally available help. Most services, whether those provided by clinical psychology or medical psychotherapy services (or both in a co-ordinated endeavour), will offer both individual and group work, some short-term, some longer-term. The range of therapeutic approaches available (for example, analytic, cognitive-behavioural, humanistic, systemic) will vary considerably, depending on local resources. Some larger clinical psychology services offer them all. With limited resources available to them, many services offer 'eclectic' psychotherapy. This term covers a multitude of meanings, from a well-informed flexibility of approach according to the needs of the individual presenting, to a 'mish-mash' based on very little understanding of anything. Some services offer psychotherapies practised by clinicians with considerable training and experience; others rely heavily on staff with very little or even no previous experience of psychotherapy – for example, doctors being trained in psychiatry – under the supervision of those with greater training and experience. Sometimes this supervision is full and frequent, but at other times it may amount to little more than infrequent consultation, with any one practitioner presenting their case for supervision in a group setting perhaps once in six weeks. There is clearly room for improvement and standardisation in the provision of supervision just as in the psychotherapies themselves.

ASSESSMENT

The assessment received in the initial consultation is of key importance to psychotherapy services within the NHS. It should be informed by an understanding of the range of different psychological therapies and their applicability to different types of difficulties and in different settings – whether in individual, group, couple or family therapies. Ideally, the assessment process should be informed by a broad understanding of human development and of the range of psychological approaches which can help in any particular case; it should be dispassionate and not biased towards any particular therapeutic orientation; it should be flexible and tailored to individual needs, and helpful in empowering people to make informed choices about which psychotherapeutic approach may best suit them. It should also be able, where necessary, to adjust psychological treatments to the individual rather than the other way round. The consultation service should further be able to offer a base for continuing flexibility during treatment if, for example, psychotherapy aims change as a result of increased understanding or changing priorities, perceptions or external circumstances.

TYPES OF PSYCHOTHERAPY PROVIDED WITHIN THE NHS

Services should aim to provide a full range of the main psychotherapies. Some of them do, and in an accessible, co-ordinated way that allows the flexibility mentioned above. Other districts or regions may have the full range, but they may be offered in differently managed units in a way which makes access to them quite a problem for patients and referrers alike. However, expertise does exist within the NHS (albeit not uniformly) in all major psychological therapies which are substantiated by sound psychological theories and/or empirical research findings. These include:

- Psychoanalytic psychotherapies which involve re-experiencing, exploring and changing feelings, assumptions and basic difficulties (especially in personal relationships) in the context of a developing relationship with a psychotherapist.
- Cognitive and behavioural psychotherapies which involve problem-solving approaches based on an analysis of how a person's experiences – and their interpretations of them – relate to how they feel and behave at any one time, and to bring about change through systematic 'real life' exercises.
- Systemic psychotherapies which are usually used in family therapy but may also be helpful in working with groups of people in a work place or other context, and also shed light on individual problems. Indeed it is sometimes the case that problems which an individual perceives as their own may best be understood as a problem within a group or organisation in which the person experiences the difficulties. In such cases it may be that, after full assessment, consultation to the group or organisation rather than the individual may be appropriate.
- Humanistic or existential psychotherapies which may use a range of approaches, including various aspects of the relationship with the psychotherapist, to help a person achieve their therapeutic goals.
- Counselling approaches which help individuals help themselves, in the context of a supportive relationship.

In some cases it may be appropriate to adopt an integrative approach where different psychotherapies may be combined, according to individual needs, so long as this is done in a way that is informed by the principles underlying these different approaches so that incompatible procedures are not mixed to brew an inherently contradictory or meaninglessly eclectic cocktail. Approaches such as cognitive-analytic therapy and some combinations of systemic with behavioural or analytic approaches are instances where therapeutic approaches may be tailored to service demands or individual needs. There has to be space within the NHS psychotherapies for innovation and development, but it is important, in my view, for its practitioners to be well grounded in the orientations they practise before combining or shortening them.

Different approaches suit different people and even different problems in the same person. They can almost all be offered on a short- or longer-term basis, in a variety of settings. These settings include individual psychotherapy with a psychotherapist; group therapy, where a number of people meet together regularly with one or two psychotherapists; couple therapy where couples meet together with one or two psychotherapists to work on their relationship difficulties (which may include sexual difficulties); and family therapy, where the whole family will meet with one or two psychotherapists. Most of these psychotherapies are offered on an 'out-patient' basis. In very severe or intransigent cases, residential or day-care psychological therapy may be recommended.

ASSESSMENT REVISITED

In short, clarifying problems and goals for NHS psychotherapy is only the start. There is then the need to determine which type of therapy (cognitive-behavioural, psychodynamic, systemic and so on), in what setting (individual, group and so forth), its frequency and its duration. Judgements must then be made about the implications of differing degrees of emotional and time commitments, and judgements too about available resources both within the NHS and within the voluntary or independent sectors, or within social services. Thorough assessment at this stage also has implications for monitoring demands on the service and how to prioritise resources, present and future.

This task of assessment is clearly broader than that available to anyone who is familiar, however deeply, with only one psychotherapeutic approach. The BPS/Royal College of Psychiatry Statement (1993) has recommended that there should be collaboration between providers of psychological therapy services, which would allow integration of assessment procedures, such that all referrals could be initially screened by a small team of those members of the service with a substantial understanding of the range of different psychological therapies available, and the respect of their colleagues in all professions. The Statement suggests that the screening team will be an important source of information and advice to other services and agencies, especially potential referrers, and will be in a good position also to identify gaps in the treatment provision and to audit aspects of the service. Such a system, following the spirit of the Patients' Charter, should be able to facilitate informed patient choice.

ORGANISATION OF PSYCHOTHERAPY SERVICES IN THE NHS

While all NHS clinical staff in mental health services use psychological skills with their patients, the two professions presently providing the bulk of formal psychotherapies are clinical psychology and medical psychotherapy. Both may also offer supervision and consultation to other NHS professionals carrying out formal psychotherapy. Some formal psychotherapy is also sometimes carried out independently of either of these two departments, by, for example, nurses or occupational therapists, with varying amounts of formal training or supervision.

Both medically organised and clinical psychology psychotherapy services (whether or not they are co-ordinated) take direct referrals from outside agencies as well as from within psychiatric and hospital services. They usually have waiting lists, either for assessment and/or for treatment. They may or may not use pre-interview assessment aids such as self-completion questionnaires.

HOW TO GAIN ACCESS TO NHS PSYCHOTHERAPEUTIC SERVICES

The usual way for a referral to be made is through a GP directly to either the consultant clinical psychologist (in adult or child services, as appropriate) or to the consultant psychotherapist (for adult services) or to child psychotherapy services (psychoanalytic only) where these exist. Different departments may have different specialities or may overlap in the service they provide. It is to be hoped that local GPs are familiar with the resources available within their local mental health services, although one cannot blame them if they sometimes become confused about which department is offering what, at what level of therapist competence. The sooner services can integrate themselves without threats to professional or psychotherapeutic identity, autonomy or status, and without any one claiming precedence over the other, the better. Easier said than done, but the present situation, as emphasised by the Joint Statement, is clearly not in the best interests of service users. Clarifying and acknowledging differences in types and levels of competencies should go some way towards minimising wasteful internecine tensions.

TRAINING IN THE PSYCHOTHERAPIES AMONGST NHS PROFESSIONALS

It might be helpful at this point to summarise the training of psychiatrists and clinical psychologists within the psychotherapies.

Psychotherapy training within the medical profession is at a general level (within training as a general psychiatrist) and at a specialist level (for training as a consultant psychotherapist) (Royal College of Psychiatrists 1990, 1991b; General Medical Council 1987). Training criteria in the psychotherapies within psychiatry are divided into that deemed appropriate for any general psychiatrist, and that required for specialist practice as a consultant psychotherapist.

Junior psychiatrists will have completed their basic medical education and have full registration as doctors, but they will not generally have received any training or experience in the psychotherapies prior to starting to practise as psychiatrists. Rather, they acquire it in the course of their 'in-service training' over a period of at least two years as psychiatrists in training.

Senior registrars in psychiatry (who will have had a minimum of two to three years of general professional training as psychiatrists) will therefore have had a minimum of eight to nine years' professional training, a minimum of two of which will have included training in the psychotherapies.

Consultant psychotherapists have had, in addition to the minimum of two to three years' training within their general professional training as a psychiatrist, a further four years' (minimum) training in a chosen psychotherapy. Consultant psychotherapists will have had a minimum of twelve years' professional training, including a minimum of six years' training in the psychotherapies.

Psychotherapy training within clinical psychology is similarly at different levels. It requires first a degree in Psychology followed by a master's or doctoral degree in Clinical Psychology (minimum three years, full-time), the core curriculum of which covers all major models in the psychotherapies (Kosviner 1992; BPS 1990).

Junior clinical psychologists (formally called 'basic grade') will therefore have had a minimum of three years' general training in the psychotherapies before starting practice as chartered psychologists in the NHS. They are expected to consolidate this by a further two years' 'continuing professional development' which, for those working in general adult or child services, includes specialist supervised practice in the psychological therapies. They are expected to continue to receive supervision in specialist psychotherapies thereafter.

Senior clinical psychologists (that is, those who have had a minimum two years' general professional experience after qualifying as chartered clinical psychologists) will therefore be required to have had a minimum of eight years' professional training, a minimum of five of which will be concerned with the psychotherapies. At this stage some may consider going on to specialist training, which takes a further minimum three to four years, depending on the psychotherapeutic orientation, and qualifies them as fully independent practitioners within a specified model of psychotherapy.

Specialist clinical psychologists in a specified psychotherapy will have had a minimum of twelve years of professional training, including a minimum of eight to nine years of psychotherapy training (Kosviner 1993).

Both professions consider 'breadth' as important as 'depth' in training in the psychotherapies. This enables those appropriately qualified to fulfil consulting roles in assessing the most suitable form of psychotherapy in any individual case. The Working Party on the Psychotherapies set up by the Joint Consultative Committee between the Royal College of Psychiatrists and the BPS will in all likelihood be addressing criteria for competence in this field in the near future.

SUPERVISION

As much NHS psychotherapy is practised at basic and intermediate as well as specialist levels, the issue of adequate standards in supervision is of paramount importance. At the present time there are guidelines within the main professions serving this field, but greater shared standards can only be a good thing. There are still inadequate numbers of either profession trained to specialist level, which is where specific expertise in particular psychotherapies (which may be held by some independent psychotherapists as well as by existing NHS professionals) should, where it is lacking, be brought into services to ensure the quality of services provided.

AUDIT, EVALUATION AND RESEARCH

The unmonitored practice of psychotherapy within the NHS is no longer acceptable. There is a need to provide more and better services within available resources, and this cannot be achieved without systematic audits of services. Measures of service relevance, equity, accessibility, acceptability, effectiveness and efficiency can be built into the process of delivering services in the psychotherapies (Parry 1992). These may include measures of psychotherapeutic outcome and process, provided that the measures used are sensitive to the variables being assessed (Fonagy and Higgitt 1989). There is a slightly dangerous tendency within the current tensions in the NHS to embrace a mock 'glasnost' about all its services, in which rapid (and sometimes meaningless) assessments have replaced thoughtful reflections about the service. The Society for Psychotherapy Research is a helpful organisation for those wishing to become more familiar with research issues in this complex field.

WHOSE CRYSTAL BALL?

We all probably have different ideas about what we think will happen to the psychotherapies within the NHS. It is reasonable to assume, in the short term at least, that there will be little increase in resources available for the psychological therapies. That means we will need to make the best possible use of all existing resources – both generalist and specialist – and so create maximum availability for the service. This, in turn, will demand improved co-ordination and organisation in any one area in order to achieve as comprehensive, effective and efficient a service as possible. We will also need enough specialists in all major psychotherapy orientations available to ensure adequate levels of supervision and quality of service. In the same way, in-service training in the psychotherapies should be encouraged and developed, with special attention paid to developing appropriate shared standards and training by specialists. The need for comprehensive assessment to be carried out by those with knowledge of all the options in the psychological therapies will be necessary to ensure the maximum effectiveness of any psychotherapy service. Consultation in the psychotherapies to medical disciplines and health-care professionals will enable these services to appreciate the psychological dimensions of physical health and illness. Finally, we need to stay grounded in an empiricism sensitive to the complexities of the service which we provide, and adequately monitor and research our services (Department of Health 1992). We need to protect the service from becoming a victim of a paradox of factuality, where what is recorded becomes more important than the actuality of what we do, and where we may lose our bearings, or, worse, our integrity, in the winds of the marketplace or political fashion.

REFERENCES

British Psychological Society (1990) *Policy Statement: Psychological Therapy Services: The Need for Organisational Change*, Leicester: BPS Publications.

British Psychological Society/Royal College of Psychiatrists (1993) *Joint Statement: Psychological Therapies for Adults in the National Health Service*.

Department of Health (1992) *Health of the Nation*, London: HMSO.

Fonagy, P. and Higgitt, A. (1989) 'Evaluating the performance of departments of psychotherapy', *Psychoanalytic Psychotherapy* 4(2): 121–53.

—— (1992) 'Psychotherapy in borderline and narcissistic personality disorders', *British Journal of Psychiatry* 161: 23–43.

General Medical Council (1987) Education Committee, *Recommendations on the Training of Specialists* (Oct.), London: GMC.

Kosviner, A. (1992) 'The psychotherapies in the curriculum of clinical psychologists', pp. 84–8 in G. Powell, R. Young and S. Frosh (eds) *Curriculum in Clinical Psychology*, Leicester: BPS (Division of Clinical Psychology) Publications.

—— (1993) *Smatterings, Standards and Snobbism in Psychotherapy and Psychology*, Psychotherapy Section Inaugural Address, BPS.

Management Advisory Services to the National Health Service (1989) *Review of Clinical Psychology Services* (Oct.), London: HMSO.

Menzies, D., Dolan, B. M. and Norton, K. (1993) 'Are short term savings worth long term costs? Funding treatment for personality disorders', *Psychiatric Bulletin* 17(9): 517–19.

Parry, G. (1992) 'Improving psychotherapy services: applications of research, audit and evaluation', *British Journal of Clinical Psychology* 31: 3–19.

Royal College of Psychiatrists (1990) *Handbook of the Joint Committee on Higher Psychiatric Training*, London: RCP.

—— (1991a) 'The future of psychotherapy services', *Psychiatric Bulletin* 15: 174–9.

—— (1991b) *Statement on Approval of Training Schemes for General Professional Training for the MRCPsych* (April), London: RCP.

Chapter 17

Psychotherapy and social services

Kenneth Kirk Smith and Jonathan Smith

Social services departments in Great Britain cost the taxpayer £5,591 million in 1991, approximately £100 for every man, woman and child. At £2 a person a week, you may be surprised it is so little. Social workers are responsible for providing a range of services (including counselling) to children and families, disabled people, the elderly, and people who are mentally ill. Social workers deal directly and indirectly with human growth and development, dependency, transference and counter-transference, and unconscious processes in individuals and organisations; yet the relationship between social work and psychotherapy is an uncomfortable one. The reasons for this, and some of the implications, will be considered in this chapter.

THE RISE AND FALL OF PSYCHODYNAMIC SOCIAL WORK

The first set of reasons is to be found in social work's own history. Social work is not a new profession. Its origins were observable in the 1870s, and it has an interesting history of which it can be justly proud. Though social conditions influence how people live and behave, individuals are unique and deal with adversity in different ways; and so both psychology and sociology are needed to understand behaviour, even if at times it is hard to hold them together in the same frame. Social work recognises this, and also the importance of the family as the social institution that creates individuals and prepares them for independent existence in the community. It has established an identity as a profession committed to helping people in need, by working with individuals, families, groups or communities.

Social work was greatly advanced in the 1950s by psychoanalytic ideas, which it took in from Dr John Bowlby and the Tavistock Clinic, from Donald Winnicott at the London School of Economics, and from the American social work profession. These ideas provided social work with the psychology that it had been looking for. The publication of Bowlby's *Forty-four Juvenile Thieves* (1946), for example, helped people to see that, in many cases, delinquents were deprived people in need of help. This psychology, which saw difficult behaviour as a way of dealing with deprivation, or as defences for the personality against anxiety and loss, provided a method that improved the practice of work with individuals, traditionally called 'case-work'.

With the addition of psychodynamic psychology, case-work became a powerful way of helping people, which was rather seductive to some members of the profession. It certainly contributed to the effectiveness of social work. In the 1950s and 1960s, social work had not caught the attention of the public, as it later would. It was an activity known only to a few; but this group, which included members of the local authority Children's Committees, judges and lawyers who knew of the work of the Probation Service, and doctors aware of the contribution made by mental welfare officers to the mentally ill, was influential. People who were aware of social work approved and some even idealised what they saw.

Psychodynamic psychology led to the 'generic principle'. Social work increasingly became aware of the common human needs underlying a variety of defensive and disruptive behaviours, and began to find the division of the profession into agencies specialising in certain kinds of client problem to be a constraint. The 1969 Children and Young Persons Act, which went a long way towards blurring the distinction between delinquent and deprived children, was an example of the application of this principle.

In pursuit of a generic approach, social workers decided to form themselves into a single professional body, the British Association of Social Workers. To achieve this, they voluntarily surrendered the smaller and highly effective organisations which supported the practice of child care and of psychiatric social work, published excellent journals, and organised well-attended annual teaching conferences. Unfortunately, BASW, the large new organisation, took some time to learn to manage itself, and for some years was not an organisation that could represent the profession and support its members. Even today, fewer people attend its Annual General Meeting than attended that of the Child Care Officers Association in 1968. This left social workers in an exposed situation when, after legislation implementing the Seebohm Report (Seebohm 1968), they found themselves working in enormous local authority departments, responsible for services to a wide range of client groups.

The Seebohm Report gave power, responsibility and independence to social work. It recommended that there should be one large social service department in each local authority, directed by a social worker, thereby confirming the high standing in which social workers were regarded at the time, and giving its assent to the generic principle.

Social workers who lived through this re-organisation will remember the chaos it brought. At a time when they were disorganised, without adequate management skills to survive in such large departments, or the practice skills to co-operate to provide a generic service, they were totally overwhelmed by legislation. The 1969 Children and Young Persons Act, an exciting and liberal piece of legislation, transferred to people who had been child-care workers the responsibility for juvenile offenders who had been the responsibility of the Probation Service. This imposed a responsibility to offer corrective relationships to young offenders onto workers who had a welfare ideology, and no experience of the creative use of authority. The skills that the Probation Service had been developing, of using a relationship sanctioned by an order to help young people in trouble, were lost. The first indication of things to come for social work was a barrage of complaints from magistrates, the police and the public, taken up in the press, that social workers had no answer to delinquency. This was followed by the Chronically Sick and Disabled Persons Act (1972), which was full of creative ideas for workers to improve the lot of disabled people, but with no offers to provide the money to do so.

Social work has found ways of coping with the constraints and opportunities of a social services setting. It has evolved new partnerships, new management and new practices, and now does work in response to community demands which would not have been possible in the 1960s. But it has never regained the confidence, the cohesion and the public approval which it once enjoyed. One aspect of this is that there is no agreed language to describe its practice. Some of the influences that led to this have been described, but there is one more significant influence to consider.

The introduction of psychodynamic psychology to social work helped it to advance, but it polarised opinion in the profession, as it has done in medicine and in society generally. As Butrym pointed out (1976), it professionalised one aspect of social work – that is, individual case-work – and it took some time for other aspects of social work practice to catch up. Group work was rediscovered in the 1960s, family therapy in the 1970s, and finally community work, mentioned in the Seebohm Report, took a higher profile after the Barclay Report (1980). Before this, however, individual case-work on psychodynamic lines had become such an interesting and powerful method that some people saw it as the whole of social work. In her classic paper, Irvine (1956) showed that psychodynamic case-work had a proper place in the repertoire of responses of social work. But other people were less accepting. Baroness Wootton (1959) attacked psychodynamic methods. Mayer and Timms (1970) questioned the relevance of case-work for working people. Radical social workers said that too much psychology detracted from the social, structural contribution to poverty and failure. A debate was in progress about the identity and practice of social work.

Unfortunately, partly due to the organisational changes going on, this debate was never finished. One result is that social work is ambivalent about, or even resistant to, psychodynamic work. Some people anticipated what was about to happen, and established a pressure group (GAPS, or the Group for the Advancement of Psychotherapy and Psychodynamics in Social Work), but it has never had more than 400 members. Another rather tragic example of the failure to resolve the contradictions inherent in providing social services is that the generic debate has never been properly dealt with, so that social services departments are even now reorganising themselves backwards and forwards from 'specialist' (based on special client groups) to 'patch' (taking all comers from a neighbourhood).

Finally, the recognition of child abuse, and later sexual abuse, in the community has created a situation which has changed social work. Since Maria Colwell, the first case to come to public notice (Department of Social Services 1974), social workers have found themselves, with the police, in the front line of services to protect children from physical and sexual abuse in their families. When this fails there is, quite properly, outrage and a demand for the allocation of responsibility, and this operates as one of the major anxieties for workers in social services departments.

To conclude this part of the argument, it is submitted that psychodynamic psychology empowered social work, and contributed to the progress that led to the creation of social services departments. Social workers evolved a form of psychotherapy which they called 'case-work' which was instrumental in helping individuals and families. At the same time, in search of the 'generic principle', social work transformed the institutions that maintained its professional identity. As a result, under the pressure of organisational change, the debate about the place of psychodynamic work was never concluded, and the profession has lost some of the practice skills and the position that it had established.

This has been a painful loss. In some ways social work has moved on, and now tackles more difficult things than it could have attempted in the 1960s, and some of the practice from that time has been shown to need improvement (Reid and Shine 1969). But in other ways it has lost cohesion and confidence, and the ability to work with people in need. It is a profession dominated by the needs of clients and employers, without a core that allows it to make its own contribution to events. Reflecting on this, and how it has happened, one can see that in the 1970s there was some idealisation and a little hubris: but there also seems to have been a kind of self-destructiveness, a determination not to form a strong professional identity, but to identify with the deprived and the outcast, in a way that contributed to its inability to speak to them.

SOCIAL SERVICES – IS ANY PSYCHOTHERAPY PRACTISED?

Social services departments are large and complex bureaucracies, with responsibilities under legislation to a range of client groups, employing a variety of professional people with different kinds and levels of training.

The range of different kinds of helping activities is considerable, and social work is only a part of the activity. Staff include foster-parents, residential and day-care workers, occupational therapists and administrators. The tasks vary from the mundane to matters of life and death, some of the work is long-term, and some of a crisis nature. Social workers are meeting the results of deprivation, delinquency, mental illness, handicap of all kinds and marital disharmony. Stress is considerable. Social work training is usually for two years, which the profession does not regard as adequate. In these circumstances, is it meaningful to talk of psychotherapy, or anything like it, in social services departments?

Our answer (this may be controversial) is a qualified 'yes'. Some social workers share with psychotherapists the belief based on experience that if dependency needs are recognised and understood, the client's growth process can continue. Understanding the client in the here-and-now of a relationship can help this to take place. This cannot be learned from a textbook, but needs to be experienced in relation to the worker's own need to be cared for and accepted. One of the most potent experiences in training to help other people is an experience of having been a patient oneself. Not everyone will want to work this way, but for those who do it is a vocation, in the sense that workers will continue to work like this whether they are sanctioned by their agency or profession, or not. Some social work training courses still prepare students to work in this way. In other cases, social workers subsidise their training by taking courses at their own expense, sometimes in psychotherapy or counselling.

Even where the demands of the agency inhibit thoughtful relationship work, workers find ways to do this by subverting the system. The study of mental health practice by Fisher et al. (1984) showed that social workers manage to keep a part of their case-load where they can do long-term work, while offering a crisis service to the majority of people for whom they are responsible.

DIFFERENCES OF SETTING

Now we can turn to the question of the differences that the setting makes to psychodynamic work in a social services agency.

The first difference is that sometimes social workers in social services departments intervene with the environment directly. This enables them to help people by providing foster-care, by financial and other kinds of help, and by engaging in community development programmes. However, it means that there are times when the social worker can no longer operate as a counsellor or psychotherapist to help a client to come to terms with and respond to difficulties in the environment, as the worker has become a part of the environment, and thus a part of the problem to be overcome. It is extremely difficult for clients to seek psychotherapeutic help from a worker who has been instrumental in removing their children. It is not easy to work with a client who needs psychological help or counselling and who also wants or needs money, unless there is a clear understanding, accepted by the client, of the circumstances, if any, in which the agency can offer financial help.

A second major difference is that usually in psychotherapy there is a contract between the worker and client, whereas, in social services departments, payment is by a third party. This could be seen as A doing something with B while C pays. This means that social workers are able to help people who need it, but could not or would not afford to pay for it. However, the price of this is a built-in confusion, as it is not always clear who C is, what he expects to happen, and even whether this is possible. At various times, C can be represented by an officer of the local authority, or by elected members, or officers or elected members of the national government, or indeed by the electorate itself. Where psychotherapy is provided in the National Health Service, it is at least fairly clear that it is psychotherapy that is being paid for. One of the disadvantages of the changes in social work described above is that it lost control of its own identity, which is now determined by a diverse variety of organisations, including employing authorities, so that what is called social work may be rather different in, say, Islington and Hackney.

A consequence of providing a free service is that it may both meet a need and uncover (or even appear to create) a demand. Some health professionals, for example, think that if people who attempt to commit suicide are given too much help with their problems, this will increase the number of attempted suicides. Without some sort of control, there is a risk that social work is either strangled by the demands arising from its own effectiveness or, alternatively, that the service may become inefficient, inappropriately defensive, and not subject to financial control. Recent legislation has made a radical attempt to clarify this. Under the NHS and Community Care Act (1991), the law separates providers or services from purchasers, devolves responsibility to a level as near the client as practical, and envisages a pluralist economy, strengthening the voluntary sector. The intention is to bring a realistic appreciation of the costs of treatments to the notice of those prescribing them, and to allow 'market forces' to exercise some control. Ultimately this may help, though there are theoretical and practical problems to deal with. In the short term, it is reducing the time available to workers in social services departments to help people themselves, and there is a real danger that it will erode even further their ability to carry out interventions that constitute clinical work.

A third major difference is that social services meet and work with people for whom psychotherapy would not be possible or helpful. Some clients want advice, information or services, and manage well enough once they have these. Others are too ill to cope with the kind of help that can be offered in regular appointments, even if they are frequent. They may need day care or support to manage at home, or even residential care or compulsory admission to hospital. Other people find ways of dealing with their problems, such as delinquency, which maintain the omnipotent defensive belief that they are all right, and it is the world that is out of step: they can only be helped with some kind of structure, court process or containing order.

DIFFERENCES OF THEORY

Now we can turn to some of the differences of theory between social work and psychotherapy, with particular reference to work with children.

Social workers are daily confronted with the realities of child abuse, deprivation and neglect in all its many and varied forms. The social worker may focus appropriately upon the parents' social situation, their here-and-now environment, and look for the factors that frequently (though not always) correlate with the problem of abuse; that is, poverty, homelessness, poor housing, racism, deprivation and inequality. These connections are valuable in helping the social worker to understand what may have precipitated the crisis.

Aware that parents are themselves desperately in need of help with their psychological as well as their social needs, social workers have at times looked hopefully to psychoanalysis and psychotherapy for maps and models to guide them in their task. It is these disciplines that have concerned themselves specifically with the subjective experience of the individual, with the feelings and emotional conflicts that reside in the psyche. Aware of the beleaguered social worker struggling to meet the demands of the desperate families on her case-load, it is to the relationship between psychotherapy and social work that we now turn.

Psychotherapy and social work are concerned with a large overlapping area of human experience, and yet their perspectives seem to be worlds apart. Communication between the two disciplines is befogged by the use of very different language and concepts. Instead of a creative cross-fertilisation of ideas they have diverged, as each has charted its own largely separate course.

There are many reasons for this. One is that professionals tend to move from social work towards psychotherapy. Social workers who go on to become psychotherapists, learning and growing on the way, with considerable expenditure of time, money and effort, must be forgiven for assuming that the end is superior to the beginning. This assumption may be reinforced if it cloaks the fact that they cease to work with the people and situations that are the most demanding, chaotic, needy and possibly least hopeful. Although psychotherapy and social work are different, and social workers are on average less trained, the task of social work is as difficult as psychotherapy, as demanding and as valuable.

The relationship between reality and fantasy, as conceived by psychotherapists, has also contributed to the divergence between the two disciplines. Whereas social work is daily confronted by the all-too-obviously painful realities of children's lives, psychotherapy and psychoanalysis have often seemed to focus attention more upon the fantasy life and imagination of the individuals who come in search of relief from their suffering.

There have been periods, however, when a cross-fertilisation of ideas between the two disciplines has taken place. Winnicott (1965), while making a significant contribution to the object relations school of psychoanalysis, shifted the focus of analysis onto the real nature of the infant–mother relationship and the traumatic effect of failures by the environment to meet the needs of the child. At the same time, Bowlby's (1969) pioneering research focused on the effects on the child of real events of separation and abandonment. (By its very nature, attachment theory focuses on the child's relationships with the primary carer.)

More recently, attachment theory researchers have begun to focus their attention on the effect of abuse on the child's attachment relationships with parents, and how the damage to the attachment relationship results in the abuse being transmitted generationally. It is unfortunate that attachment theory has had a limited reception in social work. Marris (1982) points out that it has been misunderstood as a sociological theory about family structure, rather than as a psychological theory about child development in the context of the relationship with the primary carers. It has not always found favour, for ideological reasons, with those who hold strong views either for or against the traditional family structure, and this has reduced the extent to which it has been accepted.

Alice Miller's (1985) focus upon the psychotherapist's function as advocate for the inner child, with an unequivocal focus on the realities of childhood trauma and abuse, has also made a significant contribution to bridging the gulf between social work and psychotherapy.

In the United States, Selma Fraiberg's work (1980) has raised important issues about the nature of psychotherapy with socially and economically deprived and disadvantaged groups. She raises questions about the need to change and modify the techniques of psychotherapy if clients from these groups are to be successfully engaged in psychotherapy, and to be helped in the process.

During the initial encounters with a client from such a background, the type of client who will frequently appear at the doors of a social services department, it is likely that motivation to seek psychotherapeutic assistance will be low. The psychotherapist will need to be prepared for such clients to be very difficult to engage in psychotherapy. Often a client will have experienced the involvement of statutory agencies in the family for several generations. Social workers may have intervened and removed children into care, or the client or members of their family may have been compulsorily admitted to hospital under a section of the Mental Health Act. Such a client may therefore be very wary of, or indeed hostile to, any offer of psychotherapy, and fearful that this may be yet one more intrusive and interfering intervention in their life. Furthermore there is unlikely to be much support in such a person's cultural background for the notion that psychotherapy, and the exploring of one's feelings, can be of help in life. Current external environment pressures may seem all too clearly to be overwhelming. This may sound very familiar to social workers; significantly, a psychotherapist working in a social services department will need to employ techniques and skills borrowed from social work if clients are to be successfully engaged in psychotherapy.

First, the psychotherapist will need to assume a large amount of responsibility in the process of creating and maintaining an attachment relationship with the client (Reiner and Kaufman 1959). In the initial stages of the psychotherapy, there may be repeated missed appointments and cancellations, as the client expresses uncertainty, ambivalence and hostility about the notion of engaging in psychotherapy. The psychotherapist will therefore need some understanding and acceptance of the very tenuous nature of the attachment relationship, and may need to be prepared to wait patiently for the client who fails to turn up for appointments, for several weeks, before a successful therapeutic alliance is established. It needs to be recognised that this is an important part of the work, otherwise such clients are likely to fail to engage in the psychotherapy.

Part of this process of engaging the client in psychotherapy also centres on the issue of the client's uncertainty of how far they can trust the psychotherapist. This will emerge in psychotherapy generally, whatever the setting. However, where the encounter between client and psychotherapist takes place in the particular social context described above, working through the issue of trust, recognising the effect which the social context has upon the client's doubts about how far they can trust the psychotherapist becomes a crucial issue, especially in the initial period of psychotherapy. These issues are best addressed by the psychotherapist at the first suitable opportunity.

Fraiberg gives a most graphic and telling account of the simple and straightforward, and yet highly unconventional, way in which she worked with this issue of trust, and the negative transference that had to be worked through, before one highly anxious and abusing mother was able to make use of the psychotherapeutic support that was being offered to her.

> Her past was filled with broken and disappointing relationships, meaning that a formidable negative transference had to be dealt with immediately. My acknowledgement of Beth's (the mother's) fury,

disappointment and distrust enabled her to visit me twice a week. She made constant demands on me. She changed the meeting times. I agreed. She asked for Trudy's (her baby's) hospital records. I got them. She wanted to scold the hospital administrator, I summoned him.

(1980: 223)

This example is quoted because it illustrates so clearly the kind of modification of technique and flexibility of approach that may be needed of the psychotherapist working in a social services department. It also illustrates how working therapeutically in such a context may involve combining psychotherapy with social work functions. The psychotherapist, as well as providing in-depth assistance with the client's subjective experience, with the way in which past traumatic experiences may be re-enacted in the present, also provides practical material assistance which may be in the form of financial assistance, help with food or clothing, or negotiation with other agencies such as hospitals, doctors, children's hospitals or the income maintenance services. The psychotherapist may also provide a non-didactic and supportive form of guidance in child development for those young mothers whose basic knowledge of the needs and developmental stages of babies and infants is inadequate. The provision of these forms of assistance contributes significantly to the therapeutic relationship, assisting in the formation of a therapeutic alliance, and reducing a highly self-protective negative transference. It communicates to the client in a symbolic way that the psychotherapist is there to help her find her own pathway out of her nightmare, rather than to interfere, intrude and betray her, as others are likely to have done.

The choice of location and settings may also involve the psychotherapist in adopting unconventional approaches. There are many clients whose motivation to seek therapeutic assistance is so low that they are unlikely to become engaged in psychotherapy unless the psychotherapist is prepared, initially at least, to visit them in their own homes, to conduct the psychotherapy sessions in the living room, the kitchen or the children's playroom. The psychotherapist will need to address the issue of boundaries and maintain the privacy necessary for the therapeutic work, but creative flexibility can mean that even intrusive visits by others can be worked with therapeutically. Where mothers with young children are concerned, reaching a psychotherapist's office can create practical problems and be a real disincentive to engaging in psychotherapy. This affords additional impetus for the psychotherapist to be flexible, and to find ways of conducting psychotherapy with babies or young children present, using the inter-actions between parent and child as potential material for exploring the parent's past childhood experience. Where seeing a client in her own home may create serious difficulties around the boundaries of a therapeutic relationship, then finding alternative locations near the client's home, such as a private room in a community centre or a church hall, can be considered. Such a setting would need to convey symbolically the psychotherapist's separateness from institutions that undertake statutory childcare and mental health responsibilities, which the client may perceive as intrusive and interfering.

IS PSYCHOTHERAPY POSSIBLE IN A SOCIAL SERVICES DEPARTMENT?

We have begun to touch upon an important issue: namely, whether it is possible to combine the therapeutic role with other social work functions, particularly the statutory ones; or whether it is necessary to create a separate agency and structure offering psychotherapy and other therapeutic forms of assistance, an agency that is clearly and distinctly separate from the social services department.

Events in social services in recent years have increased the likelihood of the development of an insurmountable negative transference in some of its clients. The greater awareness of the incidence of abuse, particularly sexual abuse, coupled with a number of critical inquiries into situations where children have been killed by a parent whilst being supervised by a social worker, have resulted in a concentration of resources upon the investigation and assessment of child abuse, and upon the child protection aspect of the service. The contribution of preventive or long-term supportive case-work to the field of social services has diminished appreciably, so that increasingly social services have become identified with the highly interventionist aspects of the work on child protection cases. A psychotherapist who is a social worker, or is clearly a member of a social services department, will begin by being identified as a part of this interventionist child protection service.

For psychotherapists to create the safety of the therapeutic space, they will need to be sure that the contents of the session remain completely confidential. Psychotherapists need to develop their own guidelines for breaching the confidentiality of the therapeutic space when, for example, a child's life is judged to be seriously at risk, or when there is a subpoena to give evidence in court. These guidelines are likely to be different from the procedures and policies created for social workers as part of their role in child protection, where the emphasis is of necessity more upon the sharing of information with other agencies. A single agency could not contain such differing guidelines in relation to confidentiality with any ease.

Another advantage of separating the two roles and functions can be stated as follows. There are many clients whose sense of self has been so fragmented and shattered by their experience of childhood abuse and trauma that, when they begin psychotherapy, they could not be contained in a relationship with a psychotherapist who was also clearly a member of an agency which receives children into care, or compulsorily admits people into mental hospital. The anxiety, fear and distrust of the psychotherapist would create such a formidable negative transference that the psychotherapist would be unlikely to reduce it sufficiently to engage the client in a working therapeutic alliance.

The disadvantage of separating the roles of child protection and the provision of therapeutic support into separate agencies is that collaboration between workers carrying child protection responsibility and the worker undertaking the therapeutic task remains essential. Working from separate agencies is likely to increase significantly the difficulties of facilitating a high level of collaboration between workers, and to create a barrier to the necessary continuing cross-fertilisation of ideas between social workers engaged in child protection and psychotherapists engaged in preventive work. Such a barrier would increase misunderstanding and miscommunication between workers. This is likely to occur when both workers are faced with the same client expressing very intense deeply distressed feelings (Mattinson and Sinclair 1979). Linked to this, such a separation of roles could easily increase the possibility of clients splitting into a good and a bad worker, a good and a bad agency, with all the problems of inter-agency conflict that could result if this was not dealt with successfully.

CONCLUSION

Surveying the history of social work and the relationship between social work and psychotherapy, we reached a point where a synthesis of conflicting ideas in the social work profession was much needed. For a number of reasons, the moment was lost, and social work was overwhelmed by political, social and economic forces which have sapped its vitality and strength. The need for a synthesis of ideas remains as urgent as ever, and particularly there is a need for an agreed working psychology which will contribute to the practice and language of social work, in understanding and describing work with the elderly, the handicapped, mentally ill people, and most of all, in work with children and their families.

In the field of child abuse, this is of the utmost importance. There is a need to understand and work with both the victims and the perpetrators of abuse to children, but to do this means having to manage such upsetting and conflicting emotions that it would not be surprising to see the profession and its practitioners in flight. There is a danger that 'child-protection' will dominate the concerns of employers and professionals alike, and that this will be justified in terms of scarce resources or market forces. However, social work has been creative when its practitioners established relationships with those at the margins of society who needed help, and saw them as human beings with the need for understanding, help and time. The origins of abuse are to be found in the objective social world, and subjectively in the inner world of experience. The relationship between the latter and the real events of childhood trauma need to be more fully explored and understood. This is a task of the utmost urgency, and it needs the co-operation of those who work with adults who have been abused, and of those working with the family situations where abuse is currently being perpetrated. It is in the interests of social work and its clients for there to be a strong profession of psychotherapy, with clear boundaries and high standards, and for the two professions to relate to each other with respect and understanding.

REFERENCES

Barclay, P. M. (1980) *Social Workers: Their Role and Tasks*, London: NCVO/ Bedford Square Press.

Bowlby, J. (1946) *Forty-four Juvenile Thieves: Their Characters and Home-life*, London: Baillière Tindall & Cox.

—— (1969) *Attachment and Loss: 1, Attachment*, London: Hogarth Press.

Butrym, Z. T. (1976) *The Nature of Social Work*, London: Macmillan.

Department of Social Services (1974) *Report of the Committee of Enquiry into the Care and Supervision Provided in Relation to Maria Colwell*, London: HMSO.

Fisher, M., Newton, C. and Sainsbury, E. (1984) *Mental Health Social Work Observed*, London: Allen & Unwin.

Fraiberg, S. (1980) *Clinical Studies in Infant Mental Health*, London: Routledge.

Irvine, E. E. (1956) 'Transference and reality in the casework relationship', *British Journal of Psychiatric Social Work* 3(4): 1–10.

Marris, P. (1982) 'Attachment and society', pp. 185–201 in C. M. Parkes, J. Stevenson-Hinde and P. Marris (eds) *The Place of Attachment in Human Behaviour*, London and New York: Routledge.

Mayer, J. E. and Timms, N. (1970) *The Client Speaks*, London: Routledge & Kegan Paul.

Mattinson, J. and Sinclair, I. (1979) *Mate and Stalemate*, Oxford: Blackwell.

Miller, A. (1985) *Thou Shalt Not Be Aware*, London: Pluto Press.

Reid, W. J. and Shine, A. W. (1969) *Brief and Extended Casework*, New York: Columbia University Press.

Reiner, B. S. and Kaufman, I. (1959) *Character Disorder in Parents of Delinquents*, New York: Family Service Association of America.

Seebohm, F. (1968) *Report on the Committee on Local Authority and Allied Personal Social Services*, Cmnd 3703, London: HMSO.

Winnicott, D. (1965) *The Maturational Process and the Facilitating Environment*, London: Hogarth.

Wootton, B. (1959) *Social Science and Social Pathology*, London: Allen & Unwin.

FURTHER READING

Balint, M. (1968) *The Basic Fault*, London: Tavistock Publications.

Bowlby, J. (1988) *A Secure Base*, London: Routledge.

Delozier, P. P. (1982) 'Attachment theory and child abuse', pp. 95–117 in C. M. Parkes, J. Stevenson-Hinde and P. Marris (eds) *The Place of Attachment in Human Behaviour*, London and New York: Routledge.

Yelloly, M. A. (1980) *Social Work Theory and Psychoanalysis*, New York: Van Nostrand Reinhold.

Chapter 18

Psychotherapeutic communities

The contemporary practice

David Millard and Haya Oakley

Psychotherapy is influenced by the setting in which it occurs. Nowhere among the settings considered in this section of the *Handbook* is this more true than of therapeutic communities, a defining feature of which is the deliberate attempt to use the characteristics of a residential or day-care organisation in a therapeutic way. They constitute:

> a place in which people can discover that they live IN a community. Indeed they are a constant meditation on the different ways in which this 'IN' exists – from the fact that one cannot live purely in one's 'head', to the way in which themes and issues that apply through the house are not ultimately located IN anyone.
>
> (Freidman, in Cooper *et al.* 1989: 73)

'Therapeutic community' refers to a model – or family of models – which may be applied to the organisation of residential or day-care settings. These may be either within the Health Service – namely, in-patient units, wards or 'day hospitals' more or less directed by doctors – or in hostels or 'day centres' providing predominantly non-medical accommodation and staff. In this chapter we have both in mind, but principally the non-medical settings. This reflects the current trend, in Britain as elsewhere, away from treatment in psychiatric hospitals and towards care in the wider community provided either through national or local government or by private or voluntary organisations.

HISTORICAL BACKGROUND

The term 'therapeutic community' was introduced by Main in 1946 to denote one aspect of the changes then beginning to take place in psychiatric hospitals in Great Britain. The kernel of this wide-ranging process was, perhaps, a movement from an essentially authoritarian towards a more collaborative style of staff behaviour and consequently from institutionalising and repressive residential regimes towards a more liberal, humane and participative kind of culture.

Subsequently, the partial but more general application of ideas associated with the therapeutic community became described as the 'therapeutic community approach' (Clark 1965). This influence persists, often unacknowledged, in psychiatric units employing occasional ward meetings and the like. It is to be distinguished from the therapeutic community proper, the model originally associated chiefly with the pioneering work of Maxwell Jones (1968) at the Henderson Hospital in south London. Characteristically, such communities have regular, usually daily, community meetings, one of whose functions is to examine significant events in the daily life of the community – the 'other twenty-three hours' of the residential work literature – together with an accompanying staff group and an array of other group activities: psychotherapy, work groups, creative therapies and so forth. The processes of living within the community are understood to be in themselves potentially therapeutic.

As we describe below, this places a good deal of the therapeutic influence and responsibility with the users of the service ('members', 'residents', 'patients' and so on) and constitutes, to use the title of Rapoport's (1960) classical monograph on the Henderson Hospital, the *Community as Doctor*. Jones's earlier work had been with military personnel under treatment during the Second World War for psychosomatic disorders ('effort syndrome'). Initially, he had lectured to groups of about eighty men on the dynamics of this condition, but soon discovered that they preferred to talk with one another and that the outcomes of this approach were better! This, incidentally, is an early and significant illustration of the therapeutic community principle that staff through modifying their own behaviour can change the culture even when that culture includes a good deal of active participation by the patients.

Therapeutic communities have, however, developed both within and outside the hospitals. One group exists in 'progressive' education, originally represented by the work of pioneers such as A. S. Neil, Lyward and David Wills (for contemporary examples, see Table 18.1). These had in common an emphasis on self-government, even within communities of disturbed young people. Another derives from the residential care of alcohol and drug abusers and is associated with American institutions such as Synanon and Phoenix House (Ziegenfuss 1983). These, often known as Concept Houses, have a more directive culture and frequently employ as staff members people who were themselves previously substance abusers.

Yet another derives from so-called 'alternative' psychiatry. In 1962 Dr David Cooper set up an experimental unit (Villa 21) in Shenley Hospital; he believed that breaking down the hierarchic barriers between patients and staff would enhance the understanding and treatment of the patients. This was the movement later extended and developed by the Philadelphia Association, chaired at the time by R. D. Laing, which started by setting up households where the emphasis was on ordinary living

Table 18.1 Examples of therapeutic communities classified by type of provider

Local authority social services departments

Mental health day centres;
e.g., Kensington and Chelsea (Blake *et al.* 1984); Leeds
Mental health hostels; e.g., Wandsworth; Buckinghamshire

Criminal justice system

Probation hostels; e.g., Norris 1979)
Probation day centres (Cook 1988)
Grendon Underwood Prison (Gunn *et al.* 1978)

Voluntary sector

Education and therapy; e.g., New Barns School; Peper Harow (Rose 1982);
   Thornby Hall (Worthington 1989); Cotswold Community (Whitwell 1989)
Hostels, households, etc. (mentally ill); e.g., Richmond Fellowship (Jansen
   1980); Philadelphia Association; Arbours (Berke 1982)
Residential homes (handicapped children and adults); e.g., Camphill Village
   Trust (Baron and Haldane 1992)
Crisis centres
   Will admit a person in an acute condition; e.g., Arbours Association
   Will accommodate severe crisis within their normal brief;
   e.g., Philadelphia Association; Shealin Trust

National Health Service

District-level in-patients units (may accept some day patients)
Adults (general); e.g., Oxford (Pullen 1986); Leicester, West Berkshire
Substance abusers; e.g., Alpha House; Ley Community (Donnellan and Toon
   1986)
Adolescents (Boakes 1985)
Regional or super-regional units; e.g., Henderson Hospital (Whiteley 1970b)

– hospitality rather than hospitalisation – and where people who had lost
their way would be able to wander safely and freely until they could find
their way. For nearly thirty years these ideas have evolved with experience,
and currently there are a number of such communities in London and other
parts of the country.

THE THERAPEUTIC COMMUNITY IN CONTEMPORARY BRITISH MENTAL HEALTH PRACTICE

It is not possible to enumerate accurately contemporary psychotherapeutic
communities; in the present political climate, institutions tend to open and
close, the function and model of practice of those remaining may change,
and institutions may vary in the extent to which they would describe
themselves or be recognised by others as therapeutic communities. A
fairly comprehensive *Directory* is obtainable from the Association of

Therapeutic Communities. Accounts have been published of several institutions which currently operate with some version of the model (see Reference and Notes at the conclusion of this chapter), and examples of such institutions may be classified as in Table 18.1.

A distinct feature of the British tradition in the field is the part played by the voluntary sector (see also Chapter 19 of this *Handbook*). Psychotherapeutic communities are set up by charities using government funding; for example, housing associations and local authority grants, and private means. Within the voluntary sector two approaches may be distinguished. One, as exemplified by the Richmond Fellowship, uses the treatment modality of 'community as doctor' and centres on providing a care regime aiming to care for or rehabilitate residents. The emphasis is usually to get people better so that they can rejoin society as working, valuable members. In the other type, therapeutic communities are mostly referred to as 'households' and run by organisations like the Philadelphia Association, Arbours and the Shealin Trust in Scotland; 'these communities started from a recognition of the need for places of sanctuary, asylum, refuge or dwelling felt by some people who find themselves in extreme mental distress' (Cooper *et al.* 1989: 21).

THEORY AND PRACTICE

We shall first give some introductory theory and comments on indications and contra-indications; then offer a short and perhaps rather idealised account of therapeutic community practice. The third section offers a more detailed theoretical justification for this practice, a note on effectiveness, and finally suggestions to the reader for discovering more about this type of work.

Theory I: some preliminary concepts

Institutions offering residential or day care for whatever purposes should do so in the light of explicit theories of institutional functioning (Millard 1972). This term denotes the kind of narrative which describes as precisely as possible how a particular regime actually produces the changes which it exists to bring about. Our starting point is a value assumption that such 'group care', as residential and day care may collectively be termed, is indeed to do with *change* in members, including, obviously, the minimising of deterioration where this is inevitable, and the enhancement of the quality of life, rather than *warehousing*. Theories of institutional functioning must therefore include theories about personal change. It is only on the basis of this kind of understanding that: (1) staff can be helped to see how they can best act, (2) the work of a place, including matters such as the indications for admission, can be clarified for referring agencies and others, and (3) research and the evaluation of outcomes can be conducted.

Where group care is not guided by the clear application of a theoretical model, the risk is that the problems brought by residents create such levels of anxiety in the staff that features arise in the regime, 'institutional defences' (Menzies 1960), which are often damaging both to residents and staff, and prevent the work being done most effectively. Paradoxical as it might seem, it is the professionalisation of the staff which allows the client members of a residential institution to contribute most to their own well-being. This chapter is therefore written from the perspective of the staff member.

Psychiatry is well used to the existence of a number of 'models of madness'; that is, theoretical systems for considering the fundamental nature of mental disorder. Thus, behind the use of the particular family of theories of institutional functioning underlying therapeutic community models are important theoretical notions of the nature of mental disorder. A number of models of group care are available; some are based on learning theory as applied in behaviour therapy ('token economies' and the like), others on pedagogical or pastoral theories (Arthur 1985), still others, including therapeutic community theory, on the basis that human behaviour, whether deviant or normal, is influenced by the *meanings* which people attach to their own activity and that of others. We shall return below to the significance of this viewpoint.

The variety of forms of therapeutic community practice which occur in community care settings place us firmly in the territory of Clark's (1965) *therapeutic community approach*. The differing circumstances in which community care is practised, the range of characteristics of those using such services and the constraints imposed by the parent service-delivery agencies upon individual therapeutic communities all contribute to variety within the arrangements they make. Does this then mean, as some critics have suggested, that the whole concept runs away into the sands and that we cease to be able to identify anything specific as belonging to the therapeutic community? We believe not. Manning (1989) uses the idea of a *common core* of practices. Having carefully surveyed the evolving definitions of the therapeutic community and, acknowledging the existence of some confusion among both proponents and critics of the idea, he writes:

> We can conclude from the review that, first, therapeutic communities are distinct from other therapeutic practices in terms of theoretical aims, organisational structure and process, and self identity. Second, there are three broad originating streams of therapeutic work which are beginning to converge towards one general type, most clearly related to the democratic community.* Third, that there is nevertheless, and

* Manning is here referring to what might be called the 'Maxwell Jones type' of therapeutic community.

not surprisingly, variation around this common core in terms of therapeutic ideology, client type and the purity with which the therapeutic community principles are put into practice.

(Manning 1989: 47)

We can therefore accept as falling within the scope of this chapter the application of a range of psychotherapeutic community ideas to a range of client groups; we return below to consider the balance between common and specific features.

Indications and contra-indications

People may be referred to a therapeutic community by their doctor or psychotherapist, or may refer themselves. The reasons for coming vary. Sometimes their current living conditions cannot sustain the degree of stress. Sometimes it is in order to try and prevent hospitalisation. At other times a person will wish to spend some time in a therapeutic community as a buffer between a period in hospital and ordinary living. In many communities residents are admitted or accepted for membership because their specific problem might be shared by present residents (for example, drug addiction). Some communities have a limit on length of stay; others are open-ended. Some regard participation in all the community's activities as a condition of acceptance; others leave this open to negotiation. Some therapeutic communities would wish that the whole of the treatment during the stay would be carried out within the community; others permit or encourage ongoing individual psychotherapy outside the community activities.

In general, it may be said that clients are potentially suitable if

1 their problems (whether primarily behavioural or psychological) *include or are significantly caused by psychological events* – this yields a wide spectrum, including most varieties of mental disorder, problems in social relationships and many behavioural problems, criminal or otherwise;
2 such psychological events are crucially to do with the *meaningfulness* of human experience and behaviour.

This is of course the case since therapeutic community practice aims precisely to operate on the meanings which people attribute to their experience and behaviour. It does so by providing a setting in which people are allowed in a relatively non-directed environment to 'experience' and 'behave'; then by subjecting these matters to examination, comment and interpretation, and encouraging experimentation with appropriate new behaviours and subsequent reinforcement by both fellow users and staff (Millard 1989). Communities vary in the extent to which their understanding of meaningfulness is confined to the conscious level, in which case these practices might be described largely by cognitive psychology (secondary process), or also take as essential unconscious or primary processes. Behind this statement is the obvious point that the important thing about mental disorders is that they reduce the patients' social competence.

Psychotherapeutic communities, working with psychoanalytic principles, would shift the emphasis from patterns of behaviour and reinforcement to an attempt to reach and resolve unconscious conflict via a process of psychoanalytic interpretation of what goes on between the members of the community and between them and the psychotherapist. This, as noted earlier, may take place alongside individual psychotherapy and would usually work on the understanding that the community is the patient, and that this would in turn benefit the individual members. The free development of the community is the condition of the free development of each.

The clinical categories within which such persons might fall include the more severely disabled adult neurotics; people with most varieties of personality disorder, including alcohol and drug abusers not actively taking such substances during the admission; and people with chronic disability following major psychosis, whether or not they require maintenance medication. Chronic schizophrenics, of course, form a substantial majority of those in need of long-term care. Note that this insistence on psychological meaningfulness does not exclude an organic component in the aetiology in any case.* Another clinical category is children and adolescents displaying the range of psychiatric problems which are, of course, only partly comparable to those of adulthood.

Within this large reservoir of potential users of community mental health services, two other points may be made.

1 Obviously, since this is predominantly a group technique, the clinical problem should be of a type and severity which on the ordinary criteria would require management in a group setting: most of those whose problems can be managed individually in out-patient or case-work settings are excluded. Naturally, different institutions employing the therapeutic community model will admit patients having a particular *profile* of clinical and social characteristics (Blake *et al.*, 1984).
2 Patients who need short-term, acute treatment are generally not suitable. Or to put the same point in a different way, units which are set up specifically for short-term treatment probably cannot make much use of therapeutic community models of working. This is because it is necessary

---

* Presumably, psychological function in all of us is related to the activity of whatever brain we have. We must get along as best we may in solving the everyday problems of psychosocial adjustment, whether our brain function happens to be capable of producing Nobel Prize-winning research or to be modified by whatever physiological change it is that leads to, say, schizophrenia.

for patients to be in the unit sufficiently long to be able to understand its culture and to make that culture work in a way that meets their own needs. Clinical experience suggests that this takes a minimum of three weeks' stay, but many of the users we have in mind actually require much longer. In one study of the residents in mental health hostels who for the most part were reasonably able, two-thirds needed to stay for more than a year; 80 per cent of this sample were in whole time open employment (Hewett *et al.* 1975).

An unusual exception to this generalisation are the Crisis Centres run by the Arbours Association and therapeutic communities run by the Philadelphia Association and the Shealin Trust who are prepared to take in from time to time an acutely disordered, short-term resident.

Therapeutic community practice

Therapeutic communities require a defined space: a hospital ward, a hostel or day-centre accommodation, for instance, but the characteristics of such premises are not specialised. What is needed is essentially a 'domestic' type of building: outside hospitals, something like a large flat or house, or (for a day centre) a public hall which provides rooms for large and small group meetings, cooking and communal eating, and perhaps some accommodation for creative therapies, together, of course, with sleeping and toilet arrangements if the setting is residential. It is best if the space does not have to be shared with other users. The costs of accommodation can often be relatively modest. The users of the community should be able to make a substantial contribution to their own support and the daily care of the building.

The features of therapeutic community practice may be summarised in three defining principles:

(a) therapeutic communities have a characteristic kind of social structure;
(b) therapeutic communities have a characteristic timetable for daily or weekly living;
(c) therapeutic communities have a characteristic set of expectations of the behaviour of their members – both staff and users.

In what follows we shall refer to each of these in turn.

Systems theory defines its subject in terms of *elements* and their *connections*. Figure 18.1 shows diagrammatically the principal elements in the therapeutic community model: various groups, the 'in-between' or background space/time and boundaries. These exemplify the first of the defining principles.

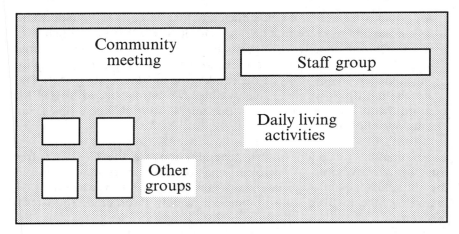

Figure 18.1 The principal elements in the therapeutic community model

(a) Community meeting

This is possibly the single most characteristic feature. Generally, such meetings are considered to have essentially two types of function (Gilman *et al.* 1987): the patient/staff administration meeting and large group psychotherapy. Other authorities distinguish a third category dealing with inter-group (or systems) analysis. These functions may be the subject matter of separate meetings, in which case important issues of boundary maintenance arise, or they may be combined. Importantly, community meetings constitute the main forum for 'feedback'; that is, they are the place where events elsewhere are reported, discussed and used for learning. As far as possible the community is self-governing, 'democratic' (to use Manning's term), both staff and users having an important measure of responsibility. Some communities operate on the principle of 'one person, one vote'; others will modify this to a variable extent.

It is impossible to differentiate entirely between the ordinary daily living, the running of the place and the psychotherapeutic input. The following illustration of a meeting in a community household may illustrate that point.

S was a young woman who had spent most of her adult life in and out of mental hospitals and various residential care settings, having been diagnosed as schizophrenic. At that time she had been living in a community for a while, convinced that all the other residents and psychotherapists were 'aliens' whilst she was the only human being. She did not formally take part in community activities, spent a great deal of time in her room, appeared periodically during meal times to take some food upstairs with her and has never sat through a whole community meeting. On the particular night a business meeting of residents and psychotherapists was discussing amongst other things some spare cash and how it would be used to redecorate the house. S was particularly agitated, and came in and out of the meeting room accusing people of being aliens, and slamming doors. The meeting decided that each resident could paint their own room the colour of their choice but that the communal space should be painted in a colour agreed upon by democratic voting procedure. Just as the vote was about to be taken someone said, 'Wait a minute, go and get S.' Someone called out and S came to the room and duly cast her vote for the colour of her choice. This was not experienced by any of the residents or the psychotherapists as a particularly unusual or dramatic event, nor would it have necessarily been listed amongst the psychotherapeutic assets of the community. However, it had a deep psychotherapeutic effect on everyone involved and in particular on S, who conceded for a brief moment that everybody else was a member of the human race that she herself could join.

A single community may also be part of a wider network sharing similar psychotherapeutic cultural elements. Cross-community activities will also affect the community's life.

(b) Staff groups

Conventionally, every community meeting is immediately followed by a staff meeting ('after-group') but staff groups often occur also at other times. From the beginnings of the therapeutic community movement it was found that the opening of communication networks and flattening of staff hierarchies created high levels of anxiety, especially among staff trained in conventional nursing or medical settings. In fact, it is virtually an axiom of residential and day care that good staff communication reduces anxiety, raises morale and improves outcomes (Revans 1976).

Although it is widely known that any psychotherapeutic team does not have to be in complete agreement and total harmony to be effective, unresolved tensions in the team will bring out the worst in the community and could even lead to occasions of serious acting out. For example: R was acutely disturbed for many months, draining the community's emotional and physical resources. The two house psychotherapists differed in their opinion as to R's future in the community, and so one of them agreed that R should stay if the other was very keen to keep him. This ambivalence was played out throughout the household, culminating in the residents 'not noticing' one day that R had wandered off in a state of confusion, only to be picked up by a totally unambivalent policeman and hospitalised.

This is a rare and extreme example, but it illustrates the need for any psychotherapeutic team to work together to understand the agreements, disagreements, competitiveness, rivalry and the multitude of anxieties and pressures generated from being involved in such a demanding and delicate field of work. Furthermore, it is known that covert staff disagreement is liable to result in high levels of disturbed behaviour among users (Stanton and Schwartz 1954).

(c) Other groups

Groups have been shown to be a defining feature of therapeutic communities (Crocket et al. 1978; Hinshelwood 1964/1987). They may be roughly classified as follows:

(i) *Verbal psychotherapy*: Group analytic ideas (Foulkes 1964) have been widely influential. Some communities will place little emphasis on individual work with members, and the small therapy group is then the most intimate and intensive site for psychotherapy.

Perhaps the most notable difference between such groups within a community and those elsewhere is the impossibility – indeed, the undesirability – in this situation of maintaining anything like a 'rule of abstinence'. Not only is there inevitably a good deal of passage of information into and out of the group and of social contact between members other than during group meetings, but often *feedback*, an account of the proceedings within a small group given to the community meeting, may be established as a community norm. A larger circle of confidentiality is therefore called for than is characteristic of ordinary group psychotherapy, and this probably induces systematic differences in the material typically communicated.

(ii) *Creative therapies*: Art therapy and drama therapy, psychodrama and related psychotherapies are widespread (McMahon and Chapman 1987); music therapy occurs in some places; movement, dance and the use of puppets have been reported; doubtless, other modalities are possible. In expert hands, these may enable the exploration of emotionally laden material to take place among members for whom exclusively verbal methods are too threatening.

'A good illustration is the story of Peter who was too fragile to participate in any verbal activity and whose first form of expression and contribution to the community life was the ability to participate in yoga classes' (Oakley, in Cooper et al. 1989: 150).

(iii) *Work groups*: Work groups which may be routine, as in shopping for and preparing community meals, and 'special occasion', to plan an outing or a party, occur widely. For these and various other types of group it is common to arrange that members, rather than staff, should take leadership roles such as convenor, reporter-back, etc. This is *sociotherapy*, the precise connotation of which is the deliberate psychotherapeutic use of the occupancy of particular roles in a social structure. It is to be sharply distinguished from *social therapy*, which may refer to no more than participation in recreational activities. The examination in small and large groups of the individual's performance in such roles forms a vital feature of most communities.

(iv) *Others*: Because of the contemporary awareness of the social tensions surrounding gender, *women's groups* (Collis 1987) and *men's groups* are frequently found in therapeutic communities. Special groups to participate in the *selection of members for admission*, or induction groups for *joiners* or preparation groups for *leavers* (Parker 1989) are not uncommon. A specific problem often arises for members where developments within the individual come into conflict with homeostatic mechanisms in her or his family, thereby tending to resist and subvert such changes; in some places, this has led to the development of *families groups*. In addition, depending on the particular client group, there may be a place for special focus groups, such as for alcohol abusers.

(d) 'In between' time

This is represented by the grey background in Figure 18.1. Here we note the significance of the structured timetable in therapeutic community practice: this is the second *defining principle* (above). The importance of this has long been recognised, such as Jones's (1968) concept of the 'living-learning' community. Recent research has pointed to it with renewed interest. In studies asking members to identify where psychotherapeutically significant happenings take place, 40 per cent identify this space/time. Van der Linden (1988), in discussing this matter, relates it to Winnicott's (1971) emphasis on the importance of play. It is also consistent with the generalisation that

> It is central to the theory of operation of therapeutic communities that no action-based programme is successful unless the gains (however small) made by patients are brought to some form of conscious recognition and verbal expression, and no verbal approach is complete unless the gains are tested and reinforced in action.
>
> (Blake *et al.* 1984: 54)

Robin Cooper (1989) tells the moving story of Richard, who was too disturbed to join the normal activities and who could not be left behind when the whole community went away for their summer holiday. Richard had been living almost as a recluse within the community as he claimed he needed complete peace to think his thoughts. On that occasion,

> he comes along bundled into the back of the Volkswagen van with his shitty mattress and stinking blankets. The cottage in fact is no more than a large converted barn, so now there is absolutely no chance of Richard getting any quiet at all. One very solitary member of the house has already pitched her tent in the nearby field, and, even on the

marshes flits between field and barn. But now there is another tent in the field – in the opposite corner of the field – and here Richard spends his days screaming at the sheep because now they are interfering with his thinking.

(Cooper *et al*. 1989: 54)

(e) Boundaries

The importance of 'background time' points to the need to define boundaries, represented by the heavy lines in Figure 18.1, including that around the community within which members need to remain to some extent. The question of boundaries is central to the life of most communities, if we allow the crude assumption that most residents are there because of some degree of inability to articulate themselves in the world. For some the task may essentially be to define their own psychic and social boundaries. We can then appreciate the importance of the acute sensibility required and attention paid to issues as mundane as: Who has which room? Can they lock it? Can you go into someone else's room? Who can visit and who says so? Who represents the law and who carries the authority?

The way in which boundaries will be defined will affect relationships both among the staff and between staff and members of the community. The extent to which detailed definitions of do's and don'ts are established, the written and unwritten rules, will also have an effect on the nature and the style of the psychotherapy which will take place in a particular therapeutic community, as well of course as the question of who defines the boundaries and who draws up the rule-book.

it was very significant that Peter chose to touch me as he did at the community household, in his room rather than mine, a private yet public place, a playground that was personal and neutral, where we were alone, yet surrounded by others whose presence was benign, where there were no tight rules about going into people's rooms or about touching them. I did not have to look over my shoulder in case a member of the nursing staff 'caught me' in the patients' dormitory. Therefore what happened remained uncluttered, a gesture of trust and closeness, an expression of genuine tenderness and love, made possible by the milieu.

(Oakley 1989: 158)

And another example:

A group of teenagers who spent most of their lives in care were used to receiving a packet of biscuits on a Friday, which they would lock away in their room. When they moved to a household with two resident workers, they took to raiding the kitchen cupboards at night only to discover it was their communal food they were eating and that there would be none there provided magically by a nameless 'big brother' administrator. They promptly demanded to join the workers on the weekly trip to the supermarket, so that they could choose the biscuits and make sure they lasted until the next trip. Youngsters from the neighbourhood were attracted to the house ('without parents'). At first they were welcomed by the residents, who rejoiced in the seemingly permanent party, only to realise their home was being abused and then decided to draw a firm boundary around it.

(Oakley, written for this chapter)

FURTHER CONSIDERATIONS

Theory II: why do we do things this way?

(a) Rule-governed behaviour

Although therapeutic communities have sometimes been stigmatised as wild and lawless places, they typically have a quite clear structure and set of social expectations. Users of the service are not required to conform to the highly structured behaviour often required of patients in institutional settings, though there may be rules about participation in meetings and so forth. Much scope is left for them to 'find their own feet' – that is, their behaviour within the therapeutic community must draw on their own resources, however inadequate these might be. This is the *third* of our *defining principles*.

How, then, does it actually work?

> In Philadelphia Association households people go to sleep when they wish. They get out of bed under their own steam and in their own time. When they are moved to, they shop, cook, eat, clean, stay in their rooms, watch television. . . . All this takes place in every household in the land. . . . What, if indeed anything, is therapeutic about this?
> (Freidman, in Cooper *et al.* 1989: 56)

No doubt, a number of mechanisms might be identified operating at various social and psychological levels of analysis. As in all psycho-therapies, the essentials must be to do with some psychological change in the user which can, so to speak, be exported from the psychotherapy. These psychological events may be thought of as having to do with the *rules* which link an individual to their social context. The central idea here is that how we act is *not* precisely in accordance with learned and fixed patterns of behaviour but rather in accordance with a stock of general principles which form (or generate) our action in particular social situations and which are therefore called *generative rules*. People are more socially competent precisely because they have generative rules which adapt them well to the demands of specific situations, but people whose stock of generative rules is somehow inadequate are those whom we recognise as disabled by one or another of the mental disorders (Millard 1981). Life in psychotherapeutic community care is therefore designed to encourage the kind of internal changes which enhance the individual's competence in social behaviour. Thus the link between a particular model of mental disorder and a particular theory of institutional functioning becomes clear.

(b) Psychotherapy and sociotherapy

The model depends crucially on a *combination of interventions* into the clients' psychological world ('psychotherapy') with those into their social world ('sociotherapy'). Edelson regards these not as alternatives, with beliefs and aims in treatment antagonistic to one another, but rather as: 'inextricably *interrelated* enterprises in any attempt to understand and influence or change persons, but enterprises *differentiated* by having different systems of intervention and analysis' (1970: 175).

Nevertheless, the technical literature generally, and perhaps inevitably, takes one orientation or the other as its starting point. On the psycho-therapy side, there are two important aspects: individual and group. Since these are the subject of other chapters in this volume, we identify here only some specific emphases.

(i) Psychotherapy

Naturally, in psychotherapeutic communities opportunities often arise spontaneously, or are contrived, for staff to sit with users as individuals or groups for formal therapeutic activities; exactly as they are found in individual case-work or in group-work settings. But among *individual* psychotherapies we note that residential and day-care settings offer uniquely the possibility of 'on the hoof' or *peripatetic therapy* (Millard 1992). This is indeed a major and insufficiently recognised skill of group-care practice. It is one in which work with individual users may be fragmented into quite short interventions, but where these accumulate in a coherent fashion over hours, days, months or even years. The technique of 'holding' such a thread is demanding. And the demand is often compounded by the need to hold several such threads simultaneously for different users, and to manage the complex ways in which they may be plaited together in the ever-shifting daily interactions of the unit.

Concerning group-work, a clear distinction must be drawn between group psychotherapy and therapeutic community practice, however much the latter may draw upon the insights and the techniques of the former. Users and staff inevitably share in the common social life. Thus, discussions primarily concerned with psychotherapy within the therapeutic community make necessary, and not incidental, reference to matters of social structure. Correspondingly, social phenomena are seen as having an essential psychological importance.

An example is worked out by Hinshelwood (1979) in the paper 'The community as analyst'. His thesis starts from the proposition that the group can offer individuals such participation in a collective defence system that they may be protected from their emotional distress and overlook it. Alternatively, by offering some form of psychotherapeutic insight and confrontation with their distress and defences against it, members can be helped to mature. Such confrontation employs the notion of transference; thus far we are in the domain of group psychotherapy. However, in a community there are not one or two psychotherapists to participate in a transference relationship but a *staff group* which is defined over against the patient group by all manner of social events in the community life. The boundary thus created between staff and patients may be used defensively to protect against anxiety or may be part of the healthy, effective structure which enables the daily life of the community to proceed in an orderly fashion. On an analogy with the analysis of transference, Hinshelwood suggests that the discussion of problems around this boundary is a crucial task for the community, and a primary tool for this purpose is the community meeting which 'exists to release and control this anxiety, not to alleviate it' (1979: 109).

(ii) Sociotherapy

Similarly, the bringing together of social events and the combined efforts of staff and residents to understand their significance, and to grow in social competence through this understanding, occur in those who take sociotherapy as their starting point.

For example: Whiteley (Whiteley *et al.* 1973) uses the term 'sociotherapy' in describing the well-known work of the Henderson Hospital. Here there exists an array of explicit social roles and tasks. Patients have the opportunity of testing themselves, in many of these supported and exhorted by a continuous stream of comments from other community members. But it will, of course, be what is learned and internalised from that experience which individuals will take away as a permanent acquisition when they leave.

Secondly, the Concept Houses, mentioned previously, employ a very rigid formal hierarchical social structure to which members are required to commit themselves completely, severing their ties, at least initially, with the outside world. Residents progress up and down (!) the hierarchy as they are able to conform to the community's morality. This is enforced by intensive group surveillance and the existence of a fearsome array of sanctions. Such communities are generally staffed by those who have themselves recovered from the problems, alcoholism or addiction, with which they deal. They usually have more conventionally qualified staff in an external, consultative role. Here also, a psychotherapeutic element is clearly present. Wilson writes:

> This rigid structure of the community seems to have the effect of enforcing the distribution of 'internal objects' along particular channels – transference is highly focused in staff, who come to represent health and the possibility of giving up addiction. Hostile and destructive inputs are acknowledged . . . initial regression is encouraged . . . [people] may complain that they are being infantilised or depersonalised . . . those who remain for long periods of time in such programmes, however, often experience a strong internal change.
>
> (1979: 98)

(c) Theory of institutional functioning: Rapoport's principles

In *Community as Doctor*, Rapoport (1960) established a framework of four principles: *permissiveness, communalism, democratisation* and *reality confrontation*, which have become widely accepted. Characteristically, users newly admitted to a therapeutic community will receive much less guidance about how they are expected to conduct themselves than they would if entering an institution of another type. This is the notion of *permissiveness*:

> the Unit's belief that it should function with all its members tolerating from one another a wide degree of behaviour which might be distressing or seem deviant according to 'ordinary' norms. Ideally, this should allow both for individuals to expose behavioural difficulties, and others to react freely so that the bases for both sides of social relationship patterns may be examined.
>
> (Rapoport 1960: 58)

The individual tends rapidly to replicate within the institution the problems experienced outside, and which are probably among the indications for admission. The extent to which the member's behaviour is constrained by the situation is modified; it does not allow, for example, the individual to fall into the stereotyped activities of the patient role. Their behaviour will be formed by whatever rules they can draw upon for guidance in only partly familiar situations.

In addition, the ideology provides that much of what goes on is regarded as public property – the user's 'symptoms' – which are likely to include both subjective (mental) discomforts as well as distorted (unsocial) patterns of behaviour, are not a private affair, to be shared only with some species of professional psychotherapist. This is the idea of *communalism*: 'the Unit's belief that its functioning should be characterised by tight-knit, inter-communicative and intimate sets of relationships. Sharing of amenities, informality (e.g. use of first names) and open communication are prescribed' (Rapoport 1960: 58).

This is an example of a therapeutic community rule. It is ethically justifiable, since all members are in the same situation; it makes an open reality of matters which are usually kept covert in other settings; and it is an essential precondition of *democratisation*: 'each member of the community should share equally in the exercise of power in decision making about community affairs – both psychotherapeutic and administrative . . . conventional hospital status hierarchies should be "flattened" to produce a more egalitarian form of participation' (Rapoport 1960: 55).

Further therapeutic community rules are implied here. Democratisation involves a conscious abrogation by otherwise powerful staff members of decision-making prerogatives in the interest of members' experimentation with revised social performances.

Thus far, nothing in this exposition points to an explicitly psychotherapeutic function nor to any notion of personal change. For these elements we need to add *reality-confrontation*: 'Patients should be continuously presented with interpretations of their behaviour as it is seen by most others' (Rapoport 1960: 63).

This is essentially the mechanism through which the meanings which individuals attach to their own experience and behaviour, and those of others, are challenged and modified. It is such modifications, translated into an improved level of social competence, which comprise the essential gain to participants in a therapeutic community regime.

Some further problems

It is not possible to make this section comprehensive, but some typical issues are noted which readers may pursue through the References list.

(a) Issues for staff

Our approach to theories of institutional functioning suggests that the characteristics of the regime should derive from the specific needs of the user group. There exist, of course, other interests which may conflict with this: public prejudice, the manager's desire to ration resources, the self-interests, legitimate or otherwise, of staff members, and the like. Some therapeutic communities will have nurses or house parents who will carry out the care function as well as doctors, social workers and other professionals who may or may not participate in the daily routine and in community meetings. Other therapeutic communities may largely be run on a daily basis by the residents, with a warden to carry out the administrative functions and a team of visiting psychotherapists. However, the task of planning the regime and, broadly, of maintaining the culture once established belongs ultimately with the staff. Therapeutic community practice will delegate such matters to users to the maximum possible extent; and thereby arises a continuing tension within which the work is done.

Typically, therapeutic communities make arrangements through some form of staff supervision or consultation to maintain the effectiveness of the staff group. These matters are widely discussed in the published literature (for example, Millard 1992).

(b) Issues for users

Whereas for some individuals being in the company of other people who share similar problems and needs can be a source of instant relief, others may initially find the close-knit atmosphere of the therapeutic community, and its push towards sharing, a little oppressive. Some may wish for greater privacy and need to form 'special' intimate relationships with a member of staff in lieu of integrating with the group as a whole. Issues of confidentiality and split loyalties to outside carers and family may also arise.

The published literature includes several accounts of experience in therapeutic communities written by users (see Mahony 1979; Hudson 1990).

(c) Issues for the community

The organisational problems of running a psychotherapeutic community are manifold and, in general, beyond the scope of this chapter. One example must suffice.

A problem familiar to practitioners of any residential care is that what constitutes a true description of events at one time may not be true at another, yet the published descriptions of communities almost necessarily have a static quality about them. Savalle and Wagenborg (1980) have given a clear description of *oscillations* with the de Spiegelberg therapeutic community in Holland. The characteristics of the periods of less effective functioning are described as: expressions of dissatisfaction and lack of confidence, with grumbling, threats to leave or aggressive outbursts; strongly increasing demands for individual treatment; increasing polarisation between staff and patients; inadequate use of treatment facilities with much irrelevant talking and absenteeism; decrease among patients of interest in one another and in care for their physical surroundings; increasing use of alcohol or tranquillisers; development of 'night-life' with many occurrences of which staff and fellow-patients are only partly aware. This author considers some of the determinants, both from within and outside, of such periods of 'low tide' in the life of a community and describes in some detail the methods available to staff for the fruitful management of such crisis periods.

Effectiveness

The therapeutic community movement in the last twenty years has been well aware of need for evaluative research, but the field combines some of the classical difficulties of psychotherapy research with that in residential or day care (Clark and Cornish 1972). Early attempts at empirical evaluation would include Whiteley (1970a) on the Henderson Hospital and Clark on the management of chronic psychotic patients in Fulbourn (Clark and Myers 1970). But methodology in the behavioural sciences has developed, and two recent examples illustrate a more sophisticated approach:

1 Dutch researchers, working with a model which is well towards the psychotherapeutic end of the therapeutic community spectrum, have used the technique of large samples and conducted a study, the NVL project (Koster and Wagenborg 1988) on a cohort of 1,340 patients admitted to eight institutions over a three-year period and assessed at intake, discharge and at one, three and five years of follow-up. The results are complex but, for instance, a global 'well-being' score rose significantly from 36.8 (s.d. 7.6) at intake to scores around 45.0 at discharge and slightly rising at follow-up.
2 Manning assessed Richmond Fellowship houses in Australia and used path-analytic statistics to demonstrate that in this instance the observed outcomes (significant improvements in cognitive and emotional functioning, general behaviour, interpersonal behaviour and performance at work) could not have been due to a combination of spontaneous improvement with a sophisticated selection of 'suitable' patients but must have been contributed to by their experience in the therapeutic community.

The broad thrust of the evidence suggests that properly conducted therapeutic community regimes are capable of producing measurably effective outcomes in a number of client groups where this question has been examined, but for further discussion of this question the reader must be referred to the technical literature.

Where to go for further information

(i) *General information*   The Association of Therapeutic Communities operates both individual and group membership, the latter to permit junior and less well-paid members of therapeutic community staff to attend conferences, and so on. This organisation is a good general source of information and publishes a *Directory of Communities* in the United Kingdom. The ATC is at 14 Charterhouse Square, London EC1M 6AX.

(ii) *Training* The Royal College of Nursing and Association of Therapeutic Communities have operated since 1986 a one-year day-release course, leading to the Certificate in Therapeutic Community Practice of the two organisations. The course meets once weekly from 2 to 8 p.m. at the Royal College of Nursing. Each session includes a formal lecture, a student-centred 'workshop' period, experience in small groups conducted by members of the Institute of Group Analysis and periodic large groups. In addition, there are two residential long weekends, operated on therapeutic community lines. The course is modular and students are able to accumulate credits towards a diploma and ultimately the BSc in Health Studies of the University of Manchester.

Among the voluntary organisations, Philadelphia and Arbours Associations run their own training programmes and there are occasional short courses based elsewhere.

(iii) *Books* The following are useful introductory texts:

Barnes, M. and Berke, J. (1972) *Two Accounts of a Journey Through Madness*, Harmondsworth: Penguin.
Cooper, R., Freidman, J., Gans, S., Heaton, J. M., Oakley, C., Oakley, H. and Zeal, P. (1989) *Thresholds Between Philosophy and Psychoanalysis*, London: Free Association Books.
Hinshelwood, R. D. (1987) *What Happens in Groups: Psychoanalysis, the Individual and the Community*, London: Free Association Books.
Kennard, D. with Roberts, J. (1983) *An Introduction to Therapeutic Communities*, London: Routledge.

In addition, the quarterly journal *Therapeutic Communities* is essential reading for serious practitioners in this field. The list of References and Notes that follows also offers an introduction to the extensive literature now available.

REFERENCES

Arthur, A. R. (1985) 'A psychotherapeutic community for religious and clergy', *International Journal of Therapeutic Communities* 6: 103–8.
Baron, S. D. and Haldane, J. D. (1992) *Community, Normality and Difference: Meeting Special Needs*, Aberdeen: University of Aberdeen Press.
Berke, J. H. (1982) 'The Arbours Centre', *International Journal of Therapeutic Communities* 3: 248–61. (See also Berke, J. H. (1990) 'Editorial: reflections of Arbours', *International Journal of Therapeutic Communities* 11: 191–5, which introduces a 'Special Issue on the Arbours Association: Twenty Years On'.)
Blake, R., Millard, D. W. and Roberts, J. P. (1984) 'Therapeutic community principles in an integrated local authority community mental health service', *International Journal of Therapeutic Communities* 4: 243–74.
Boakes, J. (1985) 'Different, or the same? Theory and practice in adolescent psychiatric units', *International Journal of Therapeutic Communities* 6: 231–8.

(See also Roosen, C. (1985) 'The psychotherapeutic community – a residential treatment for adolescents', *International Journal of Therapeutic Communities* 6: 205–18, papers among others comprising a Special Issue of this journal on work with adolescents.)

Brigland, M. (1971) *Pioneer Work with Maladjusted Children*, Birkenhead: Willmer Bros.

Clark, D. H. (1965) 'The therapeutic community concept: practice and future', *British Journal of Psychiatry* 111: 947–54.

Clark, D. H. and Myers, K. (1970) 'Themes in a therapeutic community', *British Journal of Psychiatry* 116: 534.

Clark, R. V. G. and Cornish, D. B. (1972) *The Controlled Trial in Institutional Research*, London: HMSO.

Collis, M. (1987) 'Women's groups in the therapeutic community: the Henderson experience', *International Journal of Therapeutic Communities* 8: 175–84.

Cook, R. D. (1988) 'A non-residential therapeutic community used as an alternative to custody', *International Journal of Therapeutic Communities* 9: 55–64.

Cooper, R., Freidman, J., Gans, S., Heaton, J. M., Oakley, C., Oakley, H. and Zeal, P. (1989) *Thresholds between Philosophy and Psychoanalysis*, London: Free Association Books.

Crocket, R. S., Kirk, J., Manning, N. and Millard, D. W. (1978) 'Community time structure', *ATC Bulletin* 25: 12–17.*

Donnellan, B. and Toon, P. (1986) 'The use of "Therapeutic techniques" in the Concept House model of therapeutic community for drug abusers: for whose benefit – staff or resident?' *International Journal of Therapeutic Communities* 7: 183–9.

Edelson, M. (1970) *Psychotherapy and Sociotherapy*, Chicago: University of Chicago Press.

Foulkes, S. H. (1964) *Therapeutic Group Analysis*, London: George Allen & Unwin.

Gilman, H. E., Russakoff, L. M. and Kibel, H. (1987) 'A bipartite model for community meetings: the separation of tasks', *International Journal of Therapeutic Communities* 8: 131–4.

Gunn, J., Robertson, G., Dell, S. and Way, C. (1978) *Psychiatric Aspects of Imprisonment*, London: Academic Press.

Hewett, S., Ryan, P. and Wing, J. K. (1975) 'Living without the mental hospital', *Journal of Social Policy* 4: 391–404.

Hinshelwood, R. D. (1979) 'The community as analyst', pp. 103–12 in R. D. Hinshelwood and N. Manning (eds) *Therapeutic Communities; Reflection and Progress*, London: Routledge & Kegan Paul.

—— (1987) *What Happens in Groups: Psychoanalysis, the Individual and the Community*, London: Free Association Books; first published 1964.

Hudson, P. (1990) 'We never promised you a rose garden', *International Journal of Therapeutic Communities* 11: 289–97.

* In this study of one week in 1977, among the 18 communities surveyed the distribution of groups was:

For all staff/some patients	1 to 88
For some staff/some patients	3 to 88
For patients only	1 to 15

The more group meetings, and the more time spent in groups, the more like a therapeutic community did the respondents consider themselves to be. ($r = 0.61$ (number of groups); $r = 0.64$ (time spent in groups).)

Jansen, E. (ed.) (1980) *The Therapeutic Community Outside the Hospital*, London: Croom Helm.

Jones, M. (1968) *Social Psychiatry in Practice: The Idea of a Therapeutic Community*, Harmondsworth: Penguin.

Koster, A. M. and Wagenborg, J. E. A. (1988) 'The follow-up project on therapeutic communities: a collection of measures for change', *International Journal of Therapeutic Communities* 9: 163–76. (See also the group of related papers on the NVL project in the same Special Issue of this journal.)

McMahon, B. and Chapman, S. (1987) 'Psychodrama and the therapeutic community', *International Journal of Therapeutic Communities* 8: 63–6.

Mahony, N. (1979) 'My stay and change at the Henderson therapeutic community', pp. 76–87 in R. D. Hinshelwood and N. Manning (eds) *Therapeutic Communities: Reflection and Progress*, London: Routledge & Kegan Paul.

Main, T. (1946) 'The hospital as a therapeutic institution', *Bulletin of the Menninger Clinic* 10: 66. (Reprinted in Barnes, E. (ed.) (1968) *Psychosocial Nursing: Studies from the Cassell Hospital*, London: Tavistock.)

Manning, N. (1989) *The Therapeutic Community Movement: Charisma and Routinization*, London: Routledge & Kegan Paul.

Menzies, I. (1960) 'A case study in the functioning of social systems as a defence against anxiety', *Human Relations* 13: 95–121.

Millard, D. W. (1972) 'Generic Concepts and Specialised Institutions', Lecture given at a conference on Professional Boundaries and Residential Social Work, London, 20 May 1972.

—— (1981) 'Generative rules and the therapeutic community', *British Journal of Medical Psychology* 54: 157–65.

—— (1989) 'Editorial: When is it not a therapeutic community?', *International Journal of Therapeutic Communities* 10: 192–4.

—— (1992) 'Educated intuition', *International Journal of Therapeutic Communities* 13: 83–106.

Miller, E. J. and Gwynne, G. V. (1972) *A Life Apart*, London: Tavistock Publications.

Norris, M. (1979) 'Offenders in residential communities: measuring and understanding change', *Howard Journal* 8: 29.

Oakley, H. (1989) 'Touching and being touched (the negotiated boundaries and the "extended" consulting room)', pp. 146–66 in R. Cooper, J. Freidman, S. Gans, J. M. Heaton, C. Oakley, H. Oakley and P. Zeal, *Thresholds between Philosophy and Psychoanalysis*, London: Free Association Books.

Parker, M. (1989) 'Managing separation: the Henderson Hospital leavers group', *International Journal of Therapeutic Communities* 10: 5–16.

Pullen, G. P. (1986) 'The Eric Burden community', *International Journal of Therapeutic Communities* 7: 191–200.

Rapoport, R. N. (1960) *Community as Doctor: New Perspectives on a Therapeutic Community*, London: Tavistock Publications.

Revans, R. W. (1976) *Action Learning in Hospitals*, London: McGraw-Hill.

Rose, M. (1982) 'The potential for fantasy and the role of charismatic leadership in a therapeutic community', *International Journal of Therapeutic Communities* 3: 79–87.

Savalle, H. J. and Wagenborg, H. (1980) 'Oscillations in a therapeutic community', *International Journal of Therapeutic Communities* 1: 137–46.

Siegler, M. and Osmund, H. (1974) *Models of Madness: Models of Medicine*, New York: Macmillan.

Stanton, A. H. and Schwartz, M. S. (1954) *The Mental Hospital: A Study of*

Institutional Participation in Psychiatric Illness and Treatment, New York: Basic Books.

Van der Linden, P. (1988) 'How does the large group change the individual?', *International Journal of Therapeutic Communities* 9: 31–40.

Whiteley, J. S. (1970a) 'The response of psychopaths to a therapeutic community', *British Journal of Psychiatry* 116: 534.

—— (1970b) 'The Henderson Hospital', *International Journal of Therapeutic Communities* 1: 38–58. (See also Norton, K. (1982) 'A culture of enquiry: its prevention or loss', *International Journal of Therapeutic Communities* 13: 3–26.)

Whiteley, J. S., Briggs, D. and Turner, M. (1973) *Dealing with Deviants*, London: Hogarth.

Whitwell, J. (1989) 'The Cotswold community: a healing culture', *International Journal of Therapeutic Communities* 10(4): 53–62.

Wilson, S. (1979) 'Ways of seeing the therapeutic community', pp. 93–102 in R. D. Hinshelwood and N. Manning (eds) *Therapeutic Communities: Reflections and Progress*, London: Routledge & Kegan Paul.

Winnicott, D. W. (1971) *Playing and Reality*, New York: Basic Books.

Worthington, A. J. (1989) 'The establishment of a new therapeutic community: Thornby Hall', *International Journal of Therapeutic Communities* 10(3): 165–73.

Ziegenfuss, J. T. (1983) 'The therapeutic community and addictions: a bibliography', *International Journal of Therapeutic Communities* 4: 307.

Chapter 19

Psychotherapy in the voluntary and independent sector

Sara Llewellin

The potential usefulness of psychotherapy to the voluntary sector is made evident if we look briefly at the sector's functions, history and philosophies. Equally, the obstacles to developing the interface between the two are firmly located in the sector's financing, management and, in some instances, political history.

WHAT IS THE VOLUNTARY SECTOR?

Also known as the charitable, and now part of what is known as the independent sector, the voluntary sector is made up of projects, organisations and groups running a wide variety of services. The key distinguishing feature is managerial independence from the statutory or commercial sectors, even where the statutory sector provides funding. Voluntary sector agencies are so named because the legally responsible managing body (usually the management committee or board of trustees) is entirely voluntary. This has its origins in philanthropic charity work and is still supported by the requirements of charity law. Many voluntary sector agencies have paid staff, whilst others operate entirely by the use of volunteers.

There are many thousands of voluntary sector organisations in the United Kingdom. They cover a broad spectrum of community-based and human service-based activities and needs. Some work very closely with statutory agencies, whilst some work in clear opposition to them. They range from small volunteer outfits to housing associations employing more than 1,000 staff members. The focus of their work may be agitational or practical or both. They may provide services, for example, to

- the general public (e.g., community centres, advice centres, law centres, arts or recreational groups), or
- ongoing specific client groups (e.g., play groups, pensioners' lunch clubs, after-school clubs, people with physical or mental special needs of a long-term nature), or

- groups of people in crisis (e.g., homeless people, those living with HIV/ AIDS or other life-threatening illnesses, women experiencing domestic violence or rape, people with substance dependencies), or
- groups of people fighting discrimination (e.g., black and ethnic minority people, refugees, lesbians and gay men, women).

It can be seen from this diversity that the sector has no homogeneity or common focus, which is in large part advantageous but which also leads to difficulties of documentation and strategic development. The disparate nature of the sector is a reflection of its history, an understanding of which is crucial when considering its relationship to psychotherapy.

PHILOSOPHICAL UNDERPINNINGS

The contemporary voluntary sector has its genesis in more than one philosophical base. The National Council for Voluntary Organisations (NCVO) was established in 1919 as the representative body for the voluntary sector, which was at that time (before the welfare state) operating from a base of charitable philanthropy. 'Voluntary work' was often religiously motivated or church-based and largely the domain of the middle classes 'doing good'. Still in existence, the NCVO is now in the forefront of contemporary strategic development and integration of philosophy and political ideology.

The emergence of the social and political movements of the 1960s and 1970s led to great changes in this philosophical base. Influences such as the modern women's movement, the development of black and other minority politics and more public money in the form of statutory grant aid (primarily through local authorities) led to enormous changes. The principles of autonomy, collectivism, self-determination, user participation and community-led initiatives came into the ascendancy. Concepts such as oppression, power, access and empowerment came to replace those of misfortune, assistance and succour to the poor. Above all came the integration of the demands of the grass-roots activists for equality of opportunity.

The voluntary sector mushroomed, and, during the late 1970s and eighties, especially in the inner cities and urban areas, the philosophy outlined above was prevalent. Many of these principles now form the bedrock on which practice is built.

However, we now operate under a new and different set of constraints, fraught with contradiction. As the 1990s unfold, we see the development of the contract culture where, ironically, the voluntary sector is being seen by the statutory sector as part of the private sector, now renamed jointly as the 'independent' sector. Anti-professionalism and collectivism have largely been replaced by new emphases on performance, hierarchy, cost-effective management, monitoring, evaluation, public accountability and public relations.

Agencies are now entering into negotiations for contracts with local authorities for the provision of services in line with community care legislation. Hard-pressed authorities have been squeezing and shaving grant budgets over the past five years. As the current recession has deepened, the need and demand for services has escalated. These two taken together have necessitated a return to fund-raising as an alternative, or addition, to grant aid – with all the attendant compromising which that of necessity entails. All these factors are current influences informing the internal battles of inherent contradictions.

COMPATIBILITY WITH THE HUMANISTIC TRADITION

The close resemblance between the philosophies of the humanistic therapies and those outlined above will be seen quite clearly by those familiar with either. Key parallel issues which concerned the early humanists were accessibility, autonomy, mutual consent, demystifying medical procedures, and giving people structures which they could understand and through the use of which they could effect personal change. The psychiatric and psycho-analytical traditions seemed incompatible with much of the radical thinking of the period, steeped as they were in medical mystique and hidebound by inreasingly challenged frames of reference. The humanistic psychotherapies, on the other hand, offered readily accessible models of human interaction and pathology which proved able to accommodate – and indeed promote – key concepts of rights, dignity, autonomy and self-actualisation.

The psychotherapist as an 'expert facilitator' rather than just an 'expert' placed more emphasis on process than was present in psychiatry, and more emphasis on current here-and-now functioning than was evidenced by psychoanalysis, although certainly both those traditions have undoubtedly also been influenced by developments in social and political critiques. Examples of these are Community Psychiatric Nursing (CPNs) working at the interface between psychiatry and the community, feminist psycho-analysis integrating an understanding of patriarchal structures and the social construction of femininity. Centrally important to this development is the work of Juliet Mitchell (1974, 1984), reconciling modern feminism with the legacy of the structuralist movement which integrated an under-standing of sociopolitical structures with the psychoanalytical traditions. (For further material on this, see Reading list B below.)

PHILOSOPHICAL TENSIONS

It can be seen then that there is very real historical commonality between psychotherapy and the voluntary sector. There have also been, however, philosophical tensions which proved a block to wide-scale development of the use of psychotherapy within significant parts of the sector for a number of years.

Some of these tensions had their origin in the political resistance to anything which could potentially pathologise – or appear to pathologise – the oppression or marginalisation of certain groups of people. For example, during the decade 1975–85 it was widely held in the Women's Aid Federation, which runs refuges for women leaving violent men, that any suggestion of counselling or psychotherapy carried with it the implication that violent men were not being held responsible for their actions, and women were being blamed yet again for male violence. This must be seen in the context of an emerging politic still struggling against a cultural belief system which, indeed, does 'blame' women for much of the violence they experience. However, the notion of counselling, at least, as a tool which can empower women rather than pathologise their experience has certainly been adopted now by many. At the time of writing, Camden Women's Aid refuge are advertising a post as 'Woman Counselling Worker', qualified, who 'will be providing a counselling service for CWA therefore an understanding of the complex issues surrounding domestic violence, and appreciation of the trauma associated with such violence in terms of its impact on women and children, is essential' (*Guardian*, 1993b).

There have also been philosophical tensions around the issues of money, access to knowledge, qualifications, 'professionalism' and power dynamics. The very strong anti-professional trend which dominated parts of the voluntary sector during the seventies and eighties, whilst usefully promoting access and self-determination, often had the concomitant effect of devaluing real and useful skills along with paper tigers . . . or chucking out the baby with the bathwater.

It has taken time and integrative creativity for some of the very real contradictions between need and process to begin to be resolved. Using new models and ways of working, various agencies and groups have managed to promote services which both acknowledge the concrete social realities which lie behind the historical resistance, while also skilfully tackling the needs of real people in situations of real psychological stress. These services would largely fall into the category of counselling.

COUNSELLING

Counselling services, as opposed to psychotherapy, have proliferated in the sector over the past decade and are now thoroughly well established as a legitimate and desirable part of overall provision.

The new Advice and Counselling Lead Body set up to develop national standards and incorporate them in NVQs estimates that there are 50,000 people engaged in these activities assisted by some 500,000 volunteers. A further 2 million people have the delivery of advice, guidance and counselling as an essential part of their job.

(Advice, Guidance and Counselling Lead Body 1992)

The success of many of these initiatives lies in their pro-activity in relation to the politics and philosophies of the sector. Counselling models have been determined which have creatively and sensitively addressed the thorny issues of sexual, racial, cultural and gender identity, for example, and which respond to a variety of different presenting needs. Areas covered include:

1 issue-based crisis counselling, such as bereavement, redundancy, debt, rape;
2 counselling services run by and for specific minority groups, thereby sympathetically partnering clients with counsellors whom they are predisposed to trust, and who may be less likely to hold incompatible frames of reference, such as PACE counselling service for lesbians and gay men, incest survivors' groups run by survivors;
3 general counselling services; often community-based and usually short-term – in practice therefore this often means crisis counselling, such as services based in community centres, or serving a catchment area and having a general brief;
4 issue-based counselling specifically picking up where a statutory service has left off, such as HIV/AIDS counselling services accepting referrals from on-the-spot counsellors at antibody testing centres; and
5 counselling, and in this instance often also psychotherapy, as part of a residential recovery programme designed to equip people for good-quality independent living, such as hostels for people becoming sober.

WHY COUNSELLING AND NOT PSYCHOTHERAPY?

Largely because of appropriateness, but also because of financial, organisational and operational constraints, counselling is usually the more appropriate response to crises or difficulties which may be attended to discretely, rather than requiring an examination of belief systems, behaviour and their genesis in childhood. A good illustration of this would be bereavement counselling.

In an exploration of bereavement counselling in the voluntary sector, Charlotte Sills says:

it is [my] belief that a 'normal bereavement' may not need psycho-therapy. There is a national network of skilled and experienced agencies offering support and counselling for the bereaved, which provide a more appropriate response than psychotherapy. The use of psychotherapy at a time of normal bereavement is, at best, misusing the therapist's skills and at worst appearing to pathologise and thus interfere with a normal process.

There are recognised patterns of loss that a bereaved person tends to follow. The individual experience will of course be unique. However, there will be a process starting with disbelief and acute distress and progressing over time to adjustment, and eventual acceptance. During this time a variety of emotions will be felt and expressed – for example anger, fear, despair, relief. The degree of difficulty a bereaved person experiences in 'believing in' the loss and its significance will depend on the degree of impact on his or her assumptive world. The amount of grief expressed will depend on the greatness of the loss, as well as the personality of the person and how he or she generally functions in the world. This process inevitably leads to periods of pain, disorientation or depression. However, if the process takes its normal course, the person will not need the services of a psychotherapist. What is needed is the support of someone who will help the person give time, space and recognizance to his reactions and feelings, and be a witness to the process. He can then help him re-establish the coping functions that have perhaps been temporarily overwhelmed or unsettled by the loss. In many cases, this support is provided by family and friends, but often the help of a Bereavement Service can be invaluable. Usually these services offer a trained bereavement counsellor. This may be on a short-term basis, perhaps during the early, difficult times, to help the person develop a support network for himself. Equally, counselling may take place over several months, during which time, in weekly sessions a person has a life-line to hold onto while he explores his feelings. He can then begin to build a new life, which may have to include a new sense of personal meaning – for instance the person who has always thought of himself as part of a couple and now needs to discover an identity as an individual.

Local bereavement services are organised by many organisations including Cruse, Mind, Age Concern and Local Authorities. There are also specific organisations for Gay Bereavement, Jewish Bereavement and many others. All will offer some sort of counselling. Some also offer groups for bereaved people ranging from structured, closed short-term groups led by a facilitator, informal social meetings to self-help groups.

(Sills 1992)

It should also be noted that the label 'counselling' is more acceptable to many people than anything which starts with 'psycho-', conjuring up as it can images of madness, illness, dysfunction and disorder. Whilst not entirely without a stigma factor, counselling has become far more integrated into popular culture either than it was, or than psychotherapy still is

(Clarkson and Carroll 1993). Even *London's Burning*, a television drama series about a London fire station (ITV 1992), promotes its usefulness in the modern fire service!

At the same time many people working as voluntary sector counsellors are also psychotherapists and maintain that in some circumstances the distinctions are decidedly blurred. When researching counselling in the field of HIV/AIDS in London, Andrew Henderson found the following:

> In London there are two AIDS hospices in the voluntary sector, the London Lighthouse and the Mildmay. Both employ specialist counselling teams and run a range of support groups, some of which are led by therapists. Individual counselling is mostly undertaken on the basis of time-limited contracts of a few weeks or months. However, the Lighthouse has a policy of offering some longer-term therapy. The distinction between counselling and psychotherapy is raised by AIDS in a particular form. Apart from the usual discussion amongst practitioners as to the length, intensity and depth of the work, those affected by HIV seem to fight shy of what they suspect to be the pathological implication of the psychotherapy label.
>
> This point is confirmed by other counselling/therapy services which employ some qualified psychotherapists. The Red Admiral Project is one such specialist AIDS contract-counselling service. The Terrence Higgins Trust and the Landmark Centre both offer short-term counselling. All these agencies focus on crisis counselling, while emphasising that the distinction between counselling and therapy is often hard to hold.
>
> This is especially true of the needs of partners, families and friends. Facing the life-threatening condition of a loved one will often bring to mind a previous death; the prejudice and stigma of AIDS may uncover related reactions, say, to an abortion and problems of inner rejection can emerge. An AIDS diagnosis for a child or a sibling may open up the need for family therapy.
>
> Most AIDS agencies recognise that in such instances HIV disease has been the occasion for wider therapeutic issues to emerge and will seek to refer on for generalist psychotherapy. Some agencies have their own list of private practitioners: others will use sympathetic independent and voluntary agencies. In London the Westminster Pastoral Foundation and metanoia have established links with AIDS agencies.
>
> (Henderson 1992)

He also gives a thumbnail outline of the specifics of the context in which this work has developed. In doing so he clearly illustrates both the resistance to being pathologised and the interplay between the political and the therapeutic in developing appropriate services.

The AIDS voluntary sector has developed with great speed since HIV disease emerged in the UK in the early 1980s. Perhaps because of the high level of public alarm in the face of the epidemic there seems to have been early agreement between statutory authorities and service users that community services would be most acceptably developed by the voluntary and self-help sectors. The Department of Health makes AIDS-specific grants to health and social services authorities; these authorities in turn commission a range of community services, including counselling, from voluntary organisations. So in London alone, where probably about half the UK incidence of HIV infection occurs, there are some 300 voluntary organisations and community groups. The next most significant centre of HIV disease in the UK is Edinburgh.

While current public concern in the UK tends to focus on the growing threat from HIV to the heterosexual population, the majority of those diagnosed with full AIDS continues to come from two other groups – gay men and intravenous drug users and their sexual partners. Because of the long period of latency in the body before HIV infection results in AIDS, this pattern is likely to continue for some time. The consequences for therapy and counselling support services are that the usual range of issues arising when young people face an incurable and life-threatening disease are inextricably bound up with the impact of social prejudice towards two marginalised groups.

Young people facing a life-threatening disease in a death-denying society also commonly have to contend with negative and hostile attitudes around drug use, homosexuality, sexual transmission of disease and irrational fears of contagion. The support and counselling services have focused on the crisis of an HIV/AIDS diagnosis for individuals, but from the start there has been recognition of the underlying issues outlined above, not only for those living with HIV, but also for their partners, friends and carers.

STD and specialist HIV clinics will normally undertake pre-HIV test and post-HIV test counselling, but will usually refer more long-term counselling and therapy needs to outside agencies. The same pattern is common in hospital in-patient units; crisis counselling is undertaken, but as hospital stays are typically short, longer-term support is sought from community agencies.

A further dimension of support services drawn upon by the specialist agencies are those set up to meet the needs of groups generally covered by 'equal opportunities' policies. Agencies for women, lesbian and gay people, black groups, addiction services and many others are developing AIDS awareness in their services, and particularly in the counselling dimension. For some people living with HIV, AIDS is not the most pressing issue in their lives and therapy if indicated may best be mediated through whatever organisation offers the individual most safety.

(Henderson 1992)

It would seem, then, that there is some psychotherapy taking place where the overt remit is a counselling one. There are also some voluntary sector agencies which incorporate some psychotherapeutic work in their brief, although this is still much more unusual. To give an example, Leeds Women's Counselling and Therapy Service advertised in January 1993 for a 'qualified analytical psychotherapist . . . [to head] the staff team of three psychotherapists and four counsellors . . . to provide a therapeutic service BY women FOR women in Leeds' (*Guardian* 1993a).

FINANCIAL CONSTRAINTS AND OPERATING MODELS

There can really be no doubt that (especially) one-to-one work over any sustained period of time is both expensive and often difficult to evaluate in concrete output terms, especially to the lay person. Voluntary sector funding is as precarious as it is varied. The holders of the public purse usually want tangible evidence, often in crude numerical terms, of services being provided, at what cost, to whom and with what outcome.

The context of financial insecurity in which most of the voluntary sector operates can militate against taking on long-term commitments. Funding is often on a yearly, renewable basis and this may deter the introduction of work which can require a long time.

Money is also an issue with respect to service users. Many who would seek the services of counselling or psychotherapy agencies do so because of their inability to pay in the private sector. The sector itself is largely resistant to the idea of charging commercial rates to individuals and, in many cases, to that of charging at all.

Inevitably, then, among the popular working models which keep costs down are those which involve the use of volunteers, often trainees. Hard money is then only required for administrative posts and volunteer supervision. The following is an extract from an interview with a counselling co-ordinator for a project whose counsellors are volunteers:

My role is for 15 hours per week as counselling co-ordinator for a voluntary mental health organisation. These 15 hours include administrative time. I manage a team of 10 counsellors. I do the assessment interviews of clients and then the referrals, matching them up with counsellors. I oversee/supervise the whole process. There are three groups of three counsellors, and I offer one person one-to-one supervision on a fortnightly basis. Five are training at metanoia. Of the other five, four are on courses such as Kingston Polytechnic, Windsor College and Hounslow.

On the team there are also a project co-ordinator for 28 hours per week who oversees the whole project, and a full-time Administrative Manager who works 28 hours per week.

The difference between the voluntary sector and the NHS is the high level of liaison with the many other professionals in the field in other organisations. For example, there are referrals from psychiatrists in the community, from probation officers (counselling is part of the probation requirement), and doctors. In the independent sector this level of liaison would be similar but in the voluntary sector it means that my colleagues are volunteering their time.

Our policy is that counsellors see a maximum of three and a minimum of two clients per week, with supervision in accordance with the BAC Code of Ethics which means one supervision to four hours of client contact. We ask for a minimum of two years' commitment to the Project, with three months' notice of leaving. There is a management committee, with one volunteer counsellor who represents the counselling team who is on the management committee.

We do not accept any volunteer without one year of counselling skills training of ongoing counselling skills to diploma level. Supervision is offered here but personal therapy is not a prerequisite. Supervision helps to clear up what is a therapy and what is a supervision issue.

(Moore 1992)

Other, less well-funded organisations which use volunteer practitioners pay for their external supervision. For trainees this can be an advantageous arrangement, involving them in no financial transactions at all while providing them with the clients and working environment they need in order to become qualified. This would seem to be a model equally well suited to psychotherapy trainees, although both for ethical and practical reasons the length of time committed may need to be longer and contractually more firm.

Some of the problems encountered by this model are: maintaining a slow turnover of the volunteers, quality control, and matching experience to presenting needs. The interviewee above elaborates:

We notice an increasing number of people coming for counselling who have psychiatric problems. I need to liaise with the psychiatric hospitals, but they like to keep their distance. We are inviting them to be more supportive and to liaise more closely. The volunteer counsellors are scared by the psychiatric cases who are close to suicide and very damaged. The clients have not learnt to take care of themselves psychologically and may be seen as high-risk.

(Moore 1992)

PSYCHOTHERAPY AS AN ORGANISATIONAL TOOL

Consultancy work within the voluntary sector has been a key growth area of the past five years and more. Organisational and personnel training, group or individual non-managerial supervision, crisis intervention, assertiveness training, facilitation of events, performance reviews and interpersonal skills training are some of the more common examples of consultancy bought by agencies with training and supervision budgets. The work can be one-off or ongoing.

Psychotherapeutic group skills are clearly among those most useful in this kind of work, especially since often the subtext to what is required is an external person to 'sort it all out' or mediate between people who are not communicating well. A skilled psychotherapist will be able to resist such invitations and effectively facilitate groups to take responsibility for performing these functions for themselves, even though the brief is not a psychotherapeutic one.

Some such consultancy work can be a useful addition to a private clinical caseload, requiring a different application of the same skills but in a setting, and with a contract, of a very different nature.

As a purchaser rather than a provider, I would emphasise the importance of contractual clarity as central to a useful outcome. It is also vital for working in this sector to have a good grounding in equal opportunity politics in order to facilitate people or groups to understand and resolve their own conflicts in a safe and contained way. It will be hard for a consultant to gain trust in this setting if they are not familiar with the history and development of equality critiques (see Reading list E below).

Similarly, a more positive outcome is likely if the facilitator is able to convert 'therapy language and style' into language and style in keeping with the working culture of the agency. 'How might you sabotage yourself' might draw a cynical snigger in some places when 'How might you fuck up?' will be immediately and powerfully understood (Lacey 1992).

So, because of the nature, scope and variety of work undertaken by the voluntary sector, it can be seen that there is a great potential for new collaborative initiatives between the sector and the psychotherapeutic world. Much is already happening. The key elements to be addressed for further successful development are funding packages, on the one hand, and a better popular definition (or public profile) of psychotherapy as a non-judgemental and empowering tool for the individual, on the other.

REFERENCES

Advice, Guidance and Counselling Lead Body (1992) Feasibility Study undertaken for the Department of Employment and produced February, pp. 22–6, London: AGCLB.

Clarkson, P. and Carroll, M. (1993) 'Counselling, psychotherapy, psychology and applied psychology: the same and different', in P. Clarkson, On Psychotherapy, London: Whurr (1993).

Guardian (1993a) Classified advertisements, 20 Jan., London and Manchester.

—— (1993b) Classified advertisements, 21 Jan., London and Manchester.

Henderson, A. (1992) Personal communication.
Lacey, F. (1992) Personal communication.
Mitchell, J. (1974) *Psychoanalysis and Feminism*, London: Allan Lane.
—— (1984) *Women: The Longest Revolution: Essays in Feminism, Literature and Psychoanalysis*, London: Virago.
Moore, J. (1992) Personal communication.
Sills, C. (1992) Personal communication.

FURTHER READING

List A: the origins of humanism and anti-psychiatry

Berne, E. (1968) *Games People Play*, Harmondsworth: Penguin (first published 1964).
—— (1969) *A Layman's Guide to Psychiatry and Psychoanalysis*, London: André Deutsch.
—— (1975) *What Do You Say After You Say Hello? The Psychology of Human Destiny*, London: Corgi (first published 1972).
Laing, R. D. (1969) *The Politics of the Family and Other Essays*, New York: Pantheon.
Maslow, A. H. (1962) *Towards a Psychology of Being*, Princeton, NJ: Van Nostrand.
Middleton, F. and Lloyd, S. (1992) *Charities – the New Law: The Charities Act, 1992*, Bristol: Jordons.
Perls, F. S. (1969) *In and Out the Garbage Pail*, New York: Bantam.
Perls, F. S., Hefferline, R. F. and Goodman, P. (1951) *Gestalt Therapy: Excitement and Growth in the Human Personality*, New York: Julian Press.
Rogers, C. R. (1980) *A Way of Being*, Boston: Houghton Mifflin.
—— (1980) *On Becoming a Person: A Therapist's View of Psychotherapy*, Boston: Houghton Mifflin (first published 1961).

List B: the history of the interface between psychoanalysis and sociopolitical thinking up to modern-day feminism

Althusser, L. (1964) 'Freud et Lacan', *La Nouvelle Critique* 162, 163, Paris: Larousse.
Ehrenreich, B. and English, D. (1979) *For Her Own Good: 150 Years of Experts' Advice to Women*, London: Pluto.
Eichenbaum, L. and Orbach, S. (1982) *Outside In, Inside Out: Women's Psychology – a Feminist Psychoanalytical Approach*, Harmondsworth: Penguin.
Foucault, M. (1967) *Madness and Civilisation: A History of Insanity in the Age of Reason*, London: Tavistock Publications (first published 1961).
Lacan, J. (1977) 'The Significance of the Phallus', pp. 281–91 in *Ecrits: A Selection* (A. Sheridan, trans.), New York: W. W. Norton (first published 1966).
Marcuse, H. (1969) *Eros and Civilisation*, London: Sphere (first published 1955).
Metcalf, A. and Humphries, M. (eds) (1985) *The Sexuality of Men*, London: Pluto.
Mitchell, J. (1974) *Psychoanalysis and Feminism*, London: Allan Lane.
—— (1984) *Women: The Longest Revolution: Essays in Feminism, Literature and Psychoanalysis*, London: Virago.
Showalter, E. (1987) *The Female Malady: Women, Madness and English Culture 1830–1980*, London: Virago.

List C: sociology resisting pathologising male violence/female victimisation

Dobash, R. E. and Dobash, R. P. (1979) *Violence against Wives: A Case against the Patriarchy*, New York: Free Press.

Dobash, R. E. and Dobash, R. P. (1992) *Women, Violence and Social Policy*, London: Routledge.

List D: contemporary useful texts for practitioners

Fernando, W. (1988) *Race and Culture in Psychiatry*, New York: Croom Helm.

Littlewood, R. and Lipsedge, M. (1982) *Aliens and Alienists: Ethnic Minorities and Psychiatry*, Harmondsworth: Penguin.

d'Ardenne, P. and Mahtani, A. (1989) *Transcultural Counselling in Action*, London: Sage.

Chaplin, J. (1988) *Feminist Counselling in Action*, London: Sage.

List E: 'starter kit' for understanding equality critiques

Barnes, C. (1991) *Disabled People in Britain and Discrimination*, London: Hurst (in association with the British Council of Organisations of Disabled People).

Cant, B. and Hemmings, S. (1988) *Radical Records: Thirty Years of Lesbian and Gay History*, London: Routledge.

Fryer, P. (1984) *Staying Power: The History of Black People in Britain*, London: Pluto Press.

Gay Left Collective Publications (eds) (1980) *Homosexuality: Power and Politics*, London: Allison & Busby.

Information Ireland (eds) (1985) *Nothing but the Same Old Story: The Roots of Anti-Irish Racism*, London: Information Ireland.

Moraga, C. (1981) *This Bridge Called My Back: Writings by Radical Women of Color*, New York: Persephone.

Rodney, W. (1972) *How Europe Underdeveloped Africa*, London: Bogle l'Ouverture Publications.

List F: bereavement

Bowlby, J. (1980) *Attachment and Loss: Loss, Sadness and Depression*, New York: Basic Books.

Murray-Parkes, C. (1986) *Bereavement: Studies of Grief in Adult Life* (2nd edn), London: Tavistock Methuen (hardback), and Pelican (paperback).

Murray-Parkes, C., Stevenson-Hinde, J. and Marris, P. (eds) (1991) *Attachment across the Life Cycle*, London: Routledge.

Pincus, L. (1974) *Death in the Family*, New York: Pantheon.

Worden, J. W. (1983) *Grief Counselling and Grief Therapy*, London: Tavistock (first published 1982).

ADDRESSES

National Association of Bereavement Services
68 Chalton Street
London NW1 1JR
Tel.: 071 247 0617

Feltham Open Door Project
The De Brome Building
77 Boundaries Road
Feltham TW13 5DT
Tel.: 081 844 0309

Chapter 20

Psychotherapy in private practice

Alexandra Fanning and Michael Pokorny, with additional material by Helena Hargaden

It is quite remarkable that, although in many respects psychotherapy is the same wherever it is practised, in other ways it is quite different in private practice from both the public Health Service and the voluntary sector. We shall focus primarily on these differences as they run right through the therapeutic process, from the beginning to termination. Whereas it is commonplace for there to be a definite end-point in an institutional setting, especially when the staff member moves to another job, in private practice our experience has been that the practitioner remains personally available to the former client in perpetuity. Even clients who return to their country of origin, or migrate, may expect to drop in when they visit the city of the psychotherapist. We imagine that, if we were to migrate, some of our former clients would visit us in our new location. Whether such visits are professional consultations or more in the nature of a social call will depend on the nature of the agreement at the time.

Most of the training of psychotherapists as well as most of the practice of psychotherapy takes place in the private sector. The increasing numbers of academic courses tend not to offer the clinical component that is so essential to becoming an independent practitioner. It is to be hoped that efforts now starting to bring together the private trainings and the university courses will be successful to the benefit of all the training enterprises. Training in psychotherapy has developed by groups of psychotherapists joining together to set up a clinic or a training course. The two endeavours always go together because of the need to provide clients for the trainees and to provide practitioners for the clinic clients, very often in the form of supervised trainees, who work for very low fees. In this way psychotherapy can be offered to those who could not afford to pay an economic fee. Thus a variety of training courses have sprung up, mostly in London, but now spreading all over the United Kingdom. These courses and their attendant clinics have all been staffed on a voluntary basis by practising psychotherapists, almost like the days when medicine was a private enterprise and it was usual for doctors to spend some of their time working in public hospitals run by charitable bodies. A very large segment of voluntary and low-fee psychotherapy activity has grown up inside the private sector and supports voluntary activity by private practitioners. Some of this has worked its way into the voluntary sector, where local authorities have funded specialist clinics run by psychotherapists at very low fees. Thus an important component of private practice is work in this voluntary and low-fee area.

All the committee work of actually managing the psychotherapy organisation's training and treatment is currently unpaid and usually takes place in the evening, or at weekends. It is very important to keep this feature of private practice in mind when considering all the other issues. Many people seem to believe that private practice normally excludes this area of voluntary work, which can nowadays seem so old-fashioned. We doubt whether there are many, or any, whole-time private psychotherapists who do not undertake a significant amount of voluntary professional work. It would be very interesting to conduct a survey to try to find out just how much unpaid and low-paid work is being done from private practice.

In addition to this, all the work involved in the organisation of psychotherapy as a profession is also done on a voluntary basis. Thus, psychotherapists who have to attend daytime meetings for any aspect of professional organisation, whether this is for their own organisation or for the United Kingdom Council for Psychotherapy, must juggle their commitments to their clients and at times forgo some fees.

Currently anyone with little or no training can set up in private practice in Britain. In the absence of any regulation, it is not possible to control the activities of unscrupulous practitioners. It is hoped that this will change with the introduction of the National Register of Psychotherapists, launched on 20 May 1993 by the United Kingdom Council for Psychotherapy. With regulations agreed amongst the seventy member organisations, UKCP will be able to monitor the ethical and professional conduct of its registered psychotherapists. It will also be possible to check the orientation and affiliations of any registered psychotherapist by looking them up in the register. For the first time a public document exists giving access to the range and kinds of psychotherapy available to the public.

Turning to the private practice component, we will discuss the special features of this by comparing private practice with institutional practice, whether that is in the voluntary or National Health sector. One of the main distinguishing features of private practice is its independence from medical, welfare and penal systems. With no established structures, there is neither a line manager nor organisational ethos. Private practitioners are essentially answerable to themselves, and any structures that exist must be self-created.

Thus we can start with the observation that access to the psychotherapist is much more direct and immediate in private practice than in a clinic setting. Clients can be referred direct to the psychotherapist of choice, or indeed can approach a psychotherapist themselves on the recommendation of a friend or relative. As reputable practitioners rarely advertise, that is not a usual route into psychotherapy. The advantage of direct access is that the client consults the chosen practitioner in person, and this is generally much faster than through a clinic. The most obvious disadvantage is that there is almost no way of checking the credentials of the psychotherapist. It is much easier to behave in an unethical manner in the privacy of a private consulting room, and it is much easier to practise with little or no training in a private consulting room. Whereas in a clinic the work is shared to some extent with a team, in private practice the psychotherapist works alone. There is no one to keep an eye on the health and welfare of the private practitioner. The National Register of the United Kingdom Council for Psychotherapy will make some improvement, but until there is a statutory register it may be impossible to control the activities of unscrupulous practitioners.

Psychotherapists will vary according to the type of training they have had. What follows is therefore a generalised account or outline of the common factors in private practice. It is not intended to be a definitive outline.

At the first consultation the limitation of single-handed practice means that there is a very clear limit to what can be offered to the client. One person can only offer their own capacity. It is very important that the needs of the client and not those of the psychotherapist are kept in mind at this stage. It can be hard to send a client to another practitioner or another kind of psychotherapy when one needs more work oneself.

In a clinic setting there is usually someone to answer the telephone and make an appointment. In private practice it is usually the psychotherapist who performs these tasks; some clients are very surprised by the directness of the access, and may find it rather disconcerting.

As well as ease of access, private practice offers a personal and more intimate setting than a clinic. Indeed, as many practitioners work at home, the personal aspect of the setting is very obvious. This may be experienced by the client either as cosy and warm, or as too personal and threatening. It can be felt to be intimidating to enter the home of the psychotherapist, especially if the client needs to be critical and demanding. Much more information about the psychotherapist is readily available than would be the case in a more formal setting of a hospital or clinic. The different perceptions of the available evidence are often more striking. It is a mistake to expect every client to see the same things or make the same deduction from what they see. The simplest example is that your taste in furnishings and wallpaper will, in the course of one day, be seen as wonderful and awful, with many shades in between. It is important to remember that what you are hearing is the counterpart to the phenomenon of the institutional transference. Whether you work with the transference or not, there will always be some degree of expectation of the institution in which you work, and whatever the client feels about the treatment will, to some extent, reflect their state of mind in relation to those institutional expectations. In the absence of an actual institution, those expectations will be attached to the premises and the person of the psychotherapist, in addition to the usual transference phenomena. This means that you have the advantage of carrying a greater burden of responsibility.

In addition, there is more of a problem of separating work from home life when both happen in the same premises. We think that psychotherapists who work at home develop routines to make this separation. In clinic or office practice the difference is made routinely by the journey between home and work, however short that journey may be. However, being in single-handed practice means that the clients invade the home life to some extent. The practitioner will have to decide about availability for telephone calls and for extra sessions. This takes skill in juggling personal needs for quality time with the knowledge that it might be appropriate and useful for some clients to have the opportunity for telephone contact and extra appointments. For others it might be important that the psychotherapist not be available outside the agreed session times. These boundaries have to be worked out by each practitioner; there is no automatic answer to the boundary problem. It is usual for some clients to telephone in the evenings and at the weekends – for example, to cancel or change appointments – sometimes leaving messages with various family members. This phenomenon is very unusual when working from an institutional setting. There are interesting variations in the capacity of the family to answer the phone appropriately and take clear messages, without giving away extra gratuitous information.

One of the important features of the additional responsibility of working alone is the provision of the holding function that an institution or clinic provides. In a sole private practice there is no automatic third party to give support or back-up in times of crisis, nor to provide cover when the psychotherapist is either ill or on holiday. Whereas it is quite usual to ask another private practitioner to be available for emergencies during holiday breaks or illness, it is very difficult actually to perform this function, because the emergency visit will be to new and unfamiliar surroundings just when the client is least able to cope with such strangeness. At least in a clinic, the place where the emergency consultation takes place is the same, even if the actual office used is different. The private practitioner can feel very alone when faced with an emergency, such as an attempted suicide, a sudden death or other crisis. This is all the more reason to pay attention in advance to the creation of a back-up system and a support network. A shared private practice often combines the best features of single-handed work with clinical or supportive back-up.

In the private setting the contract is at a much more personal level and continuity is as assured as it ever can be in reality. Even in private practice there is no guarantee of immortality. It is easy to see that the private practitioner must exert a sufficient degree of self-discipline in order to run an effective practice where both the clients and the psychotherapist will be looked after appropriately. It is important not to overwork nor to work unsocial hours, nor to agree to an arrangement that does not suit you, because of the needs that a client may have. Flexibility must have its limits as well as being informed by the needs of the practitioner. The isolation can be alleviated both by seeking the advice of colleagues, often known as supervision, as well as by the voluntary activities of helping in the training of others. Working in an organisation also improves the network available and helps to develop the practice.

The issue of personal safety is highlighted in private practice where the practitioner is often the only person on the premises with the client. It is therefore essential to be alert to the possibility of violence, and have some understanding of how to contain it. Often the first contact is by telephone, and from this brief contact the psychotherapist must make a decision on whether to offer the client an assessment session, or not. As well as relying on the personal 'sense' of whether this client is safe or not, it is possible to identify the referral source and check on the nature of the problem before agreeing to see the client. If there is any doubt, it is the responsibility of the psychotherapist to arrange that there is some back-up available, preferably by ensuring not only that someone else is on the premises, but also that they are aware of the possible risk.

Another element of the isolation of private practice lies in the question of contact with the client outside the psychotherapy sessions, and contact with relatives or friends of the client. There is no simple advice that will cover all these aspects.

In general, it is easier not to see or speak to friends or relatives of the client, even if the client gives permission. This is true for individual, marital or group therapy, which includes family therapy. The client group, of whatever size, should have sole right of access. However, that is not possible if you are treating a child or adolescent who is dependent on the parents, whether the parents are paying the fees or not. Equally, if you are the only psychotherapist in the town where you practise, you will have to see everybody, and cope with the problems that causes. If you practise a form of psychotherapy that requires the involvement of the spouse or partner or parent of the client, we would regard them as belonging to the client group. It may be difficult to resist the intrusion of other family members into the psychotherapy, but it is important for the psychotherapist to maintain the boundaries of the therapeutic enterprise at all times. Help from a colleague may be very welcome before responding to a request for an interview or telephone conversation. You are entitled to delay a decision by saying that you wish to think about a request. At least you will appear to be serious and thoughtful, even if the answer is disappointing.

Similarly, it is important to manage the boundaries of the treatment with regard to the possible intrusion of clients into the time of another client. Staying on after the session is over, arriving early and ringing the door-bell repeatedly, going to the lavatory after the session and spending ages so that the next session will be due to start with the previous client still in the house – all of these are ways of intruding. Any practising psychotherapist will be able to expand on this list. Of all the possible intrusions, one of the most important aspects for the client and the psychotherapist is the guarantee of safety from interruption across the external boundary. There is no simple answer to how to cope with these threats to the integrity of the space that you try to provide for your clients.

The private psychotherapist is thus responsible for all aspects of the setting and the treatment of the client. In return, the client pays the fees directly to the psychotherapist. Thus from setting up the consulting space to arranging money management, private practice covers an entire range of human work-related activities. Private psychotherapy practice is a one-person business, with all that that entails.

The first task in entering practice is to decide where you will practise and how you will arrange your consulting space. Remember that you hope to spend a lot of time in your consulting room and should therefore make sure that you are comfortable. As a simple matter of courtesy, a similar level of comfort should be provided for your clients. People vary enormously in the degree of personal or impersonal decoration that they think is appropriate to a psychotherapist's room. We think that we fall somewhere in the middle, having rooms that are far from clinical or institutional, but not containing personal memorabilia. The real problem is that the same artefacts can carry very different messages for different people. A shelf of books on fairy stories and books written in Hebrew may suggest wisdom and caring, or equally may give rise to feelings of alienation.

Having selected your consulting room and its furnishings, the question of how the clients will get in and out of the premises must be thought about. The most usual method seems to be the remotely activated door buzzer. The client presses a bell push which sounds a buzzer that is audible in the consulting room, and the psychotherapist presses a button which activates a buzzer on the door lock and allows the door to be pushed open. We think that this method is very intrusive to the client already in the consulting room. The alternative is, however, also difficult. If one answers the door-bell for each client, the clients have to arrange to ring the door-bell only at the appropriate time, as the door will not be answered during the session of another client. A different method that is more appropriate to office practice as opposed to domestic practice is to have a digital lock that the clients can operate for themselves. The client can enter and go to the waiting room in good time for the appointment. However, it may well be felt as threatening to have clients entering one's home unaccompanied.

The next question is how to start to have clients. Usually this begins during the training with the supervised clients that are an obligatory part of the training. The teachers and supervisors are generally only too glad to have another psychotherapist to whom they can refer clients once training has been completed. Although advertising to the public is considered unethical, advertising to one's professional colleagues is not. The simplest form is to circulate a notice that from a particular date one will be practising at a certain address. The inference is clear enough. Having started, it is very important to look after your sources of referral as well as your clients. Just as it matters to respond quickly to the client's request for help by making contact and fixing a date and time for a first interview, it is also important to let the referrer know what is happening – that you will see the client, that you have seen the client and what will happen next. It is helpful to inform the referrer at intervals, however briefly, about progress or lack of it. It is essential to give a brief report when the client's psychotherapy is over – first, to let the original referrer know what has become of their referral; secondly, to convey the fact that you now have a space in your timetable for another client.

However, if the client is a direct referral, some form of diagnostic or assessment interview will be needed. Whatever it is called, it will involve an assessment of the client's stage of psychological development, the severity and acuteness of the crisis and the actual or potential risk to the client or to others. If the decision is to offer psychotherapy, several criteria will have been satisfied; that a particular form of psychotherapy is the most appropriate treatment, that the client is capable of supporting it emotionally and financially, and that the practitioner will be able to carry through the psychotherapy for as long as required. The question of the inclination of the psychotherapist to work with a particular client, aside from the question of competence, raises complex difficulties. Not wanting to work with a particular client could be seen as unprofessional on the grounds that we should offer our skills equally to all who seek our help. On the other hand, to take on all comers, provided that they are suitable for our kind of psychotherapy, could be a form of omnipotent denial, a wish to be able to do anything and everything.

Continuing professional development is becoming a fashionable part of our vocabulary, partly in relation to the move to create a formal profession of psychotherapy. Under another guise it is something that most of us in private practice have been doing since we entered practice. It involves a number of activities which are designed to increase our knowledge and skills, both directly in helping our clients, and in adjacent areas of expertise. The training of a psychotherapist is never complete simply because it is only during the practitioner's day that new problems, or new versions of old problems, can emerge. It is at that point that the psychotherapist needs help with thinking about the problem. It is not possible to help anyone with a problem that they do not yet have. Unfortunately, it has become the habit amongst psychotherapists to call this process of seeking to enlarge one's range and depth of understanding by the rather inappropriate term 'supervision'. This term is easily mis-understood as belonging to student days, and is often queried by tax inspectors. In other professions it is recognised that any practitioner needs to seek the opinion of another practitioner about some cases – not necessarily difficult cases, nor must the help be sought from a more senior practitioner. Two heads are better than one. Seeking an opinion is normal in almost all walks of life. As all psychotherapists in private practice are being consulted, and therefore work as consultants, it is quite usual to consult another consultant for an opinion. As our clients are in long-term treatment with us, our seeking of another opinion has also to be relatively long-term. A one-off consultation has its usefulness and its limitations. In addition, it is vital to attend clinical and theoretical meetings in order to keep up with the thinking of one's professional colleagues, as well as to meet and chat with one's fellow professionals. It is good for the practi-tioner to be seen to be active so as to help referrers to keep a range of psychotherapists in mind during the consultation process.

Ending the psychotherapy of a client is as varied as human nature, and much has been written about it. Some clients end suddenly and without warning, some suddenly with some sort of warning. Most come to the natural end of the useful work and leave in an agreed way. When you know that you will have a vacancy at a certain date, you can let your usual referral sources know. It is important not to start a new client within six weeks of a holiday break, as it normally takes six weeks to settle in to a new place and a new routine. This is as true of job changing as of psychotherapy. You may want to arrange to see the client again after a set period or after some months. You are free to make any ethical arrange-ments that you think are needed for the welfare of the client. Follow-up is a good idea. It is, however, also important not to intrude into the life of the client once the psychotherapy is over. Some follow-up occurs by former clients writing or telephoning, or seeking an occasional session. Often such contact resolves into the sending of Christmas cards for a few years, or a letter during the early part of the New Year. We always respond to these contacts partly because of common courtesy and partly because we are glad to have news of former clients. But we keep our response to a brief and fairly formal level. The other sort of follow-up happens when one becomes involved with the training of psychotherapists and has the responsibility for the training psychotherapy. The former client becomes a colleague and the relationship changes. This can make it hard for the former client to seek further help if it should be needed. As the mind of the psychotherapist is the main tool of their trade, some further servicing may well be a good idea. As far as we know, a second personal psychotherapy is common amongst analytically trained psychotherapists, usually with a different psychotherapist from the training psychotherapist.

The vulnerability of the client is the key to a discussion of ethical practice. People seek psychotherapy because they are in psychological distress. Rogers (1951) describes the desire for psychotherapy as the wish to make the most and the best of life, instead of the least and the worst. Two extracts from Lapworth illustrate the goal of autonomy and the degree of vulnerability that precedes autonomy.

> I knew it was a process, or I knew it ought to be a process – something that I did for me with you, *not what you did to me*. And it seemed to be a process of working myself out, explaining myself to myself and sorting myself out. . . . I just knew I had to do something but I wasn't quite sure what. . . .
>
> There were a number of things about me and my situation that I wanted to sort out. I was very stuck. I was very unhappy. I was extremely frightened of everything – of the world, of other people, of change and I knew I couldn't go on being that way and so I wanted to do something to change those things.
>
> (1989: 3)

It is clear from these two extracts that the client exposes fears and vulnerability in a way that the psychotherapist does not. This power imbalance in the relationship is reflected through the process of transference and involves cultural, class, racial, economic and sexual elements; in short, all the ingredients that go towards making power relationships within the community of the world in which we all live. Professionally trained psychotherapists will subscribe to a code of ethics which will have as its focus the need to protect the client from any abuse, be this financial, moral or sexual. Accountability for this protection rests with the psychotherapist. These concerns are as relevant for the private practitioner as they are for the practitioner working in an institution of any kind. A structure conferring authority and guidance on the profession would be most welcome. It is hoped that this will be achieved by the Register of the UKCP.

A feature common to all types of psychotherapy practice, and indeed to all walks of life, is the pervasive intrusiveness of gossip. During the working day we all hear gossip about our fellow professionals. It can at times be too easy to believe what we are hearing as though it is anything other than gossip. Whereas good advice should always be passed on, gossip should be discarded as a sadistic attack on the entire profession. In order to facilitate this a courteous attitude should be maintained towards one another at all times. We are all struggling with the same problems, and may be making similar mistakes.

As private practice is a small business, it is essential to write about the money management aspect. Unhappily, that can only too easily be seen as mercenary. However, it is a nettle that must be grasped. It is striking that it receives very little attention at all either in the literature or in the training of psychotherapists. In spite of the fact that private practitioners earn their living from fees paid by clients, it seems to be thought wrong to be too interested in money and how to manage it.

There is a whole range of considerations that are applicable to all business enterprises and are not specific to psychotherapy in private practice. The practitioner will need to be aware of the pitfalls and opportunities of annual financial audit, tax returns, allowing for overheads and for renovations and repairs. The importance of keeping adequate records need not be stressed. It is also very important to be aware of being adequately insured against foreseeable misfortunes. Advice in these areas is easy to obtain if one is aware of the need to examine present and future monetary arrangements.

How much to charge for your work? There are two ways of approaching this question. What is the usual fee that your contemporaries charge (that is, the going rate)? It can be difficult to ascertain with any accuracy. We think that at present fees for psychoanalytic psychotherapy range from about £20 to about £50 per session. There are, of course, wide variations beyond these figures. Some low-cost schemes are much cheaper and some practitioners are much more expensive.

It is usually quite hard to find out how much your contemporaries are charging and there is no really established going rate. So we all have to struggle with the fact that the fee is a difficult matter for both the psychotherapist and the client. In a positive state of feeling a client may easily agree to a fee that turns out to be too high and has to be adjusted. In a negative state of mind a client may get the fee agreed at a level that turns out to be lower than usual and lower than could actually be afforded. That is difficult to adjust, and maybe even more difficult is the need to raise the fees during the course of a long psychotherapy. Without a set price there is always room for the psychotherapist to feel guilty about charging fees that, although realistic, can amount to quite a lot of money for the client. Equally, there is room for the client to feel guilty if the psychotherapist charges a fee that is obviously not enough. We have even heard of clients insisting on paying more when they felt that the psycho-therapist was under-charging. We know that money arouses very strong feelings in all of us. To set a fair price without the indignity of detailed means testing can be tricky. As the psychotherapist is both the beneficiary and the judge of fairness, there is plenty of room for discomfort. In addition, the client will often have some level of conflict between diverting finite resources to psychotherapy and protecting the needs of a family. This can also activate guilt in the psychotherapist, who may agree to a fee that is lower rather than higher, and may even be too mindful of the needs of the family of the client at the expense of the needs of the family of the psychotherapist.

All of these factors are going to have an influence on the psychotherapy, which will become clear in the transference-based psychotherapies. To feel able to take up the transference meanings of money and fees with the client can be a delicate but necessary matter. The relationship between the client and the psychotherapist can be intense and very personal. The client is dependent on the psychotherapist, who may come to represent parental figures. The introduction into the psychotherapeutic relationship of the unwelcome reality of the dependency of the psychotherapist on the fees paid by the client can be very intrusive for both parties. We think that this may induce some psychotherapists to avoid raising their fees after some time, and then to ignore the fact that the failure to re-assess fees after an interval can lead to a situation where the client is not able to discuss finances at all. Thus an important part of the transference may become hidden in an awkwardness about the reality of money and fees. Often clients are relieved if the fee is discussed from time to time. Equally often, a client may feel affronted that the size of the fee has been brought back into the sessions, even when a long time has elapsed since starting. All of these issues are much more pointed during periods of high inflation, when the real value of the fee can be eroded at an alarming rate if the psychotherapist does not take some appropriate action.

It is difficult yet essential to keep in view that what we are providing is an intense kind of emotional contact, within a setting where fees are charged. It can be felt to be a brutal reminder of the professional and fiscal nature of a very demanding and intimate experience to discuss the meaning of money or to touch upon the size of the fee in relation to the current session. We must always remember that psychotherapy is demanding of both the practitioner and the client. Thus a balance has to be achieved between the need to charge fees to earn a living, the need to provide a service that is therapeutic and the need not to let the outside world interfere too much in the psychotherapeutic enterprise. It has often been said that clients have to pay in order to benefit from psychotherapy. We have serious doubts about that. If it were true, no one would be helped by NHS, voluntary or reduced-fee psychotherapy. We know that is not true. It is possible that the idea of the client having to pay to benefit arose as a way of trying to cope with the guilt in the psychotherapist about having to charge fees of clients who are often in desperate need. If so, then it would illustrate some of the points that we have been trying to grapple with in relation to charging fees.

After many years of interesting practice, you can look forward to retirement with pleasurable anticipation, provided that you have planned carefully for it. Meantime, it is vital to plan for the unlikely event of sudden or early death which would leave your clients stranded. The usual measure is to have an agreement with a colleague who will have access to your records, see your clients and help them to come to terms with the death. The closer the colleague is, the more difficult will be the task. There is one very good article by Traynor and Clarkson (1992), but otherwise there seems to be very little written on this topic.

In conclusion, we would like to emphasise that private practice has been, and still is, an exciting challenge and a very worthwhile endeavour. The difficulties that we have outlined of being in sole charge of everything are compensated by the enormous relief of not having to accommodate colleagues or sit on endless committees. Private practitioners really can run their own working life according to their own wishes and needs. Of course, the service provided has to be excellent, but that is part of the fun of private practice. We can recommend private practice without reservation.

ACKNOWLEDGEMENTS

We are grateful for the advice that we have had from Dr R. D. Hinshelwood and Professor W. Dryden in writing this chapter.

REFERENCES

Lapworth, P. (1989) 'A customer's perspective', *ITA News* 24: 3–9.

Rogers, C. R. (1951) *Client-centred Therapy*, London: Constable.

Traynor, B. and Clarkson, P. (1992) 'What happens if a psychotherapist dies? The role of the psychotherapeutic executor', *Counselling* 3(1): 23–4, and *ITA News* (1992) 33: 20–1.

FURTHER READING

British Association for Counselling (1992) 'Code of ethics and practice for counsellors'/'Counselling skills'/'Trainers'/'Supervision of counsellors' (4 leaflets), Leicester: BAC.

International Transactional Analysis Association Training Standards Committee (1991) 'ITAA Statement of Ethics', Appendix 28, pp. 115–16 of *Training and Certification Manual for the Training and Certification Council of Transactional Analysts, Inc.*, San Francisco: ITAA.

Journal of the British Association for Counselling, 3(1).

—— 2(3).

metanoia Psychotherapy Training Institute (1990) *Code of Ethics and Professional Practice*, London: metanoia.

Turpin, M. (1991) 'Professional status', *ITA News* 30: 7.

Part V

Issues

Chapter 21

Psychotherapy and learning disability

Janet Bungener and Brendan McCormack

This chapter is primarily addressed to the psychotherapist contemplating individual work; however, some of what we say will also be relevant in the group setting. The chapter is in three main parts: context, treatment and themes. We begin with context, as this client group has a particular context, historically, culturally and within the family, out of which they have grown. Knowing something about this context can be of help clinically. We then move on to treatment. This section is to give general advice to the prospective psychotherapist and to consider communication with learning-disabled patients. In the third and final section we pick out particular themes and concepts that we have found useful and that commonly arise.

CONTEXT

The concept of learning disability

'Sticks and stones will break my bones, but names will never hurt me': this has never been less true than in relation to the names or words in the language used over the years to describe disability. No sooner has a new name been invented than it too becomes pejorative and there is pressure to change it (Sinason 1992). This naming gives a location to the disability, and giving it a location implies ownership on the one hand and disownership on the other. Disability is more safely located in someone else rather than in oneself. There have been medical, psychiatric, psychological, social, educational and legal attempts at such definitions which have changed over the years. The obsession with definitions and classifications has served more to cloud understanding of the meaning of disability, and it is in this spirit that we would like to quote a pioneer in the field, Maud Mannoni, a French psychoanalyst, who said: 'But what in fact is feeble-mindedness? . . . Quite deliberately I have chosen not to know' (1973: 15). Disability is something which can only exist in relation to something else, or someone else, and therefore it is not only a problem for one person or another, but also a problem of discourse. In other words, the location of disability could be said to be between people rather than in people (McCormack 1991a).

Historical and cultural background

Looking back at the history of psychoanalysis and psychotherapy, it seems hard not to come to the conclusion that people with learning disability have never been considered easily for therapeutic treatment. In fact it could be said that, apart from the few pioneers, this patient group has been actively avoided and considered unsuitable for treatment. There have been other groups in the past who have been similarly considered unsuitable for treatment, such as the severely deprived and the borderline. These groups are now part of the general caseloads, as techniques have developed to meet their particular needs, in line with theoretical advances in the understanding of early psychological development. The debate about treatment for people with learning disability has been around for almost as long as psychoanalysis itself. Yet, this group has still not been incorporated into the general psychotherapy caseload.

Social attitudes towards people with a mental disability must have had an impact on the way this group was considered in relation to psychotherapy. The Eugenics Movement, which was a preoccupation in Northern Europe and America in the early part of this century, was arguing very strongly in favour of segregation of the mentally deficient. The Eugenicists' main fear was that the intelligence of the race would deteriorate if the mentally deficient were allowed to reproduce (Jones 1972). After the 1913 Mental Deficiency Act in England and Wales, colonies were developed where children and adults with learning disabilities were sent to live out the rest of their days. Similar colonies were built in most Northern European countries. They were later called hospitals, and aligned with the mental hospitals, or asylums for the insane. In Nazi Germany, the mentally deficient, along with Jews, gypsies, homosexuals and the mentally ill, were sent to the gas chamber. If society in general accepted that segregation was necessary, and that nothing more could be done about mental deficiency, it should not be surprising that psychotherapists, as part of that society, should feel somewhat similarly. However, there may be other reasons too. The unconscious fear of sexuality in relation to disability could lead psychotherapists to avoid this group of patients by rationalising that they are incapable of responding to treatment (Sinason 1988).

Psychodynamics of disability

We know that psychological trauma can cause actual specific learning difficulties in children, such as sexual abuse affecting reading. This is apart from general emotional disturbance, which may affect a child's ability to concentrate and perform at school. Some psychoanalytic theory can give us insights, or help us to consider, how learning disability might come about, and subsequently be maintained. Klein (1931) has suggested that the mother's body should be felt to be well and unharmed if the infant is to develop a desire for knowledge.

Bion (1962a) describes how the development of normal thinking may be disturbed to such an extent that in the place of normal thinking, projective identification occurs as an 'evacuating' process. This interferes with the ability to learn by experience.

Sinason (1986) has described how thinking can be attacked as a defence against the memory of trauma. Janet will be describing how the psychotherapist's thinking can be attacked and Brendan will describe thinking being attacked in psychotherapy as a defence against being thought about; (see 'Sustaining gain' (page 375) and 'Counter-transference' (page 379)).

The individual and the family

Social, cultural and religious beliefs all contribute to our desires and fears about procreation. The fantasies that people have about conceiving and producing children can have a significant impact on their subsequent relationship with the child, and how they view themselves. When presented with a damaged, handicapped or disabled child, the fantasy of the idealised child is shattered. The fantasy of the woman as the producer of perfect children, and the man's potency, is also shattered. Instead, they are replaced by images or beliefs that the disability has resulted from a curse, a sin of the forefathers or 'bad sex' that produced something damaged (Sinason 1988). This can result in much guilt and blaming. Thus, rather than being associated with a sense of hope for the future, the arrival of the child can be associated with the sense of a catastrophe, about which nothing can be done.

Bicknell (1983), in her classic paper 'The psychopathology of handicap' has emphasised the impact of the arrival of a handicapped child upon the family, and the subsequent problems which can arise as a result of a failure to resolve this crisis. She emphasises the importance of loss in disability, the loss which is experienced by both the individual, and by the family, not only at the time of birth, but at all subsequent developmental stages. This loss can also be re-experienced at critical periods in the family's life cycle. Primarily, the sense of loss is about the loss of intelligence, as well as the symbolic loss of the idealised intelligent child of the parent's fantasies. Bicknell describes the common reaction to the birth of the handicapped child as being similar to that of grief, or the bereavement process. Failure to resolve the grief surrounding these losses can result in a variety of problems, such as early rejection, seeking alternative diagnoses, chronic grief and late rejection. Critical periods for families occur not only around the time of birth or diagnosis of the disability, but also later on, as the child reaches, or does not reach, developmental milestones. In addition, the grief can re-surface when other siblings who are not disabled achieve developmental milestones such as going to school, going to university, getting married. A common crisis period for a family is when their child with a disability reaches young adulthood, or the age when young adults usually leave home.

Ageing parents are reminded of the fact that they have a dependent child, who, despite being a young adult, needs some degree of supervision and care for which they feel responsible, but feel increasingly less able to provide. The parents have difficulty letting go of the child when they can see, more than anybody, the vulnerability and other problems which their child has to face. On the other hand, the child, now an adult, may be feeling frustrated at being kept as a child and not allowed the independence of non-disabled peers.

The intense mother-and-baby relationship, which is normal in the neonatal and infant period, can persist for years when a child is disabled. This can continue right into adulthood, preventing normal separation and individuation. This situation can result in a cutting-off, or excluding, of the father (Thompson 1986). It is not uncommon in clinical practice to come across a family where the father has either left at an early stage in the family's life cycle, or absents himself in some other way, by working night shifts, for instance, or working long hours during the day. We are often quick to blame the father for opting out, but further exploration sometimes reveals that the father often feels left out and frustrated, and has difficulty finding a way into the intense mother-and-child relationship. This, of course, can match cultural expectations of male and female roles, the father typically saying: 'I leave all the decisions up to her, I just provide for them.' In one such family, the father had saved £1 million for his disabled son to inherit, and meanwhile the mother was saying that father was never around and she needed more support. These problems are compounded by the way the expression of affection is made difficult for men in this culture.

Disability, death and sexuality

'The mother–child relationship in such cases [disability], will always have an aftertaste of death about it: of death denied, of death disguised, usually as sublime love, sometimes of pathological indifference, and occasionally, as conscious rejection; but the idea of murder is there even if the mother is not always conscious of it' (Mannoni 1973: 4). The result of the death wish, or the unconscious desire of the parents that the disabled child had not been born, or had died early, leaves some disabled people with a very strong sense of being an outsider, of not belonging. At worst, they may feel that they should not exist. However, if we see the death wish as a prominent issue in development, then so too is the wish for life. The wish for life must be enormous in some who have survived against all the odds.

One aspect of life for people with a disability is the extent to which they have to form, and then break, relationships with significant others. In some cases this can stretch right back to infancy, particularly for people who were in care as children. A considerable number of doctors, social workers, residential social workers, physiotherapists, occupational therapists, key-workers of various sorts and various centres may have become involved for varying lengths of time. This can make the adult with a disability wary of forming yet another significant relationship, or so-called significant relationship on offer in the form of psychotherapy.

The links between disability, death, sexuality and independence have been described by Hollins and Evered (1990). Sexuality has been a major taboo area for disabled people and the emergence of secondary sexual characteristics in adolescence, and the desire for sexual relationships in later adolescence and young adulthood, can result in considerable conflict within the family, and also within the individual.

It should be noted that a history of sexual abuse is commonly encountered in people with a learning disability who are referred for psychotherapy (McCormack 1991b). It is also increasingly recognised that the problem is widespread amongst people with learning disabilities. Children with disabilities are over-represented in groups of children who have been sexually abused. Perhaps a combination of factors contribute to this: the self-image of being damaged as a result of 'bad sex'; dependency and vulnerability exciting hostility in the abuser; poor knowledge about sex and sexuality due to lack of education; poor self-esteem, poor communication skills and a lack of an ability to protect oneself.

TREATMENT

Communication and language

Learning-disabled people have rarely been considered for psychotherapeutic treatment and, though this is changing, some common concerns still arise about undertaking such work. An immediate concern many people have is about understanding and being understood when there is a recognisable difference in IQ and verbal ability between patient and psychotherapist.

On encountering her first learning-disabled patient, a psychotherapist was faced in the early sessions with a leaden silence. She strained to think at all. There was a sense of pressure building up. She had a thought, a gaping hole, then a thought again. 'How are she and I to connect? Can I make sense to her? Can she make sense to me? How capable is she? Is there anything there? Is my treatment going to transform her? Are we going to feel very different from each other? Are we worlds apart? Oh God, is there just going to be this dumb emptiness?' Of course that was not all there was, and the meaning in the silence and concern was slowly understood by the psychotherapist and the patient. In revealing to the psychotherapist her most handicapped self, the patient showed her anxiety that she was going to be a disappointment and an unwanted burden to the psychotherapist. Although this psychotherapist has since discovered that she and the patient can understand each other, the issue about language and understanding commonly arises both prior to and at the onset of treatment.

Communication happens on more than one level. We know this from everyday experience when we look at the expression on a person's face, or listen to the tone of their voice, or even to the quality of someone's silence to discern their mood, or meaning, or state of mind. Developmental psychologists such as Stern, Bruner, Brazelton and Trevarthen have researched and described communication processes that we use unawares by studying in minute detail the patterns of interaction between infants and children and their carers (Stern 1974; Bruner 1968; Brazelton *et al.* 1974; Trevarthen and Hubley 1978). Although these forms of social experience first arise in the very early periods of our lives, they remain intact within us and between us throughout life with the potential for development. We are most aware of what goes on in the verbal domain, but we continue to relate in other domains. As psychotherapists, we can become more aware and attuned to those other domains through supervision, training, personal psychotherapy and the findings of developmental psychologists.

These different levels and forms of communication, as described by the psychologists, dovetail with the concept of 'emotional intelligence', where a person can be emotionally aware and knowledgeable despite major deficits in cognitive intelligence (Sinason 1992: 74). An encouraging common finding regarding language is that expressive abilities often increase and become more coherent in psychotherapy as the patient has an ongoing experience of the psychotherapist trying to make sense of their communications, be they verbal or non-verbal.

Another important contribution that the developmental psychologists can offer to us in this work is the growing body of understanding about the interpersonal nature of the growth of a person's mind and sense of self. Again these findings are emerging from detailed mother–infant studies and represent a move away from a simple one-person psychology to a two-person psychology which can be of relevance to the two-person situation of psychotherapy. For example, when faced with the fragility and inertness of Shona, a severely developmentally delayed four-year-old with autistic features, Janet found herself responding as a mother would to an infant a few weeks old. With the idea that Shona needed help in sustaining a sense of purpose and a sense of herself as continuous, Janet began to describe very little things Shona did in an ongoing way, speaking as perhaps Shona would have spoken herself, had she the capacity to do so.

Shona came in, sat down and looked up at Janet, smiling with an open look. Janet did the speaking. 'Hello, Mrs Bungener. Nice to see you.' Shona went to the locker and picked something out. 'I've got Plasticine.' She handed Janet some: 'Here, Mrs Bungener, I want you to have some too.' Then every tiny thing she managed to do, Janet described. 'I'm squeezing it. I can press it. Put it down, now. What can I do with it? I can put my finger in it, my nail in it, I can make a mark.'

This type of describing is like the process of 'amplifying', identified by Brazelton as a function that mothers perform for the early infant:

> Most mothers, in sum, are unwilling to deal with neonatal behaviours as though they are meaningless or unintentional. Instead, they endow the smallest movements with highly personal meaning and react to them effectively. They insist on joining and enlarging on even the least possible interactive behaviours, through imitation. And they perform as if highly significant interaction has taken place when there has been no action at all.
>
> (Brazelton *et al*. 1974: 68)

It is also like acting as the child's self-awareness, like an auxiliary ego or like a mother processing the infant's experience through alpha-function as described by the psychoanalyst Bion (1962a, 1962b). At this stage, what was important was for Shona to know that she was actually moving herself and another object and that she was capable of shaping and making an impression on the Plasticine. Ultimately, after many repetitions of similar experiences, she will be abstracting from these experiences a belief that she can shape and make an impression on life and others, including Janet.

The concern about language and intelligence is also a concern about difference. Whenever a group in society is identified as being different, it generates a concern about whether there can be a shared reality. Historically and currently, differences between people have often led to wars, injustice and exclusion. When we first meet someone, we use different types of identification as part of the process of trying to find links. One of the most immediate types of identification we use is adhesive identification; we relate to the surface qualities of a person in a two-dimensional way (Bick 1968; Bungener 1992). If the surface is very different from the surface we are used to – for example, sound of the voice, colour of the skin, shape of the body – the links or coherence we are looking for feel less within reach. We cannot avoid this level of identifying, we all make use of it and build our stereotypes from it. We also cannot avoid being faced with difference when we meet a mentally handicapped person.

Therapeutically, we can be aware of and address the issue of difference and the two-dimensional reactions we and others have to it. We can also make use of identificatory processes of a three-dimensional nature to assist in the search for the individual and not the stereotype. Later we shall describe how mentally handicapped persons themselves can make defensive use of stereotyping.

Suitability

As there are very few psychotherapists working or specialising in this field, there is, as yet, a lack of research about suitability. The best way to address this question is not so much in relation to the prospective client or patient, but in relation to the psychotherapist and what the psychotherapist can bear.

Sinason (1986, 1988, 1992) has shown that patients with severe or profound disabilities can be seen, and make use of psychoanalytic psychotherapy. It is important to remember that the process of psychotherapy is not just about speaking. Apart from this, we recommend that therapists exercise the usual caution where psychosis may be present, or where there may be risk of violence or suicide.

Technique

The best technique is the one with which the psychotherapist, through their training, feels most comfortable. As the psychotherapist gets to know the patient better, it may be that a particular emphasis or adaptation to the basic technique would be helpful. We indicate – see 'Communication and language' (page 369) and 'Counter-transference' (page 379) – where we have found some adaptation helpful such as the emphasis on the counter-transference with non-verbal patients and also, if comfortable for both psychotherapist and adult patient, providing them with materials or toys. Children of course would naturally be provided with such materials: we refer the reader to the chapters on psychotherapy with children for further details.

Boundaries

Many people with learning disabilities have grown up in an atmosphere of poor boundary keeping, where personal privacy is at a minimum. This means that the privacy normally associated with psychotherapy may be difficult to appreciate, both for client and psychotherapist. There is often pressure from carers on the normal confidentiality one would expect. This can stem from carer anxiety and a need to know.

The role of the carer in treatment

The dependency associated with disability means that many are dependent on carers to make practical arrangements for psychotherapy. This dependency affords an opportunity for carers to interfere, consciously or unconsciously, in the process. It is not uncommon, particularly in the early days, for carers to make alternative arrangements, such as a day trip for the client, so that they are unable to attend the psychotherapy. Many people working in learning disability services are working in highly stressful situations on low salaries. It should not be surprising that the luxury of individual psychotherapy should be envied. It is often helpful to acknowledge this, and to suggest ways that they might address their own needs.

It may be helpful to meet carers occasionally in order to deal with possible boundary problems, sabotage or envy. Such meetings should be carefully thought through, and discussed with the patient. Confidentiality need not be breached in such meetings, but they may be helpful in protecting the psychotherapeutic space, and in promoting understanding.

Timing

The question may be asked: how will someone with a poor appreciation of time be able to understand the regular nature of the psychotherapy, and the time of the session itself? Virtually all of us working in this field have found that a sense of time improves with ongoing psychotherapy. Sometimes it is useful to give a card to the patient, with boxes representing each planned session, and these can be shaded in, or ticked off, as the psychotherapy unfolds. This may also help in planning for termination or ending. Termination in the psychotherapy is likely to re-activate issues of abandonment, the struggle for existence and despair. Termination should be well planned to allow for working through some of these issues. Therapeutic despair, which may result from a sense of stuckness or an inability to think, may make the psychotherapist consider terminating the psychotherapy early. If this despair is encountered in the assessment stage, and not understood, it may result in psychotherapy not being offered in the first place.

Supervision

Psychotherapy is not generally available in learning disability services, and very few generic psychotherapy services are willing to take on such cases. This means that adequate supervision can be hard to come by. We would like to re-emphasise its importance and warn against taking on psychotherapy without adequate supervision. We would recommend that, in the first instance, those interested should approach local generic psychotherapy services.

THEMES

The concept of secondary handicap

One of the most important concepts of psychotherapeutic work with the learning disabled is that of secondary handicap. The handicap the psychotherapist meets is not necessarily a fixed, immovable mass. Although there may well be some primary organic damage that cannot be changed, there is the potential to move in and out of stupid states of mind caused by secondary handicapping processes. Although such fluidity in disability makes for uncertainty, it also allows scope for therapeutic change.

A secondary handicap may come after the original handicap as an exaggeration and extension of it. It may come as a newly created handicap, perhaps brought into existence as a defence against trauma and abuse. Often the secondary handicap pervades the personality to such an extent that initially, and perhaps for a long time, there is little possibility of identifying the patient's real potential. In our experience, one of the most interesting and challenging aspects of psychotherapeutic work in this field is the exploration with the patient of secondary handicapping processes. What can then be allowed to emerge is a more intelligent patient. A learning-disabled woman, for instance, managed to stay wheelchair-bound for ten years before revealing that she could walk. Undermining one's abilities or handicapping oneself is, of course, not the sole province of the disabled: our capacity to use our intelligence can vary enormously even without the burden of a disability. Days in which we perform at our best are rare for most of us, and we often do things that we regard as being stupid or forgetful.

We have found Sinason's distinction between three types of secondary handicap very useful (1992). The first is called 'mild secondary handicap', where a person with an already existing handicap exaggerates that handicap to make themselves as inoffensive and easygoing as possible. Its most distinctive feature is the handicapped smile: 'some handicapped people behave like smiling pets for fear of offending those they are dependent on' (1992: 21). It can form the so-called friendly, happy demeanour of handicapped people; their uniform, disguising underlying sadness and insecurity. In conjunction with the handicapped smile, jokey, cheery atmospheres are often created by others around handicapped people in an unconscious attempt to defend against the feelings such handicaps arouse.

The second is called 'opportunist handicap' because severe psychological disturbance in the personality takes the opportunity to use the handicap as an outlet and a home: 'The handicap can become a magnet for every emotional difficulty and disturbance the individual has. In this difficult constellation we regularly find envy of normality, hatred for parental sexuality that created them and refusal to mourn or acknowledge the loss of the healthy self' (Sinason and Stokes, 1992: 56).

An example given is where a handicapped young man waiting at a bus stop would consistently only stick out a finger to indicate his wish for the bus. As a result of course, the bus driver drove past, unable to see such a small indication. The young man could therefore continue to blame the bus driver and the world for failing to acknowledge him and meet his requests. What he was unwilling to face was his own contribution to his unmet needs and psychological immobility.

The third handicapping process is where handicap is used as a defence against the memory and knowledge of trauma and abuse. Many cases have now been treated where 'going stupid' and cutting off one's thinking are a direct result of, or greatly exacerbated by, trauma and abuse that have gone on unrecognised. With the recovery of the knowledge and memory of the sexually intrusive or violent experiences comes the retrieval of intelligence. A vivid clinical description of such a recovery is in Sinason's narrative of her treatment of eight-year-old Ali (1992: 136–77).

Sustaining gain

Ali, like many others who have suffered environmental deprivation or abuse in an extensive way, may find it very difficult to sustain the recovered intelligence in the world outside of psychotherapy if the weight of the disability, an inadequate environment and continued effects of trauma overburden an already depleted ego. When some patients come to acknowledge that they are more capable than people realise, they may also painfully feel that, outside of psychotherapy, both internal and external pressures will inevitably push them backwards into their blunted, but familiar, ways of being.

In addition to carrying their own concerns about their ability, the fears of others about stupidity and failure are often heavily projected into learning-disabled people. A competitive society like ours that places considerable value upon intelligence can use an identifiable intellectually disabled group as a repository for unwanted aspects of itself. Disability and ability in this sense are relational and fluid. The vested interest in locating all the inability in one group happens by a process of stereotyping and projection rather than struggling to own and understand the disabilities and abilities within each of us. When the projections are ongoing through-out life, the experience of damage, slowness and stuckness can take a strong hold over the personality.

The re-activating of thought processes that takes place in psychotherapy can be extremely painful. Mark was a thirty-five-year-old patient with a 'mild' learning disability. Five months on in the treatment, after a long silence in the session, he reported that his speech had been 'going funny' at work, by which he meant that he had been talking fast again and people had been finding it difficult to understand him. This had come up already in the sessions and had been discussed as one of the reasons he was regarded as handicapped or stupid. He said he had been getting feelings of anger. He was just trying to get back to his old self. The psychotherapist said it seemed as if Mark had had these kind of difficulties all his life, and he said yes, his parents never listened to him and his brother and sister never listened to him, and then he said: 'If somebody sits and listens it opens the claw in my head. It's one side of the claw says everybody is going to believe you, otherwise not at all. It's like a claw and each time I come here it goes in deeper.'

The psychotherapist felt at first as though he were being attacked for not listening to Mark. We can see, however, that the real pain was in being listened to, which is also to be thought about. Over the two years of this therapeutic relationship, much of what they thought about was indeed very painful. Thinking and memory can lead to a knowledge of trauma that is unbearable. In some cases it may not be possible to continue with the psychotherapy and the patient stops coming.

For patients fortunate enough to have good family, community or vocational support, sustaining the gains is more possible. One mother of a learning-disabled young woman noticed a subtle but important change between herself and her daughter during the daughter's third year of psychotherapy. When the daughter had returned from an outing one evening, the mother suddenly realised that she had not known exactly where her daughter had been. She was shocked, because for as long as she could remember she had acted as an auxiliary brain for her daughter, holding all information about her life, based on the belief and experience that her daughter was incapable of doing so herself. This mother had not known where her daughter was going because her daughter now knew that she had a mind of her own which could hold information, and a mother who could bear and support such separation and growth.

Fluctuations in capacity also occur within the treatment itself. In many session, patients will show an in-and-out or back-and-forth movement, in terms of being in touch with their intelligence. The job of the psychotherapist is then to work at the interface between emotional and cognitive development: the psychotherapist explores the feelings that are around as well as what happens to intelligence in the face of those feelings. It may be difficult, however, for the psychotherapist to recognise and work with the defensive loss of intelligence and to sustain a belief in more intelligence being there. At points when the patient has succumbed to 'going stupid', the psychotherapist can likewise experience in their counter-transference a thickness in their own brain and a belief that very little intelligence exists in the patient. (This experience of damage and stuckness will be discussed in more detail in the section on counter-transference.) In psychotherapeutic work, we have found that in the face of mental stuckness the psychotherapist has first of all to take into themselves the catastrophic feeling of stupidity, which means bearing a total thickness in their own brain. They need to stay with this appalling experience for some moments until they realise that it is a feeling they are dealing with rather than a fact. They then know that they have material they are equipped to work with: the treatable rather than the untreatable. It is a process of containing and transforming catastrophic feelings as described by Bion (1962a: 93–119).

Transference

There are particular, commonly occurring types of transference that arise in the work with the learning-disabled, but they are expressed in ways that are highly individual. Today transference is generally understood as being 'everything that the patient brings into the relationship. What he brings in can best be gauged by our focusing our attention on what is going on within the relationship, how he is using the analyst, alongside and beyond what he is saying' (Joseph 1988: 62).

Mannoni (1973) has described a particular type of relationship that is easily set into motion with the learning-disabled. The patient can see the psychotherapist as somebody they must try to fit in with. Through a fear of being rejected for a perceived lack in ability, the learning-disabled person seldom opposes other people and tries if they can to mould themselves to the desires of others. What can result is a neutralised patient, and a dependent relationship where everything is kept nice even though the cost is the loss of self-determination. It can feel far safer to fit in when what you represent to others is unwanted difference and damage.

Another aspect of this transference of dependency onto the psycho-therapist is not only the handing over of all self-determination, but also of the act of thinking itself. In one particular session where a patient called Dana is asked for her ideas, Dana is silent and eventually tells the psychotherapist that she has no idea, and giving the impression of complete emptiness, gazes up into the eyes of the psychotherapist, quite content. The psychotherapist comments on how Dana is looking to her for an idea. Again Dana agrees. She is passively handing over to the psychotherapist all the ability in a parasitic way and is quite prepared to inhabit the psychotherapist's mind. In situations like this there is a tremendous pull to take the easy way out; to be educative and supply the answer. Instead, the psychotherapist says to Dana that Dana finds it hard to believe that if she just looked in her own mind she might find an idea. There is a pause and Dana comes forth with her own idea. When the psychotherapist can believe in the patient's capacity to think, the patient can have some belief in herself and her ability returns. This dependency in the relationship can be a major dynamic in the maintenance of stupidity in the learning-disabled.

Envy can also often appear in the transference, though in a rather disguised form. The patient may unconsciously hand over their ability, but at the same time they can feel envious of the psychotherapist's capacities and will find ways of attacking those capacities, particularly in the form of rather 'silly' types of question. The patient described above, who was characteristically passive, at the same time began almost every session for over two years with the question, 'Aren't you speaking?', well aware of the tone of stupidity and ridicule in her voice. It was always said as the psychotherapist had just sat down, allowing no time for thoughts to develop and thus was simultaneously attacking and mocking of the psychotherapist's capacity to think and speak. It was not the patient who was to be the stupid, silent baby who could not converse with ease and intelligence, but the psychotherapist.

Lack of independence in their lives may lead learning-disabled patients to transfer into the therapeutic relationship their paranoid feelings about confidentiality. Although initially they may appear very accepting of arrangements, their actual feelings may be quite different. They may bring into the relationship an expectation of their privacy and views being disregarded.

A further regularly occurring feature that learning-disabled people bring into their relationship with a psychotherapist is the expectation of abandonment or being unwanted. This is linked with the transference of dependency already described. Before and after holidays, cancellations, absences due to illness, in fact at any breaks in the treatment, fears about abandonment are generally to be found in some form. Because handicap and disability are basically unwanted in our competitive society, those born with a disability are aware that they often represent a burden or something which has gone wrong. They are also aware that, had it been possible to detect the defect *in utero*, it is unlikely that they would have been born. With the increasing sophistication of scanning procedures and genetic research, detection of even minor abnormality is becoming possible and abortion an option that is taken for granted. Around breaks in the relationship with the learning-disabled patient, the expectation that arises is that the psychotherapist must have become tired of the burdensome patient, unable to stand them any longer. On returning from a summer holiday break, a psychotherapist found herself thinking of the treatment and relationship as monotonous and dull; very little was expressed and there seemed to be no new ideas around. After several sessions like this, the psychotherapist had a feeling that seemed unacceptable and surprising:

she did not feel pleased to be seeing her patient again. It was possible to understand the sense of boredom and displeasure in the treatment, as the patient bringing into the relationship the expectation that the psychotherapist prior to the holiday was glad to see her disabled patient go and was not pleased at seeing her back again. Once this transference was understood and recognised between the patient and psychotherapist, more alive and interested feelings and material followed.

For patients who have been abused, their experience of breaks in the treatment can have an added distressing element. Around separations, it is common for these patients to transfer the experience of abuse onto the relationship. The psychotherapist will often hear of abusive incidents in the present as well as the past, prior to or following a holiday or absence. Being left reminds the patient of the lack of protection they felt at the time of the abuse, and this can become synonymous with being abused. It is very painful to be seen as abusive and abandoning at the time of separations, but it is clinically very useful.

Counter-transference

Simply put, counter-transference could be said to be the psychotherapist's emotional response to the patient. As a concept, it has undergone considerable change since Freud. The feelings aroused in the psychotherapist used to be thought of as an impediment to the work and only indicative of the psychotherapist's psychopathology or blind spots. Today, the counter-transference is considered to be an important indicator of the patient's state of mind. It involves a process of self-analysis and struggle, where psychotherapists try to work through and discern what their thoughts and feelings are telling them about the internal world of the patient (see Brenman-Pick 1988: 34–47).

Making use of the counter-transference can be particularly important with patients whose verbal capacities are limited or non-existent, or where they fluctuate. In fact, it is one of the main therapeutic tools which makes psychotherapy possible with the non-speaking, profoundly handicapped person. The other tools are the use of materials such as toys, drawing and modelling aids, and being alert to non-verbal communications such as facial expressions, body movements, breathing, state of alertness and so on. Janet has already described working with Shona, a severely delayed young child and, for a moving and detailed description of a treatment of a profoundly handicapped, non-speaking patient, see Sinason's description of her work with Maureen (1992: 221–55).

Sinason (1992) writes of the need to work far more intensively with counter-transference feelings with non-verbal patients but also of the need to monitor carefully the patient's responses to interpretations or comments based upon counter-transference impressions. She warns, 'Sometimes, a patient can provide a nod which might be compliant rather than a sign of real agreement' (p. 251). When unsure of her impressions, she phrases her comments to take account of this uncertainty and to give the patients a sense of their right to assess for themselves whether her perception feels correct or not. It is also re-emphasised that to use one's emotional responses to patients with increasing depth and effectiveness requires supervision, personal analysis and training.

One of the most common counter-transference feelings is the experience of drowsiness or an inability to stay alert and thinking. At these times, it is helpful in the first instance simply to try to register the fact that drowsiness or heaviness is the feeling that one is experiencing because the effect of such a counter-transference is that thinking, even of the most rudimentary kind like recognising a feeling, becomes very difficult to activate. Registering the feeling is the beginning of digesting and processing the feeling in order to identify which aspects have arisen from the state of mind of the patient and why. With one moderately handicapped patient with IQ 51, a state of thickness and heaviness that arose in the psychotherapist was an important indicator that something unbearable was being experienced by the patient leading to an attack on the patient's and the psychotherapist's capacity to think. In this particular session, the patient had learned that the psychotherapist was having to cancel the next week's session. Initially the patient was able to allow herself to be in touch with the shock of the cancellation. She was able to let a difficult question develop – why was the psychotherapist not seeing her? – and she acknowledged a negative feeling that she was fed up about it. But when the psychotherapist tried to allow the negative feeling some development by saying, 'Fed up and angry with me', the patient responded flatly with 'I don't mind'. The psychotherapist then inquired, 'Now you say you don't mind?' The patient, with her eyes deadened, replied, 'Never mind.' The psychotherapist queried, 'But first you did feel fed up with me?' The patient replied, 'No I didn't, I don't mind.'

This patient had rid herself of her mind. She attacked and obliterated her intelligence in the face of a painful situation: she feared that the psychotherapist did not want to see her. However, that was not the way the psychotherapist experienced it. The psychotherapist felt as if her brain had gone into a state of seizure, it was thick and numb, and her thought was: the patient is handicapped. She knew that, from listening to what had been said, it was possible to recognise defensiveness and denial, but so powerful was the obliteration of this patient's mind that the psychotherapist believed herself to be in the presence of permanent, untreatable damage. The psychotherapist's anxiety was that if she stopped to think about it, she would get stuck in a shapeless, thick, timeless substance – a quagmire. Her urge was to forget it, to leave it behind, to keep moving. The psychotherapist struggled to stay with the feeling and process it and finally managed to resist the urge to give up and escape. The psychotherapist said, 'I think you have got rid now of that part of your mind that knew you were angry.' She made a rubbing-out movement to demonstrate. The patient, looking alert, replied, 'Like a rubber with a mistake.' With the registering and processing of the mind-numbing counter-transference, the psychotherapist retrieved her capacity to think and enabled the patient to do likewise.

The second commonly occurring counter-transference is most often found in a trio of feelings. Contempt, guilt and pity all come together to create an important set of feelings which can be difficult to detect. This arises from the situation of difference between the psychotherapist and patient, apparent as well as real: to have a nice new hairstyle, an attractive jumper, legs to walk with, to be a wife or husband, mother or father, to have a job, to be travelling independently – any attribute that the psychotherapist appears to have or have more of than the patient – can produce feelings of guilt. This guilt can be greatly exacerbated by an underlying feeling of contempt that exists unrecognised. The psychoanalyst Neville Symington writes of being confronted in the Tavistock Mental Handicap Workshop by the shocking knowledge of previously unrecognised contempt that he and other colleagues felt towards learning-disabled people (1992). On a conscious level they had only been aware of their sympathy and goodwill towards this group, but when they began to examine the detail of their practice, it emerged that in many small procedures, contempt towards the learning-disabled was lurking unawares. For example, they would accompany such a patient to the room and not do so with 'normal' patients. When they tested out whether this was based on a real perception of need or patronising care, they discovered that all their patients could make it to the room in the normal fashion; that is, by themselves. Other colleagues were brave enough to bring forth other examples such as not bothering to dress as carefully or to be as punctual for learning-disabled patients, on the unexamined assumption that they would not notice or would not mind. A further attitude which conceals this contempt is revealed in making all sorts of allowances for learning-disabled people that we would not do for 'normal' clients, letting them off being accountable or responsible for their behaviour.

Guilt is paralysing and unproductive and results in no change, no development. Symington's thesis is that the handicapped person themselves tries to induce this cycle of contempt and guilt in the psychotherapist, aided by the psychotherapist's intolerance of their own areas of disability. Omnipotently, the client believes themselves to be unwanted, and sets about to prove this to be the case; omnipotently, the psychotherapist believes that the only handicap in the room is in the client; both views seek to maintain the status quo. What is being defended against on both sides is developmental change, as it entails the working through of considerable psychic pain for the client, the retrieval and integration of disabled aspects in the psychotherapist, and a stepping into the unknown for both. Symington writes, 'We do not desire development in the person we feel sorry for, or pity' (1992: 137). He considered the recognition of contempt in the counter-transference to be a vital step in breaking out of these stagnant cycles.

CONCLUSIONS

We have shown in this chapter that it is quite possible for the generic psychotherapist to take on patients with a learning disability. It is also now a statutory requirement, under the Children Act (1989), that children with a disability must have access to all services available to children in general, which includes psychotherapy. The more generic psychotherapists assess and treat the learning-disabled, the greater the pool of knowledge will become in relation to technical and theoretical issues, as well as in our understanding of the meaning of disability. There is room also for the specialists, such as those associated with the Mental Handicap Workshop at the Tavistock Clinic, as this concentration of work and sharing of experience is helpful in advancing theory, and promoting and supporting research.

REFERENCES

Bick, E. (1968) 'The experience of the skin in early object relations', *International Journal of Psychoanalysis* 49: 484.

Bicknell, J. (1983) 'The psychopathology of handicap', *British Journal of Medicine* 56: 167–78.

Bion, W. R. (1962a) 'A theory of thinking', pp. 110–19 in W. R. Bion (1967) *Second Thoughts*, London: Maresfield.

—— (1962b) *Learning from Experience*, London: Heinemann.

Brenman-Pick, I. (1988) 'Working through in the counter-transference', pp. 34–47 in E. Bott-Spillius (ed.) *Melanie Klein Today*, vol. 2, *Mainly Practice*, London: Routledge.

Brazelton, T. B., Kolowski, B. and Main, M. (1974) 'The early mother infant interaction', pp. 49–77 in M. Lewis and L. A. Rosenblum (eds) *The Effect of the Infant on its Caregivers*, London: Wiley Interscience.

Bruner, J. S. (1968) *Processes of Cognitive Growth: Infancy*, Worcester, MA: Clark University Press.

Bungener, H. (1992) 'From link to skin', Paper given at Ninth Tavistock Model Conference, Larmor-Plage, France (Aug.).

Children Act (1989) London: HMSO.

Hollins, S. and Evered, C. (1990) 'Group processes and content: the challenge of mental handicap', *Group Analysis* 23(1): 56–67.

Jones, K. (1972) 'A history of the mental health service', Routledge & Kegan Paul: London.

Joseph, B. (1988) 'Transference: the total situation', pp. 61–72 in E. Bott-Spillius (ed.) *Melanie Klein Today*, vol. 2, *Mainly Practice*, London: Routledge.

Klein, M. (1931) 'A contribution to the psychogenesis of intellectual inhibition', pp. 219–33 in M. Klein (1975) *Love, Guilt and Reparation*, London: Hogarth.

McCormack, B. (1991a) 'Thinking discourse and the denial of history: psychodynamic aspects of mental handicap', *Irish Journal of Psychological Medicine* 8: 59–64.

—— (1991b) 'Sexual abuse and learning disabilities', *British Medical Journal* 303: 143–4.

Mannoni, M. (1973) *The Retarded Child and the Mother*, London: Tavistock.

Sinason, V. (1986) 'Secondary mental handicap and its relation to trauma', *Psychoanalytic Psychotherapy* 2(2): 131–54.

—— (1988) 'Richard III, Hephaestus and Echo: sexuality and mental/multiple handicap', *Journal of Child Psychotherapy* 14(2): 93–105.

—— (1992) *Mental Handicap and the Human Condition*, London: Free Association Books.

Sinason, V. and Stokes, J. (1992) 'Secondary mental handicap as a defence', pp. 46–58 in A. Waitman and S. Conboy-Hill (eds) *Psychotherapy and Mental Handicap*, London: Sage.

Stern, D. (1974) 'Mother and infant at play: the dyadic interaction involving facial, vocal and gaze behaviours', pp. 187–214 in M. Lewis and L. A. Rosenblum (eds) *The Effect of the Infant on its Caregiver*, New York: Wiley.

Symington, N. (1992) 'Counter-transference with mentally handicapped clients', pp. 132–8 in A. Waitman and S. Conboy-Hill (eds) *Psychotherapy and Mental Handicap*, London: Sage.

Thompson, S. (1986) Dissertation for Diploma in Family Therapy, Institute of Family Therapy, London.

Trevarthen, C. and Hubley, P. (1978) 'Secondary intersubjectivity: confidence, confiding and acts of meaning in the first year', pp. 183–229 in A. Lock (ed.) *Action, Gesture and Symbol: The Emergence of Language*, London: Academic Press.

Waitman, A. and Conboy-Hill, S. (1992) *Psychotherapy and Mental Handicap*, London: Sage.

Chapter 22

The personal and the political
Power, authority and influence in psychotherapy

Louise Embleton Tudor and Keith Tudor

THE POLITICAL AND THE PERSONAL

We write this chapter at a time in which political and psychological contexts are characterised, on a global scale, by conflict and change. Old orders are giving way as old and new conflicts emerge, often with bloody and tragic consequences. Many peoples, particularly in Eastern Europe, are dealing with rapidly changing and emerging societies that are as yet unable to establish new order, to operate and to grasp the reality of unemployment, poverty, consumerism (and other free-market commodities, such as pornography). The increase in violence and the false gods of nationalism and racism may be some reflection and acting out of the intrapsychic pain people experience in their extrapsychic new worlds. The apparent passion for destructiveness can be understood politically and sociologically in terms of alienation, anomie and divisiveness; and psychologically in terms of splitting. Such theories describe experiences which are inextricably bound up with both political and personal struggles in the world. At the same time as societies, communities, organisations, groups, families and individuals appear to be concerned with division and subdivision and smaller and smaller identifications, there are also a number of moves to negotiate how people come together in different forms of economic, political and psychological union. Alongside the horror and terror of war and conflict, there is also great excitement and potential in the changes we have witnessed in the world in recent years – perhaps exemplified in the actuality and the metaphor of the tearing down of the Berlin Wall.

This fear (terror, horror) and excitement (joy, potentiality) both characterises the diversity of response to crisis, chaos and change and represents different traditions within psychotherapy. The psychoanalytic and psychodynamic traditions tend to emphasise the destructive capacity of human beings and inevitable conflict within and between them, whereas the humanistic tend to focus more on human beings' capacity for self-actualisation, their social nature and commonality. These tensions have been significant in our own development (separately and together) as individuals and in our psychotherapeutic practice, as it has been in our respective political experience and work. Three themes have brought these issues together.

The first is represented by the 1970s slogan – 'The personal is the political' – which summarised the notion that the personal realm was the subject of (and subject to) political analysis. Influenced particularly by Marxism, feminism, both Gramsci (1971) and Althusser (1969, 1976), and books such as *Psychoanalysis and Feminism* (Mitchell 1975), *Capitalism, the Family and Personal Life* (Zaretsky 1976) and *Beyond the Fragments* (Rowbotham *et al.* 1980), we sought in different ways (and in different organisations) to advance 'the personal', through 'the political' through campaigning, being 'active' in trade unions, consciousness-raising groups and local community work. The second theme relates to the difficulty of this enterprise in the face of the rise of the political right and the Thatcher hegemony in the 1980s, and the subsequent shift of the British Labour Party to the political centre-ground. This, with the marginalisation of Marxism as a political theory and practice, particularly in Eastern Europe, and in Britain of the radical socialist tradition, together with the current political and psychological culture of the individual, means that it is difficult to adopt and pursue critical ideas as political ones. At the same time many people who were involved in politics in the 1970s and eighties turned away from confronting society to confronting themselves through the medium of various therapies, psychological or otherwise – although some, notably Holland (1979, 1985, 1990), Banton *et al.* (1985), and Hoggett and Lousada (1985), formulate and maintain some integration of *psycho*therapy practice with political commitment. The third theme, and one which currently exercises us, is the evolution of such integration in two spheres: how to maintain political perspectives and activity, particularly in our psychotherapeutic practice and the organisation(s) of psychotherapy; *and* how to influence the political world to take account of individual biography and personal distress: an integration of psyche with concerns about society.

It is significant that we begin this by contextualising our concerns about issues of power: political power, personal power and, in seeking integration of the personal and the political, the expression of power in the psychotherapeutic relationship. The issue of power in psychotherapy is, in our view, not sufficiently considered in the literature or in research, training, supervision or practice. The *abuse* of power by psychotherapists has, in recent years, been importantly highlighted by Masson (1989), Rutter (1990) and Miller (1990). However, not much has been written either on definitions of power or the positive *use* of power – what we refer to as *authority* – in psychotherapy and the impact, or *influence* this has on clients. In this chapter we explore issues of power, authority and influence in psychotherapy, outlining a framework for analysis, practice and action.

	The subjective–objective dimension	

SUBJECTIVE ————————————————————————— OBJECTIVE

The subjectivist approach to power   The objectivist approach to power

Assumptions about
Voluntarism   human nature   Determinism

Power and power relations are   *Power and power relations are*
representative of human nature,   *determined by people's*
which is autonomous and free-willed   *situation/environment*

Section I   *Human nature and child development*
Discussion – change in psychotherapy

Nominalism   Ontology   Realism
(assumptions about
the essence of phenomena)

Power is a concept/label   *Power is definable and exists*
which structures my reality   *independently as a concept*
and structure

Section II   *Unconscious and conscious processes*
Discussion – choice in psychotherapy

Anti-positivism   Epistemology   Positivism
(assumptions about
the grounds of knowledge)

I am a participant-observer in my   *Power can be studied objectively*
own power and my study of it   *through analysis of its constituent elements*

Section III   *Transference and counter-transference*
Discussion – therapeutic touch

Assumptions about
methodology
Ideographic
Nomothetic

We can only know about power   *The use and abuse of power can*
subjectively, personally through   *only be researched through*
biographies, journalistic accounts   *systematic protocol and technique, e.g. by*
and the process of research   *testing hypotheses and data analysis*

Section IV   *Psychotherapy and the notion of difference*
Discussion – the role of the psychotherapist

Figure 22.1 The subjective–objective dimension

We identify four central aspects of psychotherapeutic theory which we introduce and develop in relation to four discussions with implications for practice. The sections and discussions are framed by a conceptual schema, based on Burrell and Morgan's (1979) analysis of a subjective–objective dimension to theories and assumptions about the nature of social science (see Figure 22.1). These four aspects form the four sections in our discussion of the use of power, authority and influence in psychotherapeutic practice and its relation to the personal and the political, namely: different theories of human nature and child development; the relative emphasis on un-conscious and conscious processes in psychotherapy; transference and counter-transference and the presence of the psychotherapist; and the notion of difference. The discussions developed within each section are, respectively: change in psychotherapy; choice in psychotherapy; the use of touch in psychotherapy; and the political role of the psychotherapist in psychotherapeutic practice.

I. HUMAN NATURE AND CHILD DEVELOPMENT

One of the fundamental ideological differences between, on the one hand, psychoanalytic and psychodynamic and, on the other, humanistic and existentialist approaches rests on their respective assumptions about human nature. Within the humanistic/existential tradition philosophical assump-tions rest on the wholeness of human beings, their social nature and potential for autonomy and, crucially, the subjectivist nature of knowledge. Maslow, the founder of 'third force' psychology, identifies two main emphases of existential psychology: 'a radical stress on the concept of identity . . . [and] great stress on starting from experiential knowledge' (1968: 9). At the subjective end of Burrell and Morgan's (1979) subjective–objective dimension these assumptions are represented and reflected by humanistic views about self-concept (Rogers 1951) and self-actualisation (Maslow 1968); an existentialist emphasis on being and existence (existence comes before essence); and phenomenological streams of consciousness in which the subjective is the source of all objectivity. Psychoanalytic and psycho-dynamic critiques of such perspectives highlight such subjectivism, un-founded and unwarranted optimism and idealised bonhomie. Political critiques are more damning: 'the rejection of theory which seeks insight into objectivity in favour of subjective feelings reconstitutes a suspect Cartesian tradition in the reverse: I feel therefore I am' (Jacoby 1977: 104).

Extreme subjectivity denies the extent of power and conflict in the external world and the powerful intensity and frightening aspects of the internal, unconscious world of the client. The psychoanalytic/psycho-dynamic perspective is that human nature and child development are based on conflict. The importance of the centrality of conflict in any psychological theory, it is argued, is the link with power (and control) and the consequent implications for the theoretical and practical stance of the psychotherapist. The passion for destructiveness, for instance, can then be understood psychologically in terms of repetition-compulsion, being led by the unconscious and understood only in the transference and particularly the negative transference (see below). Such understanding may also provide insight into conflict and destruction at a political level.

More recent and more sophisticated humanistic and integrative approaches acknowledge both constructive and destructive forces: the aspirational Physis (the force of nature) quality of human nature as well as the Freudian drives, libido (the sexual instinct) and mortido (the death instinct) (Berne 1969/1981; Clarkson 1992).

It follows – from different beliefs about human nature – that there are differences about how people grow and develop from that 'first nature'. Psychoanalytic and psychodynamic approaches to child development are founded on the belief that we are born with some notion of survival, comprising *both* the capacity for love and nurturing and nourishing relationships *and* the capacity for annihilation; that is, the destruction of that love, either from without or from within, an example of which is the baby who simultaneously loves and attacks the mother's nipple. Indeed, it is argued that one thing which distinguishes psychoanalytic/psycho-dynamic theory from more humanistic approaches is its willingness to describe these important drives and early experiences. As personality is built up then, essentially in a pre-thinking phase, it is the quality of our actual experience and the environment which will determine the person-ality and character structure which emerges. The most deeply problematic aspects of people's personalities are the repression of very murderous notions and debates which actually threaten the self, either by virtue of the child's wish to assault those people considered to be threatening or by a belief that the outside world is actually hostile. Personal and social change takes place only if the murderous aspects of the human psyche are understood and brought into some sort of relation with the positive aspects. Power, therefore, is predicated upon inevitable and necessary conflict and is something about which we are all highly ambivalent – with consequent implications for the psychotherapeutic relationship (further developed below).

The implication of more humanistic approaches to child (and adult) development is that the child develops a sense of their own power(s), as well as an appreciation of the limits of those powers. This is particularly in relation to others, traditionally through the resolution of developmental processes, stages or tasks – for example, Erikson (1965, 1968) (who, from a psychoanalytic background, introduces a social element to his psychosocial description of growth and crisis in the life-cycle) and, more recently, Stern (1985), who develops a more interpersonal, process description of development. These views are predicated on a notion of power which emphasises the autonomy and negotiability of power relationships.

What both the psychoanalytic/psychodynamic and humanistic/existential traditions agree upon is that childhood is an experience of a power relationship. Nowhere is this argued more eloquently – and the destructive consequences elaborated – than in the work of the former psychoanalyst and now writer and advocate for children, Alice Miller (1985, 1987a, 1987b). The parent–child relationship is by its nature a relationship of power, authority and influence; indeed, a child cannot flourish without its parents having and using these appropriately. When power is simply equated with oppression, however, and oppression is associated with all power relationships, this leads to psychological and ideological tautology and confusion – to the extent that Masson (1989), for instance, argues against all forms of psychotherapy (except self-help therapy) on the basis of the power (structure) inherent in psychotherapy and the psychotherapeutic relationship which he regards as necessarily abusive, commenting that imbalance in power rarely leads to compassionate behaviour. The answer to this debate on power – between determinism and voluntarism – lies not in such defeatism (as Masson's); or in ignoring the existence of power; or in (the mistaken) thinking that we can share it (the logic of co-counselling), do away with it (Rogers 1957/90c), or give it away (which informs much of the discussion about empowerment in the field of mental health). Although power relationships may be inadequate, invasive and even abusive (Masson 1989; Rutter 1990), our perspective is that they are not *per se* deforming. There is, however, in some psychotherapeutic circles, a deep ambivalence about power, about owning knowledge, having skills and definable roles that distinguish one person from another – a concept of difference which we expand later. At the same time there is an ideological context to this rejection or denial of power. Certain ideas about power have prominence at certain, particular times – which brings us back to 'the political' and the extent to which the dominant culture, class, race and gender determine our thinking and beliefs as against the degree of autonomy we have and can develop for ourselves and in relation to one another.

Discussion – change in psychotherapy

People come to psychotherapy wanting a change in their lives and, indeed, can be viewed (assessed, diagnosed and so on) by the psychotherapist in relation to their stated aims or wishes for change. Often the initial stage of the psychotherapy comprises a process of mutual definition of the issues or problems and the aims of the client regarding their solution. During this process, the psychotherapist may (or, almost inevitably, will to some extent) initially be (re-)defining 'the problem/s' according to their own theoretical orientation and framework, even using concepts which have no meaning to the client or to which the client might object. Knowledge is power and the framing of knowledge has a powerful impact on practice: the psychotherapist has, by virtue of his authority and ability to conceptualise, greater knowledge in this respect than the client; and herein lies the potential both for abuse *and* for the enabling of healthy change and autonomy. The key practice issue in this respect is to what extent our own assumptions as psychotherapists about human nature (determinist or voluntarist) influence our beliefs, notions and practice about our clients' ability to change. In terms of our conceptual schema (Figure 22.1), determinist approaches to psychotherapy will rely more on diagnosis, classification and treatment, whilst voluntarist approaches (and to power relations in general) will emphasise mutual and ongoing assessment: 'if we could empathically experience all the sensory and visceral sensations of the individual, could experience his [sic] whole phenomenal field . . . we should have the perfect basis for understanding the meaningfulness of his behaviour and for predicting his future behavior' (Rogers 1951: 494–5).

Working alongside – and at times against – such power, authority and influence expressed consciously or unconsciously by the psychotherapist, we need to consider the influence of social factors on aspects of and prospects for change in psychotherapy.

Despite the encouragement and development of individual autonomy (voluntarism), there are situations and times when social disadvantage will be a (determining) factor on a client's capacity and/or options for change. To claim otherwise is at best naïve and at worst persecutory. In practice, we can consider the conceptual schema (Figure 22.1) and reflect its range: as a client denies their ability to change we can confront such denial and discounting (for example, Schiff *et al.* 1975); if they claim undue or grandiose free choice in given situations we can balance this with an appreciation of what is in some way determined.

II. UNCONSCIOUS AND CONSCIOUS PROCESSES

Freud was the first of the nineteenth-century writers who were aware of the existence of the unconscious to delineate its particular characteristics and later to distinguish three aspects of the unconscious: from the recollection of an event which was not in mind but which is easily accessed by a trigger (the preconscious); to a level where access is difficult but may or may not be accomplished after weeks, months or even years of application; to 'a mental province rather than a quality of what is mental' (Freud 1923/1973: 104), hidden from the ego. The contents of the second layer of the unconscious were generally held to relate to matters of personal experience and history which were too traumatic or threatening for the individual to remember. Jung (1954/1959) calls this the personal unconscious and added the notion of the collective unconscious, the contents of which, irrespective of historical moment, racial or ethnic group, gender, class or age, relate to (arche)typical reactions to universal human circumstances. Subsequent writers have not significantly disagreed with these definitions although they may differ in the importance they attach to these systems and phenomena in their clinical work.

A crucial question in the psychotherapeutic relationship arises in relation to the unconscious and the use of power, authority and/or influence by the psychotherapist. Whose consciousness prevails? For it is only through consciousness that the unconscious can be understood, and it is in the nature of the unconscious that its contents are obscure to the conscious. It is questionable, for instance, whether at the beginning of any psychotherapy the client is in a position to know what is being agreed in relation to the function of the psychotherapist. Whilst neither psychotherapist nor client can know what material will emerge or how, the psychotherapist at least knows about his or her own assumptions and techniques and, even at the assessment stage, can make some hypotheses about some aspects of the psychotherapy. However the client is presenting and however empathic the psychotherapist, different theoretical constructs will inevitably occur to the psychotherapist as the interaction proceeds. The psychotherapist is necessarily involved in a conscious process. However, in terms of understanding the impact of the essence of such phenomena – for example, the psychotherapist's conscious conceptual processing (let alone the psychotherapist's unconscious material) – the important question is: to what extent is the client influenced (unconsciously) by the internal processes of the psychotherapist? The answer depends partly on what we believe about power. If we believe that power is definable and exists independently as a concept and a structure (realism), then we will believe that the psychotherapist's conscious and unconscious processes will influence the client; if, on the other hand, we believe that power is a concept which we use in different ways to structure our reality (nominalism), we will believe that the psychotherapist's power, authority and influence will be questioned and mediated by the client's own sense and grasp of issues of power throughout their psychotherapy. Lukes (1974) stresses the importance of the power to define: the statement 'power is not a property, but a relation' is a nominalist definition of power which wrests it from 'objectivist' realism; and Schiff *et al.* stress the priority and necessity of understanding the patient's frame of reference, suggesting that 'the whole question, "What is really real?" is necessarily an ongoing consideration' (1975: 54). Either way (subjectivist or objectivist), there are implications for psychotherapeutic practice.

Discussion – choice in psychotherapy

This (ontological) discussion about the essence of things – which might be subtitled 'Whose reality is it anyway?' – is important in ascertaining how power is defined and how choices are made in the psychotherapeutic relationship. From choosing a psychotherapist; to the first point of contact; finding out how the psychotherapist works; what sort of person they are; even what information the client wants; through to the choices the client has within the psychotherapeutic relationship (not forgetting the occasions and situations in which there is even less or no choice in the process): all these, commonly unconscious choices and decisions, are based on assumptions about the essence of phenomena. To one client who wanted to 'get on with' her psychotherapy in the initial session the psychotherapist pointed out that she was taking a lot 'on trust' with the result that the client highlighted various (implicit) assumptions she had, particularly about the professional authority of the psychotherapist. Again, we can draw on Burrell and Morgan's (1979) conceptual schema to clarify and work with such issues as they arise in practice. Two common positions are found: in one (as in the example above), the client abdicates their reality to the psychotherapist's, often unconsciously; in the other, the client rigidly adheres to their own reality, even in the face of an objectivist 'reality'. One client's relationship with their group psychotherapist was shaken when he heard his psychotherapist define himself as black; he had hitherto and unconsciously 'seen' his psychotherapist as white and subsequently had to (re-)examine his assumptions, his relationships and his racism. Such discussion about what is 'real' (realism) and what is a concept or a label (nominalism), such defining and reclaiming is often an important stage in psychotherapy: 'it is the uniqueness of the individual that is apparent in the ancient idea of naming' (Jacobs 1985: 23). Jacobs understands naming in itself as an alternative to – and, as such, a reclaiming of the essence of – labelling.

For the psychotherapist's part, if we are aware of these largely unconscious processes and assumptions and common positions, we can respond to how our power may be viewed, being sensitive both to defining another person's reality and, equally, to rigidly defended realities. This discussion has practical implications, for instance, for diagnosis and treatment planning in psychotherapy. Rogers (1951) discusses the problems of diagnosis in terms of encouraging dependency and a reliance on an external locus of evaluation (realism). Clarkson (1992) summarises 'the case against diagnosis', referring to the dangers of alienation, reductionism and 'false certainties'. Whilst it would be a denial of our power and authority as psychotherapists to deny our experience in assessment and treatment, we need to be aware of and be explicit both about our views of human nature and about the essence of phenomena in order to be clear about our clients. One psychotherapist, in working with a client who was concerned about the process of her psychotherapy, agreed initially to answer the client's questions about his conceptualisations – thereby opening up the process as well as the content of the psychotherapy – and modelling a power-sharing which the client had not previously experienced. This also had the effect of establishing trust which, as it transpired, was a core, developmental issue for the client – reflecting the practical and conceptual link between issues of human nature and of ontology.

III. TRANSFERENCE AND COUNTER-TRANSFERENCE

For psychoanalytic and psychodynamic psychotherapists the constant examination of the transference relationship is crucial both as an expression of the client's self and as a vehicle for the negative defences central to the pathology of the client. It is thus only a transferential relationship which can stand the issue of whether the client destroyed the parent. People do not conceptually understand their internal world, it is argued, simply through thinking about it; rather, if the patient is to do so in a sustained way, they do so through an emotional experience also; namely, the vehicle of the transference. It is a criticism of more humanistic/existential approaches that they do not have this way into the destructive and negative organisation of the client's internal world.

There are implications for the person and conduct of the psychotherapist who believes in the therapeutic usefulness of the transference. The psychotherapist who adheres rigidly to a technique without paying attention to the clues from the client about exactly what was enraging, frightening or demeaning in the original responses to their anger or negativity runs the risk of compounding the original trauma; the maintenance of a 'blank screen' is one obvious example of this. It is not enough for the client to understand that their hostility against their psychotherapist derives from earlier experiences; they also need the experience of a different response in the present. At some time or other probably all psychotherapists are tempted to act as if clients only need a good experience in the present to obliterate the effects of deprivation or abuse in the past and therefore to focus on reparative interventions rather than those which facilitate the client to connect with feelings towards the psychotherapist which both might find difficult. As Casement points out: 'the analytic "good object" is not someone better than the original object: it is someone who survives being treated as a "bad object"' (1990: 87).

Whatever the orientation of the psychotherapist, they are most likely to provide a genuinely therapeutic experience for the client when they demonstrate to the client total respect for that person as an individual, a continuing interest in the relationship between themselves and the client and a commitment to examine their own defensiveness in the face of criticism from the client. This responsiveness to the individuality of the client necessitates a degree of spontaneity, flexibility, open-mindedness and creativity incompatible with over-strict adherence to any technique, whether psychoanalytic, psychodynamic or humanistic. The contributions of experienced practitioners in Dryden (1992) are examples of serious and critical self-reflection on practice, often questioning the grounds of knowledge of such practice. Such epistemological assumptions – about the grounds of knowledge – are crucial and especially so in relation to discussions about power; the challenge to Freud's seduction theory and the belief in the subjective experience and reality of the abused child represents a subjectivist (anti-positivist) knowledge based on the participation of the client in recalling and reclaiming their own experience (for example, Kelly 1988; Kelly and Radford 1990/1991) in relation to sexual abuse and violence). Abuse – and its denial or disguise, maybe as love or affection – represents a denial of the very grounds of such self-knowledge in a perverted form of (adult) 'objectivist' (positivist) knowledge.

The willingness to own and examine their own negativity and other feelings toward the client (counter-transference) will enable the psychotherapist to withstand criticism and hostility from the client without defending, retaliating or collapsing. For example, one psychotherapist was misheard by a client who then reacted to what he understood the psychotherapist to have said with sharp criticism, intending to hurt her. She was hurt. Liking the client and wanting to be liked, the psychotherapist quickly readied herself to correct the client's misunderstanding; she was also angry and formulated a retaliatory reply. Fortunately, the psychotherapist, recognising this counter-transferential invitation, was instead able to offer the client an opportunity both to acknowledge how deeply and how frequently he wanted to wound her and see her hurt, and to examine his willingness to 'hear' her make what would have been a persecutory remark. Thus, an understanding of counter-transference and continuing awareness of its impact on the psychotherapist is essential for the psychotherapist to maintain contact with the potential for the use and abuse of his power.

There is a variety of approaches within humanistic/existential psychotherapies to the concept and use of transference and counter-transference. Rogers represents one view against the use of transference:

'The client-centred therapist's reaction to transference is the same as to any other attitude of the client: he endeavours to understand and accept' . . . . acceptance leads to recognition by the client that these feelings are within her, they are not in the therapist.

(1951: 203)

This follows from Rogers' theory of personality and behaviour (1951) and theory of psychotherapy and personality change (1959/1990a, 1977/1990b). Many humanistic psychotherapists will, following this, discourage or 'cut through' the transference rather than encouraging or working in it. From a transactional perspective Berne was concerned to explore the underlying dynamics of transference transactions (Berne 1966); more recently Novellino (1984) and Moiso (1985) suggest ways of working *with* rather than *in* the transference. Clarkson (1991) offers an in-depth analysis of both psychotherapist and client transference and counter-transference. Such attempts to integrate an understanding of transference and counter-transference are not simply cognitive exercises: the symbolic meaning of the client's transference will often be realised or expressed emotionally or in behavioural terms. Schiff *et al.* illustrate their approach to transference, linking this to their understanding of power: 'Major exchanges of power occur in therapeutic relationships. Patients often wish to invest therapists with authority and responsibility . . . our policy is to accept the patients' investment of power [transference] to the extent we believe it possible to utilise that power for their welfare' (1975: 102).

Discussion – therapeutic touch

In discussing the use of touch in psychotherapy we distinguish between touch on greeting or parting; touch which the client asks for or the psychotherapist gives in an isolated incident; and touch which is part of the treatment, such as in biodynamic massage or other post-Reichian psychotherapies which focus on the body as the repository of tension and dis-ease, resulting from unexpressed or unacknowledged feelings about past traumas. The second case is less ambiguous, especially if, at or near the beginning of psychotherapy, there is discussion and agreement about the use and purpose of therapeutic touch. Nevertheless, there are implications for the power relationship if, for example, the client is undressed and prone on a massage table. For this reason biodynamic psychotherapists do not work in the transference. Southwell (1990) argues that the work is focused on the energy within the client's body and not on the relationship between psychotherapist and client. It can be argued that the degree of intimacy in the physical relationship between the biodynamic psycho-therapist and their client is such that it could not tolerate the additional intimacy of the transferential relationship: the client would have no place if the psychotherapist did not 'touch' – and the psychotherapist no way of not touching. It can be further argued that, without a place in which there is no 'touch', the client cannot fully experience the touch that is.

With some separation along these lines, whoever or whatever is evoked in psychotherapy can be explored. The technique of separation between the physical (touch) and the transferential raises the question of whether the psychotherapist acknowledges counter-transference. In an attempt to answer this, many psychotherapists using body-orientated techniques do not touch, but maintain close contact with their clients through the nature of their presence and their verbal interventions or, in accordance with their observations of the transferential processes at work, exercise considerable judgement in their use of touch. There is some evidence that Rogers, for instance, towards the end of his life, began to regard 'presence' as another 'condition' for therapeutic change (Rogers 1986; Thorne 1992). (Although Tudor and Worrall, in press, take issue with the notion of presence being viewed as a condition.) Such psychotherapists, like their psychoanalytic/ psychodynamic colleagues, may 'touch' their clients deeply with the appropriateness and usefulness of their verbal and non-verbal interventions.

A further aspect of the use of touch is the reparative need on the part of the client for being held or touched appropriately by the psychotherapist/ parent figure; to withhold this, it could be argued, only compounds the original lack or trauma and may be a lack on the part of the psychotherapist. Traditionally, psychoanalytic and psychodynamic psychotherapists perceive such reparation (or reparenting) as an avoidance of the client experiencing the original pain and as undermining of the client's ability to deal with it, although Woodmansey (1988) argues for the use of touch in treatment: as communication and as 'primary experience', suggesting contra-indications such as clients' sexual difficulties, and pointing out the need for professional responsibility. Humanistic psychotherapists have, on the whole, tended to be more open to considering touch and to touching clients, although recent research into and publicity about the abuse of such power relationships (for example, Rutter 1990) have, properly, highlighted the need for a coherent theoretical stance and consequent appropriate practice; good professional practice and ethics and, therefore, psychotherapeutic discretion; and regular supervision.

IV. PSYCHOTHERAPY AND NOTION OF DIFFERENCE

As psychotherapists the authors both come from a socialist tradition and share a belief that, as active agents in our lives and therapeutic practices, we have a view of politics which we try to relate to our understanding of our clients. As socialists we come from traditions which have an analysis of society which is essentially conflictual; traditions which, at the same time, value *inter*dependence. Yet we live in a Western society in which the value of independence (through market forces) is paramount and 'the nanny state' and *dependent* relationships are attacked. Simons (1992) points out the partiality of such attacks – as if necessary and appropriate dependence is inherently damaging. What draws these strands together is the notion of difference. The negotiation of difference, in psychotherapy, allows for some idea about ambivalence – often missing in critical politics. There *is* a structural and emotional difference between the patient and the psychotherapist, just as between many other structural differences – of class, race and gender. The difference in different psychotherapies is just how *difference* is negotiated. (Stereo)typically in the psychoanalytical tradition it is emphasised and highlighted, whereas within the humanistic tradition it is emphasised less and even ignored. In elaborating the notion of difference, we identify three areas in which psychotherapy and politics interact: psychotherapy *and* politics, politics *in* psychotherapy and the politics *of* psychotherapy.

Psychotherapy and politics

Politics, in present-day psychological and social usage, has to do with *power and control* . . . with the *locus of decision-making power*: who makes the decisions which, consciously or unconsciously, regulate or control the thoughts, feelings, or behaviour of others or oneself.

(Rogers 1957/1990c: 377)

In practising both politics and psychotherapy, one solution to such issues of power and control is to separate the two as Kopp does: 'the roots of most of women's problems are political and social. The solution to such political problems must be revolutionary rather than psychotherapeutic' (1974: 33). Certainly, such separation avoids any danger of 'psychologising' a client's politics or political involvement. However, in practice, to split off an aspect of one's life is an untenable position or – as the gay men and lesbians who entered the psychoanalytic establishment at a time when homosexuality was more widely considered pathological experienced – was and is, at the very least, a difficult road to travel.

Politics in psychotherapy

The alternative to such separation (or splitting) is the exploration and/or resolution of political issues, aspirations and ideals in and through the process of psychotherapy. This puts a client's politics on the agenda in psychological terms and therefore offers a more whole (holistic) approach to the client. In the authors' experience this is where it is possible and, indeed, necessary to explore the function and meaning of politics; power relations; the notion and experience of difference; the client's own sense of power; their relation to authority; and capacity to be influenced and to influence others. Only through such expansion and exploration is it possible to achieve a true integration – or, in Piagetian terms, a mature assimilation, rather than an immature accommodation – of the political world.

The politics of psychotherapy

As distinct from politics *in* psychotherapy, the politics *of* psychotherapy specifically puts the politics of *the psychotherapist* on the agenda and, more generally, focuses on psychotherapy from a political perspective. This first point immediately poses personal, political and ideological challenges to the psychotherapist – how much of ourselves and our views are we willing to reveal in the service of our client? How do they learn about power in the psychotherapeutic relationship? How do we negotiate our differences, whether personal, political or structural? For example, when asked in an initial interview by a lesbian client about the nature of her own sexuality and her theoretical, psychological view of the origin of lesbianism, one psychotherapist was willing to answer directly and before embarking on any exploration of the impact of her answers (or of other possible answers) on the client. By doing so, the psychotherapist intended to convey that, as a psychotherapist, she did not exist independently or isolated from social relations; and that she understood their impact on the client and that this impact would also be experienced in the psychotherapeutic relationship and process.

On the more general point, it was Reich who first developed a politics of psychotherapy both in his theoretical attempt to link his ideas about the body with what he saw as liberated societies and in practice through the establishment of his Sexual Hygiene Clinics for Workers and Employees in Germany during the 1930s: 'at this time Reich still visualised himself as a Marxist psycho-analyst, and as such he still hoped to find some measure of support for the mental hygiene work he was engaged on, in both Marxist and psycho-analytic circles' (Boadella 1985: 72). Reich was to be disappointed in and rejected by both circles. In our own personal, political and psychotherapeutic journeys we have also found it difficult to 'marry' these two worlds: within our political world and organisations to acknowledge the impact of and on the psyche; and for politics to be on the agenda within our psychological worlds.

Discussion – the role of the psychotherapist

It follows from these distinctions and brief discussions that, depending on the psychotherapist's strategy in relation to their psychotherapeutic work and politics (whether *and*, *in* or *of*), their practice and methodology will vary and differ – on Burrell and Morgan's (1979) and our analysis – from the ideographic (or symbolising) to the nomothetic (or legislative). Thus, the psychotherapist who emphasises systematic protocol and technique, typically, through diagnosis and treatment planning represents a nomothetic approach to social science and the methodology and practice of psychotherapy. A psychotherapist, on the other hand, whose method is more subjective, 'getting close to one's subject and exploring its detailed background and life history' (Burrell and Morgan 1979: 6), using, for instance, active listening, empathy (Rogers 1961) or metaphor (Kopp 1974), has an ideographic methodology. This dimension provides an understanding of debates about methodology; for instance, in psychotherapy research.

The psychotherapist's role will also vary according to their views and assumptions about the nature of society – this is another (vertical) dimension in Burrell and Morgan's (1979) work (and worthy of further consideration and development in this field). A proponent of the status quo will, however unconsciously, tend to support ways in which their client expresses their sense of social integration, of cohesion and of social order. Whereas, as an advocate of radical change, the psychotherapist/guru, 'arising in a revolutionary context . . . sets himself [*sic*] against both the traditional authority of patriarchal domination and the bureaucratic legalistic defining of power. Unintimidated by cultural expectations . . . overturning the usual ways of understanding the meaning of life' (Kopp 1974: 8).

Our own perspective is that the separation of politics and psychotherapy is a false one; and that one of our tasks and roles as psychotherapists/ activists living in a political world is to help clients understand, interpret, mediate and act on their extrapsychic as well as their intrapsychic world, to paraphrase Maslow (1968): 'intra-psychic success is not enough; we must also include extra-psychic change'. Unhappiness is informed by conflict, including conflict within power relationships: working class and ruling class, women and men, black and white, the unemployed and elderly and the productive world, children and the adult world. An ignorance or naïve understanding of such conflicts only fuels the criticism of the individualising focus and depoliticising effect of psychotherapy. A false understanding leads to attempts to substitute happiness for unhappiness, in a way in which both false humanism and commodity fetishism elevate pleasure as an end in itself, thereby minimising genuine suffering and alienation. Such naïve and unrealistic views are, in psychoanalytic terms, symbiotic organisations of and defences against the world. Just as a part of the psychotherapist's task is to confront apolitical resolutions of such crises, idealised happiness can be as destructive as rage: real health, psychologically and politically, allows for both to be expressed constructively and creatively.

Banton *et al.*, in their discussion of radical therapeutic practice, highlight the need to separate the positive and negative functions of power relations: 'radical practice must involve the subversion of discourse in a manner which maximises the positive possibilities for change' (1985: 135). They go on to argue that the (psycho)therapist's acceptance of power facilitates the opening up of experiences and connections, whilst their refusal of power leaves the client better able to integrate the connections between psychological stress and social reality and to 'maintain them independently of the therapist' (p. 139). As psychotherapists we therefore need to be able to distinguish between positive and negative power relations and to use our authority in confronting and connecting with our clients appropriately.

CONCLUSION

Lord Acton observed that 'power tends to corrupt, and absolute power corrupts absolutely' and, rather like the empirical research scientist who hung a horseshoe over the door of his laboratory as a sign of doubt and humility, perhaps Lord Acton's quotation would be well displayed or at least borne in mind in psychotherapists' consulting rooms. In this chapter, we have distinguished between the ab-use of power and the appropriate use of power – or *authority* – on the part of the psychotherapist; and have discussed the influence psychotherapy and the psychotherapist may have on the client, particularly at an unconscious level. We have suggested a conceptual framework for identifying four sets of assumptions about power and for working with issues of power, authority and influence in psychotherapy, precisely so that neither psychotherapists nor clients are corrupted by the power which necessarily and properly lies in the psychotherapeutic relationship – advocating rather that such issues are made explicit and resolved with clients and, with Banton *et al.* (1985), that this is ultimately a subversive activity, psychologically and/or politically.

In concluding, we distinguish two fallacies, the identification of which may clarify future thinking and practice in these areas: one is the fallacy of empowerment and the other, of the authoritarian nature of power – what might be referred to, respectively, as 'giving over power' and 'having power over'. Just as one cannot truly be sent for psychotherapy, one cannot truly (passively) *be* empowered; we can actively learn about power, 'own' our own power and take power: this is genuine and positive psychotherapeutic potency or authority – 'power to' and 'power for'. In response to the second fallacy – and one which also proposes a way of modelling potency ('passing on', rather than 'giving over') – Steiner objects to the concept of power being universally linked to the control of and over others and concludes poignantly that 'the greatest antidote to the authoritarian use of power . . . is for people to develop individual power in its multidimensional forms and to dedicate themselves to passing on power to as many others as can be found in a lifetime' (1987: 104).

ACKNOWLEDGEMENT

Thanks and acknowledgement to Julian Lousada for his contribution to earlier drafts of this chapter.

REFERENCES

Althusser, L. (1969) *For Marx*, London: Allen Lane.
—— (1976) *Essays in Self-Criticism*, London: New Left Books.
Banton, R., Clifford, P., Frosh, S., Lousada, J. and Rosenthal, J. (1985) *The Politics of Mental Health*, Basingstoke: Macmillan.
Berne, E. (1966) *Principles of Group Treatment*, New York: Grove Press.
—— (1981) *A Layman's Guide to Psychiatry and Psychoanalysis*, Harmondsworth: Penguin (first published 1969).
Boadella, D. (1985) *Wilhelm Reich*, London: Arcana.

Burrell, G. and Morgan, G. (1979) *Sociological Paradigms and Organisational Analysis*, London: Heinemann.

Casement, P. (1990) *Further Learning from the Patient*, London: Routledge.

Clarkson, P. (1991) 'Through the looking glass: explorations in transference and counter-transference', *Transactional Analysis Journal* 21: 99–107.

—— (1992) *Transactional Analysis Psychotherapy: An Integrated Approach*, London: Routledge.

Dryden, W. (1992) *Hard-earned Lessons from Counselling in Action*, London: Sage.

Erikson, E. (1965) *Childhood and Society*, Harmondsworth: Penguin (first published 1951).

—— (1968) *Identity, Youth and Crisis*, New York: W. W. Norton.

Erskine, R. G. (1975) 'The ABCs of effective psychotherapy', *Transactional Analysis Journal* 5: 163–4.

Freud, S. (1973) 'The dissection of the psychical personality', pp. 88–112 in J. Strachey (ed. and trans.), *New Introductory Lectures on Psychoanalysis, The Pelican Freud Library*, Harmondsworth: Penguin (first published 1923).

Gramsci, A. (1971) *Selections from the Prison Notebooks*, Q. Hoare and G. Nowell-Smith (eds) London: Lawrence & Wishart.

Hoggett, P. and Lousada, J. (1985) 'Therapeutic interventions in working class communities', *Free Associations* 1: 125–52.

Holland, S. (1979) 'The development of an action and counselling service in a deprived urban area', pp. 95–106 in M. Meacher (ed.) *New Methods of Mental Health Care*, London: Pergamon.

—— (1985) 'Loss, rage and oppression: neighbourhood psychotherapy with working class, black and national minority women', Paper presented at the Pam Smith Memorial Lecture, June, Polytechnic of North London.

—— (1990) 'Psychotherapy, oppression and social action: gender, race and class in black women's depression', pp. 256–69 in R. Perelberg and A. Miller (eds) *Gender and Power in Families*, London: Routledge.

Jacobs, M. (1985) *The Presenting Past*, Milton Keynes: Open University Press.

Jacoby, R. (1977) *Social Amnesia*, Hassocks: Harvester.

Jung, C. G. (1959) 'Archetypes of the collective unconscious', pp. 3–41 in H. Read, M. Fordham, G. Adler and W. McGuire (eds) *The Archetypes and the Collective Unconscious: The Collected Works*, vol. 9, part 1, London: Routledge & Kegan Paul (first published 1954).

Kelly, L. (1988) 'What's in a name? Defining child sexual abuse', *Feminist Review* 28: 65–73.

Kelly, L. and Radford, J. (1990/1991) '"Nothing really happened": the invalidation of women's experience of sexual violence', *Critical Social Policy* 30: 39–53.

Kopp, S. (1974) *If You Meet the Buddha on the Road, Kill Him!* London: Sheldon.

Lukes, S. (1974) *Power: A Radical View*, London: Macmillan.

Maslow, A. H. (1968) *Towards a Psychology of Being*, New York: Van Nostrand.

Masson, J. M. (1989) *Against Therapy*, London: Collins.

Miller, A. (1985) *Thou Shalt Not Be Aware: Society's Betrayal of the Child* (H. and H. Hannum, trans.), London: Pluto.

—— (1987a) *For Your Own Good*, London: Virago.

—— (1987b) *The Drama of Being a Child* (R. Ward, trans.), London: Virago.

—— (1990) *The Untouched Key* (H. and H. Hannum, trans.), London: Virago.

Mitchell, J. (1975) *Psychoanalysis and Feminism*, Harmondsworth: Penguin.

Moiso, C. (1985) 'Ego states and transference', *Transactional Analysis Journal* 15(3); 194–201.

Novellino, M. (1984) 'Self-analysis of countertransference in integrative Trans-actional Analysis', *Transactional Analysis Journal* 14(1): 63–7.

Rogers, C. R. (1951) *Client-centred Therapy*, London: Constable.

—— (1961) *On Becoming a Person*, London: Constable.

—— (1986) 'A client-centred/person-centred approach to therapy', pp. 197–208 in I. L. Kutash and A. Wolf (eds) *Psychotherapists' Casebook*, San Francisco, CA: Jossey-Bass.

—— (1990a) 'A theory of therapy, personality and interpersonal relationships, as developed in the client-centred framework', pp. 236–57 in H. Kirschenbaum and V. L. Henderson (eds) *The Carl Rogers Reader*, London: Constable (first published 1959).

—— (1990b) 'The necessary and sufficient conditions of therapeutic personality change', pp. 219–35 in H. Kirschenbaum and V. L. Henderson (eds) *The Carl Rogers Reader*, London: Constable (first published 1977).

—— (1990c) 'The politics of the helping professions', pp. 376–95 in H. Kirschenbaum and V. L. Henderson (eds) *The Carl Rogers Reader*, London: Constable (first published 1957).

Rowbotham, S., Segal, L. and Wainwright, H. (1980) *Beyond the Fragments*, London: Merlin.

Rutter, P. (1990) *Sex in the Forbidden Zone*, London: Unwin.

Schiff, J., Schiff, A. W., Mellor, K., Schiff, E., Schiff, S., Richman, D., Fishman, J., Wolz, D., Fishman, C. and Momb, D. (1975) *Cathexis Reader*, New York: Harper & Row.

Simons, H. (1992) 'There is no such thing as a free market', *Living Marxism* (June) 12–15.

Southwell, C. (1990) 'Touch and the psychotherapeutic relationship', Paper presented at the Conference of the Institute of Chiron Psychotherapy Centre, July, London.

Steiner, C. (1987) 'The seven sources of power: an alternative to authority', *Transactional Analysis Journal* 17: 102–4.

Stern, D. N. (1985) *The Interpersonal World of the Infant*, New York: Basic Books.

Thorne, B. (1992) *Carl Rogers*, London: Sage.

Tudor, K. and Worrall, M. (in press) 'Congruence reconsidered', *British Journal of Guidance and Counselling*.

Woodmansey, A. C. (1988) 'Are psychotherapists out of touch?', *British Journal of Psychotherapy* 5(1): 57–65.

Zaretsky, E. (1976) *Capitalism, the Family and Personal Life*, London: Pluto.

FURTHER READING

Clarkson, P. (1987) 'The bystander role', *Transactional Analysis Journal* 17(3): 82–7.

—— (1993) 'Bystander games', *Transactional Analysis Journal* 23(3): 158–72.

Hutcheon, L. (1989) *The Politics of Postmodernism*, London: Routledge.

Samuels, A. (1993) *The Political Psyche*, London: Routledge.

Chapter 23

Psychotherapeutic work with adult survivors of sexual abuse in childhood

Arnon Bentovim and Marianne Tranter

As professionals have become aware of the direct traumatic impact of child sexual abuse, there has also been a growing realisation of the potentially devastating long-term effects of such abuse on the adult life and functioning of victims of abuse, both male and female. It is thus not a question of whether sexual abuse may be traumatic, but to what extent and what are the factors which mitigate or potentiate such effects.

Until recently there has been a major process of denial of the phenomenon of sexual abuse in childhood. Herman (1981) outlined what she described as three historical 'discoveries' of the prevalence of sexual abuse in our society.

The first discovery of the awareness of the occurrence of sexual abuse as a traumatic experience is attributed to Freud's early psychoanalytic work when female patients revealed childhood sexual experiences with adult men in their families. Freud, using the notion of seduction theory, suggested that such experiences were causal of hysterical symptoms in adult life. He later identified such perpetrators as perhaps more likely to be other children, caretakers or distant relatives, not fathers, and he later repudiated seduction as a theory; instead he claimed that his patients' frequent reports of sexual abuse were incestuous fantasies rather than actual childhood events. Masson (1989) and others have traced the way in which such a view organised perceptions of psychotherapists for many years.

The second discovery of the prevalence of child sexual abuse was in the 1940s, when incest was 'discovered' by social scientists conducting large-scale survey studies of sexual practices, including the Kinsey study (Kinsey *et al.* 1953). Between 20 and 30 per cent of women reported having had a sexual experience as a child with a male, 1 per cent reporting sexual experience with a father or step-father. One researcher (Landis 1956) reported that 30 per cent of male participants in a survey reported childhood sexual experiences with an adult, again most typically male. Despite this description of the prevalence, the reality of the phenomenon continued to be denied by both the researchers and the public.

The third discovery of incest occurred during the 1970s, credited to the feminist movement and child abuse concern professionals who brought problems of childhood sexual abuse, together with other taboo issues, such as battering of women and rape, into public awareness. Undoing the historical legacy of denial is one of the major tasks for psychotherapists who are attempting to help victims become survivors, improve their mental health, their capacities to relate sexually, and to break the dangerous intergenerational cycle whereby abusive activities become re-enacted in the next generation.

RELEVANT EMPIRICAL RESEARCH

A variety of different approaches have now established the prevalence of childhood sexual abuse in both women and men. Finkelhor's (1979) classic study with college students revealed an incidence of 19 per cent of girls and 9 per cent of boys who had had a significantly stressful sexual experience in childhood. The review by Peters (1986) of prevalence studies in North America reported figures ranging from 6–62 per cent for female samples, and 3–31 per cent for male samples. The differences are often due to the way that sexual abuse was operationally defined, the types of activities, the characteristics of the sample studied and variations in research methodology.

Certain populations of patients have a higher rate of abuse, such as those with general psychiatric problems, anorexia/bulimia, self-mutilating behaviour, borderline and dissociative states and, particularly in those individuals, male and female, perpetrating abuse. Consistently 95 per cent of abusers are male (Bentovim et al. 1988), but there is a sub-group of women who themselves abuse (Finkelhor and Russell 1984; Tranter, 1992). Such women abuse alone or jointly with partners, creating a polyincestuous abusive context. There is a markedly high incidence of both sexual abuse and other forms of traumatic experiences in such individuals.

Children of all ages are abused in a ratio of about four girls to one boy. However, younger boys are relatively more at risk than younger girls, and boys are more at risk of extrafamilial abuse than girls. The oldest girl in a family is more at risk, as are children who have disabilities which render them more powerless and less able to communicate.

There is now a growing literature which is examining the longer-term effects of abuse, clinical and empirical (Haugard and Repucci 1988). Clinical descriptions include sexual dysfunction, depression, suicidality and guilt, isolation and disturbed interpersonal relationships, post-traumatic stress symptomatology, substance abuse, and other self-destructive behaviour and somatic complaints. Controlled studies demonstrate more marital and family conflicts, physical and sexual problems, adolescent turbulence, less sexual activity, greater amounts of sexual anxiety, sexual dysfunction, younger age of onset of problem drinking, more depression, lower self-esteem, less assertiveness: the (1989) study of Mullen *et al.* demonstrated a convincing link between abusive traumatic events in childhood and subsequent affective and phobic disorders in the adult life of women. Indeed, they put forward the view that the higher incidence of such disorders in adult women compared to men may be accounted for by abusive events in the childhood and adult life of women, compared to men. Watkins and Bentovim (1992) have brought together the literature describing the longer-term effects of abuse on men, and differences in abusive effects upon men and women.

TRAUMA ORGANISED SYSTEMS – A CONCEPTUAL MODEL TO UNDERSTAND THE PSYCHOPATHOLOGY AND LONGER-TERM EFFECTS OF ABUSE*

One way of understanding the longer-term effects of sexual abuse is to see it as a traumatic event which 'organises' subsequent emotional life and relationships. The notion of an organised system was introduced by Anderson *et al.* (1986). This is defined as a social action system which involves those engaged in communication about a particular problem. The language and way in which problems are communicated about creates the problem. In the sexual abuse field, a process of talking about the problem – such as Freud's first discovery – was replaced by silence. It is only following the phase of the third phase of discovery that the issue has fully been confronted and is now the subject of major communication and exploration. Sexual abuse is a traumatic event, and the way in which traumatic events are processed, and communicated about, is the heart of the problem. The way they are handled organises individual, interpersonal and professional relationships; the way they are represented or deleted from communication comes to determine the resulting system.

The notion of trauma suggests events of such intensity or violence that there is a breach in the defensive organisation of the organism. Helplessness overwhelms the individual; mastery, control and defence fail; there is a sense of unprotected disintegration, and acute mental pain. Helplessness and powerlessness thus become the central emotional experience. Sexual abuse represents often repeated overwhelming events, and represents a failure to respond to the core of the child's being.

There has to be a response to repeated trauma, and Bentovim and Kinston (1991) described a number of responses: the development of a self-sufficient shell; a compliant, clinging identification with the victim stance; or alternatively an angry identification with the abuser.

Flashbacks of the original event or avoidance of any contact which

* Bentovim and Davenport 1992; Bentovim 1992

reminds of the event can persist for many years. Feelings of guilt, soiling and disgust are common, fear maintains secrecy, disbelief and a sense of self-blame. Traumatic responses can be maintained in a frozen state for many years, and overwhelming feelings are deleted and the whole process obliterated leaving a 'hole' in the mind – a disaster to be avoided. This can orientate self-perception, relationships and personality development.

Finkelhor and Browne (1985) described the way in which such trauma-genic dynamics organise and create a style of perception and personality for the child who has been abused. Powerlessness is associated with the invasion of the body, absence of protection and repeated feelings of fear and helplessness. Stigmatisation is linked to the contempt, secrecy, blame and denigration so often associated with abuse. Betrayal through the manipulation of trust, violation of care and a lack of protection within the family unit, and traumatic sexualisation occurs through inappropriate responses being rewarded and an identification with victim or aggressor role activities often associated with gender effects.

Goldner et al. (1990) attempted to link psychodynamic social learning, sociopolitical and systemic notions to understand the development of abusive patterns of relating. The development of self and gender occurs during the same developmental phase. Abuse during childhood in addition gives rise to a conflict-laden layering of internalised self-representations that become the child and adult.

Gender is seen as a key concept in the development of self (see Chapter 5 of this Handbook). Boys construct themselves from a childhood negative – not being the mother, the primary caretaker. Gender structure in boys is thus threatened, and experiences such as separation conjure up echoes of the maternal bond. Women are seen as existing as reminders of what has to be given up. Girls, by comparison, see themselves as part of mother's psychological space; they identify, become empathic and claim their own voice by being the power behind the throne, the object of desire, or subject as object.

Marital violence is seen as an illusory way for males to seek personal power and psychic autonomy, to sustain the denial of dependence and dis-integration. Women have to submit to this reality, silencing their own voice and become organised into a cycle of violence, forgiveness and redemption.

For men who have experienced sexual abuse in childhood, the image of a child evokes their own experiences of powerlessness, sexual arousal and betrayal. An illusory way of seeking power and competence is to divest the self of traumatic experiences by projecting these onto a child. The child is perceived as the source of sexual interest, and the impulse to be sexual is felt to be beyond control, and addictive. A sexual orientation towards the child can take over the sexual life. Such an orientation can emerge during adolescence, and organise adult sexual patterns of relating. Alternatively, there may be a profound avoidance of sexuality since sexuality conjures up the same sense of powerlessness, and perhaps a profound fear of homosexuality in terms of a conviction that something special made the abuser choose them. The confusion of identity is even more profound for boys if the abuser is a woman in terms of who was the initiator, who the victim and who the victimiser.

Not all men who abuse have themselves been sexually abused, but there are frequent accounts of emotionally or physically abusive experiences in men who later abuse sexually. It may well be that the discovery of sexuality in adolescence provides an illusory way of creating emotional closeness out of a sense of profound emptiness and powerlessness.

There is a raised risk of homosexual activity as response to abuse in childhood for men. Eroticisation of abusive experiences may be a response which reduces the sense of powerlessness, stigmatisation and betrayal which organises thinking and feelings.

In girls who have been abused, through their identification with mother's role, they develop a conviction of being the cause of their own abuse. They are blamed for their sexual attractiveness by the perpetrator and they blame themselves. This leads to a feeling of stigmatisation, betrayal and/or powerlessness, leading to self-destructive action, anorexia/bulimia, self-mutilation and profound deficits of self-esteem, depressive mood and the danger of taking victim roles.

It is striking that the majority of women who abuse have been abused sexually themselves, but only a small proportion of women who have had abusive experiences do perpetrate abuse themselves. There is a clinical impression that women who do abuse have often been inducted into active roles, with siblings in a polyincestuous family contact. Again, as in boys, there may be an eroticisation of abuse experienced with perverse role development which encapsulates the abusive experience and maintains it in an addictive fashion.

The interlocking choice of partners is often striking. Mothers of children who have been abused by their partners describe a high level of sexual and physical abuse themselves, and both mothers and abusive fathers describe childhoods with few happy memories. Whether this is because men with an abusive orientation instinctively sense which potential partners with children can be organised into a compliant mode, or whether this is on a mutual unconscious basis, is not clear.

However, studies on families where abuse has occurred (Madonna et al. 1991) reveal that such families are characterised by high levels of marital dysfunction, parents focused on their own needs rather than their children's, being emotionally unavailable to their children; and children expected to comply with adult needs.

What becomes clear is that sexual abuse occurs in highly dysfunctional contexts, and that as a result the thinking, feeling and actions of children who are subjected to rejection, physical, emotional and sexual abuse render them vulnerable to future victim or perpetrator behaviour. There are likely to be profound effects on their functioning, self-esteem, sexual functioning, and their ability to become partners or to parent. The meaning attributed to the self is profoundly affected, and therapeutic work with such individuals has to take a broad-based view.

THE THERAPEUTIC PROCESS IN WORKING WITH THE LONGER-TERM EFFECTS OF CHILD SEXUAL ABUSE

Working with the longer-term effects of child sexual abuse into adult life implies the following:

1 The original 'frozen' effects of sexual abuse have to be processed on both an emotional and cognitive level. The core sexually abusive experience needs to be fully disclosed and shared, and a variety of therapeutic approaches are often needed to accomplish this task.
2 The effects of such experiences on the development of the individual has to be tracked, on the sort of man or woman they have become, the degree in which particular roles as partners and/or parents occur; adult functioning in the sexual field, in the relationship field, relationships with men, with women; the development of the self in terms of capacities needs to be addressed; and assessment of unrealised potential.
3 There is no one therapeutic modality which will achieve all these goals, nor therapeutic style. Just as working with sexual abuse in childhood demands individual, family and group work, with a variety of approaches – psychodynamic, behavioural, psycho-educational (Bentovim *et al.* 1988) – so work with those adults who have been abused in childhood requires a variety of therapeutic contexts and therapeutic modalities.

Draucker (1992) describes the following stages:

1 disclosing the experience of child sexual abuse;
2 focusing on the abuse experience itself;
3 addressing the context of the sexual abuse;
4 focusing on current desired life changes;
5 resolving issues of abuse.

These represent helpful stages of therapeutic work.

Disclosing an experience of child sexual abuse

Although currently an increasing number of survivors of abuse are explicitly seeking therapeutic help – for example, following accounts in the media – many cases still present in a hidden way. Both individuals seeking therapeutic help for the distressing effects of their abuse, and those who may be less aware of the connection between current symptomatology and previous experiences, may be testing the capacity of the psychotherapist to be able to hear, understand and respond in an appropriate way to such experiences. The psychotherapist's capacity to hear and know about the possibility of abuse is a major factor in the discovery of abusive experiences. Many individuals previously reported the disbelief of their psychotherapists, and the perpetuation of blame for their own abuse through the interpretation of incestuous wishes. This reinforces the attribution of guilt and responsibility for the adult's sexual interest towards them as children.

A therapeutic context of silence and waiting for disclosure may itself re-create an abusive context and reinforce the silence which accompanied abuse. Many survivors of abuse describe the silence and the secrecy of their abuse, the father who comes in the night, the silence that is taken as consent. A therapeutic silence may trigger the sense of helplessness, powerlessness and even the flashbacks of the memories of abuse that characterise the longer-term effects. Not surprisingly, the patient or client then leaves feeling retraumatised by the psychotherapist.

Children who have been abused report a positive response to a therapeutic stance which joins with them, leads rather than follows, gives them a structure of questions and activities rather than leaving uncomfortable silences. This reflects the qualities of non-possessive warmth and accurate empathy which characterise good therapeutic work (Monck *et al.* 1993). The issue is to find a therapeutic approach which meets the needs of known traumatised individuals, and also encourages the disclosure of those who may have been traumatised. It is not surprising in this particular field that group work, self-help groups and survivor groups have had an important developmental role since they conquer the sense of aloneness, isolation and conviction of responsibility for their own abuse.

Disclosing sexual abuse

Such are the multiple effects of abuse in men and women that a screening approach is necessary for the many different presentations. Direct, blunt questions such as 'Were you a victim of incest or sexual abuse?' are not helpful. It is far more useful to ask questions such as: 'Many more people with complaints similar to yours are telling us about distressing or uncomfortable experiences in their childhood – experiences which they often found themselves thinking about, and being cross that the thoughts about it remain. Have you had such experiences? As a child, for instance, were you touched in a way that felt uncomfortable, embarrassing, even frightening? As a child did anybody ever ask you to do something sexual that you did not like? Were you hurt in a sexual way? If something like that had happened would it be worse if it was somebody close in the family or someone more distant? What would be the effect of revealing something of this nature at the time or now?'

If there is a denial but if the psychotherapist feels that there are strong possibilities of abuse, it may be helpful in recalling the effects of abuse to ask about and explore such possibilities, but without the force and conviction which can inappropriately 'lead' the patient. Ellenson (1990) suggested that the following should be explored as being possibly connected with abuse:

1 nightmares of recurring catastrophe; nightmares or dreams which describe harm to the self or children, death or violent scenes;
2 intrusive obsessions – for example, to hurt one's child, to feel one's child is endangered;
3 dissociative sensations, feeling that one is a child, or one's self is experienced as a stranger, feelings of being 'spaced out';
4 persistent fears of being alone, or in physically compromising situations;
5 a variety of perceptual disturbances such as illusions of an evil entity being present; auditory phenomena being called out to; intrusion of sounds;
6 visual or tactile hallucinations, movement of objects in the peripheral vision, feelings of being touched or thrown down.

These are all reminiscent of abusive experiences which have been partially 'deleted' from consciousness – the return of the repressed.

Disclosing abuse for men is particularly difficult because of the powerful fears of homosexuality associated with their being chosen as a sexual object, in many cases by men. Associated with this is a fear of not fulfilling a masculine image, or the reverse effect, identification with the aggressor, and adopting a 'hyper'-male invulnerable stance and the development of an abusive orientation. Being treated as a thing can result in a compliant response, an angry, battling, manipulative response, or an invulnerable stonewall response reminiscent of some descriptions of borderline personality.

Struve (1990) pointed to the following issues in the abuse of males. It is necessary to think of the possibility of abuse when the following patterns are noted:

1 Dynamics of shame, based on the perceived failure to protect oneself, or the desire to achieve revenge. This can have a very real and dangerous effect; e.g., a boy of twelve who had been abused by a man who had befriended him. Some three years later such was the intensity of his feeling of shame and desire for revenge that he killed the man in a way which had obviously been planned over a period of time. A major sense of rage and angry outbursts may be associated with such experiences of abuse.
2 Major difficulties occurring with male identity, including avoiding behaviour, which may be associated with body sensations of head or body parts shrinking. The avoidance of behaviour which may be perceived as feminine, including emotional intimacy, may also be noted.

3 Difficulties with sexual identity due to fears of being perceived as passive, or associated with sexual arousal triggered by a member of the same sex.

4 Denial of feelings, a sense of unreality and invulnerability, minimisation of the effects of any contact which is reported. There is frequently a report of less traumatisation by men who have been abused by women, perhaps related to the notion that sex with an older woman is a 'macho' privilege. Associated with such a sense of invulnerability may be very poor social functioning.

Therapeutic responses to disclosure

It is essential for the psychotherapist to respond in an appropriate way when a disclosure is made. The disclosure should not be responded to as a surprise; emotional support should be given, and links made between such experiences when revealed and current disturbances in an appropriately tested way. The opportunity should be taken to point out how such childhood responses and feelings can persist in a more or less repressed way. Also an explanation needs to be given that talking and remembering is painful, and that there may well be a period of regression following the initial relief at having shared a long-standing painful matter. Tolerating memories and returning reminiscences whilst matters are talked through will require a good deal of strength and support, but is the route to real forgetting.

Without real forgetting it can be asserted that memories will recur unexpectedly; they will be triggered by somebody who looks like, or reminds the patient of, places, people and events. Thus a world of fear is created rather than one which can be controlled. Remembering, working through and 'forgetting', or at least placing in a known area of mastery, with some of the major painful affect removed, is the aim of therapeutic work. Understanding the confusions and avoidances often associated with current relationships, sexual dysfunction, parenting and partner difficulties can make a tremendous difference. It can be pointed out that the aim is 'to develop a coherent narrative of one's life, rather than one broken up with major areas of pain, distress and deletion, literally to fill the holes in the mind' (Bentovim and Kinston 1991: 284).

Such explanations form a part of the initial therapeutic contract in that it spells out the task. Until there is further exploration of the extent of abuse it is difficult to estimate the intensity of therapeutic work that would be required. There should be a contract of regular work; the individual should be living in a safe context in terms of the availability of social support outside the therapeutic context. Significant others in their lives should know that support is necessary, and enough of the reason to understand the process. There are major advantages in family meetings – for example, with siblings, supportive parents, partners and children – so that there can be proper explanations given for what is happening, and if necessary joint meetings to explore issues which are focused on the links between past and present.

Specific tasks in therapeutic work

Reviewing experiences

It is essential early in the therapeutic process that a detailed description of abusive experiences is shared. This means reviewing the duration and frequency of abuse, identity of the offender(s), the form of abuse and method used to carry out abuse – use of physical force, methods to achieve and maintain silence. Types of sexual activity need to be explored, and it is important to ask about all sexual activities which are possible with children in a way which implies that the psychotherapist is aware that children are involved in all forms of sexual activity. The psychotherapist may well need to explore such matters gently but confidently, so that the patient does not have a projected fear that the psychotherapist cannot hear or bear to think of such possibilities. The ages of child and offender need to be explored.

Contextual matters also need to be explored, which include the role of other family members in the abuse, or their response to attempts at disclosure. If disclosure did occur, what happened, how did other members of the family respond? Who was protective, comforting, blaming? Did the offender take responsibility? What happened then? Were there other important family matters in context? How did the patient make sense of what was happening, both the abuse and responses to it?

It is helpful to have such information in a factual way and to be clear that this information will form the basis of the exploration of associated feelings and beliefs which developed and which persist. Getting such information in a non-emotional way is important, and the notion of 'assumptive interviewing' is helpful in such an exploration.

Assumptive interviewing implies that the interviewer has a detailed knowledge about abusive activities, so that if the patient talks about a digital touch in the vaginal area it may be appropriate to ask not only, 'Did he touch you with any other part, such as his penis?', but 'How long was it before he started to use his penis?'

Investigative interviewing techniques need to be more cautious; for example, when interviewing children the questions would be, 'Did he touch you with any other part of his body?' rather than making assumptions about a penile touch. But to trigger memories the possibility of the fact has to be raised; also all possibilities need to be explored – oral, anal, genital – all possible abusers need also to be explored, and any use of threats, bribery, force and so on.

Exploration of feelings

It is almost inevitable that in the exploration of what actually happened, feelings will undoubtedly be aroused and such explorations can themselves be therapeutic. The essential task in exploration of feelings is to process the event emotionally in a similar way to the processing of traumatic events involved in post-traumatic phenomena. This implies the retelling of events in an emotionally supportive context to separate the event from the overwhelming accompanying defects.

Sharing feelings has a cathartic effect and can also begin to help process matters cognitively. This implies the re-editing of the distortions involved in abuse through retelling. An adult conversation automatically re-edits experiences and beliefs which emerge from childhood. Internalised conversations and beliefs about such events and about the self may have persisted for many years (White 1989). White and his colleagues introduced techniques to externalise such conversations, rather than to maintain internalised dialogues and narratives. They point out that techniques such as the following may be helpful in co-constructing a new reality and understanding:

1 Were there days you did not feel that way about what happened to you? What did you do, or what did somebody else do, that managed to make you feel differently? What could you do now that could have the same effect, and find an 'exception'?
2 Are there days when you feel more powerful than the abuse experiences, when you know that you are in control of it rather than it being in control of you? What do you do on those days that seems to make a difference?
3 If a miracle happened and all these memories and distressing events were no longer to be in control of your life, how would you know that it was the case? What would be the signs?
4 When patients report feeling less anxious, more of a survivor, they may be asked, 'When did you first realise, perhaps even years ago, you had it in you to recover, even though you felt so overwhelmed by such events for many years?'

This approach to constructing a new reality has an important application to many areas of developing survival rather than victim roles.

The advantages of doing such work in a group context may be considerable. Such groups may need to be single-sex, with individuals sharing similar experiences. They need to be theme-centred, or task-structured so that a clear brief can be developed in terms of encouraging participants to be open about experiences, to share, support and confront when necessary, and to look at specific issues in a variety of ways.

There is a major drive towards self-help survivor groups, which may indeed be extremely valuable. But it may be more difficult for such non-led groups to confront issues such as the attachment to abusers, sexual responses and wishes to resolve and forgive. Such groups can maintain a sense of anger, outrage and revenge which may give solidarity to other members of the group, but may be destructive to the individual who wishes to move on.

Dealing with traumagenic effects

Recalling experiences and discussing the details, and the feelings associated with abusive experience, will re-evoke the feelings themselves. The traumagenic effects of sexualisation, powerlessness, betrayal and stigmatisation will reveal themselves in self-description of relationship, reflected within transference/counter-transference responses with the psychotherapist, in the interactional patterns revealed between partners, and within the current and extended family revealed in family meetings.

The advantage of group contexts to share and confront traumagenic dynamic effects is very considerable. Finding a similarity of responses, and seeing reflections and mirroring, can help define them as 'not only me' responses and can begin to trigger 'new' conversations and narratives of the self as powerful, confident, normally sexual and a survivor, not a victim. Responses within the one-to-one therapeutic setting can elicit profound reflections of traumagenic effects. Indeed, there is a danger of a psychotic transference formation. The advantage of a face-to-face approach in dealing with these feelings is considerable in terms of being able to modulate and help containment rather than an escalating runaway effect.

Cole and Barney (1987) described two phases of the 'stress response cycle', and the way intense emotional responses can be regulated, to cope with severe emotional responses. These are as follows:

1 *Denial phase*: this is characterised by amnesia, repression, minimisation, withdrawal.
2 *Intrusive phase*: this is one of intense affect, perceptual experiences, hallucinations, nightmares associated with tremors, sweating, re-experiencing.

There is a therapeutic need to maintain a balance using what Cole and Barney described as the 'window' between the two states to make the situation manageable. Group work can help break through the denial phase, but may reinforce the intrusive phase. There is a need to develop coping techniques, and to structure sessions to maintain an appropriate degree of containment.

A progressive toleration of the memories of experiences and their associated affects is a key in the therapeutic process itself and the move towards survival. It is important that patients should know what to expect, and should be helped to feel in control to be able to take matters at their own pace, yet to be encouraged to move forward. Crisis services may need to be in place, linking with family and extended support networks during this phase.

The management of traumatic symptomatology

General aspects

The importance of describing and locating traumatic responses such as flashbacks is to help not to suppress them, but to recapture the original experience so that there can be a working through. This is essential in the coming to terms with the victimisation experience. However, techniques may need to be developed to help maintain control. These include the following:

(a) *Control techniques*: e.g., grounding techniques. This can consist of planting the feet firmly on the floor, grasping the chair, focusing on breathing, perhaps by breathing out and letting anxiety out by counting to three. Developing an internal conversation which asserts that one is in the present not the past.

(b) *Self-hypnotic techniques*: associated with this may be the teaching of self-hypnotic/relaxation techniques. The 'ten steps down' induction process, associated with sitting in a comfortable seat with control levers to take control of the situation, can be a helpful way of gaining control. Other possibilities are the notion of finding a warm, comfortable space to assist in coping, which has been found particularly useful when there is an urge to self-mutilate.

(c) *Cognitive techniques* restructure flashbacks and nightmares by, for instance, changing the ending, bringing in a protector in imagination.

(d) *Role-play psychodramatic techniques and/or re-editing techniques*: such techniques may be used in groups, families or individual contexts. They are intended to re-edit the context in which the traumatic symptoms originated by literally bringing in the abusing parent in imagination, role-play, the Gestalt empty chair, through letters, art forms, simulated conversations, or the use of non-verbal sculpting.

These are all means of re-editing, changing realities, creating a different belief or reality structure.

In dealing with emotional responses and/or traumatic effects, it is essential to maintain both a 'symptomatic' and 'systemic' approach. Although traumatic events have an organising effect on relationships, undoubtedly current relationships also reorganise and reshape experiences and responses. Making major changes for the individual in symptom control, re-editing or restructuring can be very valuable, but it is also important to bear in mind the way in which current relationships may have been shaped, choices of partners made, or even responses induced in the other, which can all have a reinforcing and maintaining affect on symptomatic patterns.

It is important to maintain a systemic view at all times which considers the living context and relationships of the patient, and the effects of change: improvements, worsening, competence and incompetence. Work with partners may well be indicated. Such responses include the way in which the psychotherapist is made to feel, or find themselves reflecting some of the processes. The importance of supervision and training aspects of this work cannot be stressed too greatly.

Specific traumatic symptomatology

Self-destructive behaviour

Mutilation, overdosing and substance abuse are all ways of 'avoiding' painful affects and memories by creating perhaps other sources of pain or escape. It is essential to be able to use symptomatic approaches to take control, but also to be aware of long-standing patterns of response in significant others. Similar methods need to be used to deal with self-destructive behaviour as with any other symptom as described above; for example, control techniques, cognitive, hypnotic, role-plays, re-editing, and working with the individual and significant others.

Aggression against others

Distress is an affect which can be described with ease by women, but far less easily by men. Anger is a far more difficult emotion to help women express initially, whereas for men this may have already been institutionalised as an interactional mode. Bruckner and Johnson (1987) described within male survivor groups the problem that, after disclosure, men made plans for retribution, physical assault and validation of anger. It is essential to confront and help individuals be aware of the very major danger to themselves of such assaults.

The role of retaliation as a post-traumatic effect is now being increasingly well recognised. Powerful emotional responses emerging as anger need to be managed, facilitating the development of the verbal expression of anger and the constructive use of assertion.

Substance abuse

Substance abuse, as already indicated, is an aspect of self-destructiveness based in poor self-esteem. To admit powerlessness in the face of alcohol and substance abuse may be a major problem, since it confirms the original sense of powerlessness associated with abuse. To help patients admit that they are powerless in the face of alcohol may be the first step towards taking control of the abuse itself. Alcoholics Anonymous can provide a major support for such problems, but individuals need to be aware that they will be asked to tell their stories and helped to decide how much and what is appropriate to say in the context of the AA groups. The use of detoxification as a part of the treatment will also be essential.

General self-care

A key role in the long-term effects of abuse is around the focus of self-care. There may be a drive towards obsessive, perfectionistic approaches; alternatively, the disguise of any attractiveness, whether in women or men. Women wear clothes that cover themselves up, making themselves deliberately unattractive. Group members can give positive feedback in a variety of ways, and help with self-esteem, gradual acceptance of the body and an increasing sense of attractiveness and sexuality.

Body image problems are associated with anorexia/bulimia (Oppenheimer et al. 1985), and may represent a form of avoidance, of oral reminders of abuse. Anorexic responses mean that one area of life, the body, is controlled; but feelings of the body, being the 'cause' of the abuser's interest, remain.

The link between eating disorders, the emotional aspects of borderline states as described in DSM III and early traumatic experiences is now being convincingly demonstrated.

COGNITIVE PROCESSING OF SEXUALLY ABUSIVE EXPERIENCES

The traumagenic dynamic effects which have been outlined in children and young people have a major organising effect on the young person and future adult's view of themselves. There is a maintenance of the child's views and beliefs concerning the events – such as they were to blame, they are bad, dirty, responsible for the adult's interest in them, or that any sexual responses on their part confirm their sense of responsibility.

Children generally, in fact, have fairly clear views at the time of the abuse that the abuse is not their responsibility. It may well be that secrecy or failure to process experiences can gradually result in an increasing sense of responsibility for their own abuse. Abuse may represent affection or attention. They may feel that this is a form of sacrifice of their own lives to benefit their families. A small proportion of children (5–15 per cent) feel that the abuse was a positive aspect of their lives, a normal part of family life. There may be positive feelings about the abuse earlier on, but with later development in adult life the individual may feel to be in a different role to contemporaries. A young girl of twelve felt that her father's abuse of her was a major source of affection. Later she felt outraged at the degree of his betrayal when she discovered herself to be very different from her peers. She had sexual needs they did not, she became pregnant and angry with herself. Fundamental beliefs about self and the meaning of events require a good deal of processing and reframing.

Changing fundamental beliefs: reframing abusive experiences

There are a variety of corrective questioning techniques which can be valuable in cognitively processing abusive experiences and leading to a more functional set of beliefs. Circular questioning, future questioning, questioning expecting a variety of responses can achieve these goals. A young person of fifteen felt that her parents would not have continued abusing her seriously if they had realised that it was wrong. She felt that if they had known they would have stopped. She was asked: if she had read her story in a newspaper, then hypothetically what would she say – would she say the young person was responsible? Feel angry with the parents? Introducing other realities helped her re-edit her own self. A more formal approach to achieve this goal is cognitive restructuring (Jehu 1988).

Cognitive restructuring

Jehu's approach consists of the following:

1 Giving an understanding of the way that events and experiences can result in a variety of unhelpful beliefs.
2 Identifying the beliefs that automatically accompany cues and feelings. This may require a variety of approaches, relaxation, imagery to re-experience, description of flashbacks. All these trigger beliefs; e.g., about being responsible for the adult's sexual interest in them; that there will never be a possibility of feeling sexually towards a peer; that being abused creates a sense of dirt, worthlessness, inevitable damage. Out of such responses it is possible to outline beliefs and distortions.
3 Exploring alternatives. Using a variety of resources such as videos, written information, assertions, information from other group members, the patient is encouraged to explore alternative beliefs, to build up a different view of themselves, and to experiment with their new beliefs.

Structured group approaches

A similar approach has been developed in what has been described as a psycho-educational group approach, although there is often a combination of dynamic group therapeutic approaches together with a more cognitive psycho-educational approach. There are a variety of models used in such groups, but the majority follow a more or less structured theme in terms of topics to be discussed and ways of working. They may use experiential techniques, maybe watching videos, role play, Gestalt techniques, empty chairs, writing letters to abusers, re-enacting and re-editing experiences; exploring topics such as mothers' attitudes, the abuser's attitudes, sibling attitudes, exploring issues of self-protection and difficulties of being able to protect; issues of relationships with same and opposite sex; sex education, sexual anxieties, the care of children, heterosexual and homosexual issues.

Such issues may, of course, come up spontaneously, but it may well be helpful to have a series of themes and different ways of exploring them.

THE THERAPIST ROLE AND RESPONSES

Using a clearly structured approach with a sense of purpose, an approach which understands the processes and follows through themes in a logical fashion can maintain the task of emotional and cognitive processing. The use of male and female co-therapy teams in working with families and groups may help both to enact and deal with re-experiencing within the patient–psychotherapist relationship by offering a model of a consistent male and female partnership.

At the same time, whatever approach is used – group context, individual or family work of a structured nature, a non-directive approach relying on the development of transference/counter-transference – the original traumatic experience may well be re-created and re-experienced. Patients who have been abused are often exquisitely sensitive to the therapeutic atmosphere. Feelings of rejection or abuse may be re-experienced, responses from the psychotherapist may be interpreted as enactments of abusive relationships. The sex of the psychotherapist can bring forth stereotypes of maleness and femaleness depending on how the self and other have been structured through early experience. Breaks, interruptions, time issues, all confirm feelings of powerlessness and betrayal, and the appropriate interpretations may have mutative effects.

Psychotherapists often require consultation to deal with the identification with the patient's sense of despair, damage, feelings of being soiled, sexual responses and confusion that may be experienced by the psychotherapist. Whatever may be traumatising to the patient can also awaken and put psychotherapists in touch with their own traumatic experiences. Such reflections can both help in terms of an understanding of a patient's experience, and can also have its own devastating effect. The bringing forth of responses and fantasies of a disturbing nature for psychotherapists is also a by-product of dealing with adult survivors. Transference responses which can move from neurotic to psychotic need careful monitoring.

Family work benefits greatly from having live supervision or a reflective team, but the need for openness between the observing team and the family is an essential part to avoid feelings of being traumatised through a fear of voyeurism and excitement; for example, the use by Anderson *et al.* (1986) of the reflective team.

It is also possible for psychotherapists who work extensively in this field to feel burnt-out and overwhelmed, and unable to respond to patients' distress, or to minimise and disregard feelings and experiences. When this occurs psychotherapists need the support of a team, and the opportunity for a variety of work to counter the pervasive effects of traumatic experiences and effects and supervision.

Filling the hole in the mind which is created in the face of overwhelming stress by remembering, reminiscing and working through is a highly stressful experience for both patient and psychotherapist, and needs to be held and contained towards resolution.

Dealing with the context of abuse

It is essential that connections are made between previous experiences, the way in which they have been processed and the way in which this affects current life. This is part of the process of exploring the context of the abuse rather than personal response to it.

Exploring past contexts

There are a variety of ways of exploring the original family contexts which may have played an important role in the creation of traumagenic dynamic effects. Such exploration plays an important part in the resolution of persisting feeling states. This includes explorations through geneograms with the individual and/or the convening of meetings with original family members. An example is the case described by Bentovim and Davenport (1992) of a woman abused in childhood who had a meeting with her male siblings who, it turned out, had also been abused, although less seriously, then had subsequent meetings with her mother and finally with the abuser.

Bentovim *et al.* (1988) described a sequence of treatment stages in working with the family. This commences with working on the relationship with the mother. She is often felt to have played a key role in terms of the feeling of betrayal, not listening or hearing. Work with siblings is also important in terms of the resolution of emotional cut-offs.

Work with the abuser is very much to do with final resolution of abusive experiences. This may require specific work with the abuser to assess whether there is any possibility of such a meeting. The question has to be asked: can the abuser take responsibility for his abusive action and make a real apology to the individual who has been abused?

Meetings without preparation can be counter-productive, in the sense that fresh rejection and denial can occur. Old alliances and blaming of the adult who has been abused in childhood can renew a sense of helplessness and powerlessness. It is often necessary to do some extensive individual and family work with family members to co-construct a more satisfactory resolution.

The alternative is to use a variety of techniques within a peer group or with the psychotherapist to look at previous relationships; for example, using sculpting, non-verbal techniques, using the empty chair, letters, role plays, and creating a different belief system in terms of views of self and experiences.

Current issues

Self-esteem

Self-esteem is one of the major personal issues which survivors have to deal with. Dealing with guilt and shame, the process of listening, sharing experiences, change of attributions and beliefs regarding the abuse, all play an important role in building self-esteem. A variety of different interventions are often necessary, ranging from cognitive restructuring in terms of deeply held negative views of self as worthless, blameworthy or soiled. The routine use of positive statements to one another in groups can be a helpful reinforcer in terms of building on small changes that have been made; the seeking for exceptions and exploring how this came about in order to co-construct and reconstruct different realities of the self; for example, days when the individuals felt good about themselves.

Interpersonal functioning

There are some basic major issues of interpersonal functioning which need to be considered, which include the development of trust, maintaining appropriate boundaries between self and other, maintaining an appropriate affective contact with others, and dealing with important issues such as parenting and partnering, particularly sexuality and sexual relationships.

Such issues need to be dealt with in a variety of different contexts. Trust arises through the therapeutic process itself in terms of the consistency and appropriate response of individual psychotherapists, or within group and family contexts. Work needs to be done with the individual and significant others in his or her life, whether these be partners or family members, where appropriate. It is likely that the traumagenic effects will translate into structural family interactional patterns. Even if the individual has dealt with some of the personal traumatic issues, this may be insufficient to change the interpersonal structural responses once they have been initiated. Thus marital psychotherapy and more extensive family therapy is often necessary to deal with these issues.

Sexuality and sexual functioning in women

There can frequently be an extensive abusive effect on the capacity to function sexually. There are major differences between a sexual relationship which was not sought, and one which is freely entered. Sexual contact of any nature can trigger off experiences of powerlessness or flashbacks of inappropriate experiences, and lead to major avoidance. Women need to deal with a number of stereotypes which exist in any case in society; for example, women's roles to 'please men', to be submissive, are all reinforced by abusive experiences and traumagenic dynamic effects of abuse. Such beliefs need to be changed in a variety of ways, whether this be in group contexts, individual or couples therapy.

There may need to be a classic Masters and Johnson's programme, followed by couples therapy, to help a woman regain a sense of sexual freedom and control, and to begin to change the context. It is important to ensure that those individuals who have developed a homosexual orientation are helped to reinforce their choice of partner, but at the same time to ensure that appropriate attention is paid to the re-enactment of victim/perpetrator roles within the relationship.

One of the most difficult issues for women to deal with is the fact that a sexual response can be brought forward in the sexually abusive context and may have a major effect on sexual orientation for women; for example, choice of partner, sexual response patterns and experiences. This may well be one of the most difficult issues to discuss within group contexts because it would imply acceptance and even a compliant response to abuse. Psychotherapists, whether in group contexts or individually, need to be able to show an understanding and almost an assumption that such responses are possible, and to expect sexuality to be shaped by an abusive experience.

Although the adoption of a sexually abusive role for women is a less frequent response than for men, it has now been recognised that it does occur and must be acknowledged. Work with such women needs to follow a similar sequence to work with men; for instance, identifying the cycle of abuse, what triggers an abusive impulse, the nature of abusive actions, what follows abusive action, masturbatory reinforcement, and the connection to abusive experiences.

Adult experiences may also be processed through an internal 'conversation' which leads to the development of perverse sexuality and the eroticisation of abusive context. A woman in her thirties described a split way of relating to her husband, the father of her children, who was non-sexual and caring and looked after her and her children, and her exciting lover, who was not at all parental but with whom there was an intensity of relating, considerable excitement and arousal accompanied by sadistic fantasies of a beating nature. She was a woman who had been abused more by the intense interest and voyeuristic behaviour of her step-father, and later physical contact. She was able to 'resolve' her split following an extensive piece of therapeutic work by finding a partner who 'brought together' the two men into one. She had also been able to write to her brother, to 'construct' a narrative which made sense of her experiences.

Male sexuality and sexual functioning

The sexual responses of males to victimisation is, in many ways, similar to the responses of female survivors, such as the feelings of avoidance, the danger of intense eroticisation of experiences. Flashbacks and memories of abuse may be transformed through masturbation to sexually active arousal patterns and may trigger the sexualisation of other children. Powerlessness is a particular danger for men, and power is regained by abusing others in a retaliatory fashion. There may be the reverse – total avoidance or a passive, victimised response.

The fact of being abused generally by somebody of the same sex brings in the issues of conflict with the general societal view that males are not victims. The link with later homosexual patterns and major problems of sexual identity are also evident. A form of abuse which is perhaps not so explicit is the cross-dressing of boys by mothers who both pour themselves into their child and have an intense wish for a female child. This is a common pattern (for example, Green and Money 1961; Stoller 1968) in transvestism and possibly transsexualism, with far more profound issues of identity.

The danger for men of developing a violently aggressive sexual pattern, an abuser pattern towards other children or a rapist's profile is a very real risk depending on the particular context in which the boy has grown up (Watkins and Bentovim 1992). For men, as with both sexes, dealing with sexual problems requires an exploration of orientation; understanding the details of sexual avoidance and sexual dysfunction; exploring the details of impotence, ejaculation failures, non-responsiveness or hyper-responsiveness; a detailed examination of behavioural patterns, sexual preference, use of pornography, masturbatory patterns, and an examination of both the victim cycle in terms of the response within sexual encounter, and abusive cycles if they have been initiated.

The importance of partner work where sexual dysfunction has become part of a couple's problem is important for both men and women, and it is necessary to look at various contexts to work in, such as groups for men who have been abused and have begun an offending pattern. Most practitioners feel that it is preferable to commence by working on offender patterns, before dealing with issues of empathy for victims and victim experiences. A variety of cognitive behavioural programmes, group work approaches, have been devised to 'process' and construct more functional sexual patterns.

Forgiveness and resolution

It can be helpful to work with the extended and current family in group contexts so that those who have abused take responsibility either directly or by proxy through re-enactment, role play or psychodramatic techniques. In any therapeutic process the act of forgiveness and understanding something of what led to abuse is an essential component of resolution. It is impossible to do so at an early stage in therapeutic work, and abusers who ask their victims to 'forgive them' may compound an abusive situation.

Also what can be helpful is for an abuser to say 'sorry' for any act on their part. We have found it helpful with abusers who have 'forgotten', repressed or deleted their own abusive actions, to say that they had forgotten what happened, but they are sorry for any act which they did commit. This sometimes enables situations to move on and for the possibility of the establishment of a new situation. A failure to resolve or begin to understand and forgive can have an entirely negative effect on recovery from abuse. Long-standing grievances can have a 'corrosive' effect on the self and relatedness. To be healthy and feel undamaged implies that the abuse was not so bad; it is better to be angry and feed grievances. The use of a variety of group and family contexts to 'enact' the abuser's guilt, 'grieving' the loss or absence of a caring parent, may all assist resolution.

Research on the outcome of therapeutic work with survivors of abuse is very much in its infancy. We know very little about the long-term effects of specifically organised treatment programmes since they have come into being so very recently. It is essential that we do a variety of different outcome research to know what components are the most helpful, and with whom (see Chapter 3 of this *Handbook*). It would be helpful to know who can be best helped through group work, individual work, a psychodynamic approach, a cognitive-behavioural approach, self-help groups, leader-led groups, the use of enactment, role play and psychodramatic techniques.

One suspects that carrying out such research would be extremely difficult because almost inevitably each group of practitioners who have developed and practised a particular approach to psychotherapeutic work will inevitably use what they are familiar and comfortable with.

It would be valuable if the different elements of a therapeutic programme could be looked at critically, and that there could be some agreement to be pragmatic in terms of what actually works and is helpful.

The impact on mental health of early sexual abuse is considerable, and deserves the attention now being given to the topic.

CASE STUDY: JANE

Jane, a teacher aged forty-five, referred herself to Marianne Tranter on the recommendation of a friend who had consulted her in the past.

At the first meeting Jane sketched out her current difficulties: she was cohabiting with Giles, a musician aged forty-eight with whom she had a relationship of two years' standing. Although Jane felt basically happy with Giles, she experienced some anxiety/aversive responses during lovemaking which had led her increasingly to avoid sexual contact and situations which might lead to sex, such as ordinary affectionate contact. This was creating a significant strain on the relationship, and Jane was increasingly fearful of losing Giles whom she described as 'very attractive (to women) and highly-sexed'.

Jane, mindful of this, therefore tried to overcome her apprehension of sexual contact, feeling she owed Giles a 'sexual outlet' or else he might seek one elsewhere. However, in accommodating Giles in this way she was at the same time feeling considerable resentment towards him and was also doubting herself as woman, feeling very much a failure.

In subsequent weekly sessions the following information emerged. Jane's parents had separated when Jane was three and her sister Deborah was five. Their mother, Mary, subsequently met and married Stephen, who joined the household when the girls were seven and nine and became their step-father. Within a year it became customary for the girls to have a Sunday morning 'cuddle' in the parents' bed – an experience which was remembered as 'horrid' by Jane. She began to remember with more clarity what happened: her step-father would have one girl sit next to him whilst the other sat next to mother. When it was Jane's turn, he would stroke her thighs and vaginal area and digitally penetrate her. Because of his forceful personality, although Jane tried to avoid this contact and wriggle away, he would pull her back and glare at her, making her feel terrified to say anything. She had to appear as though nothing was wrong; she was very puzzled as to whether or not her mother knew and had never felt able to tell her. She was very aware as a child of her mother's dependence on Stephen; the marriage was sometimes violent and Stephen drank excessively on occasion but her mother always appeared to make allowances for him.

Jane wondered whether her sister suffered in the same way when she was next to step-father – but she gave no clue and Jane felt unable to ask her.

Eventually, when Jane was thirteen, her mother and step-father separated. Her mother had several other partners and always enjoyed going out, even though she and her daughters were living in virtual poverty and Jane could remember having to hide from bailiffs and debt collectors.

Jane left home as a young adult and, after having one or two boyfriends, married at twenty-three. Her husband (a doctor) was very demanding sexually, and Jane assumed that she should comply with his demands because that was expected of her. She was unable to express some of her negative feelings about their sexual relationship. Her husband became very impatient with her and rather intolerant, and undermined her. She developed a depressive state, the relationship deteriorated and eventually they separated, with her husband forming a new relationship with one of Jane's friends. Jane had various other fairly short-term relationships, interspersed with periods of living on her own. She had good, close contact with a circle of women friends, although in some ways found herself seeking in them some of the closeness she felt she lacked with her mother and sister (who both emigrated fifteen years before to America).

She had had a very difficult and ambivalent relationship with her mother whom she felt had betrayed her. She could acknowledge angry feelings towards her for having 'allowed' her abuse by her stepfather, and never having stuck up for her (Jane) or herself. She could remember the fuss her mother would make of him and other male partners and her fear of being alone.

She felt her mother had over-accommodated the men in her life for fear of losing them, and could see some similarity here in her relationship with Giles. Jane felt she had had to tolerate her step-father's abuse of her for fear of rocking the boat, provoking a family row, and risking marital breakdown between her mother and step-father. Similarly she had felt she had to tolerate her husband's sexual demands and avoid causing an argument. She felt too embarrassed/intimidated/unsure of herself to confront him with how she felt, remained silent and became depressed. With Giles she had a fear that a similar pattern was repeating itself, and this had precipitated her decision to seek psychotherapy.

Continuing therapeutic work

Over the following weeks and months Jane was encouraged to explore further her memories and feelings about the abusive experiences. She felt guilty and 'dirty', and as though she were defiled by her step-father. She became contemptuous of herself (and others); she had an aversion to her own body, not liking to touch her own private parts, let alone have her lover do so. Once lovemaking progressed beyond foreplay, however, she could enjoy intercourse. The psychotherapist suggested Jane explore her own body more and engage in some masturbatory activities where touching of her genitalia could be associated with pleasure in an anxiety-free context.

Jane was also encouraged to discuss her aversion to foreplay with Giles and let him know what other erogenous zones could be touched without causing anxiety. She found that oral genital contact was more pleasurable and less anxiety-provoking than digital penetration.

She was also encouraged to take the lead sometimes in lovemaking so that she felt in control rather than passive/anxious as before, and to help construct contexts in which she could feel relaxed and anticipate sexual contact without becoming anxious. Giles was perfectly amenable to Jane's requests and alternative suggestions for their lovemaking, and responded positively to Jane's attempts to communicate more openly about their sexual relationship. The fact that he wanted sex more often than she did still posed a certain dilemma for Jane. Should she 'give in' and accommodate him, or should she let him know she 'wasn't in the mood', and so risk losing him (a constant fear) like her mother's fear of losing Stephen and others? Jane felt both indignant at being so contained, but apprehensive of 'rocking the boat' and fearing conflict and/or rejection.

Her self-esteem was quite precarious, and she had difficulty, despite her obvious intelligence and ability, in being assertive; she often 'put up' with people and situations for 'an easy life', although would sometimes be furious with herself for doing so. She blamed herself for 'putting up' with her abuse and not telling her mother, although she came to understand some of the constraints which had prevented her from doing so. When, after a year in psychotherapy, she finally found the courage to ask her sister if Stephen had ever done anything to her, she was mortified to discover that he had, and that her silence and self-sacrifice had not managed to protect Deborah as she had hoped it would. The futility of it made her suffering seem even worse. The power of secrecy (surrounding the abuse) infuriated her now whereas previously it had made her feel utterly impotent.

She veered between thinking that her mother must have known about it (how could she not have?) to finding this intolerable (why did she do nothing to stop it?), and she was unable to trust her; indeed, she had had considerable difficulty in making trusting relationships during much of her adult life and then seemed to go out of her way to develop close friendships (possibly as substitute attachment experiences). Whereas her friendships with women were based on reciprocity, her relationships with men – both personal and professional – were much less so and she often felt intimidated and bullied by them. Her birth father's rejection of her and her sister following his remarriage appears to have contributed to her sense that men did not really cherish her unconditionally but had an ulterior motive (sex or power) in relating to her. It was quite a revelation to her that Giles could accept and not reject her just because she sometimes dissented to making love.

Explaining and understanding and working through the contradictory and ambivalent feelings about her abuse and mother's failure to protect her seemed gradually to lead to some resolution of her past and current dilemmas and, at follow-up, eighteen months after psychotherapy ended, Jane remained well, was happy in her relationship with Giles, was less anxious about sex and more self-assertive. She was planning to visit her sister and mother and, with her sister's support, intended to confront her mother about her abuse and 'find out some anwers to lots of questions I still have'.

The therapist's style

The therapist was a woman (MT) with considerable experience both in working with child and adult victims of sexual abuse, and of working in marital and family therapy using a variety of related techniques. The establishment of an empathic, warm rapport created an essential context in which Jane could 'retell' and 're-edit' the traumatic experiences of her childhood, and helped to explore possible connections with them and subsequent patterns of personal development and openness.

Jane already made warm relationships with women, so the working therapeutic alliance was established with little transference distortion. Transference responses were not the focus of the therapeutic work and the shared task of resolving the effects of early abuse defined the therapeutic process.

With the use of cognitive and behavioural techniques and encouragement to feel more in control of her sexuality, Jane was helped to reconstruct a more satisfactory sexual relationship with her partner, free from the tyranny of the repetitive patterns emanating from the abuse and its context. The therapist's knowledge of the psychological consequences of such abuse enabled her to identify the patterns of traumatic sexualisation, powerlessness, stigmatisation and betrayal, and through the development of trust to begin to reverse them.

Breaking the power of secrecy, including sharing her experience with Giles (and her sister and prospectively her mother), helped Jane to create a new reality.

REFERENCES

Anderson, H., Goolishian, H. and Winderman, L. (1986) 'Problem determined systems towards transformation in family therapy', *Journal of Strategic and Systemic Therapies* 5: 14–9.
Bentovim, A. (1992) *Trauma Organised Systems – Physical and Sexual Abuse in Families*, London: Karnac.
Bentovim, A. and Davenport, M. (1992) 'Resolving the trauma organised system of sexual abuse by confronting the abuser', *Journal of Family Therapy* 14: 51–68.
Bentovim, A., Elton, A., Hildebrand, J., Tranter, M. and Vizard, E. (1988) *Child Sexual Abuse within the Family: Assessment and Treatment*, Bristol: John Wright.

Bentovim, A. and Kinston, W. (1991) 'Focal family therapy – joining systems theory with psychodynamic understanding', pp. 284–324 in A. S. Gurman and D. P. Kniskern (eds) *Handbook for Family Therapy*, vol. 2, New York: Basic Books.

Bruckner, D. F. and Johnson, P.E. (1987) 'Treatment for adult male victims of childhood sexual abuse, social case work', *Journal of Contemporary Social Work* 68: 81–7.

Cole, C. H. and Barney, E. E. (1987) 'Safeguards and the therapeutic window: a group treatment strategy for adult incest survivors', *American Journal of Orthopsychiatry* 57: 601–9.

Draucker, C. B. (1992) *Counselling Survivors of Childhood Sexual Abuse*, London: Sage.

Ellenson, G. S. (1990) 'Detecting a history of incest: a predictive syndrome (social case work)', *Journal of Contemporary Social Work* 66: 525–32.

Finkelhor, D. (1979) *Sexually Victimised Children*, New York: Free Press.

Finkelhor, D. and Browne, A. (1985) 'The traumatic impact of child sexual abuse: a conceptualisation', *American Journal of Orthopsychiatry* 55: 530–41.

Finkelhor, D. and Russell, D. (1984) 'Women as perpetrators: review of the evidence', pp. 171–87 in D. Finkelhor (ed.) *Child Sexual Abuse: New Theory and Research*, New York: Free Press.

Goldner, V., Penn, P., Scheinberg, M. and Walker, G. (1990) 'Love and violence: gender paradoxes in volatile attachments', *Family Process* 29: 343–65.

Green, R. and Money, J. (1961) 'Effeminacy in prepubertal boys', *Paediatrics* 27: 286–91.

Haugard, J. and Repucci, N. D. (1988) *The Sexual Abuse of Children*, London: Jossey-Bass.

Herman, J. L. (1981) *Father–daughter Incest*, Cambridge, MA: Harvard University Press.

Jehu, D. (1988) *Beyond Sexual Abuse*, Chichester: Wiley.

Kinsey, A. C., Pomeroy, W. B., Martin, C. E. and Gebhard, P. H. (1953) *Sexual Behaviour in the Human Female*, Philadelphia: Saunders.

Landis, J. (1956) 'Experiences of 500 children with adult sexual deviances', *Psychiatric Quarterly Supplement* 30: 91–109.

Madonna, P., Scoyk, S. and Jones, D. (1991) 'Family interaction within incest and non-incest families', *American Journal of Psychiatry* 148: 46–9.

Masson, J. M. (1989) *Against Therapy*, London: Collins.

Monck, E., Bentovim, A., Goodall, G., Hyde, C., Lwin, R. and Sharlande, E. (1993) *Child Sexual Abuse: A Descriptive and Treatment Study*, London: HMSO.

Mullen, P. E., Romans-Clarkson, S., Walton, D. A. and Herbison, G. P. (1989) 'Impact of sexual and physical abuse on women's mental health', *Lancet* 1: 841–5.

Oppenheimer, R., Howells, K., Palmer, R. L. and Chaloner, D. A. (1985) 'Adverse sexual experience in childhood and clinical eating disorders: a preliminary description', *Journal of Psychosomatic Research* 19: 357–61.

Peters, S. D. (1986) 'Prevalence', pp. 15–59 in D. Finkelhor (ed.) *A Source Book of Child Sexual Abuse*, Beverly Hills, CA: Sage.

Stoller, R. J. (1968) *Sex and Gender: On the Development of Masculinity and Femininity*, London: Hogarth Press.

Struve, J. (1990) 'Dancing with the patriarchy: the politics of sexual abuse', pp. 13–46 in M. Hunter (ed.) *The Sexually Abused Male*, vol. 1, Lexington, MA: Lexington Books.

Tranter, M. (1992) 'A study of women who abuse', Paper given to conference on Female Abusers, Westminster Hall, London.

Watkins, W. and Bentovim, A. (1992) 'The sexual abuse of male children and adolescents: a review of current research', *Journal of Child Psychology and Psychiatry* 33: 197–248.

White, M. (1989) 'The externalising of the problem and the reauthoring of lives and relationship', *Dulwich Centre Newsletter*, Adelaide: Dulwich Centre Publications.

Chapter 24

Sexual contact between psychotherapists and their patients

Tanya Garrett

LITERATURE SURVEY

Until relatively recently the issue of the sexual abuse of patients in psychotherapy had received little attention in the theoretical and research literature. It is now an established area of attention in the United States, but it is only within the past year or so that the issue has been taken up in the United Kingdom.

It is clear from North American research that sexual contact between psychotherapists and their patients is a significant problem, but that, like rape and child sexual abuse, it is under-reported.

In the United States, half the money for malpractice cases is spent on complaints regarding sexual intimacy (Pope 1991a). About 13 per cent of allegations of professional misconduct handled by the American Psychological Association (APA) insurance trust in 1981, and 18 per cent of the complaints to the APA Ethics Committee in 1982 involved sexual offences. Yet suits and complains are rarely filed, only in about 4 per cent of cases, and only half of these are completed (Bouhoutsos 1983).

The issue of therapist–patient sexual contact can be traced back over many centuries to its prohibition in the Hippocratic Oath (Bouhoutsos 1983). In more recent times, indirectly in their ethics codes the British professions have maintained this proscription by referring to, for example, the need for professional conduct which does not damage the interests of clients, or public confidence in the profession (British Psychological Society 1991). North American professions have, however, explicitly prohibited sexual contact with patients in their Codes of Conduct, and one has even produced a Position Paper on the subject (Sreenivassan 1989).

The taboo on sexual contact between psychotherapists and their patients has been raised and challenged in recent years in the context of growing sexual freedom in society (Siassi and Thomas 1973), and by articles in the popular press (Sinclair 1991). The last few decades have seen an increasing acceptance of physical and emotional intimacy between psychotherapists and their patients under the guise of humanistic approaches to psychotherapy, and a few psychotherapists have even openly advocated sexual relationships between psychotherapists and their patients (McCartney 1966; Shepard 1971).

The process of data collection in this field has been problematic. Butler and Zelen (1977) were threatened with expulsion from a professional organisation when they suggested research into the field of psychotherapist–patient sexual intimacy, and when early research was allowed, the results were suppressed (Forer 1968, cited in Bouhoutsos 1983). Not until the 1970s, at least in the United States, was concerted attention given to the problem (Bouhoutsos 1983), with a proliferation of research and theoretical papers.

Epidemiology

Until 1992, no systematic information was available in the United Kingdom for any professional or lay group of psychotherapists on their sexual contact with patients, or their attitudes towards it.

Generally speaking, the research in North America has yielded no differences in any epidemiological respect between the main psychotherapy professions of psychology, psychiatry and social work. It would therefore be reasonable to consider the surveys of different professions as a whole. No empirical evidence is available to date to indicate the extent of sexual contact between other professionals and lay psychotherapists and counsellors, and their patients.

Most surveys have found that, overall, something under 10 per cent of professional psychotherapists have had sexual intercourse with their patients. Kardener et al. (1976) indicate a figure of 6–7 per cent; Pope et al. (1979), 7 per cent; and Pope et al. (1986), 6.5 per cent. Pope et al. (1987) have more recently found significantly lower rates of sexual contact with patients than previous studies: only 1.9 per cent reported having had sex with a patient. Although Holroyd and Brodsky (1980) found that 3.2 per cent of respondents to their survey had had sexual intercourse with a patient, another 4.6 per cent engaged in other types of sexual behaviour.

As one might expect, there are large differences between male and female psychotherapists in this respect. When the overall figures are broken down by gender of psychotherapist, the percentage of male psychotherapists who engage in sexual intercourse with patients rises to around 10 per cent, and it becomes clear that women offenders form only a tiny minority of the total number. For example, Gartrell et al. (1986) surveyed US psychiatrists and found that 7.1 per cent of male and 3.1 per cent of female psychiatrists had had sex with patients. Other surveys indicate figures of 3 per cent and 12 per cent for women and men respectively (Pope et al. 1979); and 2.5 per cent and 9.4 per cent (Pope et al. 1987); and 0.6 per cent and 5.5 per cent whilst psychotherapy was ongoing (Holroyd and Brodsky 1977). The latter study found that

8.1 per cent of men and 1 per cent of women had ever had sex with patients.

The research suggests that a slightly higher number of psychotherapists have had 'erotic' non-intercourse contact with their patients. Somewhere between 3 and 13 per cent of psychotherapists fall into this category (Kardener *et al.* 1976; Pope *et al.* 1987).

Overall, according to recent research, it would appear that the rate of psychotherapist–patient sexual involvement is declining in the United States (Pope 1990).

The vast majority of North American psychotherapists have indicated in surveys that they believe sex with patients to be unacceptable. For example, Pope *et al.* (1987) found that 95 per cent of respondents believed that sexual contact with a patient is unethical, and about half believed that becoming sexually involved with a former patient is unethical. A similar result was achieved by Borys and Pope (1989).

In the light of these factors, sexual contact between psychotherapists and their patients must therefore be viewed within the broader context of gender and therefore power issues in psychotherapy. In particular, these power imbalances are demonstrated by the lack of mutuality evidenced in sexual contacts between psychotherapists and their patients or, in Claman's (1987) terms, in that the psychotherapist remains sole recipient of the mirroring and idealising in the 'relationship'.

In terms of what distinguishes offenders from non-offenders, it is clear that whilst offenders are more likely to advocate and use non-erotic touching of patients, they do not differ on most demographic variables from psychotherapists who do not have sex with their patients (Holroyd and Brodsky 1980).

There is, however, some evidence to suggest that psychotherapists who have had personal psychotherapy, or who had sexual contact with educators during professional training, may be more likely to develop sexual liaisons with their patients. Gartrell *et al.* (1986) surveyed US psychiatrists, and found that offenders were more likely to have had personal psychotherapy. This is the only study to look at this area, and the robustness of the association requires further testing.

Pope *et al.* (1986) argue that educator–student sex is a model for later psychotherapist–patient sex. For female respondents engaging in sexual contact with educators as a student was related to later sexual contact as professionals with patients, a figure of 23 per cent as compared with 6 per cent who had not had sexual contact with educators. For male respondents, the sample was too small to test the relationship. In summary, many psychotherapists who have sexual relationships with their patients were themselves sexually involved with their own teachers, supervisors or psychotherapists (Folman 1991; Pope 1989).

The earliest information about the characteristics of psychotherapists who become involved with their patients was provided by Dahlberg (1970), based on cases of psychotherapists who had had sexual relationships with their patients, whom he had treated. Usually, psychotherapists were over forty, ten to twenty-five years older than the patient; and always male. In those cases where sufficient information was available, the psychotherapist was having severe marital problems. Most psychotherapists practising at that time, Dahlberg points out, would be fairly unusual in their withdrawn-ness and introspection, studiousness and passivity, shyness and intellectualism. Having thus been unpopular with women, psychotherapists suddenly find themselves in the unusual position of having their female patients attracted to them, and thus, a fantasy fulfilled.

Gonsoriek (1987) gives information derived from the accounts of patients who have used the Minneapolis Walk-in Counselling Centre for clients who allege sexual involvement with psychotherapists. These psychotherapists were a diverse group, ranging from the uninformed (usually para- or non-professionals with little or no training in the area of boundaries and standards of care: an example of this would be the untrained 'hypnotherapist' who had sexually abused nine patients, described by Hoencamp (1990)), through those who are psychologically healthy or mildly neurotic (usually the largest category, whose behaviour is related to life stresses), the more severely neurotic or socially isolated, to those with impulsive, sociopathic or narcissistic character disorders, and psychotic or borderline personalities.

Butler and Zelen (1977) interviewed twenty offender volunteers, both psychologists and psychiatrists. Of these, 90 per cent had been vulnerable, needy and lonely in relation to marital problems at the time of the sexual contact with patients. Some psychotherapists saw themselves as domineering and controlling (15 per cent): this would be supported by a case reported by Hoencamp (1990), but most (60 per cent) saw themselves as in a paternal relationship with the passive and submissive patient. Most experienced conflicts, fears and guilt.

In terms of the motivation for initiating sexual contact with a patient, Sonne and Pope (1991) conclude that psychotherapist–patient sexual intimacy usually involves anger (battering the patient, emotionally abusing the patient or recommending activity which will harm the patient, but are ostensibly intended for the patient's benefit), power (viewing the patient in almost exclusively sexual terms, substituting the patient for a significant figure in the psychotherapist's life, attraction to pathology, authoritarian orientation, and being attracted to a physically immobilised patient) and sadism (pleasure in causing pain and sexualised humiliation). Most studies agree that power need motivates psychotherapists who have sexual contact with their patients (Bouhoutsos 1983).

In a study of an in-patient facility, Averill *et al.* (1989) found that there were two main groups of care staff who became sexually involved with patients. First, a collection of younger, exploitative individuals, and secondly, a group of older, middle-aged, isolated staff who were experiencing personal problems which triggered longings for nurturing. Both groups appear to have considered their own needs and issues at the expense of those of their patients.

It is important to note that psychotherapists who have sexual contact with one patient are at a high risk of re-offending: about 33 per cent do so, and may abuse up to twelve patients, according to a study conducted by Gartrell *et al.* (1986). Earlier studies suggest higher figures: Holroyd and Brodsky (1977) found that 80 per cent of those who had sexual contact with patients in their study had done so with more than one patient. This would accord with the 75 per cent of psychiatrists who had been sexually involved with more than one patient in a study conducted at around the same time (Butler and Zelen 1977).

Dahlberg (1970) argues that the psychotherapist who becomes sexually involved with patients is usually a shy individual who does so against a background in psychotherapy sessions of having women attracted to him and informing him of this. When psychotherapist and patient become sexually involved, the psychotherapist is acting out a fantasy of 'being young, attractive and having beautiful girls throwing themselves at you without having to take the chance of being rejected by being the one who makes the first move' (Dahlberg 1970: 119). That is, there is a fantasy of masculine omnipotence by virtue of being in a position of power as a psychotherapist and a man, in sexual terms; as well as being older than the patient. Thus, Dahlberg concludes, sexual involvement with patients would be much less common in female psychotherapists.

Claman (1987) suggests that the research evidence shows that many sexually abusive psychotherapists fit a pattern of narcissistic disturbance of the self; such psychotherapists harbour from their childhood unfulfilled longings to be mirrored and needs to merge with others. When sexual contact occurs, these needs are mirrored by the patient, who functions as a self-object. Such a pattern would fit the research finding that abusing psychotherapists' relationship patterns tend to be problematic (Zelen 1985), and could go some way towards explaining the intractable nature of this problem.

Characteristics of patients who become sexually involved with psychotherapists

The literature describing the patients who become sexually involved with their psychotherapists has identified a variety of patient characteristics. Belote (cited in Bouhoutsos 1983) found female patients who had been sexually involved with their psychotherapists to be vulnerable and high on traditional feminine attributes such as other-directedness, poor self-image, low self-actualisation and little acceptance of their own aggression. Averill *et al.* (1989) found that in their in-patient sample the typical patients who had become sexually involved with their psychotherapists were those with borderline personality disorders, a history of childhood sexual abuse (about 32 per cent – Pope and Vetter 1991) and/or rape (about 10 per cent – Pope and Vetter 1991). They were usually involved in extended treatment with maximum opportunities for transference.

On the basis that psychotherapist–patient sex involves boundary violations, it has been argued that such violations are most likely to be evoked by patients with borderline personality disorder (Gutheil 1989) because of their rage towards the psychotherapist, their neediness and dependency, their confusion of the self/other boundary, and their manipulativeness and strong feelings of entitlement. These dynamics evoke powerful counter-dynamics in the psychotherapist, which can easily lead to boundary violations. However, it is here important to caution against locating the blame for psychotherapist–patient sex exclusively with the patient, particularly as Gutheil (1989) asserts that the majority of the patients who wrongly accuse psychotherapists of sexual abuse fall within this category. Cases of false accusation should not detract from the substantial numbers of psychotherapists who have behaved in a sexually abusive manner towards their patients.

Most patients who become sexually involved with their psychotherapists are female, and a numerically small, but none the less significant minority are minors – 5 per cent in a study by Pope and Vetter (1991). When Bajit and Pope (1989) looked at cases of psychotherapist sex with child patients, 81 examples emerged. Of these 56 per cent were girls, 44 per cent were boys. The ages ranged from three to seventeen, mean 13.75, with a standard deviation of 4.12.

Pope and Bouhoutsos (1986) suggest that three major categories of patients emerge from the literature: a low-risk group who, although they are highly stressed, are essentially healthy; a middle-risk group with a history of previous relationship problems and who may be personality-disordered; and a high-risk group with a history of hospitalisation, suicide attempts, major psychiatric illness and substance abuse problems. A high percentage of the women in the latter group had also experienced childhood sexual abuse.

Certainly, the patient who enters psychotherapy after being sexually involved with one psychotherapist is at considerable risk of sexual involvement with her new psychotherapist (Folman 1991; Gartrell *et al.* 1987). However, whether this is a result of patient or psychotherapist factors remains unclear.

When does sexual contact with patients occur?

In around three-quarters of cases, psychotherapists begin a sexual relationship with their patients after termination of psychotherapy. Figures vary from 69 per cent (Gartrell *et al*. 1986) to 77 per cent (Pope and Vetter 1991). Around 18 per cent of sexual contacts occur in sessions, and 17 per cent concurrent with psychotherapy, but outside sessions (Gartrell *et al*. 1986).

Does psychotherapist–patient sexual contact get reported – and what happens when it does?

Most authors agree that sexual abuse by psychotherapists is vastly under-reported. In a study of psychologists who had treated patients who had been sexually involved with a previous psychotherapist, Pope and Vetter (1991) found that only 12 per cent of the patients filed complaints.

Although Levenson (1986) argues that professionals have an ethical obligation to intervene and to report their knowledge of unethical practice by a colleague, when Gartrell *et al*. (1986) looked at the reporting practices of psychiatrists who knew of sexual misconduct by colleagues, only 8 per cent of cases were reported, but the majority favoured mandatory reporting of such cases.

One recent report in the literature describes a case of sexual abuse of two thirteen-year-old children by a nurse who had been convicted and sentenced through the criminal justice system. The case was referred to the UKCC, where judgement was first deferred (during which time he committed further offences) and, following reprimands, the nurse was subsequently allowed to remain on the register and practice as a nurse. This case was reported by Long (1992), who criticises the UKCC for its failure to protect the public.

How many sexually abusive psychotherapists admit their behaviour or seek help?

In the two studies available in this area, a relatively high percentage (41 per cent) sought 'consultation' (Gartrell *et al*. 1986), and Butler and Zelen (1977) found a similar figure of 40 per cent who had sought help from a colleague.

UNDERSTANDING SEXUAL CONTACT IN PSYCHOTHERAPY

The relationship between sexual attraction towards patients and sexual contact with them

Freud's prohibition on kissing, other preliminaries, and sexual contact with patients has had, Pope and Bouhoutsos (1986) argue, the un-intended consequence of psychotherapists becoming suspicious of any warm feelings towards their patients, thus intensifying anxiety around psychotherapist–patient sex and inhibiting full recognition of the problem and of attempts to address it.

It is important to recognise that sexual attraction towards patients is very common, at least among psychologists; in surveys, well over half of the psychologists (more frequently men) responding admit sexual attraction towards and sexual fantasies about their patients (Pope *et al.* 1986; Pope *et al.* 1987). This can give rise to anxiety; most psychologists, whilst admitting to sexual attraction towards their patients, are concerned about this (Pope *et al.* 1986), and a substantial minority believe it to be unethical (Pope *et al.* 1987). Reluctance to acknowledge and discuss the issue may well be contributing to our difficulty in confronting the reality of the sexual abuse of patients by psychotherapists (Pope 1990), especially in the United Kingdom. We may thus be reluctant to address sexual feelings for patients in professional training courses, and in this way may miss the opportunity to prevent psychotherapist–patient sexual contact from developing (Pope 1989). So our anxiety may directly contribute to the occurrence of sexual contact between psychotherapists and their patients.

Why do most psychotherapists refrain from sexual contact with their patients?

Pope *et al.* (1986) asked participants in their survey why they did not engage in sexual contact with patients. The reasons were usually to do with ethics, values and professionalism, as well as the belief that it would be counter-therapeutic. Other motives, however, touched on issues such as the psychotherapist already being in a relationship, fear of damage to oneself as psychotherapist, fears around one's reputation or of censure, either generally or on the patient's part, in terms of retaliation.

Why do some psychotherapists engage in sexual contact with their patients?

Herman *et al.* (1987) report that 2 per cent of psychiatrists believed that sexual contact with a patient could be indicated to enhance self-esteem, as a corrective emotional experience, to treat a grief reaction, or to change a patient's sexual orientation. Slightly more, 4.5 per cent, believed that it could be useful in treating a sexual difficulty, and 4 per cent believed it could be appropriate if the patient and psychotherapist are in love. Gechtman (1989) shows that 10 per cent of social workers believed that sex with a psychotherapist may be beneficial to the patient, and Gartrell *et al.* (1986) found that most sexually abusing psychotherapists thought that the patient's experience of psychotherapist–patient sex was positive. Pope and Bajt (1988) found that in 9 per cent of cases, psychologists had argued that they had engaged in sexual relations with a patient for the treatment and welfare of that patient.

Butler and Zelen's (1977) postal survey yielded twenty psychotherapists, both psychologists and psychiatrists, who had had sexual contact with their patients and who volunteered to be interviewed. Among them, 90 per cent reported being vulnerable, needy and/or lonely as a result of relationship difficulties when the sexual contact occurred. Some psychotherapists saw themselves as domineering and controlling (15 per cent), but most (60 per cent) saw themselves as in a paternal relationship with the passive and submissive patient; 45 per cent admitted to rationalising in order to permit otherwise unacceptable behaviour during psychotherapy. Most experienced conflicts, fears and guilt.

The use of touch in psychotherapy

The psychoanalytic tradition has always maintained a taboo on physical contact with patients, on the grounds that touching introduces reality into the therapeutic relationship and consequently gratification and tension reduction, which would both render problematic the identification and understanding of transference material, diminish the range and depth of the material and reduce motivation to engage in psychotherapy. There is a recognition, however, that other therapeutic approaches which concern themselves with the patient's reality may not consider touch to be problematic in certain circumstances.

Even within psychoanalysis, there is, however, disagreement. Touch is viewed by some as acceptable in the case of patients with certain presenting problems, such as delusions, or to provide a corrective emotional experience, or dependent on the theoretical approach of the clinician. Sponitz (1972, cited in Goodman and Teicher 1988) captures the debate in asserting that the use of touch in psychotherapy should be contingent on whether it would contribute a maturational quality to the therapeutic relationship.

Most of the literature concurs that touch should be used judiciously and with caution (Edwards 1981). This is particularly true because there are many different types of touch (Edwards 1981), which can be anything from nurturing to aggressive, prompting to sexual. Particularly for more damaged patients, touch may result in a loss of inhibition, or may be experienced as a sexual promise which, when unfulfilled, can make the patient feel betrayed and abandoned. It is also important to consider the power dynamics of psychotherapy and consequently how the patient may perceive being touched by the (powerful) psychotherapist. Furthermore, it is possible that whereas a psychotherapist may not touch a patient with sexual intentions or implications, the client may either perceive it as such or have sexual feelings towards the psychotherapist.

The American Psychological Association adopted the following statement regarding physical contact with patients: 'permissible physical touching is defined as that conduct which is based upon the exercise of professional judgement, and which, implicitly, comports with accepted standards of professional conduct' (1982, cited in Goodman and Teicher 1988: 492).

The research evidence supports the view that touch should either be avoided, or used with extreme caution, and advocacy of the use of touch in psychotherapy should be treated somewhat suspiciously. Pattison's (1973) findings on the effects of touch on patients and the therapeutic relationship were that patients who were touched engaged in more self-exploration, and touch had no effects on their perception of the relationship with the psychotherapist, suggesting that touch in psychotherapy may be extremely helpful to the therapeutic process.

However, some research has demonstrated a relationship between touching patients and sexual contact with them. For example, a survey by Kardener *et al.* (1976) showed that the freer a physician is with non-erotic physical contact, the more statistically likely they are also to engage in erotic practices with patients. Holroyd and Brodsky (1980) found that psychotherapists who had sex with patients advocated and used non-erotic contact with opposite-sex patients more often than other psychotherapists. Those who had non-intercourse sexual contact, however, did not differ from other psychotherapists in their use of non-erotic touching. So, 'the differential application of non-erotic hugging, kissing and touching to opposite sex patients but not to same sex patients is viewed as a sex-biased psychotherapy practice at high risk for leading to sexual intercourse with patients' (Holroyd and Brodsky 1980: 807).

Holroyd and Brodsky (1977), in a survey of psychologists' attitudes towards erotic and non-erotic physical contact with patients, found male psychotherapists to be more likely to see benefits in non-erotic contact for opposite-sex patients. In this context, it is relevant to note that the use of physical contact with patients is a relatively common practice in psychotherapy. Results of a survey by Pope *et al.* (1987) show that a quarter of respondents had kissed a patient and 44.5 per cent hugged clients rarely, with 41.7 per cent doing so more frequently. Most were prepared to shake their client's hand and most did not consider this to be unethical. Holroyd and Brodsky (1977) found that 27 per cent of their respondents engaged in non-erotic physical contact, mostly humanistically orientated psychotherapists. In general physicians, more female practitioners than male believe in and use non-erotic touch with patients (Perry 1976).

The effects on patients of sexual contact with their psychotherapist

Systematically gathered empirical data regarding the effects of psychotherapist–patient sex have only recently become available. Traditionally, these relationships have been assumed to be harmful to patients (Marmor 1972), but some writers have more recently argued that such contact may be beneficial (for example, McCartney 1966).

Taylor and Wagner's (1976) review of every available case in the literature of psychotherapist–patient sexual contact (thirty-four in all) showed that the majority had negative or mixed effects on the patient, but 21 per cent reportedly had positive effects. However, this conclusion must be interpreted in the light of the psychotherapist's motivation, and the findings (Holroyd and Bouhoutsos 1985) that (1) psychologists who reported that no harm occurred to patients as a result of sexual encounters with their psychotherapists are twice as likely themselves to have had sex with a patient than are psychologists generally, and (2) psychologists who have been sexually intimate with patients are less likely to report adverse effects of sexual intimacy, either for patients or for psychotherapy.

In a survey of psychologists who had treated patients who had been sexually intimate with a previous psychotherapist, Pope and Vetter (1991) found that harm had occurred in 90 per cent of cases overall. Harm also occurred in 80 per cent of the cases in which psychotherapists engaged in sex with a patient after termination of psychotherapy. Butler and Zelen conclude on the basis of interviews with psychotherapists who had had sexual contact with their patients, that 'it was not a therapeutic experience for either patient or therapist' (1977: 145).

There is only one report in the literature which attempts to study as close to experimentally as possible the effects of psychotherapist–patient sex. Feldman-Sumner and Jones (1984) compared women who had had sex with psychotherapists, women who had had sex with other health-care practitioners and women who had had sex with their health professional. The first group had a greater mistrust of and anger towards men and psychotherapists, and a greater number of psychological and psycho-somatic symptoms than the third group. The first two groups did not differ in terms of the psychological impact of the sexual contacts. Severity of impacts was significantly related to the magnitude of psychological and somatic symptoms prior to treatment, prior sexual victimisation and the marital status of the psychotherapist/health care practitioner.

As a result of their work with victims of psychotherapist sexual abuse, and of growing anecdotal reports in the literature (for example, Schoener et al. 1984) of the damaging effects of psychotherapist–patient sexual contact, Pope and Bouhoutsos (1986) have developed the concept of the 'therapist–patient sex syndrome', which includes ambivalence and guilt (Schoener et al. 1984), feelings of isolation and emptiness and cognitive dysfunction (Vinson 1984, cited in Pope and Bouhoutsos 1986), identity and boundary disturbance and inability to trust (Schoener et al. 1984; Voth 1972), sexual confusion, lability of mood and suppressed rage (Schoener et al. 1984) and increased suicidal risk (D'Addario 1977, cited in Pope and Bouhoutsos 1986; Pope and Vetter 1991). Patients' symptoms are increased (D'Addario 1977, cited in Pope and Bouhoutsos 1986: Voth 1972) and hospitalisation is frequently necessary (Pope and Vetter 1991;

Voth 1972), as well as the development of disturbances in interpersonal relationships (Bouhoutsos *et al.* 1983: Voth 1972).

RECENT UK RESEARCH

An anonymous, confidential postal survey was undertaken at random of a thousand clinical psychologist members of the Division of Clinical Psychology of the British Psychological Society. A questionnaire was sent to subjects to gain epidemiological information about respondents' personal and professional circumstances, to ascertain their use of physical and sexual contact with patients, and to assess their experience of sexual contact between them as students and educators and with personal psychotherapists where applicable. Finally, questions were included about experience of treating patients who had had sexual contact with previous psychotherapists and knowledge of clinical psychologists who have become sexually involved with patients. Space was provided for further comments. The development of the questionnaire was informed by previous research in the United States.

A 58 per cent response rate (580 questionnaires) was received. For the purposes of this chapter, data are presented on 300 respondents. Many respondents did not answer some questions. The data given here exclude these non-responses; thus, for much of the data, percentages will not, when totalled, reach 100 per cent.

Among respondents 62 per cent were female and 36 per cent were male. Their mean age was thirty-nine years (range 25–77: s.d., 8.41) and the mean length of post-qualification practice as a clinical psychologist was eleven years (range 0–40: s.d., 7.74). Most respondents were married (60 per cent) or in a stable relationship (21 per cent). Many (13 per cent) were single and 4 per cent were separated or divorced, only 1 per cent describing themselves as widowed. The majority of subjects described themselves as heterosexual (96 per cent), with 2 per cent stating that they were bisexual and 1.7 per cent homosexual.

The most commonly cited influences on theoretical orientation were behavioural-cognitive-dynamic, in that order (11 per cent), or combinations thereof: cognitive-behavioural-psychodynamic (5 per cent) and psychodynamic-cognitive-behavioural (4 per cent). Just under 6 per cent of the sample identified their orientation as behavioural-cognitive-systemic, and 5 per cent as cognitive-behavioural-systemic.

Subjects gave their main area of clinical work (Table 24.1) and their main work setting (Table 24.2).

Respondents spent a mean fourteen hours per week in face-to-face patient contact (range 0–40: s.d. 7.21) and had a mean 14 per cent of patients in long-term psychotherapy (range 0–100: s.d. 22.42). Most respondents worked on a short-term basis with patients: 66 per cent of

Table 24.1 Respondents' main area of clinical work (percentages)

Adults	51.5
Children and young people	14.0
Learning difficulties	15.6
Elderly	5.3
Physical health	3.0
Neuropsychology	4.0
Other	3.7

Table 24.2 Respondents' main work settings (percentages)

National Health Service	89.7
Private practice	3.0
Social services	1.3
Voluntary agencies	0.3
Other	4.0

subjects' patients were in short-term psychotherapy (range 0–100: s.d. 30.61). A narrow majority of subjects had not undertaken personal psychotherapy (56 per cent), but a substantial minority had done so (43 per cent). Of these, women were more likely to undertake personal psychotherapy than men.

Most respondents (56.5 per cent) reported having been sexually attracted to a patient, but 42.9 per cent said that this had never happened to them. Male subjects were more likely to report experiencing sexual attraction towards patients. Of the subjects 87 per cent expressed current unconcern about the attraction, whereas 13 per cent were concerned.

Attitudes towards, and incidence of, sexual contact with patients

Although 3 per cent of the sample did not respond when asked whether they believed that patients could ever benefit from sexual contact with a psychotherapist, 3.7 per cent responded positively to this question, with 93 per cent responding negatively. Of the sample 4 per cent admitted to having engaged in what they regarded as sexual contact with current or discharged patients; 2 per cent had had sexual intercourse with a patient; and 2 per cent had engaged in other forms of erotic contact. One per cent of subjects did not respond to this question; 58 per cent of these psychologists were male, and 42 per cent were female. The male psychologists had exclusively engaged in sexual relations with female patients, and of the female psychologists, 20 per cent had had sexual contact with female patients and 80 per cent with male patients.

They were divided equally in terms of marital status between married, single and in a stable relationship. Most were heterosexual (67 per cent), a quarter were homosexual, and 8 per cent were bisexual. Of those psychologists who said that they had engaged in sexual contact with a patient, 83 per cent had done so with only one patient. For 17 per cent of these individuals, sexual contact had occurred with three patients. All of the psychologists were mainly employed in the NHS.

Of the psychologists who identified themselves as bisexual, it was a female psychologist who had had sexual contact with a male patient; of the heterosexual psychologists, 75 per cent were male having sexual contact with a female patient. Of those psychologists who identified themselves as homosexual, half were female psychologist–female patient contacts and half were female psychologist–male patient sexual involvements.

The most frequent number of occasions on which respondents had had sexual relations with patients was one (42 per cent). One individual reported three occasions, one reported four occasions, and one, ten occasions. One-third of those psychologists who had had sexual contact with patients did not respond to this question.

Over half (58 per cent) had not engaged in sexual contact with a current patient, one-third had done so with one current patient, and one individual reported sexual contact with three current patients. Fifty per cent of the sub-sample had had sexual relations with one discharged patient, and one individual had done so with three discharged patients. When those psychologists who had engaged in sexual relations with current patients were asked the circumstances in which this occurred, one did not respond, 40 per cent stated that it had happened only during psychotherapy sessions, and 40 per cent both within and outside psychotherapy sessions.

Only one of these psychologists had not disclosed their sexual involvement with patients before completing the questionnaire. Most (25 per cent) had disclosed to a colleague and friend/partner, and 17 per cent had disclosed to a colleague, manager and friend/partner. Each of the other psychologists had disclosed to, respectively, a personal psychotherapist; an unspecified individual; a colleague and a personal psychotherapist; a colleague, supervisor and friend/partner; a colleague, manager, friend/partner and personal psychotherapist; and colleague, manager, supervisor, friend/partner and unspecified individual.

The most recent patient with whom respondents had had sexual contact

When subjects were asked to consider the most recent patient with whom they had had sexual relations (if there had been more than one), 58 per cent reported that this patient had been female. One-third reported that the patient had been male, and one individual did not respond to this question. The patient's age was given by all but one subject. The mean age of patients was thirty-four years (range 19–41; s.d. 6.63).

All respondents who answered the question (92 per cent) stated that their sexual contact with the patient had been consenting and did not involve the infliction of pain on the patient. Among respondents 58 per cent considered the sexual involvement to be mutually initiated and one-third stated that the patient had initiated it. None of the subjects believed that they had exclusively initiated the sexual contact. One-third of these sexual contacts had been once-only encounters. A quarter had endured for more than five years and 17 per cent had lasted between three and eleven months. A further 17 per cent had lasted less than three months.

Most psychologists (67 per cent) reported that they had no current contact whatsoever with the patient. Eight per cent of subjects had continued social, but no sexual or psychotherapeutic contact with the patient; 8 per cent had continued therapeutic and sexual contact with the patient; and 8 per cent were married to or in a committed relationship with the patient. Although 58 per cent expressed concerns now about this sexual contact with a patient, one-third were unconcerned.

Attitudes towards, and incidence of, trainer–trainee sexual contact

Just over 22 per cent of respondents believed that trainees could benefit from sexual contact with a lecturer or supervisor, but 7 per cent did not respond to this question. Nine percent had had sexual contact as an undergraduate with a lecturer or tutor, and 8 per cent with a lecturer/tutor or supervisor, as a trainee clinical psychologist. Two per cent of those psychologists who had engaged in personal psychotherapy had had sexual involvement with their psychotherapist. Five per cent of lecturers/supervisors had had sexual contact with their trainees/undergraduates. These individuals were more likely to be male.

Information about treatment of victims of sexual abuse by psychotherapists

Twenty-two per cent of respondents had treated victims of psychotherapist–patient sex. None of these psychologists rated the effects of the sexual involvement as positive: 94 per cent believed that it had negative effects on the patient and 6 per cent viewed the effects as 'mixed'. Sixty per cent had treated one patient who had been sexually involved with a psychotherapist. The rest had treated two and five patients. Private sector psychotherapists (17 per cent) were the most commonly cited therapists who had been sexually involved with respondents' patients. Psychiatrists and 'other' psychotherapists (for example, GPs) each accounted for 16 per cent respectively of cases. Clinical psychologists, social workers and nurses made up 14 per cent each of the cases. Counsellors accounted for 4 per cent and voluntary agency psychotherapists and unknown psychotherapists had been sexually involved with patients in 3 per cent of cases.

Most of these psychotherapists (41 per cent) had not been reported to their employer, professional body, and so on, and respondents were uncertain in this respect about 28 per cent, whereas 31 per cent had been reported in some way.

Knowledge through sources other than patients or clinical psychologists who have had sexual involvement with patients

Over 40 per cent of respondents knew of clinical psychologists who had been sexually involved with patients. Most (63 per cent) knew of one such psychologist, but 30 per cent knew of two, 6 per cent knew of three and 2 per cent knew of four. Over half (52 per cent) were reported to their employer, or the British Psychological Society, 27 per cent were not reported, and for 18 per cent of offenders, respondents were uncertain whether or not they had been reported.

Well over half (61 per cent) of these psychologists known to respondents had been sexually involved with only one patient, and 39 per cent had been involved with more than one. Of respondents who knew of sexually abusive psychologists 14 per cent had taken action to report the colleague.

DISCUSSION AND RECOMMENDATIONS

If under-reporting of personal sexual contact with patients occurred here, responses to other questions may compensate for this. That is, respondents' treatment of patients who were sexually involved with previous psychotherapists, and their knowledge through other sources of clinical psychologists who had sexual contact with their patients, are alternative avenues to this information. However, there is inevitable overlap between respondents in knowledge of such psychologists, so no absolute figures may be concluded from this information.

However, the percentages of respondents who had treated patients who were sexually involved with their psychotherapists, and who knew of clinical psychologists who had engaged in sexual contact with their patients are substantial (22 per cent and 40 per cent respectively). The responses to these questions also demonstrate that many psychotherapists engage in multiple sexual contacts with patients, and that previous research findings documenting the negative effects of such sexual contact on patients, as perceived by treating psychotherapists, are supported. The questionnaire was insufficiently sophisticated to distinguish between those subjects who had themselves sexually abused patients, and those who had not, in order to control for the phenomenon of offenders reporting more positive effects on patients of sexual contact with psychotherapists.

Over half (58 per cent) of the patients with whom respondents had had sexual contact were discharged at the onset of the sexual contact. It might be argued that in these cases there are less pressing ethical problems, or even that there should be no ethical objection to such sexual contacts. This is clearly an area which could be investigated in future research but the fact that US studies have found that such contact causes harm to the patient, as well as the suggestion that psychotherapists may at times discharge a patient specifically in order to engage in a sexual relationship with them, thus giving little priority to the therapeutic needs of the patient, should be sufficient to cause psychotherapists to exercise extreme caution in this area.

It may be reasonable for the present to draw some broad conclusions from these results about the overall rate of psychotherapist–patient sexual contact in Britain, but further research is clearly required to establish whether any inter-professional differences exist in this respect. In view of the widespread practice of counselling and psychotherapy by non-professionals, and of the lack of regulation of this activity in the United Kingdom, research is required to define any differences which may exist between professional and non-professional groups in this respect. It is impossible to conclude from these results whether the British picture, as the North American, is that of a declining rate of sexual contact between psychologists and their patients: clearly, this is an area where further research could begin to contribute.

This study demonstrates that sexual contact with patients by clinical psychologists and other psychotherapists does occur in Britain and is largely perceived to be damaging to patients. Action could be taken to prevent and address the problem as follows:

1 Sexual contact with current and discharged patients should be explicitly prohibited in professional Codes of Conduct.
2 Consideration should be given to the treatment of offending psycho-therapists, and evaluated rehabilitation programmes should be considered by professional bodies.
3 Since most psychotherapists in a recent study had received little or no training about sexual attraction to patients (Pope et al. 1986), the issues of attraction to patients and sexual contact with them should be addressed in professional training courses (Thoreson 1986).
4 Folman (1991) suggests that concepts of transference, counter-transference and boundaries are fundamental for trainees to develop an understanding of attraction and intimacy between psychotherapists and their patients. Gutheil (1989) argues that training should equip psychotherapists with a knowledge of transference, with its power to produce flattering attitudes in the patient, and of counter-transference, with its potential to trigger the feeling that the psychotherapist and only the psychotherapist can save the patient. Such issues may also be raised with psychotherapy trainees in supervision.
5 A presentation of the research-based literature in the area of dual relationships as well as discussion of ethical implications of sexual contact with patients (Borys and Pope 1989) can serve to raise awareness

in training. Educational programmes for psychotherapists should aim to provide a supportive environment within which students and educators can consider their own impulses which might tempt them into unethical dual relationships (Borys and Pope 1989).

6 The recognition that inherent in the role and abilities of psychotherapists are the roots of a narcissistic disturbance (Claman 1987) leads to an understanding of the need for psychotherapists to examine personal motivation and background, particularly in training and supervision.

7 Educational establishments should take preventive and remedial action to address the problem of student/educator sexual contact (Garrett and Thomas-Peter 1992). Organisationally, the appropriate procedures should be followed, and written guidelines and standards could usefully be formed concerning dual relationships between educators and students, and procedures could be developed for avoiding conflicts of interest in monitoring and enforcing such standards.

REFERENCES

Averill, S. C., Beale, D., Benfer, B., Collins, D. T., Kennedy, L., Myers, J., Pope, D., Rosen, I. and Zoble, E. (1989) 'Preventing staff–patient sexual relationships', *Bulletin of the Menninger Clinic* 53: 384–93.

Bajit, T. R. and Pope, K. S. (1989) 'Therapist–patient sexual intimacy involving children and adolescents', *American Psychologist* 44(2): 455.

Borys, D. S. and Pope, K. S. (1989) 'Dual relationships between therapist and client: a national study of psychologists, psychiatrists and social workers', *Professional Psychology: Research and Practice* 20: 283–93.

Bouhoutsos, J., (1983) 'Sexual intimacy between psychotherapists and clients: policy implications for the future', in L. Walker (ed.) *Women and Mental Health Policy*, Beverly Hills, CA: Sage.

British Psychological Society (1991) *Code of Conduct for Psychologists*, Leicester: BPS.

Butler, S. and Zelen, S. L. (1977) 'Sexual intimacies between therapists and patients', *Psychotherapy: Theory, Research and Practice* 14: 139–45.

Claman, J. (1987) 'Mirror hunger in the psychodynamics of sexually abusing therapists', *The American Journal of Psychoanalysis* 47: 35–40.

Dahlberg, C. (1970) 'Sexual contact between patient and therapist', *Contemporary Psychoanalysis* 6: 107–24.

Edwards, D. J. A. (1981) 'The role of touch in interpersonal relations: implications for psychotherapy', *South African Journal of Psychology* 11(1): 29–37.

Feldman-Sumner, S. and Jones, G. (1984) 'Psychological impacts of sexual contact between therapists or other healthcare practitioners and their clients', *Journal of Consulting and Clinical Psychology* 52: 1054–61.

Folman, R. Z. (1991) 'Therapist–patient sex: attraction and boundary problems', *Psychotherapy* 28(1): 168–73.

Garrett, T. and Thomas-Peter, B. A. (1992) 'Sexual harassment', *The Psychologist* 5(7): 319–21.

Gartrell, N., Herman, J., Olarte, S., Feldstein, M. and Localio, R. (1986) 'Psychiatrist–patient sexual contact: results of a national survey, 1: Prevalence', *American Journal of Psychiatry* 143(9): 1126–131.

Gartrell, N., Herman, J., Olarte, S., Feldstein, M. and Localio, R. (1987) 'Reporting practices of psychiatrists who knew of sexual misconduct by colleagues', *American Journal of Orthopsychiatry* 57: 287–95.

Gechtman, L. (1989) 'Sexual contact between social workers and their clients', pp. 27–38 in G. O. Gabbard (ed.) *Sexual Exploitation in Professional Relationships*, Washington, DC: American Psychiatric Press.

Gonsoriek, J. C. (1987) 'Intervening with psychotherapists who sexually exploit clients', pp. 417–27 in P. A. Keller and S. R. Heyman (eds) *Innovations in Clinical Practice: A Sourcebook*, vol. 6, Sarasota, FL: Professional Resource Exchange.

Goodman, M. and Teicher, A. (1988) 'To touch or not to touch?' *Psychotherapy* 25(4): 492–500.

Gutheil, T. (1989) 'Borderline personality disorder, boundary violations and therapist–patient sex: medicolegal pitfalls', *American Journal of Psychiatry* 146(5): 597–602.

Herman, J. L., Gartrell, N., Olarte, S., Feldman, M. and Localio, R. (1987) 'Psychiatrist–patient sexual contact: results of a national survey, II: Psychiatrists' attitudes', *American Journal of Psychiatry* 144(2): 164–9.

Hoencamp, E. (1990) 'Sexual abuse and the abuse of hypnosis in the therapeutic relationship', *International Journal of Clinical and Experimental Hypnosis* 38(4): 283–97.

Holroyd, J. C. and Bouhoutsos, J. C. (1985) 'Biassed reporting of therapist–patient sexual intimacy', *Professional Psychology* 16: 701–9.

Holroyd, J. C. and Brodsky, A. M. (1977) 'Psychologists' attitudes and practices regarding erotic and nonerotic physical contact with patients', *American Psychologist* 32: 843–9.

—— (1980) 'Does touching patients lead to sexual intercourse?' *Professional Psychology* 11: 807–11.

Kardener, S., Fuller, M. and Mensh, I. (1976) 'A survey of physicians' attitudes and practices regarding erotic and nonerotic contact with patients', *American Journal of Psychiatry* 130: 1077–81.

Levenson, J. L. (1986) 'When a colleague practises unethically: guidelines for intervention', *Journal of Counselling and Development* 64: 315–17.

Long, T. (1992) '"To protect the public and ensure justice is done": an examination of the Philip Donnelly case', *Journal of Advanced Nursing* 17: 5–9.

McCartney, J. (1966) 'Overt transference', *Journal of Sex Research* 2: 227–37.

Marmor, J. (1972) 'Sexual acting out in psychotherapy', *American Journal of Psychoanalysis* 32: 3–8.

Pattison, J. E. (1973) 'Effects of touch on self-exploration and the therapeutic relationship', *Journal of Consulting and Clinical Psychology* 40(2): 170–5.

Perry, J. A. (1976) 'Physicians' erotic and nonerotic physical involvement with patients', *American Journal of Psychiatry* 133(7): 838–40.

Pope, K. S. (1989) 'Sexual intimacies between psychologists and their students and supervisees: research, standards and professional liability', *Independent Practitioner* 9(2): 33–41.

—— (1990) 'Therapist–patient sexual involvement: a review of the research', *Clinical Psychology Review* 10: 477–90.

—— (1991a) 'Unanswered questions about rehabilitating therapist–patient sex offenders', *Independent Practitioner* 18(2): 5–7.

—— (1991b) 'Rehabilitation plans and expert testimony for therapists who have been sexually involved with a patient', *Independent Practitioner* 22(3): 31–9.

Pope, K. S. and Bajt, T. C. (1988) 'When laws and values conflict: a dilemma for psychologists', *American Psychologist* 43: 828.

Pope, K. S. and Bouhoutsos, J. C. (1986) *Sexual Intimacy between Therapists and Patients*, New York: Praeger.

Pope, K. S., Keith-Spiegel, P. and Tabachnik, B. G. (1986) 'Sexual attraction to clients: the human therapist and the (sometimes) inhuman training system', *American Psychologist* 41(2): 147–158.

Pope, K. S., Levenson, H. and Schover, L. R. (1979) 'Sexual intimacy in psychology training: results and implications of a national survey', *American Psychologist* 34(8): 682–9.

Pope, K. S., Tabachnik, B. G. and Keith-Spiegel, P. (1987) 'Ethics of practice: the beliefs and behaviours of psychologists as therapists', *American Psychologist* 42(11): 993–1006.

Pope, K. S., and Vetter, V. A. (1991) 'Prior therapist–patient sexual involvement among patients seen by psychologists', *Psychology* 38(3): 429–38.

Schoener, G., Milgrom, J. H. and Gonsoriek, J. (1984) 'Sexual exploitation of clients by therapists', *Women and Therapy* 3: 63–9.

Shepard, M. (1971) *The Love Treatment: Sexual Intimacy between Patients and Psychotherapists*, New York: Wyden.

Siassi, I. and Thomas, M. (1973) 'Physicians and the new sexual freedom', *American Journal of Psychiatry* 130: 1256–57.

Sinclair, J. (1991) 'Article on sexual exploitation of clients by therapists', *Everywoman* (July): 27.

Sonne, J. L. and Pope, K. S. (1991) 'Treating victims of therapist–patient sexual involvement', *Psychotherapy* 28(1): 174–87.

Sreenivassan, U. (1989) 'Sexual exploitation of patients: the position of the Canadian Psychiatric Association', *Canadian Journal of Psychiatry* 34: 234–5.

Taylor, B. J. and Wagner, N. N. (1976) 'Sex between therapists and clients: a review and analysis', *Professional Psychiatry* 7: 593–601.

Thoreson, R. (1986) 'Training issues for professionals in distress', pp. 47–50 in R. R. Kilburg, P. E. Nathan and R. W. Thoreson (eds) *Professionals in Distress*, Washington, DC: American Psychological Association.

Vinson, J. S. (1987) 'Use of complaint procedures in cases of therapist–patient sexual contact', *Professional Psychology: Research and Practice* 18(2): 159–64.

Voth, H. (1972) 'Love affair between doctor and patient', *American Journal of Psychotherapy* 26: 394–400.

Zelen, S. L. (1985) 'Sexualisation of therapeutic relationships: the dual vulnerability of patient and therapist', *Psychotherapy* 22(2): 178–85.

FURTHER INFORMATION

**POPAN (Prevention of
Professional Abuse Network)**
Flat 1
20 Daleham Gardens
Hampstead
London NW3 5DA
Tel.: 071 794 3177

Chapter 25

An approach to the treatment of Post-Traumatic Stress Disorders (PTSD)

Nachman Alon and Talia Levine Bar-Yoseph

'NORMAL' RESPONSES TO EXTRAORDINARILY STRESSFUL SITUATIONS

Disastrous situations, whether naturally occurring (such as earthquakes, fires, floods and storms) or man-made (war, torture, violence, rape, child abuse), cause extreme disruption to the victims' lives. Individuals, families, groups and even whole communities experience, or are threatened with, major material, physical and/or psychological loss (Drabek 1986). This may shatter the fundamental *mental schemata* which constitute one's sense of personal, functional and interpersonal continuity and without which life is intolerable. The 'basic schemata' are the beliefs in one's invulnerability, in the trustworthiness of some people and in the predictability, manageability and meaning of the world (Horowitz 1986; Omer 1991; Omer and Alon 1994; Antonowski 1990). Such an experience evokes extreme mental anguish, as well as bodily disruption: hyper-arousal and increased sympathetic nervous system activity and reactivity to stimulation. These are evidenced by an increased EEG, alpha activity, heart and respiratory rate, and by disturbed sleep patterns (Kaplan and Sadock 1991). They may have to do with alternations in dopamine and norepinephrine levels as well as of endogenous opioids in the brain (Kolb 1987; Van der Kolk 1988).

If one's sense of personal continuity is to heal, the body has to resume balanced functioning, and the mental anguish has gradually to be processed and integrated into one's perceived world, through a pendular alternation between protective emotional numbness and constriction of interest and activity on the one hand, and painful re-experiencing of the event(s) through flashbacks, dreams and memories on the other (Horowitz 1986). Completion and integration are achieved when life before the trauma, the traumatic event itself, its meaning, the responses to it and life after, are perceived as parts of a meaningful continuum, rather than as fragmented, disconnected segments. *Personal continuity* is thus restored through cognitive and emotional working through; *functional continuity* is restored through relevant external action; while *interpersonal continuity* is restored by mutual support, trust and flexibility. Normally, advance in any one continuity facilitates advances in others, in a 'ripple effect' manner.

PTSD: FAILURES OF ADAPTATION

The Diagnostic and Statistical Manual of Mental Disorders (DSM-III-R) (American Psychiatric Association 1987) defines PTSD as follows:

(a) The person has experienced an event that is outside the range of usual human experience and that would be markedly distressing to almost anyone.

(b) The traumatic event is persistently re-experienced in at least one of the following ways:

    1 Recurrent and intrusive, distressing recollections of the event (in young children, repetitive play in which themes or aspects of the trauma are expressed).

    2 Recurrent distressing dreams of the event.

    3 Sudden acting or feeling as if the traumatic event were recurring (includes a sense of reliving the experience, illusions, hallucinations and dissociative (flashback) episodes, even those that occur upon awakening or intoxication).

    4 Intense psychological distress at exposure to events that symbolise or resemble an aspect of the traumatic event, including anniversaries of the trauma.

(c) Persistent avoidance of stimuli associated with the trauma, or numbing of general responsiveness (not present before the trauma) as indicated by at least three of the following:

    1 Efforts to avoid thoughts or feelings associated with the trauma.

    2 Efforts to avoid activities or situations that arouse recollections of the trauma.

    3 Inability to recall an important aspect of the trauma (psychogenic amnesia).

    4 Markedly diminished interest in significant activities (in young children, loss of recently acquired developmental skills such as toilet training or language skills).

    5 Feelings of detachment or estrangement from others.

    6 Restricted range of affect, e.g., unable to have loving feelings.

    7 Sense of a foreshortened future, e.g., does not expect to have a career, marriage or children, or a long life.

(d) Persistent symptoms of increased arousal (not present before the trauma), as indicated by at least two of the following:

    1 Difficulty falling or staying asleep.

    2 Irritability or outbursts of anger.

    3 Difficulty concentrating.

4 Hyper-vigilance.
5 Exaggerated startle response.
6 Physiologic reactivity upon exposure to events that symbolise or resemble an aspect of the traumatic event (e.g., a woman who was raped in a lift breaks out in sweat when entering any lift).
(e) Duration of the disturbance (symptoms in b, c and d above) of at least one month.

Onset of symptoms more than six months after the trauma is considered delayed onset. Duration for more than six months becomes chronic, and it has to do with self-aggravating family and work processes and interactions which fixate around issues of reciprocal helplessness, anger and blame (Alon 1985; Solomon *et al.* 1992). Family members may also become seriously and chronically affected by the original PTSD. The numbing aspect of PTSD is closely related to dissociative disorders and to unresolved grief disorders. In fact, it is often hypothesised that dissociative disorders, notably multiple personality disorder, have their origins in childhood trauma (Kluft 1984). PTSD may often be misdiagnosed, and inappropriately treated as factitious disorder, malingering, adjustment reaction, borderline personality disorder, schizophrenia, depression, panic disorder and generalised anxiety disorder (Kaplan and Sadock 1991).

VULNERABILITY FACTORS

The main factors determining the occurrence, duration and severity of an acute PTSD are the duration and intensity of the stressful situation (Kleber and Brom 1992). Personality factors, however, determine mainly the specific manifestation the acute PTSD will hold (Horowitz 1986) and the occurrence of a chronicity (Bernat 1991). Children and old people, as well as the economically and socially deprived, have more difficulty coping with PTSD (Kaplan and Sadock 1991). Previous traumatisation, such as child abuse or recent sudden loss, traumatic family background (for example, a family of Holocaust survivors) and previous psychological problems, as in hospitalisation or crises, are factors which predispose to acute or recurrent PTSD (Solomon 1989), while personality factors such as low perceived sense of control, lack of trust and low ego strength predispose one to difficulties in recovering from the trauma and to chronicity (Bernat 1991). Psychodynamic factors may also have a role in specific PTSD patterns, like the battered woman syndrome (Young and Gerson 1992). Child abuse may also bring about specific psychodynamic and developmental problems (Suffridge 1992). PTSD symptomatology may present even in people who have never sought help (Figley 1978; Solomon 1989).

The physical and human environment – health, physical resources, competence of leadership, availability and quality of leadership and of social support, clarity of information, roles and responsibilities, previous training and preparation, as well as early recognition of and intervention in PTSD – may be crucial, both for the prevention and overcoming of traumatic experiences (Omer and Alon 1994; Kleber and Brom 1992).

PSYCHOTHERAPY: THE CONTINUITY PRINCIPLE

Omer (1991) defined a unifying psychotherapeutic principle in treating PTSD as having the goal, whether with the individual, family, group or community, and at all stages of the problem cycle, of restoring the sense of personal, functional and interpersonal continuity that had been disrupted as the result of the traumatic experiences. Several forms of psychotherapy of PTSD conform to this principle, and it seems that most psychotherapists intuitively choose to work with it in emergency situations regardless of their habitual therapeutic approach. We will illustrate therapies of different stages of PTSD, all based on these principles.

MODELS OF PSYCHOTHERAPY OF THE ACUTE PHASE

Several models have been proposed for the treatment of acute PTSD (Ochberg 1991):

1 Individual psychotherapy. Among the influential models are Horowitz's (1986) brief psychodynamic psychotherapy and Ochberg's (1991) holistic model.
2 Behaviour therapy, based on trauma desensitization: exploration of the trauma, relaxation training with or without biofeedback, desensitization (Kleber and Brom 1992).
3 Cognitive-behaviour therapy.
4 Family therapy (Figley 1988), in which objectives are conjointly set, the problem is framed and then therapeutically reframed, and a family 'healing theory' is developed.
5 Self-help groups.
6 Group therapy (Rozynko and Dondershine 1991).
7 Milieu therapy (Solomon *et al.* 1992).

Treatment of the acute PTSD

The military front treatment of 'combat reaction', originally described by Salmon (1919), which is the most prevalent mode of treatment in many armies (Solomon and Benbenishty 1986) is based on *immediacy* – that is, treating the soldier as soon as possible after impact; *proximity* – as close as possible to the battlefield and to the unit; and *expectancy* – namely, communicating a systematic and clear expectancy for recovery and for a rapid resumption of functioning in the original unit. All may be conceived of as aspects of the continuity principle. The superiority of this 'harsh' approach to more 'soft', rear psychotherapies is well documented (Solomon and Benbenishty 1986). The basic principles apply to all forms of crisis intervention. Let us illustrate.

Case no. 1 – field treatment of an acute PTSD

In the 1973 war between Egypt and Israel a reserve officer, a psychotherapist in civilian life, was commanding a mechanised combat unit at the front line. A troop-carrier approached under light fire, and its commander, who had heard there was a psychologist around, sought the psychotherapist's help in dealing with 'a soldier who has collapsed'. The psychotherapist found the soldier lying on the floor of the vehicle, hyper-ventilating, mumbling, sweating and weeping. The crew members were standing around watching anxiously, neglecting their duties in spite of the bullet fire outside. Rapid inquiry revealed that the soldier had shown growing tension for several days. He had not eaten, slept or drunk anything except coffee. He had been smoking profusely, and had gradually become withdrawn. The psychotherapist assumed that the disruption the soldier had experienced had also become disruptive for the functioning of the whole crew. Intervention should therefore relate to the group as well as to the identified patient. A benevolent yet authoritative stance was indicated for this stressed, confused group. The commander was told emphatically to resume fighting, and to put all soldiers on duty except for two, who were to stay with the psychotherapist in order 'to learn what to do, so as to replace the psychotherapist later'. He then turned to the 'patient', starting with simple and basic questions, which grasped the soldier's attention and also helped in controlling hyper-ventilation by forcing him to talk. A simple relaxation exercise followed. The 'helper soldiers' were then told to make their friend eat and drink, while the psychotherapist continued to make the soldier talk. The 'patient' spoke of how anxious he was about his family, how difficult he found the mounting tension, how lonely and helpless he felt as his withdrawal progressed, and how affected he was by his unit's apparent helplessness with his situation. He was assured that this was a normal, universal reaction to threat, aggravated by dehydration, hunger, caffeine and nicotine, and that he would quickly recover now that his body was recovering and his mates were tending to him. After instructing the commander not to evacuate this soldier, but rather to keep him busy with much support, the psychotherapist left. Both the soldier and the crew showed an improvement on the two visits the psychotherapist made over the next three hours. Follow-up six months later showed that the intervention had allowed the soldier to resume functioning with no further problems. Maintaining the interpersonal and functional continuity by keeping the soldier with his unit rather than evacuating him were crucial in restoring well-being.

Case no. 2 – an acute family PTSD following a terrorist assault

A psychotherapist was asked to help a family whose apartment house had been attacked in a terrorist assault, resulting in several deaths and injuries. The family members – father, mother, and two sons aged six and nine – narrowly escaped, losing one another in the process. They all responded reasonably well in the following few days, until a financial crisis unrelated to the trauma occurred in the mother's family, shook the delicate balance and brought about a fully fledged PTSD to all members of the family: incessant terror, sleep disturbance, inability to resume, and avoidance of, previous study, work, domestic routines and staying alone; over-alertness, as extreme as watching the windows for hours on end looking for terrorists; and depression over the family crisis.

The first session was held in the home of the wife's family of origin. As the complex financial and social situation became clear, the psychotherapist contacted the municipal social services and secured their intervention in helping the family. Having thus achieved some peace of mind, the family held a de-briefing session in which each member recounted his or her action during and after the assault. The combined picture, which was vividly depicted in diagrams, and broadened as a result of the psychotherapist's questions to include thoughts and emotions, revealed everyone's courage and resourcefulness and delighted all, especially the proud parents.

The psychotherapist's next step was ostensibly to treat the children in this family, while indirectly helping the parents by asking them 'to serve as co-therapists and coaches for the children between sessions', thus fostering not only vicarious learning but also the resumption of habitual roles. Then freedom of movement at home was re-established by conjointly making a hierarchy of fear of the rooms, ranging from 'the most horrible, unbearable, devastating fear not to be tackled before next week' to the 'tiniest, bearable, comfortable fear that was almost no real problem to overcome'. On the door of the 'worst room', a conjointly made sign reading, 'The room of terrible fear! No entrance until next week!', and depicting a trembling Mickey Mouse, was drawn. The children were 'trained' to 'rush from the room in panic' to their parents' room, singing the 'Song of Fear', a humorously lamenting, wailing song improvised by the psychotherapist. In the following weeks they were taught self-hypnosis for relaxation and better sleep (proven by the spontaneous use of self-hypnosis for analgesia for toothache done by one of the children); then they were desensitised to the place in the house in which they had met the terrorists. This was done by playing ball near the site in such a way that the children would spontaneously run after it when it was missed. The family was then helped to resume work and study. The over-protective attitude of the father's employers, which made the father all the more depressed, had to be tackled so that the father would assume more, not less, responsibility. When the father started work again (also with a view to dealing more effectively with the family problem), the mother regained her competence at home and with the children. Each of the (ten) psychotherapy sessions would usually start with the joint family-and-psychotherapist lunch under the pretext that the psychotherapist came from a distant city and needed some refreshment. This was meant to reinforce family routine and cohesion. Since psychotherapy was overtly done with the children only, an open discussion of the parents' problems was quite limited. However, indirect discussions about children, about trauma and its implications, about the parents' image in the children's eyes, all served as an indirect suggestive psychotherapy for the parents. A two-year follow-up showed satisfactory adjustment.

An approach to treating the acute phase

Assessment

1 Assess the identified patient(s) and the family/group/community for numbing/intrusive symptoms (disruptions in personal continuity) as well as for disruptions in functioning and in relationships.
2 Assess whether others, such as family members, have been, or potentially are, affected by the problem. If psychotherapy is indicated, help with appropriate consultation/referral. When possible, give preference to working with the family/group to working with individuals.
3 Give special attention to areas of even minimal functioning: re-establishing continuities is best done on the basis of existing strengths and resources (including human resources).
4 Remember that the severity of symptoms by no means predicts the prognosis and outcome of psychotherapy.
5 The manner of appraisal should imply that the focus of attention is not 'personality-and-developmentally' focused but 'circumstances-and-present-and-future' orientated.

Milieu therapy

As far as possible, utilise and activate available material: human and organisational resources. Every person, every event can become 'therapeutic', if utilised to help the patient advance in the direction of bridging over some breach.

Communication

Establish communication on a simple level. Deal with down-to-earth matters before going to more complex issues. With the agitated or dissociated patient, the first goal is to capture their attention by whatever means, including touch.

Restoring personal continuity

(a) *Basic needs*: If necessary, allow for a medical check and for drinking, eating and sleeping. See to it that appropriate clothing, personal hygiene and other basic needs are taken care of. These actions are as therapeutic as any others, and should be a part of your therapeutic plan.

(b) *Orientation*: Orient the patient as to what has happened and what is happening now, including who you are, where he/she is and why, for how long, and so on.

(c) *Meaning*: Reframe the situation as being a 'normal, transitory process of adaptation'. Use positive expectancies without under-estimating difficulties and problems. Ascribing meaning to what has happened is vital (Figley 1988).

Processing the traumatic event(s)

(a) *Telling the story*: Have the patient(s) tell the story of the trauma repeatedly until the need to talk is exhausted and until a clear and full picture is obtained. Fill in memory gaps. Help them make an adaptive 'theory' of what has happened (Figley 1988).

(b) *Acknowledging emotions*: While recovering the facts of the event(s), name and discuss the accompanying emotions then and now, especially fear, anger, grief and guilt. If the patient finds it difficult to identify emotions and/or talk about them, make informed guesses about the emotional aspects of the event; for example, 'Most people would feel terribly guilty in this situation – how was it for you?' – so that the patient will still have a name for the emotions and will acknowledge and accept them.

(c) *Dealing with emotions*: Actively help the patient maintain a bearable level of emotional arousal (Horowitz 1986; Brown and Fromm 1986), by:

    1 Alternating between distancing tactics like exercise and acting, on the one hand, and introspection and exposure, on the other; emphasising either the observing ego or the experiencing ego stance. Useful techniques include helping the patient either to project memories on a TV screen for distancing, or to 'walk into the screen' for accessing emotions.

2 Gradually allowing the patient to move from observing to experiencing mode, thus increasing the dose of bearable pain.

3 When guilt is 'excessive' and normalisation does not decrease it, accept it and suggest symbolic reparatory ritual steps.

(d) *Overall psychotherapy structure*:

1 At this stage of psychotherapy, the frequency of such 'loaded' sessions should be as high as three to four 90-minute sessions per week.

2 Repeat the cycle in subsequent sessions until the gains are repeated and stabilised.

3 A full-blown emotional abreaction, believed in the past to be the treatment of choice, may overwhelm the patient and unnecessarily re-traumatise them. It should therefore be avoided (Brown and Fromm 1986).

4 Terminate the cycle only when the patient can comfortably discuss the events. The best indication for that stage is bodily and emotional exhaustion.

(e) *Hypnosis*: Hypnosis is an extremely useful modality for the treatment of acute PTSD, due to its power directly to stabilise bodily problems such as hyper-arousal, for relaxation and for the flexibility of thought and behaviour it fosters through suggestion and through the enhanced therapeutic rapport. The acute victim of PTSD is usually highly suggestible, and will respond favourably and promptly.

(f) *Pharmacotherapy*: At the acute phase, use pharmacotherapy only when stabilisation is not achieved by psychological interventions alone.

(g) *Functional continuity – action*: Make the patient act, even if on a very elementary level. Avoid doing things for them; preferably do things with them. Work to broaden the scope and complexity of functioning.

(h) *Interpersonal continuity – support*: Establish interpersonal support, preferably with significant others or other casualties; group work is very helpful in this respect. Mobilise whatever help you can get from others.

(i) *Psychotherapist's attitude*:

1 In all your actions, assume a benevolent yet authoritative (not authoritarian!) stance. The patient needs clarity, structure and some confidence in you; sharing your doubts with them is not useful.

2 When dealing with many casualties simultaneously, the psychotherapist should do only what others, less skilled, cannot do. The psychotherapist's time is better spent supervising others than in doing individual work.

Treating the delayed response

A delayed response may occur years, even decades, after the initial events. It may occur as a response to some stimulus which resembles or symbolises the original stimulus, or it may occur at a point of present trauma, crisis or loss. Psychotherapy has thus to deal simultaneously with both the present problem situation and the original, only partially resolved trauma. The intensity of the re-emergence of the original trauma may make it necessary to deal with this first, and to tackle the present situation only at a later time.

Case no. 3 – an acute delayed response

In 1985 Dan, a young veteran of the 1982 Lebanon war, was participating in a structured rehabilitation programme for the brain-injured in Israel. PTSD, if any, was considered to be of secondary importance in the overall serious sequelae of his head injury, which included loss of balance so severe that an urgent operation became essential. However, on arrival at hospital for the operation, he re-experienced the military field hospital in Lebanon in a hallucinatory manner with a tremendous sense of guilt and anxiety, grew extremely agitated, tore the medical equipment away and escaped from the hospital. He later announced his refusal to return to hospital, even if it cost him his health or possibly his life. A psychotherapist was called for consultation and after assessment proposed a four-hour marathon session 'to decrease re-experiencing the negative emotions from an unbearable to a bearable level, so as to enable Dan successfully to undergo the operation' – a minimalistic goal which Dan sceptically accepted.

During the marathon, the circumstances and stimuli that triggered the flashbacks were studied. Dan said that the sights and smells of the ward brought him back to that moment in the war when he had woken in hospital in severe pain from a prolonged state of unconsciousness. He could not account for the intense guilt he experienced.

He was then hypnotised and trained in projecting the memories onto a TV screen, 'to be detachedly and objectively observed while you are seated'. In this state he repeatedly watched the 'film' and became aware that each viewing brought new memories, and that emotions gradually and controllably intensified. At a certain moment, he became very agitated. He saw himself, wounded, confused and in severe pain, being carried into the hospital and noticing several casualties and corpses there. On further inquiry it became clear that when he was carried in this way, in a twilight state, he erroneously concluded that the casualties had all somehow been hit by his lorry, which in his mind had itself probably been hit by a shell and exploded. Therefore, 'he was the one to be blamed for the losses'. In defence against the mental pain he became totally amnesic to the experience, with only guilt reaching consciousness, as the flashback occurred. The psychotherapist and team now emphatically challenged this conclusion on purely logical grounds. If his lorry had exploded so violently, there was no chance of his surviving the explosion. 'His faulty conclusion was understandable in the light of his state, and in light of the human need to complete incomplete Gestalts, however irrational this may seem.' (The team believed this argument to be correct. No attempt at such persuasion could have been made had his guilt been more 'founded'.) Once Dan accepted this explanation, he experienced a tremendous relief from his guilt, was very exhausted and could enjoy profound relaxation.

Now he was ready for a desensitisation procedure. First, he learned to relax quickly and deeply. Then, while deeply relaxed, he watched alternately the war hospital and the real hospital on an imaginary TV set, having full control over the size, shape, colour and speed of the film, thus being able to control his level of anxiety. Throughout this stage suggestions were repeatedly made to the effect that he could *see* the real hospital and yet simultaneously *feel* deep comfort; 'You see the war hospital: it's in black and white, small, far away, double-speed film . . . a lot of "snow" . . . and yet your body stays deeply relaxed' – until the picture could be seen without much emotion. He then imagined being comfortably relaxed in a room in the 'real' hospital, enjoying the best of treatment and watching the shabby archive film showing the war hospital, remaining fully aware how real, friendly and caring was the real one, and how distant, far away, now unreal and 'just a memory' was the other.

He was then trained to use the mere thought of the 'real' hospital as a trigger for relaxation, and the war hospital memories as a trigger for distancing using the TV technique. After a four-hour session, he felt he could cope with the operation, and in fact did that successfully the following day.

In this case we see how personal historical continuity was damaged by loss of memory, by an unconscious thought process and the ensuing guilt which became a 'mental foreign body'. Once the personal breach was bridged over, the breach in functioning – in this case, taking care of his health – could be repaired. Considerable attention was paid to finding a balance between the need for distancing and the need for experiencing. Abreaction was actively avoided.

In another case, however, the psychotherapist chose to have the patient abreact rather than process the trauma in the manner described above. The patient in question was a young woman who, during military service, re-experienced a catastrophic childhood event in which severe family loss and a life-threatening injury took place. In spite of an overt initial alleviation of symptomatology, a separation a few months later evoked a depressive crisis, and the patient refused psychological help on the grounds that 'such help only deepens pain'. The crisis was overcome only with massive support and the formation of another relationship. In this particular case, abreaction seems to have unwittingly caused sensitisation rather than inoculation. She was exposed in psychotherapy to an overdose of pain that was beyond her ability to process. Distancing manoeuvres, as essential to psychotherapy as exposure moves (Horowitz 1986), were missing and the psychotherapy was not protective enough. This prevented her from recovering personal continuity.

TREATMENT OF CHRONIC PTSD

War and Holocaust may have far-reaching characterological and developmental effects which may turn chronic; for example, loss of modes of relatedness, pathological self-representations and impaired affective regulation (Brown and Fromm 1986). Chronicity is the outcome of a long process of ever-widening, intra- and interpersonal interacting vicious circles. For example, hyper-arousal and intrusion of memories interrupt sleep, inverting the habitual day/night cycles and causing fatigue, loss of concentration, irritability and deterioration in functioning; others react by benevolently taking responsibilities from the victim's shoulders, thus deepening the sense of helplessness, even victimisation; irritability further aggravates interpersonal friction and suspicion. Mutual self-fulfilling prophecies and rigid labelling are established. Both intra-personal and interpersonal patterns fixate and may perpetuate the situation indefinitely. Establishing a therapeutic alliance becomes very difficult, and at times only a cautious, indirect, one-down therapeutic approach can prevent an early drop-out (Alon 1985). Often only broad-spectrum, multifaceted, rehabilitative, educational and consultative teamwork can be of help (Ochberg 1991). Medication may be essential. In spite of intensive work in the field, clinical outcome research is still less than encouraging (Solomon *et al.* 1992).

Case no. 4 – a circumscribed chronic PTSD

Ruth, a forty-year-old married woman psychotherapist, a mother of two, attended a workshop on guided imagery. During a relaxation exercise she spontaneously experienced a fleeting distressing fantasy. She was a small child, walking in a field, and a tall, mean-looking man blocked her way. She came out of relaxation feeling very distressed, and sought professional help. More work revealed that as a child, she had been subjected to sexual abuse by an otherwise beloved uncle. Despite Ruth's initial unawareness of any connection, it soon became apparent that her lifelong history of unorgasmia and avoidance of sexuality, as well as her frequent nightmares and her emotional constriction in intimate relationships, originated with her childhood experiences, but these later became part of her relationships. Her husband had long ago unquestioningly accepted the scarcity of sex.

The first step in psychotherapy was to try to convince Ruth to have conjoint couples therapy. This she flatly and rigidly rejected, being afraid lest this would cause her husband, whom she conceived of as a very moralistic person, to reject her. She agreed, however, to share the problem with him privately, gradually and indirectly, as an attempt to counteract the 'conspiracy of silence'. No harm was done. In fact, to her relief, she discovered that although her husband responded at first with mild criticism of her 'over-reacting', he then became increasingly understanding and supportive on discovering that she did not withdraw resignedly from conversation. Instruction for pleasuring and sensate focusing (Kaplan 1974) turned the couple's attention away from the highly loaded field of sex into the more relaxed field of intimacy. Simultaneously, the traumatic experiences were clarified. Her guilt over her compliance to the man was counteracted, but as it did not fully subside, she was encouraged to take reparatory steps. With a great sense of mission, she volunteered to do psychotherapy in a drop-in clinic for child abuse victims, and this alleviated much of the remaining guilt. The emotional deadlock (being unable to get angry at the abusing uncle because of her love for him, and being unable fully to love him because of the resentment) was partially resolved by reframing her attitude to her uncle as 'loving the *person*, yet hating the particular *deeds*'. Under hypnosis she was then told, 'Watch little Ruth in distress with the eyes of the adult, experienced, empathic woman. . . . Knowing little Ruth better than anyone else in the world, you are able to help the little girl in the way most appropriate for her.' At that point she felt tremendous anger toward the perpetrator. In her fantasy, she prevented him by force from harming the little girl, then comforted her and established herself as an 'inner guard and counsellor' for little Ruth. An interactional 'beneficious' (as opposed to 'vicious') circle gradually evolved (Alon 1985) and enabled the couple to lead their own successful version of sex therapy. Consultation at this stage was aimed at problem-solving and at further consultation for this 'private' psychotherapy. Desensitisation to the traumatic events was then successfully achieved by controlled exposure.

In this particular case, personal continuity was enhanced by recovering memories and feelings, and by re-establishing a sense of trust via a fantasised relationship between the inner child and an inner parent. The interpersonal continuity was re-established by opening communication with the spouse and by indirectly engaging him in psychotherapy, whereas functional continuity was achieved by indirect, behaviourally orientated sex therapy.

Case no. 5 – chronic PTSD: individual treatment

Gad, a thirty-five-year-old married technician, reserve veteran and survivor of a massive bombardment in the 1982 war, was hospitalised in 1985.

He was diagnosed as suffering from atypical psychosis, and intensively treated with anti-psychotic drugs. Previously an industrious worker, Gad had started avoiding work after the war because of somatic complaints. He began to consume alcohol as a tranquilliser, to have sudden temper tantrums and depressive episodes, severe conflicts with treating agencies and occasional hallucination-like re-experiencing of his war memories. The situation at home became difficult. His wife gave up her job in order to help him and then grew bitter and frustrated when no change occurred. Hospital-isation complicated things further, not only by isolating Gad and damaging his self-esteem, but also by adding the adverse effects of medication.

The consultant suggested an alternative diagnosis of PTSD, and recom-mended release from the hospital and treatment at the out-patient clinic. The couple were relieved and hopeful. They were told that their problem was a well-known phenomenon, that most people would respond similarly to the difficult circumstances of war and its aftermath, and that although the situation was not easy to treat, it was far from hopeless, and that with determination and hard work it would improve. Stabilisation was declared to be the first goal. For several weeks, complaints were treated with anti-depressant medication and hypno-behavioural methods (Brown and Fromm 1986) – relaxation and exercise for sleep, cognitive-behavioural strategies for irritability and sleep deprivation – for the reversal of the day/night sleep patterns. Couples counselling improved the home situation to some extent, as did the fact that Gad's wife resumed work. However, Gad's perfectionist, rigid and masochistic attitudes remained a source of vulnerability.

At the time, an experimental project for the treatment of chronic PTSD casualties of the Lebanon war was initiated by the Military Mental Health Authorities (Bleich *et al.* 1992; Solomon *et al.* 1992). Gad decided to volunteer.

Case no. 6 – a comprehensive milieu treatment

The project, which Gad had joined, took place three years after the Lebanon war. The forty-five veterans with chronic PTSD who volunteered for the project were treated in a military installation for thirty days, by three platoon teams, each consisting of two psychotherapists with past mili-tary experience and behavioural training, a physical-fitness instructor with experience in rehabilitation, and two squad leaders. The basic assumptions of the project were that PTSD was based on avoidance and therefore behavioural exposure and coping skills training were the treatments of choice (Solomon *et al.* 1992).

The project schedule was tight: an early wake-up, playful morning swimming, physical education activities ranging from judo to competitive football, a group session dealing mainly with everyday events and their meaning, coping skills group training, another physical fitness lesson, individual sessions, social events, basic military retraining and a self-help group. Each soldier made his own personal behaviourally defined goals, so as to make progress measurable. *Esprit de corps* developed very rapidly. The interest shown by the military and the enthusiasm of the psychotherapists and participants alike was, for many, a corrective emotional experience. Spouses were trained in assertiveness, dealing with anger, child-rearing and so on. After the project ended, self-help couples groups continued to meet regularly for two years.

In spite of much enthusiasm among participants and staff, and in spite of marked improvement among individuals, research outcome was less encouraging. It seemed that patients were worse off at the end of the project on the intrusion dimension. In retrospect, stressing the here-and-now and avoiding dealing with the traumata, as well as exposing the patients to the military rather than to their natural civilian environment, constituted a breach of the continuity principle (Bleich *et al.* 1992).

Returning to case no. 5

Gad's depression deepened in the first two weeks of the project. The group took great pains to help him, and the concern shown was invaluable to him. Despite depression, he functioned adequately in the group, due to much encouraging and friendly pressure. It seemed that restoring functional and interpersonal continuities 'compensated', so to speak, for not dealing with the trauma. Towards the end of the project his energy and good mood rose considerably and, for the first time in three years, he was able to enjoy himself. However, his personal goals – notably, returning to work – were only partially met.

A few months after the project ended, Gad had another depressive episode after a quarrel at work. The self-help group organised a three-week home hospitalisation which helped him recover and take decisions about his career. He decided to retire on medical grounds, collect his pension and become the house caretaker, while his wife worked and provided income. This decision meant for him an end to the tyranny of macho values and the start of a new freedom. The plan was implemented with success, and in a five-year follow-up both spouses defined their present situation as 'happy'.

Dos and don'ts in treating chronic PTSD

Assessment

Assess bodily, intra-personal, interpersonal and organisational forces and vicious cycles that maintain the problems. Assess areas of undisturbed functioning and identify actual and potential support resources. Look for characterological problems and pre-morbid factors. Assess whether other family members need help.

Pharmacotherapy

Pharmacotherapy may be essential in counteracting chronic hyper-arousal. Imipramine (Tofranil) and phenelzine (Nardil) are most often reported to be useful in the treatment of PTSD. Preliminary studies reported on the effectiveness of clonidine (Catapres), propranolol (Inderal), benzodiazepines, lithium and carbamazepine (Tegretol) (Kaplan and Sadock 1991). Complement this treatment with self-hypnosis and/or biofeedback.

Stages of psychotherapy

(Brown and Fromm 1986; Alon 1985) The proposed stages should be flexibly applied. The more rigid the patient, the more useful will adherence to them be. We suggest that going from one stage to the next will be done only when the previous one has been stabilised.

1 *Establish a working alliance*. Chronic patients often appear 'resistant' due to their disillusionment with treatments, suspicion, criticism and anger. 'Resistance' is lessened when the psychotherapist (a) accepts the problem as 'normal in the difficult situation in which you have been', and (b) poses only modest, concrete goals, rejecting requests for more ambitious ones on the grounds that they have only limited power in the face of 'such a history of frustration, pain and misunderstandings'. Educating the patient and the family about PTSD is very important at this stage.
2 *Block vicious cycles and stabilise the symptom-picture*. Relief of symptoms and interpersonal frictions (functional and interpersonal continuity) at this stage takes precedence over more emotional aspects (personal continuity). Once relief is achieved, the patient will willingly go into more meaningful areas. Pay special attention to problems arising from avoidance. Target symptoms may be sleep disturbances, autonomic hyper-arousal, temper tantrums, flashbacks and/or behavioural avoidance. Preferred tools are relaxation training; physical exercise; desensitisation and exposure; coping skills (such as anger control); cognitive-behavioural tools (such as the modification of catastrophic self-talk); paradoxical interventions ('Do all you can *not* to fall asleep; instead, write down every thought so that we can cope with the sleep-preventing thinking' often leads to a good night's sleep); distraction; and directive family interventions ('I would like you to have a conjoint family dinner three times this week, so that we can better evaluate aspects of family

climate') for re-establishing family roles and routines. Self-monitoring is important in engaging the patient as a member of the therapeutic team. 'Disguising' intervention as 'diagnostic procedures' increases the likelihood of co-operation: readiness for risk-taking and commitment is higher at 'diagnosis' than at actual psychotherapy. After all, what could one resist in a diagnostic procedure?

3 *Activate 'beneficious cycles' that promote exploration and development of hitherto blocked functioning, so that change will become self-reinforcing.* Complement these cycles with skills such as assertiveness, friendship training and so on. Look for behaviours that will stimulate significant others to respond favourably, such as re-introducing the patient to long-avoided activities with the children. Often it is easier to induce significant, less damaged, others to activate such cycles than to help the avoidant, anxious patient to initiate change.

4 *Deal with the trauma in a controlled manner*, alternating between distancing and re-experiencing as suggested above. With patients who are reluctant to tackle the trauma, hold this stage until the end of the next stage.

5 *Deal with the more generalised personality and thinking patterns* – tendencies of dependency, avoidance, victimisation, somatisation and so on. At this stage the psychotherapist can deal more openly with hitherto untackled issues.

6 *Deal with long-standing psychodynamic issues when necessary.* Always be prepared for a prolonged psychotherapy, and for unexpected relapses and conflicts, especially at times of stress. Expect anniversary reactions, which may call for emergency interventions.

Teamwork

The need for co-operation with physicians, treating agencies, rehabilitation workers, law agencies, schools, vocational placement workers and other relevant people cannot be over-estimated. Without such teamwork the likelihood of getting to a therapeutic dead end becomes very high.

Relations between patient and psychotherapist

PTSD chronic patients may appear 'resistant' and 'uncooperative'. It may take considerable patience and flexibility to overcome counter-transferential reactions such as disappointment, resentment, blaming and fatigue. These have to be expected and handled, otherwise negative vicious cycles can easily occur in psychotherapy. These patients are often unaware of the positive aspects of their life, and do not volunteer positive feedback to the psychotherapist. One should therefore look for independent, 'objective' measures of therapeutic advance, to check against devaluing remarks.

A prevalent response towards patients' relapses is the assumption that the patient does not really *want* to change, or that 'What he *really* wants is compensation', and so on. This imputation of negative unconscious motivation is counter-productive. It is more appropriate to assume that the demands posed by psychotherapy were perceived by the patient as being beyond their powers, that the perceived disruption in continuity looked too deep to be bridged by that specific therapeutic move. In such cases it may be advisable to declare the relapse to be due to the psychotherapist's mistake ('I wrongly assumed that you could take more, having under-estimated your vulnerability') and either lower the demands or switch to another continuity.

Other relationship problems may include over-dependency, attempts at crossing boundaries of psychotherapy (for example, by protracted night telephone calls at times of crisis) and attempts to turn the psychotherapist into an ally in struggles with institutions on economic or practical matters. Keeping the fine balance between the necessary involvement and the no less necessary therapeutic distance becomes a special challenge, as is all the work with traumatic patients.

ACKNOWLEDGEMENT

The authors wish to thank Maggie Ridgewell for her valuable editorial assistance.

REFERENCES

Alon, N. (1985) 'An Ericksonian approach to the treatment of chronic post traumatic patients', pp. 307–26 in J. K. Zeig (ed.) *Ericksonian Psychotherapy*, vol. 2, New York: Brunner/Mazel.

American Psychiatric Association (1987) *Diagnostic and Statistical Manual of Mental Disorders (DSM-III-R)* (3rd edn, revised), Washington, DC: American Psychiatric Association.

Antonowski, A. (1990) 'Pathways leading to successful coping and health', pp. 31–63 in M. Rosenbaum (ed.) *Learned Resourcefulness*, New York: Springer Verlag.

Bernat, I. (1991) 'Pre-morbid personality factors in sustaining and recovering from combat stress reaction: their prediction value among Israeli combat soldiers in the 1982 Israel–Lebanon war', *Psychologia, Israeli Journal of Psychology* 2(2): 162–70.

Bleich, A., Shalev, A., Shoham, S., Solomon, Z. and Kotler, M. (1992) 'PTSD: theoretical and practical considerations reflected through Koach – an innovative treatment project', *Journal of Traumatic Stress*, 5(2): 265–72.

Brown, D. P. and Fromm, E. (1986) *Hypnotherapy and Hypnoanalysis*, Hillsdale, NJ: Lawrence Erlbaum.

Drabek, T. E. (1986) *Human Systems Responses to Disaster: An Inventory of Sociological Findings*, New York: Springer Verlag.

Figley, C. R. (1978) *Stress Reactions among Vietnam Veterans: Theory, Research and Treatment*, New York: Brunner/Mazel.

—— (1988) 'Post-traumatic family therapy', pp. 83–109 in F. M. Ochberg (ed.) *Post Traumatic Therapy and Victims of Violence*, New York: Brunner/Mazel.

Horowitz, M. J. (1986) *Stress Response Syndromes*, New York: Jason Aronson.

Kaplan, H. I. and Sadock, B. J. (1991) *Synopsis of Psychiatry*, Baltimore, MD: Williams & Wilkins.

Kaplan, S. H. (1974) *The New Sex Therapy*, New York: Penguin.

Kleber, R. J. and Brom, D. (1992) *Coping with Stress: Theory, Prevention and Treatment*, Amsterdam: Swets & Zillinger.

Kluft, R. P. (1984) 'An introduction to multiple personality disorder', *Psychiatric Annals* 14: 19–24.

—— (1985) 'Hypnotherapy of childhood multiple personality disorder', *American Journal of Clinical Hypnosis* 27: 201–10.

Kolb, L. C. (1987) 'A neuropsychological hypothesis explaining post traumatic stress disorders', *Psychiatry* 144: 989–95.

Lindey, J. D., Macleod, J., Spitz, L., Green, B. and Grace, M. (1988) *Vietnam: A Casebook*, New York: Brunner/Mazel.

Ochberg, F. M. (1991) 'Post-traumatic therapy', *Psychotherapy* 28(1): 5–15.

Omer, H. (1991) 'Massive trauma: the role of emergency teams', *Sihot-Dialogue: Israeli Journal of Psychotherapy* 5(3): 157–70.

Omer, H. and Alon, N. (1994) 'The continuity principle: a unified approach to treatment and management in disaster and trauma', *American Journal of Community Psychology* (in press).

Rozynko, V. and Dondershine, H. E. (1991) 'Trauma focus group therapy for Vietnam veterans', *Psychotherapy* 28(1): 157–62.

Salmon, T. W. (1919) 'The war neuroses and their lessons', *Journal of Medicine* 59.

Solomon, Z. (1989) 'A three-year prospective study of post-traumatic stress disorder in Israeli combat veterans', *Journal of Traumatic Stress* 2: 59–73.

Solomon, Z. and Benbenishty, R. (1986) 'The role of proximity, immediacy and expectancy in frontline treatment of combat stress reactions among Israelis in the Lebanon war', *American Journal of Psychiatry* 143(5): 613–17.

Solomon, Z., Bleich, A., Shoham, S., Nardi, C. and Kotler, M. (1992) 'The Koach project for treatment of combat-related PTSD: rationale, aims and methodology', *Journal of Traumatic Stress* 5(2): 175–93.

Suffridge, D. R. (1992) 'Survivors of child maltreatment: diagnostic formulations and therapeutic process', *Psychotherapy* 28(1): 67–75.

Van der Kolk, B. A. (1988) 'The biological response to psychic trauma', pp. 25–38 in F. M. Ochberg (ed.) *Post Traumatic Therapy and Victims of Violence*, New York: Brunner/Mazel.

Young, G. H. and Gerson, S. (1992) 'New psychoanalytic perspectives in masochism and spouse abuse', *Psychotherapy* 28(1): 30–8.

Chapter 26

Forensic psychotherapy

Estela V. Welldon

Crimes are directed against society; at any rate, this is what society believes. It is open to doubt whether that perception is accurate but, whether true or not, society has involved itself in the secret, sordid, domestic, run-of-the-mill situations which are the stuff of forensic psychotherapy. It is unfortunate that the focus of attention is most frequently placed exclusively on the offence and on the punishment of the offender. Any psychodynamic understanding of the offender and of their delinquent actions as a result of their own self-destructive internal and compulsive needs is automatically equated by society with their acquittal. This is an understandable but serious error.

The form of psychotherapy involved in forensic psychotherapy is different from other forms precisely because society is, willy-nilly, involved. Forensic psychotherapy has gone beyond the special relationship between patient and psychotherapist. It is a triangular situation – patient, psychotherapist, society. As Bluglass points out, 'The role of the forensic psychiatrist in confronting and trying to reconcile the differences between the interests of the law and those of psychiatry is a crucial and important one' (1990: 7).

Society, the state, authority is there looking over the end of the bed and making judgements. Analytical psychotherapy does not welcome this extra dimension in an already fraught and difficult task. But there is no option if the forensic psychotherapist is to help the patient; and of course the extra dimension is involved if the psychotherapist is to play a part in elucidating and resolving some of the painful problems with which society struggles, for the most part ineffectually.

Forensic psychotherapy is a new discipline. It is the offspring of forensic psychiatry and psychoanalytical psychotherapy. Its aim is the psychodynamic understanding of the offender and their consequent treatment, regardless of the seriousness of the offence. It involves understanding the unconscious motivations in the criminal mind which underlie the offences. This is not to condone the crime or excuse the criminal. On the contrary, the object is to help the offender and thereby to save society from further crime. One of the problems in achieving this object is that the offender attacks, through their actions, the outside world – society – which is immediately affected. Hence, concerns are rarely focused on the internal world of the offender. It is time to re-focus our concerns, at least in part. The more we understand about the criminal mind, the more we can take positive preventive action. This, in turn, could lead to better management and the implementation of more cost-effective treatment of patients.

The term 'forensic psychotherapy' has now been validated and legitimised. It is included, for example, in the final report of the Reed Committee (1992), the *Review of Health and Social Services for Mentally Disordered Offenders*.

This chapter will deal exclusively with the basic facts of forensic psychotherapy as it is practised in a National Health Service out-patient clinic, namely the Portman Clinic, where I have been working for over twenty years. Other settings such as special hospitals, medium secure units and therapeutic communities, though of great and increasing importance and relevance, are not directly addressed here, although the principles obtain in these institutions too.

The United Kingdom has from a very early stage been in the forefront of forensic psychotherapy and, within the United Kingdom, the Portman Clinic has been the leader. The history of the clinic (Rumney 1981) goes back to 1931, when a small group of men and women met in London and established an association to promote a better way of dealing with criminals than putting them in prison. It was later called the Association for the Scientific Treatment of Delinquency and Crime, a title proposed by an eminent psychoanalyst, Dr Glover, who became its first chairman (Cordess 1992a). Much later, in 1991, the original aims of the Portman Clinic were adopted by the newly established International Association for Forensic Psychotherapy. A year earlier, in 1990, the first course on forensic psychotherapy, sponsored by the British Post Graduate Medical Federation (University of London) in association with the Portman Clinic, began to train national and international professionals in the techniques of this special branch of psychotherapy. Williams (1991) describes the difficulties encountered in the successful bridging of both disciplines.

If forensic psychotherapy is the handling of three interacting positions – the psychotherapist's, the patient's and society's criminal justice system (de Smit 1992) – it follows that treatment of the forensic patient population should ideally be carried out within the National Health Service, and not within the private sector. Forensic psychotherapy has to be considered in the overall context of health care for people involved in the criminal justice process. Its aims, however, are not identical to those of the criminal justice system. There is an inevitable, and indeed necessary, conflict of values (Harding 1992). Evaluations should ideally be conducted independently, according to criteria which correspond to health-based values (Reed Report 1992).

A discipline such as this needs explanation. If we can understand the relationship between the offender and society we shall be making progress in research into the causes and prevention of crime. This is one of the tasks to which the Portman Clinic has been dedicated from its earliest days. For example, society instinctively views sexual offenders and their victims in distinct and reflex ways. Whereas the treatment of victims is encouraged and everyone is concerned about their welfare, the same does not apply to the perpetrators who are believed to be the products of 'evil forces'. Lip-service is paid to the fact that victims could easily become perpetrators, but emotional responses tend to be biased. The split is in full operation. Victims are left without the benefit of a full understanding, since generally it is expected and assumed that they are devoid of any negative, hostile feelings. The healthy expression of those feelings is not allowed and this suppression easily leads to revenge.

Another relevant stereotype is that in which women are victims and men perpetrators. When men are sexual abusers all sorts of different agencies, social and medical, intervene and very soon the police are called in. By contrast, the female 'offender' finds it very difficult to get a hearing (Welldon 1988/1992). Nobody wants to hear about her predicament, and nobody takes her too seriously. This happens even in group therapy where she finds that other patients minimise her problems. This reaction proves very anti-therapeutic, and if the psychotherapist is not ready to interpret this total denial for them, these women will never gain any insight into their problems, let alone be able to change themselves. The difficulties in acknowledging a woman's abusing power in motherhood ('they don't do those awful things') could be the result of massive denial, as a way of dealing with this unpalatable truth. Until recently, a lack of legislation on female perversion reflected society's total denial of it. The woman is thereby seen as a part-object, or just a receptacle of a man's perverse designs. The apparent idealisation of mothers prevalent in society contains a denigrating counterpart.

These are amongst the reasons for regretting that society has been slow to recognise the limited but significant contribution which forensic psycho-therapists can make to the achievement of a dynamic understanding of the causes of delinquent and criminal behaviour. A major cross-disciplinary effort should be make to understand and eradicate at least some of the more correctable reasons for crime in our society. This involves political scientists, sociologists and community leaders as well as forensic workers. An imaginative effort is required to promote discussion and to educate the general public. Forensic psychotherapists can and must play a crucial role in this, but the main burden must fall on those in the media and in politics who have special skills of communication.

A crucial point about the discipline of forensic psychotherapy is that it is a team effort. The full meaning of this phrase will emerge from the discussion which follows, but at the outset it needs to be stated that this is not an heroic action by the psychotherapist alone. The action begins with the referral agencies, which include the courts of justice. But court or no court, there is no getting away from the fact that the offender's actions are blatantly carried out against society or those principles society values, and which we all share. Accordingly, a wide range of people are inescapably involved.

It is crucial to recognise that successful treatment rests not only with the professional psychotherapist but also with a team of helpers, including psychologists, social workers, administration and the clerical staff. In the sixty years of the Portman's experience the rapport of our patients to the clinic itself, and not just to their psychotherapist, has become basic to our approach.

For the general public it is, no doubt, society which matters most; but for the professional forensic psychotherapist the prime consideration must be the patient. If forensic psychotherapy is concerned above all with the patient, it must be scarcely less concerned with the 'treater' and their training. Why? Because, if they are not properly trained, the members of the team are bound to feel confused and overwhelmed by all the dimensions involved, many of which are unpleasant and stressful. The importance of the development of this discipline in the United Kingdom as an evolving species (Adshead 1991) is our main concern. If the treater is not trained and equipped with insight into their own internal world and their own motivations, they may unwittingly react to a situation as if they were a normal member of the public. This is a very natural reaction, but unfortunately it is an abdication of responsibility: it is unprofessional.

REFERRAL OF PATIENTS AND NATURE OF THE OFFENCES

Patients are referred to the Portman Clinic and other forensic psychotherapists by various sources: external and self-referral. External sources include general psychiatric hospitals, general practitioners, probation officers, courts and other institutions. In some cases the public knowledge of a patient's sexual and/or criminal offence is very wide, as a result of that person having appeared in court – often with associated press reports. Usually, self-referrals are patients whose 'bizarre', unlawful sexual behaviour is unknown to anyone except themselves and their victims. They come to the clinic of their own free will. A very important characteristic in determining the prognosis and motivation for treatment is an intense sense of shame and despondency about the activities in which they are involved. This is reciprocated by society's response in judging and condemning them when their behaviour is detected regardless of their own feelings about their criminal actions. Both offender and society feel bewildered and unable to comprehend the motivations or symbolism attached to their deviant actions.

The criminal action is the central fact. Sometimes it has the capacity to become explosive, violent and uncontrollable, with attendant profound consequences for society. At times, it is the equivalent of a neurotic symptom. Pfäfflin (1993) describes the symptom as a constructive and healthy reaction. He adds that it is conservative, meaning that the patient needs it and keeps it until it can be properly understood and then he can give it up. At other times, it is the expression of more severe psychopathology; it is secretive, completely encapsulated and split from the rest of the patient's personality, which acts as a defence against a psychotic illness (Hopper 1991); at still other times, it is calculated and associated with professional, careerist criminality. The criminal action always appears understandable as an action against society, and yet at the same time it is a self-destructive act, with harmful effects for the offender. This aspect of criminality associated with unconscious guilt has been examined by Freud (1915), Glover (1960) and Tuovinen (1973), amongst others.

The action may be characterised by a manic defence, created against the acknowledgement or recognition of a masked chronic depression. Alternatively, it may include compulsion, impulsivity, inability to intersperse thought before action and, as mentioned earlier, a total failure to understand it.

The forensic patient is unable to think before the action occurs because they are not mentally equipped to make the necessary links (Bion 1959). Their thinking process is not functioning in their particular area of perversity, which is often encapsulated from the rest of their personality. This therefore is the work of psychotherapy; but at times the patient's tendency to make sadistic attacks on their own capacity for thought and reflection is projected and directed against the psychotherapist's capacity to think and reflect, and it is then that the psychotherapist feels confused, numbed and unable to make any useful interpretations.

Most forensic patients have deeply disturbed backgrounds. Some have criminal records and a very low self-esteem often covered by a façade of cockiness and arrogance; their impulse control is minimal, and they are suspicious and filled with hatred towards people in authority. Some rebellious and violent ex-convicts have long histories of crime against property and persons. Others may refer themselves, and in these cases are often insecure, inadequate and ashamed people. They enact their pathological sexual deviancy, such as exhibitionism, paedophilia or voyeurism, in a very secretive manner so that only their victims know about their behaviour. Some patients have a great capacity for expressing anger, yet seem shy and awkward in showing tenderness or love to anybody.

Often, forensic patients are deviant both sexually and socially. Some sexual deviations present themselves as criminal activities by definition, although some patients who indulge in these actions may never have been caught. This is a secret or secretive population who apparently lead normal lives, sometimes in both work and domestic situations. However, the links between criminal actions such as 'breaking and entering' and sexual deviations are not always obvious, at least not until the unconscious motivation is revealed. This connection has been noticed by many psycho-analytical authors, such as Zilboorg (1955), Glover (1944) and Limentani (1984).

ON THE LINKS BETWEEN CRIMINAL ACTIONS AND SEXUAL DEVIATIONS

Example 1

I will illustrate this point with a clinical vignette. A patient of twenty-eight was referred years ago by his employers, a City bank. This was, in itself, a revelation that a City bank could be so perceptive of the possibility of unconscious motivations. They had experienced a sense of bewilderment at this puzzling offence. He was the bank's 'bike' man, responsible for carrying money from and to different places. In the course of his work, he had been detected stealing spanners from other bikes' boxes. Alarm grew greatly when police found evidence of his having previously stolen 3,000 spanners. At the interview with me he tried unsuccessfully to make sense of his unlawful actions by explaining that he was a handyman and that the price of tools was subject to inflation. Obviously, such a clumsy and inadequate explanation pointed to other motivations. In describing his actions, he talked with a great deal of embarrassment mixed with excitement. In his own words:

> I'm on my bike. Suddenly I see another bike being parked and I feel taken over by an extreme curiosity to look at its box. I know this is wrong but cannot help myself. I start sweating. I feel my heart pumping and I just have to do it. I have to take the tools. Then I feel at peace, a great sense of relief surrounds me. I feel great. On my way home I start feeling confused, ashamed and guilty. I don't know any longer what to do with yet another spanner and I take it to the garage where I keep them all.

His statement is similar to that of a person suffering from sexual perversion, showing the same quality of urgency, the identical cycle which involves growing sexual anxiety, the fight against it, eventually giving in and succumbing to the action, the sexual relief, and the subsequent sense of shame and guilt.

This was a young, well-groomed man who was still living with his mother, a domineering, narcissistic woman who had never allowed him to lead his own life. When the police came to get him, her first reaction was: 'What shall I do if you take him away? I can't be on my own!' Apart from his mother he had never had any relationship of any sort and lived in complete isolation.

Our psychiatric court report briefly indicated that this man's criminal offences were the expression of his tremendous sense of social and sexual inadequacy which, in turn, were the product of a deprived and depraved early childhood. His father had been absent in the war and his mother had a severe narcissistic borderline personality. The magistrate not only found the report but also the recommendation useful. The patient was recommended to seek treatment in group psychotherapy, which, if accepted, was to be implemented immediately. The work of psychotherapy consisted of his growing awareness of the unconscious links between the sexual symbolisms and the enactment of his irresistible impulses. This unravelling made it possible for the patient to free himself from these urges.

ON OVERLAPPING OF SEXUAL PREDICAMENTS AND HIDDEN VIOLENCE

Example 2

Sometimes sexual predicaments and hidden violence overlap, as, for example, in the following brief case history. A young man of twenty-three first came to treatment because of fears of being homosexual. After a year of individual psychotherapy he left treatment having overcome that particular problem. A few years later he was back; this time, because he had experienced sudden, and unexpectedly violent, fantasies against all women, but particularly his mother, and later his girlfriend. He had achieved an intimate situation with his girlfriend but felt the urge to hurt her. In an obvious attempt to do so, he had had a one-night stand with another girl. In the following group session he described to us a recent dream. In this he had his fist inside a woman's vagina and was punching it vigorously. When he began to enjoy this process he became aware he was disintegrating: first the hand began to dissolve and later the whole body was annihilated. This dream represented his fears of being destroyed by a woman if he became close to her. His fear of homosexuality had been a protection – replaced later by a deeper fear, expressed through violent fantasies – against women who, he felt, had previously damaged him, indeed almost emasculated him.

ON THE DIFFERENT AIMS OF MALE AND FEMALE PERVERSIONS

As a clinician I have observed that the main difference between a male and female perverse action lies in the aim. Whereas in men the act is aimed at an outside part-object, in women it is usually against themselves, either against their bodies or against objects which they see as their own creations; that is, their babies. In both cases, bodies and babies are treated as part-objects (Welldon 1988/1992).

Example 3

A patient who was a practising prostitute was referred for a psychiatric assessment because of violent behaviour directed towards her second child. She had been a victim of paternal sexual abuse. Her first pregnancy came as a surprise to her. Still, she felt the need to go ahead with it, because in this way she was taking out insurance against a dread of being alone. The child could become utterly dependent on her and totally under her control. When this first child arrived, she was overcome by feelings of repulsion and revulsion against her baby. She felt ready to kick it, and after reflection she decided that in order to overcome these horrid feelings she would fix in her mind the idea of the baby being part of herself. Some days she would choose her right arm as being the baby, and at other times it would be one of her legs. In this way she felt able to master her impulses to beat up her first child. Later, with her second baby she asserted, 'There is no more room in my body for a second one. All has been used up by the first one.'

Example 4

Another woman patient was referred because of exhibitionism. She told me that her compulsion to 'flash' occurred when she became attached to a person whom she invested with idealised 'maternal' qualities. She wanted to get closer, to be noticed and to be taken care of by that particular person but she also wanted a shocked response from her 'victims'. She carefully planned the 'appropriate' clothing to wear when she was to meet that person. Usually she wore an overcoat covering only a little vest in order to respond readily to her urge. She knew this was wrong and that she would be rejected but she could not stop herself. She had a most deprived early history of being sexually abused by her mother and her siblings. It is interesting to note that, even when her exhibitionism could superficially appear to be the equivalent of her male counterpart's, this is not so. It is a well-known fact that male exhibitionists have the compulsion to 'flash' only to children and women – and women who are unknown to them – while my patient had suffered from this compulsion only with other women with whom she felt a close attachment. This is yet another remarkable difference between the genders.

In short, the sources of referral are various and the type of people who become patients even more so. But, if understanding is to occur, all patients must be treated according to a rigorous professional code in which the offender is understood whilst the crime is not condoned. This process must begin with a comprehensive assessment of the patient.

THE PSYCHODYNAMIC ASSESSMENT

The patient should be clear from the outset about the reasons for the assessment interviews. This is particularly important since the procedure could easily be taken as yet another legalistic encounter. If the purpose is the writing of a psychiatric court report this should be made clear from the start. All interviews should embody the utmost honesty. If treatment is recommended the patient should be told the length of the waiting list – especially if it is a long one – and should be informed that the assessment process may involve three or four meetings. Forensic patients usually complain and are sarcastic about the fact that an 'assessment' or psychiatric court report has been made within a mere twenty minutes of meeting a psychiatrist. They should not be allowed to get away with this caricature of a professional assessment by making sure that the allocated time is adequate for the purposes of a psychiatric report. The 'structuring of time' as coined by Cox (1978/1992b: 338) is a vital frame in forensic psychotherapy, and it is quite different as practised by forensic psychiatrists, who should be ready to be summoned at any time. Instead, forensic psychotherapists are aware that patients can only rely on those psychotherapists who keep strict timing for their sessions.

In the initial period of treatment, beginning with the first interview, it is especially important to follow firm guidelines. Never make a patient wait beyond the appointment time – neither earlier nor later; earlier will be felt as seduction, later as a sense of neglect, repeating the experience of 'nobody caring'. These diagnostic meetings should be conducted at irregular intervals in order to avoid the intensity of the emergence of transference. The meetings are not as structured as psychotherapy sessions: there is some flexibility but the timing is always to be preserved rigorously. The approach needs judiciously to combine silence and direct questioning so that the patient can feel allowed to talk freely about difficult and, at times, painful predicaments while also being expected to give, in answer to questions, more details for further clarification.

The clinician must not let the patient involve him/her in anti-therapeutic manoeuvring, such as laughing at a patient's joke. Frequently, such jokes are made at the expense of the patient's own self-esteem, with overtones of self-contempt and denigration of themselves: 'Nobody takes me seriously.'

Patients often try to engage the clinician in a jocular response. It is a serious mistake, into which inexperienced psychotherapists fall, to appear friendly and non-judgemental. No sooner has the psychotherapist laughed than a sudden realisation emerges that they are laughing *at* the patient and not *with* the patient.

During the assessment sessions, there are often attempts to re-create the original injurious, traumatic situation as experienced by the patient. Frequently, this will have been experienced as being treated as a 'part-object', and becomes vividly alive in the transference.

A sense of boundaries is crucial, amongst many other layers of need, to establish a sense of differentiation, in which 'them' and 'us' create a sense of order and justice which can be rightly acknowledged. This is one reason why patients powerfully resent the 'do-gooders'. In their eyes the 'do-gooders' try to proselytise, to infantilise, to make them believe 'we are all the same', a statement which is felt to be hypocritical, and based on double standards.

Summary of general approach in the psychodynamic assessment:

- The patient should be clear about the purpose of the meeting.
- This should be obtained in one to three sessions, at irregular intervals.
- Exact timing.
- Never engage in jocular response to the patient's 'jokes'.
- Keep a straightforward approach, neither too cold nor too friendly.
- Make it clear that information is needed for accuracy of the evaluation process.
- Listen to the patient's predicaments but if patient feels 'stuck' ask direct questions.

The psychodynamic meaning of the offence could be diagnosed as:

1 Neurotic symptoms.
2 Defence against psychotic breakdown, completely encapsulated and split from the rest of the personality.
3 'Careerist'-orientated.
4 Acting out as defined by Limentani (1989): an expression of the person's fantasy life and its motivation is at first unconscious, as a means of relieving increasing and unbearable sexual anxiety, and as a form of communication of anti-social acts.

THE CIRCUMSTANCES OF ASSESSMENT

Setting and surroundings are important – especially since the forensic patient has usually had previous experience of the judicial system, having been caught, detected and judged. In his dealings with the psychotherapist, he is likely to feel judged, charged, persecuted and subject to prejudice. If the diagnostician is not well trained, a new confrontation could easily be experienced by the prospective patient as a further condemnation of their illegal action. At times the action is symptomatic, in which the person knows it is wrong but finds themselves unable to resist it. At other times the action is an enactment which the person is not willing to admit is odd or wrong. This action has sometimes been unconsciously committed, in an attempt to obtain a response from society to the predicament of the individual offender; the action takes over, and society focuses its attention on the action and not on the person who has committed it, until, of course, it comes to condemnation.

Therefore, it is of basic importance to 'see' and to 'acknowledge' the person in their totality. For example, it is important that letters regarding all appointments are properly and formally addressed to 'Mr' or 'Mrs'. The same attitude should prevail when the patient arrives at the clinic where they are to be seen. The building should be accessible, the atmosphere warm and the attitude welcoming from the moment the patient faces the receptionist. Patients should be treated with dignity – surnames only, for example – and everything reasonable done to give them enough self-respect to face the complexities of their first diagnostic consultation with an unknown consultant. It is worth remembering that someone who has been referred for a psychiatric court report, fresh from involvement with police inquiries concerning offences, is frightened about having to face yet another figure of authority who is expected to be ready to judge and condemn.

Because of their fears of intimacy in the one-to-one situation these patients form a strong transference to the clinic as an institution. The institution treating them can become as important as, or more important than the psychotherapist themselves. A safe and containing atmosphere in which the patients feel secure and acknowledged from the moment of their arrival is essential. In short, the assessment is to be carried out like any other assessment but, if anything, with even more care and sensitivity.

Institutional setting

Forensic patients are very much in need of three structures – fellow patients, psychotherapist and institution – and family (if they have one). All are deeply related in their mental representations, which constitute a process of triangulation.

An important function provided by the institution is that of containment. It reinforces a sense of boundaries and so acts as a container for all tensions involved and allows the emergence of trust and a collective awareness of, and sensitivity to, the recrudescence of violence, reducing its likelihood.

At times of crisis, when for many reasons staff members are unable to fulfil these tasks properly, a breakdown of the system is likely – with serious consequences for all, including the patients.

Cordess (1992b) has described the application of family therapy to work with psychotic offenders and their family victims in a regional secure unit.

The topic of forensic psychotherapy and its contribution to forensic psychiatry in an institutional setting has been described by Cox (1983). The failure of psychotherapy to thrive specifically within the British special hospitals is critically examined by Pilgrim (1987).

TRANSFERENCE

It is necessary to understand the personality traits of forensic patients since they lead directly into an understanding of the transference and counter-transference phenomena, which appear from the beginning of the assessment and during the psychodynamic treatment.

An early and severe emotional deprivation is usually found in the psychogenesis of both sexes, which may include a history of neglect, abandonment, symbiotic relationship with mother, humiliation of gender identity, physical abuse, sexual abuse, wrong gender assignment at birth, cross-dressing during infancy. All the above may occur, either singly or in any combination. However, the commonest case is the victim of both seduction and neglect. There has frequently been an absence of acknowledgement of generational differences, especially in cases of incest with children being 'forced' to fulfil parental roles and victims becoming perpetrators, leading to the three-generational process.

These adult patients have experienced – as infants – a sense of having been messed about in crucial circumstances in which both psychological and biological survival were at stake. In other words, they were *actually* – in reality, not only in fantasy – at the mercy of others. These traumatic, continuous and inconsistent attitudes towards them have effectively interfered with the process of individuation and separation. There is a basic lack of trust towards the significant carer, which accompanies them all through their lives. From this early ill-treatment we can deduce some psychopathological features which will be understood in the light of the early background:

1 Need to be in control, which is apparent from the moment they are first seen and also during treatment.
2 Early experiences of deprivation and subjection to seductiveness make them vulnerable to anything which in any way is reminiscent of the original experiences.
3 A desire for revenge expressed in sadomasochism as an unconscious need to inflict harm.

4 Erotisation or sexualisation of the action.
5 Manic defence against depression.

There are very elaborate and sophisticated unconscious mechanisms which these patients have built up in themselves, which operate as a 'self-survival kit': this is 'turned on' automatically in situations of extreme vulnerability when they experience being psychically naked or 'stripped'. They use over-sexualisation in the same way, as a means to deal with an enormous sense of inadequacy and of inner insecurity. They themselves become the part-objects to be readily available and easily exploited, abused, seduced. Of course, this is no longer a unilateral, one-way system as happened when they were infants at the mercy of their parents or carers. Now, to the whole world, they appear to be adults, but, actually, much of their internal world belongs to much earlier phases of their emotional development in which an enormous sense of helplessness was acquired, and much revenge has been harboured for a long time. The one-way system has become a two-way system which is in constant dynamic activity. And here the psycho-therapist's work has to be defined. It is obvious that all these different survival mechanisms and ways of functioning will appear intermittently when the defences are down. Then alarm and the old feelings re-emerge and put the person concerned on the alert. Defence mechanisms go in waves, and when a situation of closeness is about to be achieved the person withdraws in horror. Such people loathe any new scenario which might involve or develop into trust. Thus the person could appear as a tyrannical and despotic paternal figure, who is only there to satisfy their own whims.

COUNTER-TRANSFERENCE

The forensic psychotherapist should feel safe and securely contained in caring and unobtrusive surroundings. Institutions should provide such structures, to protect the psychotherapists from the inherent anxiety produced by working with forensic patients. These patients act out sadistic and intrusive attacks on psychotherapists and on their treatment in many different ways, including on their capacity to think; this leaves psychotherapists confused and unable to offer adequate interpretations.

Money matters are important both in concrete and in symbolic terms. This is obvious with patients whose day-to-day living is provided by their own or close associates' delinquent or perverse actions. A frequent problem is the offer or 'pushing' of a gift which could at times render the psychotherapist a receiver of stolen goods.

The psychotherapists' inner knowledge that the state is paying for their professional services becomes invaluable while working with this patient population, since they are also aware of this basic fact. It reinforces both parties in the contractual agreement on which the psychotherapy is based.

The psychotherapists are debarred from blackmail, and the patients feel neither exploited nor able to exploit anybody about money matters. 'The forensic psychotherapist spends much of his time and energy waiting and witnessing, while his patients try to unravel that vitally important nodal point of experience "between the acting of a dreadful thing/And the first motion"' (Cox 1992a: 255).

The psychotherapist must listen to the patient carefully, without interrupting, however difficult or painful the material may be. Some supposedly 'unusual' or 'rare' predicaments are not that unusual: the so-called rarity is often due to the clinician's inability to listen because of the psychic pain involved. This is frequently the case with incestuous relationships. It is important to be aware of how our own feelings may be the origin, for example, of the under-recording of female perversions – such as female paedophilia and maternal incest. Patients may be ready to talk about these urges, but diagnosticians generally are not ready to listen to them. The requirement of personal psychotherapy for future treaters is of basic importance – in order to be able to discern what belongs to the treater's internal world and what to the patient. Most of these patients' material can disturb profoundly because at times it feels like dealing with dynamite. Sometimes, if unprepared, the psychotherapist could easily become irate, as if they are being 'taken for a ride', and indeed the patient often tries to be in total control of the situation. In other instances, patients succeed in making their psychotherapists become their true partners in their specific perversions. Here is a brief history of a case which illustrates the point.

Example 5

A patient came for a diagnostic interview because of his compulsive masochistic needs. These involved the hiring of prostitutes for the purpose of actively ill-treating him in a way which sexually excited him. In the course of the interview, the psychotherapist found to her horror that she had become actively engaged in a dialogue in which she began to scream at the top of her voice. She realised that every time she tried to say something to the patient he asked her to repeat it 'just a bit louder, because I'm hard of hearing'. One of the reasons the psychotherapist became aware of her own response was that at the time the patient was relating an incident in which he had secured the services of a nurse to function as a sadistic prostitute. The nurse symbolised the caring profession, which had been corrupted.

Alternatively, the treater may feel flattered by the fact that whatever positive change may have been achieved, the patients may ascribe it to the practitioner's own professional efforts. However, the flattery won't last for long; it will soon be replaced by complaints and dissatisfaction about relapses or re-offending assumed to be due to the practitioner's inefficiency and lack of 'skills', just as before the 'cure' of the problem had to do with their excellence.

In other words, there is a constant switch between idealisation and denigration. This happens because psychopathological predicaments and offending behaviour are the result of a deep, chronic, hidden depression. This turns into a manic and at times bizarrely funny acting out. There is so much pain underneath that the patient barely manages at times to confront it. They try at all costs to avoid their real feelings. The psycho-therapist could easily be caught in the counter-transference process, assuming an omnipotent role in the patient's actions regardless of whether they are law-abiding or not.

SELECTION CRITERIA FOR PSYCHOTHERAPY

It is important here to make a basic distinction between offenders who are mentally disordered and those who are not. Some offenders have a professional orientation towards their criminal activities. For example, they calculate the consequences, even going so far as to engage in a cost-benefit planning of their actions, involving such matters as how many months or years in prison they are prepared to risk. In other words, such offenders may not differ in important psychological traits from careerists generally. These two seemingly different categories do at times overlap or succeed each other. It is not unusual to find patients who have been criminal 'careerists' for a number of years but who, on reaching their thirties, begin to question the validity of what they are doing and express a deep interest in seeking professional help to change their lifestyles.

The psychodynamic assessment requires a wider understanding of all other factors concerning that particular person, their psychological growth, their family – taking it back at least three generations – their own subculture, and other circumstances. The psychotherapist needs to investi-gate the 'crimes' in detail, especially the sequence of events leading up to the action as well as the offender's reaction to it. This can give clues to early traumatic experiences, and to the unconscious ways through which an individual tries to resolve conflicts resulting from these experiences. In this way, even during the evaluation itself, the psychotherapist is able slowly to uncover layers of primitive defences and the motivations behind them – enabling us to learn about the offender's capacity or incapacity for psychodynamic treatment, as well as initiating a process whereby the offender might acquire insight into the nature of their crimes.

It is important to record how the patient interacts with the clinician and the changes observed during the series of meetings. At times it is useful to make a 'trial' interpretation to elicit the patient's capacity to make use of it, and their capacity for insight. In order to assess treatability for psychotherapy accurately in these patients, we must modify terms and concepts from those used in assessing neurotic patients. For example, when the criminal action is committed clumsily, the person is especially susceptible to detection. The criminal action has become the equivalent of the neurotic symptom. The offender may also express fears of a custodial sentence, which may in their own terms denote motivation for treatment. This could signal that it is the appropriate time to start treatment, since the patient is susceptible, however much under implied duress. They are now ready to own their psychopathology, and this may denote an incipient sense of capacity for insight. From this therapeutic standpoint, it is not unfortunate that a patient has to face persecution, but what is unfortunate is that just when they are ready for treatment they may instead have to face punishment. The patient may actually acquire a criminal record for the first time while in treatment or on the waiting list. Ironically, the very success of our treatment may produce this result. It is when the patient who has hitherto escaped detection starts to acquire some insight into themselves, they become clumsy and are detected.

The relapse in delinquent and criminal behaviour is frequently found during the first long holidays in psychotherapy. This is associated with feelings of having been abandoned by their psychotherapists at times of need. Gallwey points out that this occurrence as

> The uncovering of areas of deprivation and unfulfilled dependency can produce enormous pressure on both therapist and patient, with a speedy move into delinquent acting out, or even violence, when the patient feels let down or abandoned within the therapy. The least hazardous tactic is to contain the individual in a way which minimises the reinforcement of delinquent strategies.
>
> (1992: 359)

Delinquent adolescents also require innovative modifications of the traditional psychoanalytical therapeutic approach, as emphasised by du Bois (1992) and Scannell (1992).

It is vital to look closely at particular psychopathologies and needs, and to see if the selection criteria could be improved, either for group or individual psychotherapy. For example, given that the patients concerned present serious personality disorders and are unable to form relationships, it is obvious that some are more suitable than others for group treatment. It is important to assess certain factors in their personalities, family structure and living circumstances. For instance, the root family influence is crucial.

INDIVIDUAL ANALYTICAL PSYCHOTHERAPY

Patients who have never experienced satisfactory relationships in early life – for example, those who come from very large families with financial deprivation and emotional overcrowding – are likely to do better in individual treatment than in group treatment. Patients who are adopted or fostered react in quite different fashions, depending on whether they join a new group in which all members were 'born' simultaneously, or one with previous history and traditions. In the latter, they feel 'on trial' and closely observed by others, who are perceived as the 'old', 'legitimate', 'real' children.

Sometimes patients present themselves as 'perfect', 'ideal' patients for group therapy, but it transpires that they are rather good actors, often having been exposed previously to similar experiences in therapeutic prisons or communities. Indeed, they become good helpers but get little for themselves. This does not mean that they should not be treated in groups, but they warrant special consideration and might be treated more effectively in one-to-one psychotherapy.

Assessment of patients' present living circumstances is crucial. There are those who could benefit from group therapy but are involved in the criminal world. If they open up and talk of their own or their spouse's criminal activities, the confidentiality rule is impossible to sustain.

Example 6

Extreme secretiveness is sometimes a contraindication. For example, John, who came to the clinic because of frotteurism, was a shy, awkward married man with children who had never confessed to anyone about this perversion, and had even refused to give his address. At the first session when he admitted to his problem, the group's reaction seemed one of anxiety, covered by laughter. Everyone tried to minimise his symptom to such an extent that he felt humiliated, whereupon he became very flushed and left, never to return.

GROUP PSYCHOTHERAPY

Patients who have been subjected to an intense, suffocating relationship with one parent are suitable candidates for group therapy. Groups provide them with a much warmer and less threatening atmosphere than they can usually find in one-to-one psychotherapy, in which their sense of authority would be so intense. They can also share their experience with their peers. Often these people are still subjugated by an over-possessive mother, who will not allow them to develop any independence or individuation. Others have left home only to find themselves extremely isolated. In the group, with the help of fellow patients, they begin to express openly some rebellious, anti-authority feelings and eventually some self-assertion.

Bion (1967/1984) says that communication develops into a capacity not only for toleration by the self of its own psychic qualities, but also as a part of the social capacity of the individual. 'This development, of great importance in group dynamics, has received virtually no attention; its absence would make even scientific communication impossible' (p. 118).

Violent behaviour seems better contained and even better understood within the framework of group therapy. Freud points out that the mechanism of identification is a basic one in group formation, and he elaborates that identification not only helps to further positive feelings within the group, but also helps in limiting aggressiveness – since there is a general tendency to spare those with whom one is identified. The presence of other participants, who may notice hostility before it is expressed openly (often against the psychotherapist), gives the group a capacity to confront violent behaviour and to deal with it openly and honestly. Multiple transference provides patients with the possibility of more than just one target (as in one-to-one psychotherapy) for their anger, which they find highly reassuring.

This patient population presents a worthwhile challenge given the potential benefits of group analytical treatment for such 'anti-social' and 'asocial' people. All share an intense sense of shame and despondency about the activities in which they are involved. Group treatment often proves to be the most appropriate method of treatment if we use adequate selection criteria, are careful about the composition of the group and employ a modified technique keeping in mind the patients' particular psychopathology. The price paid for effectiveness is to give up rigid ideological psychotherapeutic principles.

Example 7

Gaining of insight and its communication are often not straightforward in working with destructive patients. A clear example of this occurred in a group session in which a member notorious for his criminal activities, which were at the service of the enhancement of his false self, told the other group members of changes he had experienced.

Herbert said, 'I am very worried about myself. I've recently noticed that when I'm about to embark on conning other people I lose my cool. For example, the other day when I went to the bank to pass some forged cheques I got scared. My heart began to pound, I got all sweaty in my hands, I avoided eye contact with the cashier. In other words, I was giving myself away.'

Another member asked, 'Do you think this *consciousness* has anything to do with this group?' Everybody showed much interest in this statement. (The term had never been used before.)

To which he replied, 'Yes. It has all happened since I came here and I am very scared.' This was an important change which had to do with his criminal activity changing from ego-syntonic to ego-dystonic. In other words, his capacity to corrupt his ego integrity was no longer so easily available, due to the formation of a new ego which had been internalised from the group, with an accompanying capacity for reflection. Perverse mechanisms in other patients were readily available. The group was split in two: some accepted this as a healthy development but others were not as generous with their response because of extreme envy.

So Adam, another member, said, 'I am extremely worried about you and the effect this group has on you if this means that you are becoming more ineffectual as a thief. Perhaps you ought to do something about that – I don't know whether you ought to leave the group or what, but be sure that the group is not affecting your skills as a thief.'

Other group members reacted to this statement in a very angry fashion, calling it cynical. They pointed out that, after all, Herbert had come to psychotherapy in order to deal with his criminal actions.

But Adam was merciless with his manic reaction, saying while laughing: 'He's not coming here to deal with his thieving problems, he's coming here because, as the doctor has remarked on many occasions, of his sense of emptiness, his deadness and his looking for excitement. So, first he'll have to know about this boredom. In the meantime he has to be careful not to get caught.'

Separation anxieties can easily produce most dangerous acting out. Psychotherapists' holidays are very distressing for group members since they feel neglected, abandoned and uncared for, just as they did when they were infants. There are often, however, signals in the sessions leading up to holidays that 'something is going on'. It is important to detect and recognise these clues, for they form part of this constellation or syndrome responsible for 'acting out' behaviour. It may be seen as a resistance to the therapeutic process (Welldon 1984).

The amount of fear, rejection and humiliation which such patients experience when confronted with their 'secrets' in a group therapy session is difficult to convey. It is not unusual for them to deal with their enormous fears of being rejected by conjuring up an image of a nagging or possessive mother who has been experienced as both frightening and rather contemptuous. They will tend to agree with one another, thus creating an atmosphere of unhealthy solidarity, with the main object of assigning that image to the psychotherapist. The psychotherapist may be trapped into situations, such as becoming a sadistic policeman who, every time they talk about their problems, will try to moralise, condemn, or put them away; or a nagging mother, who will use the group to question every patient in a persistent and repetitive way about their illegal actions, expecting them to conform to society's norms. Hence the psychotherapist has to be skilful in dealing with such interactions between patients from the outset. If collusion appears, this will create further anxieties because patients are aware that covering up brings frustrations when the psychotherapist does not intervene properly by offering adequate interpretations. Unless unhealthy expectations can be interpreted quickly as part of transference interpretations, the psychotherapist and their expertise are likely to be immobilised.

Psychotherapy aims to provide the patient with the necessary under-standing of their chosen symbolisms, and the part that the affect plays in them, but in the instance of the forensic patient this is especially relevant since this anxiety is only relieved by bizarre actions, of whose unconscious mechanisms they are aware. If they are able to gain the relevant insight, they might then interpose the thought between the urge and the action. This new link is created to overcome or to prevent succumbing to the acting out. In Bion's words, 'a capacity to think would diminish the sense of frustration intrinsic to appreciation of the gap between a wish and its fulfilment' (1967/1984: 113).

This process is highly accelerated in group psychotherapy when a group member, whose particular psychopathology is driven by a compulsive need to alleviate the increasing tension, is confronted by other group members at different stages and that member's condition is understood in some of its intricacies. At this point the rest of the group does the thinking. The learning by experience then is multiplied not only by the actual number of group members but also by their own growing process of maturation, which intrinsically involves the development of their own capacity to think.

Example 8

A patient came because of her compulsive shoplifting. She was an extremely intelligent person who, to start with, could not apprehend the complicated mechanisms involved in her self-destructive behaviour, despite her deep motivation for important inner change. Eventually she began to learn of her rage against her partner, and her desire for revenge which pervaded the acting out, that took place after angry rows with him because of her inability to tolerate frustration. It was only when she learned about it in transferential terms that she told the other group members how she had been able to resist the temptation to steal a beautiful garment in the most propitious circumstances. In her thinking she had been able to replace authority – loved/hated parents/therapist/husband – by her peer-group members. In this way she thought of what her fellow patients' actions and feelings would be after her shoplifting. She had first said to herself: 'I want this jacket very badly, and it will make me feel great.' Immediately, she recoiled from that urge by thinking of the 'afterwards': the group process involving both peer group and authority. Then she proceeded: 'I know that what I most want in my life is peace of mind and this will never be achieved by this theft, because I'm doing it in order to take revenge. As a matter of fact, the opposite will happen. Afterwards, I will feel full of shame and self-disgust.'

She had been able to interpose this thought before the action, using both her newly gained insight and the group as an auxiliary ego which stopped her, this time, from committing the action. After she had appropriately left her psychotherapy, the hope she created lived on for a long time as other members of the group talked of how deeply affected they were by her experience and how much help they had gained from her capacity to learn. Her urge to steal had to do with the aggrandisement of her false self – in order to reinforce her omnipotence versus her despondency; her discovery about herself needed to be communicated to the other members, because it constituted an important dimension of her recognition of her own true self.

Group analytical therapy may often be the best form of treatment not only for some severely disturbed perverse patients, but especially so for sexual abusers and sexually abused patients. Secrecy is the key issue in incest. It has prevailed not only in the one-to-one situation but also through collusion in the dynamics of the family situation. This being so, group analytical psychotherapy becomes the chosen treatment for these patients. The family-social microcosm which occurs in group therapy affords them a much better understanding of their problems since they are so deeply related to violence and anti-social actions that occur within the family dynamics.

This is very different to a one-to-one situation in which these patients tend to feel unique, and usually succeed in making the psychotherapist feel not only protective but also possessive about them. In some cases, this can even provoke feelings of collusion in the psychotherapist, who could easily feel cornered or blackmailed by the confidentiality clause. At other times, the psychotherapist might feel either as the consenting child or as the seductive parent in the incest situation. Either way psychotherapy – meaning internal change – is in real jeopardy.

The group setting will not allow this transferential–counter-transferential process to take place. Group members must open up and overcome the taboo of secrecy. This is because trust must lie with the peers and not only with the psychotherapist.

Sometimes these patients present problems related to violence and secrecy in the family, as in the case of incest where the fathers or mothers – yes, mothers too – have been the perpetrators of the sexual abuse. Alternatively, in the case of adult women, an undetected early history of incest accounts for a wide spectrum of problems, from chronic psycho-somatic symptoms to a very high incidence of prostitution. These are unconsciously related to those early traumatic events, which underlie the present unconscious motivations for their predicaments.

For example, I have seen female patients with a history of early incest who, while entering group analytical psychotherapy, behave from the very start as 'ideal assistants' to the psychotherapist. Even those who had previously never been familiar with the unconscious processes seem to discover immediately appropriate ways to 'help' the psychotherapist-mother-father keep the group-family together. Fellow patients often react with surprise and bewilderment, and later with competitiveness. When interpretations are made to the effect that the newcomer is repeating a pathological pattern learned early in life, fellow patients seem relieved by this understanding, but it is then the turn of the newcomer to be filled with rage at this interpretation. After all, she is 'doing her best'; why is she being so 'harshly criticised'?

Secrecy, especially in paternal incest, is at the core of the situation; each member of the family is involved, whether 'knowing' or 'unknowing', but nobody talks about it. Indeed, when paternal incest has occurred it is irrelevant whether mother acknowledges the possibility of incest or not. Had she been able to acknowledge it in the first place, incest would never have happened. Incest is committed in an effort to create ties to 'keep the family together'. Nobody 'knows' about it, or rather nobody acknowledges it.

By treating in a group the victims and perpetrators of incest and, for that matter, also both genders as perpetrators and victims, there are unexpected qualities of containment and insight to be gained which could be virtually impossible in a one-to-one situation. Also, perpetrators become deeply aware of the vast consequences of their actions when confronted by other members who correspond to their victims' mirror reflections, and they grasp how unable they are to see themselves as separate human beings, but only as parts of their parental figures. For example, each member experiences a powerful sense of belonging to the group. Expressions of self-assertion, emotional growth, independence and individuation are some of the characteristics that patients acquire during the treatment period, in which they see others and themselves developing into individuals with respected self-esteem acknowledged by others and by themselves. At times they are not only allowed but encouraged to express openly anger and frustration which has been kept hidden for long periods of time. This encouragement comes especially from other 'old' members who have gone through similar predicaments.

Workers of all sorts involved in cases of incest frequently find it difficult to maintain a detached, professional stance. They tend to take sides, usually becoming emotionally bound to the victims. Additionally, or alternatively, they feel punitive towards the perpetrators. In their distress, they lose their understanding of the dynamics of what is happening. For example, they sometimes become so indignant that they fail to see that victims who become perpetrators experience a conscious or unconscious desire to avenge the pain inflicted upon them. These victim-perpetrators believe they are creating a situation in which justice is satisfied. Actually, however, they are identifying with their aggressors. In somewhat similar ways, the professional workers often identify with the victims.

According to Davies (1992), the network could easily become corrupt, hence the therapeutic task is first to recognise the splits operating with the staff members before this could reach the patient population.

There is a strong tendency for the workers in incest cases to re-enact within their professional network the splits, denials and projections which are so characteristic of the experience of family members caught up in the dynamics of incest. In such circumstances, we professionals would do well to listen to one another, thus allowing healthy interactions in a different context. This could lead to better integration of professional workers dealing with members of a family involved in incest. So, in a sense, the patients could usefully become role models for the psychotherapists.

ACKNOWLEDGEMENTS

The author owes a great debt to Dr Limentani, one of her earliest mentors, for his valuable contribution to this chapter. She wishes to thank Dr Chris Cordess for his useful suggestions, and is grateful to Kate Brophy for her expert secretarial help.

REFERENCES

Adshead, G. (1991) 'The forensic psychiatrist: dying breed or evolving species?' *Psychiatric Bulletin/British Journal of Psychiatry* 15: 410–12.
Bion, W. R. (1959) 'Attacks on linking', *International Journal of Psychoanalysis* 40(5 and 6): 308–15.
—— (1984) *Second Thoughts*, London: Karnac (originally published 1967).
Bluglass, R. (1990) 'The scope of forensic psychiatry', *Journal of Forensic Psychiatry* 1(1): 7.
Bois, R. du (1992) 'Adolescent delinquents: psychodynamics and therapeutic approach', pp. 353–9 in *Proceedings of the 17th International Congress of the International Academy of Law and Mental Health*, Leuven, Belgium.
Cordess, C. (1992a) 'Pioneers in forensic psychiatry: Edward Glover. Psycho-analysis and crime – a fragile legacy', *Journal of Forensic Psychiatry* 3(3): 509–30.
—— (1992b) 'Family therapy with psychotic offenders and family victims in a forensic psychiatric secure unit', *Proceedings of the 17th International Congress of the International Academy of Law and Mental Health*, Leuven, Belgium.
Cox, M. (1983) 'The contribution of dynamic psychotherapy to forensic psychiatry and vice versa', *International Journal of Law and Psychiatry* 6: 89–99.
—— (1992a) 'Forensic psychiatry and forensic psychotherapy', p. 255 in M. Cox (ed.) *Shakespeare Comes to Broadmoor*, London and Philadelphia: Jessica Kingsley Publishers.
—— (1992b) 'Forensic psychotherapy: an emergent discipline', p. 338 in *Proceedings of the 17th International Congress of the International Academy of Law and Mental Health*, Leuven, Belgium (first published 1978).

Davies, R. (1992) 'The corrupt network', *1st International Congress of the International Association of Forensic Psychotherapy*, London.

Freud, S. (1915) 'Some character-types met with in psychoanalytic work', *Standard Edition*, vol. 14: 311–33.

Gallwey, P. (1992) 'Social maladjustment', pp. 359–81 in J. Holmes (ed.) *Textbook of Psychotherapy in Psychiatric Practice*, London: Churchill Livingstone.

Glover, E. (1944) *Mental Abnormality and Crime*, London: Macmillan.

—— (1960) *The Roots of Crime*, London: Imago.

Harding, T. (1992) 'Research and evaluation in forensic psychotherapy', *1st International Conference of the International Association of Forensic Psychotherapy*, London.

Hopper, E. (1991) 'Encapsulation as a defence against the fear of annihilation', *International Journal of Psychoanalysis* 72(4): 607–24.

Limentani, A. (1984) 'Toward a unified conception of the origins of sexual and social deviancy in young persons', *International Journal of Psychoanalytical Psychotherapy* 10: 383–401.

—— (1989) *Between Freud and Klein*, London: Free Association Books.

Pfäfflin, F. (1993) 'What is in a symptom? A conservative approach in the therapy of sex offenders', *Journal of Offender Rehabilitation, Department of Sex Research*, Psychiatric Clinic, Universitätskrankenhaus Eppendorf, Hamburg (in press).

Pilgrim, D. (1987) 'Psychotherapy in British special hospitals: a case of failure to thrive', *Free Associations* 11: 59–72.

Reed Report (1992) *Report of the Academic Advisory Group 1992*, London: Department of Health/Home Office.

Rumney, D. (1981) 'The history of the Portman Clinic', Unpublished monograph.

Scannell, T. (1992) 'Infant psychiatric principles in working with adolescents', *1st International Congress of the 1st International Association of Forensic Psychotherapy*, London.

Smit, B. de (1992) 'The end of beginning is the beginning of the end: the structure of the initial interview in forensic psychiatry'. *Proceedings of the 17th International Congress of the International Academy of Law and Mental Health*, Leuven, Belgium.

Tuovinen, M. (1973) 'Crime as an attempt at intrapsychic adaptation', Monograph, University of Oulu, Finland.

Welldon, E. (1984) 'The application of group analytic psychotherapy to those with sexual perversions', pp. 96–108 in T. Lear (ed.) *Spheres of Group Analysis*, Naas, Co. Kildare: Leicester Leader.

—— (1992) *Mother, Madonna, Whore: The Idealisation and Denigration of Motherhood*, New York: Guilford Press (original work published 1988 by Free Association Books, London).

Williams, T. (1991) 'Forensic psychotherapy: symbiosis or impossibility', Address given at 17th International Congress of the International Academy of Law and Mental Health, Leuven, Belgium.

Zilboorg, G. (1955) *The Psychology of the Criminal Act and Punishment*, London: Hogarth Press and Institute of Psycho-Analysis.

For further information see also the material on Grendon Underwood Prison referenced in Table 18.1 (page 316).

Chapter 27

Psychotherapy with the dying and the bereaved

Colin Murray Parkes and Charlotte Sills

A great deal of research has taken place in recent years into the problems occasioned by the loss by death of a loved person. This has clearly demonstrated that bereavement can cause serious damage to physical and mental health. It has also shown that bereavements, like other stressful situations in life, are opportunities for personal growth and maturation.

We are now beginning to understand why it is that some people emerge from the stress of bereavement stronger and wiser, while others develop lasting problems. The identification of these causal sequences not only facilitates the treatment of pathology, it also opens the door to prevention. At times of bereavement we have the opportunity to identify people who are at risk before they become mentally or physically ill and to reduce the risk by appropriate action. Random allocation studies by Raphael in Australia (1977) and by Parkes in the United Kingdom (1981) have demonstrated the reduction in pathology which can result from preventive intervention programmes offered to 'high-risk' bereaved. They provide clear evidence that the right kind of counselling, given to the right people at the right time, can be effective; and they fully justify the establishment of counselling services for the bereaved. Most bereavement counsellors in the United Kingdom are not professional psychotherapists; they are volunteers who have received a short course of basic training and a period of supervised probation before becoming fully accredited. The evidence of Parkes's study (1981) indicates that this degree of expertise is quite sufficient to enable them to reduce bereavement risk in a majority of bereaved people.

Psychotherapists who choose to do so can provide valuable support to such services by assisting in the selection, training and supervision of counsellors and by treating the minority of bereaved people who 'fall through the net', either because they fail to respond to counselling or because it is apparent from the start that their problems are of such gravity or complexity that it is unreasonable to expect a lay counsellor to take them on. Normally, a person who has suffered a major bereavement would be expected, after a short period of shock and numbness, to experience strong feelings of grief, anger, fear and anxiety which diminish over the course of one or two years. Bereavement can be said to be proceeding abnormally if there is significant disruption in this process, either by the non-emergence of these signs with, instead, some manifestation of physical or behavioural dysfunction; or by the chronic persistence of some symptom or symptoms. The decision whether to refer these people to a psychiatrist or a lay psychotherapist will depend on the nature of the problem as well as the help available. Bereavement can precipitate almost any mental illness, including schizophrenia or psychotic depression; it can increase the risk of suicide and violence, including murder. In these cases referral to a psychiatrist is imperative. In most other cases, a lay psychotherapist would be an appropriate referral.

In this chapter we shall not discuss the role of the psychotherapist in the selection, training and support of counsellors, nor shall we describe the process of bereavement counselling. These topics have been well covered elsewhere (for instance, Parkes 1986; Worden 1983). Rather, we shall focus on the psychopathology and treatment of the complications of bereavement, that group of conditions which are intimately related to the process of grieving and to the attachments which precede it.

Of course the human brain's capacity to anticipate events means that many people start to grieve before the object of their attachment is dead. Illness such as cancer, AIDS and multiple sclerosis evoke severe grief in patients and their families, and it is sometimes appropriate for psychotherapists to become involved before the patient dies. Frequently psychotherapeutic support can be offered in the context of hospices, the best of which function as therapeutic communities, in which psychosocial and spiritual help is available to families facing death. Through their Home Care Services they also reach out to the wider community of care.

For this reason we have included a brief section covering the needs of dying patients and their families. Space will not permit detailed exposition of the full range of special problems associated with these diseases, which are covered in specialist texts.

PSYCHOPATHOLOGY

Although bereavement is full of complexity, the feature which distinguishes most people who require psychotherapy at this time is the persistence of distressing symptoms or behaviour beyond the time when it would normally be expected to decline. We believe that this persistence usually results from the establishment of patterns which, once set up, perpetuate the condition.

Sometimes these patterns are established at the time of the bereavement. More often they are manifestations of patterns of coping with life that have been laid down long before.

It can be useful to think of human behaviour as occurring in cycles of experience. A cycle starts with the receiving of a stream of incoming stimuli which, after preliminary processing in the brain, are identified as *perceptions*. These, taken together, lead to conscious awareness that a particular situation exists. It is at this stage that emotions may be aroused as the individual *appraises* the situation and becomes *aware* of its implications. If the situation is appraised as problematic it will give rise to a *plan* to deal with the problem. This leads to *action*, the effects of which are then *reviewed* to determine whether or not the problem remains. If it does not, the behavioural sequence will end and the individual becomes free to pay attention to other stimuli. If the problem is not resolved, it is re-appraised and another plan considered. This sequence is repeated in many different ways. At any time, the individual is primed to pay attention to some sensations rather than others. This creates a hierarchy which is partly determined by long-established or in-born assumptions – for instance, that certain stimuli are potential indicators of danger. It is also determined by how needs have been met in the past and by long-term plans.

An example of this cycle in a newly bereaved widow (Figure 27.1) might start with her returning to an empty house. The unaccustomed absence would constitute a perception which, on appraisal, would remind her, 'My husband is missing' and give rise to a plan, 'I must search for him', which, on being put into action, leads to the classic searching behaviour of the bereaved. On reappraisal, the failure to locate the dead husband taken in conjunction with the cognitive awareness that he cannot be recovered, presses the widow towards an alternative plan. She begins to accept the permanence of the loss and is motivated to seek other ways of meeting needs for security, friendship and all the other needs that are met by relationships. Bereavement is the process of repeating such cycles in order to test reality and adjust the inner assumptive world to the new situation.

Within this larger cycle of adjustment are a myriad of smaller cycles as the person pays attention to all the demands of the current life, as well as thoughts, memories and other triggers which occur and cause the expression of feeling.

The cycle can be blocked or diverted at any stage, as indicated in Figure 27.1.

1 Some people may deny that the death has occurred. This can be done by withdrawing from society, blocking attempts by family and friends to discuss the loss, shutting away photographs or other reminders of the dead person and leaving undone any job which would formerly have been the responsibility of the dead person. In this way she avoids painful *stimuli* which would lead to an appraisal of the situation. Thus she fails to go through the individual loops of grieving which are the work of the overall cycle of coming to terms with life as it now is.

2 Many people interrupt the cycle at *appraisal*. They will acknowledge the

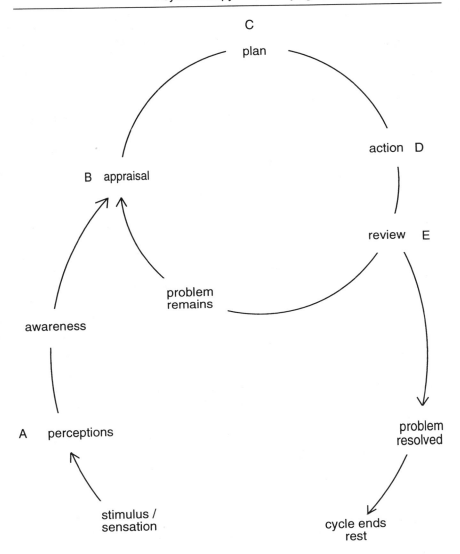

Figure 27.1 The cycle of experience

fact of death but deny its implication. They behave and feel as if their spouse were near to hand, refuse to make plans and continue to behave as if nothing has happened. The sensation is felt and correctly identified but, perhaps because of learned helplessness, an appraisal takes place in which the enormity of the change is ignored and feelings repressed.

3 For some, grief is not simply a reaction, but a sign of love. Those who have a continued sense of obligation, perhaps because they feel guilty for some failure or lack of love, may find it difficult to stop the grieving process. Far from avoiding reminders of their loss they may seek them out. This kind of self-punitive grieving may persist because it is difficult to make restitution for a wrong once a person is dead. The *plan* reached by the bereaved is calculated to perpetuate the painful duty of grieving rather than to resolve it.

4 For other people, the difficulty lies at the action stage. They may become busy with 'things to do'. This distracts the person from reminders for a time but leaves basic assumptions unchanged. Again, however, the 'mistake' was at the planning stage.

5 An example of a failure to *review* is a wife who continues to search for her husband in all his old haunts long after it should be obvious that he is not to be found. The review is not providing the correct feedback which would make her change her plan.

The way in which a person tends to interrupt the grief cycle is largely determined by pre-established patterns. Our ways of functioning grow out of our innate natural behaviour, moderated by the responses we get from the environment. This learning starts early.

Learned patterns of behaviour are established in every area of life, as the child received responses for thinking, deciding, being powerful, expressing feelings and so on. All of these patterns can affect the course of bereavement if they cause an interruption to the cycle. Those people who have learned how to deny knowledge as a way of facing stress may refuse to accept the evidence of their common sense. Those who have learned to be silent in distress may repress their grief. Those who have learned not to trust their own experience may have difficulty appraising the situation. Some have never learned to make decisions or take responsibility for their lives. All this will affect bereavement.

Each of these learned patterns can lead to an 'alternative cycle' – prematurely or unsatisfactorily closed, so that the need to grieve and to adjust is denied and the person repeats over and over the unsuccessful pattern in an attempt to achieve peace. There is thus both the natural response to the stimulus and simultaneously the defence against it in the learned response.

An example of such a fixed cycle or Gestalt (Zinker 1977) is in Figure 27.2. Here at 'appraisal' the person, whose belief about herself is that she

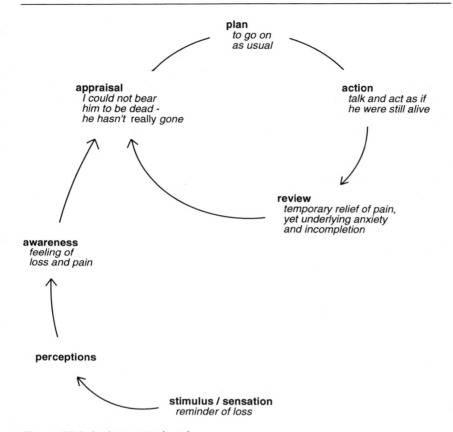

Figure 27.2 An interrupted cycle

could not survive such loss, decides 'He hasn't gone'. She forms a plan therefore to live her life as usual. At the review stage she experiences some relief at the temporary avoidance of the unpleasant truth. Yet there is, of course, still something unresolved and incomplete. Therefore she recycles this apparently satisfactory plan. She does not acknowledge the loss at appraisal, and therefore avoids the 'plan' to grieve. Somehow the bereaved person must be helped to interrupt the fixed pattern and find that healthy cycle which, though painful, will lead to resolution.

Probably the patterns which will be most significant in relation to problems with bereavement are those which are developed around attachment. Research into the relationship between pathological grief and attachment mechanisms shows that the constellation of feelings and behaviour which the child develops during the first two years of life not only influence the risk of pathological reactions but also determine the pattern that these will take (Parkes 1991; Bowlby 1988).

Grief is itself a component of the repertoire of attachment mechanisms which are inborn but modified by learning from their inception in infancy. These mechanisms include behaviours which maintain the attachment between the child and its primary carer – smiling, babbling, clinging and following – and behaviours which come into play following undue separation or when the child is frightened or distressed (crying and searching). These latter patterns, because they are essential to survival, tend to take priority over most other behavioural tendencies and to be accompanied by strong emotions. In the normal course of events they soon bring about the reunion which is their biological aim, proximity is restored and the behaviour is switched off leaving the child free to respond to other demands of lower hierarchical importance. But in the event of a lasting separation the response may persist for great lengths of time. It is this response that is grief.

Even when crying and searching do not lead to reunion they eventually die down, which psychologists cite as an example of 'extinction by non-reinforcement'. But these behavioural tendencies are easily switched on again by any reminder of the loss and, in the early stages, by any train of thought which leads back to the lost person. Hence the recurrent 'pangs' of grief that are so painful during the early stages of bereavement.

Human beings gradually learn that separations are seldom permanent and that alternative sources of support and security are available. They also learn that, to an increasing extent, they can stand on their own two feet. This enables them to tolerate longer and longer periods of separation and, eventually, to detach themselves from their parents and to make new attachments.

Research into early child development (Ainsworth 1991) has shown clearly how easily these learned behaviours are influenced by parents. Three patterns have emerged as likely to give rise to later problems. Each of them is a type of insecure attachment which easily becomes self-perpetuating.

1 *Anxious dependent pattern*. In order to survive, a child must learn what to fear. Young children are, therefore, extremely sensitive to the fears of their parents. A mother who is abnormally fearful, who gives out messages to her child that he won't survive unless he stays close to mother, will soon find that her child tends to cling and to become very intolerant of separation. Once established, this pattern becomes difficult to eradicate. In adult life a tendency to cling often evokes the very behaviour it is intended to prevent – rejection. Rejection then increases fear and evokes more clinging, a vicious circle (or cycle) which includes both anxiety and dependence.

2 *The avoidant pattern*. Some parents find it very hard to tolerate closeness. When their children cling to them they back away and may

even punish the child. The child eventually learns that clinging is dangerous and inhibits this kind of behaviour. This pattern causes children to avoid, as far as possible, situations in which they will be tempted to cling or to cry, and they become compulsively independent.

Of course, a person who has learned to avoid painful situations has no way of discovering that avoidance is no longer necessary. In later life their relationships are seriously compromised and there is a real danger that they will pass on their problems to their children because of their intolerance of closeness.

3 *The inconsistent pattern.* Both of the above patterns are adaptive in the sense that they enable the child to adapt to the demands of a particular type of parenting. But what of the parent who has no consistent style of parenting, who is responsive at one time and unresponsive at another? Mothers who suffer from recurrent depression or who frequently get to the end of their tether may swing between occasions when they are warm, caring parents who respond rapidly or appropriately to their child's smiles and tears to occasions when they are withdrawn or irritable and may be downright punitive in response to the same behaviour. The child ends up quite unable to know how to cope, and helpless in the face of any situation which evokes the need for attachment.

These are precisely the conditions which give rise to what Seligman calls 'learned helplessness' and which he has postulated as a major cause for depression in later life (1975). Faced with any threat the child withdraws into a state of numb inaction, lacking any hope that there could be a way of handling the situation, so that the situation remains unresolved and may even be aggravated. Once again a vicious circle has been established.

Bereavement is one of those life situations which makes demands upon the coping abilities of all who undergo it. It evokes powerful attachment behaviour and we cannot be surprised if people whose attachments have followed the patterns described above respond in ways which can be regarded as pathological:

(a) Anxious, dependent persons respond severely to loss. They exhibit intense separation anxiety with a tendency to panic. They may cling intensely and angrily to their children or to anyone else who is at hand, including their psychotherapist. Such behaviour, as we have seen, may evoke rejection and plunge them still deeper into chronic grief, anxiety state or panic syndrome.

(b) Avoidant persons tend to deny their need to grieve. A variety of avoidant strategies may be adopted ranging from hectic hyper-activity which enables people, by keeping busy, to drive all thoughts of loss out of their minds, to deliberate concealment of photographs or other mementoes which might remind them of the lost person and evoke a pang of grief. Others will direct their attention into a search for the lost person, half-convincing themselves that there has been a mistake and the person is not dead after all. Others seek for a scapegoat who can be punished for the death, as if this would resolve the problem and magically restore the dead person to life. In all of these cases grief is inhibited or delayed, but remains potentially waiting to be activated so that a considerable amount of mental activity needs to be devoted to the maintenance of avoidance.

(c) Persons with inconsistent patterns tend to withdraw into a state of helplessness and hopelessness following bereavement with many of the classical features of depression. Negative cognitions dominate thinking and suicide may be a real risk, although some are so helpless that they cannot even bring themselves to act upon the impulse.

COMPLICATING CIRCUMSTANCES

Thus far we have focused attention on the vulnerability of the bereaved person, but we also need to recognise that there are some bereavements that are more traumatic than others and which themselves increase the risk of pathology regardless of the personal vulnerability of the bereaved. These include the unexpected and untimely death of a spouse or child, deaths for which the bereaved feel responsible, horrific circumstances as when the survivor was a witness to mutilation, mass disasters, bereavement by suicide and bereavement by murder or manslaughter. Each of these has special aspects which lie beyond the scope of this chapter.

What they have in common is a tendency to overwhelm normal coping mechanisms. Traumatic bereavements evoke an alarm response, high levels of anxiety with hyper-vigilance and a tendency to startle. These are triggered and maintained by reminders of the loss, the memories of which remain extremely vivid, to be relived repeatedly both during waking hours (as flashbacks), and during sleep (as nightmares).

Global defences are called into operation in order to cope with these intensely painful reactions. Sufferers often shut themselves up at home avoiding anything which threatens to 'bring home' the reality of what has happened. There is a general psychic numbing or depersonalisation limiting the expression of any strong emotion, and a tendency to foster the illusion that the dead person is still near at hand. The bereaved, while recognising at one level the reality of the loss, will simultaneously say, 'I can't believe it is true'. This sense of incomprehension may persist for years, and itself reflects the difficulty which they experience in making appropriate modifications to their internal world or 'doing the grief work'.

These are the symptoms of post-traumatic stress disorder, and they have received much prominence in recent years since the syndrome was included in the *American Diagnostic and Statistical Manual* (DSM-III-R).

They are widely accepted as sufficient grounds for compensation in courts of law.

Of course, these various types of vulnerability and reaction seldom occur in pure form. It is often the case that people are vulnerable for more than one reason. Parents may evoke fear *and* punish closeness, people who are already insecurely attached may suffer traumatic bereavement. The outcome will often be a mixed picture in which anxiety, depression and avoidance coexist.

THE TREATMENT OF PATHOLOGICAL REACTIONS TO BEREAVEMENT

The above analysis of the roots of psychopathology in the bereaved may have left the reader somewhat apprehensive. How can we hope to deal with life situations which are both urgent and complex? There is a real danger that we, as well as our clients, will feel overwhelmed.

The truth is, of course, that neither we nor our clients can cope with more than a few things at a time. It may, and indeed will, be useful for us to attempt an overall view of the situation, and much of our first meeting with the client will be devoted to this kind of wide-ranging discussion but, just as the microscopist must switch back and forth between wide and narrow focus so the psychotherapist must switch between broad perspectives and the immediate problems and reactions which are occupying the client's attention at this time.

The basic assumption which underlies our psychotherapy with the bereaved is that reality-testing is worth doing however painful this may be. In other words, the bereaved have a life left to live and it is worth helping them to re-appraise this life situation in the face of this new reality.

There are, of course, exceptions to this rule. Perhaps our client is so sick that it would be kinder to encourage denial. This may be the case in a late-stage cancer patient who is in blissful ignorance of the prognosis or in a person with organic brain damage who cannot remember, from one day to the next, that their partner is dead.

With these exceptions it seems that the majority of people will make a better adjustment to life and, in the long term, will find it easier to recognise their potentialities if they bring their internal models of the world, their assumptions about the life space that impinges upon them, into line with reality. But the role of the psychotherapist is not to force people to face reality. Reality is brutal enough without our shaking it in our client's face. Rather, we must establish a secure base from which it becomes possible for the client to explore the real world. In this respect the psychotherapist is performing the same role as a good parent. We try to develop a relationship of trust which encourages clients to discover both their own strength and the extent to which they can trust us. We respect their strength without expecting the impossible, and we hope that they will learn to trust in our genuine concern for their welfare without expecting us to take control of their lives and to protect them from dangers which do not exist.

This may sound trite, but there are powerful reasons why many psychotherapists inculcate very different attitudes which do harm rather than good. These include attitudes derived from medicine in which a 'patient' is seen as sick and therefore weak, the passive recipient of the doctor's treatment. Family and friends are de-skilled by this vision and back off instead of remaining closely involved, and psychotherapists adopt authoritarian attitudes which undermine the patient's self-respect and encourage excessive expectations of and reliance on the psychotherapist.

Another, linked problem is the understandable tendency for psychotherapists to blame their clients for being dependent. '*Love*' is good, 'dependency' is bad and the client seen as 'dependent' is likely to be a nuisance. This is most likely to occur at times when, for one reason or another, the client is feeling insecure. They cling to the psychotherapist who, instead of providing support, backs away and admonishes the client. The situation is much like that of the mother who, returning from hospital with a second baby, finds herself faced with a clingy, angry first child. If she recognises the child's need for attachment and gives a little extra attention to the child the clinging will soon subside. If, on the other hand, she pushes the child away and punishes clinging she will aggravate the problems and set up a vicious circle which may become intractable.

It is often hard to handle excessive clinging. Such clients make excessive demands on our time and patience. The problem is what we and the client can do about it. The sensitive psychotherapist has an opportunity to show concern for the client not by giving in to their demands for extra time at the end of the session, for instance, but by indicating our sympathy for the pain which they suffer and expressing our confidence in their ability to come through despite it.

Equally difficult to handle is the pseudo-autonomy of the anxiously avoidant client. Compelled as children to 'stand on their own two feet' even when they 'hadn't got a leg to stand on' they back away from any interaction which might expose their underlying need for succour. We need to be most careful not to intrude or violate their personal space, but, at the same time, we must be on the lookout for ways of making contact which will minimally reduce their lonely isolation. The compulsively self-reliant are trapped in a hole in the snow; they can best be rescued by a thaw rather than a blow-torch.

In our view the only psychotherapy which has any chance of success is a specialised form of supportive psychotherapy which combines respect for our clients' strength with recognition of their fear, while simultaneously encouraging increasing autonomy and rewarding all progress, however slow, towards self-realisation.

SHORT-TERM PSYCHOTHERAPY

The establishment of basic trust in oneself and others can be a slow process, but this is not usually the case. Bereavements and other life crises are a test of strength and one which almost everyone, often to their surprise, will pass.

Bereavements also evoke support, not just from psychotherapists, but also from family and friends. In this context, although the psychotherapist may have to provide fairly frequent support in the early stages, the frequency of interviews can soon be reduced and an expectation of increasing autonomy adopted.

Regular interviews at fixed intervals are inappropriate, and it is much more consonant with the client's needs to reduce the frequency and duration of interviews as time passes. As we have implied above, the death of a loved person initiates countless cycles, behavioural and learning sequences between the initial discovery of the death and the steady state of homeostasis which can arise when the bereaved person has learned what it means to be a widow (or whatever other new roles and status are possible) and developed the new skills necessary to fill these new roles. Problems can arise in the course of any of these sequences, and it is one of the aims of psychotherapy to try to unravel them. While people are describing themselves to us, they are also describing themselves to themselves. Insight gives power, either to make different plans from a new point of view or to interrupt a recurrent cycling and move on.

The act of 'telling the story' is, therefore, psychotherapeutic, and there are many bereaved people who only need one thorough assessment interview in order to achieve sufficient insight to continue without further help. There are many others who will get all the help they need from a short series of meetings and only a small minority who need more than six sessions. Twelve sessions is long-term psychotherapy.

People with psychiatric problems after bereavement mostly perceive the world as a dangerous place. Many of them have little trust in themselves and/or little trust in others. It may be possible to achieve insight without building up a therapeutic relationship (the success of the one-off intervention and of bibliotherapy is evidence of that), but for most patients psychotherapy will be much easier if a relationship of trust has been established.

In therapy we have the opportunity to explore the nature of the attachment to the psychotherapist and to question the assumptions which are made about it. Clients have sufficient experience of relationships to realise that people are not all alike, but their ways of relating to others are likely to have created the very situations which they dread and to confirm them in a negative view of others and self. It is most reassuring to discover one situation in which this does not happen.

A CONSULTANT PSYCHIATRIST'S VIEW OF PSYCHOTHERAPY

A major issue is the extent to which the psychotherapist should actively steer the conversation towards problem areas. Working in settings in which long-term psychotherapy is seldom possible (NHS clients), one of the authors (CMP) has developed an interactive style and a structured approach to psychotherapy which differs from the approach adopted by many psychoanalysts. He does not believe that it works in *every* case and there are still a few patients who need to be referred for longer-term psychotherapy elsewhere, but it does seem to meet the needs of most clients and is cost-effective.

The approach starts in the form of a questionnaire (Parkes 1993) which clients are invited to fill in before the initial interview. This was initiated for research purposes, but turned out to be so useful that it is now used in every case, bereaved or not. It involves recalling and thinking about the client's past and present relationships and life patterns in a detailed way.

At the first meeting Parkes takes a psychiatric history using a loosely structured format. Having read and digested the referral letter and tried to figure out the reason for referral, he invites the patient to tell him what they would like from him. This leads on to a discussion of their present state and of the events which preceded it.

Bereaved people usually want to plunge into an account of the bereavement and subsequent events and feelings – all of which they are encouraged to do. He then invites them to 'tell me a little about your background' and draws a geneogram of the family while they tell him a little about each member. This leads naturally into an account of their childhood and later life up to the bereavement, with further additions being made to the geneogram (which remains the most used 'ready reference' to the background). Parkes may or may not go through the questionnaire with the patient at the first session (depending on the time available), and this sometimes makes a good starting point for the second interview. Finally, he attempts to sum up the situation as he sees it, and invites the patient to tell him if they agree or disagree with his formulation. Psychotherapist and client then develop a plan for further therapy if this seems indicated. Often this takes the form of an offer of 'a few more meetings in order to continue what we have started to do today'.

Parkes usually starts the second meeting by inviting the patient to tell him what they felt about the first. This often steers them towards issues that were not covered in the first meeting or to 'second thoughts' reflecting the fears and fantasies which patients have about psychotherapy.

Thereafter the second meeting is much less structured than the first. Issues which were not touched upon in the first session may be explored in more depth. In this and in subsequent meetings patients who have been avoiding problems often begin to feel secure enough to share them and the feelings which they evoke. Over the first few meetings a trajectory develops which makes it possible to plan for the ending of psychotherapy.

Parkes does not use contracts except in those cases where the attachment which the patient has made means that they are going to grieve for him. In these cases he sets up a fixed number of three or four further meetings (or more if the psychotherapy has been very long-term) and reminds the patient at the start of each meeting of the number of meetings left. This is usually sufficient to ensure that they will anticipate ending and do the grief work.

Because self-defeating patterns or *vicious circles* are a common cause of psychopathology, their accurate identification and termination is an important part of treatment. They often cause psychotherapy to get 'stuck' and, at such times, Parkes tends to play an active role in spelling out what he thinks is happening. Sometimes it is necessary to challenge the patient. This is particularly important in self-punitive grieving when the patient is attempting to atone by endless mourning.

The frequency of visits is reduced progressively over time. Thus the second visit may take place a week after the first, the third two weeks later and the fourth a month after that. Parkes is fairly flexible (or tries to be), but avoids the expectation of regular psychotherapy in most (not all) cases. This reduces problems at ending.

A PSYCHOTHERAPIST'S VIEW

Sills' approach differs in some respects from that of Parkes, largely as a result of the difference in the method of referral, the context of the work and the expectations of the clients. Otherwise, the work proceeds in a similar way.

Usually, the first contact is with the bereaved person herself. Sometimes this has been recommended by a GP or friend. Sometimes it is simply that the person is experiencing herself as functioning poorly or as being depressed and she has decided to come for help. The symptoms are rarely as acute as those which would necessitate a psychiatric referral. The setting is not in a hospital where people expect to 'receive treatment', and frequently they do not know what to expect from psychotherapy.

The first session is one of assessment and exploration. If the person seems to be showing signs of some severe psychiatric condition which requires medical intervention, arrangements are made for the assessment and possible involvement of a psychiatrist. Otherwise the focus is on making contact and listening to the story. In cases where the client identifies a bereavement as being the source of the problems, it is possible then to discuss a contract. Sometimes, simply the provision of information about what is to be expected during bereavement and help in planning the setting up of appropriate support is all that is needed.

Sometimes, however, it is clear that the bereaved is stuck in a more complex, fixed pattern of response which requires identifying and changing. The aim of the psychotherapy would be to establish or re-establish grieving as soon as possible. In this case, a short number of sessions would be agreed, with a specific focus. The psychotherapist would be quite explicit that bereavement would be the agenda and that the work would be likely to be difficult or painful.

With the client's agreement to this contract, the work continues. Session 2 would be likely to start with exploring the client's reactions and thoughts since session 1. Then, and in subsequent sessions, the client is invited to tell her story and her history in some depth. The psychotherapist looks for signs of where in the normal cycle of grieving the client may be blocking. Historical patterns of attachment and patterns of coping with stress are identified – including those which are manifested in the consulting room; the short-term psychotherapy is thus similar in focus, if not in style, to Davanloo (1992). Usually, beliefs are identified at the appraisal stage, of the cycle, which substantially hinders the person's ability to go forward. These beliefs may include 'I can't survive alone', 'The world is a dangerous place', or 'If I start to feel, I'll die'. Then a survival plan has been formed – for instance, to become ill in order to be looked after, to keep away from people or to keep busy. People tend at first to be unaware of these plans but begin to become aware of them in the session.

With the assumption that the client is likely to have become fixed in some self-perpetuating cycle, the aim is to intervene in any way that interrupts the maladaptive system and gives the opportunity to continue grieving. Insight and phenomenological understanding of such patterns can go some way to changing them. Work in the sessions can also help. Interventions such as work with dreams, conversations with the dead person in the imagination – with the use of an empty chair, the planning and execution of rituals, bringing of mementoes and photographs may all be used.

As termination of the sessions is approached and addressed, the psychotherapist hopes to facilitate their ending in such a way that the bereaved person can have a complete cycle – including feeling and expressing emotions, thinking over the significance, making a plan for the future in terms of setting up appropriate support, saying goodbye and leaving.

Sometimes longer-term psychotherapy is offered. There are three circumstances where this is likely. The first is when the client himself is not aware that his problems may be due to a bereavement. It is only the psychotherapist's hunch that this may be the case. She may offer that hypothesis and even receive some tentative agreement from the client, yet it is clear that this is not at all obvious to him. In this case it would seem necessary and more respectful that the initial contract be for exploring 'to see whether psychotherapy can be of any help'. The second circumstance is when the client and psychotherapist begin to identify patterns of coping with life, long before any connection is made with the loss of a specific person. Frequently again, that loss will be associated to an earlier loss or losses which need to be addressed. When this has been identified, a further contract can be made to focus on this work.

Both the above situations concern a client whose history reveals difficult patterns of coping with pain and change, but an overall level of functioning which is within the normal range. A third category of client is one in which there has been a significantly unsatisfactory way of life even before the bereavement. The client may report an excessively withdrawn life with only one close person, or a pattern of intense and unstable relationships, inability to keep employment and so on. With these clients, longer-term psychotherapy is offered (perhaps an open-ended contract). It is not unusual for a client, even at the first interview, to identify that while the present crisis is the precipitating one, they are unsatisfied with their way of being in the world. One such example was Laura, who developed symptoms of agoraphobia after her mother's death, but said that she had been agoraphobic ten years earlier while her children had been little. In both cases the phobia had served to divert her from her real feelings, and she wanted to change her way of handling life.

With other people it is during the process of identifying the patterns that this connection is made, and they express a desire to understand more and to deal with the past experiences of attachment and loss. Patricia was a thirty-five-year-old accountant, who developed problems after the death of her aunt. She found herself unable to function at work and also developed a distressing symptom of not being able to look at herself in the mirror. During the course of the first sessions she revealed a pattern of developing loose attachments to unavailable men whom she then resented and left. Her aunt, it seemed, had been the only person who had ever been faithful to her. She had very few close friends and no women friends. She realised that several sudden losses in her early childhood were affecting her present life in many ways and chose to commit herself to an open-ended psychotherapy contract.

In situations like these, bereavement therapy becomes 'ordinary' psychotherapy and proceeds at its own pace.

AN EXAMPLE OF SHORT-TERM PSYCHOTHERAPY

In the first session, John, fifty-two, told the story of his bereavement. He had been a model husband, taking care of his wife during her long and debilitating illness. After she died he lost no time in joining various voluntary groups to offer help to the disabled. Four nights a week he spent collecting people in his car and driving them around. At the weekend he helped with a centre for disabled people. He said it helped to keep busy. However, he had become seriously depressed. He refused to be involved with the local bereavement service, saying that 'it does no good to dwell'. According to him, he had lost the light of his life but he had had thirty wonderful years with her and now he was going to help those less fortunate than himself.

He saw a doctor for his depression, who persuaded him to have 'a couple of sessions' with a psychotherapist. At session 3, John began to admit that the last few years of his wife's life had been terrible for him. She had been in pain and suffered physical symptoms which he found not only distressing but revolting. Also she had become increasingly irritable. He had only admitted to himself that he would like to run away from the situation, then in guilt and self-loathing had sworn to 'stay with her to the end'. He began to see how in helping the disabled he was still 'staying with her'. When it was suggested that his reaction to the illness had been very normal he experienced palpable relief. Then he made the link to his childhood. His father had left home when he was six, and for the first year or so he had been sure that his mother would die of sadness if he left her alone. He remembered wishing guiltily that he could go out to play with the other children. John realised how much he wanted to talk about it all, and readily agreed to approach the bereavement service for counselling.

PSYCHOTHERAPY BEFORE BEREAVEMENT

Although in temporal terms, the care of the family in which someone is dying begins before bereavement, we have postponed discussion to this point because we have found it easier to conceptualise the grief of the dying patient after a full consideration of the less complex grief of the bereaved.

A major problem for families faced with life-threatening illness is uncertainty. The cycle of response described above assumed that reality-testing is possible, facts can be established and plans made. The client's internal model of the world can be revised to bring it into line with the world which now exists. Illness such as cancer and AIDS regularly face patients and their families with long periods of uncertainty. Sometimes the doctors themselves are unsure of the likely outcome, and other times doctors may have a strong expectation that a person will soon die but fail to communicate this on the assumption that 'ignorance is bliss'. At other times the medical authorities think that they have told the truth but the recipient has not understood or absorbed the message. Even so, as the disease progresses it becomes increasingly difficult to deny that something is wrong, and the patient and family enter a state in which planning is no longer possible.

Planlessness, as we have seen, gives rise to helplessness and helplessness to depression which will only be relieved when the true prognosis is declared. 'Thank goodness I know' is often the first reaction of a patient who has been given a bad prognosis; the reaction is one of relief.

Psychotherapists who work in a hospital or palliative care teams can do much to train and support staff in the arts of communication. Although we are not normally expected to break bad news, we are very likely to become involved when, for one reason or another, communication has broken down. We are then asked to take over the treatment of someone whose emotional disturbance results from their inability to escape from the cycle in which they are blocked at the planning stage. Nor can they leave this cycle for another because of the high salience of any situation which involves a possible danger to life.

In each situation we can be of great help if we provide people with opportunities to share their thoughts and feelings about the illness. We may be surprised to find that we are the only ones to invite questions; medical staff and family members may be afraid to 'rock the boat', and tend to skirt around sensitive issues of diagnosis and prognosis leaving the patient feeling that everybody is afraid of the truth.

Conversely, the psychotherapist who indicates that there is nothing that they are afraid to discuss and who accompanies that message by non-verbal reassurance (with a touch of the hand or a hug) will relieve anxiety whether or not the patient chooses to respond to the invitation to share their fears. In our experience, people seldom ask questions if they don't want answers. We should always tell the truth if we know it. If we are asked questions we cannot answer, we should not be afraid to admit our ignorance. If there are others who are better informed, we should make sure that the person has a chance to ask them. If nobody knows the answer, we must acknowledge the difficulty with which the patient is faced.

One way of dealing with uncertainty is to develop contingency plans: 'If the pain is caused by a recurrence of my cancer I shall do such and such, if not then I shall go back to work.' Even though a plan cannot be put into operation until the situation is clear, the very possession of plans for all eventualities reduces the need for endless cycling and frees the person to pay attention to other issues.

In the later stages of a terminal illness there may be very little time left. Awareness of that fact can 'concentrate the mind', and a great deal of psychodynamic progress may take place in a short space of time. Issues that have been avoided for years and secrets that have been concealed arise, and unresolved problems may be brought out of the cupboard and re-appraised. In the face of terminal illness long-standing ambivalence may be forgotten, and family members who have been avoiding one another may take advantage of a last chance to come together. This can make time spent in psychotherapy with dying people most rewarding and the psychotherapy is often an inspiration to the psychotherapist as well as the client.

Of course the problems of vulnerability that were discussed above affect the dying as well as the bereaved. Particular problems arise when it is a compulsively self-reliant person who is dying. Such people find it very hard to ask for help. They will deny pain or other symptoms rather than 'becoming a burden', and it takes considerable sensitivity to recognise that their bravado is a thin disguise for considerable insecurity.

Rather than accept the fact that their illness is worse such patients will often blame their symptoms on the drugs or other treatments which they have received. It is easier to blame the doctors and nurses than to admit the truth. Other patients adopt a combative attitude to everyone, as if by taking on the doctors they could conquer death itself. Anger is a part of grief, and we should not be surprised when patients take it out on the people around them. This can create problems in management, and it is not uncommon for the psychologist or psychiatrist to be called in, in the hope that we will make the patient behave. Occasionally staff may respond to unreasonable behaviour by themselves acting in angry or rejecting ways. This is likely further to undermine the patient's security and may aggravate the problem. It follows that the psychotherapist's role in this setting is as much concerned with reassuring and increasing the understanding and tolerance of staff as it is with the treatment of psychiatric disorders in patients. This can best be done by involving members of the caring team in psychotherapy and/or by providing detailed feedback to staff of our interactions with patients and their families.

Most psychiatrists and psychologists who serve palliative care teams are not in a position to provide intensive daily psychotherapy but attend on a weekly or less frequent basis and may be too overstretched for this. Yet there is a special urgency in the provision of care to a patient who may only have a few days to live or family members who have little time left to resolve their relationship difficulties with a dying person.

This is a further reason for involving the caring team. Strict rules of confidentiality are inappropriate in this setting, and, unless the client prohibits disclosure, it is better to assume that information and opinion can be shared within the team.

It also means that we may have to take a more active role in focusing psychotherapy on important issues and using medication to get rapid control of severe anxiety or depression than would normally be the case. We just don't have time to wait for long-term psychotherapies to take effect.

Serious illnesses have complex effects on the lives of those who suffer them, and we should seldom assume that we know better than our patients what they need from us. We may expect dying patients to be concerned about their own death, but there are many patients who are much more concerned about the welfare of a pet, the disposal of a flat or the limitations imposed by their illness. Even those who express a fear of dying will often qualify it by pointing out that it is not being dead that they fear but the process of dying. Fears of pain, fears of mutilation, fears of becoming a burden to others, fears of losing control of bodily functions, all of these are issues involving illness and its effects which are associated in people's minds with dying. They are the outcome of a 'horror comic' view of death rather than of the quiet slipping away which, in good circumstances of care, is the usual reality. Once such fears have been expressed it is usually possible to provide reassurance.

One elderly patient said, 'I wish you could tell people how good it is to die of cancer.' What she meant was that, since we all have to die of something, cancer is not a bad way to go. She had had time to wind up her affairs, say goodbye to her family and friends, and was now peacefully subsiding. Her pain had been successfully controlled and all of the passions and stresses of life seemed to be ebbing away. She had lost all of her appetites including her appetite for life itself, but this did not mean that she was suffering. 'Life,' she said, 'is like a good meal, when you've had enough you don't want a second helping.' It is not unreasonable to expect that those who are being well cared for will achieve this kind of quietness.

Those with a tendency to anxious, clinging attachments may respond well to the 'tender loving care' which they receive when very ill but badly if it is a partner who is dying. In the latter case their own need to succour may make it difficult for them to care for the patient at home and admission to a hospice or other in-patient unit may be needed in order to relieve stress in the family. In cases of this kind a full family assessment is important. If there are children it is very likely that they too will need extra support before and after the patient's death, but we should not assume that the outlook is bad. As indicated above, there is nothing like a bereavement to enable people to discover their own strength.

Similarly, people who have always viewed the world as a dangerous place will have their worst fears realised when faced with a terminal illness, but they may then find that, having faced the worst, they have nothing left to fear. The aim of psychotherapy in such cases is not to conceal the truth but to convey our own confidence that, however bad things may be, the patient or relative involved will cope. In a paradoxical way people who have always feared death may find the reality less fearful than they had imagined, they may then cope better than they or their family had expected and in doing so, become heroes. In our society opportunities for heroism are few, and those individuals who rise to the occasion by transcending their fears reassure others as well as themselves. As psychotherapists we cannot expect such transcendence to happen, we can only try to foster situations in which it is possible by adapting a matter-of-fact and accepting attitude which implies that an extraordinary situation can become quite ordinary. We neither play down the seriousness of what is happening nor do we add to the stress by excessive shows of pity or dramatisation.

It is sometimes said that psychotherapists who work with the dying have got to come to terms with their own death. This is a tall order since none of us can know until we get there whether or not we have 'come to terms' with anything of the kind. Having said that, it is reasonable to expect a psychotherapist to have a realistic view of what the passage to death is like and to have some sort of philosophy of life or religious faith which enables us to stay engaged with people who are in panic at the prospect. In the final analysis, if we can find meaning in life, then it is not unreasonable to assume that there must be meaning in death.

As in the preceding section we have not here been able to do more than to sketch out some basic principles and to highlight some of the major issues that will arise in our attempts to offer psychotherapy to the dying and the bereaved. We hope that we have said enough to encourage a few of our readers to read more widely and to enter a field of service which many find daunting but which can be so rewarding that we end up feeling that it is we who have benefited from the psychotherapy, for, in the end, we are all dying, yet somehow we can find a greater sense of living.

REFERENCES

Ainsworth, M. D. S. (1991) 'Attachments and other affectional bonds across the life cycle', pp. 33–51 in C. M. Parkes, J. Stevenson-Hinde and P. Marris (eds) *Attachment across the Life Cycle*, London and New York: Routledge.

Bowlby, J. (1988) *Attachment and Loss: III, Loss, Sadness and Depression*, London: Hogarth Press.

Davanloo, H. (1992) 'A method of short-term dynamic psychotherapy', pp. 43–71 in H. Davanloo (ed.) *Short-term Psychotherapy*, London and New Jersey: Jason Aronson.

Parkes, C. M. (1981) 'Evaluation of a bereavement service', *Journal of Preventive Psychiatry* 1: 179–88.

—— (1986) *Bereavement Studies of Grief in Adult Life* (2nd edn), London: Tavistock. Also Harmondsworth: Pelican; and New York: International Universities Press.

—— (1991) 'Attachment, bonding and psychiatric problems after bereavement in adult life', pp. 268–92 in C. M. Parkes, J. Stevenson-Hinde and P. Marris (eds) *Attachment across the Life Cycle*, London and New York: Routledge.

—— (1993) *Assessment Questionnaire*, London: St Christopher's Hospice.*

Raphael, D. (1977) 'Preventive intervention with the recently bereaved', *Archives of General Psychiatry* 34: 1450–5.

Seligman, M. E. P. (1975) *Helplessness: On Depression, Development and Death*, New York: Freeman.

Worden, J. W. (1983) *Grief Counselling and Grief Therapy*, London and New York: Tavistock.

Zinker, J. (1977) *Creative Process in Gestalt Therapy*, New York: Vintage.

* Available from Dr C. M. Parkes at St Christopher's Hospice, 51–59 Lawrie Park Road, London SE26 6DZ, at cost price.

Appendix A

Structure of the United Kingdom Council for Psychotherapy and list of its member organisations

Michael Pokorny

Registration of psychotherapists was recommended by Sir John Foster in the Report named after him (HMSO (1971)). A working party began in 1975 and reported in 1978, but its proposals led to no further action. In 1981 Graham Bright, MP, in association with others, introduced a Private Member's Bill to the House of Commons to regulate the practice of psychotherapy. It failed at second reading.

In 1982 the British Association for Counselling organised a symposium at Rugby. A working party was formed and led a second symposium at Rugby. Run on a shoestring, the so-called Rugby Psychotherapy Conference laid the foundation for the founding in 1989 of the United Kingdom Standing Conference for Psychotherapy. UKSCP had a federal structure in which different approaches and groupings of psychotherapy sorted themselves into eight Sections. In addition, there was a category of Special Member for the statutory bodies of direct relevance, and the British Association for Counselling were given a special category of their own as 'Friends of Conference', which they have continued to enjoy. Later a category of Institutional Member was added. The advent of the Register of Psychotherapists gave rise to the need for a change of name to the United Kingdom Council for Psychotherapy in 1993. UKCP is an organisation of organisations. There is no individual membership. Each member organisation may nominate two delegates to the Conference, and every position within Conference may only be held by a delegate. The gateway into the UKCP is the Section which is appropriate to the form of psychotherapy that an aspiring organisation represents or teaches. The Sections are the arbiters of their own branch of psychotherapy, and the Section criteria are open to scrutiny and acceptance or veto by the other Sections of the Council. This ensures that the criteria of any Section are sensible and within reasonable conformity with the other Sections. The central authority is the Governing Board which is composed of one representative from each of the eight Sections, one representative from each of the Special members and not more than two representatives of the Institutional members. There are also five officers and four elected members

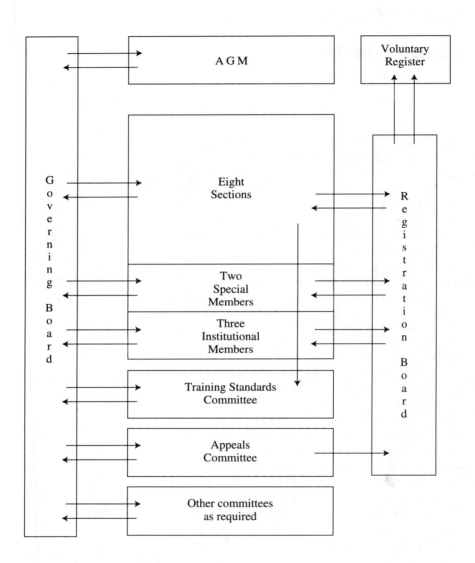

Figure A1 The United Kingdom Council for Psychotherapy

of the Governing Board. All elections are annual and there are strict limits on the tenure of office. Committees of the Governing Board are set up each year as needed. Every year at the annual meeting the Governing Board reports to the delegates of the member organisations and decisions are taken by a two-thirds majority vote. Separate from this, and not answerable to either the Governing Board or the annual meeting, is the Registration Board. Composed of delegates appointed by the Sections and the Special and Institutional members it is responsible for the Register. Only delegates of organisations recognised by their Section as a training or accrediting organisation are eligible to serve on the Registration Board.

Complaints against a registered psychotherapist are, first, the responsibility of the organisation to which that psychotherapist belongs. If the procedure there is not satisfactory the complaint goes to the Section to which the organisation belongs. Only if that also fails to resolve matters can the Governing Board become involved. Registration is through the Sections and the organisations and is not done on an individual basis. That is because the Register is voluntary. A statutory register would be managed quite differently and on an individual basis; any complaints would go to the disciplinary committee of the register.

Figure A1 shows the structure of the United Kingdom Council for Psychotherapy, and a list of its member organisations for 1995 follows. The United Kingdom Council for Psychotherapy is at:

167–169 Great Portland Street
London W1N 5FB
Tel.: 0171 436 3002

The current Chair is Professor Digby Tantam

UNITED KINGDOM COUNCIL FOR PSYCHOTHERAPY: LIST OF MEMBER ORGANISATIONS, 1995

Association of Cognitive Analytic Therapists (ACAT)
Association of Child Psychotherapists (ACP)
Association for Family Therapy (AFT)
Association for Group and Individual Psychotherapy (AGIP)
Association of Humanistic Psychology Practitioners (AHPP)
Association of Jungian Analysts (AJA)
Association for Neuro-Linguistic Programming (ANLP)
Arbours Association (ARBS)
Association of University Teachers of Psychiatry (AUTP)
British Association for Behavioural and Cognitive Psychotherapy (BABCP)
British Association of Psychotherapists (BAP)
British Association for Sexual and Marital Therapy (BASMT)
Bath Centre for Psychotherapy and Counselling (BCPC)
British Psychodrama Association (BPDA)

The Gerda Boyesen Training Centre (BTC)
Chiron Centre for Holistic Psychotherapy (CCHP)
Centre for Counselling and Psychotherapy Education (CCPE)
Centre for Freudian Analysis and Research (CFAR)
Centre for Personal Construct Psychology (CPCP)
Centre for Psychoanalytical Psychotherapy (CPP)
Cambridge Society for Psychotherapy (CSP)
Centre for the Study of Psychotherapy (University of Kent) (CSPK)
Forum for Advancement of Educational Therapy and Therapeutic
    Teaching (FAETT)
The Family Institute, Cardiff (FIC)
The Gestalt Centre, London (GCL)
Guildford Centre and Society for Psychotherapy (GCSP)
Gestalt Psychotherapy Training Institute (GPTI)
Guild of Psychotherapists (GUILD)
Hallam Institute of Psychotherapy (HIP)
Institute for Arts in Therapy and Education (IATE)
Institute of Family Therapy (IFT)
Institute of Group Analysis (IGA)
The Independent Group of Analytical Psychologists (IGAP)
Institute of Psychotherapy and Counselling (WPF) (IPC)
Institute of Psychosynthesis, London (IPS)
Institute of Psychotherapy and Social Studies (IPSS)
ISA Centre for Attachment-Based Psychoanalytic Psychotherapy (ISA)
Institute of Transactional Analysis (ITA)
Kensington Consultation Centre (KCC)
Karuna Institute (KI)
London Association of Primal Psychotherapists (LAPP)
London Centre for Psychotherapy (LCP)
Minster Centre (MC)
The Metanoia Trust (MET)
Northern Association for Analytical Psychotherapy (NAAP)
The National Register of Hypnotherapists and Psychotherapists (NRHP)
National School of Hypnosis and Psychotherapy (NSHAP)
North Staffs. Association for Psychotherapy (NSTAF)
North West Institute for Dynamic Psychotherapy (NWIDP)
The Oxford Centre for Human Relations (OCHRE)
Philadelphia Association (PA)
Psychosynthesis and Education Trust (PET)
Regent's College School of Psychotherapy and Counselling (RCSPC)
Society of Analytical Psychology (SAP)
The Sherwood Psychotherapy Training Institute (SHPTI)
Severnside Institute for Psychotherapy (SIP)
South Trent Training in Dynamic Psychotherapy (STTDP)

Tavistock Marital Studies Institute (TMSI)
University of Liverpool Diploma in Psychotherapy (ULDP)
University of Leicester Diploma in Psychodynamic Studies (ULDPS)
West Midlands Institute of Psychotherapy (WMIP)
The Women's Therapy Centre (WTC)
Yorkshire Association for Psychodynamic Psychotherapy (YAPP)

The United Kingdom Council for Psychotherapy
Ethical guidelines

ETHICAL RELATIONSHIPS IN THE CONTEXT OF PSYCHOTHERAPY

Petrüska Clarkson (Ethics Committee, British Association for Psychoanalytic and Psychodynamic Supervision) and Lesley Murdin (Ethics Committee, UKCP and Deputy Head of Training, Westminster Pastoral Foundation

These remarks are a contextualisation which we as individual professionals thought valuable and necessary as a brief frame for consideration in reading the ethical guidelines of the UKCP. This piece is *not* to be taken as official or representing the views of the various committees on which we serve. Extensive discussion is available elsewhere (P. Clarkson and L. Murdin, 1995, in press, 'Ethical relationships: the context of psychotherapy'.

The primary task of therapy is the restoration of relationship with oneself, with others, with the world. The work of the psychotherapist is conducted through relationship. Like all other relationships, it is vulnerable to the ills of exploitation or defensive practice, reductionism or betrayal, dependency or deprivation, invasion or bystanding, rigidity or lack of boundaries constellated in the delicate fabric woven from the interaction of at least two people. Because of its particular intimacy, it may be even more vulnerable.

Ethical guidelines exist as changing and developing articulations of the best moral thinking of a professional group at any particular time. Changing circumstances, special situations and exceptions as well as case law influence, shape and also change practice. Theoretical developments take place. Political/cultural currents and world events affect sensibilities in addition to challenging certainties.

The first principle in considering ethical relationships in psychotherapy is to maintain healthy and effective working relationships. Where there appear to be difficulties, the principle should be to work towards restoring the interrupted or disturbed relationship between therapist and patient if at all possible in the first place. Many problems could be prevented from the beginning if a client or patient openly discussed his or her discomforts with the therapist, giving him or her the opportunity to change, explain, seek supervision or other help as needed. Supervisors, mediators or independent consultants could perhaps effectively be involved at a next stage.

Only when such attempts at reconciliation and mutual understanding have demonstrably failed, should there be recourse to formal complaints procedures. Psychotherapy is about love and hate and cannot avoid entanglement with the most profound of human emotions. In many cases discussion, working through, insight into the complex dynamics of the therapy can resolve apparent irrevocable breakdowns. There are certain exceptions – as always – particularly in cases where sexual behaviour takes place. Sexual relationships are always wrong.

Most codes of ethics assume that their purpose is primarily to protect clients from the wrongdoing of therapists. That certainly is their major purpose. We might also consider the need of therapists for protection and help. Therapists may sometimes be particularly vulnerable to displaced feelings of vengeance or retaliation for the same complex reasons that doctors who go to help earthquake victims may be attacked. Transference theory also teaches us that clients (and others) may see us in illusional and, at times, delusional ways as the need arises for them. This is also open to misinterpretation – as well as therapeutic transformation – from both sides.

It is our hope that, as the primary function of ethical codes becomes more educational and protective of the therapeutic relationship, the policing and punitive function may in time become less important.

1 INTRODUCTION

1.1   The purpose of a Code of Ethics is to define general principles and to establish standards of professional conduct for psychotherapists in their work and to inform and protect those members of the public who seek their services. Each organisation will include and elaborate upon the following principles in its Code of Ethics.

1.2   All psychotherapists are expected to approach their work with the aim of alleviating suffering and promoting the well-being of their clients. Psychotherapists should endeavour to use their abilities and skills to their client's best advantage without prejudice and with due recognition of the value and dignity of every human being.

1.3   All psychotherapists on the UKCP Register are required to adhere to the Codes of Ethics and Practice of their own organisations which will be consistent with the following statements and which will have been approved by the appropriate UKCP Section.

2 CODES OF ETHICS

2.1   Each Member Organisation of UKCP must have published a Code of Ethics approved by the appropriate UKCP Section and appropriate for the practitioners of that particular organisation and their clients. The Code of Ethics will include and elaborate upon the following ten points to which attention is drawn here. All psychotherapists on the UKCP Register are required to adhere to the Codes of Ethics of their own organisations.

2.2   *Qualifications*: Psychotherapists are required to disclose their qualifications when requested and not claim, or imply, qualifications that they do not have.

2.3   *Terms, Conditions and Methods of Practice*: Psychotherapists are required to disclose on request their terms, conditions and, where appropriate, methods of practice at the outset of psychotherapy.

2.4   *Confidentiality*: Psychotherapists are required to preserve confidentiality and to disclose, if requested, the limits of confidentiality and circumstances under which it might be broken to specific third parties.

2.5   *Professional Relationship*: Psychotherapists should consider the client's best interest when making appropriate contact with the client's GP, relevant psychiatric services, or other relevant professionals, with the client's knowledge. Psychotherapists should be aware of their own limitations.

2.6   *Relationship with Clients*: Psychotherapists are required to maintain appropriate boundaries with their clients and to take care not to exploit their clients, current or past, in any way, financially, sexually or emotionally.

2.7   *Research*: Psychotherapists are required to clarify with clients the nature, purpose, and conditions of any research in which the clients are to be involved and to ensure that informed and verifiable consent is given before commencement.

2.8   *Publication*: Psychotherapists are required to safeguard the welfare and anonymity of clients when any form of publication of clinical material is being considered and to obtain their consent whenever possible.

2.9   *Practitioner Competence*: Psychotherapists are required to maintain their ability to perform competently and to take necessary steps to do so.

2.10 *Indemnity Insurance*: Psychotherapists are required to ensure that their professional work is adequately covered by appropriate indemnity insurance.

2.11 Detrimental behaviour

2.11.i Psychotherapists are required to refrain from any behaviour that may be detrimental to the profession, to colleagues or to trainees.

2.11.ii Psychotherapists are required to take appropriate action in accordance with Clause 5.8 with regard to the behaviour of a colleague which may be detrimental to the profession, to colleagues or to trainees.

3 ADVERTISING

3.1 Member organisations of UKCP are required to restrict promotion of their work to a description of the type of psychotherapy which they provide.

3.2 Psychotherapists are required to distinguish carefully between self-descriptions as in a list and advertising seeking enquiries.

4 CODE OF PRACTICE

4.1 Each Member Organisation of UKCP will have published a Code of Practice approved by the appropriate UKCP Section and appropriate for the practitioners of that particular organisation and their clients. The purpose of Codes of Practice is to clarify and expand upon the general principles established in the Code of Ethics of the organisation and the practical application of those principles. All psychotherapists on the UKCP Register will be required to adhere to the Codes of Practice of their own organisations.

5 COMPLAINTS PROCEDURE

5.1 Each Member Organisation of UKCP must have published a Complaints Procedure, including information about the acceptability or otherwise of a complaint made by a third party against a practitioner, approved by the appropriate UKCP Section and appropriate for the practitioners of that particular organisation and their clients. The purpose of a Complaints Procedure is to ensure that practitioners and their clients have clear information about the procedure and processes involved in dealing with complaints. All psychotherapists on the UKCP Register are required to adhere to the Complaints Procedure of their own organisations.

5.2 *Making a Complaint*: A client wishing to complain shall be advised to contact the Member Organisation.

5.3 *Receiving a Complaint*: A Member Organisation receiving a complaint against one of its psychotherapists shall ensure that the therapist is informed immediately and that both complainant and therapist are aware of the Complaints Procedure.

5.4.i.   *Appeals*: After the completion of the Complaints Procedure within an organisation, an appeal may be made to the Section on grounds of improper procedure.

5.4.ii   *Reference to UKCP Governing Board*: Appeals not resolved by the Section or those where the Section cannot appropriately hear the appeal shall be referred to the Governing Board of UKCP.

5.5   *Reports to UKCP Section*: Where a complaint is upheld the Section shall be informed by the organisation.

5.6   *Report to the UKCP Registration Board*: Member Organisations are required to report to the UKCP Registration Board the names of members who have been suspended or expelled.

5.7   *Complaints Upheld, and Convictions*: Psychotherapists are required to inform their Member Organisations if any complaint is upheld against them in another Member Organisation, if they are convicted of any notifiable criminal offence or if successful civil proceedings are brought against them in relation to their work as psychotherapists.

5.8   *Conduct of Colleagues*: Psychotherapists concerned that a colleague's conduct may be unprofessional should initiate the Complaints Procedure of the relevant Member Organisation.

5.9   The resignation of a member of an organisation shall not be allowed to impede the progress of any investigation as long as the alleged offence took place during that person's membership.

6 SANCTIONS

6.1   Psychotherapists who are suspended by, or expelled from, a Member Organisation are automatically deleted from the UKCP Register.

7 MONITORING COMPLAINTS

7.1   Member Organisations shall report to the Registration Board annually concerning the number of complaints received, the nature of the complaints and their disposition.

7.2   The Registration Board shall report annually to the Governing Board on the adequacy of Member Organisations' disciplinary procedures.

GUIDELINES FOR INCORPORATION WITHIN CODES OF PRACTICE FOR TRAINING ORGANISATIONS AND TRAINEES

This document should be read in conjunction with the Training Requirements document of UKCP and the Codes and Ethics of each individual organisation. There is a pre-supposition that the training requirements are being fulfilled.

Each training organisation is required to conduct its training in such a way as to address the needs and best interests of its trainees and of their clients. Trainees in turn are required to act in the best interests of their clients and to abide by the requirements of their training organisation.

Each organisation is advised to seek legal advice regarding its Code of Practice.

Each training organisation must therefore have a Code of Practice which incorporates the following minimum requirements:

1 Pre-course information

1.1   All prospective trainees will be fully informed of the nature and requirements of the course including its philosophy, objectives, assessment criteria and requirements for satisfactory completion.

2 Teaching

2.1   The detailed syllabus, objectives, methodology and assessment criteria for this part of the course will be clearly set out and given to all trainees.

2.2   All teachers training psychotherapists will be governed by a Code of Ethics and Practice appropriate to their work.

2.3   Teachers will respect the diversity of trainees and not discriminate on grounds of difference.

2.4   Teachers will not exploit their trainees sexually, financially or in any other relationship.

3 Clinical work

3.1   The interests of clients and trainees will be considered in establishing clinical requirements.

3.2   Requirements will be clearly set out and given to all trainees at the outset of the training.

3.3   Organisations will help trainees to make clients' interests paramount and to maintain appropriate confidentiality.

3.4   Trainees' work with clients presented for training purposes will always be closely supervised.

4 Personal and financial involvement

4.1   All prospective trainees will be clearly informed of the requirements of the course.

4.2   The degree of confidentiality will be clear. There will be safeguards to protect the confidentiality of trainees' personal material.

4.3   Training organisations will arrange for trainees to have a personal tutor and will specify the extent to which the tutor may be involved in assessment.

4.4   If an organisation wishes to change its training requirements, there must be reasonable respect for existing arrangements.

4.5   All responsibilities of costs and fees and the possibility for increases in costs during the course of training will be explicit at the outset.

5 Supervision

5.1   Organisations will ensure that supervisors are abiding by an appropriate Code of Ethics and Practice.

6 Assessment

6.1   Organisations will clearly inform trainees in writing at the outset of training of the criteria and process of assessment.

6.2   The process will be as open as possible.

6.3   Assessment processes will accord with the UKCP Training Requirement.

7 Complaints

7.1   Each organisation will clearly set out and publish a complaints procedure.

8 Appeals

8.1   Each organisation will clearly set out and publish an appeals procedure.

8.2   If a trainee or training committee is not satisfied with the organisation's internal process, complaints may be referred to the appropriate Section of UKCP and, if necessary, ultimately to the Governing Board of UKCP.

Name index

Subject index

THE UK et

kit

dition

THE UK AND EIRE
Internet
starter kit

2001 edition

ROB YOUNG

An imprint of Pearson Education
London ■ New York ■ Toronto ■ Sydney ■ Tokyo ■ Singapore
Madrid ■ Mexico City ■ Munich ■ Paris

PEARSON EDUCATION LIMITED

Head Office:
Edinburgh Gate
Harlow CM20 2JE
Tel: +44 (0)1279 623623
Fax: +44 (0)1279 431059

London Office:
128 Long Acre
London WC2E 9AN
Tel: +44 (0)20 7447 2000
Fax: +44 (0)20 7240 5771

First published in Great Britain in 2001

Pearson Education has made every effort to seek permission to reproduce the screenshots used in this book. The Publishers wish to thank the following for permission to reproduce material: Allaire Corporation, BBC Online, Big Save UK Ltd, Bonus.com, Emap Online, The Flash Team, Ginger Media Group, Ipswitch, JobSearch UK, Live Update, Look.net, LLC, Maps.com, Microsoft Corporation, Mirago, mirc.com, MoneyWorld UK Ltd, Movie Web, Naturenet, Neosoft, NetBanx Ltd, New Scientist, One Look Dictionaries, The Paris Pages, Purple Interactive, a division of Purple Trading Ltd, QXL.com plc, Qualcomm, Inc, SFA State University, Kevin Savetz, Surf.To, Peter Tanis, Tesco, Thawte.com, UK Online, UK Politics, UK Plus, Visualization Group, Yahoo!, Yellow Pages, WSGopher, WS_Ping Propack, Yorkdale Ltd (The UK Shopping City), The Zone Ltd and Mania and the United States Department of Energy, Idaho National Engineering Engineering and Environmental Laboratory.

'My Rules for Online Safety' on page 203 are from *Child Safety on the Information Highway* by Lawrence J. Magid. It is reprinted with kind permission of the National Center for Missing and Exploited Children (NCMEC). Copyright © NCMEC 1994. All rights reserved. The screenshot on page 298 is reproduced with permission of CyberDiet. © 1999 CyberDiet. The screenshots on pages 88, 171 and 242 are reproduced by permission of Lycos. © 2000 Lycos, Inc. Lycos® is a registered trademark of Carnegie Mellon University. All rights reserved. © Gamesville, Inc, a Lycos Network site. All rights reserved. The screenshot on page 61 is reproduced by permission of The Natural History Museum © The Natural History Museum, London, 2000. The WinZip screen image on page 194 is reproduced with permission of WinZip Computing, Inc. Copyright 1991-2000, WinZip Computing, Inc. WinZip is available from *www.winzip.com*. WinZip® is a registered trademark of WinZip Computing, Inc. The Top 50 UK Web Sites screenshot on page 93 is from Zebra Communications.

British Library Cataloguing in Publication Data
A catalogue record for this book is available from the British Library.

ISBN 0-13-032866-9 (pbk)

1 2 3 4 5   03 02 01 00 99

Typeset by Pantek Arts Ltd, Maidstone, Kent.
Printed and bound by Biddles of Guildford and King's Lynn.

The publishers' policy is to use paper manufactured from sustainable forests.